THE
AMERICANA
ANNUAL

1998

GROLIER

AN ENCYCLOPEDIA OF THE EVENTS OF 1997

YEARBOOK OF THE ENCYCLOPEDIA AMERICANA

This annual has been prepared as a yearbook for general encyclopedias.
It is also published as *Encyclopedia Year Book*.

© GROLIER INCORPORATED 1998
Copyright in Canada © by Grolier Limited
Library of Congress Catalog Card Number: 23-10041
ISBN: 0-7172-0229-1
ISSN: 0196-0180

Printed and manufactured in the United States of America

Contents

Feature Articles of the Year

© James Z. Huang/Sygma

© Les Stone/Sygma

© Chris Helgren/Reuters/Archive Photos

© Susan Oristaglio/Gamma-Liaison

© Steven Needham/Envision

The Alphabetical Section

Entries on the continents and major nations of the world will be found under their own alphabetical headings.

A Review of the Year 1997

I f one were to select a phrase to describe 1997, it well could be that it was a year of unusual emotion. Indeed, the tragic death of Britain's Princess Diana—who had taken on victims of land mines (*photo, right*) among her causes—led to a worldwide outpouring of grief. The death of Mother Teresa days after Diana's led India to order a state funeral for the Nobel Peace Prize winner and advocate for the poor—an unusual tribute for a non-governmental figure. Earlier, fashion enthusiasts mourned the designer Gianni Versace, who was murdered in Florida.

On another level of emotion, the transfer of Hong Kong from British to Chinese control was a time for history buffs to recall a British empire of an earlier era. The trials of Timothy McVeigh and Terry Nichols were difficult for the families of the 168 victims of the 1995 bombing of the federal building in Oklahoma City. The February announcement that a sheep had been cloned electri-

© Joao Silva/AP/Wide World Photos

fied scientists but also caused the world to pause and consider the event's ramifications. There was much concern about the safety of the astronauts aboard *Mir*, the Russian space station.

As 1997 ended, *Titanic* (*photos, page 7*)—the most expensive movie ever made—was released and drew long lines at ticket counters. With Leonardo DiCaprio and Kate Winslet (*photo*) in starring roles, the film is based on the sinking of a luxury liner on its maiden voyage in 1912. Some months before, a Broadway musical based on the same event captured a Tony as the year's best.

© Ron McMillan/Gamma-Liaison

Photos, © The Everett Collection

Although the Dow Jones industrial average ended the year 1,459.98 points above the 1996 close, it had dropped 554.26 points on "Blue Monday," October 27, causing anxiety. Markets elsewhere, including in Hong Kong (*photo, page 6, bottom*) had negative years as severe economic turmoil hit Southeast Asia.

In other Asian developments, India and Pakistan marked their 50th anniversaries; China's Deng Xiaoping died in February; and Jiang Zemin asserted his top position in China's governmental hierarchy before traveling to the United States. The Middle East peace process stagnated; a presidential election in Iran produced a surprise winner; and Iraq again challenged U.S. patience.

In Europe it was the year of Labour in Britain, NATO enlargement, and a peace agreement between Russia and the separatist republic of Chechnya.

The African nation of Zaire bid farewell to Mobutu Sese Seko and saw its name revert to the Democratic Republic of the Congo. Civil war ended in Liberia. The eruption of the Soufrière Hills volcano practically destroyed the Caribbean island of Montserrat, and a standoff between commandos and the government ended in Peru. Canadian voters returned their Liberal government.

In the United States, President Bill Clinton and Vice-President Al Gore were inaugurated for second terms and came under fire for campaign-financing practices; the president and Congress struck a major budget agreement; the states and the tobacco industry were involved in high-stakes negotiations; and all Americans were asked to volunteer.

The world's nations reached an accord on global warming; septuplets were born in Iowa; the world chess champion lost to a computer; and children collected Beanie Babies and Tamagotchis. Sports fans paid tribute to the late Jackie Robinson. The public was captivated by new images of the planet Mars and emotionally shocked by photos of starving children in North Korea.

THE EDITORS

January

5   Russia's Interior Minister Gen. Pavel Maslov announces that Russia's troop withdrawal from the separatist republic of Chechnya has been completed.

15   Israel's Prime Minister Benjamin Netanyahu and Palestine National Authority leader Yasir Arafat conclude an agreement on terms for Israel's withdrawal from most of the West Bank city of Hebron.

16   Ennis W. Cosby, the son of entertainer Bill Cosby, is shot to death on a freeway ramp in Los Angeles, CA.

19   In Austria, Finance Minister Viktor Klima is selected to succeed Franz Vranitzky as the nation's chancellor. Vranitzky had announced his resignation from the post on January 18.

20   William Jefferson (Bill) Clinton is inaugurated for a second term as U.S. president. Albert Gore, Jr., takes the oath as vice-president.

21   The U.S. House of Representatives reprimands House Speaker Newt Gingrich and fines the Georgia Republican $300,000 for bringing discredit to Congress by using tax-exempt donations for political purposes and submitting false information to the House Ethics Committee.

23   The Swiss government and Swiss banks and businesses agree to establish a fund to pay victims of the Nazi Holocaust. The fund is intended to compensate Holocaust victims who have been unable to retrieve assets that they or their relatives had deposited—or that invading Nazi forces had stolen and deposited—in Swiss bank accounts during World War II. The action is taken in response to claims that Swiss banks hold as much as $7 billion of assets that belong to Holocaust victims.

     President Clinton confers with the new United Nations secretary-general, Kofi Annan, at the White House.

24   William J. Cohen is sworn in as U.S. secretary of defense, becoming the only Republican to serve in the Clinton cabinet.

     Moldova's legislature approves a new government, led by Ion Ciubuc as premier. Petru Lucinschi, who had been elected the nation's president in December 1996, had taken office on January 15.

25   In Bangui, Central African Republic, President Ange-Félix Patasse, his opponents, and a group of army mutineers agree to end a ten-week-long uprising by mutineers as well as the accompanying violence.

26   The Green Bay Packers defeat the New England Patriots, 35–21, in professional football's Super Bowl XXXI.

February

3   In Pakistan the Pakistan Muslim League party, led by former Prime Minister Nawaz Sharif, scores an overwhelming victory in parliamentary elections. The government of Prime Minister Benazir Bhutto of the Pakistan People's Party had been dismissed on Nov. 5, 1996, on corruption charges, and the new elections were called.

4   President Clinton delivers the annual State of the Union address to a joint session of Congress.

     In a civil trial in Santa Monica, CA, a jury finds former football star O.J. Simpson liable for the 1994 stabbing death of his former wife, Nicole Brown Simpson, and her friend Ronald Goldman.

     Two Israeli helicopters collide in midair south of the Israeli-Lebanon border, killing all 65 soldiers and eight crew members aboard the two aircraft.

At the Capitol in Washington, DC, Jan. 20, 1997, William Jefferson Clinton was sworn in for a second term as president of the United States. Chief Justice William Rehnquist administered the oath; First Lady Hillary Rodham Clinton held the family bible; and Chelsea Clinton stood at her father's left. Moments earlier, Al Gore, Jr. (rear), was sworn in as vice-president.

© Doug Mills/AP/Wide World Photos

11 Fabián Alarcón, the president of Ecuador's Congress, is named to serve as the nation's interim president until August 1998. On February 6 the Congress had removed President Abdalá Bucaram Ortiz from office on the grounds of "mental incapacity."

13 Latvia's parliament approves a new government, led by Premier Andris Skele.

15 President Clinton invokes emergency powers to block a strike planned by the pilots of American Airlines.

More than 65 nations accept a global telecommunications agreement, opening their telephone markets to foreign as well as domestic competition. The agreement was negotiated under the auspices of the World Trade Organization (WTO).

17 Nawaz Sharif takes office as prime minister of Pakistan.

19 Deng Xiaoping, China's 92-year-old paramount leader, dies in Beijing.

The U.S. Department of Commerce reports a 1996 deficit of $114.23 billion in trade in goods and services.

23 The British newspaper *Observer* reports that researchers in Scotland have created the first genetic clone of an adult animal. The cloned animal is a Finn Dorset lamb called Dolly.

26 Despite Palestinian objections, the Israeli cabinet approves the development of a large Jewish settlement in a traditionally Arab sector of East Jerusalem.

28 A powerful earthquake strikes the Armenia-Azerbaijan-Iran border region, taking the lives of at least 965 persons.

March

2 *The Washington Post* reports that Vice-President Al Gore played a central role in soliciting funds for the Democratic Party in 1996, intensifying the furor over the party's fund-raising activities.

3 Harold J. Nicholson, 46-year-old former deputy station chief in Malaysia for the Central Intelligence Agency (CIA), pleads guilty to

In March, as Israel went forward with the construction of a controversial settlement in mainly Arab East Jerusalem, street confrontations between Israelis and Palestinians broke out anew, damaging the peace process.

spying for Russia. On February 28, Earl Edwin Pitts, a 43-year-old former agent of the Federal Bureau of Investigation (FBI), pleaded guilty to charges of conspiracy to commit espionage and attempted espionage for Russia.

4 South Korea's President Kim Young Sam names Koh Kun, a university president, as prime minister as the nation faces a loan scandal involving Hanbo Steel Industry Co.

11 As armed gangs in Albania continue to oppose President Sali Berisha for his role in the fall of investment schemes throughout the nation, the president names a new government.

13 A Jordanian soldier armed with an automatic rifle fires on a group of Israeli schoolgirls at a border site—killing seven girls and injuring six others, including a schoolteacher. The soldier is believed to be mentally disturbed.

14 President Clinton undergoes a two-hour knee operation at Bethesda Naval Hospital. The president injured his right knee after he slipped and fell down stairs at the Florida home of golfer Greg Norman.

15 In Zaire rebel forces capture the nation's third-largest city, Kisangani.

17 Anthony Lake withdraws his nomination to be director of the Central Intelligence Agency (CIA). Lake's nomination was facing continuing, prolonged confirmation hearings in the U.S. Senate.

Janet Jagan is sworn in as prime minister of Guyana, succeeding her husband, Cheddi Jagan, who died on March 6.

20 The Liggett Group, Inc., the smallest of the five leading U.S. cigarette manufacturers, acknowledges that tobacco is addictive and causes cancer and that tobacco companies have marketed their products to children for decades. In turn, the company is released from liability for the costs incurred by 22 states due to treating smokers' illnesses.

21 Concluding a two-day summit in Helsinki, Finland, President Clinton and Russia's President Yeltsin agree that Russia will negotiate its own partnership agreement with the North Atlantic Treaty Organization (NATO) before the alliance undergoes expansion.

22 Palestinians and Israeli soldiers engage in hostilities in Hebron as Israel's plan to build an Israeli settlement in mainly Arab East Jerusalem continues to be contested.

25 The U.S. Federal Reserve System votes to raise interest rates for the first time since Feb. 1, 1995.

26 Thirty-nine members of the Heaven's Gate cult are found dead following a mass suicide at an estate in Rancho Santa Fe, CA.

April

2   Russia's President Yeltsin and Belarus' President Aleksandr R. Lukashenko sign a treaty calling for the closer integration of their two nations. A similar 1996 agreement had not provided for full verification.

7   President Clinton confers with Israel's Prime Minister Benjamin Netanyahu at the White House.

8   Canada's Prime Minister Jean Chrétien concludes his first state visit to the United States, during which he and President Clinton announced a series of agreements easing U.S.-Canadian border crossings for commercial vehicles, combating telemarketing fraud, and facilitating searches for missing children.

9   In Zaire government troops in Lubumbashi, the nation's second-largest city, surrender to rebel troops without a struggle.

12   Pope John Paul II visits Sarajevo, Bosnia and Herzegovina. Local police report that new mines had been planted along the papal route.

13   During a visit to Albania, Italy's Prime Minister Romano Prodi states that an Italian-led multinational force will help restore order in Albania.

     Tiger Woods wins the 61st Masters Golf Tournament with a 72-hole, tournament-record score of 270—18 under par.

14   James B. McDougal, a former business partner of Bill and Hillary Clinton, is sentenced to three years in prison. He had been convicted in 1996 of 18 felony charges in connection with the Whitewater case.

15   More than 300 persons gathered for sacred Muslim rituals die as fires driven by high winds sweep an overcrowded pilgrims' encampment near Mecca, Saudi Arabia.

     Michael Bromwich, the U.S. Justice Department's inspector general, issues a report indicating "extremely serious and significant problems" at the Federal Bureau of Investigation's (FBI's) crime laboratory. According to the report, some FBI forensic operations have been sloppy and biased.

20   Hwang Jang Yop, a former top ideologue for North Korea, arrives in Seoul, South Korea—67 days after leaving North Korea and seeking asylum at the South Korean consulate in Beijing.

On April 22, members of Peru's military (below, right) were elated after staging a daylight attack on the Japanese embassy in Lima (left) and freeing 71 hostages held by the Túpac Amaru Revolutionary Movement. One hostage died of complications from a gunshot wound; 14 rebels and two soldiers were killed in the attack. During a four-month standoff between the rebels and the government, the rebels had demanded the release of 400 of the movement's jailed members or reduced prison sentences for them.

© Martin Mejia/AP/Wide World Photos

© Eugene Hoshiko/AP/Wide World Photos

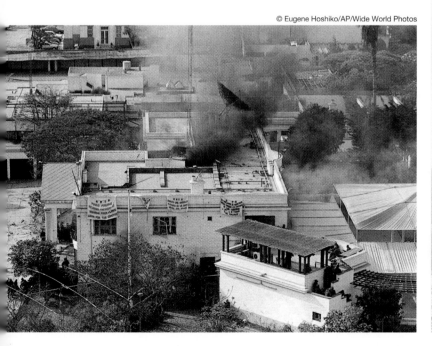

21 In India a new government—led by Inder K. Gujral, who twice has served as foreign minister—takes office. On March 30 the Congress Party had withdrawn its support of the government of Prime Minister H.D. Deve Gowda, and the Deve Gowda government was defeated on April 11.

22 President Clinton and members of his administration inspect areas of North Dakota devastated by recent flooding of the Red River.

The life of the grand jury investigating the Whitewater case is extended for six months—until Nov. 7, 1997.

24 The U.S. Senate ratifies the Chemical Weapons Convention, a global treaty banning the development, production, storage, and use of chemical weapons.

25 President Clinton and Japan's Prime Minister Ryutaro Hashimoto discuss trade and other issues at the White House.

27 President Clinton and former Presidents Jimmy Carter and George Bush assemble in Philadelphia for the Presidents' Summit for America's Future. Under the chairmanship of Gen. Colin L. Powell, the three-day conference is intended to encourage volunteerism in the United States.

29 In Aberdeen, MD, a military jury finds Staff Sgt. Delmar G. Simpson guilty on 18 rape charges.

May

2 In Great Britain, Tony Blair, the leader of the Labour Party, takes office as prime minister following the party's overwhelming victory in May 1 parliamentary elections.

The U.S. Labor Department reports that the nation's unemployment rate dropped to 4.9% in April—the lowest level since December 1973.

3 In Fort Davis, TX, a standoff between members of the Republic of Texas—a secessionist group demanding nationhood for Texas—and law-enforcement officials comes to an end as four members of the group surrender and the two remaining members flee into the nearby mountains.

5 Mousa Mohammed Abu Marzook—a political leader of the militant Islamic movement Hamas who has been jailed in New York City on suspicion of terrorism since July 1995—is deported and flown to Jordan. Under an agreement signed April 25, Abu Marzook gave up his permanent-resident status in the United States and said that he would not contest the terrorism charges that led to his detention; in return, the United States released him from solitary confinement and allowed him to return to Jordan.

6 Following two days of meetings in Mexico City, Mexico's President Ernesto Zedillo and President Clinton sign joint statements on issues involving illegal drugs and management of the U.S.-Mexican border.

7 A U.S. government report concludes that the Swiss government reneged on a 1946 agreement to return million of dollars in assets that Nazi Germany looted from European banks and Holocaust victims during World War II. The report also charges the United States with a "lack of attention" and a lack of interest in coping with the situation at the time.

A United Nations war-crimes tribunal convicts Dusan Tadic, a 41-year-old Bosnian Serb, of killing two policemen and torturing and persecuting many Muslim civilians in Bosnia in 1992. Tadic was acquitted of 20 of the 31 counts against him because of lack of evidence.

8 Meeting with the leaders of seven Central American and Caribbean nations in San José, Costa Rica, President Clinton pledges to seek a suspension in the deportation provision of U.S. immigration legislation enacted in 1996.

Tony Blair—the leader of Britain's Labour Party—and his wife, Cherie, gained the right to move into London's Number 10 Downing Street after the Labourites swept to victory in May 1 parliamentary elections. The party had been out of power since May 1979.

© Gavin Smith/FSP/Gamma-Liaison

10   At least 1,500 persons are killed and some 2,300 are injured as a major earthquake devastates northern Iran.

12   Russia's President Boris Yeltsin and Aslan Maskhadov, the leader of Chechnya, sign a peace agreement.

17   Laurent Kabila, Zaire's rebel leader, declares himself president of the Democratic Republic of the Congo—the name the nation took after its independence from Belgium in 1960. Mobutu Sese Seko, Zaire's leader since 1965, had yielded power and fled the capital on May 16.

18   In Mongolia's presidential election, Natsagiin Bagabandi, chairman of the Mongolian People's Revolutionary Party (the former Communist Party), defeats the incumbent Punsalmaagiyn Ochirbat of the Democratic Union Coalition.

19   A cyclone sweeps through the coastal region of Bangladesh, killing 108 persons and leaving 1,500 missing and 400,000 homeless.

22   U.S. 1st Lt. Kelly Flinn, the nation's first female B-52 pilot, agrees to a general discharge from the air force rather than face a court-martial for adultery, lying, and other charges.

23   Mohammed Khatami, a relatively moderate Islamic cleric, is elected president of Iran.

27   The U.S. Supreme Court unanimously rejects President Clinton's request to delay until his presidential term has ended proceedings in a sexual-harassment suit brought against him by Paula Corbin Jones.

     President Clinton and leaders of the North Atlantic Treaty Organization (NATO) join Russia's President Yeltsin in signing the Founding Act on Mutual Relations, Cooperation, and Security. The act establishes a new NATO-Russia council for consultation on security issues. It also paves the way for the expansion of the organization.

© Liz Gilbert/Sygma

Laurent Kabila, who led a successful seven-month-long rebellion against Zaire's President Mobutu Sese Seko, was inaugurated as president of the African nation—renamed the Democratic Republic of the Congo—in late May.

June

2   Canada's Liberal Party, led by Prime Minister Jean Chrétien, is returned to power—but with a reduced majority—in national elections.

3   After France's Socialist and other leftist parties gain control of Parliament in legislative elections on May 25 and June 1, Socialist Party leader Lionel Jospin takes office as prime minister. Alain Juppé had resigned the premiership following the first round of the elections.

7   The Detroit Red Wings win the National Hockey League (NHL) Stanley Cup, defeating the Philadelphia Flyers in four straight games.

12   President Clinton signs an $8.6 billion disaster-relief bill, providing aid for states devastated by floods. An earlier relief bill that contained provisions preventing government shutdowns during budget debates and prohibiting the Census Bureau from using computer-aided sampling in its census for the year 2000 had been vetoed by the president.

13   A U.S. federal jury votes unanimously that Timothy J. McVeigh should be given the death sentence for the bombing of the Alfred P. Murrah Federal Building in Oklahoma City on April 19, 1995, that took 168 lives. The 29-year-old veteran had been found guilty of 11 counts of conspiracy and murder in the case on June 2.

     The Chicago Bulls capture the National Basketball Association (NBA) championship by defeating the Utah Jazz, four games to two.

15   Croatia's President Franjo Tudjman is elected to a third term in voting that international observers call "fundamentally flawed."

22   The Summit of Eight—formerly the G-7 (the leading industrial democracies), plus the formal addition of Russia in 1997—concludes in Denver, CO. The environment, the Middle East peace process, elections in Hong Kong, and the enlargement of NATO were among issues discussed at the three-day meeting.

On June 2, Timothy J. McVeigh, a 29-year-old U.S. veteran, was found guilty of 11 counts of conspiracy and murder in the 1995 bombing of the Alfred P. Murrah Federal Building in Oklahoma City, OK, that killed 168 persons. The McVeigh trial was a media headliner for several weeks.

© Gehring/Gamma-Liaison

25   The Russian space station *Mir* loses 40%–50% of its power supply during a crash with an unmanned cargo craft during a docking exercise.

26   Bertie Ahern is chosen as prime minister of the Republic of Ireland. Final results of parliamentary elections in the republic on June 6 had revealed that the coalition led by Ahern of Fianna Fail won 81 of 166 seats, compared with 75 taken by the coalition led by the incumbent prime minister, John Bruton.

By a vote of 9–0, the U.S. Supreme Court rejects constitutional challenges to laws in the states of New York and Washington that prohibit doctor-assisted suicides. The court also declares a federal law intended to curb indecent material on the Internet to be unconstitutional.

27   By a vote of 5–4, the U.S. Supreme Court rules that the federal Brady gun-control law violates "the very principle of separate state sovereignty" by requiring state officials to conduct background checks of persons buying handguns.

28   Evander Holyfield retains his World Boxing Association (WBA) heavyweight title after Mike Tyson is disqualified for biting Holyfield's ear in the third round of a championship fight in Las Vegas, NV.

30   Turkey's President Suleyman Demirel approves a new government led by secular leader Mesut Yilmaz as prime minister. The new coalition ends Turkey's experiment with Islamic rule.

July

1   China resumes sovereignty over Hong Kong, ending 156 years of British rule.

4   An unmanned U.S. spacecraft, the Mars Pathfinder, lands on Mars to begin intensive studies of the planet. This landing is the first one on Mars since 1976.

6   Mexico's ruling Institutional Revolutionary Party (PRI) loses its majority in the Chamber of Deputies, the lower house of Congress, for the first time in 68 years.

In Cambodia, amid fighting between army factions loyal to Second Premier Hen Sen and First Premier Prince Norodom Ranariddh, Hun Sen ousts the prince from power. The two sides had announced the capture of Pol Pot, the leader of Cambodia's Khmer Rouge, in June.

8   At a summit meeting in Madrid, Spain, the Czech Republic, Hungary, and Poland are invited to join NATO.

The U.S. Senate Governmental Affairs Committee begins hearings on campaign-finance practices during 1996.

10   The nomination of George J. Tenet as director of the Central Intelligence Agency is confirmed by the U.S. Senate.

13   President Clinton completes a weeklong trip to Europe during which he visited Spain, Poland, Romania, and Denmark.

19   In Liberia, Charles G. Taylor, a 49-year-old former warlord, is elected the nation's president.

The Provisional Irish Republican Army (IRA) declares a restoration of the cease-fire in its armed campaign to end British rule in Northern Ireland. An earlier halt in the hostilities had been broken in February 1996.

23   Andrew P. Cunanan, a 27-year-old suspect in the July 15 murder of fashion designer Gianni Versace, commits suicide on a houseboat in Miami Beach, FL. The fugitive also was wanted for the murders of four other men.

Slobodan Milosevic, who is ending his second five-year term as president of Serbia, takes office as president of Yugoslavia (the federation of Serbia and Montenegro).

24   Albania's parliament elects Rexhep Mejdani to succeed Sali Berisha as the nation's president; Mejdani, in turn, designates Fatos Nano, the leader of the Socialist Party, as premier. The Socialist Party had won a parliamentary majority in elections on June 29 and July 6.

25   In India, Kocheril Raman Narayanan is the first member of the Dalits, Hinduism's lowest caste, to become president.

30   At least 13 persons are killed in two suicide bombings in West Jerusalem. A communiqué claims that the military wing of the Palestinian Islamic organization Hamas is responsible for the attacks.

A dramatic fireworks display lit the skies over Victoria harbor, Hong Kong, as part of the ceremonies marking the colony's return to Chinese sovereignty at midnight on June 30. Great Britain had ruled Hong Kong for 156 years.

August

2 Former warlord Charles G. Taylor is sworn in for a six-year term as president of Liberia. Taylor's National Patriotic Front had scored a major victory in July elections.

4 Mohammed Khatami takes the oath as president of Iran.

5 President Clinton signs legislation enacting a bipartisan plan to balance the federal budget by the year 2002.

Bolivia's Congress elects former military ruler Hugo Banzer as the nation's president.

6 Steven Jobs, cofounder of Apple Computer Inc., announces that the company's rival, Microsoft Corp., will invest $150 million in Apple and pay Apple some $100 million in a cross-licensing agreement. Apple has been losing market share to computers equipped with Intel Corp. microprocessors and Microsoft's Windows operating software.

11 President Clinton uses the line-item veto for the first time, striking three tax and spending items from balanced-budget legislation.

14 Timothy McVeigh is sentenced to death for the 1995 bombing of the Alfred P. Murrah Federal Building in Oklahoma City, OK.

18 Female students enroll at the Virginia Military Institute (VMI) in Lexington, KY, for the first time.

19 Claire Short, Great Britain's secretary for international development, announces a voluntary plan to evacuate residents from the British dependency of Montserrat. The small Caribbean island currently is threatened by the eruption of Soufrière Hills volcano.

The International Brotherhood of Teamsters union and the United Parcel Service of America Inc. (UPS) reach a tentative five-year contract agreement—ending a 15-day strike.

20 In a renewed cycle of violence between Israeli and Hezbollah forces, Israeli warplanes strike targets in Lebanon; on August 19, Hezbollah had fired rockets into northern Israel in retaliation for an attack on the Lebanese port city of Sidon.

21 Hudson Foods Inc., an Arkansas-based meat-processing company, announces a nationwide recall of 25 million lbs (11 million kg) of beef after Colorado health officials linked an outbreak of *E. coli* bacteria poisoning to hamburgers produced by the company.

22 The UN High Commissioner for Refugees announces that at least 120 people—thought to be Tutsi who had fled from eastern Congo—have been massacred at a refugee camp in western Rwanda.

24 Pope John Paul II concludes a four-day visit to France, during which he participated in the 12th World Youth Days festival.

26 South Africa's former President F.W. de Klerk steps down as leader of the National Party.

At an international conference in Geneva, Switzerland, meteorologists predict that an El Niño could lead to disastrous weather conditions in the United States, Asia, and Africa during the first part of 1998.

28 California's Proposition 209, a measure intended to eliminate state and local affirmative-action programs that was approved by the California electorate in 1996, goes into effect.

29 As the insurgency by Islamic fundamentalists against the military-supported government of President Lamine Zeroual continues in Algeria, hundreds of civilians are killed in a predawn raid in the village of Rais, south of Algiers.

30 In a special session of Mexico's Chamber of Deputies, a coalition of four opposition parties elects Porfirio Muñoz Lido of the Democratic Revolutionary Party (PRD) to a one-month term as speaker. It is the first time in 68 years that the post is not held by a member of the Institutional Revolutionary Party (PRI).

31 Diana, the 36-year-old princess of Wales, dies following a car crash in Paris, France. Emad Mohamed al-Fayed, a 41-year-old Egyptian-born film producer and friend of the princess, and Henri Paul, the 41-year-old driver of the car, had been killed instantly in the crash.

The funeral of Diana, the princess of Wales—who died following a Paris, France, car crash—was held at Westminster Abbey on September 6. The princess' brother, Earl Spencer (center), *joined members of the royal family* (right to left)— *Prince Philip; Diana's sons, Princes William and Harry; and her former husband, Prince Charles—in leading the funeral procession.*

September

3 In Phoenix, AZ, a federal jury convicts Arizona's Gov. J. Fife Symington 3d of seven felony counts of fraud. He then resigns as Arizona's chief executive.

4 Three suicide bombers kill four passersby and themselves in central Jerusalem.

5 Mother Teresa, the 87-year-old Roman Catholic nun who won the 1979 Nobel Peace Prize, dies of a heart attack in Calcutta, India.

7 Mobutu Sese Seko, 66, the president of Zaire from Nov. 24, 1965, to May 16, 1997, dies in exile in Rabat, Morocco.

At the U.S. Open tennis tournament, Australia's Patrick Rafter and Switzerland's Martina Hingis win the men's and women's singles titles, respectively.

8 A ferry sinks some 50 yds (46 m) offshore from Montrouis, Haiti, taking the lives of at least 200 persons.

11 The Scottish electorate votes to establish Scotland's own legislature for the first time since 1707.

13 Residents of Bosnia and Herzegovina vote in municipal elections.

18 A weeklong Communist Party Congress ends in China. During the gathering, an economic-reform program was enacted; Qiao Shi, a major rival of President Jiang Zemin, was ousted from power; and a new party Central Committee was selected.

U.S. businessman Ted Turner announces that he is donating $1 billion to a foundation to benefit UN causes.

Citizens of Wales vote by a narrow margin to accept London's offer to establish an elected assembly.

© T. Peternek/Sygma

With NATO troops standing guard, municipal elections were held in Bosnia and Herzegovina on September 13–14. The voting was considered a pivotal part of the Dayton peace agreement. Many voters returned to the villages where they had lived prior to the war, cast their ballots, and then were ushered away.

23 Representatives of Japan and the United States announce the approval of a new cooperative regional security agreement.

25 After an Israeli attempt to assassinate a leader of Hamas fails, a Jordanian-Israeli agreement calling for the release of more than 20 Jordanian and Palestinian prisoners in Israel results.

The U.S. Senate Finance Committee concludes three days of hearings regarding procedural problems at the Internal Revenue Service (IRS).

26 President Boris Yeltsin signs legislation restricting religious practice in Russia.

Two earthquakes strike central Italy, damaging the Basilica of St. Francis in Assisi.

29 Iranian warplanes cross into Iraqi airspace and strike two outposts of an Iraqi-based Iranian opposition group.

October

4 Members of the Promise Keepers, an all-male evangelical group, hold a rally in Washington, DC.

6 The U.S. Supreme Court begins its 1997–98 term.

8 In North Korea, Kim Jong Il—son of the nation's late founder Kim Il Sung—formally assumes the post of general secretary of the communist Korean Workers' Party.

10 The Norwegian Nobel Committee announces the awarding of the 1997 Nobel Peace Prize to the International Campaign to Ban Landmines and its coordinator, Jody Williams.

15 Cassini, an unmanned, plutonium-powered spacecraft, is launched on its mission to the planet Saturn.

17 U.S. Secretary of State Madeleine Albright visits Haiti.

18 President Clinton completes a weeklong tour of South America, during which he lobbied for expanded free trade.

20 Poland's Solidarity Electoral Action (AWS) and Freedom Union parties agree to form a coalition government with Jerzy Buzek, a 57-year-old former chemistry professor, as premier. The two parties control 261 of the 460 seats in parliament following September 21 elections.

22 South Africa's President Nelson Mandela arrives in Tripoli for meetings with Libya's President Muammar el-Qaddafi.

25 In the Republic of the Congo, Denis Sassou-Nguesso is sworn in as president. Earlier in the month, he declared victory in a four-month-old civil war against President Pascal Lissouba.

Black women from across the United States meet in Philadelphia for the "Million Woman March," a rally to promote unity among women of African descent.

26 The Florida Marlins defeat the Cleveland Indians, four games to three, to win baseball's World Series.

27 The Dow Jones industrial average of blue-chip stocks falls 554.26 points—7.18%—from the close the previous day.

Iraq orders all U.S. members of the UN arms-inspection team to leave the country within seven days.

31 U.S. Senate Governmental Affairs Committee chairman Sen. Fred Thompson (R-TN) announces that he is suspending the committee's hearings on campaign financing.

Mary McAleese, a law professor from British-controlled Northern Ireland, is declared the winner of the October 30 presidential election in the Republic of Ireland.

November

3 China's President Jiang Zemin concludes a weeklong visit to the United States, during which he met with President Clinton, congressional leaders, and business executives.

4 In off-year U.S. elections, New Jersey Gov. Christine Todd Whitman (R) wins a second term by a close margin and James S. Gilmore 3d (R) is chosen governor of Virginia.

10 President Clinton withdraws his proposal for "fast-track" authority to negotiate trade agreements, acknowledging pending defeat on the issue in the U.S. Congress.

Middlesex county, MA, Superior Court Judge Hiller B. Zobel reduces the second-degree-murder conviction of Louise Woodward to manslaughter. On October 30 a jury had found Woodward, a 19-year-old British au pair, guilty of second-degree murder in the death of Matthew Eappen, an 8-month-old boy for whom she had been caring.

WE STOPPED VIDEOTAPING OUR GET-TOGETHERS...

LOOK WHAT HAPPENED TO THE CLINTONS

© Jeff Stahler. Reprinted by permission of Newspaper Enterprise Association, Inc.

In early October the White House released video footage showing coffee gatherings President Clinton had held for Democratic Party donors. The fact that the tapes were released some months after the Senate committee investigating campaign financing had requested them caused a stir.

12 In Karachi, Pakistan, gunmen slay four U.S. businessmen and their Pakistani driver. The killings occur two days after a U.S. jury convicted Mir Amal Kansi, a Pakistani immigrant, of murdering two employees of the U.S. Central Intelligence Agency (CIA) in Virginia in 1993.

A federal jury in New York City convicts Ahmed Yousef of masterminding the plan to blow up the World Trade Center in New York City in 1993. His codefendant Eyad Ismoil is convicted of driving an explosive-laden van into the parking lot beneath the building and parking the vehicle near major supporting beams.

13 The first session of the 105th U.S. Congress adjourns.

14 In Washington, DC, President Clinton, Mexico's President Ernesto Zedillo Ponce de León, and representatives of 26 other nations belonging to the Organization of American States (OAS) sign an agreement to combat trafficking in illegal weapons.

16 Chinese dissident Wei Jingsheng, who had spent most of the previous 18 years in prison, is allowed to leave China and fly to the United States for medical treatment.

17 Seventy persons are killed when gunmen open fire on tourists at a temple near Luxor, Egypt.

A federally appointed election overseer bars Ronald Carey, president of the International Brotherhood of Teamsters, from participating in a new 1998 election. Carey's victory in a late-1996 election was annulled after it was discovered that some of his supporters had participated in illegal fund-raising.

19 In Des Moines, IA, Bobbi McCaughey, 29, gives birth to septuplets—four boys and three girls.

20 Iraq and Russia jointly announce that UN arms inspectors are free to return to Iraq. Most of the inspectors had left Iraq after the expulsion of their U.S. colleagues.

25 The annual meeting of the Asia-Pacific Economic Cooperation forum concludes in Vancouver, BC. The economic turmoil currently sweeping Southeast Asia dominated discussions at the session.

30 In Honduras, Carlos Roberto Flores Facusse of the ruling Liberal Party is elected president.

© John Gaps III/AP/Wide World Photos

In November, Bobbi and Kenny McCaughey, above, of Carlisle, IA, became the parents of septuplets and the center of attention. Kenny McCaughey's employer, a Chevy dealer, presented the considerably enlarged family with a 15-passenger van, right.

© Steve Jones/Sygma

December

2   U.S. Attorney General Janet Reno announces that she will not appoint a special counsel to investigate the fund-raising telephone calls made by President Clinton and Vice-President Al Gore during the 1996 campaign.

3   South Korea and the International Monetary Fund (IMF) agree to terms for a $57 billion financial bailout in response to that nation's severe economic crisis.

   The UN peacekeeping force that has been in Haiti since March 1995 begins to depart.

4   India's President K.R. Narayanan dissolves Parliament and calls for new elections in February 1998 after the government of I.K. Gujral falls.

   David Stern, the commissioner of the National Basketball Association (NBA), suspends for one year Latrell Sprewell of the Golden State Warriors for assaulting his coach, P.J. Carlesimo, during a team practice.

8   Jenny Shipley is sworn in as prime minister of New Zealand, succeeding Jim Bolger, who had been forced by colleagues in the National Party to resign.

9   Diplomats from North Korea, South Korea, China, and the United States gather in Geneva for the first session of talks aimed at ending the Korean War.

11 In Kyoto, Japan, delegates to the Conference of the Parties to the UN Framework Convention on Climate Change adopt the first international treaty that establishes limits on nations' emissions of carbon dioxide and five other greenhouse gases.

   The remains of M. Larry Lawrence, former U.S. ambassador to Switzerland, are removed from Arlington National Cemetery in Virginia after disclosures that Lawrence had lied about having served in the military.

   The Organization of the Islamic Conference concludes its three-day summit in Iran.

In a runoff election on December 6, Lee Brown became the first African-American to be elected mayor of Houston, TX. The 60-year-old Democrat, who had served as police chief of Atlanta, Houston, and New York City, defeated Robert Mosbacher, Jr.

© David J. Phillip/AP/Wide World Photos

13 During a two-day summit in Luxembourg, European Union (EU) leaders specifically exclude Turkey from joining the EU.

Following a request by Pope John Paul II, who is scheduled to visit Cuba in January 1998, Cuban President Fidel Castro declares Christmas a national holiday in Cuba. Christmas had not been celebrated in the Caribbean nation since 1969.

The United States and 101 other nations sign the Global Financial Services Agreement, eliminating additional barriers in the banking, insurance, and investment sectors.

15 U.S. Secretary of State Madeleine Albright concludes a seven-nation tour of Africa.

The U.S. Defense Department announces that it will vaccinate all soldiers against anthrax bacteria—one of the mostly deadly biological agents—over the next six years.

16 A panel, commissioned by U.S. Secretary of Defense William Cohen, recommends that male and female military recruits be separated during much of basic training.

18 In South Korea veteran opposition leader Kim Dae Jung is elected president.

19 In Guyana, Janet Jagan, widow of the late President Cheddi Jagan, is declared the winner of the nation's December 15 presidential balloting.

22 President Clinton visits Bosnia—four days after announcing that U.S. troops would remain in Bosnia beyond the June 1998 deadline.

Gunmen kill 45 persons in the Tzotril Indian village of Acteal in Mexico's southern state of Chiapas.

23 In Denver, CO, a federal jury convicts Terry L. Nichols of conspiracy and involuntary manslaughter for his role in the 1995 bombing of the Alfred P. Murrah Federal Building in Oklahoma City, OK.

24 The United States and Panama announce a tentative agreement under which U.S. troops would remain in Panama after the United States relinquishes control of the Panama Canal at the end of 1999.

29 In Vietnam, Lt. Gen. La Kha Phieu is named secretary-general of the ruling Communist Party.

Kenyans go to the polls in presidential elections.

31 Michael Kennedy, son of the late Sen. Robert F. Kennedy, dies following a skiing accident in Aspen, CO.

Special Features

Photo Credits: © Kimimasa Mayama/Reuters/Archive Photos (above); © James Wilson/Woodfin Camp & Associates (below)

At midyear 1997, the British flag was lowered and the Chinese flag was raised, *above*, in Hong Kong as China resumed control over the colony. China's Deng Xiaoping died in February and President Jiang Zemin visited the United States in October. All three events focused attention on China and led the editors to choose the world's most populous nation as the subject for this volume's opening feature. A look at U.S. political scandal, including campaign-financing abuses—25 years after the break-in at Washington's Watergate complex—follows.

In 1997 former Gen. Colin Powell (*page 23, top left*) served as chairman of a presidential summit held to encourage Americans to serve others; cases of sexual harassment and impropriety in the U.S. military made the headlines and led to renewed discussion about women in the service (*page 23, top right*); and Beanie Babies were the "must-have" items with youngsters (*page 23, center left*). American men and women were undergoing cosmetic surgery (*page 23, center right*) in record numbers. They also were becoming more international in their choice of food, enjoying such dishes as dim sum (*left*). Globally, more people were trying mountain climbing (*page 23, bottom*) and Jon Krakauer's book about a disaster on Mount Everest was a best-seller.

Accordingly, volunteerism, the new U.S. military, marketing to kids, cosmetic surgery, America's changing culinary tastes, and mountain climbing also have been selected as topics for feature coverage.

By John Bryan Starr

In September 1997, when the 15th National Congress of the Communist Party of China was convened in Beijing, a story circulated in the city, according to *New York Times* correspondent Seth Faison. The story went like this: "Presidents Bill Clinton, Boris Yeltsin, and Jiang Zemin each are driving down a road, and their three cars approach an intersection. Mr. Clinton turns right without signaling. So does Mr. Yeltsin. But Mr. Jiang hesitates and asks his passenger, Deng Xiaoping, which way to go. 'Signal left and turn right,' Deng replies."

For many reasons, the year 1997 might have been the turning point described in the Beijing wags' story. In mid-February occurred the long-anticipated death of Deng Xiaoping, China's paramount leader for 20 years. On July 1, China resumed sovereignty over the territory of Hong Kong, which it had ceded to Britain in the aftermath of the first Opium War in 1842. In September the National Party Congress met—a quinquennial event that in the past often has marked a major shift in national policy. Finally, in late October, President and General Secretary of the Communist Party Jiang Zemin realized a long-held goal by being received on a state visit to the United States.

In fact, however, one is struck more with continuity than with change as one looks at China in the wake of these momentous events. Although no one could "succeed" Deng Xiaoping, given the unique role he played at the time of his death, Jiang had been being groomed for the preceding eight years as China's

About the Author. John Bryan Starr's latest book, *Understanding China—A Guide to China's Economy, History, and Political Structure*, was published by Hill & Wang in 1997. His earlier books include *Ideology and Culture: An Introduction to the Dialectic of Contemporary Chinese Politics* and *Continuing the Revolution: Studies in the Political Thought of Mao.* Currently, Dr. Starr is managing director of the Annenberg Institute for School Reform at Brown University. He was president of the Yale-China Association in New Haven, CT, for a number of years and has taught at Yale, Dartmouth, and the University of California, Berkeley.

most important political figure. In the months following Deng's passing, Jiang took pains to reaffirm the pragmatic course that Deng had pursued so successfully over the preceding decades.

The transfer of sovereignty in Hong Kong, too, was uneventful, and while one could observe changes in the territory, the newly established government under the "one state, two systems" model managed to weather even a major downturn in the Hong Kong financial markets during its first months of operation. (*See* SUBARTICLE—*A Time of Change for Hong Kong*, page 27.)

It was in his speech to the 15th Party Congress that Jiang "signaled left and turned right." While he gave prominence to a "new course" featuring the privatization of substantial numbers of financially ailing state-owned enterprises, this was a solution that had been put in operation more than a decade earlier, and he cloaked it in vaguely Marxist rhetoric to make it seem ideologically correct. Finally, the Sino-U.S. summit in the late fall was only partially successful in putting the critically important Sino-U.S. relationship on a new and more secure footing.

One significant result that did emerge from the passing of these milestones was the consolidation of the position of Jiang Zemin. Despite his reputation for lacking a power base and political acumen, he succeeded in maneuvering around his potential rivals at the party congress to become the undisputed head of the party-state. His handling of himself in front of often unfriendly audiences during his trip to the United States served to modify his image as nothing more than a bland and unreflective party hack. Although it was clear that the president and party general secretary was no visionary, as the year ended he

The year 1997 was a momentous one for the People's Republic of China. Deng Xiaoping died on February 19, and the Chinese populace joined together to pay tribute to the man who had been their paramount leader for 20 years, below. Seven months later the 15th Party Congress was held in Beijing, photo, page 24. At the congress, Jiang Zemin affirmed his position as the undisputed head of the party-state.

Jiang Zemin was in the United States in late October. During the long-anticipated visit, China's president and Communist Party general secretary was greeted by President Bill Clinton on the South Lawn of the White House, right; conferred with Republican congressional leaders Rep. Newt Gingrich (above, left) and Sen. Trent Lott; and was given an IBM technology presentation in New York.

had begun to look like something more than merely a transitional figure on the Chinese political scene.

The Economy. In September the World Bank issued its first overall assessment of the Chinese economy. The report noted that the speed of China's economic development was unparalleled. Whereas it took the United States 50 years to double its per-capita income in the 19th century, China has doubled its national income twice since the late 1970s. China's gross domestic product fast was approaching $1 trillion and, while the pace of growth had slowed somewhat in recent years, the economy continued to grow at an average annual rate of about 10% per year since the late 1970s.

China's foreign trade has been increasing at twice the rate of the growth of the economy as a whole; total two-way trade in 1997 was projected to exceed $310 billion. More than one third

A Time of Change for Hong Kong

At midnight on June 30, 1997, the colony of Hong Kong reverted to Chinese sovereignty after 156 years of British rule. The vestiges of British colonialism were removed and a Special Administrative Region (SAR) under China was born. As an SAR, under China's "one country, two systems" policy, Hong Kong was to enjoy socioeconomic autonomy and some political control.

The inauguration of the Hong Kong SAR government began at that time. Tung Chee-hwa, a shipping tycoon and vice-chairman of the transitional Preparatory Committee (PC), took office as chief executive. A Provisional Legislative Council (PLC)—which had replaced the Legislative Council (Legco) that was orchestrated by Christopher Patten, the departing British governor of Hong Kong—as well as the SAR's principal officials, executive-council members, and judges also were sworn into office. A jubilant celebration to mark the handover was staged. The British flag was lowered for a final time and replaced by the Chinese flag; fireworks lit up the harbor; and various cultural performances were held. Prince Charles represented the British monarchy; President Jiang Zemin and Premier Li Peng headed the Chinese delegation. Marches of protest by ousted legislators and by persons who feared the loss of basic human rights in Chinese-controlled Hong Kong did not dampen the celebrations.

Immediate Changes. Immediately after the handover, the British crown and other colonial symbols on official buildings and uniforms were replaced by the SAR's emblem, the bauhinia flower. The word "royal" was dropped from government departments. Crown Council was renamed Government Council, and Victoria Park became Hong Kong Central Park. The queen's birthday and Remembrance Day ceased to be public holidays. Holders of new SAR passports gained visa-free access to more than 27 countries, including Canada and Britain. Almost 68,000 Vietnamese refugees had returned voluntarily to Vietnam or had been sent back forcibly before the handover. By June 19, about 2,300 remained in the region; most of them would be sent back or accepted by other countries by the end of the year.

On July 1 a Chinese Foreign Ministry Office was set up in Hong Kong and replaced Xinhua News Agency (XNA) as a channel of communication between the SAR government and China. XNA, an unofficial foreign ministry during British rule, was scaled down in its operation. Its head, Zhou Nan, retired and was replaced by Jiang Enzhu, a former ambassador to Britain. On July 11 the Preparatory Committee was disbanded. A Chinese force of 4,800 troops was stationed in Hong Kong as the SAR Garrison.

Dignitaries from Great Britain, including Prince Charles and Prime Minister Tony Blair, and from China, including President Jiang Zemin and Premier Li Peng, were on hand for the ceremonies reverting the colony of Hong Kong from British to Chinese sovereignty.

In spite of Chinese assurance of press freedom, some reporters were jittery because they had been warned to steer clear of some sensitive subjects—for example, independence for Taiwan or Tibet. The media already had started self-censorship and exercised its freedom cautiously. Most Hong Kong people believed that they still had access to objective information.

Legislation. The first task of the PLC after the handover was to deal with seven bills that had been rushed, without full discussion, through the pre-handover Legco's last sitting. At its second meeting, on July 16, the PLC succeeded in suspending the operation of the Hong Kong Bill of Rights (Amendment) Ordinance 1997, and of three pro-union bills. On October 29 the PLC abolished two pro-union bills that would protect union activists and give to employees the right to bargain collectively and amended the third pro-union bill in order to prevent union membership from using union fees for political campaigns. However, the PLC failed to freeze the other three bills—namely, the operation of the Harbour Protection Ordinance, the Occupational Deafness (Compensation Amendment) Bill, and the Employment (Amendment) No. 5 Ordinance. Throughout the month of July, some ousted legislators and union members organized marches to protest against the suspension of the bills.

The legality of the PLC was challenged in the Court of Appeal soon after the handover. However, on July 29 the three appeal-court judges unanimously concluded that the PLC was constituted legally because it was endorsed by the National People's Congress (China's parliament), and that Hong Kong courts had no right to overturn the PLC.

The Guangdong Public Security Bureau estimated that under the Basic Law—the SAR's mini-constitution—about 80,000 mainland children born to Hong Kong residents would have the right of abode in Hong Kong. The SAR government had to stop the influx of these "right of abode children" (ROAC) because they would create a strain on education, social welfare, and other facilities. Accordingly, on July 9 the PLC passed a new immigration law that requires the ROAC to obtain certificates of entitlement from the immigration department of the SAR, and attach the certificates to their one-way permits issued by the Chinese government before they are allowed to come to Hong Kong. The law was made retroactive to July 1, 1997, which meant that more than 2,000 ROAC who had entered Hong Kong illegally would face deportation. Some legal experts claimed that, although these children had entered illegally, their right of abode was guaranteed in the Basic Law. On October 9 the high court ruled that the new immigration law did not violate the Basic Law.

In August the PLC passed the proposals for the electoral system for the first elected legislature of the SAR on May 24, 1998. The elected legislature would continue to be made up of 20 persons elected by geographical constituencies, 30 by professional and trade constituencies, and ten by an election committee. The electorate for the professional constituencies will consist of groups and not individuals; hence the voter base will be reduced from about one million to 180,000 electors. On November 11 the boundaries for the five geographical constitutencies, to return 20 directly elected seats, were defined: Hong Kong Island, four seats; Kowloon East and Kowloon West, three seats each; and New Territories East and New Territories West, five seats each. The registration of voters was held in December, and the final list of voters would be published by March 15, 1998. A 424-member Election Council was formed in October to elect Hong Kong's 36 deputies to China's National People's Congress.

The Outlook. Many businesspeople in Hong Kong voiced fears that some democrats did not have Hong Kong's interests at heart, whereas some democrats charged that the business elite were interested only in their business and wealth. Despite the political wrangling, the SAR government was expected to survive and to maintain the vibrant economy of Hong Kong. The SAR may suffer a gradual erosion of autonomy, however.

China wants the policy of one country and two systems to work and wishes the SAR government to succeed because Chinese companies have invested more than $30 billion in Hong Kong. More than 70% of China's annual imports and exports were passing through Hong Kong, and about 60% of its $42 billion foreign direct investment in 1996 came from Hong Kong. Therefore, Hong Kong and China would be more integrated economically and would share the goal of building a vibrant economy in the Pearl River delta.

The United States now would play a more prominent role as the global monitor of Hong Kong's political and economic development because of its large investment of money and human resources in the region. In 1997 more than 1,200 U.S. firms and 88 U.S.-controlled factories were located in Hong Kong. In addition, Hong Kong's currency would remain pegged to the U.S. dollar.

DAVID CHUENYAN LAI, *Geography Department University of Victoria, Victoria, B.C.*

of China's exports were being produced by foreign-invested companies. Foreign investment had increased from a negligible amount in 1978 to nearly $150 billion in 1997. Were these exceptional rates of growth to continue into the 21st century, it has been estimated that China's economy would surpass in size those of both Japan and the United States to become the world's largest by 2040.

Although Chinese leaders were at pains to describe their economy as "socialism with Chinese characteristics," after 20 years of very rapid economic change there was very little in the economy that could be identified as socialist in any orthodox sense. At the outset of the reforms, the more than 900 million people living in China's rural areas farmed the land as members of regimented communes. Today, under a contract-leasing system, those who continue to farm do so as de facto landowners. And more than one third of the rural workforce has left farming altogether to take up employment in one or another of the more than 23 million factories owned by township or village collectives.

In the cities, what was once was virtually universal employment in state-owned enterprises has been supplemented with a rapidly growing collective and private sector. China's already overcrowded cities also have experienced an influx of close to 100 million rural residents who, taking advantage of the loosening of government controls, are immigrating to the cities in search of work.

These remarkable changes must be placed in context, however. China's population, while growing at a slower rate than in earlier decades, fast was approaching 1.3 billion in 1997. As a result, per-capita annual income still was very low, averaging less than $600 for the 30% of China's people who live in the city, and half that figure for the 850 million in the countryside. Moreover, some argued that efforts to slow the runaway growth of the economy in the late 1980s, accompanied as it was by crippling inflation, had been too successful, and that the Chinese economy was likely to experience a period of deflation just when accelerated growth would be needed to absorb the millions of workers who would lose their jobs as state-owned enterprises were closed or downsized. Finally, the World Bank report warned that the financial sector in China—seriously undermined by nonperforming loans, heavy international debt, mismanagement, and corruption—was ill-positioned to withstand the instability that currently beset Asian financial markets.

President Jiang's emphasis on the need to move decisively in dealing with the ailing state sector came none too soon. Some-

© Jeffrey Aaronson/Network Aspen

Since the late 1970s a system of personal responsibility has replaced collectivization on China's farms. Chinese farmers now are de facto landowners. Fruits and green beans are grown in the village of Lingnan in Hebei province, above.

Unemployed workers advertise their skills on a street in Shenyang, one of China's leading industrial cities. Although the official unemployment rate was approximately 3.5% in 1997, many Chinese had been furloughed. Underemployment was widespread.

where between one half and two thirds of the 100,000-odd state-owned enterprises were losing money, putting in jeopardy the jobs of somewhere between 50 million and 70 million workers. Although the official unemployment rate was only 3.5%, an additional 15 million to 20 million workers had been laid off or furloughed with substantially reduced wages.

Although a bankruptcy law has been on the books since 1987, the government has been reluctant to allow firms to go under, since that would result in even more urban residents being out of work. The solution proposed at the 15th Congress was to sell off the assets of all but a handful of the largest and most profitable state-owned factories to the workers in those factories. Workers would hold shares and elect a board of directors, and the "collective" thus formed would hold title to the factory and its equipment. Skeptics pointed out that this was less a solution to the problem of loss-producing enterprises than it was a transferring of responsibility for solving the problem from the government to the workers. Even if they managed to hold on to their jobs under the new ownership scheme, workers still would bear the burden of figuring out how to turn a profit so as to ensure themselves a decent wage.

Lifestyle. Alongside very rapid economic change have come substantial changes in the lifestyle of the Chinese people—particularly of those who live in the city. One of the important impulses to introduce market reforms was to increase productivity by introducing an effective incentive system. The incentives have been highly effective—too effective, some would argue. While worker productivity has increased substantially, a pervasive self-seeking individualism has taken the place of an earlier ideal of community-minded selflessness.

The close-knit family of an earlier era has been undermined by the pressures of two-career parents and the prevalence, at least in the cities, of single-child families. The high value once placed on education has given way to an instrumental view of schooling as merely a means toward the end of securing lucrative employment. One of the most pernicious manifestations of the new acquisitiveness in Chinese society has become rampant and apparently uncontrollable corruption.

In a setting in which the rule of law is only a distant goal, opportunities for extracting private gain abound and few are able to resist the temptation to take advantage of them. Extralegal fees, fines, and outright bribes were being collected by officials at every level. Favors that once could be secured for a package of cigarettes or a bag of fresh fruit now were requiring substantial sums of money or elegant gifts. And there seemed no end to the problem, since those entrusted to stamp out corruption at every level were themselves deeply corrupt. The result was a very serious undermining of public confidence in the government and the party that controls it.

Changes in the lifestyle of the Chinese people were by no means all for the worse, however. Housing, while still less than adequate in space and quality, was improving significantly for both urban and rural residents. The supply and variety of food available on farms and in city markets had increased substantially. Once-scarce consumer goods were available in abundance and were supplemented by imported products.

© Alistair B. Spooner/Gamma-Liaison

© China Features/Sygma

Members of a supervision bureau in Beijing distribute consumer-rights bulletins, left. In recent years the people of China have gained greater freedom to express their opinions. Meanwhile, an improvement in the nation's housing situation (above) was part of President Jiang's reform agenda.

© David Hartung/Gamma-Liaison

With China's economy growing at an annual rate of about 10% in the 1990s, consumer goods have become much more abundant. Although the nation's per-capita income is very low by Western standards, many Chinese can afford to purchase cars, televisions, and the latest in computers, right.

More important to the quality of life—and frequently overlooked by foreign critics of China's human-rights record—was the very significant increase in personal freedoms enjoyed by the vast majority of Chinese people. These included the freedom to change one's place of residence, the freedom to change one's employment, the freedom to express one's opinion on a broad range of issues, and access to a substantially expanded range of information and opinion. Whereas virtually every Chinese citizen once was enrolled as a member of a "unit" at his or her place of work or residence, this system was largely defunct and, as a result, the party-state had become significantly less likely to be looking over the shoulders of most people as they went about their daily lives.

Political Scene. Unfortunately, the quite remarkable economic and social changes that have taken place since the late 1970s have little or no parallel in the political system. With the exception of a very brief period in the early 1980s, when Deng Xiaoping

© James Z. Huang/Sygma

used a nascent pro-democracy movement to unseat his rivals, economic reform never has been accompanied by political liberalization. Indeed, during the 1997 party congress, and subsequently during Jiang's visit to the United States, the president expressed tight-lipped rejection of any move in the direction of political reform.

What explains this apparent contradiction? The answer is that the Chinese party-state cannot afford to take even the smallest step that would loosen its tenuous hold on the nation's society or that would bring about political instability. The party-state finds itself in this awkward position first because of the daunting array of extraordinarily serious problems confronting China in the immediate future—problems that would tax the capability of the strongest and most able of governments—and, second, because the capacity of the Chinese government is diminished severely and its capability is weak. The list of problems with which the Chinese party-state must deal in the immediate future begins with the financially ailing state sector and the pervasiveness of political corruption described above. Equally serious are the proliferating conflicts of interest among strong regional groupings and between regional and central authorities—conflicts that the central party-state is not strong enough to mediate or to control.

When the center has issued a regulation that is seen as running counter to the interests of municipal or provincial authorities, the most common response simply has been to ignore the regulation. Short of armed intervention, the center has few tools at its disposal to counteract this passive resistance.

Its lack of political legitimacy has rendered the central party-state dangerously dependent upon a strong military as the only force capable of restoring and maintaining order when push comes to shove. Some have pointed to the substantial budget increases accorded the People's Liberation Army each year as evidence of this dependency. In fact, when the small increments accorded the military during the 1980s and the exacerbating effect of runaway inflation during the same period are taken into account, the military budget has increased very little in 20 years in real terms. More telling was the situation in the spring of 1996, when China's response to Taiwan's first direct presidential election, which took the form of live missile firings in the Taiwan Strait, appeared to be directed exclusively by military, not civilian, authorities.

To this list of problems must be added the difficult task of feeding a growing population. This problem is best understood as a fraction—the numerator of which is food supply and the denominator the number of people to feed. Solving this problem involves increasing the numerator as much as possible, while simultaneously reducing the denominator. The one-child-per-family policy—now much modified, particularly in the countryside, where it encountered stiff resistance—has succeeded in slowing the growth of the population to just more than 1%, or 13 million births per year.

If addressing the denominator has proven costly in both financial and political terms for the party-state, the numerator—food supply—may prove even more intractable. Given population growth and changes in diet, it has been estimated that it will take more than 600 million tons of grain to feed the population by 2030. Not only is the population growing, but as household income increases, so does consumption of meat, poultry, and eggs. Grain production in 1996 reached the record level of 490 million tons and was likely to exceed that record in 1997. To

"The period from now to the first ten years of the next century is a crucial period in China's socialist modernization. During that period, China must actively promote fundamental shifts in economic structure and the mode of economic growth."

**New China News Agency
September 1997**

reach 600 million tons by 2030, production must increase by 4 million tons annually. But, with land being taken out of cultivation at a rate of more than 800,000 acres (324 000 ha) per year to accommodate the building of roads, railroads, factories, and housing—all of which, of course, contribute to economic growth, increased employment, and improved social welfare—conservative projections show a drop in grain output of up to 20% over the next 35 years, which would result in a grain deficit of more than 300 million tons in 2030.

Equally difficult is the problem of environmental degradation. The air in 90% of China's cities does not meet Chinese-government clean-air standards. Beijing air, on average, is 16 times more polluted than New York City air. Because soft coal accounts for three quarters of the energy used in China, China is currently the world's fourth-largest source of greenhouse gases, producing about 10% of the total.

More than one quarter of the nation's freshwater supply is polluted, and 90% of the water flowing through its major cities is impotable. While China has on the books a full set of environmental regulations, the regulations are impossible to enforce when they come into conflict with local economic-development interests. Moreover, they constitute a substantial set of unfunded mandates that local governments most frequently underfund or refuse to fund at all.

Under these difficult circumstances, it is no surprise that the party-state is loath to relax its tenuous hold on political stability. Such circumstances account for the unwavering domination it insists on maintaining over political dissidents, who either are held in the most appalling conditions of imprisonment, harassment, and torture or, when released—as was the case with the prominent dissident Wei Jingsheng in November 1997—sent into permanent exile.

"The China-U.S. relationship over the past few years can be characterized like the weather: it has its ups and downs. I think that, on the whole, relations are moving forward. But it is no easy task for the people of our two countries to really understand each other. If, through face-to-face meetings, our nations can deepen understanding, that will be a very important achievement."

China's President and
Communist Party General
Secretary Jiang Zemin
"Time" magazine
Oct. 27, 1997

International Position. Given China's extraordinary economic growth, its acquisition of foreign military equipment, and its expansive territorial claims in the South China Sea, the country is regarded on the international scene as a very significantly more important player than it was at the beginning of its era of economic reform. Far and away the most important determinant of China's foreign policy as the end of the century approaches is its interest in expanding its role in the world economy. Beijing's dominant goal is to be received into membership in the World Trade Organization, a goal it sees the United States as intent upon thwarting with the demand that the Chinese government clear ever higher hurdles. Beyond this, China seeks to be taken seriously as a world power. Issues of sovereignty and face loom large on its foreign-policy agenda.

The return of Hong Kong to Chinese sovereignty was a major achievement. Taking sovereignty over Taiwan, while infinitely more complicated to achieve, is Beijing's next major goal. It continues to fend off external assaults on what the party-state regards as "internal affairs"; the raising of issues of Tibet's religious freedom, of the human rights of China's dissident community, of the accessibility of the country's markets, of the transparency of trade and investment regulations, of the protection

Chinese troops moved rapidly into Hong Kong, above, after the colony reverted to Chinese sovereignty at midyear. Despite the numerous changes under way in China, the People's Liberation Army continues to play a key role.

of intellectual-property rights, of the recognition of self-defined boundaries around territorial waters—all of these quickly are elevated to the level of infringements upon Chinese sovereignty and occasions for the loss of face.

China has made limited progress in stabilizing its relationship with the United States in the wake of U.S. reactions to the events of June 4, 1989—when pro-democracy demonstrations were quelled at Tiananmen Square. It has settled its long ill-defined border with Russia, its large and troubled northern neighbor. It apparently has accepted Japan's newly elaborated security relationship with the United States. It has staked its claim to be taken seriously by its East Asian and Southeast Asian neighbors, and has proven its ability to assist in bringing some of its more intransigent neighbors—such as North Korea and Cambodia—to the international negotiating table. It takes its role as a world power seriously and insists that the world community take that role equally seriously.

And so China pushes forward toward the 21st century, with a rapidly growing economy, a substantially changing society, a stalemated political system, an intimidating set of problems demanding attention, and a growing assertiveness on the international scene, wishing at last to be taken seriously as a major player in world politics.

See also CHINA *in the Alphabetical Section;* OBITUARIES— *Deng Xiaoping.*

"...China and the United States share important interests that we can best advance by working together. But we also have fundamental differences, especially concerning human rights and religious freedom. I am convinced the best way to address them is directly and personally, as we did yesterday and today, and as we will continue to do until this issue is no longer before us."

U.S. President Bill Clinton
Oct. 29, 1997

Photos: © Terry Ashe/Gamma-Liaison (above); Archive Photos (right)

WHITE HOUSE SCANDAL | 25 Years After Watergate

By Robert Shogan

For 12 weeks during the summer and fall of 1997, the U.S. Senate Government Affairs Committee held hearings on campaign-finance practices during the 1996 election campaign, above. Twenty-five years earlier, a break-in at the headquarters of the Democratic National Committee had led to hearings by the Senate Select Committee on Watergate, above right, and the eventual resignation of Richard M. Nixon as president of the United States.

"I ordered that they use any means necessary, including illegal means, to accomplish this goal," President Richard Nixon confessed to his cronies in 1973 as the horrors of Watergate began to unfold. But Nixon then added: "The president of the United States can *never* admit that."

As a new batch of Watergate tapes made public on the 25th anniversary year of the unfolding of the worst political scandal in U.S. history revealed, the great Watergate cover-up that brought down the Nixon presidency was inspired by more than the desperate need to obstruct the wheels of justice. Powerful motivation also came from President Nixon's convoluted character, particularly what University of Wisconsin historian Stanley Kutler—who won a court battle to make the latest edition of tapes public—calls "Nixon's inability to confront the truth about himself."

A fuller understanding of presidential character could help to cast light not only on Watergate, but also on subsequent Washington scandals—the Iran-contra affair that tarnished Ronald Reagan's presidency and the various controversies surrounding the Bill Clinton presidency—that analysts believe have been a reflection of presidential-character defects.

Watergate. As Nixon himself later acknowledged, it was the cover-up more than the overt acts of Watergate that drove him from the White House in disgrace in 1974. And some scholars have suggested that if he early on had made disclosure of the White House's connection to history's most notorious bungled burglary, a forgiving public might have allowed him to salvage his presidency. But the Kutler tape transcriptions, included in his book *Abuse of Power*, make clear that whatever the legal and political barriers to such a course, Nixon's self-image and his identification with the presidency also stood in the way.

"You've got to be always thinking in terms of the presidency, and the president should not appear to be hiding and not be forthcoming," Nixon told White House counsel John Dean, who ultimately would abandon his efforts to shield Nixon from the scandal and become instead the most devastating single witness against his former chief.

Nixon had spent most of a political lifetime depicting himself as a paragon of middle-class values. Thus it was that even though he perceived the potentially fatal danger from trying to suppress exposure of the Watergate outrages—"Far worse than the facts here is the cover-up," he told top aide John Ehrlichman—Nixon continued to resist disclosure as a threat to his cherished reputation until the bitter end.

Watergate's origin, on June 17, 1972, was so bizarre that for a while it was dismissed as a Keystone Kops caper. Five men dressed in suits and ties were surprised in the act of rifling the office of the Democratic National Committee, their hands sheathed in surgical gloves and their pockets stuffed with sequentially numbered $100 bills. Their immediate purpose was to repair a telephone bug they had installed three weeks earlier.

Although investigators quickly established the connection of the culprits to the president's reelection committee, the White House steadfastly denied any involvement. Meanwhile, only a few days after the break-in, on June 23, 1972, Nixon had assented to a plan suggested by chief of staff H.R. Haldeman to derail the Federal Bureau of Investigation's (FBI's) investigation of the break-in by claiming that it would interfere with the Central Intelligence Agency (CIA). This taped conversation, when it became public, was the final straw in forcing Nixon to resign two years later.

Iran-Contra. If Nixon's stubborn self-delusion was a factor in his downfall, Ronald Reagan's tendency to shirk the managerial burdens of his job and to delegate authority was a major factor in Iran-contra. One part of this scandal was a scheme to trade arms to Iran in hopes of gaining the release of American hostages held in Lebanon. The other part was to use the proceeds from the weapons sales to support the contra guerrilla force fighting the left-wing gov-

About the Author. Robert Shogan, the national political correspondent in the Washington Bureau of *The Los Angeles Times*, is a long-time observer of the presidency. His books include *The Riddle of Power: Presidential Leadership from Truman to Bush* (1991) and *None of the Above: Why Presidents Fail & What Can Be Done About It* (1982). Mr. Shogan has served as an assistant editor of *The Wall Street Journal* and as a *Newsweek* correspondent.

© Lana Harris/AP/Wide World Photos

In 1987, Lt. Col. Oliver L. North, who had served as a National Security Council aide, was a key witness as U.S. House and Senate committees investigated the prime scandal of the Reagan administration—the Iran-contra affair.

ernment of Nicaragua, despite a U.S. congressional ban on such aid. Reagan professed unawareness of the details of the plan but a special investigative commission chaired by former Sen. John G. Tower (R-TX) put much of the onus on Reagan's "personal management style."

Clinton Problems. In the case of the scandals surrounding President Clinton, critics fault his tendency toward self-indulgence and his resistance to accepting responsibility when things go wrong. These traits became apparent in his 1992 campaign for the presidency—as evidenced by his response to the allegations of womanizing and draft avoidance that plagued his candidacy—and soon manifested themselves when he entered the White House. As the journalist Elizabeth Drew wrote in *On the Edge*, her chronicle of the troubled start of Clinton's presidency: "Clinton had a seemingly unshakable tendency to walk away from responsibility for things that had gone wrong....And worse, to put these things in self-pitying terms; that people didn't understand him...or that others did bad things to him."

In his first months as president, Clinton created an unnecessary headache for himself by dismissing out of hand veteran employees of the White House travel office and putting a distant cousin in charge. There also were allegations that First Lady Hillary Rodham Clinton had asserted excessive pressure to have the employees fired. The reaction to this episode, which came to be dubbed "travelgate," led to various inquiries, the rehiring of most of the dismissed staffers, and the reassignment of the president's cousin.

Other matters, particularly the Whitewater affair, were more serious for the Clinton administration. The Whitewater controversy stemmed from an investment the president and his wife had made in an Arkansas real-estate venture by that name back in 1978, shortly before he became governor. Partners with the Clintons in this venture were James B. McDougal, who also owned the Madison Guaranty Savings and Loan, a thrift that eventually failed during the savings-and-loan (S&L) collapse in 1989; and McDougal's wife, Susan. Clinton sought to dismiss the matter as nothing more than a failed effort to make a modest profit in real estate. But a subsequent investigation into allegations of mismanagement of Madison Guaranty, conducted by the Resolution Trust Corp. (RTC)—the federal agency created to clean up the savings-and-loan mess—raised serious questions. These included whether funds from the S&L had been diverted to help finance Clinton's 1984 Arkansas gubernatorial campaign and whether the president and Hillary Clinton had benefited financially or in other ways from improper management of Madison Guaranty by McDougal.

Suspicions were heightened by the seeming reluctance of the Clintons to cooperate with inquiries into the complex case. In January 1994, White House aides revealed that the Justice Department had subpoenaed documents concerning the real-estate deal from the Clintons, thus shielding this material from inquiries by Congress or the news media. In the wake of the ensuing uproar, Clinton—who previously had resisted calls for a criminal investigation—changed his mind

© Danny Johnston/AP/Wide World Photos

© Win McNamee/Reuters/Archive Photos

© Jeff Mitchell/Sygma

While in the White House, Bill and Hillary Rodham Clinton have come under fire for an investment they made in an Arkansas real-estate venture in 1978. An independent counsel was appointed to look into the case, now known as the White-water affair, and the first lady, near left, was forced to testify before a grand jury in 1997. Susan McDougal, extreme left, a partner of the Clintons in the land investment, was imprisoned after being convicted of fraud and conspiracy in connection with the case. Meanwhile, in 1994, Paula Jones, below, a former Arkansas state employee, filed a sexual-harassment lawsuit against President Clinton.

and asked Attorney General Janet Reno to appoint an independent counsel to look into his real-estate and financial dealings with McDougal. She appointed Robert Fiske, who subsequently was replaced by Kenneth W. Starr, a former Bush-administration official, after the independent-counsel law was renewed in 1994.

House and Senate inquiries into Whitewater led to the resignation of Deputy Treasury Roger Altman, the acting director of the RTC, because he had briefed White House aides on the progress of that agency's probe, but produced no clear evidence of illegality by Clinton-administration officials.

To help cover their legal expenses in the Whitewater probe, the Clintons established a legal defense fund, the first ever set up by a sitting president. Contributions also were used to help defray costs faced by the president from a lawsuit filed against him in 1994 by Paula Jones, a former Arkansas state employee. She claimed that then Governor Clinton had made sexual advances to her in a Little Rock hotel room three years earlier; Clinton denied these charges.

The Whitewater probe and the Paula Jones case both dragged on into 1997. As Starr moved into his fourth year as head of the inquiry, he told a federal judge in Arkansas that he had turned up "extensive evidence" of a possible cover-up and pressed his investigation of the unexplained delay in getting billing records for work done by Hillary Clinton when she was a private attorney in Little Rock. The records, which dealt with services the first lady had performed for Madison Guaranty Savings and Loan, supposedly had disappeared and did not turn up until two years after they had been subpoenaed.

The president's hopes that the Paula Jones affair could be resolved with a minimum of controversy were dashed in May 1997 when the Supreme Court, rejecting Clinton's claim of "temporary immunity," ruled that he is not shielded from answering questions under oath or from standing trial on sexual-harassment charges just because he is president of the United States. Jones rejected a settlement offer and a trial date was set for May 1998.

Meanwhile Clinton faced new controversies that arose in the election year of 1996. One was triggered by the disclosure that the White House had gained access to confidential files containing personal information about hundreds of Republicans. Although President Clinton called the incident, inevitably labeled "filegate," "an honest bureaucratic snafu," GOP presidential standard-bearer Robert Dole branded it a "dirt-digging expedition," and the matter was turned over to Starr's office to investigate. Of particular interest to Republicans was evidence that Craig Livingstone, the White House security official who obtained the files and later resigned, was hired at the recommendation of First Lady Hillary Clinton.

Campaign Fund-Raising. Even more serious was the furor over alleged violations of federal campaign-fund-raising regulations by Democratic Party and White House officials working for Clinton's reelection. At first, attention focused on contributions from foreign nationals and corporations, whose giving to U.S. campaigns is limited to foreigners who are legal residents of the United States and to companies with U.S. earnings. When it became apparent that these conditions had not been met in a number of cases, the Democrats began returning the funds they had received while denying deliberate intent of violating the laws.

The Republicans pounced on the disclosures. "I can imagine no greater danger than foreigners' trying to buy access to the government," House Speaker Newt Gingrich declared. The White House denied any knowledge or responsibility for any wrongdoing. And just before the election, in a much-heralded speech on campaign reform, the president proposed a ban on contributions to federal campaigns by noncitizens and by domestic subsidiaries of foreign companies—the type of donations that were the focus of the controversy over Democratic Party fund-raising.

Clinton had been too far ahead of Dole before the scandal broke for the controversy to change the outcome of the election. Nevertheless, many analysts said the fund-raising disclosures kept the president from getting the more-than-50% majority of the popular vote he sought, and also hurt Democratic efforts to regain control of the House of Representatives.

Moreover, in the wake of the election, new disclosures by the press, including *The Washington Post*, which had played such a significant role in exposing the Watergate scandal, kept the controversy alive. "Bill Clinton has personally raised campaign cash like no other figure in modern history," the *Post* reported. All through 1996, the newspaper disclosed, Clinton hosted monthly White House "coffee klatches" for substantial donors, and told his staff at one point that he wanted to meet more new donors. Rewards to contributors were doled out on a sliding scale. Those who gave $10,000 were

© CNN/AP/Wide World Photos

included in a roomful of diners with the president, while donors of up to $100,000 dined at a table with the president, although sometimes 30 people were crowded in. Big givers were asked to golf outings, appointed to honorary commissions, handed podium passes to the Democratic convention, or even invited to spend the night in the White House's Lincoln bedroom.

In their zeal to raise money, Clinton and his aides threw caution to the winds. One $20,000 donor who was invited to a White House Christmas party in December 1995 and was photographed at another event with Vice-President Al Gore turned out to be a convicted felon. And Clinton's visits with Indonesian businessman James Riady led to Republican charges, which Clinton denied, that he had let Riady influence his trade policy in exchange for political donations.

The best measure of Clinton's fund-raising success was in the Democratic National Committee's revenue from "soft-money" donors, many of whom were wooed by the White House. Unlike "hard-money" contributions, which are used directly to help candidates get elected and are limited to $1,000 per individual, soft-money donations, which are supposed to be used only for party-building activities such as issue ads rather than for promoting a specific candidate, have no limit. In the two years leading up to the 1996 election, the Democratic National Committee (DNC) took in $85 million in soft money, almost $20 million more than the Republicans, and nearly three times what the DNC collected in the 1992 election.

© White House video/AP/Wide World Photos

Late in the 1996 campaign and during 1997, questions about the fund-raising practices of the White House and the Democratic Party arose. "Coffee klatches" for substantial donors, which were taped by the White House, top, *and the activities of longtime Democratic fund-raiser John Huang,* shown above *with the president, were targets of the investigations.*

Sygma

Vice-President Al Gore visited the Hsi Lai Buddhist Temple in Hacienda Heights, CA, in October 1996, left. *A key question of the inquiry into campaign-financing practices: Did the vice-president attend a fund-raiser at the temple? The temple's tax-exempt status makes such activity illegal.*

© Dirck Halstead/Gamma-Liaison

Elaborately staged fund-raising dinners—such as the 1992 GOP one, above—long have been a tradition for both the Republican and Democratic parties. Incumbent politicians on both sides have been reluctant to change campaign-finance laws.

What was more, Bob Woodward of *The Washington Post* revealed that President Clinton himself had been part of what critics called a massive violation of at least the spirit of the law distinguishing between the uses of soft and hard money. During the campaign, the president personally had directed the use of millions of dollars of soft money for television "issue" ads, which—while they technically may not have violated the law— were intended to boost the president's image. By some estimates this artifice allowed the president to spend about $25 million more to help his candidacy than the ceilings provided by the federal election laws.

These revelations intensified the outcry for reform of the campaign-finance laws, something Congress had not done on a comprehensive scale since 1974 in the wake of Watergate. But proponents acknowledged they faced stiff resistance from lawmakers reluctant to change the rules under which they had gained office. And as the majority party in Congress, GOP legislators naturally were more resistant to change. "My job is to convince the Republicans they can fix the system and still be reelected," said Sen. John McCain (R-AZ)—cosponsor, along with Sen. Russell Feingold (D-WI), of the lead bipartisan reform proposal on the congressional docket.

Advocates of campaign reform hoped that hearings into the fund-raising controversy by the Senate Government Affairs Committee would mobilize public opinion to overcome resistance on Capitol Hill. They were to be disappointed.

Sen. Fred Thompson (R-TN), the committee chairman, who more than 20 years earlier had been a staff member on the Senate Committee investigating Watergate, started the hearings in dramatic fashion. He claimed that his investigators had uncovered evidence of a plot by the Chinese government "to pour money into American political campaigns," in order to "subvert

© Terry Ashe/Gamma-Liaison

On Oct. 7–8, 1997, former White House Deputy Chief of Staff Harold M. Ickes staunchly defended the Clinton administration's 1996 fund-raising practices before the Senate Government Affairs Committee.

our political process." This assertion got the public's attention but turned out to be a tactical error. Thompson never was able to substantiate that sensational charge, and the hearings soon degenerated into a partisan slugfest. Republicans accused the Democrats of trying to cover up the misconduct of Clinton and other party leaders. Democrats, led by Sen. John Glenn of Ohio, accused the Republicans of being more interested in slinging mud than in laying the groundwork for campaign reform. The Senate hearings adjourned in late October, and although Rep. Dan Burton (R-IN) continued a parallel investigation by the House Government Reform and Oversight Committee for a few more weeks, neither inquiry generated the momentum for which reformers had hoped.

© Joe Marquette/AP/Wide World Photos

Sen. John McCain (R-AZ), left, and Sen. Russ Feingold (D-WI) have cosponsored major campaign-finance reform. Their bill, with the provision to abolish "soft-money" contributions to political parties, became deadlocked in the Senate in 1997. Further action on the measure was expected in 1998.

Although the full Senate launched a debate on the McCain-Feingold reform bill, partisanship dominated on the Senate floor just as in the committee hearing room. Republican opponents of the McCain-Feingold bill, which was supported mostly by Democrats, countered with an amendment that would restrict donations from labor unions; the Democrats would not accept the amendment. The result was a stalemate. Senate Republican leader Trent Lott of Mississippi claimed that the Senate had not reached a consensus yet on how to deal with campaign reform and accused the Democrats of trying to divert attention from the "appalling" fund-raising tactics of the Clinton presidential campaign. The debate concluded with pledges by Lott and House Speaker Gingrich to schedule votes on the issue when Congress resumed in 1998.

But prospects for reform remained murky. Backers of change would face the same problems they encountered in 1997. And compounding the difficulties are federal-court decisions severely restricting congressional authority to regulate campaign spending, which the courts maintain is shielded by the 1st Amendment to the Constitution. Indeed, some scholars questioned whether any new legislation actually would result in a fairer system. "You are not going to stop the flow of money in American politics," claims University of Virginia political scientist Larry Sabato, coauthor of *Dirty Little Secrets*, a study of American political corruption. "So we should stop passing laws which encourage people and groups to use subterfuges."

If reformers were disturbed by the inaction on Capitol Hill, Republicans were at least as angered by the refusal of Attorney General Janet Reno to appoint an independent counsel to investigate whether President Clinton and Vice-President Gore had violated the fund-raising laws. Clinton claimed to be innocent of any wrongdoing and called upon Congress to overhaul the campaign-financing regulations.

GOP indignation had mounted in October when the White House released videotapes showing Clinton entertaining Democratic donors at White House coffees, months after such material had been requested by Thompson's committee. Although the tapes provided no clear evidence of illegality, Republicans charged that their laggardly release showed the White House's unwillingness to cooperate with investigators.

In deciding whether to appoint an independent counsel, Reno—in the face of impeachment threats if she failed to act—

Independent Counsel

Underlying the 1997 controversy over Attorney General Janet Reno's refusal to appoint an independent counsel to investigate fund-raising violations by President Bill Clinton and Vice-President Al Gore was the uniquely schizoid nature of the attorney general's job—the reason the office of independent counsel was created.

The attorney general is the guardian of the law, a posture that sets him or her apart from fellow cabinet members. But like every other member of the cabinet, the attorney general also is the instrument of the political will of the president, committed to the success of the administration and subject to dismissal at the president's pleasure. This inherent potential for conflict of interest was carved into the Constitution. But the controversies swirling around the Justice Department's massive limestone battlements ten blocks from the White House have heightened in recent decades, as the expanding reach of executive power has intensified public suspicions about the conduct of presidents and their cohorts, thus putting attorneys general on the spot.

© Dennis Cook/AP/Wide World Photos

"We have escalated the pursuit of executive malfeasance to a very high level," says Terry Eastland, former spokesman for Attorneys General William French Smith and Edwin Meese III; he attributes this attitude largely to the twin traumas of Vietnam and Watergate. "It's the modern temper."

It was during Watergate that the tension between law and politics that always has pervaded the Justice Department reached a breaking point. It occurred with President Richard Nixon's dismissal of the supposedly independent prosecutor, Archibald Cox, who had been appointed by then Attorney General Elliot Richardson to head the investigation of the scandal. Nixon's action touched off the "Saturday Night Massacre" that sealed his doom as president.

It also led Congress in 1978 to enact the first independent-counsel law. The purpose of this statute was to avoid a real or perceived conflict of interest presented by having the attorney general investigate administration officials. The law allowed for an independent counsel, operat-

ing apart from the Justice Department, to investigate some 50 officials of the executive branch. In accord with the act, the attorney general would conduct a preliminary investigation into charges of misdeeds by officials. If there then were grounds to continue the investigation, the attorney general had to ask a three-judge panel to appoint an independent counsel to pursue the case. An attorney general's decision on whether to seek such a counsel was final and could not be reviewed by the courts. A modified version of the act was reauthorized for five years in 1994.

During the Clinton presidency independent counsels have been appointed to investigate charges against three cabinet officers—Henry Cisneros, Mike Espy, and the late Ron Brown—as well as to look into the Whitewater affair, involving both Clinton and First Lady Hillary Rodham Clinton. As chief Whitewater prosecutor, Kenneth Starr during his first three years on the job obtained guilty pleas from nine people and convictions of three others who have gone to trial. Of these, only Webster Hubbell, a longtime con-

© Jeff Mitchell/Sygma

In 1997, Attorney General Janet Reno, top, refused to appoint an independent counsel to investigate whether President Clinton and Vice-President Gore had violated campaign-finance laws; and Kenneth Starr, above, at microphones, remained independent counsel looking into the Whitewater affair.

fidant of the president and a former colleague of the first lady—and once associate attorney general—was a present or former Clinton-administration official.

The independent-counsel law has come under fire from the beginning, with much of the criticism tinged with partisanship. Republicans tend to be against it when they control the executive branch, and vice versa for Democrats. Nevertheless, impartial criticism comes from lawyers in both parties. Benjamin Zelenko, a Democrat and former chief counsel of the House Judiciary Committee, has complained that the law amounts to "a confession that the Justice Department staff can't do their job as honest lawyers and would protect illegal behavior by the executive branch. I have never believed that." Republican Richard Thornburgh, attorney general under Presidents Reagan and Bush, says the independent-counsel law represents a "topsy-turvy approach" to law enforcement. "I always told my prosecutors to go where the evidence leads," Thornburgh said. "Under this statute you pick a target and try to find the evidence to make a case against him."

The ground rules give an independent counsel the opportunity to conduct unfettered, prolonged, and ultimately fruitless investigations, critics charge. They cite the Iran-contra prosecutor inquiry conducted by Lawrence E. Walsh, which consumed seven years before it finally was aborted by presidential pardons. It was in part for that reason that the 1994 reauthorization legislation put new controls on the expenses and conduct of independent counsels. And Whitewater prosecutor Starr has drawn additional criticism for risking conflicts of interest himself because of his insistence on maintaining a private legal practice even as he continued to serve as independent counsel.

To streamline the current independent-counsel law, critics suggest that the number of officials who now are under the jurisdiction of an independent counsel should be reduced to a handful, perhaps just the president and vice-president and a few key cabinet officers. They also recommend that the attorney general be given more discretion in deciding whether to refer a case for appointment. But whatever the refinements, public-interest lawyers maintain that the law needs to be on the books in some form to avoid glaring conflicts of interest.

ROBERT SHOGAN

focused on the question of whether fund-raising phone calls made by Clinton and Gore violated the Pendleton Act, an 1883 federal law prohibiting the solicitation of funds on federal property. The attorney general concluded that the calls made by the president were made from the White House residential quarters rather than from his office and, therefore, were not covered by the act. Reno concluded that Gore's calls were meant to raise soft money for the Democratic Party, not hard money for specific campaigns, and, therefore, also were not covered by the act.

In a statement on December 2, Reno promised that the Justice Department would continue to investigate wrongdoers. But critics charged that she had taken too narrow a view of the allegations, instead of looking at them as what Sen. Orrin Hatch (R-UT) called "a broad ethical question." And *The New York Times*, pointing to FBI Director Louis Freeh's disagreement with her decision, warned editorially that "demands for a counsel will persist, despite her [Reno's] desire to smother them."

Whatever the legal fine points, it seemed certain that one result of the latest in a series of presidential scandals had been to add to the already considerable store of public cynicism. A poll taken by *The Washington Post* in the summer of 1997 showed that even in the midst of economic prosperity, usually a harbinger of positive attitudes, three out of four Americans said that they did not trust their government or its leaders to do what is right.

THE NEW U.S. MILITARY

By Robert M. Lawrence

About the Author. Robert M. Lawrence is professor of political science at Colorado State University in Fort Collins, CO. He also has served as visiting professor of political science and as an affiliate of the Center for Space Law and Policy at the University of Colorado in Boulder. With arms control, the military, and defense policy as his specialties, Dr. Lawrence has written several books, including *Nuclear Proliferation: Phase II, Arms Control and Disarmament: Promise and Practice,* and *The Strategic Defense Initiative.*

The Cold War ended on Christmas Day 1991 when the United States' primary opponent in that struggle, the Soviet Union, disintegrated into 15 separate nations. Six years later, U.S. Secretary of Defense William Cohen announced a study to reconfigure the U.S. military establishment to meet the very different challenges of the 21st century.

The study effort, officially titled the Quadrennial Defense Review (QDR), was controversial. Part of the controversy resulted from the difficult task of peering into the future and accurately forecasting what the military threats to the United States would be, and then deciding how best to respond to them. Another part of the argument over the size and mission of the U.S. military derived from the fact that any national budget worth approximately $247 billion a year will generate strong feelings, some of them possibly selfish. Complicating the QDR process was the fact that both major political parties are supportive of a balanced budget and some tax relief, and that both goals impose limits upon federal spending, including that for defense.

Even though the Cold War is over, many in the United States feel that the nation must maintain a considerable military capability in order to fulfill its obligations as the world's sole remaining superpower. Just how large that capability needs to be, what it will cost, and exactly what responsibilities must be met formed the central questions the QDR was designed to answer.

The Threats. The QDR identified a number of contemporary threats against which the U.S. military might be required to respond. These included the possibility of a resurgent and expansionist Russia; a bellicose China; the so-called rogue states of North Korea, Iraq, and Iran; international terrorism from various sources; and the disruption of U.S. electronic-data systems. Particular threats associated with the rogue states and assorted terrorist organizations are from weapons of mass destruction (WMD) that are comprised of nuclear, biological, and chemical (NBC) weapons and electronic efforts to disrupt computer systems and databases.

In assessing the threats to the United States from now until 2015, Cohen noted a number of positive factors. One was that the United States is "dramatically safer than during the Cold War" and that there was little probability that the United States would be challenged militarily around the world by a "global peer competitor" such as had been the case with the Soviet Union during the Cold War. Further, he noted that it would be unlikely during the next ten to 15 years that any regional power or coalition would be able to gather sufficient conventional military force to defeat the United States once American might is mobilized and deployed to the region of conflict.

Peering into the future beyond 2015, Cohen observed that Russia and China each have the potential to become either a "great regional power" or a "global peer competitor" to the United States. However, he noted that the United States was building a partnership with Russia involving politics, economics, and security issues and that the North Atlantic Treaty Organization (NATO) had made successful efforts to integrate Russia into the "larger European security structure."

Regarding China, Cohen said that U.S. policy was to cooperate in areas of mutual interest and to try and influence Beijing to "act as a responsible member of the international community." He said tension between efforts to develop a modern market economy and the authoritarian political system could hinder the modernization of China's military establishment. In a muted reference to the possibility that China's neighbors might unite to contain aggressive Chinese action, Cohen said, "China's efforts to modernize its forces and improve its power-projection capabilities will not go unnoticed, likely spurring concerns from others in the region."

Summing up his view of the national-security future, Cohen emphasized that U.S. security rested upon two fundamental assumptions: "That the United States will remain politically and militarily engaged in the world; and that it will maintain military superiority over current and potential rivals." Failure to pursue these goals would result in the world becoming "an even more dangerous place, and the threats to the United States, our allies, friends, and interests would be even more severe."

U.S. Capabilities. In response to this array of threats, the QDR proposed that the United States maintain the forces to fight and win two major theater wars nearly simultaneously. "Such a capability is the *sine qua non* of a superpower and is essential to the credibility of our overall national-security strate-

"In the councils of government we must guard against the acquisition of unwarranted influence, whether sought or unsought, by the military-industrial complex. The potential for the disastrous rise of misplaced power exists and will persist. We must never let the weight of this combination endanger our liberties or democratic processes. We should take nothing for granted. Only an alert and knowledgeable citizenry can compel the proper meshing of the huge industrial and military machinery of defense with our peaceful methods and goals, so that security and liberty may prosper together."

President Dwight D. Eisenhower, Jan. 17, 1961

gy." The two regions where such wars could occur generally are thought to be the Korean peninsula and the Persian Gulf. In regard to the latter, Cohen was clear: "Access to oil will remain a U.S. national requirement for the foreseeable future."

To enable the United States to meet the challenge of fighting two major theater wars at about the same time, while reducing the costs of the military, the QDR proposed the following:

Army. The army would maintain ten active divisions and two armored-cavalry regiments. Reductions would include 15,000 from active units, 45,000 from the reserve, and 33,700 civilians.

© Win McNamee/Reuters/Archive Photos

U.S. Secretary of Defense William Cohen (left) and Chairman of the Joint Chiefs of Staff John Shalikashvili testified before the U.S. House Armed Services Committee regarding the Quadrennial Defense Review, a study of U.S. defense requirements for the post–Cold War era of the 21st century.

Navy. The navy would maintain 12 aircraft-carrier battle groups, and 12 amphibious-ready groups. Surface-combatant ships would be reduced from 128 to 116. The attack-submarine force would be scaled down to 50 from the current number of 73. Plans were to replace gradually the navy's current fighter/attack jet, the F/A-18C/D, with the improved F/A-18E/F model—up to a total of 548 aircraft. The personnel reductions would be 18,000 less on active duty, 4,100 less in the navy reserve, and 8,400 fewer civilians.

Air Force. The air force would maintain 12 active fighter wings, with eight wings in reserve. The F-15 fleet would be replaced gradually with F-22s, but the number would be reduced from the original 438 to 339. One hundred eighty-seven bombers would be retained. Personnel savings for the air force would be 26,900 active-duty personnel, 700 reserve, and 18,300 civilians.

Marine Corps. The marine corps would keep an active force of three Marine Expeditionary Forces, each of which is comprised of a command unit, a division, an aircraft wing, and a logistic-support group. Under the QDR proposals, the marine corps would be reduced by 1,800 active-duty personnel, 4,200 reservists, and 400 civilians.

Air Force, Navy, and Marine Joint Strike Fighter. Looking further into the future, the Department of Defense would procure 2,852 Joint Strike Fighters (JSF) for use in differing configurations by all three services. This tri-service plane would reach a maximum production rate of 194 planes in 2012. The JSF was said to be a more efficient use of resources than the development of three separate aircraft simultaneously, which the QDR stated would be "prohibitively expensive."

Nuclear Forces. Until the START II (Strategic Arms Reduction Treaty) treaty is ratified by the Russian Duma, the United States would keep its strategic nuclear forces at the START I levels, as mandated by Congress. These numbers were: 18 nuclear-powered Trident submarines carrying SLBMs; 50 peacekeeper ICBMs; 500 Minutemen III ICBMs; 71 B-52H jet bombers; and 21 B-2 jet bombers. Should the Duma approve START II, then the Bill Clinton administration was prepared to start negotiating reduction in the strategic nuclear forces in accord with START III guidelines.

Missile Defense. Protecting U.S. and allied forces against missile attack was one of the more technically daunting objectives discussed in the QDR. The problem was divided into three types of missile defense. Because of a cruise-missile threat estimated to emerge after 2000, the QDR called for increased emphasis on ways to shoot down what essentially are small and unmanned aircraft that generally are subsonic in their speed.

More demanding was the Theater High Altitude Area Defense, or THAAD, system. The objective of this program was to protect battlefield forces from ballistic-missile attack. The program has encountered technical failures that have caused it to be restructured and that "brought into serious question the program's ability to meet the 2004 target date."

President Ronald Reagan's Strategic Defense Initiative (SDI), or Star Wars concept, announced in 1983, has been downgraded over the years due to the extreme difficulty of building it. The effort now is called the National Missile Defense (NMD) program. Instead of protecting the entire U.S. population, NMD has a much less ambitious goal—to provide protection against a limited ballistic-missile attack that includes the launch of a few missiles because of human, electrical, or mechanical mistake or malfunction, or a small attack from one of the rogue nations. As noted in the QDR, the NMD effort would "remain a program with very high schedule and technical risk."

Reserve Components. Forecasts saw "no major power threatening the United States before 2010, and potential threats after that are very uncertain. Therefore, the need for a large strategic reserve has declined." Thus the QDR called for a reduction in strength of the U.S. Army Reserve and U.S. National Guard of 45,000 personnel. This would mean a reduction of 32% from Cold War levels. The smaller marine, navy, and air-force reserve units were reduced much less by the QDR analysis.

Joint Vision 2010. The QDR document "Joint Vision 2010" was developed under the supervision of then Chairman of the Joint Chiefs of Staff Gen. John M. Shalikashvili to guide the U.S. military establishment in its transition from an anti-Soviet force to one tailored for the dangers of the 21st century. Central to this transition was a concept called "Information Superiority," which is touted as an especially crucial component of what the Pentagon called the "Revolution in Military Affairs."

© Richard Sheinwald/AP/Wide World Photos

Today's U.S. National Guard frequently is called on to help alleviate the effects of natural disasters. Under the recommendations of the Quadrennial Defense Review, the strength of the National Guard would be reduced.

The seven facets of Information Superiority are referred to in the Department of Defense as C4ISR—command, control, communications, computers, intelligence, surveillance, and reconnaissance. The intent of the concept was that U.S. commanders in the future would have nearly real-time information not only on their own forces but on those of the enemy as well.

According to the Joint Vision 2010 study, there were five basic components of the evolving C4ISR capability. There would be a multisensor information grid providing knowledge of the battle space to both commanders and troops. Advanced battle-management capabilities were projected to allow use of globally deployed forces faster and with more flexibility than those of potential adversaries. Plans were for an information-operations capability able to "penetrate, manipulate, or deny an adversary's battlespace knowledge or the unimpeded use of his own forces." A joint communications grid would support communications among commanders. And defense procedures would be sufficient to protect the communications and processing network from interference or exploitation by enemy action. It was claimed that collectively, C4ISR would provide capabilities that would increase significantly "the speed of command, enabling forward-deployed and early-entry forces to take the initiative away from numerically superior enemy forces and set the conditions for early, favorable termination of the conflict."

Information on the location and movement of enemy forces would be supplied to U.S. commanders by the Joint Surveillance and Target Attack Radar System (Joint STARS). The 13 aircraft in the Joint STARS fleet would permit the round-the-clock coverage required in a major theater war. Should the United States be engaged in two simultaneous theater wars, it would be hoped that North Atlantic Treaty Organization (NATO) Joint STARS aircraft could be used as an augmentation force.

Preparing to Defend Against Asymmetric Challenges. According to the QDR, U.S. forces must be prepared to defend themselves against nuclear, biological, and chemical weapons; various types of terrorism; and information warfare. Concepts to be adopted featured the institutionalization of efforts to counter the proliferation of NBC weapons within "every facet of military activity," and the internationalization of such efforts as allies and coalition partners would be encouraged to "train, equip, and prepare their forces to operate with us under NBC conditions." Terrorism would be fought by increased training and the adoption of sophisticated detection systems. It has been predicted that a new form of warfare, information operations, would increase in scope and intensity. To combat such possibilities, the QDR called for increased efforts to obtain what is called "information assurance"—the protection, integrity, and availability of critical information systems and networks. Not content with merely protecting U.S. information systems, the QDR also called for development of means to disrupt an enemy's access to information.

Criticism of the Quadrennial Defense Review. Any program designed to transform the U.S. military from its huge Cold War configuration to one appropriate for the first part of the 21st century is bound to be criticized. So it was for the Quadrennial Defense Review.

An authoritative critique of the QDR was issued in May by the National Defense Panel, an external review group for the QDR established by Congress in the Military Force Structure Review Act of 1996. While crediting the QDR with taking "an important step down the evolutionary path that must be taken to reshape our military capability to meet the needs of the nation in the next century," the National Defense Panel expressed reservations. Most serious were questions about whether the two-major-regional-wars concept was a valid force-planning model, and a concern that the funding necessary for the QDR force structure and strategy has "more budget risk than is acknowledged by the QDR."

Later the National Defense Panel released a statement reminiscent of a statement concerning the military-industrial complex given by President Dwight D. Eisenhower as he left office in 1961. Eisenhower had provided perspective for the problem of correctly sizing the U.S. military by warning against the possibility of the military gaining "unwarranted influence" and power. In December the panel noted that maintaining the forces necessary for the two-major-regional-wars strategy increasingly served to justify the military's size and structure but not the nation's defense. As the panel downplayed the threat of

© Reuters/Archive Photos

Participating in peacekeeping operations has become a key function of the new U.S. military. During 1997, members of the U.S. military were training troops of the People's Defense Force in Uganda, left, and were part of the NATO-led force of more than 30,000 troops overseeing the peace in Bosnia, below. The Uganda soldiers were preparing to be part of a proposed African peacekeeping mission. In mid-December, President Bill Clinton announced that U.S. troops should remain in Bosnia beyond the mission's deadline of June 1998.

© J.B. Russell/Sygma

major wars, it underscored the threat from rogue states and terrorist groups. To meet the new dangers the panel suggested that a "transformation" strategy be developed to remodel the national-security establishment that was built for the Cold War.

A nongovernmental critic of the QDR was the respected Washington think tank the Center for Defense Information. In a report released in August 1997, the center charged the QDR with justifying much more military capability than is required now that the Cold War is over. The Center for Defense Information critique called for withdrawal of some U.S. forces stationed abroad with the expectation they could return rapidly if necessary. As the center's report puts it, "global reach without global presence" could be secured given the advanced warning of developing threats provided by satellites and other intelligence-collecting devices and practices.

Taking a similar view was the Government Accounting Office (GAO), Congress' funding watchdog agency. In a report released in October, the GAO said that the Pentagon could not afford all of the advanced weapons it hoped to buy and that "difficult decisions will need to be made about restructuring or terminating some programs."

> "The United States is the world's only superpower today, and it is expected to remain so throughout the 1997–2015 period."
>
> **U.S. Secretary of Defense William Cohen**

From a different perspective, there was criticism of the QDR by members of Congress who took exception to Secretary Cohen's proposals to initiate two more rounds of military-base closings. In fact, Congress refused to authorize the new rounds of base closures. Since such closures often have an adverse economic impact on their area, members of Congress suggested instead that the Department of Defense should seek monetary savings elsewhere.

A fourth criticism of the QDR was lodged by the Army National Guard, which was concerned that the 370,000 reservists would absorb more cuts in both their forces and funding. Active-duty army commanders worried that the reservists might not be trained fully for a quick response to hostilities.

Responding to the criticism that the defense secretary should reduce the Department of Defense's bureaucracy before cutting back on new weapons and troops strength, Cohen announced plans for staff cuts late in the year. Included was a reduction of his own office personnel by one third. Talking about a "revolution in business affairs," the defense secretary called for the introduction of modern business practices and information technology to the running of the world's most expensive military organization. Cohen said more of the department's business would be put out for private bid and that the Pentagon's utilities systems would be operated by the private sector.

For his part, President Clinton revised U.S. nuclear policy in November. In a Presidential Decision Directive, the president replaced the Cold War policy of planning to fight a sustained and all-out nuclear war with the Soviet Union. The new plan called for using the threat of nuclear retaliation from a downsized nuclear stockpile to deter rogue states from using nuclear, chemical, or biological weapons.

As the year ended it seemed clear that the process of transforming the U.S. military into one suited for the 21st century had begun, but that much work remained to be accomplished.

© Brad Markel/Gamma-Liaison

The Women in Military Service for America Memorial, located in Arlington, VA, was dedicated Oct. 18, 1997. The memorial recognized women's valuable contributions to the U.S. military throughout the nation's history.

WOMEN IN THE MILITARY
AN UPDATE

The dedication of the $21.5 million Women in Military Service for America Memorial in Arlington, VA, on Oct. 18, 1997, symbolized the continuing struggle of women to achieve acceptance and recognition in the U.S. armed forces. The memorial stands at the main entrance to Arlington National Cemetery across the Potomac River from Washington, DC. At the dedication ceremony, President Bill Clinton said via a videotaped message that the memorial "is a living reminder that we are all involved, men and women, when it comes to protecting America's security." He added, however, that this knowledge was "sometimes slow in coming." Perhaps the loudest roar of approval from the assembled crowd came when 102-year-old Frieda Greene Hardin, who volunteered for the navy in 1918, commented: "To those women who are now in military service, I say, 'go for it.'"

The memorial is the culmination of many years of discussion and nearly a decade of direct fundraising activity, led by retired Air Force Brig. Gen. Wilma L. Vaught. The memorial itself is composed of two parts—a fountain with a reflecting pool and a visitor's center depicting the exploits of U.S. women in the military from the nation's beginning to the present.

Since the American Revolution in the 1770s, some 1.8 million women have served in various capacities in the armed forces of the United States. In the nation's war in the Persian Gulf against Iraq in 1990–91, approximately 41,000 women served. But it has been only recently that the subject of women in the military has become a front-page issue of interest to the general public. Part of the attention now paid to women is due to a number of sexual-harassment incidents in the U.S. armed services brought to light in the 1990s, especially in late 1996 and during 1997. The other situation that has caused the public spotlight to be focused upon women in the military is the question of which jobs in the armed services are suitable for women, and which are, or should be, for men only.

Sexual Harassment. One of the most publicized cases involving charges of sexual harassment took place in 1991 at the annual convention of the Tailhook Association in Las Vegas, NV.

© Win McNamee/Reuters/Archive Photos

U.S. Air Force Lt. Kelly Flinn, left, was threatened with a court-martial in 1997 on charges relating to her affair with a married man. Air Force Secretary Sheila Widnall, above, said that Flinn, 26, would receive a general discharge rather than undergo the court-martial.

© Hagerty/Sygma

Composed of naval and marine aviators, the group took its name from the hook on the back of jet aircraft that engages arresting cables strung across the deck of an aircraft carrier and brings planes that are landing to a quick halt.

The Tailhook conventions had the reputation among those familiar with the navy as a place where the young pilots of the hottest jets, such as the F-14 Tomcat, "let their hair down" in rounds of parties. After the 1991 convention a female navy helicopter pilot, Lt. Paula Coughlin, made serious charges regarding the behavior of male pilots. Lieutenant Coughlin claimed that she and some two dozen other women, some of whom also were pilots, were sexually groped and harassed in other ways as they were pushed along a gauntlet of drunken pilots in a hotel hallway. The old tradition of "boys will be boys" suffered official rejection as information regarding the events at Tailhook became known to the public.

Reverberations of the Tailhook affair reached the top echelons of the navy in the Pentagon as charges were made that senior officers knew what went on at the Tailhook meetings and "turned a blind eye" to the goings-on. Secretary of the Navy Lawrence Garrett stated he had not participated in, nor

seen, the behavior being described by Lieutenant Coughlin. Nevertheless he left his position, writing at the time, "I hereby tender my resignation as secretary of the navy, effective immediately. In doing so, I accept full responsibility for the post-Tailhook management of my department." For his part, President George Bush stated he had "zero tolerance" for sexual harassment in the armed forces of the United States. Later, two navy admirals accused of mishandling the Tailhook investigation were retired from the service. Both claimed they were being treated unfairly. The inspector general

© David Hitch/Reprinted by special permission of King Features Syndicate of the navy who was assigned to investigate the Tailhook situation was reassigned to another position within the navy.

After the Tailhook affair, other instances of sexual harassment started coming to light. In 1993 and 1994, at both the United States Air Force Academy, Colorado Springs, CO, and the United States Military Academy, West Point, NY, the superintendents moved swiftly to punish male cadets involved in sexual-harassment situations that ran the gamut from groping to assault.

In 1997 the air force, army, and navy confronted a variety of problems arising from the increased presence of women in their forces. The nation's first female B-52 jet-bomber pilot, 1st Lt. Kelly Flinn, faced a court-martial on charges of adultery, deception, and disobedience. The matter was resolved out of court, however, when Lieutenant Flinn agreed to resign from the air force with a general discharge rather than an honorable discharge. A short time later, Defense Secretary William Cohen was criticized for following what some claimed was a double standard when he refused to disqualify Air Force Gen. Joseph Ralston from consideration for the chairmanship of the Joint Chiefs of Staff because of an adulterous affair in the mid-1980s. General Ralston later removed himself as a candidate for the Joint Chiefs of Staff position.

The army had far more sexual-harassment problems in 1996 and 1997 than did the other two services. Many of the army's difficulties arose in the context of the basic training being done at the Army Proving Ground in Aberdeen, MD. The story that emerged from courts-martial and from an investigation by the army itself indicated that male-female relationships in the military often mirrored troubled areas found in the general public regarding relations between the sexes. For example, there is considerable sociological research in the civilian field that suggests men exercising various kinds of authority, dominance, and control can use their positions of power to demand or extract sexual favors from women who are in an inferior situation. Often contributing to the power differential between such men and women is the economic insecurity of the woman, who may feel she must accede to the man's demands in order to keep her job or to be promoted to a better position.

The situation at the Aberdeen base appeared to be an example of what the civilian sociological research suggests. There the sexual-harassment

© Agence France Presse/Corbis-Bettmann

Sgt. Maj. Gene McKinney (above, center), the army's highest-ranking enlisted man, faced court-martial on 20 counts of sexual misconduct after six women publicly accused him.

cases involved drill sergeants who exercised considerable power over new female recruits. In fact, the army announced that the selection process for drill sergeants in the future would be changed to weed out potential drill sergeants who might be inclined to abuse their power over younger women recruits.

In January a criminal investigation began of Sgt. Maj. Gene McKinney, who at the time was the highest-ranking enlisted man in the army. As such, Sergeant Major McKinney was responsible for being the liaison between the 410,000 enlisted soldiers and the army's senior leadership. McKinney's problems began when Brenda Hoster, herself a sergeant major, reported that McKinney tried to grope her when the two were on official business in Hawaii. Later, five other women went public with accusations of sexual misconduct against McKinney. As the year drew to a close, he was facing a court-martial on 20 counts related to his conduct with women.

WOMEN IN THE U.S. MILITARY: 1950–96

FEMALE ACTIVE-DUTY PERSONNEL
(PERCENTAGE OF TOTAL FORCE)

	ARMY	NAVY	AIR FORCE	MARINE CORPS
1950	10,982 (2%)	5,193 (1%)	5,314 (1%)	580 (0.5%)
1960	12,542 (1.5%)	8,071 (1%)	9,326 (1%)	1,611 (1%)
1970	16,724 (1%)	8,683 (1%)	13,654 (1.5%)	2,418 (1%)
1980	69,338 (9%)	34,980 (6.5%)	60,394 (11%)	6,706 (3.5%)
1990	83,621 (11%)	59,907 (10%)	74,134 (14%)	9,356 (4.5%)
1996	69,623 (14%)	54,692 (12.5%)	84,814 (22%)	8,564 (5%)

Source: "Selected Manpower Statistics," Statistical Information Analysis Division, U.S. Department of Defense

© Les Stone/Sygma

A complicating and troubling factor in the Aberdeen cases, and the pending court-martial trial of McKinney, is race. The Aberdeen drill sergeants and McKinney are African-Americans. In the McKinney case, the defense attorney said that discrimination played a role in bringing charges against his client and that he intended to make that point in the trial, noting that white officers often are treated differently.

Late in the year a panel headed by former Sen. Nancy Kassebaum Baker (R-KS) gave its report regarding women in the military to Secretary Cohen. In addition to recommending more be done to protect women from harassment, the report suggested substantial separation of men and women during the initial periods of basic training. That step would bring the army, navy, and air force closer to the model followed by the marine corps. Cohen indicated that he would make a decision on the panel's suggestions by late spring.

Women in Combat. So far the U.S. armed forces, unlike the military establishments of other nations, have drawn a line prohibiting women from participating in direct physical combat. In 1997 this meant that women were not assigned to infantry, armor, and artillery units in the army and marines, but they were serving in support roles on or just behind the battlefields—as mechanics, truck drivers, technicians, cooks, and medics. In the navy and air force, women were flying helicopters and logistic planes, and also combat aircraft such as the F-15 jet fighter for the air force and the F-14 jet fighter for the navy. In such a context the potential combat they face does not rely upon brawn but upon brains and hand-eye

coordination. Women serve in many capacities upon naval surface ships. However, they do not serve on submarines.

The arguments against U.S. women participating in direct combat reflect American tradition, the physical differences between men and women, and—some would say—common sense. For example, there is the argument that women, the "gentle sex" as the saying goes, should not be exposed to death and injury on a battlefield or be trained to kill in such a context. A related perspective is that with women in combat, men might be less effective because they would be trying to protect their women comrades rather than focusing upon their primary responsibilities. Then there is the point about upper body strength—that women normally do not have the physical strength to engage in hand-to-hand combat. Worry also has been expressed about what could happen to American women who are captured and subjected to torture and to rape. The question has been asked—but not yet answered in the real world—would the U.S. public accept large numbers of women being killed and wounded in combat? Collectively these views, which are held by large numbers of both military personnel and civilians, amount to a modern expression of the historical view that men should do the fighting and women should do the child-raising and nursing.

Further, it has been pointed out that having young women in close proximity to young men out in field-combat conditions, where some of the norms and constraints of civilian life are missing, inevitably will lead to fraternization between the sexes that will be detrimental to the primary military mission. Additionally, it is said by some that sexual harassment is made much more frequent by conditions encountered by mixed-sex units in the field.

President Clinton's first secretary of defense, the late Les Aspin, was caught between members of the military and civilians holding traditional views regarding women in the armed services and the movement in the larger society to make positions, previously reserved for males only, available to qualified women. His response was to open up thousands of such jobs in the army and marine corps to women. As he put it, "We've made historic progress in opening up opportunities for women in all of the service....Expanding the roles for women in the military is the right thing to do, and it's also the smart thing to do." In a similar vein, Secretary Aspin opened up combat aircraft in the navy and air force and combat naval surface ships to women.

There were muted rumblings of discontent over Aspin's initiatives from the more traditionally minded, both in and out of uniform. As one retired airforce colonel said anonymously, "I don't want to ever be in a bomber that has a woman sitting in the left-hand seat," i.e., the pilot's seat. In the fall of 1994 a fatal accident involving a woman pilot of a navy F-14 jet coming in on final approach to an aircraft carrier off the coast of southern California again raised questions about the qualifications of women aviators. There was talk among naval pilots that the death of Lt. Kara Hultgreen was the result of the official effort to push women too fast into the new arena of high-speed jet-flying.

Nevertheless the policy has not changed. The clear implication of such talk was that women did not have "the right stuff" to operate an advanced jet aircraft or the killer instinct to survive and triumph in air-to-air combat. The empirical evidence needed for the final evaluation of such observations would have to wait until the next war. In the meantime, women began training to fly combat jets under Secretary Aspin's directives and were now integrated into operational combat units.

A further factor that has complicated the relations between men and women in the military is related to the physical differences between the sexes. That in turn is associated with what jobs women perform in the military. The matter came to the forefront in 1997 as male soldiers continued to complain that they must do more to meet physical-fitness requirements than women. For their part, army women and their supporters among the public note that in regard to upper-body strength—required, for example, to perform push-ups—there is in fact a physical difference between men and women, and the latter should not be penalized because of this difference. In October the army issued new physical-fitness standards that would take effect in a year. The standards were toughened a bit for both sexes, but women still did not have to run 2 mi (3.2 km) at the same speed as men, nor were they required to perform as many push-ups. Of course, there is one difference between men and women about which nothing can be done—the ability of women to become pregnant. Army policy in 1997 permitted pregnant women to stay in the service, but they were transferred to nonhazardous positions during that time.

The Future. Despite the scandals and questions raised about the role of women in the military, it is evident that women will continue to play a part in the nation's defense system. The recent scandals made the military branches more conscious of the problem of sexual harassment and forced them to take steps to correct it. At the same time, the recruitment of women, especially into the army and air force, did not decline but increased during the first months of 1997.

While no woman yet had been mentioned for membership on the Joint Chiefs of Staff, a number of women had moved up the command structures of all the services. For example, in 1997, Lt. Gen. Claudia Kennedy was the army's top intelligence officer; Marine Lt. Gen. Carol A. Mutter was deputy chief of staff for manpower and reserve affairs; and Air Force Maj. Gen. Susan L. Pamerleau was serving as commander of the Air Force Personnel Center at Randolph Air Force Base, TX.

ROBERT M. LAWRENCE

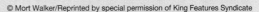

VOLUNTEERISM
A Renewed Call to Serve

By Marc Leepson

In late April 1997 former U.S. Presidents George Bush and Jimmy Carter joined President Bill Clinton in Philadelphia for the Presidents' Summit for America's Future—a three-day meeting to encourage volunteerism. While in Philadelphia, President Carter painted over a mural at an abandoned building to demonstrate the merits of working for one's community.

The subject of volunteerism in the United States received increased impetus in 1997 as Presidents Bill Clinton, George Bush, Jimmy Carter, and Gerald Ford held a three-day summit on the issue in Philadelphia, PA, in April.

According to national polls, more than 90 million Americans—from teenagers to senior citizens—spend some 20 billion hours annually helping their fellow citizens by doing some sort of volunteer work. Some 40,000 American civilians work full-time in volunteer national-service programs such as AmeriCorps, the Peace Corps, and VISTA. More than 80% of U.S. corporations sponsor volunteer programs; some 25% of corporations permit employees to take time off to do volunteer work.

These volunteer efforts vary widely. A large percentage consists of local activities sponsored by religious groups and by an assortment of voluntary community-service organizations. A report by the Corporation for National and Community Service—the independent corporation that has administered the federal government's domestic volunteer programs since 1993—

sketched the broad range of community-service activities. They include organizations "from hospices to hospital auxiliaries, from Junior League to Kiwanis, from the National Council of Jewish Women to the Urban League." Volunteers also serve, the corporation said, "as leaders of 4-H and Little League, Girl Scouts and Big Brothers, in food banks and homeless shelters, AIDS support groups and Twelve-Step mutual-help groups. Not to mention the informal help neighbor gives neighbor, worker gives worker, friend gives friend."

Historical Role. "The concept of community and the idea of service," President Clinton said in a 1993 speech, "are as old as our history." From the time the first settlers came to North America early in the 17th century, untold millions of Americans have taken part in many types of informal, nongovernmental community-service and mutual-aid activities. These include a diverse range of projects, from "the shared harvests of the early colonists to the shared burdens of the early slaves, from the barn-raisings and quilting bees of the westward migration to the city settlement houses of the great northward immigration, from the strong volunteer base of service organizations in every community in the country, to the committed participation of the civil-rights movement," as the Corporation for National and Community Service report put it.

Americans widely regarded community service as a civic ideal for the first time in the mid-1600s, when the first colonists overwhelmingly volunteered to serve in the various colonial (and later state) militias. As for civilian community service, the late 19th century was one high point—a time when the American public widely accepted the idea of "muscular Christianity," a sort of middle-class noblesse-oblige social philosophy. That movement spawned "character-building" youth organizations such as the YMCA and YWCA, which were founded in the United States in the 1850s, and the Boy Scouts and Girl Scouts, which were formed in 1910 and 1912, respectively.

Beginning in the 1930s, the federal government began sponsoring an array of community-service programs—including President Franklin D. Roosevelt's Civilian Conservation Corps (CCC), which began in 1933. During its nine years of existence the CCC sent some 2.5 million unemployed young men to rural areas to do conservation work. In his 1961 inaugural address, President John F. Kennedy called on Americans to "ask not what your country can do for you—ask what you can do for your country." With that in mind, Kennedy signed an executive order establishing the Peace Corps on March 1, 1961. By the end of that year, American volunteers were working on a variety of projects in a handful of developing countries. Participation in the Peace Corps peaked in 1966, when 15,556 volunteers and trainees were working around the globe. By 1997 some 7,500 Peace Corps volunteers were performing various developmental tasks in nearly 100 countries. The Peace Corps' domestic equivalent, VISTA, was established as part of President Lyndon B. Johnson's War on Poverty in 1965. Volunteers with VISTA (now known as AmeriCorps*VISTA) work in local antipoverty programs in all 50 states, the District of Columbia, and Puerto

About the Author. Marc Leepson, a freelance writer based in Middleburg, VA, is the author of the book *Executive Fitness,* which was published by McGraw-Hill. He has written for such newspapers as *The New York Times, The Chicago Tribune, The Washington Post,* and *The Baltimore Sun.* Mr. Leepson has been a contributor to this annual for more than a decade.

Rico. The National Health Service Corps, which began in 1978, is a federally financed effort for health-care workers, including doctors, dentists, and nurses. In return for working for four years in typically low-income rural areas, health-care workers in the National Health Service Corps receive salaries as well as funds to pay back school loans.

On the state and local levels, there are youth service-corps programs in more than half of the states. Most youth-corps programs receive funds from state or local governments and consist of volunteers (usually 17 to 23 years old) who work full-time in summer or one-year programs. The volunteers typically receive minimum-wage stipends for their efforts,

As chairman of the Philadelphia summit on volunteerism, retired Gen. Colin Powell, above, spoke to various youth groups across the United States. The former chairman of the Joint Chiefs of Staff asserted that the summit's main goal was to help at least 2 million children by the year 2000. Following the summit he formed America's Promise—The Alliance for Youth "to build a large coalition of business groups and individuals" to serve the nation's youngsters.

as well as post-service tuition credits. They perform many types of conservation and inner-city jobs, including working in homeless shelters, tutoring at-risk schoolchildren, and doing conservation work on public lands. Most of the programs also provide the volunteers with educational training.

Mandatory community service also exists in some U.S. school systems. Community service has been a graduation requirement in many private schools for many years, for example. And in recent years public schools in the city of Atlanta, the District of Columbia, and the entire state of Maryland have begun requiring that high-school students work a specified number of hours of community service before graduating. Maryland became the first state to make community service a graduation requirement in July 1992, when public high-school students were required to take part in 75 hours of public service before graduation.

1997 Campaign to Promote Volunteerism. Presidents Bush and Clinton have been strong supporters of volunteerism. President Bush in 1990 signed legislation creating the Points of Light Foundation, a federally and privately financed organization to encourage corporate and nonprofit volunteer community-service efforts across the country. That nonpartisan organization continues to work closely today with the Clinton administration's Corporation for National and Community Service. During his tenure as chief executive (1989–93), President Bush presented 1,020 Daily Points of Light Awards to individuals and organizations.

When President Clinton took office in January 1993, one of his first actions was to expand the White House Office of Community Service, and to use that office to lobby for an expanded national community-service program called AmeriCorps. That program, which was put in place in 1994, is administered by the Corporation for National and Community Service, the same group that runs the VISTA program; the National Civilian Community Corps; a college tutoring program called Learn and Service America (which currently works with more than 1 million students); and the National Senior Service Corps, which consists of some 550,000 senior-citizen volunteers working in three community-service programs: Retired and Senior Volunteers (RSVP), the Foster Grandparents Program (FGP), and the Senior Companions Program (SCP). AmeriCorps, which had some 25,000 members in 1997, has been characterized by President Clinton as "a peace corps here in America, to rebuild America." AmeriCorps' young-adult volunteers work on a variety of community-service projects. They receive an annual stipend of $7,500 and, when their tenure is complete, grants of up to $4,725 for each year of service to help pay for college or other types of educational or vocational training.

On Jan. 24, 1997, President Clinton announced that he and former Presidents Bush, Carter, and Ford would host a three-day summit meeting on volunteerism in April. The general chairman of the event—officially called the Presidents' Summit for America's Future—was retired Gen. Colin Powell, the former chairman of the Joint Chiefs of Staff. "Much of the work of America cannot be done by government," Clinton said when he announced the summit. "Much other work cannot be done by government alone. The solution must be the American people, through voluntary service to others."

The summit convened in Philadelphia on April 27. Thirty governors, more than 100 mayors, and some 3,000 government, business, religious, and community leaders and volunteers from across the country attended the event. They heard speeches from, among others, Clinton, Bush, Carter, Ford, First Lady Hillary Rodham Clinton, Vice-President Al Gore, and former First Lady Nancy Reagan—standing in for former President Ronald Reagan. The delegates also attended symposiums designed to spur a new national surge of volunteerism.

In 1997 some 25,000 members of AmeriCorps, a national community-service program set up in the early years of the Clinton administration, were working in a variety of programs. AmeriCorps volunteers may teach kindergarten—as in a Philadelphia school that was visited by First Lady Hillary Rodham Clinton, below, left—or stack wood in a needy rural area.

© Toby Talbot/AP/Wide World Photos

© Agence France Presse/Corbis-Bettmann

Colin Powell said that the summit's main goal would be to help at least 2 million children by the year 2000 by providing them with mentors, safe places to go after school, health care, job skills, and opportunities to volunteer themselves in community-service programs. To that end, Powell announced the formation of America's Promise—The Alliance for Youth, a follow-up organization to the summit that would work to "build a larger coalition of business groups and individuals."

The effort, Powell said, "is not a plea for more government programs. Nor is it a plea for just money. This is a plea for all Americans to get involved. This is the time for those who are doing well in this country to share more of their time, talent, and treasure with those who are in need, especially our most vulnerable citizens, our young people." Powell called on individual Americans to volunteer to be tutors in schools, to become mentors to at-risk young people, to increase gifts to charities, and to work with homeless shelters. "No contribution is too small," he said. "We have to help our kids one at a time." Powell and the other summit leaders also made strong pitches for American corporations to set up or expand volunteer programs for their employees.

Corporate America has responded to the call to serve. The Maxwell House Coffee Company joined Habitat for Humanity, a Georgia-based charitable organization, in launching BUILD A HOME AMERI-CA. The national volunteer initiative sought to build 100 homes for 100 families in 100 weeks.

More than 200 corporations and nonprofit groups responded by announcing new or expanded volunteer and charitable programs. LensCrafters, for example, pledged to provide free vision care to 1 million people, primarily children, by the year 2003. Honeywell, Inc., said it would encourage 8,000 employee volunteers to serve as mentors to elementary schoolchildren, 4,000 volunteers to work with the Habitat for Humanity charitable group that builds affordable housing, and 1,000 retiree volunteers to work in several different programs involving children.

The Maxwell House Coffee Company

AT&T pledged $150 million to connect 110,000 public and private elementary and secondary schools to the Internet. IBM, in conjunction with United Way of America and Ameri-Corps*VISTA, announced that it would provide computer equipment to some 2,000 community, day-care and senior-citizen centers by the year 2001. IBM volunteers would provide training for the new hardware. Kimberly-Clark announced a $2 million program to build 37 playgrounds around the nation in which employee volunteers would help with the actual construction work. The National Restaurant Association announced a plan to lobby 33,000 restaurants nationwide to help educate young people and provide jobs to those on welfare.

Support and Criticism. The summit and the new national push for volunteerism were not without critics. Several thousand demonstrators showed up in Philadelphia, for example, mostly to protest recent cutbacks in federal welfare programs. "The summit is all hoopla and propaganda, a great photo op. Charity and volunteerism, however noble, can't make up the difference in damage caused by the new welfare legislation," said Brian Becker of the National People's Campaign, a nonprofit group set up to counter the Philadelphia summit. "What I fear is the perception that these companies, or the public as a whole, can take the place of radically reduced government assistance," said Liz Krueger, associate director of New York City's Community Food Resource Center.

Summit organizers said that the push for new volunteer efforts is not designed as a substitute for the lower federal commitment to the poor that came in 1996 with large-scale revisions in the nation's federal welfare laws. Colin Powell said that arguments that the new push for volunteers is designed to substitute for governmental assistance to disadvantaged Americans were "nonsense." Before the summit he said: "There is no replacement for government help. We're partners. This is not a bipartisan effort; it's nonpartisan." "It's not either/or," added Michigan Gov. John Engler, a strong proponent of the federal and state welfare-reform measures that in recent years have reduced government's role greatly. "In many ways, the challenge for government is to get out of the way or to be a supportive partner in the back seat, not to be up front driving, and let the solutions develop. Because they will develop in [places such as] Oklahoma, Michigan, and Philadelphia."

Other critics contended that many of the corporations and nonprofit-group volunteer programs announced in April were either not new or had been planned well before the volunteer summit. The "vast majority of the commitments," *U.S. News & World Report* said in its May 12 issue, "aren't really new. Most are expansions of existing programs, and many are initiatives that companies already were undertaking—or planned to." Stuart Shapiro, the summit's chief executive officer, pointed out that while many corporations had drawn up volunteer plans before the summit, a large number of corporations increased their volunteer efforts significantly due to lobbying from the summit's organizers. "I think most corporations are doing something already," Shapiro said. "It's a matter of scale and focus."

"We challenge all the adults in America to engage in citizen service, another way of doing a good turn."

**President Bill Clinton
July 30, 1997**

"There are 15 million young Americans in need, and we should not be satisfied until we have touched the life of every one."

**Retired Gen. Colin Powell
April 27, 1997**

© Greg Lovett/"The Palm Beach Post"

Walkathons to raise funds for favorite charities have become a trend in the United States.

A Call to Give

Ted Turner, the Atlanta-based media and sports entrepreneur, announced on Sept. 18, 1997, that he would donate $1 billion to the United Nations—$100 million a year for the next ten years—for humanitarian and development activities. In announcing the bequest, Turner urged other wealthy individuals to follow suit. In all, Turner's bequest, one of the largest charitable gifts in U.S. history, shed light on a not widely known but significant section of the American social fabric—charitable giving by individuals, foundations, and businesses and corporations.

In 1996, Americans donated some $150.7 billion to charitable causes. Charitable giving increased about 5% in 1996, compared with the previous year. One reason for the increase was a healthy economy and a booming Wall Street. Some 80% of the total donated came from individual donors; nearly 70% of households made charitable contributions. The money went to churches and other religious groups, educational institutions, hospitals and other health-care providers, human-services organizations, and arts, cultural, and humanities groups.

The nation's 40,000 charitable foundations are required legally to distribute 5% of their assets over five years. With increased assets due to the meteoric rise in financial markets, foundations have had more money to give away. In 1996 the largest foundations increased giving by 16%. Analysts expected that trend to continue in 1997.

In 1996 the Ford Foundation led foundation givers, providing some $348 million in grants. Other large foundation givers included the Robert Wood Johnson Foundation, the W.K. Kellogg Foundation, the Pew Charitable Trusts, the Lilly Endowment, the J.D. & C.T. MacArthur Foundation, the Atlantic Foundation and Trust, and the Andrew W. Mellon Foundation. The largest corporate giver was IBM, which donated some $93 million in fiscal year 1996.

As for individuals, Kathryn Albertson, a supermarket heir, gave $660 million to her own foundation in 1997. The list of other large individual philanthropists included Bill Gates of Microsoft Corp. and his wife, Melinda Gates; Roberto Goizueta of the Coca-Cola Co.; Raymond Nasher, a real-estate developer; Robert H. Dedman, a sales executive, and his wife, Nancy Dedman; and Eugene M. Lang, an international businessman. Much of the money from large benefactors went to foundations and to colleges and universities throughout the nation.

Investing in nonprofit groups' business ventures has become a trend in large-scale philanthropy. For example, the Chevron Corp. has donated a gas station in Oakland, CA, to the National Association for the Advancement of Colored People (NAACP); the organization has begun running the business and supporting its programs with the profits.

MARC LEEPSON

In the three months following the summit, several large corporations announced new community-service programs. The Coca-Cola Company put forward a plan that called for spending tens of millions of dollars, mainly to train teenage mentors. The Post Cereal Company in June donated 100,000 boxes of cereal to Second Harvest, a hunger-relief agency. Post, a division of Philip Morris' Kraft Foods, also ran a series of television advertisements that month asking consumers to donate food to local food banks in grocery bags the company distributed in newspapers throughout the country.

In July the Maxwell House Coffee Company, also a division of Kraft, announced plans to use employee volunteers to help build 100 houses in 100 days in a joint venture with Habitat for Humanity. The company also said it would donate $2 million to Habitat for Humanity in the next two years and would make a series of television commercials calling on Americans to volunteer to help the organization. The first house was scheduled to be built in Mississippi in November. The 100th was to be completed early in the spring of 1998.

Colin Powell predicted that many more corporations would be putting similar efforts into effect in the future. After the Philadelphia summit, Powell began spending one day a week in his role as the head of America's Promise—the Alliance for Youth, mainly lobbying corporate boards to institute community-service programs. President Clinton spoke out periodically following the summit, urging corporations, nonprofit groups, and individuals to get involved in volunteer activities. On July 30, for example, he made those points in an address to the National Boy Scout Jamboree in Fort A.P. Hill, VA. "I ask all of you to help spread the word about good turns," he said. "Please encourage your classmates and your friends to join you in committing to community service. If every young person in America would give back to their community in the way you do, just imagine what we could do." The Boy Scouts of America, following the April summit, had pledged to provide 200 million hours of community service through the year 2000.

Will the current campaign to boost volunteerism be a success? One way to measure, said Oklahoma Gov. Frank Keating, will be to review social-welfare statistics in five years. "We can measure it through statistics," he said. "Has the level of violence gone down? Has drug abuse gone down? Are fewer kids dropping out of school? Are there fewer out-of-wedlock births?"

© Jonathan Kirn/Gamma-Liaison

Tutoring students and coaching a Little League baseball team are among the more popular ways Americans choose to volunteer.

© Dick Spahr/Gamma-Liaison

The Growing Popularity of

COSMETIC SURGERY

By Jenny Tesar

....

"How marvelous you look!
You must have had a wonderful vacation!"

....

Nowadays, that refreshed, rested appearance associated with a relaxing vacation is just as likely to result from a trip to a cosmetic surgeon. Record numbers of Americans—instead of spending their money on ski slopes or tropical islands—are paying to have wrinkles smoothed, faces lifted, tummies flattened, love handles deflated, thighs slimmed, calves enhanced, and varicose veins removed.

In part, they are doing this because of vanity. In part, it is because of the premium today's culture places on youth—an emphasis that affects not only actors' box-office receipts but also the ability of older workers to compete in the world of business. In part, the lessening stigma associated with cosmetic surgery has contributed to its increased popularity. And in part, the cost of cosmetic procedures has declined, making them affordable to people in all walks of life. The tabloids may provide details of movie stars and other celebrities who look rejuvenated after cosmetic surgery, but the number of such patients is dwarfed by the many secretaries, engineers, teachers, truck drivers, and other "ordinary folk" who go under the knife.

People of almost all ages may be appropriate candidates for specific surgeries. Surgery to correct protruding ears is performed on children as young as age 5. More than 10% of "nose jobs" are done on adolescents. At one time, procedures such as face-lifts were the domain of wealthy dowagers. But today, most

About the Author. Jenny Tesar is a freelance writer based in Bethel, CT, who specializes in a wide variety of topics involving medicine and health, computers, and science, generally. Ms. Tesar has written numerous books, including series for children on the environment, the world's wildlife, and—most recently—space exploration. She began her career as a high-school science teacher.

cosmetic surgery is done on people between the ages of 35 and 50. Another change has been the growing percentage of male patients. Some 20 years ago, only 1% of cosmetic-surgery patients were males. Today, increasingly health- and body-conscious, males account for approximately 40% of the patients. They undergo many of the same procedures as women—such as eyelid lifts to eliminate a tired look and liposuction to create firm buttocks. In addition, there are operations unique to men, including surgery to enlarge and lengthen the penis.

Most people who have cosmetic surgery are not asking for drastic changes, just for subtle improvements. They do not necessarily want other people to realize they have had cosmetic surgery, though they do want people to notice that they look terrific. If those people think it is because of a relaxing vacation, a new hairdo, or different cosmetics, that is fine.

New, Improved Techniques. Cosmetic surgery is a branch of plastic surgery, a term derived from the Greek word *plastikos*, meaning "fit for molding." The specialty of plastic surgery also encompasses reconstructive surgery, which treats birth defects, such as cleft palates; injuries sustained in accidents and wars; and changes caused by disease, such as breast loss as a result of cancer.

Plastic surgery traces its origins back thousands of years. Around 400 B.C., the Hindu surgeon Sushruta used cheek tissue to reconstruct noses and earlobes, and in the 3rd century A.D., Chinese surgeons repaired cleft lips. But Gaspare Tagliacozzi of Bologna, Italy, is considered the father of modern plastic surgery. During the 16th century, he attracted patients from throughout Europe, even though he was criticized fiercely because he "meddled with the will of God." He used arm tissue to reconstruct the tips of noses, which frequently were damaged in sword fights. He also removed a prominent hump from the nose of a famous duke, thereby restoring the man's peripheral vision. In 1597 he published the first textbook of plastic surgery, *De Curtorum Chirurgia*.

Beginning with the Napoleonic Wars, injuries suffered on battlefields were the main impetus for improved techniques. Military surgeons experimented with treating burns, reconstructing faces, and creating prosthetic devices. Progress in a broad range of other medical fields, such as the introduction of anesthetics in the 1800s and the discovery of antibiotics in the 20th century, expanded surgeons' successes and the range of procedures that were possible. Surgery for purely aesthetic purposes was introduced to the United States in 1887 by a

© Hank Morgan/Photo Researchers, Inc.

The computer now plays a major role in cosmetic surgery. Steven Pieper, above, of Dartmouth University has developed the computer-aided plastic-surgery simulator, which uses a three-dimensional scan of a patient's face. The surgeon can indicate where the incision will be placed, and the program calculates how the skin will fit together after healing. Alternative approaches then are available to the doctor and patient prior to final decisions regarding a procedure.

Rochester, NY, surgeon, who operated within the nose to improve the organ's appearance. The American Society of Plastic and Reconstructive Surgeons (ASPRS), which in the late 1990s has about 5,000 members—97% of the board-certified plastic surgeons in the United States, was founded in 1931. The American Board of Plastic Surgery (ABPS), a specialty board responsible for certifying plastic surgeons, was founded in 1937.

Cosmetic-surgery techniques continue to improve. In the past, a face-lift involved pulling up only the skin, creating a frozen, stretched look with a high hairline, raised eyebrows, and pulled-up cheeks. Today, plastic surgeons are able to produce natural-looking results by working not only on the skin tissue but also on the underlying muscles and fat. The endoscope—a long, flexible, lighted tubular instrument that can be inserted into the body through small incisions—allows surgeons to vaporize and cut internal structures, and results in less scarring and speedier recoveries than does the use of traditional scalpels. The introduction of liposuction in the 1980s and laser skin resurfacing in the 1990s has revolutionized surgeons' ability to recontour the body and resurface the face.

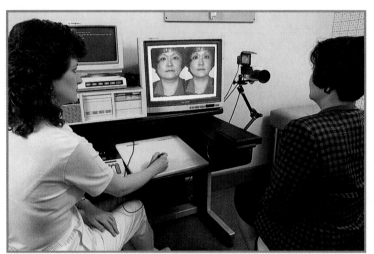

© Bachmann/Photo Researchers, Inc.

An image maker offers a person contemplating plastic surgery a preview of the results of such procedures as a face-lift.

In 1996 members of ASPRS performed more than 1.9 million cosmetic and reconstructive procedures. Liposuction was the most popular cosmetic procedure (109,353), followed by breast augmentation (87,704) and eyelid surgery (76,242). Millions of additional cosmetic procedures were performed by physicians who were not members of ASPRS. The American Academy of Cosmetic Surgery (AACS), formed in 1985 and representing approximately 1,360 physicians who perform cosmetic surgery, estimates that in 1996 a total of more than 3.3 million cosmetic procedures were done in the United States. Most popular among women were chemical peel, sclerotherapy (vein treatment), liposuction, laser resurfacing, and eyelid surgery. Among men, the most popular were hair transplantation, chemical peel, liposuction, sclerotherapy, and dermabrasion (the scraping of top layers of skin).

The Informed Consumer. For a cosmetic-surgery patient, the choosing of a physician is probably the most important factor in determining the results of such surgery. Many surgeons specialize and work almost exclusively in one type of procedure. If a patient wants a nose job, it is wiser to choose a surgeon who already has performed numerous such operations rather than one who specializes in liposuction. In recent years, many physicians whose specialties are far removed from cosmetic surgery have moved into the market, primarily for economic reasons. By doing some research, the informed consumer can feel confident that his or her physician is well trained and experienced in performing specific cosmetic procedures. Another assurance is if the physician is certified by the American Board of Cosmetic Surgeons.

A good cosmetic surgeon has been practicing cosmetic surgery for at least five years, welcomes questions about his or her background, and is more than willing to provide before and after photos of a similar procedure performed on another patient. It also is recommended that the prospective patient obtain referrals from his or her personal physician, from hospitals, and from friends who have undergone similar surgery successfully. Then the person may check with ASPRS, AACS, or the American Society for Aesthetic Plastic Surgery (ASAPS)—an organization dedicated exclusively to research and education in cosmetic surgery—to learn a surgeon's accreditation. If the operation is to be done in an outpatient facility or in a doctor's office, the patient also may wish to make sure that the place is accredited properly.

In most cases, cosmetic surgery is not covered by medical insurance. This means that patients pay the costs out of their own pockets. Furthermore, they usually are expected to pay in advance. The physicians do not have to hassle with insurers, health-maintenance organizations (HMOs), or Medicare auditors.

The best candidates for cosmetic surgery are those who have realistic expectations about what results can be achieved. Ethical physicians will not accept candidates who expect surgery to bring romance or a new lifestyle. Rather, they want candidates who are emotionally stable and in good physical health, and who do not expect the unattainable, but rather think that an improved appearance will raise their self-esteem and self-confidence. What constitutes an improvement may be obvious—recontouring a hawk nose or making ears lie flatter against the sides of the head. In many cases, though, improvements are much more subjective: What one person feels is unattractive often is unnoticeable or irrelevant to others.

Prior to any cosmetic surgery it is important for the patient to consult with physicians who meet the credentials check. The patient should discuss what changes he or she would like to see. This will help the physician determine exactly what procedure will give the best results. For instance, a person who believes his or her nose is too large may have an average-size nose but an undersized or recessed chin. Instead of a nose job, the doctor may recommend a chin implant. Prospective patients sometimes arrive at the doctor's office with photographs of people who have features they would like to have. As beauty trends change, so do the photographs. In the 1960s, a woman who wanted her nose reshaped would ask for a nose similar to that of Debbie Reynolds; today, she would be more likely to ask for a nose like that of Sharon Stone. In the early 1990s, women sought collagen injections to obtain puffy lips resembling those of Kim Basinger; today, they want full but not puffy lips, like those of Claudia

(Continued on page 73.)

Editor's Note: Members of the American Academy of Cosmetic Surgery reviewed this article for factual accuracy. The author and editors are most grateful to the Academy for its assistance.

Breast Surgery. Several types of cosmetic surgery are available for people who wish to change the shape or size of their breasts. Breast augmentation, to create larger breasts, involves the surgical implantation of sacs filled with saline solution or some other fluid. (Silicone, once commonly used, now is avoided because of concerns that it may pose health risks.) Women with large, pendulous breasts can have breast-reduction surgery, in which some of the breast tissue is removed and the nipple is moved to a new position appropriate for the newly contoured breast. Each year, thousands of men also undergo breast-reduction surgery or liposuction to treat gynecomastia (the excessive development of breasts in the male); the procedure removes excessive breast tissue that develops during adolescence but then fails to disappear naturally. Women who have sagging breasts can opt for a mastopexy, or breast lift. In this procedure, which has become more popular in the 1990s, excess skin is removed and the nipple is moved higher on the breast.

EYELID SURGERY

Chemical Peel. In this procedure, the outer layer of the skin is treated chemically with a caustic acid to erase acne scars, pigmented areas, and wrinkling such as smile lines (fine lines around the upper and lower lips and forehead) and lines around eyelids (crow's-feet). Several different chemicals are used, with the choice depending on the depth of the wrinkles to be removed. The most superficial peel uses alpha hydroxy acids such as glycolic acid. It frequently is applied by nurses or aestheticians rather than doctors; for the best results, several applications are necessary. Several treatments with trichloroacetic acid, which penetrates deeper, also may be needed. Phenol peels are the strongest—they penetrate most deeply and can get rid of deeper wrinkles; they also lighten the skin and are used to remedy hyperpigmentation; only one application is needed. However, there have been reports that phenol peels cause heart irregularities in some patients. The improved appearance resulting from mild peels may last several months; stronger peels have longer-term effects.

NOSE RESHAPING

Collagen Injections. An alternative to laser resurfacing; dermabrasion, which employs an electrical instrument to scrape away the outer

PROCEDURES

layers of the skin; and chemical peels, collagen injections "plump up" superficial wrinkles and depressions such as acne pits. The injections also are used to add fullness to lips. Collagen is a natural protein found in skin, bones, and other body tissues of humans and animals. Using a syringe with a thin needle, the surgeon injects small amounts of collagen purified from cowhide directly into a wrinkle or sunken area. The results are temporary, often lasting less than a year. The collagen gradually dissolves and additional injections are needed.

Eyelid Surgery. Known as blepharoplasty, this surgery creates a more youthful appearance by removing bags, folds, and sags that form around the eyes. The benefits typically last for several years.

HAIR TRANSPLANT OR RESTORATION

Face-lift. A face-lift, or rhytidectomy, tightens facial and neck skin and muscles, removing unsightly folds and other excess skin and eliminating some of the sagging that is a natural result of aging. In the traditional method, lengthy incisions are made inside the patient's hairline on both sides of the face; another incision may be made under the chin. The endoscopic technique involves several tiny incisions hidden within the scalp. Eyelid surgery or a forehead lift—which elevates the eyebrows and smooths out frown lines and forehead wrinkles—often is done in conjunction with a face-lift. Among older patients, rhinoplasty to correct a drooping nose may accompany a face-lift. The effects of a face-lift typically last for five to ten years, though signs of aging may begin to appear after the second year.

LIPOSUCTION

Hair Transplant or Restoration. Hair plugs, or grafts, of various sizes can be implanted into bald areas of the scalp. This procedure works best on men in their 30s and 40s who have inherited male-pattern baldness and whose hair loss has ceased; the procedure is less successful among older men whose hair has thinned as a result of age. The results may be permanent, though additional grafts may be required.

"My facelift and tummy tuck cost a fortune, but it sure is nice to be wrinkle free."

Liposuction. Its ability to remove excess fat from—and restore smooth, young-looking curves to—chins, arms, abdomens, hips, buttocks, thighs, knees, and ankles has put liposuction among the most popular cosmetic-surgery procedures in the United States. A small incision is made to allow insertion of a hollow tube called a cannula. The surgeon moves the cannula back and forth under the skin, dislodging the fatty tissue. A suction unit attached to the cannula vacuums out the fat. The results are permanent in most cases, assuming proper diet and exercise.

Nose Reshaping. Rhinoplasty can reduce or build up the size of the nose, reshape its tip, remove a hump, narrow the span of the nostrils, and change the angle between the nose and the upper lip. Unless the size or flare of the nostrils needs to be changed, all of the surgery is performed inside the nostrils, leaving no external scarring. The effects are permanent, though healing is slow and the final appearance of the reshaped nose may not be obvious for a year or more.

Skin Resurfacing. Skin resurfacing is a new technique that erases sun spots and fine wrinkles by removing the outer layers of the skin; as the skin heals, new, healthier-looking skin forms. A carbon dioxide laser, incorporated in an instrument that resembles a thick pen, is used. The physician moves the laser over the skin, vaporizing the surface tissues. The procedure is particularly effective on certain facial areas, such as that beneath the eyes. It is an alternative to dermabrasion and chemical peels. The effects are permanent, though new wrinkles can form.

Tummy Tuck. A stomach lift, or abdominoplasty, tightens the skin, removes excess skin, and repairs weakened muscles of the abdominal wall, producing a smoother, flatter abdomen. This can be a complicated operation, followed by considerable pain and a permanent hip-to-hip scar. In the 1990s, however, surgeons have found that some patients are candidates for endoscopic tummy tucks, which require only a few tiny incisions. A tuck often is teamed with liposuction. The effects of the procedure are permanent.

(Continued from page 68.)

Schiffer. Women want jawlines like Christie Brinkley's, while men want ones resembling Mel Gibson's.

Some surgeons use computer imaging to show the prospective patient how he or she might look following surgery. This can be useful for people who are unable to articulate exactly what results they would like, or who are unsure about undergoing surgery. It can improve patient-doctor communications and allows the two to work together on redesigning the patient's features. But what can be created on a computer may not be reproducible on the operating table, perhaps because of the patient's skin elasticity or bone structure. Nor is a computer image any guarantee of the surgeon's operating skills or of the final results.

The patient should learn what each procedure entails, what complications may result, how long the recovery period is likely to be, and how long the results will last. Bruising, swelling, redness, and pain that persist for weeks or even months are common. More-serious complications may include blood clots, bleeding under the skin, injury to facial nerves, infection, allergic reactions to implants and injections, and excessive scarring. A 1995 report found that about 15% of people who undergo a tummy tuck develop temporary bowel paralysis, which can cause serious intestinal complications. A 1996 report found that up to 20% of people who have eyelid lifts end up with a condition known as scleral show, in which too much of the white of the eye is exposed. Particularly controversial is penile enhancement, which can cause multiple complications, including loss of function.

Finally, the patient and doctor should discuss costs. Surgical fees for endoscopic procedures tend to be slightly higher than those for more traditional procedures. In 1996, for example, the average fee charged by ASPRS members for face-lifts was $4,407; the fee for endoscopic face-lifts averaged $4,783. The average fee for breast augmentation was $2,784, while the fee for endoscopic augmentations was $3,029. Note that these figures are the surgeon's fees; they do not include operating-room facilities, anesthesia, and other related expenses. They also do not reflect variations according to geographical area or the patient's needs. Once all these factors are considered, the total cost for a face-lift is likely to be between $5,500 and $12,000; breast augmentation may cost between $4,500 and $8,500. Typically, having related procedures done at the same time—say, a face-lift plus eyelid surgery—is less costly than having them done separately.

And the end results? Each year, there are hundreds of botched procedures that need to be redone. But much more commonly, when the surgery is done by experienced, qualified cosmetic surgeons, the end results are excellent, resulting in highly satisfied customers.

Beauty, it is said, is in the eye of the beholder. When it comes to cosmetic surgery, the most important beholder is the person looking in the mirror. If he or she believes the surgically changed image reflected by the mirror is more attractive, then the operation was indeed a success.

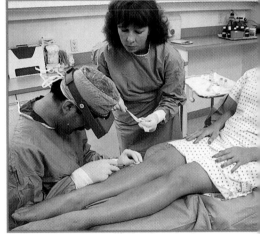

© Bachmann/Photo Researchers, Inc.

Sclerotherapy, or vein treatment, increased by more than 50% between 1984 and 1996 and accounted for some 18% of all cosmetic-surgery procedures performed in the United States in 1996. Blood clots, inflammation, allergic reaction, and scarring are among the risks associated with sclerotherapy.

MARKETING TO KIDS

© Steve Winter/Black Star

By Mel J. Zelenak

Fast-food restaurants not only cater to children with their products, packaging, and promotional campaigns but also address their advertising to the younger set. Accordingly, such restaurants are familiar to children of all ages and are among their favorite spots.

The author's daughter Lindsey, on her first day of kindergarten, was asked by her teacher to identify various corporate logos. Lindsey could not recognize any of them easily and had no idea what the "Golden Arches" were. As a result, the teacher's initial perception was that Lindsey might be "a bit slow." Very quickly the educator ascertained that Lindsey was very bright, and the instructor later learned that Lindsey was not familiar with the arches and other corporate images because her parents did not frequent "fast-food" establishments and did not watch much commercial television. The conjecture of this anecdote is that ads and logos are so pervasive in today's society that even teachers rely on these corporate images as learning tools and, in some cases at least, to evaluate a student's intelligence initially.

Societal Trends. By 1997, Lindsey was 8 years old and had learned all about McDonald's Golden Arches as well as hundreds of other corporate logos, labels, and ads. Of course, Lindsey is typical of the new generation of consumers, who are exposed to tens of thousands of commercials each year. Lindsey's generation of consumers is the largest in numbers since the baby boomers of the 1950s and 1960s. It has been estimated that by the year 2000, one in six Americans will be a child under 12 years of age.

Not only is this current generation of new consumers large in numbers, but American society has changed dramatically since the baby-boomer years. The divorce rate has increased, with more than one in two marriages now ending in divorce. The number of single-parent households continues to increase at unprecedented levels, with single mothers currently the fastest-growing poverty group in the United States. Nearly two thirds of U.S. children who have reached 16 years of age have lived with only one parent for some period in their lives. The two-career family usually requires some form of day care to take the place of the traditional parental role.

With this increased instability in the family and the associated social and psychological needs, the current generation of parents often feels the need to overindulge their children with material goods to satisfy their need to be "good" parents. Even savvy parental shoppers often do not make rational buying decisions and acquiesce once the child wants the Happy Meal, Air Jordans, Tickle Me Elmo, Beanie Babies, or Barbie. Some suggest these transformations have had dramatic consequences on buying habits and marketing trends, especially as regards the young consumer.

Youth as the Target. With the above noted changes in society, an apparently growing number of today's parents often are unwilling or unable to monitor their children's buying decisions. Prior to the 1990s, marketing of kids' products generally was geared toward the parents of children, presumably because parents ultimately purchased the products. Marketers now recognize that children control a substantial amount of discretionary income and that these children are making more of the actual buying decisions. For example, it has been estimated that children aged 4 to 12 spend approximately $15 billion a year, while teenagers spend nearly $60 billion a year. Together these groups influence an estimated $200 billion of their parents' yearly spending. Some suggest this $200 billion estimate is very conservative, and yet this figure represents as much as 40% of the total household spending of these families. In 1996, $740 million was spent on advertising during traditional kids' television programming, an all-time high. This figure was expected to increase sharply when 1997 figures were complete, although the expectation was that viewing of children's programming actually would decline.

It generally is agreed that the marketing function is to help maximize profits for the client being represented by the marketing company. It is further evident that a plethora of sophisticated marketing techniques to target children are being used in ways that would have been unimaginable a decade ago. Sometimes the marketer does not seem to care if the ads offend the parents, because the parent is not making the buying decision. In fact, some marketers suggest that it may be necessary to disaffect the parent in order to reach the target group. By not

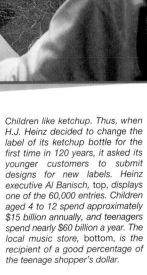

Children like ketchup. Thus, when H.J. Heinz decided to change the label of its ketchup bottle for the first time in 120 years, it asked its younger customers to submit designs for new labels. Heinz executive Al Banisch, top, displays one of the 60,000 entries. Children aged 4 to 12 spend approximately $15 billion annually, and teenagers spend nearly $60 billion a year. The local music store, bottom, is the recipient of a good percentage of the teenage shopper's dollar.

Photos: © Gene J. Puskar/AP/Wide World Photos (top); © Chuck Savage/The Stock Market (bottom)

© Carolyn Schaefer/Gamma-Liaison

Theme stores have sprung up in shopping centers and malls throughout the United States and are immensely popular with children, and with adults as well. In mid-1996 a new, 40,000-sq-ft (3 716-m²), three-story Walt Disney store, above, joined a competing Warner Brothers Studio Store amid New York City's elite Fifth Avenue shopping district.

About the Author. Mel J. Zelenak is an associate professor of consumer and family economics in the College of Human Environmental Services at the University of Missouri-Columbia. Dr. Zelenak has served on numerous professional committees and advisory boards and has written and lectured extensively on topics involving the American consumer. The 12th edition of his book *Consumer Economics: The Consumer in Our Society* was scheduled for publication in 1998.

antagonizing the parent the ad may alienate the real decision makers—the older child and teenager. Cindy Hennessy, general partner at T. L. Partnership in Dallas—whose clients include Pepsi-Cola, Frito-Lay, and Fed Ex—has noted, "Done right, teen marketing will alienate all other audiences. Done bland, you're likely to appeal to everyone except your desired target."

Market researchers such as Tom McGee—senior associate at Doyle Research, an independent marketing-research firm based in Chicago—has suggested that this prime youth market can be segmented further through the use of telephone and on-line focus groups. These marketing strategies have proven to be cost- and time-efficient and include gathering information on kids' likes and dislikes. Youth are becoming increasingly comfortable with these strategies and the seeming anonymity that they afford the youngsters.

The School Environment. Some critics feel that commercialism aimed at youth not only pervades the media but also has an undue influence in classrooms. Consumers' Union, publisher of *Consumer Reports*, updated its 1995 study *Captive Kids: Commercial Pressures on Kids at School.* The report documents a multitude of techniques that are used by commercial interests so that they are able to invade the classroom under the guise of assisting the schools with providing supplementary aids. Classroom marketing includes company perspectives on issues like the environment and nutrition and other potentially controversial topics. Promotions, contests, and school incentive programs also are very popular techniques.

Channel One, the TV-news program for students in grades six through 12, was airing in more than 12,000 schools in 1997. Channel One offers school districts the free use of satellite dishes, VCRs, and television sets. In return, nearly 20% of the 12-minute news program is devoted to promoting a multitude of products, including candy, soda, and athletic gear. These intrusions into the classroom frequently are supported by school administrators and teachers because many feel that the benefits to students compensate for the concessions that must be made. Educators often have noted that corporate support is essential, especially during difficult budgetary times.

The Internet. Much of the controversy and media involvement regarding the Internet and children in the mid-1990s has been in the area of obscene and sexually explicit material. However, little has been written or discussed about marketing toward children via the Internet, although some have suggested that this is a more pervasive and difficult problem to resolve. It was evident that this controversy would increase in intensity in the future, in part because of the expected increase in Internet use by children. By 1997 more than 4 million children had access to the Web and some 1 million of these children actively were using the service. Estimates were that these figures could quadruple by the year 2000. Virtually all commercial on-line services have established special areas aimed at children. Various corporate Web sites aim for the young in their on-line operations.

© Randy Ury/The Stock Market

The industry, the consumer watchdog, and government organizations have recognized the problem of Web-site manipulation of children and were active in 1996–97 with recommendations for Web-site use. Trade organizations—like the Direct Marketing Association, the Interactive Services Association, and the Council of Better Business Bureaus—have admitted that there are problems and that something needs to be done. These groups were contending that self-regulation is the most effective means of protecting consumers, and they have developed guidelines for Web-site marketers. In 1997 the Children's Advertising Review Unit (CARU) of the Council of Better Business Bureaus issued an updated version of "Self Regulatory Guidelines for Children's Advertising."

The Center for Media Education (CME), a Washington-based nonprofit consumer organization, published a report in 1996 entitled "Web of Deception: Threats to Children from Online Marketing." The report offers numerous examples of Web-site practices that pose a unique threat to children. The report cites the risk of invading children's privacy through the solicitation of personal information and the use of deceptive

With more than 4 million children having access to the Internet and approximately 1 million of these youngsters actively using the Web, commercial on-line services have established special Internet areas aimed at children. Parents, the government, and various groups have become concerned about what children are subjected to by way of the Web. Monitoring guidelines have been developed; new ones were being considered.

© David Young-Wolff/PhotoEdit

Teenagers enjoy shopping for their own clothes with friends. What's "in"—especially the latest designer label—has a major influence on their buying decisions.

and unfair advertising. CME and the Consumer Federation of America (CFA) issued their own suggested recommendations in 1997, entitled "Guidelines for the Collection and Tracking of Information from Children." These guidelines differ from the industry guidelines in various areas, particularly regarding privacy issues. These advocacy groups generally believe that the industry guidelines are weak. They believe the most viable protections for on-line scrutiny must come from the federal government—specifically, the Federal Trade Commission (FTC).

The FTC held hearings in 1996 and 1997 in response to the growing concerns in this area. It appeared that the Bill Clinton administration was very concerned about privacy issues as they relate to children under 12. Nonetheless, it also was evident that the FTC and the administration would move slowly in developing guidelines or standards for industry compliance.

Technological Remedies and the Future. Industry sources have indicated that there are software packages available to help parents block out unwanted electronic information and that parents should monitor their children's on-line activities. Products like Cyber Patrol, CYBERsitter, and Net Nanny are a few examples of many such programs that are available to parents. However, according to Consumers' Union, all current software can be defeated easily. Newer, perhaps more proficient, technologies, will not be available for some time.

Most surveys indicated that adults were concerned about business marketing and advertising aimed at children, although most of the concern appeared to be product related. While 80% of adults felt that advertising toward children was problematic in general, most felt it was acceptable to advertise toys, cereal, and clothing. The question remained as to whether adults would become more skeptical of the marketing tactics when new techniques surface.

TOY FADS-1997

"What do the kids want this Christmas shopping season?" is a question that for generations has brought smiles to retailers as well as smiles and frowns to the faces of accommodating parents and other gift-givers. From the Theodore Roosevelt stuffed bear made popular nearly a century ago; to the Mr. Potato Head, Play-Doh, and G.I. Joe crazes of the baby boomers' generation; to the Beanie Babies and Tickle Me Elmo rages of the 1990s, it seems that every Christmas introduces the toy that everyone wants.

Moms, dads, and other gift-givers will spend hour after hour attempting to locate that elusive

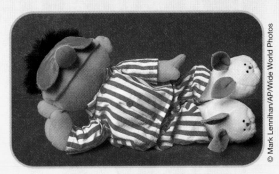

SING & SNORE ERNIE

BEANIE BABIES

popular toy of the season. The absurdity is so complete that an entire 1996 movie, *Jingle All the Way*, starring Arnold Schwarzenegger, pokes fun at the extremes parents will go to in order to purchase the year's must-have toy.

The 1997 Christmas season was no exception. A clear retail-sales hero was Sing & Snore Ernie, the sequel to the 1996 champion, Tickle Me Elmo. The 1997 Sesame Street celebrity twitters to the tune of "Twinkle, Twinkle Little Star," then snores as his abdomen moves in synch to his snoozing sounds. It had a retail-price tag of less than $30.

Although nearly 6,000 new toy products were introduced during 1997, there was little evidence to suggest that cost had any influence on the popularity of a given toy. Many of the highly desired toys were of the high-tech, electronic variety, which averaged $100 per unit. Interactive Barney, a computerized toy capable of pronouncing approximately 2,000 words and singing more than a dozen songs, had meteoric sales success despite its $100 price tag. Barney's optional tele-

vision and personal-computer (PC) kits substantially expanded its capabilities, but also increased the retail price to more than $200.

Far less costly, but very popular, were a triad of virtual pets, including Nano Pals, Giga Pets, and Tamagotchis. Each sold for $10–$15 and required the owner to care for it properly, or it could become ill or die. Even less costly were the plethora of Beanie Babies, which were popular with both children and adults. With price tags of $5 each, these became popular small gifts and stocking stuffers for many Americans.

Barbie dolls and accessories continued to be among the most sought-out toys. In fact, according to the Toy Manufacturers of America, four of the 15 top-selling toys of the 1997 Christmas season were part of the Barbie dynasty. The Barbie craze began in the late 1950s and continued to captivate both parents and children in 1997. In fact, a revamped Barbie was on the drawing board and was receiving much publicity.

Some adults are very critical of the incredible amount of money spent on toys—estimated to be as much as $100 annually for every man, woman, and child in the United States. That fact notwithstanding, one could gain some solace in the fact that not one of the year's most successful toys was considered distasteful and/or violent.

MEL J. ZELENAK

TAMAGOTCHIS

Photos, © Nova Online/Gamma-Liaison

MOUNT EVEREST

THE LURE CONTINUES

By Dunham Gooding

More people than ever are attempting to scale Mount Everest—Earth's highest point. A record number of deaths on the 29,028-ft (8 848-m) peak has drawn controversy, as high-priced guides lead inexperienced climbers onto its treacherous slopes.

With the possible exception of the Matterhorn in Switzerland and Mont Blanc in France, no other mountain peak has captured the imagination of the climbing and nonclimbing public like Mount Everest. Although the lure of Everest may have diminished for the most skilled mountain climbers in recent years, its current magnetism for the typical mountaineer is the same—if not substantially greater. In fact, the climbing season of 1996 broke all records for the most expeditions (26), the most people summiting (92), and the most people dying at the site (14). Attempts at climbing Everest continued at such high numbers in 1997—37 expeditions, 86 climbers summiting, and nine deaths.

By the end of 1997, there had been 429 expeditions attempting to climb Everest and 932 successful ascents by 726 individuals (105 people having summited more than one time). The fact that current climber Ang Rita Sherpa has summited ten times, another Sherpa seven times, and two others six times suggests the extremely important role that local Sherpa people continue to play in helping climbers reach their summit goal. Nearly all expeditions have been aided by Sherpas, who have seen far more of their people summit than those of any other culture or nationality.

The Geography. Mount Everest is the world's highest mountain, rising to 29,028 ft (8 848 m) amid other 26,000- to 27,000-ft (7 925- to 8 230-m) peaks on the Nepal-Tibet border. Known by the native Sherpa people in Tibet and Nepal as Chomolungma (Mother Goddess of the World) and recognized by them as the highest summit in the region, the mountain was not surveyed until 1849 and not determined to be the world's highest summit until 1853. The Nepalese government named the mountain—and the national park that encompasses it—Sagamartha, but the term is little used.

The Himalaya mountain range, of which Everest is a part, is the largest system of high summits in the world, reaching from the Brahmaputra River in the east to the Indus in the west, a distance of 1,600 mi (2 575 km). The area to the south of the range in Himalaya's foothills gives way to the great subcontinent of India, while to the north, the flanks of the mountains end more abruptly as they meet the high Tibetan plateau. The mountain's southwest face rises an impressively steep 8,000 ft (2 438 m) from the Western Cwm to the summit.

The Himalaya range is the youngest of the world's large mountain ranges, and its peaks still are being forced upward by the northward movement of the landmass of India. Though the range runs at high elevation throughout, it has been cut deeply by the movement of glaciers and the violent flow of rivers draining its slopes. The valleys and passes that are the product of those geological actions created routes for early trade and later exploration. It was not until 1767, when James Rennall was appointed the first surveyor general of Bengal, that a systematic survey of the region was begun. The Great Trigonometrical Survey of India began in 1800 under Maj. William Lambton; he was succeeded as superintendent by Sir George Everest (1790–1866). In his 20 years of service, Everest expanded and established systems that eventually were used to determine the great heights of the Himalayan peaks.

For many years the Survey used local people trained in the techniques of surveying to go into the vast areas still closed to Europeans. Disguised as tradesmen or travelers, these men mapped vast areas of the Himalayas and discovered several of the range's highest peaks. Surveyors did not observe Chomolungma until 1849, when it was designated "No. XV." With numerous observations to analyze, the surveyors did not make the precise calculations that revealed it to be the highest summit in the world until three years later. It finally was given the name Everest in 1865 to honor Sir George.

Historical Expeditions. The kingdom of Nepal remained closed to nonresidents until 1949, but a good political relationship between Great Britain and Tibet allowed British expeditions to attempt to climb Everest from Tibet, beginning in 1921. In that year the British Reconnaissance Expedition explored

About the Author. Dunham Gooding is president of the American Alpine Institute in Bellingham, WA, North America's largest international mountain-guide service. He has guided and taught climbing throughout the world and has served as president of the American Mountain Guides Association for six years. He has served as chairman of the National Summit Committee on Rescue and currently is president of the Outdoor Recreation Coalition of America, the trade association of the $10 billion human-powered-recreation industry in the United States.

the mountain extensively. They gained a view of the Khumbu Glacier (later used as the route for the first ascent), which they judged to be too steep and broken to be safely climbable. That expedition also climbed to the North Col, the 22,934-ft (6 990-m) pass north of the peak that would be the access route used by almost all Everest expeditions until Tibet closed its borders to climbers in 1946 and 1947.

The second British expedition to Everest, in 1922, reached the North Col and placed camps even higher; from the camps, the climbers reached 26,985 ft (8 225 m) without oxygen, and 27,297 ft (8 320 m) with oxygen. Both were remarkable feats, considering the clothing and equipment that were used. The climbers' accomplishment is placed in perspective by the fact that no one climbed a peak higher than the altitude they reached on Everest until Annapurna was summited 28 years later.

The third British Everest Expedition was in 1924. Its team of 14 climbers established a high camp at 26,772 ft (8 160 m), and from there a summit bid was made by Andrew Irvine and George Mallory. They were spotted climbing at an estimated 28,000 ft (8 423 m) before they disappeared into the clouds, never to be seen again. Their mysterious disappearances captured the imagination of the world. British expeditions followed in the mid-1930s and in 1947. In 1950 an American party of five and in 1951 a British party of six scouted the western approach to Everest through Nepal, using the Khumbu valley and glacier. In 1952 a Swiss expedition with eight climbers succeeded in climbing via the Khumbu Glacier up to and above the South Col. However, it was the British Everest Expedition of 1953 that brought mountaineers to the world's highest point. Composed of 14 members, including New Zealander Edmund Hillary, the expedition approached the mountain through Nepal and climbed via the Khumbu and South Col. The expedition's first bid for the top failed, but a second team, composed of Hillary and the Nepalese climber Tenzing Norgay, reached the summit on May 29. Sherpas sped a coded message with the news down the mountain to a remote Indian radio post in Namche Bazaar, from which it was transferred to the British embassy and then to the *Times* of London.

© Paul Souders/Gamma-Liaison

Base camps, including the ones at Mount Everest and at Mount McKinley, above, form the control centers of expeditionary climbs. From such points, mountaineers haul food and equipment to successively higher camps in preparation for the summit attempt.

Everest was climbed for the second time in 1956, by a Swiss expedition, and possibly again in 1960, by the Chinese, in an ascent that still is disputed. But it was the third confirmed ascent, by an American expedition in 1963, that set a new Himalayan standard for technical achievement and the search for greater challenge on unclimbed routes. America's first successful team, comprised of Jim Whittaker and the Nepali Nawang Gombu, made the biggest headlines in the United States, but it was the second team that achieved something truly new. Willi Unsoeld and Tom Hornbein reached the summit via the West Ridge and descended via the South Summit and South Col, completing the first technical ascent of the mountain as well as its first traverse. Other major accomplishments on the mountain include Italy's Reinhold Messner's non-oxygen-assist-

MOUNTAIN CLIMBING— THE SPORT TODAY

© Susan Oristaglio/Gamma-Liaison

Indoor climbing has grown extremely popular. In 1997 some 2,400 walls were found everywhere from school gyms to health clubs throughout the United States.

Mountaineering, rock climbing, and ice climbing—the three basic types of activities associated with mountain climbing—are part of a general U.S. trend toward more active lifestyles. They are among the fastest-growing outdoor sports, with nearly 9 million people hitting the heights in 1997. As people continue to seek challenging recreational activities, mountain climbing is expected to continue its growth in popularity.

Rock Climbing. Rock climbing—the most popular form of climbing—involves the ascent of one or more pitches (rope lengths) on a crag, cliff, or wall. The term "cragging" is sometimes used to differentiate one- to three-pitch rock climbs from longer ascents. In rock climbing, the primary focus is the difficulty and skill required to surmount technical challenges over moderate distances—although "big wall climbs" of ten, 20, or more pitches also are done. Difficulty is graded by a decimal system that originally ran from 5.0 to 5.9. As equipment and techniques improved, however, it was expanded to accommodate ever-harder climbs; today climbers have pushed the limits into the 5.14 range. The difficulty of upper-limit climbs is differentiated further by letters such as 5.12a, 5.12b. Recreational climbers most commonly climb in the 5.7 to 5.10 range.

Rock climbers protect themselves from falling with 150- to 165-ft (46- to 50-m) elastic ropes run through anchors (called "protection" or "pro"), which can be placed in and removed from cracks. These artificial chocks include wired nuts, stoppers, hexes, and camming devices. Carabiners—snap links through which the rope can run—are clipped to these chocks. Permanent bolts and hangers are common on faces lacking cracks. The use of pitons—once the most common anchor—has declined greatly except as permanent protection, because the constant hammering in and removal sap time and energy and damage the rock. Special lightweight shoes, which fit like a second skin, have soles of soft, sticky rubber. Rock climbing is a warm-weather sport, so clothing is light and allows for full freedom of movement.

The sport is done worldwide, including in nearly every U.S. state. Some famous climbing areas are Yosemite Valley, Joshua Tree, and Owens River Gorge (California); Smith Rock (Oregon); Leavenworth (Washington); Squamish (British Columbia); The Needles (South Dakota); City of Rocks (Idaho); Estes Park and Eldorado Canyon (Colorado); the desert towers and canyons of Utah; the Shawangunks (New York); and New River Gorge (West Virginia).

A recent aspect of rock climbing called "sport climbing" focuses exclusively on making individual, athletic moves on extremely difficult, short routes. On sport routes, anchors usually are pre-placed bolts into which the climber clips the rope while ascending, without expending energy placing anchors.

Ice Climbing. Water-ice climbing is similar to rock climbing in its focus on difficult, athletic moves over moderate distances. Climbs are done on frozen flows of water from seeps or waterfalls. Ice climbs are graded WI 3 to WI 6; WI 5 is predominantly vertical.

Ice climbers wear crampons—devices that are strapped onto boots with ten steel points facing down and two forward—and wield two short ice axes to make their way up the steep ice. Ice screws and occasionally rock protection on adjoining rock surfaces are used to anchor the rope. Popular North American ice-climbing areas include Valdez (Alaska), Banff (British Columbia), Ouray (Colorado), and North Conway (New Hampshire).

Mountaineering. The goal of mountaineering is to reach the summit of a peak, whether it be a small, accessible mountain that can be climbed in one day or a large, remote summit requiring days or months of climbing.

When mountaineering—which can involve rock, ice, and snow climbing—is done on an especially large peak, it usually is referred to as an expedition or expeditionary climbing. Ski mountaineering is done on peaks pitched moderately enough to be ascended on skis.

Mountaineers typically layer their clothing to allow for wide changes in body temperature due to weather and exertion. Rugged leather boots with knobby rubber soles are worn for climbs primarily on rock; double plastic boots are used on snow and glacier climbs. Crampons are worn on frozen snow, ice, and glaciers, while a 28-inch (70-cm) ice axe provides balance and security. A protective system of ropes is anchored to rock, snow, and ice with a variety of devices similar to those used in rock and ice climbing.

The European Alps—the birthplace of modern mountaineering—still are one of the most heavily used climbing areas. Popular North American ranges include those in Alaska, the Rockies, the Cascades of Washington, the Sierra of California, and the Tetons of Wyoming. The newest mountaineering frontier involves making highly technical rock and ice ascents under the harsh conditions of expeditionary peaks, such as Great Trango Tower in Pakistan's Karakoram Range and the ice-capped rock towers of Cerro Torre and Fitzroy in Argentine Patagonia.

Indoor Climbing. Those wishing to try their hand at rock climbing have it easier than ever because of indoor climbing walls and "rock gyms." During 1997 thousands climbed at the 2,400 U.S. indoor walls, without having to invest in equipment or go to the mountains. During 1997, rock walls were found in health clubs, school gymnasiums, Boys and Girls Clubs, and YMCAs. By year's end some 255 U.S. rock gyms were devoted exclusively to the sport.

Built of wood, cement, or plastic resin over a wooden frame, indoor climbing walls—pitched at various angles and reaching from 20 ft (6 m) to 100 ft (31 m) high—have various sized artificial hand- and footholds of cast resin and sand, which can be moved to change difficulty.

This convenience has created a new danger, however, when people used to the controlled environment of the gym take to the real cliffs, where holds break, rocks fall, anchors fail, and the weather is unpredictable. Rock-climbing injuries were up in 1997. More instruction in outdoor, traditional climbing seemed to be required.

DUNHAM GOODING

ed solo climb of the mountain in 1980 and a five-man Australian team's unsupported, non-oxygen-assisted first ascent of the Great Couloir on Everest's North Face in 1984.

From the 1950s through the 1970s, the number of Everest expeditions grew from one every four years to two per year. An average of five climbers summited each year there was an expedition, and one climber died for every six making the summit. The 1980s saw an average of more than 12 expeditions per year, while summit successes jumped 17 per year and the fatality rate rose to one death for every three climbers summiting.

The Climbers. The type of person attempting to climb Mount Everest has changed significantly in the 20th century. In the 1920s and 1930s, expeditions primarily were composed of upper-class Britons. By the 1950s, expedition teams were more likely to include recreational climbers from a variety of professions with significant alpine-climbing experience. A radical increase of government peak fees in the 1990s has had an immense impact on the type of person now traveling to Everest. Fees charged by the Nepalese government were revised upward from

$10,000 in 1991 to $70,000 in 1996. The fee covers seven climbers, with $10,000 charged for each additional person. These fees largely eliminated the low-budget, grassroots expeditions of experienced climbers that had become well represented on the mountain. In their place came a strong presence of commercially operated trips run by professional guides who offer positions on their expeditions to those who will pay their $40,000 to $60,000 fee. Criticism has been leveled at those commercial operations for taking climbers who are much better equipped financially than they are in the skills of high-altitude expeditionary mountaineering.

Many members of the mountaineering community have argued that it is not possible to "guide" Everest. The fundamental characteristic of the guide/client relationship is the provision, by the guide to the client, of a significant margin of safety that clients would not be able to attain on their own. The argument suggests that on Everest, the proportion of unpredictable problems to foreseeable challenges is so bad and the overall magnitude of hazard is so high that it is impossible for a guide to fulfill his or her normal role. Weather is the most commonly cited example. On a mountain on the scale of Everest, storms are typically severe. They can develop rapidly and with little warning.

© J. Tuholske/AP/Wide World Photos

Experienced Everest guide Scott Fischer (above) *and guided client Doug Hansen* (below), *both of Washington state, died on separate commercial expeditions in May 1996—one of Everest's deadliest climbing seasons.*

Predictions of disaster for the scores of guided clients attempting Everest were realized in the spring climbing season of 1996. On two commercial expeditions, six guides and clients died high on Everest and ten others came extremely close to doing so. Among those who died, guide Andy Harris' oxygen apparatus apparently malfunctioned, and with an abrupt loss of oxygen, he gradually became disoriented while trying to assist other climbers. Client Doug Hansen summited and then had difficulty descending because of exhaustion and possibly due to running out of oxygen. Guide and expedition leader Rob Hall tried to assist Hansen, ran out of oxygen, and died of exposure. Guide and expedition leader Scott Fischer exhausted himself trying to get clients to the summit, developed altitude illness, and died of exposure. Client Yasuko Namba managed to climb down to the South Col but died of exposure when she and her companions could not find their tents in the storm that had enveloped the mountain. Her ten unsheltered companions, clients, and guide nearly died. The deterioration of weather is what ultimately killed the climbers, but they were caught in its trap by having too many people on the route at one time and too many people moving slowly because of their lack of depth in climbing skills and dependency on their guides.

With the Nepali government's need for expedition fees, it is unlikely that it will limit the number of simultaneous expeditions or persons attempting to climb the mountain, despite the clear dangers that the high numbers bring. Nonetheless, the thought of possibly having success in meeting all of Everest's complex challenges gives to the prospective climber the lure of an achievement on a scale that will not be found in any other aspect of life. Everest still has an unmatched fame and mystique.

© "Valley Daily News"/AP/Wide World Photos

America's Changing
Taste Buds

By Phyllis Louise Harris

About the Author. Phyllis
Louise Harris—a cookbook
author, food writer, and
cooking teacher who spe-
cializes in Asian foods—is
food editor of *Asian Pages*,
a biweekly newspaper
reaching five states in the
upper Midwest. She holds
certificates from the Culinary Institute of America,
the California Culinary
Academy, and the China
Institute in America in New
York City, and completed
the China Institute's chef
seminars in China. She is
founder of Asian Culinary
Arts Institutes, Ltd., in
Edina, MN, which is dedi-
cated to the preservation,
understanding, and enjoy-
ment of the culinary arts of
the Asian Pacific Rim.

Pass the salsa and soy sauce! America's melting pot is boiling
over with "new" tastes that are, in reality, centuries old. In this
land where meat and potatoes have reigned supreme for more
than 300 years, tacos, sushi, stir-fry, and curry are satisfying
Americans' growing demands for exotic flavors and lighter fare.
The 1990s is the Decade of Flavor—and, it seems, the hotter the
better.

From Fusion to Flavor. During the 1950s and 1960s, Chinese
dishes were the ethnic foods of fashion. U.S. President Richard
Nixon's historic trip to China in 1972 expanded this fascination
with "Oriental" flavors, touching off a flood of Chinese cookbooks. But the recipes featured were for the most part not
based on traditional Chinese cooking. This was fusion food,
adjusted for Americans who had come to like chop suey and
chow mein. Chinese food authority Florence Lin remembers the
time well. As food consultant to *The Cooking of China*, part of
Time-Life's Foods of the World series published in 1968, she
created and tested all the recipes for the book. "When the edi-

tors kept asking me, 'Where is the sauce?' in many of the dishes, I explained that Chinese cooking doesn't always include sauces," Lin recalls. But sauce was what Americans expected, so sauce they got.

The 1960s and 1970s were also a time when home cooks were adding French and Japanese dishes to their party fare. Quiche, crepes, tempura, and teriyaki began appearing in national food magazines, on home menus, and in ethnic restaurants.

The 1980s saw Tex-Mex sweep the country, along with the nouvelle California and Pan-Asian cuisines. By the 1990s, Americans were searching for even more exotic flavors and embracing the ethnic foods of India, Japan, Thailand, Vietnam, Korea, and China (with or without sauce); anything containing chilies was especially popular. At the same time, the growing Latino community fueled interest in Latin cooking, with a further push from the nation's supermarkets, where special merchandising of Chinese and Mexican kitchenware and accessories was designed to increase ethnic-food sales. Now cooks everywhere had easy access to woks, chopsticks, tortilla griddles, rice cookers, and nacho skillets, as well as to all the ingredients for cooking these "new" foods at home.

With American taste buds becoming more international in the late 1990s, more and more Mexican favorites are being prepared in the home (page 86); Indian dishes and spices (above, left) are attracting new enthusiasts; stir-fry sauces (above) can be purchased not only in U.S. specialty stores but in supermarkets as well; and the tortilla chip with salsa (left) is a favorite snack. Salsa, an uncooked sauce, is a staple of Mexican and Southeast Asian cuisines. Mexican salsas usually contain chilies and often tomatoes; Southeast Asian salsas often are made from fresh fruits and vegetables with seasonings such as lime juice, fish sauce, mint leaves, and cilantro.

Meat and Potatoes, Plus! While meat and potatoes (mainly burgers and fries) continue to be America's favorite foods, those old standbys are being replaced with foods that are light, low-fat, easy, fast, fresh, and flavorful.

In the late 1970s, Americans were consuming 97.7 lbs (44.3 kg) of beef per person per year. In the 1980s, America's per-capita beef consumption decreased by 15%, with consumption of other meats, fish, and poultry remaining level. Today, while beef still accounts for 42% of supermarkets' meat sales, it is taking on new shapes and flavors. Leaner, preseasoned, ready-to-cook meat entrees now appear in 94% of U.S. supermarkets,

(Continued on page 90.)

Favorite "Exotic" Foods

Dim Sum

These small dumplings—which are filled with seasoned meat, seafood, or vegetables—originally were created by Chinese teahouse chefs more than 1,000 years ago during the Sung dynasty. They were served to men who came to *Yum Char*—"take tea"—while they gossiped, conducted business, or enjoyed other pleasures. Restaurants throughout the world now offer more than 100 types of dim sum, or "heart warmers"; they can be baked, deep-fried, steamed, stir-fried, barbecued, or boiled, and are served at any time of day, with or without tea.

Spring Rolls

These thin pancakelike wrappers filled with seafood, meat, and vegetables are really Chinese sandwiches; they are deep-fried and served with sweet-sour sauce and hot mustard. They are known as egg rolls in the United States, where wrappers often have been made from egg sheets. The more typical Shanghai wrapper includes only flour and water. Shaped like antique Chinese gold bars, spring rolls are considered symbols of prosperity and often are served at Chinese New Year banquets. Each Asian Pacific Rim cuisine has its own version of egg rolls. In the Philippines they are long and narrow, and are filled with pork and carrots. In Vietnam they are often vegetarian and contain noodles, or they may be fresh spring rolls, which are not fried but instead are served cold.

Fried Rice

This ubiquitous Asian hot dish is made with leftovers of cold, cooked rice stir-fried with any combination of eggs, bits of cooked meat, seafood, vegetables, fruit, and seasonings. China's *ch'ao fan*, Indonesia's *nasi goreng*, and Thailand's *khao phat* are just a few Asian stir-fry dishes made from precooked rice. Indians, Burmans, and Malaysians stir-fry raw rice before cooking it in water with the other ingredients and seasonings.

Sashimi

Paper-thin slices of fresh fish in season make this Japanese dish delectable. Frozen, iced, or even refrigerated fish never are used in good sashimi, for once the fish is chilled, its fresh flavor is lost forever. Served with grated daikon, wasabi, and a soy-mirin sauce, sashimi is Japanese cuisine at its best. Fresh, simple, light, healthful, and served with exotic flavors, it is Japan's most popular food.

Sushi

One of Japan's most popular dishes, sushi was created by accident. Salted carp once was stored on top of vinegared rice. When someone accidentally tasted the rice and liked the new flavor, sushi was born. Sushi is actually the name for cooked rice flavored with vinegar and sugar and cooled to room temperature. Functioning like the bread in an open sandwich, portions of sushi are hand-shaped into small "buns" and topped with raw, pickled, smoked, or cooked fish. It may be rolled around fillings of fish, pickles, mushrooms, or other vegetables and can be encased in egg or bean curd. Sushi is a meal in itself, no matter what form it may take.

Pad Thai

The national noodle dish of Thailand, pad Thai is finding a growing following among American chefs and diners. Cooked rice noodles are stir-fried with shrimp, fresh bean sprouts, crushed peanuts, and scallions, then seasoned with lime juice, chilies, and fish sauce. This is just one of the selections available from the many noodle shops, stalls, vendors, and hawkers in Bangkok—forerunners of the increasingly popular Asian noodle shops in America.

Raita

A flavored yogurt (milk curd), raita is served at most meals in India to soothe the burning sensation of chilies and potent curry spices. It is used as a condiment or a salad, and also as a marinade for meats before they are charcoal grilled or baked in tandoors. One popular raita served in America combines yogurt with grated cucumber and chopped mint leaves. In Kerala, at India's southwestern tip, the most popular raita is yogurt flavored with fresh coconut, chilies, mustard seeds, curry leaves, and fresh pineapple.

Curry

The name was coined during the British occupation of India; curry is actually any dish that is made with a sauce. Often these sauces are seasoned with fresh curry leaves, which have a very subtle citrus flavor, and the name was applied to all dishes with a "curry" flavor. Seasonings for curries (sauces) are as varied as the ingredients available and the inclinations of the cook. Ground cumin, coriander, and turmeric often are used. Sometimes the combination can be dozens of spices, sometimes just one or two. American diners have become accustomed to the flavor of Madras curry powder, which is made exclusively for export and never is eaten in India. And, because many Indian restaurants in the United States add chilies to their curry seasonings, Americans have come to believe that "curry" equals "hot." This is not necessarily true—curry is hot only if it contains chilies.

Satay (saté)

Skewers of bite-sized pieces of marinated meat, fowl, or seafood, satays are a favorite street food in Malaysia, Indonesia, and Thailand. Vendors cook the mini kabobs over charcoal grills. Peanuts and coconut are predominant flavors in Malaysian marinades, sweet soy sauce is used in Indonesia, and coconut cream with fish sauce is popular in Thailand. America's love of barbecued anything has made satays almost an instant hit in the United States. Often served with peanut sauce, satays are showing up on non-Asian menus around the country.

Tempura

This popular dish—consisting of seafood, meat, or vegetables barely coated with a light batter, deep-fried in vegetable oil, and served with a sauce of mirin, soy sauce, and dashi (fish broth)—was introduced to the Japanese by 16th-century Portuguese missionaries and sailors. When celebrating Ember Days, the *quattuor tempora*, on the Roman Catholic calendar, the Portuguese abstained from eating meat and instead deep-fried and ate the local Japanese prawns. *Tempora* eventually became Japanese tempura, which now includes a wide variety of ingredients.

(Continued from page 87.)

with packaged ready-to-eat meat products appearing in 65%—thus turning meat departments into meal departments. Turkey breasts stuffed, seasoned, and ready for the oven; stir-fry meat packaged with vegetables and seasonings ready for the wok; marinated chicken breasts to pop in the microwave; kabobs of trimmed meat and vegetables all cut and skewered, ready to marinate and grill—these are just a few of the items designed to meet Americans' search for more flavor, less fat, and no fuss.

Hamburgers still appear on 77% of U.S. restaurant menus and usually are served with French-fried potatoes. But today's menus often feature such variations as teriyaki burgers, burgers and peppers, and burgers with salsa. In fact, tomato salsa has become such an American favorite that, by 1992, it had surpassed ketchup as the number-one-selling condiment in the United States. Even French fries now come in new spicy flavors.

Meanwhile, hot dogs' 100-year-old position as the favorite food of fans at baseball games across the country is being challenged by variety foods such as nachos—crispy corn tortilla chips smothered with cheese sauce and sometimes with chili peppers or salsa as well. Mexican in inspiration, nachos are fast becoming an American classic. While one major-league stadium in the Midwest sells about 12,000 to 13,000 hot dogs during a game, it also sells 10,000 to 12,000 orders of nachos. And the hot dog is no longer a plain old wiener on a bun. Offerings include chili dogs, dogs and jalapeños, hot dogs and salsa, and dogs that have chilies mixed right into the meat—truly hot hot dogs.

Among fans at ballparks and sports stadiums across the United States, nachos now are as popular as the all-time classics—hot dogs and peanuts.

Food-service publications featuring the newly popular foods in their trend predictions are providing recipes to commercial chefs for ethnic dishes such as pad Thai, churrasco with chimichurri sauce, shrimp diablo, and red-onion relish in the Latin style. Restaurant chains such as Country Kitchen and Applebee's that cater to middle-American tastes now consider Mexican-inspired dishes to be menu staples, with taco salads and quesadillas leading the way. Perkins, originally a Midwestern chain of pancake houses, today offers a burrito breakfast, chicken and cheese quesadillas, tortilla sandwiches, and salads, in addition to more standard fare. Marie Callender's—a restaurant chain out of California that specializes in pot pies, pot roast, and hand-carved roast turkey—also serves "Cabo San Lucas" chicken Caesar salad; "Cinco de Mayo Picnic," featuring quesadillas and guacamole; and teriyaki-mushroom burgers. Stir-fry vegetables and rice with all sorts of Asian and non-Asian seasonings have replaced peas and potatoes as side dishes in hotel dining rooms from coast to coast.

With all of this interest in ethnic foods, it is no wonder that, in 1996, the James Beard Foundation's Rising Star Chef of the

Year was Douglas Rodriguez, owner of New York City's Latin restaurant Patria. Or that the hottest restaurants in the United States include the Japanese Noba in New York City, Susanna Foo's Chinese restaurant in Philadelphia, Thai Rain in New York City, and the French-Vietnamese Le Colonial in New York City, Los Angeles, and Chicago.

As Americans continue their trend toward eating out more than ever before and buying ready-made foods in record quantities, exposure to flavorful new dishes will only increase. According to the U.S. Department of Agriculture's (USDA's) tenth annual food-consumption survey in 1994, 56% of Americans ate away from home at least once a day. This figure does not even include take-out food eaten at home or food that is delivered to one's house.

Combining traditional fried tortillas, chilies, and salsa from Mexico with ground beef, cheese, and sour cream—all of which came originally from Europe—tacos are filled with shredded lettuce, chopped tomatoes, cucumbers, carrots, and scallions for a "meal in a shell."

Hot and Healthy in a Hurry. America's search for variety in its menus is accompanied by a growing desire to eat more healthful foods. While in many cases this preference for healthy food may have been lip service practiced only on occasion, those occasions are increasing in frequency as national publications such as the *Berkeley Wellness Letter* tout the healthful aspects of diets low in meat. In 1993, this journal advised readers that a semivegetarian diet with rice as its basis, such as is eaten commonly in China, is a healthy diet, resulting in less heart disease and colon cancer in China than in the United States. Today, America's vegetable and grain consumption is on the rise with stir fries, Asian noodles, and Mexican tacos helping to lead the way. Not far behind are the flavor-filled, healthful cuisines of India, featuring vegetable curries, varieties of flat bread, basmati rice, seasoned yogurt, and tandoor chicken.

But it is the fiery flavors of chilies that Americans of the 1990s seem to crave the most. Christopher Columbus is said to be the first European to have tasted chilies, when he bumped into the "West Indies" in 1492. And it was Columbus who erroneously named them "peppers." Since he could not bring Spain's Queen Isabella the precious black pepper of India he had promised her, he would do the next best thing and bring her these New World chili "peppers," hoping they would be an intriguing substitute. They were, and Spanish cuisine changed forever. So did cuisines in much of the rest of the world, as Spanish traders exchanged the chilies for spices and silk throughout Southeast Asia. Only northern Europeans resisted the new flavors and, except for Hungarians, showed little interest in incorporating the fiery tastes into their rather bland fare.

If the trend toward exploring and assimilating international foods continues—as certainly seems likely—the old line "as American as hamburgers, hot dogs, and apple pie" (none of which were originally American) may soon become "as American as tacos, sushi, stir-fry, and curry." The "global kitchen" is approaching U.S. shores rapidly and will be a fixture in American homes.

The Alphabetical Section

As with any year, varied anniversaries were marked during 1997. Fifty years earlier, the U.S. Air Force was established as a separate branch of the U.S. military; Lawrence Bell of Bell Aircraft congratulated Capt. Charles E. Yeager after a Bell X-1, with Yeager at the controls, broke the sound barrier *(below)*; and the United States was facing a housing shortage. In answer to the latter, William J. Levitt began mass-producing small, inexpensive homes on former potato fields in Nassau county on Long Island, NY *(page 93, bottom)*. In the 50 years since Levittown's birth, the trees had grown and the homes had ceased to resemble their original designs *(page 93, bottom, insets)*.

© SRA Billy Johnson/U.S. Air Force

To celebrate their milestones, the U.S. Air Force staged a "Golden Air Tattoo" at Nellis Air Force Base near Las Vegas, NV, in April 1997 *(above)* and Yeager broke the sound barrier one more—and one last—time over the California desert in October 1997 before announcing that he had "decided to go out on top" *(bottom)*.

Special musical revues were staged at Cinderella's Castle for a yearlong 25th-birthday party at Disney World *(page 93, top left)*.

Although the exact location of John Cabot's 1497 landing in the New World is unknown, Britain's Queen Elizabeth and Prince Philip were in Bonavista, Nfld., in late June 1997 to watch as a replica of Cabot's ship *Ye Matthew* *(page 93, top right)*—with a crew of 19 members—completed a seven-week journey from Bristol, England, and reenacted the landing.

© Archive Photos

© Sam Mircovich/Reuters/Archive Photos

© Stan Godlewski/Gamma-Liaison

© Keith Gosse/AP/Wide World Photos

Photos, Courtesy, Century
21-Dallow Realty

© UPI/Corbis-Bettmann

ABORTION

Women seeking abortions met with few new obstacles in 1997. However, the controversy that developed after the U.S. Supreme Court legalized the procedure in *Roe v. Wade* in 1973 continued. In December the federal Centers for Disease Control and Prevention announced the number of U.S. abortions had dropped by 20% between 1980 and 1995, citing the use of contraceptives as the reason.

Legislation. Rather than openly challenge a woman's right to abortion, antiabortion forces focused their efforts on barring a specific procedure they called "partial birth" abortion. Performed typically in the second or third trimester of pregnancy, intact dilation and extraction involves inducing labor, delivering the fetus feetfirst, and then collapsing the skull to facilitate passage through the birth canal. Public-opinion polls showed widespread disapproval of the procedure, and Congress had banned it in 1996. But President Bill Clinton vetoed the ban, arguing that the bill failed to protect the woman's life. In 1997 both houses of Congress again banned the procedure, except when needed to save the woman's life. The measure (HR 1122)—vetoed by Clinton on the same grounds in October—would have fined and sentenced for up to two years doctors who perform the operation, while exempting the woman from criminal prosecution.

Conservative Republicans postponed further action on the measure until 1998, in hopes of gaining the two-thirds majority needed to override the president's veto in the Senate, which was three votes shy of that margin in 1997. Republicans reportedly hoped to capitalize on public opposition to late-term abortions in their party's quest to gain seats in the 1998 elections, when the entire House and one third of the Senate would face elections.

Antiabortion forces campaigned heavily against pro-choice Republican Christine Todd Whitman's reelection as governor of New Jersey, following her 1996 veto of a state ban on partial-birth abortion, and promised to derail her prospects for national office. Whitman narrowly won reelection. In October antiabortion activists announced plans to press the Republican National Committee to withhold campaign funding from any candidate who opposed a ban on late-term abortions.

Several other bills contained language restricting abortion. Most controversial of these were a broad foreign-operations spending bill (HR 2159) that would pay $819 million of more than $1 billion in unpaid U.S. dues to the United Nations and a bill that would reorganize the State Department (HR 1757). Passage of both measures was held up by clauses—sponsored by Rep. Christopher H. Smith (R-NJ)—that barred U.S. funding of any organization that funds or promotes abortion, even with its own money. Included were overseas family-planning groups offering contraceptive services as a way to reduce the incidence of abortion. The use of U.S. funds to perform abortions already was banned. Clinton promised to veto any measure that included the more restrictive language, first introduced in 1984 by former President Ronald Reagan in an executive order that Clinton overturned shortly after taking office.

Other abortion-related bills included a $25.2 billion appropriations bill for the Treasury Department and other agencies that prohibited federal workers' health plans from paying for most abortions; a ban on abortions in U.S. military hospitals overseas contained in a Defense authorization bill; and the inclusion in a Labor, Health and Human Services, and Education spending bill of a ban on federal funding for abortions except in cases of rape, incest, or to save the woman's life.

The effectiveness of several state laws that imposed waiting periods on women seeking abortion was questioned by a study reported in the *Journal of the American Medical Association*. Researchers found that requiring women to wait 24 hours before an abortion reduced the abortion rate in Mississippi, but drove more women to go out of state to seek the procedure. Mississippi's waiting period also caused more women to seek late-term abortions.

RU-486. While abortion opponents focused on legislative restrictions, pro-choice advocates looked forward to the arrival on the U.S. market of a drug that would enable women to terminate pregnancies at an earlier stage than is possible with surgery. Mifepristone, known popularly as RU-486, was declared safe and effective by the Food and Drug Administration (FDA) in 1996, but final approval awaited completion of plans for manufacturing the drug. The Population Council—a New York City nonprofit family-planning group that acquired the rights to RU-486 from its French manufacturer, Roussel Uclaf—announced in February that it had created a new company, Neogen, to sell RU-486. But in June a European company that had agreed to produce the pill backed out, delaying its introduction until 1998.

MARY H. COOPER
"The CQ [Congressional Quarterly] Researcher"

ACCIDENTS AND DISASTERS

AVIATION

Jan. 9—A twin-engine turboprop commuter plane en route from Cincinnati to Detroit crashes outside of Detroit as it prepares to land; all 29 persons aboard are killed.

Feb. 4—Two Israeli military helicopters collide in midair during a routine mission just south of the Israel-Lebanon border; 73 are killed in the crash.

March 18—A Russian passenger airliner explodes and crashes shortly after taking off from Stavropol, killing all 50 persons on board.

May 8—A passenger jet en route from Chongqing to Shenzhen, China, crash-lands and explodes into flames during a thunderstorm in Shenzhen, killing at least 30 persons.

July 11—A Cuban plane carrying 44 crashes into the Caribbean off Cuba's coast, killing everyone aboard.

Aug. 6—A jumbo jet en route from South Korea to Guam crashes as it attempts to land in Agana, Guam's capital; 225 persons are killed, but 29 miraculously survive.

Sept. 3—A Vietnamese jetliner crashes and burns in Cambodia on its approach to Phnom Penh's airport, killing 65 on board the plane.

Sept. 13—Two military aircraft—one from Germany and one from the United States—apparently collide in midair in the South Atlantic Ocean off the coast of Angola; as many as 33 persons are feared dead.

Sept. 26—An Indonesian passenger plane crashes into a ravine in northeastern Sumatra, killing all 234 on board.

Oct. 10—An Argentine passenger plane crashes and explodes in severe weather conditions near Nuevo Berlín, Uruguay, killing all 75 aboard.

Dec. 6—Sixty-seven persons are killed when a large Russian military-transport plane crashes into an apartment complex near Irkutsk, in central Siberia in Russia.

Dec. 15—A charter flight en route from Tajikistan crashes into the desert as it prepares to land at Sharja airport in the United Arab Emirates; 85 persons are left dead.

Dec. 17—Some seventy persons are killed when a Ukrainian plane crashes while trying to land at Salonica, Greece.

Dec. 19—A Singaporean jet carrying at least 104 persons crashes on the Indonesian island of Sumatra shortly after takeoff from Jakarta, killing all aboard.

FIRES AND EXPLOSIONS

Feb. 23—Fire sweeps through temporary shelters being used by Hindu pilgrims near Baripada, India, killing at least 200.

March 11—Over the course of a week, several explosions in three separate, privately run coal mines in Pingdingshan county, central China, kill a total of 86 miners.

April 15—More than 300 persons are killed when fire sweeps through 70,000 tents at an encampment outside Mecca, Saudi Arabia, where some 2 million Muslims had gathered for the annual pilgrimage to the holy places of Islam.

April 30—An explosion occurs in an underground ordnance depot in Selize, Albania; at least 27 persons are killed.

June 13—Fire breaks out in a crowded movie theater in New Delhi, India, killing some 60 persons.

July 11—Ninety persons are killed when fire rips through a 17-story resort hotel in Pattaya, Thailand.

Sept. 14—At least 28 workers are killed when four fuel tanks explode in a petroleum refinery in Vishakhapatnam, India.

Sept. 29—Fire destroys a building at a home for the mentally retarded near Colina, Chile; 30 residents are killed.

LAND AND SEA TRANSPORTATION

Jan. 14—A crowded bus speeds off a bridge and into the Nile River near Cairo, Egypt, killing at least 39 persons.

Feb. 20—A boat carrying ethnic Tamil refugees from Sri Lanka to India overturns and sinks 35 mi (56.3 km) off the Sri Lankan coast, killing 165 persons.

March 3—A 17-car runaway passenger train crashes near Khaniwal, Pakistan, leaving at least 125 persons dead.

April 29—At least 60 persons are killed in Rongjiawan, central China, when a passenger train crashes into another train stopped at a station.

May 4—More than 100 Rwandan Hutu refugees die from suffocation or crushing and hundreds are injured in an overcrowded train carrying the Hutu from a refugee camp in Zaire to be airlifted to their own country.

Aug. 26—Two riverboats collide near Port Harcourt, Nigeria, sinking one of the boats and leaving about 100 persons dead.

Sept. 4—Two passenger buses collide on a highway in northwest Turkey, and one bus then rolls down an embankment; 33 persons are killed.

Sept. 8—At least 200 persons are feared dead after a crowded ferry sinks off the coast of Haiti while traveling between the mainland and the island of La Gonave.

Sept. 14—At least 77 are killed when a crowded train derails as it crosses a bridge near Raigarh, India.

Sept. 16—A truck carrying children to their work picking cotton in government-owned fields overturns into a canal in the village of Maseer, Egypt, trapping the children inside and causing 29 to drown.

Sept. 26—A Caribbean-registered supertanker collides with an Indian cargo vessel in the Strait of Malacca, between Indonesia and Malaysia; 29 on the cargo ship are killed.

Oct. 13—A bus carrying senior citizens on a holiday outing plunges off a rural highway and down a hill in St.-Joseph-de-la-Rive, Quebec, Canada, killing 43 persons.

Oct. 14—At least 58 persons are killed when an overcrowded bus plunges off a bridge and into a canal near Tangail, Bangladesh.

Nov. 18—At least 29 schoolchildren are killed when their overcrowded school bus plunges off a bridge and into a river near New Delhi, India.

STORMS, FLOODS, AND EARTHQUAKES

Feb. 4—At least 88 are killed when two earthquakes hit northeastern Iran.

Feb. 28—A strong earthquake centered in Baluchistan province, Pakistan, kills at least 60 persons.

Feb. 28—Some 965 persons are killed and tens of thousands are left homeless when a powerful earthquake and some 200 aftershocks strike Ardabil province in northwestern Iran.

March 1–2—Tornadoes and torrential rain and flooding leave at least 49 persons dead as they sweep through Texas, Arkansas, Mississippi, Tennessee, Kentucky, Ohio, and West Virginia, with Arkansas experiencing the most damage.

May 10—More than 1,500 persons are killed when a magnitude-7.1 earthquake strikes northeastern Iran near the Afghanistan border.

May 19—A strong cyclone featuring 125-mph (201-km/hr) winds hits the southern coast of Bangladesh; at least 400,000 homes are destroyed and 108 persons are feared dead.

May 27—Several powerful tornadoes tear through central Texas, killing at least 25 persons in the town of Jarrell.

July 2—Powerful thunderstorms roll through Indiana, Ohio, and Michigan, touching off tornadoes and killing at least 16 persons in Michigan's Lower Peninsula.

July 9—The northeastern coastal region of Venezuela is struck by that nation's worst earthquake in 30 years, which leaves at least 81 persons dead.

Aug. 3—Heavy flooding in Poland and the Czech Republic kills more than 100 persons.

Aug. 17–18—Typhoon Winnie hits Taiwan with heavy rains and winds of up to 92 mph (148 km/hr), killing at least 37 persons; the storm then strikes China, leaving at least 200 dead.

Aug. 27—Unusually heavy monsoon rains and resultant severe flooding have killed at least 945 persons in India since the monsoon season began in June.

Sept. 26—Eleven persons are killed when the Umbria region of central Italy is shaken by two strong earthquakes several hours apart.

Oct. 10—The Pacific coast of Mexico is hit hard by Hurricane Pauline, which triggers landslides and flash flooding that kill some 118 persons.

Nov. 4—At least 132 persons are killed when the southern coast of Vietnam is hit by Typhoon Linda.

Nov. 15—A month of heavy rains in Ethiopia causes the Juba and Shabelle rivers—which flow into Somalia—to flood, killing more than 2,000 persons in the latter country.

MISCELLANEOUS

Feb. 18—At least 250 persons are killed in southern Peru when a mud slide buries two mountain villages.

March 26—An avalanche buries at least 100 persons walking along a highway in northern Afghanistan.

June 25—In Montserrat, the Soufrière Hills volcano—which became active in July 1995—erupts, killing at least 19.

July 30—A landslide strikes a popular ski resort at Thredbo, in New South Wales, Australia, destroying and burying two lodges under tons of rubble; 18 persons are left dead.

Sept. 5—A crowded covered stadium in Ciudad del Este, Paraguay, collapses in strong winds, killing at least 36.

ADVERTISING

The U.S. advertising industry began and ended 1997 on a tumultuous note, but nonetheless managed to post its strongest year ever. The placid economic story, however, masked an array of controversies and a massive restructuring that dramatically reshaped the industry.

The lines separating advertising from editorial content continued to blur in 1997. One example was an ill-fated marketing alliance between the American Medical Association (AMA) and medical-products marketer Sunbeam that brought the AMA's objectivity into question and ultimately led to its reorganization. The Magazine Publishers of America and the American Association of Magazine Editors, meanwhile, joined to establish strict guidelines separating advertising and editorial decisions among member magazine companies. The move was inspired by pressure from major marketers that wanted to screen or change editorial content before they ran ads. One of those marketers, Chrysler Corp., reversed its policy in 1997.

Spending Growth. Despite comparisons to 1996—which saw incremental spending from media coverage of the Atlanta Olympics and the presidential election—U.S. ad spending rose at a higher rate in 1997. Ad agency McCann-Erickson projected that spending would reach nearly $187 billion by year's end. At that rate, it was estimated that the advertising business would have outpaced U.S. economic growth by nearly a percentage point.

Growth came primarily from a continued shifting of marketing budgets back to ad media from promotional spending—particularly retail trade and price promotions that had fallen into disfavor among marketers.

Controversies and Innovation. The year began with the airing of one of 1997's most controversial ad campaigns—a TV commercial, run by hotel chain Holiday Inn during the Super Bowl, that depicted a transsexual attending his (now her) class reunion.

While few other campaigns generated that degree of public outcry, several were surrounded by controversy for other reasons. A 1996 TV ad for Home Box Office (HBO), for example, elicited enormous industry attention when it was nominated for and won the first-ever Emmy Award for a TV commercial.

The placement of ads in unconventional media environments perhaps captured the greatest attention in 1997. Advertisers who ran commercials during the episode of ABC's *Ellen* in which the title character disclosed her homosexuality were threatened with boycotts. The Ford Motor Co. used sensitive TV topics to create a showcase for its messages, becoming the exclusive sponsor of NBC's uninterrupted airing of the Holocaust film *Schindler's List* as well as a controversial episode of CBS' *Murphy Brown* dealing with the title character's breast cancer.

Tobacco Advertising. Of all the controversies surrounding the ad business in 1997, tobacco marketing loomed largest. The year saw a landmark settlement by the tobacco industry, which included numerous advertising and marketing concessions intended to stave off legal action from attorneys general of the states. (*See* BUSINESS AND CORPORATE AFFAIRS—*The Tobacco Industry*.)

By midyear the U.S. Food and Drug Administration (FDA) finalized its new tobacco-advertising rules, which further restricted the media and methods cigarette marketers could use, including extremely stringent prohibitions on media reaching audiences under the legal smoking age of 18.

In a move that appeared to signal the end to an era of tobacco marketing, R.J. Reynolds retired controversial brand icon Joe Camel.

Internet Advertising. Advertising's newest "established" medium, the Internet, grew into a full-fledged media form in 1997. Major marketers began moving into more sophisticated forms of on-line advertising, including interstitial programming and, in an ironic return to the early days of TV, sponsor-driven Web programming. NBC and Levi Strauss & Co., for example, adapted the popular "They Go On" Levi ads into a Web-based series.

Despite stepped-up on-line ad spending, Web advertising was estimated to have totaled significantly less than $1 billion in 1997, or less than a percentage point of media spending.

Agencies. Amid this volatile backdrop, ad agencies faced enormous upheaval and restructuring. Cordiant, the parent of Saatchi & Saatchi, approved and implemented the "de-merger" of its agency holding company, thus splitting it into three independent agencies: Saatchi & Saatchi Advertising, Bates, and Zenith Media. The Leo Burnett agency, meanwhile, experienced major account losses that led to a radical restructuring, effectively breaking it up into many smaller agencies.

Moving in the opposite direction, True North Communications acquired independent Bozell, Jacobs, Kenyon & Eckhardt, forming one of the largest agency networks in the world, following a failed attempt by French-owned Publicis to acquire True North.

JOE MANDESE, *"The Myers Reports"*

AFGHANISTAN

In 1997, Afghanistan's civil war remained a stalemate, but a November agreement on the mutual release of prisoners inched opponents closer to talks. Harsh theocratic rule prevailed over much of the land.

Civil War. During 1997 defections and betrayals marked the civil war between Taliban—an organization of Pashtun religious zealots—and the National Liberation Front of Afghanistan, a loose alliance of Tajiks, Uzbeks, and Hazaras. On May 24, Taliban occupied the northern center of Mazar-e-Sharif—site of the largest, best-equipped opposition force—after the mutiny of Gen. Abdul Malik Pahlawan, deputy to Uzbek leader Gen. Abdul Rashid Dostam. Malik surrendered hundreds of Dostam's troops as well as Tajik leader Ismail Khan. Dostam escaped to Turkey, however, while Mazar-e-Sharif citizens and Malik's own Uzbek soldiers—outraged by Taliban religious fanaticism, ethnic prejudice, and the demand that Uzbek troops disarm—killed 300 occupiers. Malik then changed sides again and helped drive Taliban forces south almost to Kabul. Ahmad Shah Massoud, defense leader of the opposition government that fled Kabul in 1996, and Hazara chief Karim Khalili attacked retreating Taliban flanks, but did not win a decisive victory; Taliban still controlled 75% of the country.

Economy. Inflation continued, with unemployment at more than 50%. Some 57% of Afghans suffered malnutrition. The war dimmed prospects for a planned $2 billion pipeline from Turkmenistan to Pakistan via Afghanistan. Although agriculture—the mainstay of the Afghan economy—was hurt by some 10 million unremoved land mines, opium exports jumped by 25% to 2,800 tons. Afghan opium accounts for 50% of the world's heroin, and Taliban lands produced some 93% of Afghan opium. Although Taliban prohibited hashish, alcohol, and tobacco, it did not restrict opium exports until October, after six months of negotiations with the United Nations (UN). In November, Taliban pledged to uproot new opium-poppy crops in Kandahar province and destroy the country's heroin laboratories.

Society. Taliban's Department for Promoting Virtue and Preventing Vice enforced the world's harshest Islamic theocracy. Women were confined to the home unless accompanied by a male relative, forced to wear head-to-toe burkas when in the open, forbidden to wear high heels or walk "loudly," denied most education, and restricted to such jobs as nursing other women. Men had to grow full, untrimmed beards; wear turbans; and attend prayer sessions five times daily. Music, movies, videos, television, the photographing of anything alive, and clapping were outlawed, as were paper bags—which might contain recycled Korans. Medieval punishments—including amputations, stonings, whippings, and public executions—were common. Some of the executed were left on display for days, with vendors, often children, selling candy to onlookers. A UN International Children's Emergency Fund (UNICEF) survey of 300 Afghan minors—aged 8 to 18—showed severe traumatic stress: 72% had experienced a death in the family (of these, 40% had lost a parent); almost all had witnessed wartime violence; two thirds had seen mutilated bodies or parts of bodies; half had witnessed mass deaths from rockets; and 90% believed they would die in the war. Reversing a trend of refugee repatriation, more than 1 million Afghans, many well educated, fled again to Pakistan, depriving Taliban of professionals needed for effective government.

Foreign Affairs. Each warring faction had powerful but unacknowledged foreign backers. Russia supported the Tajiks and Uzbeks; Iran the Hazaras; and Pakistan and Saudi Arabia, the Taliban. In October, Norbert Holl, outgoing UN special envoy to Afghanistan, said that UN peace efforts were hopeless without agreement among combatants' foreign sponsors. Only three nations recognized Taliban as Afghanistan's legitimate government—Pakistan, Saudi Arabia, and the United Arab Emirates. While the United States contributed $3 billion to a UN mine-removal program, in August it suspended Afghan embassy operations in Washington. In November, U.S. Secretary of State Madeleine Albright called Taliban treatment of women "despicable."

ANTHONY ARNOLD
Freelance Writer on Afghanistan

AFGHANISTAN • Information Highlights

Official Name: Islamic State of Afghanistan.
Location: Central Asia.
Area: 250,000 sq mi (647 500 km²).
Population (mid-1997 est.): 22,100,000.
Chief Cities (1988 est.): Kabul, the capital, 1,424,400; Kandahar, 225,500; Herat, 177,300.
Government: No functioning government as of December 1997.
Monetary Unit: Afghani (3,000 afghanis equal U.S.$1, principal rate, June 1997).
Gross Domestic Product (1995 est. U.S.$): $12,800,000,-000 (purchasing power parity).

AFRICA

In 1997 two long-standing, repressive former leaders—Hastings Kamuzu Banda of Malawi and Mobutu Sese Seko of Zaire—died. In a transparent move to maintain power, Kenya's President Daniel arap Moi, 74, made last-minute reforms to allow opposition parties in the December 1997 general election. Liberia's national election in July, the first since 1985, was deemed free and fair by international observers; rebel leader Charles Taylor was elected president. Military takeovers occurred in Congo, Sierra Leone, and Zaire (renamed the Democratic Republic of the Congo), contributing to widespread cynicism about the long-term chances for African stability and democracy. An attempted coup in Zambia on October 28 led to the declaration of emergency rule and the detention of opposition leaders, including Zambia Democratic Congress (ZDC) leader Dean Mung'omba and former President Kenneth Kaunda. Increasing Hutu violence against Tutsi in Rwanda raised fears of a renewed ethnic war.

U.S. Secretary of State Madeleine Albright paid her first official visit to Africa in mid-December. The trip was aimed at developing closer ties with leaders who were embracing democratic reforms. She cited South Africa as an example for the rest of the continent.

Kenya. In November, President Moi's government lifted a ban on the country's Safina opposition party, a coalition of pro-democracy organizations with support from different ethnic groups, thus opening the way for its participation in the December 29 general election, in which some 9 million Kenyans voted. The decision meant that candidates from other opposition parties also could participate. Safina saw it as a move to further splinter opposition already split along ethnic lines, and feared that Moi would win as he had in 1992, when he received only 38% of the vote. More than a dozen opposition candidates ran for president. On Jan. 4, 1998, Moi was declared the official winner of the balloting, in which he took about 40% of the vote.

Liberia. In July, Liberia held its first truly free election since it became a colony for freed U.S. slaves in the 1840s. Ironically, Charles Taylor—who in 1989 had started the deadly civil war in which an estimated 150,000 had been killed, more than 700,000 had been exiled, and several hundred thousand had lost their homes—won by a landslide. While 13 political parties contested the elections, Taylor and his National Patriotic Front won 75% of the votes cast. The Unity Party, led by Ellen Johnson-Sirleaf, was a distant second with 9%. Many voters—believing Taylor would continue the civil war if not elected—voted for him to avoid further bloodshed. On August 2, Taylor was sworn in, and by mid-August he had appointed all 19 cabinet members and made such key appointments as governor of the central bank.

Zaire/Congo. In May rebels of the Alliance of Democratic Forces for the Liberation of Congo (ADFL), led by Laurent Kabila, overthrew the government of President Mobutu Sese Seko and renamed Zaire the Democratic Republic of the Congo. While there was international approval for the removal of Mobutu, in the months after Kabila took power there was little evidence of economic improvement or greater democracy. In addition, Kabila and his followers were accused of massacring Rwandan Hutu

Property damage was heavy in Brazzaville, the capital of the Republic of the Congo, as a result of a civil war that began in June 1997. Much of the city was left without water and electricity as a result of the conflict.

refugees as Kabila's forces swept across the country earlier in the year. Rwandan Tutsi continued to occupy key roles in Congo's military. In December, under international pressure and after five months of delay, Kabila allowed the United Nations (UN) to investigate the alleged killings. Kabila's initial efforts to unite the deeply divided country were unsuccessful. In November more than 20 died in clashes over the arrest of an ADFL commander, Anselme Masasu Mindaga.

Former President Mobutu, 66, who ruled the country from 1965 until his ouster in mid-May, died on September 7.

Republic of the Congo. On June 5 fighting began between soldiers loyal to Congolese President Pascal Lissouba and the militia of Gen. Denis Sassou-Nguesso, former military ruler of the country. Lissouba had tried to arrest Sassou-Nguesso and disarm his militia prior to the scheduled July 27 presidential elections. The Cobras—a military group loyal to Sassou-Nguesso—consolidated control over the devastated capital city of Brazzaville and the port city of Pointe-Noire early in October. Lissouba went into exile in Burkina Faso, and Sassou-Nguesso—who had been president from 1979 to 1992—declared himself president. The Marxist Sassou-Nguesso often was referred to as a "Champagne Marxist," and was reputed to have appropriated some of the country's vast oil revenues; this loss in revenue, combined with lavish spending, had brought the Congo Republic close to bankruptcy in 1990. In this latest takeover, Sassou-Nguesso—who in 1991 had been forced by trade unions and other pressure groups to organize a "national conference" to bring about reforms, including a democratic national election—was said to have had strong military backing from the Angolan military because Lissouba was seen as a supporter of Jonas Savimbi's rebel movement, the Union for the Total Independence of Angola (UNITA). Some observers maintained that Lissouba had promised Sassou-Nguesso a place in his government prior to the 1992 election but reneged after winning. Sassou-Nguesso had supported Lissouba's opponents in the 1992 election, primarily in the north of the country. He also was said to have had the support of French oil companies, concerned about their lucrative interests in the country.

Sierra Leone. Democracy in Sierra Leone came to an abrupt end on May 25, 1997, when President Ahmad Tejan Kabbah's government—elected in a free and fair 1996 election—was toppled by low-ranking officers dissatisfied with Kabbah's policies toward the

© Sasa Kralj/AP/Wide World Photos

On Aug. 26, 1997, F.W. de Klerk, above, the 61-year-old former president of South Africa, announced that he was resigning as leader of the National Party and retiring from politics.

military. Sierra Leone had been under military rule from 1992 to 1996. Kabbah was replaced by Maj. Johnny Paul Koromah. There was no support or recognition for the military takeover, and Western and African nations saw the coup as a major attack on democracy in Africa. Nigerian troops, which were in Sierra Leone as part of an agreement with President Kabbah, refused to accept the legitimacy of the junta and took military action against it for the remainder of the year. The British Commonwealth suspended Sierra Leone's membership, and the Economic Community of West Africa (ECOWAS) imposed trade sanctions. In October the military rulers agreed to a peace plan, negotiated with the foreign ministers of neighboring nations, whereby the president would be restored to power in April 1998.

South Africa. In August, Nobel Peace Prize cowinner and former President F. W. de Klerk announced that he was resigning as leader of the National Party (NP) and from politics. De Klerk was said to have been unhappy about internal disputes over the future of the party and suggestions by the Truth and Reconciliation Commission of his complicity in some of the atrocities committed during the apartheid era. Marthinus van Schalkwyk, a 37-year-old political scientist, succeeded him.

The Truth and Reconciliation Commission, under the leadership of Archbishop Desmond Tutu, continued its hearings. Those who testified before the commission included cabinet and military leaders from the apartheid era as well as prominent members of the African National Congress (ANC). Several dozen witnesses implicated Winnie Madikizela-Mandela, former wife of President Nelson Mandela, in various murders and assaults.

Nelson Mandela stepped down as leader of the ANC at the end of 1997 and reaffirmed that in 1999 he would retire as the president of South Africa. He said that his chosen successor was Deputy President Thabo Mbeki, in whom he had the utmost confidence. On December 16, Mandela made his last speech as president of the ANC before 3,000 delegates in the Northern Cape town of Mafeking. In his speech, he said that the achievement of equality was far from complete and that many whites continued to resist change and oppose important policies such as affirmative action. At the same time, he was critical of the increasing corruption in the country, of the media, and of donor agencies. His harshest remarks were reserved for opposition parties such as the National Party, the Democratic Party, and the newly formed United Democratic Movement (UDM). The next day the ANC delegates, not surprisingly, chose Mbeki as leader of the party. Some observers believed Mandela's strident attacks reflected many of Mbeki's views. The same day, Winnie Madikizela-Mandela withdrew her name for consideration as deputy president of the ANC, because it was clear that only a handful of the delegates supported her. Jacob Zuma, the party's national chair, was elected ANC deputy president.

Zimbabwe. Widespread strikes by workers in many different sectors of the economy—who were dissatisfied with government mismanagement and corruption, as well as soaring prices for basic commodities—plagued Zimbabwe during 1997. Veterans of the country's liberation war prevented President Robert Mugabe from making a speech at the Heroes Day celebration because they had not received promised benefits. The International Monetary Fund (IMF) refused to extend loan payments to the government due to its continued resistance to the implementation of economic reforms.

At the end of the year, Mugabe threatened to appropriate, without adequate compensation, more than 1,700 white-owned farms for redistribution to landless African farmers. His demands that the British government provide compensation to dispossessed white farmers was rejected by British Prime Minister Tony Blair, because there was no plan to ensure that the land would be allocated to farmers. In the past, top politicians and military leaders had received much of the land earmarked for redistribution. On December 9 the first nationwide general strike since the country gained independence was held. It was accompanied by sporadic violence, especially in the capital city of Harare.

Somalia. In November the Egyptian government brought together the warring Somali National Alliance (SNA), under the leadership of Hussein Aideed, and Ali Mahdi's Somali Salvation Alliance (SSA) in Cairo. While past peace efforts had failed, there was some promise the new talks would reach a settlement because of the devastating floods that had deluged the country. Some 1,300 had been killed in the floods, while thousands were left homeless. In addition, crops, farmland, and livestock herds were destroyed. At the Cairo meeting there appeared to be consensus on a future government that would include a council of presidents.

Malawi. At the end of November former Malawi President Banda, who had led what formerly was known as Nyasaland to independence in 1964, died of respiratory failure in a Johannesburg hospital. Although his exact age was unknown, he was rumored to have been in his late 90s. Banda's rule was characterized by a mixture of benevolent dictatorship and repression. In 1971 he declared himself "president for life," but in 1994 he was ousted from power after instituting democratic reforms under pressure from foreign donors and governments. Soon thereafter, he was placed on trial for allegedly authorizing the murders of three cabinet ministers and a member of parliament ten years earlier. He subsequently was acquitted of the charges.

Sudan. In 1991 three commanders of the Sudan People's Liberation Army (SPLA)—Riak Machar, Lam Akol, and Gordon Kong—split from the movement because of differences over priorities and leadership. In 1996, Machar signed a peace agreement with the Islamic government of Sudan; since April 1997, he had chaired the Southern Sudan Coordinating Council, which essentially governed ten states in the south and had agreed to hold a referendum in the next four years to determine whether people in the south wished to join or secede from a united Sudan. In April other rebel factions of the SPLA signed

© David Guttenfelder/AP/Wide World Photos

Although the Supreme Court of Cameroon ruled that 81% of the electorate had reelected President Paul Biya overwhelmingly on Oct. 12, 1997, many journalists found the voting stations deserted—especially in opposition strongholds such as Bamenda, above.

an agreement with the government, and in September, Akol, commander of the SPLA-United, also signed a peace agreement with the government. Col. John Garang, leader of one of the largest factions of the SPLA—whose goal is full self-determination for the south—accused Akol of selling out. Early in the year the government indicated willingness to talk with Garang. A scheduled meeting between Sudan President Omar Hassan Ahmed al-Bashir and Garang in South Africa, to be hosted by Nelson Mandela, did not take place, however. Instead, the government agreed to accept the 1994 Declaration of Principles (DOP)—an Inter-Governmental Authority on Drought and Development (IGADD) negotiation arrangement previously accepted only by opposition forces. IGADD is comprised of leaders of East African states actively working for a resolution to the Sudanese conflict.

Further negotiations in September, in which regional foreign ministers from Kenya, Uganda, Eritrea, and Ethiopia participated, were a hopeful sign that the conflict might be resolved. Talks between the government and these groups continued in October.

Angola. In October the UN Security Council imposed sanctions against UNITA. The sanctions included removal of diplomatic privileges and a ban on flights into territory under UNITA control. The rebel movement was obliged to dismantle its military and surrender the towns of Andulo and Bailundo by the end of October, under the terms of the 1994 Lusaka peace accords. Although UNITA's Savimbi was unwilling to meet the terms of the Lusaka agreement, there were 70 UNITA members in the Angolan parliament. Some commentators thought there were now two factions of UNITA—one seeking to continue the war and another working within the political process. UNITA continued to use profits from the rich diamond-producing areas it holds to fund its operation.

Rwanda. What began as sporadic attacks by Hutu rebels against Tutsi in 1996 escalated during the last six months of 1997, particularly in northwest Rwanda near the border with Congo, where rebels were alleged to be camped. The rebels were mostly former Rwandan Hutu soldiers who had fled the country earlier, fearing reprisals for the 1994 Hutu massacre of hundreds of thousands of Tutsi. One of the worst attacks occurred on December 11 at a refugee camp where more than 230 Tutsi were murdered. Both Amnesty International and the UN estimated that as many as 6,000 had been killed by both Hutu and Tutsi in Rwanda during 1997.

PATRICK O'MEARA and N. BRIAN WINCHESTER
Indiana University

AGRICULTURE

Farmers and agribusinesses around the world continued to provide an increased supply of food, cotton, and other natural fibers to a growing world population in 1997, despite increased environmental restrictions and unfavorable weather in parts of Australia, Indonesia, China, and other important agricultural areas.

International

Feed Grain. World feed-grain production dropped an estimated 2.4% below that of 1996, but was slightly more than offset by increases in wheat and rice crops. Grain production rose in Eastern and Western Europe and the former Soviet Union, but declined in North America, China, and Australia in response to adverse weather. Several countries in Eastern Europe and the former Soviet Union moved from importing to net-grain-exporting positions. A decade earlier the former Soviet Union had been one of the largest foreign markets for U.S. grain.

World feed-grain stocks as a percentage of annual use were projected to remain near 1995 levels that triggered a dramatic rise in grain prices, while food-grain stocks as a percentage of annual consumption were modestly above 1995–96 levels. Concern over possible adverse impacts on global grain production stemming from El Niño weather developments and global warming caused increased volatility in grain prices. El Niño's negative impacts on crop production, however, were relatively small, and were felt mainly in Australia and parts of eastern Asia.

The southern two thirds of Africa continued to present the largest challenge to agricultural productivity due to rapid population growth, low incomes, low prices for agricultural produce, and restrictive government policies. Low incomes also limited the ability of African consumers to augment their food supplies through imports.

Livestock. Global poultry and pork production continued their long-term upward trend, responding to increased consumer income and the desire for more dietary protein in Asia, Latin America, North Africa, the Middle East, and other areas. Nonetheless, severe diseases caused sharp reductions in the swine herds of Taiwan and the Netherlands. In Taiwan swine inventories were nearly 40% less than in 1996, as herds were slaughtered to halt a foot-and-mouth-disease epidemic. In the Netherlands the herd was reduced about 25% due to a severe outbreak of hog cholera. Both countries had been experiencing serious environmental problems because of highly concentrated livestock production and dense populations. Downsized pork industries in these countries were more than offset by sharply expanding pork production in the United States and Canada, where population densities are much lower and environmental impacts are less severe. Canadian livestock production also was encouraged by the loss of long-standing freight subsidies that previously had supported central-prairie-province grain prices. In some cases, expanded livestock production came from Taiwanese producers who relocated to Canada but continued to supply their established Japanese customers.

Concern over bovine spongiform encephalopathy (BSE) remained high in Europe, restraining the demand for beef and causing continued action to prevent British beef from entering the European continent. British agricultural authorities proposed an extensive slaughter plan that would eradicate all animals born before controls were adopted, when BSE infection was possible.

United States

Crop Production. U.S. farmers harvested a bumper wheat crop that caused shortages of storage space in the central Great Plains, despite a very unusual mid-spring freeze that initially appeared to damage winter-wheat production. Nearly ideal spring and early summer weather allowed the crop to recover, however, and the total U.S. production of winter and spring wheat was 1% more than the large harvest of 1996, despite a 6% decline in the total area harvested. A cool, wet spring in the northern plains, severe flooding in parts of North Dakota and Minnesota, and more attractive prices for oilseed crops contributed to the reduced amount of cropland devoted to wheat. Lack of storage space was aggravated by a major railroad merger that limited the number of railroad cars used to move grain to terminal elevators.

The nation's corn crop slightly exceeded that of 1996, and the soybean crop was up about 14%. The planted area of some crops declined in response to the Freedom-to-Farm Act implemented in late 1996, which removed certain government production controls and income-protection payments. Crops affected included sorghum, barley, and cotton.

Citrus-fruit production also exceeded that of 1996, and supplies of most other fruits and vegetables were ample. The U.S. apple crop was about 1% larger than in 1996, while the peach crop increased 28% and sweet-cherry and pear production rose 24%. Production of almonds, pecans, walnuts, apricots, prunes, and plums also was well above the 1996 total. U.S. grape production rose by an estimated 20%, due to favorable weather in 1997. The nation's potato crop declined about 8% because of disappointing 1996 prices and reduced area planted. A sharp increase in area and yields boosted lentil production by an estimated 71% over 1996.

Livestock. Some concern was expressed over possible BSE in U.S. beef supplies early in the year, but extensive tests failed to identify a problem. Of mounting concern, however, was the extensive use of antibiotics in food-producing animals. Studies by the Food and Drug Administration Center for Veterinary Medicine and the Centers for Disease Control and Prevention (CDC) showed a significant risk that such use could lead to the development of antibiotic-resistant microbes and the reduced effectiveness of antibiotics in human medicines. A bill introduced in Congress late in the year called for a review of antibiotic use in the U.S. poultry industry.

Extreme winter weather in the northern plains from January through March caused severe losses for cattle ranchers—especially of younger animals and calves. Federal disaster assistance tempered the financial impacts and helped ranchers obtain private financing to cover some of the lost income and large feed bills. In late October an unexpectedly heavy snowstorm struck major cattle-feeding areas of Kansas, Nebraska, and Colorado, which caused extensive cattle deaths. Some estimates placed the toll at more than 100,000 animals.

Trade Issues. Several major U.S. agricultural groups were disappointed by Congress' failure to pass "fast-track" legislation that would allow the administration to negotiate new trade agreements with other countries, and then present them to Congress for approval or disapproval as a single package rather than voting on separate details. Agricultural trade is vitally important to U.S. agriculture because production capacity far exceeds domestic demand for most major farm products. Fast-track legislation was proposed in part to help facilitate renegotiation of the agricultural section of the Uruguay Round of the General Agreement on Tariffs and Trade. It also was expected to facilitate negotiations to add other nations to the North American Free Trade Agreement (NAFTA).

Agricultural groups continued to express concern about nontariff barriers allegedly used by the European Union (EU) to restrict U.S. imports—particularly livestock products—such as differing U.S. and EU sanitary requirements. Many U.S. groups said such requirements need to be based on sound science. EU import-license requirements also were considered by some to be a form of nontariff barrier for U.S. cheese and other dairy products. Other trade issues related to subsidies on agricultural exports, particularly from the EU.

Environmental Concerns. Environmental impacts and regulation changes were debated in several important agricultural states. A proposed Senate bill would establish nationwide standards for manure handling in medium- and large-sized livestock operations. The impact on aquatic life in the Gulf of Mexico caused by nitrate concentrations in the Mississippi River watershed was another environmental concern. To reduce potential groundwater contamination, the bidding process was revised for the Conservation Reserve Program (CRP)—established in 1986 to focus on long-term removal of environmentally sensitive fields or portions of fields from production, as well as those best suited for wildlife habitat. The new process would allow landowners to enroll new property into the program, or reenter land under an expiring CRP contract.

Technology. The first fruits of the biotechnology revolution had a positive impact on U.S. grain yields and crop productivity. Slightly less than 10% of the nation's corn crop was planted with varieties containing *Bacillus thuringiensis* (BT), a naturally occurring insect deterrent transferred into crop plants through recombinant DNA techniques. BT enables corn plants to resist the widespread insect pests known as corn borers, which damage stalks—weakening plants and reducing yields. BT corn can eliminate the need for costly and environmentally damaging insecticides typically used to control such pests. Agriculturalists warned farmers that the new seed should be used along with conventional varieties to avoid the development of insect strains resistant to BT corn.

"Round-Up–ready" soybeans—soybeans that are resistant to the broad-spectrum herbicide Round-Up—also were used more extensively by U.S. farmers than in 1996, and were being considered by South American farmers. Round-Up kills a wide range of grasses and broadleaf weeds, as well as older varieties of soybeans. The altered soybeans allow farmers to control yield-reducing weeds more effectively, eliminating the need for repeated herbicide treatments. Industry estimates based on seed sales indicate that up to 10 million acres (4 million ha)—17% of the total planted area—are Round-Up–ready soybeans. Agriculturalists noted that the use of this and other yield-increasing technologies was important, since global population expands by more than 2% each year, while cropland in many countries shrinks.

South American governments authorized the importation of limited amounts of these two genetically altered crops, while Western Europe and Egypt continued to express concern about the safety of foods made from these crops. Scientific studies indicated such products should pose no added health risks for consumers.

U.S. high-oil corn—another product of genetic modification—also gained acceptance in the world livestock-feeding industry. The oil content of this product tends to be about double that of conventional corn, providing higher energy and more rapid weight gain in livestock than conventional corn.

Geographic Information Systems (GIS) were used increasingly by farmers as a tool for maximizing efficiency in grain and oilseed production. GIS technology uses computers on harvesting equipment to monitor crop yields continuously, utilize satellite signals to determine location within the field, and create topographical yield maps. Farmers use the maps to examine agronomic conditions in low-yielding areas, adjust fertilizer rates, change weed-control programs, and make other management adjustments.

Structural Changes and Productivity. Structural changes continued to move agriculture and agribusiness toward fewer and larger firms. Changes were most rapid in the hog-pork industry, with substantial increases in the number of large confinement farrowing and finishing facilities. The sale of land to larger operations by retiring grain farmers led to an increase in the average size of a grain farm. In some areas, there also was strong interest in large-scale dairy farms. Mergers and joint ventures resulted in fewer but larger businesses in the farm-input and agricultural-credit industries as well.

A partnership of farmers, agribusiness supply and marketing firms, and public and private research and educational institutions has made sustained increases in productivity possible. Productivity increases continued in 1997, despite a shrinking cropland base, environmental constraints, and a declining number of farmers worldwide.

ROBERT N. WISNER, *Iowa State University*

ALBANIA

During 1997, Albania was shaken by armed rebellion against the government of President Sali Berisha. The unrest followed the collapse of fraudulent investment schemes in which more than half of the population lost their life savings. Calm returned after general elections brought the Socialists back to power.

Public Revolt. During the first half of 1997, Albania was crippled by a mass armed rebellion against the central government, sparked by the dissolution of several "pyramid" schemes that had swindled investors of their life savings. Observers estimated that about half of Albania's 3 million people had lost money. The authorities in the capital, Tiranë, rapidly lost control of large areas of the country as military and police forces rapidly disintegrated. Rebels demanded that Berisha—whose government was accused of benefiting directly from the failed schemes—resign. Tiranë asserted that opposition Socialists orchestrated the unrest in order to overthrow the government. Hundreds died as rebels and ordinary citizens captured arms from military stocks; by March the entire southern part of the country was controlled by local militias, criminal gangs, or armed citizens defending themselves against looting and banditry.

To prevent the outbreak of an all-out civil war, Berisha declared a state of emergency and appointed an interim government of national reconciliation headed by Socialist Bashkim Fino. He also agreed to hold early general elections in June and promised to compensate victims of pyramid schemes. The administration appealed for an international military force to restore law and order, and in April a multinational force of 7,000 arrived. Mandated by the United Nations (UN) Security Council to protect the delivery of humanitarian assistance and to avoid confrontations with armed civilians, the Italian-led force stayed only four months.

Despite poor security conditions, the Organization for Security and Cooperation in Europe (OSCE) declared the June elections acceptable by international standards. The Socialists overwhelmingly won, gaining 100 of the 155 parliamentary seats. A number of smaller parties allied with the Socialists took 17 seats, giving the coalition more than a two-thirds majority and enabling it to change the constitution to weaken presidential powers. The ruling Democratic Party was decimated and Berisha resigned. Parliament elected Socialist Rexhep Mejdani as president, and Socialist leader Fatos Nano became prime

In Albania the collapse of a fraudulent investment scheme led to rebellion against the government of President Sali Berisha in 1997. A state of emergency was declared. General elections—in which the Socialists were returned to power—helped restore calm.

© Yannis Behrakis/Reuters/Archive Photos

minister. In a public referendum held at the same time, more than 60% opted to keep Albania a republic, rejecting the creation of a monarchy; King Leka Zogu had returned to the country but was unable to muster any significant support.

The new government set three priorities for rebuilding the country: to reestablish law and order, rebuild paralyzed government institutions, and reconstruct the shattered economy. The government began efforts to reform and rebuild the discredited police and security forces and restore public confidence in national institutions. The state of emergency was lifted, an amnesty was offered to citizens who surrendered captured weapons, and several of the most threatening gangs were disarmed by security forces.

ALBANIA • Information Highlights

Official Name: Republic of Albania.
Location: Southern Europe, Balkan peninsula.
Area: 11,100 sq mi (28 750 km²).
Population (mid-1997 est.): 3,400,000.
Chief City (1990 est.): Tiranë, the capital, 244,200.
Government: *Head of state,* Rexhep Mejdani, president (took office July 1997). *Head of government,* Fatos Nano, prime minister (took office July 1997). *Legislature* (unicameral)—People's Assembly.
Monetary Unit: New lek (145.170 leks equal U.S.$1, market rate, July 1997).
Gross Domestic Product (1995 est. U.S.$): $4,100,000,000 (purchasing power parity).
Economic Index (1996, 1992 = 100): *Consumer Prices,* all items, 275.5; food, 263.0.

The Democratic Party—now in opposition—reelected Berisha as party leader and asserted its intention to push for early general elections. The Democrats also claimed that the Socialists were conducting purges in all governmental, educational, and judicial institutions and failing to compensate pyramid-scheme victims. Socialist leaders asserted that they simply were depoliticizing all official bodies and restoring public trust in the government.

Economic Rebuilding. The Nano government signaled a commitment to strict fiscal discipline to reduce the budget deficit and introduce free-market reforms based on the privatization of state-owned enterprises. It, however, was unable to repay investors their losses because of a lack of available funds, and analysts warned that the large-scale printing of cash to compensate citizens would spark hyperinflation.

In September, parliament approved a new tax law and introduced price hikes on a range of products, including tobacco, alcohol, and fuel, to improve revenues and currency reserves. The projected 1997 inflation rate of 50% was acceptable to international advisers. The World Bank provided funding to help Tiranë carry out its financial-transparency process and close down the remaining pyramid schemes. In October authorities signed an agreement with the International Monetary Fund (IMF) in which $12 million would be made available for economic reconstruction. Further aid from donor countries was made conditional, based on the progress of fiscal reform and cuts in the budget deficit.

International Relations. While the Italian-led UN mission helped the Nano government restore a sufficient measure of security, Italian, Greek, and Turkish military advisers remained to help train and organize the police and the military. North Atlantic Treaty Organization (NATO) Secretary-General Javier Solana signed an agreement with Prime Minister Nano to help rebuild the Albanian armed forces. The Western European Union—the European Union's (EU's) military arm—also launched a six-month police-training mission. NATO officials expressed concerns that disturbances in Albania could destabilize the Albanian population of Kosovo in neighboring Serbia as well the Albanian regions of Macedonia. Indeed, reports surfaced that weapons from Albania were finding their way to armed groups in both locations.

JANUSZ BUGAJSKI
Center for Strategic and International Studies

ALGERIA

The violence that had wracked Algeria since 1992 continued throughout 1997. National parliamentary elections in June and local elections in October did little to restore the legitimacy of the military-dominated regime. After a string of gruesome massacres in the summer, one of the armed Islamist opposition groups declared a cease-fire, but violence continued.

Elections. With the constitution revised by referendum in November 1996, the government organized parliamentary elections to restore the National Assembly that was dissolved during the 1992 military coup. In January it was announced that the new assembly would have 380 seats, filled by a system of modified proportional representation. President Lamine Zeroual declared that he would form a new political party called the National Democratic Rally (RND) to promote his views during the electoral process. Abdelhak Benhamouda—an outspoken critic of the Islamist movements—was assassinated on January 28 by an Islamic terrorist group, after the press reported that he would resign as head of the General Workers' Union (UGTA) to assume leadership of the new presidential party. Benhamouda was the most prominent victim of a wave of car bombs and raids that claimed more than 250 lives in and around Algiers during January. President Zeroual denounced the attacks on television, claiming that "foreign interests" were responsible for the unrest in Algeria.

In February, Zeroual appointed a little-known former ambassador, Abdelkader Ben

© Benito/Gamma-Liaison

Parliamentary elections in June 1997 did little to improve the political situation in Algeria. A UN observer group criticized various aspects of the voting process. Meanwhile, violence continued to rock the nation.

Salah, to serve as head of the RND, which was destined to replace the discredited National Liberation Front (FLN) as the party of the governing regime. The government formed an independent national commission to monitor the legislative elections in the politically and socially volatile setting. A new election law that prohibited political parties based upon religion barred the Islamic Salvation Front (FIS). FIS had won the 1991 election, but was not allowed to rule. The Islamic Society Movement (Hamas) changed its name to the Movement of a Society for Peace (MSP) to comply with the law. Some 39 political parties ultimately fielded candidates in the June 5 election.

The major opposition parties—including Hamas, the Socialist Forces Front (FFS), the Rally for Culture and Democracy (RCD), and the Workers' Party (PT)—all protested the commission's handling of the elections, accusing it of censorship and favoritism toward the RND. PT leader Louisa Hanoun was refused television time, and the FFS was prohibited from circulating certain election materials. On May 26, Hamas threatened to boycott the election over the commission's heavy-handedness. A United Nations (UN) observer group later criticized many aspects of the electoral process, including a lack of transparency in counting the votes.

RND won the most seats—156—while the FLN, now realigned with President Zeroual, won 62 seats, giving the government a comfortable majority of 218 of the 380 seats. Hamas won 69 seats, while another Islamic party, La Nahda, won 34, giving the Islamists 103 seats. The two Berber-based parties—FFS and RC—won 20 and 19 seats, respectively, giving them about 10% of the assembly membership. The remaining 20 seats were scattered among the PT (four), several smaller parties, and independents. Party leaders such as Mahfoud Nahnah (Hamas) and Said Sadi (RCD) accused the government of fraud, while FFS chairman Seddik Debaïli denounced the "total opaqueness" of the process. Despite much discontent, the new assembly began to operate, providing a forum that had been absent from the political system since 1992. Ahmed Ouyahia was reappointed prime minister; his new government was composed of 21 ministers from the RND, seven from the FLN, and seven from Hamas. The major ministries (foreign affairs, interior, finance, justice) continued to be held by the same officials.

The October local elections produced even stronger expressions of outrage. Despite an apparently feeble turnout, the Ministry of the Interior declared that 66% of eligible voters had cast ballots. The official results gave RND 55% of the seats on the town and city councils—well ahead of the FLN (22%) and Hamas (not quite 7%). Large demonstrations protesting this "massive fraud" were held in Algiers on October 27 and October 30.

Violence. While terrorist violence never had subsided, the scale and savagery of attacks on villages south of Algiers from July through September were unprecedented. Nighttime raids were estimated to have killed 1,000. The attacks—at least one just outside Algiers—followed the July 15 release of top FIS leader Abassi Madani. On September 1, Madani—who spent six years in a military prison—was rearrested after he called for UN involvement in mediating Algeria's civil war. Despite his renewed detention, the military branch of the FIS—the Islamic Salvation Army—unilaterally declared a cease-fire on October 1. Violence continued, however, largely attributed to the Armed Islamic Group (GIA), a radical FIS splinter faction.

Economy. Aided by rising energy prices and production, the balance of payments ran a surplus in 1996, according to figures released in 1997. By April, Algeria held more than $5 billion in reserves, and other economic indicators were the most positive in years. The minister of mines and industry announced that 1997 oil-production capacity would be between 850,000 and 900,000 barrels per day. Natural-gas exports—up 9.5% in 1996—were expected to rise another 25% to 52 billion cubic meters; among these were the first shipments by trans-Mediterranean pipeline to Portugal. A severe drought in western Algeria during February and March badly damaged the annual cereals harvest.

ROBERT MORTIMER, *Haverford College*

ALGERIA • Information Highlights

Official Name: Democratic and Popular Republic of Algeria.
Location: North Africa.
Area: 919,591 sq mi (2 381 740 km²).
Population (mid-1997 est.): 29,800,000.
Chief Cities (1987 census): Algiers, the capital, 1,507,241; Oran, 628,558; Constantine, 440,842.
Government: *Head of state,* Lamine Zeroual, president (took office January 1994). *Head of government,* Ahmed Ouyahia, prime minister (named Dec. 31, 1995). *Legislature* (unicameral)—National Assembly.
Monetary Unit: Dinar (59.346 dinars equal U.S.$1, official rate, July 1997).
Gross Domestic Product (1995 est. U.S.$): $108,700,000,000 (purchasing power parity).
Economic Indexes: *Consumer Prices* (1995, 1990 = 100): all items, 334.6; food, 347.1. *Industrial Production* (1996, 1990 = 100): 80.
Foreign Trade (1995 est. U.S.$): *Imports,* $10,250,000,000; *exports,* $10,240,000,000.

ANTHROPOLOGY

Among the 1997 highlights in anthropology were genetic tests indicating Neanderthals were not ancestors of modern humans, the discovery of the oldest fossil footprint of a modern human, and the possible discovery of a new *Homo* species.

Neanderthal DNA. In an unprecedented achievement, a team of German and U.S. scientists extracted a small segment of mitochondrial DNA, genetic material inherited only through the mother, from a Neanderthal fossil found in Germany in 1856. Differences between the ancient genetic sequence and corresponding sequences in modern people indicated that Neanderthals were not ancestors of *Homo sapiens*, the researchers reported. The Neanderthal sequence was equally unlike DNA samples of Africans, Europeans, Asians, Native Americans, Australians, and Pacific Islanders. If European Neanderthals had interbred with modern humans, as some researchers think, they should exhibit a closer genetic match to people now living in Europe than to those in other parts of the world. Neanderthals died out some 30,000 years ago.

Statistical analyses of the ancient DNA and human genetic material suggested that Neanderthals split from the human evolutionary line about 600,000 years ago, whereas fully modern humans emerged in Africa around 150,000 years ago. Debate over modern human origin continued, however, as scientists awaited the isolation of further DNA samples from Neanderthals and prehistoric humans.

Ancient Footprints. Researchers working in South Africa discovered the oldest known footprints of any anatomically modern human. Preliminary estimates placed their age at about 117,000 years old. At that time, a person apparently walked down a sand dune toward a lagoon shortly after a rainstorm. The moist sand held three footprints intact. Wind then blew dry sand into the tracks and covered them with material that eventually turned to rock, which slowly eroded over tens of thousands of years. Found along Langebaan Lagoon, 60 mi (97 km) north of Cape Town, the footprints each measure 8.5 inches (21.6 cm) long. Comparisons with feet of modern hunter-gatherers in southern Africa indicated that the ancient human stood between 5 ft (1.5 m) and 5′ 4″ (1.6 m) tall. The researchers suspect the footprints may have been made by an adult female.

Spanish Fossils. Fossils discovered in a Spanish cave could belong to a new species in the human evolutionary family, some scientists argued. Dubbed *Homo antecessor*, the approximately 800,000-year-old species may have served as the last common ancestor of Neanderthals and modern humans. However, anthropological opinion about the identity of the ancient bones was divided. Some investigators assigned the fossils to a species already uncovered in Germany, *H. heidelbergensis*,

Researchers discovered the oldest known footprints of an anatomically modern human on the shore of a lagoon in South Africa in 1997. The footprints are reported to be 117,000 years old.

while others refrained from designating a species to any *Homo* remains from that general time range.

The Spanish bones display an unusual mix of modern and primitive features that justify their inclusion in a new species, according to their discoverers. For instance, the facial area is relatively flat, as in modern humans, without the jutting jaw typical of Neanderthals. At the same time, the braincase, lower jaw, and teeth in some ways resemble those of human ancestors who lived in eastern Africa close to 2 million years ago.

Ancient Apes and Monkeys. An animal that lived more than 20 million years ago may be the ancestor of living apes, humans, and gibbons, according to scientists excavating the find in Uganda in 1997. Assigned to a new genus, *Morotopithecus*, the creature was capable of a relatively upright posture. Researchers contended that the fossils show the earliest evidence for an apelike body plan in the primate fossil record.

A 15-million-year-old ape found in Kenya, known as *Kenyapithecus*, also may have held a close evolutionary relationship to modern apes and humans. Another find in Kenya, the skull of an ancient monkey belonging to the genus *Victoriapithecus*, is the oldest known monkey skull in the Old World. While the creature clearly was a monkey, parts of the face look as though they belong to a smaller version of an orangutan.

BRUCE BOWER, *"Science News"*

ARCHAEOLOGY

Evidence that urban planning occurred more than 4,000 years ago and the discoveries of the world's oldest known hunting weapons and of the flagship of the pirate Blackbeard were among 1997 highlights in archaeology.

Eastern Hemisphere

Turkish City. Excavations of an ancient city in southeastern Turkey yielded evidence of surprisingly modern urban planning more than 4,000 years ago. Titus Hoyuk, a 125-acre (51-ha) walled site, rose and fell rapidly between 2500 B.C. and 2200 B.C., leaving its original structures relatively unobscured by later construction. Investigators uncovered groups of houses in two residential neighborhoods. Analysis indicated that builders first had installed rock-paved streets, followed by identical dwellings constructed according to standardized plans. One neighborhood had slightly larger, fancier houses. Extended families apparently lived in the homes. Each featured several cooking areas, as well as stone crypts for seven to nine deceased family members.

Hunting Spears. A German coal mine yielded the world's oldest known hunting weapons, a trio of wooden spears produced some 400,000 years ago. The spears, which ranged in length from 6 ft to 7 ft (1.8–2.1 m), were uncovered among sharpened stone tools and animal bones, including the remains of more than ten butchered horses. Investigators theorized that the spears were used for hunting and not simply to drive predators away from carcasses.

Careful planning went into making the spears. Each was carved from a 30-year-old spruce tree; the sharpened tips were made from the base of the trunk, where the wood is hardest. The weighted shaft is shaped much like a modern javelin, suggesting that the spears were made to throw at animals from a distance.

African Hunters. The earliest undisputed *Homo sapiens*, whose bones have been uncovered in caves at the mouth of South Africa's Klasies River and date to about 100,000 years ago, hunted with more skill and success than previously assumed. That conclusion was reached through an analysis of animal bones found with the ancient human remains. A microscopic study of more than 5,400 of these bones found that nearly one in five bears butchering marks. The marks appear on animals of all sizes and cluster at major skeletal joints, where an animal is easiest to cut apart. Many bones came from prime meat-bearing areas, such as the upper legs.

A broken spear tip was found still embedded in the neck bone of an extinct giant buffalo, one of southern Africa's largest Stone Age game animals. Early humans who used the Klasies River caves may have formed hunting parties that drove large game into pits studded with pointed stakes and ran smaller game off nearby cliffs.

Ancient Ships. The largest concentration of deep-sea ancient shipwrecks ever found was discovered 2,500 ft (762 m) beneath the surface of the Mediterranean Sea. The eight sailing ships were detected by a research team in a U.S. Navy nuclear submarine equipped with long-range sonar. After locating the ships, the team inspected the wrecks with a remote-controlled vehicle, retrieving 115 items by means of mechanical arms.

Five ships sailed at the time of the Roman Empire and may have plied trade routes from

Rome to North Africa. The oldest vessel dates to around 100 B.C. Storage areas in the 100-ft (31-m)-long ship held large clay jars known to have been used as shipping containers. Another Roman ship from the 1st century A.D. held large stone columns and blocks, perhaps parts of a temple being shipped to a construction site. The wreckage covers 20 sq mi (52 km²) and includes three ships about 100 to 200 years old.

Stone Age Arrowhead. Close examination of human remains from a 13,000-year-old burial in a Sicilian cave revealed a small piece of flint, apparently part of an arrowhead, embedded in a female hipbone. X-ray images indicated the flint was part of a small blade that may have been one of several attached to the end of an arrow shaft to form a point. Investigators suspect that the woman, who most likely survived the wound, was the victim of a violent attack. Only one other arrowhead of comparable antiquity ever has been found.

Western Hemisphere

Early Agriculture. Domestication of squash in the Americas began as early as 10,000 years ago—more than 4,000 years before the earliest evidence of maize and bean cultivation—according to a reanalysis of material previously found in a Mexican cave. This finding suggests that the adoption of an agricultural way of life probably began around the same time in Mexico as in the Near East and China. Six seeds and three stems from squash plants were assigned radiocarbon dates that ranged from about 8,000 to 10,000 years old; all exhibit signs of domestication—such as rinds and stems that are much thicker than those of wild squash. Although evidence of human occupation of the Mexican cave has been placed at about 9,000 years old, the squash remains previously were thought to be no more than 5,000 years old.

Colonial Gunboat. A sunken vessel, part of a 15-ship squadron led by Benedict Arnold in a losing battle with a British fleet on Oct. 11, 1776, was discovered during a survey of the bottom of Lake Champlain, bordering New York and Vermont. The ship's 50-ft (15-m) mast and a large bow cannon still were intact. During the battle, Arnold lost two ships within several hours. That night he tried to slip the remaining ships past a British blockade, but one was captured and another sank. The next day, the remaining 11 ships engaged the British in a second battle, but lost again. Investigators suspect that the newly discovered gunboat is the one that sank while attempting to run the blockade.

Blackbeard's Flagship. Investigators think they have found the flagship of the pirate Blackbeard lying in 20 ft (6 m) of water about 2 mi (3 km) off the North Carolina coast. The sunken vessel contained more than 15 large cannons, two anchors, a bronze bell inscribed with the date 1709, and part of an oak hull. Based on the ship's location and attributes, it was identified provisionally as *Queen Anne's Revenge*, Blackbeard's flagship. Edward Teach, or Blackbeard, pillaged Atlantic-coast and Caribbean settlements beginning in 1716. *Queen Anne's Revenge*, a 200-ton merchant ship built in 1710, participated in a series of raids before it ran aground on a sandbar near North Carolina.

Maya Site. Archaeologists discovered the ruins of an approximately 1,300-year-old Maya settlement, known as La Corona, in Guatemala. The site contains an inscribed panel that refers to a ruler at Site Q, a mysterious Maya city from the same time period that is known only from writings on sculptures held in various museums and private collections. La Corona features a main plaza flanked by two tall structures, an acropolis, and scattered nearby mounds. Looters have plundered much of the site, but left several carved tablets, one with a partially legible inscription describing a political allegiance between La Corona and another Maya city.

Mound Builders. A scientific team concluded that hunter-gatherer groups constructed an array of 11 earthen mounds in northern Louisiana more than 5,000 years ago as part of a seasonal base camp. If this date holds up, the site will predate by 2,000 years what previously was considered to be the oldest mound site, also in northern Louisiana.

The new dating, at a site known as Watson Brake, suggests that prehistoric hunter-gatherers exhibited a flair for massive construction projects and complex culture usually attributed only to later farming societies, in which a few powerful people had access to slave labor. New excavations at Watson Brake, which first had been discovered more than 30 years earlier, yielded evidence of intensive bead production and numerous bones of aquatic and land animals. Charred seeds at the site represent wild versions of edible plants domesticated in North America beginning around 4,500 years ago. Hunter-gatherers occupied Watson Brake each spring and summer to exploit plants and animals that lived near now dried-up rivers, according to investigators.

BRUCE BOWER, *"Science News"*

ARCHITECTURE

A number of influences such as globalization and preservation strongly affected architecture during 1997. The American Institute of Architecture (AIA) revised criteria for its yearly Honor Awards.

Globalization. The 1997 Pritzker Prize, the top international award in architecture, went to Norwegian Sverre Fehn, who, at 72, intended to go on practicing his consistent, quiet Modernism. Fehn said that his designs, which utilize the effects of daylight and the conflict between the natural and man-made environments, are influenced particularly by the severe Norwegian climate.

Architectural exchange among countries continued to increase. Patkau Architects of Vancouver, BC, was awarded a contract to design the University of Texas' $55 million Nursing and Biomedical Science Building, while the Museum of Decorative Arts in Montreal opened redesigned galleries by U.S. architect Frank Gehry. Ralph Lerner, dean of Princeton's School of Architecture, was selected to design the 1.5-million-sq-ft (139 000-m²) Indira Gandhi Center for the Arts in New Delhi, India.

A global view also was evidenced at the 1997 AIA Honor Awards, previously the top award for U.S. projects. Recipients included Rafael Vinoly Architects for the Tokyo International Forum performing arts and convention center; Comunitas Architecture for Parco San Giuliano in Mestre, Italy, a large park and transportation center; and Skidmore, Owings & Merrill for the Saigon South Master Plan of a new city for up to 1 million inhabitants.

Preservation. The preservation of historic structures took on new dimensions. One large-scale government project to create an attractive environment for tourism in major Cuban cities involved the wholesale renovation of thousands of structures dating as far back as the 16th century. The project was financed by the Cuban government and foreign governments and corporations. A large-scale U.S. restoration, that of the Library of Congress in Washington, DC, opened on May 1 after some 16 years of work. The project's architects, Arthur Cotton Moore/Associates and Einhorn Yaffee Prescott, worked under the auspices of the Architect of the Capitol's office.

The movement of preservation into mainstream popularity was exemplified by the opening of many projects instigated by communities and minority ethnic groups. Among them were the restoration of rural adobe churches by Latinos in New Mexico, under the guidance of Cornerstone Community Partnerships; the salvaging of slave-built structures in Georgia, by the African-American Historic Preservation Committee; and the conversion of an 1882 AME Church for the Baltimore Urban League, by architects Kelly, Clayton & Mojzisk.

The restoration of Dresden's Baroque Frauenkirche, destroyed by Allied bombing in World War II, began with the help of computer software usually used for aircraft design. The software was used to build a three-dimen-

Photos, The Pritzker Architectural Prize/The Hyatt Foundation

Norwegian architect Sverre Fehn, above, was awarded the 1997 Pritzker Prize for architecture that "is a fascinating and exciting combination of modern forms tempered by the Scandinavian tradition and culture from which it springs." His works include the Brick House Baerum, Norway, left, which was built in 1986.

sional model on which the surviving original stones could be placed by analyzing their shapes.

Security.   Security from terrorist attacks was a priority of the U.S. federal government in awarding the commission to design a replacement for the Alfred P. Murrah Federal Building in Oklahoma City, OK—destroyed by a bombing in 1995—to Ross Barney and Jankowski, teamed with local architects The Benham Group. The solution was to design low, spread-out buildings that hopefully would be less inviting to would-be saboteurs. Meanwhile, negative reaction to the new, bunker-like U.S. embassy building in Peru continued. Little concern for security was evidenced in the General Services Administration's own awards, however, which went to an interesting cross section of projects—including Kohn Pedersen Fox's U.S. Courthouse at Foley Square, New York City; and Skidmore, Owings & Merrill's U.S. Court of Appeals in San Francisco, CA.

Return to Mainstream Design.   After almost two decades of discussion about the appropriate direction of architectural design, the AIA revised the criteria for its 1997 Honor Awards to honor projects commissioned to address community concerns by ordinary, rather than elite, clients. Although Modernism predominated, the recipients represented a broad range of design languages. Criteria were not always applied evenly, however, and at least one award's juror thought the new criteria did not set a high enough standard. One seemingly inappropriate award went to the renovation of Memorial Hall for Harvard University, certainly a prestigious client. Designed by Venturi, Scott Brown and Associates in association with Bruner/Cott and Associates and Robert Neily Architects, the project, however, did restore a much-neglected 1874 Gothic space by creating an efficient dining facility for students. It also provided a badly needed student common in an underutilized basement.

Similarly, the Neurosciences Institute in San Diego, CA, designed by Todd Williams, Billie Tsien and Associates in association with Joseph Wong Design Associates, did not quite fit the new rules. Its angled sculptural concrete-wall planes, arranged around a court-yard open to the Pacific Ocean, recalled the landmark Salk Institute by Louis Kahn, although the scheme was far freer and less formal. Several large houses that won also did not seem to match the criteria.

More in tune with the program's intent, the Paul Cummins Library for the inner-city Crossroads School in Santa Monica, CA, was designed by Steven Ehrlich Architects to be a straightforward structure enlivened by bright colors and contrasting materials. Another community-based project was the Bellevue Regional Library in Bellevue, WA, designed by the Zimmer Gunsul Frasca Partnership as a large shedlike building that mediated between commercial and residential districts. Several projects provided sorely needed housing. The Manville Hall Student Apartments in Berkeley, for the University of California, were housed in two cubelike buildings to present a smaller massing to the street than one block would have done. David Baker Associates, in association with Crosby Helmich Architects, also gave the buildings contrasting bright colors to complement the vibrant neighborhood. Laureola Oaks, a complex of 16 below-market-rate residential units in San Carlos, CA—by Seidel/Holzman for a non-profit developer—was arranged in traditional peaked-roof "houses" around a common courtyard to encourage community interaction. More typical of the high-style award recipients of the past was a 2,000-sq-ft (186-m^2) guest house for the Delta & Pinelands Company in Scott, MS, by architect Walter Chatham. Raised on pilings above its flood-plain location to allow the natural flow of water underneath, it was sheathed in brightly polished corrugated metal inside and out, creating a shaded interior of luminescent reflections.

While the design press and professional organizations continued a 50-year tradition of promoting Modernist design—with a few notable exceptions, such as the historic style of Robert Stern—a growing number of respected architects were rediscovering the popular appeal of classical principles. "One need not be an antiquarian," wrote noted practitioner Alvin Holm, "to observe that earlier eras produced, in abundance, finer, nobler buildings than we in our time."

Fantasy.   Respected architecture critic Ada Louise Huxtable examined in her book *The Unreal America: Architecture and Illusion* the possibility that such make-believe environments as Disneyland, where many well-known practitioners have worked, might be valid architecture. Meanwhile, the construction of the Paris Las Vegas casino in Nevada led architects Robert Venturi and Denise Scott Brown to publish their earlier book, *Learning from Las Vegas*, which concluded that the local billboard is a suitable design element.

CHARLES K. HOYT, *Fellow*
American Institute of Architects

ARGENTINA

In 1997 the ruling Peronist Party (PJ) lost ground. High unemployment persisted, but foreign investment and economic growth were robust. North America and Europe sought trade arrangements with the Southern Cone.

Politics and Government. In the October 26 midterm elections for half of the 257 lower-house congressional seats, the governing PJ party lost 12 seats to a hastily built alliance of the Radical Civic Union (UCR) and the Front for the Country in Solidarity (Frepaso). Although the PJ lost its majority, it retained a plurality in the chamber. An emerging figure in the 1999 presidential contest was Graciela Fernández Meijide, 67, a former French teacher who forged the UCR-Frepaso alliance and won her third election in as many years. Meijide—who lost a son during the repressive military rule (1976–83)—was known for her human-rights activities. The alliance vowed to fight corruption, inequality, and police brutality while supporting the government's economic model. In losing Buenos Aires province, Gov. Eduardo Duhalde saw his presidential ambitions dimmed, leaving the PJ—which received less than 18% of the votes cast in the nation's capital—without a clear presidential candidate.

José Luis Cabezas, a photojournalist for the crusading weekly *Noticias*, was murdered on January 25 after being threatened for photographing Alfredo Yabrán, who was running a postal service and reputedly was linked to a criminal organization. Yabrán—a prime suspect in Cabezas' murder—had benefited from President Carlos Saúl Menem's privatization programs and allegedly was the president's friend. Menem denied any connection, but police had traced 35 calls between Yabrán and Menem's private office. Federal Justice Minister Elías Jassan resigned on June 26 over his connection to Yabrán.

Economy. New privatizations included those of airports, postal services, and a national mortgage bank. Frustrated by congressional delays in approving such legislation, Menem began to issue executive decrees—which were declared unconstitutional. On August 27 he issued a decree of "urgency and necessity"— the most powerful and controversial legal tool available to him; it also was rejected. A decree signed on March 24 authorized the sale of the state-owned postal service. A consortium of Argentine capital and the Bank of Galicia, the country's largest private bank, won a 30-year concession on July 31 to take over the country's largest mail service. It would pay the state nearly $52 million every six months after taking over in September. Sale of the $4 billion national mortgage bank to fund construction and public works drew opposition. Opponents speculated that distribution of gains from the sale before a congressional election in October would favor incumbents, and the sale was postponed.

In August the foreign debt topped $100 billion, with Moody's—the international risk-rating agency—predicting $130 billion by year's end. Debt service in 1997 was nearly $4 billion.

During a mid-October 1997 visit to Argentina, U.S. President Bill Clinton and Argentina's President Carlos Menem (right) conferred on a wide variety of subjects, including defense matters and trade issues.

ARGENTINA • Information Highlights

Official Name: Argentine Republic.
Location: Southern South America.
Area: 1,068,297 sq mi (2 766 890 km²).
Population (mid-1997 est.): 35,600,000.
Chief Cities (1991 census): Buenos Aires, the capital, 2,960,976; Cordoba, 1,148,305; San Justo, 1,111,811; Rosario, 894,645.
Government: *Head of state and government,* Carlos Saúl Menem, president (took office July 8, 1989). *Legislature*— National Congress: Senate and Chamber of Deputies.
Monetary Unit: Peso (0.9999 peso equal U.S.$1, financial rate, Dec. 5, 1997).
Gross Domestic Product (1995 est. U.S.$): $278,500,000,-000 (purchasing power parity).
Economic Index (1996, 1988 = 100): *Consumer Prices,* all items, 321,965.8; food, 274,354.9.
Foreign Trade (1996 U.S.$): *Imports,* $23,733,000,000; *exports,* $23,773,000,000.

With obligations of $17.5 billion due, Congress authorized raising up to $8.5 billion on the bond market. The International Monetary Fund (IMF) and the World Bank demanded Argentina make fiscal and judicial reforms.

With mineral exports outstripping imports by $100 million, Argentina experienced a boom in mining investments. After four years in development and an input of more than $1 billion, the Bajo la Alumbrera open-pit mine in Catamarca province began operations. With an expected 190,000-ton annual copper production and 730,000 troy oz (22 705 000 g) of gold, Argentina would become the ninth-largest producer of copper and 14th-largest producer of gold. Australian and Canadian firms also were developing mines in the northwestern provinces. The surge in mineral exploration was attributed to changes in the 1993 mining law.

In December 1996, Menem decreed labor reforms after Congress did not move to facilitate the hiring of more people by companies in order to force down the 17% unemployment rate. The decree, which provoked a general strike, was rejected by the judiciary. Menem threatened to impeach the judge responsible, but another judge then endorsed the decree. The country was awash in social protests between April and July, largely because of Menem's neoliberal economic program. Paradoxically, Menem's economic plan resulted in an 8% economic-growth rate (from July 1996 to July 1997), but joblessness declined by only one point, to 16%.

To stem an unfavorable 1997 trade balance with Argentina of more than $1 billion, Brazil announced in March that it no longer would finance imports for 180 to 365 days. Argentine pressure caused Brazil to modify the ruling so that Argentine exports of less than $40,000 could be financed for up to 120 days. Both countries agreed to consult before future trade-regulation changes, and in April hammered out a mutual agreement concerning the manufacture and shipment of automobiles.

Foreign Relations. President Bill Clinton and his wife, Hillary Rodham Clinton, visited Argentina in October, when the U.S. chief executive announced "non-NATO-ally" status for Argentina, making it eligible for funds to fight terrorism and buy arms. Clinton said Argentina need not abandon Mercosur—the Southern Cone common market—to participate in a prospective Free Trade Area of the Americas (FTAA). In a bow to Argentine pressure, Clinton agreed to negotiate Mercosur's entry into FTAA as a bloc. Clinton gained Argentine support for a plan that binds developing countries to limits on greenhouse-gas emissions. Accords were reached on airspace, cooperation on the national-park system of Argentina, and a restructuring of the Argentine judiciary. Clinton pressed his host for greater press freedom and an end to harassment of journalists.

During a March visit, French President Jacques Chirac praised Mercosur, suggesting a summit between European and Latin American heads of state to consider a future free-trade zone. Chirac also condemned excesses committed during the 1976–83 "dirty war," in which French workers were killed.

On October 7 a Spanish court ordered the detention of former Argentine naval officer Adolfo Scilingo for crimes committed during the "dirty war." An international arrest order was issued for ten other high-ranking Argentine officers in connection with the disappearance of 600 Spaniards in Argentina during military rule. A Spanish judge had ruled in March that Leopoldo Galtieri, former Argentine president (1981–82), be placed in prison for human-rights abuses. Since amnesty was decreed in Argentina, none of the accused served any prison time at home.

Erich Priebke, 83, who fled to Argentina following World War II, was convicted in Rome on July 22 of participating in the 1944 slaying of 335 civilians in Italy as part of the occupying Nazi army. His 15-year sentence was reduced to five years.

A December 1996 agreement created a special oil-licensing zone covering 6,948 sq mi (18 000 km²) along the border dividing British and Argentine territorial claims near the Falkland Islands. Menem's suggestion that Argentina and Britain share sovereignty of the disputed territory was rejected, but in November, Britain invited Menem to bilateral relations talks in London.

LARRY L. PIPPIN, *University of the Pacific*

ART

Museum construction and attendance at art exhibits continued their recent boom in 1997. The art world suffered major losses as important fresco paintings were damaged by earthquakes in Italy. Death claimed abstract-expressionist master Willem de Kooning (*see* SIDEBAR, page 119), and pop-art painter Roy Lichtenstein (*see* OBITUARIES).

Losses, Recovery, and Restoration. Fresco paintings by the 13th-century master Cimabue on the ceiling of the upper church of St. Francis of Assisi in Assisi were damaged severely by the second of two earthquakes that ripped through central Italy on Sept. 26, 1997. Cimabue is considered a key figure in the late-medieval revival of large-scale figure painting that preceded and led to the Renaissance. Italy had suffered other damage to its precious artistic patrimony in April, when fire struck the San Giovanni Cathedral and its Guarini Chapel, which houses the Shroud of Turin. The Turin cathedral is a masterpiece of baroque architect Guarino Guarini.

For the first time, state museums in France began to acknowledge those works that entered their collections after World War II as returned war booty plundered by the Nazis from the collections of French Jews. U.S. journalist Hector Feliciano focused attention on the story behind these works in his book *The Lost Museum* in 1997.

New York City's Metropolitan Museum of Art returned two sculptures to Cambodia after learning that the 10th- and 11th-century sandstone heads had been stolen from the Angkor Wat temple area. The British Museum in London again balked at the return to Athens of the Elgin Marbles, masterpieces of ancient Greek art's Classical Period, removed from the Parthenon and Erechtheum temples in 1816 in a deal between British ambassador Lord Elgin and the Ottoman emperor. Greece long has sought to repatriate the sculptures and has plans to install them in a new museum to be constructed near the Acropolis. Russian officials continued to refuse to return to Germany works of "trophy art" confiscated from German collections by the victorious Red Army during and after World War II.

After lengthy restoration, Rembrandt's great "Danae" went back on view at the Hermitage Museum in Leningrad. The painting depicts the naked beauty Danae in her bed, about to be visited by the Greek god Zeus disguised as a shower of gold. Badly damaged by an acid and knife attack in 1986, the picture retains evidence of damage, of its former glory, and of the continuing struggle to preserve art against its natural and human enemies.

Exhibitions. The well-funded J. Paul Getty Center planned to inaugurate its new 100-acre (40.5-ha) facility near Los Angeles, designed by architect Richard Meier, with an exhibition of ancient art from its collection—"Beyond Beauty: Antiquities as Evidence." The show was to run from mid-December through October 1998.

"The Glory of Byzantium" at the Metropolitan Museum of Art showed some 350 works created from the 9th to the 13th century, including glowing mosaics and highly detailed manuscripts, some never before seen outside of their sacred shrines. "Art That Heals: The Image as Medicine in Ethiopia," which originated at the Museum for African Art in New York City and was shown at Baltimore's Walters Gallery of Art, also featured spiritually charged works. The first exhibition in America of Italian Renaissance master

Lent by the Department of the Interior Museum/National Museum of American Art, Washington, DC/Art Resource

"Grand Canyon of the Yellowstone," left, an 1872 painting by Thomas Moran, was purchased by the U.S. Congress that same year and was instrumental in Yellowstone being declared a national park. The first retrospective of Moran's paintings opened at Washington National Gallery of Art in September 1997.

National Gallery of Art/AP/Wide World Photos

Pablo Picasso's 1906 self-portrait was shown at an exhibit of his early works, which was organized by the National Gallery in Washington and the Museum of Fine Arts in Boston.

Lorenzo Lotto was seen at the National Gallery of Art in Washington. Baroque painter Giambattista Tiepolo was afforded a 300th-birthday exhibition at the Metropolitan.

The light of Impressionism and of the Mediterranean drew large crowds to the Kimbell Art Museum, Fort Worth, TX, and the Brooklyn (NY) Museum of Art to see "Monet and the Mediterranean," featuring about 65 paintings deriving from Claude Monet's trips to the French and Italian coasts and to Venice. French Impressionism is noted less for penetrating portrayals of people than for glorious landscapes. Yet portraits by another Impressionist master, Auguste Renoir, highlighted a show organized by the National Gallery of Canada, Ottawa, which was seen at the Art Institute of Chicago in 1997 and was to travel to the Kimbell Art Museum in 1998. "The Private Collection of Edgar Degas" opened at New York City's Metropolitan in October.

The Museum of Modern Art (MoMA) in New York City showed some 150 of Austrian Expressionist Egon Schiele's psychologically charged works, drawn from the Leopold Collection in Vienna. German Expressionist Gabriele Münter, a member of the "Blue Rider" group centered in Munich before World War II, was presented in an exhibition

organized by Reinhold Heller of the University of Chicago for the Milwaukee Art Museum. "Exiles and Emigrés, 1933–1945," organized by Stephanie Barron for the Los Angeles County Museum of Art, featured the work of artists driven out of Europe by the rise of Nazism and World War II.

Perennial hunger for Picasso was sated by "Picasso: The Early Years, 1892–1906," jointly organized by and seen at the National Gallery in Washington and the Museum of Fine Arts, Boston. A show of Picasso's rarely seen photographs was organized by the Musée Picasso in Paris and seen at Houston's Museum of Fine Arts. Members of America's "first family of art," the Peales of Baltimore, were featured in "The Peale Family: Creation of an American Legacy." Works by Charles Willson Peale (1741–1827) and his artistically named and inclined children were seen at the M.H. de Young Memorial Museum in San Francisco and the Corcoran Gallery of Art in Washington, DC.

Thomas Moran's 19th-century paintings of the Yellowstone area helped to earn it national-park status. The first Moran retrospective, coinciding with the 125th anniversary of Yellowstone National Park, was organized by the National Gallery of Art, Washington, and seen there. It was to travel to the Gilcrease Museum in Tulsa and the Seattle Art Museum. Early works by American high-society portraitist John Singer Sargent (1856–1925)—such as the successfully scandalous "Madame X"—were seen at the Sterling and Francine Clark Art Institute in Williamstown, MA. "Fame and Misfortune: Andy Warhol's Portraits," organized by Pittsburgh's Andy Warhol Museum and the Akron Art Museum, showed more than 100 flattering portraits by the late pop artist. A Warhol disciple, the downtown graffiti ace Keith Haring (1958–1990), was much in evidence uptown in New York, as his vibrant paintings were afforded a retrospective at the Whitney, while New York's Public Art Fund installed a number of his sculptures on Park Avenue.

The Solomon R. Guggenheim Museum in New York City presented a huge retrospective of the collages, assemblages, photographs, and sculptures of prolific contemporary American artist Robert Rauschenberg. More than 400 works created from 1949 to 1997 occupied the entire spiral of the museum's landmark Fifth Avenue building as well the museum's newer SoHo branch. American minimalist sculptor Richard Serra placed his massive rolled-steel "Torqued Ellipses" on display in the new galleries opened by the Dia Center for the Arts

The Georgia O'Keeffe Museum, dedicated to the works of American artist Georgia O'Keeffe (1887–1986), opened in Santa Fe, NM, in July 1997. One hundred and seventeen pieces were on view at the museum's opening exhibition.

in the Chelsea neighborhood on New York City's West Side, to which many SoHo galleries have moved.

New York City's Whitney Museum of American Art held its 69th Biennial Exhibition, devoted to the most recent work by prominent and emerging artists. The show featured an international group of artists working in America, including Italian painter Francesco Clemente, Russian installation artist Ilya Kabakow, and Pakistani graphic artist Shahzia Sikander. Other large group exhibitions of contemporary art included the massive Documenta X in Kassel, Germany; the venerable Venice Biennale in Italy; the much-praised "Sculpture Projects" in Münster, Germany; and the inaugural Neuberger Museum Biennial for Public Art in Purchase, NY, where veteran sculptors Louise Bourgeois and George Rickey were honored.

Facilities.   The big news in museum construction was in the otherwise obscure Basque city of Bilbao, Spain, where the Solomon R. Guggenheim Foundation—overseers of the Solomon R. Guggenheim Museum in New York City and an increasing number of satellites—unveiled the Guggenheim Museum Bilbao, designed by West Coast architect Frank O. Gehry. The 256,000-sq-ft (23 783-m²) building features undulating walls and dramatic horizontal projections reminiscent of the prow of a ship, and verticals that shimmer like a candle's flame. Clad in limestone, titanium, and glass, the building was hailed by critics as a masterpiece of form prior to its opening. A much smaller, 7,000-sq-ft (650-m²), Guggenheim branch—designed by New York archi-

tect Richard Gluckman—opened in Berlin in November. The 13,000-sq-ft (1 208-m²) Georgia O'Keeffe Museum, also by Gluckman, opened in Santa Fe, NM, where the American painter lived and worked from 1949 to 1986.

New York City's MoMA moved forward with its expansion plans, first exhibiting the proposals submitted in competition by ten architects, and then announcing the three finalists—the Swiss team of Jacques Herzog and Pierre de Meuron, Japan's Yoshio Taniguchi, and Bernard Tschumi of the United States. The Art Institute of Chicago opened new galleries for contemporary art, while New York City's Metropolitan opened its renovated and expanded galleries of Chinese art. The Contemporary Arts Museum, Houston, reopened after a six-month renovation, while the eight facilities of the Baltimore City Life Museums—including the first museum building in the United States, the Peale Museum—closed due to financial difficulties.

Staffing.   New museum directors in 1997 included: Arnold Lehman, Brooklyn Museum of Art; Peter Sutton, Wadsworth Atheneum, Hartford; Elizabeth Ferner, Austin Museum of Art; Samuel Sachs II, Frick Collection, New York; Daniel T. Keegan, Kemper Museum, Kansas City; and Roslyn A. Walker, National Museum of African Art, Washington, DC. Marla Prather was named curator of 20th-century art at the National Gallery, and Joachim Pissarro moved from the Kimbell Museum in Fort Worth to the Yale University Art Gallery as curator of European and contemporary art.

PETER CHAMETZKY, *Adelphi University*

Art Market

The year 1997 someday may be remembered by historians as the birth of a new era in the art market. Christie's and Sotheby's, the world's largest auction houses, started investing their own money in art in a big way during the year. The usually cautious firms—both are public—got aggressive, perhaps not surprisingly, just as the market showed early signs of a boom.

American paintings are perhaps the best bellwether of the art market: They were the first to take off in price in the mid-1980s, the first to nose-dive later that decade, and the first to recover in the 1990s. June 1997 saw new records for several U.S. artists, including Andrew Wyeth and Winslow Homer. A Wyeth portrait of Christina Olson brought $1.7 million, while Homer's "Home Sweet Home" notched $2.64 million. In the December auctions, John Singer Sargent's "In the Garden, Corfu" brought $8.36 million. Although not a record, this obviously was a substantial price in a sale that brought $43.66 million overall—a sum that made it the highest-grossing U.S. art auction since May 1989.

Impressionist and Modern art started 1997 off with a bang when Estee Lauder executive

"Madame Cézanne au Fauteuil Jaune," below, a portrait of his wife by French artist Paul Cézanne (1839–1906), sold at auction at Christie's in May 1997 for $23.1 million.

© Christie's Images

Ronald Lauder paid about $50 million for Paul Cézanne's "Still Life, Flowered Curtain, and Fruit" in a private transaction. In the spring, Sotheby's privately brokered the sale of Pierre-Auguste Renoir's "Au Moulin de la Galette" for almost $50 million—$10 million more than it was worth in 1990, but $28.1 million less than a fevered buyer paid for it that year. In May's Impressionist and Modern auctions, a rare Cézanne portrait of the artist's wife brought $23.1 million, and a self-portrait by Edouard Manet reached $18.7 million. A Gustav Klimt landscape estimated at $5 million to $7 million sold for $14.74 million—a record for the artist that lasted until October, when another landscape notched $23.5 million.

The November Impressionist and Modern auctions racked up $366.6 million, by far the most realized in one season since the 1990 peak. The highlight of the week was a group of Pablo Picasso paintings from the Victor and Sally Ganz collection. Of the group, "The Dream," a portrait of one of Picasso's mistresses, brought $48.4 million. Overall, the exceptionally strong Ganz collection of Picassos and contemporary works brought $206.5 million, the most one collection ever has fetched at auction. It had been projected to bring about $125 million. Christie's had a financial interest in the artworks.

In a similar move, Sotheby's bought into the middling collection of the late Evelyn Sharp; however, it apparently pushed too hard with the estimates. The sale was expected to bring more than $60 million but reached only $41.2 million; the shortfall would wind up costing Sotheby's at least $3 million. To be sure, the market was strong; the next night, Sotheby's sold a Renoir bather for $20.9 million. Buyers, however, were choosy about quality.

Contemporary-art sales increased significantly and seemed finally to have recovered from a long slump. The November auctions brought out some quality paintings, with prices to match. The San Francisco Museum of Modern Art paid $5.94 million for Mark Rothko's brooding, ethereal "No. 14, 1960"—64% more than any Rothko had fetched before. And in the Ganz auction, a 1970s Jasper Johns painting, "Corpse and Mirror," brought $8.3 million.

Following the buoyant auctions, one dealer said, "Rich people like to spend real money. They're not happy unless it's real money." If that statement was true, there surely were many happy collectors heading into 1998.

ANDREW DECKER, *Contributing Editor*
"ARTNews Magazine"

Willem de Kooning (1904–97)

Willem de Kooning, one of the United States' foremost artists, died on March 19, 1997, at the age of 92. De Kooning was an originator of abstract expressionism—a school of painting in which the works are spontaneous and nonobjective and reflect the inner life of the painter. De Kooning's works, which often included distorted human forms, were distinguished by bold strokes and swirling paint patterns. Although the works often appear to be ferocious and violent, they also are comical and beautiful. In the years following World War II, de Kooning, along with Jackson Pollack and other abstractionist artists, helped make New York City the art capital of the Western world.

Background. Willem de Kooning was born in Rotterdam, the Netherlands, on April 24, 1904. An artistically talented youngster, he found work in a commercial art and design studio before entering his teen years and, while employed, studied at night at the Academy of Fine Arts in Rotterdam. In 1926 he stowed away on a ship bound for the United States. First in Hoboken, NJ, and later in New York City, de Kooning worked as a housepainter, sign painter, and carpenter, but in 1935 he landed a job painting murals for the Works Progress Administration's Federal Arts Project, which gave work to artists during the Great Depression. Also in that year, he did his first easel painting.

In New York City, de Kooning was influenced by Arshile Gorky, an abstractionist painter, as well as by Pablo Picasso's Cubism and Joan Miró's surrealism. Soon, de Kooning's own works were becoming less figurative and more abstractionist. Many of his early works were black-and-white; some of these were seen at his first one-man show in New York, in 1948. It is said that this show marked the birth of abstract expressionism, which is also called action painting.

In the early 1950s, de Kooning began his Woman series—oil and pastel paintings of women. Beginning in the early 1960s, when he moved to a new studio in East Hampton, NY, he began painting colorful landscapes. Although he suffered from Alzheimer's disease from the 1980s on, he continued to paint, helped by assistants. These later paintings were exhibited in San Francisco in 1995 and at New York City's Museum of Modern Art in early 1997. De Kooning was elected to the National Institute of Arts and Letters in 1960 and was awarded the Presidential Medal of Freedom in 1964.

WILLIAM E. SHAPIRO

ASIA

Political drama and economic turmoil marked Asian regional affairs in 1997. The Association of Southeast Asian Nations (ASEAN) expanded its membership to include nine of the ten Southeast Asian states. Currency and stock-market crises spread throughout the Asia-Pacific, threatening the region's economic growth and possibly its political stability. Late in the year the Asia-Pacific Economic Cooperation (APEC) forum met in Vancouver, Canada, to grapple with these issues and formulate an international response.

ASEAN Expansion. Asia's oldest political-economic group, ASEAN, founded in 1967, added two new members—Myanmar and Laos—in its quest to include all ten Southeast Asian states. Only Cambodia still remained outside; its entry was postponed until its internal political situation stabilized. North America, Europe, and some ASEAN members continued to harbor serious reservations about human-rights violations by Myanmar's military government and its decision to nullify the 1990 elections that would have thrown it out of office. The Philippines, Thailand, and Singapore all expressed concern over adding an illegitimate regime to ASEAN but ultimately acquiesced. It was hoped that ASEAN's multiple political and economic activities gradually would liberalize the Myanmar regime. Moreover, the move was considered a strategic necessity. Over the past decade, China had made significant political and economic inroads into Myanmar, dominating its trade and becoming the sole supplier of its armed forces; Myanmar's membership would provide an alternative to Chinese hegemony. ASEAN relations with Europe suffered, however, with the European Union (EU) refusing to permit any delegation from Myanmar to attend the ASEAN-EU meeting scheduled for 1998.

ASEAN was prepared to admit Cambodia's dual government in Phnom Penh, led by Prince Norodom Ranariddh and former Khmer Rouge Hun Sen. A bloody coup, however, was carried out by Hun Sen against Ranariddh only days before the ASEAN decision was to be made in July, leading the association to postpone its decision. Ranariddh continued to claim authority from exile, while the United Nations (UN) left Cambodia's seat vacant during the 1997 General Assembly rather than seat Hun Sen. Meanwhile, ASEAN asked that the Cambodian elections scheduled for May 1998 be fair and free, involving the full participation of all political parties under international supervision. While Hun Sen seemed to have accepted these stipulations in principle, no practical measures were undertaken. Hun Sen insisted that Ranariddh would be arrested and tried on criminal charges, should he return to Cambodia.

Economic Turmoil. East Asia's economic juggernaut seemed to falter in 1997 when a July financial crisis in Thailand spread throughout the region. While most qualified observers agreed that the underlying factors for Asia's long-term success—which include a high savings rate and a hardworking labor force—persisted, the crisis revealed a number of serious weaknesses throughout the region, from the ASEAN states to Korea and Japan. The states most seriously affected were among the region's top performers—Thailand, Indonesia, and South Korea—while financial pressures also slowed economic development in Malaysia and the Philippines. Japan's economy faltered also, although Tokyo's problems had more to do with secrecy and corruption in its banking system than with regional contagion.

The underlying problems for most of these economies included overextended bank loans, particularly in vastly overvalued commercial real estate, and corruption between the banks and political leaderships. Loans to political cronies often were made for projects that were not commercially viable. Indonesia and Thailand required multibillion-dollar bailout packages backed by the International Monetary Fund (IMF), plus funding from Japan, the United States, Singapore, Malaysia, and China. Beijing saw the economic crisis as an opportunity to demonstrate its common interest in maintaining regional stability and as a way of countering its less favorable image with respect to its political ambitions in the South China Sea.

In November financial officials from the East Asian states, the United States, and Canada met in Manila to reach an agreement on how financial aid and reforms would be coordinated. An attempt by some Asian states to create their own fund—outside IMF scrutiny and pressure for reforms—was abandoned. Instead, it was agreed that the IMF would be the lead institution, with enhanced abilities to respond more swiftly to national crises. In exchange, the countries accepting bailout packages must enact more-prudent economic policies. These principles subsequently were endorsed at the APEC annual summit in Vancouver.

Sheldon W. Simon, *Arizona State University*

ASTRONOMY

The spectacular Hale-Bopp comet was visible for a large part of 1997 (*see* SIDEBAR, page 123). The Mars Pathfinder landed on the Red Planet's surface, followed by the orbiting Mars Global Surveyor. Evidence of black holes and a 3,000-light-year-long fountain of antimatter were discovered in our own galaxy, while stars were found to exist between galaxies. In Arizona the world's largest telescope mirror was cast.

The Solar System. Spectacular images from orbiting spacecraft provided evidence that Earth is pelted by 5 to 30 "mini-comets" per minute. These house-sized icy bodies are vaporized in the extreme upper atmosphere—their water falling gently to Earth. They may contribute much of Earth's water or even organic compounds.

Two newly discovered objects—1996 TL$_{66}$ and 1996 TO$_{66}$—are believed to be the largest of the 43 bodies known in the distant Kuiper Belt of comets. Calculations suggested that some are as large as 310–370 mi (500–600 km) across, and may be the first of a new class of objects within our solar system. The asteroid 3671 Dionysius, an Earth-crossing asteroid in a 3.25-year orbit, was found by astronomers to have a moon that orbits the asteroid every 28 hours, blocking Dionysius' light from our view.

In June the Near-Earth Asteroid Rendezvous (NEAR) flew within 745 mi (1 200 km) of the asteroid 253 Mathilde, taking hundreds of close-up images. The asteroid—only about 37 mi (60 km) in diameter—is cratered heavily, with at least five craters more than 12 mi (19 km) across.

Astronomers using the Hubble Space Telescope (HST) found a crater that is 286 mi (460 km) wide and 8 mi (13 km) deep on the asteroid Vesta—itself only 360 mi (580 km) in diameter. Vesta is the only known parent of a class of meteorites called basaltic achondrites; the impact that formed this giant crater might help explain the meteorites' origins.

On July 4—21 years after Viking landed on Mars—Pathfinder touched down on the planet's red soil. A stereo camera revealed that the craft was in the mouth of an ancient river channel, named *Ares Valles*. A six-wheeled rover named Sojourner was deployed to traverse the surface and return information about its chemical and geological properties. A battery of meteorological equipment recorded weather data.

The Mars Global Surveyor entered orbit some 248 mi (400 km) above the Martian surface on September 11. Photographic mapping of the planet for a full Martian year (687 Earth days) was scheduled to begin in March 1998 and should reveal images as small as 5 ft

The Hubble Space Telescope's Near Infrared Camera and Multi-Object Spectrometer photographed one of the brightest stars, left, in our galaxy in September 1997. Appearing as the bright white dot in the center of the image, the star is hidden at the galactic center, behind obscuring dust. It glows with the radiance of 10 million Suns.

(1.5 m) across. Meanwhile, photographs by the Jupiter-orbiting Galileo spacecraft showed that that planet's ice-covered moon Europa has eruptions that seem to be ice volcanoes, and revealed evidence that beneath Europa's 0.6–1.2-mi (1–2-km)-thick ice sheet lies a global ocean.

Amid antinuclear protests, the plutonium-powered Cassini was launched aboard a Titan rocket on October 15. After its seven-year flight to Saturn, Cassini will photograph the planet's rings, moons, and clouds from orbit and will deploy the Huygens probe, which will set down on the surface of Saturn's largest moon, Titan. The spaceborne Solar and Heliospheric Observatory (SOHO) discovered "rivers" of hot plasma flowing beneath the surface of the Sun. These features seem to be related to the 11-year sunspot cycle.

Searching for Extra-Solar Planetary Systems. Astronomers photographed a gigantic disk of dust, some 620 billion mi (1 trillion km) across, surrounding the faint binary star system BD+31643 in the constellation Perseus. It was only the second such circumstellar disk found; this dust may be caused by collisions between rocky asteroid-type objects in orbit nearby.

Other astronomers found evidence that planets orbit distant stars. One, they believe, is a Jupiter-sized body that circles the star Rho Coronae Borealis every 40 days. Only 25 million mi (40 million km) from the star, the body has a temperature thought to be 500°F (300°C). Another planet, possibly 1.7 times the mass of Earth, may orbit the pulsar known as Geminga, in the constellation Virgo.

The Galaxy. The HST produced the first direct visible-light image of an isolated neutron star. A highly compressed sphere of neutrons no more than 17 mi (27 km) across and 400 light-years distant, the star has a temperature of 1,200,000°F (670,000°C). Deep near the heart of our own Milky Way galaxy, astronomers found the most luminous star ever. Known as the "Pistol Star" because of its location inside the Pistol Nebula, it apparently emits 10 million times more energy than the Sun—producing in six seconds the amount of energy put out by our Sun during its entire 5-billion-year lifetime. This superstar is believed to be only 1 million to 3 million years old.

Astronomers from Northwestern University, observing highly energetic gamma radiation, found a 3,000-light-year-long fountain of antimatter near the center of the Milky Way. They believe this radiation is produced when an electron and its antimatter counterpart, a positron, merge and annihilate each other.

New evidence that black holes exist within our Milky Way galaxy was beginning to accumulate. Astronomers have determined that binary star systems that emit powerful X rays consist of normal stars orbiting black holes. One such system is located 10,000 light-years away and has been named V404 Cygni by astronomers.

Beyond the Milky Way. Deep in the heart of the active galaxy NGC 6521, astronomers found what appears to be a warped, dusty disk swirling around a supermassive black hole. This was the first opportunity for astronomers to gain a direct line of sight to the immediate environs of a black hole. Astronomers also found evidence that stars may exist in the space between galaxies. About 600 stars—each 1 billion times too faint to be seen with the naked eye—were discovered about 1 million light-years east of the giant elliptical galaxy M87.

For three decades, astronomers have puzzled over the nature and origin of highly energetic gamma-ray bursts. Evidence gathered from spacecraft and ground-based telescopes in 1997 suggested these mysterious bursts might originate within galaxies billions of light-years away. If the findings are correct, then the outbursts produce in one second as much energy as the Sun has emitted during the last 5 billion years.

The faintest, most distant galaxy ever seen was found by the HST in a cluster of galaxies some 13 billion light-years away in the constellation Ursa Major. The galaxy's light, which appeared as an unusually red arc, was believed to be stretched by the gravitation of a foreground cluster.

Astro-Technology. The world's largest telescope mirror—27.5 ft (8.4 m) across—was cast at the University of Arizona's Steward Observatory Mirror Lab in Tucson. It will be part of the two-mirrored Large Binocular Telescope (LBT).

Astronauts from the space shuttle *Discovery* paid a service call to the HST. During five space walks, they made several equipment upgrades, repaired the telescope's protective insulation, and installed two new instruments. One of the instruments, the Near-Infrared Camera and Multi-Object Spectrometer (NICMOS), is capable of exploring the heat emissions of the universe. The other, the Space Telescope Imaging Spectrograph (STIS), can gather the spectra of many objects simultaneously.

DENNIS L. MAMMANA
Reuben H. Fleet Space Theater and
Science Center

Comet Hale-Bopp

On the night of July 22, 1995, professional astronomer Alan Hale of New Mexico and amateur astronomer Thomas Bopp of Arizona each independently discovered a comet outside the orbit of Jupiter. Although Alan Hale is one of the top visual comet observers in the world and had seen some 200 comets, this was the first comet discovery for both men.

Designated C/1995 O1, the newly found comet was named Comet Hale-Bopp in honor of its codiscoverers. But Comet Hale-Bopp soon turned out to be more than "just an ordinary" comet. After calculating its orbit, astronomers realized that the body had an orbital period around the Sun of nearly 2,400 years, and that it still was two years away from its closest approach to Earth. In fact, it was the farthest comet ever discovered by an amateur, and appeared 1,000 times brighter than Halley's Comet did at the same distance.

By the time Hale-Bopp reached its closest approach to the Earth in March 1997—121 million mi (194 million km)—it already had become the sensation of the decade. Comets are ancient chunks of ice and rock left over from the birth of the solar system nearly five billion years ago. Because these fossilized cosmic time capsules hold many secrets to the early days of the planetary family, astronomers soon aimed nearly every available telescope toward Hale-Bopp. Millions of sky watchers ventured out under country, mountain, and desert skies in hopes of gaining a pristine view of this celestial wanderer.

Astronomers found that the comet's icy nucleus had a diameter of between 19 and 25 mi (30 to 40 km), more than six times larger than that of a "typical" comet. They learned that it was an extremely active body, spewing gases and dust from vent holes at a prodigious rate. In its more than two years of visibility, Comet Hale-Bopp proved to be one of the brightest and most spectacular comets ever visible in the skies of planet Earth.

Beyond the scientific researchers and the cosmically curious, the comet captured the imaginations of those on the fringes of science and paranoia. Groups touted the comet as a herald of the end of the world; some believed it would collide with Earth and destroy all life; and some—most notably 39 members of the Heaven's Gate cult near San Diego, CA—took their lives to join a spacecraft they believed was following the comet.

DENNIS L. MAMMANA

© Frank Zullo/Photo Researchers

© Rick Rycroft/AP/Wide World Photos

Residents of Sydney celebrated with an elaborate fireworks display on Dec. 31, 1997. Australia's largest city—which continued to be an important tourist destination—was looking toward 2000, when it was to host the XXVII Summer Olympic Games.

AUSTRALIA

The second year of Liberal Prime Minister John Howard's Liberal Party–National Party coalition government was marked by improved economic performance and a program of massive debt reduction from the sale of public assets. Many contentious issues came to the fore in 1997, and there was a widely held perception that the government was losing credibility.

Domestic Affairs. Political tensions rose as the government moved to resolve the issue of native land titles, following a December 1996 High Court ruling that focused on pastoral leases covering 40% of the country. Known as the Wik judgment after the Queensland Aboriginal people who initiated the case, the ruling overturned the assertion that pastoral leases automatically extinguished land claims based on native title. The court ruled that pastoral leases and native title could coexist on the same land, but confused the issue by adding that, in the event of conflict between them, the leaseholder's right should take precedence. The House of Representatives passed a ten-point Native Title Amendment Bill to clarify Australian land tenure after Prime Minister Howard warned that its rejection could precipitate a general election involving both houses. The bill—which would limit native rights and aroused heated opposi-

tion from churches and Aboriginal groups—did not pass the Senate.

The task of reconciling black and white Australians grew more difficult as indigenous leaders and the Howard government traded accusations. Governor-General Sir William Deane publicly urged that hopes of a true national reconciliation be kept alive.

Details were announced for a "people's convention" to meet in February 1998 to discuss whether Australia should become a republic and sever constitutional ties with the British monarchy. The government named 75 prominent citizens to the convention; another 75 were chosen in a national postal ballot. Howard—indicating his intent to vote for nonrepublican candidates—said Australia long had been a crowned republic, with the effective head of state an Australian since 1965. Australians, he believed, would embrace change only when there was a "safe, stable, workable, and secure alternative."

Public-opinion polls and a state election in South Australia revealed a general drift away from the party in office. Howard's leadership—seen as lacking direction or inspiration—faced increasing criticism.

In October the Australian Labor Party (ALP) gained strength from the new allegiance of the Democrats' high-profile leader Cheryl Kernot, after she resigned from the Senate to join the ALP. In the ALP's efforts to reposition itself on sensitive issues, it faced sharp factional differences. Opposition leader Kim Beazley cautiously moved away from the party's "deregulation" approach. The *Australian Financial Review* was unimpressed by revised ALP policy, calling it a return to "government force-feeding to pump up the economy in ways that fuel inflation and increase the risks of the old boom-bust cycle."

Independent (former Liberal) parliamentarian Pauline Hanson—buoyed by the attention she received for disparaging comments on immigration and multiculturalism—launched the One Nation party. After early support, the party's ratings dropped sharply.

As a result of 1996 gun-control legislation, more than 300,000 firearms were surrendered and their owners compensated. The federal parliament passed legislation to override the Northern Territory's controversial Terminally Ill Act after three people used the voluntary euthanasia law to end their lives.

The Economy and Financial Matters. Treasurer Peter Costello's 1997–98 budget, presented in May, was predicated on 3.75% gross-domestic-product (GDP) growth and 2% inflation. Revenue of more than A$10 billion from privatization of government businesses supported a A$6.4 billion surplus. Provision was made to repay A$5.2 billion of debt—the first installment of a total of A$25 billion over four years, which would cut government debt as a proportion of GDP from 19% to 10%. In November, A$1 billion of the A$14 billion received from the public sale of one third of Telstra, the national telecommunications operator, went to fund major environmental projects.

Prevailing business hesitancy and rural difficulties, including drought, kept unemployment above 8%. Wages moved up by 5% and increased household borrowing helped maintain consumer demand that contributed to a balance-of-payments deficit above A$12 billion. Manufacturing continued to feel pressure from imports. While overall industrial output increased, results from individual sectors were spotty. Concerned about the danger of further job losses, the government slowed the process of tariff reductions in the automotive, textile, footwear, and clothing industries.

Lending for house building showed a 12-month rise of 8%, while house prices in favored residential areas rose strongly—up 20% in leading suburbs of Sydney and Melbourne. On the fringes of the big cities, however, house prices generally fell.

The stock market rose to record levels before the Southeast Asian financial crisis

---

AUSTRALIA • Information Highlights

Official Name: Commonwealth of Australia.
Location: Southwestern Pacific Ocean.
Area: 2,967,896 sq mi (7 686 850 km²).
Population (mid-1997 est.): 18,500,000.
Chief Cities (mid-1993 est., metro. areas): Canberra, the capital, 325,400; Sydney, 3,719,000; Melbourne, 3,187,500; Brisbane, 1,421,700.
Government: *Head of state,* Elizabeth II, queen; represented by Sir William Deane, governor-general (took office February 1996). *Head of government,* John Howard, prime minister (took office March 1996). *Legislature*—Parliament: Senate and House of Representatives.
Monetary Unit: Australian dollar (1.5380 A$ equal U.S.$1, Dec. 31, 1997).
Gross Domestic Product (1995 U.S.$): $405,400,000,000 (purchasing power parity).
Economic Indexes (1996, 1990 = 100): *Consumer Prices,* all items, 116.1; food, 116.1. *Industrial Production,* 108.
Foreign Trade (1996 U.S.$): *Imports,* $65,443,000,000; *exports,* $60,498,000,000.

---

caused a retreat; afterward share prices quickly steadied. Australia contributed to International Monetary Fund (IMF) rescue packages for Thailand and Indonesia. Privatization caused a significant rise in ownership of shares of stock, to one in four of the adult population for the first time.

Reserve Bank Governor Ian Macfarlane told a Senate committee in November that economic expansion was continuing, with employment growth responding.

Some 5 million visitors made tourism an important part of the economy. The most dynamic growth was from Great Britain and other parts of Europe, with modest increases from Asia. There generally were fewer migrants due to tighter visa requirements in view of labor surpluses.

The gap between rich and poor widened as incomes for the most affluent 20% rose. There was sharpened political disagreement on key issues, including the appropriate level of government intervention in economic affairs and labor relations.

Foreign Affairs and Defense. Prime Minister Howard—who defined Australia's political alignments as "Asia first, not Asia only"—visited China in April with the aim of strengthening economic ties. Howard said China would undertake a feasibility study for a A$1 billion iron-ore-processing plant using liquefied natural gas from Western Australia.

A review of Australia's defense needs found that, to maintain its "knowledge edge," Australia must embrace new military information technologies. Defense Minister Ian McLachlan said that Australia's Defense Force would be prepared to deploy troops throughout Asia and the Pacific.

R.M. YOUNGER
Author, "Australia and the Australians"

AUSTRIA

Domestic issues dominated the Austrian political scene in 1997.

Domestic Affairs. Franz Vranitzky stepped down as federal chancellor and chairman of the Social Democratic Party of Austria (SPÖ) on Jan. 18, 1997. The decision led to a change of leadership in the SPÖ and a reorganization of the government. Vranitzky had headed five different coalition governments of the SPÖ and the Christian Democratic Austrian People's Party (ÖVP) since 1986. Viktor Klima, who had served as minister of public industry and transport (1992–96) and as minister of finance (since early 1996), succeeded Vranitzky as chairman of the SPÖ and federal chancellor. A number of ministerial appointments were made by the SPÖ, which continued its coalition with the ÖVP. Vice-Chancellor and Foreign Minister Wolfgang Schüssel was serving as chairman of the ÖVP.

As in 1996, the federal government pursued a restrictive budget policy in order to meet European Union (EU) requirements for participating in the initial phase of the introduction of a single EU currency, the Euro, in 1999. The EU criteria, which include reduction and limitation of government deficits, were established by the Maastricht Treaty on European Union. The reduction of federal spending and the deficit-management programs resulted in a drop in the deficit from 4.6% of the gross domestic product (GDP) in 1996 to 3% in 1997. The Austrian government endorsed equally austere 1998 and 1999 draft budgets, projecting a further deficit reduction to 2.6% of the GDP—enough to meet EU requirements.

Austria's fiscal policy is a prime example of how EU procedures directly affect the domestic policies of member states. In particular, Austria—with a rapidly aging population—must finance its relatively expensive social-welfare and retirement systems under conditions of budgetary austerity. In the not-so-distant future, there will not be enough taxpayers in the active labor force to support the system's generous programs. A broad debate on reforming the institutions of the Austrian welfare state had produced a wide variety of proposals and a fair amount of anxiety among the population at large. The problems of reforming social-welfare and retirement systems undoubtedly would play a major role in the future in Austria's domestic political scene.

Austria experienced modest economic growth in 1997—1.4%—comparable to other EU member states. The lackluster performance of the tourist industry in recent years has been a source of growing concern. Inflation remained low at less than 2%, and unemployment was relatively stable at 7%.

Foreign Affairs. Austrian domestic debate about the meaning of neutrality in light of the processes of European integration remained inconclusive. There, however, seemed to be a gradual shift of opinion toward recognizing that Austria should participate, in some capacity, in a European regional security organization, such as the Western European Union (WEU) or the North Atlantic Treaty Organization (NATO).

In 1997, Austria proceeded with the implementation of the Schengen Agreements, conceived to reduce border controls for persons traveling within the EU. This placed greater responsibility on Austria to maintain a substantial part of the EU's "external border," thereby preventing illegal immigration to the EU as a whole.

In October a routine traffic-control stop led to the arrest of Franz Fuchs, 48, an unemployed engineer from a small village in Styria, suspected in a series of bombings. Following Fuchs' arrest, a massive amount of evidence was collected, suggesting he had planned and executed a series of six letter and pipe bombings since 1993. These attacks were directed at foreigners and at proponents of the integration of foreigners into Austrian society. In letters to the authorities, an organization calling itself a "Liberation Army" took credit for the attacks, but Fuchs apparently acted alone. His apprehension ended a three-year investigation, during which authorities screened thousands of suspects—mostly from right-wing circles—with negligible results.

LONNIE JOHNSON, *Author*
"Central Europe: Enemies, Neighbors, Friends"

AUSTRIA • Information Highlights

Official Name: Republic of Austria.
Location: Central Europe.
Area: 32,375 sq mi (83 850 km²).
Population (mid-1997 est.): 8,100,000.
Chief Cities (1995 est.): Vienna, the capital, 1,539,848; Graz, 237,810; Linz, 203,044; Salzburg, 149,976; Innsbruck, 118,112.
Government: *Head of state,* Thomas Klestil, president (took office July 8, 1992). *Head of government,* Viktor Klima, chancellor (took office January 1997). *Legislature*—Federal Assembly: Federal Council and National Council.
Monetary Unit: Schilling (12.247 schillings equal U.S. $1, Nov. 3, 1997).
Gross Domestic Product (1995 U.S.$): $152,000,000,000 (purchasing power parity).
Economic Indexes (1990 = 100): *Consumer Prices* (1996): all items, 119.4; food, 113.7. *Industrial Production* (1995): 112.
Foreign Trade (1995 U.S.$): *Imports,* $66,272,000,000; *exports,* $57,540,000,000.

AUTOMOBILES

With sales of domestic-built cars and trucks holding at or near all-time record levels in 1997, the strong U.S. economy produced peak profits for the world's two largest vehicle producers—General Motors (GM) and Ford. The buoyant market persisted as total U.S. vehicle registrations surpassed the 200 million mark for the first time.

Overall, as Japanese and German automakers shifted more production to U.S. plants, the market posted its fourth consecutive year of 15 million retail deliveries of both domestic and imported brands. Of total sales, more than 13 million emanated from domestic plants in the United States, Canada, and Mexico. Domestic brands had eclipsed the 13 million mark in only four other years—1996, 1995, 1994, and 1978. Sales of vehicles assembled overseas have been on a steady decline since 1986, when 4.1 million imports were sold in the United States for the all-time high. Increased penetration of the American market by "transplant" manufacturing facilities through the 1980s and 1990s accounted for the trend, reducing the import volume to 1.4 million in 1996 and to some 1.5 million in 1997.

Transplant growth was extended in 1997 by the opening of a Mercedes-Benz utility-vehicle-assembly plant in Vance, AL, and would continue in 1999 with the debut of full-size pickup-truck production at a new Toyota plant in Princeton, IN. These two facilities would raise the number of North American plants producing foreign-nameplate vehicles for the U.S. market to 16, covering eight of the nine Japanese brands and including a BMW car-assembly point that opened in Greer, SC, in 1996. Three transplant plants are in Canada and one in Mexico.

The impact of strong domestic-vehicle sales was reflected in the record earnings of GM and Ford for the second quarter of 1997. High-profit trucks, vans, and utility vehicles—generally lacking competition from foreign-owned plants in North America—lifted GM to a net income of $2.1 billion in the June quarter and Ford to $2.5 billion, compared with $1.9 billion for each in the comparable period of 1996. GM said it would have earned $2.2 billion in the second quarter had it not been for strike-related production losses, and both GM and Ford attributed the results to the effect of continuing high-volume sales on the truck side, buoyed by introductions of GM's new four-door minivans and Ford's Lincoln Navigator luxury utility vehicle.

During the first eight months of 1997, a total of 10,323,952 new cars and light trucks were sold in the United States, down 0.8% from 10,408,759 in the comparable period of 1996. Cars took 55.4% of the 1997 sum and trucks, 44.6%—compared with 57.2% and 42.8% in the previous year. A relatively low value for the Japanese yen against the U.S. dollar, permitting Japanese new-car prices to remain unchanged from 1996 to 1997 models, was credited with reducing GM's penetration from 31.7% to 30.8% and Chrysler Corp.'s from 16.4% to 15.3%, while Ford gained minimally from 25.1% to 25.2%. The Japanese-brand share, paced by Toyota and Honda, rose to 23.9% and the European penetration to 4.8%. Prolongation of labor disruptions by United Automobile Workers (UAW) local unions at GM stemmed from demands by the workers for the cessation of outsourcing of parts work to nonunion suppliers with lower labor costs, as well as for continuation of jobs that the corporation feels are redundant from a cost standpoint.

New 1998 car models making headlines included the completely redesigned Cadillac Seville, left, and the new Dodge Durango. With optional seating for eight persons, the Durango became the largest compact sports utility vehicle on the market.

Courtesy, Cadillac   Courtesy, Dodge

The Air Bag

Of all the automobile-safety systems mandated by the U.S. government, none has become more controversial than the front-seat air bags that have been installed on passenger cars since 1986. According to data from the National Highway Traffic Safety Administration (NHTSA), while an estimated 2,000 lives have been saved by air bags deploying in front-end collisions, at least 40 children and 27 small adults have died after being struck by the supposedly protective bags. Smaller front-passenger-seat occupants have sustained life-threatening impacts because the bags deploy at forces equivalent to 150–200 mph (241–322 km/hr). The fatality toll, concentrated in the period 1992–96 on occupants of front passenger seats, gave rise in 1997 to a debate over corrective action involving the overseeing NHTSA, a unit of the Department of Transportation; vehicle producers, and consumer interests.

Under pressure from Congress, the NHTSA took steps to issue a rule allowing car and truck owners to deactivate their bags with an optional on-off switch. The proposal was opposed vehemently by the American Automobile Manufacturers Association, insurance companies, and consumer activists; industry forces were fearful of damage-liability exposure if inadvertent switch turnoffs keep air bags from deploying when needed in crash situations. Consumerists argued that a requirement that the bags deploy at less velocity would be preferable to ending the passive-restraint capability that air bags possess.

Late in 1997 the NHTSA gave automakers the option of reducing the deployment force of bags by 20% to 35%. NHTSA experts warned, however, that—while the reduction in bag-activation force would be less harmful to children and small adults—adults who fail to wear seat belts could be endangered either in the driver's or the passenger's seat. The 1998-model year brought further installations of side-mounted air bags, designed to protect the driver or front passenger from side-impact injuries. Volvo was the first automaker to offer side-mounted air bags, in 1996, and most luxury manufacturers added them to their 1998-model passenger cars.

As a result of the fatality toll to children since air bags were introduced on the front passenger side of autos in 1993, the NHTSA urged that infants and children up to the age of 8 be seated only in the rear of vehicles.

MAYNARD M. GORDON

Chrysler's drop in market share and earnings, after a 1996 showing that included record second-quarter earnings of $1.7 billion, also was ascribed to a UAW strike. In this case the walkout occurred at an engine plant. Chrysler's new-car sales declined 12% in 1997's January–August period in the face of stepped-up competition from other domestic producers and transplants.

Ever since the first Japanese-brand assembly plants were opened in the United States by Nissan and Honda in 1981 and 1982, respectively, the UAW has been able to organize only in four plants in which the Japanese company shared production with a Big Three automaker—GM-Toyota at Fremont, CA; Ford-Mazda, Flat Rock, MI; Chrysler-Mitsubishi, Normal, IL; and Ford-Nissan, Avon Lake, OH. A concerted effort to organize the Nissan plant at Smyrna, IL, had failed in 1989 by a two-to-one vote and the union suffered a second rebuff in September 1997, when fewer than 2,000 of Smyrna's 5,000 workers signed union cards asking for a collective-bargaining election. BMW's plant in South Carolina also remained nonunion, although all German auto plants by law recognize a union for their workers in Germany.

The franchise system of selling vehicles through individual investors began with the arrival of the Oldsmobile and the defunct Duryea Brothers models in the late 1800s and remained basically unchanged for a century as literally hundreds of U.S. automakers came and went, with only Chrysler Corp., Ford, and Olds-owning GM left. But late in 1996, after the first-ever public stock offering was registered by a dealership group—Cross-Continent Auto Retailers of Amarillo, TX—a large conglomerate in Fort Lauderdale, FL, Republic Industries, launched a buying spree unparalleled in the U.S. industry. A creation of Florida billionaire H. Wayne Huizenga, who had sold Blockbuster Video for $8.4 billion, Republic Industries purchased more than 150 retail car dealerships through 1997 to forge the largest "megadealer" network in the United States. Republic's holdings also included the AutoNation USA chain of used-car "superstores," an entity competing with other new department-store-like superstore networks called CarMax and Driver's Mart.

The 1998 and 1999 Models. A redesigned and enlarged Honda Accord featured a radical "flexible" platform for differing widths as well as lengths. Car platforms always had been "stretchable" from sedans to minivans, and the '98 Accord used a unique set of adjustable subframe brackets to allow narrower widths for Japanese and European streets or wider axles for North America. New minicompact entries introduced in Europe and South America by Ford—the Ka—and Mercedes-Benz—the A-Class and Smart—were being projected for the U.S. market as early as 1999.

The 1998-model Cadillac Seville was ushered in with a total redesign—side air bags mounted to the front seats and "adaptive" front seats with sensors that can be adjusted to conform to fit drivers' seating postures. GM's Saturn division and Honda introduced small electric cars, the EV1 and EV Plus, respectively, on a limited-edition basis in California and Arizona. Electric-powered offerings of the Ford Ranger pickup and Toyota RAV4 utility vehicle were set for introduction in 1998. Daewoo, one of South Korea's five automakers, announced it would introduce

Courtesy, Honda

The Japanese automaker Honda introduced its sixth-generation Accord for 1998. The redesigned and enlarged Accord featured a radical "flexible" platform for differing widths and lengths.

the midsize Leganza car in the United States in early 1998 through a network of department stores with service centers or at factory-owned outlets.

Chrysler added the art-deco Plymouth Prowler to its sporty Dodge Viper lineup; both models were limited-production roadsters sold only by large-volume dealers. Dodge dealers got their first utility vehicle, the Dodge Durango. Five poor-selling Ford models—the Aerostar minivan; the Korean-assembled Aspire minicompact; the Thunderbird and Cougar midsize sports coupes; and the Probe two-seater—were dropped. Buick discontinued the Skylark compact series after a run that began in the 1960s. Chevrolet phased out the Geo name it had used for its Suzuki-designed Tracker, Prizm, and Metro entry-level line since 1989.

Globalization. In line with intensive efforts by all automakers to expand production and sales efforts on a worldwide basis, the U.S. Big Three were pursuing international initiatives hotly. GM broke ground for a new Buick car-assembly plant in Shanghai; Ford increased its control over Mazda by having installed a company vice-president, Henry Wallace, as the first foreigner to head a major Japanese company; and Chrysler reported record overseas sales—60,575 vehicles in the second quarter.

GM's Saturn division said it would assemble its midsize car, derived from an Opel platform, in Wilmington, DE, starting in 1999. Nissan planned to relocate its Sentra compact-car production from Smyrna, TN, to Mexico by the year 2000. Sentra, therefore, would become the only car line sold in the United States that is assembled fully in another country.

MAYNARD M. GORDON, *Senior Editor*
"Ward's Dealer Business Magazine"

WORLD MOTOR VEHICLE DATA, 1996

Country	Passenger Car Production	Truck and Bus Production	Motor Vehicle Registrations
Argentina	269,439	43,711	5,903,466
Australia	302,615	19,423	11,207,000
Austria	97,386	8,703	4,368,126
Belgium	367,536	69,062	4,754,544
Brazil	1,466,900	345,700	15,160,689
Canada	1,279,312	1,117,731	16,667,612
China	381,510	1,074,670	10,400,029
Comm. of Ind. States	857,550	178,973	23,494,600*
Czech Republic	263,327	8,684	4,601,987**
France	3,147,622	442,965	30,295,000
Germany	4,539,583	303,326	43,561,316
India	395,844	365,648	6,550,000
Italy	1,317,995	227,370	32,806,500
Japan	7,863,763	2,482,023	66,853,500
Korea, South	2,264,709	548,005	8,468,901
Malaysia	180,000	0	2,594,896
Mexico	797,682	421,742	12,150,000
The Netherlands	145,206	33,000	6,290,000
Poland	352,750	47,921	3,935,800
Portugal	119,042	12,952	3,439,100
Romania	76,948	23,490	2,390,256
Spain	2,213,102	199,207	17,283,880
Sweden	367,799	95,362	3,953,046
Taiwan	264,943	101,083	4,950,000
Turkey	207,757	68,990	4,040,923
United Kingdom	1,686,134	238,263	27,941,957
United States	6,083,227	5,715,678	200,446,000***
Yugoslavia (former)	8,600	1,200	1,325,191
	37,318,281	14,194,882	646,759,108#

Source: American Automobile Manufacturers Association.

Other countries with more than one million registrations include Bulgaria, 1,805,299; Chile, 1,357,787; Colombia, 1,700,000; Denmark, 2,027,098; Egypt, 1,647,528; Finland, 2,181,239; Greece, 3,076,000; Hungary, 2,487,000; Indonesia, 3,750,000; Iran, 2,145,900; Iraq, 1,040,000; Ireland, 1,230,578; Israel, 1,394,323; Morocco, 1,278,033; New Zealand, 2,010,810; Norway, 2,066,683; Pakistan, 1,045,000; Saudi Arabia, 2,817,800; South Africa, 5,990,000; Switzerland, 3,528,488; Thailand, 5,000,000; and Venezuela, 1,997,030.

*Former Soviet Union.

**Includes Slovakia.

***U.S. total does not include Puerto Rico, which has 1,670,000 vehicles.

#World total includes 477,010,289 cars and 169,748,819 trucks.

BALTIC REPUBLICS

The Baltic republics of Estonia, Latvia, and Lithuania spent 1997 engaged in international political maneuvering in a collective quest to join the North Atlantic Treaty Organization (NATO) and the European Union (EU). Russian opposition to NATO expansion was a particular concern to the Baltic leaders. Lithuanian domestic politics were dominated by a presidential race, while Estonia and Latvia suffered bouts of political instability. Economically, Estonia continued to soar ahead of its neighbors, but the Latvian and Lithuanian economies also made progress.

Foreign Relations. Driven mainly by security concerns over their giant neighbor, Russia, the Baltic states lobbied intensively in European capitals to be among the first postcommunist states admitted as part of NATO and EU expansion. There was tacit agreement that, while all three republics would continue to cooperate in their campaign to join the international structures, each could fashion individual national approaches. Lithuania argued that at least one Baltic state should gain early admission to NATO, and—dispatching emissaries to NATO's Brussels headquarters, Washington, and other European diplomatic centers—presented itself as the most suitable candidate. Estonia positioned itself for EU membership, insisting that as the economic "little tiger of the Baltics," it was best qualified.

Russia—which was concerned about NATO expansion in the region, especially into the Baltic states—lobbied vigorously against it. At the U.S.-Russian March summit in Helsinki, Finland, Russian President Boris Yeltsin offered security guarantees to the Baltic republics as an alternative to NATO. Although Baltic leaders declined the offer and pressed on with their campaign, Poland, the Czech Republic, and Hungary were chosen. As consolation, U.S. Secretary of State Madeleine Albright, en route to the summer NATO meeting in Madrid, met with Baltic representatives in Vilnius, Lithuania, to assure them of continued U.S. support for their NATO aspirations.

Estonia, however, was named among the first new EU members. In order to extract more concessions for the large ethnic Russian minority in Estonia, Russia had tried to block its early entry by delaying the Russian-Estonian border treaty that had been ready for signature in late 1996. Although the EU requires that all border issues be settled, it recognized Russia's delaying tactic for what it was. Estonia would not be integrated fully into the EU until 2002, but its acceptance was an important step for the country and the region.

Politics. In Lithuania shared power between a leftist president, a conservative government—led by Prime Minister Gediminas Vagnorius—and a parliamentary coalition was not working. In late 1996 conservative parties had won the parliamentary elections, leaving President Algirdas Brazauskas, a former communist leader, politically isolated. Conservatives strengthened their position by dominating the nationwide local elections of February 1997. Nonetheless, the president remained the country's most popular politician, and began campaigning in early 1997 for the December presidential election. Other strong contenders were conservative Speaker of the Seimas (parliament) Vytautas Landsbergis, a former president; former Deputy Prosecutor-General Arturas Paulauskas; and Valdas Adamkus, a Lithuanian-American environmental specialist whose candidacy was complicated by constitutional residency requirements.

In the fall, however, Brazauskas, who was leading in the opinion polls, withdrew, citing frequent policy conflicts with the government and the Seimas, his Communist Party background—which he felt might be an international detriment to Lithuania—and his age. The president, 65, argued that it was time for a younger man, and his supporters adopted Paulauskas, who immediately became the front-runner. In the first round of voting on December 21, Paulauskas garnered 45% of the vote, followed by Adamkus with 27%, which put the two in a runoff election in early 1998.

	Nation (in millions)	Population (sq mi)	Area (km²)	Capital	Head of State and Government
Estonia	1.5	17,413	45 100	Tallinn	Lennart Meri, president Mart Siiman, prime minister
Latvia	2.5	24,749	64 100	Riga	Guntis Ulmanis, president Guntars Krasts, prime minister
Lithuania	3.7	25,174	65 200	Vilnius	Algirdas Brazauskas, president Gediminas Vagnorius, prime minister

BALTIC REPUBLICS • Information Highlights

Domestic politics in Estonia and Latvia were marred by scandals, shaky coalitions, and governmental instability. After barely surviving a no-confidence vote in Estonia's Riigikogu (parliament) in early 1997, Prime Minister Tiit Vahi and his ministers resigned over allegations of corruption during housing privatization in the capital, Tallinn. President Lennart Meri—after consultations with the ruling coalition in parliament—appointed Mart Siimann to form a new government, which basically continued to stress economic stabilization and EU acceptance.

During the summer a Finnish politician proposed that Estonia adopt a bilingual policy, similar to Finland's concession to Swedish, with Russian as a second official language. Estonia's leadership, usually sensitive to criticism of its treatment of its Russian minority, almost unanimously rejected the idea.

After 14 Estonian soldiers drowned in a military training accident, Defense Minister Andrus Oovel resigned.

In Latvia, Prime Minister Andris Skele resigned on two separate occasions. In January the independent prime minister and his government quit over allegations concerning the new finance minister, and uncertain support among the ruling coalition parties in the Saeima (parliament). Less than a week later, however, after consultations with parliamentary leaders, President Guntis Ulmanis reappointed Skele. But by summer, the new government's support in the Saeima had weakened critically, and Skele once again resigned. This time the president asked Guntars Krasts, a former economics minister, to form a new government. Prime Minister Krasts, a conservative, did so successfully, but by mid-November political instability returned. Krasts said that the limits of trying to form a stable government from the incumbent parliament had been reached, and that early elections might be necessary.

Economy. Estonia's economic development in 1997 continued to outstrip that of its neighbors. By midyear, growth roared ahead at 11.7%, inflation had fallen to 12%, unemployment was only 4%, and exports were up by 30%. An International Monetary Fund (IMF) delegation visiting in November warned the Estonian leadership against the dangers of an overheating economy and recommended slowing growth and domestic demand. In response, Estonia included a reserve fund for the first time in its prospective 1998 budget. Estonia remained the most successful and the most open economy of the region, with a stable currency, the kroon, and

© Alexander Demianchuk/Reuters/Archive Photos

The Baltic presidents (l-r)—Estonia's Lennart Meri, Latvia's Guntis Ulmanis, and Lithuania's Algirdas Brazauskas—reviewed such issues as NATO expansion in Estonia in May 1997.

the most foreign investment—led by Finland, Sweden, Russia, the United Kingdom, the United States, and Singapore. It also had a policy of free trade and planned to reduce the corporate flat tax from 26% to 15% in 1998.

Latvia continued its journey toward a full market economy with counsel and funding from the EU on harmonizing Latvian legal and administrative procedures with European standards, and with the assistance of World Bank loans. Still, internal debate between protectionism and free trade remained unresolved. The Latvian economy continued to benefit from the great volume of Russian goods passing through its Baltic ports. The Lithuanian economy—the laggard of the region—made some progress with the support of international financial institutions. As the schedule for privatizing state-owned banks and media was stepped up, Lithuania gradually attracted more foreign investment, with the United States, Germany, Sweden, Britain, and Luxembourg its heaviest investors.

ROBERT SHARLET, *Union College*

BANGLADESH

Political turmoil continued to dominate events in Bangladesh in 1997. Sheikh Hasina Wajed's Awami League (AL) government made progress toward settling unrest in the Chittagong Hill Tracts and was able to push for increased foreign investments.

Politics. A change in government from the Bangladesh Nationalist Party (BNP) to the AL in 1996 did not stop political unrest. Perhaps taking its cue from the AL, the BNP used strikes, demonstrations, and parliamentary boycotts as political weapons. Among BNP accusations was that the AL rigged the June 1996 elections, sold out national interests to India, and conducted political repression. The BNP boycotted parliament, and its strikes and demonstrations often were violent, leading to clashes between police and protesters. In September strikes and demonstrations were banned in Dhaka, but the ban was ignored. By November there were instances of violence between contenders for seats on rural councils. Elections for the Union Parishads (district councils) began as scheduled in early December and continued through the month. Despite some violence, turnout was heavy, especially among women. Although these were nonpartisan posts, political parties took an active interest. Meanwhile, in November some suppliers of foreign aid threatened to link assistance to the resolution of domestic political problems.

In April charges were brought against 20 persons—many of them former army officers—in the 1975 murder of Sheikh Mujibur Rahman, Sheikh Hasina's father. The AL long had held that the BNP shielded the alleged killers, giving some "cushy" foreign postings.

The Public Administration Reforms Commission moved to streamline public services, making them more accessible and accountable to the public. Disposition of files was required within a month, an ombudsperson office was opened to hear public complaints, and the number of years of service needed for voluntary retirement with full benefits was reduced from 25 to 20.

An agreement with Santi Bahini (Peace Army) insurgents in the Chittagong Hill Tracts was signed on December 2. Although the agreement—which would end more than 20 years of armed conflict—was praised widely, the BNP called it "a black treaty" and accused the government of compromising national security. Some 100 were injured in three BNP-led nationwide strikes held to protest the agreement.

Economy. Political turmoil affected economic performance. Total foreign investment in Bangladesh was only $206 million in the 1997 fiscal year—much of it in the Export Processing Zones of Dhaka and Chittagong, where investors were given tax holidays, infrastructure, duty-free imports, a three-year income-tax exemption, and cheap labor. International donors pledged $1.9 billion in aid for 1997–98—less than the requested $1.27 billion—noting the slow pace of reforms and the inability to utilize previous aid due to unrest and bureaucratic inertia.

Although officials forecasted a growth rate slightly above 5%, few felt it could be attained. However, as the country privatized telecommunications and increased gas, oil, and mineral exploration with foreign collaboration, investments were expected to increase. This also should help ease the $15 billion external debt.

Social Issues. To make exports more palatable to the West, Bangladesh banned child labor. Many industries fired underage workers; it was unclear what impact this had on the families of the youngsters involved. Investments in building hurricane shelters appeared to have paid off as weather-related deaths declined despite two storms in which 300 died and property damage was high. This was a considerable drop from previous years, when thousands of people often died in a single storm.

Foreign Relations. Effort was devoted to resolving refugee problems. The treaty with the Chittagong tribes included provisions with India prohibiting either nation from sheltering insurgents. Rohinga (Muslim) refugees from Myanmar remained an issue, and avenues for further regional economic cooperation were sought.

ARUNA NAYYAR MICHIE
Kansas State University

BANGLADESH • Information Highlights

Official Name: People's Republic of Bangladesh.
Location: South Asia.
Area: 55,598 sq mi (144 000 km²).
Population (mid-1997 est.): 122,200,000.
Chief Cities (1991 census): Dhaka, the capital, 3,637,892; Chittagong, 1,566,070; Khulna, 601,051.
Government: *Head of state,* Shahabuddin Ahmed, president (took office October 1996). *Head of government,* Sheikh Hasina Wajed, prime minister (sworn in June 1996). *Legislature*—unicameral National Parliament.
Monetary Unit: Taka (44.10 takas equal U.S.$1, official rate, July 1997).
Gross Domestic Product (1995 est. U.S.$): $144,500,000,-000 (purchasing power parity).
Economic Indexes (1996, 1990 = 100): *Consumer Prices,* all items, 125.8; food, 125.7. *Industrial Production,* 159.
Foreign Trade (1996 U.S.$): *Imports,* $6,615,000,000; *exports,* $3,297,000,000.

BANKING AND FINANCE

While U.S. banks continued to report record profits in 1997, the nation's banking industry waited in vain for financial-modernization legislation to pass in Congress. Commercial-bank-merger activity spread increasingly to nonbank financial companies.

Legislation. On Aug. 5, 1997, President Bill Clinton signed into law the Taxpayer Relief Act of 1997. This act made changes in existing individual retirement accounts (IRAs) and created two new individual retirement accounts, the Roth IRA and the education IRA. The new law affects traditional IRAs by raising the income limits for contributing to an IRA, allowing spouses of pension-plan participants to make contributions, and permitting penalty-free (but not tax-free) withdrawals for first-time home purchases and college expenses. The new Roth IRA, which was named after Sen. William V. Roth, Jr. (R-DE), is nondeductible at the time of contribution but withdrawals are tax-free if the account is held five years or longer. First-time home buyers can make withdrawals of up to $10,000 both tax- and penalty-free. Education IRAs were created as a means of saving for college. Parents or others can contribute up to $500 per year to benefit a person under 18. If the funds are used to pay for college expenses before the beneficiary is 30, the withdrawals are tax-free.

A bill that would have changed banking and its relationship with other financial-service companies significantly, the Financial Services Competitiveness Act of 1997, never was brought to a vote in the House. The bill would have allowed affiliations among banking, securities, and insurance firms, and would have merged the bank and thrift charters and the regulators and insurance funds. Congress was expected to continue working on this bill in 1998.

The issue of bankruptcy reform came under discussion in Congress in the fall, when the National Bankruptcy Review Commission presented its final report with 170 recommendations for legislative action. Personal-bankruptcy filings in 1997, while slowing, still were expected to set a record—estimates ranged from 1.3 million to 1.4 million filings—for a second consecutive year. The commission's report was considered controversial, as creditors and some commission members felt the proposed revisions were not strong enough to stop the growth in bankruptcy filings. Congressional hearings on the topic were expected in 1998.

Court Cases. The U.S. Supreme Court opened its fall session by hearing arguments in the case of *National Credit Union Administration (NCUA) v. First National Bank and Trust Co. of Asheboro, NC.* At issue in this case was whether the NCUA acted properly in 1982 when it expanded the "common bond" for federal credit unions. As defined in the Federal Credit Union Act of 1934, credit unions were to be organized to serve one occupation or association as a "common bond." In 1982 the NCUA allowed federal credit unions to include unrelated groups as long as each group had its own common bond. The U.S. Court of Appeals for the District of Columbia ruled in 1996 against the NCUA. The arguments before the Supreme Court focused on whether the NCUA was correct in its interpretation of "common bond," and whether banks and the banking industry had standing to challenge the regulation. A decision was expected in 1998.

Regulatory Agencies. President Clinton's appointments of Edward Gramlich, former public-policy dean of the University of Michigan, and Roger W. Ferguson, a banking consultant with McKinsey & Co., to the board of governors of the Federal Reserve were approved by the Senate at the end of October. Also, Ellen S. Seidman, former special assistant for economic policy to President Clinton, was sworn in as director of the Office of Thrift Supervision (OTS) in October. She would be responsible for supervising the 1,300 savings institutions that are regulated by the OTS. Finally, Ricki Helfer resigned as chairman of the Federal Deposit Insurance Corporation in June. Helfer had served since October 1994 and was the first woman to head a federal banking regulatory agency. In November, President Clinton nominated Donna A. Tanoue, former Hawaiian commissioner of financial institutions, to complete Helfer's term.

The Federal Reserve, in its monetary-policy role, raised the federal-funds-rate target that commercial banks charge each other for overnight loans from 5.25% to 5.5% in March. The nation's largest banks followed the Fed's lead and increased the prime rate from 8.25% to 8.5% that same month.

Mergers. Banks were active acquirers in 1997, not only of other banks and savings institutions but also of other financial-services companies. The two largest bank-merger deals in U.S. history took place in the fall when NationsBank of North Carolina purchased Barnett Banks of Florida for $15.5 billion and First Union of Charlotte, NC, bought

Debit Cards

Debit cards, sometimes called check cards, are machine-readable, magnetically encoded plastic cards that are issued to checking-account holders and directly linked to a user's checking account. Although the first debit-card pilot program was conducted by the Bank of Delaware in 1966 and First Federal Savings and Loan installed debit terminals in Hinky Dinky supermarkets in Lincoln, NE, in 1974, explosive growth of debit cards did not begin until the 1990s. Transaction volume has doubled between 1995 and 1997—from 1.6 billion in 1995 to more than 3.2 billion in 1997. The number of debit cards in the United States has risen to 220 million. Debit cards are accepted readily by many retail merchants.

© Mark Foley/AP/Wide World Photos

There are two kinds of debit cards, on-line and off-line. They fundamentally differ only in the procedures for paying at the place of purchase and the time it takes the bank to remove the funds from the user's checking account. An on-line debit card has direct access to a consumer's checking account in the same manner as an automated teller machine (ATM) card does. Indeed, many ATM cards can be used as on-line debit cards. In making a purchase with an on-line debit card, the consumer passes his or her card through a point of sale (POS) terminal and keys in his or her personal identification number (PIN) as he or she would at an ATM. The transaction is authorized electronically, and the funds are deducted almost immediately from the checking account. On-line debit card use in 1997 accounted for 1.4 billion transactions in the United States.

Off-line debit cards are more like checks in the time it takes the funds to be removed from the customer's checking account—two to three days—and more like credit cards in their use. In an off-line debit-card purchase, the user's card is cleared by the same card readers and networks as a credit-card transaction. No identification or PIN is required. The user signs a receipt as he or she would a credit-card slip. With 1.8 billion transactions in the United States in 1997, off-line debit-card transactions outnumbered on-line ones.

One reason debit-card growth has soared is the advantages debit cards offer over other methods of payment. Consumers find debit cards convenient and faster at the checkout than writing a check, and debit cards are safer than carrying cash. Consumers also like having their debit-card transactions listed on their monthly checking-account statements, having no interest charges to pay as they might with a credit card, and being able to use their debit card at ATMs and merchant locations throughout the country. On the other hand, since debit cards are linked to a user's checking account, consumers risk overdrawing their accounts and owing their bank overdraft fees. Also, if a debit card is lost or stolen, the consumer is liable for some losses. Off-line debit cards, where no identification or PIN is required at the point of sale, are especially vulnerable to fraud.

In response to consumer and congressional concerns about debit-card liability, Visa, MasterCard, and several large banks announced during the summer of 1997 that they would limit cardholders' liability to $50 or less, no matter when they are notified of the loss or theft. Thus the major debit-card companies have established policies that are broader than what the federal government requires under the Electronic Funds Transfer Act. Under that act, consumers' liability is limited to $50 only if the debit-card company is notified within two business days after the loss or theft. If the consumer waits or does not know his or her card has been stolen, the liability increases to $500 if the lost card is reported in the first 60 days, and is unlimited after that. Prior to adjourning in 1997, Congress was considering legislation that would limit debit-card liability to the same amount as credit cards ($50).

ANN KESSLER

Corestates of Pennsylvania for $17.1 billion. Other important mergers of the year included: First Bank System of Minnesota's purchase of U.S. Bancorp of Portland, OR; Washington Mutual's acquisition of Great Western Financial Corp. in California; First Union's deal to buy Signet Banking Corp. of Virginia; Wachovia Corp. of North Carolina's move into Virginia with the addition of Central Fidelity Banks and Jefferson Bankshares; and Banc One Corp. of Ohio's agreement to buy First Commerce Corp. of Louisiana.

Commercial banks also bought securities firms, investment banks, and other financial-service companies to a greater extent than ever before in 1997. Bankers Trust of New York bought Alex Brown & Sons of Baltimore, an investment bank, for $1.9 billion. Other commercial banks acquiring investment banks or securities firms included Nations-Bank's purchase of Montgomery Securities, First Union's acquisition of Wheat First Butcher Singer Inc., and Fleet Financial Group's deal for Quick & Reilly, the third-largest discount broker. With these additions, banks continued to diversify their financial-services holdings.

While banks were acquiring nonbank financial firms, brokers and insurance companies were applying for thrift charters in 1997 before the proposed financial-modernization legislation restricted the powers of these unitary thrift holding companies. Among the companies applying to own a savings institution were A.G. Edwards, Merrill Lynch, State Farm, Transamerica, and Travelers Group. Since the Travelers Group, an insurance company, already owns the Smith Barney Inc. brokerage firm and has acquired the investment bank Salomon Inc., it would be the first company to offer banking, securities underwriting, and insurance in one diversified financial-services company.

Bank and Thrift Profitability. For the first two quarters of 1997, commercial banks reported record profits. Banks earned $29.1 billion in the first half of 1997, $3.6 billion more than during the same period of 1996. However, the annualized net charge-off rate of credit-card loans—the percentage of loans that are written off as bad debts—was 5.22% in the second quarter, the highest quarterly charge-off rate in 14 years. Losses on credit-card loans totaled $2.9 billion, or 66.4% of all loans charged off in the second quarter.

As of the second quarter of 1997, there were 9,308 commercial banks and 89 new banks had been chartered. The number of bank branches had risen to 57,788 by the end

© NationsBank via "The Charlotte Observer"/AP/Wide World Photos

Hugh L. McColl, Jr., above, the chief executive officer of NationsBank Corp., was to remain CEO after the North Carolina bank merged with Florida's largest bank, Barnett Banks.

of 1996, and no bank or thrift had failed since August 1996. The large number of mergers in the second quarter of 1997—198—in part reflected the impact of the Riegle Interstate Banking and Branching Efficiency Act of 1994, which took effect on June 1, 1997. After that date, bank-holding companies were allowed to merge subsidiary banks in different states into one bank with branches in other states, thus reducing the total number of banks.

Savings institutions earned $4.8 billion in the first six months of the year and had the highest equity-capital ratio (a measure of financial strength), 8.53% of assets, since 1951. The number of savings institutions decreased to 1,852 in the second quarter. This decline was indicative of a migration of savings institutions to the commercial-banking industry. Not only did commercial banks acquire 33 savings institutions in the first half of 1997, but 22 savings institutions converted to commercial-bank charters. These 55 institutions accounted for more than $38.1 billion in assets. A total of 81 thrifts had been absorbed by the commercial-banking industry since August 1996, when the Small Business Job Protection Act removed some tax liability from thrifts converting to or being acquired by commercial banks.

Under 1996 legislation, Congress authorized the federal government to convert all payments, except tax refunds, made by the federal government from checks to electronic-funds transfers by Jan. 1, 1999. Social Security recipients will be the group most affected.

ANN KESSLER, *American Bankers Association*

BELGIUM

Economic ups and downs and concern over police and judicial effectiveness marked the year 1997 in Belgium.

Economy. Workers demonstrated in January against government austerity moves aimed at qualifying Belgium to participate in the single European currency—the Euro. Public employees marched in Brussels to protest the elimination or privatization of government jobs. In Tubize, 80,000 workers took to the streets after the Walloon government refused to subsidize the reopening of the Forges de Clabecq steel mill.

The greatest shock was French carmaker Renault's decision to close its 3,100-worker Vilvoorde assembly plant in July. Renault—which had invested $288 million to modernize the profitable plant three years earlier—wanted to shift manufacture to Spain, where costs were lower. Belgium's Prime Minister Jean-Luc Dehaene called the move "brutal and unacceptable" and took the matter to Belgian and European Union (EU) courts. The government, seconded by the European Commission, contended that Renault failed to abide by EU directives requiring large companies to consult with employees "in good time with a view to reaching an agreement."

In response to layoffs and unemployment, Belgium passed incentives for employers to hire more workers and ruled part-time early retirement was possible, even when not provided for in a collective-bargaining agreement. An incentive of $4,230 per year was approved for each new position, while graduated reductions in employers' social-security contributions over two or three years were granted for small businesses hiring second or third employees.

To fulfill a European Council regulation, Belgium introduced a three-month parental leave that guarantees the employee his or her job upon return. Business social-security contributions for laborers were cut by $564 per year, while discrimination between genders for night work was abolished.

In general, the Belgian economy fared well in 1997. Gross domestic product (GDP) grew steadily and was expected to rise by 2.25% for the year. The current-account surplus of the Belgo-Luxembourg Economic Union (UEBL) was 5.75% of GDP—the best level within the European Union. The inflation rate was down, predicted to reach only 1.8% for the year. Belgium's new small capitalization market was inaugurated, while plans were made to merge the Antwerp and Brussels stock exchanges. Government budget cuts of up to 1% of GDP—linked with predicted revenue improvements—suggested that the budget deficit would fall to 2.7% of GDP, qualifying Belgium for participation in the planned economic and monetary union (EMU).

Justice. Public concern continued to focus on the uncovering of a widespread child-sex syndicate. Officials were accused of inefficiency and lack of effort, while citizens demonstrated against alleged police incompetence.

On January 31, Marc Dutroux—who already had admitted kidnapping six girls—was charged with murdering two others and an accomplice. On March 5 police found the body of a girl, missing since 1992. Patrick Derochette admitted guilt in that crime.

In mid-April the preliminary report of a 15-member all-party parliamentary investigative commission stated that grave police and judicial incompetence may have permitted four avoidable deaths. Rivalry between police and judicial divisions caused a "flagrant failure" to share information. Rumors insisted that Dutroux received high-level protection, but investigators found little proof. Further investigation was promised, but the June publication of a book by a former member of the commission about its inner discussions may have compromised its confidentiality and ability to gain information. Commission recommendations included the creation of an integrated national police force to replace the present local, judicial, and national police. Its order that all dossiers on missing people be reopened led to the discovery of more bodies in October and public shock that complaints filed in 1987 and 1992 against the alleged murderer—clergyman Andreas Pandy, 70—were not better investigated.

JONATHAN E. HELMREICH, *Allegheny College*

BELGIUM • Information Highlights

Official Name: Kingdom of Belgium.
Location: Northwestern Europe.
Area: 11,780 sq mi (30 510 km²).
Population (mid-1997 est.): 10,200,000.
Chief Cities (Dec. 31, 1994): Brussels, the capital (incl. suburbs), 951,580; Antwerp (including suburbs), 459,072; Ghent, 227,483; Charleroi, 206,491; Liège, 192,393; Bruges, 116,273.
Government: *Head of state,* Albert II, king (acceded Aug. 9, 1993). *Head of government,* Jean-Luc Dehaene, prime minister (sworn in March 7, 1992). *Legislature*—Parliament: Senate and Chamber of Deputies.
Monetary Unit: Franc (36.08 francs equal U.S.$1, commercial rate, Nov. 21, 1997).
Gross Domestic Product (1995 est. U.S.$): $197,000,000,-000 (purchasing power parity).
Economic Indexes (1996, 1990 = 100): *Consumer Prices,* all items, 115.0; food, 104.6. *Industrial Production,* 99.
Foreign Trade (1996 with Luxembourg, U.S.$): *Imports,* $152,791,000,000; *exports,* $165,807,000,000.

BIOCHEMISTRY

Cancer research remained in the forefront of biochemistry in 1996–97.

Cancer. Since 1994 biochemists had discovered that the function of two genes, BRCA-1 and BRCA-2, is critical to the prevention of breast cancer. Women who inherit a single defective copy of either of the genes are significantly prone to developing breast cancer in their lifetime. In addition, BRCA-1 mutations predispose women to ovarian cancer and mutations in BRCA-2 predispose men to prostate cancer. When initially discovered, the two genes were considered to be classical tumor suppressors, which normally hold cell proliferation in check but, when mutated, can lead directly to tumor formation.

In early 1997 several teams of scientists working independently reported that the proteins encoded by BRCA-1 and BRCA-2 play a critical role in enabling cells to repair their DNA when damaged. This indicated that the tumor-promoting effects of BRCA-1 and BRCA-2 are indirect—they disrupt DNA repair and allow the cells to accumulate mutations, including those that promote cancer. Two lines of evidence supported this mode of action. Proteins encoded by BRCA-1 and BRCA-2 bound strongly to a known cellular repair protein called RAD51—as would be expected—and cells containing inactivated BRCA-1 and BRCA-2 failed to recover from radiation damage. The latter point suggested that women who have breast cancer due to BRCA mutations might be good candidates for radiation therapy.

Two competing research teams identified another tumor-suppressor gene, whose inactivation leads to brain, prostate, and other cancers. One team, led by Ramon Parsons of Columbia University, named it P-TEN, while the other, led by Peter Steck of M.D. Anderson Cancer Center in Houston and Sean Tavtigian of Myriad Genetics in Salt Lake City, called it MMAC1. Unlike some 16 other tumor-suppressor genes, the single protein encoded by P-TEN/MMAC1 has two biological functions. One segment of the protein resembles tyrosine phosphatase, which is an enzyme that removes phosphate from the amino acid tyrosine of the target proteins; another segment resembles tensin, a protein that connects the cell's internal skeleton of protein filaments to the protein matrix outside the cell.

The tyrosine phosphatase directly counters the actions of another set of enzymes called tyrosine kinases, which add phosphate to tyro-sine and make cells cancerous when they are mutated into an overactive form. Resemblance to the protein tensin indicated that P-TEN/MMAC1 might help cells stay in their normal location within a tissue, and its loss might add to the ability of the tumor cells to spread to other parts of the body. The discovery of P-TEN/MMAC1 was expected to provide guides to better cancer therapies.

Apoptosis. The immune system's activated T lymphocytes are known to kill some cells while sparing others. The T cells perform this function by delivering the death signal to their target cells and causing them to commit suicide. This process, called apoptosis, involves interaction between two chemicals—Fas and FasL—located on cell surfaces. When a cell bearing FasL comes in contact with another cell bearing Fas, the interaction between Fas and FasL triggers a series of events inside the cell bearing Fas that leads to its suicide. The T cells contain both Fas and FasL on their cell surfaces and this allows them not only to kill their target cells bearing Fas by apoptosis but also to turn this molecular weapon on each other to restrain the immune response.

In 1997 a team of Swiss scientists discovered how melanoma cells (cancerous pigmented cells of skin and other tissues) protect themselves against attack by the body's T cells. It was found that melanoma cancer cells carry FasL but not Fas, and thus can deliver the death signal to T cells (which carry Fas) rather than receiving such a signal from T cells, because they do not carry Fas themselves. Apparently, melanoma cells—and perhaps cells of other cancers—defend themselves against immune attack by acquiring the ability to produce FasL. Researchers were looking for ways to overcome those defenses as a way of controlling cancer.

Niemann-Pick. Niemann-Pick (NP), a neurological disorder, involves the inability of cells to process cholesterol, causing them to become gorged with that water-insoluble molecule. Nerve cells are the first to die, so that the patient becomes physically disabled; death ensues at an early age. Scientists discovered that the gene responsible for NP is located on chromosome 18 and encodes a protein, NPC1. In its normal form, NPC1 senses a cell's level of cholesterol and helps shuttle it from one part of the cell to another. Apparently, NPC1 protein causes disease when it is disabled and cannot shuttle cholesterol within a cell. Researchers were expected to use cell cultures and mouse models to screen for drugs that might slow cholesterol buildup in NP patients.

PREM P. BATRA, *Wright State University*

Biography

A selection of profiles of persons prominent in the news in 1997 appears on pages 138–49. The affiliation of the contributor is listed on pages 591–94; biographies that do not include a contributor's name were prepared by the staff. Included are profiles of:

ALBRIGHT, Madeleine K.

Early in President Bill Clinton's first term, when then Joint Chiefs of Staff Chairman Colin Powell firmly resisted launching U.S. air strikes against the Bosnian Serbs, Madeleine Albright, then U.S. ambassador to the United Nations (UN), had a blunt question for the country's top soldier: "What's the point in having this superb military you're always talking about if we can't use it?"

"I thought I would have an aneurysm," recalled Powell, who stuck to his guns and got his way, for awhile. But eventually, Albright's view prevailed and the use of U.S. airpower helped pave the way for a cease-fire and the 1995 Dayton Accord that brought a measure of peace to that strife-torn corner of the globe. Such forthrightness helped Albright make her mark as the U.S. ambassador to the United Nations and helped her gain acceptance when Clinton picked her at the start of his second term to head the State Department; she was the first woman to hold that job.

Though Albright is respected by her peers as a consummate professional, it was a personal revelation that dominated her start as secretary of state. Soon after she got her new job, Albright—the daughter of Czechoslovakian refugees from Nazism—discovered that her parents, who raised her in the Roman Catholic faith, had been born Jewish, and that more than a dozen of her relatives might have been killed in the Holocaust. Soon thereafter, she returned to her Prague birthplace, where—on the wall of a local synagogue—she saw inscribed the names of her paternal grandparents, who had perished in the Nazi death camps. "Their image will forever be seared into my heart," she said.

In helping to implement U.S. foreign policy during 1997, Albright played a key role in the negotiations leading up to the expansion of the North Atlantic Treaty Organization (NATO), in trying to ease the Middle East tensions between Israel and the Palestinians, and in dealing with the still-troublesome Serbs. During one encounter, Serbian President Slobodan Milosevic tried to unsettle her by saying with a patronizing smile: "Madam Secretary, you're not well informed." Albright, who had spent three years in Belgrade as a child, shot back: "Don't tell me I'm uninformed, I lived here." Milosevic's smile vanished.

Meanwhile, Albright acted quickly to establish control of her own agency. When the substance of important meetings about China policy was leaked to the press, she summoned her senior officials, looked them in the eye, and said: "You have a choice. You can have a good and trusting relationship with me. Or you can have an undisciplined relationship with the press." The grapevine soon carried the word: Madam secretary was a take-charge guy.

Background. Madeleine Korbel was born on May 15, 1937, in Prague, Czechoslovakia. She came to the United States when her parents were granted asylum after the communist takeover in Czechoslovakia. A graduate of Wellesley College, she earned graduate degrees from Columbia University before working as a congressional aide and on the National Security Council staff in the

© Robert Giroux/Reuters/Archive Photos

Madeleine K. Albright

Jimmy Carter administration. She taught from 1982 to 1993 at Georgetown University's School of Foreign Service, where students four times voted her best teacher. She was foreign-policy adviser to Democratic standard-bearers Walter Mondale in 1984 and Michael Dukakis in 1988, as well as Clinton in 1992. She served as ambassador to the United Nations throughout Clinton's first term.

Her marriage to journalist Joseph Albright ended in divorce after the couple had three daughters. She is the author of several books and numerous articles on foreign affairs.

ROBERT SHOGAN

ANNAN, Kofi

In late 1996 the United States vetoed the reelection of Boutros Boutros-Ghali of Egypt as secretary-general of the United Nations, but failed to name its preferred candidate as his successor. Yet it was no secret that the mild-mannered chief of the UN peacekeeping department, Kofi Annan of Ghana, was Washington's choice to be secretary-general.

It would have been a handicap for Annan had it appeared that the world's major superpower was imposing him on other members. In this case, however, most Security Council members agreed that Annan—known as part technocrat, part politician, and part mediator—was a candidate for a period in history when the world was leaving behind outmoded rules and dogma and preparing for the 21st century. But a new secretary-general was being chosen at a time when the United Nations' morale was as depleted as its finances. The failure of the U.S. Congress to appropriate payment on the $1.5 billion the United States owed the UN for its regular dues and for peacekeeping contributed to the decline of the UN's morale. Dues would be paid, Congress said, when United Nations reforms were implemented. Annan was seen as a vehicle for such reform.

After being elected for a five-year term on Dec. 17, 1996, Annan invited the world to applaud the United Nations when it prevailed, correct it when it failed; but, above all, he pleaded, do not let this indispensable institution perish "as a result of governments' indifference, inattention, or financial starvation." If anyone could convert the unconverted to the cause of UN reform, Annan was considered the one. As someone who had worked with him explained: "Every post he has held throughout his career prepared him for this role [UN secretary-general]. He paid his dues and earned his credentials from the ground up." In fact, he was the first secretary-general who had risen to the top through the UN system.

Background. Kofi Annan was born on April 8, 1938, in the small town of Kumasi, Ghana. He studied at Kumasi's University of Science and Technology; did undergraduate work in economics at Macalester College in St. Paul, MN; took graduate courses in economics at the Institut Universitaire des Hautes Etudes Internationales in Geneva; and—as a Sloan Fellow—was awarded a master of science degree in management from the Massachusetts Institute of Technology (MIT).

Annan first joined the UN staff in 1962, when he became an administrative and budgetary officer at the World Health Organization (WHO). From then on, he rose through various UN positions, primarily involving personnel management and budget planning. In 1992 he was appointed first UN assistant secretary-general for peacekeeping and the following year became undersecretary-general for peacekeeping. From Nov. 1, 1995, to March 1996, he was the secretary-general's special representative to the former Yugoslavia. From 1974 to 1976 he had taken a break from the UN to serve as managing director of the Ghana Tourist Development Company.

The most urgent task facing Annan as the UN's seventh secretary-general would be to streamline and rejuvenate the world organization. During 1997, Annan unveiled a two-track reform package. Track one, announced in March, would reduce the UN budget for 1998–99 by $123 million, eliminate 1,000 jobs, cut administrative costs from 38% to 25% of the budget, and consolidate three economic and social departments into one. Track two, announced in July, called for the appointment of a deputy secretary-general and the establishment of a revolving fund to tide the UN over during times of financial difficulties. Although the General Assembly approved Annan's reform program in November, the U.S. Congress voted against paying even part of the amount it owed the UN. Annan then declared that the UN now "must take serious stock of its financial difficulties." (*See also* UNITED NATIONS.)

Secretary-General Annan is married to the former Nane Lagergren, a Swedish lawyer and artist. They are the parents of three children.

RUTH PEARSON

BLAIR, Anthony Charles Lynton (Tony)

After Tony Blair led Great Britain's Labour Party to a landslide victory in the general election on May 1, 1997—a few days short of his 44th birthday—he became Britain's youngest prime minister since Lord Liverpool in 1812. Perhaps even more striking than Blair's youth was the speed with which he had transformed his party's policies and public image after being elected Labour leader in 1994.

Described by the historian Ben Pimlott as "an attractive politician in the mold of JFK," Blair moved swiftly to distance the party he began calling "new Labour" from its

© Stan Honda/Agence France Presse/Corbis-Bettmann

Kofi Annan

long-standing socialist policies. In a series of bold moves, he persuaded the party to drop its commitment to the fair distribution of the means of ownership, production, and exchange and the nationalization of industry; warned trade unions that they no longer could expect to enjoy decisive influence over Labour Party policy; abandoned unilateral nuclear disarmament; declared his party to be a friend of the business community; and adopted a cordial stance toward the European Union (EU). All of these actions ran against long-established Labour policies.

Blair's education and family background—his father was a lawyer and Conservative Party politician on the local level—mark him as middle-class. The handicap this might have posed for a leader of a traditionally working-class movement was canceled out by Blair's popularity with the British public. Soon after his election as Labour leader, a

Tony Blair

© Alain Buu/Gamma-Liaison

Gallup poll indicated that 45% of the voters favored him as prime minister as against 15% for the incumbent, John Major.

In jousts with Major in the House of Commons, Blair, who was trained as a barrister (legal advocate), established himself as a nimble debater keen to promote policies hard to distinguish in some cases from those of his Conservative opponents. Among critics, his eagerness to move away from old Labour policies earned him the sobriquet of "Tony Blur." He promised to be "tough on crime and the causes of crime," denied that Labour under his leadership was a "tax and spend" party, and poured scorn on the government's hard-line EU policies that he said had alienated Britain from its European partners. From early 1995 he maintained pressure on the Conservatives as a succession of leading government supporters were accused of political or financial corruption.

Background. Anthony Charles Lynton (Tony) Blair was born on May 6, 1953, in Edinburgh, Scotland, the son of Leo and Hazel Blair. He was educated at Durham Cathedral School; Fettes College, Edinburgh; and St. John's College, Oxford. At Oxford, Blair initially showed little interest in politics but was active as a Christian social idealist. He played guitar in a university rock group called Ugly Rumours and wore his hair like Mick Jagger. He joined the Labour Party in 1975 and became a barrister in Lincoln's Inn, London, in 1976.

He first was elected a member of Parliament for Sedgefield in 1983 and joined Labour's shadow cabinet in 1988. He was opposition spokesman on home affairs (1992–94) when he was elected Labour Party leader on the death of John Smith. Today, Blair describes himself as more a social democrat than a socialist.

In 1980 he married Cherie Booth, whom he met while at Oxford. The couple have three children. He is a High Anglican but attends Mass with his Roman Catholic wife. Mrs. Blair also is a barrister, with the elevated rank of Queen's Counsel, and continued to appear as an advocate after Blair became prime minister.

Tall, slim, and good-looking, Tony Blair was described by one political commentator as being "a man whose tongue is as sharp as his suit."

ALEXANDER MACLEOD

BROOKS, Garth

In August 1997 country-music idol Garth Brooks scheduled a free concert in New York City's Central Park to coincide with the release of his new album. Although the album's release was postponed, the concert went on as planned, attracting a crowd estimated by police at 250,000. New York's Gov. George Pataki was among those in the crowd, which went wild when pop star Billy Joel—whose style Brooks cites as a strong influence on his own—came onstage for a duet. The concert was underwritten by Brooks and Home Box Office (HBO), which televised the event.

People traveled long distances to attend the New York concert, attesting to Brooks' popularity. In fact, in 1996, Brooks had become the top-selling solo artist in U.S. history, surpassing the likes of Billy Joel, Elton John, Michael Jackson, and Elvis Presley. In the years since his debut in 1989, Brooks had sold more albums—62 million—than anyone else except the Beatles, who needed 32 years to sell 71 million. With the 1997 release of the album *Sevens*, Brooks was expected to overtake even the beloved British quartet.

His "good ol' country boy" demeanor is scorned by some as a marketing ploy, but there is no denying his astonishing success, which goes far beyond his sales figures. His third album, *Ropin' the Wind*, became the first country album ever to go straight to the top of the Billboard pop chart. He has been the recipient of dozens of awards, and is the youngest member ever inducted into the Grand Ole Opry, earning that honor in 1990. His concerts usually sell out in a matter of hours, if not less.

Background. Troyal Garth Brooks was born in Tulsa, OK, on Feb. 7, 1962, the second child of Troyal Raymond Brooks, an oil-company engineer, and Colleen Carroll

Brooks, who briefly was a recording artist in the late 1950s. He was raised in Yukon, a suburb of Oklahoma City, along with four half siblings.

It was not until just before entering college that Brooks decided what he wanted to do. Driving in his car one day, he heard George Strait's "Unwound" on the radio. "That's the exact moment it all changed. I became a George wanna-be and imitator for the next seven years." Matriculating at Oklahoma State University on a track scholarship, Brooks majored in advertising and journalism, earning his bachelor's degree in 1984. While attending OSU, he held various jobs, including that of a bouncer at a local nightclub. One evening he was called to eject a woman from the club following an altercation. He did so; the woman later became his wife.

After Brooks was graduated from OSU, he began performing at a club for $600 per week. In 1985 he went to Nashville to seek his fortune, but soon returned, disillusioned, to Oklahoma. "I thought the world was waiting for me, but there's nothing colder than reality." Two years later, Brooks and his wife risked their last $1,500 to return to Nashville and try again. This time he was discovered by a Capitol Records scout in a newcomers' showcase in a local club; the rest is history.

Today Brooks lives outside Nashville, TN, with his wife, Sandy, and their three daughters. He is known as an unabashed lover of both his art and his family; the entire Brooks clan travels with him when he tours.

BRUCE JACOBY

COHEN, William Sebastian

When former U.S. Sen. William S. Cohen was selected to run the Department of Defense at the start of President Bill Clinton's second term, the choice was hailed widely on Capitol Hill, where Cohen, a Maine Republican, had served for 24 years. He was confirmed by a vote of 90–0 and took office as the nation's 20th secretary of defense on Jan. 24, 1997.

However, even Cohen's admirers conceded that, while the veteran lawmaker had demonstrated his grasp of defense issues and politics, he had little training in the management skills that are needed to run a bureaucratic behemoth like the Pentagon. "When you move from the Hill to the Pentagon you have to stop being a legislator and begin being C.E. [chief executive] of one of the largest, most complex organizations in the world," former Joint Chiefs of Staff Chairman Colin Powell remarked about the difficult transition Cohen faced.

The task was made harder by the nature of the problems Secretary Cohen faced, particularly the issues arising from the military's struggle to cope with changing standards for relations between the sexes in an age of political correctness. In June, Cohen was forced to accept the withdrawal of Air Force Gen. Joseph Ralston, his personal choice to be the next chairman of the Joint Chiefs of Staff, because of an adultery scandal. One reason Ralston's previous adultery prevented his promotion was that his name came to the fore right after a female U.S. Air Force pilot, 1st Lt. Kelly Flinn, was forced to resign because of her own adulterous affair. Cohen also had his hands full dealing with sexual-harassment charges against the army's top enlisted man, Sgt. Maj. Gene McKinney. In October the army announced that it would court-martial McKinney on charges that he had propositioned and assaulted six female service members.

Another major challenge was defining a suitable role for the U.S. military in the post–Cold War world, where a variety of new perils loomed. That problem was illustrated by Cohen's decision to cancel the promotion of Air Force Brig. Gen. Terryl J. Schwalier on grounds that he had not done enough to prevent the 1996 truck bombing of a housing complex in Saudi Arabia that killed 19 U.S. servicemen. In July the defense secretary had to accept the resignation of the air force's chief of staff, Gen. Ronald R. Fogelman, in protest against the Pentagon's decision to discipline Schwalier. (*See also* FEATURE SECTION, pages 44–57.)

Background. William Sebastian Cohen was born on Aug. 28, 1940, in Bangor, ME. After being graduated from

Bowdoin College and Boston University Law School, he practiced law in Bangor and taught at the University of Maine. He served as a member of Bangor's city council (1969–72) and as Bangor's mayor (1971–72). In 1972 he won election to the first of three terms in the U.S. House of Representatives. In 1978 he was elected to the first of three terms in the U.S. Senate. One of the most influential lawmakers on defense and national-security issues, Cohen was a longtime member of the Senate Armed Services and Intelligence committees. He was chief Senate sponsor of the GI Bill of 1984, was involved heavily in drafting the defense-reorganization act of 1986, and helped foster the development of the military's Rapid Deployment Force.

Secretary Cohen is married to the former Janet Langhart; the couple have two grown sons, Kevin and Chris. He has written or cowritten eight books—two poetry collections, three novels, and three works of nonfiction.

ROBERT SHOGAN

© Diana Walker/Gamma-Liaison

Katharine Graham

GRAHAM, Katharine

As publisher of *The Washington Post* and chief executive officer (CEO) of The Washington Post Company, Katharine Graham successfully directed one of the world's leading publishing companies. In 1997 she turned her attention to a different phase of publishing, becoming a best-selling author. Her autobiography, *Personal History*—which she wrote herself with some editorial help but without the usual ghostwriter—not only was well received by the critics but also was a fixture on the best-seller lists for numerous weeks. Graham, once described as the most powerful woman in America, marked another milestone in 1997. On June 16 she celebrated her 80th birthday.

Background. Katharine Meyer was born on June 16, 1917, in New York City, the daughter of Eugene Meyer, a financier, and Agnes Elizabeth Ernst Meyer, an author and philanthropist. One of five children, she was raised in an atmosphere that encouraged public responsibility. After attending Madeira School in Virginia, outside of Washington, DC, she studied at Vassar College before earning her bachelor's degree from the University of Chicago in 1938. She then went to California and became a reporter for the *San Francisco News*. The following year she returned to the East Coast, joining the circulation staff and editorial department of *The Washington Post*. Her father had purchased the financially troubled paper for $825,000 in 1933.

On June 5, 1940, she married Philip L. Graham, a graduate of Harvard Law School and clerk for two Supreme Court justices. During World War II, he served in the U.S. Army Air Force and she continued to work for the *Post*. After his discharge from the army, he joined the *Post* at his father-in-law's persuasion and soon was appointed publisher. In 1948 the Grahams became the paper's majority owners. Katharine, meanwhile, devoted herself to raising their four children, as her husband—who was the "fizz" in their lives—oversaw the expansion of The Washington Post Company. In 1961 the corporation purchased *Newsweek* magazine and in 1962 it joined the Los Angeles Times Company in establishing an international news service. Philip Graham, however, was suffering from severe manic depression and committed suicide on Aug. 3, 1963.

Mrs. Graham assumed the presidency of the company the following month. Although lacking executive editorial experience as well as self-esteem, she was determined to preserve the family nature of the publishing company and to maintain the integrity of the *Post* and the company's other publications. Under her tutelage the company continued to grow, acquiring a 45% interest in the *Paris* (now the *International*) *Herald Tribune* and expanding its radio and television operations. Graham also appointed top journalists, including Benjamin C. Bradlee, to various editorial positions at the *Post* and raised the paper's editorial budget significantly.

In June 1971, Graham gave the go-ahead for the *Post* to publish excerpts from the Pentagon Papers, a classified government study of U.S. policy in Southeast Asia from the end of World War II to 1968. At the time, the U.S. Justice Department had gone to court to prevent the *Post* and The *New York Times*—which earlier had printed the first installment of a planned series from the study—from publishing additional excerpts. On June 30 the U.S. Supreme Court dissolved its temporary injunction against both newspapers and ruled that the study could be published. The case was considered a victory for freedom of the press.

The *Post* also played a leading role in exposing the excesses of the Richard Nixon administration in the Watergate affair. The paper and Graham personally came under attack from the administration for the *Post*'s investigation of the case. Watergate ended with Nixon's resignation as president and with numerous accolades, including a Pulitzer Prize for meritorious service for the *Post* and its prime Watergate reporters, Bob Woodward and Carl Bernstein.

Graham turned over the positions of publisher and CEO to her eldest son, Donald, in 1979 and 1991, respectively, but remained the company's chairwoman until 1993. At that time, she became chair of the executive committee. Throughout her years in Washington, Graham has served as a trustee or board member for numerous organizations and committees. She also has been a fixture on the capital's social scene, befriending members of both major political parties. The Black and White Ball, which the late author Truman Capote gave in her honor at New York City's Plaza Hotel in November 1966, was called the social event of the "year, decade, or century."

GREENSPAN, Alan

Alan Greenspan, who has served as chairman of the powerful board of governors of the Federal Reserve Board (the Fed) since Aug. 11, 1987, refused to hit the brakes hard on the U.S. economy in 1997.

It would have been easy for chairman Greenspan to ask his policy-making colleagues at the Fed for a modest hike in short-term interest rates—beyond the hike of one quarter of one percentage point imposed in March 1997—as a "preemptive move" against inflation. After all, U.S. unemployment by October had slipped to 4.7% of the labor force—the lowest rate since 1973. Many economists believe that at this level, a tight labor market will bring higher wage costs and push prices upward. But 1997 statistics showed declining, not rising, inflation.

The husky economy, Greenspan could see, had helped in virtually eliminating the federal budget deficit. It was providing those at the bottom of the economic ladder a better chance to move up that ladder. Indeed, many economists praised Greenspan for guiding the United States into a "golden age" of rising prosperity without inflation. Greenspan also has proven he has guts in the way he deals with stock-market slumps. Two months after taking office as Fed chairman in 1987, Greenspan saw the Dow Jones industrial average plunge 508 points, or 22.61%, on October 19. The Fed leaped to the market's assistance, promising Wall Street there would be adequate credit and pumping money into the economy.

Nothing like that happened in 1997. For one thing, in December 1996, Greenspan had questioned whether stock prices were showing "irrational exuberance." He was speaking of the danger that the United States might follow in the footsteps of Japan, where a huge bubble developed in both stock and real-estate prices in the 1980s. When the bubble burst, Japan's economy slumped into a long recession. So it was likely that Greenspan shed no tears when stock prices fell by nearly 7% over several days in August 1997.

Not even the more dramatic 554-point (7.18 percentage points) drop in the Dow on Monday, October 27, ruffled the chairman—at least visibly. Only four weeks earlier, Greenspan again had hinted that stocks were ripe for a tumble. On October 29, after a sharp snapback in prices the day before, the chairman gave modest assurance to the nation of the solidity of the economic expansion. "It is quite conceivable," he testified before the Joint Economic Committee of Congress, "that a few years hence, we will look back at this episode, as we now look back at the 1987 crash, as a salutary event." Greenspan and other senior U.S. officials that make up a body known as the President's Work Group on Financial Markets had decided to interfere little in the financial crisis that was reverberating around the globe.

Background. Born in New York City on March 6, 1926, Alan Greenspan was an only child whose parents were divorced when he was very young. Before devoting himself to economics, he spent two years at the Juilliard School of Music in New York City, studying the clarinet. He then toured with a swing band before continuing his education. He obtained his bachelor's (1948), master's (1950), and doctoral (1977) degrees from New York University. In 1954, Greenspan joined bond trader William Townsend in founding Townsend-Greenspan & Co., a leading economic-consulting shop in New York, and served with the company from 1954 to 1974 and from 1977 to 1987. He was chairman of the Council of Economic Advisers (1974–77) under President Gerald Ford and chairman of President Ronald Reagan's bipartisan National Commission on Social Security Reform (1981–83).

The chairman is not seen as a Keynesian, a monetarist, or a supply-sider, but as a free-enterprise economist. Ayn Rand, author of *Atlas Shrugged* and an advocate of laissez-faire capitalism and "rational selfishness," once said of her longtime friend: "Alan is my disciple philosophically, but his career as an economic analyst is his own achievement."

On April 6, 1997, Greenspan and NBC News correspondent Andrea Mitchell, 50, were married after a 12-year courtship.

DAVID R. FRANCIS

© Mike Theiler/Reuters/Archive Photos

Alan Greenspan

GWYNN, Tony

During the 1997 Major League Baseball season, Tony Gwynn of the San Diego Padres enhanced his reputation as the game's best hitter. He did this by winning his eighth batting title—tying Honus Wagner's National League (NL) record—and leading the league in hits for a seventh time. In 1997, Gwynn won his fourth consecutive hitting crown with a .372 average, while also topping the NL with 220 hits and 152 singles. Though held to 149 games by injuries, he had 49 doubles, second in the circuit, while reaching career peaks with 17 home runs and 119 runs batted in. On the open market, such numbers would command compensation far beyond the 1997 contract extension that pays him $4.2 million a year through 2000, but Gwynn has no desire to leave San Diego.

The 5'11" (1.8-m), 220-lb (100-kg), left-handed hitter has been a National League All-Star 13 times—even though he has been hobbled by three operations on his left knee, another for a partially torn right Achilles tendon, and assorted other ailments. An opposite-field-singles hitter before 1997, Gwynn added power to his résumé after a conversation with Ted Williams. The Hall of Famer told Gwynn that a good hitter meets the inside pitch in front of the plate—advice Gwynn applied after recovering from a 1996 heel injury.

Background. Anthony Keith Gwynn was born on May 9, 1960, the second son of Charles Gwynn, Sr., a warehouse worker for the state of California, and Vendella Gwynn, a U.S. postal employee. Tony starred in both baseball and basketball at Long Beach Polytechnic High School, then attended San Diego State on a basketball scholarship. Although his school record for assists still stands, he decided to concentrate on baseball because he thought his height was insufficient for the National Basketball Association (NBA). Still, Gwynn was drafted on the same day by the San Diego (now the Los Angeles) Clippers of the NBA as well as by the Padres.

A third-round amateur-draft choice in June 1981, Gwynn reached the majors 13 months later. He broke in with a 15-game hitting streak. During a rare 1983 slump, Gwynn learned to analyze his swing by watching videotapes, becoming a pioneer in baseball video analysis. The video work paid off, as he had a club-record 25-game streak late in that season. In 1984, his first full season, Gwynn led the NL in batting (.351), on-base percentage (.410), and hits (213) as the Padres won their only pennant. Although no one has hit .400 since Ted Williams finished at .406 in 1941, Gwynn came closest, with a .394 mark in the strike-shortened 1994 campaign.

Two years later, after his two-run single at Los Angeles on the next-to-last day of the regular season gave San Diego its second postseason berth, Gwynn called it the "biggest hit" in a career that includes Padres records for average, hits, runs, runs batted in, and stolen bases.

Tony Gwynn
© Susan Sterner/AP/Wide World Photos

Another career highlight was the chance to play with his brother Chris—a former San Diego State All-American—for the Padres in 1996. Tony also has won five Gold Gloves for fielding excellence.

During the off-season, Gwynn follows a rigorous weight-lifting regimen and works at a San Diego baseball school where he is co-owner. The Padres standout relaxes by playing video games, golfing, and fishing. He also is active in civic life, receiving the 1995 Branch Rickey Award for outstanding community service by a major-league player. Gwynn and his wife, the former Alicia Cureton, are the parents of Anthony II, born Oct. 4, 1982, and Anisha Nicole, born Aug. 8, 1985.

DAN SCHLOSSBERG

HERMAN, Alexis

When negotiations between the Teamsters Union and United Parcel Service (UPS) broke down during a 1997 summer strike that all but crippled the thriving mail-cata-logue industry in the United States, it was Secretary of Labor Alexis Herman who spent hours persuading the two sides to resume talks. The new cabinet member then took up residence in the same Washington hotel as the union and management negotiators, meeting with them count-less times until the 15-day strike was settled.

The tense bargain was a trial by fire for Herman, and its resolution was a triumph for the former White House offi-cial, whose nomination to the cabinet post by President Bill Clinton initially stirred little enthusiasm from the ranks of labor, as well as troublesome questions about possible ethical violations from Congress. The questions arose because of indications that Herman might have used her widespread contacts—made as an official of the Demo-cratic National Committee—to boost the fortunes of the consulting business she ran before taking her White House job under Clinton. But when Senate investigators were unable to find any solid evidence of wrongdoing, Herman gained Senate confirmation by a vote of 85–13. She took office on May 1. And then she let her performance in the UPS strike answer her critics in the labor movement, who claimed she lacked the experience with unions and issues important to working families that was necessary to play an effective role in the Clinton cabinet.

John T. Dunlop, who was secretary of labor under Presi-dent Gerald Ford, said the strike gave Herman a valuable opportunity to establish the kind of clout necessary to get things done in Washington. "In future disputes, her com-ments will be taken more seriously than they would other-wise be," said Dunlop, currently a professor of economics who specializes in labor issues. And as the secretary her-self acknowledged, there would be no lack of challenges for her at the helm of a department that has had to strug-gle for influence and respect in the face of the conservative tide that has dominated Washington since the 1980s.

"I hope it will spotlight the issues we care about," she said of the strike settlement, "whether it is lifelong learning or the challenge of moving people from welfare to work or retirement security for young women and girls." In pursuing these objectives, Herman would rely on the same skills she used in the negotiations. And as Herman—the first African-American to hold the labor post—told an aide, these tal-ents had been acquired "growing up black in the South and learning to walk in other people's shoes."

Background. That process started in Mobile, AL, where Alexis Herman was born on July 16, 1947, and where the future labor secretary returned to help desegregate her old high school in 1969, after being trained as a social worker at Xavier University in New Orleans.

Herman's experience in developing training programs for jobless youth and other unskilled workers, and her con-tacts in Democratic politics, won her appointment from President Jimmy Carter as director of the Labor Depart-ment's Women's Bureau in 1977. Leaving government, she established a consulting business that advised corpora-tions and local governments on job training and creation. After serving on the staff of the Democratic National Com-mittee, she was director of the White House Office of Pub-lic Liaison during Clinton's first term.

ROBERT SHOGAN

JOSPIN, Lionel

"These are the tears of 1997...they're very different from the tears of 1993," said France's Socialist Party leader Lionel Jospin as he comforted a weeping party activist the night of the left's upset victory in the second round of leg-islative elections on June 1. A few months earlier, no one in France would have predicted Jospin would lead the Social-ists to triumph after their crushing repudiation just four years earlier.

Jospin, who took office as premier of France on June 3, is neither flamboyant nor charismatic. Yet in this very awk-wardness may lie the key to his popularity. His terrible earnestness and his manifest honesty are the by-products of a certain Protestant rigor that contrasts with the style of most French politicians. After more than a decade of Presi-dent François Mitterrand's machiavellianism and two years of President Jacques Chirac's clannishness, the French sought more transparent leadership.

Background. Lionel Jospin was born on July 12, 1937, in Meudon, just west of Paris; he was the second of four children. His mother was a midwife and his father was a socialist activist who ran a school for adolescents in diffi-culty. Following a year of studying political science at the influential Sciences-Po institute in Paris and military service in Germany, Jospin enrolled in the prestigious Ecole Nationale d'Administration, the seedbed for much of France's political and economic elite. After being graduat-ed in 1965, he joined the foreign service as a foreign-min-istry economic-affairs officer. He left the diplomatic corps after the "events" of 1968 to teach college economics—a phase that left him with an indelibly professorial style.

Jospin did not join the Socialist Party until 1971. Mitter-rand quickly drew him into his "circle of experts," and with-in two years, Jospin held the first of a series of positions in the party's national leadership. His relationship with Mitter-rand remained very close, and when Mitterrand ran for president in 1981, Jospin was chosen to head the Socialist Party. He was appointed education minister in 1988, but already had begun marking his distance from what he saw as the excessively free-market orientation of Mitterrand's second term, and the internal squabbles of the Socialist Party.

In 1993 he left the party's national leadership but partici-pated in renovation efforts. In 1995 he announced his can-didacy for president. An unprecedented internal primary designated him the party candidate and, in a breathtaking upset, Jospin won the first round of voting and garnered a healthy 47.3% of the ballots in the second round.

Alexis Herman
© Mike Theiler/Reuters/Archive Photos

© Evan Agostini/Gamma-Liaison

Christopher Plummer

Jospin has held a number of elective offices, including Paris city councillor, representative in the National Assembly, European parliamentarian, and local assemblyman.

The French premier is married to philosophy professor Sylviane Agacinski and has three children, two from a previous marriage.

SARAH CHAYES

KHATAMI, Mohammed

Mohammed Khatami, who became the fifth president of Iran on Aug. 3, 1997, was comparatively little known before his surprising and clear-cut victory in the presidential election of May 23. His victory certainly was gained at the expense of the hard-line Islamic forces in Iran—who had ruled it for 18 years—and portended some policy changes in a liberal direction; but their extent, especially in foreign relations, remained uncertain. In policy-making, Khatami would be hampered by his position as constitutionally second to the conservative Ayatollah Ali Akbar Hoseini Khamenei, Iran's spiritual leader. (*See* IRAN.)

Background. Mohammed Khatami was born on Sept. 29, 1943, in Ardakan, in the central Iranian province of Yazd. He was the son of the respected Ayatollah Ruhollah Khatami. His earliest schooling was near home; in 1961 he went to the Theology School in Qum, the leading Iranian center of religious studies. He earned his bachelor's degree in philosophy at the University of Isfahan. He studied educational methods at Tehran University but returned more than once to pursue progressively higher theological studies at Qum. Khatami became a faculty member and then a professor at the Qum seminary, which was his career base until 1978.

During the 1960s, Khatami was engaged in low-level opposition—mostly the writing and distribution of pamphlets—directed against the rule of the shah. Some of the material was written by the Ayatollah Khomeini, who later brought about the revolution destroying the monarchy. Khatami and Khomeini became friends as well as political allies.

Khatami was appointed director of the Islamic Center in Hamburg, Germany, in 1978, returning to Iran in 1980 immediately after the revolution. He represented his home district of Ardakan in the first postrevolution Majlis (legislature) in 1980, and held concurrent appointments as head of the Kayhan Institute and—from 1982 to 1992—as minister of culture and Islamic guidance. During Iran's war with Iraq (1980–88), he also had various war-related duties. He was much in demand as a thoroughly reliable administrator.

Khatami's years as minister of culture and Islamic guidance gave a clear guide to his thinking. He relaxed censor-ship, permitted live concerts, and controlled—with only a light hand—the distribution of books, films, and periodicals. In 1992 he was forced to resign from the cabinet for being too permissive and was relegated to honorable obscurity as head of the National Library. He also served as a cultural adviser to the moderate President Ali Akbar Hashemi Rafsanjani.

He entered the presidential race only in March 1997, being one of the four candidates vetted and approved by the Council of Constitutional Guardians. It generally was assumed that Ali Akbar Nateq-Nouri, speaker of the Majlis, would win easily. However, Khatami's campaign, which was supported by Rafsanjani and called for wider civil liberties within the Islamic framework, as well as his call to improve relations with the Arab countries and Europe, resonated with the young. Khatami gained 20,078,178 votes, or about 70% of the votes cast; Nateq-Nouri took about 25%.

Khatami has been married since 1974 and has two daughters and a son. In addition to Farsi, he speaks Arabic, German, and English. As a direct descendant of the Prophet Mohammed, Iran's new president is entitled to wear the black turban that is the badge of respectability.

ARTHUR CAMPBELL TURNER

MALONE, Karl Anthony

Despite the incredible popularity and continued elite play of Michael Jordan, Karl Malone emerged as the National Basketball Association's (NBA's) most valuable player (MVP) for the 1996–97 season. Malone, the 12-year power forward for the Utah Jazz, barely won the coveted award, beating out four-time winner Jordan in the second-closest voting in MVP history. It was an extraordinary accomplishment for the hardworking Malone, who has labored most of his career in the shadow of NBA superstars who play in much more high-profile markets.

Winning the MVP was an emotional experience for Malone, who was not sure his superior play during 1996–97, coupled with Utah's rise to the top of the league's Western Conference, would be enough to overcome the sensational Jordan. But voters rewarded Malone not only for a wonderful season—he averaged 27.4 points, 9.9 rebounds, and 4.5 assists and finished second in the league in scoring and 11th in rebounding—but for a career of achievement. As one of the NBA's hardest workers and most solid citizens, he long has been admired for his standards and his consistent performances. Season after season, Malone, a rock of a man at 6'9" (2.06 m) and 250 lbs (113.4 kg), has produced consistent statistics and the kind of leadership that has kept the Jazz among the league's best teams for most of his tenure with the franchise. Teaming with long-time friend John Stockton, Malone had hoped to bring the Jazz their first NBA title in 1997, but Utah was eliminated by Chicago in the final play-off round after six games.

Background. Karl Anthony Malone was born July 24, 1963, in Summerfield, LA, the youngest of eight children of J.P. and Shirley Malone. His father abandoned the family when Karl was 4, forcing his mother to take on a series of jobs—including operating a forklift and working as a poultry cutter—to support the family. Malone was raised within a strongly conservative, religious atmosphere that stressed hard work and gratitude for the small things in life. After Malone led his high-school team to three straight Louisiana state titles, his mother urged him to attend nearby Louisiana Tech in Ruston rather than the University of Arkansas. After sitting out his freshman season because of academic problems, he put together three outstanding years at Louisiana Tech, where he picked up the nickname "Mailman" because he could deliver points, rebounds, and blocked shots whenever needed.

He passed up his senior year of college and made himself available for the 1985 pro draft. He lasted until the 13th pick, when he was taken by a grateful Jazz, who never expected him to be available. By his second season, after teaming up with Stockton, Malone emerged as one of the NBA's premier forwards, using his considerable strength and bulk to score consistently close to the basket. Since then, he has become a model of predictability, always among the league's top scorers and rebounders. A perennial all-star and all-league selection, he played on both the 1992 and 1996 U.S. basketball teams—the so-called Dream Teams—that won Olympic gold medals. During the 1996–97 season, he joined Wilt Chamberlain, Kareem Abdul-Jabbar, Moses Malone, and Elvin Hayes as one of five players in NBA history to score 25,000 points and grab 10,000 rebounds.

Malone, who is married and the father of two daughters and a son, owns a small trucking company, an extension of his longtime fascination with 18-wheelers. He does considerable charity work in the community. He lives in Utah and also has a 195-acre (79-ha) cattle ranch in Arkansas where he rides horses.

PAUL ATTNER

PLUMMER, Christopher

Christopher Plummer, a Canadian-born actor whom some have called the best actor in the English-speaking theater, won his second Antoinette Perry (Tony) Award in 1997. Plummer received the award for leading actor in a play—for his portrayal of the Shakespearean actor John Barrymore in *Barrymore* by William Luce.

In *Barrymore*, Plummer plays the flamboyant classical actor near the end of his life as he tries to recreate a legendary performance of *Richard III*. As a young actor, Plummer—who played roles ranging from Mark Antony in *Julius Caesar* to the title role in *Henry V*—knew Barrymore and even has been compared to him on occasion in regard to both looks and lifestyle. Plummer's career has included performances in more than 80 plays, television shows, and films. He is best known for his Shakespearean roles.

Background. Arthur Christopher Orme Plummer was born in Toronto, Ont., on Dec. 13, 1929, to Isabella Mary Abbott Plummer, the granddaughter of Canada's first native-born prime minister, and John Plummer, secretary to the dean of science at McGill University, in Montreal, Que. His parents divorced when he was 1 year old. He grew up with his mother in Montreal. Plummer began his association with the theater while in high school when he served as lighting designer for a production of *A Midsummer Night's Dream*. He began acting in high school and began acting professionally after his high-school graduation.

In 1950, Plummer joined the Canadian Repertory Theatre in Ottawa. Two years later he joined the Bermuda Repertory Theatre and in 1954 made his Broadway debut as George Phillips in *The Starcross Story*. His Shakespearean premiere came in Stratford, CT, in 1955, when he played Mark Antony in *Julius Caesar*. This was the inaugural pro-

duction of the American Shakespeare Festival. The actor returned to Canada in June 1956 to play Henry V in the eponymous play at the Shakespearean Festival in Stratford, Ont. In 1961 he took his talents to Stratford-upon-Avon and London, England, as a member of the Royal Shakespeare Company. He earned the Evening Standard Award as best actor of the year for his portrayal of King Henry II in *Becket*.

The stage was not Plummer's only acting venue. He also made a name for himself on television in both Canada and the United States. He starred in the NBC production *Hamlet at Elsinore* and was Oedipus in *Oedipus Rex*, among others. His film career took off in 1965, when he played the role of Captain Von Trapp, opposite Julie Andrews as Maria, in *The Sound of Music*. He spent most of the next decade working in film despite a bevy of poor reviews. Plummer returned to the theater in 1971 and in 1974 earned his first Tony Award for his performance as Cyrano in the musical of the same name. He received an Emmy Award as outstanding lead actor in a limited series for his 1976 role in television's *The Moneychangers*.

Like Barrymore, Plummer has been married several times. His first marriage, to actress Tammy Grimes, ended in 1960 but only after they had a child, Amanda Plummer, who became a Tony-winning actress. His second marriage, to Audrey Lewis, a British journalist, also ended in divorce. In 1970 he married Elaine Regina Taylor, a former actress and dancer with the London Festival Ballet.

KRISTI VAUGHAN

ROBINSON, Mary

In September 1997, Mary Robinson resigned as president of Ireland nearly three months before her term expired to become the United Nations high commissioner for human rights—a post that had been a hornet's nest of controversy since it was created in 1993. She succeeded José Ayala-Lasso—who had resigned in March, with more than a year remaining in his term, to become foreign minister of Ecuador.

Like other major human-rights organizations, Amnesty International welcomed Robinson's appointment. It urged her to "seize the opportunity to make human rights a cornerstone of the UN's work for the next millennium." Earlier, Amnesty had criticized the record of Ayala-Lasso, the first high commissioner, as "disappointingly mixed."

In naming Robinson to the post in June, UN Secretary-General Kofi Annan called it "one of the most important appointments" that he would make during his tour of duty. Queried by a reporter about the challenges she faced, Robinson said: "The word I like to use is 'daunting.'" The Geneva-based human-rights center, which she would direct, was being restructured to achieve better integration with other parts of the UN bureaucracy. Her major challenge, however, would come from using what she called a "moral voice"—one that is "impartial but not neutral"—to cope with the old and new human-rights crises throughout the world. In her early consultations with foreign ministers, including Qian Qichen of China, she expressed a human-rights approach that embraced a country's social and economic gains as well as its progress in civil and human rights.

Background. Mary Bourke was born on May 21, 1944, in Ballina, County Mayo, Ireland, the only girl of five children in an upper-middle-class family. She earned both her bachelor's and law degrees from Trinity College in Dublin in 1967 and went on to take a master's in law from Harvard Law School. At the age of 24, she joined the law faculty of her alma mater, becoming the youngest professor in Trinity's history. In a male-dominated academic environment, she broke precedent by running for one of the three seats allotted to the college in the upper house of Parliament, the Seanad (Senate). Her election in 1969 made her the youngest member of the Seanad and the first Catholic ever to represent the college there. During 20 years as a senator, she championed various controversial causes: For example, she introduced legislation to legalize the sale of contraceptives—a measure that became law in a restricted form in 1979.

Mary Robinson
© Paul McErlane/AP/Wide World Photos

In 1989 she accepted the Labour Party nomination for the presidency of Ireland, which for 17 years had been filled without a contest, and never by a woman. Dublin oddsmakers listed her as a 1,000-to-1 underdog. For six months, however, she stumped from town to town to the strains of her campaign song, "Mrs. Robinson." She won an upset victory in runoff elections in November 1990. Although largely a ceremonial office, the presidency became her platform for promoting civil- and human-rights causes, both in Ireland and in Europe at large. She also focused attention on the needs of developing countries.

In 1970, Mary Bourke married Nicholas Robinson, a former Trinity classmate. The couple have three children.

ROBERT A. SENSER

SAMPRAS, Pete

During 1997, Pete Sampras ruled the center courts of the tennis world with a scorching serve and disarming efficiency. With straight-set triumphs over Spain's Carlos Moya at the Australian Open and France's Cedric Pioline at Wimbledon, Sampras upped his collection of major titles to ten—only two short of the record set by Australia's Roy Emerson. En route to a 55–12 match record for the year, Sampras notched a total of eight tournament wins and his fifth consecutive top ranking.

But while such achievements left little doubt that Sampras would be remembered as the dominant player of the 1990s, he had not been shielded from disappointment and criticism. During the 1997 season, for example, Sampras continued an annual disappearing act in Paris, falling in the third round of the French Open. Tennis cognoscenti—Sampras included—stated that his place among the all-time greats could not be secured without a win on the clay at Roland Garros Stadium. In addition, Sampras' outstanding season ended on a down note as a pulled calf muscle forced him to withdraw from Davis Cup singles competition. Sweden went on to take the cup.

Some critics asserted that Sampras never would measure up to the titans of past ages because he played—albeit brilliantly—in an era of lesser talents. Other detractors complained that his unflamboyant court style had failed to galvanize fans. Yet it was this workmanlike devotion to mastering serve-and-volley tennis that lifted Sampras to the top of his sport. With a 120-mph (193-km/hr) serve, surprising speed, uncanny shot-making, and an ability to play through injury and exhaustion, Sampras has shown no signs of winding down his quest for a place in the record books.

Background. Peter Sampras was born on Aug. 12, 1971, in Washington, DC, the third of four children. Soon after the family moved to southern California, Sampras began taking tennis lessons at a local racquet club. He demonstrated such a precocious knack for the game that his parents hired a private coach when he was only 8. By the time he was 12, Sampras had decided he would become a tennis pro. In his early teens, Sampras emerged as one of the top junior players in the nation. Rather than idolizing the brash pro personalities that dominated the sport at the time, he aspired to emulate Rod Laver, an Australian legend who dominated tennis in the 1960s with masterful shot-making and a businesslike court demeanor. In 1988, Sampras felt confident enough about his tennis skills to drop out of high school and turn professional.

Following two unremarkable, but solid, seasons, Sampras and his game hit the big time at the 1990 U.S. Open, where he rolled over marquee competition with startling ease. In the final rounds, he dispatched two established stars—Ivan Lendl and John McEnroe—before crushing another young American, Andre Agassi, in a straight-set victory in the finals. Only a few weeks past his 19th birthday, Sampras became the youngest male winner in the history of the prestigious tournament. Although he continued to solidify his position as one of the top players in the game, Sampras did not win another major tournament until 1993. That summer, he won his first Wimbledon championship and the U.S. Open, and ended the year as the Number 1 player for the first time. He held onto this ranking in 1994 with a dominating 77–12 match record and major victories in Australia and at Wimbledon. In 1995 he captured his third straight Wimbledon and the U.S. Open; he took his fourth U.S. Open, while assembling a 65–11 match record, in 1996.

Sampras lives in Tampa, FL, where he tries to maintain a low profile and pursue his love of golf.

PETER A. FLAX

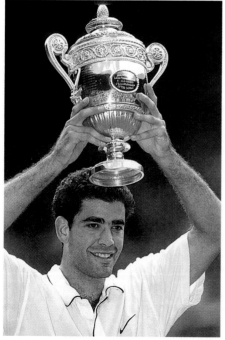

Pete Sampras

© Ross Kinnaird/Allsport

SEINFELD, Jerry

The ability to laugh at everyday occurrences—particularly everyday annoyances—has propelled comedian Jerry Seinfeld's career from his early days as a stand-up comic on the college and nightclub circuits to his current status as producer, writer, and star of the Number 1 television show, NBC's *Seinfeld*.

Seinfeld and cocreator Larry David based the series on the daily lives of four single friends living in New York City in the 1990s. The focus is on "observational humor"—dissecting the little details of life: losing a car in a parking garage, getting served in a soup restaurant, and experiencing the trials and tribulations of dating. This formula is so successful that the reach of the show, which in fall 1997 entered its ninth season, is felt far beyond its Thursday-night slot. Seinfeld's three costars—Julia Louis-Dreyfus, Jason Alexander, and Michael Richards—in 1997 demanded then-unheard-of salaries of $1 million each per episode. The network agreed to pay the actors approximately $600,000 each—about $300,000 to $500,000 more than many other TV stars.

A number of shows that initially aired in the time slots before or after *Seinfeld* have become hits, in some cases due in large part to the nearly guaranteed audience they picked up from their *Seinfeld* association. Ironically, *Seinfeld* itself did not become a true hit until 1993, when it was put in the Thursday-night slot following *Cheers*.

Because of its vast popularity, particularly among high-spending 18- to 34-year-olds, *Seinfeld* is the first TV series to obtain the "Super Bowl" status of commanding more than $1 million per minute for advertising. *Seinfeld* has won an Emmy Award for outstanding series, a Peabody Award, a Golden Globe Award, and a Screen Actors Guild Award. In December 1997, Seinfeld announced that the show's current season would be its last, saying that he wanted the series to end "from a point of strength."

Background. Jerry Seinfeld was born in Brooklyn, NY, on April 29, 1954. He is the younger of two children of Kalman and Betty Seinfeld. After being graduated from Queens College in 1976 with a bachelor's degree in theater and communications, Seinfeld performed in New York City comedy clubs for four years before moving to Los Angeles and working briefly as a joke writer for the television sitcom *Benson*.

In 1981 a talent scout for *The Tonight Show* saw Seinfeld's act at a comedy club; the comedian subsequently appeared on *Tonight* many times. In 1982 he also became a regular on *Late Night with David Letterman*. His first solo TV credit came in 1987, with *Jerry Seinfeld: Stand-Up Confidential* on HBO. In 1988 he was named funniest male stand-up comic at the American Comedy Awards; the same year, he was approached by NBC and Castle Rock Entertainment executives regarding a series. *Seinfeld's* pilot episode aired in July 1989.

Jerry Seinfeld, who is single, splits his time between New York City and Los Angeles. His 1993 book *SeinLanguage* was a best-seller.

KRISTI VAUGHAN

© Barry King/Gamma-Liaison

Jerry Seinfeld

STEWART, Martha

Martha Stewart, America's "doyenne of domesticity," by 1997 was an established presence on U.S. airwaves and in other media, dispensing a seemingly endless supply of advice on how to add gracious touches to one's entertaining and to one's everyday lifestyle, and establishing a possibly unattainable standard of domestic perfection. Stewart continued her reign during the year, taking several steps toward establishing her business as a multimedia brand—with a presence in books, on television, and on the Internet, and merchandise ranging from linens to paints. She also was investigating the possibility of issuing public stock in Martha Stewart Living Omnimedia, a publishing, television, and retailing empire that generates some $150 million to $200 million yearly.

Not only did Stewart succeed in February 1997 in buying out the profitable Martha Stewart Living Enterprises from Time Inc., but in the fall she expanded her ten-year-old deal with Kmart to the point of establishing her own store within a store. Known as Martha's World, this domestics department would include the Martha Stewart Everyday collection of sheets and towels, house paints, and, in the future, garden tools and seeds.

In September, Stewart made the jump from a twice-weekly guest spot on NBC's *Today* to a weekly spot on CBS' *This Morning*. She also had a daily TV show, *Martha Stewart Living*, on CBS; a daily national radio program,

askMartha; and a syndicated newspaper column. In addition, her Web site (www.marthastewart.com) premiered in September, and the Martha by Mail catalog was released in November. Stewart also was working on creating home-planning software.

Background. Martha Kostyra was born in Jersey City, NJ, in 1941 or 1942, the second of six children of a pharmaceuticals salesman and a schoolteacher. The family moved to Nutley, NJ, when she was 3. She has told biographers that she was brought up unpretentiously and learned cooking from her mother and grandmother and gardening from her father. She catered her first party when still a high-school student. She paid her way through Barnard College in New York City by modeling. She married Andrew Stewart in 1961 and was graduated from Barnard in 1963. Stewart's only child, a daughter, Alexis, was born in 1965.

After several successful years at a small Wall Street brokerage firm, Stewart turned to restoring the 1805 farmhouse she and her husband had bought in Westport, CT. She also honed her culinary skills and in 1976 opened a catering business—which within a decade was earning $1 million a year.

In 1982, *Entertaining*, the first of Stewart's dozen books, was published. By the late 1980s she had made several TV specials and a series of videotapes. In 1990 she launched *Martha Stewart Living*, a bimonthly magazine—then financed by Time-Warner—featuring how-to ideas and instructions on all things domestic. The magazine's circulation had reached 2.3 million by 1997.

Stewart owns homes in Connecticut; East Hampton, NY; and Maine. Her marriage ended in divorce in 1989. Although she has been the subject of several parodies and has been criticized sharply for her upscale style, she insists that she works to bring style and information to the average woman.

KRISTI VAUGHAN

Martha Stewart

© Frank Capri/SAGA/Archive Photos

TENET, George John

On July 31, 1997, George J. Tenet, 44, was sworn in as director of the U.S. Central Intelligence Agency (CIA), ending several months of speculation and political infighting to fill the post, which had been vacant since December 1996. Tenet became the fifth CIA director during the 1990s, and the third under President Bill Clinton.

Tenet had been the number-two man at the CIA under John M. Deutch, and had been its acting director since Deutch's resignation. An earlier nominee to succeed Deutch, Anthony Lake, withdrew in March after contentious Senate hearings regarding his appointment. Tenet's nomination, at first applauded by Democrats and Republicans alike, nevertheless was delayed by an inquiry

© Ira Schwarz/Reuters/Archive Photos

George J. Tenet

by the Justice Department into his personal finances. After Tenet was cleared by the Justice Department, the U.S. Senate approved the nomination by voice vote without opposition on July 10.

The post of director of Central Intelligence includes running the CIA as well as coordinating a dozen other intelligence organizations. Tenet's empire includes some 80,000 employees and a fiscal 1998 budget of $26.6 billion. As CIA director, Tenet was given cabinet rank.

Background. George John Tenet was born on Jan. 5, 1953, in Flushing, NY, the son of Greek immigrants who came to the United States in the mid-1940s. After being graduated from the Georgetown University School of Foreign Service in 1976, Tenet received a master's degree from the School of International Affairs at Columbia University. Following a stint as international programs director for the Solar Energy Industries Association, he joined the staff of Sen. John Heinz (R-PA). He worked for more than three years on Heinz's staff, specializing in national security and energy issues and serving as legislative director.

In 1985 he joined the staff of the Senate Select Committee on Intelligence, becoming its staff director in 1988. In 1993 he took over as senior director for intelligence programs at the National Security Council, helping to write secret presidential directives setting post–Cold War priorities for U.S. intelligence. He served in that post until he was named deputy CIA director.

Tenet is known as a tireless worker—one whose lifestyle habits underwent a change after he developed heart problems in 1994. He is married and has one child, a son.

BRUCE JACOBY

THOMPSON, Fred

As chairman of the Senate Governmental Affairs Committee investigating the 1996 campaign-finance scandal that engulfed the White House and the Democratic Party, Sen. Fred Thompson (R-TN), a sometime Hollywood actor and former Watergate counsel, faced the toughest challenge of his career in 1997.

When the Senate hearings opened on July 8, 1997, Thompson, an imposing 6′ 6″ (2-m) Southerner with a baritone drawl, shocked the public by saying investigators had information that China tried to buy its way into the U.S. political process during the 1996 political season. By the time Thompson concluded the hearings on October 31, the senator and his Republican colleagues had failed to show that China had funneled money into the 1996 presidential or congressional campaigns. Instead, the chairman of the Senate panel was left with a tangled web of accusations and no proof that laws were broken.

Key witnesses demanded immunity and refused to testify without it. The hearings often broke down in a maze of

partisan bickering. Complicating the Senate investigation was the Justice Department, which began its own probe into what happened in the 1996 presidential campaign. And Thompson, one of only a few Republicans supporting campaign-finance reform, turned his committee's attention from investigating the alleged abuses to how to change the system of financing federal elections. Speaking positively of the hearings, he noted that the sessions had pulled "the curtain back a little bit for the American people and let them see how the government operates."

Although Thompson denied that he has any interest in running for president, his name often has been mentioned as a possible GOP contender for 2000. Ironically, his hearings focused on one of his potential rivals for the office—Al Gore. The Democratic vice-president had attended a fundraiser at a Buddhist temple in Los Angeles and acknowledged that he made fund-raising phone calls from his office at the White House. (*See* FEATURE SECTION, page 36.)

Background. Born in Sheffield, AL, on Aug. 19, 1942, Fred Thompson married his high-school sweetheart, Sara; the couple had three children. The future legislator worked his way through Memphis State University and Vanderbilt Law School while supporting his family. He first received acclaim as the top staff lawyer for then Sen. Howard Baker during the Senate Watergate Committee hearings in 1973–74. It was Thompson who questioned White House aide Alexander Butterfield when he revealed that Richard Nixon had a secret taping system in the Oval Office.

After practicing law in both Tennessee and Washington, DC, and appearing in supporting roles in 18 Hollywood films—including *The Hunt for Red October* and *In the Line of Fire*—Thompson was elected to the Senate in 1994 to fill the final two years of Gore's Senate term. Calling himself "Ole Fred," he had campaigned in Tennessee, driving a red pickup truck and often wearing a plaid shirt to symbolize his status as an outsider. But Thompson was as much an insider as anyone. He had practiced law in Washington, worked as a lobbyist, and served as a special counsel to various Senate committees. He ran for the Senate again in 1996 and easily won a full six-year term.

Thompson and his wife were divorced in 1984.

JUDI HASSON

WEIL, Andrew

By 1997, the bearded countenance of physician and author Andrew Weil had become the face of the United States' growing fascination with alternative medicine. His messages promoting herbal remedies, holistic therapies,

Fred Thompson

© Richard Ellis/Sygma

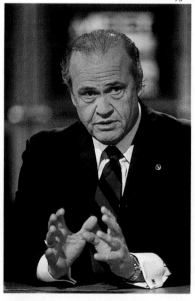

and healthier lifestyles were absorbed by an audience of millions. In another corner, however, were many in the mainstream U.S. medical community, who pointed an accusing finger at Weil and his tendency to advocate untested treatments.

Despite the criticism, it was obvious that Weil—who commanded such appellations as best-selling author, doctor, educator, television personality, and Internet entrepreneur—had tapped into a growing public distrust of the conventional technology-based, pharmaceutical approach to health care. The scope of the movement was phenomenal; in 1996, U.S. consumers spent an estimated $14 billion on alternative treatments.

Weil enjoyed an unprecedented following in 1997. Two of his most recent books, *Eight Weeks to Optimum Health* and *Spontaneous Healing*, remained on best-seller lists for much of the year. In both books, Weil offered his trademark doctrines about the body's inherent healing abilities and the need for preventive, self-administered care. Among his other projects were a Web site, a public-television series, and a collection of recorded meditations. Along with straightforward advice about nutrition, exercise, and moderately common therapies such as acupuncture and hypnosis, Weil also offered controversial promotions of herbal remedies that many doctors, scientists, and government regulators insisted could be dangerous.

But although Weil had plenty of criticism for the medical mainstream, he hardly had abandoned it. Rather, he advocated the concept of integrative medicine—combining the preventive strengths of alternative treatments with the disease-fighting power of modern medicine. To that end, in 1997, Weil launched the Program in Integrative Medicine at the University of Arizona's College of Medicine to teach doctors integrative techniques.

Background. Andrew Thomas Weil was born on June 8, 1942, in Philadelphia, PA. He was graduated in 1964 from Harvard University, where he majored in biology. Weil entered Harvard Medical School, where, during his his final year, he was thrust into the national spotlight with his involvement in one of the earliest credible studies to determine the medical effects of smoking marijuana. The study's conclusions—that the drug did not cause serious medical problems or psychotic reactions—caused a national stir.

After his 1968 graduation, followed by an unproductive stint at a government health agency, Weil decided to focus on writing and traveling. Between 1971 and 1975, he traveled in Latin America and Africa as a fellow of the Institute of Current World Affairs, studying curative herbs, psychoactive plants, and meditation and yoga. He chronicled

© Claus Guglberger/Black Star

Andrew Weil

his travels in *The Marriage of the Sun and Moon*. From 1971–84 he was on the research staff of the Harvard Botanical Museum.

In his influential 1983 book *Health and Healing*, Weil offered a prescient appraisal of rising health-care costs and a persuasive call for new approaches. Ten years later, he founded the Center for Integrative Medicine in Tucson, AZ, dedicated to promoting a union between traditional and alternative medicine. Weil, who lives near Tucson, was married to Sabine Kremp from 1990 to 1997. The couple had a child in 1991.

PETER A. FLAX

YELLEN, Janet Louise

On Feb. 13, 1997, Janet L. Yellen, a 50-year-old economics professor who had been serving on the board of governors of the Federal Reserve System (the Fed), was sworn in as chairman of President Bill Clinton's Council of Economic Advisers (CEA). Yellen had been named to the post by Clinton in December 1996. At the time, the president called her an "esteemed writer and thinker." Treasury Secretary Robert E. Rubin noted that the White House "wanted someone [for the post] who could bring a rigorous analytic approach to the issues and who could work well with others."

Yellen, in turn, acknowledged that she was "very fortunate" to be joining the administration "at a time when the economy is in extraordinary good health with strong job creation and low inflation." During her Senate confirmation hearings, she stated, however, that she was not satisfied with 1996's growth rate of some 2.5% and that the government should be "focusing on trying to pursue policies that raise the growth rate." In terms of philosophy, the CEA chair described herself as a "nonideological pragmatist."

Background. Janet Louise Yellen was born on Aug. 13, 1946, in Brooklyn, NY. She was graduated from Brown University summa cum laude with a degree in economics in 1967 and earned a doctorate in economics from Yale University in 1971. She served as an assistant professor of economics at Harvard University from 1971 until 1976, taught at the London School of Economics, and was an economist at the Federal Reserve Board (1977–78). In 1980, Yellen joined the faculty of the University of California, Berkeley, becoming a full professor at its Haas School of Business in 1985 and Bernard T. Rocca professor of international trade in 1992.

She took a leave from Berkeley in 1994 when President Clinton appointed her a member of the Fed's board of governors. At the Fed, Yellen gained a reputation as a thoughtful policy maker and publicly supported the policies of chairman Alan Greenspan. She believed that the Fed should look for "the broader forces affecting the economy."

Janet Yellen married George Akerlof, also an economist, on July 8, 1978. The Akerlofs have written numerous economic reports together. For example, in 1985 they presented a paper showing that policy can be effective provided that prices and wages tend to remain at existing levels. This "rational expectations" theory was in opposition to the prevailing beliefs of the Keynesian school.

The Akerlofs are the parents of one son.

Janet Yellen

© Richard Ellis/Sygma

BIOTECHNOLOGY

Although developments involving cloning (*see* SPECIAL REPORT, page 151) dominated 1997 news in biotechnology, other important findings were reported and considered.

Human Artificial Chromosome. H.F. Willard and his colleagues at Case Western Reserve University and at the biotechnology company Athersys in Cleveland, OH, announced that they had been able to cause the formation of an artificial human chromosome within cells growing in tissue culture. Their experiment began with the synthesis of the three essential DNA components of a chromosome—telomeres, which form the ends of every chromosome; centromeres, which are the attachment sites for the protein fibers that move each chromosome to an end of a cell during cell division; and a section of easily identifiable human DNA. The components were added as separate units to cultures of human cells. The cells absorbed the units and combined them into single DNA molecules to which they added the chromatin proteins normally found in chromosomes. Each artificially formed human chromosome was maintained in a cell and was able to self-replicate, thereby furnishing a copy of itself to each daughter cell during the 240 cell divisions of the six-month experiment.

If the formation of artificial human chromosomes can be developed to include genes whose absence or malfunctioning is involved in genetic diseases (for example, cystic fibrosis), gene therapy may become the treatment of choice for these diseases.

Hemoglobin in Plant Growth. Hemoglobin (Hb), in its various forms, is found throughout the animal kingdom. Bacteria and even some plant species also contain genes for the production of this oxygen-carrying compound. The bacterium *Vitreoscilla* has a gene that produces a type of hemoglobin (called VHb) when the organism is cultured in oxygen-limiting conditions, and some of the cereal-plant species have a hemoglobin gene that is expressed only in seed and root tissues when oxygen is in poor supply.

In order to determine what effect the introduction of a hemoglobin gene would have on the growth and development of a plant that does not normally have this gene, L. Bülow and his colleagues in Lund, Sweden, transferred the VHb gene from *Vitreoscilla* to *Nicotiana tabacum* (tobacco) plants. Compared to controls, the transgenic tobacco plants exhibited an enhanced growth and a shortened time period (50% less) for seed germination. Associated with the increased growth, transgenic plants contained on average 30%–40% more chlorophyll than did controls. If such results can be obtained by transferring the VHb gene to food crops, food production could be increased significantly.

Phytoremediation. The technology that uses plants to absorb pollutants is called *phytoremediation*. Following the 1986 explosion at the Chernobyl nuclear facility in the Ukraine, the surrounding area was contaminated with large amounts of the radioactive elements cesium-137 and strontium-90. The U.S. phytoremediation company Phytotech, in Monmouth Junction, NJ, has used floating gardens of sunflowers (*Helianthus cucumerifolius*) to absorb the radionuclides from the ponds and lakes at the Chernobyl site.

The plants are positioned so that their roots dangle in the water and suck up the radioactive atoms. The company disposes of the plants as radioactive wastes after a three-week period and replaces them with new floating gardens. However, to avoid seepage of additional radioactive elements into the water, the land nearby must also be decontaminated. Phytotech scientists have been removing cesium and strontium from the soil at the Chernobyl site by growing Indian mustard (*Brassica juncea*) plants that function on land in the same way as sunflower plants do in water. Similar procedures are used to decontaminate the groundwater and land around U.S. uranium-processing plants.

Fetal-Cell Analysis. The procedures that inform expectant parents whether their developing child carries the genotype for a genetic disease require the insertion of a needle into the uterus of the mother to obtain fetal cells. This use of a needle carries an infrequent, but possible, danger to the developing child. Y.W. Kan and others at the University of California at San Francisco have developed a new technique for obtaining the required fetal cells. During gestation, a small number of fetal red blood cells pass into the bloodstream of the mother. Some of these cells contain nuclei that are extruded from the cells as they mature. A sample of blood is taken from the mother and is mixed with antibodies that are specific for nuclei-containing red blood cells. These are collected and exposed to a second antibody that attaches only to those cells that possess fetal proteins on their cell membranes. Using this approach, the scientists are able to collect enough fetal cells for genetic analysis. It was not known when this new method would become available to the public.

LOUIS LEVINE, *City College of New York*

Spotlight on Cloning

Cloning refers to any natural or artificial process that produces genetically identical organisms. In the Feb. 27, 1997, issue of the journal *Nature*, Dr. Ian Wilmut and his colleagues at the Roslin Institute, Edinburgh, Scotland, announced that they had cloned a lamb, which they named "Dolly"—using, for its genetic constitution, the nucleus of a cell from the mammary gland of an adult sheep. All nuclei of an individual contain the same genes. Therefore, Dolly and the adult female sheep from which she was derived were genetically identical; hence they constituted a clone. The cloning announcement electrified both the scientific and nonscientific communities.

The Procedure. The process of cloning occurs naturally in many organisms. In single-celled species—for example, bacteria, protozoa, and yeasts—that reproduce asexually through cell division, each population that is derived from a single ancestral cell constitutes a clone. Even in sexually reproducing species, humans included, clones may be produced under special conditions. Each set of identical siblings (twins, triplets) represents the formation of a clone as a result of the splitting, one or more times, of a very early embryo and the subsequent independent development of each of the masses of cells. Identical sets or siblings also occur naturally in other mammalian species. In addition, identical sets of siblings can be produced artificially by taking an embryo 7–10 days old (about 60–100 cells) from the uterus of a female and surgically dividing the embryo into two or more parts. Each part then is placed in a tissue-culture medium, where, through cell division, the lost cells are replaced. Subsequently, each reconstituted embryo is placed into the uterus of a different surrogate mother, where it completes its development. Using this technique, many genetically identical sets of sheep, pigs, cattle, and horses have been produced. There is no record that any identical sets of human siblings ever have been produced using this or any other artificial procedure.

Scientists and biotechnologists are extremely interested in the production of both plant and animal clones because, except for environmentally caused variations, all the members of the clone have precisely the same characteristics. Therefore, if—as a result of genetic engineering or a breeding program—a particularly desirable plant or animal is produced, cloning becomes the most efficient way of obtaining large numbers of organisms with the same traits.

Cloning of medically important human genes has been practiced commercially for some 25 years. It involves the transfer, through genetic-engineering techniques, of such genes as those for insulin, growth hormone, and others to a bacterium or yeast. Subsequently, as the organisms duplicate their own genes prior to cell division,

© Murdo Macleod/FSP/Gamma-Liaison

Dolly, left, a lamb that had been cloned by using, for its genetic constitution, the nucleus of a cell from the mammary gland of an adult sheep, became a media celebrity in 1997.

they duplicate the transferred human genes as well. In addition, the bacteria and yeast cells produce human insulin, growth hormone, and others, which they do not use and which, therefore, are available for harvesting for medical purposes.

The procedure used to clone Dolly is called "nuclear transplantation." Nuclei from cells of one individual are transferred to unfertilized eggs whose nuclei have been removed, and each egg cell with its "foreign" nucleus then is stimulated to divide, thus beginning its development. Nuclear-transplantation experiments date back to 1952, when Dr. Robert Briggs and Dr. Thomas J. King of the Medical College of Pennsylvania in Philadelphia experimented with producing clones of frogs. They found that the success rate depended on the stage of development of the donor individual. When nuclei from cells of an early embryonic stage (blastula) were used, development was normal and clones of adults were obtained. This showed that each of the cells of the blastula retains the ability to utilize all its genes and, therefore, is able to undergo normal development. However, there was a progressive increase in death among the developing frogs as nuclei from more advanced embryonic stages (gastrula, for example) were used. This seemed to indicate that more and more of the cells of progressively older embryos become irreversibly specialized and no longer have the ability to use all of the genes needed for normal development. When nuclei from adult cells were used, the mortality rate was 100%. The same pattern of results was obtained in nuclear-transplantation experiments involving mammals.

It therefore came as a complete surprise when the birth of Dolly, which actually had taken place on July 5, 1996, was announced. The success of this experiment appears to have resulted from placing the donor cell initially into a tissue-culture medium, which is devoid of almost all nutrients, for a period of five days. This procedure, which involves a partial starvation of the mammary-gland cell, seems to have the effect of reactivating all of the adult cell's genes, thereby returning the adult cell to an early embryonic condition. This permits the complete development of the subsequently produced artificial "fertilized egg." The so-called "reconstructed" cell was stimulated to divide by the administration of a mild electric shock and, after a six-day period in a tissue-culture medium during which many cell divisions occurred, the multicellular embryo was transferred to the uterus of a surrogate mother sheep.

The birth of Dolly came only after many failures. The scientists had fused a total of 277 donor cells to enucleated eggs. Of these, only 29 developed into embryos that could be implanted into the uteri of surrogate mother sheep. Only one of these 29 embryos developed into a healthy lamb. Many of the implanted embryos were stillborn. A few were born deformed or with other problems and died shortly after birth. A success rate of one in 277 trials raised serious questions about the feasibility of any realistic development of the procedure.

The Debate. The birth of Dolly also led to an emotional debate on cloning. The immediate question raised was whether human beings could be cloned. Everyone seems to agree that, from a theoretical point of view, this should be possible. This being the case, there were those who urged that research on all aspects of cloning of human material be outlawed. The arguments against human-cloning experiments, especially any that involve cloning of a total individual, deal with a number of issues. One is the high rate of failure in sheep and what is expected to be a comparable experience in humans with inevitable tragic disappointments. There is the objection that it is an "unnatural" method of human procreation. There also are questions about the biological and legal relationship of the cloned individual to the person who provided the donor cell.

In response to the objections raised against experiments involving human cloning, U.S. President Bill Clinton banned all federal funding of research in this area. He also asked the National Bioethics Advisory Commission (NBAC) to prepare a report for him on the legal and ethical issues involved in human-cloning techniques. NBAC's report, issued in June 1997, concluded that "it is morally unacceptable for anyone in the public or private section...to attempt to create a child." The commission recommended that the ban on federally sponsored human-cloning research be continued. It also recommended that the U.S. Congress pass legislation that would prohibit the cloning of a human being by anyone in the private sector as well. Such legislation reached congressional committee status in 1997.

The NBAC report also stressed that the ban the committee recommended should be applied only to attempts to produce a total individual. The committee emphasized that the cloning of human DNA or the cloning of human-cell lines should be free to continue under current federal guidelines and regulation. A similar committee involving various European countries and Japan also favored prohibiting the cloning of a human being. However, the committee recommended that all animal cloning and the cloning of human organs be continued.

LOUIS LEVINE

BOLIVIA

In 1997, Bolivia chose retired Gen. Hugo Bánzer, a former military dictator whose iron-fisted autocratic rule had extended from 1971 to 1978, as its president.

Election and Coalition. Bánzer, of the Democratic Nationalist Action (ADN) party, finished first in a confused and lackluster election held on June 1. The contest was marked by a multiplicity of candidates and no clear electoral message. Bánzer received only 22.3% of the popular vote, slightly more than the candidate of the governing Nationalist Revolutionary Movement (MNR) party, Juan Carlos Durán. In a subsequent runoff in the national Congress, mandated by Bolivian law, Bánzer handily defeated Durán; he was inaugurated on August 6.

He succeeded Gonzalo ("Goni") Sánchez de Losada, a U.S.-educated president, who was barred constitutionally from seeking reelection. Sánchez de Losada had been victorious four years earlier, receiving 34% of the vote. He took office when Bánzer, who ran second, conceded defeat a few days after the election and instructed his supporters in Congress to vote for Sánchez. Bánzer similarly had aided in the selection of Jaime Paz Zamora in 1989. Under a constitutional amendment passed before the 1997 election, Bánzer was to serve five years as president.

The Bánzer presidency was made possible when he signed an agreement with three other parties—the Revolutionary Left Movement (MIR), led by Paz; the Civic Solidarity Union (UCS); and the Conscience of the Fatherland (CONDEPA). Together, the coalition members effectively controlled the Congress, holding 24 of the 27 seats in the Senate and 96 of the 130 seats in the Chamber of Deputies. Jorge ("Tuto") Quiroga, a U.S.-trained economist, who reportedly was well-liked in Washington, was elected vice-president. As a reward for his efforts in helping to form the coalition and because of his close ties to the United States, Quiroga was given control of the formulation of economic policy by Bánzer. The new president also created a new ministry of foreign trade and investment and named Jorge Crespo, a former ambassador to the United States, to that post.

Bánzer's Agenda. As minister of economy under President Paz Estenssoro in the 1980s, Sánchez de Losada was the author of the stabilization and reform plan that had freed Bolivia from runaway inflation that reached 20,000% a year. As a result, at the beginning of his presidency he enjoyed strong popular

BOLIVIA • Information Highlights

Official Name: Republic of Bolivia.
Location: West-central South America.
Area: 424,162 sq mi (1 098 580 km²).
Population (mid-1997 est.): 7,800,000.
Chief Cities (mid-1993 est.): Sucre, the legal capital, 144,994; La Paz, the administrative capital, 784,976; Santa Cruz de la Sierra, 767,260; Cochabamba, 448,756.
Government: *Head of state and government,* Hugo Bánzer, president (took office August 1997). *Legislature*—Congress: Senate and Chamber of Deputies.
Monetary Unit: Boliviano (5.245 bolivianos equal U.S.$1, market rate, July 1997).
Gross Domestic Product (1995 U.S.$): $20,000,000,000 (purchasing power parity).
Economic Indexes (1996): *Consumer Prices* (1991 = 100): all items, 163.8; food, 170.5. *Industrial Production* (1990 = 100): 131.
Foreign Trade (1996 U.S.$): *Imports,* $1,635,000,000; *exports,* $1,137,000,000.

support. During his four-year term, however, the support disappeared as his government failed to make a dent in the country's endemic poverty. At the end of his term, the average family income still was only $800 per year, adult illiteracy hovered around 20%, and life expectancy was only 60 years. Economic growth had averaged 3.9% a year, but largely was swallowed up by a population increase of 2% annually.

Bánzer, in his inaugural speech, pledged to continue Sánchez de Losada's reform efforts but also promised a drive to create jobs and to boost wages. Key priorities, he said, would be to pursue Bolivia's partnership with Mercosur, the Southern Cone free-trade arrangement, and to attract increased foreign and local investment.

Bánzer also promised to rid Bolivia of all surplus coca leaf and to crack down on drug trafficking. That effort was expected to meet with difficulty because of lack of funds to indemnify coca growers and because of the strength of coca growers in Bánzer's political coalition. A leader of the coca growers in the Chaparé region, Evo Morales, was elected to Congress in 1997. According to U.S. Ambassador Curtis Kamman, the Sánchez de Losada government had promised to clear 17,290 acres (7 000 ha) of coca plantings in 1997, but had eliminated only 8,460 acres (3 425 ha) successfully.

RICHARD C. SCHROEDER
Freelance Writer

BOSNIA AND HERZEGOVINA

The North Atlantic Treaty Organization's (NATO's) Stabilization Force (S-FOR) maintained the cease-fire in Bosnia and Herzegovina during 1997. However, little progress was made in reintegrating Bosnia's two entities and in reconciling divided ethnic communities. Nationalist forces continued to dominate among all three ethnic groups and there were growing fears that, with the planned withdrawal of NATO in 1998, war could restart.

Political Segregation. Although the 1995 Dayton Accords that ended the hostilities in the Balkans were premised on the principles of state integrity, pluralism, and democracy, the onus was placed on the three conflictive parties—the Croats, the Serbs, and the Muslims—to rebuild a single state voluntarily. However, the Bosnian government and the Serb leadership displayed two diametrically opposed conceptions for the future of the country. While the predominantly Muslim authorities considered the Dayton Accords to be a guarantee for reintegrating Bosnia and Herzegovina under a viable central government, Serb leaders viewed the agreement as a legitimation of the Serb entity and a stepping-stone for partition.

All sides complied with Dayton's military components, but in the civil and political arena, compliance proved much more problematic in 1997. At the local level, nationalist Serbs and Croats resisted the reintegration of communities deliberately divided by the war. Many local political leaders and criminal syndicates were launched into power by ethnic war and division and were reluctant to dilute their control. They controlled the major political parties, economic networks, and media outlets. Even the Muslim side had become increasingly radicalized as a result of the war and elements of the leadership supported the creation of an essentially Muslim state in response to Serb and Croat separatism.

It took several months of negotiations before the Bosnian government at the central level finally was formed. The first session of the two-chamber Bosnian parliament took place in early January after months of obstruction by Serb representatives. The parliament confirmed nominations for the central-government Council of Ministers, which were allocated among Muslims, Croats, and Serbs. The two joint prime ministers (or cochairmen) were to rotate on a weekly basis. The power-sharing arrangements demonstrated that ethnic proportionality, combined with the separatist objectives of Serb and Croat representatives, ultimately would paralyze the central governmental institutions.

The parliament of the Muslim-Croat Bosnian Federation maintained limited powers in the Croat-majority areas as the "Herceg Bosna" parallel administration continued to function despite repeated promises by Croat leaders that it would be disbanded. The municipal elections in September provided another endorsement for separatist nationalism. Even though the civic parties scored some success in such cities as Sarajevo and Tuzla, the ruling nationalists gained control over the majority of local councils. Their control over the security forces and economic resources also consolidated ethnic exclusivity and authoritarianism. Because refugees voted in large numbers, some towns elected nationalist parties from rival ethnic groups.

Serb Conflicts. Escalating political conflicts in the Serb entity threatened to split the region into two. The position of the hard-line faction around indicted war criminal Radovan Karadzic, based in Pale, was challenged by the more moderate and pro-Dayton leadership of Bosnian Serb President Biljana Plavsic, based in Banja Luka. Conflicts—particularly for control over the army, police forces, and the mass media—intensified during the summer and fall. Two rival power centers emerged and the ruling Serbian Democratic Party in effect split. Plavsic created her own party in Banja Luka and attracted some former Karadzic loyalists. NATO forces intervened to prevent firefights between the two groups and gained control of television transmitters controlled by the hard-liners in Pale. NATO troops also shot dead one indicted Serb war criminal and apprehended another suspect, thus increasing pressures on Karadzic to surrender to the Hague tribunal.

In July, Plavsic dissolved the Serb Assembly and planned to hold new elections in the Serb entity. The elections were approved by the Organization for Security and Cooperation in Europe (OSCE). The November 22–23 balloting, in which about 55% of the electorate participated, showed that Karadzic's party had lost its parliamentary majority but

---

BOSNIA AND HERZEGOVINA
Information Highlights

Official Name: Republic of Bosnia and Herzegovina.
Location: Southeastern Europe.
Area: 19,781 sq mi (51 233 km²).
Population (mid-1997 est.): 3,600,000.
Chief Cities (1991 census): Sarajevo, the capital, 415,631; Banja Luka, 142,644.
Government: *Head of state,* Alija Izetbegovic (Muslim), Momcilo Krajisnik (Serb), Kresimir Zubak (Croat), presidents. *Head of government,* Haris Silajdzic, Boro Bosic, co-prime ministers. *Legislature*—Assembly of Bosnia and Herzegovina: House of Peoples and House of Representatives.
Monetary Unit: New dinar (143.31 dinars equal U.S.$1, 1995 average).
Gross Domestic Product (1995 est. U.S.$): $1,000,000,000 (purchasing power parity).

remained the most-powerful political faction. An attempt by the international community to use the election as a way of removing Karadzic from the political scene failed. The new Bosnian Serb Assembly held its inaugural session on December 27. The hard-liners asserted their power by cutting off live television coverage of the session, annoying Western observers. The dispute frustrated Plavsic's attempt to nominate a moderate for the prime ministership.

Fresh elections to the Bosnian Serb presidency and for the Serb member of the collective Bosnian presidency were scheduled for early 1998. Observers feared that two rival governments could emerge on Serb territory. This would lead either to a territorial split between the western and eastern Serb Republic or to an all-out armed conflict.

Regional Factors. By initialing the Dayton Accords, Serbian (and later Yugoslav) President Slobodan Milosevic cast himself in the role of peacemaker. He calculated that, through acceptance of the agreement, further Serb territorial losses in Bosnia and Herzegovina would be prevented and the autonomous status of the Serb Republic would be recognized internationally. Milosevic attempted to mediate in the power struggle between Plavsic and Karadzic, and the Yugoslav government signed a pact formally establishing relations with the Bosnian Serb Republic.

Croatia's President Franjo Tudjman concluded that Zagreb would benefit greatly from the Dayton pact. The Bosnian Federation would be able to establish closer economic, political, and military ties with Croatia, while Zagreb could maintain the option of annexing Croatian-controlled territory in western Herzegovina and central Bosnia if the federation with the Muslims were to collapse. Moreover, Croatia and Herceg Bosna would obtain significant financial assistance, while Tudjman's international standing and Croatia's candidacy for European integration would be enhanced substantially.

Both Milosevic and Tudjman harbored long-term aspirations toward Bosnia that contradicted their pledges at Dayton. Indeed, the two leaders reportedly held several secret meetings to discuss the partition of the country and their own territorial ambitions. They calculated that, by the time any substantial NATO force left the country, both the Serb Republic and Herceg Bosna would have sealed their distinctive status and ethnic homogeneity. They then would be in a position to press for closer ties with Serbia and Croatia, respectively. At that point, the international community would have precious few levers at its disposal to prevent secession.

Although Milosevic's relationship with the leadership of the Serbs deteriorated during the war, the quasi state ultimately was dependent on Belgrade for military and economic support. Moreover, all major political forces in the Serb Republic, including the opposition parties, supported a separate Serb-dominated entity that one day would merge with Serb-dominated Yugoslavia. The main differences between them appeared to be over timetables and tactics rather than objectives. Similarly, leaders of most of the major opposition parties in Serbia itself indicated their support for a Greater Serbia even as they paid lip service to Bosnian integration.

Tudjman's ties with the separatist Bosnian Croats remained close. Indeed, several members of his inner circle were from the region and supported the Greater Croatia project. While Tudjman has been cooperative with the international community and has expressed his support for the Bosnian Federation, he has reserved the long-term option of Herceg Bosna's unification with Croatia. Nonetheless, unlike the situation in Serbia, the strongest opposition parties in Croatia itself have opposed Tudjman's hidden agenda and remained openly committed to an integral Bosnia and Herzegovina.

The international community had provided millions of dollars in aid to Bosnia and Herzegovina since the signing of the Dayton Accords. But there were persistent complaints that funds had been misused and primarily benefited the ruling nationalists. No major boost in production had been registered, and production was estimated at less than half of prewar levels. The Serb entity in particular remained pauperized and devoid of any significant reconstruction assistance because of the obstruction of nationalist politicians. NATO planned to scale down its Bosnian mission substantially by the summer of 1998. Some Western leaders proposed creating a D-FOR (Deterrence Force) under NATO's auspices to help maintain peace in the country. There were fears that without a significant NATO presence, the war in Bosnia could restart. U.S. President Bill Clinton was in Bosnia in December to show support for U.S. troops stationed there and to encourage the Bosnians to reach a definitive peace. Earlier the White House had announced that the president wanted U.S. troops to remain in Bosnia beyond the June 1998 deadline.

JANUSZ BUGAJSKI
Center for International and Strategic Studies

BRAZIL

Despite corruption and social problems in 1997, President Fernando Henrique Cardoso's approval ratings remained high thanks to the sound economic management that tamed inflation. Recent constitutional changes would allow Cardoso, in 1998, to become the first Brazilian chief executive in four decades to stand for reelection.

Politics. Cardoso remained the favorite to recapture the presidency in 1998, despite divisions besetting his Brazilian Social Democratic Party (PSDB). One such rift occurred in September, when São Paulo Gov. Mário Covas, a leading Social Democrat, said he would not seek reelection in Brazil's wealthiest state. Covas' decision grew in part from Brasília's having cut state taxes on export goods. While stimulating sales abroad, the action diminished revenues available to the governor for social and educational programs.

Cardoso's political problems were pale in comparison to those of his major adversary, Luiz Inácio (Lula) da Silva, the bearded standard-bearer of the Labor Party (PT) whom Cardoso trounced in the 1994 election. PT disunity—the party encompasses a wide array of disparate groups—in the face of economic stability made Cardoso three times more popular than da Silva.

In late 1997 unrest among landless peasants, who demanded that affluent landowners provide them with their uncultivated lands in Brazil's interior, ignited violence when members of the Landless Rural Workers' Movement squatted on ranches in several states. The campesinos and their advocates insisted that most large property owners live luxuriously in cities while earning tax breaks from their vast, undercultivated estates. Ranchers called for changing the law that prevents the ousting of squatters until police obtain permission from governors and human-rights groups.

In Brazil the richest 20% own 90% of the land, while the bottom 40% hold just 1%. Land reform loomed as an issue that Cardoso must address in his reelection campaign.

Economics. Brazil had a mixed economic record in 1997. Gross domestic product (GDP) climbed 5% amid modest price increases, while the January–July trade deficit exceeded the entire 1996 shortfall.

Cardoso named Gustavo Franco, who in 1994 helped implement a stabilization plan and new currency (the real), to head the Central Bank. Franco shared the same views as Cardoso and Finance Minister Pedro Malán on the need for tight fiscal policies and foreign investment. In his previous post as director of the Central Bank's international-affairs department, he courted entrepreneurs responsible for $15 billion in direct investment—up $6 billion from 1996. Brazil attracted 60% of all investment funds that flowed to Latin America in 1997.

The Brazilian Association of Port Terminals identified Brazilian ports as the single biggest "brake" on foreign trade. Santos, Brazil's largest port, was loading 12 containers an hour for $580 per container. In contrast, Buenos Aires, Argentina, was loading 22 containers an hour at $150 each. That was one reason why foreign commerce accounts for 20% of Argentina's GDP, but for only 8% of Brazil's GDP. In 1993, Congress agreed to privatize 31 ports over 25 years. But private operators faced two enormous challenges: a bloated workforce, reputedly Latin America's

Residents of Rio de Janeiro welcomed Pope John Paul II to Brazil in early October 1997. It was the pontiff's third visit to the Latin American nation.

least productive dockworkers, whose unions resist the layoffs inherent in modernization; and a shortage of resources with which to expand and streamline port facilities. Such expansion likely would facilitate an additional $5 billion yearly in exports and create 250,000 jobs throughout the economy.

Despite the problems of privatization, Cardoso and Congress accelerated the sale and leasing of inefficient government enterprises. By year's end, the telecommunications ministry confirmed that services controlled by Telebrás, the federal holding company for telecommunications, would be split into 13 companies before being placed on the auction block. Government economists estimated that wholesale privatizations could generate upward of $80 billion over the next three years. Meanwhile, former Planning Minister José Serra and current Communications Minister Sérgio Motta voiced concerns about Cardoso's policies. They favored a shift from restrictive monetary and fiscal approaches to more expansionist economic policies.

Throughout 1997 debate raged over whether to devalue the currency, deemed by many economists to be overvalued by 5%–30%. Devaluation proponents called the action essential to reducing a current-account deficit of 2%–4% of GDP. Opponents warned that devaluation would drive up the modest 12% inflation rate, while rewarding currency speculators. Meanwhile, Brazil was enjoying better conditions than those besetting Mexico during its Christmas 1994 "peso crisis"—inflation remained relatively low, there were substantial hard-currency reserves, and the country had attracted a favorable blend of long-term investment and short-term capital.

Nevertheless, in November the government reacted to investors' fears that Brazil—facing the same pressures that were besetting Asian economies—would be forced to devalue the real. To allay such concerns, Brasília announced a program of tax increases and spending cuts aimed at trimming an estimated $18 billion from the budget deficit. The action occurred just weeks after the central bank doubled interest rates to stop an outflow of dollars.

Foreign Affairs. In late September, Pope John Paul II visited Rio de Janeiro, where in a packed soccer stadium, he excoriated abortion as an "abominable crime," and said that poverty "destroys the family...corrupts and damages...the health of young people and adults." Cardoso, who has downplayed his atheism in recent years, warmly received the pontiff and concurred with "the pope's cry for

---

BRAZIL • Information Highlights

Official Name: Federative Republic of Brazil.
Location: Eastern South America.
Area: 3,286,473 sq mi (8 511 965 km²).
Population (mid-1997 est.): 160,300,000.
Chief Cities (mid-1993 est.): Brasília, the capital, 1,673,151; São Paulo, 9,842,059; Rio de Janeiro, 5,547,033; Salvador, 2,174,072.
Government: *Head of state and government,* Fernando Henrique Cardoso, president (sworn in Jan. 1, 1995). *Legislature*—National Congress: Federal Senate and Chamber of Deputies.
Monetary Unit: Real (1.1129 reales equal U.S.$1, Dec. 19, 1997).
Gross Domestic Product (1995 est. U.S.$): $976,800,-000,000 (purchasing power parity).
Economic Indexes: *Consumer Prices* (1996, 1992 = 100): all items, 84,767.8; food, 81,894.4. *Industrial Production* (1996, 1990 = 100): 112.
Foreign Trade (1996 U.S.$): *Imports,* $56,947,000,000; *exports,* $47,762,000,000.

---

justice," but cordially disagreed on abortion, the pace of antipoverty initiatives, and other controversial issues.

The October visit of U.S. President Bill Clinton dominated the nation's foreign affairs. Upon Clinton's arrival, reporters forced him to comment on a U.S. embassy report to potential investors criticizing corruption as "endemic" in Brazilian society. Clinton sidestepped the charge by indicating that it applied to previous administrations, heaping praise upon Cardoso's war on corruption. The two leaders signed pro forma accords on education, nuclear power, energy technology, public administration and judicial reforms, and joint endeavors in space.

Nonetheless, Cardoso did not fix a date for Brazil's joining a Free Trade Area for the Americas (FTAA)—an expansion of the North American Free Trade Agreement (NAFTA) to 34 countries of the Western Hemisphere. While agreeing to Brazil's eventual FTAA membership, Cardoso said that his priority was strengthening the Mercosur economic pact, embracing Southern Cone nations. Clinton praised Mercosur, saying Mercosur was "good for Brazil, for the member countries, for stability, growth and cooperation throughout the region, so it's good for the U.S., too." Furthermore, the U.S. president, Secretary of State Madeleine Albright, and Commerce Secretary William Daley said that asking Mercosur nations to choose between their regional trading bloc and the FTAA was a "false choice," calling Mercosur a priceless stone in an ultimate FTAA mosaic. Meanwhile, Mercosur announced that talks for a trade arrangement with the European Union (EU) would begin in 1998.

GEORGE W. GRAYSON
College of William & Mary

BULGARIA

After months of unrest, Bulgaria elected a new government in April 1997 that declared its commitment to fast-paced market reform and European integration. Although the impact of the economic reforms was felt painfully by workers in state industries, the new administration held broad public support.

Political Revolution. The increasingly isolated Socialist-led government of Premier Zhan Videnov had resigned in December 1996 following several months of widely supported demonstrations. As 1997 began, many people were angry with rapidly declining living standards amid reports of widespread government corruption. Newly inaugurated President Petar Stoyanov called for early parliamentary elections, which were held in April. The Union of Democratic Forces (UDF) scored an overwhelming victory, gaining 52% of the vote and 137 of 240 parliamentary seats. The Socialists received 22% of the vote and won 58 seats. UDF leader Ivan Kostov was appointed prime minister.

The UDF-dominated legislature passed a number of important measures to root out corruption among state officials and industrial managers. A new law passed in September prohibited former communist bureaucrats from obtaining high civil-service positions for five years. Parliament also approved the opening of secret police files to determine which top officials had collaborated with the communist-era State Security Service—a move indicating that authorities favored openness in government operations. Some former Socialist officials were believed to have embezzled millions of dollars in state funds, and investigations into such corruption were launched.

Economic Transformation. Bulgaria was determined to pursue radical economic reforms in order to avert a major financial crisis. In consultation with the World Bank, Sofia launched a major stabilization program that lifted most price controls, pegged the national currency—the lev—to the German mark, and established a Currency Board to help control government spending. As a result, the inflation rate dramatically decreased. Parliament also approved a new budget that cut state spending and the subsidization of unprofitable industries. A far-reaching privatization program was launched in which some 40% of state-owned enterprises were to be sold by the end of the year. Social unrest—a continued threat should living standards drop sharply because of austerity measures—could be exploited by unreformed socialists, populists, and nationalists in an effort to unseat the incumbent government.

The economic reforms were approved by international financial institutions; Bulgaria obtained new loans from the World Bank, the International Monetary Fund (IMF), and the European Bank for Reconstruction and Development (EBRD). Although the country's gross domestic product (GDP) was expected to fall by some 2% in 1997, longer-term projections indicated that Bulgaria could expect economic growth if it kept its reform program on track.

International Reorientation. The new government was determined to pursue Bulgaria's integration into Euro-Atlantic institutions. In particular, President Stoyanov declared that Bulgaria was seeking membership in the North Atlantic Treaty Organization (NATO) and that it was willing to undertake the necessary reforms of its military structure. The pro-NATO policy dismayed Russia, and relations between Sofia and Moscow grew tense. Russian representatives were not invited to participate in a Sofia meeting of southeast European defense ministers in which the United States took part. The Bulgarian media attacked the Russian ambassador for engaging in extensive espionage activities in Bulgaria, while the interior minister accused Moscow of racketeering through its manipulation of gas prices and control over Bulgarian energy supplies. Bulgaria's pro-Western policy was welcomed in Washington and the Bill Clinton administration indicated that Bulgaria was a serious contender for future NATO membership. (*See also* SPECIAL REPORT, page 235.)

JANUSZ BUGAJSKI
Center for Strategic and International Studies

BULGARIA • Information Highlights

Official Name: Republic of Bulgaria.
Location: Southeastern Europe.
Area: 42,823 sq mi (110 910 km²).
Population (mid-1997 est.): 8,300,000.
Chief Cities (Dec. 31, 1992 est.): Sofia, the capital, 1,114,476; Plovdiv, 341,374; Varna, 308,601.
Government: *Head of state,* Petar Stoyanov, president (elected November 1996). *Head of government,* Ivan Kostov, prime minister (elected April 1997). *Legislature* (unicameral)—National Assembly.
Monetary Unit: Lev (1,718.6 leva equal U.S.$1, June 1997).
Gross Domestic Product (1995 est. U.S.$): $43,200,-000,000 (purchasing power parity).
Economic Indexes (1996, 1990 = 100): *Consumer Prices,* all items, 10,273.2; food, 11,462.7. *Industrial Production,* 59.
Foreign Trade (1995 U.S.$): *Imports,* $5,026,000,000; *exports,* $5,091,000,000.

BURMA.   *See* MYANMAR.

BUSINESS AND CORPORATE AFFAIRS

Big things—big mergers, downsizings, write-offs, losses, legal settlements, and even scandals—happened in the U.S. business and corporate world during 1997. Companies maneuvered and experimented, tried bold new concepts, and even changed the entire nature of their operations. It was the same in the executive suite, where large corporations switched leadership at a rate that quickened as the year progressed.

In most instances, the rumblings could be traced to changes in markets, where a premium was placed on innovation as well as on quality and style; increased competition from the developing global marketplace, from entrepreneurs, deregulation, and new technology; and pressure from a growing shareholder class for continued strong profits. Symbolic of change was the near-final transformation on December 1 of Westinghouse Electric Corp., a premier industrial concern, to CBS, whose sole focus would be radio and television.

Mergers and Acquisitions. Much larger in dollar terms were corporate changes involving mergers and acquisitions. The scale was unparalleled, totaling more than $700 billion, at least half of it involving stock rather than cash. While critics commented that some shares were inflated by a robust stock market, it deterred neither buyer nor seller.

Reflecting upheavals in telecommunications, WorldCom Inc., a smaller and relatively upstart Mississippi company with no significant profits in 1996, outbid British Telecommunications and GTE Corp. for MCI Communications Corp., the second-largest U.S. long-distance phone carrier. The winner offered $51 a share in November, equal to $37 billion in WorldCom stock. If finalized, it would be the biggest merger ever.

Within a few days, First Union Corp. agreed to buy CoreStates Financial Corp. for about $17 billion, which would make it the dominant retail bank in the northeastern United States. When completed, the takeover would be First Union's ninth acquisition of a financial institution in less than seven years, with total assets of $153.9 billion.

Billion-dollar deals were common, provoking comment of a new Industrial Revolution. Regional telephone giants Bell Atlantic Corp. and Nynex Corp. combined in a $25.6 billion exchange of stock. Starwood Lodging Trust beat out Hilton Hotel Corp. for the ITT Corp. in a largely stock deal of more than $13 billion. Ernst & Young and KPMG Peat Mar-

wick LLP, private firms, joined to create the world's biggest accounting firm. America Online swallowed CompuServe, its chief rival in on-line services. On Wall Street the Morgan Stanley Group Inc., a premier investment bank, merged with retail broker Dean Witter, Discover & Co. in a $10.2 billion stock swap that was the biggest in Wall Street history. In another Wall Street merger, Travelers Group, a conglomerate of financial companies, announced that it would buy Salomon Inc., the holding company of Salomon Brothers investment bankers, for $9 billion, merging it with its Smith Barney Holdings. And in the arms industry, the Lockheed Martin Corp. bought the Northrop Grumman Corp. for $8.3 billion. Another giant merger, that of Office Depot Inc. and Staples Inc., was considered doomed after the Federal Trade Commission (FTC) rejected the merger and a federal judge issued an order to block it.

Write-offs, Layoffs, and Downsizings. Fundamental, massive changes occurred in other ways, too. Late in the year, Eastman Kodak Co. said it would cut 16,600 jobs and take a fourth-quarter restructuring charge of $1.5 billion. Citing plant closings, among other things, General Motors Corp. said it planned a $2 billion to $3 billion charge against net income. Boeing Corp. said it would write off $1.68 billion.

Citicorp, the nation's second-largest bank, took a third-quarter charge of $889 million to restructure back-office operations, and it announced plans to eliminate 8% of its 90,000 jobs. And in November, Kimberly-Clark said it would dismiss 5,000 workers and sell or close as many as 18 plants. Earlier, deregulation brought intense competition to airlines, caused buyers to bid high prices for prime radio-station properties, and made wireless and mobile phones must-own items for millions. In some states deregulation even brought competition to electric utilities.

New Concepts and New Ferment. On-line stock trading forced down brokerage fees. G. Wayne Huizenga's Republic Industries bought up new- and used-car dealers with total revenues in the billions of dollars. Amazon Books, a Seattle-based on-line bookseller, claimed to be the nation's biggest bookstore, and was considered the hottest retail site in cyberspace.

The ferment produced victims, and for a variety of reasons. Tandy Corp. gave up on its Incredible Universe stores, huge units filled with everything electronic. Though the biggest fast-food restaurateur, McDonald's lost mar-

(Continued on page 163.)

The Tobacco Industry

The 40-year war between the U.S. tobacco industry and antismoking advocates reached a critical stage in 1997, with an unprecedented agreement to settle scores of lawsuits over the damage caused by smoking and the costs of treating tobacco-related diseases. Since the first surgeon general's report linking smoking with disease in 1964, the tobacco industry adamantly had denied any such link. In recent years, however, tobacco litigation had expanded continuously, setting the stage for the landmark agreement.

Under the June 20 agreement, tobacco companies promised to pay the states, plaintiffs, and public-health organizations $368.5 billion over 25 years—a sum that was expected to raise the cost of a pack of cigarettes by 62 cents. They also promised to restrict advertising, pay fines if smoking among young people failed to drop by at least 60% over five years, and accept regulation of nicotine by the Food and Drug Administration (FDA). In return, companies would be protected from future class-action lawsuits. Individuals still would be allowed to sue tobacco companies, but not for punitive damages. The tobacco companies would pay no more than $2 billion a year in total damages.

Following the settlement, the focus of the smoking debate shifted from the states to Congress. Since some of the agreement's terms required changes in existing law, it could not go into effect without the approval of Congress and the president. Assigned the task of codifying the agreement, with or without modifications, Congress essentially was charged with formulating a national tobacco policy, expected to emerge in 1998.

The tobacco industry—already a leading spender on lobbying efforts in Washington—poured millions more into its effort to convince lawmakers to approve the settlement as written, and hired former Senate Republican majority leader Howard H. Baker, Jr., and Senate Democratic majority leader George J. Mitchell, as well as former Texas Gov. Ann Richards, to strengthen its hand in Congress. Most of the money went to Republican lawmakers, viewed as more tolerant of the industry; but a Republican-backed provision in the balanced-budget agreement that would have granted a $50 billion tax credit to tobacco companies later was repealed.

Initially welcomed by most parties to the debate over smoking, the tobacco settlement drew criticism as it came under closer scrutiny, and divided the public-health community. Shortly after the settlement was announced, the American Cancer Society, the American Medical Association, and other antismoking groups formed a coalition—Effective National Action to Control Tobacco (ENACT)—to encourage approval of the agreement. But other public-health advocates,

© James Leynse/SABA

Although smoking remained the leading cause of death in the United States, some 48 million Americans—about 25% of the adult population—still smoked. The campaign to encourage teenagers not to smoke intensified in 1997.

including the American Lung Association, denounced the settlement terms as too soft on the tobacco industry and not protective enough of public health. The division deepened among health professionals in October, when former Surgeon General C. Everett Koop, an outspoken anti-smoking advocate, declined to be a spokesman for ENACT.

Clinton Proposal. Among the critics was President Bill Clinton, who on September 17 asked Congress to impose stricter terms on the industry. The president cited the fact that most adult smokers began the habit as teenagers and focused his proposal on discouraging smoking among young people. He called for a price increase of $1.50 a pack, in hopes of making tobacco prohibitively expensive for teenagers, if teen-smoking rates failed to drop. In addition to proposing stiffer terms, the Clinton administration laid claim to part of the money the states won under the June agreement. The Health and Human Services Department argued that the federal government usually gets a share of Medicaid-related awards won by states because it pays for more than half of all expenses related to Medicaid, the federal-state program that provides health care to the poor. In November, 47 state attorneys general rejected that claim, saying that not all the tobacco lawsuits involved Medicaid issues and that the citizens of the states were entitled to all proceeds of the litigation settlement.

As the year drew to a close, several lawmakers offered alternative proposals that were likely to frame negotiations leading to a final tobacco law in 1998. In November, Sen. John McCain (R-AZ) introduced what was expected to be the industry-endorsed bill because it included virtually the same terms as the original agreement. The bill also set aside $28.5 billion in aid for tobacco farmers who could suffer as a result of eventual tobacco legislation.

A bill by Senate Judiciary Committee Chairman Orrin Hatch (R-UT) raised the industry's payment by $30 billion and increased industry penalties if underage-smoking-reduction targets were not met. Sen. Frank Lautenberg (D-NJ) attached a provision to the spending bill that would bar the federal government from promoting U.S. tobacco products overseas.

The strongest antismoking proposal came from Sen. Edward Kennedy (D-MA), whose bill almost would double the industry's payment, to $650 billion over 25 years. The measure would impose a $1.50-a-pack tax increase over three years, assist farmers hurt by the deal, and rescind the industry's protection from litigation—the main benefit

to tobacco manufacturers included in the June agreement.

Other Litigation. Meanwhile, tobacco litigation continued, offering hope for both sides of the smoking debate. The industry appeared to take a cautious stance when it settled two multibillion-dollar cases brought by Mississippi and Florida, seeking reimbursement for smoking-related health-care costs. Both lawsuits were settled in accordance with the terms of the June tobacco settlement. A $14 billion suit brought by Texas was postponed.

The prospects for some 24 state-level class-action suits pending against the tobacco industry were left in doubt following two actions in October. These cases arose following the failure in 1996 of a nationwide class-action suit known as the Castano case. Antismoking advocates were encouraged by a New York state court's decision to allow a class-action suit on behalf of allegedly addicted smokers seeking recovery of money they had spent on tobacco products. That suit was based on a state law allowing consumers to recover the cost of products bought from companies engaged in deceptive trade practices. Most courts had denied class-action suits against tobacco companies related to nicotine addiction, however, saying individual smoking patterns were too diverse to justify a class action. The industry received a boost when a federal judge in Philadelphia dismissed another class-action suit, brought to recover the cost of future health monitoring and medical treatment for some 2 million Pennsylvania smokers.

The tobacco industry settled a class-action suit filed on behalf of 60,000 airline flight attendants who claimed that secondhand smoke had caused their lung cancer and other illnesses. (Smoking was allowed on domestic flights until 1990.) Although the tobacco companies did not admit that secondhand smoke caused disease and did not pay the plaintiffs directly, they agreed to set up a $300 million foundation to study illnesses associated with tobacco smoke.

While states made headway in efforts to recover billions of dollars spent to treat smoking-related illnesses, the tobacco industry continued to fend off suits brought by individuals holding cigarette makers responsible for their illnesses. In October a Jacksonville, FL, jury found that R.J. Reynolds was not responsible for a former smoker's lung cancer. As in some previous suits, the plaintiff had quit smoking before filing suit. That weakened her argument that the manufacturer had sold her cigarettes knowing that they were addictive.

Health News. Smoking continued to be the leading cause of death, disease, and disability in the United States. The annual death toll from tobacco-related diseases exceeded 400,000. Still, some 48 million Americans—about 25% of the adult population—continued to smoke. That number was virtually unchanged since 1990.

Evidence of tobacco's damage to human health mounted. British researchers had reported in December 1996 that smoking may damage sperm, increasing the risk of cancer among children of smoking fathers, even if the children themselves are not exposed to tobacco smoke. A California study reported evidence that second-hand smoke can cause not only cancer and heart disease, but a number of other diseases, including sudden infant death syndrome, cervical cancer, and more-severe childhood asthma.

Another study found that light, low-tar, and filter-tipped cigarettes—about 75% of the cigarettes sold in the United States—actually caused an increase in cancers deep inside the lungs because smokers of such cigarettes inhale more deeply to increase the nicotine dose. Adenocarcinomas, rare in the 1950s before filters and low-tar cigarettes were introduced, had become more common than squamous-cell carcinomas. Previously the most common type of smoking-related cancer, squamous-cell carcinomas occur in the bronchi.

The argument that smoking greatly increases overall health costs—by some $50 billion a year in the United States, according to government estimates—was questioned by a Dutch study released in October. Since smokers were likely to die prematurely of lung cancer, heart attack, or emphysema, the researchers found, they actually pose less of a long-term burden on the health-care system than nonsmokers, who were more likely to die of chronic diseases after years of costly nursing-home care.

Smoking Trends. A central goal of tobacco policy continued to be the effort to curtail smoking among young people. The FDA introduced a national program to reduce teenage smoking that included restrictions on young people's access to cigarettes and on tobacco advertising. A number of states also launched extensive campaigns—raising prices, cracking down on sales to minors, and restricting advertisements aimed at young people.

The most controversial advertisements, R.J. Reynolds' Joe Camel ads, seemed likely to disappear. Under the June agreement, tobacco companies agreed to refrain from advertising their products using "human figures and cartoons."

Joe Camel's demise seemed likely to occur even faster in California, where under a settlement with 13 cities and counties, all Joe Camel ads were to be removed by the end of 1997.

The results of state and local efforts to curb teen smoking were mixed. Local California ordinances barring cigarette machines in retail stores were credited with reducing cigarette sales to minors by as much as 80%. But the effectiveness of most campaigns remained in doubt, as smoking rates among young people nationwide failed to drop. Between 4.5 million and 6.7 million children aged 12–17 smoked, and about one third of tenth- and 12th-graders said they had smoked in the past month, according to a University of Michigan survey of smoking trends. Smoking among eighth- and tenth-graders had increased by nearly half since 1991. A Massachusetts study found that even when 82% of retailers restricted sales to minors, teenagers continued to buy cigarettes from noncompliant retailers, and smoking rates failed to drop significantly.

Meanwhile, smokers found it harder than ever to find places to light up. In August, Clinton signed an executive order banning smoking in all federal buildings, and most states and localities had imposed or were considering similar measures. As restrictions spread, some companies bucked the trend. A number of airports, including Dulles International Airport in Washington, DC, opened smoking lounges in their otherwise smoke-free terminals.

Outlook. Although the struggle between cigarette manufacturers and antismoking advocates was far from over by year's end, the tobacco industry no longer could count on its traditional clout in Washington to persuade Congress to accept the June agreement as the final word. Even Rep. Thomas J. Bliley, Jr. (R-VA), chairman of the House Commerce Committee and a long-standing industry champion, in December forced the industry to turn over hundreds of documents that were expected to show whether it had suppressed information on tobacco's addictiveness and toxicity, or face a subpoena.

If approved as written, the tobacco settlement, although costly, was not expected to damage the industry's long-term profitability seriously. Financial analysts predicted that the biggest companies would suffer a reduction in 1998 profits of no more than 15%—far less than the threat posed by continuing litigation. If Congress approved a price increase much higher than the 62 cents a pack envisioned under the settlement, however, industry losses could be more onerous.

Mary H. Cooper

(Continued from page 159.)

ket share. Under fire from the National Labor Relations Board, jeans maker Guess?, Inc., shifted operations to Mexico. Faced with competition in the jeans market, Levi Strauss closed plants and cut jobs. Dow Jones & Co., owner of *The Wall Street Journal* and other media properties, came under heavy shareholder criticism for slow growth. Rising credit-card delinquencies caused Sears, Roebuck stock to fall sharply. Both Prudential and Metropolitan insurance companies remained under fire, allegedly for misleading sales practices. Even the strong economy claimed a victim: Union Pacific Railroad succumbed to massive traffic jams on its 36,000 mi (57 935 km) of track, resulting in economic losses said to be in the billions of dollars.

Columbia/HCA Healthcare Corp. came under criminal investigation into whether it defrauded the federal government on patient claims; it announced a restructuring plan that could include selling off more than 100 hospitals. In fact, the entire health-care industry was attacked by critics and state regulators for having, it was said, garnered too much power over medical decisions and patient needs.

Executive Changes. The business ferment produced major changes in the executive suite. AT&T directors chose C. Michael Armstrong, chairman of Hughes Electronics, to head the giant telecommunications company and named Vice-Chairman John D. Zeglis to be president. Simultaneously, AT&T announced the imminent resignation of Robert E. Allen, who had held the top job for nine stormy years. During that time the company incurred billions of dollars in losses on a computer venture and then was split into three independent units. The choice of Armstrong followed the resignation of John R. Walter when the board reneged on year-earlier indications it would name him chief executive officer (CEO). At the Chrysler Corp., Thomas T. Stallkamp, head of the company's auto-parts-purchasing division and known as a cost-cutter, was elevated to the presidency. The move made Stallkamp the heir apparent to Robert J. Eaton, the chairman and chief executive. Leadership also changed at another of America's elite corporations, Coca-Cola. Roberto C. Goizueta, 64, who as Coca-Cola chairman since 1981 had helped raise the company's market value from $4 billion to $150 billion, died of lung cancer. Goizueta, who thought globally and proved its benefits by raising the company's sales on every continent, was succeeded by M. Douglas Ivester, 59, his deputy chairman and "partner."

Other big changes included the resignations of Columbia/HCA CEO Richard Scott and President David Vandewater; Thomas F. Frist, Jr., was named to head the company. Michael Smith replaced Armstrong at the helm of GM's Hughes Electronics division. Robert S. Morrison resigned as CEO of Philip Morris' Kraft Food division to replace William Smithburg as chief of Quaker Oats Co. H. John Greeniaus retired as chairman of Nabisco Holdings Corp. and was replaced by James Kilts, once executive vice-president of Philip Morris. Leo F. Mullin was named CEO of Delta Air Lines.

Directors of Weyerhaeuser Co. lured Steven Rogel from the top job at rival Willamette Industries Inc. In one of the more unusual arrangements, Steve Jobs, cofounder of Apple Computer, returned to the company's board of directors and to virtual command, but without a title. He remained head of Pixar Animation Studios, which he also had founded. And in a sign of the changing times, Laura Ashley Holdings, whose clothing and home furnishings symbolized a way of life in the 1970s and 1980s, dismissed its chief, Ann Iverson, after a six-month $7.6 million loss.

Executive Income, Corporate Payout. "Big" applied widely—in executive pay, legal cases and settlements, profits and losses, and even scandals. A September Internal Revenue Service (IRS) report stated that, from 1980 to 1995, tax-deductible senior executive compensation rose by 182%, while corporate revenues rose by only 129.5%.

Michael Eisner, Walt Disney Co. chief, seemed to top big earners, having received options of 8 million shares, which compensation specialists valued at $196 million. But Disney and Eisner were not alone; enticed by a soaring stock market, many corporations granted options to top executives in lieu of pay hikes. In a sense, Eisner's view of income was matched in other ways, especially in the $250 million suit with Jeffrey Katzenberg, who was passed over for the presidency of the Walt Disney Co. in 1994. The suit was settled for an unspecified sum in November.

Again, Disney was not alone; big settlements were the rule throughout business when top executives were replaced. John R. Walter of AT&T, for example, walked away with almost $26 million in July after serving as president for only nine months.

The Justice Department in November charged that Bill Gates' Microsoft Corp. violated a 1995 antitrust settlement by compelling computer makers to install its Internet Explorer browser with Windows 95,

Microsoft's dominant operating system. Critics feared Microsoft could gain a monopoly position, but the company compared the action to a lynching.

Scandal pushed its way into the big picture. Bre-X Minerals Ltd., a tiny Canadian mining firm, convinced some of finance's biggest names that its remote Indonesian operation possibly held Earth's largest gold vein. But in early May an independent investigation found the site and story a scam. The stock, at one time more than $200 a share, evaporated before the eyes of brokers who had lent customers hundreds of millions of dollars.

JOHN CUNNIFF
Business News Analyst, The Associated Press

CAMBODIA

A violent takeover in July 1997 undermined the groundwork for peace and democracy laid by the United Nations (UN) in 1993. Although the coalition-government framework of Cambodia remained, Second Premier Hun Sen held most power and ruled by intimidation. The regime faced renewed warfare from resistance troops. The economy slid toward recession, and Cambodia's international position suffered.

Politics. Second Premier Hun Sen staged a violent military putsch on July 5–6, ousting First Premier Prince Norodom Ranariddh, son of King Norodom Sihanouk, while he was in France. At least 40 opposition members were killed and hundreds were injured, arrested, or in hiding during the battle for power. Police harassment shut down the opposition press. The takeover followed escalating tension between the Cambodian People's Party (CPP) and Prince Ranariddh's United National Front for an Independent, Neutral, Peaceful, and Cooperative Cambodia (FUNCINPEC), which had formed separate alliances with smaller parties in anticipation of a national election scheduled for 1998.

The situation worsened when CPP members were blamed for killing at least 16 people and injuring more than 100 in a grenade attack against an opposition demonstration in March. Ranariddh publicly called Hun Sen a dictator and blamed the CPP for the growing drug trade, corruption, and political assassination. Hun Sen claimed he took power in July to prevent Ranariddh from bringing Khmer Rouge (KR) hard-liners into the capital to support FUNCINPEC.

After Hun Sen established control, the National Assembly approved an arrest warrant for Ranariddh and installed Foreign Minister Ung Huot as first premier. The government still faced serious political problems. FUNCINPEC factionalism contributed to the Assembly's rejection in September of a controversial cabinet shuffle that would have removed four Ranariddh loyalists. Tension allegedly was growing within the CPP as members worried about the impact of Hun Sen's political moves. King Norodom Sihanouk initially provided lukewarm support to the regime but by October was frustrated over Hun Sen's refusal to accept his offer to mediate peace talks. The king's repeated requests to abdicate were denied.

Sihanouk left Cambodia for China in October and returned in December, when he declared that he would pardon Ranariddh. In the northwest unpaid government troops fought but did not defeat resistance elements, which included Ranariddh's supporters, other opposition-party members, and KR guerrillas. More than 50,000 displaced civilians fled to Thailand for safety.

The KR, nearly a spent force in late 1996, changed dramatically. The guerrillas, who had ambushed government negotiators in February, agreed by June to end their resistance and support the constitution. Serious divisions between KR leader Pol Pot and senior officials over political plans led to skirmishes between members, the murders of top official Son Sen and his family, kidnappings, and eventually Pol Pot's arrest. The remaining group distanced itself from Pol Pot, whom they denounced and sentenced to life imprisonment during a public show trial on July 25. Khieu Samphan and younger, educated members assumed control and renamed the group the National Solidarity Party.

Revolutionary leader Ta Mok, who remained an adviser, blamed an unrepentant Pol Pot for killing hundreds of thousands during past atrocities and now claimed to support a liberal democracy. Ieng Sary, who led a large

---

CAMBODIA • Information Highlights

Official Name: Kingdom of Cambodia.
Location: Southeast Asia.
Area: 69,900 sq mi (181 040 km²).
Population (mid-1997 est.): 11,200,000.
Chief City (1991 est.): Phnom Penh, the capital, 900,000.
Government: *Head of state,* Norodom Sihanouk, king (acceded Sept. 24, 1993). *Head of government,* Ung Huot, first premier (named August 1997); Hun Sen, second premier (named Sept. 24, 1993).
Monetary Unit: Riel (3,750.0 riels equal U.S.$1, September 1997).
Gross Domestic Product (1995 est. U.S.$): $7,000,000,000 (purchasing power parity).
Foreign Trade (1995 est. U.S.$): *Imports,* $630,500,000; *exports,* $240,700,000.

In August 1997 thousands of Cambodian civilians fled to Thailand to escape the fighting that had broken out between troops loyal to Second Premier Hun Sen and those supporting First Premier Prince Norodom Ranariddh. Thailand had opened its border to Cambodians in light of the violence.

© Apichart Weerawong/Reuters/Archive Photos

KR faction that defected in 1996, announced during his first trip to Phnom Penh since 1979 that he supported Hun Sen's regime.

Economy. The economy was in disarray after looting in July caused millions of dollars in damage to businesses and violence prompted hundreds of foreigners to evacuate. Before the putsch, international economists had predicted economic growth would be about 7%, but predictions of 0% to 3% growth were common by year's end. Cambodia was hit hardest by the suspension of foreign—including U.S., Australian, and German—developmental aid, which normally covered about half of the budget, and by the decisions of the International Monetary Fund (IMF) and the World Bank to freeze financial support. Some investors, including foreign oil firms, temporarily suspended operations.

The Cambodian riel, which had been valued at about 2,500 per U.S. dollar since 1995, depreciated sharply to 3,750 per dollar in September. Foreign-exchange difficulties and sinking investor confidence produced trade problems, increased inflation to double digits, and led to a rise in unemployment. The government's financial position was damaged further by sharply declining revenues. Government attempts to reverse the economic decline failed despite cuts in government expenditures, continuing assistance from Japan—the largest aid donor—and the introduction of more favorable tourist and investment policies.

Foreign Affairs. The violent takeover cost the government international support and divided the international community on Cambodian policy.

The Association of Southeast Asian Nations (ASEAN) in July postponed Cambodia's admission into the regional group. The United Nations (UN) left Cambodia's seat vacant until it could judge the credentials of two rival delegations vying for representation. China, Russia, and ASEAN supported the regime retaining the UN seat, but the United States and Norway blocked Hun Sen's delegation from participating. The UN compromised to avoid explicit condemnation of Hun Sen's actions, while endorsing ASEAN mediation efforts. The United States appointed former U.S. Rep. Stephen Solarz as a special envoy to help seek a solution to the crisis.

Most ASEAN countries continued assistance to Phnom Penh, but Washington pressed donors, who earlier pledged $450 million, to suspend all but humanitarian aid to Cambodia. Cambodia's relations with other Asian countries became more complex. Thai and Vietnamese leaders declared support for the new government. Thai border officials, however, allegedly had close ties to resistance elements, and the king accused Vietnam of occupying parts of southeast Cambodia.

China played a balancing act between encouraging budding relations with the CPP and supporting traditional ties to Sihanouk and the KR. Despite the king's links to North Korea, Phnom Penh established full diplomatic relations with South Korea in November in an effort to boost Seoul's economic support. Taiwan rejected Hun Sen's request to reopen its Phnom Penh office, which was closed after Taipei was accused of supporting Ranariddh.

CHRISTINE VAN ZANDT
U.S. Government Analyst on East Asian Affairs

Canada

Canada's economy improved in 1997 as unemployment fell a little. Quebec separatism faded slightly but regionalism dominated the 36th general election. Canadians spread their support among five parties and gave Jean Chrétien's Liberal government only a narrow victory. While Ottawa supported a court challenge to unilateral secession and talked of potential partition, nine provincial premiers agreed that Quebec is unique—but no better than the other provinces.

The Economy. Most economic indicators rose in 1997, as Canada experienced some of the fastest growth among nations belonging to the Organization for Economic Cooperation and Development (OECD). Inflation was tamed, and deficits were under control and likely to disappear by 2001. Mortgage rates were at 30-year lows. The prosperity of 1996 continued in the West and Ontario and cautiously moved into Quebec. Job creation exceeded the official 1% drop in unemployment to 9%, showing that discouraged workers were flocking back to be counted in the labor force. Canadian investors shared in the mutual-funds boom, and consumer confidence buoyed the retail sector. Prime Minister Chrétien, who is considered pro-business and pro-labor, began 1997 with his third "Team Canada" visit to Asia. Nine premiers, including Quebec's separatist (Parti Québécois) leader, Lucien Bouchard, joined 600 business leaders, academics, and officials to sign more than C$2.6 billion in deals.

One sign of prosperity was a modest rise in labor militancy. In 1996, 3.3 million worker days were lost to strikes—double the number in 1995—and 1997's total would be higher still. Wage settlements rose 1.8% compared with under 1% in 1995 and 1996. Unions won some strikes and lost others battling for part-time workers. In Ontario the government avoided major clashes with hospital and institutional workers but teachers were on the picket lines in October. Eaton's, Canada's most famous department-store chain, closed 17 of its 87 stores and sought bankruptcy protection. And investors, who had begun the year wondering who would gain most from Bre-X's fabulous gold find at Busang, Indonesia, ended it knowing that they were victims of massive "salting" of core samples, allegedly by a geologist who had committed suicide. Newfoundland's Hibernia oil field got its C$5.8 billion offshore oil platform, but development of the huge Voisey Bay nickel deposits was slowed by the demands of 5,500 local Inuit and 1,600 Innu.

Despite prosperity, many Canadians felt worse off, with higher taxes and fees and reduced public services. Average disposable income was C$36,679 in 1996, down from C$37,787 in 1993. And, fearing renewed inflation, the Bank of Canada moved in October to raise interest rates.

The Liberals insisted that their four years of bitter medicine had saved the economy. In a budget introduced in February, Finance Minister Paul Martin declared that he would "hold the line" to wipe out the deficit by 2000. The C$610 billion national debt—up from C$508 billion in 1993—represented 74.5% of

On June 2, 1997, Jean Chrétien, right, led Canada's ruling Liberal Party to election victory but with a decreased majority. Commenting on the results, the prime minister said: "When you have a majority and you have four parties located in different parts of Canada, with some who are on the right, some on the extreme right, and some on the left, it's not a difficult political problem to run a government."

© Canapress Photo Service

The 36th Canadian General Election

Parties	Liberal	Reform	BQ	NDP	PC	Ind
Newfoundland	4	0	0	0	3	0
Nova Scotia	0	0	0	6	5	0
Prince Edward Island	4	0	0	0	0	0
New Brunswick	3	0	0	2	5	0
Quebec	26	0	44	0	5	0
Ontario	101	0	0	0	1	1
Manitoba	6	3	0	4	1	0
Saskatchewan	1	8	0	5	0	0
Alberta	2	24	0	0	0	0
British Columbia	6	25	0	3	0	0
Yukon	0	0	0	1	0	0
Northwest Terr.	2	0	0	0	0	0
1997 TOTAL	**155**	**63**	**44**	**21**	**20**	**1**
1993 TOTAL	**177**	**54**	**52**	**9**	**2**	**1**

Canadian General Elections, 1984–1997

Party	Seats				% of Votes			
	1984	1988	1993	1997	1984	1988	1993	1997
PC	211	169	2	20	51	43	16	19
Liberal	40	82	177	155	29	32	41	38
NDP	30	43	9	21	19	20	7	11
BQ	0	0	54	44	0	-	13	11
Reform	0	0	52	60	0	2	19	19
Other	1	1	1	1	1	3	4	2
TOTAL	282	295	295	301	100	100	100	100

gross national product (GNP) in 1996, but would be 71.2% by 1998. There would be no tax increases—though opposition members reminded voters that increases voted earlier would hit in 1997, and huge premium increases and lower benefits designed to keep the Canada Pension Plan solvent would affect people's purses. Other ministers promised a C$600 million national child benefit, a "Health Transition Fund" to experiment with home-care and drug programs, and more generous terms for educational savings plans and repayment of student loans.

Politics. Four years into a five-year mandate, the Liberals called an election. Far behind in the polls, opposition parties almost conceded defeat. In March the Bloc Québécois (BQ), which had finished second in the 1993 voting, replaced its leader, Michel Gauthier, with Gilles Duceppe. The new leader is a former hospital worker, former Communist, and committed separatist. Reform Party leader Preston Manning shed his denim shirts and glasses for tailored suits, contact lenses, and styled hair, as part of his response to Reform's extremist image. An erosion of able backbenchers also hurt the opposition. The Reform Party seemed to be in trouble. With only two seats, the Progressive Conservatives (PCs) threatened to disappear, especially when leader Jean Charest failed to get solid endorsement from Tory provincial Premiers Mike Harris of Ontario and Ralph Klein of Alberta. As for the New Democratic Party (NDP), its unpopularity in traditional strongholds, Ontario and British Columbia, had cut into its support.

However, the Liberals had problems, too. Legislation to control rifles and other firearms was unpopular in rural areas, especially in western Canada. Bill C-71, which would regulate tobacco products, angered organizers of cultural and sporting events, especially in Quebec. Attempts to link Brian Mulroney to a kickback scandal involving Swiss banks and sales of aircraft to Air Canada utterly collapsed in January, leaving the former prime minister to collect an apology and $2 million in costs. The attempt to stop the 1993 handover of Toronto's international airport to Conservative supporters proved equally costly in the courts. Even the prime minister's attempt to impose able women on winnable Liberal ridings produced protests. A 1993 promise to eliminate the unpopular goods and services tax (GST) could be kept only in three Atlantic provinces, and at a cost of $1 billion in compensation. The new 15% "harmonized sales tax" (HST) won few friends, particularly after national retailers forced Ottawa to back down from plans to hide the tax in the price.

Despite some misgivings from party pollsters, the Liberals postponed the tobacco-regulating bill for a year and called an election in April, confident of surviving the campaign and even of making gains in Quebec and the West. Critics noted that Chrétien's opening campaign speech was weak; meanwhile, Manitobans, facing their worst flood in a century, were angry. Manning's new style drew crowds and attention; so did Jean Charest, once handlers focused on him and not his Harris-style program. On April 23 polls told the Liberals their support had dropped to the low 30s.

Led by Preston Manning, below, the Reform Party overtook the Bloc Québécois (BQ) in the balloting, becoming the official Opposition. As expected, Reform candidates did well in the West.
© Canapress Photo Service

Employment figures were supposed to help: They showed a continuing unemployment rate of 10%. Among Liberal's opponents, only Duceppe stumbled, looking absurd in a photo opportunity and firing his bus driver when aides sent him by the wrong route.

On May 8 former Quebec Premier Jacques Parizeau burst into the campaign with his memoirs, boasting that France would have recognized Quebec days after a 1995 referendum victory by the BQ. National unity became an issue. Was Chrétien to blame for nearly losing the 1995 contest? Who could do better? In nationally televised debates in May, Charest was strong in French and English; Liberals and the NDP declined; the BQ sank. Reform had blamed Chrétien for "almost losing Canada"; now it issued ads denouncing Quebec domination, lumping Chrétien, Charest, Bouchard, and Duceppe together. The Reform Party bounced up in the West, was down in Ontario, and was going nowhere with a few token candidates in Quebec. There, the BQ recovered. Liberals attacked Charest, too—as a survivor of the hated Mulroney government. As opinion polarized in Ontario and

Quebec, Charest support frayed. Weak candidates, organization, and funds could not support his initial gains. The NDP leader, Alexa McDonough, stuck to economic issues and focused on 26 winnable ridings. In the final weeks, nervous Liberals contemplated big promises and heavy spending. Their pollsters told them to "stay the course" and they did, recovering slowly.

On June 2, 67% of the Canadian electorate voted, the lowest turnout in years. Another near sweep of Ontario gave Liberals a nine-seat margin. The West made Reform the official opposition and the BQ ran third. The NDP won seats where it barely ever had made a showing—in Nova Scotia and New Brunswick. Charest's gains were in the same region and in Quebec. Both parties regained official standing in the House of Commons.

After the election, Manning debated whether to occupy the official residence of the leader of Opposition—which he once had threatened to turn into a bingo palace. He moved in, chiefly to try to normalize his party as a contender for power. Shaken by near defeat and anxious about a nine-vote margin against four opposition parties, Chrétien replaced the defense and health ministers in his cabinet—both of whom had lost to the NDP—and his party planned programs it had promised before and during the campaign.

When Parliament met in September, the speech from the throne encouraged Canadians to think about the dividend they could enjoy when the deficit disappeared. Conservatives and Reformers demanded tax cuts, but Liberals wanted some of the benefits to go to Canada's struggling health system and the elderly, with plans to ease the cost of prescription drugs and home care. By mid-October opposition parties had made little headway, beyond exposing an investigation by the Royal Canadian Mounted Police into Liberal fund-raising in Quebec.

Federal-Provincial Relations. The regionalism of the new Parliament led the government to renew promises of closer partnership with the provinces. One test would be how Ottawa acted on Newfoundland's September 2 referendum, ending religious control of the province's schools.

Even before Justice Horace Krever's report on Canada's AIDS-tainted blood system was released, Ottawa and most provinces reluctantly agreed to replace the Red Cross with a national blood agency. Only Quebec proposed to continue with the Red Cross. The historic agency seemed likely to be buried in lawsuits.

THE CANADIAN MINISTRY

Jean Chrétien, prime minister
David Anderson, minister of fisheries and oceans
Lloyd Axworthy, minister of foreign affairs
Ethel Blondin-Andrew, secretary of state for children and youth
Don Boudria, leader of the government in the House of Commons
Martin Cauchon, secretary of state for the Federal Office of Regional Development—Quebec
Raymond Chan, secretary of state for Asia-Pacific
David Collenette, minister of transport
Sheila Copps, minister of Canadian heritage
Herb Dhaliwal, minister of national revenue
Stéphane Dion, minister of intergovernmental affairs and president of the Queen's Privy Council for Canada
Ronald Duhamel, secretary of state for science, research and development, and western economic diversification
Arthur Eggleton, minister of national defense
Hedy Fry, secretary of state for multiculturalism and the status of women
Alfonso Gagliano, minister of public works and government services
Ralph Goodale, minister of natural resources and minister responsible for the Canadian Wheat Board
Alasdair Graham, leader of the government in the Senate
Herbert Gray, deputy prime minister
David Kilgour, secretary of state for Latin America and Africa
Lawrence MacAulay, minister of labor
John Manley, minister of industry, the Atlantic Canada Opportunities Agency, and western economic diversification, and minister responsible for the Federal Office of Regional Development—Canada
Sergio Marchi, minister of international trade
Diane Marleau, minister of international cooperation and minister responsible for Francophonie
Paul Martin, minister of finance
Marcel Massé, president of the Treasury board and minister responsible for infrastructure
Anne McLellan, minister of justice and attorney general of Canada
Fred Mifflin, minister of veterans affairs and secretary of state for the Atlantic Canada Opportunities Agency
Andrew Mitchell, secretary of state for parks
Gilbert Normand, secretary of state for agriculture, agri-food, and fisheries and oceans
James Peterson, secretary of state for international financial institutions
Pierre Pettigrew, minister of human-resources development
Lucienne Robillard, minister of citizenship and immigration
Allan Rock, minister of health
Andy Scott, solicitor general of Canada
Christine Stewart, minister of the environment
Jane Stewart, minister of Indian affairs and northern development
Lyle VanClief, minister of agriculture and agri-food

A long-simmering U.S.-Canadian salmon-fishing dispute made headlines in 1997. In July, British Columbian fishermen blockaded an Alaskan ferry in Prince Rupert for three days.

© Ian Lindsay/"Vancouver Sun"

Quebec's sovereignist government was an awkward partner. Since the Atlantic provinces got $1 billion for adopting the HST, Quebec was entitled to compensation for doing the same in 1991. When Ottawa offered modest funds to alleviate child poverty, Quebec promptly calculated the maximum possible amount, announced a program to spend it, and blamed Ottawa when the whole sum was not forthcoming. In some fields—retraining and forest management—there was more cooperation. Intergovernmental Affairs Minister Stéphane Dion also caused friction by making it clear that separation would not be easy. If Canada could be divided, so could Quebec. When Quebec City lawyer and former *péquiste* (member of the Parti Québécois) Guy Bertrand challenged his province's claim to unilateral secession, Ottawa turned the case into a reference to the Supreme Court of Canada. An angry Bouchard government refused to plead, claiming it was not Ottawa's business, nor the court's. Hearings were set for 1998.

If Ottawa talked tough about Quebec, some provincial premiers sought accommodation. At their annual meeting in St. Andrew, N.B., in August, New Brunswick's Premier Frank McKenna and Saskatchewan's Premier Roy Romanow pressed the issue. Alberta's Premier Ralph Klein, who was reelected overwhelmingly on March 11, was sympathetic; British Columbia's Premier Glen Clark, at war with Ottawa and eastern Canada on a number of fronts, was not. Bouchard stayed away from a second meeting in September in Calgary, but the nine premiers struggled to an agreement. As a "framework," they accepted that Quebec was unique—but insisted that all provinces had to be equal. To win Reform leader Manning's support, even this had to be discussed with voters. While Bouchard raged that the offer "belittles us, holds us back, reduces us," polls found most Quebeckers thought it worth pursuing.

Foreign Affairs. It was a rocky year for Canada-U.S. relations. Foreign Minister Lloyd Axworthy visited Cuba in January and denounced the Helms-Burton Act—U.S. legislation that punishes nations that trade with Cuba. In Oslo in September, the United States rejected Canadian pleas to join a world ban on antipersonnel mines. However, collapse of the 1985 Canada-U.S. Pacific Salmon Treaty caused the hottest exchanges. Mindful of the devastation of the Atlantic fishery, British Columbians denounced Alaska and

---

CANADA • Information Highlights

Official Name: Canada.
Location: Northern North America.
Area: 3,851,792 sq mi (9 976 140 km²).
Population (mid-1997 est.): 30,100,000.
Chief Cities (1991 census): Ottawa, the capital, 313,987; Toronto, 635,395; Montreal, 1,017,666.
Government: *Head of state,* Elizabeth II, queen; represented by Roméo LeBlanc, governor-general (took office February 1995). *Head of government,* Jean Chrétien, prime minister (took office Nov. 4, 1993). *Legislature*—Parliament: Senate and House of Commons.
Monetary Unit: Canadian dollar (1.4204 dollars equal U.S.$1, Nov. 24, 1997).
Gross Domestic Product (1995 est. U.S.$): $694,000,-000,000 (purchasing power parity).
Economic Indexes: *Consumer Prices* (1996, 1990 = 100): all items, 113.5; food, 110.6. *Industrial Production,* 109.
Foreign Trade (1996 U.S.$): *Imports,* $174,962,000,000; *exports,* $201,636,000,000.

West Coast fishing fleets for scooping salmon heading to Canadian rivers to spawn and causing massive depletion of stocks. Premier Clark raged that Ottawa's quiet diplomacy had failed and threatened to close the Nanoose weapons-testing range to both U.S. and Canadian navies. In July fishermen in British Columbia blockaded an Alaska ferry in Prince Rupert for three days. Clark praised their "courageous resistance," placed ads on U.S. television, and launched lawsuits against the province's neighboring U.S. states. Axworthy, in turn, had to pay contrite visits to U.S. congressmen. As the year ended, it was not clear if Canadians would be exempted from stringent new U.S. border controls.

Another premier, Quebec's Lucien Bouchard, visited Paris to seek support for Quebec sovereignty. He got less than his predecessors—a nuanced reply from President Jacques Chirac and polite indifference from Socialist Premier Lionel Jospin.

Defense. It was a hard year for the Canadian military forces, too, with cuts to strength, reorganization, base closures, and revelations of past scandals. A senior general was fired for expense-account fraud and the commander of Canadian peacekeepers in Haiti was removed for using excessive force on a civilian. After costing Canada $500 million, the rest of the force withdrew from the Caribbean nation in December, leaving behind a weak, inexperienced Haitian National Police. Defense Minister Douglas Young refused to extend the two-year-old Commission of Inquiry into the Deployment of Canadian Forces into Somalia. On March 1, Young promised that the 90,000-member Somalia force would be reformed. Such reforms included better-educated officers, pay raises, and improved ethics training. In July the Somalia commission's report denounced virtually every senior officer associated with the 1992–93 Somalia operation, including acting Chief of the Defense Staff Vice-Admiral Larry Murray.

Defeated for reelection on June 2, Young was replaced as defense minister by former Toronto Mayor Arthur C. Eggleton, who downplayed the Somalia report. He also bypassed Murray and appointed Gen. Maurice Baril, currently the land-forces commander, as the new chief of the defense staff. Critics denounced Baril, a former adviser to the UN secretary-general, for failing to prevent massacres in Rwanda in 1993.

Justice. Though murder was up 6% in 1996, most crime continued a five-year decline. Still, the majority of Canadians thought crime was growing, and law and order was prominent among Reform Party issues.

With the Supreme Court figuring increasingly in decisions affecting Canada's constitution and Charter of Rights, the prime minister's prerogative to make appointments to the nine-member bench was criticized. In October, Michel Bastarache, 50, a barrister, legal scholar, and appeal-court judge, replaced fellow New Brunswicker Gérard La Forest, becoming the Supreme Court's youngest member.

First Nations. After several years of confrontation and standoff under Ovide Mercredi, the Assembly of First Nations chose Manitoba chief Phil Fontaine as its new leader. In turn, the government announced that it would involve Fontaine in implementing recommendations of the C$60 million report of the Royal Commission on Aboriginal People, published in 1996. While the commission had urged native self-government, corruption in band administration was as much a theme of Native concern as the grim problems of violence, substance abuse, and poverty.

Environment. Most Canadians would remember 1997 as a year of a hard winter; a long, dry summer; and a beautiful autumn. The year opened on the west coast with the "storm of the century." Massive power failures and blocked roads resulted, and the army was called out to rescue motorists and transport the sick. In April in Manitoba, it was the "flood of the century," as the Red River devastated more than 494,000 acres (200 000 ha) of the province's best farmland and drove 28,000 people from their homes. Dikes and a C$63 million diversion ditch, built after the 1950 flood, saved most of Winnipeg. So did 6,000 soldiers. Meanwhile, engineers could boast following the opening of the Confederation Bridge, an 8-mi (13-km) span linking New Brunswick and Prince Edward Island.

It was a bad-news year for environmentally complacent Canadians. An environmental report released by the North American Free Trade Agreement (NAFTA) put Ontario third, behind Texas and Tennessee, as a continental polluter; Quebec was 12th. The Chrétien government confessed that Canada had fallen short of the emission targets it had accepted at the 1992 Earth Summit in Rio de Janeiro, Brazil. Ontario Hydro announced that seven of its troubled CANDU nuclear reactors would be shut down and the remaining 12 would have to be reengineered at a total cost of $8 billion.

DESMOND MORTON, *Director*
McGill Institute for the Study of Canada

Provinces and Territories

ALBERTA. Premier Ralph Klein's Progressive Conservative (PC) government was reelected easily for a second term in March 1997, winning 63 of the province's 83 seats. The Liberals, under leader Grant Mitchell, won 18 seats; the socialist New Democrats, under leader Pam Barrett, garnered two. Going into the election, the PCs had held 54 seats, the Liberals 29, and the New Democrats none. Klein had campaigned on his record of restraining spending, balancing the budget, paying off the accumulated debt, and eventually cutting taxes. He also had a tough law-and-order agenda. The PCs now had ruled Alberta since 1971, making them the longest-reigning provincial government in the nation. Mitchell later announced his intent to resign from the Liberal leadership.

Budget. Provincial Treasurer Jim Dinning in February unveiled a C$14 billion budget that fulfilled the government's promise of no tax increases and ensured that Alberta remained the only province without a sales tax. The budget contained a C$128 million increase in health-care spending, C$91 million more in education spending, and C$52 million extra for transportation and utility upgrading. These increases came after several years of controversial cuts. But the big budgetary news came later in the year, when newly appointed Provincial Treasurer Stockwell Day announced in August that Alberta's budget surplus might top C$1.2 billion; Premier Ralph Klein said that the rest of the province's net debt, currently C$3.7 billion, now might be paid off by the end of 1999. The government had estimated in 1993 that it would take until 2010 to pay off the net debt. However, several years of soaring oil revenues, a vibrant economy, and spending cuts had given the province the best financial balance sheet in Canada. Day even spoke of major tax cuts or a onetime tax "dividend" check for Albertans.

Labor. An 11th-hour settlement in March between the government and the United Nurses Association of Alberta prevented a threatened illegal strike by its 12,000 members. Nurses claimed that a 5% wage cut imposed by the government in 1994, and the lack of increases since then, had made it impossible for them to survive. Statistics reportedly showed that, because of downsizing, there now were 26% fewer full-time nursing positions in the province than in 1993. Under the complex settlement, which included generous severance packages to employees being let go, nurses won salary increases of 7.4% over three years. The threatened strike was one of a number of labor confrontations fought during the year between the government and provincial and municipal employees over downsizing and salary cutbacks.

Gambling. Worry and discontent swept across Alberta over the installation of video lottery terminals (VLTs) in bars, hotels, and newly opened casinos. Since 1994, when the provincial government legalized VLTs, some 5,500 VLTs had been installed. With them came stories of men and women who lost their life savings to the machines, of marriages ruined, and even of suicides. Reports showed that, in 1996, C$1.8 billion was plugged into the VLTs, with much of it going to the government. When the government refused to hold a province-wide plebiscite on whether VLTs should be banned, citizens' groups forced local votes on the issue, and VLTs were voted out in a number of rural communities. Amid the widespread movements for local plebiscites, the Alberta Urban Municipalities Association (AUMA) passed a motion calling on the provincial government to change legislation banning such votes. The AUMA claimed the province should not be allowed to dump controversial provincial issues on local governments.

PAUL JACKSON
"The Calgary Sun"

BRITISH COLUMBIA. A salmon-fishery dispute with Alaska virtually overshadowed all else in British Columbia (BC) politics during 1997. Meanwhile, northern BC experienced economic problems.

Government and Politics. Tensions over Canada–U.S. salmon catches following the collapse of talks to renew the 1985–92 Pacific Salmon Treaty escalated to alarming proportions in 1997, illustrated by Premier Glen Clark's threat to terminate the lease on the Vancouver Island Nanoose Bay weapon-testing range used by the U.S. Navy and the blockade of an Alaskan ferry at Prince Rupert by BC fishers.

At home, the New Democratic government began the year with a mini cabinet shuffle after the December 1996 resignation of Moe Sihota, former education and labor minister. Throughout the year, opposition groups debated the possibilities of electoral mergers. The attempted renewal of the BC Reform Party in the wake of the national Reform Party's successes in the June federal election and the selection of a new provincial leader were overshadowed by a Liberal Party victory in the September Surrey–White Rock by-election, as well as by the defection of one of the two Reform members of the Legislative Assembly (MLAs) to the Liberal Party.

Government support of expanded gambling opportunities and the installation of slot machines in casinos exacerbated the conflict between the provincial government and local municipalities seeking control over new gaming. Preparations began for recall campaigns against two government MLAs; meanwhile a court challenge to the validity of the 1996 provincial general election on the grounds of electoral fraud continued.

Public Policy. Arguments surrounding the 1996–97 budget raged on with revision of the balanced-budget forecast to a C$395 million deficit. The 1997–98 budget cut operating expenditures to an estimated C$20.6 billion and forecast an operating 1997–98 deficit of C$185 million. Total direct debt of C$11.1 billion would increase by an estimated C$530 million. New legislation included the establishment of a Fisheries Renewal BC Crown corporation and legal recognition of the rights of same-sex couples. Business opposition forced the withdrawal of proposed Labour Relations Code amendments.

The Economy. The provincial government embraced a job-creation strategy for 40,000 new jobs. Surplus hydroelectric power from the Columbia River Treaty would be available at discounted prices under a Power for Jobs Initiative. A jobs and timber accord with industry envisaged the creation of more than 22,400 new forestry jobs by 2001. By year's end, however, while Vancouver hosted the 18-nation Asia-Pacific Economic Cooperation (APEC) conference, economic downturns in Japan and elsewhere had continuing dire consequences for employment in forestry and the pulp and paper industry. Difficulties in the economy of northern BC attracted regional policy attention, and the provincial government intervened to restructure the Prince Rupert pulp-mill operations of Skeena Cellulose in an effort to maintain that company's 2,400 jobs.

NORMAN J. RUFF, *University of Victoria*

MANITOBA. Two items dominated Manitoba news in 1997: flooding on the Red River, and the federal general election. Connecting the two was Canada's Prime Minister Jean Chrétien. Despite a request from the province's political leaders for a delay, he called an early federal election. Supporters of his Liberal government distanced themselves from Chrétien's apparent lack of concern for the province.

Flooding. During the winter of 1996–97, Manitoba received double the normal amount of precipitation. High groundwater content, combined with an unexpectedly quick snowmelt, led to wide apprehension about potential flooding.

On April 6 there was an ice blizzard in the upper reaches of the Red River, which shut down Winnipeg almost completely. A rapid melting of snow and ice in the next two weeks produced flooding in Grand Forks, ND, on April 19. The Red River crested there 4 ft (1.2 m) higher than predicted, causing widespread damage when the dikes broke. Manitoba was better prepared than North Dakota, having built a floodway in the 1960s. The floodway had saved Winnipeg in both 1979 and 1996, but now endured a more severe test.

To prevent the floodwaters from doing an "end run" around the floodway's west end, 300 pieces of heavy equipment were brought in to build an additional, 25-mi (40-km) dike. It was built in three days of 24-hour work, using 3,000-lb (1 361-kg) "super-sandbags." In the end, only one town—the small community of Ste-Agathe, which had gaps in its dike—was flooded. Isolated farms and houses also suffered damage, and about 20,000 people were evacuated. No one was killed. Total damages ran to more than C$150 million.

Federal Election. During the flood, the federal election practically was ignored. There had been demands that it be suspended for 90 days, but the chief electoral officer, Jean-Pierre Kingsley, decided not to postpone the vote. In the event, the voter turnout in Manitoba was much the same as in other provinces.

The election resulted in many upsets. The Liberals, who had held all but two of Manitoba's 14 seats, lost two to the New Democrats, two to the Reform Party, and one to the Progressive Conservatives (PCs). The vote split was close; the Liberals got 35%, the New Democratic Party and Reform 24% each, and the PCs 18%.

In provincial politics, the Liberals fared even less well. Two of their three members of the legislature bolted, accusing new leader Ginny Hasselfield of arrogance. She threatened to sue one of them for slander, but decided instead to put her leadership up for review in 1998. The PCs remained dominant, with 31 seats out of 57.

MICHAEL KINNEAR, *University of Manitoba*

NEW BRUNSWICK. New Brunswick's Premier Frank McKenna fulfilled a ten-year-old promise Oct. 7, 1997, by resigning.

Government and Legislation. McKenna had led the Liberals to lopsided victories in three straight elections.

After his first win—Oct. 13, 1987, when the Liberals swept all 58 legislative seats—he had expressed the belief that no premier should serve longer than ten years. "I'm here now to keep my promise to the people of New Brunswick," he told the Fredericton news conference where he announced his resignation as premier and Liberal member of the Legislative Assembly (MLA) for Miramichi–Bay du Vin. One week later, Ray Frenette was sworn in to replace McKenna on an interim basis.

The leadership of the Conservatives, the official opposition party, also changed hands in 1997. On October 18, at a convention in Fredericton, Moncton lawyer Bernard Lord beat out three other contenders for the job, which had been relinquished earlier in the year by Edmunston MLA Bernard Valcourt.

Under a revised Education Act, elected school boards would be replaced by a system of advisory groups. The House also passed a Clean Air Act providing stiffer penalties for polluters, and a bill to establish a blended federal-provincial sales tax.

Other News. Recurring problems at the Point Lepreau nuclear-power plant yielded up a victim February 5, when Energy Minister Albert Doucet was forced to resign. He later was suspended from the Liberal caucus for publicly refuting government statements that he had quit the position for health reasons.

Despite burgeoning growth in the advanced-technology sector, and a fiscal climate that enabled the provincial government to post a C$125 million budgetary surplus in 1996–97, New Brunswick's population of about 760,000 remained virtually stagnant.

JOHN BEST, *"Canada World News"*

NEWFOUNDLAND. The 500th anniversary of John Cabot's landfall was celebrated in Newfoundland during 1997. On June 24 a replica of Cabot's ship, the *Matthew* (*see* photo, page 93), sailed into Bonavista harbor to be welcomed by Great Britain's Queen Elizabeth II and Prince Philip, honored guests, and hundreds of thousands of cheering visitors. The queen later visited St. John's, Labrador, and Ottawa.

Quincentennial Celebrations. The *Matthew* had been reconstructed in Poole, England, and its voyage across the Atlantic could be watched via direct-satellite feed on television and the World Wide Web. The exact location of Cabot's landfall is uncertain, but, by mere assertion, Newfoundland seemed to win the challenge over

CANADIAN PROVINCES AND TERRITORIES • Information Highlights

Province	Population (in millions)	Area (sq mi)	Area (km²)	Capital	Head of State and Government
Alberta	2.8	255,286	661 190	Edmonton	H.A. Olson, lieutenant governor Ralph Klein, premier
British Columbia	3.9	365,946	947 800	Victoria	Garde Gardom, lieutenant governor Glen Clark, premier
Manitoba	1.1	250,946	649 950	Winnipeg	Yvon Dumont, lieutenant governor Gary Filmon, premier
New Brunswick	.76	28,355	73 440	Fredericton	Marilyn Trenholme Counsell, lieutenant governor Ray Frenette, interim premier
Newfoundland	.57	156,649	405 720	St. John's	Arthur Maxwell House, lieutenant governor Brian Tobin, premier
Northwest Territories	.07	1,304,903	3 379 700	Yellowknife	Don Morin, government leader
Nova Scotia	.95	21,425	55 491	Halifax	J. James Kinley, lieutenant governor Russell MacLellan, premier
Ontario	11.3	412,580	1 068 580	Toronto	Hilary M. Weston, lieutenant governor Mike Harris, premier
Prince Edward Island	.14	2,185	5 660	Charlottetown	Gilbert R. Clements, lieutenant governor Pat Binns, premier
Quebec	7.4	594,857	1 540 680	Quebec City	Lise Thibault, lieutenant governor Lucien Bouchard, premier
Saskatchewan	1.0	251,865	652 330	Regina	John N. Wiebe, lieutenant governor Roy Romanow, premier
Yukon	.03	186,660	483 450	Whitehorse	Piers McDonald, government leader

Labrador, Cape Breton, and Maine. In the 46 days following the rebuilt *Matthew*'s arrival, the ship sailed around the island and was greeted at every port by historical pageants, music, and crowds.

Other aspects of the celebrations included conferences on all manner of subjects, as well as an international "Summit of the Sea" on the world's fisheries and oceans.

Natural Resources and the Economy. The Hibernia oil platform was towed successfully from its construction site to its final offshore location on the Grand Bank. At Voisey's Bay, the giant nickel mine in Labrador, difficulties over environmental issues and native land claims seemed closer to settlement by the close of 1997.

Whatever the promises in the future from natural resources, in the meantime the province was having to deal with declining transfers from Ottawa and a continued high unemployment rate. The budget brought down in March forecast a deficit of C$29.2 million. While this was the lowest deficit since 1965–66, it still meant a 20% cut in municipal transfers and a reduction in public service of some 1,100 jobs over the next three years.

Government and Politics. Premier Brian Tobin announced in November that an agreement had been reached between the federal and provincial governments and the Labrador Inuit Association. Still left to be settled was an agreement with the Innu (Indian) Nation.

Educational reform—an issue many thought had been settled by a provincial referendum in 1995—reawoke in 1997. The Roman Catholic and Pentecostal churches challenged the interpretation of the constitutional amendment in court and won an injunction that seemed to return the whole process to the earlier status quo. To break the impasse, Tobin announced in August that a second referendum would be held on September 5. This time the question was whether to end completely the churches' role in any aspect of educational administration, leaving religious instruction in place with a curriculum designed by the provincial Department of Education. The proposed amendment was approved by 73% of those voting. Once again the province would be asking the Canadian Parliament to amend the constitution; school reform would be delayed until September 1999.

SUSAN McCORQUODALE, *Memorial University*

NORTHWEST TERRITORIES. During 1997 preparations continued for the division of the eastern and western portions of the Northwest Territories (NWT) into two new territories on April 1, 1999, and for the opening of Canada's first diamond mine in 1998.

Nunavut. A controversial proposal for gender parity in the new legislative assembly of Nunavut, as the new eastern territory was to be called, was rejected by voters in the Eastern Arctic in May. The controversial proposal called for an equal number of men and women to be seated in the legislative assembly. Supporters of the idea claimed that an equal-gender legislature was more in keeping with traditional Inuit culture.

Budget and Elections. Finance Minister John Todd, in his January 29 budget address, proposed spending cuts of some C$100 million for the 1997–98 budget. This followed C$80 million in spending reductions in the 1996–97 budget. If budgetary targets for 1997–98 were met, the NWT could wind up with a C$ 8.9 million surplus, to be applied toward the territories' accumulated debt, which stood at about C$65 million by late 1996.

NWT voters chose two women to represent the territories in the federal government. Winning a third term as the Western Arctic's member of Parliament (MP) was Ethel Blondin-Andrew, while Nancy Karetak-Lindell overwhelmingly won as MP representing Nunavut. In Yellowknife mayoral elections in October, incumbent Dave Lovell defeated Matthew Grogono by six votes.

Mining. In January, former Canadian Prime Minister John Turner dropped a legal challenge to block the proposed C$750 million BHP diamond mine. The action—brought by Turner on behalf of World Wildlife Fund Canada, of which he is a director—was meant to ensure better protection of the central Arctic wilderness. Turner announced that he was ending the legal action because of the positive steps the federal and territorial governments had made toward designating wilderness areas to be protected from future mining and industrial development.

Late in the year, territorial officials were mounting a lobbying campaign to locate a diamond-sorting plant in the Northwest Territories. The lobbyists held that the facility not only would bring jobs to the territories, but also would build confidence in the North as a place of investment. While the federal government indicated its support, the final decision rested with BHP.

PATRICIA BEHAN

NOVA SCOTIA. During 1997, Nova Scotians got a new premier, followed several high-profile court cases, and enjoyed a brisk economy.

Legislation and Government. In March, Premier John Savage—by announcing his decision to quit public life—opened a leadership race in the Liberal Party. The party's involvement in this race was so intense that Savage's last legislative session was the shortest of his four-year rule. Fourteen bills were enacted, however. These included a law pertaining to the distribution of natural gas; an amendment to the Motor Vehicle Act, providing stiffer penalties for violations; and changes in the Residential Tenancy Act, to streamline procedures for settling landlord-tenant disputes. During the session, the provincial government—for the first time in 25 years—brought a C$8.3 million surplus budget.

In July, Russell MacLellan won the leadership of the Liberal Party and became the 24th premier of Nova Scotia. He improved the party's image by distancing himself from the policies of the Savage government. He announced his determination to alter the Savage government's blended sales-tax deal with the federal government; provided relief from highway tolls; and negated the previous government's decision to open 42,000 acres (17 000 hectares) of Cape Breton's bog for mineral exploration. Such measures improved the Liberals' chances of holding onto power in the spring 1998 election. They won two of the four by-elections held on November 4.

Court Cases. On the legal front, Nova Scotians were focused on some high-profile court cases. In a mercy-killing case, Halifax respiralogist Dr. Nancy Morrison was charged with murdering a terminally ill patient. In another case, former Premier Gerald Regan was charged in 18 sex-related complaints involving 13 women from 1956–78. Nova Scotians were shocked when Martin Smith sued the provincial government, alleging that residents at the government-run Shelburne School for Boys had been abused physically and sexually by counselors in the 1960s and 1970s. The fact that officials, despite their knowledge of such abuse, had failed to take any action embarrassed the government.

Energy. Nova Scotians were thrilled when a federal-provincial review board approved a Mobil Oil–headed C$3 billion production and pipeline project to extract Sable Island natural gas. The project was expected to produce 13 million cu ft (368,119 m³) of gas per day and would create 4,500 jobs during its construction phase.

Economy. The provincial economy was humming along in 1997, recording its strongest performance in more than eight years. Since September 1996, employment had grown by 9,500, and the unemployment rate in some areas had fallen by 10% over the previous eight months. Although manufacturing shipments and exports

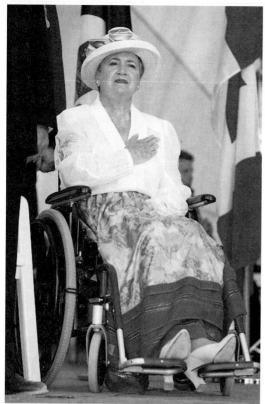

© P. Roussel/Publiphoto

Lise Thibault, above, was sworn in early in 1998 as Quebec's first woman lieutenant governor. Thibault, 57, was admired for her work on behalf of the province's disabled population.

were off the pace set in 1996, retail sales of durable goods were up 5% late in the year over the first half of 1997. Activity in the forest sector remained buoyant, and Nova Scotia's paper mills announced capital-expansion plans.

R. P. SETH, *Professor Emeritus*
Mount Saint Vincent University, Halifax

ONTARIO. Despite growing opposition, Premier Mike Harris' Conservative government forged ahead in 1997 with a drastic restructuring of Ontario's public sector.

Education and Social-Welfare Reform. In January the province decided to assume the cost of primary and secondary education, in return shifting about C$5.3 billion of social and health services to the municipalities, which now would be responsible for welfare, public health, and public housing, all of which had been funded by the province. Due to opposition from the Association of Ontario Municipalities, the scheme was modified: The province would pay 80% of welfare costs and allow municipalities to keep 50% of education property taxes, which now would be set by the province, not the school boards.

In June the welfare system was overhauled. New measures were introduced to combat fraud; to extend "work for welfare," already in place in 23 cities, to include single parents of school-age children; to enable direct government payments to utilities and landlords; and to establish new definitions of disability.

To save money, most school boards were amalgamated into larger ones and many hospitals were scheduled to be closed. The seven boroughs in the metropolitan Toronto area were amalgamated into a "super-city"; the government ignored the opposition of local politicians, as well as a referendum in which 70% of voters were opposed to the plan. Mel Lastman was elected mayor of the new city of Toronto, now the sixth-largest government in Canada.

The hospital closings became a national unity issue when the commission proposed closing the province's only French-language teaching hospital.

Strikes and Energy Issue. Fearing serious economic consequences, Ontario's cabinet surprisingly modified a bill to prevent public-services workers and teachers from striking while new contracts were being negotiated with the newly amalgamated regulatory bodies, after public-sector unions threatened to strike.

Public-school teachers struck illegally in October—leaving 2.1 million students without classes for two weeks—over legislation giving the government power to set class size, determine teacher-preparation time, and lengthen the school year. The government refused to back down, claiming its aim was to improve the quality of education; the teachers, however, saw the bill as a device to cut funding and eliminate jobs.

Ontario Hydro was embarrassed by having to shut down nine of its nuclear reactors during the year. The company was to lose its monopoly and would be split into three separate utilities.

PETER J. KING, *Carleton University*

PRINCE EDWARD ISLAND. Prince Edward Island's (PEI's) long-anticipated fixed link to the Canadian mainland became a reality on May 31, 1997, when traffic began to flow across the brand-new Confederation Bridge between PEI and New Brunswick. The 8-mi (13-km), two-lane structure replaced a ferry service that had operated for more than a century. The bridge was built by a Calgary-based consortium at an estimated cost of close to C$1 billion. The federal government will buy it from the consortium over a 35-year period.

Meanwhile, PEI's only other ferry service to the mainland was expanding. On February 25, Northumberland Ferries, which operates between PEI and Nova Scotia, announced a C$3 million project to upgrade its loading facilities. A new and larger ferry was to enter service in 1998.

Other News. A task force that had spent 16 months studying how best to protect PEI's land resources released its report September 3. Among other things, the 162-page report called for mandatory crop rotation, a watchdog review board on farming practices, and a ban on livestock access to waterways. Premier Binns promised action on at least some of the recommendations made by the task force.

Reacting swiftly to a ruling of the Supreme Court of Canada, the Binns government announced September 19 that it would establish an independent commission to set provincial judges' salaries. The high-court ruling said that a 1994 rollback of judges' salaries by the province was unconstitutional.

Under the Conservative government's first budget, presented April 8, big business and high-income earners were hit by tax increases, while social-assistance recipients were treated to a little extra help.

JOHN BEST

QUEBEC. It took just 24 hours for the independence-minded Parti Québécois (PQ) government to reject a national-unity framework put together by nine of Canada's provincial premiers in fall 1997. The product of a closed-door, 11-hour meeting of provincial leaders in Calgary September 14, the framework established a set of principles to guide negotiations on unity. The key provision called for recognition of French-speaking Quebec's "unique character," while affirming the equality of all ten provinces. The package quickly was endorsed by Canadian Prime Minister Jean Chrétien. Just as quickly, on September 15 it was denounced by Quebec Intergovernmental Affairs Minister Jacques Brassard as an "empty shell."

Meanwhile, a 1997 decision by the Supreme Court of Canada could cause problems for the PQ as it prepared to stage another independence referendum, should it win reelection. In a unanimous ruling October 9, the court struck down sections of the Quebec referendum law that limit campaign spending by parties other than the official "Yes" side and the official "No" side, finding them to infringe freedom of expression. The Bouchard government denounced the ruling as "an attack on democracy," and vowed to seek ways to override it.

Job-Training Measure and Election Results. For one day in Quebec City in early spring, the struggle between Quebec's separatist government and the federal government in Ottawa seemed all but forgotten. It happened April 3, when Premier Bouchard and Prime Minister Chrétien put their signatures to an agreement giving Quebec control over job training, together with the money necessary to finance it. Despite the aura of goodwill, Bouchard could not resist suggesting that the approach of a federal election had something to do with Ottawa's willingness to conclude the deal. "We have to recognize the role played by Quebec voters in this affair," he stated.

In the ensuing national election on June 2, Chrétien's Liberals won 26 of Quebec's 75 House of Commons seats, up from 19 in 1993. Bouchard's federal allies, the Bloc Québécois, dropped from 54 seats to 44, while the Conservatives took five seats.

De Gaulle Statue. The unveiling of a statue of Charles de Gaulle demonstrated that the late French president still had the capacity to inflame passions. The crowd of about 2,000 that gathered for the July 23 ceremony in Quebec City was divided evenly between separatists and Canadian federalists. The two groups squared off in a battle of flags—the maple leaf and Quebec's fleur-de-lys—and staged shouting matches and heated debates. The C$150,000 bronze statue, paid for by the PQ government, commemorated de Gaulle's visit to Quebec City on July 23, 1967. The next day, in Montreal, de Gaulle had uttered his unforgettable "Vive le Québec libre" cry.

Population Drop. Statistics Canada reported that Quebec's share of the Canadian population had dropped to 24.7%. It was the first time since Canada was born in 1867 that Quebec's share had fallen below one quarter.

Bus Accident. On October 13 a tour bus loaded with senior citizens on a Thanksgiving outing plunged down an embankment in the Charlevoix region 65 mi (105 km) northeast of Quebec City, after failing to negotiate a curve in the road. Forty-four persons lost their lives in the worst traffic accident in Canadian history.

JOHN BEST

SASKATCHEWAN. Saskatchewan residents, who had been carrying one of Canada's highest tax burdens under a New Democratic Party government determined to get its fiscal affairs in order, were rewarded in 1997 with a cut in the provincial sales tax (PST).

Budget and Finances. Finance Minister Janice MacKinnon announced the PST reduction, which would cost the treasury an estimated C$180 million, in her budget of March 20. The two-percentage-point decrease brought the tax to 7%—the lowest rate in any province except Alberta, which does not have a PST.

MacKinnon's fourth straight balanced budget forecast total revenues of C$5.073 billion and a slight surplus of C$24 million for 1997–98. She projected continued balanced budgets at least until 2000–01. Former Health Minister Eric Cline replaced MacKinnon as finance minister in a June cabinet shuffle; he was expected to continue her policies.

The government's Public Accounts, released in early September, showed that the province had a higher-than-expected budget surplus for 1996–97 of almost C$407 mil-

lion, helped by a booming resource sector. The surplus helped pay down Saskatchewan's accumulated debt by C$1.3 billion, reducing it to C$12.4 billion as of March 31.

Public Utilities. After an extensive review of the publicly owned major utilities, the government decided in June that it would not privatize its telephone, electrical, natural-gas, and auto-insurance companies. Instead, it created new, independent boards of directors to oversee operations of the Crown corporations and made the Crown Investments Corporation minister accountable for them. Consultations had revealed that while taxpayers wanted to retain ownership of Crown corporations, they wanted better public accountability from the companies.

Judicial News. The major news from the justice system in 1997 was the Saskatchewan government's apology and offer of compensation to David Milgaard, 43, who was convicted wrongly of murdering Saskatoon nursing assistant Gail Miller in 1969 and had spent 23 years in prison. Milgaard, who was released in 1993 on a Supreme Court order, was exonerated in July, based on DNA evidence. Justice Minister John Nilson appointed retired Judge Alan Gold to mediate a settlement with Milgaard and gave the wronged man C$250,000 as an interim payment on a final package worth millions.

SARATH PEIRIS
"The Star-Phoenix,"Saskatoon

YUKON. The year 1997 was one of slow progress in the territory's economy and in devolution talks as the New Democratic Party (NDP) completed 14 months in power.

Political News. New Democrat Robert Bruce finally regained his seat in the legislature after winning a by-election in April. Bruce originally had won the seat in a draw, following the September 1996 general elections. But the Yukon Party had challenged the vote, and the territorial Supreme Court had overturned the election results. Following his April victory, Bruce was named legislature speaker. In May, however, he revealed that he was an alcoholic, and sought treatment later in the year.

In other government news, first-term legislature member Patricia Duncan was chosen to lead the Liberal Party. She succeeded Ken Taylor, who had served for two and one-half years, but had lost his seat in the 1996 election.

Budget and Economy. The NDP government announced in November that the budget deficit was expected to reach C$22.6 million during the 1998 fiscal year, about C$12.7 million higher than originally expected. Total government spending was expected to exceed C$476 million. Finance Minister Piers McDonald said the accumulated surplus could drop to C$19 million.

Yukon's economy stayed in the doldrums throughout 1997. At the beginning of the year, the unemployment rate was at 14.7%; it climbed to a high of 15.7% in March. By November unemployment was down to 11.3%, but was still almost 3% higher than the national average. Spurred on by demands of the opposition Yukon Party to spend on capital projects and establish a winter-works program, the government passed the Oil and Gas Act and unveiled an export-development strategy. It also established a Community Development Fund.

Government. In February the federal government announced that it would transfer authority for natural resources to the territory by April 1998. The transfer to the Yukon government would place the territory, in effect, in the position of having fully responsible government, similar to that of the ten provinces.

Devolution negotiations between Ottawa, the territorial government, and Yukon's First Nations people continued slowly through the year. Two land-claim and self-government agreements were signed, and several other agreements neared completion.

PATRICIA BEHAN

The Arts

Two Canadian cultural icons said good-bye in 1997. After nearly 25 years of presenting Canada to itself, Peter Gzowski—considered a living national treasure—gave his last radio show on May 30. Gzowski's *Morningside* had debuted in 1982; his earlier show, *This Country in the Morning*, began in the early 1970s. Also in 1997, Karen Kain, Canada's prima ballerina, embarked on a farewell tour. Meanwhile, as government funding dwindled and corporate money became increasingly important, many members of the Canadian arts community expressed dismay over a federal-government plan to outlaw tobacco-company sponsorship.

Television. Ken Finkleman's half-hour comedy *The Newsroom*, which premiered in October 1996 on the Canadian Broadcasting Corporation (CBC), was considered widely to be the sharpest—and blackest—satirical show ever seen on Canadian television. In contrast, the nostalgic pull of Atlantic Canada (for many Canadians the area is like that country's Old South) meant that the maritime provinces continued to be the setting of many of the CBC's shows, including the dramatic series *Black Harbour*, which is filmed in Nova Scotia. *Gullage's*, a new half-hour comedy, featured a hapless taxi driver in St. John's, Nfld., and *Emily of the Moon*, the latest series drawn from Lucy Maud Montgomery's books, was set near Summerside, P.E.I.

U.S. broadcast-network shows continued to dominate the Canadian ratings. Nevertheless, the proliferation of new cable programming allowed Canadians to see a greater variety of Canadian-made television than ever before. Series such as *The Passionate Eye* on Newsworld, *Discovery @ Canada* on Discovery, and Vision's remarkable and harrowing three-part documentary on Rwanda, *Chronicle of a Genocide Foretold*, all testified to the growth in homegrown Canadian television.

Visual Art. During 1997, Vancouver photo-conceptual artist Jeff Wall continued his remarkable climb to the heights of the art world. After a show at the Jeu de Paume in Paris and representation at the Whitney Biennial, he prepared an exhibition of his large backlit cibachrome photographs to be shown at the Museum of Contemporary Art in Los Angeles. Wall is part of a small group of conceptual artists in Vancouver that has gained international acclaim; a younger member of this group of artists, Rodney Graham, was chosen in 1997 to represent Canada at the Venice Biennale.

In group shows, regionalism reigned. The Vancouver Art Gallery's "Topographies: Aspects of Recent BC Art" spoke to British Columbians' growing interest in their local history and environment. The work of three curators, it contained more than 100 works by 40 artists. In Ontario the Art Gallery of Hamilton, the Art Gallery of Windsor, and the London Regional Art Gallery together mounted a show called "1996," which was meant to provide "a critical snapshot of the end of millennium mood" in Canada's most-populated province. In addition, "Renoir's Portraits: Impressions of an Age" drew large summer crowds to Ottawa's National Gallery.

Music. In the field of popular music, Canadian women continued to achieve extraordinary success. In 1997, Alanis Morissette's place in the sun was shared with Sarah McLachlan, considered to be Canada's preeminent singer-songwriter. In the summer, McLachlan created "Lilith Fair," a critically acclaimed traveling women's musical show that went across both the United States and Canada and outsold male-dominated shows such as "Lollapalooza."

Terri Clark, fellow Albertan Paul Brandt, and Shania Twain were three of the most notable members of what in 1997 began to be seen as a Canadian invasion of Nashville. And in the jazz field, Diana Krall, a singer from Nanaimo, BC, won a nomination for best jazz vocalist at the Grammy Awards in February. Her third album, *All for You*, met with critical and popular success, and Krall had been voted third in *Down Beat* magazine's late 1996 Reader's Poll.

Film. The number of films made in Canada continued to increase. Even though Vancouver and Toronto now are important centers of film and television production, the domestic film industry remained plagued by problems with funding and distribution.

Canadian movies could be seen, however, at the Toronto International Film Festival, which has become one of the world's major venues for new films. The 1997 Canadian highlight was Atom Egoyan's movie *The Sweet Hereafter*, which took three awards at the Cannes Film Festival. Because of its emotional impact, *The Sweet Hereafter* was considered widely to be a breakthrough film for Egoyan, whose work has been criticized for its chilliness. *Le polygraphe*, Robert Lepage's second film after his brilliant *Le confessional*, opened to very mixed reviews. As with Lepage's acclaimed theater work, *Le polygraphe* explored artistic deception and the distortions of memory.

duction—one that featured nude angels and an eerie, ghost-story atmosphere.

High Life, a dark comedy about four would-be bank robbers written by Lee MacDougal and directed by Jim Miller, stole the show when it premiered in 1996 at Toronto's du Maurier World Stage Festival. The play went on to New York, then returned to Canada late in 1997. It featured an especially brilliant performance by Brent Carver as a thief with a talent for teasing bills out of bank machines.

The Shaw Festival, under longtime artistic director Christopher Newton, successfully continued to combine middle-of-the-road British entertainments with productions of great plays such as 1997's *The Seagull*, in which the role of Arkadina was played exquisitely by Fiona Reid. The year's English entertainments included Martin Vale's 1935 murder mystery *The Two Mrs. Carrolls* and a reprise of 1996's crowd pleaser *Hobson's Choice*.

As always, the Stratford Festival put on a musical—*Camelot*, directed by Richard Monette in a production exceptional for its energy. Cynthia Dale, best known to Canadians for her role in the CBC drama series *Street Legal*, stood out as a convincing and lively Guenevere. In *The Taming of the Shrew*, directed by Richard Rose, Lucy Peacock took firm hold of the role of Katherina, Petruchio's wife, and gave a blistering performance. Marisha Chamberlain's sensitive adaptation of *Little Women* was directed wonderfully by Marti Maraden. The play preserved the 19th-century bloom of Louisa May Alcott's story. Finally, audiences got to see an anthropologically correct production of *Oedipus Rex*, complete with a comic playlet as its prequel. The actors, wearing enormous platform shoes and huge, deeply carved masks, came across as both stately and emotionally imposing.

Toronto's Canadian Stage Company presented David Young's new play about Antarctic exploration, *Inexpressible Island*.

Dance. *The Trilogy of Sable/Sand* was perhaps 1997's outstanding dance event. A work from Toronto-based Dancemakers, created by Serge Bennathan, it featured haunting Arabic music and nine dancers under a scouring sun. In February, James Kudelka's Mozart-inspired *Musings* was performed by the Paris Opera Ballet. And in April the Firehall Arts Centre in Vancouver presented *The Blind Musician*, a composite of film, abstract text, and spoken movement.

See also LITERATURE—*Canadian*.

BRUCE SERAFIN
Founding Editor, "The Vancouver Review"

© Jat Blakesberg/Retna

Sarah McLachlan created "Lilith Fair," a successful show featuring a rotating lineup of 61 women singer-songwriters that traveled to some 30 U.S. and Canadian cities during the summer.

Two low-budget comedies found audiences. *Kitchen Party*, a raucously entertaining film by Calgary writer-director Gary Burns, was received well both at the Toronto Festival and at the Vancouver Film Festival. And *The Planet of Junior Brown*, directed by Clement Virgo, promised to become a small classic. It told the story of a fat, gentle, black teenager— an aspiring pianist—who has to play in silence because his controlling mother has cut the strings of his piano in a fit of anger.

Opera and Theater. Building on previous work by directors Robert Lepage and Atom Egoyan, Canadian opera in 1997 placed a strong emphasis on theater and, in so doing, experienced something of a renaissance. Signaling the new emphasis, Canadian Opera Company's (COC's) *Béatrice et Bénédict*, directed by Robin Phillips, dazzled audiences not just with its excellent singing but with its fluid, audacious acting. The COC commissioned film director François Girard (*Thirty-Two Short Films about Glenn Gould*) to direct two works by Igor Stravinsky—*Symphony of Psalms* and *Oedipus Rex*. And in February acclaimed theater director Morris Panych put on Carlisle Floyd's contemporary opera *Susannah* in a daring Vancouver Opera pro-

CARIBBEAN

The Caribbean region continued to show relatively minor economic growth in 1997. All but three of the island nations—Cuba, Haiti, and Suriname—made small advances in total gross domestic product (GDP), and only five countries failed to show some growth in per-capita income.

Tourism prospered as the area came through the year without major hurricane damage. With a few scattered exceptions—drought in the Dominican Republic, volcanic eruptions in Montserrat (*see* SIDEBAR, page 179)—the year was similarly positive for agriculture. Caribbean banana growers, however, were dismayed by a ruling from the World Trade Organization (WTO) that the European licensing system for banana imports discriminated against Latin American and U.S. producers of the fruit. Some 65% of Europe's bananas come from Latin America, while only 8% are imported from the Caribbean.

Caricom Summit. The Caribbean Community and Common Market (Caricom) held its 18th annual summit meeting in Montego Bay, Jamaica, in early July. At that meeting, the members recommitted themselves to establishing a Caribbean common market by the year 1999 and to a single Caricom currency at some time in the future. In addition, Haiti was admitted conditionally as the organization's 15th member.

Haiti. The glaring exclusion to the mildly favorable Caribbean outlook was Haiti. In 1997 the United Nations Conference on Trade and Development (UNCTAD) downgraded Haiti's development rating from "less-developed country" (LDC) to "economy in regression." UNCTAD explained that per-capita income fell by 45% in Haiti between 1980 and 1994, while in the LDCs as a whole, it increased by 4%. Investment fell by 46% in the first five years of the 1990s. On a more positive note for Haiti, the country's conditional acceptance as the 15th member of Caricom gave it a chance to participate in the single Caribbean market being created by Caricom members.

Haiti's Prime Minister Rosny Smarth resigned on June 9, citing chaos in the National Assembly and its failure to hold elections as scheduled. After a successor was named but rejected by the legislature, Smarth agreed to stay on until the post was filled, but he quit again on October 20. At year's end, Haiti had no prime minister.

Meanwhile, the United Nations (UN) contingent of 150 police and 50 soldiers left Haiti late in the year, but 300 civilian police and 500 U.S. troops remained.

Tragedy struck on September 8 when a ferryboat capsized with 250 persons aboard. Some 148 bodies were recovered from the wreck, and officials said at least 172 had drowned.

Dominican Republic. A severe drought afflicted the Dominican Republic for much of the year, creating power outages because of lowered reservoir levels and causing a food crisis. The price of bananas quadrupled, and the country had to import sugar, beans, rice, cooking oil, and other items it formerly exported. The government subsidized the import of an additional 500,000 lbs (226 800 kg) of chickens for consumption by the poor. When heavy rains finally came in October, electric grids were disrupted by downed power lines.

Status Questions. The issue of political status weighed heavily for the island of Nevis. Nevis, the smaller of the two islands in the St. Kitts-Nevis federation, opted to seek independence when its five-man legislature voted unanimously in October to end its federation with St. Kitts. The vote called for a referendum in which the 9,000 people of the island can ratify or reject the move. If they accept it, Nevis, with only 36 sq mi (93 km²), would be one of the world's smallest nations.

Nevis reportedly had about 8,000 offshore businesses registered there. They operate under strict secrecy laws, and more than half have been opened in the past three years. Critics say the secrecy laws aid drug traffickers and other criminal enterprises.

The U.S. Congress considered a bill requiring that a plebiscite be held to determine Puerto Rico's preferred status—statehood, independence, or the current status of commonwealth. The debate over status is a perennial feature of Puerto Rican politics. The last status referendum was held in 1993 and the commonwealth plan won a slim plurality. In the face of Republican opposition, Congress deferred action on the issue until 1998.

Deaths. Michael Manley, the former prime minister of Jamaica, died on March 6 in Kingston. He was 72 years old. Manley was the son of Jamaican national hero Norman Manley. He became prime minister of Jamaica in 1972, lost to Edward Seaga in 1980, and was returned to office in 1989, serving until his retirement in 1992. Sir Eric Gairy, who was Grenada's prime minister from 1967 to 1979, died on August 23 at the age of 75.

RICHARD C. SCHROEDER
Freelance Writer

Montserrat

The tiny—39-sq-mi (101-km²)—British colony of Montserrat, 350 mi (563 km) southeast of Puerto Rico, was once a lush, green paradise known as "The Emerald Isle." In 1995, when the long-dormant Soufrière Hills volcano on the southern part of the island awoke from 400 years of slumber, paradise was lost.

With increasing frequency, the volcano spewed rivers of lava, rock, and ash onto villages below. On June 25, 1997, pyroclastic flows of molten rock and lava reaching 950°F (510°C) burst from the volcano's 3,000-ft (915-m) dome and rushed down the slopes at speeds of up to 100 mph (161 km/hr), killing 19 persons, in the largest eruption to date.

By late 1997, showers of rocks and billows of smoke and ash were plunging the sky into darkness about every 12 hours. Some two thirds of the land had been destroyed and Plymouth, the capital, was a ghost town. A new $20 million hospital collapsed before it ever was used and a medical school had closed its doors. Hotels and tourist facilities all were destroyed. The airport was gone, and the only access to Montserrat was by ferry or helicopter. The market, government offices, and hundreds of homes in the island's southern two thirds had been swept away.

More than half the 11,000 inhabitants were gone. The remaining 4,000 were crowded into homes and shelters on the northern third of the island. Some refugees reached England and parts of the United States, including the Virgin Islands and Puerto Rico, but most—an estimated 3,000—found temporary shelter 30 mi (48 km) north, on the island of Antigua. There they represented almost 5% of that island's population of some 100,000; officials said that they were straining Antigua's ability to provide housing, education, medical treatment, jobs, and other social services.

The British offered Montserrat's people free passage anywhere they could go legally, and put them up in Antiguan hotels while they awaited flights. The British also were willing to give evacuees money—the exact amount not yet determined—to help them start over elsewhere. But many resisted leaving the island, fearing they never would be able to return. Some even believed that Britain wanted to evacuate the island completely so it could wash its hands of the devastation. Others demanded a substantial payment from Britain—up to $15,000 for each head of a household—to relocate. But as the volcano kept rumbling and living conditions deteriorated further, it might only be a question of time before everyone was forced to leave the lost paradise of Montserrat.

See also GEOLOGY.

RICHARD SCHROEDER

© Kevin West/Gamma-Liaison

CENTRAL AMERICA

In May 1997, after more than one full term in office, U.S. President Bill Clinton made his first visit to Latin America. With his wife, Hillary Rodham Clinton, and eight cabinet members, he traveled to Mexico, then to San José, Costa Rica, where he met with the heads of state of Belize, Costa Rica, El Salvador, Guatemala, Honduras, Nicaragua, and Barbados. (Panama's absence probably reflected only the uniqueness of its relationship with the United States.) The Central Americans' chief concern seemed to be the changes taking place in U.S. immigration policy.

During the 1980s much of Central America suffered from civil war and bitter political unrest. Encouraged by the Ronald Reagan and George Bush administrations, thousands of Central Americans fled to the United States for asylum. Most of these refugees had legal, but not permanent, status. Now an estimated 300,000 people faced the likelihood of deportation, presenting the possibility of great distress in several of the Central American republics. Their return seriously would upset the labor market and welfare programs, and governments feared that some of the younger men had organized or joined gangs while away and might bring new criminal habits home with them.

Perhaps more important, many of the exiles had found jobs in the United States and habitually sent portions of their earnings back to relatives in Central America. The loss of these funds could prove disastrous to many families as well as to their governments. President Clinton could promise only that there would be no mass deportations and that he would raise the issue with Congress on his return to Washington. In October the U.S. House of Representatives reopened the deportation process and seemed amenable to changing some of the harsher provisions, but no new legislation was enacted at that time.

Also raised at the San José conference was the question of trade. Generally, Central American leaders sought greater access to U.S. markets, even talking of measures similar to those enjoyed by Mexico under the North American Free Trade Agreement (NAFTA). But membership in that association seemed no closer for Central Americans than in 1996. In September leaders of the seven republics of Central America and the Dominican Republic met at Managua, Nicaragua, and discussed the latest of the notions of political union—a plan under which each nation would retain its sovereignty but that would bring about closer economic, cultural, and environmental ties. Little had come from similar schemes in the past. More practical was the decision of the Inter-American Development Bank in March to study means of financing the modernization of the Pan-American Highway throughout Central America.

Belize. In March, President Clinton had listed Belize as one of the nations he could not "certify" as doing its share in the war on drugs. Specific charges were that prison terms were too short and bail often was set too low for drug traffickers in Belize. The action greatly distressed the government of Belize, but it took steps to remedy the conditions. In June representatives of the United States, Colombia, and Mexico met in Belmopán, the

Unfavorable weather conditions led to a smaller-than-usual coffee crop in Central and South America in 1997. Consequently the price of coffee hit a 20-year high in May.

CENTRAL AMERICA • Information Highlights

Nation	Population (in Millions)	Area (sq mi)	(km²)	Capital	Head of State and Government
Belize	0.2	8,865	22 960	Belmopán	Sir Colville Young, governor-general Manuel Esquivel, prime minister
Costa Rica	3.5	19,730	51 100	San José	José María Figueres Olsen, president
El Salvador	5.9	8,124	21 040	San Salvador	Armando Calderón Sol, president
Guatemala	11.2	42,042	108 890	Guatemala City	Alvaro Arzú Irigoyen, president
Honduras	5.8	43,278	112 090	Tegucigalpa	Carlos Roberto Reina, president
Nicaragua	4.4	49,998	129 494	Managua	Arnoldo Alemán Lacayo, president
Panama	2.7	30,193	78 200	Panama City	Ernesto Pérez Balladares, president

capital of Belize, to draft measures to aid Belize in policing the many thousands of cays, so easily used as pickup spots in drug delivery.

Belize continued to be a center of both environmental activities and studies of antiquity. In February the UNESCO World Heritage Committee designated the nation's barrier reefs as "places of outstanding universal value." Several international agencies worked closely with the nation and with scientists from many parts of the world to study the rain forests. Near the Mexico-Guatemala border, archaeologists continued to find more cities and tombs dating back some 15 centuries and revealing ever more about the preconquest lives of the natives of Belize. A tomb at Dos Hombres seemed to verify the existence of a considerable amount of ancient commerce between Belize and other areas of what is now Central America. International agencies granted Belize about $10 million in funds to aid the growth of the infrastructure and help combat poverty.

Costa Rica. In mid-1998, Costa Rica would hold elections for the presidency, as well as for the national legislature and 81 municipal governments. Officially, campaigns began in November 1997, but by October the ruling National Republican Party already had nominated its candidate for president, José Miguel Corrales, a lawyer and former congressman. Corrales had little to suggest about reducing the large foreign debt, but in early talks he stressed an anticorruption campaign. The United Christian Socialists nominated Miguel Angel Rodríguez, also a former legislator. Early polls showed voter indecision.

Evaluations of the economy were mixed. Inflation had been reduced significantly, but there was little economic growth. Unemployment had risen slightly, but preliminary figures indicated that exports might make a significant improvement for the year. Coffee prices were good, but urbanization was driving up the cost of land. An international poll rated Costa Rican business the least corrupt in all of Latin America.

During his Central American trip, President Clinton visited Costa Rica's Braulio Carrillo National Park to inspect the rain forest. He used the occasion to call upon the world to reduce the danger of greenhouse gases, and to praise Costa Rica for its efforts to preserve the forests. The high quality of Costa Rica's educational system brought new rewards in 1997. Competing with nations from Israel to Thailand, Costa Rica won out in a bid for a new Intel Corporation plant that was expected to create 3,500 jobs and result in billions of dollars in export revenue. Government and corporate officials all stressed the quality of Costa Rican education—from high school to graduate programs—as the major reason for the choice. In May, Hillary Rodham Clinton and Central American first ladies participated in a seminar sponsored by the Inter-American Bank designed to acquaint women with the opportunities for credit to help start small businesses, especially in the home.

El Salvador. In March, El Salvador held elections for the national legislature as well as municipalities. It was the second national election since the civil war ended in 1992. International agencies heavily monitored the campaign of 1994, but not this time. Both campaign and election were fairly peaceful, although a few participants were shot by unknown parties. In the National Assembly the Farabundo Martí National Liberation Front (FMLN) captured 27 of the 84 seats, an increase of six. The ruling Nationalist Republican Alliance (ARENA) dropped from 39 to 28 seats. Both parties had splinter groups, accounting for many other seats. No party possessed an absolute majority, indicating the increased acceptance of the former rebels, but also posing new problems of governance.

The municipal elections proved even more encouraging for the FMLN, which won 54 mayoralties, compared with only 13 in 1994. ARENA dropped from 210 to 155 mayoralties, and even lost the important city of San Salvador. Great voter dissatisfaction with the conservative ARENA party was obvious,

© Scott Sady/AP/Wide World Photos

U.S. Maj. Herminio Torres (right) was part of the 155-member UN mission that was sent to Guatemala in 1997 to supervise the cease-fire agreed to by the government and rebel forces in 1996.

drawn and 155 UN troops were sent to Guatemala to supervise the cease-fire, presumably for three months.

The declassification of thousands of U.S. Central Intelligence Agency (CIA) documents revealed some unsavory plans of the United States to overthrow the government of Jacobo Arbenz Guzmán in the 1950s, even going so far as to plan the assassination of a number of Guatemalans. The murders apparently did not take place, but the role of the United States in Arbenz' overthrow now was documented fully.

The return of peace encouraged the economy of Guatemala. Tourism in 1997 was up 20%, new roads were being built to tourist centers such as Chichicastenango and Flores, and much of Guatemala City was being renovated. But renewed tourism and busy shops did not remove the dangers of social unrest. The matter of land titles was unresolved; thousands of Mayans returned from Mexico after the war to find their lands occupied by others. Titles were recorded badly. Many landless tried to take over unused land or cut the invaluable rain forest to create new farms. Squatters even were occupying national preserves; a leading supporter of the Petén preserve was murdered. An estimated 2% of the nation's farmers still owned two thirds of the land. The peace treaty provided machinery to settle land disputes, but few persons had tried to utilize the methods.

In August a commission began an investigation into the hundreds of massacres that occurred in Guatemala's 36 years of civil war.

Honduras. Honduras chose a new president in 1997. In a late-November election, Liberal Party candidate Carlos Flores, president of the National Congress, defeated National Party candidate Alba Nora Gunera. Cesar Castellanos of the National Party won the important mayoralty race in Tegucigalpa.

In March the Honduran congress approved a bill to provide stiff penalties for threats or insults "offensive to public authorities"; punishment could be as much as six years in prison if the "offended authority" were the president. The Inter-American Press Association joined with the Honduran press in a clamor for repeal, calling the measure a muzzle on the press. The law probably was triggered in part by a general strike in February.

The economy received an unexpected boost. Supported partly by prolonged drought in much of Central America, the world price of coffee rose some 17% over 1996. As a result, Honduran exports rose 30%, so great an increase that the crop's value might exceed

although only 40% of the 2.6 million eligible voters cast ballots. According to the U.S. Immigration and Naturalization Service, El Salvador ranked second only to Mexico in the number of illegal aliens in the United States, amounting to some 335,000, or 6% of the total. They had fled their homeland beginning in the 1980s, and they faced a change in the attitude of the U.S. public, which now saw the refugees as a burden on the economy and felt that they should be deported. At year's end, legislation still was pending in Washington about this problem.

According to the Catholic Church of El Salvador, right-wing death squads were still active. As many as 40 murders were attributed to these groups, with the church calling the killings vigilante action. Three policemen were arrested for their part in the crimes.

A new United Nations (UN) study ranked El Salvador 36th poorest among developing nations; only Guatemala and Haiti ranked lower in Latin America.

Guatemala. Late in 1996 the government of Guatemala and the leaders of major rebel forces agreed upon peace terms to bring an end to Central America's longest civil war. But the transition from guerrilla warrior to peacetime voter was not proving easy, for most cultural and political differences had not been settled and thousands of persons still were listed as missing. Maintaining the cease-fire proved to be a new challenge. China vetoed a UN Security Council vote to monitor the cease-fire until Guatemala promised not to support a Taiwan bid for UN membership. When Guatemala agreed, the veto was with-that of the banana in unprecedented fashion. Tensions with El Salvador rose again. Honduras claimed that 100 or more trucks, guarded by armed former guerrillas, daily were crossing the border, cutting timber, and hauling it off to tiny Salvadoran farms for firewood. Ominously, these incursions were in the same border region where the war of 1969 broke out.

Large-scale crime became epidemic in 1997. The major city of San Pedro Sula suffered especially from extortions, kidnappings, and youthful gang wars. The chief targets were banks and manufacturers whose owners paid hundreds of thousands of dollars in ransom or protection. In August, protesting against squalid conditions in two prisons, 700 men rioted, set fires, and escaped. Most were captured within a few days, but the episode stimulated greater demand for police reform. Run by the military for many years, the police had little professional standing, and their corruption even prompted suggestions that the archbishop be appointed chief of police.

Perhaps even more sobering was the revelation of health officials that some 300,000 Hondurans were suffering from endemic Chagas' disease, transmitted to humans by blood-sucking bugs. While not always fatal to adults, the disease is especially hard on children. World health organizations were trying to ameliorate the effects, but there is no known cure.

With major help from the Inter-American Bank, the government of Honduras provided food coupons to more than 300,000 mothers and children in 1997. Families, desperate for the dollar a day the children can earn, send them to work on large plantations during harvest season. Mothers receive a $3 a month voucher if their children remain in school.

Nicaragua. Arnoldo Alemán Lacayo was sworn in as president of Nicaragua on Jan. 10, 1997, replacing Violeta Barrios de Chamorro. Alemán had defeated former President Daniel Ortega Saavedra in the election of October 1996. Between the election and the inauguration of Alemán, the Sandinista-dominated National Assembly passed much legislation designed to weaken the new president, but the Supreme Court invalidated most of it. A coalition of conservative parties held a plurality in the new assembly.

As usual, much disorder was caused by land-tenure problems. In the 1970s and 1980s the Sandinistas seized more than 100,000 properties and gave them to party supporters. Among the properties was the 6,500-sq-ft (604-m^2) home occupied by Ortega. Now many former owners were demanding the return of their homes. President Alemán promised to return all property or provide compensation to the previous owners. In September the new government announced that an agreement had been reached with the Sandinistas to provide land titles to thousands of peasants for some 2.5 million acres of land. Implementation of the plan would be an enormous task for the future.

As elsewhere in Central America, drought cut the Nicaraguan coffee crop in 1997, but the shortage of the commodity pushed the price to the highest level in 20 years. The outgoing Chamorro government claimed to have reduced the foreign debt from $12.7 billion to $3.86 billion in six years. New immigration law in the United States could impact heavily upon Nicaragua. As many as one third of the 200,000 or more Nicaraguans living in Florida faced deportation. In May, 40,000 of them filed suit in a Miami federal court to prevent the expulsion; a restraining order postponed the action only briefly.

Panama. President Ernesto Pérez Balladares spent much of 1997 attempting to change the Panamanian constitution to permit his own reelection. Current law requires the president to sit out two terms before running again. A national plebiscite must approve any such change by congress. Panama Canal matters continued to dominate public concern. Each month more former U.S. property was being turned over to Panama, and there was much pressure to find uses for the many buildings and huge land parcels available. By the end of 1997, about one third of the change already had taken place. In addition, Panamanians talked of converting one large fort into a great university and research center; and a Spanish-Mexican consortium acquired the former School of the Americas and planned to remodel it into a five-star hotel. But many citizens complained that conversion was being handled sloppily—that concessions were made and revoked or poorly planned. Many Panamanians also complained that President Pérez Balladares had appointed too many relatives and friends to the board of directors that would run the canal after the United States leaves in 1999. More critical was the danger posed by leftover American ordnance, including land mines.

As for the canal itself, it was breaking records annually; in 1996, 13,700 ships paid $486 million in tolls. A major expansion was under way. The vast majority of employees were now Panamanians.

THOMAS L. KARNES, *Arizona State University*

CHEMISTRY

Chemical developments in 1997 included a major study of the chemistry of a short-lived artificial element and resolution of a controversy over the names of artificial elements.

Artificial Elements. The transuranium element seaborgium—element 106, named after U.S. chemist and Nobel Prize winner Glenn Seaborg—falls in the same group of the chemical periodic table as the more familiar elements molybdenum and tungsten. Hence one normally might expect it to behave chemically like those elements. However, two other transuranium elements—with atomic numbers 104 and 105—have shown differences in chemistry from their common relatives, and scientists have been uncertain about what to expect from 106. The task of finding out has been hampered by the fact that element 106 can be produced only a few atoms at a time, using a particle accelerator. Once created, the fragile atoms exist for only a few seconds before disintegrating.

In 1997 the challenge of deciphering the chemistry of element 106, which first was created in 1974, was met by an international group of scientists working at an accelerator laboratory in Darmstadt, Germany. The team produced seven atoms of element 106, about one per hour, by bombarding a curium target with a stream of neon atoms. They then subjected the newly created atoms to a stream of gas containing reactive substances, such as chlorine and oxygen, and analyzed the products with special instruments. The reaction products showed that seaborgium behaves chemically in a manner similar to molybdenum and tungsten, confirming the general predictive power of the periodic table.

For several years conflicting claims by teams from Germany, Russia, and the United States had held up the official naming of elements 101 through 109. These elements, including seaborgium (106), are created in particle accelerators and typically exist for only brief periods of time. Normally scientists who first produce or discover an element are given the privilege of naming it. However, because these elements have such elusive natures, priority disputes over their true discoverers have been rather common. In September 1997 the International Union of Pure and Applied Chemistry settled on a compromise set of names that appeared to satisfy almost everyone. In order, the names are mendelevium, nobelium, lawrencium, rutherfordium, dubnium, seaborgium, bohrium, hassium, and meitnerium. Most of these names honor scientists, but two—dubnium and hassium—recognize the locations of the accelerators in Russia and Germany where the discoveries were made. This step opened the way for the naming of elements 110, 111, and 112.

Ultrafast Pictures. For decades chemists have utilized technological advances to study chemical reactions and other molecular events at shorter and shorter timescales. Since the late 1980s the ability to create ultrafast laser-light pulses has allowed examination of events as short as a few femtoseconds. (A femtosecond is a billionth of a millionth of a second.) Heretofore, the studies have been somewhat indirect, however, since researchers have had to infer information about the time courses of the molecular phenomena from changes in the spectra of the participating species. In 1997 several groups reported that, by preparing ultrashort pulses of electrons and X rays, they had developed more direct means for studying these events. Employing the phenomena of electron and X-ray diffraction, these groups obtained the equivalent of consecutive flash "snapshots" of the species during the course of various events.

In one example, Ahmed Zewail and his coworkers at the California Institute of Technology in Pasadena reported that they had obtained snapshots of diiodomethane, CH_2I_2, as one of its C-I bonds disassociated. They did this by first using a laser pulse lasting a few femtoseconds to initiate the bond's breakup. This light pulse was followed by a pulse of electrons lasting about 10 picoseconds—a picosecond is a millionth of a millionth of a second—which then gave the diffraction snapshots. By delaying the electron pulse for varying fractions of a second after the initial light pulse, the Caltech workers could observe the loss of the iodine atom from the CH_2I_2 as it took place over a period of about 70 picoseconds. Although faster electron pulses will be needed to get an entirely accurate picture of chemical bond-breaking, the scientists were encouraged that an important step in that direction had been taken.

In a second example, researchers at the University of Chicago and the European Synchrotron Radiation Facility in Grenoble, France, cooperated to obtain snapshots of the release and subsequent recombination of carbon monoxide with the protein myoglobin. In this case the researchers took advantage of the synchrotron facility's ability to provide extremely short, bright X-ray bursts. Such studies promise that more direct information on chemical processes will be forthcoming.

PAUL G. SEYBOLD, *Wright State University*

CHESS

In 1997, in a feat that computer scientists had envisioned for decades, an IBM RS/6000 SP computer named Deep Blue beat the world's leading chess champion, Russia's Garry Kasparov, $3\frac{1}{2}$ to $2\frac{1}{2}$, in a six-game match in New York.

Deep Blue. The Kasparov–Deep Blue match was the first time that a computer had bested a chess champion in a traditional match, and the first time that the 34-year-old Kasparov had lost a multigame match against an individual opponent. C.J. Tan, Deep Blue project manager, said that the match demonstrated "what technology can do for man and how far we can take it."

In their first meeting, in 1996, Kasparov had defeated Deep Blue, 4–2. Following that match, IBM engineers upgraded the computer, enabling it to examine some 200 million positions per second. In addition, new software allowed programmers to make adjustments easily and quickly during the match.

Kasparov appeared to self-destruct in the final game of the 1997 match. Playing black, he opened with the Caro-Kann defense, which forced Deep Blue to sacrifice a knight. But he made a serious error on move seven and resigned after just 19 moves. Nonetheless, Deep Blue's win was controversial, with some chess experts suggesting the match was an unfair contest in which the computer was programmed to beat Kasparov specifically. Lev Alburt, a former U.S. champion, commented: "If they want to prove it was more than a show, let them play anyone but Garry. If it would play against, say, Grandmaster Boris Gulko, who is not even among the top 50, I am willing to bet $10,000 the computer would lose."

The 1997 World Championship. Kasparov became the world chess champion in 1985. He left the World Chess Federation (FIDE) in 1993, however, and started his own chess sanctioning body, the Professional Chess Association. FIDE then awarded its championship to Anatoly Karpov, also of Russia. For the 1997–98 FIDE World Championship Tournament in Lausanne, Switzerland, FIDE seeded both Kasparov and Karpov into the semifinals. Kasparov, however, refused to play, leaving Karpov the only seeded player. Karpov and Viswanathan Anand of India tied 3–3 for the lead, forcing a blitz play-off. Karpov handily won the two tiebreaker games to retain his title and earn the $1.3 million first prize.

Other Tournaments. In late 1997, ten of the world's best women players qualified from the Interzonal at Kishinev, Moldova. The top two, Alisa Galliamova of Russia and Xie Jun of China, were scheduled to play a further match to decide who would challenge Zsuzsa (Susan) Polgar of Hungary, the current women's world champion, in 1998.

Major events sponsored by the U.S. Chess Federation—the nation's official sanctioning body for tournament chess—included the 98th Annual U.S. Open Championship, which was won by Alex Yermolinsky with 10.5 out of a possible 12 points.

Joel Benjamin, who was a consultant for Deep Blue during its match with Kasparov, won the 1997 Interplay U.S. Championship, beating Gregory Kaidanov, $2\frac{1}{2}$ to $\frac{1}{2}$, and Larry Christiansen, $3\frac{1}{2}$ to $2\frac{1}{2}$, in successive matches. Esther Epstein became the new U.S. Women's Champion after scoring seven out of a possible nine points to finish first in the Interplay U.S. Women's Championship. The U.S. Junior Open was won by 19-year-old Shearwood McClelland III, who scored $5\frac{1}{2}$ out of six points to lead the field of more than 100 players.

JENNY TESAR, *Freelance Writer*

Russian chess grandmaster Garry Kasparov (left) was defeated in a rematch with International Business Machines (IBM) Corp.'s Deep Blue in New York City in May 1997. It was the first time that a chess champion had been defeated by a computer in a regular contest.

CHICAGO

Chicago's housing market boomed in 1997, while the Bulls won the National Basketball Association (NBA) title. In April the Vatican named Archbishop Francis George of Portland, OR, to succeed Cardinal Joseph Bernardin, who died in 1996, as archbishop of Chicago. George was installed in a May 7 ceremony at Holy Name Cathedral. Renovation of Orchestra Hall was completed and it became part of Symphony Hall.

Meigs Field. Meigs Field—a 76-acre (31-ha) lakefront airport—was reopened for five years, following an agreement between Chicago Mayor Richard M. Daley and Gov. Jim Edgar (R-IL). The airfield, used mainly by private pilots and politicians, was closed by Daley in 1996 to make way for a $27 million park and nature preserve. After the five years, the park project will proceed.

Economy and Government. A growing housing market added to Chicago's robust economy. Builders started nearly 5,000 housing units, more than double the 1995 starts. Just seven years earlier, only 600 to 700 units were built each year. Realtors said many of the new home owners—as many as one third in some developments—were suburbanites returning to the city.

Much of the new housing was in trendy and upper-income neighborhoods; other parts of the city continued to crumble. Mayor Daley—who had committed $187 million annually since 1989 to upgrade the city's infrastructure—now would spend $333 million per year for three years on the "Neighborhood Alive" project. The money would go toward 124 blocks of street work, 320 new alleys, 80 mi (129 km) of water mains, new park buildings, libraries, and expanded community policing. "The goal is clear," said Daley. "We want to ensure that every neighborhood is one in which people want to live and work and raise a family."

In November, Chicago Police Superintendent Matt Rodriguez stepped down after it was disclosed that he had violated a rarely enforced police-department rule against associating with convicted criminals. The highly regarded Rodriguez—who was credited for introducing community policing and other improvements during more than five years as superintendent—was a friend of former gas-station owner Frank Milito, who once had been convicted of mail fraud and tax evasion.

The Bulls. Chicago's hometown heroes—the Chicago Bulls, featuring Michael Jordan—claimed their fifth NBA title in seven years by

ARCHBISHOP FRANCIS GEORGE

In April 1997 the Vatican surprised many Chicagoans by naming the Most Rev. Francis E. George, the archbishop of Portland, OR, to succeed the popular Cardinal Joseph Bernardin, who died in 1996, as archbishop of Chicago. Following the announcement, the archbishop promised "to preach the faith as Cardinal Bernardin preached it. There may be some difference in style...but there'll be no difference in substance."

Francis E. George was born in Chicago on Jan. 16, 1937, and was ordained there in 1963. A member of the Oblates of Mary Immaculate, he studied at the University of Ottawa, Canada, and Catholic University of America in Washington, DC. He holds doctorates from Tulane University in New Orleans, LA, and the Pontifical Urban University in Rome, Italy.

George taught philosophy at Creighton University in Omaha, NE, and was the Oblates' provincial for the Central United States in St. Paul, MN. He was named Bishop of Yakima, WA, in 1990 and was appointed archbishop of Portland, OR, on April 30, 1996.

In early 1998 he was one of two U.S. bishops to be designated a cardinal by Pope John Paul II.

© Sue Ogrocki/Reuters/Archive Photos

defeating the Utah Jazz, four games to two, in the play-off finals. "I didn't enjoy this journey," Bulls Coach Phil Jackson said of his troubled season. "It was filled with injuries and suspensions. But we had a great ride, didn't we? It was wonderful."

ROBERT ENSTAD
"Chicago Tribune"

CHILE

While much of Chile's 1997 foreign policy dealt with U.S. trade relations, the domestic economy grew and inflation dropped.

Free Trade. Chile has inched closer to free trade with the United States since democratic rule was restored in March 1990. In late February 1997, Chilean President Eduardo Frei Ruíz-Tagle met with U.S. President Bill Clinton to discuss membership in the North American Free Trade Agreement (NAFTA) and other issues. Frei—perhaps cautious because of three years of Chilean congressional foot-dragging—expressed interest but little urgency in pressing Chile's case. Frei said his country had an "attractive alternative" in Mercosur, the Southern Cone common-market arrangement.

In September, Clinton sent to the U.S. Congress his long-awaited proposal for authority to negotiate new trade accords—including a possible expansion of NAFTA—under the so-called "fast-track" provision, which would bar amendments to the initiatives. The administration insisted such authority was crucial to successful trade negotiations. Fast-track legislation faced strong opposition in Congress—especially among Democrats, including House Minority Leader Richard Gephardt. With opposition also from labor unions and environmental groups, fast-track legislation was defeated.

The Canada-Chile free-trade agreement, approved by the Chilean Congress on July 2, abolished duties on 90% of Chilean exports to Canada and 70% of Canadian imports to Chile.

Economy. Gross national product (GNP) grew at a rate of 4.9% for the first half of 1997. Central Bank President Carlos Massad estimated that year-end growth would be close to the official 5.5% target—considerably below the 1996 rate of 7.2%. Finance Minister Eduardo Aninat projected yearly inflation at 5.5%, more than a point less than 1996's 6.6% rate. Industry growth was led by mining (14%) and transport and communication (10%).

Chile's foreign-trade surplus for the first half of the year was $657 million, 41% greater than in 1996. The international reserve position was a strong $17.6 billion.

Despite the favorable economy, Chile's income remained badly skewed. According to the National Statistical Institute, the poorest 10% of the population had an average income of $220 per month, while the wealthiest 10% averaged about $4,500 per month. Planning Minister Roberto Pizarro said that 3.3 million Chileans are classified as poor—22% of the total population of almost 15 million. In June the government announced plans to reduce poverty, targeting the 6.5% of the population affected by "hard-core" poverty.

The Chilean government moved in May to close the Lota coal mine, after 150 years of operation. The mine was nationalized in 1970 and placed under control of the state-owned Empresa Nacional de Carbón. The government said the mine lost $40 million per year and that the $150-per-ton production costs could not compete with high-grade imported coal at $45 per ton.

Politics. In March former President Patricio Aylwin said he had been wrong to support the September 1973 military coup that ousted and killed President Salvador Allende. Aylwin said he had "overestimated" the military's dedication to democracy and human rights. He charged military chief Augusto Pinochet with responsibility for thousands of deaths and disappearances in Chile. Military leaders denounced Aylwin's statement as "an aggression against the armed forces."

In early April, Washington eased the ban on high-tech arms sales to Latin America. The Chilean military's plan to purchase F-16 fighter jets from the United States raised some fears of a regional arms race.

In June the government was unable to muster the 28 votes needed in the Senate to amend the constitution to eliminate the eight so-called *designados*—holders of Senate seats appointed by the military regime. Only one in six adults registered to vote in December congressional elections. Of the 20 Senate seats up for election, the government lost one. The Independent Democratic Union (UDI), a small group of conservative Catholics that had been aligned with Pinochet, did well.

RICHARD C. SCHROEDER, *Freelance Writer*

CHILE • Information Highlights

Official Name: Republic of Chile.
Location: Southwestern coast of South America.
Area: 292,259 sq mi (756 950 km²).
Population (mid-1997 est.): 14,600,000.
Chief Cities (June 30, 1995 est.): Santiago, the capital, 5,076,808; Concepción, 350,268; Viña del Mar, 322,220.
Government: *Head of state and government,* Eduardo Frei Ruíz-Tagle, president (took office March 1994). *Legislature*—National Congress: Senate and Chamber of Deputies.
Monetary Unit: Peso (439.75 pesos equal U.S.$1, official rate, Dec. 30, 1997).
Gross Domestic Product (1995 est. U.S.$): $113,200,-000,000 (purchasing power parity).
Economic Indexes (1996, 1990 = 100): *Consumer Prices,* all items, 205.2; food, 207.5. *Industrial Production,* 148.
Foreign Trade (1996 U.S.$): *Imports,* $17,828,000,000; *exports,* $15,353,000,000.

CHINA

Deng Xiaoping, China's paramount leader for 20 years, died in mid-February 1997. As the country began to sort out what a "post-Deng" era might look like, attention started to turn from effecting a "soft landing" for the overheated economy of the late 1980s and early 1990s and focus instead on how to avoid a period of economic deflation.

Economic growth in 1997, initially projected at 10%, came in just under 9%; the inflation rate, at less than 2%, fell well below the 6% target set early in the year. Foreign direct investment, on the rise for the previous eight years, fell 35% short of 1996's figure.

It was assumed widely that Executive Vice-Premier Zhu Rongji would be named premier, succeeding the unpopular Li Peng, at the National People's Congress (NPC) in March 1998. At year's end, Zhu was turning his attention to reforming China's banking system as a bulwark against the adverse influence of Asia's growing financial problems.

Party General Secretary Jiang Zemin devoted much of his keynote speech at the 15th National Party Congress in September to the problem of transferring ownership of all but a handful of government-owned factories into the hands of their employees. Simultaneously, the party-state was attending to the mounting social and political consequences of the parlous fiscal condition of the state sector. While the official unemployment figure stood at less than 4%, very large numbers of workers in loss-producing government-owned factories had been laid off on reduced wages. In many cases, even the reduced wages had gone unpaid for months on end. A major and immediate task for local and central authorities was to reknot a safety net that was independent of the failing state sector and that could provide the housing, health care, and retirement income that once were received from their employers by all workers in the state sector.

A milestone was passed in the construction of the controversial Three Gorges Dam on the Yangzi River when a barrier was closed on November 8, diverting the river so that construction on the dam itself could proceed. The 600-ft (183-m)-high dam would create a 350-mi (563-km)-long reservoir, displacing more than 1 million people from their homes and workplaces. To facilitate their relocation, much of the area has been incorporated into the municipality of Chongqing, which henceforth—like Beijing, Shanghai, and Tianjin—would be administered as the equivalent of a province and assigned the complicated task of resettlement. The cost of the dam project was estimated at $25 billion. The dam will produce 18,200 megawatts of electric power; it takes 50 million tons of coal to produce the equivalent amount of thermal-generated power.

Politics. The National People's Congress (NPC), meeting in March, enacted a new criminal code that eliminated the crime of "counterrevolution" and "crimes by analogy"—prosecution for crimes that are not on the statute books; moved toward an adversarial system where defense and prosecution both present evidence; and expanded the defendant's right to legal counsel. These positive steps toward establishing a rule of law in a political system notable for its absence were counterbalanced by the unexpected downturn in the fortunes of their champion, NPC President Qiao Shi.

The 15th Party Congress elected a new Central Committee, which, in turn, appointed a Politburo and its Standing Committee. The

Wei Jingsheng (center), China's most prominent dissident, who had spent nearly 18 years in prison for his pro-democracy views, was released and allowed to fly to the United States in November 1997. The 47-year-old former electrician at the Beijing Zoo underwent medical treatment at a Detroit hospital.

seven members of the new Standing Committee were Jiang Zemin, Li Peng, Zhu Rongji, Li Ruihuan, Hu Jintao, Wei Jianxing, and Li Lanqing. The Standing Committee, which meets weekly, "forms the nucleus of the handful of individuals" who set policy for the party-state. Absent from the new inner circle was Qiao Shi, who might have acted as a rival contender for Jiang's position as China's undisputed leader.

The party-state has used the rationale that political stability is the absolute prerequisite for economic growth. Two threats to political stability manifested themselves during the year. One was a series of protests by workers laid off from their jobs in failing state enterprises and deprived of their pay. The largest of these that was reported in the press took place in the inland city of Nanchong in March, when 20,000 workers took to the streets to protest for the nonpayment of six months' back wages. The second was an even more threatening sequence of demonstrations and bombings by Muslim minorities in Yining, Ürümqi, and Beijing itself in February and March.

Foreign Relations. The year was marked by a spate of visits designed to revive and reorient a Sino-U.S. relationship that began the year in decidedly ill health. U.S. Secretary of State Madeleine Albright visited Beijing in February and was followed in March by Vice-President Al Gore and Speaker of the House of Representatives Newt Gingrich. The reestablishment of contact between the Chinese and U.S. military establishments, postponed at the time of the Chinese saber rattling in the Taiwan Strait in March 1996, was effected by an exchange of visits by Chinese Minister of National Defense Chi Haotian (late 1996) and Chairman of the Joint Chiefs of Staff Gen. John Shalikashvili. Chinese Foreign Minister Qian Qichen spent three days in New York and Washington in the spring, and the long-awaited state visit by President Jiang took place in October.

The Chinese side had high hopes that this sequence of high-level meetings would result in U.S. agreement to China's admission to the World Trade Organization. The U.S. side sought major progress by China on human-rights issues, nuclear nonproliferation, and the mounting U.S. deficit in Sino-U.S. trade. Progress was thwarted, however, by an ongoing investigation into allegations that the Chinese government had sought to buy influence by channeling money into the Bill Clinton presidential campaign in 1996.

A second damper on progress in the relationship was what Beijing regarded as a campaign in the United States to vilify China as a potential threat to U.S. security and, indeed, to the Christian faith. Christian conservatives focused their attention on what they described as a Chinese-government campaign of persecution of "underground" Protestants and Catholics who refuse to affiliate with government-sponsored churches. A third obstacle to improved relations was Beijing's grave concern over a U.S.-Japanese military-cooperation agreement signed in April—concern that deepened when a senior Japanese official acknowledged in August that the territory to be defended under the agreement includes Taiwan.

Although Congress was unable to overturn the president's recommendation that China's most-favored-nation status be renewed for another year, the administration announced in August that China's unwillingness to open its markets to foreign penetration precluded its being admitted to the World Trade Organization in the near term.

The Chinese regarded their relationship with Russia to be a bright spot on their foreign-policy horizon. President Jiang visited Moscow in April, and Russian President Boris Yeltsin returned the visit in November. The two reached final agreement on the delineation of the long-contested eastern sector of their common border, agreed to expand trade, and laid plans for a pipeline that would link Siberian natural-gas fields to consumers in coastal Chinese cities.

Regarding Korea, China persuaded Pyongyang to drop its demand for the withdrawal of U.S. troops from Korea as a prerequisite to four-way talks among Pyongyang, Seoul, Washington, and Beijing aimed at a long-overdue peace treaty to end the Korean war.

See also CHINA—A NEW ERA BEGINS; OBITUARIES—*Deng Xiaoping.*

JOHN BRYAN STARR, *Brown University*

CHINA • Information Highlights

Official Name: People's Republic of China.
Location: Central-eastern Asia.
Area: 3,705,809 sq mi (9 598 000 km²).
Population (mid-1997 est.): 1,236,700,000.
Chief Cities (Dec. 31, 1990 est.): Beijing (Peking), the capital, 7,000,000; Shanghai, 7,830,000; Tianjin, 5,770,000.
Government: *Head of state,* Jiang Zemin, president (took office March 1993). *Head of government,* Li Peng, premier (took office Nov. 1987). *Legislature* (unicameral)—National People's Congress.
Monetary Unit: Yuan (8.3100 yuan equal U.S.$1, Dec. 30, 1997).
Gross Domestic Product (1995 est. U.S.$): $3,500,000,-000,000 (purchasing power parity).
Foreign Trade (1996 U.S.$): *Imports,* $138,944,000,000; *exports,* $151,197,000,000.

CITIES AND URBAN AFFAIRS

The demographic and socioeconomic characteristics of U.S. urban areas did not change appreciably in 1997. People of low income—frequently members of minorities—huddled at the core of the city, while more-affluent whites continued to find homes in growing suburban jurisdictions where crime and failing schools are news reports, not daily occurrences. Yet, despite continuing stark disparities and little new assistance from the federal government, the mood in many cities had become more upbeat. A new take-charge atmosphere was epitomized in 1997 by a number of big-city mayors who were eschewing partisanship and ideology in governance and instead were taking steps to make city living more civil. They emphasized cooperation and feasibility, and the 1997 mayoral-election returns seemed to demonstrate the wisdom of their philosophy.

A fortuitous economy—with very low unemployment—a nationwide drop in violent crime, and the greater willingness of those with capital to invest in the inner city contributed without question to the more upbeat mood in many central cities. Whether these underlying circumstances and the new mode of pragmatic governance seriously could alter significant regional disparities remained to be seen. Also in the offing was the end of the longtime welfare system. New time limits and work requirements would affect the many recipients of Aid for Families with Dependent Children (AFDC) who live in central cities, where remunerative unskilled positions have declined precipitously in recent years. Despite these caveats, the notion of cities as ungovernable was no longer as operative, and a mood of guarded optimism best described the urban politics of 1997.

The Positive Municipal Agenda. In decades past, various scholars derided the concept of great men determining history, stressing instead economic and social forces. Certainly, economic trends—especially globalization and deindustrialization—as well as the effects of institutional racism have contributed to an urban landscape of inequity. U.S. central cities increasingly have become repositories of minorities and the poor, while middle-class and business flight have stripped the urban tax bases. Political polarization along racial lines frequently has become the norm. Yet, in the late 1990s, a different politics—practiced by both black and white mayors—of "let's get the job done" has arisen. This new pragmatism has changed the discourse and conveyed

a mood of greater optimism. It has been affirmed at ballot boxes in many cities. These new mayors work with each other, share ideas, and eschew old notions of partisanship and competitiveness. A look at a few of these mayors illustrates the nature of the change.

In Philadelphia, Edward Rendell, a former district attorney and longtime Democrat who was in his second term as mayor, had restored the city's bond rating, closed substantial deficits, carried out some privatization, and tamed some very strong local unions. A champion of downtown development, he also advocated renovating historic buildings for needed hotel space....Thomas Menino of Boston became the city's first non–Irish-American mayor in the 20th century in 1993. He championed "the big dig," taking an obtrusive aboveground freeway and placing it underground. Although Boston has made the transformation to the postindustrial age better than most U.S. cities, it has had its problems. Irish-working-class south Boston has seen growing despair among its young because of the erosion of traditional lifestyles. Menino's approach found many adherents; he ran unopposed for reelection in 1997.

Dennis Archer was reelected mayor of Detroit in November with more than 80% of the vote. During his first term, Archer made great strides in restoring cooperative relationships with suburban jurisdictions and the business community. He facilitated a musical-chairs exchange of office space to keep General Motors headquartered in Detroit. Under the plan, GM would move to the Renaissance Center, while city offices would be located in the historic midtown GM complex. New stadiums were planned for downtown Detroit; expensive single-family homes were going up in the city; and gentrification was beginning to occur.

Cleveland's Michael White won reelection in 1997 handily. He had presided over the 1995 opening of the Rock and Roll Hall of Fame and Museum, which helped to trigger a successful new downtown entertainment district. New middle-class housing was going up, and White began tackling the city's troubled school system....Chicago's Richard M. Daley had made a beleaguered school system his particular reform target. The Illinois legislature gave him power to appoint the school board and the system's chief executive officer. Standards were strengthened so that students no longer could be passed on from grade to grade if they could not do the work. Market-rate housing was going up everywhere, even in some neighborhoods that had been written

The J. Paul Getty Center, left, which includes a major museum and allied facilities, overlooking Los Angeles, opened in December 1997. The $1 billion arts center was designed by Richard Meier. Throughout the United States, cities were turning to the arts as a way to save their downtown areas. Accordingly, all types of cultural facilities were being built or remodeled nationwide.

© David Rohmer/Gamma-Liaison

off years before. Retail chains also were locating operations in poor minority areas.

In traditionally liberal and Democratic New York City, Rudolph Giuliani, a Republican, resoundingly won a second term. Giuliani had concentrated his initial months as mayor on restoring civility to the nation's largest city. He freed motorists from the intimidation of "squeegee men" and made parks safer for residents to enjoy. He benefited from New York's significant crime drop and increased his share of the minority vote. He also made a dent in New York's cumbersome education bureaucracy. Other mayors of a similar ilk reelected in 1997 were Richard Riordan in Los Angeles, Tom Murphy in Pittsburgh, and Sharon Sayles Belton in Minneapolis.

Atlanta has been an exception. Incumbent Bill Campbell won a November 25 runoff against longtime city-council president Marvin Arrington. Campbell's mayoralty had been marked by administrative misadventures, including an almost nonfunctioning wastewater system. Arrington had flirted with conflict-of-interest and corruption charges in the past. In St. Louis, Clarence Harmon, an African-American and former police chief, defeated the city's first black mayor, Freeman Bosley, Jr., in the Democratic primary and won out over two white challengers in the spring election. In Miami former Mayor Xavier Suarez defeated fellow Cuban-American Joe Carollo, the incumbent.

A New Developmental Emphasis. Newark, NJ, has struggled against increasing odds since a 1967 race riot. Joining with the state government, the city has gambled on the new New Jersey Performing Arts Center, located in Newark's downtown area, to turn the city's image around and bring people back. This use of culture as a redevelopment tool was growing in American cities. Arts aficionados will travel and will spend. Chicago gained many tourist dollars from the Monet exhibit at its Art Institute. Cleveland also had used an arts center as a developmental catalyst, and Detroit had renovated Orchestra Hall and built a new home for the Michigan Opera Theatre. The Chicago Symphony itself expanded its facilities and successfully refurbished its acoustics. Los Angeles was preparing for the opening of the massive J. Paul Getty Center. Homes for artists, such as loft dwellings in abandoned warehouses, can aid development further. Kansas City was trying to revive its historic jazz district.

Meanwhile, discussion about ending sprawl was becoming widespread. Portland, OR, already had a "stop growth" law in place.

LANA STEIN, *University of Missouri–St. Louis*

COINS AND COIN COLLECTING

For U.S. coin collectors, 1997 was a milestone year. They were rewarded not only with three worthwhile commemorative issues, but also with a new platinum bullion coin and the prospect of a special series of circulating quarter dollars.

In February the U.S. Mint introduced a silver dollar celebrating the 175th anniversary of the nation's oldest continually operating botanic garden, located at the foot of Capitol Hill in Washington, DC. Limited to a mintage of 500,000 specimens, the issue quickly sold out, with a portion of the proceeds earmarked for preservation of the historic landmark. Of particular interest to numismatists was the U.S. Botanic Garden Coinage and Currency Set, which featured the commemorative dollar coin along with a new 1997 $1 bill and an uncirculated 1997 Jefferson nickel. The matte-finish nickel was obtainable only in this special offering, limited to 25,000 sets.

Upon the public opening of the Franklin Delano Roosevelt Memorial in Washington, DC, in May, the Mint issued 100,000 gold $5 coins bearing a profile of President Roosevelt. Surcharges from the sale of the coin were slated to defray the costs of constructing and maintaining the memorial.

To mark the 50th anniversary of the end of racial segregation in Major League Baseball, the U.S. Mint struck silver $1 and gold $5 coins picturing Jackie Robinson, the legendary Brooklyn Dodgers player who broke the "color barrier." (*See also* SIDEBAR, page 473.) Released in July, the dollar was the first U.S. silver coin in 43 years to depict an African-American, while the $5 was the first U.S. gold coin ever to do so. Legislation provided for up to 100,000 gold coins and not more than 200,000 silver coins, with a percentage of the proceeds to go to the Jackie Robinson Foundation, a nonprofit organization that

© U.S. Mint

Two coins featuring baseball legend Jackie Robinson were introduced in 1997 to mark the 50th anniversary of his breaking of Major League Baseball's "color barrier."

provides scholarships to minority youth. However, some $1 million—or almost 20% of the funds raised—was earmarked for support of the botanic garden.

The first U.S. platinum bullion coins—intended to compete with the precious-metal investment products of other nations—went into production in 1997. The 1-oz (28-g) piece has the highest denomination of any U.S. coin: $100.

The numismatic community was abuzz in summer 1997 over the possibility of a new series of circulating commemorative quarters; they would be the first since the bicentennial quarter in 1976. A proposal submitted to Treasury Secretary Robert E. Rubin called for the striking of 50 circulating quarters over a ten-year period, each commemorating a U.S. state. Rubin said he would not oppose such a program; as of mid-September, the proposal was awaiting congressional approval.

The redesign of the U.S. $50 bill, unveiled in June 1997, includes high-tech features to discourage counterfeiting, as well as an enlarged portrait of President Ulysses Grant. When a tiny printing flaw was discovered, however, release of the new bills was delayed until October.

BARBARA J. GREGORY
American Numismatic Association

A modernized U.S. $50 bill—incorporating features to prevent counterfeiting—was released in 1997. This was the first change in the bill's design since 1929.

© Bureau of Engraving and Printing

COLOMBIA

In 1997, Colombia continued to be a mixed bag of violence, political chicanery, drugs, and deft political maneuvering. Relations with the United States were at a low ebb after Colombia's 1996 decertification as a U.S. partner in the war against drugs. U.S. officials continued to vilify President Ernesto Samper, while a dispute over importation of Colombian flowers into the United States escalated. Colombia's refusal to amend its constitution to permit retroactive extradition of drug traffickers to the United States also provoked strong reaction. The nation's economy, which had been performing admirably, began to show signs of weakness.

Politics. Throughout 1997, President Samper—unable to shed completely charges that his 1994 electoral campaign was financed by the Cali drug cartel—was subject to domestic and international pressure to resign before the August 1998 presidential elections; this prospect grew increasingly unlikely. The year marked the emergence of several major candidates for president in 1997. Alfonso Valdivieso, a former minister of education who had become the public prosecutor of drug traffickers, led in early polls. Another major candidate was Antanas Mockus, the former mayor of Bogotá and a former professor of philosophy at the National University. Both candidates maintained ties to the Liberal Party but chose to run as Independents. The Liberal Party probably would run Interior Minister Horacio Serpa. The leading candidate for the Conservative Party appeared to be former Foreign Minister Noemi Sanin.

Perhaps Samper's boldest move in 1997 was on July 24, when he asked for the resignation of Chief of the Armed Forces Harold Bedoya—a public critic of Samper's dialogue with the two main guerrilla groups: the National Liberation Army (ELN—*Ejército de Liberación Nacional*) and the Revolutionary Armed Forces of Colombia (FARC—*Fuerzas Armadas Revolucionárias de Colombia*). The guerrillas, sometimes in league with drug producers, have been responsible for a high level of violence in the countryside. In securing Bedoya's resignation, Samper reasserted the tradition of civilian control over the military.

Results of the September 26 municipal elections showed that 8.9 million of 20.4 million eligible voters—approximately 45%—cast ballots, despite efforts by guerrillas to intimidate them. Voter turnout was heavy in the cities, but low in rural areas. Some 7.7 million voted for a Samper peace initiative on the

---

COLOMBIA • Information Highlights

Official Name: Republic of Colombia.
Location: Northwest South America.
Area: 439,734 sq mi (1 138 910 km²).
Population (mid-1997 est.): 37,400,000.
Chief Cities (mid-1995 est.): Santa Fe de Bogotá, the capital, 5,237,635; Cali, 1,718,871; Medellín, 1,621,356; Barranquilla, 1,064,255.
Government: *Head of state and government,* Ernesto Samper Pizano, president (took office August 1994). *Legislature*—Congress: Senate and House of Representatives.
Monetary Unit: Peso (1,291.92 pesos equal U.S.$1, Dec. 31, 1997).
Gross Domestic Product (1995 est. U.S.$): $192,500,000,000 (purchasing power parity).
Economic Indexes (1996, 1990 = 100): *Consumer Prices,* all items, 363.6; food, 326.0. *Industrial Production,* 125.
Foreign Trade (1996 U.S.$): *Imports,* $13,674,000,000; *exports,* $10,572,000,000.

---

ballot. His Liberal Party garnered 19 of the 32 governorships, while the opposition Conservatives managed just four wins. Liberal mayors would govern 412 municipalities, 100 more than the Conservatives.

In early December the lower house of Congress passed a bill that would grant early release to prisoners, including drug-cartel chiefs, with good conduct who have completed 60% of their sentences. Bill supporters said that it was intended to ease prison overcrowding, since Colombia had 42,000 inmates in prisons designed to hold 28,000. In mid-December the Senate passed its bill, allowing imprisoned drug lords to go home on weekends and holidays and to take 15 annual vacation days. The bill was considered a compromise to the one passed by the House; differences between the two were to be reconciled.

Economy. The Colombian economy did not register the gains of previous years, but continued to function at an acceptable level, with gross national product (GNP) predicted to grow by 3.5%. An inflation rate of 18% was forecast by the ministry of development, while the National Department of Statistics (DANE) estimated a 14.91% rate. In spite of the U.S. decertification, trade with that country increased. Exports to the United States amounted to $2.1 billion, with petroleum, coffee, and flowers leading the list. But Colombia continued to suffer a negative trade balance, with U.S. imports to Colombia amounting to $2.7 billion.

ERNEST A. DUFF
Randolph-Macon Woman's College

COMMONWEALTH OF INDEPENDENT STATES. *See* RUSSIA AND THE COMMONWEALTH OF INDEPENDENT STATES.

COMPUTERS AND COMMUNICATIONS

Information technologies, a broad arena encompassing the computer and telecommunications industries, enjoyed continued growth during 1997. Much of the credit could be given to the popularity of the Internet, a global network of computer networks that most users access via a collection of standards and protocols known as the World Wide Web, or simply "the Web." Power, speed, ease of use, and portability were the prime selling points of new computers. Portability also was stressed in the telephone sector.

The Internet and Other Networks. By September 1997 an estimated 26 million computers were connected permanently to the Internet, up from 14.7 million a year earlier. And in the United States alone, according to a survey conducted by Computer Intelligence, more than 31 million personal computers (PCs) accessed the Internet regularly—an increase of 108% from a year earlier. The most common uses of the Internet were for E-mail and Web browsing, followed by the downloading of software and electronic commerce, including financial services and shopping. A survey by IntelliQuest found that 42% of Internet users spent five hours or more per week on-line.

Each World Wide Web site has an address in the format http://www.grolier.com. As demand for addresses soared—there were almost 1 million by mid-1997—the Internet community debated how to increase the supply. One solution would be to increase the number of top-level domains, or address endings. The addresses of all U.S. Internet sites are classified into six domains: *.com* for commercial businesses, *.edu* for educational institutions, *.org* for nonprofit organizations, *.net* for networks, *.gov* for government bodies, and *.mil* for military sites. Seven additional domains were proposed; these would not affect existing addresses, but would be used for addresses applied for in the future.

The technology used to build the Internet also can be used to build private networks. Intranets—networks within organizations— were enjoying tremendous growth in 1997, thanks to their ease of use. Intranets can be expanded easily, are very useful to telecommuting employees, and can provide employees with quick access to Web-based company information. With multimedia hardware, intranets also allow videoconferencing.

In 1997 one of the hottest buzzwords was "extranet"—an extended intranet that connects not only a company's employees but also select customers, suppliers, and partners. For example, Mobil's lubricant distributors worldwide can submit purchase orders via an extranet, speeding delivery and saving millions of dollars in phone charges.

Variations on a Theme. Standard PCs were challenged on several fronts during 1997. Web-TV devices, also known as set-top boxes, blended elements of PCs and TVs. Geared for nontechnical users and touted as being easy to use, Web TV lets people use remote-control devices to surf the Web via their TV, doing such things as checking E-mail while watching a favorite TV show.

A new wave of handheld PCs (HPCs), small enough to tuck into a jacket pocket, reached the market. They came equipped with Microsoft's Windows CE, designed to run on systems with limited memory and processor power. When used with a modem, an HPC can be connected to the Internet. And with a serial cable or infrared port, the HPC can be connected to a Windows 95 or Windows NT desktop and can exchange files.

Taking aim at corporate intranets, about a dozen manufacturers introduced network computers, or NetPCs, which have many of the features of regular PCs but have "sealable" or sealed chassis and do not store programs or data. Instead, applications reside on server computers and are delivered on demand to the NetPCs. This gives network administrators more control over the applications that users can access; allows system information to be updated even when the NetPCs are not being used; and, say supporters, can reduce administrative costs drastically. NetPCs were designed to compete not only with PCs but also with the Java-based network computer (NC) introduced in 1996 and backed mainly by IBM, Sun Microsystems, and Oracle.

Many industry observers had expected that the rise of PCs and network computing would mean the demise of mainframes. But after years of decline, sales of high-end computers boomed in 1997 as organizations looked for ways to store very large quantities of data centrally for quick access by large networks. Highly scalable modular server systems were of particular interest, since average data-storage requirements are doubling every year.

Ever Faster and More Powerful. At the beginning of 1997, Intel—which produces 85% of the microprocessors used in PCs— introduced a Pentium chip with MMX technology, at speeds of 166 and 200 megahertz (MHz); later in the year a 233-MHz version

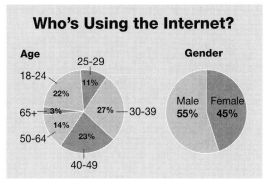

Who's Using the Internet?

Age

- 18-24: 22%
- 25-29: 11%
- 30-39: 27%
- 40-49: 23%
- 50-64: 14%
- 65+: 3%

Gender

- Male: 55%
- Female: 45%

Source: Louis Harris & Associates

came on the market. MMX enhances a PC's video, audio, and animation capabilities, making it particularly attractive for multimedia applications. Another new family of Intel processors was the Pentium II, in iterations of 233, 266, and 300 MHz. Intel also announced that a technological breakthrough enabled it to make memory chips that can store two bits of data on a transistor instead of one, thereby doubling the storage capacity of the chips.

People who depend on modems to connect their computers to the Internet via a phone line have had to be content with rates of no more than 33.6 kilobytes per second (Kbps), the top speed possible on analog phone lines. In 1997, however, manufacturers introduced 56-Kbps modems, which take advantage of the digital connections of most on-line-service providers to download data at speeds approaching 56 Kbps. Data moving in the other direction, however—from an individual computer to the Internet—remains limited to 33.6 Kbps. In contrast, users with cable modems—which connect a PC to the outside world through the same wires that carry cable TV—can cruise the Internet at speeds of up to 40 megabytes per second (Mbps). Cable modems were expected to become more widely available in 1998. Meanwhile, phone companies were fighting back by offering customers digital modems that could receive at up to 10 Mbps and transmit at 640 Kbps.

PC CD-ROM drives with a 24x transfer rate arrived in 1997. Most new PCs, including at least 85% sold for the home market, were equipped with a CD-ROM drive as standard equipment. However, it was predicted that by the year 2000, CD-ROMs would be succeeded by the next generation of technology—DVD- (digital video disk) ROM. A DVD-ROM can hold more than 9 gigabytes of data—13 times as much as a CD-ROM—enabling it to store massive data files such as high-quality films. Manufacturers promised that DVD-ROM drives—which became available in 1997—

would be "backward-compatible," thus letting people continue to use CD-ROMs.

The Year 2000 Headache. Beginning decades ago, designers of computer operating systems and applications software—eager to conserve precious memory and disk space—began using only two digits to represent a year. For example, the year 1901 was recorded as 01, in a six-digit format: YYMMDD (March 24, 1901, being 010324). Until now, the system has worked well; however, computers that depend on this two-digit shorthand are unable to interpret the correct century. Many of these machines—if they use applications involving long-term planning—already have run into problems because they are unable to distinguish between the years 1900 and 2000.

If this problem goes uncorrected, the potential impact could be immense. A 1997 guide from the U.S. General Accounting Office noted that federal payments to disabled veterans could be delayed severely, systems that track student loans could generate erroneous information, and tax systems could be unable to process returns. In addition, banks might be unable to calculate mortgage and credit-card payments correctly, automated systems controlling buildings' heating and cooling could refuse to work, corporate-inventory systems could break down, and so on. Furthermore, erroneous data produced by the computers could lead to lawsuits and bankruptcies.

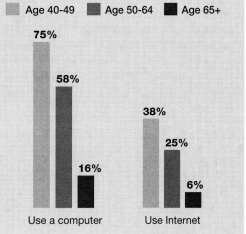

Mature Computer Users

The number of computer users aged 40 and older is growing rapidly. An October 1997 survey shows the percentage, by age group, who use computers and who access the Internet.

- Age 40-49
- Age 50-64
- Age 65+

Use a computer
- Age 40-49: 75%
- Age 50-64: 58%
- Age 65+: 16%

Use Internet
- Age 40-49: 38%
- Age 50-64: 25%
- Age 65+: 6%

Source: Louis Harris & Associates

The Internet—Legal Issues

By 1997 the global computer network known as the Internet had placed mass-media publishing capabilities into the hands of ordinary citizens. For the relatively low price of personal-computer equipment, individuals could disseminate messages to thousands of people. The network seamlessly spans national borders, allowing people worldwide to share ideas and information. But this new technology has challenged laws written with older communications media in mind.

Freedom of Speech. In 1996 the U.S. Congress passed legislation to ban "indecent speech" from the Internet. "Indecent speech" might include vulgar language, information on sexual topics, erotic literature, or artistic depictions of nudity; all of these forms of speech are protected constitutionally, but may be inappropriate for children. The legal arguments in favor of the statute rested upon a comparison with broadcast media, which Congress has had broad constitutional latitude to regulate. However, in a landmark opinion hailed by some and maligned by many, the U.S. Supreme Court declared the statute unconstitutional. According to the court, the Internet enjoys the same broad constitutional protection from censorship as do printed materials. The court therefore found that the government lacks the authority to ban indecent speech on the Internet. This ruling ensured that information posted on the Internet would receive the highest degree of constitutional protection, and made the issue of what information children can access a matter of individual responsibility.

Copyrights. Copyright law protects authors and artists against unauthorized reproduction, distribution, adaptation, and public performance or display of their works. Copyright law covers a wide range of creative works, including music, books, software, films, and photographs. Today, all of these can be transformed easily into a digital format. Thus the Internet poses a difficult problem: It is simple and inexpensive to make unauthorized copies of copyrighted works and distribute them electronically. Authors and publishers are seeking new laws to prevent such digital copying. However, librarians and consumer advocates are concerned that such legislation might curtail the public's 1st Amendment right to quote, criticize, and comment upon copyrighted works.

Commercial Law. The Internet promises to speed consumer and business transactions. But before electronic commerce can blossom, the integrity of on-line transactions must be assured. Consumers may be afraid to send payments over the Internet unless they are sure their credit-card numbers cannot be intercepted. Businesses may be reluctant to enter into on-line transactions if they cannot tell whether purchase orders are legitimate. Many such difficulties can be solved through the use of public-key cryptography, which utilizes mathematical principles to encode messages in an unbreakable cipher that can be decoded only by someone possessing the key. This helps ensure security. Public-key cryptography also can be used to create "digital signatures" that verify the identity of a message's sender. The laws covering contracts and commercial transactions are being rewritten to accommodate such new forms of commerce.

Privacy. Because the Internet is a network of computers, information about the on-line activities of Internet users readily can be recorded, stored, and analyzed. For example, Internet merchants might track patterns of consumer purchases and build up a profile of individual consumers' buying preferences. Some consumer advocates are seeking legislation to curtail such practices. Other citizens fear that the government, rather than corporations, will use electronic surveillance to monitor individuals' on-line activity. Cryptography could provide security against governmental snooping, but law-enforcement officials worry that unbreakable cryptography also would allow criminals to communicate securely, without fear of government wiretaps. U.S. law-enforcement agencies therefore are pressing Congress for legislation requiring cryptographic software to permit covert governmental access to encrypted messages. Civil-liberties organizations object that such a law could facilitate unconstitutional government surveillance of electronic communications.

International Conflict of Laws. Because the Internet spans borders, differences in national laws can lead to conflicts. For example, German authorities have attempted to block the access of German citizens to U.S. World Wide Web sites that contain neo-Nazi propaganda. Such writings are illegal under the German constitution, but are protected political speech under the U.S. Constitution. Such policy conflicts will become increasingly common as more and more people around the world use the Internet.

DAN L. BURK

The Gartner Group, a technology consulting company, estimated that as many as 90% of mainframe applications will fail as time goes on because of invalid date computations, if corrective measures are not taken. The company's estimate of the cost of fixing the problem worldwide has run as high as $600 billion or more.

Two basic approaches to remedying the problem have been developed. One involves expanding the year-date field in files, programs, and databases from two digits to four. The second approach changes program logic to enable it to supply the century's two missing digits. In either case, all noncompliant computer code must be identified and updated. By 1997 most companies had in place teams of employees and consultants working to solve the problem.

Wireless Telephone Services.   Digital phones have come to dominate the cellular-phone market in many parts of the world and are beginning to take hold in the United States, where the vast majority of the 38-million-plus cellular users still are using first-generation analog networks. But even as U.S. cellular carriers finally are upgrading to digital service, the industry is focusing on third-generation technology, named IMT-2000 (International Mobile Telecommunications for the 2000s), expected to be realized early in the coming century. IMT-2000 is being designed to integrate different types of existing mobile communications services into a single service comparable to an ISDN wire-line network. This will enable worldwide roaming and high-rate data transmission (up to 2 Mbps) with a pocket handset.

Similar to a digital cellular system is PCS (personal communications service). However, PCS operates at different frequencies than do cellular systems. In the United States, for example, cellular systems operate at 824 to 849 MHz, and PCS at 1850 to 1990 MHz.

In 1997 manufacturers launched the first "dual-band" handsets, which work on two digital standards. Owners of such phones could use them as they traveled from one continent to another, assuming the infrastructure for the specific networks was installed.

Turbulent Markets.   Mergers, acquisitions, joint ventures, and other deals were rampant in the information-technology industry in 1997 as companies strove to build market share and compete in an ever-changing marketplace. In February, 68 nations agreed to end state telephone monopolies and open their telecommunication markets to all players. The agreement was expected to lead to declines in the cost of international calls and to speed the spread of new technologies.

The Federal Communications Commission (FCC) approved new rules that partly deregulated the U.S. telephone industry. A major issue left unsolved was how to provide affordable phone service to rural areas without government subsidies.

Microsoft announced that it would invest $1 billion in Comcast, the fourth-largest U.S. cable operator, and would spend $425 million to acquire WebTV Networks, a company that delivers Internet information to TV sets. Microsoft also agreed to invest $150 million in its longtime rival, Apple Computer. Apple, once the PC-industry leader, captured only 4% of U.S. PC sales in the first quarter of 1997. Later in the year, by purchasing the Macintosh business of Power Computing, Apple ended a two-year-old strategy of attempting to grow by allowing other manufacturers to clone its Macintosh computers.

Microsoft ran into problems in October when Sun Microsystems filed suit against it. Sun was objecting to Microsoft's claim that its Internet Explorer 4.1 is Java-compatible. Microsoft later countersued, asking for the right to terminate Sun's license to Microsoft's Java technology. Meanwhile the U.S. Justice Department in December won a court order to force Microsoft to stop requiring installation of its Explorer Internet browser on all Windows 95 machines.

Worldcom, which controls approximately 5% of the U.S. long-distance-telephone market, acquired CompuServe for about $1.2 billion in stock. It kept CompuServe's high-speed phone lines and Internet gateways and sold the firm's on-line service to America Online. The latter had no immediate plans to merge CompuServe's 2.6 million subscribers with its own membership of some 9 million.

The big telephone battle of 1997 developed as companies tried to position themselves as major players in handling burgeoning data and Internet traffic. It began when British Telecommunications made a $19.9 billion cash-and-stock offer for MCI Communications. Worldcom then bid $30 billion in stock for MCI, and GTE followed with a $28 billion cash bid. In November, MCI accepted Worldcom's offer of almost $37 billion in cash and stock. MCI Worldcom would control about 25% of the U.S. long-distance market, behind AT&T with 50%, and would be one of the world's largest carriers of Internet traffic. The merger remained subject to FCC approval.

JENNY TESAR, *Author*
"The New Webster's Computer Handbook"

CONGO, DEMOCRATIC REPUBLIC OF THE

The violent reaction to government policy begun in the refugee camps in eastern Zaire escalated to a full-scale civil war, sweeping Zaire's longtime president, Mobutu Sese Seko, and his corrupt regime from power in 1997. Rebel leader Laurent Désiré Kabila then took control of the government and changed the nation's name back to Democratic Republic of the Congo.

The Refugee Problem. The massacres of Tutsi and subsequent civil war in Rwanda, in conjunction with intertribal problems in Burundi in the mid-1990s, caused a massive influx of refugees into eastern Zaire. By late November 1996 more than 1 million refugees inhabited 40 squalid camps under United Nations (UN) supervision. Armed Hutu controlled most of these refugee camps. Regular army units were too few to provide law and order. Many of the Zairian soldiers, underpaid and without supplies, added to the chaos by looting villages.

Attempts to persuade the refugees to return home were difficult because of fear of retribution and the control exercised by the armed Hutu. Mobutu's attempts to expel them were only partially successful. He could not starve the camps because of UN pressure and his army was not strong enough to force them to leave. Nevertheless, by December 1996 more than 500,000 refugees had left. One

of the major reasons for this was the onset of fighting between forces loyal to Mobutu and those of Kabila.

The Civil War. Kabila had led a relatively obscure guerrilla movement based in the southeast for 30 years. The breakdown of government control increased the numbers of dissidents and Kabila, with support from Uganda and Rwanda, struck at the Zairian army in October 1996 and soon had seized Bukavu. The rebels, at first primarily Tutsi, then seized Goma. By January they controlled the three main airports in eastern Zaire. The collapse of the road network during the Mobutu regime made it difficult for the government to mount successful counterattacks. Lack of a unified central government also aided the rebels. Suffering from cancer, Mobutu was in France for treatment. Many of the relief camps were pillaged, and the refugees fled.

The rebel forces gained more adherents with each success, and what at first was a localized rebellion became a general war to overthrow Mobutu. Kabila rejected international calls for a cease-fire and on February 21 called upon Léon Kengo wa Dondo, then prime minister, to get rid of Mobutu—who, although ailing, had returned to Zaire in December and was trying frantically to rally support. Kabila announced the creation of a new state, the Democratic Republic of the Congo, for areas he had seized. By mid-February his forces were advancing on three fronts and were threatening Zaire's third-largest city, Kisangani. The city fell to Kabila

Amid civil war in Zaire, the nation's President Mobutu Sese Seko (second from left) and rebel leader Laurent Kabila (second from right) met aboard a naval vessel on May 4, 1997. The peace talks, overseen by South Africa's President Nelson Mandela (center), failed; Mobutu's government fell; and Kabila became leader of Zaire, renamed the Democratic Republic of the Congo.

on March 15. With the fall of Kisangani it was obvious that Mobutu's army—even bolstered by mercenaries—could not halt what had become a popular movement throughout the nation. Lubumbasha, Zaire's second-largest city, was captured on April 9.

To try to strengthen the government's position, Parliament appointed Mobutu's political adversary, Étienne Tshisekedi, to the prime ministership. Mobutu, however, disavowed the appointment and named Gen. Likulia Bolongo to the post. Subsequently, Tshisekedi led a general strike against Mobutu; by then, Kinshasa, the capital, was in chaos. Meanwhile, South Africa's President Nelson Mandela sought to intervene to secure a peaceful settlement between government and rebel forces. Peace talks between Mobutu and Kabila did occur on May 4 on a warship in the Congolese port of Pointe-Noire, but failed. The nation's military elite said that it could not defend Kinshasa and urged Mobutu to resign. On May 16, Mobutu yielded power and fled. Kabila declared himself president of the Democratic Republic of the Congo, the name the nation took when it gained independence from Belgium in 1960, and began to form a government. (Desperately ill for some time, Mobutu died in Rabat, Morocco, on September 7.)

Post–Civil War Developments.   Kabila announced his new government system while his ragtag army—bolstered by regular army units from Rwanda and Angola—was disarming the remnants of the Zairian army and securing the capital city. Kabila abolished the post of prime minister and declared himself to be president, with full powers of governing. The key executive positions were filled by loyal members of his alliance. He excluded Tshisekedi and other members of the anti-Mobutu parties in Kinshasa. Political activity in Kinshasa was banned, which effectively prohibited political organization.

The new government brought immediate protests from the supporters of Tshisekedi, who maintained that he was the chosen leader and that Kabila was establishing a dictatorship. A large crowd demonstrating for Tshisekedi was dispersed by Kabila's troops. Subsequently the government banned all public meetings and strikes. Kabila made it clear that he would not rush into general elections. His most pressing problem was economic.

Ravaged by Mobutu's misrule, the economy had been damaged further by nine months of war. The road and river transport systems needed costly repairs; the inflation rate was astronomical; prices of commodities were high; and the currency was almost worthless. High unemployment was made worse by members of Kabila's army, who now expected rewards. His security forces—made up of a conglomerate of anti-Mobutu civilians, mainly young men—were not adequate to police the new state. Kabila had to depend largely on Angolan and Rwandan troops for this.

The new government made some progress in solving several short-term problems. A new currency was adopted and new contracts with foreign companies for copper and cobalt mining were signed. Partially to mollify his critics in the United States, Kabila issued a 15-point constitutional decree. Although it confirmed him with full executive, legislative, and military power, it did promise a Constituent Assembly, which would draw up a new constitution. The good relations with Rwanda and Uganda were capped by a two-day conference in August hosted by him. Inflation did drop, and railroad repair began.

The refugees remained in many camps and scattered throughout the east despite abortive plans to airlift many back to Rwanda. A more serious problem regarding refugees threatened to halt much-needed loans to the desperately cash-poor state. As early as March, rumors reached Kinshasa that Kabila's forces were guilty of massacring thousands of Hutu refugees as the regime consolidated its hold in the east. The worst case was that of an alleged 1,500 killed at Musenge in January. The UN requested permission to investigate these rumors but was hampered. The United States and other creditor nations were wary of loaning money to the new state because of the failure of Mobutu's government to pay previous debts. A conference of potential lenders convened in August and decided against any major loans until the human-rights questions had been answered. Under such pressure and after much hesitation, Kabila agreed to allow the UN commission to proceed to the interior to investigate the charges.

Harry A. Gailey, *San Jose State University*

CONGO • Information Highlights

Official Name: Democratic Republic of the Congo.
Location: Central equatorial Africa.
Area: 905,564 sq mi (2 345 410 km²).
Population (mid-1997 est.): 47,400,000.
Chief City (1987 est.): Kinshasa, the capital, 2,500,000.
Government: *Head of state and government,* Laurent-Désiré Kabila, president (took office May 1997).
Monetary Unit: New zaire (66,610.0 new zaires equal U.S.$1, 3d quarter 1996).
Gross Domestic Product (1995 est. U.S.$): $16,500,000,-000 (purchasing power parity).
Foreign Trade (1995 U.S.$): *Imports,* $397,000,000; *exports,* $438,000,000.

CONSUMER AFFAIRS

It was a mixed year for consumers in 1997. The U.S. economy was booming, the stock market hit all-time highs before causing some uneasiness late in the year, inflation and unemployment were under control, and many consumer organizations appeared to flourish once again. In addition, despite decreasing interest in involving the federal government in consumer affairs, various substantial laws and regulations were considered during the year. However, numerous marketplace problems—old and new—faced the U.S. consumer. Personal bankruptcies hit all-time highs, while fraud perpetrated on consumers appeared to increase in many areas, including telemarketing, the Internet, and the financial-planning industry.

Auto Leasing and Financial Matters. The automobile-leasing industry, which involves more than 30,000 new-car and leasing companies, has been besieged with deceptive practices, mainly the result of inaccurate or incomplete disclosures. As a result, the Federal Reserve Board revised its regulations, which now provide for clearer and more substantive disclosures to consumers who lease automobiles.

In October major amendments to the Fair Credit Reporting Act (FCRA) became law. This law, which was passed originally in 1970, ensures that inaccurate and obsolete information must be removed from the consumer's credit file. The amendments require credit bureaus and other credit-reporting agencies to investigate disputed items within 30 days. These agencies must then disclose corrections to the consumer within five days after the investigation.

Credit agencies no longer are allowed to insert previously deleted, adverse information unless the creditor has certified its accuracy, and the consumer has been notified of the reinsertion. The credit bureau must then allow the consumer to add an explanatory statement.

Credit reports requested by the consumer are free to consumers in numerous specified cases, and a minimal charge (typically $8) is allowed in all other cases. Employers now must get written permission from the prospective employee before information is gathered as part of the employment process. Further, there are increased monetary penalties for creditors who violate the law.

As of July, state agencies were given the principal authority to oversee financial planners with assets of less than $25 million, there-by placing most planners under the scrutiny of state law. Many felt that state government would do a better job at oversight than the Securities and Exchange Commission (SEC). The SEC, however, continued to regulate financial planners with assets in excess of $25 million.

In July banks for the first time were allowed to change their out-of-state auxiliary operations into branch offices. This allowed banks to expand their operations more easily.

Government Action. The U.S. Office of Consumer Affairs (OCA) had a very difficult year in 1997. OCA—the federal consumer agency that was established in February 1971—sponsored National Consumers Week, offered a toll-free help line for consumers, and provided various other assistance to consumers. The office was "zeroed out" of existence by a Congressional Conference Committee in September. A resolution was passed in early October that temporarily saved the agency, but Congress later voted to eliminate it. A January 1998 closing date was scheduled. Presumably, OCA efforts would be taken over by other federal agencies; but skeptics believed this was a further dismantling of the consumer voice in Washington.

The impact of the U.S. Food and Drug Administration (FDA) on public health was changed by a reform bill enacted in 1997. The act cuts the time for approval of new drugs substantially, offers gravely ill patients easier access to experimental drugs, and expands the FDA's program to streamline the approval of new therapies for serious or life-threatening conditions.

MEL J. ZELENAK
University of Missouri-Columbia

CRIME

Despite grisly violence and mounting concern over terrorism in 1997, serious crime continued to decline in the United States. According to the Federal Bureau of Investigation's (FBI's) report for 1996—its most recent figures—there were 13.5 million crimes in 1996, down 3% from the year before; this was the fifth consecutive decrease. The 19,645 murders represented a 9% decrease from the year before. The murder rate of 7.4 per 100,000 people was the lowest since 1969. The decline was due largely to a 31% drop in juvenile murder arrests since 1993, although the adult rate also has declined slowly since 1991. The total crime rate—5,079 per 100,000—was the lowest since 1984.

Attorney Roy Black met the press after his client Marv Albert, center, pleaded guilty in Arlington County (VA) Circuit Court on Sept. 25, 1997, to misdemeanor charges of assaulting a woman during a sexual encounter in a hotel room. The plea occurred amid a trial in which the NBC sportscaster faced more-serious felony charges. Subsequently, Albert, who was dismissed by NBC, received a 12-month suspended sentence.

© Ken Cedeno/Reuters/Archive Photos

Experts credited the drop to the aging of the baby-boom generation, longer jail terms, and tougher law enforcement. "Many baby boomers are now in their 40s and have mellowed out. They are not committing the high-risk violent and property offenses they did ten years ago," said Jack Levin, director of the Program for the Study of Violence at Northeastern University in Boston. Other contributing factors cited by Levin were the jailing of more violent prisoners, the practice of going after those who commit small offenses, smaller numbers of guns on the streets, partnerships between police and residents, and grassroots efforts in major cities.

But James Alan Fox, dean of criminal justice at Northeastern, warned that a 15% growth in the teenage population by 2005 could reverse the trend. The new figures are "a very good five-year trend, but the improvements are still marginal," said Rep. Bill McCollum (R-FL), chairman of the House Judiciary subcommittee on crime. "We are very far from an acceptable level of violent crime....Even with these declines, it is still nearly four times more likely that you are going to be raped, robbed, assaulted, or murdered than it was in 1960."

The FBI report listed 1,682,278 violent crimes in the United States in 1996, down 6.5%. The violent-crime rate fell to 634 per 100,000, the lowest since 1987. The South had the most violent crimes, with 707 per 100,000; it was followed by the West with 692, the

Northeast with 555, and the Midwest with 537. The 11.8 million property crimes were 2% fewer than in 1995, with 4,445 per 100,000. The South led again with a rate of 5,020 per 100,000, followed by the West with 4,837; the Midwest with 4,127; and the Northeast with 3,343.

The 95,769 forcible rapes were the fewest since 1989, and 2% less than in 1995. The rate was 71 per 100,000 women. Robberies declined 7% to 537,050, or 202 per 100,000 people. There were 2.5 million burglaries, down 3.6%—the fewest in more than 20 years. Aggravated assaults were down 1%, to 1 million; thefts fell 1.3%, to 7.9 million; and motor-vehicle theft fell 5.2 %, to 1.4 million.

More than half of murder victims were reported to have known their assailants, reversing a recent trend of murders committed by strangers. The report noted that 30% of female murder victims were slain by husbands or boyfriends, while 3% of murdered males were killed by wives or girlfriends. A Justice Department study said the drop in the murder rate appeared to be related to a drop in crack-cocaine use.

Experts praised city police programs that targeted guns. Other tactics included "zero tolerance" policies and giving police the authority to stop and frisk youths in high-crime neighborhoods for offenses like playing loud radios. These tactics have made youngsters more wary of carrying guns. Charleston, SC, offered a bounty for reporting guns.

President Bill Clinton attributed lower crime rates in part to the 1994 crime bill that toughened sentences and paid for 57,000 new local police officers in community-oriented programs.

The rate of youth arrests for violent crimes plunged 9.2% in 1996—the second straight drop (2.9% in 1995) after an escalating seven-year juvenile crime wave. In 1996, for every 100,000 youths 10 to 17 there were 464.7 violent-crime arrests, down from 511.9 in 1995 and 527.4 in the peak year of 1994. Rates had spiraled up from 311.3 arrests per 100,000 in 1987 as drug gangs recruited teenage couriers, arming them with automatic weapons.

The drop in crime since 1990 helped slow the growth of America's adult prison population in 1996–97, according to the Justice Department. After a ten-year surge that more than doubled the number of inmates, the state and federal prison population rose by only 5% in 1996. There were 213 state and federal prisons built from 1990 to 1995, bringing the total number to 1,500. (*See also* PRISONS.)

In a finding the Justice Department said indicates domestic violence is underreported, nearly half the 1.4 million victims of violence or suspected violence who were treated in emergency rooms in 1994 knew their attackers. Among the victims of abuse by spouses or former spouses—7% of the total—women victims outnumbered men nine to one. Nearly 10% were hurt by a boyfriend or girlfriend; women were almost eight times more likely than men to fall into this category. Almost one in five was hurt by a spouse, former spouse, or current or former boyfriend or girlfriend.

In a high-profile case, NBC sportscaster Marv Albert, 56, pleaded guilty in September to misdemeanor assault and battery, in a case brought by a woman he had known for ten years. Due to Albert's guilty plea, a more serious charge of forcible sodomy was dropped.

Law-enforcement officials were concerned about the growing incidence of "road rage"—angry motorists who explode in violence over minor traffic infractions. A study commissioned by the American Automobile Association (AAA) Foundation for Traffic Safety in Washington, DC, found 10,037 incidents nationally of violent, aggressive driving between Jan. 1, 1990, and Aug. 31, 1996. The report only included offenses reported in the news or to police and assumes many more actually occurred. At least 218 persons were killed and another 12,610 injured as a result of the documented incidents. A particularly horrifying case occurred in Adelphi, MD, when Joy Estrella Mariano Enriquez, 19, was shot

to death by a bicyclist after bumping him with her car. Alajandra Jose Grant, 26, was charged with murder.

By mid-October more executions had taken place in U.S. prisons than in any year over the past four decades. The pace was expected to quicken further, since the appeals process was streamlined and legal-aid funds were cut back. Gary Lee Davis, 53, became the 59th convicted murderer put to death in 1997 when he was executed by lethal injection in Colorado; it was the state's first execution in 30 years. The annual U.S. total was the highest since 1957, when 65 people were executed.

Major Crimes. A federal jury in Denver condemned Timothy J. McVeigh to death for the April 19, 1995, bombing of a federal office building in Oklahoma City that killed 168 persons and injured 850 others. McVeigh, a 29-year-old Persian Gulf war veteran, was accused of gathering materials for a bomb, which he placed in a rented Ryder truck that he drove from Junction City, KS. In the fall, jury selection was under way in the trial of Terry Nichols, also accused in the case. (*See also* TERRORISM.)

Suspected serial killer Andrew Cunanan, 27, shot himself to death in Miami Beach, FL, after reportedly gunning down fashion designer Gianni Versace. Four earlier killings in three states were attributed to Cunanan, who did not leave a suicide note when he shot himself aboard a houseboat on July 23.

Jesse Timmendequas was sentenced to death in Trenton, NJ, for the rape and murder of Megan Kanka, 7, whose name became synonymous with new laws that require that communities be notified when convicted sex offenders move into a neighborhood. Lawyers for Timmendequas pleaded for mercy, contending the killer himself was a victim of severe childhood abuse.

In Pearl, MS, Luke Woodham, 16, was charged with murder in the stabbing death of his mother and the deaths of two classmates in a shooting spree at the town's high school. Seven others were injured. Six other teens, described as friends of Woodham, were jailed on suspicion of plotting murder. Among those killed in the rampage was Christina Menefee, 16, who had dated Woodham.

In Sonora, CA, Ellie Nesler, who ignited a national debate about vigilante justice after killing her son's alleged molester, was freed after serving four years in prison. Originally sentenced to ten years, she was granted a retrial due to juror misconduct and was released after pleading guilty to voluntary manslaughter. Nesler, 45, shot Daniel Mark

The FBI under Fire

The Federal Bureau of Investigation (FBI), the nation's storied crime-fighting agency, came under unusual attack in 1997. But by year's end, despite a series of embarrassments—from bungling by its crime laboratory to misconduct and cover-ups—FBI Director Louis J. Freeh said the agency had patched its image and was well on the way to regaining public confidence.

The Crime Lab. A review of the bureau's crime lab by the inspector general of the Justice Department discovered shoddy procedures, management bungling, and testimony slanted to favor prosecutors—but no criminality. Three crime-lab supervisors were transferred to jobs outside the laboratory, and scientist-agent Frederic Whitehurst, whose allegations had prompted the year-long probe, was suspended with pay.

FBI officials responded to the findings by ordering the lab to revise outdated procedural manuals and seal corridors once open to nonlab agents, as the laboratory applied for its first certification by outside experts. In October, Donald M. Kerr, Jr., 58, a nuclear-weapons physicist who formerly ran the Los Alamos National Laboratory, was appointed to head the crime lab. FBI officials cited Kerr's scientific background and experience in nuclear weapons—now considered an emerging threat to law and order—as reasons for his selection.

Sen. Charles E. Grassley (R-IA), whose Judiciary subcommittee oversees the FBI, remained unconvinced that the lab had solved its problems, and ordered Capitol Hill hearings to explore the difficulties. The problems opened the door for a number of cases to be reopened and retried.

The Olympics Bombing and Ruby Ridge. The FBI was lampooned for the way it handled the July 27, 1996, bombing at the Olympics in Atlanta, GA—particularly the agency's highly public accusation of Richard Jewell, a 34-year-old guard at Centennial Olympic Park in Atlanta. Jewell first was hailed as a hero for helping clear people away from the bomb before it exploded, killing one person and injuring more than 100. Within days, however, he had become the focus of the FBI's investigation, a fact that was reported widely in the media. The Justice Department later cleared Jewell in the bombing, and the FBI was left with its image badly bruised.

Although Attorney General Janet Reno offered Jewell an apology for the leak of his name as a suspect in the bombing, she did not apologize for a ruse that FBI agents used to get him to waive his right to counsel during questioning or for a search of his home that Jewell said was based on little evidence. Jewell also accused the FBI of tapping his phone illegally, harassing his friends and relatives, and violating his constitutional rights.

The Justice Department suspended three FBI officials for their roles in a deadly 1992 siege at Ruby Ridge, ID, and its aftermath. Senior FBI officials were accused of trying to cover up misconduct following a shoot-out at the mountain cabin of white separatist Randy Weaver. Weaver's wife and son and a U.S. marshal died in an exchange of gunfire, sparking widespread resentment against the FBI and charges that it had used excessive force.

The case led to the removal of Larry Potts, Freeh's second in command, and two others. Another FBI supervisor, E. Michael Kahoe, pleaded guilty to obstruction of justice for destroying a document after the incident, and was sentenced to 18 months in prison.

Director Freeh and the Agency's Reputation. The FBI again attracted negative headlines when Freeh and Reno appeared to be at odds over her resistance to calling for an independent prosecutor to investigate Democratic fund-raising. Freeh was reported widely to favor the independent investigation, but the two top officials denied there was a rift. Freeh had come in for some criticism earlier over reports that he had failed to give President Bill Clinton a full accounting of alleged Chinese efforts to sway U.S. elections.

Earl Pitts, the second FBI agent ever convicted on espionage charges, admitted to spying for the Russians during and after the Cold War and was sentenced to 27 years in prison. But the FBI, which caught the 44-year-old Pitts in a sting investigation that lasted about 16 months, won praise for exposing him.

Early in the year, Freeh told reporters that he gave thought to resigning. By autumn, however, he said his optimism was renewed after the FBI played key roles in the conviction of Timothy McVeigh for the 1995 Oklahoma City bombing and the capture of Mir Aimal Kansi of Pakistan, suspected in a 1993 shooting outside of the headquarters of the Central Intelligence Agency (CIA) that left two dead and three injured. Kansi was convicted of ten charges in November.

JIM RUBIN

Driver five times in the back of the head on April 2, 1993. Driver had been charged with molesting four boys, including Nesler's son.

In a case that caused a stir on both sides of the Atlantic, Louise Woodward, a 19-year-old British au pair, was found guilty by a jury in Middlesex county, MA, of the second-degree murder of Matthew Eappen, an eight-month-old baby for whom she had been caring. In response to a motion by her attorneys requesting that the verdict be overturned, Superior Court Judge Hiller B. Zobel reduced the conviction to manslaughter and sentenced her to 279 days in jail—the amount of time she already had spent in prison.

In Toms River, NJ, a 15-year-old boy accused of sexually assaulting and strangling a neighbor, Eddie Werner, 11, was said to be the victim of molestation himself by a man he met on the Internet. Werner was selling candy and wrapping paper door-to-door for a school fund-raiser. Local school officials suspended fund-raisers after the killing.

The United States pressed Israel to extradite Samuel Sheinbein, 17, who fled there after he and a friend allegedly killed Alfredo Enrique Tello Jr., 19. Members of Congress threatened to cut aid to Israel if the teenager was not returned to the United States. Tello's burned and dismembered body was found in Wheaton, MD. Sheinbein's father, Shlomo, 53—a lawyer, former Pentagon employee, and Israeli citizen—was charged in Israel with obstructing justice by helping his son flee the United States.

A Republic of Georgia diplomat, Gueorgui Makharadze, 36, pleaded guilty to involuntary manslaughter and aggravated assault in the Washington, DC, drunken-driving death of Jovianne Waltrick, 16, of Kensington, MD. The incident sparked international controversy that led Makharadze's government to waive his diplomatic immunity.

In Boulder, CO, the investigation into the murder of JonBenet Ramsey, the 6-year-old beauty queen found strangled in her home the day after Christmas in 1996, continued into the final months of 1997.

Organized-crime boss Vincent "Chin" Gigante, 69, who prosecutors said dodged prosecution for nearly three decades by feigning mental illness, was convicted in New York City of plotting to kill rival leader John Gotti. Although the conviction was overturned on a technicality by a federal judge, Gigante's racketeering conviction was upheld.

A federal jury in New York City convicted Autumn Jackson of trying to extort $40 million from Bill Cosby, claiming the comedian was her father. The jury rejected her defense that she was involved in a lawful negotiation to obtain support from Cosby, who admitted to having an affair with Jackson's mother. In Los Angeles, Mikhail Markhasev, 18, was charged with the January 18 killing of the entertainer's son, Ennis. Police said Markhasev intended to rob Cosby, who had stopped to change a tire.

In New Jersey, Melissa Drexler, 18, was charged with murdering her infant son after giving birth while attending her senior prom. Jennifer Garcia, 19, was charged with killing her newborn baby girl and dumping the body in a garbage can outside her home in a Los Angeles suburb. Linda Chu, 20, a sophomore at the University of Southern California, was accused of strangling her newborn baby girl and putting her in a trash chute. Some experts said that, despite their notoriety, such cases are rarer now than before legalized abortion.

John E. Du Pont, heir to a chemical-company fortune, was convicted in Pennsylvania of the 1996 killing of Olympic gold-medal wrestler David Schultz on the grounds of the country estate Du Pont had turned into a private training camp. The jury convicted him of third-degree murder and found him to be mentally ill, confining him to a state hospital.

Former Black Panther leader Elmer Pratt was released on bail after 27 years in prison on what he said was a trumped-up murder charge. A judge in Los Angeles ruled that prosecutors withheld crucial evidence in the 1968 robbery-homicide case.

Mir Aimal Kansi, 33, of Pakistan, was convicted of the 1993 murders of two employees of the Central Intelligence Agency (CIA) outside the agency's suburban Virginia headquarters. A four-year manhunt led the FBI to Kansi in a Pakistani hotel in June.

In Stamford, CT, Alex Kelly, a 30-year-old former high-school wrestling star, was found guilty of raping a 16-year-old girl in 1986. He was sentenced to 16 years in prison. An earlier trial in the case had ended in a mistrial. Kelly also faced charges that he raped a 17-year-old girl four days after the incident for which he was convicted. Kelly had returned to the United States in 1995 after eight years avoiding prosecution by living as a fugitive in Europe.

Convicted rapist Lawrence Singleton was charged with murdering prostitute Roxanne Hayes in Tampa, FL. Singleton, 69, who raped a teenage hitchhiker and chopped her arms off with an axe in California in 1978, was paroled in 1987.

JIM RUBIN, *The Associated Press*

CROATIA

Although the reelected government of President Franjo Tudjman was accused increasingly of authoritarian tendencies, Croatia's domestic politics remained relatively stable through 1997.

Political Centralism. Croatia held both parliamentary and presidential elections in 1997—only the second general elections since the country gained independence with the breakup of Yugoslavia in 1991. In elections to the upper house of parliament in April, the ruling Croatian Democratic Union (HDZ) won 42 of the 63 seats. The oppositionist Croatian Social-Liberal Party obtained only 11 seats. In the June presidential elections, Tudjman was reelected president with 61.4% of the vote. His nearest challenger, Zdravko Tomac of the Social Democratic Party, gained 21%; and Vlado Gotovac, leader of the Social-Liberals, obtained 17.5%. Only 57.7% of voters went to the polls.

The Organization for Cooperation in Security and Cooperation in Europe (OSCE) declared the elections to be "free but not fair." Both the opposition and observers charged that the HDZ dominated the state-controlled mass media and gave Tudjman an unfair advantage. Moreover, there were reports of intimidation and harassment; for example, Gotovac, the Liberal candidate, was assaulted by an army captain during a rally.

The Croatian government was criticized on a broad range of domestic issues, including the absence of full press freedoms, the creation of a personality cult around Tudjman, and the nonimplementation of minority rights for the large Serb population. The United Nations scaled down its operations in Eastern Slavonia, the last region still occupied by Serb guerrillas. The region was due to be reintegrated into Croatia at the end of 1997. However, Zagreb was criticized for not doing enough to build confidence among the Serb population and to promote social reintegration with the Croatian majority.

Economic Stability. The Croatian economy remained relatively stable in 1997, with a low inflation rate and a small budgetary deficit. Growth in the gross domestic product (GDP) was projected at about 6%. However, Zagreb needed to implement a range of economic reforms, including a transparent process of privatizing state industries, in order to gain any significant Western investment. There also were concerns that falling living standards among some sectors of the population could precipitate strikes and demonstrations.

CROATIA • Information Highlights

Official Name: Republic of Croatia.
Location: Southeastern Europe.
Area: 21,829 sq mi (56 538 km²).
Population (mid-1997 est.): 4,800,000.
Chief Cities (1991 census): Zagreb, the capital, 706,770; Split, 189,388; Rijeka, 167,964; Osijek, 104,761.
Government: *Head of state,* Franjo Tudjman, president (took office May 1990). *Head of government,* Zlatko Matesa (took office November 1995). *Legislature*—Assembly: House of Districts and House of Representatives.
Monetary Unit: Kuna (6.166 kuna equal U.S.$1, June 1997).
Gross Domestic Product (1995 est. U.S.$): $20,100,000,-000 (purchasing power parity).
Economic Index: *Consumer Prices* (1996, 1990 = 100): all items, 58,710.6; food, 55,861.6.
Foreign Trade (1996 U.S.$): *Imports,* $7,788,000,000; *exports,* $4,512,000,000.

The Dayton Process. Following intensive U.S. pressure, Zagreb ensured the surrender of ten indicted Bosnian Croat war criminals to the Hague War Crimes Tribunal. But serious questions remained about whether this indicated a genuine commitment to the Dayton process or was merely a concession to cushion against further international criticism. Washington leaned on its European allies to suspend Croatia from the Council of Europe because of its human-rights violations and repeated failures to implement the Bosnian accords.

The Tudjman government had the opportunity to buttress Bosnian integration and to discard its claims to Bosnian territory. Zagreb exercised substantial control over the Bosnian Croat areas and over politicians who resisted the creation of a multiethnic state. Reintegration had to take place at four levels—security, political, economic, and social. The melding of the Croat-Muslim Federation military structure and the creation of joint combat units were behind schedule. Police forces were divided by ethnic membership and party loyalty.

Government bodies of the federation had little authority, as real power lay at the cantonal and municipal levels, where nationalists continued to dominate. The federation was not a single economic unit but was divided into two parallel systems that simply consolidated division and separatism. Indeed, not only did Croatian areas operate as separate economic entities, but they were tied more closely to Zagreb than to the Bosnian capital of Sarajevo. Croatian officials exclusively controlled customs, port, and railway fees along Bosnia's southern border with Croatia. Revenues from all these services should have flowed into Bosnia's federal coffers. Several foreign-financed federal business ventures also were blocked by Croatian separatists.

JANUSZ BUGAJSKI
Center for Strategic and International Studies

CUBA

Cuban economic recovery slowed and a housing shortage developed in 1997. Tourism was up, and relations with the United States remained cool and received international attention.

The visit of Pope John Paul II to Cuba—scheduled for Jan. 21–25, 1998—also drew international interest. Businesslike negotiations with the Vatican concerning details of the papal stay indicated that the government thought the visit would enhance its prestige and legitimacy at home and abroad. Cuba announced that, for the papal visit, it would permit a Miami cruise ship with U.S. worshipers to dock in Havana and would allow direct flights from the United States to land at Havana's airport.

Economy. Cuba's recovery from economic woes following the 1991 collapse of the Soviet Union slowed down noticeably in 1997. Gross national product (GNP) grew by about 2.5%—5% less than in 1996—according to Carlos Lage, Cuban deputy prime minister in charge of the economy. Lage blamed the U.S. Helms-Burton Act, adverse weather—which seriously damaged agriculture—and administrative mismanagement. The United Nations (UN) Economic Commission for Latin America and the Caribbean—which predicted the 1997 decline—reported that living standards still were below those of 1989, when Cuba last received Soviet assistance.

Housing became a problem in 1997. Havana said that more than half of its 560,000 dwellings were in need of repair and some 60,000 had to be demolished. The situation was worse in the provinces, from which some 28,000 migrate annually to Havana seeking better living conditions. One bright spot was tourism, with more than 1 million foreigners visiting the island in 1997. In addition, thousands of Cuban exiles—mostly from the United States—traveled to their homeland, spending or giving to relatives some $800 million. Tourism was endangered temporarily during the summer after a dozen small bombs exploded in various Havana hotels, killing an Italian-Canadian businessman and wounding several other foreigners. The bombings stopped in September after the Cuban police arrested a young Salvadoran who, according to Havana, confessed to placing six of the bombs. The accused said that he was paid $4,500 for each incident by anti-Castro exiles. Cuba accused the Miami Cuban American National Foundation of masterminding the scheme, a charge the foundation denied.

© Alain Nogues/Sygma

In October 1997 a Cuban schoolboy carried a portrait of Che Guevara during a large-scale national funeral for the late guerrilla leader. Guevara's remains had been found in Bolivia.

U.S. Relations. The 1996 Helms-Burton Act punishes foreign companies investing in Cuba, especially in U.S. properties nationalized in 1960. Although Havana said that foreign investments grew by 25% in 1997, large conglomerates showed little interest in investing substantially in Cuba—a nation of 11 million with limited natural resources and a Marxist regime. To facilitate foreign commerce, the government created a Cuban Central Bank, which operates along traditional Western lines. Havana said that U.S. efforts to deny Cuba access to long-term, low-interest foreign loans adversely affected Cuba's economic recovery. As a result, Cuba could obtain only expensive, short-term funds, diminishing its ability to buy vitally needed goods abroad. Cuba also had to pay higher prices for oil and received lower prices for sugar—its principal export. Only 4.2 million tons of sugar were produced—250,000 tons less than in 1996.

U.S. policy toward Cuba, influenced by the Miami-based Cuban-exile lobby, was subject to criticism. "The American strangulation of Cuba," said a February *New York Times* editorial, "is a Cold War anachronism." Elizardo Sánchez Santacruz, a dissident who spent nine years in Cuban jails and who lives in Havana, wrote in an April article, "I am convinced that...efforts to pressure and isolate Cuba simply give the leaders a pretext to continue their repression and allow them to divert attention from their failures. The vast majority of us on the island who oppose the [Castro] government believe that a dialogue and a relaxation of tension would better facilitate a transformation." Sánchez Santacruz advocated lifting travel restrictions to Cuba and ending the embargo on sales of food and medicines—calling it a "prohibition that violates international law and hurts the people of Cuba, not the regime."

In November, after its annual discussion of Cuban-U.S. relations, the UN General Assembly once more passed a resolution—143–3, with 17 abstentions—asking Washington to end its Cuban embargo. Japan, which abstained in 1996, joined all 15 European Union (EU) members, Australia, Canada, New Zealand, Mexico, Brazil, and Argentina in supporting the resolution. Only Israel and the former Soviet republic of Uzbekistan sided with the United States. Helms-Burton also was criticized strongly in November during the final statement of the seventh summit of the Ibero-American nations held in Venezuela.

While Havana bitterly complained about Helms-Burton, Washington was embroiled in controversy over the law with European governments and Canada, which considered it illegal and a violation of the free-trade agreement signed by the United States. Canada's foreign minister criticized the law during a visit to Havana and was rebuked publicly by the U.S. State Department. Throughout 1997, Washington negotiated the issue with the European Union to avoid a complaint to a court of world trade under the auspices of the World Trade Organization, where the United States could suffer an embarrassing rebuff.

Washington gave Stet International, an Italian telecommunications firm, the green light to invest in Cuba after it agreed to pay the New York–based International Telephone and Telegraph (ITT) $24 million for the use of its confiscated Cuban properties. For the first time in 30 years, Washington permitted U.S. media to open news bureaus in Cuba. The growing popularity of Cuban music in the United States prompted the Bill Clinton administration to issue visas to Cuban musicians, who performed before large audiences in various U.S. cities.

CUBA • Information Highlights

Official Name: Republic of Cuba.
Location: Caribbean.
Area: 42,803 sq mi (110 860 km²).
Population (mid-1997 est.): 11,100,000.
Chief Cities (Dec. 31, 1993 est.): Havana, the capital, 2,175,995; Santiago de Cuba, 440,084; Camagüey, 293,961; Holguín, 242,085.
Government: *Head of state and government,* Fidel Castro Ruz, president (took office under a new constitution, December 1976). *Legislature* (unicameral)—National Assembly of People's Power.
Monetary Unit: Peso (1.0 peso equals U.S.$1, noncommercial rate, April 1997).
Gross Domestic Product (1995 est. U.S.$): $14,700,000,-000 (purchasing power parity).
Foreign Trade (1995 est. U.S.$): *Imports,* $2,825,000,000; *exports,* $1,600,000,000.

Political Affairs. The October 8–10 Congress of the ruling Communist Party of Cuba, the first since 1991, emphasized the political and economic status quo. The 71-year-old Castro delivered a nearly seven-hour speech, belying rumors he was seriously ill. He said that while he liked the Chinese economic model, Cuba could not adopt it because of the relentless U.S. hostility that China did not face. He indicated, however, that the limited operating space that a market economy has at present would be retained.

While Castro and his brother, Raúl, remained the country's top leaders, the party's Politburo was reduced by three members, to 24, and its Central Committee was cut by 75, to 150. There was a drastic generational changeover in both bodies, whose newly appointed members were mostly in their 30s and 40s. Raúl Castro explained the streamlining by pointing out that membership in the committee should be based "not only on representatives but also skill." He also noted that it was necessary to "elect a Central Committee that will keep the revolution immune from ideological viruses" like those that affected the USSR and Eastern Europe in the 1980s.

Also in October, Cuba paid tribute to Ernesto Che Guevara, one of the most honored heroes of the Cuban revolution, whose remains were brought from Bolivia to be placed in a mausoleum in Santa Clara. The Argentine-born revolutionary—after the Castro brothers, the highest figure in early days of the revolutionary regime—had tried unsuccessfully in 1967 to organize a peasant guerrilla movement in the Bolivian mountains. Wounded by soldiers, Guevara was taken prisoner and later was shot by his captors. His remains and those of some of his Cuban and Bolivian guerrillas had been discovered earlier in the year.

GEORGE VOLSKY, *University of Miami*

CYPRUS

In 1997, Cyprus remained split as the result of a 1974 Turkish invasion and occupation of about 40% of the island's northern territory. In 1983, Turkish-occupied lands had been designated as the Turkish Republic of Northern Cyprus. The southern part, inhabited by Greek Cypriots, continued as the Republic of Cyprus. United Nations (UN) peacekeepers continued to patrol the Green Line—a buffer zone that separated the two. Great Britain, the island's former colonial ruler, retained its military bases at Akrotiri and Dhekelia.

Rivalries. The Greek Cypriot president of Cyprus, Glafkos Clerides, and his government steadfastly refused to recognize the formal existence of the Turkish Republic of Northern Cyprus, or that the Turkish Cypriot Rauf Denktash was its president. Only Turkey recognized the Denktash regime.

Since 1974 numerous initiatives to bring together the Greek and Turkish Cypriots in some kind of compromise over the island's governance had been totally unsuccessful. Some 200,000 Greek Cypriot refugees from the north remained in the south, with their status in abeyance. In the north, now populated heavily by Turkish Cypriots and resettled mainland Turks, the Turkish government stationed strong military forces. The situation remained fraught with tensions, and the two sides seemed irreconcilable. With the Greek government vigorously supporting the Greek Cypriots, and the Turkish government supporting the Turkish Cypriots, relations between those two countries were strained severely.

Reconciliation Efforts. Under UN auspices, Clerides and Denktash met several times during 1997, and particularly major discussions were held at a resort area some 90 mi (145 km) from New York City in July and in Switzerland in August. These talks basically indicated how far apart the two sides were.

During 1997 the United States showed strong willingness to assist the Cypriots in resolving their disputes. In the U.S. State Department, Thomas Miller held the position of special coordinator for Cyprus, and in June the highly respected U.S. diplomat Richard Holbrooke was appointed as President Bill Clinton's special emissary for Cyprus. In November, Holbrooke visited Cyprus and arranged a four-and-one-half-hour meeting in the UN buffer zone at Nicosia between Clerides and Denktash. This followed separate meetings between Holbrooke and the two leaders. Holbrooke later was quoted as saying that the two men had incompatible positions on several essential matters, but were willing to discuss them. Holbrooke's initiative was praised not only by Cyprus but by the Greek and Turkish governments.

In May a "peace" concert was staged in the buffer zone at Nicosia, under UN auspices with the concurrence of the Clerides government. It was held to bring Greek and Turkish Cypriot young people together in harmony.

Despite these efforts, the end of 1997 brought no resolution to the problems of Cypriot division.

The European Union. Clerides' government continued its quest to make Cyprus a part of the European Union (EU). Denktash, however, voiced strong objections, saying that EU accession could not be negotiated without formal Turkish Cypriot representation. Meanwhile, the economy in the Greek Cypriot south vigorously flourished, while Turkish Cyprus lagged far behind.

GEORGE J. MARCOPOULOS, *Tufts University*

CYPRUS • Information Highlights

Official Name: Republic of Cyprus.
Location: Eastern Mediterranean.
Area: 3,571 sq mi (9 250 km²).
Population (mid-1997 est.): 700,000.
Chief Cities (Dec. 31, 1993 est.): Nicosia, the capital, 186,400; Limassol, 143,400.
Government: *Head of state and government,* Glafkos Clerides, president (took office March 1, 1993). *Legislature*—House of Representatives.
Monetary Unit: Pound (0.539 pound equals U.S.$1, official rate, July 1997).
Gross Domestic Product (1995 est. U.S.$): $7,800,000,000 (purchasing power parity).
Economic Indexes (1996, 1990 = 100): *Consumer Prices,* all items, 129.8; food, 131.9. *Industrial Production,* 100.
Foreign Trade (1996 U.S.$): *Imports,* $3,977,000,000; *exports,* $1,386,000,000.

CZECH REPUBLIC

In 1997 the Czech Republic—among the most stable and prosperous of the postcommunist countries—experienced serious political and economic problems. Shaken by financial and banking scandals in the spring, the government of Prime Minister Václav Klaus resigned in November.

Politics. In June the ministers of finance, education, and trade and industry were replaced, and the government won a vote of confidence by just two votes. Twenty-nine percent of those surveyed in September supported the opposition Social Democrats; 25% supported Klaus' Civic Democratic Party. Klaus' coalition partners, the People's Party and the Civic Democratic Alliance, called for a new government program in October. In late October, Foreign Minister Josef Zieleniec resigned and was replaced by Jaroslav Šediv, a former dissident. In November, Klaus' government was forced to resign, and on December 16, President Václav Havel appointed a nonaffiliated economist, Josef Tošovsky, 47, as prime minister.

In response to Organization for Security and Cooperation in Europe (OSCE) criticism, parliament abolished a section of the criminal code that imposed a two-year jail sentence for slandering the president. In August the U.S. Helsinki Committee criticized the Czech citizenship law. Many Roma—or gypsies—applied to immigrate to Canada in response to a very positive television show about Roma life in that country. In October, Canada reimposed visa requirements for Czech citizens. Czech officials in the city of Ostrava discussed giving Roma free air tickets to immigrate. Many Roma also have emigrated to Britain. The government considered a special report on Roma issues and promised to take action to improve their situation. In September the Council of Europe criticized the citizenship law and a law that bans former communist officials from certain government positions.

In October parliament passed a law establishing 14 regional governments, as called for in the constitution. One of every five families lost child-care payments in September, due to social-welfare reforms. The shift from a universal to a need-based benefit system also reduced other benefits. In November the trade-union federation held a rally against the government's economic and social policies.

Economy. Growth rates decreased significantly in the first six months of 1997. Financial and banking scandals caused the Czech koruna to drop. Inflation increased to 10.3% in September, while unemployment reached a post-1989 high of 4.8%. Officials anticipated a budget deficit of $554 million. The state budget narrowly passed by parliament envisioned a further decrease in spending, particularly on agriculture and pensions. Foreign debt increased to $19.6 billion by September. Czech leaders enacted a series of banking and other financial reforms in November to regulate investment funds and stimulate the stock market. The trade deficit decreased between January and September.

Serious floods in July and August caused $1.8 billion in damage and contributed to the economic problems. Some 50 people died in the floods, which affected more than one third of the country. The Czech government aided citizens who lost their homes. Outside organi-

---

CZECH REPUBLIC • Information Highlights

Official Name: Czech Republic.
Location: East-central Europe.
Area: 30,387 sq mi (78 703 km²).
Population (mid-1997 est.): 10,300,000.
Chief Cities (Jan. 1, 1996 est.): Prague, the capital, 1,209,855; Brno, 388,899; Ostrava, 324,813.
Government: *Head of state,* Václav Havel, president (took office Jan. 1, 1993). *Head of government,* Josef Tošovsky, prime minister (appointed Dec. 16, 1997). *Legislature—* National Council: Senate and Chamber of Deputies.
Monetary Unit: Koruna (34.64 koruny equal U.S.$1, commercial rate, Dec. 31, 1997).
Gross Domestic Product (1995 est. U.S.$): $106,200,000,-000.
Economic Index (1996, 1991 = 100): *Consumer Prices,* all items, 175.9; food, 167.7.
Foreign Trade (1996 U.S.$): *Imports,* $26,835,000,000; *exports,* $21,924,000,000.

---

zations such as the European Bank for Reconstruction and Development (EBRD) and the European Union's (EU's) Phare program also provided assistance. The opposition and some deputies from the ruling coalition refused to support an income tax to balance the budget after the floods.

Foreign Affairs. The Czech Republic was identified as a candidate for the first round of North Atlantic Treaty Organization (NATO) expansion at the Madrid NATO Summit in July. It was also among six postcommunist countries invited in June to EU accession talks, which began in September. In preparation for joining NATO, Czech defense officials agreed with their Hungarian and Polish counterparts in October to coordinate their policies and military purchases. Public support was stronger for joining the EU than for joining NATO. NATO membership was backed by about one third of Czech citizens and opposed by one third; another third were undecided. Czech leaders began a campaign to increase support for NATO membership. (*See also* EUROPE—*NATO Expansion.*)

Czech-Slovak relations worsened as a result of the Czech decision to give part of the gold confiscated from Slovak Jews in World War II to a Jewish foundation. President Havel's criticism of Slovak Prime Minister Vladimir Mečiar's attitude toward NATO expansion contributed to poor relations. In October, Mečiar and Prime Minister Klaus agreed to settle part of their nations' mutual debts by bank transfers.

In February and March both houses of parliament approved the declaration of reconciliation that Czech and German leaders signed in January. In October, Czech and German leaders agreed to establish a joint discussion forum and fund for Nazi victims.

SHARON L. WOLCHIK
The George Washington University

DANCE

Established masters like Jerome Robbins, Merce Cunningham, and Paul Taylor still created superior works in 1997, but their younger colleagues seemed adrift. The tendency of U.S. and foreign choreographers was to work in modes they already had made familiar—even when ballet companies experimented with modern-dance ideas, such as Lar Lubovitch's *Othello* for American Ballet Theatre (ABT) and Angelin Preljocaj's *La Stravaganza* for the New York City Ballet. In each case, a choreographer transferred to new terrain the signature style he had used in his own troupe.

Audiences remained loyal to their favorite companies and choreographers. There were a few new faces, such as Diana Vishneva, 21, the rising star of the Kirov Ballet, who was introduced to New York at a gala with other young Russian dancers. Carlos Acosta—a Cuban-born principal with the Houston Ballet—promised to be ballet's next superstar, and Darcey Bussell, a better-known English ballerina, triumphed as she led the Royal Ballet at the Lincoln Center Festival '97.

Ballet. The season's highlight was *Brandenburg*, Robbins' first major work in several years for the New York City Ballet. Set to excerpts from Bach's *Brandenburg Concertos*, the ballet's retrospective tone used familiar devices made to look fresh. The good humor of Bach's concertos was reflected in the playful ensembles, but the central encounter was a duet in which Nikolaj Hubbe and Lourdes Lopez initially avoided contact and resembled sleepwalkers. Hubbe and Damian Woetzel alternated in *A Suite of Dances* at the City Ballet, a Bach solo that Robbins created in 1994 for Mikhail Baryshnikov.

In another premiere, *Schoenberg/Wuorinen Variations*, Richard Tanner used the two-piano arrangement that U.S. composer Charles Wuorinen made of Arnold Schoenberg's *Variations for Orchestra*. The choreography mirrored the music's dissonance.

City Ballet Director Peter Martins again tried to stimulate choreography with the 1997 Diamond Project, a sequel to similarly named 1992 and 1994 showcases. French modern-dance choreographer Preljocaj created the brilliant and mysterious *La Stravaganza*, which contrasted two ensembles. An Old World group in 17th-century Dutch dress used weighted gestures, while a sextet in contemporary costumes displayed ballet virtuosity. The project's other premieres, in City Ballet's familiar neoclassical style, were Kevin O'Day's *Open Strings*, Christopher d'Amboise's *Circle of Fifths*, Miriam Mahdaviani's *Urban Dances*, Christopher Wheeldon's *Slavonic Dances*, and Robert LaFosse's *Concerto in Five Movements*. Merrill Ashley, one of the company's most popular ballerinas, retired after 31 years and gave a farewell performance at the opening of City Ballet's fall season.

American Ballet Theatre's new three-act *Othello* also was performed by coproducer the San Francisco Ballet. The production was designed spectacularly by George Tsypin,

"Brandenburg," below—Jerome Robbins' first major work in several years for the New York City Ballet—premiered in January 1997 and was a highlight of the ballet season. It is set to excerpts from Bach's "Brandenburg Concertos."

A Renaissance in Irish Dance

Throughout 1997, there was a resurgence of popularity around the world—and particularly in the United States—of all things Irish. The most notable feature of this trend was the phenomenal international success of *Riverdance*, an explosive show that brought to the forefront an energized form of Irish dance, as well as the powerful rhythms of Irish step-dancing music.

Traditionally, Irish step dancing uses a technique sometimes called "fire and ice," in which dancers perform vigorous, complex, high-stepping routines with their lower bodies while keeping their upper bodies as still as possible. The new, more audience-friendly form of step dancing seen in *Riverdance* and its offshoot, *Lord of the Dance*, is largely the creation of Chicago-born Irish-American champion step dancer Michael Flatley, 38. He and fellow dancer Jean Butler first performed the untraditional program in 1994 in a seven-minute television piece entitled *Riverdance* and shown as part of the widely viewed Eurovision talent contest. Eurovision's producer, Moya Doherty, commissioned composer Billy Whelan to write a dance piece and Flatley to choreograph and perform in it. *Riverdance*'s spectacular success led to its being expanded into a full two-hour extravaganza with a company of 85 dancers. By mid-1997 the show was maintaining two touring companies and had

a successful video, and its best-selling soundtrack had won a Grammy Award. A television version of the concert raised more than $10 million when shown during a Public Broadcasting System (PBS) pledge drive.

Flatley, however, left *Riverdance* in October 1995 for reasons that are disputed, and established a rival Irish-dance extravaganza, *Lord of the Dance*, which opened in Dublin in July 1996 and toured the United States during 1997. It features 40 dancers, with Flatley as the lead, performing to a score by Ronan Hardiman. *Lord of the Dance*, although suffering in comparison to *Riverdance* in many reviews, experienced a runaway success even more remarkable than that of its predecessor.

Meanwhile, other expressions of Celtic culture were discovering renewed popularity, which was sparked further by the rejuvenated, rock- and flamenco-influenced version of step dancing. One music chain, Michigan-based Harmony House, reported that its Celtic-music sections had tripled in size over recent years. So-called "authentic Irish pubs" were popping up across the United States at the rate of one per week. And Frank McCourt's book *Angela's Ashes*, a prizewinning memoir of growing up poor in Ireland, had been on best-seller lists for a year.

MEGHAN O'REILLY FIERO

© Joan Marcus

A resurgence of interest in Irish culture—particularly in Celtic music and dance—was engendered by the international popularity of "Riverdance," left, and "Lord of the Dance," both of which showcased an updated, sensual version of Irish step dancing.

whose plastic decor suggested slabs of cracked glass. Working with the composer Elliott Goldenthal, Lubovitch produced vivid theatrical choreography that owed more to his expressive modern-dance roots than to conventional British and Russian ballets. Two new smaller works were Nacho Duato's *Remanso* and Jean-Christophe Maillot's *In Volo*.

ABT's *The Merry Widow*, a ballet version of Franz Lehar's operetta that Ronald Hynd choreographed for the Australian Ballet in 1975, was a smash hit. The troupe's dance power—embodied in Julio Bocca's hilarious bravura—gave the comic ballet new life. Frederic Franklin's fresh production of *Coppélia* had a gentler charm.

Choreographer Eliot Feld changed the name of Feld Ballets/NY to Ballet Tech, to identify the company with his ballet school. His dancers—younger and less classical than their predecessors—were energetic and disciplined, and Feld's new choreography was geared to their talents. *Yo Shakespeare* successfully fused break dancing and ballet, but Feld's fondness for gimmicks was visible in premieres such as *Juke Box*, *Shuffle*, *Joggers*, and *Re: X*. *Evening Chant* featured lights on the costumes, and *Umbra Blues* consisted of shadow play. Feld fared better in *Industry*, Buffy Miller's sexy contortionist solo.

The Boston Ballet drew interest with an appealing version of *Cinderella* by English choreographer Michael Corder. Its colorful production of *Le Corsaire*, a 19th-century spectacle based on a Bolshoi Ballet version, was renamed *The Pirate*.

Dance Theatre of Harlem introduced Alicia Graf, a striking young dancer, and South African choreographer Vincent Sekwati Mantsoe. His ballet *Sasanka* shared the bill with Robert Garland's *Crossing Over* and John Alleyne's *Adrian (Angel on Earth)*. Company ballerina Virginia Johnson retired after 28 years.

At the Houston Ballet, Ben Stevenson's full-evening *Dracula* attracted attention. Audiences at the Kennedy Center for the Performing Arts in Washington got a taste of company star Carlos Acosta's effortless technique and warm personality in *Don Quixote*.

Modern Dance. Garrison Keillor, host of the radio show *Prairie Home Companion*, was a hilarious master of ceremonies for a fund-raising tribute to Merce Cunningham at the Brooklyn Academy of Music. Mark Morris and Bill Irwin created affectionate parodies of Cunningham's works. Cunningham's premieres for his own season at the academy were *Installations*, *Windows*, *Rondo*, and *Scenario*, for which fashion designer Rei Kawakubo stuffed costumes with padding. Cunningham's use of a computer as a compositional tool seemed to make his choreography flatter than in the past.

Paul Taylor's *Eventide* was one of his most beautiful pieces, an ode to love and loss expressed in the quiet passion of five couples; his *Prime Numbers* proved minor. Twyla Tharp's touring company added *Roy's Joys*, one of her best jazz pieces, set to Roy Eldridge recordings. Morris paid tribute to composer Lou Harrison in *Rhymes with Silver*. His company premiered *I Don't Want to Love*. Baryshnikov's White Oak Dance Project featured *Unspoken Territory*, a fine, frieze-like Baryshnikov solo by Dana Reitz, and *Journey of a Poet*, said to be a posthumous work by Erick Hawkins. Meg Stuart's *Remote* was a poorly received piece about alienation.

The Limón Dance Company celebrated its 50th anniversary with revivals of José Limón works as well as Donald McKayle's *Heartbeats* and Jiri Kylian's *Evening Songs*. The last two played at the Jacob's Pillow Dance Festival in Becket, MA, where executive director Sali Ann Kriegsman resigned and was succeeded by Ella Baff of the University of California at Berkeley.

New Alvin Ailey American Dance Theatre works were Donald Byrd's *Fin de Siècle*, George Faison's *Slaves*, and Earl Mosely's *Days Past, Not Forgotten*. More on the cutting edge were Ralph Lemon's *Geography* and John Jasperse's *Waving to You from Here*.

Foreign Companies. The Royal Ballet presented Kenneth MacMillan's 1989 version of Benjamin Britten's undanceable ballet score, *The Prince of the Pagodas*, in which Darcey Bussell proved dazzling. She also triumphed in Frederick Ashton's exquisite 1948 *Cinderella*, a Ravel program that featured Ashton's *La Valse* and *Daphnis and Chloe*, and Wheeldon's *Pavane pour une Infante Défunte*. Diana Vishneva appeared with Russian dancers at a Lincoln Center tribute to impresario Serge Diaghilev. Experimental dance from abroad was represented best by Pina Bausch's *Der Fensterputzer*, Anne Teresa de Keersmaeker's *Woud*, and Angelin Preljocaj's *Annonciation*, presented by Preljocaj's own troupe.

Awards. Edward Villella received the Kennedy Center Honors. Anna Halprin received the Samuel H. Scripps/American Dance Festival Award. The Capezio Dance Award went to Mark Morris.

ANNA KISSELGOFF, *"The New York Times"*

DENMARK

During 1997 support for a "yes" vote in the 1998 referendum on Danish ratification of the European Union (EU) Amsterdam Treaty grew. Fiscal policy was tightened twice to prevent the Danish economy from overheating.

European and Foreign Affairs. Social Democratic Prime Minister Poul Nyrup Rasmussen announced in October that the referendum on the ratification of the new EU Amsterdam Treaty would be held on May 28, 1998. That date was chosen to allow the Supreme Court to deliver a verdict in a relevant appeal case from the District Court, which had rejected the claim by 11 Danish opponents of the Maastricht Treaty that it is unconstitutional and, hence, that the referendum is irrelevant.

Denmark was the only country voting on the new Amsterdam Treaty. The Danish government had said that it would not attempt to renegotiate the terms, as it did with the Maastricht Treaty in 1992, if the Danes were to reject it. The government had not said that Denmark would leave the EU in the event of a "no" vote, only that the relationship with the EU would become very uncertain.

Polls indicated that the government would not be put to the test. Throughout 1997 support for the Amsterdam Treaty grew, so that by October, those in favor held a lead of between 15% and 16%, with 25% of the voters undecided. The decisive swing came from the prime minister's own party, where a majority for the first time declared they would vote yes. Conservative and liberal voters increasingly declared their opposition, but the numbers were too small to have a serious impact on the outcome.

The growing support for the Amsterdam Treaty was not reflected in support of Danish accession to the economic and monetary union (EMU), which would require another referendum. This meant that Denmark would not be among the founding EMU members, despite the fact that it meets all the criteria. But the Danish currency, the krone, would be linked to the new EU currency, the Euro, by a special agreement stipulating that exchange rates may vary only within a narrow band—perhaps between 1% and 2%—giving Denmark virtual membership.

U.S. President Bill Clinton visited Denmark in July and congratulated the Danes for their efforts on behalf of the Baltic states. His presence in Denmark strengthened Danish ambitions to have a special relationship with the United States.

DENMARK • Information Highlights

Official Name: Kingdom of Denmark.
Location: Northwest Europe.
Area: 16,629 sq mi (43 070 km^2).
Population (mid-1997 est.): 5,300,000.
Chief Cities (Jan. 1, 1996 est.): Copenhagen, the capital, 476,751; Århus, 279,759; Odense, 183,564.
Government: *Head of state,* Margrethe II, queen (acceded Jan. 1972). *Head of government,* Poul Nyrup Rasmussen, prime minister (took office Jan. 1993). *Legislature* (unicameral)—Folketing.
Monetary Unit: Krone (6.7450 kroner equal U.S.$1, Dec. 2, 1997).
Gross Domestic Product (1995 est. U.S.$): $112,800,-000,000 (purchasing power parity).
Economic Indexes (1996, 1990 = 100): *Consumer Prices,* all items, 112.6; food, 109.8. *Industrial Production,* 117.
Foreign Trade (1996 U.S.$): *Imports,* $43,221,000,000; *exports,* $48,775,000,000.

Denmark continued to protest human-rights violations in China, which prompted China to shelve Danish participation in a number of commercial projects and to cancel ministerial- and trade-delegation visits. By the fall, however, there were signs of a quiet normalization of relations.

Politics. The opposition Conservative Party chose a new leader, Per Stig Moller, after the former leader, Hans Engell, resigned following a drunken-driving incident. The scandal was compounded when it was learned Moller had received a 20-day sentence for drunk driving as a young student—a fact he initially tried to deny. The governing coalition, reduced by the departure of the Centre Democrats in the final days of 1996, published its long-term plan to make Denmark an economic model for Europe. During the next eight years, foreign debt was to be eliminated completely, and the national debt was to be reduced from 67% to 40% of gross domestic product (GDP).

Economy. The GDP rose by more than 3% in 1997 and was expected to rise by a little less than that in 1998. The gain was in response to two mild doses of fiscal tightening. The first, in May, nominally increased the price of cars for environmental reasons. The second, in October, imposed compulsory savings at the rate of 1% of earnings in 1998. Unemployment dropped to 8.1% of the labor force, while exports and business investment provided the main growth stimuli. Denmark's largest bank, Den Danske Bank, was an active participant in creating an integrated Nordic financial market, and bought the Swedish Ostgota Enskilda Bank.

Coca-Cola chose Carlsberg Breweries as its Nordic production and distribution partner—an agreement accepted by the EU Commission.

LEIF BECK FALLESEN, *"Boersen," Copenhagen*

DRUGS AND ALCOHOL

Victories and setbacks marked the 26th year of the U.S. "war on drugs." Alcohol use declined in 1997 among 12- to 17-year-olds.

Drugs. There was a good deal of wrangling over the best way to combat the importation and use of illegal drugs—primarily marijuana, cocaine, and heroin. Ramifications of 1996 ballot initiatives in California and Arizona in which voters approved legalizing marijuana use for medical purposes were debated hotly. Antidrug groups and law-enforcement officials said the initiatives promoted greater use of marijuana. Many who advocated these initiatives "are pushing for legalization of drugs, plain and simple," said retired U.S. Army Gen. Barry R. McCaffrey, director of the Office of National Drug Control Policy.

Advocates of the laws, such as financier and philanthropist George Soros, argued that they were a first step toward more-effective drug policies. "I am not for legalizing hard drugs. I am for a saner drug policy," Soros said. He also stated that "criminalizing drug abuse does more harm than good, blocking effective treatment and incarcerating far too many people." Counteracting the 1996 initiative trend, voters in Washington state in 1997 rejected a proposition that would have legalized the medical use of marijuana and other drugs.

Also in dispute was the effectiveness of the 26-year war on drugs, which has cost an estimated $290 billion in federal, state, and local funds. The fiscal-year 1997 federal drug-control budget was more than $16 billion, including a $195 million antidrug advertising campaign aimed at young people. "The drug war is the number one growth industry in federal funding, but we've spent most of the money on a policy that basically doesn't work," said Mathea Falco, a former U.S. State Department narcotics official who is president of Drug Strategies, a nonprofit policy group in Washington.

Falco and others pointed to significant failures in the war. In 1997 cocaine and heroin imported into the United States were purer, cheaper, and more plentiful than ever before, while international production was at an all-time high. Despite the death in July of Amado Carrillo Fuentes, one of the world's most powerful drug traffickers, the multibillion-dollar cocaine trade continued to flourish in his country, Mexico. Colombian drug cartels—aligned with Russian and Nigerian organized crime—continued large-scale international cocaine-smuggling and money-laundering operations. In the United States a vast amount of marijuana was grown largely uncurtailed; at the same time, heroin use climbed drastically among teens and adults, with an estimated 600,000 addicts.

On the positive side, nationwide surveys released in 1997 indicated that, while drug use among teenagers and young adults remained steady, marijuana use declined slightly for the first time in five years. The federal government's 1996 National Household Survey on Drug Abuse, released on August 7, reported that 7.1% of 12- to 17-year-olds said they used marijuana monthly, compared with 8.2% in 1995. Drug use among 18- to 25-year-olds, however, continued to increase. The survey found that 15.6% of that age group reported using an illegal drug the previous year, compared with 14.2% in 1995 and 13.3% in 1993.

Alcohol. The same survey indicated a continuing decline in alcohol use among those 12 to 17 years of age. Nearly 19% said they used alcohol in the previous month, compared with a high of 32.5% in 1990. Alcohol, however, continued to be an extremely costly and dangerous social and health problem among older teens and adults.

Alcohol was involved in 40.9% of the nearly 42,000 fatal driving accidents in 1996, according to the National Highway Traffic Safety Administration, leading Mothers Against Drunk Driving (MADD) to characterize these deaths as "the nation's most frequently committed violent crime." International attention focused on the issue after autopsy tests revealed that Henri Paul—the driver of the car in which Diana, the princess of Wales, and Dodi Fayed were killed—had a high blood-alcohol level.

Binge drinking, another serious and widespread threat to health, was brought to public notice after the alcohol-induced deaths of two college fraternity pledges—20-year-old Benjamin Wynne of Louisiana State University in August and 18-year-old Scott Krueger of the Massachusetts Institute of Technology in September. Both deaths were brought about by binge drinking—imbibing at least four to five drinks in a row in a short period of time. Harvard School of Public Health surveys indicated that some 44% of college students and more than 85% of college fraternity-house residents took part in binge drinking. Late in 1996 the spirits industry ended a longtime voluntary ban on hard-liquor advertising on television. In April, President Bill Clinton called on the Federal Communications Commission (FCC) to study instituting a mandatory ban.

MARC LEEPSON, *Freelance Writer*

ECUADOR

Political developments dominated 1997 news in Ecuador.

The Presidency. The congress of Ecuador dismissed President Abdalá Bucaram Ortiz in February, in the midst of widespread popular demonstrations. Bucaram was dismissed only six months after his August 1996 inauguration. As president, he had acted as clownish as he had throughout his colorful political career. The populist politician had disappointed some supporters by retaining many policies and several ministers from the administration of his conservative predecessor, Sixto Durán Ballén.

Bucaram advocated pegging the currency to the U.S. dollar, as Argentina had done with great success; but with Ecuador's inflation accelerating to an annualized triple-digit rate, Argentina's success could not have been repeated in Ecuador. The public was more angered by the president's nepotism and corruption. According to his successors, one third of all the spending in the Bucaram administration took place during his last week in office, which suggested that much of the money had been stolen. By early 1997 surveys showed that more than 90% of the public disapproved of Bucaram's performance.

On February 5 and 6, an alliance of union leaders, indigenous organizations, women, and peasants called a national civic strike. This strike mobilized thousands of citizens in all regions of the country. Although the striking groups had different grievances, they all demanded the removal of Bucaram from the presidency. In response to this peaceful mobilization, the congress on February 6 declared the presidency vacant on the grounds of Bucaram's "mental incapacity" and chose the president of the congress, Fabián Alarcón Rivera, as interim president. But Bucaram refused to recognize his dismissal, and to complicate matters further, Vice-President Rosalía Arteaga claimed that she was the legitimate president under the constitution. Ecuador made worldwide headlines for having three presidents. Congress resolved the dispute by recognizing Arteaga's claim on February 9 and then, two days later, replacing her with Alarcón. The armed forces refused to take sides during the confusion. However, military leaders, the congress, and the supreme court were unanimous in insisting that Alarcón leave office in August 1998.

The New Administration. Alarcón called a referendum in May that created the impression of strong popular support for his replacement of Bucaram and for a series of constitutional reforms. The acting president then called for the election of a constituent assembly. Elections for a National Assembly were held on November 30, and deliberations on a new constitution began in December.

Acting on the referendum's mandate, the congress dismissed the Supreme Court and its president, Carlos Solorzano, and replaced them with justices who reflected the partisan composition of the congress more faithfully. These acts put an end to Solorzano's corruption charges against Alarcón and the speaker of congress, Heinz Moeller. One of Alarcón's first acts as president was to abolish the ministry of ethnic affairs that Bucaram had set up. Leaders of the social movements complained that the new president had turned his back on those who had brought him to power.

The government wished to restructure its foreign debt, as debt service was consuming 45% of the budget. To reassure creditors, the government first had to reduce the inflationary budget deficit, which amounted to at least 5% of the gross domestic product (GDP). To this end, Alarcón announced that he would cut the budget by 10%, improve tax collection, and renew various temporary taxes. By year's end this promise proved overoptimistic. The new government also abandoned all plans to peg the sucre to the dollar.

Relations with Peru. Little progress was made in the peace negotiations regarding the border war with Peru. Talks continued intermittently in Brazil and the United States. In June and July the Peruvian press warned that Ecuador was planning to launch a new attack while the popularity of Peru's President Alberto Fujimori was low, but these rumors subsided in August after Alarcón and Fujimori met during a summit in Bolivia.

MICHAEL COPPEDGE
University of Notre Dame

ECUADOR • Information Highlights

Official Name: Republic of Ecuador.
Location: Northwest South America.
Area: 109,483 sq mi (283 560 km²).
Population (mid-1997 est.): 12,000,000.
Chief Cities (mid-1995 est.): Quito, the capital, 1,401,389; Guayaquil, 1,877,031; Cuenca, 239,896.
Government: *Head of state and government,* Fabian Alarcón Rivera, interim president (took office February 11, 1997). *Legislature* (unicameral)—National Congress.
Monetary Unit: Sucre (4,330.00 sucres equal U.S.$1, floating rate, Dec. 8, 1997).
Gross Domestic Product (1995 est. U.S.$): $44,600,000,-000 (purchasing power parity).
Economic Index (1996, 1990 = 100): *Consumer Prices,* all items, 648.8; food, 605.8.
Foreign Trade (1996 U.S.$): *Imports,* $3,724,000,000; *exports,* $4,890,000,000.

EDUCATION

U.S. education policy never skipped a political beat in 1997 as it went from being a centerpiece of the 1996 presidential campaign to being one of the most controversial issues between Congress and the White House.

Declaring that education would be the highest priority of his second term, President Bill Clinton early in the year proposed a number of new initiatives. None, however, caused as much debate and confrontation as did the White House plan to develop voluntary national tests to be taken by fourth-grade students in reading and by eighth-grade students in math. The yearlong battle over the testing idea not only crossed party lines on Capitol Hill, but also split the education community.

The Clinton administration initially funded development of the tests from existing programs, bypassing Congress. It said the tests were needed to encourage states and districts to set higher standards and to provide uniform expectations for students. Republican education leaders in the House of Representatives said the tests were a federal intrusion on state and district prerogatives and were unnecessary; the House prohibited the administration's investment in the tests' development. The Senate approved the idea by a wide margin, but gave the White House an unacceptable trade-off in the process, unexpectedly passing a block-grant proposal for most education programs at the same time. In late October the House and Senate agreed on a compromise whereby money would be allocated to develop the tests and allow states to adopt them voluntarily, but House and Senate education committees would evaluate the tests and make the decision on whether they would be implemented fully. Clinton signed a spending bill containing the provisions in November.

The Republican-controlled House also narrowly approved a voucher program for the District of Columbia; the program would permit the distribution of tax-financed vouchers to poor Washington families, enabling them to send their children to private or religious schools of their choice. Policy watchers considered the approval the opening wedge for the passage of a more general voucher bill.

State Policies. State policy makers had their own controversies in 1997. As states became more insistent on accountability for results in student achievement, the takeover of "academically bankrupt" districts and schools became an issue. In 1997 more than 20 states had such takeover authority. Some urban districts also had tried to reorganize failing schools, but the problems with this policy became more evident in 1997.

An Education Commission of the States analysis of state takeover actions found that none of them had resulted in significant improvement in student achievement despite the fact that some districts, such as New Jersey, had been under state control for up to seven years. Even though the District of Columbia schools now were headed by a retired U.S. Army general appointed under emergency procedures, the schools still did not open on time in fall 1997; opening was delayed for three weeks due to uncompleted repairs.

Still, states felt compelled to do something about the consistent failure of public schooling. When Maryland state officials realized that as many as 50 schools in Baltimore failed to meet student-achievement targets, they sought legislative approval for a reorganization plan that avoided taking over the schools. Meanwhile the superintendent of Philadelphia's school district tried to reorganize two schools but was stopped by a teachers'-union grievance that said proper notice had not been given. After trying other interventions, Hartford, CT, asked state officials to step in; and the Ohio legislature approved shifting governance of the Cleveland schools to the mayor's office. (In contrast, the Baltimore plan took authority away from the mayor.)

Meanwhile, state development of higher content standards—as required by Title I and often funded under Goals 2000 legislation—was completed, at least for the first round, but development of new assessments lagged behind. Analyses by both the National Center for Fair and Open Testing and the American Federation of Teachers (AFT) found that most state assessment programs did not match higher content standards. The assessments continued to rely on multiple-choice items and many of them were still norm-referenced. The former group listed Vermont as the only state meeting criteria that judge assessments on the basis of how well they support high-quality teaching and learning. Assessment systems in 17 states, it said, needed a complete overhaul.

One noncontroversial but important policy interest at the state level concerned investment in early childhood learning. Spurred by emerging neurological research on the importance of early brain development, many governors and legislatures started or expanded programs for infant and early-childhood care emphasizing quality standards and staff training. In some states, however, quality had to compete with quantity as officials scrambled to find enough child-care slots for mothers leaving the welfare system.

In California a scramble was taking place to find space and teachers for a reduced-class-size initiative, introduced by Gov. Pete Wilson in 1996, that funded ratios of 20–1 in up to four grades (K–3). Districts had had only a few weeks between approval of the plan and the opening of school in September 1996 to put it into effect, but 95% of the eligible districts participated. The effort brought classroom ratios down from an average of 29–1. State school districts hired more than 18,000 new teachers. Most, however, were inexperienced, and urban districts hired larger percentages of teachers with emergency certificates. More than half the new classroom space came from portables. The governor and legislature added $1.5 billion to the program in 1997 to expand it to four grades, cover more costs, and help districts with facilities. Added to the $1 billion already funded, this made the effort probably one of the largest school-reform investments ever made.

Teacher Issues. One of the purported reasons for Governor Wilson's class-size initiative in California was to keep state surplus monies dedicated to education spending and out of the general fund, where they probably would have gone to boost teachers' salaries. This reflected an animosity toward teachers' unions that ran strongly through the rhetoric of conservative politicians and causes across the country. At the same time, there were indications of changing directions by the unions, at least at the top. National Education Association (NEA) President Bob Chase signaled a "new unionism" in a major speech that laid out his plans for greater attention to professionalism and school improvement. His speech came within days of the death of Albert Shanker, who headed the American Federation of Teachers for more than 20 years and was respected widely for his efforts on standards-based school reforms. His successor, Sandra Feldman—who also would continue as head of the United Federation of Teachers of New York City—indicated she would continue to push Shanker's causes as well as to emphasize teacher-quality issues. The statements of the NEA and AFT leaders aligned their policies closer than in the past and set the stage for further discussions about merging the two unions. Policy makers and critics of the unions questioned the sincerity of the commitment to new directions, however, citing continuing adversarial actions by local

© Gino Domenico/AP/Wide World Photos

New York City teenagers, above, prepare to attend the funeral of their teacher, Jonathan Levin, 31. The son of Time Warner's chief executive officer (CEO) had been shot—allegedly by one of his students. The murder raised the issue of how deep a commitment teachers should have toward their pupils. Levin was known to spend free-time hours assisting those he taught.

units. Chase noted that it would take a long time to retrain negotiators accustomed to traditional union bargaining.

An emerging trend in 1997 was a new definition of quality professional development for teachers. Rather than relying on traditional workshops or courses unrelated to a school's problems, staff-development experts were encouraging teachers to use student work as the basis of developing consensus about content standards. Asking teachers to analyze the quality of student work was the strategy used to develop New Standards, a major assessment program that was adopted as a core assessment program by the New York City and San Diego school systems. In Kentucky teachers became more expert at using student work as the focus of professional-development activities. Also, at least 12 states became partners with the National Commission on Teaching & America's Future to redesign the teaching profession to make it standards-based.

Another important step toward a standards-based profession concerned school administrators. An interstate consortium finished its work on standards for school leadership. Five of the six standards dealt with instructional, not management, skills. Developed as assessments by the Educational Testing Service, the standards were used for the first time to evaluate candidates seeking principal certification in Mississippi; other states indicated they would be using the assessments for their principal-certification systems.

School Governance Issues. Despite some evidence that standards and teacher-quality reforms were taking hold, dissatisfaction with public schooling was expressed in 1997 through a continuing demand for charter schools. President Clinton announced additional support for charter schools. More than 500 charter schools were operating under legislation passed in 25 states and the District of Columbia; this was more than double the number in 1996.

The first report from a long-term study of charter schools conducted by the U.S. Department of Education (DOE) provided baseline data about the schools. It found that charter schools tended to enroll fewer students than did traditional public schools; enrolled about the same percentage of minority students, but fewer students with special needs; and faced considerable problems over start-up funds and facilities. The principal reasons given for starting a charter school were a common vision among those associated with the school, the preference for a smaller school environment, and the desire for more autonomy. The DOE-sponsored study did not report results, but another study—by the conservative Hudson Institute—used self-reporting from parents to claim that students were performing better in charter schools than in their previous schools.

A voucher program in Milwaukee, WI, was prevented by the courts from expanding to include parochial schools, but a similar program in Cleveland was allowed to continue while opponents challenged it in court. Researchers lined up on both sides of the issue, with some claiming benefits to students using vouchers and others disputing these benefits. Nonetheless, an annual Phi Delta Kappa/Gallup poll indicated a dramatic change in public opinion about using "government" funds to attend private schools. About 48% approved of the idea in 1997, compared with only 24% three years earlier.

In another church-state issue, the U.S. Supreme Court reversed a 1985 decision in *Aguilar v. Felton* and permitted public-school teachers to provide Title I services on the premises of parochial schools. The earlier decision had resulted in costly solutions for public schools. New York City, where the issue first arose, spent about $6 million a year to comply with *Aguilar*.

New York City has been a leader among urban districts in creating smaller schools within the public-school system, financed partially by an Annenberg Challenge grant given to supporters of smaller schools. However, Chancellor Rudy Crew, using greater authority granted him by the state legislature, announced plans to clamp down on the small schools, requiring them to have higher enrollments and to substitute principals for teacher-directors.

Student Issues. The disappointing performance of U.S. eighth graders on the Third International Mathematics and Science Study (TIMSS), released in 1996, was countered to some degree by the reports of fourth-grade performance released in 1997. These results showed that U.S. students were behind only those in Korea on science performance and were above the international average in math. Researchers attributed some of the better results at the elementary level to the infusion of higher math and science standards and to investments in improving teacher skills.

The National Assessment of Educational Progress (NAEP) science report card indicated that, by the end of high school, most students have some grasp of scientific facts and

© Susan Lapides/Gamma-Liaison

Geography was receiving renewed attention in U.S. schools in 1997. Several states had mandated geography courses in middle school or had in place a geography requirement for university admittance, and geography was an increasingly popular college major.

principles and can carry out simple experiments, but that students do poorly at applying scientific facts to a new situation or designing an experiment themselves. These higher-order skills appeared on the science assessment for the first time. The NAEP also reported that girls did almost as well as boys in science, but that the gap between white and African-American students was significant at all three grade levels that were assessed and was larger than on previous assessments. A Data Book released by the Education Trust also documented a widening gap in achievement in various subjects between white students and students of color.

Videotapes comparing eighth-grade math instruction in the United States, Germany, and Japan—based on the TIMSS study—became a popular professional development tool and were analyzed by researchers for clues as to why U.S. students did so poorly at this level. Teenagers also provided some hints themselves. A Public Agenda survey found that American high-school students believed standards should be higher; two thirds said they could do much better in school if they tried. Focus groups with the students revealed lax standards imposed by schools. One of those standards—a promotion policy—was found to be almost nonexistent in 80 districts studied by the AFT. No district had an explicit policy endorsing social promotion, but it was implicit in most districts because holding students back was considered an option of last resort, according to the AFT.

A dispute about student discipline between advocates of disabled students and education groups was resolved after several years of debate. Congress approved changes in the Individuals With Disabilities Education Act (IDEA), allowing schools to place students receiving IDEA services in alternative settings for a limited time.

Another issue—how children learn to read—took on national proportions. President Clinton proposed a national campaign to enable all children to read at grade level by the end of third grade, relying on training volunteers to supplement in-school reading instruction. Congress, however, seemed more likely to approve a greater investment in teacher training for early reading instruction than in volunteer training. Research results in 1997 regarding the 20% of children considered problem readers called for increasing professional skills, particularly in diagnosing reading problems; and providing the right balance between direct instruction (including phonics) and reading comprehension.

Opponents of bilingual education in California started a campaign in the fall of 1997 to put a ballot initiative before the state in 1998 that would require all students to be taught in English. About half of the 2.3 million U.S. students who cannot speak or understand English fully enrolled in schools in the last decade; 70% of them live in California, Texas, and three other states. Rather than endorse one method of teaching non-English-speaking children over others, a major report from the National Research Council recommended that research and policies should identify a variety of approaches, depending on local needs and resources. Meanwhile, the Teachers of English to Speakers in Other Languages released language standards for English as a Second Language (ESL) students to bridge their instruction to the higher standards expected of all students.

In 1997 several reports were released to determine the impact of changes on students enrolled in school-to-work programs. The federal program began in 1994 through grants to every state to plan school-to-work systems, followed by grants to implement approved plans. The first evaluations indicated that the programs were helping to bridge academic and occupational learning and were drawing employers into involvement with schools. However, the programs still were reaching few students and did not yet reflect the development of a "system" of school-to-work transitions like the ones in European countries after which the effort was modeled.

Higher Education. The elimination of affirmative-action policies in admission to California state campuses and the banning of affirmative-action policies in Texas public-college admissions was reflected in the applicant pools for law schools in both states. The result alarmed higher-education and other officials. As the fall 1997 term began, substantial reductions were seen in the number of minority students enrolled at the University of Texas Law School and at California's state law school. In Texas this result led to new legislation requiring state universities to accept all applicants who graduate in the top 10% of their high-school classes, regardless of their standardized test scores. Similar changes were being considered in California. In other admissions news, a study by FairTest found that at least 280 four-year college and university campuses were using options other than just ACT or SAT scores for admission decisions; this reflected an increase of 100 schools since 1994.

ANNE C. LEWIS
Education Policy Writer

EGYPT

Despite tension with Israel's new Likud government, Egyptian President Hosni Mubarak remained an important intermediary in the Middle East peace process. The ruling National Democratic Party (NDP) gained local-council seats, while a land-reform program sparked unrest among tenant farmers. Seventy people died in a terrorist attack.

Domestic Affairs. The April 7 local-council-seat election was one of the quietest in 20 years, despite Muslim Brotherhood charges that the government had detained hundreds of its followers to prevent their participation. Two days before the election the state security prosecutor arrested several journalists affiliated with the Brotherhood.

Few candidates competed against the NDP and it won, unopposed, 44.4% of the 47,382 local seats. Several seats remained unfilled due to a lack of candidates, while Wafd and Muslim Brotherhood party boycotts created close races between rival NDP factions. Human-rights groups and opposition newspapers reported that ballot boxes were stuffed, monitors expelled, and ballots cast for the NDP in the names of dead voters.

Prime Minister Kamal Ahmed al-Ganzouri brought an unusually large number of corruption cases to Egyptian courts—the most prominent against the former chairman of the

In November 1997, 70 persons were killed when gunmen opened fire on visitors to a temple near Luxor, one of Egypt's leading tourist attractions. The government of President Hosni Mubarak, shown at right inspecting the site, was believed to be the target of the attack.

Engineering Holding Company, Abdel-Wahab Habbaq, who was accused of placing millions of dollars from kickbacks into numbered Swiss bank accounts. It was believed that Ganzouri—who also brought charges against state television and four parliament members—sought to prevent those accused from sabotaging his privatization program. According to Transparency International, which reports on business bribery, corruption in Egypt was worse than in Mexico and Brazil but not as bad as in Indonesia, India, Russia, China, or Nigeria.

In July, Ganzouri concentrated his power in the 32-member cabinet by moving several cabinet functions to his office. Three ministers left, four new ones were appointed, and six were reassigned. The new cabinet included Egypt's first environmental-affairs minister, Nadia Riyad Makram Ebeid, from a well-known Christian family.

In February the parliament overwhelmingly approved a presidential decree extending emergency legislation—in force since President Anwar el-Sadat's 1981 assassination—that permits extralegal measures against terrorism. The Egyptian Organization for Human Rights said 17,000 people had been arrested in connection with militant activity since 1989.

Despite increased police activity against Islamic militants, terrorist attacks continued on government officials, Coptic Christians—who make up about 10% of the population—and European tourists. In areas with the largest Christian populations, gunmen attacked Coptic stores, churches, and other institutions. The Muslim Brotherhood and Egypt's leading Islamic authority—the sheikh of al-Azhar mosque, Mohammed Tantawi—denounced the attacks, while the Coptic Church's Pope Shenouda III warned against reckless talk of a religious war.

In November gunmen at Luxor, a 3,400-year-old temple and major tourist attraction, killed 70 people—60 of them tourists—in the deadliest act of terrorism since Islamic militants began their campaign to overthrow the government in 1991.

Census Results and the Economy. In June the Central Agency for General Mobilization and Statistics released 1996 census figures showing that the total population had reached 61,452,382—an increase of 11 million since the 1986 census. The rate of population growth decreased from 2.8% to 2.1%, and average family size went down to 4.6 people from 4.9 in 1989—the result of a successful family-planning campaign. For the first time

EGYPT • Information Highlights

Official Name: Arab Republic of Egypt.
Location: Northeastern Africa.
Area: 386,660 sq mi (1 001 450 km²).
Population (1996 census): 661,452,382.
Chief Cities (July 1, 1992, est.): Cairo, the capital, 6,800,000; Alexandria, 3,380,000; Giza, 2,144,000.
Government: *Head of state,* Mohammed Hosni Mubarak, president (took office October 1981). *Head of government,* Kamal Ahmed al-Ganzouri, prime minister (took office Jan. 2, 1996). *Legislature*—People's Assembly.
Monetary Unit: Pound (3.3985 pounds equal U.S.$1, free-market rate, Dec. 30, 1997).
Gross Domestic Product (1995 est. U.S.$): $171,000,000,-000 (purchasing power parity).
Economic Index (1996, 1990 = 100): *Consumer Prices,* all items, 191.6; food, 176.5.
Foreign Trade (1996 U.S.$): *Imports,* $13,041,000,000; *exports,* $3,540,000,000.,000.

in recent history migration to cities declined; urban population had decreased from 44% to 43% of the total since 1986. Illiteracy had dropped from 49.6% to 38.6%, but it was harder to find work. The percentage of young married couples living with parents because they could not afford homes increased from 1% in 1986 to 3.9%.

In October the 1992 Law 96—which established a new system of agricultural rents—went into effect, permitting landlords to charge tenant farmers the market rate for agricultural-land rent. Affected were some 6 million farmers—10% of the population—who now had to pay up to three times their previous rents. Many with two- or three-acre plots, who survived just above the subsistence level, were threatened with losing farms they had tilled for 50 years. While the agricultural ministry set up a fund to help tenants purchase land, the amounts offered were considered too low, and the leftist opposition Tagammu and Nasserite parties began to organize tenant committees to confront landlords. Some committees urged tenants to obtain guns to prevent eviction.

In January, Mubarak initiated the Toshka Canal—a massive new irrigation project the press called "The Next Pyramid." When completed in 2017, it will pump water from Lake Nasser to a desert region west of the Nile River. This "New Valley" will receive nearly 6 billion gal (23 billion l) of water daily. The first stage should irrigate 500,000 acres (202 500 ha) of new farmland, with huge electric pumps lifting water from Lake Nasser into a canal that will stretch 140 mi (225 km) northwest across the Western Desert. With the population expected to reach 85 million by 2015, Mubarak projected that the New Valley would relieve pressure on the Nile Valley—4% of Egypt's land area—where 90% of Egyptians were living. The government put the cost at about $2 billion, but foreign companies had not yet submitted bids.

Egypt—committed by an International Monetary Fund (IMF) agreement to privatize one third of its 314 public-sector enterprises by mid-1997—had trouble finding buyers for the less attractive firms with large workforces and major debts; the massive public sector—with more than 6 million employees—continued to slow the economy.

Foreign Affairs. Mubarak repeatedly called on Israel to halt construction of Jewish settlements in the West Bank, which were regarded by Egypt as an obstacle to peace. In retaliation for the establishment of these settlements, the Arab League in March renewed its boycott of Israel. Relations with Israel were exacerbated further by charges that its intelligence agents were active in Egypt.

Relations with the United States were strained when Egypt refused to support U.S. steps to force Iraqi compliance with United Nations (UN) resolutions. Cairo called the U.S. action a violation of international law and an infringement on Iraq's sovereignty and territorial integrity. Cairo also resisted U.S.-led efforts to impose sanctions on Sudan and called for relaxation of the UN blockage against Libya.

See also MIDDLE EAST.

> DON PERETZ, *Professor Emeritus*
> *State University of New York, Binghamton*

ENERGY

During 1997, U.S. energy consumption continued to grow, reflecting a strong economy, low energy prices, and a growing population. Total energy consumption for the year was likely to exceed the 1996 record of almost 90 quadrillion British thermal units (Btu). Domestic production of oil—the leading U.S. energy source—continued to decline, forcing increased reliance on imported oil. The pace of electric-power-industry deregulation quickened, while concern mounted over the impact of U.S. energy consumption on the global environment.

Oil. America's recent taste for sport-utility vehicles and big cars contributed to a slight increase in consumption of oil, which accounted for 38% of the energy consumed in the United States. The country continued to grow more dependent on foreign oil—more than 60% was imported—as domestic reserves gradually ran down.

A buoyant U.S. economy and low gasoline prices fueled the thirst for gasoline, the main product of crude oil used in the United States. One gallon of regular gasoline cost on average about $1.25 in 1997. Adjusted for inflation, the price was virtually unchanged since 1990, and was about half the 1981 level. Heating oil and propane were cheaper than usual because the relatively warm winter of 1996–97 left utility companies with large supplies of these fuels.

Changes in the international oil market cast doubt on the reliability of future supplies. The United States lessened its vulnerability to sudden disruptions in supply by shifting to sources outside the volatile Persian Gulf, such as Venezuela and Mexico. The Persian Gulf accounted for only about 17% of total oil imports, down from about 25% in the early 1990s.

While the United States tried to diminish its dependence on Persian Gulf oil, the region continued to be the leading source of world oil supplies—a fact that occasionally undermined U.S. foreign-policy objectives. The oil industries of France, Russia, and Malaysia challenged a U.S.-led economic embargo against Iran—imposed to thwart the country's alleged support of international terrorism—by signing a deal to develop a huge oil field there.

Iraq, chafing under seven-year-old United Nations (UN) trade sanctions that were imposed when Iraqi troops invaded Kuwait, obtained some relief when the UN Security Council eased the restrictions in August. Under the "oil-for-food" plan, Iraq was allowed to sell $2 billion worth of oil every six months, provided it used the proceeds to buy food and other vital supplies for its citizens.

In October the first Caspian Sea crude oil in decades was shipped through a new pipeline linking the port of Baku in the former Soviet republic of Azerbaijan and the Russian port of Novorossiysk on the Black Sea. With proven reserves of about 40 billion barrels and potential exports of several million barrels a day, the Caspian basin—which includes Kazakhstan and Turkmenistan—eventually was expected to rival the Persian Gulf. Western oil analysts feared that Russia, which had halted most oil production in the region during the Soviet era as it exploited Russian oil reserves in Siberia, may try to control the flow of Caspian oil and natural gas. To gain a foothold in this vital region, oil companies from around the world intensified investments there. In August four American oil companies signed an agreement to invest $8 billion in Azeri oil fields. This and other U.S. investments were backed by President Bill

Clinton as steps to reduce Russia's dominance over the region.

The search for new domestic oil deposits continued, with drilling companies planning to tap what geologists believed could be a number of oil deposits under Lake Michigan. Each deposit—estimated to be worth about $10 million—was expected to yield some 500,000 barrels. The underwater deposits, located in an environmentally sensitive region, posed challenges to drillers. In Alaska, home to the largest untapped domestic oil reserves, opposition by environmental groups appeared to be outweighed by oil-company plans to begin drilling in the 23.4-million-acre (9.5-million-ha) National Petroleum Reserve, the country's largest undeveloped public-land holding. New technology enabled companies to discover new reserves in Alaska's North Slope that promised to slow the decline in U.S. oil production.

Natural Gas. The production of natural gas—which accounted for 24% of U.S. energy sources—continued at the level of the past two decades, about 19 trillion cu ft (532 billion m³). But 1997 demand, especially by industry and home owners, continued to grow, exceeding 21 trillion cu ft (588 billion m³). To bridge the gap, the United States imported more than $5 billion worth of gas from Canada, where competition among natural-gas companies mounted in a race to build pipelines linking Canadian gas fields to Chicago and other lucrative northern U.S. markets.

The growing U.S. reliance on imported natural gas was not a matter of deep concern, since virtually all the imports came from North America. But the international market for natural gas, like that for oil, posed significant policy problems for the Clinton administration. In September the French oil company Total announced that it would invest $2 billion in Iran's offshore gas fields, in defiance of U.S. policy isolating Iran. In October the British-Dutch conglomerate Shell followed suit by entering into negotiations with Iran to build a $2.5 billion gas pipeline there. Because of its strategic location between the Caspian Sea and the Persian Gulf, Iran was seen as an essential player in the scramble by world energy companies to gain access to Caspian-basin gas.

Much of the pressure to open new routes to Caspian Sea oil and gas fields came from Asia, where rapid economic growth spurred demand for new energy sources. At a November summit in Beijing, Russian President Boris Yeltsin and Chinese President Jiang Zemin agreed to build a $12 billion pipeline to carry natural gas from Siberia to China, South Korea, and Japan.

Coal. Coal, the only fossil fuel with abundant U.S. reserves, continued to play a key role in the domestic energy mix and was the only fuel for which exports exceeded imports. The main downside of coal burning—air pollution—was not serious enough to prevent coal consumption from exceeding the 1996 level of 20.5 quadrillion Btu.

Coal accounted for 22% of the U.S. energy market, with some 90% burned for producing steam to generate electricity. The advent of efficient scrubbers on utility smokestacks helped filter out some of the sulfur dioxide emissions that cause acid rain and contribute to summertime smog. But recent laws, such as the 1990 Clean Air Act Amendments, induced coal-burning utilities to reduce harmful emissions further by switching from high-sulfur Appalachian coal to low-sulfur coal, mined principally in Montana and Wyoming. As a result, Western coal prices rose as prices for Appalachian coal fell. Overall coal production was likely to exceed the 1996 level of more than 1 trillion tons.

Nuclear. There was little change in the nuclear-energy market. The United States' 110 operating power plants accounted for about 20% of electricity generated in the country and 8% of all energy sources. With no construction permits pending for new plants since 1983, the prospects for expanding the 40-year-old industry appeared dim.

Despite its shrinking role in the U.S. energy mix, nuclear power continued to generate controversy. The main issue was what to do with some 30,000 tons of highly radioactive nuclear waste stored at temporary sites across the United States. Western lawmakers continued to block completion of a central repository for spent nuclear fuel at Yucca Mountain, 100 mi (161 km) from Las Vegas, NV, that Congress had approved in 1982. Because of construction delays, lawmakers later called for a temporary repository at the same site, which also faced strong opposition. Clinton said he would veto a bill that approved the temporary site, pending completion of an ongoing study of Yucca Mountain's suitability as a permanent nuclear-storage facility.

The issue of nuclear safety also surfaced in Canada, which had continued to build new nuclear-power plants into the late 1980s. Following reports of widespread management lapses, Ontario Hydro shut down seven of its 20 nuclear reactors in August, pending a costly review of the company's compliance with safety standards.

U.S. manufacturers of nuclear-power equipment received a boost in early November when Clinton, during a Washington visit by President Jiang, lifted a decade-old ban on U.S. sales of nuclear-power technology to China. In its search for new energy sources to fuel its fast-growing economy, China also acquired nuclear technology from Canada, France, and Russia.

Utility Deregulation. U.S. electric-power companies prepared for major upheaval as Congress considered legislation that would dismantle the industry's monopolistic power as early as 1998. But even in the absence of federal action, electric-utility deregulation was proceeding apace as states dismantled legislation governing the industry. A number of states introduced so-called "retail wheeling," in which large industrial customers could buy power from any source and receive that power over the local utility's transmission lines. California took the lead in electric-utility deregulation with a plan set to take effect Jan. 1, 1998, that would allow all customers to choose their power providers, much as they choose long-distance-telephone providers. Unlike some states, California also planned to set aside revenues from electric bills for research and development of renewable energy sources.

Environmental Concerns. A small but perhaps promising segment of the U.S. energy mix, the renewable energy sources—including hydropower and newer technologies to harness energy from the Sun, wind, underground pockets of steam, plant material, and even garbage—accounted for 8% of all energy sources, but were expected to play a greater role in years to come.

Pressed by tighter clean-air regulations to find an alternative to gasoline—a major contributor to urban ozone and smog—automakers intensified efforts to produce an affordable, efficient, nonpolluting car. California regulations requiring that, by 2003, 10% of all cars sold be zero-emission vehicles prompted General Motors to introduce a battery-driven electric car to California drivers. But the two-seater EV1—available only through a $400-a-month lease—attracted just a few hundred customers in 1997. The car also drew complaints for its short range between recharges and limited passenger space.

Other automakers concentrated on the next generation of electric cars, driven by pollution-free hydrogen-fuel cells. Long stymied by the high cost of producing cells, manufacturers made several breakthroughs in 1997. Canada's Ballard Power Systems Inc., a world leader in fuel-cell development, produced cells for buses that entered into service in Vancouver. At a September auto show in Frankfurt, Germany, German automaker Daimler-Benz and Japan's Toyota Motor Corp. introduced passenger cars powered by hydrogen-fuel cells. Toyota also planned in December to begin selling a new hybrid car fueled by both gasoline and electricity to Japanese consumers. Because of high prices, however, analysts doubted whether the Toyota Prius or other alternative-fuel cars would sell widely in the United States as long as gasoline prices remained low.

The biggest push for greater reliance on renewable energy in the long term seemed likely to come from ongoing negotiations to curb global emissions of carbon dioxide and other gases implicated in global warming. Released by burning fossil fuels, these gases widely are believed to trap the Sun's heat inside Earth's atmosphere, causing a gradual but potentially devastating warming of surface temperatures around the world.

As the biggest emitter of carbon dioxide, the United States assumed a lead role in setting the terms of a treaty to reduce emissions after the UN-sponsored 1992 Earth Summit in Rio de Janeiro, Brazil. But negotiations quickly bogged down. Developing countries wanted to be exempted from requirements to curb fossil-fuel use, arguing that they had not created the problem and needed to use these fuels to industrialize their economies. The United States and other developed countries responded that China, India, and some other rapidly industrializing countries soon would emit more carbon dioxide than the developing countries and therefore should be included in any strategy to reduce emissions.

The controversy deepened in October, when the Clinton administration proposed a plan that would stabilize U.S. carbon emissions at 1990 levels between 2008 and 2012. A U.S. coalition of automakers, energy companies, and conservative think tanks sharply criticized the proposal, saying it would drive up energy costs and harm the economy. European countries and Japan—where energy costs were much higher than in the United States—rejected the plan as inadequate and proposed more-stringent restrictions on fossil-fuel use. In December, Earth Summit participants met in Kyoto, Japan, to hammer out terms of a global-warming treaty. (*See also* ENVIRONMENT—*Global Warming: A World Solution?*.)

MARY H. COOPER
"The CQ [Congressional Quarterly] Researcher"

ENGINEERING, CIVIL

The year 1997 showed certain parts of the world to be the last frontier for truly large-scale engineering and environmental challenges. In the United States engineers were building fewer huge public-works projects and instead were focusing on fine-tuning technologies designed to augment and maintain an aging infrastructure.

Philippine Dike Project. Besides the massive Three Gorges Dam project in China, the most ambitious engineering effort under way in 1997 was the Pasig-Potrero Outer Dike project in the Philippines. When completed, the 37-mi (59-km)-long, 33-ft (10-m)-high concrete-armored dike would protect a number of towns from the destructive floods of water and volcanic debris, called lahar, that spill off Mount Pinatubo and the Pasig-Potrero River. Whether the $1.45 billion project would be completed remained a question in 1997. Setbacks such as earthquake-induced cracks and an 82-ft (25-m) breach that opened, inundating five towns, delayed the project. The Philippine government took over work from 13 slow-moving contractors to ensure that the project would be finished.

New Bridge in Sweden. The year ended on a high note with the completion of the Hoga Kusten Bridge in northern Sweden. The Hoga Kusten carries European Interstate Highway E4, which runs along the east coast of Sweden and crosses the Ångerman River near its mouth at the Gulf of Bothnia. The main span of the four-lane bridge is 3,970 ft (1 210 m)— the seventh-longest main span of any suspension bridge in the world; it joins together side spans of 1,017 ft (310 m) and 919 ft (280 m). Its navigation height is 131 ft (40 m), while the maximum water depth is 295 ft (90 m). The 591-ft (180-m)-high pylons, founded on bedrock, reach 59 ft (18 m) below the water. A welded steel-box girder measures 72 ft (22 m) wide and 13 ft (4 m) high and features a corrosion-preventing dehumidification system inside the box. The girder is continuous through the pylon, extending 5,906 ft (1 800 m) from abutment to abutment.

Center clamps located between the girder and the main cables fix the girder in the longitudinal direction. Expansion joints allow the girder to move as much as 6 ft (1.84 m) at abutment. Hydraulic buffers, designed to reduce the traveling distance of the expansion joints and bearings, take asymmetric live loads, loads from breaking forces, and wind loads, while allowing slow movements resulting from temperature changes in the girder and cable system, effectively increasing the life cycle of these components.

Transshipment Terminal in Oman. The sultanate of Oman was preparing to become the owner of a new state-of-the-art container transshipment terminal at Port Raysut. The terminal—together with a planned industrial and free-trade zone—would establish Oman as a major gateway for container traffic in the Middle East. Its first two berths, designed to accommodate the largest containerships afloat, were scheduled to be in operation by the second quarter of 1998. The sultanate was funding the project's $128.7 million dredging and infrastructure costs directly. A total of 170 million cu ft (4.8 million m³) of material would be dredged to widen and deepen the approach channel and turning basin. When completed, four berths totaling 4,003 ft (1 220) m in length would have a combined capacity of more than 1 million lifts per year. Dockside facilities were to include 12 high-speed, 50-ton-capacity container cranes designed to load ships up to 18 containers wide; 27 rubber-tired gantry cranes; and four top loaders.

Riverbank Erosion. The New England Power Co. (NEP) installed erosion-control mats along one section of the Connecticut River in North Walpole, NH, to stem severe riverbank erosion. A preliminary inspection indicated that the mats were beginning to work and were exceeding expectations. Sixty erosion-control mats were placed and anchored along the New Hampshire shoreline 40 ft (12 m) below the surface at a cost of $250,000. The mats, developed in Europe, had not been used before in a riverine environment. Previously, control mats have been successful in stemming erosion in coastal environments, particularly along the North Sea.

Constructed of a specially formulated polypropylene film, each mat measures 16 ft (5 m) by 13 ft (4 m) and consists of nearly 22,000 individual strands of film. As the mat is deployed and anchored, these strands assume a floating upright position, rising to a height of 5 ft (1.5 m) and establishing a structure analogous to natural sea grass. As local currents transport sediments through the strands, velocities diminish and silt is deposited on the mats and is compacted by the motion of the strands. Ultimately, the mats create a natural, fiber-reinforced berm to protect the riverbank. As much as 100,000 lbs (45 360 kg) of silt can be held down per mat. As one mat fills up, another can be anchored on top to develop a barrier.

HARRY GOLDSTEIN
Science and Technology Writer

ENVIRONMENT

In the United States during 1997, the sharp partisan divisions between Republican and Democratic legislators over environmental issues faded and were replaced by regional battles on such issues as clean air and global warming.

On the world scene—five years after the "Earth Summit" in Rio de Janeiro, Brazil—representatives from more than 150 nations gathered in Kyoto, Japan, to consider an international framework to reduce greenhouse emissions. Argentina's Raúl Estrada-Oyuela served as chairman of the negotiations. (*See* SPECIAL REPORT, page 229.)

Changes on the Political Front. Election-year grandstanding by both U.S. political parties on the environment in 1996 earned Republicans public distrust over their all-out effort to revise major environmental laws. Acknowledging that it had gone too far, the GOP pledged to take a slow approach to environmental policy, pushing incremental—rather than major—policy shifts. This lower profile for Republicans in 1997 did away with much of the rhetoric about remaking the federal bureaucracy and national environmental laws. No longer were the Republicans the easy target of Democrats and environmental groups.

In the fall, for example, Republicans pushed through the House a series of relatively minor bills dealing with the grazing of livestock on federal land and the limiting of presidential authority to protect environmentally sensitive federal property under the 1906 Antiquities Act. While the measures were opposed by environmental groups, many Democrats, and the White House, they did not cause the stir that the more comprehensive Republican legislation of the previous year did. The GOP also refused to move forward on major issues without strong bipartisan backing, allowing a number of issues to languish. Efforts to overhaul the superfund hazardous-waste program and the Endangered Species Act sputtered yet again.

A multibillion-dollar maintenance backlog at the U.S. National Park System drew considerable press attention, but no attempt was made to overhaul park-system management or significantly address the backlog. There were some signs that the clout of environmental groups had diminished—a point driven home in the fall after U.S. Sen. Dirk Kempthorne (R-ID) assembled an impressive bipartisan coalition behind a bill to rewrite the 1973 Endangered Species Act. The Kempthorne bill, which was put at the top of the 1998 Senate agenda, drew the backing of key Senate Democrats, moderate Republicans, and, most importantly, President Bill Clinton. Environmentalists, who argued that the bill would gut one of the nation's premier environmental laws, failed to generate much headway. They gave Kempthorne high marks for selling his bill in environmentally friendly terms and persuading colleagues that the bill would enhance species recovery and restore habitat. "We are completely changing the dynamics of the act by making it work better and smarter, so that we recover species without putting communities at risk," Kempthorne declared during the official bill-introduction ceremony on September 17. "Our strategy changed," declared U.S. Rep. George Radanovich. The California Republican added, "The challenge has been, how do we 'out green the greens'?"

The politics of the environment shifted in more fundamental ways as well. By far the two biggest issues in 1997 were stringent new clean-air rules issued by the Clinton administration and a new international treaty to stem global warming. On clean air, the administration issued two rules in July to clamp down on ground-level ozone and tiny particles. Then in mid-December, the administration signed the international framework to reduce greenhouse emissions such as carbon dioxide. Both issues deeply divided the Democratic Party and forced Clinton and Vice-President Al Gore to decide between warring factions. Democrats from midwestern and oil states joined forces with Republican opponents of the clean-air rules and the climate treaty, because power plants, refineries, and automobile users in their states could be subject to new costs. Hundreds of cities and counties feared they would be in violation of the clean-air rules; Democrats warned of devastating effects on local economies. "We cannot survive the new regulations," said Rep. Ron Klink. According to the Pennsylvania Democrat, "I can tell you this is an issue we will go to war on."

If there was a single figure who demonstrated the changing dynamics of environmental policy in 1997, it was John Dingell of Michigan. As the senior Democrat on the House Commerce Committee, Dingell railed against Republican environmental positions in 1996 and was a tireless critic of the Republican-led effort to overhaul the superfund hazardous-waste program. But in 1997, Dingell led the charge against a Democratic president on both clean air and global-climate change.

"The proposal was asinine," said Dingell, a longtime supporter of the automobile industry, which opposed the new clean-air rules. "A, the Clean Air Act is working, and B, this disrupts the public trust of the statute. It will incur virtually no benefits in terms of clean air and the environment," noted Dingell. The political turnabout was largely attributable to the fact that in 1996 the Clinton administration and its environmental allies were on the defensive, while in 1997 they were on the offensive—seeking to strengthen environmental laws, not just defend them. "Typically, the standing dynamic is that when the anti-environmentalists are on the offensive, more Democrats are with us," said Carl Pope, executive director of the Sierra Club.

Clean Air. The fight over the November 1996 U.S. Environmental Protection Agency (EPA) proposal of two stringent new rules to regulate ozone—the main component of smog—and microscopic particles known as "particulate matter" began heating up almost immediately after the new year. The proposals, which alarmed many in industry, were supported strongly by environmental groups and many governors and elected officials whose states were downwind from pollution threats addressed by the rules. A major lobbying battle went on all winter and spring, with opponents spending millions of dollars on television advertisements. They sought to pressure the White House by building support in Congress. The U.S. House Commerce Committee, for example, waged an all-out effort to punch holes in the scientific evidence behind the rules, playing up the lack of agreement among EPA's own scientific advisory board. Opponents tried to humanize the issue, alleging that the rules would stifle basic freedoms such as shooting fireworks on the Fourth of July and summer backyard barbecues. Both activities, they contended, would be limited under the new regulations.

EPA Administrator Carol M. Browner and environmental groups strongly disputed these claims, also seeking to wrap their case in emotionally charged arguments. Browner testified repeatedly on the Hill that the rules would benefit the most vulnerable citizens, including asthmatic children and the elderly. One television commercial, paid for by the proponents, showed a wheezing child being rushed to the emergency room. Children also appeared at press conferences, to demonstrate their inhalers.

On July 16 the administration announced the final rules, which hewed closely to the EPA's original proposal. The existing standard

© Richard Hutchings/PhotoEdit

Opponents of new proposals by the U.S. Environmental Protection Agency to regulate ozone claimed that they would hinder such pleasures as fireworks on July 4 and backyard barbecues.

© Alan Oddie/PhotoEdit

for ozone was changed to .08 parts per million measured over eight hours, instead of the existing standard of .12 parts per million measured over one hour. A new regulation was put in place to monitor particles as small as 2.5 microns in diameter; the smallest particles regulated under existing rules are 10 microns.

Browner made clear that the regulations were aimed at smokestack industries and utilities. She said that each year the rules would prevent about 15,000 premature deaths, 350,000 asthma attacks, and 1 million major cases of reduced lung function in children. The ozone standard would go into effect in 2004, the particles rules in 2005. While environmentalists cheered the decision, opponents asserted that the Clean Air Act was working well as it stood. They said the new regulations were based on flimsy science and that the EPA would impose millions of dollars in compliance costs on industry with no appreciable benefit. The bipartisan coalition of opponents also argued that job losses would ensue.

With nowhere else to turn, opponents looked to Congress to block the new rules, seeking to gain support for a bill (HR 1984) to impose a four-year moratorium on the standards and call for more scientific studies. But supporters of the moratorium faced an uphill fight, with the president sure to veto such legislation, and a two-thirds vote required to overcome a veto. It was a politically difficult struggle as well. It would be hard for any member of Congress to vote to block rules that the president was sure to argue would aid sick children. As Congress adjourned for the year, the effort to block the regulations appeared to have sputtered.

Dolphin-Safe Tuna. The United States finally signed off on a new international agreement aimed at protecting dolphins from deadly tuna nets in the eastern tropical Pacific Ocean. The 1995 agreement known as the Panama Declaration—an international agreement that protects dolphins, conserves tuna fisheries, and reduces the unintentional taking of other marine species—was allowed to go into effect in August, after President Clinton signed implementing legislation. This legislation, the International Dolphin Conservation Program Act (IDCPA)—a compromise reached after more than a year of U.S. congressional wrangling—provides $10.5 million to fund dolphin-health studies and lifts tuna embargoes for signatory countries.

A 1972 U.S. law has barred Mexico, Venezuela, and other Latin American nations since the 1980s from access to the $1.4 billion U.S. canned-tuna market because their fishermen have used encircling nets that snag and kill dolphins. To qualify for the U.S. market, these countries must adopt measures to protect dolphins and fully ratify the Panama Declaration. To obtain the U.S. canners' "dolphin-safe" tuna labels—considered essential to entering the U.S. market—their boats must be inspected by the U.S. National Marine Fisheries Service.

Under the new law the definition of the dolphin-safe label also would be changed. Tuna now is considered dolphin safe if it is caught without using encircling nets. The bill initially tightens the definition by prohibiting the use of encircling nets and the use of other fishing methods that could kill or seriously injure dolphins. However, as early as March 1999 the U.S. commerce secretary could change the definition to allow use of encircling nets as long as no dolphins were killed or injured. Also under the bill, as many as 5,000 dolphins could be killed each year in the eastern tropical Pacific Ocean, with the objective of eliminating dolphin deaths entirely through the setting of annual limits. The conditions drew fire from Latin American fishermen, who argued that they already had revised the encircling fishing method to better protect dolphins and that U.S. fishing boats are relatively unsupervised compared to Latin American boats, which carry inspectors from the Inter-American Commission on Tropical Tuna on board. This commission's goal of reducing the number of dolphins killed in the eastern Pacific to 5,000 actually was surpassed in 1993 when 3,600 were killed; by 1996 the number dropped to 2,500.

Wildlife Refuges. At the start of the 105th Congress in 1997, the Clinton administration and the Republican Congress were at an impasse over how to manage the nation's wildlife refuges. But by early spring, Republicans and the White House had forged a deal on major legislation that put the 92-million-acre (37-million-ha) National Wildlife Refuge on firmer footing. The new law puts in place the first clearly defined legal mission for the federal system, a sprawling and diverse network designed to protect plants and wildlife and provide recreation for millions of Americans. The law, which establishes conservation and restoration of fish, plants, and wildlife as the refuge's basic mission, was supported broadly by environmental groups. The law also recognizes hunting and other recreation as a priority, and is aimed at striking a balance between environmentalists—intent on protecting fish, wildlife, and their habitats—and hunters and other recreational users, who fear being barred from the refuge system because they trample on conservation goals. It was such divisions, pitting green groups against hunting and recreational users, that had scuttled previous efforts to revise the system.

ALLAN FREEDMAN, *Environmental Reporter*
"Congressional Quarterly"

Global Warming: A World Solution?

The nations of the world hardly agree on anything, let alone something as daunting as an accord to address the worldwide problem of global warming.

But from Dec. 1–11, 1997, in Kyoto, Japan, representatives from more than 150 nations met at the United Nations (UN) Climate Change Conference for one last round of talks on global warming. The result was a historic agreement. Industrialized countries—including European nations, the United States, and Japan—agreed to shake hands on an international treaty to stem the emissions of so-called greenhouse gases blamed for warming the climate. Under the Kyoto Protocol, the United States and Japan agreed to cut emissions of carbon dioxide and other greenhouse gases to 7% below 1990 levels by 2012. Europe agreed to an 8% cut.

Global warming is caused by the increasing buildup of carbon dioxide, methane, and other gases from the burning of fossil fuels, such as oil, coal, and natural gas. Those gases collect in the atmosphere, wrapping Earth in a layer of insulation and heating the climate. Scientists predict that a warming of Earth's atmosphere will have devastating impacts, including severe droughts, intense hurricanes, and rising sea levels that will gobble up shorelines. Reducing emissions is not accomplished easily. Because there is no technology to reduce carbon dioxide emissions, the only way for industry to meet the target will be to burn less fuel.

Most environmental groups hailed the agreement as a big first step toward cutting emissions, arguing that economic growth and energy efficiency can coexist. By encouraging more fuel-efficient vehicles, for example, the United States could lessen its dependence on foreign oil. Many power plants could save energy simply by running more efficiently.

But a difficult road lay ahead for the Kyoto treaty. Industry groups immediately opposed the agreement, contending that meeting the targets would lead to a devastating slowdown in the U.S. economy. Chief among their concerns was that the treaty did not include developing nations such as China and India. Under the accord, those nations would not have to comply with any firm limits, as the United States would. Developing nations argued that it was the world's industrial countries that produced the bulk of the pollution in the first place, so they should take the first big step toward reducing their emissions. But U.S. businesses were worried that the developing nations would gain an economic advantage by not having to adhere to strict environmental controls, and that energy prices would rise at home and cause jobs to move to other countries, where energy would be cheaper. Gail McDonald, president of the industry-supported Global Climate Coalition, predicted that the accord would "result in devastating job losses and skyrocketing energy prices."

Unless Third World countries commit to stricter controls on their emissions, the Kyoto treaty appeared to have little hope of being approved by the U.S. Senate, which must ratify the agreement by a two-thirds vote. "I would urge President Clinton not to submit the treaty to the Senate for ratification until developing countries have agreed to participate in a meaningful way," said Senate Minority Leader Tom Daschle of South Dakota.

The Clinton administration was following that advice. Vice-President Al Gore said the treaty would not be submitted for ratification until after the administration hammered out more agreements with developing nations. Those negotiations were expected to continue into 1998, which likely meant that a treaty would not be submitted to the Senate for ratification until 1999 at the earliest. Given political opposition in Congress, the Clinton administration and its allies in the environmental community said that a vigorous campaign to focus the public's attention on global warming was needed. As they look to the midterm elections in 1998 and the presidential race in 2000, Gore and the Democrats also will face some tricky internal politics as they try to bridge differences between labor unions that fear the agreement would lead to job losses, and environmental groups that support it. In the meantime, President Clinton planned to support a series of modest steps to reduce greenhouse-gas emissions, such as tax incentives to encourage new, more fuel-efficient technology.

"To get the Senate in a position ready to sign on to this, you're going to have to have meaningful participation by developing countries," said Sen. John Kerry (D-MA), a supporter of the treaty. "No one in their right mind is going to say it's OK for the U.S. to make these significant changes and allow our competitors to remain free of them."

ALLAN FREEDMAN

ETHIOPIA

In 1997, Ethiopian prosecutors charged more than 5,000 officials of Ethiopia's former military government with genocide, murder, and war crimes. In domestic affairs, Ethiopia initiated the development of a multiplicity of projects to expand its water supply. Internationally, the nation used its growing regional clout to involve itself in diplomatic activity in the various Central African disputes.

Political Affairs. Ethiopian special prosecutor Girma Wakjira in February charged 5,198 officials of the former Marxist Dergue government with genocide, war crimes, and murder. The charges related to the killing and torture of 14,200 people during the rule from 1974 to 1991 of Col. Mengistu Haile Mariam—himself one of those charged, albeit in absentia. According to Girma, "extrajudicial executions, torture, and enforced disappearance of innocent people were rampant throughout the country during the era of the Dergue." He specifically accused the defendants of "systematic human-rights violations." One of those charged was Mamo Wolde, a 1968 and 1972 Olympic medalist in marathoning. The exact charges against the former athlete were not made public, and he declared that he was innocent. Trials of the accused were to occur over a three-year period.

In late 1996 deputy prime minister, defense minister, and member of parliament Tamrat Layne was dismissed from office for "gross misconduct." Prime Minister Meles Zenawi stated that Tamrat had acted "contrary to the principles" of Ethiopia and had "fallen prey to the corrupting comfort of city life."

Development of Water Resources. In a move helpful to its ongoing attempt to increase its water supply and to upgrade and expand the storage capacity of dams to generate electric power, Ethiopia in 1997 accepted funds from the United States to develop seven small dams in Tigre province.

The government also produced development plans to utilize more water flowing from the Blue Nile, in Ethiopia's highlands, for the construction of dams and for hydropower projects. More than 200 dams that use 624 million cu yds (477 million m³) of Nile water per year already had been completed, and hundreds more were being constructed for irrigation purposes. These dams, however, would reduce neighboring Egypt's flow of water radically. At a hydrologists' conference held in Addis Ababa in early summer, one participant maintained that Egypt and Ethiopia were set "on a collision course" over the use of water discharging from the Blue Nile.

Ethiopia contracted with U.S., Italian, Dutch, and French engineering firms in 1997 to develop a master plan of Ethiopia's future water needs. With drought and famine intermittent visitors to Ethiopia throughout its history, the government finally was attempting to gain some control over nature.

Foreign Affairs. Throughout the year, Ethiopia used its growing regional authority to involve itself in the settlement of African disputes. In midsummer, Ethiopia's Prime Minister Zenawi attended a summit meeting in Kinshasa, the capital of the Congo (formerly Zaire). The summit was held in support of Congolese President Laurent Kabila, who in May had toppled Congo's former ruler Mobutu Sese Seko from power; Mobutu died in exile in September. Ethiopia (and Eritrea) had supported Kabila's revolt. The summit's participants denounced the United Nations' attempt to investigate claims against Kabila for human-rights violations. Among those attending the meeting were the leaders of Uganda, Zimbabwe, Namibia, the Central African Republic, Zambia, Eritrea, Rwanda, and Gabon.

In April, Ethiopia had participated—with Tanzania, Kenya, Uganda, Zambia, and Rwanda—in a meeting with Burundi's military leader Maj. Pierre Buyoya to discuss those nations' embargo against Burundi, imposed in an effort to push Buyoya into talking to opposing Hutu rebels and restoring democracy. The summit, held in Arusha, Tanzania, concluded with the Tutsi leader agreeing to take the participants' demands into account. The embargo remained in place, but the sanctions were softened somewhat.

PETER SCHWAB, *Purchase College State University of New York*

ETHIOPIA • Information Highlights

Official Name: Federal Democratic Republic of Ethiopia.
Location: Eastern Africa.
Area: 435,184 sq mi (1 127 127 km²).
Population (mid-1997 est.): 58,700,000.
Chief Cities (1994 census): Addis Ababa, the capital, 2,112,737; Dire Dawa, 164,851; Harar, 131,139.
Government: *Head of state,* Negasso Ghidada, president (took office May 1995). *Head of government,* Meles Zenawi, prime minister (took office May 1995). *Legislature*—Federal Parliamentary Assembly: Council of the Federation and Council of People's Representatives.
Monetary Unit: Birr (6.604 birr equal U.S.$1, April 1997).
Gross Domestic Product (1995 est. U.S. $): $24,200,000,-000 (purchasing power parity).
Economic Index (1995, 1990 = 100): *Consumer Prices,* all items, 183.9; food, 198.6.
Foreign Trade (1994 U.S.$): *Imports,* $1,033,000,000; *exports,* $372,000,000.

ETHNIC GROUPS, U.S.

Issues of racial preferences in drawing electoral districts, hiring, granting college admissions, and awarding public contracts attracted considerable attention and formed public policy during 1997. Leaders of both major political parties made race a matter of national debate.

In June, President Bill Clinton announced a yearlong initiative to discuss racial tensions in the United States and to propose measures to help minorities gain firmer economic and educational footholds in U.S. society. In acknowledging that race remained a festering sore in American culture, the president promised to hold four town-hall meetings and form a presidential advisory board to focus sustained national attention on racial issues. Speaker of the U.S. House of Representatives Newt Gingrich responded by calling for the Clinton administration to do away with quotas, preferences, and set-asides and to stop "obsessing on race."

During 1997 religious and civil-rights organizations and leaders renewed calls for self-help as the key to racial progress. Such an emphasis was exemplified best in the numerous follow-up measures nationwide after the April 1997 summit on volunteerism and the October "Million Woman March" that brought hundreds of thousands of African-American women to Philadelphia to promote racial unity and a rededication to social activism. At its annual meeting in July, the National Association for the Advancement of Colored People (NAACP) reported that it had eliminated its debt and restored its moral credibility after several years of mismanagement and scandal, pledged a new economic-development program to promote black

entrepreneurship, and pushed for higher minority-voter turnouts in local elections. In November, Martin Luther King III was elected to succeed the Rev. Joseph E. Lowery as president of the Southern Christian Leadership Conference (SCLC).

Race-Based Election Issues. In a series of decisions since 1993, the Supreme Court had ruled unconstitutional efforts by states or local governments to draw election districts in ways intended primarily to preserve or boost the voting power of racial or ethnic minorities. The trend continued in 1997. Following the court's lead, a panel of federal judges in February ordered the New York legislature to redraw the 12th District—which, the panel stated, had been drawn solely to elect a Hispanic representative. Also in February, a panel of federal judges declared the black-majority 3d District in Virginia unlawful because it was drawn too heavily along racial lines. In June the Supreme Court decided by a 5–4 vote that Georgia might retain only one black-majority district among its 11 U.S. House districts.

In May the court by a 7–2 vote in a case from Bossier Parish, LA, ruled that the U.S. Justice Department in 1993 acted improperly in its denial of approval of a Louisiana school-district plan. Then in November, in a decision with wide implications for local-government elections, the court struck at U.S. Justice Department efforts to increase local minority-voting power when it reversed by a 7–2 vote lower-court rulings that had objected to the at-large majority system for electing the mayor and city council in Monroe, GA. The court allowed the at-large system to continue.

In ballot questions in 1997, minorities showed voting solidarity to protect their own interests and ensure minority representation.

On Oct. 25, 1997, black women from throughout the United States participated in the "Million Woman March" in Philadelphia. A 12-point platform was endorsed for the rally, which was intended to encourage unity among women of African descent.

The importance of maintaining access to the ballot was pointed out in January, when the Sentencing Project released a report that found nearly one in seven black men of voting age had lost their right to vote because of being convicted of a crime. The report ignited much discussion about the mobilization for minority voting rights. In September, Cuban-Americans rallied to defeat a proposal to abolish the city of Miami and merge it with the Dade county government, where Hispanic voters no longer would form a majority. In the same referendum, Miami voters approved a change in Miami's representation from an at-large to a district system, making it likely that the city commission would have at least one black commissioner. Houston voters agreed to keep that city's affirmative-action plan, and in December elected Lee Brown as the city's first black mayor.

Affirmative Action. In February the U.S. Supreme Court refused to hear the city of Philadelphia's appeal of a lower-court ruling that had struck down the city's minority-set-aside program for awarding contracts. By letting the lower-court decision stand, the court in effect ended an eight-year court battle over the constitutionality of such municipal minori-ty-set-aside programs. Meanwhile, the fate of statewide affirmative-action programs came under review. In March protests and marches greeted the first effort to implement California's Proposition 209, approved in 1996, which banned racial and gender preferences in college admissions, state employment, or public contracts in the state. The California move against affirmative-action programs was considered a bellwether for state actions elsewhere on the question—so much so that civil-rights groups, federal governmental agencies, and the courts struggled to clarify its meaning and application. In April a three-judge federal appeals court unanimously upheld the California ban, stating the voter-approved Proposition 209 was neutrally applied law and "no doubt" constitutional. In August the U.S. Court of Appeals for the 9th District refused to reconsider the judges' decision. Finally, in September the U.S. Supreme Court, without comment or dissent, made final the lower court's ruling that the California ban was constitutional. The court's action, however, left open questions about the obligation of municipalities and state agencies to enforce their own antidiscrimination codes and laws and to abide by federal antidiscrimination rules. It also cleared the way for anti-affirmative-action ballot initiatives pending in 22 other states. The court's action also suggested that proponents of affirmative action would not be able to rely on the federal courts to protect the principle and would have to win electoral battles in the various states to do so.

The Clinton administration attempted to preserve a "race-conscious" system of awarding federal contracts and a commitment to affirmative-action principles in federal employment. In May the administration announced it would use statistics to determine whether African-Americans, Hispanics, Asians, and Native Americans were excluded unfairly from obtaining government work. By establishing federal "industry-specific benchmarks" in awarding contracts, the administration argued it could use "race-conscious measures" that would give advantage to "socially and economically disadvantaged businesses."

The elimination of affirmative-action initiatives in California and Texas led to a radical drop-off in law-school admissions at the University of California Boalt Hall law school, the University of California at Los Angeles law school, and the University of Texas law school, officials reported in July. Likewise, in November the Association of American Medical Colleges cited anti-affirmative-action measures to explain an 11% drop in applications from minorities seeking admission to medical schools nationwide.

In a case with major potential significance for establishing new standards for affirmative action in the workplace, the Supreme Court in June rejected the advice of the Clinton administration to avoid taking up the case of *Board of Education v. Taxman*, an affirmative-action dispute arising from a Piscataway, NJ, school-board decision in 1989 to lay off a white teacher rather than a black teacher, solely based on race. In August the court accepted legal briefs in the case. In November the NAACP Legal Defense Fund, the Black Leadership Forum, and the SCLC joined the Piscataway school board in an agreement to help pay for an out-of-court settlement of the case, thereby averting an expected defeat for affirmative action by the U.S. Supreme Court.

In Washington the politics of affirmative action stalled the Senate confirmation of Bill Lann Lee, a Chinese-American civil-rights lawyer and proponent of affirmative action whom President Clinton had nominated in June to head the civil-rights division in the Justice Department. After the grueling confirmation process, during which anti-affirmative-action groups charged Lee with backing "preferential rights," the Senate Judiciary Committee declared the nomination "dead" in November. In December the president named Lee acting attorney general for civil rights and said that he would resubmit the nomination for Senate approval in 1998.

Antidiscrimination Issues. In February the U.S. Supreme Court in a unanimous decision expanded the scope of federal civil-rights law by giving new legal protection to workers who contend that their former employers wrote bad job references or took other retaliatory action against them for filing discrimination claims. Also in February, the Justice Department brought the first housing-discrimination suit against a nursing home, charging an Akron, OH, facility with an unlawful pattern of discrimination in refusing to rent rooms to African-Americans. In June the NAACP announced it would organize a national boycott of the Holiday Inn, Best Western, and Motel 6 hotel chains to protest alleged discrimination against African-Americans in hiring, promotion, and room rental.

Despite several years of efforts by regulators to end discrimination in home insurance and mortgage lending, disparities continued. In March, Nationwide Insurance reached an agreement with the Justice Department to change its policies for insuring inner-city homes and to provide $2.2 million a year for six years to help minority home buyers with down payments, closing costs, home-owner-ship counseling, and below-market mortgages. In August the Federal Financial Institutions Examination Council issued its annual review, showing that lending institutions had turned down 48.8% of applications for home-purchase loans from African-Americans but only 24.1% from whites in 1996.

Business. *Black Enterprise* magazine and the Travelers Group agreed in March to create jointly a multimillion-dollar equity-investment fund to finance established minority businesses. A growth in minority businesses was revealed in a ten-year study released in August by the National Foundation for Women Business Owners; the study showed that business start-ups for African-American, Latino, and Asian women proprietors more than tripled the rate of U.S. businesses overall between 1987 and 1996.

Native Americans. The clarification of treaty rights continued to concern Native Americans. In May lawyers for the state of Alaska filed suit in federal court against the Athabascan Indians of Alaska, in an effort to reverse a federal appeals-court ruling that gives Indian tribes the power to tax companies extracting natural resources from Indian lands or transporting goods across those lands. At issue is the meaning of "Indian country."

The case, which the Supreme Court agreed to consider, has far-reaching implications.

In June the attorney general of Missouri filed suit in state court to block the Coeur d'Alene tribe of Idaho and its partner, UniStar Entertainment, from operating and advertising an on-line gambling business in Missouri. Also in June the U.S. Supreme Court ruled that the Coeur d'Alene tribe of Idaho could not bring suit in federal court regarding land claims in the state, arguing that a state could not be sued under the 11th Amendment and sending the Indians to the state court to seek relief.

In a dispute over mismanagement of tribal trust funds, the U.S. government considered ways of paying Indian tribes hundreds of millions of dollars to avoid lawsuits. In March a presidential investigation of the Bureau of Indian Affairs (BIA) headed by Paul Homan recommended stripping the BIA of its trust-fund management role. Indian tribes also struggled with the meaning of federal welfare reform, which with its work requirements was forcing Native Americans to leave tribal lands where no work was available and go to urban areas where it was. Various tribes insisted that treaty guarantees for education, health care, and other services overrode the new work rules. At the same time, numerous tribes tightened definitions for membership, thereby removing mixed-tribe Indians and others from their rolls and increasing the per-capita federal and tribal money distribution for full-blooded tribal members.

The role of Indian money in politics became news in February, when a leader of the Oneida tribe of Wisconsin admitted donating $103,000 to the Democrats in 1996 in order to gain access to the White House; and in March, following revelations that the Cheyenne-Arapaho Indians of Oklahoma had donated almost $108,000 to President Clinton's campaign in hopes of getting the federal government to return Indian lands. In December the Justice Department expanded its inquiry into allegations that Interior Secretary Bruce Babbitt had rejected the application by three bands of Chippewa to open a casino in Wisconsin, in deference to other Chippewa who wanted to prevent competition with their casino and who had donated more than $230,000 to the Democratic Party.

Navajo tribal members in Arizona, Utah, and New Mexico in November voted down a measure to introduce casinos on America's largest Indian reservation.

RANDALL M. MILLER
St. Joseph's University, Philadelphia

EUROPE

Developments related to the issue of unity dominated European affairs in 1997.

The Intergovernmental Conference. At the December 1996 six-month summit meeting of the European Union (EU), held in Dublin, the organization's heads of state and government laid down the agenda for the EU's activity in 1997. Primarily they postponed action on the EU's five most pressing problems—institutional change, budgetary and farm reforms, unemployment, admission of new members, and adoption of a common currency.

EU had agreed at the Maastricht summit in 1991 to appoint an Intergovernmental Conference (IGC) to revise the Treaties of Rome to make the institutions more effective and to prepare machinery for implementing common foreign and security policies and collaboration on justice and home affairs. Beginning in March 1997, IGC struggled to reduce the voting power of smaller members, to cut the size of the European Commission, to reform the European Parliament, and to restrict the powers of the European Court of Justice. But its work was hampered by a split between those—led by Britain—unwilling to increase the EU's supranational powers, and those—led by Germany—that wished to increase them, as well as by the smaller states' refusal to see their voting rights made more proportional to their populations.

At a June 1997 summit in Amsterdam, the IGC presented a new treaty that was accepted by the heads of state and government, and the IGC then disbanded. But, again, crucial decisions on reform were postponed, with the proviso that they would be taken up when entry negotiations with new members were almost completed. Until then, no changes in voting procedures or in the powers of the EU's institutions were to be made. The relatively unimportant secretary-general of the Council of Ministers was to be the EU's spokesperson on common foreign and security policies, and plans pushed by France for making the Western European Union (WEU) the defense arm of the EU were shelved. The EU would establish common policies on immigration and would become responsible for the Schengen agreement, which individual members had drawn up in 1990 to abolish frontier controls among them. Britain and Ireland, however, retained the right to maintain their border inspections.

Budgetary and Agricultural Policies. Arguments over relative national contributions to the EU's budget, which in 1997 was not permitted to exceed 1.27% of gross national product (GNP), revived. Germany complained that its contribution of 60% of the EU budget was excessive. However, Greece, Ireland, Portugal, and Spain—which all received large subsidies from the budget—refused to have their benefits lessened, and even argued that the budget ceiling should be raised when new members were accepted.

Reform also was demanded in the way the budget was spent. Although improvements in the Common Agricultural Policy (CAP) and, in particular, reduction of some price supports had ended the accumulation of vast stockpiles of unsold produce, the CAP still absorbed almost half of the budget, while two fifths went to various structural payments. Unless changes were made in agricultural and structural subsidies, many members felt that the cost of admitting new members from Eastern Europe would be prohibitive. To begin negotiations on the needed reforms, the European Commission proposed in July an austerity program called Agenda 2000, which it claimed would make possible admission of new members without further budgetary increases.

Unacceptable Unemployment. The cost of the EU's intractable unemployment directly hindered financial reforms. Although growth in the GDP of the EU had reached a healthy 2.9% by midyear, unemployment rose to 18 million, of whom 4.5 million were in Germany. Average unemployment in the union was above 10%. Moreover, in comparison with the United States and Britain, where unemployment was falling, unemployment in continental Europe was structural and was caused by rigidities in the labor market, the high social costs of hiring workers, and lack of deregulation. The most dramatic proposals by national governments for reducing unemployment—the offers by newly elected Socialist Prime Minister Lionel Jospin in France and center-left Prime Minister Romano Prodi in Italy to reduce the workweek in coming years to 35 hours without loss of pay—were received skeptically by most economists. In October the European Commission endorsed new employment targets—notably the creation of 12 million new jobs in five years—and it produced recommendations for cutting tax and other welfare costs to employers hiring new workers, which were discussed at an employment summit of heads of government in November.

Delaying Admission of New Members. At their 1993 Copenhagen summit, the EU's leaders had defined the criteria that new members must meet—stable democratic government, a

NATO Expansion

Intense debate about expanding the North Atlantic Treaty Organization (NATO)—the mutual-defense pact of North American and European countries that was created in April 1949 at the height of the Cold War—to include nations from the former Eastern bloc occurred during 1997.

Early History and after Communism. Although Greece and Turkey joined the original 12 nations—the United States, Canada, Belgium, Britain, Denmark, France, Iceland, Italy, Luxembourg, the Netherlands, Norway, and Portugal—as NATO members in 1951, expansion was slow and cautious. West Germany's rearmament and entrance in 1955 led the Soviet Union to organize the Warsaw Pact as a communist military alliance counterbalancing NATO, thereby institutionalizing the East-West conflict as a confrontation of two military blocs. Spain, admitted to NATO in 1982, was the only new state to enter the organization before the 1989–90 collapse of Soviet and Eastern European communism led to the 1991 disbandment of the Warsaw Pact. Rather than disband NATO, however, members decided to expand its role—while, at the same time, reducing its forces. In addition to guaranteeing member security, NATO began playing a wider role in safeguarding newly democratic regimes and undertaking limited peacekeeping operations, as in the former Yugoslavia.

As early as 1991, NATO foreign ministers proposed close cooperation with former Warsaw Pact states and declared that "coercion or intimidation" of countries in Eastern Europe would be "of direct and material concern" to NATO. By 1997, 27 countries—including Russia and many former Soviet states and neutral countries—had joined with NATO in Partnerships for Peace, jointly training for, planning, and engaging in common military exercises. Most Eastern European countries wanted, by 1996, full membership in NATO—either before, or at the same time as, membership in the European Union. NATO members agreed that some expansion was necessary.

Problems Arise. The number and variety of applicants posed problems, however. Admittance of Estonia, Latvia, and Lithuania would alienate an already distrustful Russia, while doubts arose about the democratic stability of Slovakia, Albania, Bulgaria, and Romania. Macedonia and Slovenia were too small to be of military significance; however, France—annoyed at U.S. unwillingness to permit a European commander to replace an American in NATO's southern subcommand—supported the entry of Slovenia and Romania. Only Poland, Hungary, and the Czech Republic seemed to all members to meet the criteria for membership—stable democratic government, a market economy, civilian control of armed forces, and ability to fulfill the military duties of membership. Another problem was the cost of extending NATO's military infrastructure, modernizing the new members' military, and preparing new task forces for immediate defense of the enlarged territory. Finally, Russia viewed NATO expansion as a direct threat to its own security.

Agreements. On May 27, 1997, after long and difficult negotiations between NATO Secretary-General Javier Solana and Russian Foreign Minister Yevgeny Primakov, Russian President Boris Yeltsin and 16 NATO leaders signed the Founding Act on Mutual Relations, Cooperation, and Security in Paris. A NATO Russia Permanent Joint Council was established to discuss such matters as terrorism, military doctrine, and nuclear safety, and Russia was assured that NATO did not intend to station nuclear weapons or large combat forces on the territory of the new members. Russian opposition was assuaged, without NATO having to give Russia the veto power over the organization's significant decisions that it wanted.

Meanwhile, members of NATO continued to argue over which applicants to accept. The NATO foreign ministers meeting at Sintra, Portugal, in June were split between a U.S.-led camp favoring only Poland, Hungary, and the Czech Republic and a French-led group supporting Romania and Slovenia as well. The U.S. view triumphed at the July summit meeting of NATO leaders in Madrid, not least because of worry over the costs of expansion, which even for three new members could exceed $27 billion. Poland, Hungary, and the Czech Republic will become members by NATO's 50th anniversary in 1999, providing that the expansion is ratified by the legislatures of the 16 NATO members and the three prospective members. At that point, a new summit will consider further expansion of the alliance. NATO's 16 members also joined in Madrid with the 27 members of the Partnerships for Peace in founding a new Euro-Atlantic Partnership Council, as another attempt to ensure that NATO, through ever-increasing institutional ties, would be a stabilizing influence beyond the borders of its members.

F. Roy Willis

functioning market economy, and ability to conform to the rules of the single market. In 1997, 12 countries were formal applicants for EU membership. Turkey's application was shelved because of worries over its ethnic problems and its political instability. Slovakia's democratic system seemed questionable. Romania and Bulgaria also had ethnic problems and wavering economies. Cyprus, which had been approved as a candidate by the European Commission, was unlikely to be accepted without some solution to the embattled relations of its Greek and Turkish communities. Of the three Baltic states (Estonia, Latvia, and Lithuania), only Estonia had firm support because of its dynamic economy. By far the strongest candidates for EU membership were the Czech Republic, Hungary, and Poland—which also were accepted for NATO membership in July—as well as small but prospering Slovenia.

In Agenda 2000, the commission recommended that, in addition to the approval of Cyprus, talks begin with the leading five candidates only—the Czech Republic, Estonia, Hungary, Poland, and Slovenia. This choice was endorsed at the Luxembourg summit in December. Negotiations were likely to be slow and difficult. Even the wealthier of the new applicants were likely to be a drain on the EU budget. Major constitutional changes in the EU would be needed for a community of 20 members to function efficiently. Deep reforms would be needed in the common agricultural and regional policies.

Toward a Common Currency. In the Maastricht Treaty, the EU's leaders had agreed to create a common currency, named the Euro in 1995, by Jan. 1, 1999, at the latest. This currency was to replace the national currencies in 2002, and was to be used as an instrument of public debt beginning on Jan. 1, 1999. Only countries that met specific standards, however, would be permitted to join this economic and monetary union (EMU). For example, the budget deficit was not to be more than 3% of GDP and the public debt must not exceed 60% of GDP. Long-term interest rates must be low and exchange rates for the national currency stable.

Since the achievement of these goals required considerable fiscal austerity, a widespread debate occurred over the desirability of having a common currency at all. The arguments in favor were numerous. Since the opening of the single European market in January 1993—when the majority of obstacles to free movement of capital, labor, goods, and services had been removed—the principal obstacle remaining to consolidation of this stimulating free market was the existence of national currencies and, by implication, the continuation of competing national monetary policies. The existing Exchange Rate Mechanism (ERM), through which national currencies were supposed to remain within fixed relationships to each other, had virtually collapsed in 1992–93. Discipline to control inflation and encourage growth would be imposed upon irresponsible governments by the European Central Bank.

With the value of the common currency certain, investment within the EU would be stimulated. There even would be substantial savings on the cost of doing business. Nevertheless, Britain, Denmark, and Sweden declared their intention of not participating, at least in the initial group of countries creating the Euro. They felt that Europe lacked the homogeneity of economic conditions that was needed for a common monetary policy to be successful. German financial circles shared that concern, and to satisfy them—as well to appease German public opinion, which was massively opposed to losing the stable German mark—the German government insisted that a stability pact accompany introduction of the new currency. At both the Dublin and Amsterdam summits, France argued in favor of a more flexible approach. In particular, it urged that a group representing the national governments should be created to supervise the European Central Bank.

By midyear it seemed probable that the common currency would be created on schedule. In 1995 only Luxembourg was meeting the criteria for membership. In 1997, the commission reported in October, every country except Greece had brought its budget deficits within acceptable limits. Denmark, Ireland, and Luxembourg were setting high standards by showing net surpluses in their budgets. The German government, which had attempted unsuccessfully to revalue its gold reserves as subterfuge for meeting the criteria, was able to bring down its deficit to 3%. Despite doubts about its enthusiasm for the Euro, France's Jospin government brought down its deficit by imposing new corporate taxes and by cutting spending. In Italy, when the former Communists threatened to bring down the Prodi government in protest against spending cuts needed to reduce the Italian deficit, protest from their own supporters compelled them to vote for the budget that made Italy eligible for the monetary union.

F. ROY WILLIS
University of California, Davis

The Marshall Plan—50 Years Later

On June 5, 1947, U.S. Secretary of State George Marshall, speaking at the Harvard University commencement, startled the world with the generosity of his offer of massive U.S. financial aid to all the countries of Europe—West and East alike—to restore their economies, which were decimated by World War II. Between 1948 and 1952, $13 billion ($88 billion in current dollars) was distributed through the European Recovery Program, or the Marshall Plan. Fifty years after that speech, on May 28, 1997, President Bill Clinton met at The Hague with Dutch Prime Minister Willem Kok and other leaders of countries that had been aided by the Marshall Plan. A colorful pageant of dancing children, trumpets, and drums accompanied videotaped scenes of war destruction and recovery, while speakers shared personal accounts of how the aid had affected them and called for similar aid to Eastern Europe in the late 1990s. Later, thousands in Rotterdam rallied as President Clinton *(below)* dedicated a plaque to Marshall.

Although Marshall had specified that his plan was not directed against any country or doctrine, the Soviet Union refused to accept certain conditions—such as coordinating economic planning and providing detailed information on its economy—required to become a recipient. Eastern European countries were forced to go along with the Soviet refusal. Sixteen Western European countries ultimately formed the Organization for European Economic Cooperation (OEEC) to work with the United States in administering the aid. Britain received the largest share, $3.2 billion; France got $2.7 billion; and Iceland received the smallest amount, $29 million. Because Western Europe already had a trained workforce and resources, the aid brought about positive results rather quickly. Recipients' gross national products jumped 25%, while industrial production rose 35%. Industries targeted for investment, such as steel and chemicals, showed great increases in productivity. Best of all, trade among OEEC countries increased 70%, as Europeans became accustomed to collaboration.

There were some disappointments for American planners, however. Tariffs barely were reduced, and capital and labor did not move freely across frontiers. To bring about the collaboration that Marshall had proposed, new European organizations were needed. Former administrators of the Marshall Plan—for example, Paul-Henri Spaak of Belgium and Jean Monnet of France—led Europe from OEEC directly into true economic integration, by creating the European Coal and Steel Community in 1952 and the European Economic Community in 1958.

F. ROY WILLIS

FAMILY

The issue of dual-career families took center stage in the United States in 1997.

Working Women and the Child-Care Issue. Growing attention to child care came as the number of women joining the workforce increased at a rapid rate. An estimated 63% of all married women with children under age 6—some 8 million mothers—were working in 1997. This was up from 18.6% in 1960 and 58.9% in 1990.

The White House responded to what First Lady Hillary Rodham Clinton called a "silent crisis" by hosting an October conference that sought solutions to the problems of quality, availability, and financing of child care. Working against such solutions were the economics of the industry—low-paid workers, high staff turnover, and parents unable to pay more. Government subsidies were reaching only one in ten eligible children. At the conference, President Bill Clinton pledged a $300 million measure to improve training and pay for child-care workers.

A study by the National Institute of Child Health and Human Development found that, although children in high-quality day care had some advantage in language and learning abilities, the impact of day care was less important than was the quality of home life.

Meanwhile, with a stay-at-home mother a reality in fewer U.S. families, businesses attempted to help working parents by offering increasingly flexible schedules. Gaining in popularity were emergency leave, job sharing, and paid-time-off programs, which gave workers greater control over days off. An estimated 60% of U.S. companies offered some job flexibility in 1997, according to Catalyst, an advocacy group for working women.

The Woodward Trial. In fall the United States—and the world—watched a Massachusetts trial in which a young English au pair stood accused of murdering her nearly 9-month-old charge. The charge against 19-year-old Louise Woodward, who was accused of shaking Matthew Eappen to death, brought out strong reactions, as did the trial's outcome. Some thought Woodward was being accused unfairly; some questioned whether young au pairs were trained adequately to care for young children; and some blamed the boy's parents for leaving him in another person's care. Although a jury found Woodward guilty of murder, the judge reduced the sentence to involuntary manslaughter and gave her a prison term equal to the 279 days she already had served.

Income and Poverty. U.S. median household income rose 1.2% more than inflation between 1995 and 1996, according to the U.S. Census Bureau. The median income for working women rose to an all-time high of 74% of what men earned for comparable work.

On the negative side, the number of Americans with incomes of less than half the poverty threshold rose to 14.4 million in 1996. The proportion of people with incomes less than the poverty rate fell to 13.7% in 1996 from 13.8% in 1995. The highest poverty rate was among Hispanics, at 29.4%; the rate among African-Americans was 28.4%; among Asian-Americans, 14.5%; and among whites, 11.2%.

Lifestyles. The percentage of U.S. households composed of married couples continued its decline, according to the Census Bureau, decreasing to 53.7% of households in 1996, compared with 70.5% in 1970. The nation's high divorce rate, meanwhile, raised concern among lawmakers. In Arizona legislation was pushed to reduce marriage-license fees for those getting premarital education, while in Michigan a bill was introduced to extend the marriage-license waiting period for those who did not receive premarital counseling. And Louisiana passed a "covenant marriage" law, giving couples a choice between a traditional marriage license or one mandating counseling and making it more difficult to divorce.

While Americans had more leisure time than in the past, much of it came in short increments and apparently was spent watching television. Studies by John Robinson and Geoffrey Godbey, authors of *Time for Life*, found that close to 40% of free time went to watching TV.

Teens. Studies released in 1997 found that teens' sexual activity had declined for the first time in more than 20 years. The National Center for Health Statistics reported that 50% of girls 15 to 19 years old had had sex, compared with 55% in 1990. A study of boys by the National Institute of Child Health and Human Development found a drop in the percentage who had had sex from 60% in 1988 to 55% in 1995. Physical and sexual abuse among teens, however, was high; two studies showed that one in four adolescent girls reported having been abused sexually or physically.

Adults' faith in the younger generation, meanwhile, was apparently low, with only 37% surveyed by Public Agenda saying they believed that today's children will make the country a better place. Many cited a failure of children to learn fundamental moral values.

KRISTI VAUGHAN, *Freelance Writer*

FASHION

In 1997 the operative word in regard to fashion was "casual." Once, it was possible to guess what city an airport was located in from the way people dressed as they waited for planes. In San Francisco, they wore neatly tailored suits; in Minneapolis, it was tweeds; and in New York, outfits that were carefully coordinated. Now, however, women as well as men were dressing for ease and comfort. The T-shirt, with or without printed messages, remained the article of choice, paired with jeans or chinos, whether one was at the airport, at a shopping mall, at school, or even at work. This was increasingly true for people of all ages and in most countries.

Fashion designers continued to suggest alternatives to the casual trend. Couturiers, especially the makers of custom clothing in Paris—traditionally considered the pacesetters in the world of fashion—offered elaborate designs embellished with feathers and beads. Most women were amused by the pictures of these styles in magazines and on television, but did not consider them appropriate for their lives. They continued wearing T-shirts wherever possible.

Ironically, press coverage of fashion shows was increasing, yet this had little effect on what people actually wore. The casual style was not limited to young people. Older women also wore T-shirts, as well as sweaters, baseball jackets, khakis or chinos, and sneakers. Sedate "old lady" fashions virtually had disappeared. Fashion now was perceived as entertainment. The single designer who did the most to forge this link was Gianni Versace, who was killed in July 1997 (*see* SPECIAL REPORT, page 241). It was said that the fashion business was changing more dramatically in the 1990s than at any time since the invention of the sewing machine in the 19th century.

Designers.   One prominent sign of the dramatic changes in the industry was the decision of two major companies, Donna Karan and Ralph Lauren, to go public. The stock offerings of both designers were received warmly, at least initially. Donna Karan's stock prices began to falter when a contract with Designer Holdings to produce her jeans collection under a licensing arrangement fell through, and the company's earnings were less than anticipated. In 1997's second quarter, a loss of $14.7 million was reported, and Karan herself stepped down as the company's CEO. Ralph Lauren's stock fell off a bit after an initial flurry but remained fairly stable. It was considered a well-run company and a good investment. Designer stocks, even though the names

© M.L. Sinibaldi/The Stock Market

© Ronnie Kaufman/The Stock Market

The professional, pulled-together look of a suit remained in favor among working women in 1997. Skirt lengths varied from mid-thigh to ankle-grazing. Pantsuits owed their increasing popularity to their style, ease, and comfort.

Athletic wear made specifically for women and appropriate for a wide variety of sports was increasingly available in 1997; for dressier occasions, women had the option of a trendy leather pantsuit by designer Richard Tyler.

were well known, were subject to the same market forces as were industrial stocks; it was agreed, however, that they were there to stay.

In fact, designer names now were considered brands, much as in the toothpaste or automobile businesses. One name that was revived with much hoopla was Halston. Roy Halston Frowick (he used only his middle name in business) was a darling of the 1970s. He was one of the first designers to capitalize on his dealings with show-business figures. Martha Graham and Liza Minnelli were often in the front-row seats at his shows. But he also was a favorite of society women, who wore his jersey dresses to big charity balls and his Ultra-suede dresses to lunches and other daytime events. Ultra-suede was a synthetic leather Halston called "leatherette" and said could be thrown in a washing machine.

Halston died in 1990 at the age of 57, but a company called Tropic Tex International and run by two Israeli brothers, Marc and Jack Setton, felt the Halston philosophy could be revived for today's fashion industry. Randolph Duke, known for his swimsuits, was named design director. Carmine Porcelli, who worked with Oscar de la Renta, was business manager. They planned 22 collections, ranging from sportswear to evening clothes. These would include accessories, menswear, furniture, and sleepwear. Halston was perceived as a worldwide brand with a potential sales volume of $500 million within five years.

Trends. At a time when mid-thigh and ankle lengths were both acceptable, trends were far less dictatorial than in the past. Still, there were some noteworthy developments in 1997. By fall, store buyers were ordering more pantsuits than jackets with skirts. Pants were skinny, lightly flared near the hem ("boot leg"), or occasionally full. Thirty years after

(Continued on page 243.)

Gianni Versace

The 1997 death of Gianni Versace, the prominent Italian fashion designer, sent tremors through the industry in Europe, the United States, and even the Far East. The 50-year-old Versace was shot on July 15 outside his home in South Beach, FL, a part of Miami he had helped turn into an American St. Tropez, a gathering place for photographers, models, and those who liked to vacation among the "beautiful people."

Versace was known not only for his dazzlingly sexy clothes, but because he managed to merge the world of fashion with that of entertainment. He designed costumes for La Scala and for the opera in San Francisco, as well as for the popular 1980s TV series *Miami Vice*. He filled his runways with supermodels and ringside seats at his shows with personalities like Elton John and Sylvester Stallone. He entertained lavishly at his homes in Lake Como, Italy; Florida; and New York.

The "Versace look" was sexy and elaborate, the opposite of the quiet elegance of Giorgio Armani, the other major Milan designer. Versace was known for his bold prints and his dresses made of gold or silver mesh. In recent years, however, his designs were becoming subtler and more sophisticated and had been winning growing critical acclaim.

Due to Versace's celebrity, his violent death made headlines in newspapers worldwide until the suicide of his alleged assailant, multiple murderer Andrew Cunanan, nine days after the killing. The press coverage continued through the fall, as monthly magazines readied appreciations of his work. His sister, Donatella, who had worked with him, was to be in charge of new collections. She had been designing Versus, a lower-priced collection. Her daughter, Allegra, was his main heir.

In addition to his sister and niece, he was survived by his brother, Santo, who handles the company's business affairs. There are 300 Versace boutiques around the world. The company had 1996 sales of more than $1 billion. Like Gucci and Chanel, important fashion houses that continued despite their founders' deaths, the house of Versace was expected to survive. A public stock offering had been scheduled for mid-1998, with the aim of finalizing the house's transformation into a global brand name; the offering was postponed after Versace's death, however.

Background. Gianni Versace was born in Reggio di Calabria, Italy, in 1946. He learned his future trade in his mother's dressmaking salon. In

© P. Castaldi/AP/Wide World Photos

1972, Versace moved to Milan, where a fashion center was developing. He designed collections for a number of manufacturers. Even before he opened a collection of ready-to-wear under his own name in 1978, he was recognized as a design talent.

He introduced his first couture, or made-to-order, collection in 1990, and chose to present it at Paris' Ritz Hotel, inviting comparisons to French haute couture. The clothes were sexy, extravagant, and very well made. They were greeted with respect, which grew in later years when the styling became more adventurous and the workmanship remarkably refined.

Through the 1990s, Versace produced two ready-to-wear and two couture collections a year, as well as men's styles. He also designed accessories collections and casual clothes under the Versace Jeans Couture label. His ad campaigns were shot by top fashion photographers, and his clothes were worn by Madonna, Elton John, Princess Diana, and actress Elizabeth Hurley.

BERNADINE MORRIS

"Designermania"

At the height of Pierre Cardin's company's fame in the 1960s and 1970s, the French couturier had contracts with 612 manufacturers worldwide to sell products bearing his name. This was the high-water mark for a single fashion house, but the idea has spread since then. Fashion designers are branching out. Not only have they explored every angle of the fashion field, from underwear to eyeglasses, but they also are attacking the world of home furnishings and even the food market. Donna Karan has her name on tea, while Ralph Lauren has paint.

Background. Licensing, as it is called, started with the Paris couture houses in the 1930s. Chanel No. 5 perfume—a result of the early foray into sidelines—is still with us. Designers discovered that women who could not afford their extravagantly priced made-to-order fashions would be happy to flaunt designer names on perfume or cologne. Scarves and costume jewelry soon followed.

The concept got a big boost in the 1960s as couture designers added ready-to-wear collections produced by manufacturers outside their companies. Now customers did not have to go to Paris and wait for weeks to have private fittings. They simply could drop into a neighborhood department store or boutique—whether in Columbus, OH, or Tokyo—and buy an Yves Saint Laurent dress off the rack.

The Licensing Process. The basic licensing concept still holds. The market for the most expensive fashions is limited, though the prestige of designer names is great. Some of this prestige rubs off on lower-priced styles—as long as they carry a famous designer's name.

The designer receives a royalty, usually 10% of the wholesale price, for each article sold. There is often a sizable fee for signing the contract with a manufacturer in the first place. This fee can amount to a substantial sum: Approximately 90% of Calvin Klein's $2.5 billion volume worldwide is estimated to be in licensed products.

However, there is no way for consumers to know just how much input a designer has on a product bearing his or her name. Some are more conscientious than others, supplying sketches and trying to supervise the final product. "We like to try out our new ideas in house to be sure we do it right," says Donna Karan, who, as of 1997, had only six licensees. "Once we are satisfied, we may pass them along to manufacturers who might have better production facilities." In recent years some designers' reputations have been damaged by a flood of mediocre-quality licensed merchandise.

© Allan Tannenbaum/Sygma

Designers often open their own boutiques, as did Christian Lacroix, right, to display their clothing as well as the array of other items emblazoned with their names. The majority of many designers' profits derive from the sale of licensed nonclothing products.

"Designermania" Reigns. Like a number of other fashion designers—including Ralph Lauren, Geoffrey Beene, Calvin Klein, and Adrienne Vitadini—Bill Blass currently is working on furniture. "He's doing it all himself," says Gail Levenstein, Blass' license director. "He's already done lamps, sheets, and towels. Now he feels ready to attack furniture, upholstered and otherwise." Furniture · represents yet another field for fashion designers to conquer—as well as yet another area of stores where their name can be promoted.

Calvin Klein says that furniture, dishes, and home ornaments provide another outlet for his "modern design sensibility." As he opens his own megastores in Europe and the Far East as well as in the United States, it also gives him more products to sell in those stores.

A visit to any large department store will demonstrate how widespread the licensing procedure has become. Throughout the furniture, bed and bath, home-decoration, and kitchenware departments, designer names are prominent. In the fashion departments, the same names appear among underwear, active sports clothes, mid-priced fashions, and the stellar top-priced collections. And finally, designer names pop up yet again in the perfume and cosmetics department. What an ego trip—and revenue builder—for today's designers. And as long as consumers seem willing to snap up just about any product bearing their favorite designer's name—whether it be for perceived good quality or simply for the cachet—"designermania" will continue flourishing.

BERNADINE MORRIS

Yves Saint Laurent suggested that trousers be treated as serious fashion for women, his point seemed to have been accepted.

Another growth area for women's fashion was the active sports field. Increasing interest in women's basketball and other team sports such as hockey and softball encouraged manufacturers to offer special styles for women. Sneaker manufacturers like Nike and Adidas were in the forefront of this development. Women athletes, many of whom had been wearing men's styles, now could find shorts and tops designed to fit their bodies. These active sports clothes were also appropriate for biking and in-line skating. Stretch fabrics and bright colors were important components.

Stretch fabrics also were used for nonathletic wear because they improved the fit and increased the comfort quotient. Skirts, pants, blouses, and jackets all were made with stretch fabrics. When properly constructed, they permitted the body to move freely and also had a neat, pulled-together look.

While a little bit of decoration in the form of beads and embroidery was permissible for evening, the prevailing style was clean and simple. Flounces and ruffles were considered passé, and minimalism was still the dominant look. Women wanted their clothes to be simple and practical. It was not a time for flights of fancy or clothes that distorted the body. This was the attitude not only of women in the United States and in Europe, but globally.

Fashion was changing because women had less time to devote to it. Not only did they have less time for shopping, but they had less time for upkeep of their wardrobes. They were working at more upscale jobs than a generation ago. They had families and less, if any, household help. They wanted to look smart, but they wanted clothes on their own terms. That explained why the suit remained the dominant article of apparel. With pants or a skirt, the suit was versatile. And it did not go out of fashion in a season. The idea of fashion obsolescence was dying a natural death.

BERNADINE MORRIS
Freelance Fashion Journalist

"Casual" was the fashion watchword throughout 1997; men and women of all ages were looking to stay comfortable in T-shirts, sweaters, chinos or jeans, and soft-fitting knits.

FINLAND

The Finnish economy was on a strong growth path in 1997. Political support for making Finland the only Nordic country to embrace the new European Union (EU) currency, the Euro, in 1999 was reinforced.

European Affairs. Polls showed that a majority of Finns did not want to give up their national currency, the markka, in favor of the Euro. And a government-sponsored working group of academics concluded in April that there were no compelling economic reasons to advocate or to reject Finnish membership in the European economic and monetary union (EMU). But the politicians had made up their minds. The Finnish government and a large majority in the Finnish parliament were determined that Finland should become the only Nordic country to participate in EMU from its start in 1999.

Stronger integration into the EU was seen as enhancing Finnish sovereignty in terms of neighboring Russia and would give Finland leverage in advancing the cause of Estonia's membership in the EU. Popular support of the EU remained high, partly for security reasons, but also because EU membership had caused food prices in Finland to fall by 13%.

Politics. The five-party coalition government—led by Paavo Lipponen of the Social Democratic Party and with a majority of 143 seats in the 200-seat Finnish parliament, the Eduskunta—continued to demonstrate relative unanimity. The coalition was called the "rainbow government" because it included parties ranging from the right to the Leftist Alliance to the environmentalist Green Party. Its broad base was credited with creating bipartisan support for tight fiscal policies, including cutbacks in unemployment benefits. As leader of the opposition, former Prime Minister Esko Aho of the Center Party had questioned Finland's membership in the EMU, but he would not want to revoke it if he were to lead the next government.

A controversial proposal that Finland should buck the Nordic trend toward alternative sources of energy and build another nuclear-power plant created divisions.

Economy. Finland had become the economic success story of the Nordic economies, bringing about a major turnaround during the 1990s. The economy grew by more than 5% in the first half of 1997. Although unemployment was a high 14.7%, it was down from more than 18% in 1994. It was expected to drop to 13.8% in 1998 and to 12.5% in 1999, assuming economic-growth rates of about 4%.

Most of the revival was due to better export performance. The end of the Cold War and communism led to the collapse of Finnish exports to Russia and Eastern Europe—the equivalent of 13% of gross domestic product (GDP). However, in 1997, exports accounted for almost 40% of GDP, up from 22% of GDP in 1991. In the first half of 1997 exports rose by 10%, while imports rose only 8%, further improving the trade balance. Inflation was 1% in 1997—one of the lowest inflation rates in Europe. It was sustained by a tight budget for 1998.

Europe's first cross-border merger between retail banks was initiated in October by Finland's largest bank, Merita Bank, and targeted Nordbanken, Sweden's fourth-largest bank. The merger would create a bank with assets of more than $100 billion and almost 6.5 million customers. The new bank was expected to seek merger partners in Denmark and Norway. The merged bank would use the Euro, thereby indirectly introducing the new EU currency in non-Euro countries.

The government decided in October to merge two government-owned financial institutions—the postal bank Postipankki and Finnish Export Credit—creating a financial institution in Finland second only to Merita.

LEIF BECK FALLESEN, *Editor in Chief*
"Boersen," Copenhagen

FINLAND • Information Highlights

Official Name: Republic of Finland.
Location: Northern Europe.
Area: 130,127 sq mi (337 030 km²).
Population (mid-1997 est.): 5,100,000.
Chief Cities (Dec. 31, 1995 est.): Helsinki, the capital, 525,031; Espoo, 191,247; Tampere, 182,742.
Government: *Head of state,* Martti Ahtisaari, president (took office March 1, 1994). *Head of government,* Paavo Lipponen, prime minister (took office April 13, 1995). *Legislature* (unicameral)—Eduskunta.
Monetary Unit: Markka (5.3740 markkaa equal U.S.$1, Dec. 10, 1997).
Gross Domestic Product (1995 est. U.S.$): $92,400,000,-000 (purchasing power parity).
Economic Indexes (1996, 1990 = 100): *Consumer Prices,* all items, 112.6; food, 92.9. *Industrial Production,* 121.
Foreign Trade (1996 U.S.$): *Imports,* $29,271,000,000; *exports,* $38,442,000,000.

FOOD

During 1997 per-capita world grain production declined slightly from the previous year. The world grain harvest increased less than one tenth of 1%, while the world population rose by slightly more than 2%. Reductions in reserve grain carryover stocks helped compensate for the production shortfall. With the below-trend harvest, grain stocks by mid-

1998 were expected to drop slightly below minimum standards necessary to maintain global food security.

The trend toward low stocks reflected cost-cutting policies in the United States, Canada, and Europe that eliminated formerly large government grain-storage programs. Low stocks brought increased volatility in retail costs of foods that have a small amount of processing. In industrialized countries price volatility is tempered because processing, transportation, labor, advertising, and overhead expenses account for much of the retail-food cost. These expenses do not fluctuate with the size of the harvest. In contrast, retail costs for rice, wheat flour, and vegetable oil in developing nations fluctuate almost as much as farm prices, except where protected by government subsidies. These commodities are major dietary components in many developing countries. Greatly increased volatility of farm prices thus tended to create greater burdens for consumers or their governments—through subsidies to stabilize prices—in developing nations than those in developed nations.

Food-Safety Concerns. Food safety was an important issue in Japan, Europe, Canada, and the United States in 1997. *E. coli* contamination of ground beef in Japan caused the deaths of schoolchildren. The same contamination was documented in ground beef in the United States and Canada. These problems and governmental measures to reduce food-borne illnesses were accompanied by increased efforts to educate consumers about proper handling and meat-preparation methods. In December the U.S. Food and Drug Administration (FDA) approved irradiation of meat for preservation and for reduction of food-borne illnesses. However, the U.S. food industry was not expected to use this newly approved process in the immediate future.

In Western Europe bovine spongiform encephalopathy (BSE) remained a concern. British agricultural leaders developed a plan involving the slaughter of all cattle having a risk of BSE. In the United States the live-stock-meat industry and the Department of Agriculture monitored cattle for possible BSE problems. None was found.

In the United States multistate hepatitis infections in schoolchildren originated from contaminated fruit, reinforcing the need for increased efforts to protect against unsanitary food handling.

Genetically Altered Foods. European, Egyptian, and some American consumers expressed serious reservations about the safety of foods produced from genetically modified farm products. Several such products, including the Flavr Savr tomato, have become available in recent years in the United States. Products bringing the issue to the forefront were a type of corn producing a naturally occurring chemical toxic to corn borers (BT corn), and Roundup-ready soybeans, which are immune to the normally toxic effects of the herbicide Roundup.

Roundup-ready soybeans made up about one tenth of the 1997 U.S. soybean crop and would comprise a larger share in the next few years. BT corn may provide one fourth or more of the U.S. corn supply within two to four years. U.S. corn and soybeans are exported worldwide, thus affecting global food supplies. While scientific evidence indicated these crops are safe, a late-1997 survey of European Union (EU) consumers revealed 70% were unsure of the safety of such products.

ROBERT N. WISNER, *Iowa State University*

The Bagel

Historically, the bagel was merely a round piece of bread with a hole in the middle. It was a hard, crusty circle of delight, produced by a laborious process of kneading, hand-rolling, refrigerating, boiling, and baking, and destined to be enjoyed at room temperature with lox and cream cheese. It could be purchased only at traditional Jewish bakeries or delicatessens.

Much of that has changed as the bagel has become a $2.6 billion business in the late 1990s.

Not only have frozen bagels been available for a number of years, but fresh bagels can be purchased at many supermarkets and are part of the menu at all types of restaurants. In addition, retail shops specializing in just the bagel have proliferated across the United States. Such stores offer their diverse clientele all types of bagels, including pumpkin, blueberry, sun-dried tomato, and jalapeño pepper. A bagel with cream cheese already in it even made its debut at a chain of warehouse-type stores in 1996.

Photo by © George Mattei/Envision

FRANCE

In 1997, France suffered a bitter cold snap that blanketed even balmy Provence with snow. Spring followed hot and dry; then temperatures plunged again, killing crops. This erratic weather was an accurate harbinger of a year full of surprises and shifts in fortune. The biggest was the Socialist-led left's upset victory in legislative voting held a year ahead of schedule. Socialist Party leader Lionel Jospin (*see* BIOGRAPHY), who succeeded Alain Juppé as prime minister, retained the confidence of most French citizens throughout the year— walking a narrow line between the tenets of "realistic" socialism and the demands of activists on his coalition's left.

Domestic Affairs. On February 9 the National Front won municipal elections in the Mediterranean coast town of Vitrolles. An openly racist political party, the Front favors "national preference" in jobs and housing, and would rescind the French citizenship of certain naturalized immigrants. In the four towns they control, National Front mayors were most active in 1997 in the cultural domain. They interfered with acquisitions at

© J. Bourguet/Sygma

public libraries, cut subsidies to music festivals, and attacked the well-known avant-garde dance theater Chateauvallon.

The National Front victory in Vitrolles, coupled with brewing opposition to a draft law tightening France's immigration policies, produced an explosion of public protest in February. "Intellectuals," led by 60 filmmakers, launched an appeal for civil disobedience. Soon, Paris dailies were publishing special sections with thousands of signatures of people who rejected laws they said were inspired by National Front ideas. The protest forced a modification of the most controversial provision of the immigration legislation and, some say, contributed to the Socialists' electoral victory three months later. But on February 27 the new immigration law sailed through the National Assembly, where conservatives still enjoyed a four-fifths majority.

In one of the most fateful political moves of his career, President Jacques Chirac announced the dissolution of Parliament on April 21. French presidents traditionally exercise this power only in moments of political crisis, or just after their election if the Parliament is dominated by the opposing political party. Chirac told the nation that he judged, "in conscience," that the national interest required early elections, because the changes

Following the victory of the Socialist Party in French parliamentary elections in May and June 1997, Lionel Jospin, below center, formed a new cabinet and Philippe Seguin, left, succeeded Alain Juppé, the previous premier, as leader of the neo-Gaullist Rally for the Republic (RPR) party.

© Alexis Orand/Gamma-Liaison

his team had initiated—including a military overhaul, a reduction in public spending, and health-care and pension reform—needed more time to bear fruit. He also said that a newly confirmed government would give France weight in upcoming European negotiations. But the decision was viewed widely as tactical—a way to catch the opposition left off guard and to face the voters before taking further austerity measures like those that sparked the massive public-sector strikes of 1995.

The brief election campaign began amid indifference. Dominating the 577-member National Assembly with 464 seats, Chirac's conservative coalition seemed assured of retaining a majority. The Socialist Party platform, which included the abrogation of the new immigration laws and a plan to create 350,000 jobs in the public sector, sparked some interest. Still, voters interviewed at the polls during the first round of voting on May 25 voiced disillusionment and often said they voted only out of a sense of duty.

The first-round results took France by surprise. Chirac's conservative coalition garnered only 31% of the popular vote, its lowest percentage since World War II. The Socialists, allied with the Communist and Green parties, won more than 40%, and the National Front 15%. Voter turnout was low. The following day, Prime Minister Juppé announced that he would resign, no matter how the second round turned out. This unheard-of move by President Chirac's longtime friend and political ally was interpreted as a sign of panic.

The suddenly exciting campaign ended on June 1 with a solid victory for the left in the second round of voting. The new ruling coalition consisted of the Socialist Party and its allied groups, with 274 seats in the National Assembly; the Communist Party, with 38; and the environmentalist Green Party, with 7, for a total of 319 seats. The number of seats held by the then-ruling conservative coalition of the neo-Gaullist Rally for the Republic (RPR) and the Union for French Democracy (UDF) practically was cut in half, to 242.

Named prime minister on June 2, Lionel Jospin quickly appointed a 26-member cabinet, from which the Socialist old guard was noticeably absent. The cabinet included eight women and, for the first time, four Communists in key positions. Martine Aubry was second only to Jospin in the powerful employment and solidarity ministry. Green Party leader Dominique Voynet was appointed minister of the environment and regional development.

FRANCE • Information Highlights

Official Name: French Republic.
Location: Western Europe.
Area: 211,208 sq mi (547 030 km²).
Population (mid-1997 est.): 58,600,000.
Chief Cities (1990 census): Paris, the capital, 2,175,200; Marseilles, 807,726; Lyons, 422,444.
Government: *Head of state,* Jacques Chirac, president (took office May 1995). *Head of government,* Lionel Jospin, prime minister (took office June 1997). *Legislature*—Parliament: Senate and National Assembly.
Monetary Unit: Franc (5.9863 francs equal U.S.$1, Dec. 8, 1997).
Gross Domestic Product (1995 est. U.S.$): $1,173,000,-000,000 (purchasing power parity).
Economic Indexes (1996, 1990 = 100): *Consumer Prices,* all items, 113.8; food, 107.1. *Industrial Production,* 100.
Foreign Trade (1996 U.S.$): *Imports,* $274,073,000,000; *exports,* $289,351,000,000.

Though his RPR went through a period of severe post-defeat infighting, President Chirac seemed oddly at ease with his new Socialist partners, only expressing occasional reservations as their legislative program took shape. In July the RPR elected former parliamentary speaker Philippe Seguin as its party leader, replacing former Prime Minister Juppé.

Like 1994, 1997 was a year marked by World War II–era history. Amid an international scandal about Nazi gold and Holocaust victims' assets still held by Swiss banks, similar revelations concerning paintings in French museums and buildings owned by the City of Paris stirred controversy. Prime Minister Juppé appointed a commission to trace the previous ownership of all public property acquired in dubious circumstances during the war.

Just a week after the French Catholic Church publicly spoke out against its silence during the World War II persecution of Jews, former Vichy-government official Maurice Papon went on to trial for his role in deportations from the Bordeaux area. His signature had been found on arrest and logistics orders concerning ten trainloads of Jews sent to the French concentration camp of Drancy and then to Auschwitz. Papon had gone on to a successful government career, culminating in his position as budget minister under President Valéry Giscard d'Estaing. He was the only Vichy official ever to stand trial for crimes against humanity, and the proceedings reopened still-painful arguments about the French state's contribution to the "Final Solution."

Economic Affairs. The number 3 dominated economic debate in 1997. According to the Maastricht Treaty on European Union, the budget deficit of countries seeking to join the single currency could not exceed 3% of their gross domestic product (GDP). Most international forecasts agreed that neither France nor Germany would make it in time. It was this economic constraint that prompted President Chirac to call early elections, before another round of budget-cutting measures—made unavoidable, he thought, by the 3% limit. The then-opposition Socialists denounced the limit, calling it overly rigid; ill-adapted to the low-growth, high-unemployment period all Europe was traversing; and not even literally required by the Maastricht Treaty.

Once in power, the Socialists gave their European partners a scare. In a series of June summits, they continued to contest the 3% figure, withholding their final approval of a monetary-stability pact that established punishments for countries that exceed the limit after the single currency is adopted. Germany, preoccupied by the strength of the new Euro, had sponsored the pact. The French Socialists reiterated their opposition for the benefit of the left-most segment of their electorate. But as long-fervent supporters of the European-unification process, they quickly accepted the German position in exchange for a European jobs summit held in November. The budget approved by the end of the year provided for a deficit at 3% of GDP by 1998.

The domestic economic program included several iconoclastic elements. The first law the new Parliament approved, for example, provided for the creation of 350,000 public-sector jobs for young people. Critics accused the government of increasing the public sector's already large share in the French economy. But the measure was so popular that even some conservative parliamentarians abstained rather than go on record against it. Analysts noted that the cost, 2.5 billion francs (about $440 million), was relatively insignificant compared with France's total budget of some 50 billion francs (about $8.7 billion) devoted to employment measures. Most said the idea's success or failure would depend on how energetically the young beneficiaries sought to exit the system by obtaining other work.

On October 10, Prime Minister Jospin convened a summit on jobs, wages, and working conditions. At the end of a full day of talks among government ministers, labor unions, and business associations, Jospin announced he would introduce legislation stipulating a gradual reduction in France's legal workweek from 39 to 35 hours by the year 2000, as a means of combating unemployment. The measure was to be accompanied by incentives for businesses negotiating the reduction sooner. Though this idea long had been champi-

oned by the Socialist Party and was an explicit element of its campaign platform, the powerful National Council of French Business Executives swore it had been duped and promised conflict with the government and unions.

With the sale of 20% of France Telecom in October, the Socialist government launched France's largest-ever partial privatization of a public enterprise. After a direct offer of shares to individuals and institutional investors, the company was floated on the Paris and New York stock exchanges on October 20.

On November 3, truck drivers went on strike and set up roadblocks in a repeat of a similar action in 1996. Truckers said their employers had not respected the terms of the agreement that ended the 1996 strike; they called for a minimum monthly salary for a set number of hours, to curtail unpaid overtime. France's European neighbors berated Paris for not ensuring the free circulation of merchandise. But France argued that the European Union (EU) was partly to blame because it had promoted competition in the trucking industry without establishing common rules. The government said it would push for European norms on wages and working conditions in the road-transport industry. An agreement was signed on November 7.

Foreign Affairs. The lightning conquest of Zaire by forces loyal to Laurent Kabila in May had important implications for France's Africa policy. With close ties to the ousted Zairian dictator, Mobutu Sese Seko, France at first had called for international intervention. This appeal went unheeded by the international community, much of which saw it as a last-ditch effort to prop up Mobutu. France, undermined by criticism of its support for the genocidal Hutu regime in nearby Rwanda, kept a relatively low profile during the Zairian crisis. France's support of Mobutu Sese Seko, who would die of prostate cancer in September, led Zaire—now renamed Democratic Republic of the Congo—to shun a November meeting in Hanoi, Vietnam, of some 50 nations in which French is spoken. These nations agreed to add a political and economic dimension to their loose bloc, heretofore dedicated to promoting French culture.

France's new modesty on Africa took clearer shape after the left's election victory. At his maiden press conference, Overseas Development Minister Charles Josselin criticized France's past policy toward Africa as a "cross between interference and incapacity." He announced a more equal and transparent

During a four-day visit to China in mid-May 1997, French President Jacques Chirac and China's President Jiang Zemin (extreme left) signed a declaration pledging closer ties between their two nations.

"partnership" with a new generation of African elites. The clearest manifestation of the new policy was the decision in July to review all French military-assistance accords with African nations. Troop presence was sharply reduced in the Central African Republic. Still, critics pointed to underlying continuities with the earlier approach. A flurry of media reports on France's "loss" of Africa to Anglophone American influence revealed that archaic analyses still held sway.

On May 27, Paris hosted a landmark summit at which members of the North Atlantic Treaty Organization (NATO) signed a cooperation pact with Russia. The agreement gave Russia an observer's role at future NATO meetings, forbade NATO to amass weapons at Russia's borders, and set up mechanisms for regular consultations between NATO and its new partner on joint operations. It allowed for NATO's expansion to include three former Warsaw Pact countries, admitted on July 9. But the Socialist-led government slowed France's steps toward complete integration of NATO's military-command structure.

In late September, Total Oil Company sparked a transatlantic minicrisis by signing a major gas-field-exploration contract with Iran, despite a U.S. law that provided for sanctions against foreign companies that do business with Iran or Libya. Total's move was a test, and received the backing of the European Commission. The EU long had maintained that the U.S. position violated international law. Washington did not impose sanctions.

Amid rising tensions over Iraq's obstruction of UN weapons monitoring, France expressed solidarity with the United States. On November 14, after Baghdad expelled U.S. monitors, President Chirac "regretted the Iraqi leader's obstinacy." France, however, remained opposed to a military solution to the situation. Paris long had favored a gradual lifting of the UN embargo against Iraq, arguing that it was detrimental to the Iraqi population without destabilizing Hussein.

The year 1997 was a particularly terrible one in the former French colony of Algeria. Targeted assassinations of individuals—police officers or women without veils—gave way to atrocious massacres of entire village neighborhoods. Islamic extremists struggling to take power said they had committed the killings. But the apparent passivity of Algerian armed forces during the worst massacres, in late August and late September, prompted growing questions internationally about the government's attitude and possible complicity. Citizens of France, the foreign country with the closest ties to Algeria, urged their government to "do something." Paris broke its silence in early November, declaring, "The international community needs to know what's going on in Algeria, and legitimately seeks to understand what the authorities are doing to protect their population." On November 10, tens of thousands demonstrated across France in solidarity with the Algerian population.

Diana. The death of Britain's Princess Diana, after a high-speed chase in the midnight streets of Paris on August 31, blanketed world headlines for days. (*See* OBITUARIES.)

SARAH CHAYES, *Contributing Reporter, Paris* *National Public Radio*

GAMBLING

By 1997, fundamental questions had arisen regarding the wisdom of the rapid expansion of legal gambling in recent years. The National Gambling Impact Study Commission, which came into existence as a result of a 1996 federal law, was charged with addressing some of these questions by 1999.

Revenues. The U.S. commercial gaming industries racked up another record year, with total revenue of $47.6 billion in 1996—about 0.7% of national personal income.

The non-Indian casino industry generated gross revenues of $19.1 billion in 1996 and employed more than 341,000 individuals. Major new properties opened in 1996 and 1997 in Las Vegas, Mississippi, Missouri, and Indiana. In general, casinos experienced moderate growth in 1997.

Lotteries recorded sales (handle) of $42.9 billion and revenues after prize payment of $16.2 billion. Video lottery terminals (VLTs) generated more than $884 million in revenues, a 47% increase over the prior year. However, year-over-year growth of other lottery revenues was only 5.0%, and 15 states, as well as Washington, DC, experienced declines.

Revenues generated by pari-mutuel wagering on horses and dogs declined by 0.8% in 1996 to about $3.7 billion. On-track revenues from live racing fell by 14.0%. One racecourse, Arlington Park in Chicago, announced it would not reopen in 1998. Because of their declining performance, many racetracks were permitted to offer casino-style gaming.

Indian Gaming. Indian gaming increased 12.2% to $5.4 billion in 1996. The largest and probably most profitable casino in the world—Foxwoods in Connecticut—generated slot revenues of more than $600 million in 1996 and overall gaming revenues of about $1 billion.

Major legal battles over tribal gaming continued in some states. In New Mexico, Indian casinos finally were compacted after years of disputes. In California negotiations continued through 1997 between one tribe and the governor. In Kansas a tribe proposed building a casino on a tribal burial ground in Kansas City. In Wisconsin one tribe claimed the Bill Clinton administration had blocked its casino after other tribes with casinos made election contributions to the Democratic National Committee.

Regional Markets. Las Vegas and Atlantic City had record revenue years through mid-1997, with gross gaming revenues of $5.4 billion and $3.8 billion, respectively. However, both experienced declining profit margins due to increased competition.

Riverboat casinos had expanded operations in Indiana and Missouri, but competition and possible market saturation were issues in some markets. Riverboats in western Louisiana performed well, but casinos in New Orleans continued to disappoint. The bankrupt Harrah's Jazz land-based casino in New Orleans made no progress toward completion by late 1997, and the last downtown riverboat casino in New Orleans closed in October.

Michigan, which authorized three casinos in Detroit in a November 1996 referendum, advanced on the bidding process in 1997 to award those licenses. The Canadian province of Ontario expanded government-owned "border" casinos. The province also awarded licenses for 44 "charitable casinos."

WILLIAM R. EADINGTON
University of Nevada, Reno

Illegal Sports Betting

The last major gambling activity generally prohibited in the United States in 1997 was betting on sporting events. Under 1992 federal legislation, wagering on sporting events is prohibited in all states except Nevada—which has relatively unrestricted sports-wagering operations—and Oregon and Delaware.

It is extremely difficult to estimate the size of illegal U.S. sports-betting markets. However, when most forms of gambling are legal, sports betting is small in comparison. In Nevada sports betting generated $2.5 billion in wagers in 1997, with operators retaining $90 million, just over 1% of gaming revenues. Thus, it is unlikely illegal betting generates gross revenues in excess of $3 billion or $4 billion, if that much.

A recent development in sports betting is Internet gambling. There are offshore Web sites that offer sports wagering, though their legality was challenged. Some Indian tribes have tried unsuccessfully to establish sports-betting and casino-gaming sites on the Internet under the cloak of sovereignty. In 1997 legislation was introduced in Congress to prohibit Internet gambling in the United States and by U.S. citizens.

WILLIAM R. EADINGTON

GARDENING AND HORTICULTURE

The All-America Rose Selections (AARS) Committee picked "Roses Take Center Stage from Dawn 'til Dusk" as the theme for the introduction of its 1998 honorees. The winners for 1998 were "Fame!," "Opening Night," "First Light," and "Sunset Celebration."

"Fame!"—a grandiflora with lightly scented dark pink 4.5-inch (11-cm) blossoms with 30 to 35 petals supported on upright, spreading canes with dark green, glossy foliage—was judged as a vigorous plant with bushy habit and abundance of bloom. "Fame!," introduced by Bear Creek Gardens, Medford, OR, was hybridized by Keith Zary from a combination of "Tournament of Roses" and "Zorina." "Opening Night," the first true red hybrid tea rose to win an AARS award in 14 years, also was introduced by Bear Creek Gardens and hybridized by Keith Zary. "Opening Night"—with pointed buds opening to reveal 4.5-inch (11-cm) flowers with 25 to 30 petals and a slight fragrance—comes from a combination of "Olympiad" and "Ingrid Bergman."

"First Light"—a landscape rose with a rounded, compact growth habit—requires much less space than earlier shrub-rose varieties. With clusters of spicy fragrant, light pink flowers of five to seven petals each and contrasting purple stamens, "First Light" was hybridized by Stanley and Jeanne Marciel and introduced by DeVor Nurseries, Watsonville, CA. "Sunset Celebration"—a hybrid tea rose with fruity fragrant, 4.5-inch to 5.5-inch (11-cm to 14-cm) blossoms on long stems with deep green foliage—is capable of changing colors. The colors are apricot burnished with cream, amber-orange blushed with pink, or, occasionally, a warm rich peach. "Sunset Celebration" was introduced by Weeks Wholesale Rose Grower Inc., in Upland, CA, and hybridized by Gareth Fryer from "Pot O' Gold" and an unnamed seedling.

Other Winners. The All-America Selections (AAS) committee announced its 1998 award winners for bedding plants—Impatiens F-1 "Victorian Rose" and Petunia F-1 "Prism Sunshine"—as well as its vegetable award winners: lemon basil "Sweet Dani" and Swiss chard "Bright Lights."

"Victorian Rose," introduced by Goldsmith Seeds, is the first impatiens with consistently semidouble flowers. This impatiens' characteristics include earlier bloom than comparison varieties (eight to ten weeks from seed), season-long bloom whether grown in garden soil or containers, and prolific blooming. As with all impatiens, "Victorian Rose"

"Fame!"—a 1998 All-America Rose Selection

performs best in partial shade and when grown in the garden. It needs only sufficient water to provide abundant color. Petunia F-1 "Prism Sunshine," a grandiflora flower introduced by Floranova, was selected for its staying power of color. "Prism Sunshine"'s pure yellow, 3-inch (8-cm) flowers are produced on compact plants with a spread of up to 20 inches (51 cm); the plant is tolerant to heat and drought once established in a full-sun garden. "Victorian Rose" and "Prism Sunshine" also were recognized by Fleuroselect as gold-medal winners—Europe's equivalent of AAS.

Lemon basil "Sweet Dani," introduced by Pan American Seed, is an aromatic herb featuring culinary and ornamental uses. This heavily scented basil—a result of intentional breeding of high essential oils and citral—releases its lemon fragrance with the slightest touch. Swiss chard "Bright Lights," introduced by Johnny's Select Seeds, Albion, ME, produces stems of yellow, orange, gold, pink, violet, and striped, as well as the standard red and white.

The Perennial Plant Association named salvia "May Night" (*Mainacht*)—which was bred and introduced by German plantsman Karl Foerster in 1956—as the perennial plant of 1997. "May Night" has the typical square stem of mints; a delightfully fragrant, slightly blue-gray foliage; and upright spikes of florets of deep, rich indigo-black, outlined with delicate purple bracts.

RALPH L. SNODSMITH, *Ornamental Horticulturist*

GENETICS

The first report of genetic imprinting linking genes on the human X chromosome with social behavior was among 1997's high points in the science of genetics.

Genetic Imprinting and Social Behavior. With certain genetic traits, the effects of the gene vary depending on whether it was inherited from one's mother or from one's father. A study was made of Turner Syndrome (TS) individuals—females who have only one X chromosome, which can be inherited from either parent. TS affects about one in 3,000 females. Affected persons are characterized by short stature, infertility, and an extra thickness of skin around the neck.

D.H. Skuse and his coworkers at the Institute of Child Health in London, England, compared the I.Q. scores and social behavior of 55 TS individuals whose X chromosomes came from their mothers with those of 25 TS persons whose X chromosomes came from their fathers. The scores on I.Q. tests fell within the normal range and were the same for both groups. However, TS females with paternal X chromosomes were found to have an easier time making and keeping friends—and to get along better with their teachers and family members—than those whose X chromosomes came from their mothers.

Natural and Experimental Speciation. One of the modes of speciation in plant evolution is the crossing of two species, followed by the establishment of the hybrid form. After a number of generations, the hybrid form becomes incapable of crossing to either parental species, and thereby becomes an independent species. There is good genetic evidence that this occurred about 100,000 years ago in the western United States with the crossing of two sunflower species, *Helianthus annuus* and *H. petiolaris*. The resultant hybrid evolved into the species now known as *H. anomalus*.

L.H. Rieseberg and colleagues in the department of biology at Indiana University, Bloomington, reported on their experiment to repeat the formation of *H. anomalus*. They crossed the parental species to produce a hybrid form. The hybrid form, in separate lines, then was bred to each of the parental species—and, in addition, to itself—for a number of generations. Surprisingly, when the three experimental lines were examined for a wide variety of genetic traits, it was found that the plants had about 68% of their genes in common with one another and with the existing species *H. anomalus*. It appeared that the plants had repeated the process that led to the evolution of the original *H. anomalus*.

Neanderthal versus Modern DNA. The human fossil record contains skeletons of now extinct forms that at one time coexisted with humanity's direct ancestors. One such group was Neanderthal, which lived in Europe and the Middle East for at least 100,000 years, becoming extinct only about 30,000 years ago. The coexistence of Neanderthal and direct human ancestors allows the possibility that the two forms mated with one another, resulting in the presence of Neanderthal genes in some modern human populations.

Svante Pääbo and his colleagues at the University of Munich, Germany, and elsewhere studied the DNA found in cells of one of the Neanderthal fossil skeletons. They analyzed the sequence of nucleotides in a 379-nucleotide section of the mitochondrial DNA in the fossil bone cells and compared it with the same section in modern humans. They found that whereas modern humans showed an average of eight differences in nucleotides from one another, Neanderthal mitochondrial DNA showed an average of 26 differences from that of modern humans. These differences are so great that it is highly unlikely that modern humans mated with Neanderthals.

Parallel Evolution in the United States and England. Moths of the species *Biston betularia* may be pale white in color (recessive gene) or completely black (dominant gene). Those collected in the areas around Liverpool, England, and Detroit, MI, before the establishment of factories were overwhelmingly pale white. Their color blended in with that of the tree trunks on which they rested, thereby providing the moths with camouflage. Subsequent industrial development resulted in the air surrounding both cities becoming filled with soot and dirt, which settled on all vegetation. By the year 1959, the black forms of the moths made up 94% of the *B. betularia* population in the Liverpool area and 92% in the Detroit area.

Clean-air legislation was enacted in England in 1956 and in the United States in 1963. A study of the moths was undertaken in 1994 and 1995 by B.S. Grant of the College of William and Mary in Virginia and colleagues in England. They found that the black-body types had dropped to 18% in the Liverpool area and to 20% in the Detroit area. These studies demonstrated the occurrence of parallel changes in the genetic composition of populations, in separate parts of the world, in response to parallel changes in environment.

Louis Levine, *City College of New York*

GEOLOGY

New geological evidence in 1997 indicated that part of the Baja drifted north millions of years ago and that Earth's crust can move substantial distances along earthquake faults even when there is no earthquake activity. A series of earthquakes plagued Iran, while a volcano continued to devastate the Caribbean island of Montserrat.

Earth's Crust. During the year, geophysicists reported new evidence that a chunk of North America migrated north from what is now Baja, CA, and became part of Canada and Alaska. Carried by the motions of Earth's tectonic plates, the wandering crust reached its present position sometime between 83 million and 45 million years ago, the scientists determined. Some geologists, however, were reluctant to accept this scenario because nobody has found the remains of ancient faults, similar to the San Andreas fault zone, that the wandering crust must have slid along during its journey.

Scientists used precise satellite measurements to show that after a magnitude-7.6 earthquake at Honshu, Japan, the ground continued to creep slowly east along the earthquake fault, traveling as far in the following year as it had during the actual quake. The new observations of the creepy crust beneath Honshu would help solve the long-standing mystery of why computer simulations predict more tectonic-plate movement along earthquake faults than actual earthquakes can account for globally. The Honshu quake showed that "afterslip"—a period of fault motion not accompanied by perceptible ground-shaking—may account for a significant portion of the missing motion.

Inner Earth. Seismologists offered new evidence to buttress the theory that pieces of tectonic plates that dive into Earth's interior at subduction zones can end up near the bottom of the mantle, the planet's hot middle layer of rock. Subducted plates are recycled in the mantle, but scientists disagree on whether or not the plates can plunge all the way to its base at a depth of 1,800 mi (2 900 km). To help resolve the question, two teams of seismologists used earthquake vibrations ringing through Earth's interior to take unusually clear snapshots of the lower mantle—much as a CAT scan uses X rays to construct a picture of the body's interior. Both teams captured shadowy images that are interpreted as cold, subducted oceanic crust deeper down in the mantle than had been thought possible. One slab—located by both teams as well as a third, independent, team—is believed to be the Farallon Plate, thought to have raised the Rocky Mountains as it subducted beneath North America beginning about 100 million years ago.

Paleontology. With the 1995 discovery of *Giganotosaurus carolinii*, a predatory dinosaur from South America, *Tyrannosaurus rex* lost its long-held title as biggest killer on the block. But one *T. rex* may have been the most foul-tempered. Scientists examined the fossilized bones of "Sue," a nearly complete *T. rex* from Montana, and found evidence of gout, a painful condition that affects bones and joints. Ultimately, Sue proved her worth despite her ailments; after eight minutes on the auction block, she fetched $8.4 million,

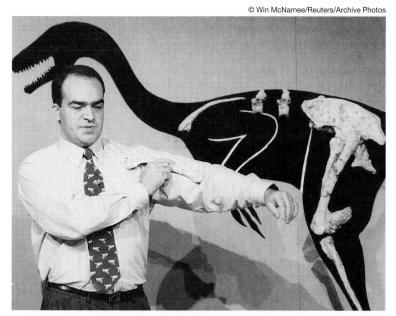

Paleontologist Fernando E. Novas, left, displayed the fossil bones of a birdlike dinosaur that he discovered in Argentina's Patagonian region. The dinosaur, "Unenlagia comahuensis," was said to be the most birdlike dinosaur ever found.

paid by Chicago's Field Museum and a group of sponsors.

Paleontologists in Argentina unveiled the most birdlike dinosaur ever found, a meat-eater that lived 90 million years ago in the Cretaceous period. The upright-walking *Unenlagia comahuensis*, or "half bird from northwest Patagonia," was 7 ft (2 m) long. According to its discoverers, the shoulder-joint design suggests that it could flap and fold its forearms in an avian style. The scientists believe that *Unenlagia*'s ancestors branched off from the dinosaur family tree just prior to the lineage that led to *Archaeopteryx*, the oldest known ancestor of modern birds. Thus, even though *Unenlagia* lived some 55 million years after *Archaeopteryx*, the animal offers a possible glimpse of the transition between dinosaurs and birds.

Paleontologists reexamining the bones of the reptile *Coelurosauravus jaekeli*, which lived 250 million years ago, uncovered a strange chapter in the history of animal flight. The scientists found that the squirrel-sized creature used flaps of skin to glide through the air, but strangely, the flaps were reinforced with spiny bones that were not attached to its body. In contrast, bats, birds, and other flying vertebrates have all achieved flight by modifying existing equipment, typically arms and hands.

Earthquakes. Iran was plagued by repeated earthquakes beginning February 4, when a magnitude-6.4 earthquake struck the border region of Iran and Turkmenistan, killing at least 88 persons and injuring nearly 2,000. On February 28 a magnitude-6.0 earthquake rocked the Ardabil area of northwestern Iran, killing an estimated 965 persons and injuring 2,600. On May 10 an even more deadly quake shook Iran, this time in the east. The powerful magnitude-7.1 earthquake caused the deaths of 1,567 persons and injured 2,300. It was felt strongly over an area of more than 190,000 sq mi (500 000 km²). In another multiple event, a trio of earthquakes rocked southern Xinjiang, China, on January 21, April 5, and April 11. The third shock, at magnitude 6.1, was the largest. At least 44 persons were reported killed by the quakes, which took a considerable toll in homes damaged or destroyed and livestock killed.

On September 26 a double earthquake rattled the historic Umbria region of Italy. A magnitude-5.6 earthquake struck first, followed by a magnitude-6.0 temblor nine hours later, killing ten persons. The quake, centered at the town of Foligno in central Umbria, was felt in Rome, 90 mi (150 km) to the south-west. The dead included two monks struck down by rubble from collapsing frescoes in the historic Church of St. Francis in Assisi. The damaged fresco paintings were by the master Cimabue.

On July 21 a magnitude-3.3 earthquake caused the collapse of the Hartebeesfontein gold mine in South Africa's North West province, killing at least 15 persons and injuring 46. Although the tremor was relatively moderate compared to the major earthquakes of the year, it was centered a mere 500 ft (153 m) from where miners were working 1 mi (1.6 km) beneath the surface. It was the third South African mine collapse triggered by earth tremors in 1997. The previous two killed 13 miners and rendered three permanently disabled.

Volcanoes. Volcanic eruptions filled the skies with thunder and ash across the globe, but it was the drama on the Caribbean island of Montserrat that drew most of the headlines. In its third year of eruptions, the Soufrière Hills volcano on Montserrat reached a new and deadly level of activity, killing at least 19 and virtually destroying Plymouth, the island's capital. The volcano's first-ever eruption in recorded history began on July 18, 1995.

The 19 victims died on June 25, 1997, after entering the evacuated zone of the island's south side. They were engulfed by pyroclastic flows and surges—fiery avalanches of debris, ash, and gas that travel down volcanic slopes at highway speeds, burning everything in their path. In August the flows reached Plymouth, setting homes and businesses alight. By August 6, Plymouth was in ruins, with more than 80% of its buildings damaged or destroyed.

In early September scientists warned that more large explosions and pyroclastic flows were likely. The lava dome, a plug of congealed molten rock in the mouth of the volcano, continued to grow rapidly. By the first week of October, explosions from the volcano's summit came as frequently as every nine hours—each followed by pyroclastic flows, rock avalanches, and clouds of ash. As the explosions continued, scientists and the remaining holdouts on the island maintained a wary vigil. The rate at which explosive, gas-rich lava rose to the surface waxed and waned but increased steadily. Scientists believed that eruptions at Montserrat could persist for an undetermined number of years. (*See also* CARIBBEAN—*Montserrat*.)

DANIEL PENDICK, *Contributing Editor*
"Earth Magazine"

GERMANY

With the 50th anniversary of the Federal Republic two years away, Germans had little reason to celebrate in 1997. Record-high unemployment, ballooning budget deficits, increasing crime, underfunded schools, and political gridlock in Bonn fostered growing self-doubt about the German model of social and economic consensus.

The Economy. Fueled by a surge in exports and increased domestic demand, the economy grew in 1997 by 2.4%, as compared with only 1.4% in 1996; but unemployment reached a post–World War II record of 11.4%. Faced with high labor costs, many employers invested in technology to increase output without adding workers. German business in 1997 also outsourced production to low-wage countries in Eastern Europe, Asia, and Latin America.

In the former East Germany, unemployment jumped to more than 18%. For the first time since the 1990 unification, economic growth in the East (2%) lagged behind that in the West (2.4%). One of the few bright spots was a continued low inflation rate of less than 2%.

The record-high unemployment was the top item on Chancellor Helmut Kohl's agenda. In January a major overhaul of the tax system—designed to reduce the tax burden on business and stimulate investment—was introduced. The plan also lowered the top tax bracket for individual taxpayers from 53% to 39%. The opposition Social Democratic Party (SPD) and Greens opposed the plan as a giveaway to the rich. Since the SPD controlled the second parliamentary chamber, the Federal Council (Bundesrat), it was able to veto the legislation. The Kohl government charged the SPD with pursuing an irresponsible "blockade" policy to the detriment of all Germans. Later in the year the government was able to pass legislation that would reduce the costs of pensions.

Another major policy issue was the planned European economic and monetary union (EMU). The high costs of unification and the country's generous welfare system made it difficult to reduce budget deficits to the 3% level needed for EMU admission. The government planned to meet the criteria in 1998, but many economists were skeptical.

Kohl was the chief champion of the currency union within Germany and Europe. Barring any unforeseen developments, Germany and France expected to lead a core group of 11 countries into the EMU, and the new currency—the Euro—will debut on Jan. 1, 1999. While about 70% of Germans did not want to give up the Deutsche mark, a similar number considered the Euro inevitable, and all major parties supported joining the EMU.

Germany's efforts to meet EMU membership criteria led to increased interest rates and a major conflict between the government and the Bundesbank—the powerful central bank responsible for monetary policy. In May the government attempted to reduce the budget deficit by revaluing the nation's gold reserves. The move was criticized strongly by the Bundesbank as an accounting trick that would undermine the independence of the bank and public confidence in the currency union. The controversy drew international attention, and an embarrassed Kohl government eventually backed down.

The economic problems caused many Germans to doubt the validity of the social-market economy, which combines free-market

© Netshaut/Sygma

Germans formed a human chain to protest the nation's high unemployment rate in 1997—some 12% for the nation as a whole, and about 18% in East Germany.

GERMANY • Information Highlights

Official Name: Federal Republic of Germany.
Location: North-central Europe.
Area: 137,931 sq mi (356 910 km²).
Population (mid-1997 est.): 82,000,000.
Chief Cities (June 30, 1994 est.): Berlin, the capital, 3,477,900; Hamburg, 1,703,800; Munich, 1,251,100.
Government: *Head of state,* Roman Herzog, president (took office July 1994). *Head of government,* Helmut Kohl, chancellor (took office Oct. 1982). *Legislature*—parliament: Bundestag and Bundesrat.
Monetary Unit: Deutsche mark (1.7987 D. marks equal U.S.$1, Dec. 31, 1997).
Gross Domestic Product (1995 est. U.S.$): $1,452,200,-000,000 (purchasing power parity).
Economic Indexes (1996): *Consumer Prices* (1991 =100): all items, 116.5; food, 109.2. *Industrial Production* (1990 = 100): 96.
Foreign Trade (1996 U.S.$): *Imports,* $455,925,000,000; *exports,* $521,008,000,000.

capitalism with the welfare state. The elaborate and generous pension, health, and welfare systems; high wages and fringe benefits; and large government subsidies for declining industries such as coal, steel, and shipbuilding now were seen as luxuries the country could not afford. But efforts to cut these programs prompted strong opposition. When the government attempted to phase out subsidies for the coal industry—which cost taxpayers about $60,000 annually for each of the 90,000 mining jobs and made German-mined coal three times more expensive than the world-market price—angry miners marched on Bonn, demanding that the government preserve their jobs. Earlier in the year steelworkers staged a similar protest over the planned merger of two major companies.

In November students at 50 of the country's 230 colleges and universities went on strike to protest budget cuts and the proposed introduction of tuition charges. Later that month, more than 40,000 students demonstrated in Berlin, Frankfurt, and Bonn; it was the largest demonstration since the massive protests of the late 1960s.

The once vaunted consensus now was viewed as paralysis. In April, President Roman Herzog criticized political parties and interest groups for their inability to deal with the challenges of globalization and the coming EMU. A leading business figure attracted wide attention when he called for fundamental changes in the political system, such as a reduction in the power of the Bundesrat, to end the deadlock.

Unification Problems. Many economic difficulties stemmed from the expensive unification process. According to an August government assessment of the first seven years of a unified Germany, the enormous costs of unification have matched its achievements.

Between 1991 and March 1997 some $600 billion was transferred from West Germany to East Germany—about 5% of the yearly West German gross national product (GNP), or about $1,100 per capita. The annual range of transfers had been from $78 billion in 1996 to an estimated $72 billion for 1997. About 25% of the money came from the federal government, with the remainder coming from the United States, the European Union (EU), and heavy government borrowing.

These transfers helped build or rebuild 2.1 million apartments in the former East Germany, install 5 million telephone connections, and build 3,100 mi (5 000 km) of railroad tracks and 6,831 mi (11 000 km) of streets and highways. A variety of employment and retraining programs kept 2 million East Germans off the unemployment rolls, although unemployment remained high, at about 18%. West German transfers also quadrupled the pension benefits of retired East Germans; in some cases, because of a longer work history, East German pensions exceeded those in the West.

An impressive display of internal German unity occurred in July, when the "flood of the millennium" along the Oder River—which divides Germany from Poland and the Czech Republic—riveted the nation's attention. For more than three weeks, 50,000 residents, military personnel, and volunteers from throughout Germany worked to shore up a 110-mi (177-km) stretch of the river, successfully maintaining most dikes. While the flooding killed 120 in Poland and the Czech Republic, no one died in Germany.

Politics. During 1997 the two major parties, the Christian Democratic Union (CDU) and the SPD, prepared for the 1998 national election. On his 67th birthday in April, Kohl ended speculation, announcing that he would seek an unprecedented fifth term. Later in the year he named his choice as successor—Wolfgang Schäuble, the CDU's parliamentary leader—renewing speculation that Kohl would not serve out the entire four-year term if reelected. Kohl, the longest-serving head of government in Europe, was determined to remain in office until the currency union is complete.

The opposition SPD remained divided in 1997 over its candidate for chancellor and the program it would present to the voters. The SPD leader and chief executive of Lower Saxony, Gerhard Schröder—who led the polls—wanted to move the party to the center for the 1998 election. Schröder had established close ties with many of Germany's business elite and, like Britain's Prime Minister Tony Blair, promised both economic growth and the retention of the welfare state. His rival, Oskar Lafontaine, the losing 1990 candidate, was the favorite of the party faithful, who still favored large welfare programs to deal with the unemployment problem.

The two small parties in parliament, the Free Democrats (FDP) and the opposition Greens, also focused their efforts on the upcoming campaign. The FDP—junior partner in the governing coalition—pushed for a reduction in the "solidarity surtax" that Germans paid to cover unification costs. The Greens, who hoped to become the SPD's partner in a new government, continued to moderate their once-radical program, now supporting Germany's North Atlantic Treaty Organization (NATO) membership. The Greens also tried to establish ties to the business community. Their leader, Joschka Fischer, hoped to become foreign minister in a new government after the election.

Human Rights. In 1997, Germany continued to deal with human-rights issues arising from its Nazi and communist past. In August a Berlin court sentenced Egon Krenz—the last East German hard-line communist leader—to six years in prison for his role in the deaths of people trying to cross the Berlin Wall. Two other former top-level communist leaders were given three-year terms. Since unification, some 100 soldiers, military officers, and government officials had been charged with responsibility for the "shoot to kill" order at the wall, which killed more than 900 East Germans between 1961 and 1989. Most of the 55 who were convicted received short or suspended sentences. Krenz and others argued that the trials were a violation of their rights, since the actions they took as representatives of a then-sovereign state were not illegal at the time. All three planned to appeal.

Responding to the pressure of Jewish organizations and the U.S. Congress, Germany passed legislation in November that ended a 50-year policy of providing disability and pension support to veterans suspected of being Nazi war criminals. It was estimated that some 50,000 former soldiers, including former Waffen SS members, were drawing benefits.

Social Issues and the New Capital. Violent crime continued to increase in 1997. In Berlin it had jumped by 20% since 1994. Drugs were sold openly at the major cities' main railroad stations—once models of cleanliness and order. Since the end of the Cold War, organized crime—based largely in Eastern Europe and the former Soviet Union—also has been active in Germany. A large and efficient market in stolen cars destined for Poland and Russia was a major problem for the police. Governmental officials, mindful of Nazi police repression, were reluctant to adopt the hardline zero-tolerance approach to crime associated with countries like the United States.

Foreign residents comprised almost 10% of the Federal Republic's 82 million inhabitants. Two million Turks—as well as thousands of Croatians, Serbs, Spaniards, Italians, and Russian Jews—have made Germany a multicultural society. Yet even foreigners born in Germany had a difficult time becoming citizens, since Germany had based citizenship on bloodlines. In November the SPD and Greens, together with the FDP and younger members of Kohl's CDU party, proposed legislation granting dual citizenship at birth to the offspring of foreign residents, who then could choose their citizenship when they reached 18. Kohl, however, saw dual citizenship as a threat to German identity.

© Patrick Piel/Gamma-Liaison

Plans continued to go forward in 1997 to return the German government to Berlin. In September, Chancellor Helmut Kohl (at podium) laid the cornerstone for the new Berlin chancellery building.

© R. Bossu/Sygma

In January 1997, Chancellor Kohl conferred with Boris Yeltsin in Moscow. Three months later the Russian president (above, second from right) was in Germany for a meeting with the chancellor. NATO enlargement was a focus of their talks.

In September, Kohl laid the cornerstone for the new Berlin chancellery building. By June 1998 the first of nearly 50,000 politicians, civil servants, diplomats, lobbyists, and journalists would begin work in the many new buildings nearing completion. The political center of the country would move from a small town near the Belgian border to a booming metropolis of 4 million, some 50 mi (81 km) from Poland. Some were apprehensive about the change, since Bonn symbolized West Germany's new beginning after World War II, while Berlin was the center of Nazi power. Supporters, however, pointed to Germany's 50-year record of democratic stability and commitment to peaceful relations with its neighbors. The move would cost more than $10 billion and should be completed by 2000.

Foreign Policy. Germany continued to be Russia's strongest advocate within the European Union (EU) and NATO. In January, Kohl visited Moscow and assured President Boris Yeltsin that the eastward enlargement of NATO would respect Russian security concerns. Kohl and Yeltsin had developed a close relationship, and Kohl was the last Western leader to visit Yeltsin before his 1996 heart surgery. He was also the first to call on him when the Russian leader returned to the Kremlin.

Germany's traditionally close ties with Iran and Turkey took a turn for the worse in 1997. In April a Berlin court convicted an Iranian and three Lebanese of murdering Kurdish dissidents at a local restaurant. The court ruled that the assassins were acting on orders from Iran's highest authorities—the first time a Western court directly linked Iran's leadership to the murder of Iranian dissidents who sought refuge in Europe. The parliament also approved a resolution condemning Iran for ordering the killings. Before the trial, Germany had tried to maintain a "critical dialogue" with Tehran and, unlike the United States, had not imposed sanctions. In response to the ruling, the leader of an extremist Shiite fundamentalist group threatened Germany with suicide bombings if it did not apologize. By May the situation had eased. German leaders, seeking to avoid further confrontation, announced there would be no investigations of top Iranian leaders such as the prime minister and president. An arrest warrant for Iran's intelligence minister, however, still remained in force.

Earlier in the year a Frankfurt court alleged that high-ranking Turkish officials, including Turkish Foreign Minister Tansu Ciller, were connected with drug trafficking. The Turkish government protested and sought an apology from the foreign ministry, but the Kohl government, citing the independence of the judiciary, took no action. German-Turkish relations were strained further when Kohl and Foreign Minister Klaus Kinkel questioned Turkey's fitness to join the EU.

DAVID P. CONRADT
East Carolina University

GREAT BRITAIN

Great Britain saw extensive political change in 1997, with the May 1 election of a Labour government (*see* SPECIAL REPORT, page 261). The new administration—with Tony Blair as prime minister—vowed to modernize Britain. The Conservatives—ousted after 18 years—chose William Hague, 36, to replace John Major as party leader. Shaken by public reaction to the death of Diana, princess of Wales (*see* OBITUARIES—*Diana*, page 385), Buckingham Palace promised to review the monarchy's role. Scotland and Wales voted for their own legislative bodies, while the Northern Ireland peace process resumed after the Irish Republican Army (IRA) renewed its cease-fire.

Domestic Politics. Major's attempt in early 1997 to persuade Britain that his government deserved five more years was undermined by a Conservative rift over the issue of Europe; some 250 of more than 600 Conservative candidates rejected Major's "wait and see" approach. Blair took advantage of the divisions, using the months before the election to outline his policies—which analysts sometimes found difficult to differentiate from those of the Conservatives.

With the election won, the new administration lost no time in making it clear that Labour had ideas of its own. Within days of taking office, Gordon Brown, chancellor of the exchequer, surprised London's financial district by transferring power to vary interest rates from the government to the Bank of England. The new government also promised a crackdown on juvenile crime, promised the creation of an independent food-standards agency, and offered the House of Commons a free vote on a ban on the private possession of handguns. The Commons voted for a ban. In July, Brown confirmed the imposition of a windfall tax on the profits of public utilities privatized by the Major government; most of the £5.2 billion ($8.8 billion) raised would be used to put unemployed youths back to work.

Blair did show signs of caution. Labour's plans to reform the House of Lords were delayed. Single parents—who received state benefits under the previous government—were told to seek work. In the House of Commons, 47 Labour members of Parliament (MPs) voted against a bill to reduce welfare benefits to single parents. Despite a promise to outlaw blood sports, the government initially did not support an antihunting bill. In late November, however, a bill banning the hunting of foxes and other wildlife was given initial approval by the House of Commons.

Blair's first significant political setback was in early November, when the government proposed to exempt Formula One motor racing from a ban on tobacco sponsorship and advertising in sports. In the ensuing uproar it emerged that Bernie Ecclestone, head of Formula One racing in Europe, had given the Labour Party £1 million ($1.7 million) before the election and had been asked for a further £500,000 ($841,900) after May 1. Blair apologized on television for his government's handling of the affair, and Labour agreed to return Ecclestone's donation. The *Daily Telegraph* compared the incident to Watergate.

In a Sept. 11, 1997, referendum in Scotland, 74% of the voters approved plans to establish a 129-member Scottish parliament. In a second question, voters agreed to grant the new legislature some taxation powers.

© Tom Kidd/FSP/Gamma-Liaison

© Colin MacPherson/Sygma

In June 1997, 36-year-old William Hague, a member of Parliament since 1989 and former cabinet member, was elected to succeed John Major as leader of Britain's Conservative Party. Major had resigned the post after the Tory defeat in May 1 elections. Hague's fiancée Ffion Jenkins joined him for the party's annual conference in October, right.

© Dave Caulkin/AP/Wide World Photos

As new Conservative leader, Hague announced that his party would oppose British participation in a single European currency for at least ten years. Senior Conservatives—including Kenneth Clarke, the former chancellor, and Michael Heseltine, the former deputy prime minister—disagreed, and Clarke suggested joining a "cross-party coalition." Hague justified his strategy, claiming that a majority of Conservative voters opposed participating in the single currency.

Neil Hamilton, a senior Conservative accused of accepting cash for political favors under the Major government, was defeated in the general election by Martin Bell, a former television reporter who ran as an independent. An inquiry later reported adversely on Hamilton's activities, and a parliamentary committee supported most of its findings.

Constitutional Affairs. The Labour government fulfilled its promise to offer voters in Scotland and Wales parliamentary assemblies of their own—a policy bitterly opposed by the Conservatives. On September 11, Scots voted decisively for a parliament with tax-raising powers. A week later, Welsh voters opted, by a small margin, for an assembly lacking such powers. While Conservatives said that Scotland was on "the slippery slope to independence," and that the Welsh vote was indecisive, Blair promised to work toward early elections in both regions. Blair also confirmed that London—which had lacked a central urban government since the early 1980s—would have an opportunity to elect a "strategic authority" and its own mayor.

The government also announced that the European Charter of Human Rights would be incorporated into British law, so that Britons challenging court decisions no longer would have to appeal to the European Court of Human Rights in Strasbourg. The decision was made on the same day that the Strasbourg court upheld the 50th complaint by a British citizen that the country's laws had infringed the European Charter.

Monarchy. Queen Elizabeth II and her family remained at the center of debate about the future of the monarchy. On August 31— with the nation shocked by the death of Diana, princess of Wales—the queen and members of her family, including Prince Charles, Diana's former husband, remained at the royal holiday residence in Balmoral, Scotland, resisting public demands that they return to the capital and that the Union flag be flown at half-mast from Buckingham Palace. When they did appear in London, they were confronted by public outcry—fanned by mass-circulation tabloid newspapers—over the queen's alleged insensitivity. Against all

---

GREAT BRITAIN • Information Highlights

Official Name: United Kingdom of Great Britain and Northern Ireland.
Location: Island, western Europe.
Area: 94,525 sq mi (244 820 km²).
Population (mid-1997 est.): 59,000,000.
Chief Cities (mid-1994 est.): London, the capital, 6,967,500; Birmingham, 1,008,400; Leeds, 724,400; Glasgow, 680,000; Sheffield, 530,100.
Government: Head of state, Elizabeth II, queen (acceded Feb. 1952). Head of government, Tony Blair, prime minister and First Lord of the Treasury (took office May 1997). Legislature—Parliament: House of Lords and House of Commons.
Monetary Unit: Pound (0.6054 pound equals U.S.$1, Dec. 31, 1997).
Gross Domestic Product (1995 est. U.S.$): $1,138,400,-000,000 (purchasing power parity).
Economic Indexes (1996, 1990 = 100): Consumer Prices, all items, 121.1; food, 118.5. Industrial Production, 108.
Foreign Trade (1996 U.S.$): Imports, $287,503,000,000; exports, $262,099,000,000.

The Year of the "New" Labour

Great Britain's Labour Party had been in opposition continuously for 18 years—since May 1979—when it swept to power in national elections on May 1, 1997. By winning 419 of 659 seats in the House of Commons, Labour had scored its best-ever general-election performance.

Throughout the six-week election campaign, opinion polls had put Labour well ahead of Prime Minister John Major's Conservative Party, but a few hours before the landslide dimensions of the victory were known, Labour leader Tony Blair still refused to forecast the outcome. There were good reasons for caution. Five years earlier, Labour under its then leader Neil Kinnock had seemed poised to win power, but in the final week of the campaign, voters swung back to the Conservatives.

Another long spell in the political wilderness gave Labour time—and reason—to rethink the policies, particularly in the field of taxation, that had contributed to its fourth successive electoral failure. The party replaced Kinnock with John Smith, a canny right-of-center Scots lawyer, who began to move Labour away from its attachment to the trade unions and its preference for centrist government dedicated to high public-sector spending. Smith launched a nationwide Labour Party recruitment drive. When he died suddenly of a heart attack in 1994, Labour chose Blair as leader.

New Party Philosophy. Sensing that the Major administration was running out of energy and ideas and that the electorate was of a mind for political change, Blair—working closely with his shadow chancellor of the exchequer, Gordon Brown—began calling his party "New Labour" and accelerated the process of policy reform that Smith barely had had time to begin.

Peter Mandelson, a member of Parliament (MP) and key party strategist, advised the leadership that one lesson to be learned from Labour's 1992 debacle was that former Conservative Prime Minister Margaret Thatcher's 11-plus years in power had produced a transformation in British society. The rapid growth of a "new" middle class, consisting largely of blue-collar and moderate-income office workers who had benefited from the Thatcher administration's attempt to make Britain a property-owning democracy, made it increasingly difficult for a party dedicated to socialism to win power. Mandelson advised

Labour to court the middle classes by appealing to their middle-classness. In pursuit of this strategy, Labour spokespersons were required to adhere strictly to policy briefs calculated to appeal to voters who had supported the Conservatives in 1992. It says much for Blair's powers of leadership that even old-style party stalwarts accepted the "New Labour" line.

Senior party figures began courting leaders of industry in a bid to persuade them that a Labour government would further their interests. Instead of rejecting the European Union's (EU's) "social chapter" on workers' rights, which the Major government had shunned, Labour undertook to make it part of British industrial legislation. It also promised the people of Scotland and Wales refer-

In the midst of a successful campaign to gain the prime ministership, Labour leader Tony Blair informed the voters that Britain had slipped further down the World Prosperity League.
© Agence France Presse/Corbis-Bettmann

WORLD PROSPERITY LEAGUE	
1	Luxembourg
2	United States
3	Switzerland
4	Hong Kong
5	Norway
6	Iceland
7	Japan
8	Denmark
9	Singapore
10	Canada
11	Belgium
12	Austria
13	Germany
14	Netherlands
15	France
16	Australia
17	Italy
18	Sweden
19	Ireland
20	Finland
21	United Kingdom
22	New Zealand
23	Spain
24	Taiwan
25	Portug

endums on whether they wanted their own elected assemblies; promised to incorporate the European Convention on Human Rights into British law and to pass a Freedom of Information Act; and worked hard to increase the number of female Labour candidates seeking places in the House of Commons. (In fact, in the 1997 voting, 101 Labour women were elected—double the number in the previous Parliament.)

The 1997 Campaign. Among sophisticated election techniques—some borrowed from the 1992 and 1996 U.S. presidential campaigns of Bill Clinton—Labour issued voters plastic "credit cards" promising to cut school-class sizes, introduce fast-track punishment for persistent young criminals, improve the national health service, create jobs for 250,000 young unemployed, and eschew a rise in income-tax rates for two years. Labour urged voters: "Keep this card and see that we keep our promises." One election slogan described "new" Labour as a party of the "radical center."

The public mood fostered by Labour's confident, modernizing approach found expression in opinion polls that put it well ahead of the Conservatives from the moment Blair became leader. But without a series of disasters that befell the Major administration over the same period, Labour's election victory might not have been as stunning as it turned out to be. Within weeks of being returned to office in 1992, the Conservatives broke an election pledge not to impose value-added tax on domestic fuel. The decision to tax electricity and gas bore heavily on pensioners and others on fixed incomes.

From 1992, Major began to be plagued by splits in the ruling party, and even within his own cabinet, over policy toward Europe. Enjoying only a modest parliamentary majority, he was put under pressure by "Euroskeptics" to reject the single European currency the EU had pledged to introduce in 1999. Major met these demands by proposing a "wait and see" policy on monetary union.

Temporary suspension of a group of Euroskeptic MPs failed to stem the criticism. So did Major's decision to offer himself for reelection as Conservative Party leader in July 1995. He won by a large majority, but John Redwood, a cabinet minister who had resigned and opposed him for the leadership, emerged as a de facto leader of the Euroskeptics in and outside Parliament. During the 1997 campaign some 200 Euroskeptic Conservative MPs openly rejected Prime Minister Major's policy of deferring a decision on a single currency until 1999 and declared themselves hostile to monetary union.

Finally, British political life was rocked in the last two years of the Major government by a series of political and financial scandals involving Conservative ministers and backbenchers that Labour was able to exploit to great advantage. The *Guardian* newspaper played a leading part in revealing examples of what the media described as "sleaze." Neil Hamilton, an MP who was accused of receiving money for tabling parliamentary questions and wrongfully accepting hospitality from the chairman of Harrod's department store, became a cause célèbre in his own right. Hamilton was obliged to resign a ministerial post. When, however, he insisted on contesting his parliamentary seat on May 1, the Labour and Liberal Democrat candidates pointedly withdrew from the electoral contest. Martin Bell, a distinguished war correspondent with the British Broadcasting Corporation, stood as an independent and won handsomely.

Election Results and Aftermath. When it became clear that the Conservatives had won only 165 seats and gained a mere 31% of the vote—their lowest share since 1832—Major declared: "When the curtain falls, it is time to get off the stage."

The election outcome thus left Blair with a commanding parliamentary majority and facing a weakened Conservative Party, many of whose leading figures—including Michael Portillo, widely fancied as a future Conservative leader—had lost their parliamentary seats. As the new government moved rapidly to introduce budgetary measures, including a windfall tax to pay for putting jobless young people back to work, the Conservatives elected William Hague, 36, as Major's successor. Hague, who had held the post of secretary of state for Wales for the last two years of the Major administration, campaigned for the leadership on a markedly Euroskeptical platform, and was elected with support from Baroness Thatcher. His first shadow-cabinet appointment was of Lord [Cecil] Parkinson as Conservative Party chairman. Former Chancellor Kenneth Clarke, Hague's defeated rival for the leadership and a leading "Europhile," declined to serve in the new shadow cabinet.

Commenting on Hague's leadership victory, *The Economist* magazine said the Conservatives had "leapt into the unknown." The new Labour government, it said, would face "a fractious, traumatized party" until Hague forged a united shadow cabinet. To have a realistic hope of returning to power, the Conservative Party would need to acquire "a sense of direction, ruthlessness, and political acumen."

ALEXANDER MACLEOD

precedent, the queen delivered a live tribute to Diana on television. During the funeral, the flag appeared on the palace flagstaff. Anthony Holden, who writes about the British monarchy, called the flag incident "typical of insensitive palace officials mired in protocol."

Early reports that Diana's car had been pursued at high speed by "paparazzi" unleashed demands to curb the activities of these freelance photographers and for British newspapers to refuse their pictures; the Press Complaints Commission (PCC) met in emergency session to map out a stricter code of self-regulation. (*See also* PUBLISHING—*The Paparazzi.*) The national mood was stirred further when Diana's brother, Charles—the Ninth Earl Spencer—asserted that the press had "a direct hand" in her death. At the funeral, Spencer appeared to criticize the queen for depriving Diana of the appellation "Her Royal Highness" after she and Prince Charles were divorced.

In November the queen confirmed that she and her advisers were working on plans to make the monarchy "less formal" and "more closely in touch with the people." The cost of the monarchy for 1998–99, a palace spokesman said, would be £41.2 million ($70 million), some 40% less than in 1990. A November poll indicated that only one in five young people thought the monarchy important, while overall backing dropped from 65% in 1983 to 32% in 1997.

On November 20 a 50th-wedding-anniversary celebration was held for Queen Elizabeth and Prince Philip. Although it was the largest gathering of royalty since the queen's 1953 coronation, it was termed a "people's banquet," since Prime Minister Blair had insisted that the guest list include many ordinary citizens. The royal yacht *Britannia* was decommissioned and the government decided not to replace it. In addition, the queen's Christmas message, which was broadcast worldwide and on the Internet, was considered more personal and emotional than previous ones. In the address, the queen spoke of the sorrow of Diana's death and of the joy of her 50th wedding anniversary.

Economy. Prime Minister Blair and Chancellor Brown benefited politically from an economic recovery that began in mid-1996, although inflationary pressures remained a problem and necessitated a series of interest-rate hikes in the second half of 1997. In November the unemployment rate was reported to have fallen to 5.2% of the workforce, compared with 7.2% a year earlier—lower than any European country except Switzerland. Economic success boosted the pound sterling in relation to other European currencies and the U.S. dollar by 20% between August 1996 and August 1997, while export volumes grew strongly.

Although Labour took office promising to hold government spending to levels fixed by the outgoing administration for two years, in July, Chancellor Brown said an extra £1 billion ($1.7 billion) would be spent on education and a further £1.2 billion ($2 billion) on health in 1998. He left income tax unchanged but increased stamp duty on property sales. House prices continued to recover from the deep slump of the late 1980s, with banks and building societies reporting yearly price rises of between 6% and 12% as of September.

On Nov. 20, 1997, Queen Elizabeth II and Prince Philip celebrated their 50th wedding anniversary with a "service of thanksgiving" at Westminster Abbey. A "people's banquet" followed.
© R. Chambury/Alpha/Globe Photos

Foreign Affairs. The central foreign-policy issue facing Britain remained relations with the European Union (EU), with Blair steadily shifting toward a more positive approach to the economic and monetary union (EMU). Aware that the Conservatives were moving in the opposite direction, he stressed that Britain wished to play "a leading role" in Europe.

In October, however, conflicting media accounts appeared. London's respected *Financial Times* reported that Britain might decide to join a single currency in the "first wave" in 1999. Other stories suggested that Blair firmly would rule out early EMU membership. On October 27, Chancellor Brown told the House of Commons that Britain would not be part of the first wave and was unlikely to join EMU in the current Parliament. Thereafter, Britain would join only if the single currency was successful and the economic case for joining was "clear and unambiguous." When Hague affirmed that his policy of a ten-year waiting period would remain unchanged, two pro-EMU Conservative front-bench spokesmen in the Commons resigned from their posts.

A key element in Blair's political strategy was to portray Britain as a modern state determined to play a dynamic role in the world. The government threw its support behind a plan to build a giant dome on London's outskirts to celebrate the millennium year, and at a British Commonwealth conference in Edinburgh, Scotland, Blair treated visiting leaders to a video presentation of modern Britain and had a band greet the queen—who is head of the Commonwealth—with a rock version of the national anthem.

Foreign Secretary Robin Cook broke new ground in July by announcing that Labour's foreign policy would be conducted according to an ethical code, curbing arms sales to countries with unacceptable human-rights records. The sale of Hawk jet military aircraft to Indonesia would go ahead, he said, because contracts negotiated by the previous government could not be canceled. In a late-summer meeting with Indonesian officials, however, Cook said the £151 million ($256 million) deal would be based on the new criteria.

Northern Ireland. Before July, chances for the peace process regarding Northern Ireland appeared bleak, with sporadic violence in the province. Attempts by Marjorie Mowlam, the new Northern Ireland secretary, to achieve a breakthrough appeared to suffer a setback after she ordered security forces to protect a seasonal march by Protestants through the Catholic Garvahee Road area.

Blair issued a warning to Sinn Fein, political wing of the IRA, that "the settlement train" would leave the station if the IRA failed to declare a cease-fire soon. A week later the IRA obliged. Sinn Fein President Gerry Adams agreed in September to subscribe to principles of nonviolence, and Sinn Fein took its place at the negotiating table, despite Unionist protests.

The multiparty talks proved difficult. Martin McGuinness, Sinn Fein's chief negotiator, said the IRA would refuse to surrender "a single bullet"; but the Ulster Unionist party, having sounded the views of its grassroots members, decided to stay in the talks. The *Belfast Newsletter*, widely regarded as a mouthpiece of unionism, advised unionist leaders to "have the confidence to get in there and negotiate." On December 11, Adams met with Blair at his 10 Downing Street office—the first meeting between an IRA leader and a British prime minister since 1921.

In late December violence aimed at derailing the peace process broke out. Billy Wright, one of the most-feared Protestant guerrilla leaders in Northern Ireland, was shot and killed in a top-security prison, allegedly by members of the Irish National Liberation Army. A Catholic man, who had been convicted of murdering Protestants in the 1970s, was killed in retaliation.

Other News. The British Broadcasting Corporation (BBC) launched a 24-hour television news service and committed itself to a costly program of digital television and radio broadcasting....Rolls-Royce Motor Cars was up for sale, with strong indications that a German carmaker would acquire the company. A British-made jet car, *Thrust*, broke the world land-speed record and shattered the sound barrier in the United States.

The government said it was not opposed to lowering the age of consent for homosexuals from 18 to 16, but continued to oppose homosexuals in the armed forces....British Waterways—which owns 2,000 mi (3 218 km) of English and Scottish canals—came under study as a candidate for privatization. Britain's transport department indicated that parts of the London Underground also might be sold to private investors....Foreign Secretary Cook announced a review of Britain's relations with its overseas dependencies, following a dispute between London and the government of Montserrat over measures to assist islanders rendered homeless by an active volcano (*see also* CARIBBEAN—*Montserrat*).

ALEXANDER MACLEOD
"The Christian Science Monitor"

GREECE

The Panhellenic Socialist Movement (PASOK), a political party led by Prime Minister Costas Simitis, continued to control Greece's parliament with a large majority in 1997, while the country faced economic and foreign-policy issues.

Politics. Simitis strengthened his position within PASOK. His moderate policies lacked the flamboyant, sometimes anti-U.S. stance of PASOK's founder, the late Andreas Papandreou. The chief parliamentary opposition came from the New Democracy Party, which in March chose Costas Karamanlis—nephew of former Prime Minister and President Constantine Karamanlis—as its leader. The elder Karamanlis founded the New Democracy Party and piloted development of the current Hellenic Republic.

Foreign Affairs. Greece continued to have serious and sometimes critical problems in its relations with neighboring Turkey. Turkish occupation of part of Cyprus had been a source of friction since 1974. Disputes relating to territorial waters and the continental shelf around Greece's Aegean islands that border Turkey were also often acrimonious. How to proceed with handling the dispute over the ownership of the Aegean islets of Imia—a question that almost led to war in 1996—remained unresolved. The conditions of Turkey's eventual accession to the European Union (EU) also were an issue, and blunt statements by Greek Minister of Foreign Affairs Theodoros Pangalos were called intemperate by the Turkish authorities.

In the Greek parliament, Simitis declared that Greece and Turkey had no need for outside mediation to resolve their differences. Simitis' short private meeting with Turkish Prime Minister Mesut Yilmaz at a Southeastern European Summit, held on the island of Crete in November, led to no modification in relations between the two nations. At the summit, leaders from the major Balkan states—with the exception of Croatia and Slovenia, which were not represented—issued a declaration that their countries would work to promote peace, security, and stability in the region. Equally, a communiqué signed at Madrid in July by Simitis and President Suleyman Demirel of Turkey about Greek-Turkish relations fundamentally changed nothing.

Nicholas Burns—former U.S. State Department spokesman—became the new U.S. ambassador to Greece at the end of 1997. The designation of a high-ranking State Department official to the post indicated strong U.S. interest in the complicated relationships of Greece, Turkey, and Cyprus.

Greece remained adamant that it would not accept the name of Macedonia used by one of its neighboring states, but continued to refer to the country as the Former Yugoslav Republic of Macedonia (FYROM). Greece's position held that its neighbor unjustly was expropriating the glories of the classical era of Greek history and misusing the name of the province of Macedonia in northern Greece. All attempts at compromise failed.

The Economy. The government labored in 1997 to build up the Greek economy to a standard nearer that of other EU members. In November, National Economy Minister Yiannos Papantoniou presented a 1998 budget that aimed to bring Greece into the European economic and monetary union (EMU) by 2001. But he said that the Greek currency—the drachma—would not be part of the exchange-rate mechanism (ERM) until after Greece had entered the EMU. His assertions, based on the hope of maintaining a strong drachma without devaluation, brought mixed response—especially since the projected 1998 budget was, like 1997's, austere. A nationwide strike by labor unions occurred in December during parliament's budgetary debate, but the budget later was passed.

Despite government efforts to privatize, about 60% of the Greek economy remained under state control, while foreign investment was not being attracted to Greece easily.

Culture. Salonika—the second-largest Greek city—was designated by the EU as the 1997 Cultural Capital of Europe, succeeding Copenhagen. Athens was chosen to be the site of the 2004 Summer Olympics. Aside from the ancient beginnings of the Olympics in Greece, the first modern Olympiad was held in Athens in 1896.

GEORGE J. MARCOPOULOS, *Tufts University*

GREECE • Information Highlights

Official Name: Hellenic Republic.
Location: Southeastern Europe.
Area: 50,942 sq mi (131 940 km²).
Population (mid-1997 est.): 10,500,000.
Chief Cities (1991 census): Athens, the capital, 772,072; Salonika, 383,967; Piraeus, 189,671.
Government: *Head of state,* Costis Stephanopoulos, president (took office March 1995). *Head of government,* Costas Simitis, prime minister (took office January 1996). *Legislature* (unicameral)—Chamber of Deputies.
Monetary Unit: Drachma (282.30 drachmas equal U.S.$1, Dec. 31, 1997).
Gross Domestic Product (1995 est. U.S.$): $101,700,000,-000 (purchasing power parity).
Economic Indexes (1996, 1990 = 100): *Consumer Prices,* all items, 207.0; food, 190.2. *Industrial Production,* 99.
Foreign Trade (1994 U.S.$): *Imports,* $21,489,000,000; *exports,* $9,392,000,000.

HONG KONG. *See* CHINA: A NEW ERA BEGINS—*A Time of Change for Hong Kong.*

HOUSING

The U.S. housing market operated at a high level in 1997, although growth of the housing sector slowed from the rapid pace of 1996. Home sales edged up to an all-time high. Starts of conventionally built housing units remained around the high levels of 1996, while the residential remodeling market posted modest growth in real (inflation-adjusted) terms. Placements of mobile homes declined moderately. Home prices rose significantly in most parts of the country, while the regional composition of national housing activity shifted more toward the Northeast and West. In the process, the home-ownership rate in the United States reached a new record high.

On the international scene, Canada recorded a major housing expansion for the second consecutive year, while Great Britain outpaced other major European nations. Housing investment contracted sharply in Japan, however, as that nation's overall economy faltered badly.

Market Segments. Strong growth in employment and income, falling mortgage rates, and high levels of consumer confidence fueled home-buyer demand throughout the United States. Sales of conventionally built single-family homes (excluding mobile homes) rose by nearly 4% to a record 5 million units—4.2 million previously occupied homes and 800,000 new units sold by merchant builders. In addition, about 300,000 custom homes were built on lots already owned by the occupants. In total, builders started nearly 1.15 million new single-family homes in 1997, down a bit from 1996, and inventories of unsold new homes were drawn down to some degree to meet consumer demand.

In 1997, 330,000 apartment units in new multifamily structures (containing two or more units) were started during the year, up nearly 5% from 1996. Four fifths of these units were built for the rental market, while the balance were condominiums—individual units owned by their occupants, with common ownership of some open space and facilities.

Shipments of mobile homes (from factory to dealer) slipped a bit in 1997 to 350,000 units, and placements for residential use weakened even more as inventories of unsold mobile-home units accumulated during the year. Several partnerships between very large builders of conventional single-family homes and very large producers of mobile homes were announced. These partnerships were aimed at improving the distribution systems for mobile homes in the United States.

Residential remodeling amounted to an estimated $117 billion, up about 2% from 1996. Roughly 35% of this total represented maintenance and repair expenditures on single-family and multifamily structures, while the balance were improvements to existing structures—including additions, alterations, and replacements of major items such as roofs or heating systems.

New-Housing Characteristics. The average size of new single-family homes continued to trend upward in 1997, rising to 2,150 sq ft (200 m²). One third of new homes had at least four bedrooms, half had at least 2.5 bathrooms, and almost four fifths had garages for two or more cars. On-site "stick-built" construction represented 94% of new homes, while the remainder were made with factory-built modular components or panelized kits shipped to building sites.

The characteristics of apartment units in newly constructed multifamily structures changed little in 1997. The average size of new units held at about 1,100 sq ft (102 m²). Nearly three fourths of the new units had at least two bedrooms, and about half had at least two bathrooms.

The average size of mobile homes continued to increase, reaching 1,400 sq ft (130 m²). This trend reflected the declining position of traditional single-wide units—to 45% of the market—and growth in the shares of double- and triple-wide units. Indeed, 85% of new mobile homes had three or more bedrooms, and more than 75% had factory-installed central air conditioning.

Regional Patterns. The regional distribution of U.S. housing starts shifted somewhat in 1997. The Northeast (New England and the Middle Atlantic census division) regained some share of the national housing market as all states except Maine, Vermont, and New York posted solid increases in housing starts. New Jersey led the way with a 14% increase from 1996.

The Midwest lost market share as both the East North Central and West North Central divisions lost ground. All Midwest-region states experienced significant declines in housing starts, with the exception of North Dakota, which was up slightly.

The South picked up some share of the national market, as slippage in the East South Central division was more than made up by gains in both the South Atlantic and West

South Central divisions. Solid growth in housing starts was recorded in Florida, North and South Carolina, West Virginia, Texas, and Oklahoma. The West gained some share of the national market as the Pacific division finally moved up, more than offsetting slippage in the Mountain states. Colorado was the only state in the Mountain division to show a significant increase in housing starts, while California paced the Pacific division with a 17% gain from 1996.

Home-Ownership Record. The home-ownership rate for the United States continued to increase, reaching a record 66% by the third quarter of 1997, narrowly exceeding the previous high in the third quarter of 1980.

The increase continued a strong upswing that began in 1995, following the 1994 announcement of the National Homeownership Strategy by the Bill Clinton administration. The upswing was broad-based in regard to income, age, race, and geographic area, although a good deal of disparity in home-ownership rates persisted in 1997. On a regional basis, the Midwest posted the highest rate (70%), while the West had the lowest (60%). In terms of age, households aged 55 to 64 continued to have the highest rate of home ownership (80%), while those under 35 continued to lag well behind (39%).

Income continued to be a major determinant of home ownership. Households with incomes equal to or greater than the median family income had a home-ownership rate of 81%, while households below the median family income had a rate of only 50%. Striking disparities across racial and ethnic classes also persisted. Whites had the highest rate (72%), blacks were at 45%, and Hispanics were at 43%.

The ongoing aging of the U.S. incumbent population, and the prospects for higher home-ownership rates among minority and immigrant groups, should continue to raise the home-ownership rate in the United States. Indeed, the goal announced by the Clinton administration for the U.S. home-ownership rate by the year 2000—67.5%—certainly seemed attainable.

Tax Preferences Enhanced. Tax preferences for housing in the U.S. tax code were enhanced by the Taxpayer Relief Act of 1997. This law virtually eliminated the taxation of capital gains on sales of principal residences, exempting gains under $500,000 for married couples ($250,000 for single persons) and permitting use of the exemption as often as every two years, regardless of the age of home sellers. The law also broke new ground for first-time home buyers, permitting penalty-free withdrawals from tax-deferred individual retirement accounts (IRAs) if the proceeds were used for down payments on first homes. This new provision applied not only to withdrawals by home buyers but also to withdrawals by parents and grandparents.

International Comparisons. In the United States the real (inflation-adjusted) value of residential fixed investment—including production of new housing units as well as remodeling of the existing housing stock—grew by 2.5% in 1997, following an expansion of nearly 6% in 1996. This modest growth allowed the ratio of housing investment to total national investment (both public and private) to slip to 21%, although the ratio of housing investment to gross domestic product (GDP) held near 4%.

Housing investment posted positive growth during 1997 in some of the other major industrialized countries, but some reversals also were recorded. In Europe growth was slow or negative in Germany, France, and Italy, while growth of 5.9% was posted by Great Britain. Expansion was most robust in Canada (14%), while housing investment contracted by a dramatic 15.5% in Japan, following strong growth in 1996.

The share of housing in total national investment was similar to the U.S. share in Canada, France, Great Britain, and Italy—ranging from 20% in France to 28% in Italy. This ratio was the highest in Germany, where housing continued to account for one third of total national investment. The ratio of housing investment to GDP was also the highest in Germany, remaining slightly above 7% for the fourth consecutive year.

In Japan, where housing investment faltered badly in 1997, the housing share of GDP slipped to 4.5%. Furthermore, the housing share of total national investment fell to 15.1% in Japan—the lowest for the major industrialized countries.

Home-ownership rates generally were stable or rising in most of the industrialized nations in 1997. Home-ownership rates were comparable to those in the United States in Great Britain, Canada, and Japan, as well as in Finland and Norway. The rate remained higher than in the United States in Italy, Spain, Australia, New Zealand, Ireland, and Israel, exceeding 70% in some cases. Lower home-ownership rates continued to prevail in France, Germany, Austria, Sweden, and the Netherlands.

DAVID F. SEIDERS
National Association of Home Builders

HUMAN RIGHTS

Systematic violations of human rights continued to plague many countries throughout the world in 1997. The governments of China, Nigeria, and Myanmar again evoked the greatest concerns. The principle that basic human rights apply universally came under renewed attack. At the same time, a new campaign protesting religious persecution in China and elsewhere escalated (*see* RELIGION—*Overview*).

U.S. Global Survey. In the U.S. State Department's 1997 report on human rights, which covered 194 countries and territories, China received the most attention by far—most of it critical. Despite "economic pragmatism and increasingly robust ties of trade and commerce with the United States and many other countries," China's government persisted in "widespread and well-documented human-rights abuses...stemming from the authorities' intolerance of dissent, fear of unrest, and the continuing absence of laws protecting basic freedoms," the report said.

In response, the State Council in Beijing charged that the U.S. report was an "old trick," using fabrications and distortions to interfere in China's internal affairs. From another perspective, an Amnesty International representative said that the report's tough China section highlighted the contrast between the administration's words and its actions, particularly its "rolling out the blood-red carpet to honor [those] who personally organized the Tiananmen Square massacre." The report did not spare U.S. friends. It provoked irritation in Germany for its criticism of an officially sanctioned campaign of discrimination against members of the Church of Scientology, which Germany does not regard as a religion.

United Nations. In March and April more than 2,000 governmental and nongovernmental representatives crowded the Palais des Nations in Geneva for the annual six-week session of the UN Commission on Human Rights. For the first time, the 53-member commission passed a resolution urging governments to consider abolishing capital punishment. For the seventh year in a row, China escaped censure, mainly because of divisions among Western governments. Despite the opposition of African countries, except South Africa, the commission called on Nigeria to release all "trade-union leaders, human-rights advocates, and journalists currently detained," and ordered a special investigation into arbitrary detentions and executions there. The commission passed milder resolutions on the human-rights situations in Cuba, Guatemala, Indonesia, and Myanmar.

Away from the Geneva sessions, the commission also subjected the United States to scrutiny. Bacre Waly Ndiaye of Senegal, a commission expert, visited California, Florida, New York, and Texas for two and one half weeks in September and October to investigate U.S. capital-punishment practices.

In a meeting with members of the UN Security Council in mid-September, Pierre Sané, secretary-general of Amnesty International, emphasized how armed conflicts cause human-rights atrocities and vice versa. He urged the council to regard human-rights work in troubled places, such as Cambodia and the Congo, as part of peacekeeping efforts rather than as an impediment. He also called on nations to adopt the International Code of Conduct on Arms Transfers as a means of combating the "destructive effects of the unregulated arms trade."

Mary Robinson, an attorney and human-rights advocate, gave up the presidency of Ireland—some three months before her term expired—to become the new UN high commissioner for human rights. (*See* BIOGRAPHY.)

On the fringes of the July meetings in Kuala Lumpur, Malaysia, between top officials of the Association of Southeast Asian Nations (ASEAN) and other Asian and Western powers, Malaysian Prime Minister Mahathir bin Mohamad touched off a controversy by proposing that the UN Declaration of Human Rights be "reviewed." He said that the 1948 declaration should not remain "a common standard of achievement for all peoples and all nations." U.S. Secretary of State Madeleine Albright expressed a "relentless" opposition to any dilution of the charter.

Public Awareness. In its 1997 *World Report*, Human Rights Watch called attention to a positive influence of the global economy: "By establishing new and immediate connections among distant peoples," globalization has "produced a surprising new source of support for the human-rights cause." Since goods imported from an authoritarian country may be made by victims of oppression, "the very act of consumption can be seen as complicity in that repression." As a result of public reactions in the United States and Europe, some companies left Myanmar, for example.

A directory compiled by the American Association for the Advancement of Science listed nearly 400 World Wide Web sites devoted to human-rights issues.

ROBERT A. SENSER
Editor, "Human Rights for Workers"

HUNGARY

Hungary's coalition government remained relatively stable despite losing some popularity in 1997, while the opposition began gearing up for 1998 parliamentary elections. In major foreign-policy developments, Hungary was included in the first round of North Atlantic Treaty Organization (NATO) enlargement and specified for future European Union (EU) membership.

Politics. The Socialist-Liberal coalition maintained itself despite eroding public support. Although evidence emerged of a scandal—linked with the privatization process—in which transfer payments were made to companies linked with the governing parties, the opposition was unable to benefit greatly. Nevertheless, public-opinion polls indicated that the coalition had lost ground to the Alliance of Young Democrats (Fidesz) and the Smallholders Party. Fidesz emerged as the major opposition force in parliament, following the dissolution of the Christian Democratic People's Party, and was poised to be the major contender in general elections scheduled for the spring of 1998.

The political-reform process continued. In July parliament approved a judicial-reform bill, together with amendments to the penal code increasing the independence of courts and establishing a new court of appeals. Budapest was praised widely for its policy of guaranteeing cultural, educational, and linguistic rights to the country's small ethnic minorities. The government launched a program to compensate surviving Jewish victims of the Holocaust; hundreds of thousands of Hungarian Jews had perished at the hands of Nazis and their collaborators during World War II. Budapest also agreed to return property to the Catholic Church that had been confiscated by the communists after the war.

© Zoltan Asztalos/MTI/AP/Wide World Photos

Prime Minister Gyula Horn, above, campaigned in favor of a referendum supporting Hungary's membership in NATO. Voters overwhelmingly approved the initiative in mid-November 1997.

Economy. Hungary's economy continued to improve in 1997, with gross domestic product (GDP) projected to grow by 3.5%. Unemployment and inflation remained stable and relatively low, while the number of private companies continued to increase. Despite corruption scandals, the privatization of large state-owned enterprises continued. A United Nations (UN) report showed that Hungary attracted more foreign investment than did any other former Soviet-bloc state. From 1990 to 1997, more than $14 billion was invested in Hungary, out of $46 billion for the entire region. In order to buttress the reform process, the World Bank approved a $225 million loan to help restructure the country's banking sector.

International Affairs. Hungary's relations with most neighboring states improved, and in March, Hungary hosted the first visit by a Romanian prime minister since the fall of communism. The two states agreed to establish a commission to monitor the implementation of their basic treaty, signed two years earlier. Budapest and Bucharest also decided to establish a joint battalion for peacekeeping operations.

Hungary, Italy, and Slovenia agreed to create a joint military brigade and to hold regular joint maneuvers. Relations with Slovakia, however, remained strained during the year. The Hungarian government complained that Slovak authorities had failed to implement the provisions of the bilateral basic treaty that

---

HUNGARY • Information Highlights

Official Name: Republic of Hungary.
Location: East-central Europe.
Area: 35,919 sq mi (93 030 km²).
Population (mid-1997 est.): 10,200,000.
Chief Cities (Jan. 1, 1994 est.): Budapest, the capital, 1,995,696; Debrecen, 217,706; Miskolc, 189,655.
Government: *Head of state,* Arpád Goncz, president (elected August 1990). *Head of government,* Gyula Horn, prime minister (took office July 1994). *Legislature* (unicameral)—National Assembly.
Monetary Unit: Forint (201.26 forints equal U.S.$1, Dec. 16, 1997).
Gross Domestic Product (1995 est. U.S.$): $72,500,000,000 (purchasing power parity).
Economic Indexes (1996, 1990 = 100): *Consumer Prices,* all items, 382.8; food, 356.9. *Industrial Production,* 89.
Foreign Trade (1996 U.S.$): *Imports,* $15,854,000,000; *exports,* $12,647,000,000.

guaranteed the rights of the large Hungarian minority. In October, Slovak Prime Minister Vladimir Mečiar outraged Hungarian politicians when he suggested that members of the Hungarian minority could leave Slovakia at any time.

In July, Hungary—together with Poland and the Czech Republic—was included in the first round of NATO enlargement at the NATO summit. In a mid-November referendum, Hungarians overwhelmingly approved NATO membership; earlier, parliament had voted unanimously in favor of accession (*see also* EUROPE—*NATO Expansion*).

In addition, the EU named Hungary as one of five East European countries to be included in negotiations for the next stage of EU expansion. The decisions signaled that Hungary was considered to have largely completed its process of transformation from communism to democracy and from a command economy to capitalism.

JANUSZ BUGAJSKI
Center for Strategic and International Studies

ICELAND

Iceland's economic recovery continued in 1997, with more growth predicted. A diplomatic incident involving Taiwan occurred.

Economy. The economic recovery of 1995–96 continued, with further improvement predicted for 1998. The 1996 gross domestic product (GDP) was about $7 billion—up 5.7% over 1995. Figures for 1997 indicated that GDP would be about $7.5 billion, up 3.5%. By mid-1997 inflation was running at about 1.5%, with unemployment down slightly to 4.5%. Exports amounted to $1.8 billion in 1996 and imports were $1.9 billion, with figures for the first half of 1997 outstripping those for the first half of 1996.

ICELAND • Information Highlights

Official Name: Republic of Iceland.
Location: North Atlantic Ocean.
Area: 39,768 sq mi (103 000 km²).
Population (mid-1997 est.): 300,000.
Chief City (December 1996): Reykjavík, the capital, 105,487.
Government: *Head of state,* Ólafur Ragnar Grímsson, president (took office August 1996). *Head of government,* David Oddsson, prime minister (took office April 1991). *Legislature* (unicameral)—Althing.
Monetary Unit: Króna (71.19 krónur equal U.S.$1, selling rate, October 1997).
Gross Domestic Product (1996 est. U.S.$): $7,000,000,-000.
Economic Index (1996, 1990 = 100): *Consumer Prices,* all items, 121.7; food, 110.1.
Foreign Trade (1996 U.S.$): *Imports,* $1,900,000,000; *exports,* $1,800,000,000.

In 1996, Iceland had its smallest budget deficit since 1984—about $28 million, less than 0.5% of GDP—largely due to cuts in health spending. The government hoped to reach a surplus of about $2 million in 1998.

Guarded optimism was attributable partly to brighter prospects in the fisheries, which provide more than 70% of Iceland's export earnings. For the second consecutive year, the allowable quota for cod, Iceland's major commercial fish, was raised. A total catch of 218,000 tons was permitted for the 1997–98 season, up from 186,000 tons. After more than ten years of strict controls, cod stocks had improved, and surveys indicated they still were growing. The additional cod could yield up to $60 million, while the overall fish catch was expected to be up about 0.5%.

Quotas for other species, such as haddock and saithe, still were being cut to preserve stocks, and Icelandic ships sought opportunities to fish in international waters, such as on the Flemish Cap off Newfoundland and in the Barents Sea. The fish-processing industry also aimed to produce higher-value export products from the fish. The value of the total fish catch remained at about $715 million in both 1995 and 1996, while the value of fish exports rose about 10%. Fishing in international waters was expected to yield only about $100 million in 1997—nearly $50 million less than in 1996.

In October, Icelandic Aluminum, a subsidiary of the Swiss Alusuisse Lonza conglomerate, opened an extension to its smelter—Iceland's biggest industrial plant. The addition increased capacity from 100,000 tons to 162,000 tons annually and provided 80 new jobs. The plant became the third-largest aluminum smelter in Europe. Another aluminum plant, owned by Columbia Ventures of Canada, was due to open at Grundartangi, west Iceland, in 1998. Its initial production capacity would be 60,000 tons a year, with the potential for 180,000 tons.

International Relations. Iceland was at the center of a diplomatic furor in October, when Taiwan Vice-President Lien Chan visited and Beijing demanded the visit be terminated. Iceland refused and held informal meetings with Chan. After Chan's departure, Iceland sent a peacemaking mission to Beijing.

In July, President Ólafur Ragnar Grímsson and his wife made an official visit to the United States and met with President and Mrs. Bill Clinton. They observed the launch of the space shuttle *Discovery,* which had Iceland's Bjarni Tryggvason aboard.

ANNA YATES, *Freelance Writer, Reykjavík*

INDIA

Aug. 15, 1997, marked the 50th anniversary of India's independence—an appropriate time to evaluate the nation's accomplishments and failures. The accomplishments included maintaining its territorial integrity despite several secessionist movements, the institutionalization of a democratic tradition, development of the world's sixth-largest economy, some social progress, and the potential settlement of long-standing disputes. Continuing problems were those of instability as coalition politics have become the norm, perceptions of political opportunism replacing leadership, public corruption, persistent poverty, and lagging development of basic social needs.

Politics. The potential for cabinet instability was heightened when Deve Gowda's ten-month-old coalition government led by the Janata Dal (JD) party fell on March 30, 1997. The Congress Party—which was not a coalition member but a parliamentary ally—withdrew support when doubts about the prime minister's secular commitment and basic policy disagreements became an issue. Some felt the move was a bid by Congress President Sitaram Kesri to become prime minister in order to forestall further inquiries into corrupt party practices and to stem growing Congress infighting.

India's President Shankar Dayal Sharma gave the Gowda government a week to establish its majority. When it failed to do so, Sharma disregarded requests by the Congress and Bharatiya Janata (BJP) parties that they each be permitted to form the government, and allowed the Janata coalition to negotiate with its supporters to choose a new prime minister. Gowda attempted to continue as coalition head, but when Congress refused to accept him, members of his own party began looking for alternatives.

After much debate, Inder Kumar Gujral—JD member of the Rajya Sabha (upper house) representing Bihar state—was sworn in as prime minister on April 3. Although Gujral had a long and distinguished career in both Congress and JD administrations, he had no popular base of his own and presented no threat to other regional coalition leaders. Moreover, his integrity, commitment to secular rule, and effectiveness in negotiating with China, Bangladesh, and Pakistan made him an attractive candidate.

Gujral reiterated the Gowda administration's goals of economic liberalization and growth with a "human face." He vowed to

Prime Minister I. K. Gujral addressed Parliament as India, a nation of nearly 970 million people, marked the 50th anniversary of its independence on Aug. 15, 1997. Maintaining its territorial integrity and a democratic tradition are among the nation's hallmarks.

© Pablo Bartholomew/Gamma-Liaison

INDIA • Information Highlights

Official Name: Republic of India.

Location: South Asia.

Area: 1,269,340 sq mi (3 287 590 km²).

Population (mid-1997 est.): 969,700,000.

Chief Cities (1991 census): New Delhi, the capital, 301,297; Mumbai (Bombay), 9,925,891; Delhi, 7,206,704; Calcutta, 4,399,819.

Government: *Head of state*, Kocheril Raman Narayanan, president (elected July 1997). *Head of government*, Inder Kumar Gujral, prime minister (took office April 21, 1997). *Legislature*—Parliament: Rajya Sabha (Council of States) and Lok Sabha (People's Assembly).

Monetary Unit: Rupee (39.036 rupees equal U.S.$1, official rate, Dec. 16, 1997).

Gross Domestic Product (1995 est. U.S.$): $1,408,700,-000,000 (purchasing power parity).

Economic Indexes (1996, 1990 = 100): *Consumer Prices*, all items, 179.6; food, 188.0. *Industrial Production*, 142.

Foreign Trade (1996 U.S.$): *Imports*, $37,378,000,000; *exports*, $33,057,000,000.

continue the battle against public corruption, refusing to intervene in inquiries against fellow JD member, and former chief minister of Bihar, Laloo Prasad Yadav—currently in custody. He also did not interfere in the November bribery trial of former Prime Minister P. V. Narasimha Rao. Gujral opened a special office to handle allegations of corruption by bureaucrats and elected officials. Gujral met with Prime Minister Nawaz Sharif of Pakistan within two weeks of taking office to lay the basis for dialogue to resolve long-standing problems between the two countries.

Despite the energetic start, the Gujral government lasted only seven months. In November the Congress again withdrew its support due to the tabling of a preliminary report on former Prime Minister Rajiv Gandhi's assassination in 1991. The report implied the Tamil Nadu–based Dravida Munnetra Kazaghan Party (DMK) may have given "tacit support" to Sri Lankan Tamil Tigers believed to have carried out the assassination. The Congress demanded the DMK be dropped from the United Front (UF), which the latter refused to do, stating the report was only preliminary. Given the volatile climate of shifting alliances, no party wanted to go to the polls. However, as no compromise could be worked out between the UF and Congress, and the BJP was unable to attract enough members from other parties, President K.R. Narayanan, on a recommendation from the UF, dissolved Parliament on December 4. Elections were scheduled for February 1998.

Routed in the February state elections in Punjab by an unlikely coalition of the BJP and the Sikh-based Shiromani Akali Dal (Badal faction), the Congress Party's own fortunes continued to decline. In its traditional stronghold of Uttar Pradesh state, its strength had dropped to 37 members (out of 425) after elections in the fall of 1996. In October 1997, 19 of those defected to form their own splinter party and joined a BJP-led coalition with the anti-high-caste Bahujan Samaj Party (BSP). In a novel arrangement, the BJP and BSP agreed to rotate the chief ministership every six months. BSP leader Mayawati took the first turn, during which she confiscated land from higher castes and granted it to Dalits (low castes). She also transferred or suspended officials assumed to be friendly with other parties, including the BJP, Congress, and her Dalit rival—the Samajwadi Party. In October, when BJP leader Kalyan Singh assumed the chief ministership, he began inquiries into the Mayawati administration's activities, which caused the BSP to withdraw support. Left as a minority government, the BJP welcomed legislative support regardless of party affiliation. With the Congress defections, along with support from 13 BSP defectors, several smaller parties, and independent legislators, Singh won a majority. Uttar Pradesh now had the largest cabinet in India's history, 93 members.

The Congress and BSP parties pressed the central government to dismiss the Singh administration and impose president's rule to be followed by fresh elections—under Article 356 of the constitution—on the grounds that the BJP-BSP coalition had lost a legislative mandate. Under existing laws, defectors should be disqualified. Congress also threatened again to withdraw support from the UF. The pressured Gujral government forwarded a recommendation to the president to dismiss the Singh administration over the alleged opposition of Home Minister Inderjit Gupta, who observed that the situation had strong parallels to the fall of the Gowda government. The president refused to acquiesce and the Singh government retained power. Notably, many UF regional leaders, who had been victims of Article 356 in the past, also objected to its use.

These government changes at the central level and in Uttar Pradesh raised issues concerning the constitution and the role of the president. Article 356, originally meant to be used in times of economic or political emergency, had been used since the late 1950s as a political weapon. There was an almost unanimous consensus that safeguards need to be included to prevent its partisan use. Newly elected President K.R. Narayanan was praised for not bowing to partisan pressures.

Other political concerns were the increase in defections and parties who were unwilling to face the electorate for new mandates.

Instead, as the BJP actions indicate, all parties had decided to use the "divide and rule" principle in legislative politics. The BJP national leadership made it clear that its strategy would be to split the Congress by encouraging defections and thus to bring down the UF government. The government was considering strengthening laws against defections.

Narayanan's election in July was the first time India chose a Dalit as president. Narayanan, from Kerala state, who had been vice-president since 1992, succeeded Sharma, a high-caste Brahmin. Detractors said the choice was based on caste rather than merit, but Narayanan, a lawyer, holds a degree from the London School of Economics, served in the foreign service, was ambassador to Beijing and Washington, and served in Parliament and in former Prime Minister Rajiv Gandhi's cabinet before becoming vice-president. Narayanan is known for his integrity.

England's Queen Elizabeth and Prince Philip were among the dignitaries visiting India in October for the independence-year celebrations. Although the trip was largely successful in its purpose of underscoring the historical ties between the two countries, it was not without controversy. The royal pair paid a visit to Jallianwala Bagh in Amritsar city, the scene of a massacre of Indian freedom fighters in 1919. Although the queen laid a wreath at the memorial, some wanted a royal apology. In addition, Prince Philip evoked memories of British imperial racism when he questioned the number of people killed, using as his source the son of Gen. Reginald Dyer, who ordered the shooting.

The death of Mother Teresa of the Sisters of Charity resulted in national mourning not seen since the deaths of Gandhi and Nehru. Thousands of Indians and foreign dignitaries attended her state funeral—only the second given to someone not a head of state or prime minister. (*See also* OBITUARIES.)

The Economy. Annual economic-growth rates of 6%–7% during the 1990s—a vast improvement over previous 3%–4% averages—were expected to continue. Foreign investment—which increased from $150 million in 1991 to more than $2 billion in 1995–96—was expected to top $3 billion in 1997.

Individual and corporate taxes were lowered in the hopes of increasing productivity, consumer demand, and taxable collections. Still, India had not been able to reduce deficits below 5.4% of the GDP or reduce its government payroll—largely due to political pressures. A central-government pay commission recommended modest upward revisions in pay scales, which public-service unions were able to embellish considerably. Pressure also forced the government to retain subsidies to rural areas amounting to 15% of the GDP and increase the amount of subsidized food distributed to low-income people through the Public Distribution System (PDS).

Despite considerable pressure to provide more funds to the states, it turned out that many states had not spent funds from the previous year. Such states cited a lack of the administrative capability to carry out designated projects. Additionally, several states had not been able to absorb foreign-aid funds earmarked for specific projects. With such continued dependence on the center for program implementation, the new "federalism"—called for in 1996—appeared doomed.

Even with the healthy growth rates of the 1990s, poverty remained the lot of nearly 50% of India's population. Official figures put the poverty rate at about 35%, which was disputed by virtually all researchers and observers. Illiteracy also was hovering at 50%, and a World Bank study ranked India last among ten similar developing countries in reducing infant mortality. Regional inequalities persisted. The richest 42% of the population—who lived in the wealthiest northern and southern states—accounted for about 49% of GDP.

Actually, the bulk of India's population would not benefit from lower taxes or economic liberalization. Labor statistics showed that only 3% of all active workers were in jobs employing ten or more people, with 6% in the public sector. The rest were in the vast "informal" economy. Without considerable increases in human-resource development, the income gap was expected to widen, and India would not live up to its potential as the world's second-largest emerging market.

Social Issues. In December 1996, India's Supreme Court upheld previous bans on child labor and instructed local governments to ensure compliance. While several manufacturers began using "child labor free" tags on their products, government "spot checks" on industries known to employ children were able to turn up very few. As word spread, employers temporarily or permanently sent children home, leaving families with less income. Observers felt solutions lay in combining work with education rather than in simple bans. Moreover, bans did not affect the vast number of children hired as domestics or in small tea shops and restaurants that were out of view of law enforcement.

Education continued to cause concern in 1997. Although more than 95% of India's children were starting school, only half were finishing fourth grade and only 40% of boys and 20% of girls were attending secondary school. Studies indicated extremely low attendance rates at all levels. In addition, there were not enough teachers and they were trained inadequately. Many had attendance records as poor as those of their students—especially in rural areas—and teachers often were paying more attention to fee-paying tutorial students than to the other children. The quality of many postsecondary institutions, colleges, and universities also had declined, largely because of an exponential increase in their numbers, coupled with stagnant funding and the loss of teachers to higher-paying private-sector jobs. Tuition had not increased since the 1950s, and as the government sought to reduce spending, studies were being conducted to find alternative funding sources. One suggestion was to increase tuition drastically according to an income-based sliding scale, while tapping the private sector to fund endowments.

In 1996, India's courts were instructed by the central and state governments to enforce environmental laws strictly, especially those dealing with auto emissions, industry, and mining. But lead-free gasoline was not readily available, and the government was not keeping its vehicles well-maintained. In addition, alternative sites needed to be found for polluting industries, while some assistance should be made available for small businesses to pay for emission-reducing technologies.

Foreign Affairs. New bilateral talks between India and Pakistan on outstanding disputes, including the Kashmir border question, raised cautious optimism in both countries. Although no specific resolutions were reached, the Gujral administration proposed a "no war" treaty that could provide a basis for resolving thornier issues. Despite an October shooting incident across the Kashmiri border, both governments stated their intention to maintain a dialogue.

India continued to lobby the international community for inclusion in an expanded United Nations (UN) Security Council. Russia and the United States expressed sympathy for India's position. However, Japan remained a serious competitor—especially if expansion is based on geographic representation.

Although India still refused to sign the Nuclear Test Ban Treaty (NTBT), it ratified the Chemical Weapons Convention and for the first time revealed the existence of a chemical-weapons program. India held that, unlike the NTBT, the chemical-weapons ban treated all parties equitably. Many were surprised when India refused to sign the landmine treaty that was negotiated in Oslo, Norway, in 1997.

India continued to press for membership in the Asian Pacific Economic Cooperation (APEC) forum. Despite India's participation in groups such as the South Asian Association for Regional Cooperation (SAARC) and the Association of Southeast Asian Nations (ASEAN) Regional Forum, APEC membership remained elusive. APEC countries maintained that India's economy still was too restrictive of foreign investment. In addition, the magnitude of the Indian economy potentially could dominate those of other members.

ARUNA NAYYAR MICHIE
Kansas State University

INDONESIA

The ruling Functional Group Party (Golkar) easily won the 1997 national elections, held before a regional economic crisis—which began in Thailand in July—reached Indonesia.

Politics. On May 29 nearly 113 million votes—representing more than 90% of the 124 million registered voters—were cast in Indonesia's sixth national election since President Suharto came to power in 1966. At stake were 425 of the 500 House of People's Representatives (DPR) seats. Ethnic and religious violence—rooted in social and economic grievances—marked the campaign and continued after the election, with Dayak attacks on Madurese settlers in West Kalimantan in July and anti-Chinese rioting in Sulawesi in September.

Golkar won 74.5% of the vote, assuring it 325 DPR seats—a significant increase from its 1992 total of 68% of the vote and 282 seats.

INDONESIA • Information Highlights

Official Name: Republic of Indonesia.
Location: Southeast Asia.
Area: 741,097 sq mi (1 919 440 km²).
Population (mid-1997 est.): 204,300,000.
Chief Cities (Dec. 31, 1995, est.): Jakarta, the capital, 9,160,500; Surabaya, 2,701,300; Bandung, 2,368,200; Medan, 1,909,700.
Government: *Head of state and government,* Suharto, president (took office 1966). *Legislature* (unicameral)—House of People's Representatives.
Monetary Unit: Rupiah (5,675.00 rupiahs equal U.S.$1, Dec. 16, 1997).
Gross Domestic Product (1995 est. U.S.$): $710,900,000,000 (purchasing power parity).
Economic Indexes (1996, 1990 = 100): *Consumer Prices,* all items, 165.2; food, 171.1. *Industrial Production,* 111.
Foreign Trade (1996 U.S.$): *Imports,* $42,929,000,000; *exports,* $49,814,000,000.

The Islamic Development Unity Party (PPP) gained 22.5% of the vote and 89 DPR seats, while the big loser was the Indonesian Democratic Party (PDI), with 3% of the votes and 11 seats—the legal minimum to be represented. Before PDI won the 11th seat in North Sumatra, the government was looking for ways to give PDI a Golkar seat to allow it to maintain its DPR presence. Since the government-sponsored internal PDI coup in July 1996 against the leadership of Megawati Sukarnoputra, daughter of Indonesia's first president, the PDI had been split. Megawati's supporters refused to support PDI leadership, benefiting both the Golkar and PPP parties.

With Golkar and the military's backing already announced, there was no doubt that Suharto would be unopposed if he decided to run for a seventh five-year term in 1998. Speculation and political jockeying were focused on the vice-president's post. One possible candidate was the president's oldest daughter, Siti Hardiyanti Rukmana—better known as Mbak Tutut—who emerged in 1997 as the leading political figure in Golkar.

Economy. In the midst of a region-wide financial crisis, the Indonesian currency—the rupiah—lost 50% of its value by the end of the third quarter. Real economic growth of 5% or less lagged behind the projected 8%. Rupiah devaluation caused the current-account deficit to balloon, despite a reduction in imports, while inflation pushed toward double digits.

In September, Indonesia announced its own rescue package, focused on export promotion, spending cuts, lower interest rates, and new taxes. But major structural reform had serious political implications because of the entrenched position of monopolistic Suharto family–related enterprises, and the government's effort to restore confidence did not succeed. In October it was forced to turn to the International Monetary Fund (IMF) and the World Bank for advice on fiscal policy and long-term debt relief. On October 31 a rescue package for Indonesia was announced. With $23 billion from multilateral sources and a second line of defense of $15 billion in bilateral standby credits—including $3 billion from the United States—the $38 billion plan was second in scope only to the 1995 Mexican bailout.

The economic picture was clouded further by a worsening drought that threatened domestic food supplies, and by massive forest fires that choked the air with smoke as far away as Singapore, Malaysia, and south Thailand.

© Denis Paquin/AP/Wide World Photos

In May 1997, President Suharto joined 90% of Indonesia's electorate in voting. Golkar, the ruling party, did well, as 425 seats in the House of People's Representatives were contested.

Foreign Affairs. In July, South African President Nelson Mandela tried to jump-start negotiations concerning Indonesian rule in East Timor. With Suharto's permission he visited jailed East Timorese leader Xanana Gusmao. Another round of United Nations (UN) talks between Indonesia and Portugal on East Timor began in October. Indonesia's stated flexibility excluded independence or self-determination for the former Portuguese colony, now an Indonesian province.

U.S.-Indonesian relations were complicated by the emergence of James Riady of Indonesia's Lippo Group business conglomerate as a key figure in the U.S. campaign-fundraising controversy. More significant was Indonesia's May 1997 decision to cancel its purchase of U.S. F-16 fighter jets and its refusal to participate in the U.S. International Military Education and Training program. The decision was a clear expression of resentment at continuing U.S. criticism of Indonesia's human-rights record.

DONALD E. WEATHERBEE
University of South Carolina

INDUSTRIAL PRODUCTION

Refined, redesigned, and equipped with modern electronic technology, U.S. industry in 1997 displayed hefty and long-anticipated improvements in productivity that spread benefits—including price stability and improved incomes—through the entire economy. Late in the year, the total gain in industrial production was at an annual rate of 5%—the best increase since the 5% gain also registered in 1994. The 1995 and 1996 industrial-production increases were 3.3% and 2.8%, respectively.

Improvements. The improvements were diffuse throughout U.S. industry, with gains in nonfarm productivity reaching an annual rate of 4.1% in the third quarter—the highest quarterly rate in five years. However, the most impressive showing was in manufacturing. Spurred by gains in output of electricity, trucks, computers, and aircraft, that sector's productivity soared 9.3% in the third quarter—the largest jump since a 12.5% gain in the second quarter of 1982. Even before these numbers were reported, the National Association of Manufacturers (NAM) had begun a campaign to dispel what it called the popular myth of manufacturing's decline. "The facts clearly show," said Jerry Jasinowski, the NAM president, "that manufacturing is the most important and dynamic sector of the U.S. economy in terms of productivity, technology, trade, and the American standard of living."

Economists remarked on how rare it was for productivity gains to continue so long into an economic expansion. Even Alan Greenspan, the Federal Reserve chairman, who is noted for his careful objectivity, seemed surprised; he commented that huge investments in computers and other high-tech equipment had helped put the economy on the threshold of "once or twice in a century" productivity gains. It helped, he said, to explain the low level of inflation.

The source of the gains—much of them in the output and use of long-term durable goods—was encouraging, particularly to economists, and suggested that more improvements might be forthcoming. Production of durable goods—such as business equipment, electrical machinery, and industrial machinery and equipment—far outstripped output of consumer items. Late in the year, both electrical and industrial machinery were being produced at an annual rate nearly 15% higher than a year earlier, reflecting the high priority American business was placing on lowering costs to compete in a global economy.

In some instances, production gains were deceptive. The output of iron and steel, for example, grew by less than 3%, but it was the sixth straight year of improvement for an industry that, in the popular mind, had been written off as a relic of the old smokestack past. But, modernized and efficient, U.S. steel mills had returned quietly to competitiveness. Similarly, the coal industry, which had shrunk in terms of employment, produced a record 1.08 billion tons during 1997.

Transformations, Weaknesses, and Efficiencies. Entire industries were in transformation during 1997. Seeking to spur the application of digital high-definition television (HDTV), the Federal Communications Commission (FCC) awarded an additional channel to about 1,500 TV stations. The expectation was that they would return their old analog-channel space in 2006, when the change to HDTV was to be complete. But the latter became questionable due to congressional legislation that would allow stations to keep both spaces if 15% of their market still was using analog.

INDUSTRIAL PRODUCTION

	Canada	France	Germany	Great Britain	Italy	Japan	United States
	Major Industrial Countries 1992 = 100 (seasonally adjusted)						
1987	101.6	93.0	86.4	96.6	92.4	86.4	93.1
1988	106.9	97.3	89.8	101.2	97.9	94.5	97.3
1989	106.8	100.9	94.0	103.4	100.9	99.9	99.0
1990	103.2	102.4	98.9	103.1	101.1	104.2	98.9
1991	98.9	101.2	101.7	99.6	100.2	106.1	96.9
1992	100.0	100.0	100.0	100.0	100.0	100.0	100.0
1993	104.5	96.2	92.5	102.2	97.6	95.8	103.4
1994	111.8	100.0	95.6	107.6	102.6	97.0	108.6
1995	115.6	102.0	96.6	110.0	108.2	100.2	112.1
1996	117.6	102.4	96.8	111.2	106.4	102.9	115.2
1997*	124.2	107.5	99.6	113.8	109.8	105.6	121.5

*August preliminary

Source: National data as reported by Department of Commerce

There were weaknesses from the previous year in some industries and actual declines in others, but they were rare and generally caused by special situations. Hurt by the shift to lower-wage non-U.S. production, apparel output continued to fall. Printing and publishing—hurt by electronic inroads—barely kept pace with the year before. The most significant weakness, however, was in the continuing but slowing decline in defense and space equipment for the eighth straight year. The industry in 1997 had shrunk to only two thirds its 1989 size, and companies that had been its mainstay since World War II had merged or were producing peacetime products.

But even among relatively slow-growth industries—such as utilities and mining—the numbers were deceptive. As in other industries, their effectiveness was to be measured by the increased efficiency of output as well as by total production. Reflecting this, commodity prices remained stable and producer prices of finished goods actually fell.

One of the most illustrative examples of these efficiencies was found in the automotive industry, where sales rose to an annual rate of 15.2 million vehicles in November, slightly ahead of the year-earlier pace. In the five years through 1997, the industry sold 74 million vehicles—second only to the 76 million units sold in the five years that ended with 1984. In the view of some in the industry, a saturation point was approaching that would compel carmakers to put increasing emphasis on improvements in design and technology. Anticipating that, carmakers were designing and testing cars by computer, based on three-dimensional images that could be varied at the touch of a key. Industry reports indicated that vehicles completely redesigned, in some instances without paper blueprints, could be readied in as little as 28 months, less than half the time required in 1990. And savings throughout the automotive industry could be measured in billions of dollars. The new techniques were made use of quickly in satisfying a quirky consumer market that at times demanded more small trucks than cars. (*See also* AUTOMOBILES.)

Electronic Items and New Products. Equally innovative applications could be found throughout industry. One of the fastest growing electronic items was the sub-$1,000 personal computer (PC), and the size of some PCs actually shrank to suit-pocket size. Technology changed or was about to change not just basic industrial production but the type and variety of products, too. Medicine—one of the fastest growing of the service industries

that made up a growing share of the nation's output—was being transformed by the introduction of analytical and imaging devices.

Automobiles came equipped with cellular telephones, and farm tractors had computers and satellite-guidance systems. E-mail pay systems were being readied for airports, to stand side by side with coin phones and bank "smart cards," which stored cash in a microchip and updated the owner's account balance after each transaction.

Some of the new products were of questionable value, and many—including smart cards, credit cards, cellular phones, and even the increasingly common automatic store checkout counters—intruded on personal privacy. For other reasons, many people considered of questionable value Philip Morris' smokeless cigarette system—a battery-operated, pager-size, handheld device into which a cigarette was to be inserted before inhaling.

See also UNITED STATES—*The Economy.*

JOHN CUNNIFF, *The Associated Press*

INDUSTRIAL PRODUCTION—MAJOR MARKET GROUPS

(1992 = 100; monthly data seasonally adjusted)

	1987	1991	1997*
Consumer Goods			
Total	93.7	97.0	114.2
Durable	93.9	93.0	133.0
Nondurable	93.6	98.1	109.6
Equipment			
Total	92.7	98.4	129.5
Business	85.1	95.7	143.2
Defense and space equipment	117.5	106.7	75.7
Intermediate Products			
Total	100.7	97.5	113.2
Construction	104.7	96.2	120.7
Business supplies	98.4	98.3	108.7
Materials			
Total	90.4	95.9	129.9
Energy	96.2	100.8	106.1
Primary Metals			
Total	97.8	96.7	124.8
Iron and steel	95.4	96.0	122.6
Fabricated Metal Products	101.9	96.2	121.9
Industrial Machinery and Equipment	86.0	95.4	182.4
Electrical Machinery	75.6	89.6	191.6
Transportation Equipment			
Total	96.1	96.5	118.6
Motor vehicles and parts	94.9	88.5	136.4
Lumber and Products	104.9	94.5	112.4
Nondurable Manufactures			
Apparel products	105.5	97.8	96.1
Printing and publishing	102.5	99.1	100.7
Chemical products	87.0	96.4	113.3
Food	93.5	98.4	108.6

*October preliminary

Source: Board of Governors of the Federal Reserve System

INTERIOR DESIGN

While casual elegance in the form of eclecticism again described the majority of interior design in 1997, there also was a movement toward more formality. The bottom line, though, was this: Consumers continued to be more comfortable with their own design decisions, following their hearts when furnishing personal spaces.

Styles. Dominating the style scene were two distinct design directions—classic Mission from the Arts & Crafts school and Mediterranean, a style that had been out of the spotlight since the 1970s. Mission-style furnishings were represented beautifully not only by line-for-line reproductions found at L. & J. G. Stickley but also by adaptations found at Michael Thomas, among a wealth of others.

Meanwhile, Mediterranean style in its new incarnation was anything but overdone; also referred to as southern European, it was both restrained and refined. The influences of Spain, Italy, and even the Greek isles added subtle romance to these newly created pieces; all the original details were still present (bombé shapes, intricate carvings, and nailhead trim, for instance) but they were toned down to make a more sophisticated statement. There was another big difference as well: The new Mediterranean furnishings were finished in light, dry tones as opposed to the dark, shiny glosses used the last time the style was in favor. Some of the best examples came from Hickory Chair's San Marino Collection, Lane's Hearst Castle Collection, and Century's Caspian Collection.

Equally important, however, were lifestyle furnishings that best could be described as simple, clean, and casual. Offered by the likes of Crate & Barrel and Pottery Barn, these pieces were embraced particularly by the baby boomers. Some of the most successful licensee programs also appealed to the baby boomers—the Nautica line from Lexington and Eddie Bauer from Lane, for instance. The attraction of licensees was not limited to only one segment of the population, though; just as desirable to consumers were products from the Bill Blass Collection from Pennsylvania House and the Pinehurst Collection from Drexel Heritage.

Finally, size itself was an issue in design circles. While overscaled, overstuffed comfort still had been very much in evidence in 1996, the scale of furniture in general finally seemed to have peaked. The gargantuan frames characteristic of recent years started to shrink during 1997.

Colors. As consumers continued to put an eclectic spin on furniture, color trends also took several different directions. Green continued to be a hot color in 1997, but it moved away from the hunter and sage shades of 1996 and into newly fashionable hues of kiwi, citrus, spring, and—for the really daring—chartreuse.

Likewise, rainbow hues came onto the horizon in the form of bright oranges, striking reds, brilliant blues, and sunny yellows. As for the new neutrals, bark, basil, and truffle proved important but most fashion-forward were the various forms of black—including onyx, slate, silver, gray, platinum, and licorice. Used as background colors or as accents, they invariably imparted a special coolness to a design scheme.

Fabrics. Some favorite fabrics, especially in the area of leather, were holdovers from 1996. In addition to the already popular broken-in bomber-jacket styles, many leathers got new twists such as tufting and antiquing.

Overall, though, there was a move to dressier fabrics in upholstery, even though casual design remained the dominant force. Dress-up looks were back and elegance was in, but with a late 1990s twist; there was a sheen and shine due to the increasing use of calendered finishes (a new word for chintz). In addition, there was a resurgence of prints, with florals, paisleys, and ethnic patterns among the most popular of these.

Texture, too, remained important. Chenille retained its predominance from 1996 and was joined in 1997 by velvet, bouclé, and wide-wale corduroy. Plus, there were a number of apparel applications in fabric such as seersucker, Polarfleece, and even jersey.

With the use of so many soft textures, fabrics in general had no hard-edged feeling. Whether chenille, velvet, prints, or workhorse fabrics like denim and chambray were used, soft was the operative word. Napped, sueded, fluffed, and sanded surfaces were the rule, not the exception. Even faux-washed fabrics joined the parade, creating similar textural effects through weaving, printing, and new technology.

Materials and Finishes. In 1997 wood finishes started to show a shift back to formality, with a bit of gloss and glimmer returning to case goods. Even more obvious, however, was a concentration on texture here as well. Cane, wicker, rattan, stone, and plenty of carving gave new products as much tactile quality as they had had in many a season.

HEATHER J. PAPER
Freelance Interior Design Writer

INTERNATIONAL TRADE AND FINANCE

It was a big year for world trade and financial markets in 1997. Amid an Asian economic crisis, the United States and more than 100 other countries signed a global trade agreement in December that dismantled hundreds of barriers and opened up Latin America and Asia to banks, insurers, and investment companies. The Dow Jones industrial average plunged a record 554.26 points to 7,161.15 on "Blue Monday," October 27, followed the next day by a record surge in points—337.17.

The Crisis in Asia. The troubles in Southeast Asia began May 14 in Thailand, when investors—prompted by Thailand's political instability, declining economic growth, and inflated levels of debt—saw its currency, the baht, as overvalued, igniting financial flash fires throughout Asia. The Thai government abandoned its promise to keep the baht pegged to the U.S. dollar on July 2, and the baht promptly fell 20%; by November 12 it had fallen 36.2%. Other currencies feeling the heat were the Indonesian rupiah, down 31.6%; the Malaysian ringgit, down 27.3%; the Philippine peso, down 23.9%; the South

Korean won, down 15.4%; the Taiwan dollar, down 14.1%; and the Singapore dollar, down 9.7%.

Moreover, Asian stock markets took a beating. When the Hong Kong market fell in late October, it frightened investors and markets tumbled in Europe, Latin America, Canada, and the United States. But the International Monetary Fund (IMF), working in cooperation with industrial nations, strove to keep Asia's financial fires from spreading. The IMF put together a $22 billion rescue package for Thailand, $40 billion for Indonesia, and $1 billion for the Philippines. South Korea—the world's 11th-largest economy, roughly as big as those of Indonesia, Malaysia, and Thailand combined—was next. On November 21 its government announced it would seek $20 billion from the IMF, plus an open line of credit, in case that was insufficient. The IMF's subsequent $57 billion rescue package imposed strict reforms on Korea's economic and financial systems. "The Asian miracle"—the extraordinarily rapid move of many of the region's nations from poverty to prosperity—was tarnished badly. In a nationally televised speech, South Korean President Kim Young Sam apologized. But most econo-

President Clinton was host to the leaders of the Group of Seven (G-7) industrial nations at the annual G-7 summit in Denver in June 1997. Since Russia formally became a member of the group, the meeting was renamed the Summit of the Eight.

mists predicted that Asia's economic advance would resume.

If the Korean troubles did not affect Japan, they were not expected to damage the U.S. economy seriously. Still, the effects would not be "negligible," as Federal Reserve Chairman Alan Greenspan (*see* BIOGRAPHY) pointed out in congressional testimony. But stock prices moved up again. During the remaining days of 1997 the Dow Jones industrial average recovered much of its "Blue Monday" losses and ended the year 22.64% above 1996's close. (*See also* STOCKS AND BONDS.)

Meanwhile, most Asian nations were patching up their banking systems. The Japanese government had announced three economic packages by December. The last contained $76 billion to help sort out its financial situation—although it was not immediately clear if the money would be used directly to bail out banks, which were carrying some $920 billion in bad loans. As the most important country in Asia to the United States, Japan takes 12% of U.S. exports. Economists said its revival depended on its dealing adequately with the aftermath of the collapse of Japanese stock prices in 1989 and real estate in 1991.

In an unusual move, the Japanese government allowed the nation's tenth-largest commercial bank, Hokkaido Takushoku Bank, to go under on November 17. Soon afterward, Yamaichi Securities Co.—a huge Japanese brokerage house—failed. In late December, Merrill Lynch announced it would hire some 2,000 former Yamaichi employees and acquire up to 50 branch offices. Earlier in November the medium-sized Sanyo Securities Co. failed when it was unable to repay mounting debts.

On November 19 the South Korean government tripled to $10 billion a special fund to write off some of the $26 billion in bad loans held by its banks. It also indicated it would force mergers among debt-ridden merchant banks. In Thailand and Malaysia, collapsing real-estate prices hurt the banks. The operations of some 58 financial institutions were suspended in Thailand during the summer.

The Indonesian government agreed to shut down some broken banks as part of an IMF loan package reform deal. In China state-run banks—forced by the government to lend some $200 billion to failing state-owned companies—had little hope of recovering all of these loans. At a mid-November meeting of China's top leaders, the government indicated it would overhaul the financial sector during the next three years.

Capital Flows. One mixed blessing for the Asian economies was a massive inflow of capital from the industrial nations. It was not entirely a good thing because some of the money had helped finance new skyscrapers and plants that were surplus to immediate needs. These skyscrapers and plants turned out to be financial liabilities.

The Institute of International Finance (IIF)—with members including some 270 of the world's largest financial institutions from 50 nations—estimated in September that net private capital flows to leading emerging market economies would total $261 billion in 1997, down from $281 billion in 1996. The Asian financial crisis, however, was causing money to leave the region, and it seemed unlikely those expectations would be met.

While international investment in Asia was in trouble in 1997, during 1996 multinational companies spent a record $129 billion in developing nations—up 34% from 1995, according to the United Nations (UN) World Investment Report released in September. U.S. and British firms led the way.

Global acquisitions and expansions by "transnational companies" (TNCs) in the developed world remained high at $208 billion—on a par with 1995. Total foreign direct investment in plants, equipment, and offices rose 10% to $349 billion in 1996—including $12 billion in Central and Eastern European former communist nations. When use of internal and other funds raised by the affiliates themselves were included, these 44,000 TNCs and their foreign affiliates may have invested up to $1.4 trillion in 1996, the UN report said.

The United States—the largest host for TNC money—received $85 billion. It also invested $85 billion abroad, more than any other country. For the first time, a developing country, China, was the second-most-desirable country for foreign direct investment, drawing $42.3 billion. The attraction of foreign investment was growing in developing countries, where the top 50 TNCs increased their foreign assets to $79 billion in 1995—up 280% from 1993.

Cross-border mergers and acquisitions continued to increase—about 45 exceeded $1 billion in 1996. The total value of majority-held cross-border mergers and acquisitions reached $163 billion in 1996.

The Economic Picture. Despite the Asian trouble, the world economy was its strongest in a decade, growing at a 4.25% real rate in 1997, according to an October IMF report. The expansion was underpinned by continued solid growth and low inflation in the United States and Britain, a strengthening recovery in Canada, and a broadening recovery across continental Western Europe. High European unemployment remained a problem, however. In the United States the economy grew about 3.6%, taking into account 2.4% inflation, according to the average forecast of economists. The Federal Reserve nudged short-term interest rates up 0.25 percentage point in March as a preemptive move against unseen inflation, but did not act for the rest of the year.

By the end of 1997, the U.S. economic recovery was 81 months old—the third longest since World War II—and still was going strong. There was evidence of an end to the decline in output, and perhaps a beginning of growth, in Russia and other former communist countries, the IMF report concluded.

Developing countries grew at about a 6% real rate on average, but that figure may have been reduced by the Asian crisis. Africa's overall growth was a disappointing 3.75%, the IMF estimated. Industrial nations showed few signs of the tensions and imbalances that usually precede business downturns. Global inflation remained subdued, averaging 2.5% in 1996. During 1997 there was talk of deflation in the United States and in Japan, the world's two most powerful economies. On November 18, Japan announced another package of 120 measures to revive its long-faltering economy, including incentives to coax the private sector into financing infrastructure and to revitalize the moribund property market. Most economists did not expect a dramatic pickup anytime soon.

There was uncertainty about whether the economic and monetary union (EMU) in Europe actually would take place by January 1999. Britain's new Labour government announced in the fall it would not join at that date. Nonetheless, key European nations, such as France, Germany, and Italy, continued efforts to reduce budget deficits to the EMU qualifying level. Interest rates in the prospective members showed some convergence, suggesting that financial markets expected the project to go ahead.

The U.S. federal government deficit shrank to $22.6 billion in the fiscal year that ended September 30—far short of the $126 billion forecast by the Bill Clinton administration in February. A surplus in local and state governments close to or exceeding $30 billion meant that government as a whole enjoyed a budget surplus. Some economists expected that surplus to continue into 1998. A bustling economy, booming stock market, and the continued impact of the George Bush and Clinton budget packages were credited.

Federal revenues rose to 20% of the nation's total output of goods and services, a historically high level compared with 17%–18% a few years earlier. A large chunk came from the affluent, who had been getting richer, while others saw little or no gains. Federal spending consumed about 20% of gross domestic product (GDP), down from 22.5% in 1991.

G-7 Summit. The annual summit of the Group of Seven (G-7) industrial nations, held in Denver in June, was called the Summit of the Eight because of the presence of Russian President Boris Yeltsin as a nearly full member. Its June 22 communiqué included a call for a worldwide ban on human cloning and a warning to China to retain democracy in Hong Kong after its July 1 takeover. Although Clinton boasted that U.S. entrepreneurial capitalism proved itself as a model for how an economy should be organized, some Europeans saw it as hard-hearted because of its treatment of the poor and its large inequity in incomes.

World Trade. In November, President Clinton was forced to withdraw the "fast-track" legislation that would have allowed him to negotiate trade deals and bring them to Congress for a yes or no vote without the possibility of amendment or delaying tactics. Foreign nations dislike negotiating a pact with the United States, only to see it weakened by Congress. Clinton had hoped to broaden the North American Free Trade Agreement (NAFTA) among the United States, Canada, and Mexico to include other Latin American nations, but could not muster support within his own party; some 80% of House Democrats voted against the measure, encouraged by organized labor and environmentalists. The defeat had negligible impact on the stock market, since NAFTA and the last worldwide trade deal under the General Agreement on Tariffs and Trade (GATT) still were reducing tariffs and other trade barriers.

World trade continued to grow solidly. In 1996 the volume of trade in goods and services increased by 6.3%, down from 9.5% in 1995. According to IMF estimates, it grew 7.7% in 1997. The value of world exports of merchandise reached $5.1 trillion, up from $4.9 trillion in 1995, the World Trade Organization (WTO) estimated. The value of trade in commercial services rose 5%, from $1.17 trillion in 1995 to $1.2 trillion in 1996. The barriers to world trade and investment continued to fall, and "globalization" moved ahead at a steady pace.

DAVID R. FRANCIS
"The Christian Science Monitor"

IRAN

The year 1997 was probably the most important one for Iran since the collapse of the regime of the shah in 1979. The indications were that Iran was modifying its behavior in the sphere of international relations so as to conduct itself in a more normal fashion, as one state among many—and less as the champion and embodiment of a Shiite Islamic revolution. In domestic affairs, similarly, a new era of openness, of more latitude in individual behavior, and in expression of opinions appeared to be dawning gradually.

Two 1997 events—the surprising result of the May presidential election and the Islamic Conference Organization meeting held in Tehran in December—pointed in this same direction. Simultaneously, a number of incidents showed that there was plenty of fight left in the upholders of the rigid theocratic orthodoxy that had prevailed in Iran for 18 years.

Presidential Election and New Administration. Iran's President Ali Akbar Hashemi Rafsanjani did not seek any constitutional change that would have permitted him to run for a third term. Four aspirants to be his successor emerged, having been approved by the Council of Guardians. It generally was expected that the speaker of the Majlis (parliament)—Ali Akbar Nateq-Nouri, a conservative often at odds with Rafsanjani—would be easily victorious. Mohammed Khatami (*see* BIOGRAPHY), a moderately prominent cleric who had been minister of culture for some ten years prior to 1992, when he was ousted as too liberal, entered the race only in March.

Khatami scored a resounding and unexpected success in the May 23 election, gaining about 70% of the votes cast, while Nateq-Nouri garnered only some 25%; the other two candidates went nowhere. Khatami had been supported by Rafsanjani, but his clear-cut victory was, above all, testimony to the discontent of the nation's young people toward a rigid regime. Many of the young now were quite prosperous.

As the year rolled on, the perception grew that Khatami was a very shrewd and canny politician, who had been underestimated consistently. After the election, cautious observers maintained that Khatami's ability to make changes would be very limited, in view of the fact that in the constitutional hierarchy he was merely second to the supreme spiritual leader, the rigidly orthodox Ayatollah Ali Akbar Hoseini-Khamenei. Next it was said that he would find it impossible to obtain the necessary parliamentary approval for cabinet members whom he would wish to appoint. It also was supposed that, even if he were to speak out and even effect some changes in internal matters, he never would dare make alterations in the sphere of foreign relations.

All these negative prognostications, however, were to prove wide of the mark. On August 20 the Majlis approved all of the 22 persons whom Khatami had named for his cabinet. This was a clear victory for Khatami and implied a strengthening of his authority. It was of interest that the two-day debate on the nominations was televised nationwide, with some strong criticism of his choices. This was especially the case with regard to the approval of Ataollah Mohajerani as minister of Islamic culture and guidance, and of Abdollah Nouri as interior minister. The outcome of the voting was influenced by Khatami's speech to the Majlis on August 20, when he urged that members should "admit that differences of opinion exist," and advocated "greater cultur-

Mohammed Khatami (center), a 54-year-old cleric who had served as Iran's minister of culture (1980–92), won a surprising victory in the nation's presidential election in May 1997. His campaign particularly appealed to Iran's young people.

IRAN • Information Highlights

Official Name: Islamic Republic of Iran.
Location: Southwest Asia.
Area: 636,293 sq mi (1 648 000 km²).
Population (mid-1997 est.): 67,500,000.
Chief Cities (Oct. 1, 1994, est.): Tehran, the capital, 6,750,043; Mashad, 1,964,489; Esfahan, 1,220,595; Tabriz, 1,166,203.
Government: *Head of state and government,* Mohammed Khatami, president (elected May 1997). *Legislature* (unicameral)—Islamic Consultative Assembly (Majlis).
Monetary Unit: Rial (3,000.00 rials equal U.S.$1, official rate, Dec. 31, 1997).
Gross Domestic Product (1995 est. U.S.$): $323,500,000,-000 (purchasing power parity).
Economic Index (1996, 1990 = 100): *Consumer Prices,* all items, 455.3; food, 506.3.
Foreign Trade (1994 est. U.S.$): *Imports,* $13,000,000,000; *exports,* $16,000,000,000.

al openness." Novel also were the appointments by Khatami of two women to noncabinet posts—Aazam Nouri as deputy culture minister and Masumeh Ebtekar as one of the eight vice-presidents.

New Era Dawns. The loosening of restrictions under Khatami's presidency made itself felt with surprising speed in a wide variety of aspects of life. Of course, large numbers of the Iranian population had been restive under the prevailing regime. Its restrictions were being challenged, or ignored, for some years previously. Many women evaded the restrictions on dress; television satellite dishes, although forbidden, existed. But now the thaw had arrived in unmistakable, and perhaps irreversible, fashion. Films were being made that would have been vetoed earlier. Bookstores had a wider variety of publications available. The atmosphere of fear had dissipated.

Demonstrably freer behavior reached a climax when, on September 29, the national Iranian soccer team defeated the Australian team in Australia and thus won a place in 1998's World Cup. It would be Iran's first appearance in the competition since 1978. There were great crowds and dancing in the streets of Tehran at the time of Iran's victory. A general atmosphere suggestive of a liberated city prevailed.

However, the conservative mullahs mounted a strong counterattack in the late fall. In Tehran in November, there were street demonstrations by bazaar merchants who supported the mullahs and opposed President Khatami. Also, the distinguished but dissident cleric Ayatollah Hossein Ali Montazeri—who had been in and out of house arrest for years—was harassed by militants and his house burned, in reprisal for remarks criticizing Ayatollah Khamenei. The most prominent of Montazeri's supporters, Ebrahim Yazdi, was jailed in December.

Iran continued to have many problems. Economic problems, including unemployment and inflation, were chronic, caused in large measure by the rapid increase in the population. These problems had outstripped the government's capacity to provide adequate services. Earthquakes again caused loss of life and property.

Foreign Relations. A seven-month crisis in relations with the European Union (EU) dragged on from April to November. In April a German court in Berlin held that the Iranian leadership had been responsible for an act of terrorism—the 1992 murder in a Berlin restaurant of four Iranian Kurds. EU ambassadors (except for the Greek ambassador) were withdrawn from Tehran in protest. This minor crisis dealt a serious, perhaps mortal, blow to the major European powers' policy of "critical dialogue" with Iran. This policy had been pursued since 1992 and was determinedly different from U.S. policy. The EU, however, carefully disavowed any intention to introduce sanctions against Iran. This dispute ended when most of the ambassadors came back to Tehran in mid-November.

Relations between Iran and Greece became particularly friendly in 1996–97. Iranian Vice-President Hasan Habibi paid a very successful visit to Athens in February 1997. Iran's policy toward Greece, however, was only one example of the nation's recent attempt to create a wider network of friendly relations with neighboring states, including Saudi Arabia. Iran's relations with those states have been chronically strained. Foreign Minister Kamal Kharazi made a weeklong tour of the Gulf states in early November. Iranian media hailed the trip as a turning point in relations. Also in 1997, Iran tried to mediate conflicts in other neighboring regions, as in Afghanistan and Tajikistan.

This extending of olive branches, perhaps, had two main related purposes—to underline the growing perception that the United States was alone in trying to isolate Iran; and to lay the groundwork for a successful Islamic conference in December. As to the first point, France, Germany, and Russia increasingly were bent on trading with Iran—and were pushing ahead with deals. The European powers chose to ignore Iran's continuing arms buildup, its support and arming of Hezbollah in Lebanon, and the fact that the *fatwa* decreeing death for author Salman Rushdie had not been withdrawn.

Islamic Conference. In 1997, Iran assumed the presidency of the Islamic Conference Organization for a period of three years, and was host of the 55-member group's eighth conference, December 9–11. About 30 heads of state and thousands of delegates and visitors attended. Representation included Middle East states that are U.S. allies. No such gathering had occurred in Iran for 19 years.

In two sharply contrasting addresses to the conference, Ayatollah Khamenei made a typical sharply anti-U.S. speech, while President Khatami took a much more moderate line. The new president went even further in a press conference on December 14, when he expressed "great respect" for the American people, and hoped for the beginning of a "thoughtful dialogue."

ARTHUR CAMPBELL TURNER
University of California, Riverside

IRAQ

From the point of view of Saddam Hussein, 1997 was a good year. The Iraqi dictator remained in power, and in virtually complete control of his country. The opposition to him—what there had been—was in complete disarray. Although it was six years since the end of the Persian Gulf war—in which Hussein's forces had been driven out of invaded Kuwait and defeated decisively—armistice conditions laid down by the United Nations (UN) in regard to the elimination of weapons of mass destruction, and ending the possibility of creating chemical and biological weapons, remained unfulfilled. There seemed to be a diminishing probability that decisive action would be taken to enforce compliance. Iraq's defiance in the last two months of the year showed that the overwhelming international coalition that had come together in 1990–91 was frayed and seemingly incapable of concerted action; up to the end of the year, Iraq's contemptuous actions toward the UN and the United States remained unchastised.

Internal Affairs. Since December 1996 a limited amount of Iraqi oil had been piped through Turkey and sold abroad under terms of an agreement with the UN. The agreement allowed Iraq to export $2 billion worth of oil each six months for badly needed food and medical supplies. The agreement was renewed twice—in the summer and late in the year. Iraq would have liked permission to sell a larger amount of oil, with less surveillance of the uses to which the funds were put, but the year-end discussions showed little prospect of that in the near future. The arrangement made a small contribution to alleviating the miseries of ordinary Iraqis. It also was notori-

ous that a considerable but unknown quantity of Iraqi oil was making its way to world markets in small ships sneaking out by way of Iran's territorial waters.

Saddam Hussein's eldest son, Uday Hussein, who had been wounded in an attempt on his life in December 1996, surfaced again in a television interview on March 10. Rumor had exaggerated the extent of his injuries, but it seemed likely he would have a permanent limp. Uday was a man widely disliked and feared. His assailants remained unknown. The 60th birthday of Saddam Hussein on April 28 was celebrated with enthusiasm.

A Russian plane carrying five tons of medical supplies and more than a score of Russian legislators flew to Baghdad, with UN permission, on December 25; passengers and crew received a heroes' welcome.

As 1997 ended, the U.S. State Department said it had "credible reports" that Iraq summarily had executed "hundreds, if not thousands" of political detainees recently.

Northern Iraq. Iraq's brief incursion in late August and early September 1996 into northern Iraq, and its occupation of Erbil in support of Massoud Barzani's Kurdish Democratic Party (KDP) in its perennial conflict with Jalal Talabani's Patriotic Union of Kurdistan (PUK), had served Saddam Hussein well. Large numbers of the Iraqi opposition based there were executed, forced to flee into exile, or totally demoralized. Western activities in the region also were disrupted fatally. Attempts by the United States to bring about reconciliation between the KDP and the PUK continued, although without much success. Leaders of the two factions held a U.S.-sponsored meeting in Ankara on May 14.

However, perhaps the most important long-run aspect of the complex situation in northern Iraq was the intervention by Turkey, which was battling forces—located across the border—of the Kurdistan Workers Party (PKK), the semiterrorist organization of Turkish Kurds in chronic revolt against the Ankara government. Turkish cross-border incursions had occurred in earlier years. Two

---

IRAQ • Information Highlights

Official Name: Republic of Iraq.
Location: Southwest Asia.
Area: 168,754 sq mi (437 072 km²).
Population (mid-1997 est.): 21,200,000.
Chief City (1987 census): Baghdad, the capital, 3,844,608.
Government: *Head of state and government,* Saddam Hussein, president (took office July 1979). *Legislature* (unicameral)—National Assembly.
Monetary Unit: Dinar (0.311 dinar equals U.S.$1, principal rate, July 1997).

Saddam Hussein continued to dominate events in Iraq during 1997. His 60th birthday on April 28 was celebrated with lavish street entertainment, left.

© Scott Dan Peterson/Gamma-Liaison

distinctive features in 1997 were the tight control of information about events and the apparent size of the intervention. Estimates held that between 25,000 and 50,000 Turkish troops were involved, with appropriate air support. The Turkish troops acted with support of the KDP—and also to some extent of the PUK. The Turkish presence inside the Iraqi border was so consistent a feature of the year that it was possible there was an intention to create a Turkish "security zone" there.

Forbidden Flights and Oil Deals. In defiance of a vaguely worded sanctions ban on air traffic into or out of Iraq, on April 9 an Iraqi aircraft carried more than 100 pilgrims to Saudi Arabia, landing at Jiddah. On April 13, Iraq defiantly claimed the right to operate civilian aircraft abroad.

Also in April, Iraq and Russia signed a major oil deal. Russia would invest $200 million over three years to develop a new oil field, to which it would have privileged access for 22 years. Russia maintained the deal did not breach sanctions, as no money would change hands before sanctions were lifted—but also undertook to work to that end. A similar deal with China was pending, and it seemed likely others would follow.

End-of-Year Confrontation. Beginning at the end of October, Iraq embarked on a daring series of sanctions-testing actions. These concerned UNSCOM, the UN Special Commission charged with carrying out inspections into the Iraqi arms program. On October 29, Iraq declared that Americans no longer would be permitted to work on the UNSCOM team of inspectors; they were given one week to leave. When they withdrew to UNSCOM's base in Bahrain, the UN withdrew all its team members. The United States augmented its already strong forces in the Gulf, and tension

mounted. On November 12 the UN Security Council instituted a travel ban on Iraqi officials who did not cooperate with the inspections. But it was clear that if any military action were taken against Iraq, it probably would be taken by the United States alone. Iraq declared it would shoot down any spy plane over its territory; but no such threat was carried out.

On November 19 a surprise agreement was concluded in Moscow between Russia and Iraq that seemingly defused the near crisis by permitting the return of the inspectors. On its side, Russia undertook to press for the end of sanctions. However, the next obstacle Iraq threw in was to declare that certain so-called presidential palaces and "sovereign areas" never would be open to inspection. These appeared to number around 70, but up to the end of the year no precise list had been provided by Iraq, nor in fact had the inspectors been hampered in their work.

The basic difficulty in shaping any strong response was that in the Security Council the United States, though supported by Britain, was really the sole enthusiast for increasing or even maintaining sanctions. France and Russia had opposed sanctions for years. The resolutions passed by the Security Council on the subject continually had to be watered down from the preferred U.S. versions to make it possible for them to be passed. Typically, the one passed on December 23 said that failure to allow the inspectors into any site was "unacceptable and a clear violation of the relevant resolutions"; but, at the insistence of Russia, the statement did not "condemn" Iraq's action.

See also MIDDLE EAST.

ARTHUR CAMPBELL TURNER
University of California, Riverside

IRELAND

In 1997, Ireland witnessed a major change of government and underwent a presidential election.

Politics. The erosion of support for John Bruton's Fine Gael, Labour, and Democratic Left coalition government came to a head at the June 6 elections. Although Fine Gael increased its Dail seats from 43 to 54, Labour lost 14. The leading opposition party, Fianna Fail—led by Bertie Ahern—formed a coalition government with the Progressive Democrats and a number of independents. Among the leading members of Ahern's cabinet were Progressive Democrat leader Mary Harney, Ray Burke, David Andrews, Mary O'Rourke, Charlie McCreevy, and John O'Donoghue.

Ahern, 46—who first entered the Dail in 1977 and was minister of finance (1991–94)—promised to press for a peaceful solution in Northern Ireland and said he intended to lower taxes and reduce crime. For the first time in the republic's history, a winning candidate from Sinn Fein, the political wing of the Irish Republican Army (IRA), took up his Dail seat. Unlike previous Sinn Fein representatives who refused to serve, Caoimhghin O Caolain actively engaged in his parliamentary duties.

A major political scandal erupted in April when Ben Dunne, the wealthy former chairman of Dunne's Stores, a chain of supermarkets, admitted he had doled out some $4.3 million to his favorite politicians over the course of ten years. The leading recipient—reportedly more than $2 million—was former Prime Minister Charles Haughey, longtime leader of Fianna Fail. Haughey, who previously denied receiving the money, said on July 15 that he had forgotten about the payments. Although the electoral law of Ireland permits cash donations to politicians, tax questions remained. In October, Haughey put his vacation retreat—the island of Inishvickillane—up for sale to help pay taxes and legal bills stemming from the donation. Further investigations were planned.

On February 27 the government removed the last obstacle to legalizing divorce. Under the new law, those seeking divorce must prove irreconcilable differences and that they have lived apart for four of the previous five years.

In October, Foreign Minister Ray Burke resigned over allegations that he was involved in several financial scandals. In November, Dick Spring announced his resignation as leader of the Labour Party. On November 13, Ruairi Quinn was elected to replace him, defeating Brendan Howlin 37 to 27. Quinn said he was interested in Labour's joining a coalition government after the next general election.

Presidential Election. On March 12, President Mary Robinson announced she would not seek another seven-year term. The highly respected Robinson left for Geneva in mid-September to take up duties as the United Nations (UN) high commissioner for human rights. (*See also* BIOGRAPHY—*Robinson, Mary.*)

The presidential-election campaign began in August with rumors that former Prime Minister Albert Reynolds and Social Democratic and Labour Party (SDLP) leader John Hume might run, but within a month the field was down to four women and one man. With only 47.6% of Irish voters turning out on October 31, the Fianna Fail candidate, law professor Mary McAleese, won with 48.7%. Mary Banotti of the Fine Gael—a member of the European Parliament—garnered 41.3%. Trailing behind were pop-music star Dana (Rosemary Scallon) and Labour candidate Adi Roche. McAleese, a Catholic from Northern Ireland, was considered more conservative than Robinson. At her November 11 inauguration in St. Patrick's Hall, Dublin Castle, she promised to build bridges across the divisions of class and religion and help reconcile the "two traditions" in the north.

The North. Widespread consensus about the need to resolve the Northern Ireland conflict peacefully spurred the IRA in mid-July to renew its cease-fire after one and a half years of sporadic violence. Irish and British politicians hailed the decision as the long-awaited precondition of peace talks. Despite some hard-line Unionist holdouts, peace talks in Belfast resumed in September, raising hopes for an end to the 28-year-old conflict in which

---

IRELAND • Information Highlights

Official Name: Ireland.
Location: Island in the eastern North Atlantic Ocean.
Area: 27,135 sq mi (70 280 km²).
Population (mid-1997 est.): 3,600,000.
Chief Cities (1991 census): Dublin, the capital, 915,516 (incl. suburbs); Cork, 174,400; Limerick, 75,436.
Government: *Head of state,* Mary McAleese, president (took office Nov. 11, 1997). *Head of government,* Bertie Ahern, prime minister (elected June 26, 1997). *Legislature*—Parliament: Senate (Seanad Eireann) and House of Representatives (Dail Eireann).
Monetary Unit: Pound (0.7004 pound equals U.S.$1, Dec. 31, 1997).
Gross Domestic Product (1995 est. U.S.$): $54,600,000,-000 (purchasing power parity).
Economic Indexes (1996, 1990 = 100): *Consumer Prices,* all items, 115.1; food, 112.5. *Industrial Production,* 171.
Foreign Trade (1996 U.S.$): *Imports,* $35,763,000,000; *exports,* $48,154,000,000.

some 3,200 had died. (*See also* GREAT BRITAIN.)

The Economy. Ireland's rising productivity, falling unemployment, increase of some 14% in government revenue, and projected 7% to 8% growth in gross national product (GNP) drew praise from *The Economist*, *The Wall Street Journal*, and *Fortune*, and earned the Irish economy the label "Celtic Tiger."

In December, Finance Minister Charlie McCreevy said Ireland would meet debt requirements for membership in the European single currency by 2000. Despite signs of prosperity, high living costs in the greater Dublin area created pockets of hard-core poverty.

Famine Anniversary. Various ceremonies were held to recognize the 150th anniversary of the worst year of the Great Famine—"the Black '47." At a May concert in Millstreet, County Cork, the actor Gabriel Byrne read a statement from British Prime Minister Tony Blair expressing regret that Britain had failed to provide adequate relief at the time.

L. PERRY CURTIS, JR., *Brown University*

ISRAEL

Prime Minister Benjamin Netanyahu of Israel faced several domestic and foreign-policy crises during 1997. Charges of corruption led to the investigation of several ministers and recriminations within Netanyahu's Likud Party and among the eight-party government coalition. Relations with American Jewry were embittered by disagreements over the authority of Israel's Orthodox rabbinate. Although agreement was reached with the Palestinian Authority on Israel's withdrawal from most of Hebron, the peace process was endangered by terrorist bomb attacks and by Israel's continued construction of housing for Jewish settlers in Jerusalem and the West Bank. U.S. efforts to restart peace talks proved difficult, despite Secretary of State Madeleine Albright's visit to the region. Israel's relations with Jordan—its closest Arab ally—were strained after a failed assassination attempt by Israeli intelligence agents in Amman.

Domestic Affairs. Netanyahu's January agreement with Palestinian Authority President Yasir Arafat to withdraw from the West Bank city of Hebron became the focus of a major political scandal. An Israeli journalist reported that Netanyahu appointed Roni Bar-On—a friend of Aryeh Deri—as attorney general in exchange for the ten Knesset votes of Deri's Shas party in support of the Hebron agreement. Bar-On, in turn, was believed to have agreed to accept a plea bargain from Deri, who was charged with bribery.

The day after Bar-On's appointment, he resigned, and Deri, Netanyahu, and others were investigated by the new attorney general, Elyakim Rubinstein. After several weeks, sufficient evidence was found to indict only

Benjamin Netanyahu went on TV after Israeli federal prosecutors announced on April 20, 1997, that there was not sufficient evidence to pursue charges against the prime minister concerning allegations connected with his appointment of an attorney general.

© Zoom 77/AP/Wide World Photos

Ehud Barak, 55-year-old former army chief of staff, visited the Wailing Wall on June 4, 1997—the day he was chosen to succeed Shimon Peres as leader of Israel's Labor Party.

Deri. Several cabinet members threatened to withdraw support from the government because the scandal could have resulted in a call for new elections.

The Hebron agreement, opposed by militant nationalist factions in Likud and Jewish West Bank settlers, precipitated the resignation of Science Minister Benjamin Begin, son of former Prime Minister Menahem Begin. In June, Finance Minister Dan Meridor—a longtime Netanyahu rival for Likud leadership—resigned over differences with Netanyahu regarding financial policies, Hebron, and the Bar-On affair.

By November quarrels within Likud between supporters of Netanyahu and those opposed to his policies threatened to disrupt the party. The disaffection was brought to a head when Netanyahu attempted to replace the primary system for choosing Likud candidates for the Knesset with selection by the much smaller Central Committee. The upheaval led to the resignation of the Russian-born director general of the prime minister's office, Avgdor Lieberman.

Israel and the Palestinian Authority initialed the January 14 Hebron protocol, which provided for withdrawal from 80% of Hebron. Occupied by some 500 mostly Orthodox Jewish settlers, Hebron is home to some 150,000 Arabs. The disputed tomb of the patriarchs, revered by Jews and Muslims, was to remain under Israeli control, although Muslims would be given access. Israeli troops would continue to guard the Jewish settlers. The agreement also called for three further pullbacks during 1997–98 from West Bank areas designated by Israel as Palestinian.

About 9% of the West Bank was controlled by the Palestinian Authority, with 27% under joint Israeli and Palestinian rule. The rest of the territory was controlled by the Israeli army. The Israeli cabinet voted for the Hebron agreement 11 to 7 on January 16, while the Knesset approved it 87 to 17, with one abstention and 15 absent. A few days later, Arafat paid his first visit to Hebron since Israel occupied the city in 1967.

Relations between the Israeli government and Arafat began to deteriorate soon after the Hebron deal. Netanyahu announced that he initially planned to withdraw from only a small sector of the West Bank, sparking unrest among Palestinians, who had expected to receive up to 80% of the occupied area. The crisis intensified during March after the suicide bombing of a Tel-Aviv cafe by a Palestinian from the Muslim fundamentalist group Hamas. More Hamas bombings in Jerusalem during July and September brought the peace process to a halt. Relations between Netanyahu and Arafat were severed; Israel imposed strict restrictions on Palestinian travel in the West Bank—banning Arab laborers from entering Israel—and cut off payment to the Palestinian Authority of funds due under the Oslo agreements.

Relations worsened further when the prime minister ordered construction of a new Jewish development at Har Homa, Jerusalem, and the extension of a West Bank housing project in or near Jewish settlements. Palestinians charged that the additional construction violated the Oslo agreement. Netanyahu insisted that Israel was within its rights to build in Jerusalem, its capital, and to provide more homes for expanding population in the Jewish settlements.

As a result of U.S. pressure, Netanyahu called for a halt in August to the plans of an

---

ISRAEL • Information Highlights

Official Name: State of Israel.
Location: Southwest Asia.
Area: 8,019 sq mi (20 770 km²).
Population (mid-1997 est.): 5,800,000.
Chief Cities (Dec. 31, 1994, est.): Jerusalem, the capital, 578,800 (including East Jerusalem); Tel Aviv–Jaffa, 355,200; Haifa, 246,700.
Government: *Head of state,* Ezer Weizman, president (took office March 1993). *Head of government,* Benjamin Netanyahu, prime minister (sworn in June 18, 1996). *Legislature* (unicameral)—Knesset.
Monetary Unit: Shekel (3.5275 shekels equal U.S.$1, Dec. 31, 1997).
Gross Domestic Product (1995 est. U.S.$): $80,100,000,-000 (purchasing power parity).
Economic Indexes (1996, 1990 = 100): *Consumer Prices,* all items, 203.4; food, 176.6. *Industrial Production,* 151.
Foreign Trade (1996 U.S.$): *Imports,* $30,603,000,000; *exports,* $20,474,000,000.

American Jewish millionaire for developing property in the Arab district of Ras al-Amud, Jerusalem. Netanyahu's decision was attacked by several members of Likud.

Israel's three religious parties—with 23 of the 120 Knesset seats and four of the 18 cabinet posts—began to pressure the government to pass into law the traditional "understanding" that gave the Orthodox Jewish rabbinate control of personal-status matters, including marriage, divorce, and conversions to Judaism. Control by the Orthodox rabbinate excluded Reform and Conservative rabbis from officially performing these functions within Israel. The Orthodox demand drew strong protests from U.S. Jews, most of whom are Reform or Conservative. Not wanting to alienate American Jewry, but needing Orthodox votes, Netanyahu appointed a commission to find a compromise. The Orthodox rabbinate refused to accept the commission's recommendation, however, and the issue awaited further action.

Israel's economic ministers predicted a tepid performance in 1997 and 1998. After the economy grew by 6% during most of the 1990s, they expected the growth rate to fall to about 2.5% in 1997 and 1998. The World Economic Forum's 1997 Global Competitiveness Report ranked Israel 24th among the 53 economies it rated, behind Ireland and Thailand. The report also ranked Israel 44th in "government," citing high taxes, government spending and regulations, an overevaluated exchange rate, and subtle trade barriers. However, Israel did receive a high credit rating and in April was added to the International Monetary Fund (IMF) list of 23 industrialized nations.

In November, when unemployment reached a four-year high of 8.1%, Finance Minister Yaacov Neeman warned that "unemployment is the number-one problem in Israel today." Nevertheless, the labor ministry pointed out that there were between 150,000 and 200,000 imported foreign workers in Israel, about half of them illegally. They came mainly from the Third World and economically depressed countries of Europe.

In May, Israel's Labor Party voted down a proposal to designate former Prime Minister Shimon Peres for the new post of party president. In June recently retired Army Chief of Staff Ehud Barak was elected, with 57% of the vote, to lead the party; he thus became the probable next challenger to Netanyahu.

Foreign Affairs. Deteriorating relations with the Palestinians caused low-level diplomatic contacts with Yemen and Morocco to be suspended, and there were harsh words from Egypt and Jordan. After Israel's decision to build at Har Homa, King Hussein wrote a letter to Netanyahu warning that he could not continue as a friend and partner when "I sense an intent to destroy all I worked to build between our peoples and states."

Relations were strained further in March when a Jordanian soldier shot and killed seven Israeli schoolgirls participating in a class visit to a border site known as the Island of Peace. Hussein sought to make amends by personal visits to the victims' parents.

Israel-Jordan relations were brought to the breaking point in September following a failed attempt by Israeli secret service (Mossad) agents to assassinate Hamas leader Khaled Meshal in Amman. Israel had accused Meshal of planning the Jerusalem suicide bombings. Hussein said the attempt infringed on Jordan's sovereignty and threatened to cut all ties with Israel, but behind-the-scenes negotiations prevented a breakdown. In exchange for Jordan's release of the Mossad agents, Israel ended the eight-year imprisonment of Hamas founder Sheik Ahmed Yassin and released 22 other Palestinian prisoners.

The United States attempted to rescue the peace process during Secretary of State Albright's September visit to the region. Albright criticized Netanyahu for policies that undercut the process and Arafat for insufficient measures to deter terrorism. She called on Netanyahu to take "time out" on construction in the occupied territories. After Albright left Israel, U.S. Ambassador Dennis Ross was able to restart low-level meetings between Israel and the Palestinians.

Israel attempted to strengthen its position in the region through close military ties with Turkey. Talks in April between Israeli Foreign Minister David Levy and the chief of the Turkish general staff, Gen. Ismail Hakki Karadayi, reinforced a $600 million plan for Israel to modernize the Turkish air force. In October, Poland signed an agreement to buy several million dollars' worth of Israeli-made military equipment.

DON PERETZ
Professor Emeritus, Binghamton University

ITALY

During 1997 the chief tasks facing Premier Romano Prodi's coalition government—formed after parliamentary elections in April 1996—were revising the 1947 constitution and cutting expenditures so that Italy's deficit

ITALY • Information Highlights

Official Name: Italian Republic.
Location: Southern Europe.
Area: 116,305 sq mi (301 230 km²).
Population (mid-1997 est.): 57,400,000.
Chief Cities (Dec. 31, 1993): Rome, the capital, 2,687,881; Milan, 1,334,171; Naples, 1,061,583.
Government: *Head of state,* Oscar Luigi Scalfaro, president (sworn in May 28, 1992). *Head of government,* Romano Prodi, prime minister (sworn in May 18, 1996). *Legislature*—Parliament: Senate and Chamber of Deputies.
Monetary Unit: Lira (1,767.00 lire equal U.S.$1, Dec. 31, 1997).
Gross Domestic Product (1995 est. U.S.$): $1,088,600,-000,000 (purchasing power parity).
Economic Indexes (1996, 1990 = 100): *Consumer Prices,* all items, 132.6. *Industrial Production,* 105.
Foreign Trade (1996 U.S.$): *Imports,* $206,912,000,000; *exports,* $250,992,000,000.

would not exceed 3% of gross domestic product (GDP)—the European economic and monetary union (EMU) requirement. By December, Italy's strong economy made 1999 EMU charter membership a likely prospect.

Politics. The cornerstone of the center-left "Olive Tree" coalition was the Democratic Party of the Left (PDS)—led by Massimo D'Alema, and made up of former communists. D'Alema, who prudently refrained from taking any ministerial post for himself, insisted that the premiership go to Prodi. Prodi was a distinguished economist and broadly acceptable Catholic leader of the Italian Popular Party (PPI)—heir to the left wing of the old Christian Democratic Party. Prodi's center-left coalition also included a few Greens and independents.

Prodi's coalition government lacked a clear parliamentary majority and depended for survival on 35 deputies in the far-left Refounded Communist Party (PRC) led by Fausto Bertinotti—which chose to stay outside the government and resisted most government efforts to bring about a radical overhaul of Italy's costly pension system.

The opposition center-right bloc "Freedom Alliance" was led by Milan media tycoon and former Prime Minister Silvio Berlusconi and his Forza Italia Party. It also included the post-Fascist National Alliance Party, and the right wing of the old Christian Democratic Party.

Mayoral elections in April, May, and November produced impressive victories for the Olive Tree coalition. By year's end, it controlled nine of Italy's ten leading cities. Milan was the exception. In the same elections, the secessionist Northern League (LN) suffered humiliating defeats in Mantua, Pavia, Goriza, and Venice.

Another important Olive Tree triumph occurred in a November by-election near Florence, when Antonio Di Pietro won a seat in the Senate by a landslide. Di Pietro, the best known of the magistrates who five years earlier launched the "clean-hands" campaign that overthrew Italy's old political establishment, was being mentioned as future president under an amended constitution.

On May 6, Prodi won a confidence vote linked to a proposed minibudget. In backing the government, the Chamber of Deputies approved a controversial $9.1 billion budget package, which contained spending cuts and onetime tax hikes designed to help Italy qualify for the proposed EMU.

After a national referendum on June 16 attracted an unusually low turnout, politicians called for stricter rules governing referenda. Only 30% of eligible voters cast ballots in the June referendum, which dealt with such varied topics as hunting, privatization, the media, and the role of magistrates. A 50% turnout was required for the results to become legally binding. In recent years the frequency of referenda in Italy had mushroomed, to the growing annoyance of voters.

On October 10 the small PRC brought down the government for a few days, arguing that Prodi's tightfisted, pro-Europe policies were a betrayal of the working classes and a sop to globalized capitalism. But when confronted by popular indignation over the fact that the fall of the government would bring about an explosion of the budgetary deficit and prevent Italy from qualifying for EMU membership, the Communists beat a quick retreat. On October 14 they allowed the government to be reinstated after it agreed to reduce the proposed $2.5 billion in welfare cuts by $290 million in the 1998 budget, and promised to introduce legislation to reduce the legal working week from 40 hours to 35 hours by the year 2001. "In this crisis there were no winners or losers," Prodi told a news conference on October 14. "Italy and good sense won." Many observers doubted that the workweek will be cut to 35 hours by 2001.

Northern League. The LN—led by Umberto Bossi, an erratic figure who sought independence for Italy's prosperous industrial north—stood apart on the political right. In September 1996, Bossi had proclaimed the "independent" state of "Padania" in the northeast, with its "capital" at Mantua. The league's program tapped into the resentment in the affluent northeast over Rome's use of its tax revenues to subsidize the economically depressed regions of southern Italy. League supporters believed that an independent Padania, where Italy's most efficient indus-

Italian troops were part of a UN peacekeeping force that was dispatched to Albania as the East European nation was rocked by violence and political chaos early in 1997. Italy's participation in the mission had been a subject of parliamentary debate as the Romano Prodi government survived confidence motions in both chambers of Parliament on the issue.

© Luca Bruno/AP/Wide World Photos

tries were located, could compete successfully with northern European countries.

By mid-February 1997, Bossi moderated his demands, referring to the need for "consensual secession." He indicated that a series of referenda could decide whether northerners supported his program.

On May 9, armed separatist rebels who advocated political independence for Venice scaled and occupied the 300-ft (91.5-m) bell tower in the city's central Piazza San Marco. They timed the seizure to coincide with the 200th anniversary of the 1797 fall of the 1,000-year-old Venetian Republic to Napoleon Bonaparte's French forces. Italian paramilitary forces raided the tower seven hours later and took eight separatists into custody. No one was hurt and no shots were fired. Bossi distanced himself from the episode, declaring, "This is no way to stage a revolution."

As a result of judicial rulings on June 9 and June 23, Bossi was ordered to stand trial in March 1998 on charges of having ordered his supporters to "identify and pursue right-wing voters," and of having insulted President Oscar Luigi Scalfaro in public statements made in 1996.

Pension Reform and the EMU. On November 1 the government pushed through modest pension reform. In the past, Italy's unusually generous pension system absorbed 14% of GDP, against the European Union's (EU's) average of 10%. Under the new reforms, the cost would be $2.3 billion, down from the $2.9 billion in the original budget. Italians still could retire at age 53, provided they had made insurance contributions for 35 years. In 2008 the retirement age would rise to 57.

Meanwhile, the European Commission in Brussels revised downward its 1997 deficit forecast for Italy from 3.2% to 3% of GDP, bringing it under the ceiling set by the Maastricht Treaty for entry into the new EMU. In 1996, Italy's deficit stood at 6.8% of GDP, one of the highest percentages in Europe.

Germany, whose currency was Europe's strongest, long had been dubious about Italy's ability to cut its deficit sufficiently to qualify for EMU membership. Most Italians—who were enthusiastic about EMU membership—expected participation to bring lower interest rates and a more efficient banking system.

Proposed Constitutional Reforms. In November the *bicamerale*—a 70-member parliamentary advisory commission for reforming the 1947 Constitution of the Italian Republic—made its report after many compromises, recommending a number of major changes, all of which would require final approval from both chambers of Parliament. The reforms—which would be put to a popular referendum following parliamentary approval—would make Italy a federal state, with the central government controlling foreign policy, defense, education, the environment, and justice, while being responsible for collecting less than one half of total tax revenues. There would be a semipresidential system, whereby the president of the republic—previously elected by both houses of Parliament—would be chosen by the people for a six-year term. The president would select the prime minister and would be in charge of foreign policy and defense. In addition, the lower house of Parliament would have 400 to 500 deputies instead of 630. The Senate—to be composed of 200 elected members and the same number representing Italy's 20 regions—would have less power than it currently did. A reform of the judiciary would split the self-governing body of the magistrates into two equal groups—one half for judges, the other half for prosecutors.

Meanwhile, Italy's major political parties reached agreement to rescind a clause in the present constitution that bars exiled male descendants of Italy's last king, Umberto II (1946), from returning to Italy; this allowed Vittorio Emanuele, the heir to the nonexistent throne, to return after his 51-year exile.

A new law to regulate the voting system for Parliament provides for a combination of single-member constituencies plus some proportional representation of political parties.

Foreign Affairs. On April 10 and 12, Prodi's government survived confidence votes in the two chambers of Parliament. Scalfaro had called for these votes in response to a series of divisive debates over proposals to send 2,500 Italian troops to Albania as part of a European peacekeeping force of 6,000. Although the PRC had refused to support such a mission, Bertinotti decided at the last moment not to let the issue bring down the Prodi government. (*See* ALBANIA.)

In an official report on August 8, the government confirmed that paratroopers of Italy's Folgore brigade had tortured Somali civilians during a United Nations (UN) mission in Somalia in 1993. The abuses included sexual assaults and murders of unarmed local people. The panel concluded that Italian soldiers had committed the atrocities, and it suggested that nonmilitary observers should accompany soldiers on future peacekeeping missions. The case had caused an uproar in Italy, partly because the Folgore unit was part of the peacekeeping force in Albania.

Other News. The government's campaign against organized crime chalked up more successes when some 70 Mafia members were arrested in Sicily in March, while others were nabbed in Calabria. On June 6, Pietro Aglieri, reputedly the most wanted man in the Sicilian Mafia, also was arrested.

On July 22 an Italian military court in Rome convicted and sentenced Nazi war criminal Erich Priebke, 83, and a codefendant, Karl Hass, 84, for their participation in the World War II massacre (March 24, 1944) of 335 Italian civilians in the Ardeatine Caves near Rome. Both were former SS officers. In 1996 an Italian military court had found Priebke guilty of the massacre (a crime to which he openly had confessed), but not guilty of "cruelty and premeditation." An Italian statute of limitations resulted in Priebke's being released after the 1996 trial. Public outrage at his release led to a second trial in 1997 in another Rome military court on charges of "crimes against humanity"—a category not subject to any statute of limitations. This time Priebke was given a 15-year sentence, but because of a long-standing amnesty law, this was reduced to five years. He actually served only 18 months because of time he already had spent in jail. Hass was sentenced to ten years and eight months, but his sentence was suspended under the amnesty law.

On December 4 former Prime Minister Berlusconi was convicted of falsifying the price of a film company bought by his Fininvest company, in order to create a slush fund.

On April 11 a fire damaged Turin's San Giovanni Cathedral and its Guarini Chapel, which housed the Shroud of Turin, believed by many to be the burial cloth of Jesus Christ. The shroud was saved by a fireman who broke through four layers of bulletproof glass to reach the relic.

Two earthquakes with magnitudes of 5.5 and 6.0, respectively, struck central Italy on September 26, killing at least ten persons and injuring more than 100. Badly damaged was the Basilica of St. Francis in Assisi, which contained priceless 13th- and 14th-century frescoes by Giotto di Bondone and Giovanni Cimabue. There were more than 400 aftershocks. About 100,000 residents were forced to camp outside for weeks in cold weather. The government set aside $500 million to help the victims.

Vittorio Mussolini, eldest son of Fascist dictator Benito Mussolini, died on June 12 at the age of 81. On July 15, Gianni Versace, 50, an internationally famed Italian fashion designer, was gunned down in front of his mansion in Miami Beach, FL. (*See also* FASHION—*Gianni Versace.*)

CHARLES F. DELZELL, *Vanderbilt University*

JAPAN

In 1997, as Japan celebrated the 50th anniversary of its constitution, Prime Minister Ryutaro Hashimoto's ruling Liberal Democratic Party (LDP) strengthened its position in the nation's parliament, dealt with a shaky financial system, and sought to improve trade relations with the United States and relations in general with Russia and China.

Domestic Affairs

In 1997 the conservative LDP, which had dominated politics from 1955 to 1993, regained control of the important lower house of the Diet, Japan's parliament.

Party Politics. On January 20 the Diet opened its session by hearing Prime Minister Hashimoto's annual address. Prominent in a plurality was the LDP. As a result of a general election for the (lower) House of Representatives in October 1996, the LDP had made progress in its bid to return to full power. Even with some independents recruited in early 1997, however, the party still fell short of a majority of seats. Nor did it enjoy a majority in the (upper) House of Councillors. To pass legislation, the LDP relied on its informal allies, the Social Democratic Party (SDP) and the New Party (Sakigake), who agreed to support the LDP on a bill-by-bill basis. Arrayed against the coalition were the New Frontier Party (Shinshinto) and the Democratic Party of Japan (DPJ). When cooperating, they formed a formidable opposition (193 seats in the lower house). Of course, the Japan Communist Party (JCP), with 26 seats, often voted against the LDP cabinet. After the 1996 election, the LDP-led coalition reelected Prime Minister Hashimoto. In his January policy speech, Hashimoto sketched a program of deregulation and pledged to slash central- and local-government deficits to 3% of gross domestic product (GDP) by fiscal year 2005. It was estimated that Japan's long-term public debt reached $3.8 trillion by the end of March. On April 1 citizens felt the first impact of the government plan, when the national consumption tax was raised from 3% to 5%.

When the Diet adjourned in June, the coalition successfully had navigated through an impressive legislative agenda. Bills passed included revision of the antimonopoly law and the commercial code, privatization of the Nippon Telegraph & Telephone Corp. (NT&T), the $649 billion fiscal 1997 budget, and amendment of a 1952 law providing land for U.S. forces based on Okinawa. On April 17 the Diet had passed legislation enabling the state to override opposition by some 3,000 landowners to renewal of leases for 12 bases used by the U.S. military. The action came a week before the prime minister's scheduled summit meeting in Washington and saved him embarrassment. On April 22 the lower house passed a parallel resolution urging the government to make every effort to persuade the United States to scale down bases on Okinawa, where 27,000 troops were stationed.

Workers tried to prevent crude oil from drifting ashore at the Edo River after a Japanese-owned supertanker gashed its hull in Tokyo Bay in early July 1997. Japan had been struck by an earlier oil spill, caused by the breakup of a Russian tanker, in January.

© Shizuo Kambayashi/AP/Wide World Photos

Executives of Yamaichi Securities met the press in late November 1997 after the securities firm, one of Japan's largest, announced that it was closing as the result of a liquidity crisis.

The strangest aspect of this episode was the fact that two opposition parties, the New Frontier Party and the DJP, supported the LDP initiative, while a member of the informal coalition, the SDP, opposed it.

On September 5 the LDP returned to majority status (251 seats) in the lower house for the first time in four years. The gain was attained by recruiting independents and welcoming members of the opposition who earlier had defected from the LDP. Hashimoto immediately began a campaign to be renamed president of the LDP. Unopposed, he was endorsed officially in a party meeting on September 11, becoming the first leader to be reelected since 1984. The same day, the prime minister reorganized the cabinet with attention to the powerful factions within the LDP. He retained Finance Minister Hiroshi Mitsuzuka, Health Minister Junichiro Koizumi, and Defense Agency chief Fumio Kyuma. Conspicuously absent was the outspoken Seiroku Kajiyama, who had served as chief cabinet secretary.

Responding to a strong lobbying effort by the faction headed by former Prime Minister Yasuhiro Nakasone, Hashimoto named Takayuki (Koko) Sato as chief of the Management & Coordination Agency to supervise reform and deregulation. Sato had served 11 terms in the lower house but had never been a minister because of a suspended sentence for bribery in the Lockheed payoff scandal of the

1970s. Only 12 days after taking office, Sato resigned to save face for Hashimoto.

Economy. Although the Japanese continued to feel the effects of a stubborn recession, Tokyo was encouraged by an Organization for Economic Cooperation and Development (OECD) June estimate that the economy would grow at a 2.3% rate in 1997. In fact the GDP in the April–June quarter, according to the Economic Planning Agency (EPA), shrank from that of the previous quarter at an annualized rate of 11.2% in real terms. Part of the decline, the EPA noted, was caused by a slump in sales after a buying spree just before the tax rise. Despite the sag in private consumption, employment and income trends appeared to be favorable. The annualized real-term value of goods and services totaled $3.9 trillion.

At the end of fiscal 1996 (March 31, 1997), however, the unemployment rate stood at 3.3%. By May it matched a record-high 3.5% (2.44 million jobless)—still a modest level compared with those in other G-8 industrial nations. Similarly, inflation remained low by world standards. In August the consumer-price index (CPI) stood at 102.1 (1995=100); but by September, Tokyo prices—among the highest in the world—had risen 2.1% in only one year. They reflected the lingering effects of the tax increase as well as increased costs of medical insurance shifted to individuals.

Meanwhile, the Diet had become engaged in a debate over a budget package compiled in December 1996. In January, Ichiro Ozawa, former LDP member and now president of the New Frontier Party, criticized the plan as incapable of dealing with the "abnormal economic situation." In fact, opposition weakness made possible an early passage of the $649 billion budget on March 28, a few days before the start of the new fiscal year. The public

---

JAPAN • Information Highlights

Official Name: Japan.
Location: East Asia.
Area: 145,882 sq mi (377 835 km²).
Population (mid-1997 est.): 126,100,000.
Chief Cities (Oct. 1, 1995 census, metropolitan areas): Tokyo, the capital (city proper), 7,967,614; Yokohama, 3,307,136; Osaka, 2,602,421; Nagoya, 2,152,184.
Government: *Head of state,* Akihito, emperor (acceded Jan. 9, 1989). *Head of government,* Ryutaro Hashimoto, prime minister (took office January 1996). *Legislature*—Diet: House of Councillors and House of Representatives.
Monetary Unit: Yen (130.42 yen equal U.S.$1, Dec. 31, 1997).
Gross Domestic Product (1995 est. U.S.$): $2,679,200,-000,000 (purchasing power parity).
Economic Indexes (1996, 1990 = 100): *Consumer Prices,* all items, 107.1; food, 106.0. *Industrial Production,* 98.
Foreign Trade (1996 U.S.$): *Imports,* $349,173,000,000; *exports,* $410,924,000,000.

would supply an additional $75 billion through increases in taxes and medical bills. And despite austerity, the package allocated $49 billion in defense-related expenditures, up 2.1% from the previous fiscal year.

During the year, the LDP moved to reduce traditional pump-priming measures such as public works and personal-income-tax cuts in favor of revival by deregulation and reform. On May 15 the cabinet announced its Action Plan for Economic Structural Reform and Creation, with the goal of cutting costs to international competitive levels by 2001.

On July 30, Finance Minister Mitsuzuka imposed severe penalties on Dai-Ichi Kangyo, the nation's third-largest commercial bank, and on Nomura Securities, one of the nation's four largest brokerage firms, for payoffs to corporate racketeers. But a more intense shock to the financial system occurred in November, when Yamaichi Securities, Japan's oldest brokerage firm, announced that it was going out of business—a move that would leave behind some $24 billion in liabilities to customers and add 7,000 people to the unemployment rolls. The firm's downfall was the result of the disclosure that it too had made payoffs to corporate racketeers, causing customers to move their accounts elsewhere. Following this event, shares of some leading banks fell heavily, and there were fears that the OECD growth-rate prediction of 2.3% for 1997 was overly optimistic.

In mid-December the prime minister announced a $15.4 billion income-tax cut to revive the economy. The sale of government bonds would finance the one-year cut.

Society. A significant if subtle aspect of Japanese life was underlined by a Management & Coordination Agency report released September 14. Elders (age 65 or older) reached a total of 19.73 million (15.6% of the population). Earlier, on May 3, Children's Day, the agency had reported that the number of children (age 15 or under) had dropped to 19.52 million, the lowest level since the first national census of 1920.

The Japanese were shocked to learn of assaults on three primary schoolchildren and the murder of two others in Kobe. One involved the gruesome killing of an 11-year-old by a 14-year-old. A judge ordered the 14-year-old boy to a psychiatric facility.

In 1997, Japan experienced two serious oil spills. One, on January 2, came from the breakup of a Russian tanker in the Japan Sea and spread about 1 million gallons (3.8 million l) of fuel onto Shimane prefecture's shore. The other, on July 2, resulted from a Japa-

© Agence France Presse/Corbis-Bettmann

U.S. Secretary of State Madeleine Albright was greeted by Japan's Prime Minister Ryutaro Hashimoto in Tokyo in February 1997. Trade and security issues were topics of discussion.

nese-owned supertanker running onto a shoal in Tokyo Bay. Some 400,000 gallons (1.5 million l) of cargo washed over the harbor of Yokohama. A third environmental disaster occurred in March, when a fire followed by an explosion caused a substantial increase in radiation at a state-run nuclear-waste-reprocessing center at Tokai.

Foreign Affairs

On September 5 the USS *Independence* cruised into Otaru harbor on Hokkaido. This was the first civilian-port call by a U.S. aircraft carrier since the end of World War II. The visit symbolized Japan-U.S. security ties.

U.S. Relations. The reciprocal visits of important persons during 1997 demonstrated the significance to Washington and Japan of their security pact. On February 24, Madeleine Albright, on her first trip to Asia as U.S. secretary of state, emphasized the priority assigned to the alliance as "key to the American military presence in Asia." The subject of U.S. forces on Okinawa was mentioned obliquely.

When U.S. Vice-President Albert Gore was in Tokyo in March for talks with the foreign minister, he was direct in stating the U.S. position: U.S. forces should remain in Japan to guarantee security in the Asia-Pacific region. He specifically added that the marine garrison on Okinawa should remain intact because of the threat on the Korean peninsula. On April 17 the Diet passed the base-lease law, just prior to the prime minister's summit meeting with U.S. President Bill Clinton in Washington on April 25. Even more sensitive was the bilateral move to update the 1952 security agreement, a plan launched by a U.S.-Japan subcommittee in Honolulu and released by the Security Consultative Committee in New York on September 23. The draft defined peacetime cooperation, joint response to an armed attack against Japan, and Japan's support in case of a conflict in "areas around Japan." The last, an undefined clause, triggered vigorous debate: Critics claimed that the change would violate the no-war constitution; the prime minister responded that revision would clarify the role of the Self-Defense Forces (SDF) in an emergency. In a December referendum, voters in the Okinawan town of Nago rejected plans for a new U.S. military base. The United States and Japan had been planning the base for more than a year. The referendum was an embarrassment to the prime minister, but was not binding legally.

During the year trade issues, which regularly had plagued foreign relations, did not completely surrender the stage. The finance ministry announced that, in 1996, Japan's current-account surplus dropped 30.9% (from 1995) to $59.8 billion. At the Denver G-8 summit, however, Clinton expressed concern to Hashimoto over the 1996 U.S. deficit with Japan ($35.3 billion). And by August, Tokyo revealed that in the January–June period, the surplus had jumped 40.4% over the same six-month span in 1996. U.S. Trade Representative Charlene Barshefsky pointed to three sectors where Japan needed to increase deregulation and to apply market-opening measures: harbor practices, automobile sales, and "open skies" in aviation. On September 4 the U.S. Federal Maritime Commission began levying sanctions of $100,000 per Japanese vessel entering U.S. ports, the first trade penalty in a decade. The move was in retaliation for restrictive practices by the politically powerful Japan Harbor Transport Association. On October 17 a tentative agreement was reached to lift future sanctions but levied fines remained untouched.

On the positive side, on October 1, Ambassador Barshefsky did not include Japan's auto market on the Super 301 watch list for retaliation. A long-simmering aviation dispute also was resolved tentatively, on October 10. Additional carriers were authorized on both sides and "beyond rights" (of flights to third nations) expanded, subject to a four-year negotiation. All these problems would come under the scrutiny of a new U.S. ambassador, Thomas Foley.

Russian Relations. Japanese welcomed the results of a meeting between Prime Minister Hashimoto and Russian President Boris Yeltsin, held November 1–2 in Siberia. They had hoped it might introduce some thaw into a frosty relationship. Conferring in Krasnoyarsk (halfway between Tokyo and Moscow), the leaders seemed to fulfill promises to pursue a new "Eurasian diplomacy." The achievements were far greater than those expected from "an official summit," Foreign Minister Keizo Obuchi said. Prime Minister Hashimoto had launched an initiative in a meeting with Yeltsin on June 20 during the Denver summit. He had hoped that reciprocal visits could improve bilateral relations based on three principles: trust, mutual benefits, and long-term perspective. These could be applied to an interminable dispute, the "Northern Territories" border problem.

At issue were four small islands in the southern Kurils, historically recognized as Japanese territory but occupied by the Russians since 1945. Tokyo and Moscow had normalized relations in 1956 but a formal peace treaty ending World War II awaited resolution of the island dispute. In May, Japanese media had hailed pledges made by visiting Russian Defense Minister Igor Rodiono to Defense Chief Fumio Kyuma. The Russians were prepared to cut garrisons stationed on the islets and to cease deploying missiles aimed at Japan. Even more encouraging was a proposal by retired Gen. Alexander Lebed, former security adviser to Yeltsin and now a prospective presidential candidate in Russia's next election in 2000. Lebed favored a plebiscite in Russia to try to sway opinion toward settlement of the islands dispute. Discouraging was his prediction that 20 years might be needed to find a solution. The Hashimoto-Yeltsin talks suggested that a shorter time might do. The two leaders agreed to make every effort to sign a peace treaty, after solving the territorial dispute, but by the year 2000.

China. September marked the 25th anniversary of Japan's establishment of diplomatic ties with China. In Beijing on September 4–5, Prime Minister Hashimoto drew a distinction between thriving economic relations and problematic political attitudes. Thus Japan had become China's biggest market, and China, Japan's second-biggest trading partner. Tokyo had given Beijing $17.5 billion in low-interest loans. All this was not enough to avoid political friction.

Ties continued to bog down in historical disputes over Japan's recognition of its war role; Japanese politicians' visits to Yasukuni Shrine, where war dead (and war criminals) are interred; China's own territorial claims (over the Daioyu islands, called the Senkaku chain by Japanese); and Japan-U.S. security coordination (especially as it impacts on Taiwan). True, on the August 15 anniversary of Japan's surrender in 1945, the prime minister expressed remorse for Japan's aggression and condolences to victims, particularly Asian neighbors. And he did avoid an official visit to the Yasukuni Shrine. Nevertheless, when President Jiang Zemin began his state visit to the United States with a stop in Hawaii on October 26, he deliberately chose the Arizona National Memorial to memorialize those killed in Japan's attack on Pearl Harbor.

Moreover, on August 22 in a speech in Kuala Lumpur, Malaysia, China's Premier Li Peng declared that earlier remarks made by Japan's Chief Cabinet Secretary Seiroku Kajiyama were completely unacceptable. Unilaterally interpreting Japan-U.S. security guidelines, Kajiyama had predicted that in case of U.S. involvement in conflict between China and Taiwan, Japan's SDF would support U.S. forces. Taiwan, Li countered, is an "inalienable part of China." Hashimoto then devoted much of his time during his Beijing visit in September reassuring officials that the guidelines were not aimed at China.

The Two Koreas. Prime Minister Hashimoto found himself in hot water on January 25, when he hosted South Korean President Kim Young Sam at a hot spring in Beppu, Kyushu. Designed to improve bilateral relations, the encounter centered on yet another offhand comment by Hashimoto's cabinet secretary. Kajiyama had stated that "comfort women" (a polite term for prostitutes), often forcibly mobilized by Imperial forces on the mainland during the Pacific War, merely reflected a "social background." At the time, he stated, Japan licensed prostitution. Two days later the secretary apologized for this bizarre interpretation of history.

Japan had only informal contact with North Korea. On August 22 in Beijing, negotiators from Tokyo and Pyongyang agreed to reopen talks toward normalization of relations. On October 11, North Korea thanked Japan for the contribution through the UN of $27 million in food to combat famine in North Korea.

ARDATH W. BURKS, *Rutgers University*

JORDAN

It was a difficult year for the Jordanian monarchy. Worsening relations between King Hussein and his prime minister led to the latter's replacement; foreign policy had to tread

---

JORDAN • Information Highlights

Official Name: Hashemite Kingdom of Jordan.
Location: Southwest Asia.
Area: 34,445 sq mi (89 213 km²).
Population (mid-1997 est.): 4,400,000.
Chief Cities (Dec. 31, 1991 est.): Amman, the capital, 965,000; Zarqa, 359,000; Irbid, 216,000.
Government: *Head of state,* Hussein I, king (enthroned May 2, 1953). *Head of government,* Abdul Salam Majali, prime minister (took office March 19, 1997). *Legislature*—National Assembly: House of Notables and House of Representatives.
Monetary Unit: Dinar (0.70751 dinar equals U.S.$1, Dec. 31, 1997).
Gross Domestic Product (1995 est. U.S.$): $19,300,000,-000 (purchasing power parity).
Economic Indexes (1996, 1990 = 100): *Consumer Prices,* all items, 131.2; food, 135.1. *Industrial Production,* 120.
Foreign Trade (1996 U.S.$): *Imports,* $4,428,000,000; *exports,* $1,817,000,000.

---

an even more difficult tightrope than ever; and the question of the king's health again led to speculation about the future.

Domestic Affairs. On March 19, King Hussein dismissed Abd al-Karim al-Kabariti as prime minister and replaced him with Abdul Salam Majali, who had been prime minister from 1993 to 1995. Various policy differences had developed between the king and Kabariti in the past months. The prime minister reportedly had favored a tougher policy than did the king toward Israel, and he had supported stringent economic measures that had proved unpopular and from which the king had retreated. The king was also unhappy with disaffection encouraged by what he called "the yellow press." On May 17 the new government put forward and the king endorsed a series of restrictive amendments to the 1993 press law. There also were some indications of possible actions against the all-too-political activities of professional associations.

During this period of political change, the king underwent prostate surgery at the United States' Mayo Clinic on April 5. While there, he was visited by both U.S. President Bill Clinton and Israeli Prime Minister Benjamin Netanyahu. A general election for the 80-member lower house of the Jordanian parliament was held on November 4. The election went smoothly, with supporters of the monarchy securing a comfortable majority. Tribal leaders loyal to the king took at least 45 seats. Some 55% of the electorate voted. But since the Islamic Action Front and other leftist groups boycotted the election, it did not really function as a forum on policy issues.

External Relations. From the start, Jordan's conclusion of a peace treaty with Israel in October 1994 engendered considerable opposition among the Jordanian population, which was now more than half Palestinian.

After seven Israeli schoolgirls were killed by a Jordanian soldier while on a field trip in Jordan in March 1997, King Hussein (left) personally visited the homes of the victims to express his condolences.

The number of such opponents was increasing perceptibly in 1997 as the Netanyahu government, in power in Israel since May 1996, espoused policies that all but halted the Israeli-Palestinian peace process. A number of incidents demonstrated this. The most striking of these occurred on March 13, when a Jordanian soldier, Corp. Ahmad Dakamsa, 26, killed seven Israeli schoolgirls on a field trip in Jordan. King Hussein was appalled by this event, all the more so since it had been committed by a member of the Jordanian army, traditionally tightly disciplined and nonpolitical. The news found the king in Spain, where he had conferred with Spain's Foreign Minister Juan Matutes. According to Matutes, on that same day the king had urged the European Union (EU) to exercise a greater role in the Middle East peace process.

Hussein immediately returned to Jordan. He expressed "a deep sense of shame and anger that this thing should have happened," and also telephoned messages of condolence to the Israeli president and prime minister. Crown Prince Hassan, the king's younger brother and designated heir, promised a full investigation of the incident. On March 16, Hussein, in a gesture without precedent in Arab-Israeli relations, visited—escorted by Prime Minister Netanyahu—all seven families of the victims.

It remained true, however, that two days before the massacre there had been made public an exchange of letters in which the king sharply criticized Netanyahu's policies as destructive of peace efforts. At a news conference on March 16, the king said that the letter never was meant for publication. There had been no offense intended, he said, only a genuine concern for the process of peace in the region. This letter was only the first of several tart responses made by King Hussein during the year to actions of the Netanyahu government, either in letters to the prime minister or in comments to the media. There was evident a disappointment with an Israeli administration whose advent the king had welcomed the previous year.

Other Jordanians reacted differently than did the king to the murders by Dakamsa. The same day as the king's condolence visits, a group of activists opposed to normalization of relations with Israel visited Dakamsa's family, offering them various forms of support, including free legal support from members of the Jordanian Bar Association. However, on July 19 a military court found Dakamsa guilty of the seven murders, and he was sentenced to life imprisonment.

In a somewhat similar but less deadly incident on September 22, two Israeli security guards attached to the Israeli embassy in Amman were wounded in a drive-by shooting by unknown assailants. A spokesman for the group Hamas, opposed to peace with Israel, disclaimed responsibility.

On September 25, Israeli agents operating in Amman made an unsuccessful and rather farcical attempt to assassinate the Hamas leader Khaled Meshal, believed to be behind the horrific terrorist actions that killed 19 persons in Jerusalem in July and September. The furious king was able to exact—as the price of freeing two Israeli agents—the return to Gaza of the Hamas leader Sheik Ahmed Yassin, who had been in Israeli jails for eight years, as well as the release of some 20 Palestinian and Jordanian prisoners.

ARTHUR CAMPBELL TURNER
University of California, Riverside

KENYA

In December 1997, Kenyan President Daniel arap Moi was reelected easily with 40% of the popular vote, and the 25% in five of the eight provinces that was needed to avoid a runoff election. Moi's victory, and the chaotic handling of the election, did not bode well for a stable political future.

The Election. Opposition candidates showed early signs of unity with the establishment in April of an Opposition Alliance. By introducing sweeping electoral reforms before the December vote, however, Moi appeared to rob them of their unity, and the field was divided among four key players. The Democratic Party candidate, former Vice-President Mwai Kibaki, led the opposition with 1.8 million votes (31%) to Moi's 2.4 million, followed by Raila Odinga of the National Development Party and the Social Democratic Party's Charity Ngilu—the first woman to run for president in Kenya. In parliament the ruling Kenya African National Union (KANU) lost its comfortable majority.

Widespread flooding made some polling stations inaccessible, while not enough ballots arrived at others, leading the Electoral Commission to extend some polling to a second day. Some voters refused to vote if they were not paid, while some recounts led first-time losers to win by wide margins. Both opposition candidates and KANU called the voting rigged.

Government and Opposition. Moi continued to make decisions that showed an unwillingness to deal with corruption. In January he announced that Nicholas Biwott would join the cabinet, while he demoted KANU reformists Simeon Nyachae, William Ntimama, and Kipkalya Kones. Biwott was minister of energy during construction of the Turkwel Gorge dam. World Bank condemnation of the project led to a ten-year halt in investment in the energy sector, resulting in current electricity shortfalls. In 1990, Biwott had been implicated in the murder of Foreign Minister Robert Ouko, who was investigating high-level corruption.

In June the High Court dismissed on technical grounds all charges in the Goldenberg fraud case, in which more than $430 million—10% of Kenya's gross national product (GNP)—was exported illegally by individuals close to KANU. The International Monetary Fund (IMF) then suspended a meeting of Kenya's donors and reversed an April decision to disburse $37 million—the second installment of $216 million in assistance.

Early in the election campaign, opposition moved from parliament to the campuses and streets. On February 23, Solomon Muruli—who had led student demonstrations to protest police shootings of three students in December 1996—died when his room at the University of Nairobi exploded. He was reported to have been kidnapped and tortured prior to his death, and journalists accused the police of murder.

Opposition demonstrations in June shut down the Nairobi and Mombasa central business districts. Police used tear gas and ax handles against worshipers praying for free speech and accountable government in All Saints Anglican Cathedral. Students calling for constitutional reforms took control of one of Nairobi's major thoroughfares for several hours. Violence in Mombasa drove hundreds of thousands from their homes, none of whom could vote if they did not return. Moi's meetings with opposition and church leaders were denounced by the Executive Council of the National Convention.

The Economy. While official estimates predicted a growth rate of 5.2%, the World Bank said even 4% was too high. Agricultural production rebounded from a 25% drop due to drought in 1996, but more than half of Kenya's farmers remained subsistence, rather than commercial, producers. Despite plans to privatize the Kenya Post and Telecommunications Corporation and the electrical-power industry, privatization was said to be slow, and relations with the IMF remained strained. Tourism plummeted 60% due to political unrest. Election-related costs and other public expenditures left the government with little reserves. Nearly half of all Kenyans were living in abject poverty, without basic needs.

WILLIAM CYRUS REED
*The American University in Cairo
and Indiana University*

KENYA • Information Highlights

Official Name: Republic of Kenya.
Location: East Coast of Africa.
Area: 224,961 sq mi (582 650 km²).
Population (mid-1997 est.): 28,800,000.
Chief Cities (1990 est.): Nairobi, the capital, 1,505,000; Mombasa, 537,000.
Government: *Head of state and government*, Daniel T. arap Moi, president (took office Oct. 1978). *Legislature* (unicameral)—National Assembly.
Monetary Unit: Kenya shilling (65.917 shillings equal U.S.$1, principal rate, August 1997).
Gross Domestic Product (1995 est. U.S.$): $36,800,000,-000 (purchasing power parity).
Economic Index (1996, 1990 = 100): *Consumer Prices*, all items, 324.3; food, 339.7.
Foreign Trade (1996 U.S.$): *Imports*, $2,852,000,000; *exports*, $2,067,000,000.

KOREA

The two overriding concerns in both South and North Korea in 1997 were the economy and the selection of the top political leadership. In a surprising economic reversal, South Korea went into a financial nosedive and sought an emergency bailout from the International Monetary Fund (IMF) in late November. The IMF imposed strict reforms on Korea's economic and financial systems. Another surprise was the first victory of an opposition leader in December's heated presidential race. In North Korea crippling economic woes continued unabated, despite gradually increasing offers of help from the international community to mitigate the grave food shortage. Kim Jong Il's long-awaited assumption of the top party post on October 8 brought no immediate changes in personnel or policy.

Republic of Korea (South Korea)

Politics and Society. Throughout 1997 the popularity of President Kim Young Sam plummeted. The year hardly had begun when opposition politicians joined forces with labor unions to denounce the new labor law that had been rammed through the legislature in the closing days of 1996. Nationwide strikes and demonstrations forced Kim to promise amendments. Labor issues quickly were pushed to the sidelines, however, as the first of a series of major business failures grabbed headlines. The brand-new Hanbo iron and steel mill—still partly under construction—went bankrupt in late January, spawning allegations of bribery, embezzlement, influence-peddling, and poor business judgment. The National Assembly conducted a lengthy televised hearing into the case that was largely inconclusive. The second son and close confidant of the president, Kim Hyun-chol—as well as several powerful politicians, business leaders, and bank officials—faced the investigation panel. Most—including the junior Kim—subsequently were indicted, convicted, and imprisoned.

The Kim Hyun-chol affair was only the beginning of the rapid decline in the president's political fortunes. President Kim appointed one of his former premiers—Lee Hoi-chang—to the top position in the ruling New Korea Party (NKP), but chose not to play an active role in the acrimonious intra-party fight to select the candidate for the presidential elections in December. Lee obtained the support of a plurality at the party convention in August, but the strained party unity led to the formation of a splinter group, the New Party by the People (NPP). NPP nominated Rhee In Je, the runner-up in the August convention vote, while the main opposition party—the National Congress for New Politics (NCNP)—nominated veteran opposition leader Kim Dae Jung, known as DJ.

Early in November, DJ—making his fourth run for the presidency—managed to forge an alliance with the smaller opposition group, the United Liberal Democrats, headed by Kim Jong Pil, or JP. The two Kims agreed to a power-sharing scheme whereby JP would support DJ's candidacy in exchange for a major role in DJ's administration. They also

© Yun Jai-hyoung/AP/Wide World Photos

© Seolyong Lee/Gamma-Liaison

Nearly 81% of South Korea's electorate went to the polls on Dec. 18, 1997, and elected Kim Dae Jung ("DJ") of the National Congress for New Politics party as president.

agreed to work for constitutional change that would introduce a parliamentary cabinet system in lieu of the current presidential system, as JP earlier had advocated. Within the ruling NKP, Lee became increasingly alienated from President Kim, whose longtime followers began to defect to the maverick Rhee. Lee bolstered his position by merging the NKP with the small Democratic Party, renaming it the Grand National Party (GNP). On the same day, President Kim gave up his party membership, but Lee was unable to counter the negative effect of his past association with the president.

The 1997 election campaigns were peaceful and orderly, revolving around a series of televised debates and media advertisements. The new election law forbade the massive and costly outdoor rallies that, in the past, had mobilized huge crowds who were paid to attend. The three major candidates represented different generations: DJ was 72; Lee, 62; and Rhee, 49. DJ's primary support lay in the Cholla provinces in the southwest, augmented by JP's popularity in the central Chungchong provinces. Lee inherited the support of Kyongsang-province voters, who had stood behind some of his colleagues in the GNP, while Rhee courted younger voters by advocating a generational change in the political leadership. By and large, their platforms differed little, and the contest focused more on personalities than issues. There was considerable mudslinging, especially toward the close of the three-week campaign period, but no violence or flagrant cases of fraud.

The December 18 vote showed that the people were dissatisfied with politics as usual. DJ won with 40.3%—10,326,275 votes. Lee received 38.7%, or 9,935,718 votes, while Rhee finished with 19.2%, or 4,925,591 votes. Although the 390,557-vote margin of victory was narrow, the losers promptly conceded and vowed to cooperate with Kim in resolving the ominous economic emergency. Kim promised faithful implementation of the IMF bailout accord, and—although he had suffered torture, death-row imprisonment, and exile at the hands of previous military regimes—publicly committed himself to reconciliation without retribution. He endorsed presidential amnesty by year's end for the two former generals turned presidents, Chun Doo Hwan and Roh Tae-woo.

Student demonstrations, a perennial part of the South Korean sociopolitical landscape, hit another violent peak in June, resulting in two deaths and the erosion of public support. A government crackdown against the leader-

SOUTH KOREA • Information Highlights

Official Name: Republic of Korea.
Location: Northeastern Asia.
Area: 38,023 sq mi (98 480 km²).
Population (mid-1997 est.): 45,900,000.
Chief Cities (1995 census, preliminary): Seoul, the capital, 10,229,262; Pusan, 3,813,814; Taegu, 2,449,139; Inchon, 2,307,618.
Government: *Head of state,* Kim Young Sam, president (formally inaugurated Feb. 25, 1993). *Head of government,* Koh Kun, prime minister (appointed March 4, 1997). *Legislature* (unicameral)—National Assembly.
Monetary Unit: Won (1,737.6 won equal U.S.$1, Dec. 15, 1997).
Gross Domestic Product (1995 est. U.S.$): $590,700,000,000.
Economic Indexes (1996, 1990 = 100): *Consumer Prices,* all items, 141.8; food, 144.8. *Industrial Production,* 163.
Foreign Trade (1996 U.S.$): *Imports,* $150,676,000,000; *exports,* $130,346,000,000.

ship of the radical student organization Hanchongryon seemed to be effective.

Amid a cloud of economic malaise and the often petty partisan political debates, South Koreans sought relief in cheering Chan Ho Park of the Los Angeles Dodgers, the first Korean starting pitcher in the U.S. major leagues. Chan became a national hero with his 14 wins during the regular season. South Korean sports fans also were elated that their national soccer team qualified, with a 6–1–1 record, to compete in the 1998 World Cup Soccer match in Paris.

The August 6 crash of a Korean Airline jumbo jet, only miles from the Agana airport on Guam, cost 225 lives.

Foreign Affairs. South Korea's foreign policy focused on trade and economic relations with the United States. The ongoing U.S. demands for easier access to South Korean markets, especially for automobiles and telecommunication equipment, aroused South Korean resentment. On October 1, South Korea was designated for "priority foreign country practice" (PFCP)—subject to Super 301 sanctions under the Comprehensive Trade Act. Seoul threatened to take the matter to the World Trade Organization (WTO). South Korea embargoed bacteria-infected U.S. beef as a nationwide citizens' campaign to protest and boycott U.S. goods spread. South Koreans also suspected the United States of masterminding the stringent IMF demands.

On December 9–10 a four-party conference that Kim and U.S. President Bill Clinton had proposed in April 1996 to seek solutions to the political and military problems on the peninsula convened in Geneva after four rounds of preparatory sessions in New York. The high-level meetings of delegates from the United States, China, and North and South

© Paul Barker/Reuters/Archive Photos

As 1997 drew to a close, South Koreans were focused not only on the presidential election but also on the nation's economic crisis, which led to an International Monetary Fund (IMF) bailout.

ruptcy of the giant Hanbo steel and iron mill exposed fundamental defects in South Korea's industrial and financial structures. Excessive reliance on borrowed capital to build costly and redundant production facilities, illicit liaisons between business and politics, and mismanagement and corruption in banking and business were largely responsible for the sudden reversal of South Korea's economic fortune. When foreign investors and creditors began to divest and recall their loans, the financial roof collapsed, and a severe foreign-exchange shortfall developed in November. The value of South Korea's currency fell precipitously from 842.7 won to the U.S. dollar on January 4, to 1,737.6 won by December 15. The benchmark South Korean stock-market index stood at 799.54 on June 18 but fell to 385.80—a ten-year low—by December 15. A dozen or more major business groups—including Jinro, Haitai, Kia, Halla, and Ssangyong—became insolvent, threatening a complete business breakdown. The deputy premier in charge of economic affairs resigned on November 19. Two days later his replacement requested an international bailout. On December 3, South Korea signed an agreement with the IMF that provided emergency aid totaling $57 billion. In return, South Korea agreed to streamline its financial structure, open its financial markets to foreign investors, cut its current-account deficit to less than 1% of annual gross domestic product (GDP), and slow the economic growth rate from an estimated 6% or more in 1997 to 2.5% in 1998. By the end of 1997 the IMF pronounced the fundamentals of the South Korean economy—the 11th largest in the world—to be sound. South Korea's commodity trade showed a surplus of $600 million in November, and labor productivity—which had been rising since 1994—reached its highest point in the second half of 1997, 15.1% higher than in 1996. South Koreans were shocked to learn that their past economic success had been built on a shaky foundation, and that they now had to accept a life of austerity and dependency on foreign institutions. They referred to December 3, the date of the IMF bailout accord, as a day of "national humiliation."

Democratic People's Republic of Korea (North Korea)

Politics. The formal succession of Kim Jong Il to the official posts left vacant by his father, Kim Il Sung, began in 1997—more

Korea produced little beyond an agreement to hold a second meeting on March 16, 1998. This was the first time the four major combatants of the Korean War had met since the 1953 armistice. A spin-off from the New York meetings was a direct Washington-Pyongyang dialogue that became almost routine as the year progressed. Despite U.S. assurances, South Korea remained unconvinced that such a dialogue was not detrimental to its interests.

Months of negotiations failed to produce a new fishery treaty with Japan, partly due to the two nations' conflicting territorial claims on the contested Tokdo Island group. On October 29, Cambodia became the 183d nation to establish diplomatic relations with South Korea. Prominent foreign visitors to Seoul included Canadian Prime Minister Jean Chrétien, U.S. Vice-President Al Gore, and Russian Foreign Minister Yevgeny Primakov.

Economy. A labor strike in January was primarily political in nature, but the bank-

than three years after the "Great Leader"'s death—amid renewed debate in the outside world about the impending collapse of this communist regime. On October 8, Radio Pyongyang broadcast a special report, made jointly by the Central Committee and the Central Military Committee of the Workers' Party of Korea, expressing respect to Kim Jong Il as general secretary of the party. The announcement came after a series of provincial party committees and party chapters in the government offices and the People's Army had adopted resolutions honoring Kim as the formal party head. At the same time, North Korea began to use a new Juche (self-reliance) calendar that placed 1912 (the year of Kim Il Sung's birth) as Year 1 of the Juche era. Furthermore, the senior Kim's birthday, April 15, was designated as the "Festival of the Sun." The reasons for delaying the junior Kim's assumption of the top party post, for forgoing the formal election process in the party central committee, and for continuing to leave the state presidency vacant remained unexplained. It was clear that Kim Jong Il was in firm control of North Korea, as he had been for at least the previous three years. The personality cult centered on the Kims continued, and the appellation "Great Leader" now was used for the younger Kim as well.

While North Korea's policies and rhetoric remained largely unaltered, some noteworthy events took place. The dramatic February defection of Hwang Jang Yop—the party secretary in charge of international affairs—in Beijing and his subsequent arrival in Seoul shattered the myth of the monolithic unity of the party. The death of Defense Minister Marshall Choi Kwang in February, and that of his top deputy later the same month, further reduced the ranks of the old leadership, fueling rumors of a possible wholesale political reshuffle. Another high-level defector was Pyongyang's ambassador to Egypt, Chang Sung Gil, who sought refuge in the United States and was said to possess valuable information on North Korea's missile sales to Arab countries. While North Korea merely denounced Hwang, it demanded Chang's extradition on the criminal charge of embezzlement. When this demand was ignored by the United States, Pyongyang boycotted, in late August, the ongoing negotiations with Washington on limiting the production and sale of missiles and related technology.

In November the Japanese press reported the public execution of the North Korean party secretary in charge of agriculture, So Kwan Hui, together with 17 other party and military personnel. Pyongyang ignored the report.

More and more hungry families sought dangerous passage to South Korea. About 180 North Koreans made it to the South in 1997. Nevertheless, there were no reports of large-scale social unrest.

Foreign Affairs. North Korea continued its cautious probes aimed at establishing diplomatic relations with the United States and Japan. The joint U.S.–North Korean search for Americans missing in action (MIAs) from the Korean War era continued without fanfare. In October a few representatives of U.S. veterans' groups were invited to North Korea to observe the operation. Pyongyang also hosted a growing number of U.S. visitors—including former Sen. Sam Nunn, former ambassador to Seoul James Laney, seven members of the House Intelligence Committee, the first U.S. government team to study the North Korean food situation, and U.S. journalists.

In return, the United States continued its leadership role in the Korean Peninsula Energy Development Organization (KEDO) project for construction of light-water reactors at Simpo, on the country's east coast. Washington also took measured steps to lift economic sanctions against North Korea, always with an eye on Seoul's reaction. Chang's defection to the United States—allegedly with the help of the Central Intelligence Agency (CIA)—caused only a temporary rupture in relations. By the end of 1997 a visit to the State Department by the deputy foreign minister of North Korea was treated as a routine news item by the U.S. press.

North Korea removed a stumbling block to normalizing relations with Japan by permitting some Japanese women married to North Koreans and residing in North Korea to visit Japan. Fifteen made a weeklong trip in November and surprised the Japanese press by praising "the paradise on earth" in their adopted land. Reopening formal negoti-

---

NORTH KOREA • Information Highlights

Official Name: Democratic People's Republic of Korea.
Location: Northeastern Asia.
Area: 46,540 sq mi (120 540 km²).
Population (mid-1997 est.): 24,300,000.
Chief Cities (1986 est.): Pyongyang, the capital, 2,000,000; Hamhung, 670,000.
Government: *Head of state,* president (vacant as of Dec. 31, 1997). *Head of government,* Hong Song-nam, acting prime minister (took office 1997). *Legislature* (unicameral)—Supreme People's Assembly. The Workers' Party of Korea (Communist Party): General Secretary, Kim Jong Il.
Gross Domestic Product (1995 est. U.S.$): $21,500,000,-000.

ations for normalization was considered a matter of time by the end of 1997.

North Korea's relations with China remained correct and delicate. Hwang's defection and subsequent one-month stay in the North Korean consulate in the Chinese capital was a source of embarrassment to the Beijing government. China insisted on observing strictly the customary rules on political refugees and allowed Hwang to depart only for the Philippines, and not directly for South Korea. On the occasions of the Chinese Communist Party conference in September affirming Jiang Zemin's leadership and of Kim's accession to the top party position, fraternal greetings were exchanged between Pyongyang and Beijing. Goodwill missions, including of party and military officials, also were exchanged. At the first meeting of the four-party Geneva conference, the chief Chinese delegate finessed a delicate position, supporting Pyongyang's demand for a peace treaty on the one hand, while urging a direct North-South dialogue as Seoul had advocated. Protests from South Korea and worldwide antinuclear groups stalled the controversial export of radioactive waste from Taiwan to North Korea.

Although Pyongyang's foreign policies showed cautious steps toward more open relations with the outside world, especially the United States, it remained defiant when it faced a frontal challenge. When the United Nations (UN) human-rights office requested relevant information, Pyongyang angrily rejected the demand and withdrew its acceptance of the 1947 UN Declaration on Human Rights.

Economy and Famine. North Korea's economy had been declining since 1990. Pyongyang's 1995 statistics showed a sharp reduction in the per-capita gross national product (GNP), from $868 in 1988 to $239 in 1995. The Bank of Korea in Seoul estimated a 3.7% reduction in the GNP of North Korea and a per-capita GNP of $910 for 1996—considerably higher than Pyongyang's estimate. But even the higher figure placed North Korea, with a nominal GNP of $214 billion for a population of 23.6 million, among the poorest nations of the world. The dismal 1997 fall harvest of about 1.14 million tons—half of what was expected—contributed to the economic deterioration and prolonged a serious food shortage. A 1997 drought afflicted the primary grain-growing areas of western North Korea, which had been ravaged by flood during 1995 and 1996. Pyongyang continued to appeal for outside assistance. Foreign governments, private relief agencies, and the UN responded, but efforts were uncoordinated, while conflicting estimates of local production and domestic need rendered any discussion of foreign aid tentative at best. The lack of transparency on North Korea's part compounded the problem. World news coverage of the widespread famine depicted graphic scenes of emaciated children, reminiscent of the Ethiopian and Somalian disasters. Pyongyang already had launched a campaign for "two meals a day," and the daily ration of grains reportedly was reduced to an average of 100–150 g (3.5–5.3 oz) per day, compared with 600 g (21.2 oz) per day at the beginning of 1995. After the fall harvest, a UN World Food Program (WFP) source reported a slight

© Allyson Thirkell/Oxfam/AP/Wide World Photos

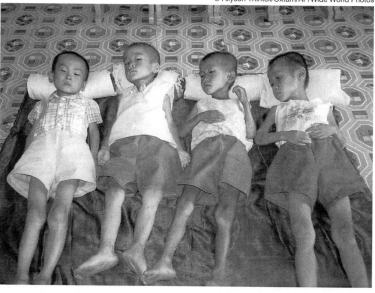

Graphic photographs of emaciated North Korean children shocked the Western world and led various agencies to send assistance. The UN World Food Program distributed some 400,000 tons of food.

Representatives of the United States, South Korea, China, and North Korea gathered in New York City in August 1997 for preliminary talks regarding peace negotiations on the Korean peninsula.

© Jeff Christensen/Reuters/Archive Photos

improvement. The WFP had distributed 400,000 tons of food, and a roughly equal amount had been pledged by foreign governments to help cover a shortfall of about 1.3 million tons. In December the situation was reported to be very bad, but not critical.

Inter-Korean Relations

Considering the political uncertainty and the pressing economic needs that preoccupied the two Koreas, they managed to maintain a surprisingly active level of contact—mostly in nonpolitical arenas. Throughout 1997, however, there were occasional events reminiscent of the Cold War, such as Chang's defection to the United States and Hwang's dramatic escape to the Korean consulate in Beijing, accompanied by another high party official, Kim Dok-hong. After days of tense diplomatic standoff, Pyongyang accepted Hwang's departure to South Korea. Once in Seoul, Hwang denounced Kim Jong Il as an "arrogant dictator" and warned that Pyongyang already had decided on and prepared for an all-out war against South Korea.

A defection from South to North Korea also occurred, when the former head of the indigenous Korean religion Chondogyo, Oh Ik-jae, slipped into Pyongyang from Beijing in August and publicly paid tribute to Kim Jong Il. Oh was a former consultant to the opposition NCNP and allegedly had met Kim Dae Jung on one or two occasions, but his defection failed to become an election-campaign issue. Equally surprising was the arrest of a well-known Seoul National University professor, Koh Young-bok, as a North Korean spy. Koh, a sociologist, often had been a consultant to the Seoul government and a member of official South Korean delegations that had visited Pyongyang in the early 1970s.

Sensational as these revelations were, they seemed to have no impact on economic exchanges. The joint KEDO project to build "safe" nuclear reactors at Simpo, North Korea, proceeded apace and a formal ceremony on August 19 marked the beginning of the construction by combined North and South Korean crews. The head of the huge Daewoo conglomerate, Kim Woo Jung, made his second trip to North Korea in September, at about the same time that a group of South Korean journalists were permitted to enter the North. In October a North-South joint venture to manufacture pharmaceutical products at a plant near Pyongyang was announced.

It also was common to find fish, farm produce, and other primary North Korean products for sale in South Korean supermarkets. Official statistics announced in Seoul in October showed a 25% increase in inter-Korean trade in 1997, up to $150 million. Also announced was an agreement to open the skies over North and South Korea to civilian airliners beginning on April 23, 1998. Despite these transactions, 1997 did not produce serious inter-Korean political dialogue—a situation that South Korean President-elect Kim pledged to change once in office. He expressed interest in a North-South summit.

HAN-KYO KIM, *University of Cincinnati*

LABOR

In the United States in 1997, unemployment dropped to a 24-year low; Alexis Herman (*see* BIOGRAPHY) took office as U.S. secretary of labor; a major strike by United Parcel Service (UPS) workers occurred in August; and labor was influential in obtaining the defeat of "fast-track" trading authority. On the international scene, unemployment remained high in Germany and Italy; the leader of Mexico's modern labor movement died; and Canada was hit by a postal workers' strike.

United States

Employment and Unemployment. The U.S. economy continued to show strength in 1997. Employment in November increased by 3 million over November 1996. Unemployment totaled 6.2 million, down by 1 million from 12 months earlier. The unemployment rate declined to 4.6%—a 24-year low. Despite the low unemployment rate, inflation was lower than in November 1996, at 2.1%. The tightened labor market did spark an increase of 4.1% in earnings, which meant a rise of 2% in real earnings when adjusted for inflation.

Lower unemployment held for all categories of workers. The rate for adult men in November was 3.8%; for adult women, 4%; and for teenagers, 15%. Unemployment was 9.4% for black workers. The largest improvement was for Hispanic workers, whose unemployment rate of 6.9% was down from 8.3% in November 1996.

By region, the jobless rate declined most in the West, reaching 5%, from 6.3% in 1996. Other regional rates were 5.1% in the Northeast, 4.2% in the Midwest, and 4.5% in the South.

Teachers' Union President. Albert Shanker, 68, longtime president of the 900,000-member American Federation of Teachers and the 85,000-member New York United Federation of Teachers (UFT), died in February. In 1968, Shanker had led a strike of New York City teachers that closed most schools for 55 days in three citywide stoppages. The issue was the transfer of 13 white teachers, against their wishes, out of a largely black school district. The union's claim that the transfers were illegal and a violation of civil-service laws and union contracts was upheld in court, but political leaders refused to restore the teachers in the racially charged conflict. The strikes ended when the state education commissioner suspended the district school board and appointed a trustee to oversee the return of the union teachers. Shanker spent 15 days in jail for calling the strikes in violation of a state law.

Shanker was succeeded as president of the national teachers' union by Sandra Feldman, president of the New York United Federation of Teachers since 1986. She was expected to step down from the UFT position and devote full time to the national job. Feldman favored high standards for teachers and was opposed to using vouchers that channel students and dollars from public to private schools.

The American Federation of Teachers, affiliated with the American Federation of

U.S. EMPLOYMENT AND UNEMPLOYMENT

A COMPOSITE

	Nov. 1997	Nov. 1996
Labor Force	136,800,000	134,800,000
Participation Rate	67.1%	66.9%
Employed	130,600,000	127,600,000
Unemployed	6,200,000	7,200,000
Unemployment Rate	4.6%	5.4%
Adult Men	3.8%	4.5%
Adult Women	4.0%	4.8%
Teenagers	15.0%	17.0%
White	3.8%	4.6%
Black	9.4%	10.6%
Hispanic	6.9%	8.3%

Armed forces excluded

Source: U.S. Bureau of Labor Statistics

U.S. UNEMPLOYMENT RATE

All civilian workers; seasonally adjusted

Labor–Congress of Industrial Organizations (AFL-CIO), represents mostly teachers in large cities. In 1997 it was the second-largest teachers' union, after the 2.3-million-member independent National Education Association.

Teamsters' Union Election. A federal election overseer overturned the December 1996 reelection of Ron Carey as president of the International Brotherhood of Teamsters and ordered a new election. She found that the Carey campaign had received more than $700,000 in illegal contributions that might have influenced Carey's narrow victory over James P. Hoffa, the son of the legendary former Teamsters leader.

The ruling detailed several schemes in which Carey's aides and campaign consultants had channeled money from the Teamsters treasury into his campaign through intermediaries. Carey denied knowing anything about the illicit financing, but a court-appointed election officer found that Carey knew of and approved the use of the illegal funds. The officer barred Carey from running in the rerun election to be held in spring 1998. Carey's appeal of the disqualification was denied. Federal election monitors were investigating charges that Hoffa also engaged in improper fund-raising during the election, raising the possibility that he also might be disqualified from the rerun election.

New York Philharmonic–Musicians' Union Agreement. In December the New York Philharmonic and Musicians Local 802 negotiated an unprecedented six-year labor contract. This was the longest agreement ever negotiated for a symphony orchestra, and was portrayed as a reaction to a recent wave of orchestra strikes in Atlanta, San Francisco, and Philadelphia that crippled performance schedules and outraged audiences.

The contract covered 104 members of the orchestra and provided for a minimum weekly salary of $1,980 by 2004—an increase over the current salary of $1,560. Additional stipends assured that every player would earn at least $2,000 a week, 52 weeks a year, by the end of the contract. Pensions would rise from $43,500 per year to $53,000.

Strikes. The year was marked by several major strikes and strike threats. The most important involved the Teamsters' Union and United Parcel Service (UPS), which closed down 2,400 UPS depots staffed by 185,000 package loaders and sorters. The major issues in the strike—which involved more workers than any other strike in the 1990s—were the union demand that the company convert 10,000 part-time jobs to full-time over the

© Peter Morgan/Reuters/Archive Photos

The late-1996 reelection of Ron Carey (above) as president of the International Brotherhood of Teamsters was overturned after it was revealed that he had received illegal contributions.

next four years, and the company's proposal to establish a new pension plan to replace the existing multi-employer plan in which UPS was by far the biggest contributor.

The August strike was settled after 15 days on terms widely recognized as favorable to the union. UPS agreed to convert 2,000 part-time jobs a year to full-time, for a total of 10,000 over the five-year term of the contract, and to remain in the multi-employer plan with benefit increases. Wages were to be increased over five years by $4.10 an hour for part-time workers and $3.10 an hour for full-time workers. Starting pay for part-time loaders would rise to $8.50 from $8.00 per hour. After the settlement, part-timers still represented more than 50% of UPS workers. In turn, the company gained more flexibility in managing its workforce and increasing labor efficiency.

After almost two years on strike, the 2,000 reporters, editors, pressmen, mailers, and drivers at *The Detroit Free Press* and *The Detroit News* offered to return to work unconditionally. The strike had started to keep the newspapers from buying out several hundred union jobs and reorganizing the papers' distribution system. The newspapers—operating with 1,300 replacement workers—insisted that the former strikers would return to work only as vacancies occurred. The workers also would have to accept a new wage scale and

© A. Tannenbaum/Sygma

Some 185,000 unionized United Parcel Service workers were on strike for 15 days in August 1997. Issues involving part-time workers were a focus of the walkout. The Teamsters and the package-delivery company reached a five-year agreement on August 19.

new work rules adopted by the companies before and during the strike.

The strikers' only hope resided with the National Labor Relations Board, which was considering union charges that the companies engaged in unfair labor practices during negotiations leading up to the strike. If charges were upheld, strikers would be entitled to back pay for each day the companies deny them their old jobs back.

After a brief strike in February, American Airlines and its pilots' union reached agreement on a new contract. The pilots did not achieve their objective that they, rather than pilots at the American Eagle subsidiary, should fly small jets that American plans to buy. However, the pilots were granted an improved compensation package that included raises totaling 9% through 2001.

Negotiators reached agreement between Wheeling Pittsburgh Steel and the United Steelworkers union to end a ten-month strike by 4,500 workers in August. The agreement included a raise, a signing bonus, and a guaranteed pension plan amounting to $1,600 per month for an employee with 40 years of service. In return, the company received improved workplace efficiency and some job reductions. The company also agreed to keep open two plants in West Virginia that the

company had planned to close, which would have eliminated 200 jobs.

Strikes over issues of staffing, outsourcing of work to independent suppliers, and health and safety closed down several GM plants for short periods. GM was committed to long-run restructuring, which might eliminate 50,000 to 70,000 of some 220,000 hourly jobs. GM, which in the 1960s built three fifths of all automobiles sold in the United States, was down to about 30% and was trying to remain competitive with Ford and Chrysler as well as with overseas car manufacturers. GM claimed that in the second quarter of 1997 alone, strikes had cost it $490 million—enough to build a new state-of-the-art factory. The company was struggling to negotiate agreements with local unions at a number of plants nearly a year after it reached agreement with the national UAW in 1996.

AFL-CIO Organizing Agenda. The new leadership of the AFL-CIO focused on recruiting new members in an effort to arrest the 20-year slide in union membership. Membership had sunk to 14.5% of the labor force, as compared with 35% in the 1950s. At its winter meeting in February, AFL-CIO President John Sweeney proposed a $60 million advertising effort to burnish labor's image. Organizing 20,000 strawberry workers in California and thousands of construction, hotel, and health-care workers in Las Vegas, NV, was at the top of labor's agenda. The Teamsters and the Farm Workers were cooperating in a drive to organize 40,000 fruit pickers and warehouse workers in Washington state's $1 billion annual apple harvest. Growers said that their business was largely a family industry with narrow profit margins, reliant on low-wage entry workers in a state with an acute labor shortage. On average, warehouse workers earned about $7.50 per hour, working about ten months a year. Adjusted for inflation, the wage had not changed in more than ten years.

In the biggest union election in private industry, nearly 10,000 reservation takers, gate agents, and ticket sellers at U.S. Airways voted to join the Communications Workers of America (CWA). The CWA hoped to use the U.S. Airways victory as a springboard to unionize 14,000 passenger-service workers at United Air Lines. Some 60,000 passenger-service workers in the airline industry did not belong to unions. Only at Northwest Airlines and Trans World Airlines were these workers represented by unions.

Legislation. In their biggest legislative victory in years, labor unions were a major factor in the defeat of President Bill Clinton's effort to expand his power to negotiate free-trade agreements, known as "fast track." The president wanted Congress to give him the same authority that previous presidents had had to negotiate trade agreements without the possibility of amendments by Congress. Labor opposed fast track on the grounds that it would result in agreements that could cause the loss of U.S. jobs and allow developing countries to maintain substandard wages, working conditions, and environmental-protection measures. Unions worked closely with environmental, consumer, and civil-rights organizations that also were opposed to fast track.

In March the House of Representatives approved a bill that would change the Fair Labor Standards Act of 1938, so employees could choose between overtime pay and 1.5 hours of compensatory time for every hour over 40 worked in a week. The Senate was expected to vote on the bill in 1998. Although the bill stipulated that compensatory time be voluntary and would make employers liable for damages if they coerce employees, the legislation was opposed by labor unions. AFL-CIO head Sweeney said that "employees are not well-protected against employer pressure."

International

Western Europe. According to the U.S. Bureau of Labor Statistics, Americans worked more hours per week for less than did workers in Germany, France, and Italy. Only British workers earned less per hour than did production workers in the United States. Weekly hours in manufacturing in Germany averaged 29, followed by France with 31.7, Italy with 35, Britain with 35.6, and the United States with 37.9. Hourly compensation of production workers in Germany averaged $31.87, outstripping French workers at $19.34 and Italian workers at $18.08. U.S. workers earned $17.74 per hour, and workers in Britain lagged behind at $14.19. Unemployment in the United States was 4.6%; in Britain, 5%; in Germany, 12%; and in Italy, 13%.

Politicians and union leaders in Germany and Italy were searching for ways to reduce unemployment without reducing wages. In Italy the government pledged to trim the maximum legal workweek to 35 hours from 40 by the year 2001. The French made a similar vow. But other members of the 15-member European Union (EU) rejected as ineffective the idea of reducing hours of work in order to increase employment. They argued that shortening work hours should be negotiated on a company-by-company basis, with cuts in pay if necessary. The main objective, they said, should be to increase productivity in order to compete effectively in the global market.

Mexico. Fidel Velázquez Sánchez, who helped create Mexico's modern labor movement—which he led with an iron fist for more than 50 years—died in June at the age of 97. Velazquez was one of the few public figures in Mexico with sufficient power to exert influence on the Institutional Revolutionary Party (PRI), which has governed Mexico without interruption since 1929. He long was considered the second-most-important political figure in Mexico; his Confederation of Mexican Workers has 6 million members. Velazquez was instrumental in obtaining legal recognition of the right to strike. He succeeded in getting wage increases that substantially improved the standard of living for Mexican workers. In the 1980s and 1990s, however, he was willing to go along with government and business in arrangements that placed the burden for Mexico's economic recovery on workers, who still had not regained the buying power they had in 1981. He supported the North American Free Trade Agreement (NAFTA) and encouraged the government to sell off hundreds of state-owned enterprises.

Democratic changes in Mexico's political system aroused hope for democracy in labor unions. As a result, isolated labor disputes flared among the long-suffering working population. A survey conducted by an independent labor federation concluded that 95% of Mexico's organized workers belonged to unions that they had no voice in choosing. Workers seeking to transfer union jurisdiction from a PRI-backed union to one of their own choosing risked dismissal or violence.

Canada. In the largest teachers' strike ever in Canada, 126,000 public- and Catholic-school teachers in Ontario walked out in October. The strike kept 2.1 million students in 4,742 schools from attending classes. The teachers were protesting a provincial-government proposal to overhaul the education system by weakening local school boards and giving the government the power to determine class size and tax rates. Teachers' preparation time would be cut, and noncertified instructors would be allowed to teach some subjects. Teachers feared that as many as 10,000 positions might be lost. The teachers returned to work after two weeks without getting the government to withdraw its plans.

Canadian postal workers went out on strike in November over wages and work rules. They returned to work after 17 days when the government passed a law granting workers a 5.15% increase over three years. The union, which had sought a 10% raise, said its members would refuse to check postage on mail because of the holiday overload.

France. For the second year in a row, French truck drivers blocked highways across the country in November. Their action disrupted freight shipments across Europe just as a similar 12-day strike in 1996 had. The strikers set up 150 barricades across the country and stopped all intercity truck traffic, making European countries from Portugal to Poland hostage to the French labor dispute. The issues at stake in the 1997 strike were mostly unresolved grievances from 1996. At that time the country's 300,000 truck drivers had won the right to retire at age 55, a reduction in working hours from 275 to 200 hours a month, and a $500 bonus, but few of them said they actually had received the promised benefits. In the 1997 strike, they were asking for a raise in average gross pay of up to 7%, to about $1,750 a month. This was considerably less than drivers in Germany and some other European countries earned. With a new Socialist government in power, the truckers hoped to achieve at least some of their demands. The 1997 strike lasted only five days, less than half the duration of the previous year's strike. The biggest union, the French Democratic Labor Federation, representing approximately 80% of the drivers, approved the settlement offer of trucking companies of a 6% raise and a minimum annual salary of $21,000 for experienced drivers within three years.

Israel. A nationwide strike of 700,000 workers, called by the Histadrut labor federation, shut down Israel's airports, seaports, banks, and stock exchange for five days in early December. The shutdown was estimated to have cost the Israeli economy about $32 million a day. The main issue was a pension agreement signed by the previous Labor government shortly before it was voted out of office by the conservative Likud Party. The new government had balked at honoring the agreement, arguing that it had been a last-minute political maneuver by the outgoing government. The settlement was a compromise put forward by the president of the Labor Court.

Union Membership Worldwide. Labor-union membership had dropped in most industrial countries between 1985 and 1995, according to the annual report of the International Labor Organization, a Geneva-based arm of the United Nations (UN). Union membership declined in 70 of the 92 countries surveyed. The sharpest decreases—from 21.8 million in 1985 to 14 million in 1995—took place in Central and Eastern Europe, largely as a result of the end of compulsory unionism. Union membership plunged by 46% in Poland and by 51% in the Czech Republic.

The report said, however, that despite the drop in membership, labor remained at least as influential as before in Scandinavia, Germany, the Netherlands, and Ireland, as well as in much of Eastern Europe, where unions remained a full partner with government and business in three-way negotiations that determined wages and working conditions in many industries. Unions helped elect left-of-center governments in Italy, France, and Germany.

There was strong growth in union membership in several industrial and developing countries. From 1985 to 1995, membership climbed by 127% in South Africa, 92% in Spain, 90% in Chile, 69% in the Philippines, and 61% in South Korea.

In Great Britain union membership had fallen by 25% since 1985, due to antiunion legislation under former Prime Minister Margaret Thatcher. Only 26% of British workers belonged to unions in the mid-1990s.

JACK STIEBER, *Michigan State University*

LAOS

The Lao People's Revolutionary Party reaffirmed its commitment to the authoritarian, one-party system during a Central Committee meeting in September 1997.

Politics. President Nouhak Phoumsavan and Prime Minister Khamtay Siphandon maintained political stability and emphasized traditional values before legislative elections in late 1997. The National Assembly passed laws on natural-resource use to encourage foreign investment and advance the transition to a market-driven economy. In Warsaw, Poland, Lao and Polish students demonstrated for free elections and a United Nations (UN) human-rights review in Laos.

Economy. By midyear, Laos' currency—the kip—lost more than one third of its value due to monetary factors and links to Thailand. Thailand—which suffered a recession—normally provides about half of Laos' foreign investment and trade. Rising inflation appeared likely because of foreign-exchange problems, reliance on imported consumer goods, and a poor harvest in the predominantly agrarian nation. Inexperienced management posed problems for tourism.

A nearly 80-mi (129-km)-long bridge in Khammouane province opened, highlighting long-term infrastructure development that included road improvements, bridges, plans for a railroad, and progress in the demarcation of the Thai border. Vientiane approved more than 20 dam projects—many dependent on Japanese assistance—to fulfill contracts for increased power to Thailand and Vietnam by 2006. World Bank support remained unclear for the largest dam—Nam Theun 2—which would flood 175 sq mi (453 km²) and cost about $1.5 billion.

Foreign Relations. With UN Development Program support, Laos met admission criteria to become an Association of Southeast Asian Nations (ASEAN) member in July. Vientiane expanded relations with India and other nations to attract aid and investment and reduce dependence on Thailand.

Vietnamese Prime Minister Vo Van Kiet visited in August, the 20th anniversary of the bilateral-cooperation treaty between the two nations. Vientiane signed bilateral trade and investment agreements with the United States to encourage passage of U.S. legislation granting Laos most-favored-nation status, but criticized the United States for a Lao-language version of Radio Free Asia.

CHRISTINE VAN ZANDT
U.S. Government Analyst on East Asian Affairs

LAOS • Information Highlights

Official Name: Lao People's Democratic Republic.
Location: Southeast Asia.
Area: 91,430 sq mi (236 800 km²).
Population (mid-1997 est.): 5,100,000.
Chief City (March 1995 census): Vientiane, the capital, 528,109.
Government: *Head of state,* Nouhak Phoumsavan, president. *Head of government,* Khamtay Siphandon, prime minister. *Legislature* (unicameral)—National Assembly.
Monetary Unit: New kip (920 new kips equal U.S.$1, 1995).
Gross Domestic Product (1995 est. U.S.$): $5,200,000,-000.
Foreign Trade (1995 est. U.S.$): *Imports,* $587,000,000; *exports,* $348,000,000.

LATIN AMERICA

In 1997, Latin American economies were characterized by moderate growth based on large inflows of external capital, while some observers thought Mexico would experience its highest annual growth in 16 years. U.S. President Bill Clinton made two trips to Latin America and attempted to win congressional approval for a hemisphere-wide free-trade pact early in 1998. He also reversed a long-standing ban on the sale of high-tech weapons to Latin American countries, selling advanced jet fighters to Chile.

In October, Latin stock markets were jolted by a worldwide downturn. The Latin American loss was proportionately greater than that experienced in the United States. Hardest hit was Brazil, which was forced to adopt austerity measures in November to avoid currency devaluation—more than doubling interest rates.

An emerging El Niño—a warm ocean current off the west coast of South America that wreaks havoc with global weather—raised worldwide speculation about its potential effects. Drug trafficking remained a serious concern for U.S. policy makers, but the source of drugs seemed to vary widely, from synthetic designer drugs produced in Mexico to more traditional drugs such as cocaine, produced in the Andean countries.

Economy. The growth of Latin America's gross domestic product (GDP) was expected to reach 4.5% in 1997, according to United Nations Economic Commission for Latin America and the Caribbean (ECLAC) estimates. The rate was up from 3.5% in 1996 and well above the annual 3.7% average from 1991–94.

ECLAC also estimated that the inflows of external capital should have reached $70 billion by the end of 1997, compared with $63 billion in 1996. External capital flows—consisting of direct foreign investment, private and public loans, grants, and other funds transfers—would more than compensate for the balance-of-payments deficit on the current account, which in 1997 was expected to reach some $55 billion. That figure represents approximately 3% of GDP, a proportion similar to that in 1993–94.

The single greatest economic achievement of recent years was the taming of inflation, which fell from 26% in 1995 to 18% in 1996 and was estimated at 12% in 1997—the lowest level in 50 years. In 1997 inflation in 15 of the 23 ECLAC-surveyed countries was 10% or less. As recently as 1993, the average region-wide inflation rate was 888%. Some individual countries posted truly remarkable inflation records. Before the October stock-market crisis, Brazil—which had rung up four-digit price rises in the late 1980s and early 1990s—brought inflation to the 12% range. Mexico, where inflation recently had flared up again, pared it back to 28% in 1996 and 17% in 1997.

The favorable trends were not matched in the labor market, where urban unemployment reached its highest level of the 1990s. In Argentina and Mexico job creation failed to keep pace with economic recovery. Only in Chile and Peru did unemployment continue to decline.

Latin American exports continued to grow in both 1996 and 1997. The region's 1997 exports increased by about 11% over the previous year, but imports climbed by 11% to 20%—leaving an ever-widening current-account deficit. Fortunately, this deficit was more than offset by the inflow of external capital.

On October 27, U.S. and Latin American stock markets suffered heavy losses in response to a continuing crisis in Asia. The Mexican Bolsa took its largest one-day dive in a decade, plummeting 13.4%. In Brazil the São Paulo Exchange—Latin America's largest—dropped almost 15% in the fourth-largest decline in history. In Argentina the Merval index suffered a 13.7% loss on the Buenos Aires exchange. All three markets recovered the next day. Mexico closed up 11.69%, while São Paulo regained 6.4% and Buenos Aires posted a 6.07% rise. Investors remained skittish, however, over potential currency instability and the possibility of higher interest rates. On October 30 there was another significant drop, with shares in Brazil losing 10% and in Mexico 3.5%. On November 7, losses of 10% and 5% were registered in São Paulo and Buenos Aires, respectively, and on November 10 the Merval lost 5.7%, while the Bolsa lost 2.6%.

The recent resumption of economic growth in Latin America had relatively no effect at all on the equitable distribution of income and resources. According to a document presented in April to a United Nations (UN) conference in São Paulo, Brazil, only Uruguay showed an improvement in income distribution in the previous five years and only in Argentina and Uruguay did fewer than 15% of the households live below the poverty line. Chile, Costa Rica, and Panama were in the mid-range, with 15% to 30% living in poverty. Five countries—Brazil, Colombia, Mexico, Peru, and Venezuela—had between 31% and 50% of their populations living in poverty. In countries such as Bolivia and Honduras, half or more of the people were poor. Still, the study reported that the overall assessment for the first six years of the 1990s was "positive," since eight of 12 countries recorded lower levels of poverty than at the start of the decade. Compared with 1980, however, only Brazil, Chile, Panama, and Uruguay showed lower levels of poverty, while Argentina, Honduras, Mexico, and Venezuela were higher.

Foreign Affairs. U.S. President Bill Clinton made two trips to Latin America in 1997—in May to Mexico and Central America, and in October to Venezuela, Brazil, and Argentina. He planned to visit Santiago, Chile, in April 1998 to attend the second Summit of the Americas, where the principal agenda item was to be the creation of a free-trade zone for the hemisphere.

To facilitate free-trade talks, Clinton sought renewal of his lapsed authority to negotiate trade pacts without the possibility of Congress amending them—a power available to every president since Gerald Ford. This so-called "fast-track" arrangement—opposed by a strong coalition of organized labor, environmentalists, and liberal Democrats—was shelved in November.

On September 29, UN Secretary-General Kofi Annan announced that Colombia Finance Minister José Antonio Ocampo would replace Guatemalan economist Gert Rosenthal as ECLAC's executive secretary.

The Organization of American States (OAS) adopted a draft inter-American convention against illicit trafficking in firearms, ammunition, and explosives. OAS Secretary-General Cesar Gaviria said that homicides were a "potentially devastating phenomenon" for Latin America, where the murder rate was twice that of Africa and the Middle East. In Colombia and Jamaica the rate was seven times that of the United States.

RICHARD C. SCHROEDER, *Freelance Writer*

Law

From cases involving assisted suicide to the powers of the U.S. Congress and the president, the U.S. Supreme Court's 1996–97 term was filled with rulings of unusual, sweeping impact. In recent years, commentators often have described the high court in other terms, pointing to fewer rulings and incremental change as hallmarks of a generally conservative trend. But in late June the justices wrapped up their session with a flurry of momentous decisions that reminded the nation of the power vested in the court.

The term was not particularly noteworthy for any ideological shift, as Chief Justice William H. Rehnquist marked his 25th anniversary on the court and 11th year as chief justice. As the leader of the conservative majority, he was generally on the prevailing side in close cases. In some of the most dramatic rulings, the justices were unanimous. Conservative Justices Antonin Scalia and Clarence Thomas voted together in all but one of the high court's 80 signed opinions. Justices Sandra Day O'Connor and Anthony M. Kennedy remained pivotal votes, with Justice Kennedy dissenting only four times. The more liberal bloc—Justices John Paul Stevens, David H. Souter, Ruth Bader Ginsburg, and Stephen G. Breyer—dissented in eight of the 17 cases decided by 5–4 votes.

In the lower courts, there were significant developments regarding affirmative action, abortion regulation, and the drive to hold cigarette companies legally responsible for the deaths of smokers (*see* SPECIAL REPORT, page 163). Lawyers battled in Tennessee courts over efforts to force a trial in the case of the man convicted of killing the Rev. Dr. Martin Luther King, Jr. A civil jury found O.J. Simpson liable for the 1994 deaths of his former wife, Nicole Brown Simpson, and her friend Ronald L. Goldman (*see* SIDEBAR, page 315).

Youths who commit grown-up crimes increasingly were being treated like adults in court, and some members of Congress called for even stricter treatment of young offenders. One proposal would provide financial incentives for states that try juveniles as young as 14 in adult criminal court. Another bill would allow prosecutors in federal cases, not judges, to decide whether a juvenile would be tried in adult court. In recent years, virtually all states have decided to make more of the most serious youthful offenders stand trial as adults. Ironically, juvenile arrests for violent crimes continued to decline in 1996.

Also on Capitol Hill, Republicans were moving slowly to confirm President Bill Clinton's judicial appointments to the federal bench. With about 100 vacancies on the feder-

In 1997 the U.S. Supreme Court included (bottom row, l-r): *Antonin Scalia, John Paul Stevens, William Rehnquist, Sandra Day O'Connor, Anthony Kennedy;* (top row, l-r): *Ruth Bader Ginsburg, David Souter, Clarence Thomas, and Stephen Breyer.*

al bench by the fall, the president accused the GOP of threatening to "let partisan politics shut down our courts and gut our judicial system." Clinton said that Republicans were stalling on his nominations to fill most of the empty judges' seats. Republicans said that they were being cautious to assure judges were well qualified and not committed to carrying out an activist political or social agenda. Clinton had appointed 204 federal judges to lifetime jobs in his first four-year term.

Cases derived from the collapse of the former Yugoslavia remained paramount in international law.

United States

Supreme Court. In a hectic conclusion to its term, no case attracted more widespread attention than the justices' unanimous ruling that states may ban assisted suicide (*Vacco v. Quill* and *Washington v. Glucksberg*). The ruling left it to the states and "democratic society" to decide whether medical assistance for the terminally ill should be legalized. The ruling left open the possibility that a future case could provide the basis for a right to a doctor's assistance to hasten death for those enduring intractable pain.

In another dispute involving due-process rights (*Kansas v. Hendricks*), the justices voted, 5–4, to permit states to keep some violent sex offenders in mental hospitals after they have served criminal sentences. A 6–3 ruling barred states from adopting laws that deprive parents of appeals in parental-termination cases just because they are too poor to pay the court fees (*M.L.B. v. S.L.J.*).

A 9–0 ruling held that President Clinton could not postpone proceedings in a sexual-harassment suit until he leaves office (*Clinton v. Jones*). The justices said that Paula Corbin Jones, a former Arkansas state employee, was entitled to her day in court to force Clinton to answer charges he propositioned her in a hotel room when he was governor. The high court also ordered White House lawyers to give the Whitewater prosecutor notes of their conservations with Hillary Rodham Clinton, refusing to hear the Clinton administration's appeal of a lower-court ruling (*Office of the President v. Office of Independent Counsel*). The president won a victory when the justices, voting 7–2, rejected a challenge to a law that gives the chief executive so-called line-item veto power (*Raines v. Byrd*). The ultimate constitutionality of the law was not decided, as the court held that the six members of Con-

gress who challenged the new law lacked legal standing to bring the suit.

The court curtailed congressional power, striking down the Religious Freedom Restoration Act of 1993 that attempted to give additional protection to religious observances (*City of Boerne v. Flores*). The 6–3 ruling held that Congress went too far by making a substantive change in the Constitution. The justices also overturned a portion of the Brady gun-control law that required local law-enforcement officials to perform background checks on prospective handgun purchasers (*Printz v. United States*). The 5–4 decision said Congress may not force states to help administer federal programs.

In a key religion case, the court reversed a 1985 ruling and said public-school teachers may teach special federally financed remedial classes on the grounds of parochial schools (*Agostini v. Felton*). The 5–4 decision could signal new willingness by the majority to allow government aid to parochial schools.

Breaking new ground, the court supported freedom of speech in cyberspace. It struck down the Communications Decency Act of 1996, an attempt by Congress to prevent indecent material on the Internet from being seen by minors (*Reno v. American Civil Liberties Union*). The court said the attempt to keep sexually explicit material from children would infringe on the rights of adults.

The justices handed the broadcast-television industry a victory by upholding a federal law that requires cable-television systems to carry the signals of local over-the-air broadcast stations (*Turner Broadcasting v. Federal Communications Commission*). The 5–4 ruling rejected the cable industry's claims that the 1992 law violated its free-speech rights. In a case involving the free-expression rights of abortion opponents, the court voted 6–3 to uphold a lower-court order keeping protesters 15 ft (5 m) from entrances to abortion clinics (*Schenck v. Pro-Choice Network*). But the ruling allowed demonstrators to approach clinic patients outside the 15-ft zone. In another test related to freedom of expression, the court ruled, 6–3, that states are not required constitutionally to permit candidates to appear on more than one political party's ballot line (*Timmons v. Twin Cities Area New Party*). The justices, by a 5–4 margin, allowed the federal government to force crop growers to help pay for generic advertisements that promote an industry (*Glickman v. Wileman Bros.*). The court upheld a court-ordered redistricting plan that reduced from three to one the number of black-majority congressional districts in

Criminal v. Civil Law

The U.S. government's failure in 1995 to convict former football star O.J. Simpson of the murder of his former wife, Nicole Brown Simpson, and her friend Ronald Goldman did not keep the victims' families from suing and receiving a civil-jury verdict of $33.5 million in 1997. The two trials of Simpson, one criminal and one civil, struck many people as unfair and even as a violation of the prohibition of double jeopardy. Yet, U.S. law is clear that criminal and civil proceedings are completely distinct, and an acquittal in a criminal case does not preclude a subsequent civil suit.

Lawsuits brought by the federal government or state governments to prosecute a person for violating a law are termed "criminal cases." Although people can file complaints with the police, only the government can initiate a criminal case. Government officials called prosecutors decide whether to file criminal charges in court against a person. Federal prosecutors generally work in the U.S. Attorney's office, part of the U.S. Department of Justice. At the state level, prosecutors are usually part of the district attorney's office.

The term "civil suit" refers to a case brought by a person or group of people against another person or people, or against a business, or even against the government, in order to recover compensation for injuries or to halt injurious practices. If a person sues a doctor for making a mistake (a malpractice suit), a civil suit is filed. A legal action to obtain a divorce is a civil suit also. Whenever people sue each other for money or for an injunction (a court order commanding certain behavior to cease), a civil suit is used. Any person can file a civil suit in court. Even the government can file a civil suit when it wants to collect money it believes it is owed.

In a criminal case, the government must prove its case beyond a reasonable doubt. In a civil case, the plaintiff need only prove its case by a preponderance of the evidence; that is, the jury need only conclude that it is more likely than not that the defendant is liable. This, in part, explains why successive criminal and civil actions are allowed: The government's failure to prove guilt beyond a reasonable doubt should not preclude those injured from attempting to establish liability by the less onerous standard of preponderance of the evidence. Also, in criminal cases at the federal level and in 48 states (all but Louisiana and Oregon), jury verdicts must be unanimous. In most states, civil-jury verdicts do not need to be unanimous. A criminal case, if there is a conviction, can result in a prison sentence, probation, or a fine to be paid to the government. A civil case, if the defendant is deemed liable, can result in money damages or an injunction.

Often the same events can give rise to both criminal and civil actions when the government prosecutes the wrongdoing and the victim sues to recover compensation for injuries. In the Simpson case, the government prosecuted O.J. Simpson for murder. Although the jury acquitted Simpson, the murder victims' families still could sue to recover money damages. The civil jury found Simpson responsible for the victims' deaths and assessed $8.5 million in compensatory damages and $25 million in punitive damages.

ERWIN CHEMERINSKY

© Axel Koester/Sygma

As O.J. Simpson's civil trial progressed during early 1997, public emotion ran high. Outside the courtroom, spectators held signs detailing their opinions on Simpson's guilt or innocence. On February 4 the jury found Simpson responsible for the deaths of his former wife and her friend.

Georgia, ruling the plan did not violate the federal Voting Rights Act (*Abrams v. Johnson*).

In the area of criminal law, the court ruled unanimously that police who have stopped a motorist for a traffic violation can proceed to ask the driver for permission to search for drugs. The police are not required to tell motorists they can decline to be searched, the justices said (*Ohio v. Robinette*). By a 7–2 vote, the court held police may routinely order passengers out of a car when they stop cars suspected of traffic violations (*Maryland v. Wilson*). The court said the police need not show they suspect the passenger is engaged in criminal behavior or poses a danger. The justices struck down a Georgia law requiring candidates for public office to be tested for drugs (*Chandler v. Miller*). The justices were unanimous in ruling that police armed with search warrants must knock and announce their presence even when searching for drugs (*Richards v. Wisconsin*).

The court, voting 5–4, barred retroactive application of a 1996 law that limits federal-court appeals by prison inmates, shielding prisoners who already had such petitions pending (*Lindh v. Murphy*). The justices split, 5–4, on limiting the ability of death-row inmates to challenge their sentences on grounds jurors were not told they could impose a life sentence without parole (*O'Dell v. Netherland*).

By a 5–4 vote, the justices refused to extend the partial immunity from prisoner lawsuits enjoyed by public employees to workers with private companies that are hired by state and local governments to run prisons (*Richardson v. McKnight*). The court threw out a $1.3 billion award against asbestos manufacturers, ruling, 6–2, that the settlement did not protect the interests of all plaintiffs (*Amchem Products v. Windsor*).

In an important environmental decision, the justices unanimously allowed use of the Endangered Species Act by those seeking less, not more, federal protection for animals and plants. The decision allows people to sue based on claims they suffered economic harm from enforcement of the law (*Bennett v. Spear*). A 6–3 ruling backed the federal government in its long-running boundary dispute with Alaska, extending federal environmental protection to some coastal areas targeted for oil and gas drilling (*United States v. Alaska*). The court upheld, 6–3, the Securities and Exchange Commission's broad interpretation of insider trading (*United States v. O'Hagan*). Investors can be guilty of insider trading with-

out having formal ties to the company whose stock they acquired.

Local Law. California was allowed to implement its new law, Proposition 209 or the California Civil Rights Initiative, limiting affirmative action. The measure, which was approved by California voters in 1996, made the state the first to eliminate race and sex as factors in numerous programs, including hiring, education, and contracting. Campaigns to curtail or abolish affirmative action were under way in many states. The 9th U.S. Circuit Court of Appeals had cleared the way for the law to take effect, setting the stage for a likely Supreme Court test. In a related development, the University of Texas School of Law abandoned affirmative action after the 5th U.S. Circuit Court of Appeals barred the school from using race as a factor in admissions and scholarships. The Supreme Court had declined to review the ruling.

In Tennessee a federal judge expressed deep misgivings but upheld a 1994 federal law that is designed to protect women against violence. The Violence Against Women Act makes crimes motivated by gender a violation of civil rights, potentially opening the federal courts to a broad class of domestic-relations suits. The Tennessee case attracted particular notoriety because of the prominence of the couple. Laurel Seaton won the right to sue her husband, Kenneth Seaton, a wealthy businessman, for from $47 million to $87 million. Other challenges to the law were working their way through federal courts.

A federal judge in Houston threw out most of a record $222.7 million libel verdict against Dow Jones & Co. in a case that media lawyers viewed as a potentially major restraint on freedom of the press. The ruling by U.S. District Judge Ewing Werlein erased $200 million, the punitive damages awarded to the investment firm of MMAR Group Inc. Dow Jones, publisher of *The Wall Street Journal*, continued the fight to have the rest thrown out. A seven-member jury had decided that five sentences in a 1993 *Journal* article were false and defamatory.

A federal judge in North Carolina slashed a $5.5 million jury award to Food Lion against Capital Cities–ABC Inc. The supermarket chain was ordered to take just $315,000. A jury had awarded the larger sum to punish ABC for the ways its *PrimeTime Live* news show assembled a 1992 undercover report accusing the supermarket chain of selling rotten meat. The jury cited network reporters for lying to get jobs at Food Lion.

JIM RUBIN, *The Associated Press*

International Law

During 1997 there were significant developments in international environmental law, international humanitarian law, international trade law, and the law governing the use of force. In December more than 150 nations signed the Kyoto Protocol in Kyoto, Japan. Under the agreement, the United States and Japan agreed to cut greenhouse-gas emissions to 7% below 1990 levels by 2012; Europe agreed to an 8% cut. (*See* ENVIRONMENT— *Global Warming: A World Solution?*.)

War Crimes. In May the International Criminal Tribunal for the former Yugoslavia (ICTY) found Dusan "Dusko" Tadic guilty of war crimes and crimes against humanity—the first such decision since the Nuremberg trials of the 1940s. In finding Tadic responsible for torture, ethnic cleansing, and other acts of persecution against civilians, the tribunal established a number of important legal precedents, including some that proved controversial. The critical issues were the nature of the conflict and the test for attributing responsibility for acts committed by combatants to those linked to, but not formally in control of, the actual perpetrators.

International law is far more extensive, and places greater obligations on individual states to prosecute offenders, in cases of international armed conflict than in cases of internal struggle. But in many cases it is difficult to categorize a conflict as purely international or purely internal.

In the Tadic case, a majority of the three-judge trial chamber decided that the Bosnian conflict was transformed from an international to an internal conflict when the government of the Federal Republic of Yugoslavia (Serbia and Montenegro) formally announced the withdrawal of Yugoslavia National Army units deployed in Bosnia. The majority also concluded that acts of the Bosnian Serbs could not be attributed to Yugoslavia unless the Bosnian Serb forces "were acting as de facto organs or agents of that state for that purpose or more generally"—even though Yugoslavia continued to support and exercise some control over Bosnian Serb forces. The immediate effect was dismissal of counts against Tadic alleging violations of the grave breaches provisions of the Geneva Conventions Relative to the Protection of Civilian Persons in Time of War. More broadly, the tribunal set a high threshold for establishing the existence of an international armed conflict and for imputing responsibility to outside participants.

International Criminal Court. Wide dissatisfaction with the ad hoc nature of the war-crime tribunals for the former Yugoslavia and Rwanda gave renewed impetus to a 50-year effort to establish a permanent International Criminal Court (ICC). Unlike the International Court of Justice (ICJ)—which hears cases between states—the ICC would have jurisdiction to try individuals for grave violations of international criminal law such as genocide, war crimes, and crimes against humanity. Although major disagreements still must be overcome before the ICC is created, substantial progress was made at 1997 preparatory conferences. Supporters hoped the ICC would be established in 1998.

Land-Mines Convention. Delegates from some 90 countries met in Oslo to approve a treaty banning the use of antipersonnel land mines and requiring countries to clean up mines already deployed. The United States— reluctant to forgo the use of land mines in Korea—unsuccessfully tried to craft an exception and became one of the few major powers to refuse to sign.

The agreement was the first time states had outlawed an active weapons system since the banning of poison gas some 70 years earlier. International attention was focused on the issue when the Nobel Peace Prize was awarded to the International Campaign to Ban Landmines and its coordinator, Jody Williams.

Use of Force. The United Nations Security Council continued to take an expansive reading of its coercive powers under the UN Charter, maintaining and tightening sanctions on Iraq to achieve compliance with the weapons-inspection program it established after the Persian Gulf war. The council also authorized a group of West African states to use force to promote the restoration of an elected government in Sierra Leone.

International Trade. The World Trade Organization (WTO) decided a number of important trade disputes in 1997. The WTO found invalid Canadian restrictions on the importation of certain U.S. periodicals, European restrictions on importation of meat treated with certain hormones, and European restrictions on importing and distributing bananas. Such decisions raised important compliance issues, as states were forced to confront an effective dispute-resolution system that greatly reduced opportunities to delay or block resolution of disputes raised under the General Agreement on Tariffs and Trade (GATT).

DAVID WIPPMAN
School of Law, Cornell University

LEBANON

In 1997, Lebanon remained less a sovereign state than a Syrian province. There were some 35,000 Syrian troops in Lebanon, and perhaps 1 million Syrians working in Lebanon. The political leaders of Lebanon had at best a limited autonomy. Meanwhile, the ambitious rebuilding of Beirut was going on apace.

Hezbollah and Strife in the South. The anti-Israeli, Iran-supported guerrilla organization Hezbollah in recent years had broadened its base of operation, run hospitals and social programs, and attained parliamentary memberships. But in 1997, Hezbollah came under heavy flank attack from its left, led by the fiery Sheikh Sobhi Tufayli, the organization's former secretary-general. On July 4 in the town of Baalbek, the sheikh addressed a crowd estimated at 10,000, protesting neglect of the average citizen.

The "security zone" in the south held by Israel and its ally, the South Lebanon Army, still provided incidents of violence and casualties. Hezbollah's arms, provided by Iran, were increasing, and the number of Israeli casualties was rising. A midair crash of two Israeli helicopters just south of the Israel-Lebanon border on February 4 took the lives of 73 Israeli soldiers. An Israeli commando raid on September 5 mounted by sea was intercepted by chance south of Sidon; 12 Israeli commandoes were killed in the attack. Mortar attacks by Lebanese guerrillas in the Israeli buffer zone killed nine Lebanese civilians in late November. Four anti-Israeli guerrillas had died in an earlier skirmish with Israeli forces. Militiamen commanded by an ally of Syria had killed at least six civilians in the port city of Sidon in mid-August. Under the terms of the peace agreement, formalized in 1996, all sides involved in the hostilities were not to attack civilians.

Internal Affairs. The Lebanese budget, which had an unfortunate tendency to be an optimistic work of fiction, was approved by parliament, after skeptical debate, on February 3. It envisaged a deficit of nearly $1.6 billion, or about 36% of total expenditures. The actual deficit in 1996 had been 51% of total expenditures.

The ruling triumvirate bickered often and agreed sometimes. President Elias Hrawi is a Maronite Christian; Prime Minister Rafik al-Hariri is a Sunni Muslim; and parliamentary speaker Nabi Birri is a Shiite Muslim. They agreed in April on setting dates for municipal and parliamentary elections. Local-council elections would be held for the first time since 1963 by April 1998. The next general election, due in summer 2000, would be postponed for eight months. Four members of parliament lost their seats in May when the Constitutional Council ruled that their 1996 elections involved fraud.

On May 9, Samir Geagea, leader of the Christian militia during the nation's civil war and the only such leader to be prosecuted for wartime actions, was found guilty and sentenced to death for a 1991 attempt to murder the then defense minister. The sentence was commuted to life imprisonment; he already was serving two such sentences.

Foreign Affairs. Madeleine Albright, on her first visit to the Middle East as U.S. secretary of state, made a brief stop in Lebanon on September 15. She stated that the freeing of the country from foreign occupation was a U.S. objective. In July, Albright had lifted the ten-year-old travel ban that forbade Americans to visit Lebanon.

The arrest on February 18 of a number of Japanese members of the Red Army terrorist groups occasioned a minor diplomatic contretemps with Japan. Japan wanted the men extradited; instead, they were put on trial on June 9 in Beirut on a series of minor, rather technical, charges. They enjoyed much support in Lebanon because their actions had been anti-Israeli.

Papal Visit. Pope John Paul II visited Lebanon on May 10–11. It was his first visit to the Middle East, the first visit by any pontiff to Lebanon, and the first papal trip to the region since 1964. Pope John Paul met with both Christian and Muslim leaders and called for "a restoration of national sovereignty" for Lebanon. More than 300,000 attended an outdoor papal Mass near Beirut—reportedly the largest gathering in Lebanon ever.

ARTHUR CAMPBELL TURNER
University of California, Riverside

LEBANON • Information Highlights

Official Name: Republic of Lebanon.
Location: Southwest Asia.
Area: 4,015 sq mi (10 400 km²).
Population (mid-1997 est.): 3,900,000.
Chief Cities (1982 est.): Beirut, the capital, 509,000; Tripoli, 198,000.
Government: *Head of state,* Elias Hrawi, president (took office November 1989). *Head of government,* Rafik al-Hariri, premier (named Oct. 22, 1992). *Legislature* (unicameral)—National Assembly.
Monetary Unit: Lebanese pound (1,527.00 pounds equal U.S.$1, Dec. 31, 1997).
Gross Domestic Product (1995 est. U.S.$): $18,300,000,000 (purchasing power parity).
Foreign Trade (1996 est. U.S.$): *Imports,* $7,568,000,000; *exports,* $1,014,000,000.

LIBRARIES

Libraries in North America faced numerous challenges in 1997. Foremost among these were finding alternative ways of funding and providing access to the Internet.

Funding. Microsoft founder Bill Gates and his wife, Melinda, established the Gates Library Foundation in June. The foundation was to disburse $200 million in cash and $200 million in computer equipment and software to public libraries, especially those in low-income communities in the United States and Canada. The foundation's program director, Christopher Hedrick, said his goal is for all citizens to "think of the public library as the champion of books and patrons of knowledge, as well as a major access point to the benefits of the digital age."

Before Congress adjourned in late October 1996, it established the Library Services and Technology Act, replacing the 32-year-old Library Services and Construction Act. More than $140 million would be made available to libraries in fiscal year 1998. The majority of the funds would be allocated to the states for library technological innovation and outreach activities. Also in October 1996, Congress enacted a law switching federal responsibility for U.S. libraries from the Department of Education to the newly created Institute of Museum and Library Services.

Outsourcing became a catchword in 1997 after Hawaii's state public-library system announced its dissatisfaction with its contract with book jobber Baker & Taylor to provide all book selection and cataloging. State librarian Bart Kane canceled the year-old agreement in July, alleging that the company had defaulted. Critics of outsourcing said that ceding responsibility for core library operations to a for-profit company would result in poor service to patrons. More controversy was stirred up in July when the Riverside County (CA) Public Library outsourced its management operations to the private firm Library Systems & Services, Inc.

The Internet. On May 5 the Federal Communications Commission (FCC) unanimously voted to give libraries and schools up to $2.25 billion annually in discounts on telecommunications services. The new rules mandated discounts ranging from 20%–90%, with deeper discounts for libraries in rural, high-cost, and low-income communities.

Librarians, computer users, and civil libertarians scored a decisive victory June 26 when the U.S. Supreme Court ruled that the Communications Decency Act was an unconstitutional violation of free-speech rights. Librarians had been concerned that the law would subject them to criminal prosecution for posting materials on-line that are legal in other media.

Parental concern over unexpurgated Internet access in public libraries swept the nation in 1997, resulting in the installation of filtering software in several libraries and pledges from others to monitor minors' World Wide Web use. Opponents of filtering software claimed that it was impossible to screen out everything objectionable without denying access to legitimate social, medical, and sexual sites. Proponents contended that it was not the library's place to provide pornography, and that filtering allows librarians some control over what comes into the building and the context in which it may be used or viewed by an adult patron. (*See also* SPECIAL REPORT, page 197.)

Associations. The 116th annual conference of the American Library Association (ALA), held June 26–July 2 in San Francisco, drew more than 23,000 attendees. ALA President Mary Somerville presided over the event, which had "Kids Can't Wait" as its theme. Barbara J. Ford, director of the Virginia Commonwealth University library, was inaugurated as ALA's new president.

"Reinventing Libraries" was the theme of the Canadian Library Association's 52nd annual conference, which was held June 18–22 in Ottawa.

The Third National Conference of African-American Librarians was held July 31–August 3 in Winston-Salem, NC; the conference's theme was "Culture Keepers III: Making Global Connections."

GEORGE M. EBERHART
"American Libraries" magazine, Chicago, IL

LIBRARY AWARDS IN 1997

Beta Phi Mu Award for distinguished service to education for librarianship: Charles A. Bunge, School of Library and Information Science, University of Wisconsin at Madison

Randolph J. Caldecott Medal for the most distinguished picture book for children: David Wisniewski, *Golem*

Grolier Award for unique contributions to the stimulation and guidance of reading by children and young people: Patricia R. Scales, director, Greenville (SC) Middle School Library

Joseph W. Lippincott Award for distinguished service to the profession of librarianship: Richard M. Dougherty, professor, School of Information, University of Michigan

John Newbery Medal for the most distinguished contribution to literature for children: Elaine L. Konigsburg, *The View from Saturday*

LIBRARY INTERNET LINKS

American Library Association: http://www.ala.org/
Canadian Library Association: http://www.cla.amlibs.ca/
Internet Public Library: http://www.ipl.org/
Mexican Library Association: http://cuib.unam.mx/ambac/ (English version available)
Special Libraries Association: http://www.sla.org/
Tips for Parents: http://www.ssdesign.com/ALAkids/

LIBYA

A ban on Libyan air travel, imposed in 1992 to pressure the government into surrendering two men implicated in the bombing of a U.S. airliner, remained in effect during 1997. Libya periodically defied the embargo, while critics of the strategy urged Great Britain and the United States to accept one of the compromises offered by Libya.

Foreign Relations. Libya had refused to turn over for trial in Great Britain or the United States two intelligence agents alleged to have sabotaged a Pan Am flight that exploded over Scotland in December 1988, killing 270 passengers. Alternatives proposed by Libya during 1997—permitting British and U.S. judges to monitor a trial in Libya conducted under international law, holding the trial in a neutral country, or bringing the case before the International Court of Justice—elicited no response. The Arab League, the Organization of the Islamic Conference, the Organization of African Unity, and the Non-Aligned Nations Movement all supported these proposals, as did South African President Nelson Mandela—who traveled to Libya in October—and Russian Foreign Minister Yevgeny Primakov.

Libya's mission to the United Nations also sent letters in June to the families of the crash victims, stressing its government's desire to engage in negotiations regarding a trial, but this also failed to produce results. The lingering controversy ensured the frigidity of U.S. relations with Libya, whose classification as a "terrorist nation" precluded U.S. firms from doing business there. The Bill Clinton administration's efforts to discourage foreign businesses from investing in Libya provoked several European allies to condemn U.S. interference in international commerce.

As the search for a solution dragged on, Libya occasionally defied the air-travel ban.

In March planes belonging to the national airline flew Libyans to and from Saudi Arabia to participate in the annual Muslim pilgrimage to Mecca. In May a fleet of Libyan planes flew Col. Muammar el-Qaddafi and a large entourage to and from Niger and Nigeria on state visits. In September the Arab League urged its 22 members to disregard the sanctions, asserting that official Libyan delegations, pilgrims, and Libyan workers employed in other countries should not be prevented from air travel.

Libya was more cooperative regarding a second bombing incident, allowing French officials preparing to try several Libyans accused of blowing up a French airliner over the Sahara in 1989 to conduct investigations in Tripoli. Another long-standing case moved toward resolution when German prosecutors announced in February that they would try five suspects—one of them Libyan—for the deaths of two U.S. servicemen and a Turkish woman in the 1986 bombing of a Berlin discotheque.

Regional Relations. As Libya won increasing regional support for ending the sanctions, its government emphasized its commitment to Arab unity. In July, Libyan officials organized a march to the Egyptian border to mark the 45th anniversary of the 1952 Egyptian Revolution that brought Gamal Abdel Nasser to power. Nasser's advocacy of Arab unity inspired Qaddafi, who always has regarded unity essential for regional development and advancement, and has seen himself as Nasser's ideological heir.

Ironically, a complicating factor in Libya's relations with other Arab countries was its treatment of Palestinians, whom Qaddafi had ordered to leave in 1994 to symbolize his rejection of the Palestinian Authority's peace agreement with Israel. Although he subsequently withdrew the order, many Palestinians lived in a crowded camp on the Egyptian-Libyan frontier. Most wanted to leave Libya, but other countries were unwilling to accept them.

In January a military court ordered the execution of eight persons charged with spying for the United States and plotting a 1993 coup. Although rumors of organized opposition to Qaddafi persisted throughout 1997, the regime's effective management of information—particularly concerning domestic political and economic conditions—made it difficult to assess the strength or viability of such movements.

KENNETH J. PERKINS
University of South Carolina

LIBYA • Information Highlights

Official Name: Socialist People's Libyan Arab Jamahiriya ("state of the masses").

Location: North Africa.

Area: 679,359 sq mi (1 759 540 km²).

Population (mid-1997 est.): 5,600,000.

Chief Cities (1988 est.): Tripoli, the capital, 591,062; Benghazi, 446,250.

Government: *Head of state and government,* Muammar el-Qaddafi (took office 1969). *Legislature* (unicameral)—General People's Congress.

Monetary Unit: Dinar (0.386 dinar equals U.S. $1, official rate, July 1997).

Gross Domestic Product (1994 est. U.S.$): $32,900,000,000 (purchasing power parity).

Foreign Trade (1994 est. U.S.$): *Imports,* $6,900,000,000; *exports,* $7,200,000,000.

Literature

Overview

Dario Fo, a little-known and very controversial Italian playwright and performer, won the 1997 Nobel Prize for literature....Robert Pinsky was named U.S. poet laureate....Miller Williams, an Arkansas poet, read at U.S. President Bill Clinton's second inauguration....The memoir remained the prevailing literary form....Poet Adrienne Rich rejected the 1997 National Medal of Arts.

Nobel Prize. It was a surprise to many, including the recipient, when the 1997 Nobel Prize for literature went to Dario Fo, 71. Though Fo has written about 70 plays—many of them one-man productions in which he also is the performer—he is not well-known outside his homeland. As a longtime member of the Communist Party, he was, for many years, refused entry into the United States under an old law denying visas to those who participated in antigovernment activities or were members of the Communist Party. Fo, with his wife and collaborator Franca Rame, frequently choose the Roman Catholic Church and various controversial subjects for their plots, offending governments and the Vatican alike.

In announcing the $1 million prize, the Swedish Academy compared Fo to a medieval court jester. The academy noted, "With a blend of laughter and gravity, he opens our eyes to abuses and injustices in society and also the wider historical perspective in which they can be placed. Fo is an extremely serious satirist with a multifaceted oeuvre."

In his native Italy, Fo's popularity peaked in the mid-1970s but he has continued to draw both friends and foes with his political views. His best-known play, *Accidental Death of an Anarchist*, was written in 1979 and was successful in Italy and Britain. It had only a short run on Broadway in 1984, however. His one-man tour de force, *Mistero Buffo*, was performed at the Joyce Theater in New York City and the Kennedy Center Theater in Washington, DC, in 1986.

U.S. Poet Laureate. Robert Pinsky, a prizewinning poet and professor in the graduate creative-writing program at Boston University, was named poet laureate of the United States by the Library of Congress in March 1997. His predecessor, Robert Haas, served a two-year term and would be remembered for lecturing on literacy and doing poetry read-

© Grazia Neri/Sygma

Dario Fo

ings. The promotion of public awareness of poetry is one of the duties of the poet laureate. In accepting the honor, the 56-year-old Pinsky said that he would like to address the fading of poetry from high-school and college curricula and make an addition to the poetry readings stored in the Library of Congress archives. Regarding the latter, he said he might ask people who are not poets or scholars to read and record their favorite poems.

Pinsky was born in Long Branch, NJ, and earned his doctorate in English from Stanford University. His own work includes five poetry collections—including *The Figured Wheel: New and Collected Poems, 1966–1996*; several books of essays; two books of nonfiction; and an acclaimed translation of Dante's *Inferno*. He also is the poetry editor of the Internet magazine *Slate* (http://www.slate.com).

National Medal of Arts. Adrienne Rich, 68, who has published more than 15 volumes of poetry, refused the 1997 National Medal of Arts when it was offered to her. Rich stated that she was against "a government where so much power is concentrated in so few hands." She is believed to be the first artist to decline the award, which is given annually to 12 people. In a letter to Jane Alexander, chairwoman of the National Endowment of the Arts, which administers the awards, Rich wrote, "the very meaning of art, as I understand it, its incompatible with the cynical politics of this [the Bill Clinton] administration." Rich's most recent volume of poetry is *Dark Fields of the Republic: Poems, 1991–1995*.

Kristi Vaughan

American Literature

The personal memoir continued to be wildly popular in 1997. It was so popular, in fact, that there was a so-called "memoir backlash" in which many authors and reviewers proposed a retreat from what they saw as mere narcissism and exhibitionism and encouraged, in its place, a resurgence of the well-made novel, story, and poem. Many consciously crafted works of literature appeared in 1997, although it seemed that the reading public's interest in the tawdry tell-all was far from being exhausted.

Novels. Two much-honored veterans not only sustained but extended their reputations as master craftsmen who consistently serve up a big, important, well-crafted tale. Indeed, Thomas Pynchon's *Mason & Dixon* and Don DeLillo's *Underworld* were just the kind of novels the anti-memoir crowd was calling for. *Mason & Dixon* is about the two English surveyors who drew the line that later would separate the North from the South. The ostensible subject is slavery,

Courtesy, Henry Holt and Company, Inc.

although there are frequent flourishes of whimsy as well as an undercurrent of Pynchon's trademark paranoia. *Underworld* begins with a 1951 baseball game and ends after the collapse of the Soviet empire. Its subject is nothing less than the American psyche during the Cold War years. It is DeLillo's longest, most ambitious, most complicated novel to date, and many critics believed it to be his best.

Meanwhile, a trio of old hands turned in competent performances; Saul Bellow's *The Actual*, Norman Mailer's *The Gospel According to the Son*, and Philip Roth's *American Pastoral* were admired if not exalted by reviewers. The critics were less kind to John Updike's *Toward the End of Time* and Joyce Carol Oates' *Man Crazy*. Cult figure Kurt Vonnegut gave himself a negative notice for *Timequake*, calling it "junk" and saying it would be his last novel.

The South continues to be a rich region for fiction, and 1997 was no exception. Ellen Gilchrist writes with the kind of intimacy often associated with the memoir, although her work is always consummately well crafted.

It is not hard to see why she has such a loyal following; her 1997 novel, *Sarah Conley*, is a classic tale of passion and betrayal, although Gilchrist's feisty heroine is triumphant in the end. A handsome but suspect stranger shakes up the inhabitants of a little North Carolina town in the 1950s in Clyde Edgerton's hilarious *Where Trouble Sleeps. Cold Mountain* by Charles Frazier paints a grimmer picture, yet one lightened often by the surprise appearance of dozens of interesting minor characters; it is the story of a Confederate soldier who quits the battlefield to walk hundreds of miles and find his lost sweetheart. The novel, Frazier's first, won the National Book Award for fiction.

Among other first novels, Dawn Turner Trice's *Only Twice I've Wished for Heaven* stands out as a moving description of an encounter an 11-year-old black child from Chicago has with a world that threatens her, yet helps her grow.

As in any year, there were a certain number of near misses in 1997, but even these showed the novel's rich potential. Kirsten Bakis' *Lives of the Monster Dogs* is the story of a group of dogs who were trained to walk upright and speak by a mad scientist but have rebelled against being turned into soldiers; if the writing is sometimes uninspired, at least the premise is ingenious. And although occasionally weakened by implausi-

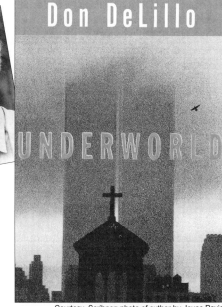

Courtesy, Scribner; photo of author by Joyce Ravid

AMERICAN LITERATURE
MAJOR WORKS • 1997

NOVELS

Adams, Alice, *Medicine Men*
Askew, Rilla, *The Mercy Seat*
Bakis, Kirsten, *Lives of the Monster Dogs*
Barthelme, Frederick, *Bob the Gambler*
Beattie, Ann, *My Life, Starring Dara Falcon*
Bellow, Saul, *The Actual*
Busch, Frederick, *Girls*
Collignon, Rick, *Perdido*
Corn, Alfred, *Part of His Story*
DeLillo, Don, *Underworld*
Eberstadt, Fernanda, *When the Sons of Heaven Meet the Daughters of the Earth*
Edgerton, Clyde, *Where Trouble Sleeps*
Frazier, Charles, *Cold Mountain*
Garcia, Cristina, *The Agüero Sisters*
Gilchrist, Ellen, *Sarah Conley*
Goldman, Francisco, *The Ordinary Seaman*
Graver, Elizabeth, *Unravelling*
Gurganus, Allan, *Plays Well With Others*
Hall, Brian, *The Saskiad*
Johnson, Denis, *Already Dead: A California Gothic*
Johnson, Diane, *Le Divorce*
Jones, Louis, B., *California's Over*
Just,Ward, *Echo House*
Kelley, Thomas, *Payback*
Leithauser, Brad, *The Friends of Freeland*
Mailer, Norman, *The Gospel According to the Son*
Mallon, Thomas, *Dewey Defeats Truman*
Moody, Rick, *Purple America*
Nunn, Kem, *The Dogs of Winter*
Oates, Joyce Carol, *Man Crazy*
Prose, Francine, *Guided Tours of Hell: Novellas*
Pynchon, Thomas, *Mason & Dixon*
Rhodes, Jewell Parker, *Magic City*
Roth, Philip, *American Pastoral*
Strong, Albertine, *Deluge*
Thurm, Marian, *The Clairvoyant*
Trice, Dawn Turner, *Only Twice I've Wished for Heaven*
Updike, John, *Toward the End of Time*
Vonnegut, Kurt, *Timequake*
Watson, Larry, *White Crosses*

SHORT STORIES

Baxter, Charles, *Believers: A Novella and Stories*
Boyd, William, *The Destiny of Nathalie X and Other Stories*
Carlson, Ron, *The Hotel Eden: Stories*
Davis, Lydia, *Almost No Memory*
Eisenberg, Deborah, *All Around Atlantis: Stories*
Gilbert, Elizabeth, *Pilgrims*
Giles, Molly, *Creek Walk: and Other Stories*
Hempel, Amy, *Tumble Home: A Novella and Short Stories*
Hynes, James, *Publish and Perish: Three Tales of Tenure and Terror*
Lattimore, Steve, *Circumnavigation*
Malamud, Bernard, *The Complete Stories*
Mattison, Alice, *Men Giving Money, Women Yelling: Intersecting Stories*
McKnight, Reginald, *White Boys: Stories*
Nevai, Lucia, *Normal*
Ozick, Cynthia, *The Puttermesser Papers*
Powell, Padgett, *Aliens of Affection*
Stone, Robert, *Bear and His Daughters: Stories*
Theroux, Paul, *Collected Stories*
Weaver, Gordon, *Four Decades: New and Selected Stories*
Woodman, Allen, *Saved by Mr. F. Scott Fitzgerald and Other Stories*

HISTORY AND BIOGRAPHY

Ambrose, Stephen E., *Citizen Soldiers*
Beschloss, Michael R., *Taking Charge: The Johnson White House Tapes, 1963–1964*
Blotner, Joseph, *Robert Penn Warren: A Biography*
Bosworth, Patricia, *Anything Your Little Heart Desires: An American Family Story*
Cifelli, Edward M., *John Ciardi: A Biography*
Ellis, Joseph J., *American Sphinx: The Character of Thomas Jefferson*
Farrow, Mia, *What Falls Away: A Memoir*
Graham, Katharine, *Personal History*

Gray, Spalding, *It's A Slippery Slope*
Harrison, Kathryn, *The Kiss*
Hellmann, John, *The Kennedy Obsession: The American Myth of JFK*
Heyrman, Christine Leigh, *Southern Cross: The Beginnings of the Bible Belt*
hooks, bell, *Wounds of Passion: A Writing Life*
Kertzer, David I., *The Kidnapping of Eduardo Mortara*
Kincaid, Jamaica, *My Brother*
Kloefkorn, William, *This Death by Drowning*
Lukas, J. Anthony, *Big Trouble: A Murder in a Small Western Town Sets Off a Struggle for the Soul of America*
Lyden, Jacki, *Daughter of the Queen of Sheba*
Lynn, Kenneth S., *Charlie Chaplin and His Times*
Mailer, Adele, *The Last Party: My Life With Norman Mailer*
McPherson, James M., *For Cause and Comrades: Why Men Fought in the Civil War*
Oates, Stephen B., *The Approaching Fury: Voices of the Storm, 1820–1861*
Rampersad, Arnold, *Jackie Robinson: A Biography*
Robertson, James I., *Stonewall Jackson: The Man, the Soldier, the Legend*
Suarez, Virgil, *Spared Angola: Memories from a Cuban-American Childhood*
Tanenhaus, Sam, *Whittaker Chambers*

CULTURE AND CRITICISM

Baxter, Charles, *Burning Down the House: Essays on Fiction*
Botstein, Leon, *Jefferson's Children: Education and the Promise of American Culture*
Bryant, J. A., Jr., *Twentieth Century Southern Literature*
Cantor, Norman F., *The American Century: Varieties of Culture in Modern Times*
Delbanco, Andrew, *Required Reading: Why Our American Classics Matter Now*
Goodwin, Doris Kearns, *Wait Till Next Year*
Hoffman, Andrew J., *Inventing Mark Twain: The Lives of Samuel Langhorne Clemens*
Kazin, Alfred, *God and the American Writer*
Lynch, Thomas, *The Undertaking: Life Studies From the Dismal Trade*
Momaday, N. Scott, *The Man Made of Words: Essays, Stories, Passages*
Muske, Carol, *Women and Poetry: Truth, Autobiography, and the Shape of the Self*
Pells, Richard, *Not Like Us: How Europeans Loved, Hated, and Transformed American Culture Since World War II*
Perrin, Noel, *A Child's Delight*
Shipler, David K., *A Country of Strangers: Blacks and Whites in America*
Straus, Dorothea, *The Paper Trail: A Recollection of Writers*
Trow, George W. S., *Within the Context of No Context*
Walker, Alice, *Anything We Love Can Be Saved: A Writer's Activism*
Wallace, David Foster, *A Supposedly Fun Thing I'll Never Do Again: Essays and Arguments*

POETRY

Algarín, Miguel, *Love Is Hard Work: Memorias de Loisaida*
Applewhite, James, *Daytime and Starlight*
Balaban, John, *Locusts at the Edge of Summer: New and Selected Poems*
Bang, Mary Jo, *Apology for Want*
Barr, John, *The Hundred Fathom Curve*
Bell, Marvin, *Ardor: The Book of the Dead Man Series (Volume 2)*
Bidart, Frank, *Desire*
Bierds, Linda, *The Profile Makers*
Clampitt, Amy, *The Collected Poems*
Crane, Hart, *O My Land, My Friends: The Selected Letters*
Hernandez Cruz, Victor, *Panaramas*
Kumin, Maxine, *Selected Poems, 1960–1990*
Lindsay, Sarah, *Primate Behavior*
Macdonald, Cynthia, *I Can't Remember*
Meredith, William, *Effort at Speech: New and Selected Poems*
Moore, Marianne, *The Selected Letters of Marianne Moore*
Muske, Carol, *An Octave Above the Thunder*
Nelson, Marilyn, *The Fields of Praise: New and Selected Poems*
Orlen, Steve, *Kisses*
Price, Reynolds, *Collected Poems*
Sarton, May, *May Sarton: Selected Letters, 1916–1954*
Schuyler, James, *The Diary of James Schuyler*
Waring, Belle, *Dark Blonde: Poems*
Wright, Charles, *Black Zodiac*

ble writing, Jewell Parker Rhodes' *Magic City* is an eye-opening fictional account of an actual race riot in 1920s Tulsa.

Short Stories. Increasingly, short-story writers seek to create a kind of architecture within their collections, seeking a unity of subject or speaker or locale that perhaps is meant to give their work the solidity of longer narratives. Thus Molly Giles gives voices to complex female characters in *Creek Walk: and Other Stories*. Another "theme" collection—this one by a much-praised novelist, Robert Stone, working with the shorter form—

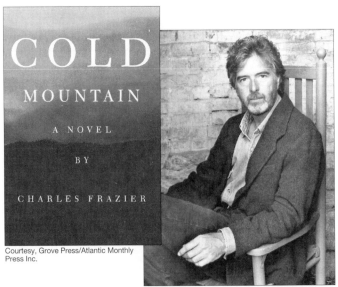

Courtesy, Grove Press/Atlantic Monthly Press Inc.

Courtesy, Atlantic Monthly Press Inc., photo by Marion Ettlinger

is *Bear and His Daughter: Stories*. Stone's characters like drugs, and if some of these pieces tumble off into something resembling a junkie's woozy self-absorption, the best ones more than compensate for any lapses.

But in *The Destiny of Nathalie X and Other Stories*, William Boyd bucks the trend toward unity with stories involving a variety of characters in Los Angeles and Lisbon, and in Germany and France. All of the separate pieces are stamped with wit, intelligence, and erudition. Another worthwhile collection is Charles Baxter's *Believers: A Novella and Stories*. A writer's writer, Baxter long has been admired by his peers for the craft and originality evidenced in his five earlier books. On the surface, the pieces in this new gathering are not connected, although each is concerned intimately with its characters' inner lives, sensibilities, and perceptions. The work of a younger writer, Allen Woodman, deserves a wider readership; his *Saved by Mr. F. Scott Fitzgerald and Other Stories* engages and charms with its portraits of offbeat Southerners.

Of course, the work of a master writer needs no design other than genius. The appearance of Bernard Malamud's *The Complete Stories* makes it possible for older readers to reread their favorites and younger ones to see if the stories, written in the 1950s through the 1970s, hold their own against contemporary fare. (They do.)

History and Biography. The bombshell memoir of 1997 was Kathryn Harrison's *The Kiss*, an account of the author's adult affair with her father. While some observers criticized Harrison for excessive frankness, reviewers generally praised the book for its courage, honesty, and fine writing. In *What Falls Away*, Mia Farrow describes her marriages to Frank Sinatra and André Previn and

her life with her biological and adopted children. However, readers likely will be more interested in her disastrous relationship with Woody Allen than anything else. The memoir craze may have reached its nadir in Adele Mailer's *The Last Party: My Life With Norman Mailer*, a laughably ill-written book, nonetheless valuable for its insights into the mind of a woman curiously enthralled by an abusive spouse.

Not every tell-all autobiography is about familial dysfunction, however. For example, William Kloefkorn's *This Death by Drowning* is a quirky, funny, moving account full of unforgettable characters and rare moments of pure stylistic magic. Mixing poems, stories, and essays, novelist Virgil Suarez' *Spared Angola* is a charming, intricate self-portrait of an exile's progress from Cuba to Spain to the United States. Feminist writer and scholar bell hooks looks at gender, class, and race in academia and beyond in *Wounds of Passion: A Writing Life*. And in *Daughter of the Queen of Sheba*, National Public Radio correspondent Jacki Lyden writes richly of her mother's manic depression and its effect on the family but also the woman's courage and will as she struggled against her disorder.

It has been said that, when Robert Penn Warren and Cleanth Brooks founded *The Southern Review* in the 1930s, they moved the center of literary criticism in the West from the left bank of the Seine to the left bank of the Mississippi; Joseph Blotner's *Robert Penn Warren: A Biography* is the definitive life of one half of this extraordinarily influential pair. Warren is the only writer to win the Pulitzer Prize for both fiction and poetry—the latter twice—and seems to have been that rare creature among celebrated artists, a genuinely decent person.

Culture and Criticism. In this age of the memoir, Andrew Delbanco champions timeless works in *Required Reading: Why Our American Classics Matter Now*. The person perhaps the closest to the ideal of "the great American author" is Mark Twain, whose several personae are examined in Andrew J. Hoffman's *Inventing Mark Twain: The Lives of Samuel Langhorne Clemens*. J.A. Bryant, Jr., looks at African-American and women writers as well as postmodern and contemporary writers in *Twentieth Century Southern Literature*. Bryant gives special attention to Robert Penn Warren, calling him "the supreme summary figure of the century."

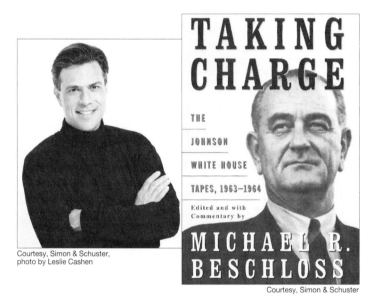

Courtesy, Simon & Schuster, photo by Leslie Cashen

Courtesy, Simon & Schuster

Still, some of the most engaging critical works of 1997 had an intimacy that appealed to readers. In *Burning Down the House*, Charles Baxter examines Jane Smiley's novel *A Thousand Acres* and Richard Nixon's memoirs as well as the differences between and similarities of poets and prose writers. (Both, for example, use "stutter memories" to repeat key ideas for effect.) In *The Man Made of Words: Essays, Stories, Passages*, the dean of Native American writers, N. Scott Momaday, looks at American Indian culture but also at figures as diverse as Isak Dinesen, Edmund Wilson, and Billy the Kid. At 1,000-plus pages, David Foster Wallace's 1996 novel *Infinite Jest* left some readers wondering whether there was anything to Wallace's approach other than sheer bulk, but the nonfiction pieces gathered in *A Supposedly Fun Thing I'll Never Do Again: Essays and Arguments* reveal an acute and mentally agile observer at

work as he ranges over film, television, and other aspects of American culture.

Poetry. James Dickey, who was the Dylan Thomas of the South—the hard-living carouser whose poetry was rooted deeply in the soil; the boozy celebrity who was a larger-than-life, if occasionally embarrassing, advertisement for his native region—died on Jan. 19, 1997. He had a successful career in advertising before becoming a teacher at various universities and poet-in-residence at the University of South Carolina in 1969. His writings included criticism, screenplays, children's books, and, of course, *Deliverance* as well as two other novels—*Alnilam* (1987) and *To the White Sea* (1993). The 1965 collection *Buckdancer's Choice and Other Poems* won the National Book Award for poetry. Dickey will be remembered largely for poetry bold in subject matter and extravagant in diction—work that begins in the personal yet transcends it.

A quieter voice in the poetry of the South is that of Reynolds Price, whose *Collected Poems*—dealing with religion, dreams, and the "eel" (a cancerous tumor that threatened his life for years)—were published in 1997. John Ciardi (1916–86) was a major poet in the 1940s and 1950s, and in 1997 the University of Arkansas Press published *The Collected Poems of John Ciardi* as well as Edward M. Cifelli's *John Ciardi: A Biography*. In his prime, Ciardi was considered a peer of Robert Lowell, Elizabeth Bishop, and others whose work still shapes American poetry. Ciardi's own work is little known now, although he created a place for himself in literary history with his translation into English of Dante Alighieri's *Divine Comedy*. Many experts consider it the best translation of the masterpiece by far.

Collections of letters by several major American poets, including *The Selected Letters of Marianne Moore* and *May Sarton: Selected Letters, 1916–1954*, appeared in 1997. However, the most engaging gathering was *O My Land, My Friends: The Selected Letters of Hart Crane*, which throbs with the intensity of a fever. During his brief life—he killed himself at 32—Crane epitomized the excesses of the Jazz Age.

DAVID KIRBY, *Florida State University*

Children's Literature

Two trends dominated children's publishing in 1997: books that were bold in the subjects they tackled, such as depression and pedophilia; and the commercialization of children's literature, in which publishers endlessly looked for a tie-in between a book and a product, such as a doll, T-shirt, or stuffed animal.

Young-adult literature revived in 1997 with controversial titles. Brock Cole's *The Facts Speak for Themselves* is a first-person account by a 13-year-old girl involved in a sexual relationship with a middle-aged man—an affair that leads to murder. Norma Fox Mazer's *When She Was Good* details the mental and physical abuse of one sibling by another, and Han Nolan's *Dancing on the Edge* describes a girl's self-mutilation and descent into madness. Although these books were written commandingly by some of today's most skillful writers, many questioned the appropriateness of such bleak topics for this audience.

Merchandising potential seemed to dominate preschool and middle-grade titles. Even classics such as the Beatrix Potter books were being spun off into everything from cookbooks to paper dolls. Marc Brown's "Arthur" books, about an appealing aardvark and his family, hit the jackpot with their adaptation as a PBS television show that zoomed ahead of *Barney* in popularity and spun off everything from games to pajamas.

Other divisions of children's literature seemed to follow the path of adult publishing

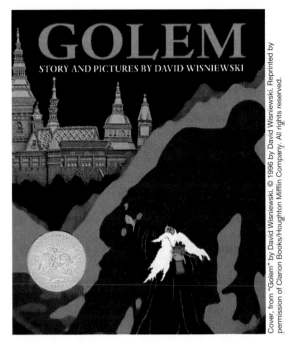

"Golem," which was written and illustrated by David Wisniewski, was awarded the 1997 Randolph J. Caldecott Medal as the most distinguished picture book for children.

Sharleen Collicott used an airbrush-like technique in illustrating Laura Numeroff's "The Chicken Sisters." The 32-page story was published by HarperCollins and is for those aged 4–7.

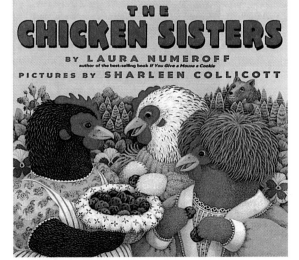

by concentrating on established names or newcomers who had the potential to hit it big, rather than on midlist authors.

Veteran author E. L. Konigsburg, who won her first Newbery Award in 1968, won a second Newbery in 1997 for *The View from Saturday*, the story of six students who learn about themselves and their teacher as they prepare for an academic bowl. The Caldecott Medal for most distinguished artwork went to David Wisniewski for the paper-cut illustrations in his book *Golem*, the legendary tale of a rabbi who shapes a giant man of clay to protect the Jews of Prague, but unleashes an uncontrollable force in the process.

Picture Books. Picture books remained the domain of established artists. Diane Stanley, best known for her illustrated middle-grade biographies, offered the amusing feminist fairy tale *Rumplestiltskin's Daughter*. Richard Egielski set another fairy tale, *The Gingerbread Boy*, in New York City, while Paul O. Zelinsky offered a beautiful new version of *Rapunzel*. *December*, an original fantasy by Eve Bunting about an unusual Christmas angel, was illustrated strikingly by Caldecott winner David Diaz.

Middle-Grade Books. Middle-grade series books, such as the "Goosebumps" stories, still were in retreat, causing the focus to shift to the many quality single-title fiction and nonfiction books. These included Jerry Spinelli's

SELECTED BOOKS FOR CHILDREN

Picture Books

Ehlert, Lois, *Cuckoo*
Fleming, Denise, *Time to Sleep*
Hearne, Betsy, *Seven Brave Women*
Lindbergh, Reeve, *The Awful Aardvarks Go to School*
McDermott, Gerald, *Musicians of the Son*
Numeroff, Laura, *The Chicken Sisters*
Pyle, Howard, *Bearskin*
Shapiro, Arnold, *Mice Squeak, We Speak*
Stadler, John, *The Cats of Mrs. Calamari*
Wells, Rosemary, *Bunny Money*

The Middle Grades

Billingsley, Franny, *Well Wished*
Cooper, Ilene, *The Dead Sea Scrolls*
Fleischman, Paul, *Seedfolks*
Freedman, Russell, *Out of Darkness*
Giblin, James, *Charles A. Lindbergh*
Herkes, Kevin, *Sun & Spoon*
Oughton, Jerrie, *The War in Georgia*
Reeder, Carolyn, *Across the Lines*
Stevenson, James, *The Unprotected Witness*
Tillage, Leon Walter, *Leon's Story*
Wick, Walter, *A Drop of Water*

Young Adults

Fine, Anne, *The Tulip Touch*
Haas, Jessie, *Westminster West*
Hampton, Wilborn, *Kennedy Assassinated*
Klause, Annette Curtis, *Blood and Chocolate*
McGuigan, Mary Ann, *Where You Belong*
Mazer, Harry, *Twelve Shots*
Naidoo, Bevley, *No Turning Back*

Wringer, about a boy who does not wish to take part in a pigeon shoot; Phyllis Reynolds Naylor's *Saving Shiloh*, the final book in a trilogy about a boy and his dog; and *Ella Enchanted*, a retelling of the Cinderella story by first-time author Gail Carson Levine.

Junior High and High School. Sophisticated titles and fantasy dominated the young-adult field in 1997. Jess Mowry's *Babylon Boyz* is a tough-talking book that takes place in the ghetto, while Barbara Wersba's *Whistle Me Home* and M. E. Kerr's *"Hello," I Lied* both deal with the lives of young gay men. Fantasies included *The Subtle Knife*—the second book in Phillip Pullman's trilogy "His Dark Materials"—and *Rose's Daughter* by Robin McKinley.

ILENE COOPER, *Editor, Children's Books "Booklist" Magazine*

Canadian Literature: English

While Canadians, as always, watched mostly U.S. motion pictures and television, the interest in homegrown writing that has marked Canadian culture for a number of years became an unmistakable trend in 1997.

Fiction and Poetry. Although 1997 did not produce the bumper crop of novels that appeared in 1996, many notable books were published. Carol Shields' *Larry's Party* takes readers deep into the puzzle of maze designer Larry Weller's life and mind as he plans a dinner party. *Barney's Version* is Mordecai Richler's vulgar, satirical, and poignant account of a life very similar to his own. It won the Giller Prize. Nino Ricci's *Where She Has Gone* completes his trilogy about Italian-Canadian life. In *The Underpainter*, which took the Governor-General's Award for fiction, Jane Urquhart provides a romantic look at a man's life and loves in Ontario and New York.

A number of works featured British Columbia settings and authors. *Traplines*, by Eden Robinson, tells four terrifying, blackly comic stories about young Native Canadians living in Vancouver and on a reserve in the interior of British Columbia. Fred Wah's *Diamond Grill* combines fiction and memoir in a brilliantly written book about the restaurant Wah's Chinese-Canadian father ran in Nelson, BC. British Columbia author Shani Mootoo's *Cereus Blooms at Night* is a lush, yet controlled, novel praised by critics.

Two established Canadian writers published short-story collections in 1997. Sandra Birdsell's *The Two-Headed Calf* contains densely written stories about the Canadian prairies—stories that at their best generate an extraordinary power. *Dust to Dust*, by Timothy Findley, explores the subject of mortality, often with a welcome light touch. Among books of poetry, George Stanley's *Gentle Northern Summer*, published in late 1996, stands out. By combining immediately accessible depth of feeling with penetrating intelligence, Stanley offers an entirely fresh picture of the frontier culture of the British Columbia interior.

Nonfiction. Biographies once again seized the imaginations of Canadians in 1997. *Glenn Gould: The Ecstasy and Tragedy of Genius* is Peter Ostwald's sensitive portrayal of the life of the great Canadian pianist. In *Sir Wilfred Laurier and the Romance of Canada*, Laurier La Pierre offers a clear account of the visionary prime minister's career. Catherine Dunphy has produced an exhaustive history of the fight for abortion rights in Canada in her biography of activist Henry Morgentaler, *Morgentaler: A Difficult Hero*. Anthony Bianco provides exceptional insight into the Reichmann family in *The Reichmanns: Family, Faith, Fortune, and the Empire of Olympia and York*. In *The Antagonist: Lucien Bouchard and the Politics of Delusion*, Lawrence Martin takes a long, hard look at the leading Quebec separatist.

Carol Shields, the chancellor of the University of Winnipeg and a prizewinning novelist, looks into the mind of an ordinary guy planning a dinner party in her 1997 work, "Larry's Party."

Two literary biographies offered moving portrayals of the tragic lives of Canadian poet Milton Acorn and novelist Margaret Laurence. Chris Gudgeon's biography of Acorn, *Out of This World*, deftly sketches the poet's life of self-destruction. *The Life of Margaret Laurence*, by James King, thoughtfully evokes Laurence's unhappiness and complexity.

A number of notable memoirs were published during the year. William Weintraub's *City Unique: Montreal Days and Nights in the 1940s and 1950s* renders a loving, clear-eyed, bittersweet look at the days when Montreal seemed to have it all. In *No Previous Experience*, literary biographer Elspeth Cameron titillates readers with her explanation of why she herself has entered a lesbian relationship. *A Leaf in the Bitter Wind* by Ting-xing Ye is a harrowing, enthralling depiction of the events leading to Ye's emigration from a brutal China and her subsequent ten-year separation from her daughter. *The New Yorker* humorist Bruce McCall depicts his Canadian childhood as years spent in a stagnant, backwater world yearning for the excitement of the United States in *Thin Ice: Coming of Age in Canada*.

Two widely read books described the changing makeup of Canada. *Boom, Bust and Echo*, by David K. Foot with Daniel Stoffman, explains how a fundamental demographic shift is transforming Canada's social and economic life. Michael Adams' *Sex in the Snow* puts forward the idea that as Canada's baby boomers enter middle age, they are becoming self-motivated individuals who are increasingly autonomous and skeptical of authority.

BRUCE SERAFIN
Founding Editor, "The Vancouver Review"

English Literature

Some of 1997's most compelling English fiction, frequently cast in modes of the historical, supports a claim that the historical serves as the basis of today's literary plots much as myths did for the ancient Greeks. In the realm of nonfiction, the 50th anniversary of the independence of India and Pakistan prompted several English publications. In English poetry, the year saw strong voices, some familiar and some new.

Fiction. John Banville's *The Untouchable*, based on the real "Cambridge spies"—Philby, Burgess, and Maclean—presents them and their deeds in thin disguise as a novel. However, authorial imagination may seem moved less by muse than by research. Banville masterfully uses incidents and characters that have become legendary if not mythical in recent British history. In another, quite different work, the mix of fiction and fact can hardly be more dense: In Harriet Waugh's novel *The Chaplet of Pearls*, a young scholar reconstructs the life of the historical Victorian novelist Charlotte M. Younge, but is challenged persistently by a small society of her elderly admirers. Also, Tim Parks' *Europa*, through the extended metaphor of a bus ride, examines the impending prospects of European unification. Several vantage points of political, economic, and social consequence are posed adroitly in an engagingly personal narrative. The intricately layered and lyrical third novel of Paul Wilson, *Do White Whales Sing at the Edge of the World?*, recounts four separate stories deliberately interwoven and conveyed in beautiful prose. The novel is centered, not too strangely, in a mental asylum, where some inmates reenact a 17th-century story of Arctic exploration against the backdrop of how they themselves arrived at the institution, along with the story of the asylum's imminent closing, which coincides with the misdeeds of the religious order that runs the institution.

But style compels aesthetic motive in fiction as well, as can be seen in John Burnside's *The Dumb House*, in which attractive use of language plays against the horror of what Burnside records—a fictionalized modern experiment on the living to determine if language is innate or acquired. In another powerful novel, Jonathan Coe dazzles readers with his prose in *The House of Sleep*. Ian McEwan's *Enduring Love* portrays a couple, Joe and Clarissa, securely in love, who come to be threatened by a third party after a ballooning accident. Helen Dunmore's collection of short stories, *Love of Fat Men*, deftly written with a poet's hand, memorably reveals place, character, and motive in a still-welcome genre.

India's Arundhati Roy, 37, was awarded the prestigious Booker Prize for the internationally best-selling *The God of Small Things*. Other novels on the Booker shortlist were Nick Jackson's *The Underground Man*, *Quarantine* by Jim Crace, *The Essence of the Thing* by Australia's Madeleine St. John, *Grace Notes* by Ireland's Bernard MacLaverty, and Parks' *Europa*.

Anthologies, however limited, still reveal brief, yet instructive glimpses of fiction that range between the sheerly imaginative and the concretely political. Of particular note, Salman Rushdie and Elizabeth West—in *The Vintage Book of Indian Writing 1997*—provide a sampling of Indian fiction since independence. *The Flamingo Book of New Scottish Writing, 1997*, edited by Douglas Gifford, contains short fiction that shifts among rural subjects to stories of communal crises. *Irish Short Stories 1997*, edited by David Marcus, displays works of several contemporary Irish writers who previously were unpublished.

Given the popularity of the genre, perhaps one should not overlook a crime novel of note, Craig Smith's compellingly and tightly written *Silent She Sleeps*, which portrays a young academic sleuth who takes a university position to help herself solve the long-ago campus murder of her mother. Finally, either in experimentation or as an indication of new directions, a different mode of authorship and of publication are striking. *Finbar's Hotel* is a novel in which the stories of a hotel's employees and its transient guests were written collaboratively by seven authors, including Dermot Bolger, Roddy Doyle, and Anne Enright. It leaves readers puzzled as to which of the identified authors wrote the various parts of the work. And Online Originals, a new electronic-publishing venue, appeared on the World Wide Web and had a few fiction titles in 1997—such as *The Paternoster Bead* by Rayne Arnaud and Patricia le Roy's *The Angels of Russia*—with the promise of more.

Nonfiction. Among the works published to coincide with India's and Pakistan's independence anniversaries was Sunil Khilnani's *The Idea of India*, an examination of the origin and persistence of India's secular state. *The Princes of India in the Endgame of Empire, 1917–1947*, by Ian Copland, exposes long-term British mismanagement and betrayal of the Indian princely establishment. In *Jinnah, Pakistan and Islamic Identity, the Search for Saladin*, Akbar S. Ahmed examines the com-

© Stefan Rousseau/AP/Wide World Photos

Arundhati Roy, a 37-year-old resident of New Delhi, India, was awarded the 1997 Booker Prize for her first novel, "The God of Small Things." It was an international best-seller.

plex roles played by the first ruler of Pakistan. *Nehru, A Tryst with Destiny* by Stanley Wolpert and B. R. Nanda's *Jawaharlal Nehru, Rebel and Statesman*—both published before 1997—explore the life and decisive governing acts made by the practical architect of the modern state of India. Finally, one finds a first among the several books whose appearance coincides with the positive vote of September 1997 to establish a Scottish parliament: a new translation of the Bible into Glaswegian, *A Glasgow Bible*.

Poetry. Among the year's strong voices in poetry, some were new and others were familiar. In *Collected Poems*, John Fuller displays fluency and wit over a broad range of themes; meanwhile, the *Collected Poems, 1956–1994* of Thomas Kinsella convincingly secures the Irish poet's place with particular lyrical insistence. In *The Bounty*, Nobel Prize winner Derek Walcott—now a lyrical but thoughtful praise-singer of his native island of St. Lucia—suggests that all is not well in his Eden.

The Marble Fly, the third book of poems by Jamie McKendrick, reexplores veins of the rich lode of classical mythology with surprising invention. David Harnett's new collection of poems, *At the Wood's Edge*, contains poems of acknowledgment to masters, extended conceits, and meditations on various locales. Among the new voices in Indian poetry (in English), a new edition of Imtiaz Dharker's *Postcards From God* treats themes of exile from the personal medley of Dharker's Islamic and Hindu cultural past; and *Point No Point* by Sujata Bhatt reveals by nuance and textured image the vast subcontinental diaspora.

DONALD L. JENNERMANN
Indiana State University

World Literature*

In 1997 the West Indies and India led the way in a superb literary year that saw virtually every major Western literature and several Eastern ones produce at least one runaway critical and popular success.

The Caribbean and India. From the Anglophone Caribbean came *The Nature of Blood*, by Caryl Phillips of St. Kitts, a brilliant evocation of the Holocaust experience told in flashback through the voice and discontinuous memories of a young female Jewish death-camp survivor; undercutting and occasionally glossing this main narrative line are such improbable interpolations as a retelling of *Othello* in the Moor's own voice and an account of the persecution of Jewish moneylenders in 15th-century Italy. Nobel laureate Derek Walcott of St. Lucia brought out *The Bounty*, his first collection of new verse since the 1990 epic poem *Omeros*. It reveals anew his unmatched talent among today's English-language poets for creating dazzling verbal textures and the richest imagery imaginable. The work was announced in late 1996 but was not released until early 1997.

From the Francophone Caribbean came wonderfully original novels by two younger writers from Martinique. *Urban Chimeras*, by Raphaël Confiant, recasts his own 1985 Creole novel of socioeconomic exploitation, survival, and assimilation in early colonial times in and around the island's capital, Fort-de-France; and *The Old Slave and the Mastiff*—by Patrick Chamoiseau, the winner of the 1992 Prix Goncourt for *Texaco*—recounts an archetypal tale of slavery, attempted escape, and pursuit and recapture by the oppressive forces of darkness and dominion.

Perhaps the single biggest literary sensation of 1997 was the young South Indian writer Arundhati Roy's debut novel, *The God of Small Things*, a sensuously magical and intricately dreamlike tale of sexual and caste conflict in the exotic, communist-infiltrated Kerala of the late 1960s. Another brilliant first novel, A. Sivanandan's *When Memory Dies*, moves majestically through three generations of a Sri Lankan family—from the subservient 1920s, to independence in 1948, to the neoliberal communalism of the 1980s. In the stories of *Love and Longing in Bombay*, Vikram Chandra followed up the explosive novelistic success of 1995's mythic/exotic *Red Earth and Pouring Rain* with a series of chronicles about glitzy urban sophisticates, high finance, high society, and generally high times.

*Some titles are translated.

Asia and Eurasia. Two important mid-1980s novels from China made their first appearance in the West in 1997. *The Castle*, by southeastern regionalist writer Jia Pingwa, weaves a complex tale about the doomed efforts of a talented and energetic young entrepreneur to reopen an abandoned antimony mine and turn it into the provincial town's biggest economic success in more than a century. *Virgin Widows*, by Gu Hua, follows its vibrant and vital heroine through an oppressive failed marriage and her subsequent attempts to achieve both economic independence and cultural-social liberation from traditional restraints against the remarriage of widows and against assertive women in general.

Japan witnessed a recurrence of "Banana-mania" in 1997 with the publication of Banana Yoshimoto's latest novel, *Amrita*. It is yet another earnest and quirkily ingenious foray into the adolescent soul-searchings of a Generation-X "20-something"—in this case, a woman trying to come to terms with the sudden death of her actress sister. The dialogue rarely rises above comic-book level, but an effortless lyricism infuses the work with an often surprising weightiness and charm.

Two of Israel's premier writers—A.B. Yehoshua and Amos Oz—brought out superb new works in 1997. Yehoshua's novel *Voyage to the End of the Millennium* looks backward rather than forward, to the end of the first millennium—specifically, the year 999—as it tracks the relationship between a prosperous Jewish merchant of Tangier and his beloved nephew and commercial partner, a young European Jew who sells the merchant's exotic wares in Paris and the Rhineland. Through these two characters the novelist meditates on the nature and future of Jewish identity. Oz' *Panther in the Basement*, set in 1947 Jerusalem, chronicles the adolescence of a precociously word-obsessed 12-year-old called "Proffy" (short for "Professor"), particularly his "fraternizing" with the British occupiers and the question of whether such close contact constitutes treason or betrayal of his people and their heritage.

In Turkey, Orhan Pamuk's novel *The New Life* was a best-seller despite the surrealistic phantasmagoria of its story line and the extended ambiguity of its narrative, which charts the metamorphoses in the life of a young engineering student following his perusal of a certain book.

Africa. Among a good crop of 1997 releases by African authors, two stood out, as much for their strong sociopolitical relevance as for their artistic merit. *The Lily and the Flamboy-*

ant, by the Francophone Congolese writer Henri Lopes, purports to be an account of the life and career of the beautiful and talented African-born mulatto singer Kolélé, as told by her former lover, the African-Chinese-European writer Victor Houang. Houang's manuscript is rejected by French publishers, however, since one "Henri Lopes" had published his own version of this story nearly 20 years earlier. Still, one gets to read Houang's manuscript, and even to compare it with "Lopes'" predecessor, which it significantly updates and expands into a treatise focused primarily on the new latter-day hybridization of African identity and the corruption, pretensions, and hypocrisy of most modern African rulers. In the short stories of *Awaiting Court Martial*, prizewinning Nigerian author Festus Iyayi paints a horrific portrait of human irrationality, immorality, and cruelty. His is a world where the prominent may kill with total impunity, where kindly little old grandmothers decoy unsuspecting good Samaritans into traps for armed robbers, and where supposedly loving relatives circle a patriarch's deathbed in anticipation of their inheritance.

The Romance Languages. From the Romance-language literatures of Europe and the Americas came several outstanding new works of fiction in 1997. The Russian-born French writer Andrei Makine dazzled readers and critics alike with *Dreams of My Russian Summer*, a haunting semiautobiographical novel of hardship in early 20th-century Russia and in Western exile. The work was the first to win both the Prix Goncourt and the Prix Médicis. J.M.G. Le Clézio's new novel, *The Golden Fish*, recounts in the first person the kidnapping, sale, and peripatetic experiences of a young North African woman who endures the harsh realities of exclusion and prejudice on three continents (Africa, Europe, North America) before her return to and rediscovery of her true African origins.

In *News of a Kidnapping*, Colombian Nobel laureate Gabriel García Márquez combines the precision of first-rate journalism with the imaginative flair of the finest fiction writing to produce a classic and compelling narrative of several fateful political kidnappings orchestrated by the late Medellín drug king Pablo Escobar. Portugal's Jose Saramago, in *The History of the Siege of Lisbon*, weaves a cryptic, ingenious tale about two humble yet whimsically subversive proofreaders who rewrite one of the seminal events of early Portuguese history through the smallest and most subtle of alterations in the standard texts on which they are assigned to work.

Elsewhere in Europe. Austria's Peter Handke returned to the storytelling ways of his earliest novels and novellas with *On a Dark Night I Left My House*, a wonderfully light and inventive account of a fantastic journey into alien territories beyond the "border," undertaken by a lonely but resourceful pharmacist. In *The Rumors*, Flemish author Hugo Claus follows a military deserter back to his native village, where the young man's return sparks a series of highly mysterious incidents. And in what may well be two of the last original works of Yiddish fiction—both first published in 1983 but not translated until 1997—*Ship of the Hunted* and *The Empire of Kalman the Cripple*, Polish-born Canadian rabbi Yehuda Ellberg paints vivid portraits of life in Poland during World War II and of the world of the 19th-century Central European shtetl.

The late Nobel Prize–winning poet Joseph Brodsky was honored with the posthumous release of his last unpublished poems, together with a good many earlier selections, in *Landscape with Floods*. It is a collection that is nothing short of outstanding in the richness of its lyric expression and the depth and originality of its content. Hungarian author Péter Nádas' monumental 1986 novel *A Book of Memories* finally made its debut in English in 1997, introducing a wealth of new readers to the stylistic brilliance and Joycean linguistic virtuosity of this multilevel bildungsroman, which moves seamlessly from the revolutionary days of 1956 to the mid-19th century and back in charting the growing-up experiences of its three very different protagonists.

The Life of Insects, by the Russian writer Victor Pelevin, is set entirely within the fetid subworld of mosquitoes, flies, cockroaches, ants, and dung beetles, a seedy and lawless sphere beset by cynicism, raw self-interest, authoritarian bullying, and the unchecked brutality of rapacious capitalists and petty hoodlums. Never strictly fable-like, parabolic, or even satiric in any sustained manner, the work fashions a universe wholly unto itself, though one that possesses definite similarities to post-Soviet Russia.

And lastly, in *Spiritus*, Albania's Ismail Kadare again attempts to come to terms with the unspeakably evil and oppressive nature of the dictatorship (1944–85) of Enver Hoxha in an imaginative and solidly constructed work focusing on several secret-service operatives enthralled with the power of their electronic eavesdropping equipment and the secrets they are able to unearth through its use.

WILLIAM RIGGAN, *"World Literature Today"*

LOS ANGELES

A lackluster 1997 election year in Los Angeles returned many incumbents to office. A new police chief and school superintendent were appointed, while voters approved a large school-bond measure. A civil jury found O.J. Simpson liable in the slayings of his former wife, Nicole Brown Simpson, and her friend Ronald L. Goldman (*see* Law—*Criminal v. Civil Law*). The $1 billion J. Paul Getty Center opened in December (*see* Cities and Urban Affairs).

Political News. Little interest was aroused by the city's election even though 1960s activist State Sen. Tom Hayden ran against wealthy Mayor Richard Riordan. The near-record-low 24% turnout appeared to be due to a lack of perceived relevance to everyday life. Riordan received 61% of the vote in the five-person contest. Eight of the 15 council seats up for election were filled by seven incumbents. The remaining seat went to a former incumbent's aide. A ballot proposal to increase elected officeholder slush-fund accounts above the current $10,000 annual limit was defeated. The mayor continued his effort to run the city as a business, causing occasional anger from council members. In August, Councilman Mike Hernandez was arrested for felony cocaine possession. He pleaded guilty and was admitted to a treatment center.

Political leaders in the San Fernando Valley, where some voters urged withdrawal from the city, lent support to Mayor Riordan's attempts to revise the 1925 city charter in order to increase the administrative powers of his office. But since labor-endorsed candidates won control of an official charter commission, with power to put its proposed changes on the ballot, funding for the commission's operation remained in limbo.

Personnel. The mayor appointed S. David Freeman as general manager of the Department of Water and Power, made Bernard C. Parks chief of police, and filled several other key positions. During his controversial term, Police Chief Willie L. Williams raised public approval ratings of the police department, but internal morale remained low. A series of errors cost him the support of the civilian police commission; he never had the backing of the rank and file. When his five-year contract was not renewed, Williams threatened to sue the city and settled for $375,000. Although a nationwide search was conducted, politics dictated a replacement from within. The mayor and the council approved Parks, a veteran of 32 years on the force. The board of education named Deputy Superintendent Ruben Zacarias, a 31-year veteran of the district with Latino support, superintendent.

Schools. For the first time in 26 years, voters approved a school-bond measure. The $2.4 billion for school repair received strong support from Latinos, white conservatives, and the mayor. It passed by 71%—the largest such proposal ever approved in the nation—but immediately raised controversy over how the money would be spent and who would control it. In national standardized tests, district schools ranked in the bottom quarter in reading and the lower third in mathematics.

Transportation. Construction of the Metropolitan Transportation Authority's $5.9 bil-

Bernard C. Parks (left), a 53-year-old, 32-year veteran of the Los Angeles police department, took the oath as the city's chief of police in August 1997.

lion-plus subway remained deep in controversy over huge cost overruns, slow progress, and shoddy work. The agency head left in January, and two men who were offered the job refused it. In addition, the state tightened fiscal rules and the federal government demanded more realistic planning.

CHARLES R. ADRIAN
University of California, Riverside

MACEDONIA

Although Macedonia itself was surrounded by turmoil, the Balkan republic remained relatively stable during 1997. The major source of conflict revolved around the aspirations of the large Albanian minority.

Political Continuity. The government of President Kiro Gligorov did not face any major challenges to its authority despite the political turmoil that rocked neighboring Albania, Bulgaria, and Serbia. Following the collapse of a major pyramid investment scheme in which thousands of citizens lost their deposits, Prime Minister Branko Crvenkovski reshuffled his cabinet and launched an anticorruption drive among state officials. The scheme's owner and the governor of the National Bank were arrested in connection with the scandal. The government's actions, especially the National Bank's pledge to reimburse investors, helped to avoid public unrest.

The country's stability also was buttressed by a reasonable economic performance. The gross domestic product (GDP) grew slightly for the first time since Macedonia achieved independence, while inflation remained in single digits.

Ethnic Tensions. Skopje's major internal problems were with the Albanian minority. Albanians campaigned for their own university and the use of their own flags in public places. In July two Albanians were killed and several dozen were wounded in the town of Gostivar during clashes with the Macedonian police. The riots erupted when policemen pulled down Albanian flags that had been hoisted on the city hall. Rufi Osmani, the ethnic Albanian mayor of Gostivar, was arrested on charges of inciting unrest and promoting ethnic hatred.

The government sought to avoid further ethnic polarization and proposed a draft law to give minorities the right to use their own national symbols in any private, cultural, or sporting events. They, however, would not be able to fly their flags over public buildings.

MACEDONIA • Information Highlights

Official Name: The Former Yugoslav Republic of Macedonia.
Location: Southeastern Europe.
Area: 9,781 sq mi (25 333 km²).
Population (mid-1997 est.): 2,100,000.
Chief City (1994 census): Skopje, the capital, 444,299.
Government: *Head of state,* Kiro Gligorov, president (took office Jan. 27, 1991). *Head of government,* Branko Crvenkovski, prime minister (took office Sept. 4, 1992). *Legislature* (unicameral)—Assembly.
Monetary Unit: Denar (38.8 denar equal U.S.$1, December 1995).
Gross Domestic Product (1995 est. U.S.$): $1,900,000,000 (purchasing power parity).
Economic Index (1996, 1993 = 100): *Consumer Prices,* all items, 270.2; food, 241.9.
Foreign Trade (1995 U.S.$): *Imports,* $1,719,000,000; *exports,* $1,204,000,000.

Albanian parliamentarians urged compromise with the government, but a radical faction sought greater confrontation with the state. Gligorov feared that too many concessions on the question of autonomy would provoke demands for separatism. His difficult balancing act was acknowledged by the special envoy of the United Nations (UN) Human Rights Commission to the former Yugoslavia, Elizabeth Rehn. She stated that Macedonia had improved human rights but that concerns remained over police abuses and the plight of the Albanian minority.

International Factors. During the uprising in Albania, which occurred as a result of people losing their savings in pyramid schemes, Macedonia placed its military in a state of alert, fearing a mass influx of refugees. The threat subsided by the end of the summer after elections in Albania. Nevertheless, the defense ministry remained concerned over border incidents between Albanian bands and Macedonian security forces. To underscore the importance of preserving Macedonian stability, the UN extended the mandate of its peacekeeping force even though the number of troops was to be reduced.

JANUSZ BUGAJSKI
Center for Strategic and International Studies

MALAYSIA

In 1997, Malaysia was hit by the economic crisis that swept through Asia. The year also witnessed some undistinguished behavior on the part of the country's long-standing prime minister, 71-year-old Mahathir bin Mohamad.

Economy and Politics. Malaysia's economy was in crisis for much of the year. Between March and November, the stock market lost 50% of its capitalization. In July the ringgit, the national currency, hit a 24-year low against

© Mark Fallander/AP/Wide World Photos

An economic crisis and a great haze caused by fires on Borneo and Sumatra were problems for Malaysia's Deputy Prime Minister and Finance Minister Anwar Ibrahim during 1997.

the U.S. dollar. The country faced a large current-accounts deficit; the possibility of growing inflation, helped by 3% unemployment; and overexpanded credit equal to 170% of gross domestic product (GDP).

Malaysia's 1998 budget, released in October, did little to restore confidence in the economy. Economic-growth estimates were reduced to 7% for the year. The government put $65 billion in infrastructure projects on hold, including the multimedia corridor near Kuala Lumpur, the national capital, and the Bakum dam in Sarawak. In early December the Kuala Lumpur Stock Exchange restricted trading activities of five brokerage firms. An austerity plan also was announced in December.

Mahathir was intent on blaming someone other than himself and his government for the collapse of the ringgit and the stock market. He settled on international-currency trader George Soros and Jewish currency traders—whom he alleged had an agenda to block Muslim progress. Then, he declared that currency trading was immoral and should be out-

lawed. Worse still, Mahathir approved a ban on the short selling of leading stocks.

Although the ban was lifted quickly, the ringgit and the stock market plummeted. Deputy Prime Minister Anwar Ibrahim stepped in to calm the financial community. He held the reins of government in June and July, while Mahathir was on vacation. The appearance in August of a *surat layang* ("flying letter") alleging that Anwar was both a homosexual and unfaithful to his wife did nothing to negate his strong performance in the country's hour of need.

Muhammad Muhammad Taib, chief minister of Selangor, was forced to resign after being caught leaving Australia with $900,000 in undeclared pocket money.

Society. Signs of militant Islam appeared throughout the country. Muslim men were banned from bodybuilding, while three women were arrested for entering a beauty contest. It became easier for Malay men to take a second wife. The federal government was preparing to amend the constitution, making it a crime for Muslims to renounce Islam.

Environment. Uncontrolled fires on the islands of Borneo and Sumatra brought "the great haze" to Malaysia. In October the pollution index in Kuching, the capital of Sarawak, East Malaysia, exceeded 800. The U.S. considers anything more than 100 as dangerous. The federal government in Kuala Lumpur ordered cloud seeding to clear the air and banned teachers and scientists in all state universities from commenting on the problem because their comments would hurt tourism. Malaysia also faced serious long-term problems from auto and industrial emissions.

Foreign Relations. Relations with Singapore became strained in March when comments by Singapore's former Prime Minister Lee Kuan Yew became public. Lee had referred to Malaysia's Johor state as rampant with muggings, carjacking, and shootings. Lee's apology was of little avail. Traffic across the causeway between the two countries was slowed to a snail's pace, owing to increased vehicle inspections by Malaysian officials. Then, plans for Malaysia's high-speed train service into Singapore ran into trouble.

Kuala Lumpur was the venue for the second Association of Southeast Asian Nations (ASEAN) informal summit in mid-December. The heads of state borrowed language from Mahathir to announce the ASEAN Vision 20/20, a regional blueprint for the future.

PATRICK M. MAYERCHAK
Virginia Military Institute

MALAYSIA • Information Highlights

Official Name: Malaysia.
Location: Southeast Asia.
Area: 127,317 sq mi (329 750 km²).
Population (mid-1997 est.): 21,000,000.
Chief Cities (1991 census): Kuala Lumpur, the capital, 1,145,342; Ipoh, 382,853; Johor Baharu, 328,436.
Government: *Head of state,* Sultan Jaafar bin Abdul Rahman, king (selected February 1994). *Head of government,* Mahathir bin Mohamad, prime minister (took office July 1981). *Legislature*—Parliament: Senate and House of Representatives.
Monetary Unit: Ringgit (Malaysian dollar) (3.9013 ringgits equal U.S.$1, Dec. 31, 1997).
Gross Domestic Product (1995 est. U.S.$): $193,600,000,-000 (purchasing power parity).
Economic Indexes (1996, 1990 = 100): *Consumer Prices,* all items, 125.6; food, 133.6. *Industrial Production,* 187.
Foreign Trade (1996 U.S.$): *Imports,* $78,429,000,000; *exports,* $78,258,000,000.

Medicine and Health

The surge of infectious diseases continued to worry health officials during 1997, as new and drug-resistant strains developed. Late in the year, for example, a strain of chicken influenza began to affect humans in Hong Kong. It was the first influenza virus known to jump from birds to humans without first passing through other animals. In an effort to contain the virus, Hong Kong destroyed some 1.2 million chickens. The incidence of noninfectious diseases, such as diabetes and certain cancers, also climbed.

Americans were living longer than ever, with life expectancy topping 76 years. A profile tracking the government's Healthy People 2000 objectives found that targets for the awareness of high blood cholesterol and consumption of fruits and vegetables for the year 2000 already had been met, while the incidence of obesity, physical inactivity, and insufficient dietary calcium had increased since 1990. New techniques to combat vision and dental problems were introduced. Mental-health experts presented studies on the roots of bulimia and on how people react to grief, while medical ethicists continued to debate patient-assisted suicide—an issue under review by the U.S. Supreme Court. President Bill Clinton proposed a "bill of rights" that would establish federal standards for health plans and insurance companies.

ing the coming decade. The U.S. Agency for International Development (USAID) said that as a result of AIDS deaths, 40 million children in developing countries would be without one or both parents by 2010. A review by a National Institutes of Health (NIH) committee of clean-needle exchanges, safe-sex education, and drug-abuse treatment found these programs to be powerful weapons against the spread of AIDS, but also found that, in many countries, moral and government objections limited their effectiveness.

Another NIH committee warned that about 4 million Americans were infected with hepatitis C, a viral disease that can lead to cirrhosis of the liver. The virus is spread most commonly through needle sharing by intravenous drug users; having sexual relations with a virus carrier also is a significant risk factor. The virus may produce no obvious symptoms for many years following infection, and about 15% of those affected recover without medical help. The rest develop a chronic infection; about a fifth of these people develop cirrhosis and may require liver transplants to survive. Indeed, chronic hepatitis C infec-

Food safety was a major health issue in 1997. In August, Burger King pulled all products of Hudson Foods from its restaurants after an outbreak of E. coli bacteria poisoning was linked to hamburgers produced by the meat-processing company.

© Kevin Moloney/Gamma-Liaison

Overview

Infectious Diseases. By June 1997 more than 612,000 AIDS cases and almost 380,000 AIDS deaths had been reported to the U.S. Centers for Disease Control and Prevention (CDC) since the disease first was recognized in 1981. A 19% decline in AIDS deaths in the first nine months of 1996, compared with the same period in 1995, was expected to continue, thanks to new drug therapies that combat HIV—the virus that causes AIDS—and the pathogens that cause opportunistic infections to develop as HIV weakens a person's immune system.

Worldwide, more than 30 million people were believed to be infected with HIV, although less than 5% were aware of their infection. The epidemic was particularly severe in Africa and Asia, and was expected to become widespread in Latin America dur-

© Kuni Takahashi/Impact Visuals

In 1997 the U.S. Food and Drug Administration approved a medical device intended to reduce epileptic seizures. It involves the implanting of a pacemaker-like electrode that sends seizure-blocking signals to the brain through a nerve in the user's neck. The user can activate the electrode through a special wristband.

tion is the main reason for liver transplants. The NIH committee estimated that about 8,000 Americans die each year from hepatitis C, and that this number will triple by 2017.

Clinical tests found that three doses of a new vaccine for Lyme disease provided 100% protection against the deer-tick-borne illness in people under age 60. The incidence of Lyme disease fell 36% in 1997, probably because of natural fluctuations in tick populations. Meanwhile, scientists discovered another virus carried by deer ticks. It was not clear whether this virus causes disease in humans, but related viruses in Europe can be deadly.

The mosquito that carries Plasmodium, the protist that causes malaria, increased its range, migrating into higher elevations in Latin America, central Africa, and Asia. Between 300 million and 500 million people are infected annually, and as many as 3 million—mostly children and pregnant women—die. Efforts to develop a vaccine have been unsuccessful, and drugs used to treat the disease are losing their effectiveness as resistant Plasmodium strains evolve.

Drug-Resistant Bacteria. The rise of bacterial strains able to withstand antibiotics was creating a critical public-health problem, as some of the world's deadliest infectious diseases evaded traditional therapies. In 1997 a new strain of the *Staphylococcus aureus* bacterium was discovered in Japan and a similar strain later showed up in the United States. These bacteria were resistant to vancomycin, a powerful antibiotic that long had been used when other antibiotics proved ineffective. Staph bacteria are the main cause of infections developed by patients in U.S. hospitals, and are blamed for about 13% of the nation's 2 million hospital infections each year.

A strain of *Enterococci* also had become resistant to vancomycin; once a minor problem, this intestinal bacterium now posed a lethal danger to some hospital patients. A strain of *Salmonella* resistant to ampicillin and tetracycline became the second-most-common type of salmonella poisoning in Britain, and reached the United States. In Madagascar a strain of bubonic plague was found to be resistant to all antibiotics normally used to treat the disease.

Scientists investigated new ways to attack fast-evolving bacteria, and physicians were warned that they were contributing to the problem by misusing antibiotics. Researchers at the University of Colorado found that 51% of patients diagnosed with colds, 52% of those with upper-respiratory-tract infections, and 66% diagnosed with bronchitis were treated with antibiotics, even though antibiotics gave little or no benefit for these diseases.

Another factor was the failure of many patients to complete a prescribed regimen of antibiotics. As a result, not all the bacteria that caused the patients' illnesses are killed; those that survive have an opportunity to mutate and become more virulent. The practice of taking antibiotics only until one feels better—or no longer can afford the medicine—was a factor in the development of a strain of tuberculosis that was virtually untreatable. The World Health Organization (WHO) reported that untreatable cases of tuberculosis accounted for 2% to 14% of the world total, and could increase rapidly because only one in ten patients received appropriate medical care.

Cancer. A National Cancer Institute review of more than 100 studies on the medical effects of silicone breast implants found no evidence the implants cause breast cancer. A Harvard School of Public Health group examining blood provided by nurses during a long-term health study found that levels of

DDT and PCBs in the blood of 240 women who subsequently developed breast cancer were comparable to those in women who did not develop breast cancer.

A University of Arizona study directed by Larry C. Clark found that patients previously treated for skin cancer who took daily supplements of 200 micrograms of selenium for ten years had 63% fewer prostate cancers, 58% fewer colorectal cancers, and 45% fewer lung cancers than did patients who received a placebo.

Scientists at Johns Hopkins University School of Medicine reported that broccoli sprouts contain 30 to 50 times the concentration of isothiocyanates as mature broccoli—chemicals previously shown to be powerful anticancer agents. Researchers at the University of Illinois at Chicago discovered a substance in grapes called resveratrol, which appears to inhibit the formation and spread of malignant cells.

Work by Esther John of the North California Cancer Center suggested that brief daily exposure to sunlight can lower the risk of breast cancer by 30% to 40%. The skin uses the sun's ultraviolet rays to make vitamin D, which, according to other studies, helps protect against breast cancer. Excessive exposure to sunlight, however, causes skin cancer.

Melanoma, the deadliest skin cancer, was the fastest-growing cancer in the United States; 1 in 84 Americans could expect to develop melanoma—up from 1 in 600 in 1960 and 1 in 1,500 in 1935. An estimated 7,300 Americans died of the disease in 1997. Trials of two vaccines designed primarily to prevent recurrence of melanoma in early- and intermediate-stage patients got under way. Previous attempts to develop cancer vaccines were unsuccessful, but an improved understanding of how the immune system responds to cancer made scientists cautiously optimistic.

"The good news is that the death rate from childhood cancer has declined dramatically. But an equally dramatic rise in the overall number of kids who get cancer threatens to overshadow the gains we have made," said Carol M. Browner, head of the U.S. Environmental Protection Agency (EPA). Each year cancer is diagnosed in an estimated 8,000 U.S. children under age 15. Acute lymphoblastic leukemia and brain cancer are the most common childhood cancers, and both are occurring at higher rates than just a few decades ago. The EPA established an Office for Children's Health Protection, designed to be a clearinghouse for research and to stimulate cooperative efforts among scientists and oth-

ers concerned with children's environmental health. The senior adviser to the office, Philip J. Landrigan of the Mount Sinai School of Medicine in New York City, said that the increases in childhood cancers were "too rapid to reflect genetic changes, and better diagnostic detection is not a likely explanation." He and other scientists recommended investigating the estimated 75,000 synthetic chemicals introduced in the past 50 years, as well as chemicals in foods, drinking water, and car emissions. The toxicity and cancerous effects of many of these chemicals are unknown.

Sickle-Cell Disease. A U.S. National Heart, Lung and Blood Institute study was ended 16 months early because of unexpectedly promising results that showed regular blood transfusions reduced the risk of strokes by 90% in children with sickle-cell disease—an inherited disorder characterized by an abnormal form of hemoglobin, the oxygen-carrying molecule in red blood cells. The hemoglobin contorts the cells into shapes that can block and damage blood vessels. About 10% of children with sickle-cell anemia—the most common form of the disease—are at high risk for strokes. The institute urged doctors to identify these children and consider transfusion therapy as a preventive measure.

Diet Drugs and the Heart. More than two decades ago, the U.S. Food and Drug Administration (FDA) separately approved two drugs for short-term use as diet aids: an appetite suppressant called fenfluramine (trade name Pondimin) and an amphetamine called phentermine. Neither was particularly effective, but in 1992, Michael Weintraub,

The popular diet aids fenfluramine and dexfenfluramine were removed from the market during 1997 after it was discovered that they may cause heart-valve abnormalities.

© Yvonne Hemsey/Gamma-Liaison

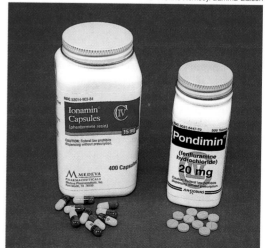

then at the University of Rochester, published the results of a four-year study of 121 obese patients who took the two in combination and lost an average of 30 pounds. Suddenly, everyone wanted "fen-phen," and doctors began writing thousands of prescriptions for the drugs, which never were approved to be taken in combination or for long periods. In 1995 the FDA was asked to approve dexfenfluramine (trade name Redux), a more effective form of fenfluramine, and to allow it to be labeled for indefinite use. Approval was granted in 1996, with the proviso that labels caution that studies of its effects had lasted only one year. Within a year some 2 million Americans were taking the drug. In mid-1997 new data submitted to the FDA suggested that fenfluramine and dexfenfluramine may cause heart valve abnormalities in up to 30% of people using the drugs. Both were withdrawn from the market, and the FDA and other federal agencies urged people who had taken either of the drugs to undergo medical checkups. They also recommended that all users consider an echocardiogram, to look for evidence of leaky heart valves, even if they had no symptoms. Deprived of fenfluramine and dexfenfluramine, some doctors began mixing and marketing other combinations as diet aids. Some advertised "phen-pro"—a combination of phentermine and Prozac—while others prescribed a mix of phentermine and chromium picolinate. Neither the safety nor the efficacy of such combinations had been established.

The FDA also warned about the possible dangers of herbal diet supplements that contain ephedrine, a stimulant sold under names such as ephedra and ma huang. Ephedrine had been blamed for at least 20 deaths and more than 800 adverse reactions since 1993. It can cause heart attacks, strokes, seizures, and high blood pressure.

Diabetes. According to the CDC, the number of Americans diagnosed with diabetes increased six-fold since 1958, from 1.6 million to a record 10.3 million in 1997, in addition to an estimated 5.4 million undiagnosed cases. The increasing number of overweight, physically inactive, and older people was considered the main reason for the rise. There was a dramatic increase of Type 2 (non-insulin-dependent) diabetes among children. In this disease, the body fails to use insulin properly; it usually develops in overweight adults. A study conducted at the Arkansas Children's Hospital found that nearly all the children with Type 2 diabetes were obese and more than 30% had high blood pressure.

The FDA approved troglitazone (trade name Rezulin), a drug that offers patients with Type 2 diabetes the possibility of reducing or even ending their need for insulin shots. Troglitazone was the first of a new class of drugs called insulin sensitizers, which in yet-unknown ways resensitize the body so that it makes better use of pancreatic or injected insulin.

New guidelines issued by the American Diabetes Association recommended lowering the diagnostic number on the most commonly used test for diabetes—possibly resulting in up to 2 million more diagnosed cases. The test, fasting plasma glucose (FPG), is a simple blood-glucose test done after not eating for eight hours. The previous value of 140 mg/dl on the FPG, which was considered evidence of diabetes, was lowered to 126 mg/dl. A value of 110 mg/dl on the FPG was defined as the upper limit of normal blood glucose.

Vision. Over the past decade, a laser procedure called photorefractive keratectomy (PRK) has been performed on thousands to correct mild to moderate nearsightedness by reshaping the patients' corneas. In 1997 an FDA panel backed an advanced new procedure, laser in situ keratomileusis (LASIK). LASIK can correct more-severe nearsightedness and, unlike PRK, does not injure the clear membrane covering the cornea. Therefore postoperative pain is reduced, healing is faster, and the patient recovers vision more rapidly. The Emory University developers of LASIK studied the procedure on 1,048 eyes and found that patients had a greater than 95% chance of seeing 20/40 or better without glasses or contact lenses. The procedure is complex, however, requiring great skill on the part of the surgeon.

During 1997 scientists reported that they had identified several genes that lead to vision loss, which may lead to new treatments. Two of the genes account for some forms of retinitis pigmentosa, which causes legal blindness by damaging the retina's light-sensing rods and cones. The disease usually develops in childhood or early adulthood and affects 100,000 to 200,000 Americans.

Another gene is responsible for primary congenital glaucoma, which causes blindness in an estimated one of every 10,000 births. Still another is linked to age-related macular degeneration, the major cause of vision loss in people over age 65; more than 11 million Americans had signs of this disease, and about 200,000 new cases are diagnosed annually.

Dentistry. Some 40 million Americans avoid or postpone dental visits because they fear the pain of drilling and other procedures. A variety of new products have been designed to eliminate these fears. Noven Pharmaceuticals introduced DentiPatch, which releases the anesthetic lidocaine into the gums, numbing them for about 40 minutes without the use of a needle. An electronic anesthesia from 3M involves the placement of pads on the cheeks that, when turned on, send a numbing electric current into the jaw.

The FDA approved the first laser for treating tooth decay in adults. The erbium-YAG laser, developed by Premier Laser Systems, removes cavities without the pressure and vibration of a drill, eliminating most patients' need for local anesthesia. This shortens the length of the procedure, since dentists do not need to wait for the painkiller to take effect. The laser also makes a smaller hole than a drill, thus requiring a smaller filling.

Oral-medicine specialists reported that many common medications can cause serious tooth decay and gum disease. Up to 20% of people who take calcium channel blockers for high blood pressure and heart disease develop gum inflammations, and similar problems are caused by anti-epilepsy drugs and some amphetamines used to treat hyperactivity in children. More than 400 drugs cause dry mouth, which increases the risk of cavities, fungal infections, and other problems.

Americans drink almost 3 billion gallons of bottled water a year, and dental experts were concerned that some people—especially children—did not get enough fluoride, a chemical added to public water supplies to strengthen teeth and prevent decay. Bottled water tends to lack fluoride, as does water that passes through some home water filters. The American Dental Association said that relying solely on other sources of fluoride, such as toothpaste, rinses, and certain foods, "is not an effective or prudent public-health practice."

In 1997 the FDA approved Colgate Total, the first toothpaste shown to prevent gum or periodontal disease—which can develop undetected over a long period of time and can lead to the loss of teeth. Researchers also reported that more appears to be at stake than inflamed gums. They suspect that gum disease can contribute to clogged arteries, diabetes, and premature births.

Fertility. In November, Bobbi McCaughey, 29, of Carlisle, IA, gave birth to three girls and four boys—the first time that a U.S. woman ever has given birth to living septuplets, and only the second time it has occurred in the world. The babies, about two months premature, weighed from 2.5 lb to 3.4 lb (1.1 kg to

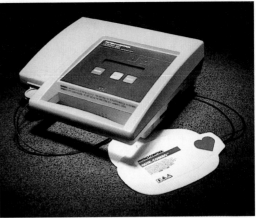

Courtesy, Physio-Control Corporation

Cardiologists now believe that wider availability of defibrillators, like the one above—which deliver an electric shock to restart the heart—would save more victims of cardiac arrest.

1.5 kg). McCaughey had taken a fertility drug because she and her husband had trouble conceiving. Specialists caution women about carrying so many fetuses to term, pointing out that almost all women with five or more fetuses either miscarry and lose them all or give birth to babies with severe mental and physical problems.

Reproductive Biology Associates, a private clinic in Atlanta, GA, reported that they had thawed and fertilized frozen human eggs, then implanted them into a woman who had no eggs of her own. The woman became pregnant and gave birth to healthy twin boys. The procedure could allow a woman diagnosed with cancer and scheduled to undergo chemotherapy, which can damage the ovaries, to save her eggs for later use. A study led by researchers at Laval University in Quebec found that even mild cases of endometriosis, a disease of the uterine lining, can cause infertility in women. Endometriosis affects up to 10% of women of childbearing age. Since mild cases often are asymptomatic, the study suggested that women with unexplained infertility should be examined for the disease.

JENNY TESAR, *Freelance Science Writer*

Health Care

After two years of partisan charges and countercharges over the future of the popular but financially ailing Medicare program for the elderly and disabled, the Bill Clinton administration and the Republican-controlled Congress in 1997 agreed on changes projected to keep the program solvent until 2010. The Medicare deal was enacted into law as part of

© Marilynn K. Yee/NYT Permissions

Mary Mundinger (left), dean of the Columbia School of Nursing, meets with nurse practitioners who have opened an office in midtown New York City. Such practices—in which the nurses treat common medical complaints and refer serious problems to specialists—are growing in number across the United States.

the Balanced Budget Act signed by President Bill Clinton on August 5. That bill included major changes to the joint state-federal Medicaid program and a new program to cover up to half the estimated 10 million uninsured U.S. children. The children's program was the largest single health-insurance-coverage expansion since the creation of Medicare and Medicaid in 1965.

Lawmakers introduced reams of bills but took little concrete action on the growing backlash by patients and physicians over "managed-care" plans. Many bills required health plans to cover items such as mandatory hospital stays for women undergoing mastectomies for breast cancer, while others banned practices such as "gag clauses" that limited doctor-patient communications. But Congress never really engaged the managed-care debate before leaving for the year. Mean-

while, Clinton endorsed a patient "bill of rights" in November, crafted by a commission he appointed in the spring. The document included many items in the congressional bills, such as the right to confidential medical records, freer access to specialists, and better information about health plans.

Medicare. The biggest change in health care in 1997 was the financial rescue and redirection of Medicare, which served an estimated 38 million elderly and disabled Americans. In April the program's trustees reported that, without changes, Medicare's Hospital Insurance Trust Fund would run out of money in 2001. It was the nearest the program had been to insolvency since its creation in 1965. By trimming payment increases for doctors, hospitals, and health plans, and increasing costs for patients, however, the balanced-budget legislation breathed life into the trust fund until 2010. Coincidentally, that was when the first of the massive "baby boom" generation would become eligible for Medicare at age 65.

Many in Congress wanted to use the opportunity to seek even longer-term changes. The Senate voted to raise Medicare eligibility to age 67 and also voted to charge higher premiums for high-income beneficiaries. The latter proposal was endorsed at various times by both Democrats and Republicans over the previous decade. But in the end, Clinton and the Congress decided to defer decisions on long-term Medicare changes to a bipartisan commission charged with reporting back in 1999.

Congress, however, did take steps to steer the program in a radically new direction, by giving beneficiaries greater choices of private managed care and other plans that would accept the financial risk for their care. Managed care already was growing rapidly in Medicare; by the end of 1997 an estimated 14% of beneficiaries voluntarily had joined managed-care plans, which frequently offered richer benefits than traditional Medicare. These plans, however, reduced choices of doctors, hospitals, and other health-care providers. The legislation simultaneously made managed care more attractive to beneficiaries, by allowing less-restrictive types of managed-care plans to be offered through Medicare, while making Medicare more attractive to the plans, primarily by boosting payments in rural areas and other parts of the country where fees had been too low to spur interest. The legislation also authorized "provider-sponsored networks"—groups of hospitals, doctors, and other health-care providers that could band together to offer

Medicare coverage without the participation of an insurance company.

The bill also authorized other forms of private coverage for Medicare, including Medical Savings Accounts (MSAs), which combined high-deductible insurance with tax-preferred accounts from which beneficiaries could pay routine medical costs themselves. Advocates argued MSAs could help hold down health-care costs by making patients more sensitive to the actual costs of care. But opponents argued that the accounts would draw the healthy and wealthy out of traditional Medicare, leaving the poor and sick behind.

Medicaid. Increasing managed-care enrollment was also the likely outcome of congressional changes to Medicaid, the federal-state health-insurance program for some 35 million low-income Americans. Unlike Medicare's optional managed care, many states required Medicaid recipients to join managed-care plans. By 1997 more than a third of Medicaid beneficiaries were in managed-care plans, according to the Henry J. Kaiser Family Foundation's Commission on the Future of Medicaid.

The Balanced Budget Act made it much easier for states to move Medicaid patients into managed care—primarily by eliminating a requirement for state governments to apply to federal officials to receive a "waiver" of certain Medicaid rules. The legislation also allowed "Medicaid only" plans, by eliminating the requirement that managed-care plans serving Medicaid patients have at least 25% of their patients come from outside the program.

Backers of the new rules argued that they would make Medicaid more cost-efficient, and that managed care actually could offer better, more coordinated health care than the traditional program, where patients often had a hard time finding doctors willing to treat them for the low Medicaid rates. But advocates for the poor worried that the law eliminated important consumer protections that prevented plans from providing less care than might be necessary.

Children's Health. Among the most far-reaching provisions of the budget bill was a program to provide states with $48 billion over ten years to help broaden efforts to provide health insurance to children. Most analysts agreed that children made up about 25% of the 40 million Americans who lacked health insurance. Under the plan—which was to be funded partially by an increase in the cigarette tax—states could choose to either expand existing Medicaid programs to children in families otherwise earning too much to qualify, or devise new, children-only insurance plans.

The federal program actually built on what many states had done already. Florida, Pennsylvania, and New York, in particular, were covering tens of thousands of children from working families who could not afford private coverage. Republicans in Congress initially resisted broad plans to use federal dollars to pay for health insurance, with some warning that it represented a first step toward national health insurance. But in the end the public demand to help cover low-income children overcame doubts about the program.

Managed Care. The budget bill also took some first steps to address the managed care "backlash"—complaints about practices some consumer advocates said put company profits ahead of patient care. Among other things, the bill required health plans covering Medicare beneficiaries to pay for hospital-emergency-room care if a patient had symptoms that a "prudent layperson" would deem to require such care.

But Congress failed to pass any of the bills that would extend that and other protections to patients in private-sector insurance programs. Insurance companies and business groups complained that many of the bills, as well as the "bill of rights" devised by the president's Advisory Commission on Consumer Protection and Quality in the Health Care Industry, would increase costs to the point that many people with insurance would lose their coverage.

JULIE ROVNER, *Health-Policy Writer*

Bioethics

The year 1997 saw more publicized debate in bioethics than ever before. In fact, bioethics issues seemed to come to the fore continually during the year.

New Kinds of Reproduction. Couples seeking new ways to have families saw remarkable new options take shape in 1997. While adoption of children from war-torn nations continued to increase, the success rates of in vitro fertilization in the United States were controversial. The U.S. Centers for Disease Control and Prevention released a major report on the success rates for assisted reproduction. Success rates as low as 15% per attempt, at an average cost of $6,000, were a source of alarm as bioethicists questioned the value of a $1 billion national expenditure for assisted reproductive services.

In Oregon, Barbara Coombs Lee (left), a chief sponsor of the state's 1994 law permitting physician-assisted suicide, and fund-raiser Margaret Surguine shared congratulations after learning that Measure 51—a motion to repeal the law—was defeated on Nov. 4, 1997.

Meanwhile, in February, Scottish veterinary biologist Ian Wilmut announced the successful birth of a cloned sheep, made when his team transplanted the DNA from an adult sheep's mammary cell into another sheep's egg. In March scientists at the Oregon Regional Primate Research Center announced that they had transplanted the nucleus of a fertilized monkey embryo cell into another embryonic cell, producing a clone of a primate embryo. The news excited many in veterinary and agricultural settings, and promised to speed research on human pharmaceuticals by providing identical test animals. However, it was apparent that at some point in the future it might be possible to clone a human using the same or similar technology. Such a possibility gave rise to various legal and ethical issues. (*See also* BIOTECHNOLOGY—*Spotlight on Cloning.*)

Ethicists worried that cloning would present the opportunity for families to replicate rather than reproduce, and that families with cloned children thus would not allow their children to have the freedom to explore their own horizons. Others suggested that while cloning might be appropriate for some families, allowing cloning technology to be governed by the marketplace seemed fundamentally unfair. Still other policy analysts and ethicists worried about the possibility that cloning technology might be used by tyrants or small military forces to create engineered humans. However, ethicists emerged who were willing to defend human cloning. It was argued that cloning is less morally problematic than families created by sperm or egg dona-

tion, because cloned children are at least products of their families' DNA. Others claimed that cloning to produce children for families needing a bone-marrow transplant might be appropriate. The debate about the cloning of humans emerged as a major area of future study, as many feared the possibility that this technique might be used by someone irresponsibly. Doubts also emerged about the ability of anyone to police biotechnology.

It also was discovered in 1997 that infertility treatments and gestation may be possible for postmenopausal women of advanced age. It was revealed that Arceli Keh, 63, had lied to a University of Southern California reproduction clinic and was able to carry a child to term successfully, giving birth to a child in November 1996. Ethicists wondered whether or not menopause should be a barrier for gestation, and some speculated that pregnancy among women in their 50s and 60s might be a moral problem since the mother is unlikely to live past the child's adolescence. However, others argued that elder males become fathers with some frequency and that, if safety turns out not to be an issue, there should be no age barrier.

In November septuplets were born to a couple in Iowa. Shortly after their infertility treatment had resulted in multiple gestations—a common result of such treatment— the couple determined that they would not "selectively reduce" the number of fetuses but instead would attempt to carry all seven to term. The children were born uneventfully and given critical care in an Iowa hospital. Many supported the parents' decision and

Neil Adkins, left—whose mother, Janet, gained Dr. Jack Kevorkian's help in ending her life—was among those who supported the repeal of Oregon's physician-assisted-suicide law. Although Oregon voters refused to repeal the law, physician-assisted suicide would remain a topic of debate throughout the United States.

© Don Ryan/AP/Wide World Photos

various donations were given. However, the medical costs were expected to top $5 million in the first year, prompting many ethicists to ask again at what cost infertility treatment should be provided.

Assisted Suicide. The debate about the legality of physician-assisted suicide and euthanasia reached a new level as the U.S. Supreme Court ruled on two appellate court cases, *Vacco v. Quill* and *Washington v. Glucksberg*. In overturning both appellate-court decisions, the court dealt a significant blow to those who had argued for a constitutionally protected right to assistance in suicide. The court held that the constitution and its framers, as well as common law dating back to the beginning of recorded history, do not support either the idea that suicide is a constitutionally protected activity, or that assistance in suicide can be derived from a more general right to privacy.

The court left it open to the states—including Oregon, where a law authorizing assisted suicide again was reaffirmed by referendum—to establish new laws pertaining to assisted suicide. Meanwhile, retired Michigan pathologist Jack Kevorkian continued to participate in assisted suicides in 1997, two of which were reviewed for prosecution by Michigan grand juries.

Alternative Medicine. Bioethicists also debated the rights of patients to insurance reimbursement for alternative therapies, and the need for standards for their use. Several studies focused attention on psychoactive alternative medicines—including St. John's wort and gingko biloba—and their potential use in treating depression, memory loss, and Alzheimer's disease. However, the lack of standards for their use prompted worry that healthy Americans would engage in unsafe experiments with enhancement drugs. Several other alternative therapies, including acupuncture and crystal healing, were included formally in managed-care health-insurance plans in the United States.

GLENN MCGEE, *University of Pennsylvania*

Mental Health

A rare study of bulimic women not being treated for the eating disorder helped investigators narrow down the factors implicated in its emergence. Excessive grief was linked to a variety of health problems, possibly even cancer, while depression was linked to cellular activity in the brain.

Roots of Bulimia. Bulimia sufferers often held extremely negative views of themselves during childhood, had parents who maintained minimal contact with them but demanded high levels of achievement, and battled obesity early in life, according to a research team headed by Christopher G. Fairburn of the University of Oxford in England. In addition, periods of depression or other psychiatric disorders often afflicted these women before the appearance of bulimia.

An estimated 1% to 3% of females in many Western countries develop bulimia as teenagers or young adults. The condition involves binges of food consumption that alternate with fasting, self-induced vomiting, or other efforts to lose weight. Many possible causes, such as childhood sexual abuse, have been proposed, based on studies of women receiving some form of treatment for bulimia.

Fairburn's team interviewed females aged 16 to 35 who lived in urban and rural parts of southern England and fell into one of three groups—bulimia sufferers, those diagnosed with some other psychiatric disorder, and those with no psychiatric problems and no history of mental illness.

The findings suggested that bulimia was most likely to develop in female dieters who were prone to becoming obese and to developing psychiatric disorders in general.

Severe Grief Reaction. Some people suffer from an extreme form of bereavement that raises the likelihood of developing a number of physical and mental ailments up to two years after a spouse's death, researchers reported. Surviving partners who long had experienced insecurities regarding intimate relationships were particularly apt to display this grief response, dubbed "traumatic grief" by Holly G. Prigerson of Yale University School of Medicine and her colleagues.

Prigerson says psychotherapy can help diminish the symptoms of traumatic grief, which include sleep problems; mental anguish; suicidal thoughts; increased alcohol, tobacco, and food consumption; high blood pressure; heart trouble; and possibly even cancer.

Grief after a loved one's death often includes feelings of depression and despair. But traumatic grief involves searching and yearning for the deceased, disbelief that a partner really is dead, avoidance of reminders of the spouse, bitterness and guilt over the death, and hallucinations of seeing or hearing the lost partner. Prigerson's group tracked 92 women and 52 men for two years after their spouses had died of serious illnesses for which they had been hospitalized. Most participants had been married at least 20 years. A variety of health problems occurred more frequently in the 33 who exhibited traumatic grief, including the emergence of new cases of cancer. Larger studies need to explore this possible link. Preliminary studies of adults suffering from traumatic grief, also conducted by Prigerson, found large drops in the responsiveness of disease-fighting immune cells.

Memory in Schizophrenia. New evidence suggested that working memory—which temporarily keeps several pieces of information in mind as people speak or perform other mental operations—seriously malfunctions in schizophrenia, which affects 1 in 100 people with debilitating disruptions of thought and emotion.

Schizophrenics have trouble clearing the working memory of information irrelevant to mental tasks at hand, and also immediately forget useful material if it is no longer in plain view, according to researchers at the National Institute of Mental Health in Bethesda, MD. Working-memory problems may contribute substantially to the confusion and communication difficulties often observed in schizophrenia, they suggested.

The investigation was based on the Stroop task—a 60-year-old experimental technique that shows that people take longer to name the color of an ink used to print the word for a contrasting color than to name the same color when it spells out a nonsense word. Color naming occurs most quickly if ink color and color word match.

In two experiments, schizophrenics and people with no history of psychiatric disorders watched a computer screen that showed random combinations of color names printed in white and colored rectangular patches. Words either preceded patches by fractions of a second, appeared simultaneously with them, or followed patches by fractions of a second. A patch that preceded a clashing word by one-tenth of a second caused the biggest delays in color naming for healthy volunteers. Schizophrenics took longest to name colors when patches preceded clashing words by one-twentieth of a second. Longer pauses between viewing patches and reading clashing words eliminated delays in color naming only for schizophrenics, apparently because they forgot the distracting information once it was out of sight.

Inside Depression. Cell activity in a particular part of the brain spells success or failure for attempts to treat depression with medication, reported Helen S. Mayberg of the University of Texas Health Science Center at San Antonio. Depressed individuals who respond to antidepressant drugs display elevated neural responses in a small structure called the cingulate gyrus, Mayberg said. Depressed volunteers underwent scanning by a brain-imaging device that measures energy use by brain cells, a sign of how hard they are working. Ten depressed patients who improved after six weeks of drug treatment exhibited high cingulate activity from the start; low cingulate activity characterized eight patients whose mood did not brighten after the same treatment. The finding could lead to the use of brain-scan data in diagnosing and treating depression.

BRUCE BOWER, *"Science News"*

METEOROLOGY

An unusually strong El Niño and the activities of important new satellites were among the meteorological highlights of 1997.

El Niño. A new El Niño—the cycle of oceanic warming across the eastern tropical Pacific—began early in 1997. By mid-July it had surpassed typical peak values, usually not seen until November. Although El Niño weakened after September, it was one of the three strongest such events since modern records began in 1950. Unusual worldwide storms, floods, and droughts were credited to its effects.

Although the 1997 El Niño was documented by an unprecedented array of satellites, day-to-day forecasts continued to demand all the skill that meteorologists could muster. El Niño was linked to such diverse events as seal starvation along the California coast and the coral bleaching in the Florida Keys.

Satellites. After an April launch, the Geostationary Operational Environmental Satellite dubbed GOES-10 was "parked" over the central United States. The Japanese Advanced Earth Observing System (ADEOS), launched in August 1996, fell victim to an electrical failure in late June after transmitting data for several months. The National Aeronautics and Space Administration (NASA) Scatterometer (NSCAT) aboard ADEOS set a new standard observing wind velocity over the global ocean before the outage.

NASA's Sea-Viewing Wide Field-of-View Sensor (SeaWiFS) was launched on a commercial satellite in August. By observing ocean color, SeaWiFS helped monitor biological activity—key to understanding the ocean's role in governing global atmospheric carbon dioxide. The Tropical Rainfall Measuring Mission (TRMM)—a three-year joint U.S.-Japan project to provide three-dimensional information on precipitation—was launched in November. TRMM carried the first satellite-borne meteorological radar as part of its instrumentation.

Other Technology. NASA's ER-2 high-altitude research aircraft were modernized to increase capability and make them lighter and more fuel-efficient. The operational ceiling was raised above 70,000 ft (21 350 m) and the payload volume doubled. The National Oceanic and Atmospheric Administration (NOAA) began to operate a Gulfstream 4SP jet, for high-altitude flights over Atlantic hurricanes and tropical storms.

In May the first observations of a tornado were made using a dual Doppler radar sys-

© Agence France-Presse

U.S. Vice-President Al Gore discussed the effects of global warming with Dr. Dan Fagre (left) of the U.S. Geological Survey while inspecting Glacier National Park in Montana in 1997.

tem. The twin Doppler on Wheels (DOW) consisted of 8-ft (2.4-m) radar dishes mounted on flatbed trucks. The DOWs were guided to positions a few miles apart in the vicinity of tornadic storms to capture details of air motions inside the tornado vortex.

The last of the WSR-88D Doppler radars was installed at the National Weather Service (NWS), and installation began of the first 21 operational Automated Weather Interactive Processing System (AWIPS) units. AWIPS are flexible computer systems that Weather Forecast Offices use to store, analyze, and display the data sets available to make forecasts.

During 1997 both the NWS and the Canadian Meteorological Centre (CMC) tested numerical-forecast models with a spacing between grid points of 6.2 mi (10 km); the goal was to capture the fine detail of precipitation in mountainous terrain and around severe thunderstorms.

Stratospheric Ozone. The Antarctic ozone "hole"—somewhat smaller than in recent record years—made its annual appearance from October to December; but attention was focused in the Arctic, where record-low values—40% below the 1979–82 average for March— occurred. This record was associated closely with unusual wind patterns that reinforced the very cold conditions needed for rapid ozone destruction. The Photochemistry of Ozone Loss in the Arctic Region in Summer (POLARIS) field study was conducted from April to September to study the annual fluctuation of ozone.

Some good news was that the ocean degrades methyl bromide more quickly than previously estimated. In the stratosphere, this methyl bromide releases bromine, thought to be about 50 times as effective as chlorine in depleting ozone. It was estimated that man-made sources of methyl bromide account for some 3%–10% of ozone destruction; production was being phased out by international treaty.

Climate Change. Debate continued over the proper interpretation of long-term observations and numerical model results. Global land temperatures continued to increase—mostly at night and not as the result of increasing urbanization—while satellite Microwave Sounding Unit (MSU) data appeared to show decreases over the oceans.

While the Bill Clinton administration pushed for specific caps on greenhouse gases in the United Nations (UN) accord finalized in Kyoto, Japan, in December, critics pointed to these uncertainties and likely economic costs as grounds for delay.

The role of aerosols in delaying global warming was investigated in the second Aerosol Characterization Experiment (ACE-2). Atmospheric aerosols are particles or droplets smaller than 0.39 in (1 mm) in diameter from smog, smoke, and sea spray. Aerosols typically cool the atmosphere by reflecting sunlight.

Polar Ice. Several studies were undertaken to better understand the polar ice caps. An analysis of whaling records appeared to show a 25% reduction in Antarctic sea ice between the mid-1950s and the early 1970s. Satellite data since then showed fairly consistent sea-ice coverage. The Canadian Space Agency began satellite-borne radar surveys to provide quantitative information on the volume and structure of the Antarctic ice cap. A new observing effort also began in Greenland, where a four-person team set up a year-round camp at the apex of the ice sheet to observe a wide variety of meteorological variables.

Summary of Weather Events. Hurricane activity in 1997 was markedly different than in the previous few years. Only seven named storms occurred in the Atlantic, of which three were hurricanes. In the eastern Pacific, there were 16 named storms, of which eight were hurricanes. Hurricane Danny was the only Atlantic tropical storm to affect the continental United States, causing $100 million worth of damage from the central Gulf Coast to New England. In the eastern Pacific, remnants of Ignacio and Linda brought rare record rains to north-central and southern California. Nora, Olaf, and Pauline buffeted coastal southwestern Mexico, with Pauline also hitting Arizona. Tropical cyclone Drena caused extensive damage to New Caledonia and northern New Zealand, while typhoon Linda became the most destructive storm to hit Southeast Asia in the 20th century.

U.S. precipitation tended to be above average in the West (*see* SPECIAL REPORT, page 347), and below average in the East. Parts of the Mid-Atlantic states suffered significant summer drought, but rains returned to normal or above normal during the fall. Overall, temperatures were cool, although several notable summer heat waves hit the West. Several outbreaks of Arctic air in the spring brought damaging freezes to the Midwest and a storm that blanketed Boston, MA, with a record April snowstorm.

Tornado activity in the United States was less than in previous years, but still greater than the long-term average. The U.S. tornado death toll of 69 for the year nearly matched the long-term average of 82 and was much higher than in the previous two years. The powerful F5 twister that swept through Jarrell, TX, in May killed 27 and caused some $20 million in damage.

Persistent drought in Southeast Asia, Indonesia, and Papua New Guinea and drought during the first half of the year in large parts of eastern Africa and southern South America were attributed to El Niño. The South American drought was broken by strong storms that brought unusually heavy snows to the Andes starting in June. A damaging June freeze in the Brazilian coffee-growing region drove up worldwide coffee prices. In eastern Africa drought was replaced by flooding and storms that brought the first snow to Swaziland in more than 30 years. The European and central Asian winter was colder and snowier than usual. North Korea's continued drought exacerbated its economic crisis. Heavier-than-usual summer monsoons caused heavy death tolls along the Pakistan-India border.

GEORGE J. HUFFMAN
Science Systems and Applications, Inc.

A Year of Unusual Floods

Floods—natural weather events that occur every year—struck with unusual frequency and severity in 1997, raging through sections of North America, Europe, and Africa. The spring flooding along the Red River from North Dakota into Canada was of a magnitude that occurs only once every 500 years. Floods along the Oder River in Europe also were the worst in centuries. In Africa flash floods following a drought killed thousands.

Red River. Residents of the Red River Valley—which covers portions of North Dakota, Minnesota, and Manitoba—were warned in March that the river was primed for major flooding. Thirteen snowstorms had dumped 150% of normal precipitation during the winter. The flat, gradually sloping countryside was suited perfectly to widespread water pooling should snow suddenly melt and ice jams choke waterways. By mid-April floods were under way, and officials struggled to keep up. At Grand Forks, ND, each of several flood-crest predictions fell short of the actual crest, which was more than 5 ft (1.5 m) above the old record set in 1979. Many other locations saw the river rise about 2 ft (0.6 m) above previous records. An analysis of the forecasts underscored the difficulty of predicting an event that exceeded all previous such events, as well as a need for better information on barriers to flood flow in the vicinity of Grand Forks.

Levees and other permanent protective features were almost uniformly inadequate for containing the massive flood, as were temporary dikes, whose design and construction was governed by the local-crest forecasts. In addition to their force, the prolonged floods saturated, softened, and eroded structures over a long period of time, and the massive flood-control efforts slowly lost to the river by attrition.

Some 100,000 U.S. residents were forced to evacuate their homes, many for weeks or months, while nearly 4.5 million acres (1.8 million ha) were inundated, as far as 40 mi (64 km) from the normal banks of the Red River. Adding insult to injury, several blocks in Grand Forks' downtown burned on April 19–20 because the waters prevented effective fire fighting. Total damage in the vicinity of Grand Forks alone was put at between $1 billion and $2 billion, while 11 persons died in the flooding.

The flood continued north into Canada, inundating several small towns and outlying areas around Winnipeg. However, the natural decrease

© Scott Takushi/"St. Paul Pioneer Press"/Sygma

The overflowing Red River forced all 50,000 residents of Grand Forks, ND, to evacuate on April 19, 1997. The Red Cross estimated that the flood destroyed 10% of the town's homes and damaged another 40%.

Chauncey, OH, was among the towns affected by the flooding in the Ohio River Valley in February and early March. Thirty-eight persons lost their lives in the disaster.

© Shannon Stapleton/Sygma

in the power of the flood as it moved farther from its source, together with the advance warning provided by the U.S. flooding that allowed Canadian officials to take stronger actions, spared Winnipeg the fate of Grand Forks.

Response to the disaster came from many different quarters. The bulk of the actual work fell on those directly affected, while some aid came from private groups. The U.S. government pitched in with $488 million in disaster relief; in recognition of the widespread devastation, President Bill Clinton directed the Federal Emergency Management Agency (FEMA) to reimburse 100% of the immediate cleanup effort, instead of the usual 75%.

Pacific Northwest. The week surrounding New Year's Day 1997 saw a series of "pineapple express" storms barrel out of the central Pacific and slam the Pacific Northwest. Some stations measured up to 24 in (61 cm) of rain during the week. The prolonged rain combined with unusual snowmelt to cause widespread flooding that set record or near-record levels on 15 rivers across the Northwest. Flood-control reservoirs were only partially successful in controlling the waters, because they already had absorbed heavy winter-storm runoff. Many levees in California were breached. The total damage was estimated in the range of $2 billion–$3 billion. Thirty-six persons were killed. The bulk of property damage occurred in northern California, while 19 of the deaths were reported in Washington.

Ohio River. The early-March flooding in the Ohio River Valley and its tributaries was triggered by a severe storm complex. Tornadoes caused widespread damage and killed 29 across Arkansas, Mississippi, and Tennessee. Meanwhile, very heavy rain fell in a swath from Arkansas to West Virginia. Louisville, KY, set an all-time state record of 10.48 in (27 cm) in 24 hours, with a storm total of 13.04 in (33 cm). The soil already was saturated from prior storms, so floods developed very quickly. For a time, Cincinnati's Riverfront Stadium was surrounded totally by water, although it sustained only superficial damage. The Ohio River crested at 16 ft (5 m) above flood stage at Louisville, KY. Total damage was expected to exceed $1 billion, with 159 counties declared federal disaster areas. Thirty-eight deaths were attributed to the flooding. Northern Kentucky sustained the most damage and was where the most deaths occurred. The effects of the flood were much worse than during the region's last major event in 1964, because of the dense development that had occurred in the intervening three decades. Still, flood-control barriers were moderately successful in averting even worse problems.

Oder River. Plentiful wintertime snows across central Europe left water tables high after the spring melt. A series of three very heavy rainstorms during July drove rivers over their banks in Germany, Poland, the Czech Republic, and Austria, breaking a three-century-old record along the Oder River. As with the Red River, the persistence of the flooding was particularly hard on levees, since most of them were not designed to stand up to prolonged stress. The levees protecting land along the Oder River on the German-Polish border were particularly hard-pressed. Some 500,000 acres (202 500 ha) in Poland were reported to be inundated. Estimates of damage throughout central Europe ranged from $6 billion to $10 billion, with more than 100 deaths reported. In December the World Bank approved a

As 1997 began, heavy snows and rains struck the U.S. Pacific Northwest. The rains caused a 100-ft (30-m)-wide highway intersection to plunge into a deep ravine in the Seattle suburb of Shoreline.

© Jeff Vinnick/Reuters/Archive Photos

$200 million Emergency Flood Recovery Project loan to Poland.

Other sites in Europe—including Russia, the British Isles, and northern Italy—also experienced flooding.

Eastern Africa. At the beginning of 1997 the watchword in eastern Africa was "drought." Flamingos that normally frequent Lake Nakuru, Kenya, were migrating to the Rift Valley in search of water. Dar es Salaam, Tanzania, was without water for weeks, and brushfires were widespread. However, a series of heavy rains leading to flash floods moved north, hitting Zimbabwe in early March, Tanzania in early April, and Somalia in early May.

In late October and November, three weeks of intense rain began in much of eastern Africa, eventually causing the two main rivers in Somalia to merge into a huge temporary lake. Crops and livestock in much of the country were wiped out, leading to fears of a new Somalian famine. The death toll was estimated to be in excess of 2,000, and hundreds of thousands were left homeless. Meteorologists considered these events unusual, not only because of their severity and persistence, but because the African region normally would experience drought in the year that an El Niño begins.

GEORGE J. HUFFMAN
Science Systems and Applications, Inc.

© Corinne Dufka, Pool/AP/Wide World Photos

Rainfall was considerably above normal levels in the African nations of Kenya, Ethiopia, and Somalia late in 1997. In Somalia, left, two main rivers merged in mid-November, leaving 60 sq mi (155 km²) of land underwater.

Porfirio Muñoz Ledo (center) of the Democratic Revolutionary Party (PRD) was chosen speaker of Mexico's Chamber of Deputies following July 1997 elections, in which the Institutional Revolutionary Party (PRI) lost control of the body for the first time since 1929.

MEXICO

Although the governing Institutional Revolutionary Party (PRI) suffered stinging setbacks in elections, Mexico's President Ernesto Zedillo Ponce de León's popularity increased in 1997, thanks to robust economic growth, decreasing inflation, and his assertive action during an October hurricane.

In December the nation was shocked by the massacre of 45 unarmed Indians in a village in Chiapas state. Survivors accused the PRI of involvement in the killings, and among those arrested were the village's mayor and his deputy, both PRI members.

Politics. The PRI—in power since 1929—had hoped to bounce back from late-1996 reverses in the states of Coahuila, Hidalgo, and México, pinning its hopes on Mexico City, where voters elected their mayor for the first time in modern history on July 6. The PRI candidate, Alfredo del Mazo, however, commanded only 25.5% of the vote, finishing far behind the nationalist-left Democratic Revolutionary Party's (PRD's) Cuauhtémoc Cárdenas, who received 47.7%. Carlos Castillo of the center-right National Action Party (PAN) took third place with 15.9%. Despite PAN's anemic performance in the capital, it picked up two governorships—Nuevo León and Querétaro—bringing its total to six. In Querétaro the outgoing PRI governor had compiled

an impressive record and the PRI nominee was expected to win. The PRI controlled the governorships of Campeche, Colima, Sonora, and San Luis Potosí. While tranquility and a notable lack of irregularities characterized most contests, in Campeche the loser—PRD candidate Layda Sansores, who had deserted the PRI three months before—raised substantial postelection claims of fraud. To its dismay, the PRI lost its once-unassailable grip on the Chamber of Deputies, winning only 238 of 500 seats. Moreover, the opposition—led by the PRD (125 seats) and the PAN (122 seats)—rejected an alliance with the PRI in favor of a loosely structured "Bloc of 4," embracing two minor parties.

While disagreeing on many points, the Bloc of 4 pledged to cooperate on achieving several goals. These included dismantling the "state party" regime, in which the president manipulates the PRI to attain his objectives; diminishing the power of the president; combating corruption in Mexican society; and enlarging public funds earmarked for state and municipal governments. Few observers, however, believed the disparate coalition would remain intact when its participants vied for ten governorships in 1998. Meanwhile, the PRI watched its majority in the upper house dip from 95 to 77—a loss that could have been worse if more than a quarter of the 128 Senate seats had been up for grabs.

MEXICO • Information Highlights

Official Name: United Mexican States.
Location: Southern North America.
Area: 761,602 sq mi (1 972 550 km²).
Population (mid-1997 est.): 95,700,000.
Chief Cities (March 1990 census): Mexico City (Federal District), the capital, 8,235,744; Guadalajara, 1,650,042; Nezahualcóyotl, 1,255,456.
Government: *Head of state and government,* Ernesto Zedillo Ponce de León, president (took office Dec. 1, 1994). *Legislature*—National Congress: Senate and Chamber of Deputies.
Monetary Unit: Peso (8.1020 pesos equal U.S.$1, floating rate, Dec. 8, 1997).
Gross Domestic Product (1995 est. U.S.$): $721,400,000,-000 (purchasing power parity).
Economic Indexes: *Consumer Prices* (1996, 1994 = 100): all items, 301.8; food, 295.5. *Industrial Production* (1996, 1990 = 100): 113.
Foreign Trade (1995 U.S.$): *Imports,* $45,977,000,000; *exports,* $47,056,000,000.

The elections left many PRI factions jostling for influence. Two mutually antagonistic groups stood out. The "renovators"—including presidential aspirants Sens. Esteban Moctezuma and Elba Esther Gordillo—shared Zedillo's belief that PRI reverses argued strongly for democratizing the party's internal operations; advancing the president's neoliberal economic agenda; and recruiting new constituencies, such as women, environmentalists, and young people. Some 82% of younger voters backed opposition parties in the capital elections.

The PRI traditionalists—spearheaded by Govs. Manuel Bartlett (Puebla), Roberto Madrazo (Tabasco), Diodoro Carrasco Altamirano (Oaxaca), and outgoing Gov. Manlio Fabio Beltrones (Sonora)—advocated only cosmetic changes, seeing no need to reshape their party's governance, structure, policies, ideology, or target constituencies. They contended that PRI's resurgence lay in nominating better candidates, waging tougher campaigns, yielding no quarter to political foes, pressuring the media for positive coverage, and deploying the patronage and assets at their disposal to reward loyalists and mobilize voters.

Rank-and-file PRI activists—who agreed with this "governors' cartel"—articulated the virtues of an activist government; manipulated revolutionary symbols such as preserving the oil industry as a state enterprise; and trumpeted nationalist values at a time when Zedillo had trimmed the huge bureaucracy, impelled Mexican integration in the global economy, and welcomed foreign investment. Hard-line governors also won praise for registering impressive victories in their own states. Bartlett, for example, kept Puebla's legislative and congressional delegations firmly in the

PRI column, while Madrazo not only garnered a lion's share of congressional seats on July 6, but also captured all 17 October municipal elections held in Tabasco. This sweep caught the attention of party militants around the country, because Tabasco is the home of PRD president Manuel Andrés López Obrador. In fact, had the PRI held a democratic convention to nominate its next presidential candidate in late 1997, Madrazo or Bartlett would have been the odds-on favorite. However, the actual selection will not occur until 1999, and it remained to be seen whether Zedillo would attempt to name a successor, or would keep his promise to foster an open selection process.

In the face of internal divisions, Zedillo played an ever more vigorous role in party affairs, despite a campaign pledge to maintain a "healthy distance" from the PRI. In mid-September he named the new party president, Mariano Palacios Alcocer, a former Querétaro governor with a long résumé of PRI elective and appointive posts. The choice was an attempt to stem defections by party notables, while Zedillo and Government Secretary Emilio Chuayffet Chemor endeavored to build bridges between feuding elements. Even after the naming of Palacios, other important players jumped to the PRD—former attorney general Ignacio Morales Lechuga, to improve his chances of running for governor of Veracruz state, and Deputy Sergio Valdés, to advance his own political agenda.

The PRI's declining fortunes contrasted with Zedillo's surging popularity, which was due to improved economic conditions, an image of honesty, and decisive management of relief efforts after Hurricane Pauline lashed Acapulco and neighboring states in October. During the hurricane, Zedillo sent the army to distribute aid, rather than leaving it up to "sticky-fingered" politicians.

Economy. Gross domestic product (GDP) grew 6%, powered by construction, manufacturing, exports of *maquiladoras* (plants where foreign components are assembled into completed parts), and oil sales. Finance Secretary Guillermo Ortiz Martínez, another presidential hopeful, took particular pride in a projected 18.8% rise in the consumer-price index, down from a 27.7% increase in 1996. During the first eight months of 1997, the country ran a trade surplus of just more than $2 billion as exports ($70.9 billion) outstripped imports ($68.8 billion). In mid-October hard-currency reserves reached the reassuring level of $25.4 billion, and the International Monetary Fund (IMF) required only an $800 million remittance on Mexico's $2.7 billion debt in 1997. The upswing generated labor demand, and employment rose 12.5% from January to August, according to the Mexican Social Security Institute. Nevertheless, private-sector analysts reckoned that real wages increased only 1%–2% for the year, after tumbling 21.9% during the 1995–96 economic crisis.

Organized Labor. The uncertain economic climate discouraged strikes, and the union movement continued to fragment and lose influence. The biggest blow was on June 21, when Fidel Velázquez Sánchez, the 97-year-old patriarch of the Confederation of Mexican Workers (CTM), died after a half century of authoritarian leadership. Although he was out of touch with Mexico's imperative for competing in a global market, the grizzled Velázquez—more than any of the ten presidents with whom he served—had preserved social peace. Due in large part to his heavy-handed guidance, Mexico's government had evolved from a protracted, bloody revolution early in the century to a civilian-run regime, boasting a record of stability and orderly power transfers unmatched in the Third World. But Don Fidel—as he was known to friends and foes alike—had lost much of his political influence before he died, by making no effort to eradicate the ubiquitous CTM corruption, tying organized labor's fate to a single party—the PRI, and not enlisting the mushrooming number of service workers and employees of the 2,000-plus *maquiladora* assembly plants concentrated just south of the U.S. border.

Leonardo Rodríguez Alcaine, 78, head of the Electrical Workers' Union, succeeded Velázquez until the CTM could elect a permanent secretary-general in March 1998. The interim secretary-general enjoyed neither Don Fidel's legendary stature nor the late leader's squeaky-clean image. According to press reports, Rodríguez Alcaine had amassed a fortune from an insurance company, land holdings, automobiles, and jewelry. His critics even claimed that millions of pesos had disappeared from his union's mutual fund. Still, Rodríguez Alcaine probably would beat back any other challengers within the CTM.

A greater threat to labor unity originated with Francisco Hernández Juárez, head of the affluent Telephone Workers' Union, who in late November 1997 joined with Antonio Rosado García, chief of the 300,000-member Union of Social Security Workers, and Agustín Rodríguez Fuentes, secretary-general of the 8,000-member National Autonomous University Workers, to create the National Workers' Union (UNT) as a new labor central. UNT's prospects remained clouded, however, because Senator Gordillo—a PRI leader and the moving force behind the 1.2-million-member teachers' union—refused to affiliate with the new confederation lest she compromise her chance to obtain the ruling party's presidential nomination. The problem within the existing labor movement, said Gordillo, "is not one of centrals, but of a plural, democratic culture."

Meanwhile, Cárdenas and the opposition in Congress could hasten the decline of the old labor order. The new Mexico City mayor pledged to expose hundreds of pliable "letter-head unions" in the capital, formed by industrialists and allegedly countenanced by local CTM kingpins in exchange for secret payments. Federal lawmakers also planned to hold muckraking hearings on pervasive illegal, unethical, and undemocratic union practices.

Foreign Affairs. In the spring, the U.S. White House recertified Mexico as a cooperative ally in combating the drug trade—a process abhorred by Mexican officials as an intrusion into Mexico's domestic affairs. In mid-May, when U.S. President Bill Clinton visited Mexico City, Zedillo provided him with a report showing that, in 1996 alone, local authorities had arrested 11,283 reputed narcotics traffickers—including 28 suspected big shots in drug cartels; this was up 14% from 1995. Also highlighted was the seizure of 1,006 tons of marijuana, a jump of 15%. Cocaine interdiction rose only 6%. Such information did little to assuage the U.S. government's growing concern about Mexico's "Colombianization." News reports indicated that Mexico's major drug cartels had expanded their role from merely transporting cocaine through Mexico across the Rio Grande, to becoming wholesale providers to major segments of the U.S. market.

U.S. Sen. Jesse Helms, chairman of the Senate Foreign Relations Committee, used Clinton's nomination of former Massachusetts Gov. William Weld as ambassador to Mexico to spotlight the drug issue. Since Weld favored the medicinal use of marijuana, Helms insisted that the Massachusetts politician would be an ineffective combatant in the war against drugs. When Weld's prospects for confirmation dimmed, he withdrew his nomination. The two-month saga grabbed front-page coverage in Mexico City newspapers.

GEORGE W. GRAYSON
College of William and Mary

MICROBIOLOGY

For microbiology, the year 1997 meant important new findings regarding parthenogenesis—the development of unfertilized eggs into adults; the influenza virus; and plant growth patterns. Microbiologists also discovered that the lung disease hantavirus pulmonary syndrome (HPS) can be transferred from person to person.

Infective Parthenogenesis. Depending on the particular species, the process of parthenogenesis produces either males or females. It long has been assumed that parthenogenesis is a genetically controlled phenomenon that has evolved in each of the various groups of animals in response to that group's particular way of life.

R. Stouthamer and M. Schilthuizen at the Wageningen Agricultural University, the Netherlands, reported that infection of female wasps belonging to the genus *Trichogramma* by the bacterium *Wolbachia* leads to the parthenogenetic production of all-female wasp strains. This, in effect, does away with the need for males and results in the wasps reproducing asexually. The bacterium accomplishes this transformation by infecting the ovaries of the wasps and, in some unknown fashion, causing the unfertilized eggs to duplicate their one set of chromosomes and develop into females.

Whether a similar type of infection could cause some mammals, humans included, to form parthenogenetic all-female populations remained purely speculative in 1997. It did not appear that *Wolbachia* could accomplish this, as all forms of the bacteria found were temperature-sensitive and could not survive inside warm-blooded animals.

1918 Influenza Virus. In 1918 there was a worldwide influenza epidemic that killed about 21 million people. Although lung tissues from victims of that epidemic have been preserved in various laboratories, a study of the genes of the 1918 influenza virus became possible only in the mid-1990s. Jeffrey K. Taubenberger and his colleagues at the Armed Forces Institute of Pathology in Washington, DC, studied the infected lung tissue of a U.S. Army private who died of the disease in 1918. They were able to isolate and analyze the nucleotide sequences of five of the organism's genes. It was found that the sequences resembled those of a virus that infects pigs. This finding, announced in 1997, indicated the need to study the influenza viruses of the world's pig populations for indications of possible future human epidemics. Most surveillance efforts for new flu strains have been restricted to the monitoring of people.

Bacterial Determination of Plant Growth Patterns. Among the bacteria there are two groups whose members are extremely small in size, lack a cell wall, and cannot be grown in the laboratory. They are all obligate parasites of other cells. Those that infect animal cells form a group called mycoplasma; the plant-associated equivalent is called phytoplasma.

One phytoplasma that has been studied by Ing-Ming Lee and his colleagues at the U.S. Department of Agriculture laboratory in Beltsville, MD, parasitizes the poinsettia plant. Poinsettias that are not infected by phytoplasma develop into tall, straight plants with typically deep-red flowers at the tops of their stems. Phytoplasma-infected poinsettias develop into short, bushy forms with their floral parts close to the ground.

In experiments designed to test the transmissibility of phytoplasma, the scientists connected the transportation system of an infected poinsettia to that of an uninfected one. Within four months, the well-branched uninfected poinsettia began to turn bushy. Although it had not been proven by late 1997, it was believed that the phytoplasma causes its effects on the poinsettia's growth pattern by controlling the plant's growth hormones.

Hantavirus Transmission. The severe lung disease HPS occurs worldwide and has a 50% mortality rate. The viral infection causes flu-like symptoms that worsen with time. The patient's lungs become filled with fluid and the heart slows down, sending the individual into shock. Prior to 1997, it was believed that people became infected with the virus only if they inhaled microscopic bits of rodent urine or feces containing the virus.

In 1997, Dr. C.J. Peters of the Centers for Disease Control and Prevention in Atlanta reported on the first known cases in which HPS was spread from person to person. These cases occurred in the coastal town of El Bolsón in Argentina in 1996. However, subsequent cases involved some people who had contact with El Bolsón residents but who never had visited the town. These included a physician in Buenos Aires to whom an early victim of the disease had traveled for treatment. Although it was believed that the original viral infection resulted from inhalation of rodent particles, it seemed clear that the virus had mutated in some fashion that permitted its transfer from person to person. This meant that humans have become potential reservoirs for the spread of the HPS virus.

LOUIS LEVINE, *City College of New York*

MIDDLE EAST

Changes, and portents of greater changes to come, abounded in the Middle East in 1997. Long-standing relationships in some cases were manifestly less firm; and some chronic hostile relationships also appeared ready to be muted or ended. Thus, strikingly in the first category was the grouping usually called by Washington "the allies"—the United States and the major Western countries—a coalition that had acted in 1990–91 against Iraq effectively, accepting U.S. leadership. This company now had become an awkward squad indeed, and the ability of the United States to achieve the results it desired was impeded. This pattern of behavior was highlighted sharply by the events of the last two months of the year—Iraq's actions and the response to them. The close relationship between the United States and Israel also was under strain, as the Benjamin Netanyahu government repeatedly took steps that Washington thought unhelpful to the prospects of peace.

New Links and Leaders. On the other hand, one could not fail to notice the beginnings of a thaw in the 19-year-old hostile relationship between Iran and the United States—a development with the possibility of changing totally the anatomy of politics in the Middle East. Another profoundly important development was the working strategic alliance, dating only from February 1996, of Israel and Turkey. The year showed this link strengthening significantly and with remarkable speed—a course of events of great concern to the neighbors of both states.

At the level of personalities, too, change either had arrived or was a clear possibility. In the most important U.S. ally in the Gulf region, Saudi Arabia, the ailing King Fahd essentially had ceded his power, though not the throne, to Crown Prince Abdullah. The latter was known to favor a more austere financial policy, which could imply fewer purchases of U.S. military hardware. Abdullah attended the Islamic Conference Organization meeting in Tehran in December—though, earlier, Iranian-Saudi relations were strained; and he had spoken in favor of reconciling Iran and the United States. Syria's President Hafiz al-Assad and King Hussein of Jordan both had health concerns that posed grave questions about succession, and indeed about the future of their countries.

At the core of Arab-Israeli relations, the two protagonists—Yasir Arafat, leader of the Palestinian National Authority, and Israel's Prime Minister Netanyahu—were both in shaky positions, though for quite different reasons. And in Iran, Mohammed Khatami, the surprise victor in 1997's presidential election, undertook totally new and welcome initiatives toward the United States.

The New Geopolitics. It also must be noted that ideas about what constituted the Middle East necessarily were undergoing revision. "Middle East" never has been a technical term with a precise meaning. Until 1914 it—or the alternative, "Near East"—was thought of as also embracing the Balkan Peninsula, on the grounds that most of that region still was ruled by the Ottoman Empire. In the 1990s the boundaries of the region connoted by the term Middle East expanded again—in another direction, into Central Asia.

The 1991 breakup of the Soviet Union released into independent statehood the 19th-century colonial conquests in Central Asia, and permitted the creation of five new independent, sovereign states: Kazakhstan, Kyrgyzstan, Tajikistan, Turkmenistan, and Uzbekistan. To these perhaps should be added—on the other side of the Caspian—Azerbaijan, since its capital is the great oil port of Baku. The five new states, predominantly Islamic, are not noticeably peaceful. Several have had years of ethnic civil strife. For example, a peace treaty to end a five-year civil war in Tajikistan was signed in June 1997. Nor are they necessarily democratic. These states also have remained poor, but their economic potential is almost impossible to exaggerate. The Caspian region, in general, is thought to contain about one third of the world's reserves of oil and natural gas. Some of this already is being exploited. Baku has become a boomtown. (*See also* RUSSIA AND THE COMMONWEALTH OF INDEPENDENT STATES.)

Iran, Turkey, and, of course, Russia all eagerly were attempting to establish links with the region. The question of routes, for pipelines to world markets, was a major issue. Routes might run through Russia, Turkey, or Iran. Iran so far had been the most active in this area. A railroad had been built from Turkmenistan to Bandar Abbas, on the Gulf, and its traffic was increasing steadily. Iran claimed, with some credibility, that this was the natural corridor for Central Asian goods seeking an outlet to the world. On December 29, President Khatami of Iran—making his first trip outside Iran since his May election—traveled to Turkmenistan to inaugurate a new gas pipeline. It was hoped it would become part of a large regional network sending natural gas to Europe.

Major Issues. The most important ongoing issues in the Middle East were, as for some years, three in number—Arab-Israeli relations, developments in Iraq and Western reaction to them, and relations between Washington and Tehran. In terms of Arab-Israeli relations, a virtual deadlock prevailed throughout the year. There appeared to be an unbridgeable gap between Arafat and Netanyahu. The Israeli prime minister's overriding emphasis has been on Israeli security—a concentration reinforced by the killing of Israeli civilians by terrorists in July. His argument has been that until Arafat would show greater zeal in controlling terrorists, Israel must not be expected to make more concessions, especially territorial. As for the issue of new Jewish settlements, he pointed to the fact that settlements are not even mentioned in the basic 1993 accords that began the now-stalled "peace process."

One positive 1997 step toward peace was the agreement on Israel's withdrawal from Hebron, made in January. Both leaders had domestic constituencies to appease; both had a somewhat tenuous hold on power. Also, Arafat was obviously in poor health throughout the year. Politically, he was threatened by the growing influence of the Hamas organization, whose explicit aim has been to destroy the peace process. Arafat did not—probably could not—crack down on Hamas. Indeed, in August he held a conference with Hamas in Gaza City, where he clearly was angling for the organization's support and spoke the language of confrontation toward Israel. Frequent Israeli border closures kept Palestinian workers from their Israeli employments. The Palestinian economy had plummeted since 1993.

The defection of Netanyahu's foreign secretary as 1998 began left the prime minister with a paper-thin majority of one in the Knesset. The voting position in the Knesset perhaps exaggerated the weakness of Netanyahu's political position. He, after all, was

In late 1997 tensions between Iraq and the United States mounted over the issue of United Nations arms inspections in Iraq. The United States increased its military presence in the Persian Gulf, left, at the height of the dispute.

Benjamin Netanyahu, shown waving to supporters, began his second year as head of Israel's government in June 1997. Throughout the year, Israeli security was at the very forefront of his policy in dealing with the Arabs.

elected directly as prime minister of Israel—the first to be so—and there certainly was nothing in the events of 1997 to make the ordinary Israeli less concerned with security.

Both Arafat and Netanyahu made several trips to Washington in 1997, and U.S. special envoy Dennis Ross visited the Middle East several times to confer separately with the two leaders, but with slight progress. Both Netanyahu and Arafat were due in Washington in January 1998 to confer with President Bill Clinton.

Internationally, the position of the Israeli government was strengthened by the 1996 military-cooperation agreement with Turkey. In 1997 it was underpinned by ratification of a trade agreement. The Turkey-Israeli military pact was disliked by Syria and other Arabs, as well as by Iran, and was looked at askance by the Europeans; but Turkey, having had its application for membership in the European Union (EU) summarily rejected in December, was not in a conciliatory mood. On Jan. 7, 1998, the Turkish and Israeli navies carried out joint exercises in the Mediterranean, accompanied by a U.S. destroyer and a high-level Jordanian observer. The maneuvers, in fact, were concerned mainly with search-and-rescue operations. Egypt had been invited to send an observer, but declined.

The provocative actions of Iraq late in the year concerning weapons inspections within its border as dictated by the United Nations following the Gulf war were not new in kind, though perhaps with an enhanced degree of self-confident effrontery. The episode, which continued into 1998, had the outline that had become normal—some daring Iraqi action in violation of sanctions; then, when pressure built against Iraq, a partial or total retreat. On January 8 the spokesman for the U.S. Defense Department said that the United States would continue to keep two carrier battle groups in the Persian Gulf, poised near Iraq, as long as Iraq refused to comply fully with UN arms sanctions.

However, the West had retreated from its earlier proclaimed intentions in northern Iraq, which—from 1991 on—was supposed to provide a safe haven for Kurds and Iraqi dissidents. Iraq ceased to do anything of the kind in late August–September 1996, when its forces invaded the area. And, in a little-noted action, "Operation Provide Comfort" ended at the end of 1996 or, strictly, was continued in a much-attenuated form, without French cooperation. Ground forces of the United States and other Western powers were withdrawn from northern Iraq.

In 1997 it became the accepted wisdom that the U.S. policy of "dual containment" regarding Iraq and Iran—proclaimed in 1993 and enunciated again by Secretary of State Madeleine Albright in 1997—had become tattered, if it had not failed outright. Certainly, France, Germany, and Russia were eager to make deals with Iran and Iraq, and already had made a number; certainly Iraq had indulged in belligerency; and neither the Europeans nor any Gulf state were eager for a military clash with Iraq. However, it could be argued that neither Iran or Iraq, in fact, had done anything truly outrageous on the international scene for some years—a result that well might have had something to do with an active and vigilant U.S. military presence in the Gulf area.

A Tale of Two Conferences. There was a marked and significant contrast between two conferences—one held in Qatar in November; the other in Tehran in December. The fourth annual Middle East and North Africa Economic Conference (MENA), held under U.S. auspices and opened by Secretary Albright on November 16, was the least successful of that promising series. The series of conferences was intended to further economic development of the region, unite Israelis and Arabs in fruitful cooperation, and foster deals—as indeed had happened on the three previous occasions. Most Arab states boycotted the Qatar conference in protest of Israel's 1997 actions. Syria played a major part in engineering the boycott. The refusal of Egypt to attend was a blow to the underlying idea, and indeed to U.S. prestige.

In contrast, the Islamic conference in Tehran in December saw Sunni and Shiite Muslims from more than 50 countries attending. It also marked the return of Iran to the world political scene. It, perhaps, was interesting most of all for the olive branch extended by Iran's President Khatami to the American people—though not to their government. His approach was repeated a few days later in a news conference and again in a January 1998 television interview. The U.S. government responded in a cautiously courteous fashion. The U.S. view was that there were major problems to be resolved, requiring government-to-government contact.

Yemen. Among the lesser countries of the Middle East, Yemen has one of the most important strategic locations, poised as it is on the eastern side of the strait of Bab el Mandeb, the southern exit of the Red Sea. Yemen hardly has been a happy country in recent years. As 1997 ended, however, there seemed some possibility of improvement within Yemen, though negative factors remained.

Among these various negative factors were the extremely high rate of population growth—at 3.7% per year, one of the highest in the world—and the progressive deterioration of the ancient system of water storage and use. Yemen has a limited rainfall, but one better than in other parts of the Arabian peninsula. During 1997 the normal summer rains came late, and thus destroyed much of the harvests of sorghum, the nation's principal crop, and coffee.

The present Republic of Yemen was created peacefully in 1990 by the union of the two very different regimes that existed in place of the one Yemen of the historic past—the Yemen Arab Republic and the People's Democratic Republic of Yemen, which commonly, if inaccurately, were referred to as North Yemen and South Yemen. Discovery of oil occurred in the 1980s, promising potential wealth, but the union did not settle down smoothly. A two-month civil war erupted in 1994 as south Yemeni leaders attempted to secede. The attempt failed, but the war cost thousands of lives and did much damage to Aden, which under British rule had been one of the greatest ports of the Middle East.

In a general election on April 27, 1997—the first since the civil war—the ruling General People's Congress, the party of longtime President Ali Abdullah Saleh, whose power base is in the north, won a clear nationwide victory, gaining 187 seats in the 301-seat parliament. Some opposition parties boycotted the election, but ten parties did field candidates. International election monitors said on April 29 that the elections had been relatively free and fair.

In 1997, Yemen saw an increase in small-scale violence. Car bombs—a novelty in Yemen—exploded in both San'a and Aden. There was a wave of road blockades and kidnappings (usually of foreigners) in the north, mostly as a protest against increases in fuel prices. The kidnapped persons were released after some time. For example, a U.S. oil executive in San'a was kidnapped by six gunmen on October 30, and released on November 28.

Two ongoing territorial disputes continued to simmer. There was a border dispute with Yemen's more powerful neighbor, Saudi Arabia, which had led to skirmishes over several years. At the end of November a visit to Riyadh by Yemen's foreign minister—in which he met King Fahd and Crown Prince Abdullah—produced no settlement. In the other dispute, Eritrea had seized Hanish al Kabir (Greater Hanish Island), at the mouth of the Red Sea, in December 1995 from Yemeni troops stationed there.

Following a meeting in Brussels on June 18–19 of Yemen's finance minister and representatives of the World Bank and the EU, Yemen received an undertaking of $1.8 billion over three years for an economic-reform program. It would promote flood control as well as improvements in education, electricity, and transportation. The loan was in part a reward for Yemen's success in bringing down inflation and reducing budgetary deficits.

ARTHUR CAMPBELL TURNER
University of California, Riverside

MILITARY AFFAIRS

The year began with newly appointed U.S. Secretary of Defense William Cohen (*see* BIOGRAPHY), a former Republican senator from Maine, announcing that changed conditions in the world—most notably the end of the Cold War—required a review of U.S. defense policy. The announcement set in motion the Quadrennial Defense Review—a reassessment of U.S. defense strategy, force structure, modernization programs, and infrastructure (*see* FEATURE SECTION, page 44). A new chairman of the Joint Chiefs of Staff was appointed in 1997, and a major chemical-weapons-disarmament treaty went into effect.

New Appointments. In October, Army Gen. Henry H. Shelton replaced Army Gen. John M. Shalikashvili as chairman of the Joint Chiefs of Staff—the third consecutive chairman to be selected from the army since Gen. Colin Powell took on the job in 1989. The chairmanship traditionally rotates among the army, navy, and air force, and early in the year many expected a member of the air force to be the new chairman. In the summer, however, Air Force Gen. Joseph W. Ralston removed himself as a candidate when it was learned that he had been involved in an adulterous relationship in the mid-1980s.

Also in October, Army Chief of Staff Gen. Dennis Reimer removed the army's top enlisted man, Sgt. Maj. Gene C. McKinney, from his duties pending trial at a court-martial on sexual-misconduct charges. Robert Hall became the army's new sergeant major.

Arms Control and Disarmament. A major disarmament treaty banning the production and use of poison gas went into effect in April. The Chemical Weapons Convention, which also requires that existing chemical-weapons stocks be destroyed in ten years, now carried the signatures of 167 nations. More importantly, 102 countries, including the United States, had ratified it by late 1997. An important ratification was obtained in November when the Duma—the lower house of the Russian legislature—gave overwhelming support to the ban. Russia, however, does not have the economic resources to build the needed plants to neutralize the nearly 40,000 tons of gas left over from the Cold War. At the time, it was not known to what extent the United States and other nations would assist the Russians financially.

It was hoped in Washington that the Russian action on the Chemical Weapons Convention would presage similar acceptance of the START II treaty, designed to reduce further the number of nuclear weapons possessed by Russia and the United States. That treaty had been stalled for several years in the Russian Duma.

Although U.S. President Bill Clinton had called for a ban on antipersonnel land mines before the United Nations (UN) in 1994, the United States did not sign such a treaty produced by a special conference held in September in Oslo, Norway. The conference was held shortly after the death of Diana, princess of Wales, whose visits to areas ravaged by mines in Africa and Bosnia highly publicized the possibility of a land-mine treaty. Russia and China also did not sign the treaty, which would be submitted to nearly 100 countries for ratification. Signers would agree to never use, develop, produce, acquire, stockpile, retain, or transfer antipersonnel land mines; to destroy current land-mine stocks and remove mines that had been placed; and to render assistance for the care and rehabilitation of those harmed by land mines. Signatory nations have the right to withdraw from the treaty with six months' warning unless they are at war when the six-month period expires.

In announcing that the United States would not sign the treaty, President Clinton said, "As commander in chief, I will not send our soldiers to defend the freedom of our people and the freedom of others without doing everything we can to make them as secure as possible." Washington had tried unsuccessfully to modify the treaty to permit the use of antipersonnel land mines to protect antitank mines, and to delay the effective date of the treaty for nine years. Both provisions were based on Washington's view that antipersonnel land mines were needed for the next few years to protect South Korea from invasion by North Korea.

In November, Defense Secretary Cohen announced a new tactic in U.S. efforts to keep modern weapons from so-called "rogue states"—in this instance, Iran. According to Cohen, the United States secretly bought 21 MiG-20 jet fighters from the former Soviet republic of Moldova, after Moldova informed the United States that Iran had shown substantial interest in the jets. Pentagon officials said that 14 of the planes were the most advanced models, capable of carrying nuclear missiles. The former Soviet warplanes were transported to Wright-Patterson Air Force Base in Ohio.

Questions About the B-2 and the F-22. In 1988 the B-2 was unveiled as the most potent long-range jet bomber ever to fly. The claim was based on the radical "bat-wing" design,

GEN. HENRY (HUGH) SHELTON

Gen. Henry (Hugh) Shelton—shown below with President Bill Clinton and Defense Secretary William Cohen (*center*)—took office as chairman of the U.S. Joint Chiefs of Staff on Oct. 1, 1997. He succeeded Gen. John M. Shalikashvili.

Born on Jan. 2, 1942, in Tarboro, NC, Shelton possesses a bachelor's and a master's degree. Commissioned a second lieutenant in the U.S. Army in 1963, he served two tours of duty in the Vietnam war. After his Vietnam service, for which he was awarded a Bronze Star and a Purple Heart,

he rose in rank and commanded various infantry units. Shelton was deputy operations director at the Joint Chiefs (1987–89), was connected with the 101st Airborne Division during the Persian Gulf war, and was joint task-force commander during the 1994 U.S. invasion of Haiti. He subsequently served as commanding general of the XVIII Airborne Corps at Fort Bragg, NC. In February 1996, Shelton was appointed commander in chief of U.S. Special Operations Command at MacDill Air Force Base in Florida.

© Doug Mills/AP/Wide World Photos

---

which offers less surface to reflect radar, and the bomber's outer covering, or "skin," which does not reflect radar. Together these attributes give the plane its "stealthy," radar-evading designation. But from the beginning—even before the end of the Cold War—the $44.7 billion price tag for the first order of 21 planes had been unpopular with cost-conscious members of Congress and nongovernmental critics. Some observed that the B-2 costs roughly three times its weight in gold. In August the Government Accounting Office (GAO) issued a report that questioned whether the plane's skin can retain its radar-evading qualities when operating in "extreme climates." The study also pointed out that repairs to the bomber's special skin must be made in climate-controlled hangars that exist at present only in the United States. In late September, as Congress debated the defense-spending bill, the decision finally was made against building nine additional B-2s.

Another costly and controversial plane is the F-22. Designed to replace the current top-of-the-line air-force F-15 jet as an air-

superiority fighter for the beginning of the 21st century, the new plane was flown successfully in the fall. But as with the B-2, critics questioned the purpose of the F-22 in the aftermath of the Cold War. The air force responded that the F-22 could be needed for future national-security contingencies that are not currently visible.

The Military Budget. President Clinton and the Republican-controlled Congress agreed to spend $247.5 billion on defense for fiscal year 1998, which began in October. An important facet of the bill was that funds for the U.S. forces in Bosnia were to expire on June 30, 1998, unless the president asked for an extension by May 15. In response to a Freedom of Information suit filed by the Federation of American Scientists, the Central Intelligence Agency's (CIA's) annual budget of $26.6 billion was released to the public for the first time in 1997. Since the creation of the agency in 1947, CIA spending had been one of the "black budget" secrets.

ROBERT M. LAWRENCE
Colorado State University

MOROCCO

Moroccans voted twice in 1997—once for local officials and once for the lower house of a new bicameral legislature. A painstaking negotiation process resulted in an accord on the Western Sahara.

Elections. The electoral year was ushered in by a novel "honor pact"—negotiated and signed by the interior ministry and 11 political parties. Under its terms the authorities promised not to falsify vote counts and the opposition promised to accept the results. Falsifying votes was believed common in Morocco, where the ruling party regularly won 99% of the vote.

Only 75% of registered voters turned out for the pact's first test—the June 14 local elections. They cast ballots in transparent plastic urns to symbolize the new era. Roughly one third of the 24,000 town councillors elected belonged to the government coalition, and one third to opposition parties. Some 24% of the vote went to "centrist" parties supporting the coalition. The opposition decried vote-buying and government interference but accepted what they called "honorable results."

On November 14, Moroccans directly elected the 325-member House of Representatives for the first time. King Hassan II presented the vote as "an historic step" in establishing democratic institutions to ensure the transition of power after his reign. Although Islamist parties were outlawed, 142 candidates with known fundamentalist leanings ran as centrists; nine were elected. The outcome mirrored the results of the June election, with no one coalition achieving a majority. The opposition remained split over whether to seek a place in the new government; it was clear the palace would determine its makeup.

MOROCCO • Information Highlights

Official Name: Kingdom of Morocco.
Location: Northwest Africa.
Area: 172,413 sq mi (446 550 km²).
Population (mid-1997 est.): 28,200,000.
Chief Cities (1994 census): Rabat, the capital (incl. Salé), 1,385,872; Casablanca, 2,940,623; Fez, 774,754; Marrakech, 745,541.
Government: *Head of state,* Hassan II, king (acceded 1961). *Head of government,* Abdellatif Filali, prime minister (appointed May 1994). *Legislature* (bicameral)—Chamber of Councillors and House of Representatives.
Monetary Unit: Dirham (9.902 dirhams equal U.S.$1, official rate, July 1997).
Gross Domestic Product (1995 est. U.S.$): $87,400,000, 000 (purchasing power parity).
Economic Indexes (1996): *Consumer Prices* (1991 = 100): all items, 138.0; food, 143.5. *Industrial Production* (1990 = 100): 115.
Foreign Trade (1996 U.S.$): *Imports,* $9,718,000,000; *exports,* $6,736,000,000.

Government Crackdown. Hoping to avoid the kind of violence perpetrated in neighboring Algeria by Islamic extremists during Ramadan in January, Morocco's King Hassan cracked down on striking students at the University of Casablanca. Most of the students—who walked out to demand better housing and transportation—belonged to Justice and Charity, a militant Islamist organization, so the regime perceived a political undercurrent beneath the concrete demands. During demonstrations in several cities, police beat protesters; 24 students were arrested and sentenced to prison terms ranging from two months to five years. Eight university rectors were replaced.

Western Sahara. During March, United Nations (UN) Secretary-General Kofi Annan—determined to resolve the Western Sahara conflict—appointed former U.S. Secretary of State James Baker to launch a negotiating process. After an intense series of talks, an accord was signed by Morocco and the Polisario Front in mid-September. It established a set of five restrictive criteria to determine who will vote in a referendum on Western Saharan independence, scheduled for summer 1998. Morocco had encouraged its citizens to settle there to counterbalance the votes of the native Saharans. The Polisario Front wanted only the 74,902 inhabitants counted by the Spanish colonial government in 1974 to be eligible. The Baker plan also included provisions on the return of refugees encamped for years south of the Algerian town of Tindouf, and restrictions on 65,000 Moroccan soldiers in the Western Sahara.

The Stock Market and Foreign Affairs. International confidence in the Casablanca stock exchange grew as privatization continued, along with efforts to modernize and regulate transactions. The World Bank incorporated Casablanca into its International Finance Corporation (IFC) index of emerging markets. The market's average shot up by more than 50% in 1997; analysts said it could sustain a 10%–20% annual rate of increase.

On May 23, Zaire's ousted dictator Mobutu Sese Seko, 66, was allowed to enter Morocco. The ailing strongman died of cancer on September 8 at the Rabat military hospital....On December 18, French Prime Minister Lionel Jospin visited Morocco, where talks on bilateral development, immigration, and Morocco's bid to solidify its links with the European Union (EU) were termed "particularly warm and friendly."

SARAH CHAYES, *Contributing Reporter, Paris National Public Radio*

MOTION PICTURES

The average cost of making and marketing a Hollywood movie had climbed to $60 million in 1997, according to Jack Valenti, chairman of the Motion Picture Association of America, which represents the major studios. The figure clearly reflected the expense lavished on formula productions in the quest for financial blockbusters and the corresponding lack of interest in less costly films that might appeal to audiences preferring more realistic stories and characters.

There were exceptions—many of which were showcased by studios and independents at the major film festivals, such as Cannes (*see* Sidebar, page 363), Berlin, Toronto, New York, and Sundance. Of the many fine films produced and distributed, some reached large audiences while others were confined to more selective patrons in the major cities. The 1997 awards demonstrated a greater appreciation for films that in other years might have lost out to more conventional choices.

At the Academy Awards, nine Oscars were lavished on the unusual romantic adventure drama *The English Patient*, including one for best picture; one to Anthony Minghella for directing the film, based on a novel by Michael Ondaatje; and one for best supporting actress to French star Juliette Binoche, who already had been chosen best actress by the Berlin Film Festival. The only film in the "typical" Hollywood category to receive a major Oscar was *Jerry Maguire*, for which Cuba Gooding, Jr., was judged best supporting actor.

Broad Choices. One of the most talked-about films of the year was *L.A. Confidential*, which was showcased at Cannes, the Toronto Film Festival, and the New York Festival before its release. Hailed as a contemporary version of 1940s film noir, it crackled with sharp characterizations, cynical treatment of police corruption, and fine acting by Kevin Spacey, Russell Crowe, Guy Pearce, Kim Basinger, and Danny DeVito. The huge Toronto Festival highlighted *In & Out*, a comedy about attitudes toward homosexuality that starred Kevin Kline, Tom Selleck, and Matt Dillon. The film also gave picture-stealing Joan Cusack the chance to show off her dynamic talent with one of the year's most appealing performances as the intended bride left at the altar.

The subject of pornography went mainstream with Paul Thomas Anderson's acclaimed *Boogie Nights*, first seen at the Toronto and New York festivals. Mark Wahlberg, formerly known as model and rap singer Marky Mark, starred as a youth who becomes a porn star in the 1970s. Burt Reynolds earned praise for his characterization of a director who thinks his sleazy films are artistic, and Julianne Moore was poignant as a drug-addicted porn actress. Columbia TriStar got new mileage from Milos Forman's 1996 drama about pornography and 1st Amendment rights with the international launch of *The People vs. Larry Flynt*, which won the top Golden Bear award at Berlin.

The lives of unhappily married adults and their often puzzled children were examined with disdain in director Ang Lee's *The Ice Storm*, with key performances by Kevin Kline and Joan Allen. A high-profile Canadian film, leading off the Toronto Festival, was Atom

Peter Fonda gave a top performance as a Florida beekeeper who looks after his two granddaughters while his son is in prison and his daughter-in-law struggles with drug addiction in "Ulee's Gold."

Kevin Kline (extreme right), Joan Cusack, and Debbie Reynolds are featured in "In & Out," the tale of a high-school teacher who is called gay by a former student during an Oscar-awards ceremony.

The Everett Collection

Egoyan's *The Sweet Hereafter*, about a British Columbia rural community wracked by the death of children in a bus accident and the machinations of a lawyer, impressively portrayed by Ian Holm.

Peter Fonda gave a particularly strong performance in *Ulee's Gold*. The tender tale of a lonely beekeeper—written and directed by Victor Nunez—it is a prime example of a film that focuses on people with whom audiences can empathize. Robert Duvall donned the many hats of executive producer, screenwriter, director, and star for *The Apostle*, which profiles a charismatic preacher wanted by the law. Robin Wright Penn and Sean Penn

Kevin Spacey (left), Russell Crowe, and Guy Pearce are cops fighting corruption in Los Angeles during the 1950s in the much-discussed "L.A. Confidential." Curtis Hanson directed the film.

The Everett Collection

were moving as a troubled couple in *She's So Lovely*, directed by Nick Cassavetes from a screenplay by his late father, John. Other acting standouts included Al Pacino and Johnny Depp in *Donnie Brasco*, Pacino in *Devil's Advocate*, Julia Roberts in *My Best Friend's Wedding*, Brad Pitt in *Seven Years in Tibet*, Kevin Bacon in *Telling Lies in America*, and Michael Douglas in *The Game*.

Washington Square, a film version of the Henry James book, starred Jennifer Jason Leigh, Ben Chaplin, and Albert Finney. Directed by Agnieszka Holland, it was closer to the novella but less dynamic than director William Wyler's classic *The Heiress*. Another James-based film, *The Wings of the Dove*, was directed beautifully by Iain Softley and featured excellent performances by Helena Bonham Carter, Linus Roache, and Alison Elliott.

One British import that overcame the distribution problems of special films was *The Full Monty*, a good-natured comedy about a group of unemployed men who decide to earn money to support their families by staging a male strip show. Another fine British film, *Brassed Off*, lionized miners trying to keep their lives together during the era of pit closings by rallying around the town's brass band in a national competition. British history provided the backdrop for the compelling *Mrs. Brown*, in which Queen Victoria—touchingly played by Judi Dench—is coaxed from depression after her husband's death by an unlikely friendship with a brash servant, played by Billy Connolly.

Ideas on Film. A number of 1997 films attempted to say something about the human condition. *In the Company of Men*—a nasty but riveting satire on the role of men in the

Cannes Film Festival Turns 50

Despite the proliferation of film festivals over the years, the Cannes Film Festival—which was held for the 50th time in May 1997—remains the most important. Founded by the French government in 1939 to compete with Italy's Venice Festival, it was suspended immediately during World War II and really did not get started until May 1946. Every year it is a glamorous, celebrity-packed event, attended by representatives of every facet of the motion-picture industry.

Journalists and critics flock to cover Cannes' overflow screenings, lavish parties, multimillion-dollar deals, and competition for awards. At the anniversary celebrations held May 8–18, 1997, some 25,000 persons were accredited, including 4,000 members of the press. Seventy-five films from 34 countries were screened officially, 20 of those in the main competition; about 1,000 others played in commercial-market screenings. One highlight was the official celebration dinner held on May 11 in a tent outside the Festival Palais.

Beyond the lure of its Côte d'Azur location—offering sun, sand, restaurants, and a jet-set image—Cannes is successful for many reasons. Hollywood uses the festival to launch overseas distribution and Cannes awards provide international cachet. In addition, no festival gets more international coverage, with controversy and gossip frequently whipping interest to a frenzy.

The top Palme d'Or (Golden Palm) award for 1997 was shared by *Taste of Cherry,* which was directed by Abbas Kiarostami of Iran, and *The Eel,* which Shohei Imamura of Japan directed. The former initially was banned by Iran as offensive. Sean Penn took the award for best actor in *She's So Lovely,* directed by Nick Cassavetes from a script by his late father, John Cassavetes. Kathy Burke won best actress for *Nil by Mouth.* James Schamus won best script for his adaptation of Rick Moody's novel *The Ice Storm.* Wong Kar-Wai of Hong Kong took top honors as best director for *Happy Together.* The runner-up Grand Prize went to Atom Egoyan's Canadian film *The Sweet Hereafter.* A 50th Anniversary Prize was awarded to the Egyptian film *Destiny* and the Jury Prize went to the French film *Western.* A special Palme d'Or was awarded to Swedish director Ingmar Bergman, who did not attend.

French star Isabelle Adjani headed the jury; such notables as Bruce Willis, Demi Moore, Kim Basinger, Danny DeVito, Kevin Spacey, Michael Jackson, Robert De Niro, Sylvester Stallone, and Claudia Schiffer kept the paparazzi busy.

WILLIAM WOLF

competitive workplace and their attitudes toward women and each other—was written and directed by Neil LaBute, and was a hit at the New Directors/New Films series at the Museum of Modern Art in New York. Michael Winterbottom's *Welcome to Sarajevo,* starring Woody Harrelson, Marisa Tomei, and Stephen Dillane, conveyed the horrors of the Bosnian conflict. Spike Lee, whose 1996 *Get on the Bus* was honored with a special mention at the Berlin Festival, made the documentary *4 Little Girls,* about the children killed in the 1963 racist bombing of a Birmingham, AL, church. Kevin Smith's *Chasing Amy* boldly depicted the youthful problems of finding one's sexual identity. What can happen when science gives prospective parents a genetic profile of what their baby will be like was the subject examined in *The Twilight of the Golds,* based on the Broadway play by Jonathan Tolins.

In *Contact*—based on a book by late astronomer Carl Sagan and starring Jodie Foster as a dedicated scientist determined to make contact with life beyond our planet—director Robert Zemeckis probed the conflicting relationship between science and religion. Director Errol Morris pondered the ways of the world in *Fast, Cheap & Out of Control,* his very unusual documentary about an animal trainer, gardener, mole-rat specialist, and robot scientist. In the ominous hospital drama *Critical Care,* director Sidney Lumet lampooned the way money and medicine often intertwine at the expense of patients' welfare. Terrence McNally's play *Love! Valour! Compassion!,* about the struggles of a group of gay men coming to terms with their lives and the specter of AIDS, was directed effectively for the screen by Joe Montello. In *Cop Land,* Sylvester Stallone had the opportunity to stretch his screen persona in a laid-back role as an ethical New Jersey sheriff trying to do the right thing amid police corruption.

The Action Market. Fans of special effects and action (*see* SPECIAL REPORT, page 367) rushed off to see the profitable rerelease of the *Star Wars* trilogy and Steven Spielberg's *Jurassic Park* sequel, *The Lost World: Jurassic Park,* which took in nearly $100 million at the

The Japanese film "Shall We Dance?"—with Koji Yakusho and Tamiyo Kusakari—was marketed by Miramax and went on to become one of 1997's more popular foreign-language films.

box office in its first five days of release. In general, however, box-office results for this genre were very mixed. *Con Air* was an action blast about a revolt by convicts being transported on a plane. In *The Peacemaker*, from the new DreamWorks studio, George Clooney and Nicole Kidman teamed up to thwart nuclear terrorists. Demi Moore shaved her head and endured grueling military training to join a select U.S. Navy unit in *G.I. Jane*. Harrison Ford was a very physical U.S. president who conquered terrorists aboard *Air Force One*. Oliver Stone's *U-Turn* provided a defiant twist as a bloody melodrama with a comic edge reminiscent of film noir.

As usual, the end of the year saw a diverse crop of late arrivals. In *Mad City*, directed by Costa-Gavras, Dustin Hoffman played a television reporter exploiting a hostage situation involving a museum security guard, played by John Travolta. Francis Ford Coppola returned to direct *The Rainmaker*, based on John Grisham's book. In *Red Corner*, Richard Gere battled to free himself from a murder frame-up while traveling in China. Martin Sherman's play *Bent*, about Nazi persecution of homosexuals in World War II, became an extremely powerful movie under the astute direction of Sean Mathias, with affecting performances by Clive Owens and Brian Webber. Steven Spielberg directed *Amistad*, about an 1839 slave-ship revolt. Robert Redford direct-

ed and starred in *The Horse Whisperer*, adapted from the popular novel.

Titanic, reputed to cost some $200 million, set sail in late 1997, while a much more intimate film, *The Winter Guest*, teamed celebrated actress Emma Thompson and her mother, Phyllida Law, as daughter and mother. Woody Allen's *Deconstructing Harry* was a comedy that dissected the life of a complicated writer. Others due before year's end included *The Postman*, Kevin Costner's opus about a postapocalyptic drifter; Alan Rudolph's *Afterglow*, which teamed Nick Nolte and Julie Christie; and Martin Scorsese's *Kundun*, about turbulent events in Tibet.

Foreign-Language Films. The year's breakthrough foreign-language import was *Shall We Dance?*, a delightful tale from Japan about a man who secretly takes dance lessons. Miramax marketed it without a hint that the film had subtitles—a move that helped it to reach a wider audience than is usual for foreign-language films. A very special experience was provided by *Marcello Mastroianni: I Remember*, a documentary ode to the late Italian actor by his companion, Anna Maria Tato. Among the directors bringing new life to French cinema was Cedric Klapisch, whose charming *When the Cat's Away* was a favorite at the New Films, New Directors series in New York. Hungarian director Janos Szasz' *The Witman Boys*, a strong drama of alienation, highlighted the many films unveiled in that country's Film Week. The remarkable, philosophical Iranian film *Taste of Cherry*, directed by Abbas Kiarostami, was acquired for U.S. distribution. Despite films of quality, foreign-language films still reached a comparatively limited U.S. audience.

Controversy. The Hollywood blacklist that existed during the McCarthy era of the 1950s left many writers without screen credit because their names were dropped or replaced by others. In an effort to rectify these injustices, The Writers Guild of America decided to have names restored on new film prints and video releases, as well as in the record books.

A new version of the novel *Lolita*, directed by Adrian Lyne and starring Jeremy Irons and Dominique Swain, had trouble finding anyone in the United States willing to brave the controversial subject and distribute the film, even though it was playing in Europe. *Crash*, David Cronenberg's expertly made but distasteful film about people who find car accidents erotic, was stalled before Ted Turner reluctantly allowed his Fine Line company to release it.

WILLIAM WOLF, *New York University*

MOTION PICTURES • 1997

ABSOLUTE POWER. Director, Clint Eastwood; screenplay by William Goldman, based on the novel by David Baldacci. With Clint Eastwood, Gene Hackman. E.G. Marshall, and Ed Harris.

AIR FORCE ONE. Director, Wolfgang Petersen; screenplay by Andrew Marlowe. With Harrison Ford, Gary Oldman, Dean Stockwell, and Glenn Close.

ALIEN RESURRECTION. Director, Jean-Pierre Jeunet; screenplay by Joss Whedon, based on characters by Dan O'Bannon and Ronald Shusett. With Sigourney Weaver, Winona Ryder, Ron Perlman, and Dan Hedaya.

AN AMERICAN WEREWOLF IN PARIS. Director, Anthony Waller; screenplay by Tim Burns, Tom Stern, and Waller. With Tom Everett Scott, Julie Delpy, Vince Vieluf, and Phil Buckman.

AMISTAD. Director, Steven Spielberg; screenplay by David Franzoni and Steven Zaillian. With Morgan Freeman, Anthony Hopkins, Djimon Hounsou, and Matthew McConaughey.

ANASTASIA. Codirectors, Don Bluth and Gary Goldman. With the voices of Meg Ryan, John Cusack, Angela Lansbury, Christopher Lloyd, Hank Azaria, Bernadette Peters, and Kelsey Grammer.

THE APOSTLE. Written and directed by Robert Duvall. With Robert Duvall, Miranda Richardson, and Farrah Fawcett.

AS GOOD AS IT GETS. Director, James Brooks; screenplay by Mark Andrus and Brooks, based on the story by Andrus. With Jack Nicholson, Helen Hunt, and Greg Kinnear.

BATMAN AND ROBIN. Director, Joel Schumacher; screenplay by Akiva Goldsman, based on characters created by Bob Kane. With Arnold Schwarzenegger, George Clooney, Chris O'Donnell, Uma Thurman, and Alicia Silverstone.

BEAN. Director, Mel Smith; screenplay by Richard Curtis and Robin Driscoll. With Rowan Atkinson, Peter MacNicol, Pamela Reed, Harris Yulin, and Burt Reynolds.

BEAUMARCHAIS THE SCOUNDREL. Director, Edouard Molinaro; screenplay by Molinaro and Jean-Claude Brisville. With Fabrice Luchini.

BENT. Director, Sean Mathias; screenplay by Martin Sherman. With Lothaire Bluteau, Clive Owen, Brian Webber, Ian McKellen, and Mick Jagger.

BLOOD AND WINE. Director, Bob Rafelson; screenplay by Nick Villiers and Alison Cross. With Jack Nicholson, Stephen Dorff, and Jennifer Lopez.

BOOGIE NIGHTS. Written and directed by Paul Thomas Anderson. With Mark Wahlberg, Julianne Moore, Burt Reynolds, and Don Cheadle.

THE BOXER. Director, Jim Sheridan; screenplay by Sheridan and Terry George. With Daniel Day-Lewis and Emily Watson.

BRASSED OFF! Written and directed by Mark Herman. With Pete Postlethwaite, Tara Fitzgerald, and Ewan McGregor.

BREAKDOWN. Director, Jonathan Mostow; screenplay by Mostow and Sam Montgomery, based on a story by Mostow. With Kurt Russell, J.T. Walsh, Kathleen Quinlan, and M.C. Gainey.

CAPITAINE CONAN. Director, Bertrand Tavernier. Screenplay by Tavernier and Jean Cosmos, based on the novel by Roger Vercel. With Philippe Torreton, Samuel Le Bihan, and Bernard LeCoq.

CAREER GIRLS. Written and directed by Mike Leigh. With Katrin Cartlidge and Lynda Steadman.

CHASING AMY. Written and directed by Kevin Smith. With Ben Affleck, Joey Lauren Adams, and Jason Lee.

CITY OF INDUSTRY. Director, John Irvin; screenplay by Ken Solarz. With Harvey Keitel, Stephen Dorff, Timothy Hutton, and Wade Dominguez.

CON AIR. Director, Simon West; screenplay by Scott Rosenberg. With Nicolas Cage, John Cusack, and John Malkovich.

CONSPIRACY THEORY. Director, Richard Donner; screenplay by Brian Helgeland. With Mel Gibson, Julia Roberts, and Patrick Stewart.

CONTACT. Director, Robert Zemeckis; screenplay by James Hart and Michael Goldenberg, based on the novel by Carl Sagan. With Jodie Foster, Tom Skerritt, Matthew McConaughey, and Angela Bassett.

COP LAND. Written and directed by James Mangold. With Sylvester Stallone, Harvey Keitel, Ray Liotta, Robert De Niro, and Janeane Garofalo.

CRASH. Written and directed by David Cronenberg. With James Spader, Holly Hunter, Elias Koteas, Deborah Kara Unger, and Rosanna Arquette.

CRITICAL CARE. Director, Sidney Lumet; screenplay by Steven Schwartz. With James Spader, Kyra Sedgwick, Helen Mirren, Anne Bancroft, and Albert Brooks.

THE DAYTRIPPERS. Written and directed by Greg Mottola. With Hope Davis, Stanley Tucci, Anne Meara, Pat McNamara, Parker Posey, and Liev Schreiber.

DECONSTRUCTING HARRY. Written and directed by Woody Allen. With Woody Allen, Caroline Aaron, Kirstie Alley, Bob Balaban, Richard Benjamin, Eric Bogosian, Billy Crystal, Judy Davis, Hazelle Goodman, Amy Irving, Judy Davis, Demi Moore, Elisabeth Shue, Stanley Tucci, and Robin Williams.

DEVIL'S ADVOCATE. Director, Taylor Hackford; screenplay by Jonathan Lemkin and Tony Gilroy, based on the novel by Andrew Neiderman. With Keanu Reeves, Al Pacino, Charlize Theron, and Craig T. Nelson.

THE DEVIL'S OWN. Director, Alan J. Pakula; screenplay by David Aaron Cohen, Vincent Patrick, and Kevin Jarre, based on a story by Jarre. With Harrison Ford, Brad Pitt, Margaret Colin, Natascha McElhone, and Ruben Blades.

DONNIE BRASCO. Director, Mike Newell; screenplay by Paul Attanasio, based on the book by Joseph D. Pistone with Richard Woodley. With Al Pacino, Johnny Depp, Michael Madsen, and Anne Heche.

THE EDGE. Director, Lee Tamahori; screenplay by David Mamet. With Anthony Hopkins, Elle Macpherson, and Alec Baldwin.

EVE'S BAYOU. Written and directed by Kasi Lemmons. With Samuel L. Jackson and Lynn Whitfield.

FACE/OFF. Director, John Woo; screenplay by Mike Werb and Michael Colleary. With John Travolta, Nicolas Cage, Joan Allen, and Nick Cassavetes.

FAIRY TALE: A TRUE STORY. Director, Charles Sturridge; screenplay by Ernie Contreras, based on a story by Albert Ash, Tom McLoughlin, and Contreras. With Florence Hoath, Elizabeth Earl, and Harvey Keitel.

FAST, CHEAP AND OUT OF CONTROL. Documentary. Director, Errol Morris. With Dave Hoover, George Mendonca, Ray Mendez, and Rodney Brooks.

THE FIFTH ELEMENT. Director, Luc Besson; screenplay by Besson and Robert Mark Kamen, based on a story by Besson. With Bruce Willis and Gary Oldman.

FLUBBER. Director, Les Mayfield; screenplay by John Hughes and Bill Walsh. With Robin Williams.

FREE WILLY 3: THE RESCUE. Director, Sam Pillsbury; screenplay by John Mattson. With Jason James Richter, August Schellenberg, and Annie Corley.

THE FULL MONTY. Director, Peter Cattaneo; screenplay by Simon Beaufoy. With Robert Carlyle, Tom Wilkinson, Mark Addy, and Steve Huison.

The Kobal Collection

Danny DeVito (right) *and Matt Damon star in "The Rainmaker," the latest film to be based on a best-seller by John Grisham.*

THE GAME. Director, David Fincher; screenplay by John Brancato and Michael Ferris. With Michael Douglas, Sean Penn, and Deborah Kara Unger.

GATTACA. Written and directed by Andrew Niccol. With Ethan Hawke, Uma Thurman, Gore Vidal, Ernest Borgnine, and Blair Underwood.

GEORGE OF THE JUNGLE. Director, Sam Weisman; screenplay by Dana Olsen and Audrey Wells, based on a story by Olsen and characters developed by Jay Ward. With Brendan Fraser, Leslie Mann, and Richard Roundtree.

G.I. JANE. Director, Ridley Scott; screenplay by David Twohy and Danielle Alexandra. With Demi Moore, Viggo Mortensen, and Anne Bancroft.

GOOD WILL HUNTING. Director, Gus Van Sant; screenplay by Ben Affleck and Matt Damon. With Robin Williams, Matt Damon, Ben Affleck, Minnie Driver, and Stellan Skarsgard.

GREAT EXPECTATIONS. Director, Alfonso Cuarón; screenplay by Mitch Glazer, based on the novel by Charles Dickens. With Ethan Hawke, Gwyneth Paltrow, Anne Bancroft, and Robert De Niro.

GROSSE POINTE BLANK. Director, George Armitage; screenplay by Tom Jankiewicz, D.V. DeVincentis, Steve Pink, and John Cusack, based on a story by Jankiewicz. With John Cusack, Minnie Driver, Alan Arkin, and Joan Cusack.

GUANTANAMERA. Directors, Tomas Gutierrez Alea and Juan Carlos Tabio; screenplay by Eliseo Alberto Diego, Alea, and Tabio. With Carlos Cruz, Mirtha Ibarra, and Raul Eguren.

THE HOUSE OF YES. Written and directed by Mark Waters, based on the play by Wendy MacLeod. With Parker Posey, Josh Hamilton, Tori Spelling, Freddie Prinze, Jr., Genevieve Bujold, and Rachael Leigh Cook.

THE ICE STORM. Director, Ang Lee; screenplay by James Schamus, based on the novel by Rick Moody. With Kevin Kline, Sigourney Weaver, Christina Ricci, and Elijah Wood.

I KNOW WHAT YOU DID LAST SUMMER. Director, Jim Gillespie; screenplay by Kevin Williamson, based on the novel by Lois Duncan. With Jennifer Love Hewitt, Sarah Michelle Gellar, Ryan Phillippe, and Freddie Prinze, Jr.

THE IMAX NUTCRACKER. Written and directed by Christine Edzard. With Miriam Margolyes, Heathcote Williams, and Benjamin Hall.

IN & OUT. Director, Frank Oz; screenplay by Paul Rudnick. With Kevin Kline, Joan Cusack, Tom Selleck, Debbie Reynolds, Wilford Brimley, and Bob Newhart.

IN THE COMPANY OF MEN. Written and directed by Neil LaBute. With Aaron Eckhart, Stacy Edwards, and Matt Malloy.

THE JACKAL. Director, Michael Caton-Jones; screenplay by Chuck Pfarrer. With Bruce Willis, Richard Gere, and Sidney Poitier.

JACKIE BROWN. Written and directed by Quentin Tarantino, based on a book by Elmore Leonard. With Pam Grier, Samuel L. Jackson, Robert Forster, Bridget Fonda, Michael Keaton, and Robert De Niro.

KISS OR KILL. Written and directed by Bill Bennett. With Matt Day and Frances O'Connor.

KISS THE GIRLS. Director, Gary Fleder; screenplay by David Klass, based on the novel by James Patterson. With Morgan Freeman and Ashley Judd.

KUNDUN. Director, Martin Scorsese; screenplay by Melissa Mathison. With Brad Pitt and Richard Gere.

L.A. CONFIDENTIAL. Director, Curtis Hanson; screenplay by Brian Helgeland and Hanson, based on a novel by James Ellroy. With Kevin Spacey, Russell Crowe, Guy Pearce, and Kim Basinger.

LIAR LIAR. Director, Tom Shadyac; screenplay by Paul Guay and Stephen Mazur. With Jim Carrey, Maura Tierney, Jennifer Tilly, and Swoosie Kurtz.

LOST HIGHWAY. Written and directed by David Lynch. With Bill Pullman, Patricia Arquette, Balthazar Getty, Robert Loggia, and Robert Blake.

THE LOST WORLD: JURASSIC PARK. Director, Steven Spielberg; screenplay by David Koepp, based on a novel by Michael Crichton. With Jeff Goldblum, Julianne Moore, and Richard Attenborough.

LOVE! VALOUR! COMPASSION! Director, Joe Mantello; screenplay by Terrence McNally, based on his play. With Jason Alexander, John Glover, Stephen Bogardus, John Benjamin Hickey, Stephen Spinella, Justin Kirk, and Randy Becker.

MAD CITY. Director, Costa Gavras; screenplay by Tom Matthews, based on the story by Matthews and Eric Williams. With Dustin Hoffman, John Travolta, and Alan Alda.

THE MAN WHO KNEW TOO LITTLE. Director, Jon Amiel; screenplay by Robert Farrar and Howard Franklin. With Bill Murray, Peter Gallagher, and Joanne Whalley.

MEN IN BLACK. Director, Barry Sonnenfeld; screenplay by Ed Solomon, based on comics by Lowell Cunningham. With Will Smith, Tommy Lee Jones, and Rip Torn.

MIDNIGHT IN THE GARDEN OF GOOD AND EVIL. Director, Clint Eastwood; screenplay by John Lee Hancock, based on the book by John Berendt. With Kevin Spacey and John Cusack.

MIMIC. Director, Guillermo Del Toro; screenplay by Del Toro and Matthew Robbins, based on the short story by Donald Wollheim. With Mira Sorvino, Jeremy Northam, Josh Brolin, Alexander Goodwin, and F. Murray Abraham.

MOUSE HUNT. Director, Gore Verbinski; screenplay by Adam Rifkin. With Nathan Lane and Lee Evans.

MR. MAGOO. Director, Stanley Tong; screenplay by Pat Proft and Tom Sherohman. With Leslie Nielsen.

MRS. BROWN. Director, John Madden; screenplay by Jeremy Brock. With Judi Dench and Billy Connolly.

MURDER AT 1600. Director, Dwight Little; screenplay by Wayne Beach and David Hodgin. With Wesley Snipes, Diane Lane, Alan Alda, and Dennis Miller.

MY BEST FRIEND'S WEDDING. Director, P.J. Hogan; screenplay by Ronald Bass. With Julia Roberts, Dermot Mulroney, Cameron Diaz, and Rupert Everett.

MY MOTHER'S COURAGE. Written and directed by Michael Verhoeven, based on the writings of George Tabori. With Pauline Collins, Ulrich Tukur, and Natalie Morse.

THE MYTH OF FINGERPRINTS. Written and directed by Bart Freundlich. With Blythe Danner, Roy Scheider, and Noah Wyle.

NIGHT FALLS ON MANHATTAN. Written and directed by Sidney Lumet, based on a novel by Robert Daley. With Andy Garcia, Ian Holm, and Richard Dreyfuss.

ONE NIGHT STAND. Written and directed by Mike Figgis. With Wesley Snipes, Nastassja Kinski, Kyle MacLachlan, Ming-Na Wen, and Robert Downey, Jr.

OSCAR AND LUCINDA. Director, Gillian Armstrong; screenplay by Laura Jones, from the novel by Peter Carey. With Ralph Fiennes, Cate Blanchett, Ciaran Hinds, Tom Wilkinson, and Clive Russell.

OUT TO SEA. Director, Martha Coolidge; screenplay by Robert Nelson. With Jack Lemmon, Walter Matthau, and Dyan Cannon.

PARADISE ROAD. Written and directed by Bruce Beresford. With Glenn Close, Pauline Collins, and Frances McDormand.

THE PEACEMAKER. Director, Mimi Leder; screenplay by Michael Schiffer. With George Clooney, Nicole Kidman, and Armin Mueller-Stahl.

THE POSTMAN. Director, Kevin Costner; screenplay by Eric Roth and Brian Helgeland, based on the book by David Brin. With Kevin Costner, Will Patton, Larenz Tate, Olivia Williams, James Russo, and Tom Petty.

PRIVATE PARTS. Director, Betty Thomas; screenplay by Len Blum and Michael Kalesniko, based on the book by Howard Stern. With Howard Stern, Robin Quivers, Mary McCormack, Jackie Martling, and Fred Norris.

THE RAINMAKER. Written and directed by Francis Ford Coppola, based on the novel by John Grisham. With Danny DeVito, Matt Damon, Claire Danes, Jon Voight, and Mickey Rourke.

RED CORNER. Director, Jon Avnet; screenplay by Robert King. With Richard Gere, Bai Ling, and James Hong.

SCREAM 2. Director, Wes Craven; screenplay by Kevin Williamson. With David Arquette, Neve Campbell, Courtney Cox, and Sarah and Jamie Kennedy.

SEVEN YEARS IN TIBET. Director, Jean-Jacques Annaud; screenplay by Becky Johnston, based on the book by Heinrich Harrer. With Brad Pitt, David Thewlis, and B.D. Wong.

SHALL WE DANCE? Written and directed by Masayuki Suo. With Koji Yakusho, Tamiyo Kusakari, Naoto Takenaka, and Eriko Watanabe.

SHE'S SO LOVELY. Director, Nick Cassavetes; screenplay by John Cassavetes. With Sean Penn, Robin Wright Penn, John Travolta, and Gena Rowlands.

SPEED 2. Director, Jan De Bont; screenplay by Randall McCormick and Jeff Nathanson from a story by De Bont and McCormick, based on characters created by Graham Yost. With Sandra Bullock, Jason Patric, and Willem Dafoe.

STARSHIP TROOPERS. Director, Paul Verhoeven; screenplay by Ed Neumeier, based on the book by Robert A. Heinlein. With Casper Van Dien, Dina Meyer, Denise Richards, Jake Busey, Neil Patrick Harris, Patrick Muldoon, and Michael Ironside.

THE SWEET HEREAFTER. Written and directed by Atom Egoyan, based on the novel by Russell Banks. With Ian Holm, Sarah Polley, Bruce Greenwood, Tom McCamus, and Gabrielle Rose.

TELLING LIES IN AMERICA. Director, Guy Ferland; screenplay by Joe Eszterhas. With Kevin Bacon, Brad Renfro, Maximilian Schell, and Calista Flockhart.

THAT OLD FEELING. Director, Carl Reiner; screenplay by Leslie Dixon. With Bette Midler, Dennis Farina, and Paula Marshall.

A THOUSAND ACRES. Director, Jocelyn Moorhouse; screenplay by Laura Jones, based on the novel by Jane Smiley. With Michelle Pfeiffer and Jessica Lange.

TITANIC. Written and directed by James Cameron. With Leonardo DiCaprio, Kate Winslet, Kathy Bates, Frances Fisher, Bernard Hill, Jonathan Hyde, Danny Nucci, David Warner, and Bill Paxton.

TOMORROW NEVER DIES. Director, Roger Spottiswoode; screenplay by Bruce Feirstein. With Pierce Brosnan.

TROJAN EDDIE. Director, Gillies MacKinnon; screenplay by Billy Roche. With Richard Harris, Stephen Rea, and Aislin McGuckin.

ULEE'S GOLD. Written and directed by Victor Nunez. With Peter Fonda, Patricia Richardson, Jessica Biel, and Vanessa Zima.

U-TURN. Director, Oliver Stone; screenplay by John Ridley, based on the book *Stray Dogs*. With Sean Penn, Billy Bob Thornton, Jennifer Lopez, and Jon Voight.

WAG THE DOG. Director, Barry Levinson; screenplay by Hilary Henkin and David Mamet. With Dustin Hoffman, Robert De Niro, Anne Heche, Denis Leary, and William H. Macy.

WASHINGTON SQUARE. Director, Agnieszka Holland; screenplay by Carol Doyle, based on the novella by Henry James. With Jennifer Jason Leigh, Albert Finney, Ben Chaplin, and Maggie Smith.

WELCOME TO SARAJEVO. Director, Michael Winterbottom; screenplay by Frank Cottrell Boyce, based on a book by Michael Nicholson. With Stephen Dillane, Woody Harrelson, and Marisa Tomei.

THE WIND IN THE WILLOWS. Written and directed by Terry Jones, based on the novel by Kenneth Grahame. With Steve Coogan, Eric Idle, Terry Jones, and Nicol Williamson.

WINGS OF THE DOVE. Director, Iain Softley; screenplay by Hossein Amini, based on the novel by Henry James. With Helena Bonham Carter, Linus Roache, and Alison Elliott.

THE WINTER GUEST. Director, Alan Rickman; screenplay by Sharman MacDonald and Rickman. With Emma Thompson and Phyllida Law.

Special Effects

When *Star Wars* was released in 1977, it quickly became an enormous international success. Even so, it was too early to predict accurately the profound impact it would have—spawning a new generation of films that depended upon ever-escalating special effects enhanced by rapidly expanding technology. The 20th-anniversary rerelease of the *Star Wars* trilogy—including the original film's two successors, *The Empire Strikes Back* and *Return of the Jedi*—came in a year filled with would-be blockbusters dependent upon the latest in special effects to lure audiences. This 1997 release, with heightened special effects, fattened the overall *Star Wars* trilogy box-office receipts, which totaled some $1.3 billion worldwide.

History. By now, movie lore includes the tale of how Twentieth Century–Fox, not expecting great things from the original *Star Wars*, gave producer-director George Lucas the sequel and merchandising rights instead of a $500,000 directing fee. The film's success enabled Lucas to expand his Industrial Light & Magic special-effects emporium, part of today's billion-dollar Lucasfilm empire. It is the reigning company in the field of providing producers with the effects that they need. Industrial Light & Magic, headquartered on Lucas' sprawling Skywalker Ranch north of San Francisco, was born of necessity in 1975 because Lucas could not find anyone else to create what he wanted for *Star Wars*.

Of course, the art of special effects did not begin with *Star Wars*, but dates to the early days of cinema. As early as 1902, French filmmaker George Méliès employed imaginative effects in his *A Trip to the Moon*, while Fritz Lang's futuristic 1927 classic *Metropolis* made impressive use of special effects. Film buffs fondly remember the climax in *King Kong* (1933), when the great ape clings to the top of the Empire State Building batting away airplanes.

Stanley Kubrick's memorable *2001: A Space Odyssey* (1968) dazzled filmgoers with its simulation of travel through the universe, while the *Star Trek* television series—which spun off a series of films—fired the imagination. But in the 1990s, advances in computer and digital technology have made it possible to take gigantic leaps, enabling films to simulate convincingly treacherous tornadoes as seen in *Twister*, dinosaurs for

Rapidly advancing technology gave Steven Spielberg the ability to mix robotics and computer-generated effects in his 1997 film "The Lost World," below—the sequel to the dinosaur epic "Jurassic Park," which is the largest-grossing movie ever.

The Everett Collection

the *Jurassic Park* movies, and alien space creatures for such films as *Men in Black*.

The Technology. If a script calls for fantastic occurrences and settings—in space, beneath the sea, or in combat—experts can make things happen in convincing ways that once were impossible. But special effects are labor-intensive—as a glance at the credits scrolling by at the end of a movie will attest. Although special effects are expensive, they also can save considerable money by eliminating the need for constructing elaborate physical settings. Digitally created environments are made by breaking film down into digital components, which then are manipulated with high-powered computers before being put back onto film again.

Actors can be shown in the midst of elaborate scenic setups created with such digital technology. It is also possible to fashion characters by computer instead of relying on actors. In addition, live actors now can interact with artificially created actors or animals in ways far superior to Gene Kelly's groundbreaking dance with a mouse in *Anchors Aweigh* (1945)—long a standard for human/animation interaction. Even mass crowd scenes can be created by multiplying extras with the aid of computers.

It is possible to perpetrate considerable mischief with the new technology, as in *Forrest Gump* (1994), in which Tom Hanks shakes hands with an image of President John F. Kennedy. This raises some serious ethical issues. While having fictional characters interact with real persons in movies is not a problem in itself, it becomes possible to mislead audiences about serious matters using these special-effects techniques.

The challenge of working in special effects is primarily one of doing what is seemingly impossible to stimulate audience excitement and generate box-office receipts. And the craft grows ever more sophisticated. While the lifelike dinosaurs of Steven Spielberg's *Jurassic Park* (1993) were a striking feat of technology, by the time the sequel—*The Lost World: Jurassic Park*—was released in 1997, the ability to mix robotics and the computer-generated effects by Industrial Light & Magic was even more impressive. The mix created scenes that added spice to the rather simple story.

Robert Zemeckis' *Contact* (1997) posed challenging requirements for its fanciful story involving communication from life in space and philosophical questions about science versus religion. Sony Pictures Imageworks used some 350 visual-effect shots to blend with live-action photography. Ken Ralston, who previously was with Industrial Light & Magic and now heads Imageworks, was in charge of the sleight of hand, which used digital computer techniques as well as models and miniatures.

Today and the Future. *Mimic*, another 1997 release steeped in special effects, had giant mutated insects roaming through Manhattan's subway tunnels and other underground passages. The producers called upon Rick Lazzarini and his team of technicians to use puppetry, animatronics, and prosthetics to develop the creatures. Digital effects were provided by Hybrid Technologies and C.O.R.E. Digital Pictures, as well as by other expert individuals and companies. "Fundamentally we used the same techniques that were used on *Jurassic Park*, combining puppets, miniatures, and wholly computer-generated creatures," explained Brian Jennings, the film's visual-effects supervisor.

Much of the credit for what can be done today is traced to the pioneering work of Lucas but, inevitably, his success has spawned competition. There now are about a dozen others tapping into special effects based on new technology. One such company, Pixar, achieved recognition for the 1995 movie *Toy Story*. DreamWorks SKG, which Spielberg formed with Jeff Katzenberg and David Geffen, is an example of a company that prefers to develop its own special effects. Other companies also see potential in developing their own know-how and facilities.

This reliance on advanced technology puts special demands on actors, who must work out their movements in relation to nonexistent characters or scenery, and cannot realize fully the impact of their work until they see it on the screen.

Some audience members already are complaining that movies have become oversaturated with effects at the expense of good stories with substantial characters. Also, big-budget failures give producers second thoughts, while the high costs incurred by the effects companies has led to cutbacks, layoffs, and closures. For example, Warner Digital Studios closed and Boss Film Studios, which worked on *Air Force One*, shut down after 14 years in business. But with each new technological possibility comes the temptation to experiment further. Apparently we have not seen the last of *Star Wars*. George Lucas has promised three more related epics, concerning the 40 years before the original *Star Wars* setting. He plans to start the first in 1999, and told *Newsweek* that the new films will be more tragic and darker than the previous *Star Wars* films. You can bet that the special-effects techniques will be up to the minute.

WILLIAM WOLF

Music

Overview

In 1997 everyone in the music business was reading *Who Killed Classical Music? Maestros, Managers, and Corporate Politics* by Norman Lebrecht, a British critic and journalist. Lebrecht writes in a rollicking and gossipy manner, and he is not meticulous about fact-checking. Nevertheless, he hits his target—commerce, the friend and enemy of art. Concert audiences are graying and dwindling; record companies are retrenching; performers, presenters, and ensembles struggle to survive in a hostile financial and political environment. Meanwhile freak phenomena like performances by the Three Tenors are taking millions of dollars out of the cultural economy without putting very much back.

The Pulitzer Prize for music went to Wynton Marsalis for his jazz oratorio *Blood on the Fields*. Elton John's "Candle in the Wind" made pop-music history.

Classical

Certainly 1997 provided many additional examples proving critic Lebrecht's point. Major media attention of a kind rarely generated by concert music went to the world tour of the Australian pianist David Helfgott, whose inspiring battle against mental illness was the subject of the popular film *Shine*. Live, on the concert stage, Helfgott proved unable to play with technical consistency or musical coherence, but audiences loved him anyway. Critics and music lovers gnashed their teeth, admiring the man but not the musician and certainly not the market forces that cashed in on Helfgott as a freak attraction.

The Helfgott controversy played out in the television news and magazine shows in a way that the stories of Leif Ove Andsnes, who won the Gilmore Award; Jon Nakamatsu, who won the Cliburn Competition; or Max Levinson, who won the Dublin Competition, never could hope to. The young Helfgott had wanted to become a great musician. Instead he became a great celebrity, which is something different.

If Evgeny Kissin could become a best-selling superstar for one major company, it was incumbent upon others to find brilliant young Russian pianists. The year 1997 brought the arrival of Arcadi Volodos, thanks to Sony Classical. An even more striking instance of lemming thinking was the response to the continuing phenomenon of mezzo-soprano Cecilia Bartoli, whose major career was built

San Francisco's War Memorial Opera House, a 1932 Beaux Arts landmark in the Civic Center, was rededicated on Sept. 5, 1997, following a two-year $88.5 million renovation. The gala concert also marked the 75th anniversary of the San Francisco Opera.

not just by her own beauty of voice and charm of person—in 1997 she sang in the Metropolitan Opera's first production of Rossini's *La Cenerentola*—but also by her record company in collaboration with the bewitched media. Bartoli has become the most popular singer of her generation, and a big moneymaker. In 1997 managements and record companies, hoping to duplicate Bartoli's success, introduced prominent appearances and recordings by Olga Borodina, Sonia Ganassi, Susan Graham, Lorraine Hunt, Vesselina Kasarova, Angelika Kirchschlager, Jennifer Larmore, and Eva Podles. Bartoli's success also led to a renewed triumph for such established mezzos as Anne Sophie von Otter.

On the other hand, the Helfgott controversy made it clear that music still matters to many people, and it brought Rachmaninoff's "Third Piano Concerto" to people who, otherwise, never would have heard it. The florescence of mezzos provided another indication that lack of new talent never will be a problem.

It also is a mistake to identify New York's Lincoln Center, Washington's Kennedy Center, and other prestigious venues with the musical world. The YMHA in New York may have had to abandon its plan to present the complete works of Schubert in a cycle stretching over several years, culminating in the 1997 bicentennial of the composer's birth, but outside the limelight of the U.S. musical capital, the collaborative pianist John Wustman quietly and successfully completed the presentation of Schubert's 634 songs to audiences in a university town in Illinois—a feat unduplicated in any musical capital. Meanwhile, Boston's Emmanuel Music confidently embarked on the second year of a seven-year, 51-concert Schubert survey.

New Works. The Grawemeyer Award went to British composer Simon Bainbridge's *Ad Ora Incerta*, which was premiered by the BBC Symphony in 1995.

New works of quality included Bernard Rands' *Cello Concerto* and Augusta Read Thomas' *Chanson*—both written in commemoration of the 70th birthday of Mstislav Rostropovich, which was celebrated with hosannas around the world; Leon Kirchner's oratorio *Of things exactly as they are* and Henri Dutilleux' *The Shadows of Time*—in part inspired by and dedicated to the memory of Anne Frank, and performed by the Boston Symphony; Sofia Gubaidulina's *Viola Concerto*; Lawrence Rapchak's *Scetas*; Aribert Reimann's *Violin Concerto*; Leif Segerstam's *February*; Jay Alan Yim's *Rough Magic* for

the Chicago Symphony; Elliott Carter's *Allegro scorrevole*; John Adams' *Century Rolls*—a concerto for piano and orchestra for the Cleveland Orchestra; Esa-Pekka Salonen's *LA Variations*; Chen Yi's *Qi*; Larry Lipkis' *Harlequin* and Anders Hillborg's *Meltdown Variations* for the Los Angeles Philharmonic and its New Music Group; Olly Wilson's *Shango Memory* and Andre Previn's *The Magic Number* for the New York Philharmonic; Domenick Argento's *Valentino Dances and Reverie (Reflections on a Hymn Tune)*; David Szubay's *Sun Moon Stars Rain*; David Evan Thomas' *Elegy for a Singer* for the Minnesota Orchestra; Aaron Jay Kernis' *Concerto for Violin and Guitar* for the St. Paul Chamber Orchestra; and John Corigliano's *Red Violin Rhapsody* for the San Francisco Symphony.

Ellen Taaffe Zwilich's *Peanuts Gallery*, based on Charles Schulz' comic strip, proved a popular work for children, and the little music-theater pieces Robert Kapilow composed on texts from children's books were among the most widely performed new works in any category. In 1997, James Thurber's *Many Moons* joined its predecessors based on books by Dr. Seuss. Tan Dun's *Symphony 1997*, commemorating the transfer of Hong Kong from British to Chinese sovereignty, reached a worldwide audience on recording and so did Paul McCartney's huge tone-poem *Standing Stone*. Dun's opera *Marco Polo* won admiration at the New York City Opera.

The centennial of U.S. composer Henry Cowell and the 80th birthday of living national treasure Lou Harrison were celebrated widely. London saw the premiere of Leonard Bernstein's *A White House Cantata*, which rescued music from his 1976 flop Broadway collaboration with Alan Jay Lerner, *1600 Pennsylvania Avenue*. The mentioned composers demonstrate how much more open to diversity classical music has become in recent years; the works themselves demonstrate an astonishing and resourceful plurality of styles.

The Operatic World. The new operas of 1997 included Thomas Ades' *Powder Her Face* (performed at Aspen); Peter Lieberson's *Ashoka's Dream* (Santa Fe); *Black Water*—John Duffy's collaboration with novelist Joyce Carol Oates that is based on the 1969 Chappaquiddick drowning incident (American Musical Theater Festival); the modish and heartless *Jackie O* by Michael Daugherty and librettist Wayne Koestenbaum (Houston Opera Studio, and recorded by Argo); and *Amistad* by Anthony Davis, on a libretto by Thulani Davis (Chicago Lyric Opera). Philip Glass' second opera based on the work of

Doris Lessing, *The Marriages Between Zones Three, Four and Five*, had its premiere in Europe.

There were several prominent American premieres and revivals as well. Britain's Royal Opera brought Hans Pfitzner's *Palestrina* to the Lincoln Center Festival. Les Arts Florissants under the direction of William Christie brought a spectacular production of Rameau's *Hippolyte et Aricie* to the Brooklyn Academy of Music, and the Boston Early Music Festival attracted attention with a staging of Luigi Rossi's *L'Orfeo*, created in collaboration with Sweden's Drottningholm Court Theater. The early-music revival found another form of confirmation when the dazzling countertenor David Daniels became the first singer in this category to win the Richard Tucker Award. Mirella Freni, 62, brought old-time diva grandeur to the New York Metropolitan Opera in Giordano's melodrama *Fedora*.

Deborah Voigt made headlines, not just for some splendid dramatic soprano singing but for losing 80 lbs (36 kg). The year saw the American premieres of Schubert's *Fierrebras* (by the Collegiate Chorale and the Orchestra of St. Luke's), von Einem's *The Visit of the Old Lady* (New York City Opera), and the original version of Cherubini's *Medee*, as well as the first revival in decades of *Koenigskinder*—another fairy-tale opera by Engelbert Humperdinck, the composer of *Hansel and Gretel*—(Sarasota Opera). The New England Conservatory gave the stage premiere of *The Padrone*, an opera in verismo style written in 1912 by George Whitefield Chadwick and submitted without success to the Metropolitan Opera, which, more than 80 years later, requested a copy of the score.

Milestones and Real Estate. The Vienna Philharmonic, after 155 years, admitted its first full-time woman player to membership. Valery Gergiev's appointment as principal guest conductor of the Metropolitan Opera was the biggest surprise of the year and brought speculation about how much longer James Levine would continue as artistic director of the company. Andrew Davis was named music director of Chicago's Lyric Opera. Peter Oundjian, longtime first violinist of the Tokyo Quartet, began a new career as a conductor and director of the Caramoor Festival in Katonah, NY. Pianist Leon Fleisher made headlines by leaving his post as artistic director of the Tanglewood Music Center, the prestigious summer institute for advanced musical training sponsored by the Boston Symphony. Fleisher left angrily protesting Boston Symphony music director Seiji Ozawa's attempt to

© Jack Vartoogian

In 1997, Deborah Voigt, a soprano star, sang the role of Sieglinde in "Die Walkure" at the New York Metropolitan Opera.

overhaul and revitalize the school. At an emotional concert at Tanglewood, Robert Mann, a founding member of the Juilliard Quartet, retired after 49 years as first violin; he was succeeded by Joel Smirnoff.

San Francisco's War Memorial Opera House reopened after an $88.5 million renovation. Chicago completed a $110 million renovation of its Orchestra Hall, which now is part of Symphony Center. The Santa Fe Opera played its final season in its celebrated indoor-outdoor theater. It would be replaced by an all-indoor facility.

The year also saw important new biographies of composers Johannes Brahms by Jan Swafford, Virgil Thomson by Anthony Tommasini, and Ruth Crawford Seeger by Judith Tick. The latter is of particular significance because it focuses attention on the life of a neglected modernist composer and a pioneer in the folk-music revival. It also considers how she reconciled these complementary activities with her responsibilities as wife and mother. Gunther Schuller's *The Compleat Conductor* read the riot act to careless musicians, naming names and citing the recorded evidence. A musicologist from the University of Northern Iowa, David J. Buch, created a stir by arguing that parts of two little-known Viennese fairy-tale operas, *The Philosopher's Stone* and *The Beneficent Dervish*, were written by Mozart in his desperate final years.

RICHARD DYER, *"The Boston Globe"*

Popular and Jazz

The $12 billion popular-music business weathered a rocky 1997 characterized by relatively flat sales. To a certain extent, the year was a sobering aftermath to the industry's dramatic growth during the 1980s and early 1990s—an expansion spurred on by the introduction of the CD, plus the growth in popularity of country and rap music. The industry now looked to superstars like U2 and Mariah Carey to revive sluggish sales and hoped that electronic dance music would fill the void left by the decline in popularity of "grunge rock." This did not happen; instead, the success of No Doubt made ska, the rhythmic style that preceded Jamaican reggae, the pop-dance beat of the year.

The lackluster sales environment left record chains suffering from the effects of overexpansion. Strawberries, a 133-unit chain, filed for bankruptcy in 1997, while the largest chain, Musicland, navigated choppy financial waters. Retailers complained about electronic merchandisers selling superstar releases at bargain prices and were increasingly wary that the Internet might be used by major labels as

Elton John, who rewrote his hit "Candle in the Wind" as a tribute to Princess Diana, gave the only live performance of the new song at Diana's funeral, below.

© Pool/FSP/Gamma-Liaison

well as artists to sell music directly to consumers. The sales picture also prompted job cuts at most major record labels, including 550 positions at Polygram. Britain-based EMI shuttered its U.S. namesake, shifting some of the acts to its Capitol label.

Best-sellers. The biggest single of the year was Elton John's "Candle in the Wind 1997," which he sang at the funeral of Diana, princess of Wales. The tune was a rewrite of an earlier Elton John–Bernie Taupin song about Marilyn Monroe. Recorded shortly after Princess Diana's funeral and produced by George Martin of Beatles fame, "Candle in the Wind 1997" debuted at the top of the U.S. singles chart. In mid-October the song became the biggest-selling single in recording history, with some 31.8 million copies distributed worldwide. Profits were earmarked for charities favored by the late princess.

The year's other top single, "I'll Be Missing You"—by Puff Daddy and the Family and based on the Police hit "Every Breath You Take"—was also a memorial, this one for the rapper Notorious B.I.G. (Christopher Wallace), who was shot dead in Los Angeles in March. The murder, like the 1996 shooting of Tupac Shakur, remained unsolved late in 1997. The two rappers had been point men in a public feud between their respective record labels—Sean "Puff Daddy" Combs' Bad Boy Entertainment and Shakur's Death Row Records. Authorities suspected street-gang involvement in both shootings.

A few months after Notorious B.I.G.'s funeral, his chillingly titled *Life after Death...'Til Death Do Us Part* debuted at the top of the charts. The future of the controversial "gangsta" style of rap remained unclear, but with its two biggest stars both gunned down in the streets, fans could not help but notice that both were killed by the lifestyles that their music celebrated.

Other hits were bigger surprises. Some industry observers lately had complained that few records appealed to young teens. The year saw two acts, however, that did draw widespread interest from the teenage market: the Spice Girls and Hanson. The Spice Girls, a female quintet from Britain, had an international hit with "Wannabe," a perky single that promoted what the group called "girl power." Hanson consists of a trio of brothers ranging in age from 13 to 16. With help from proven songwriters and trendy producers, the trio recorded a slick album that exploded on the strength of the hit single "MMMBop."

There were more predictable hits in 1997 as well. Celine Dion won the pop-album

Grammy for *Falling Into You,* which sold more than 8 million copies. Fleetwood Mac reunited to celebrate the 20th anniversary of one of the biggest-selling albums of all time, *Rumours,* and scored another hit with a live album consisting of earlier hits, drawn from an MTV special. The band then played a successful concert tour. Arguably the hippest pop star of the year was Beck, whose folk-rock-tinged hip-hop album *Odelay* won the Grammy for best alternative performance.

Tours. Concert tours in 1997 met with mixed success. U2's *PopMart* stadium tour was less than a sellout, while the Rolling Stones filled many of the same venues on their third concert tour in a decade. Established summer package tours like Lollapalooza and the H.O.R.D.E. Festival faced stiff competition from other warm-weather tours. The most successful event of the summer turned out to be the Lilith Fair tour; organized by Canadian singer-songwriter Sarah McLachlan, it featured an all-female program highlighting such performers as Jewel, Sheryl Crow, Fiona Apple, Paula Cole, Tracy Chapman, Joan Osborne, and Shawn Colvin (*see* CANADA—*The Arts.*)

Conspicuous in her absence from Lilith Fair was the most independent female in popular music, Ani DiFranco, a singer-songwriter whose music is a canny mix of folk and new-wave influences. DiFranco has released nine solo albums on her own label, with each album selling more than the previous one—a track record that has attracted lucrative offers from virtually every major label. She has declined, fearful of losing her artistic independence. In lieu of Lilith Fair, DiFranco spent much of the summer touring with Bob Dylan, who won critical kudos for his first new music of the 1990s, *Time Out of Mind.* Meanwhile, Dylan's son Jakob became a rock star when his band, the Wallflowers, scored a major hit with its second album, *Bringing Down the Horse.*

Country. Country music, a genre whose audience is thought to have peaked following its recent rise in popularity, had its own youth movement in LeAnn Rimes, whose album *Blue* was at the top of the country charts for much of 1997. The 15-year-old Rimes also hit Number 1 with an album recorded before *Blue* and entitled *Unchained Melody/The Early Years.* Rimes' popularity is largely due to the fact that her voice recalls that of the late country legend Patsy Cline.

Some in Nashville's country community grumbled when Lyle Lovett—scarcely a presence on country radio—won the Grammy for best country album for his *The Road to Ense-*

© Christopher Berkey/AP/Wide World Photos

Young country sensation LeAnn Rimes, 15, was named Female Star of Tomorrow at the 1997 TNN–Music City News Country Awards show, where she also performed, above.

nada. Still, his victory reflected the fact that, to the pop-oriented audience, country music is not necessarily what comes from Nashville. Indeed, pop critics praised a number of rock acts with country leanings, including Son Volt, Wilco, BR5-49, and the Bottle Rockets.

Jazz. *Blood on the Fields,* a long-form musical piece by trumpeter Wynton Marsalis that explores the issue of slavery, was the first jazz work to win the Pulitzer Prize in music. The piece, which also was performed live at New York's Lincoln Center, drew mixed reviews from jazz critics, some of whom questioned the judgment of the Pulitzer judges. Marsalis himself would agree that jazz legends such as Duke Ellington should have been awarded a similar honor.

Singer Cassandra Wilson, who performed in *Blood on the Fields,* consolidated her position as the day's leading female jazz singer with the Grammy-winning *New Moon Daughter.* While Wilson had expanded her audience by adding pop-oriented tunes to her repertoire—even performing at Lilith Fair—she also did a series of Lincoln Center concerts focusing on the music of Miles Davis. Other high-profile jazz events of 1997 included a duet recording pairing bassist Charlie Haden and Pat Metheny, and one that paired keyboardist Herbie Hancock and saxophonist Wayne Shorter.

Sound Tracks. The music industry continued to look to movie sound tracks as a way to ride the coattails of highly promoted films that might become lucrative hits. Conversely,

John Denver

Singer-songwriter John Denver, whose folk-pop songs celebrated romantic sentiments and the pleasures of nature, died Oct. 12, 1997, when the plane he was piloting plunged into California's Monterey Bay. Denver, a longtime pilot, was alone in his Long EZ plane. The ultralight fiberglass two-seater is classified as an experimental craft, although it has an excellent safety record. Denver was 53 years old.

Born Henry John Deutschendorf, Jr., in 1943 in Roswell, NM, Denver started playing folk songs after his grandmother gave him a 1910 Gibson guitar. He dropped out of Texas Tech to pursue a music career in Los Angeles. There he took his stage name and, in 1965, replaced Chad Mitchell in the Chad Mitchell Trio. Denver's first mainstream success came four years later when Peter, Paul & Mary had a Number 1 hit with one of the songs he wrote, "Leaving on a Jet Plane."

© Deborah Feingold/Archive Photos

Denver hit the pop charts himself with 1971's million-selling "Take Me Home, Country Roads" and soon moved to Aspen, CO. Songs like "Rocky Mountain High" and "Sunshine on My Shoulders" made him hugely successful during the 1970s and even prompted Colorado's governor to name him the state's poet laureate in 1977. Denver's popularity was impervious to criticism characterizing his songs as simplistic and saccharine. His 1973 *Greatest Hits* album had sold more than 10 million copies by 1997.

During the mid-1970s, Denver was a ubiquitous presence not only on the pop charts, but on television; in addition to his frequent specials, Denver hosted several Grammy presentations. He also costarred with George Burns in the 1977 film *Oh God!* By the end of the 1970s, ten of his albums each had sold more than 1 million copies worldwide.

Denver's popularity waned in the 1980s; his last major hit was 1981's "Perhaps Love," a duet with Plácido Domingo. However, he remained active in humanitarian and environmental activities. He cofounded the Hunger Project, was active in UNICEF, and established an environmental-research foundation, Windstar. In 1993 he was presented with the Albert Schweitzer Music Award for humanitarian work.

Two arrests for drunken driving—in 1993 and 1994—tarnished Denver's reputation. It was revealed after his death that Denver had been flying without the required medical certificate, which was suspended as a result of the arrests. The father of three also had gone through two bitter divorces. But when Denver's plane went down in Monterey Bay, his fans remembered only the smiling troubadour who sang of clear blue water and sunny skies.

JOHN MILWARD

---

movie producers looked to sound tracks as a way to promote their films through videos produced for MTV and other outlets. The extent to which sound tracks had been embraced by the business was evident on the Billboard chart of April 12, 1997, when 27 sound tracks were listed among the Top 200 albums.

Whereas sound tracks of an earlier era consisted of the instrumental music used in a film, they are now more often a seemingly random compilation of pop tunes. (The instrumental score is released separately, if at all.) Such a format often is seen as a good one in which to launch the career of a new artist. Toni Braxton, for example, became known through the hit soundtrack to *Boomerang* before her debut album went on to sell more than 8 million copies. Braxton's second album, *Secrets*, was released in 1997. The Cardigans' debut album, *Lovefool*, was helped similarly by the group's appearance on the hit sound track to the film *Romeo + Juliet*.

DVD. In 1997 the recording business started touting what was said to be the audio format of the future: digital versatile disc, or DVD. Expected to reach the market in about two years, DVD would replace the two-speaker stereo recording—the standard format for the past 35 years—with a multichannel format employing six speakers. While electronics manufacturers and record labels have a vested interest in pushing DVD, that hardly guarantees a successful launch. In the 1970s, consumers rejected four-channel quadraphonic systems that aimed for a similar "surround sound" effect; more recently, digital audiotape (DAT) never gained acceptance. The industry contended, however, that DVD would stand a better chance because DVD machines would be able to play existing CDs.

JOHN MILWARD, *Freelance Writer and Critic*

MYANMAR

The State Law and Restoration Committee (SLORC)—the junta that had ruled Myanmar since 1988—was replaced in November 1997 by the State Peace and Development Council (SPDC). Comprised of the four top generals and 15 commanders of the country's various military regions, the SPDC gave no indication that the military was ready to relinquish the absolute authority with which it had ruled.

In early 1997 the government cracked down on the largest, best-organized student protests since 1988 by closing major universities for most of the year. The Internet became a potent weapon for regime opponents in the United States, forcing Myanmar's government to respond to FreeBurma.org with its own Web site.

A March anti-Muslim rampage by Buddhist monks in Mandalay quickly spread to other cities, but not all believed the riots were caused by Buddhist rage at the 4% Muslim population. Some speculated the monks were really disguised soldiers, loyal to junta factions eager to scuttle Myanmar's entry into the Association of Southeast Asian Nations (ASEAN). Ostensibly, they were concerned that ASEAN might have unwanted influence in internal policies. The riots, however, did not derail admission into ASEAN in July, although anticipated perks of membership—aid and investment—did not increase substantially.

Terrorist bombs continued to threaten junta member Army Chief of Staff Lt. Gen. Tin Oo. On April 6 his adult daughter was killed by a package bomb presumed to be for him. Oo also survived a Dec. 24, 1996, assassination attempt that left five dead and 17 wounded.

Ethnic Relations. The government blamed the Karen National Union, an antigovernment ethnic group, for the December 1996 bombing. There were signs that cease-fires with other ethnic insurgents might be fraying as well. In February the military began an offensive against the Karen driving nearly 15,000 refugees into Thailand. Thailand, which has been an unenthusiastic sanctuary for opponents of the SLORC regime over the years of its rule, sent back thousands of male refugees in 1997 as it sought to improve economic relations with the junta.

Economy. In January, Myanmar had only three weeks' worth of hard-currency reserves. The nation retained its notorious distinction as the world's largest exporter of heroin. There also were troubling signs that drug

---

MYANMAR • Information Highlights

Official Name: Union of Myanmar.
Location: Southeast Asia.
Area: 261,969 sq mi (678 500 km²).
Population (mid-1997 est.): 46,800,000.
Chief Cities (1983 census): Yangon (Rangoon), the capital, 2,513,023; Mandalay, 532,949.
Government: *Head of state and government,* Gen. Than Shwe (took power April 23, 1992). *Legislature* (unicameral)—People's Assembly.
Monetary Unit: Kyat (6.174 kyats equal U.S.$1, June 1997).
Gross Domestic Product (1995 est. U.S.$): $47,000,-000,000 (purchasing power parity).
Economic Index (1996, 1990 = 100): *Consumer Prices,* all items, 384.1; food, 420.7.
Foreign Trade (1996 U.S.$): *Imports,* $1,361,000,000; *exports,* $691,000,000.

---

addiction and the number of AIDS cases were soaring.

In April, U.S. President Bill Clinton implemented a 1996 law that tied new contracts to improved human rights. Many U.S. companies had pulled out already, but Unocal—the single largest U.S. investor, with 28% of a joint French-Myanmar pipeline—resisted, and also pumped millions of dollars in additional loans to the discredited regime. Exiled Burmese critics sued Unocal for benefiting indirectly from forced labor used to build the pipeline infrastructure.

Canadian and U.S. economic sanctions against Myanmar—where both countries had modest investments—raised controversy over continued ties to China, which had similar human-rights violations. The European Union (EU) had been among the first to use sanctions, but ASEAN nations, sensing "fire-sale" opportunities, muted criticism. The regime declared the sanctions were having no negative impact. One possible sign the sanctions might be working, however, was the mixed responses the SLORC made to its chief opposition, the National League for Democracy (NLD).

Although NLD members continued to be harassed and jailed, in September the SLORC offered to hold talks with NLD member Aung Shwe. The NLD refused unless talks were held with NLD leader and Nobel Peace Prize winner Aung San Suu Kyi. The SLORC then accused the NLD of being held hostage to the "whims of one person." The SLORC, however, did allow the NLD to hold its Ninth Party Congress in its leader's home. More than 800 assembled from September 27–29 without junta interference, but they could do little, since the junta never had permitted the NLD's 1990 election victory to be implemented. Still, Aung San Suu Kyi praised the junta for allowing the congress and held out hope for future dialogues.

LINDA K. RICHTER, *Kansas State University*

NETHERLANDS

The year 1997 was a quiet one for the Netherlands, as the Dutch reaped the rewards of austerity programs that brought their budget within the parameters established for joining the projected European economic and monetary union (EMU).

The Economy. The Dutch economy was growing faster than those of France, Britain, and Germany, with a midyear unemployment rate of 6.5%. Foreign companies were increasing their office space in the industrial/shipping complexes of Rotterdam and Amsterdam. Consumer spending was mounting as shoppers took advantage of newly extended store hours, the result of legislation passed in 1996 permitting many stores to be open after 6 P.M. and on Sundays. Critics noted that 37% of Dutch workers were earning only part-time wages. Although new jobs were appearing at a rate of 100,000 per year, most were of a part-time or temporary nature. Since many families included two part-time workers and temporary jobs now could last longer than six months, complaints were not high. In part, this was because, by law, such jobs included health and vacation benefits and, after six months, pension contributions.

To attract women into the job market, the government had deregulated work hours, permitting part-time and temporary contracts that in previous years were banned to maximize full-wage positions. Many people also had been forced back to work by cuts in unemployment benefits. New laws shifted the burden of handling sick pay from the government to employers, and the latter monitored such cases more closely than in the past. The Dutch attributed their success to a workable mixture of a vigorous free market with humane and reasonable social benefits.

In May the Organization for Economic Cooperation and Development praised the manner in which the Dutch had reached their compromise through a "consensual process" involving all partners in the society and avoiding threats to social cohesion. Essentially the formula skirted ideological confrontation by focusing on practical programs. A chief architect of the consensus was Prime Minister Willem Kok. As a labor leader in the early 1980s, he persuaded unions to accept only limited annual wage increases (about 2%) in return for more jobs and shorter workweeks. As a result, domestic and foreign firms have been willing to invest in the Netherlands. Negotiations over reduction of fringe benefits, nevertheless, were bitter at times.

Observers questioned whether the current harmony could last as the population of the aged expanded in comparison to the number of active workers supporting its social benefits. Moreover, though the number of workers receiving disability pay declined by more than 100,000 in three years, some 735,000 workers still were drawing such pay. Welfare dependency by single parents, however, had fallen to less than 30%.

Other News. U.S. President Bill Clinton was in Rotterdam in May to mark the 50th anniversary of the Marshall Plan. The Dutch used the occasion as an opportunity to thank the United States for the plan (*see* SIDEBAR, page 237)....In February the government launched an inquiry regarding missing gold, taken by German National Socialists during World War II. According to Dutch figures, 145.6 metric tons were looted from the Dutch treasury. Slightly less than half that amount was recovered after the war.

A new study of physician-assisted suicides in the Netherlands asserted that caregivers were moving to end patients' lives without their permission. That conclusion was challenged promptly by other authorities....In August, Shell Netherlands closed part of the Pernis oil refinery near Rotterdam, Europe's second-largest refinery. This unexpected closing quickly forced gasoline prices up by 20%.

JONATHAN E. HELMREICH, *Allegheny College*

NETHERLANDS • Information Highlights

Official Name: Kingdom of the Netherlands.
Location: Northwestern Europe.
Area: 14,413 sq mi (37 330 km²).
Population (mid-1997 est.): 15,600,000.
Chief Cities (Jan. 1, 1994): Amsterdam, the capital, 724,096; Rotterdam, 598,521; The Hague, the seat of government, 445,279.
Government: *Head of state,* Beatrix, queen (acceded April 30, 1980). *Head of government,* Willem Kok, prime minister (took office Aug. 22, 1994). *Legislature*—States General: First Chamber and Second Chamber.
Monetary Unit: Guilder (2.0100 guilders equal U.S.$1, Dec. 10, 1997).
Gross Domestic Product (1995 est. U.S.$): $301,900,000,-000 (purchasing power parity).
Economic Indexes (1996, 1990 = 100): *Consumer Prices,* all items, 116.8; food, 109.4. *Industrial Production,* 110.
Foreign Trade (1996 U.S.$): *Imports,* $180,642,000,000; *exports,* $197,245,000,000.

NEW YORK CITY

With the results of the November 1997 mayoral race never really in doubt, New York City Rudolph W. Giuliani was reelected in a landslide to a second four-year term.

The Election and Rent Control. Running as the nominee of the Republican and Liberal parties, Giuliani defeated Ruth W. Messinger, a Democrat and the borough president of Manhattan, to become the first Republican since Mayor Fiorello H. LaGuardia in the 1930s to get a majority of the votes. Newly effective term limits also meant he would be the city's first official lame-duck mayor.

Enrolled Democrats outnumber Republicans in the city by a margin of five to one, but the election was largely nonideological. During his first term, Giuliani reaped the benefits of a boom on Wall Street and double-digit declines in reported crime. He presided over a revivified city—in which once-tawdry Times Square was being transformed into a mecca for family entertainment—but one still bedeviled by overcrowded and underachieving schools and by high unemployment rates.

If the mayoral election seemed foreordained, the fate of the city's legacy of rent regulation was not. Only after fierce debate in the state capital did state Republicans abandon their goal of phasing out controls entirely. The legislature lifted some rent ceilings for the most expensive apartments and for the wealthiest tenants and limited succession rights to an apartment when the tenant dies.

Crime. Crime declined but did not disappear. A former student was accused of torturing a Bronx public-school teacher, Jonathan Levin, for his bank-card access code, then murdering him; the crime was magnified because the teacher was the son of the chairman of Time-Warner. Betty Shabazz, the widow of Malcolm X and a civil-rights leader in her own right, died from injuries suffered in a fire set by her 12-year-old grandson in her home in nearby Yonkers. New York icons figured in two other cases. A 69-year-old teacher from Gaza, protesting the plight of Palestinians, shot seven persons—killing one—before killing himself on the observation deck of the Empire State Building. A federal jury, concluding what was probably the last major trial stemming from the 1993 bombing of the World Trade Center, convicted Ramzi Ahmed Yousef, the accused mastermind of the plot to punish the United States for its support of Israel. The jury also convicted a second man, Eyad Ismoil, who was accused of driving the van that carried the bomb. Six people were killed in the terrorist attack.

Federal prosecutors closed another case: A man who had been acquitted of state charges was convicted in federal court along with another defendant on charges stemming from the murder of a Hasidic Jew during the Crown Heights racial rioting in 1991. Still, one mystery was unresolved: The Federal Bureau of

© Lawrence Schwartzwald/Gamma-Liaison

The political future of Rudolph Giuliani, above, became a topic of speculation by commentators and the public after New York City's Republican mayor easily won a second term in 1997.

Investigation (FBI) said it had suspended its investigation after finding no evidence of sabotage in the explosion of TWA Flight 800 over Long Island, which killed 230 people in 1996. Safety investigators still were seeking a mechanical cause for the crash.

Among the most spectacular crimes was one in which police officers themselves were accused: the torture of a Haitian immigrant, Abner Louima, in a Brooklyn station house. The Louima case renewed a debate over whether more-aggressive policing was responsible not only for the decline in reported crime but for complaints of police brutality and abuse. The case also was a reminder of the vulnerability of immigrants in a city where their numbers continued to increase. Just a month earlier, the police announced arrests related to what was described as a ring of illegal immigrants who smuggled deaf Mexicans into the city and then forced them into what amounted to indentured servitude.

Other News. New York dedicated a new Museum of Jewish Heritage at Battery Park in lower Manhattan and celebrated the 50th anniversary of the integration of modern Major League Baseball. Country-music superstar Garth Brooks performed in Central Park in August.

SAM ROBERTS, *"The New York Times"*

NEW ZEALAND

The first year of modern peacetime coalition government, 1997 was marred increasingly by friction between the two partners—National and New Zealand First. Dissatisfaction with their performance soared to 90% in October. In November, Prime Minister Jim Bolger was ousted in favor of Jenny Shipley, 45, a former teacher and cabinet minister. She thus became New Zealand's first woman prime minister. The economy tended downward, and there was widespread unrest over cuts to the public hospital system.

Politics and Domestic Issues. While National support slipped from 39% to 30%, that for New Zealand First plummeted to 1%, whereas the opposition Labour Party's polls rating peaked at 52%. This, combined with Bolger's lack of perceived firm leadership, led to his downfall and that of his deputy, Don McKinnon, in a well-executed internal coup. However, Shipley left the composition of the cabinet virtually intact, although Bolger was excluded. McKinnon remained foreign minister. Indications were that major policy initiatives in health, welfare, education, transport, and privatization would be unveiled early in 1998.

In July the first national referendum conducted by mail was held on a compulsory-retirement-funding scheme. The 74% that turned out rejected the plan 92% to 8%. Public health was a primary concern; some 80% believed that health care was underfunded. A lengthy commission of inquiry—known as the Winebox—into corporate fraud and tax avoidance found no evidence of business conspiracy or corruption among the government agencies involved. An Organization for Economic Cooperation and Development (OECD) study revealed a variety of shortcomings in higher education, with only 45% of secondary-school graduates going on to universities or institutes of technology.

Economic Affairs. Early in 1997, New Zealand's currency was at the highest level it had reached in eight years—with NZ$1.00 equaling U.S.$0.70.9. Consumer and business confidence steadily evaporated, however, in the face of adverse indicators. The external deficit jumped to NZ$6 billion by June 30—6.4% of gross domestic product (GDP)—the highest since 1986. Later the dollar dropped to a two-year low. It stood at U.S.$0.582 as the year ended.

The first budget of Deputy Prime Minister and Treasurer Winston Peters promised abolition of the retirement surcharge, as well as of income and asset testing for long-stay hospital care, if an economic-growth rate of 4.2% was attained. Accelerated tariff reductions and modest privatization of state enterprises were matched by sizable supplements to education and health, which consumed 55% of the NZ$34 billion expenditure. However, the forecasted budget surplus slipped to NZ$1.5 billion, bringing into question any future radical tax cuts.

Foreign Policy and Other Matters. Prime Minister Bolger attended the South Pacific Forum meeting and the Commonwealth Heads of Government conference. New Zealand also hosted successful peace talks between the Papua New Guinea government and secessionists from the island of Bougainville. Foreign Minister McKinnon presided over the signing of an immediate truce.

In September the government bowed to pressure from farmers and lifted its ban on rabbit calcivirus disease (RCD). The disease—developed and used widely in Australia to eradicate the rabbit pest problem—had been smuggled into New Zealand by farmers, who had been using it illegally for several weeks. In July university and agricultural research scientists identified STAT5b, a key gene in stimulating growth in human males.

GRAHAM BUSH, *University of Auckland*

NEW ZEALAND • Information Highlights

Official Name: New Zealand.
Location: Southwest Pacific Ocean.
Area: 103,737 sq mi (268 680 km²).
Population (mid-1997 est.): 3,600,000.
Chief Cities (March 1994 est.): Wellington, the capital, 326,900; Auckland, 1,002,000; Christchurch, 312,600; Hamilton, 151,800.
Government: *Head of state,* Elizabeth II, queen, represented by Sir Michael Hardie-Boys, governor-general (sworn in March 21, 1996). *Head of government,* Jenny Shipley, prime minister (took office Dec. 8, 1997). *Legislature* (unicameral)—House of Representatives.
Monetary Unit: New Zealand dollar (1.7182 N.Z. dollars equal U.S.$1, Dec. 31, 1997).
Gross Domestic Product (1995 est. U.S.$): $62,300,-000,000 (purchasing power parity).
Economic Indexes (1996, 1990 = 100): *Consumer Prices,* all items, 113.4; food, 104.5. *Industrial Production,* 114.
Foreign Trade (1996 U.S.$): *Imports,* $14,725,000,000; *exports,* $14,442,000,000.

NIGERIA

Despite pressure from the United States and Commonwealth countries, the government of Nigerian strongman Gen. Sani Abacha remained defiant and continued its slow progress toward civilian control in 1997.

Internal Affairs. The Abacha regime continued to suppress political opponents. Some

22,000 prisoners in 148 prisons awaited trial, many for alleged political offenses. Eight distinguished civilians associated with the opposition National Democratic Coalition (NADECO) were arrested in March. Three others living in exile—including the government's most vocal critic, 1986 Nobel Prize winner Wole Soyinka—were to be tried in absentia. Several bombs exploded on military bases between January and April. Old tribal rivalries in eastern Nigeria flared on March 22 when Ijaw tribesmen, protesting the relocation of local-government headquarters, seized 127 Shell Oil employees. The hostages soon were released, but the Shell closure reduced Nigeria's oil production by an estimated 10%. Lagos' main telephone exchange had burned earlier, disrupting an already poor system for seven months; the exchange cost $1 billion to restore.

In keeping with the timetable for a return to civilian control by August 1998, local-government elections were contested in March among the five recognized political parties. Monitors reported little violence and a high turnout. Voter turnout was low, however, as Nigerians chose 1,000 state legislators in December. Later that month, Lt. Gen. Oladipo Diya, deputy head of state, and 11 others were arrested for plotting a coup against Abacha.

Economic Affairs.   A slightly improved economy remained dependent on oil. Food was in short supply and the Farmers Association warned of the continued threat of famine. The Society of Engineers warned of an imminent electrical-supply-system collapse, while the oil-delivery system nearly did collapse at midyear, causing widespread fuel shortages in major cities. The government appropriated $2.4 million in August to upgrade refineries. Inflation stood at 28%, down from 78% in 1996, but unemployment in cities remained very high. The economy's estimated growth was 3.25%, with federal revenue at $4.9 billion, of which $2.9 billion came from petroleum sales. External debt was $28 billion.

The Report on Banking in Africa criticized Nigerian banks for instability, ineptitude, and incompetence. In February the economic situation worsened when the United States decertified Nigeria and promised to oppose loans from international sources because of the nation's poor human-rights record and lack of cooperation in drug enforcement. This cut off military and economic aid.

Foreign Affairs.   Relations with the United States deteriorated after aid was halted; the ill will was underscored in September when

---

NIGERIA • Information Highlights

Official Name: Federal Republic of Nigeria.
Location: West Africa.
Area: 356,668 sq mi (923 770 km²).
Population (mid-1997 est.): 107,100,000.
Chief City (1993 unofficial est.): Abuja, the capital, 250,000.
Government: *Head of state and government,* Gen. Sani Abacha, military leader (took over November 1993). *Legislature* (suspended)—National Assembly: Senate and House of Representatives.
Monetary Unit: Naira (83.2 naira equal U.S.$1, August 1997).
Gross Domestic Product (1995 est. U.S.$): $135,900,-000,000 (purchasing power parity).
Economic Index (1995, 1990 = 100): *Consumer Prices,* all items, 687.9; food, 379.9.
Foreign Trade (1994 U.S.$): *Imports,* $6,517,000,000; *exports,* $9,376,000,000.

---

police invaded a reception for the departing U.S. ambassador. Britain also ceased aid programs and in May refused to allow Nigerian aircraft to land on its soil. The dispute with Cameroon over the Bakassi Peninsula remained unresolved, while border disturbances with Chad continued even after a conference between leaders was held.

Despite its problems, Nigeria remained the dominant power in the Economic Community of West African States (ECOWAS). Abacha presided over its annual meeting in August. Nigeria sent more than 6,000 men to police ECOWAS policy in the Liberian civil war—a major factor in ending that conflict. Abacha visited Liberia for the inauguration of its new president, Charles Taylor, and received him on a state visit to Nigeria in August. Nigeria also sent troops to Sierra Leone to counter a coup that overthrew the elected government. Some troops caught in the factional fighting escaped after Nigerian ships bombarded the coup leaders' headquarters on June 2. The Nigerian garrison was reinforced and remained in Freetown.

HARRY A. GAILEY, *San Jose State University*

NORWAY

A new minority government led by the Christian People's Party took over from the Social Democratic Party in Norway after the September 1997 general election. Major new oil and gas finds were reported.

Politics.   The Labor government of Thorbjoern Jagland resigned in October after his party failed to obtain 36.9% of the vote in the September 13 elections. The Labor Party attracted 35% of the vote, but Jagland had made it a cardinal point that Labor should gain at least what it mustered in the 1993 election if it was to continue in office. The

Kjell Magne Bondevik, parliamentary leader of Norway's Christian People's Party, and party chairperson Valgerd Svarstad Haugland (left) enjoyed a celebratory cake after the party nearly doubled its number of parliamentary seats in September 1997 elections. Bondevik later headed a new coalition government.

© Per Lochen/AP/Wide World Photos

strongest gain in the election was the advance of the right-wing Progressive Party of Carl I. Hagen, which went from ten to 25 seats in the new Storting—Norway's parliament. The Christian People's Party, headed in parliament by the charismatic Kjell Magne Bondevik, 50, almost doubled its number of seats—to 25—and formed a coalition government with the Centre Party and the Liberal Party. The Norwegian Labor Party, however, remained the country's largest political party, and the new government controlled only 42 of the 165 parliament seats.

The key cabinet posts of finance and energy went to Marit Arnstad of the environmentalist Centre Party, which—campaigning on a platform calling for the reduction of oil production by 10%—lost heavily in the election. Norway remained the world's second-largest exporter of crude oil after Saudi Arabia, producing more than 3 million barrels of oil per day. Hilde Frafjord-Johnson of the Christian People's Party became minister for development and human rights.

The new government intended to increase spending on foreign aid by 50%. Norway has been the world's largest per-capita donor nation, spending more than 1% of gross domestic product (GDP) on foreign aid. The new coalition was prepared to spend more oil money and to increase taxes to pay for the foreign aid and for improvements in social-welfare programs.

Economy. Growth in the Norwegian economy slowed from 4.8% in 1996 to 3.8% in 1997 and was expected to slow to 3.4% in 1998. Excluding oil, the underlying growth remained at about 3% and was predicted to be a little lower in 1998. Unemployment was expected to drop to 4.2% in 1998, from 4.5% in 1997. Norway had the lowest unemployment rate among Nordic countries. The official long-term-planning report forecast a stable GDP-growth rate of about 2.7%. The State Petroleum Fund's assets would rise to $57 billion by 2001 and to about $110 billion by 2007. The yield was scheduled to finance the aging Norwegian population, beginning in the middle of the 21st century. About half of the oil assets might be invested in foreign equities, which would make Norway one of the world's largest equity investors.

European Affairs. Norway clashed with the European Union (EU), which wanted a special duty on Norwegian salmon exports to the EU in order to protect Scottish salmon. In 1997, Norway was Europe's largest producer of farmed salmon, accounting for 40% of the total. Scotland was the second-largest producer. In June a compromise, including minimum prices and export ceilings, was negotiated. The billion-dollar salmon industry employed 16,000 Norwegians.

LEIF BECK FALLESEN, *Editor in Chief*
"Boersen," Copenhagen

NORWAY • Information Highlights

Official Name: Kingdom of Norway.
Location: Northern Europe.
Area: 125,182 sq mi (324 220 km²).
Population (mid-1997 est.): 4,400,000.
Chief Cities (Jan. 1, 1995 est.): Oslo, the capital, 483,401; Bergen, 221,717; Trondheim, 142,927; Stavanger, 103,590.
Government: *Head of state,* Harald V, king (acceded January 1991). *Head of government,* Kjell Magne Bondevik, prime minister (took office October 1997). *Legislature—* Storting.
Monetary Unit: Krone (7.3560 kroner equal U.S.$1, Dec. 31, 1997).
Gross Domestic Product (1995 est. U.S.$): $106,200,000,-000 (purchasing power parity).
Economic Indexes (1996, 1990 = 100): *Consumer Prices,* all items, 113.9; food, 106.8. *Industrial Production,* 134.
Foreign Trade (1996 U.S.$): *Imports,* $35,087,000,000; *exports,* $49,331,000,000.

Obituaries

HARRIMAN, Pamela

British-born socialite, U.S. political fund-raiser, and diplomat. b. Farnborough, England, March 20, 1920; d. Paris, France, Feb. 5, 1997.

Pamela Digby Churchill Hayward Harriman—who enjoyed a life of exceptional power, wealth, and social status—died on Feb. 5, 1997, after suffering a cerebral hemorrhage following a swim in the pool of the Ritz Hotel in Paris. Having become a naturalized U.S. citizen in 1971, she was the U.S. ambassador to France at the time of her death. In the 1980s and early 1990s, Harriman had helped revive the Democratic Party, raising millions of dollars for it. She was national cochair of the 1992 Bill Clinton–Al Gore campaign.

Background. Born into British aristocracy and educated privately at the Downham School in Hertfordshire and at the Sorbonne in Paris, Pamela Digby was presented at court in 1938. The following year, at the age of 19, she married Randolph Churchill, who soon was serving in World War II. A son, her only child, was born in 1940 and named Winston, after his grandfather. During the war, she served as a confidante to her father-in-law, the prime minister. Her marriage ended in divorce in 1945.

She then joined the staff of Lord Beaverbrook's *Daily Express and Evening Standard*, reporting on politics, the arts, and the social scene from various international locales. The future ambassador later lived in Paris and was involved romantically with several international figures. In 1960 she married Leland Hayward, the producer of the Broadway hit *South Pacific*. Following Hayward's death in 1971, she married W. Averell Harriman, the former governor of New York and a member of every Democratic administration since Franklin Roosevelt's. They had met during World War II.

The couple became prime fund-raisers for the Democratic Party, especially after Ronald Reagan's and the Republican Party's overwhelming victory in 1980. Following Governor Harriman's death at the age of 94 in 1986, Pamela Harriman remained active in the Democratic Party—both as a fund-raiser and as a member of its national committee (1989–93). Her homes in the Georgetown section of Washington and in suburban Virginia were the scenes of major party gatherings.

Pamela Harriman

© Diana Walker/Gamma–Liaison

When the Democrats regained the White House in 1992, the new president, Bill Clinton, named Harriman ambassador to France. She took up the post in May 1993 and gained respect as a successful diplomat. She spoke French fluently.

JAMES E. CHURCHILL, JR.

DENG Xiaoping

Chinese leader: b. Paifang, Sichuan province, China, Aug. 22, 1904; d. Beijing, Feb. 19, 1997.

Deng Xiaoping led the world's most populous nation through an unprecedented transformation of its economy. In 1978, when he began this formidable task, the Chinese economy was characterized by central planning, state ownership, low productivity, and stagnant growth. Today that economy is perhaps the world's third largest—after that of the United States and Japan—and second largest by some estimates. It is one in which most decisions are driven by market forces, ownership is shared with vigorous and growing private and collective sectors, productivity is increasing, and growth rates are high. Deng began leading this undertaking at the age of 74 and he accomplished it without a grand design.

His career was remarkable for its longevity. He was active in Chinese Communist Party work for more than 70 years, occupying top leadership positions for much of that time. His career also was remarkable for its instability.

Deng Xiaoping

On three occasions he was dismissed from office and publicly vilified, and in each case he rebounded to assume more powerful positions. In his latter years he came to be known as China's "paramount leader."

From the moment he returned to power in 1977, Deng's first priority was to develop China's economy as rapidly as possible in order to improve the standard of living of the Chinese people. He firmly believed that this process could take place successfully only under conditions of political stability. Proceeding from this assumption, his strategy proved to be the reverse of the one followed in the former Soviet Union, where *perestroika* (political restructuring) preceded economic transformation. Deng began with the economy and never quite made it to political reform. Indeed, his reputation at home and abroad as a liberal reformer—always an inaccurate one—was dealt a death blow when, on the night of June 3, 1989, he gave the order that brought troops and tanks into the streets of Beijing to clear them of student demonstrators calling for political change.

Although it was Mao Zedong, not Deng, who was responsible for initiating China's opening to the outside world, Deng bolted through the door that Mao had opened—normalizing relations with the United States, repairing China's long-troubled relations with the Soviet Union, and engineering China's full participation in the world economy. He also assisted in negotiating the agreement that returned Hong Kong to Chinese sovereignty in 1997.

Background. Deng was born on Aug. 22, 1904, of landlord parents in the village of Paifang in Sichuan province. When he was 16 years old, his father sent him off to join a work-study program in France. While there, he was befriended by Zhou Enlai, who later served for many years as China's prime minister. Zhou introduced Deng to membership in the Chinese Socialist Youth League and, sub-sequently, in the Chinese Communist Party. After five years in France, Deng returned to China via Moscow, where he spent close to a year in military and ideological training.

Once back on Chinese soil, he rose rapidly in the Chinese Communist Party, becoming secretary to the Central Committee in 1927. He spent the next 20 years deeply immersed in the civil war and the anti-Japanese struggle, serving as a political commissar and party official. Following the establishment of the People's Republic of China in 1949, he joined the central government's Economic Commission and later was named finance minister. In 1956 he was appointed secretary-general of the party, a post he held for the next ten years.

His first fall from power had come in 1933, when he was removed from office because of his support of Mao Zedong, then competing for ascendance within the party. His second setback came in 1966, when, at the onset of the Cultural Revolution, he was criticized by Mao as the "the Number 2 party person in authority taking the capitalist road" and dismissed from office. Thanks to the patronage of Zhou Enlai, Deng managed to sit out the Cultural Revolution in a tractor factory in Jiangxi province.

By 1973, with the leadership in disarray as the Cultural Revolution ground to a halt, Deng was brought back to Beijing—at Zhou's behest and with Mao's reluctant acquiescence—to help pick up the pieces. This second reincarnation was a brief one. The so-called Gang of Four surrounding Mao was opposed unalterably to Deng, and when Zhou died in January 1976 these men engineered Deng's third fall from power, accusing him of having fomented a demonstration in Tiananmen Square. But the ascendancy of the Gang of Four was short-lived. Soon after Mao died in September 1976, its members were arrested, tried, and sentenced, and Deng began his third return to power and his remarkable transformation of the Chinese economy.

Deng Xiaoping was married three times. His first wife, Zhang Xiyuan, died in childbirth in 1930. He was divorced from Jin Weiying, his second wife, in 1933. In 1939 he married Pu Zhuo Lin, with whom he had five children. He was a lifelong chain-smoker and an enthusiast for the game of bridge. Indeed, at his death, his only formal position was that of honorary chairman of the Chinese Bridge Association. In failing health for several years, Deng died from complications of Parkinson's disease on Feb. 19, 1997. He was survived by his wife and all of his children.

JOHN BRYAN STARR

COUSTEAU, Jacques-Yves

French oceanographer and filmmaker: b. St.-André-de-Cubzac, France, June 11, 1910; d. Paris, June 25, 1997.

"The best way to observe fish is to become a fish," wrote Jacques Cousteau, the explorer whose lifelong fascination with the sea and its creatures was matched by a desire to share his passion. His many books and documentaries about the ocean and sea environment made Cousteau a household name.

Cousteau's first major contribution to oceanography came in the early 1940s, when he coinvented the Aqua-Lung, or scuba (*self-contained underwater breathing apparatus*). Prior to its invention, divers had to remain in watertight diving bells or wear helmeted suits connected to an air supply on a nearby boat. In 1950, Cousteau bought a former minesweeper and converted it into a research vessel he christened *Calypso*. Living *Calypso*'s motto—"We must go and see for ourselves"—he sailed the world, often using underwater cameras he built himself to photograph wonders previously unseen by humans.

By 1974, concerns about the ocean environment and its degradation led Cousteau to found the Cousteau Society, dedicated to marine conservation. He added his voice to those who warned that humans would be the losers if they continued to misuse the ocean.

Background. Cousteau learned to swim at age 4 and made his first dive at age 10. He made his first home movie at age 13. He was a lackluster student, however, and was expelled from high school after breaking 17 of the school's windows. In 1930, Cousteau entered the French Naval Academy. He trained to become a combat pilot but an automobile accident at age 26 disqualified him from flying. He was posted to a naval base on the Mediterranean, where he swam daily. During World War II, he was active in the French Resistance.

Cousteau's first book, *The Silent World* (1953), sold more than 5 million copies in 22 languages. A documentary version of the book won an Oscar. In the following decades, he wrote or cowrote more than 80 books, produced nearly 100 films, and hosted several television series. The documentary television series *The Undersea World of Jacques Cousteau* was seen in more than 100 countries.

Cousteau's awards included three Oscars, ten Emmys, and the U.S. Presidential Medal of Freedom. He was survived by his second wife and three children.

JENNY TESAR

STEWART, James

U.S. actor: b. Indiana, PA, May 20, 1908; d. Beverly Hills, CA, July 2, 1997.

No matter what role he played, beloved actor James (Jimmy) Stewart could be counted on for a combination of qualities that made him a Hollywood legend. His acting skill—first evidenced on the stage and then honed in some 80 movies—was enhanced by a larger-than-life image that critics and audiences alike perceived as reflecting decency, honor, and the solid-citizen attributes romantically associated with small-town America. The lanky, unpretentious actor with the often-imitated drawl never looked or sounded much different from one film to another, but he imbued each character with an aura of truthfulness and sincerity capable of making audiences believe in his portrayals.

He spoke modestly of his achievements with such comments as "I don't act, I react." He delighted in recounting homespun incidents like the time his father phoned upon hearing about Stewart winning "some kind of an award"—an Oscar—and said he had better bring it back to put in the window of the family hardware store.

One of Stewart's favorite roles was his depiction of the unassuming, troubled banker George Bailey in *It's a Wonderful Life* (1946)—Frank Capra's sentimental film about the difference a decent person can make. It became one of the most popular films of all time. There were many standouts among Stewart's movies. He won an Academy Award for *The Philadelphia Story* (1940) and Oscar nominations for his performances in *Mr. Smith Goes to Washington* (1939), *It's a Wonderful Life*, *Harvey* (1950), and *Anatomy of a*

Jimmy Stewart

© UPI/Corbis-Bettmann

Murder (1959). He portrayed bandleader Glenn Miller in *The Glenn Miller Story* (1954) and Charles A. Lindbergh flying across the Atlantic in *The Spirit of St. Louis* (1957).

His many leading ladies included Marlene Dietrich in the spirited Western *Destry Rides Again* (1939) and Grace Kelly in Alfred Hitchcock's *Rear Window* (1954). Hitchcock cast Stewart with Doris Day in *The Man Who Knew Too Much* (1956) and with Kim Novak in the thriller *Vertigo* (1958). The actor also appeared on Broadway in the 1947 production of *Harvey* and in its 1970 revival.

Background. James Maitland Stewart was one of three children born to parents of Scotch-Irish descent. The family had a successful hardware store in the western Pennsylvania town of Indiana, for which Stewart enjoyed a lifelong fondness. He went to prep school at Mercersburg Academy in Pennsylvania and in 1932 was graduated from Princeton University with a degree in architecture. His life took a crucial turn when college pal Joshua Logan, later a Broadway director, prompted him to join a summer-stock company, the University Players, in Falmouth on Cape Cod, MA. Henry Fonda was in the company and became a lifelong friend, despite their differing political viewpoints. Stewart's first major stage part was in *Yellow Jack* (1934), which proved to be a path to an MGM contract a year later and to his Hollywood future.

When World War II approached, Stewart joined the U.S. Air Force. He flew 20 combat missions as a pilot based in England and won numerous military honors; after the war he served in the Air Force Reserve until 1968, eventually becoming a brigadier general. In 1985 he was awarded the Presidential Medal of Freedom.

His professional honors included a special 1985 Academy Award for 50 years of acting and "his high ideals both on and off the screen," the American Film Institute's Life Achievement Award (1980), and Kennedy Center honors for lifetime contributions to the performing arts (1985). He also drew attention as a writer with his book *Jimmy Stewart and His Poems* (1989).

His 1949 marriage to former model Gloria Hatrick McLean lasted until her death in 1994. The Stewarts raised two sons from Mrs. Stewart's previous marriage—one of whom, Ronald, was killed in the Vietnam war. They had twin daughters, Judy and Kelly, who survived Stewart, as did his stepson Michael McLean.

WILLIAM WOLF

BRENNAN, William Joseph, Jr.

U.S. Supreme Court justice: b. Newark, NJ, April 25, 1906; d. Arlington, VA, July 24, 1997.

"The most important responsibility the [U.S. Supreme] Court has," wrote Associate Justice William Brennan, "is to see to it that individual rights as provided in the Constitution are enforced." In his nearly 34 years on the nation's highest bench, Brennan wrote numerous landmark rulings in defense of individual rights. With his intellect and legal acumen and his personal warmth and charm, Brennan helped bring about great social and political change, especially during the late 1950s and 1960s. Conservative critics condemned him as representing all that is wrong with an "activist court." Admirers considered him a hero.

Background. William Joseph Brennan, Jr., was born in Newark, NJ, the second of eight children of Irish immigrants. After graduating from the Wharton School of Finance and Commerce at the University of Pennsylvania and Harvard Law School, he practiced labor law with a Newark law firm, taking time out during World War II to serve as a legal officer in the U.S. Army. Beginning in 1949, he was a judge in the New Jersey Superior Court, Appellate Court, and Supreme Court. In 1956, President Dwight D. Eisenhower named Brennan, a Democrat, to the U.S. Supreme Court. Reportedly, Eisenhower, a Republican, later would regret the decision.

On the Supreme Court, Brennan's opinions on such issues as abortion, religion, and freedom of speech were consistently liberal. In *Baker v. Carr* (1962), for example, he ruled that federal courts could require states to ensure the one person–one vote principle. In *New York Times Company v. Sullivan* (1964), he reaffirmed the principles of the 1st Amendment by concluding that public officials could not sue for defamation unless they could prove that actual malice was involved. And he wrote the majority decision in a 1989 case that ruled that the burning of the American flag is protected by the Constitution's free-speech guarantees. Beginning in 1969, the court became more conservative and Brennan became the spokesman for the liberal minority, espousing such causes as the abolition of the death penalty. He resigned from the court on July 20, 1990.

Brennan's first wife, Marjorie, with whom he had two sons and a daughter, died in 1982. The following year, he married Mary Fowler, his longtime secretary.

WILLIAM E. SHAPIRO

DIANA

Princess of Wales: b. Sandringham. England, July 1, 1961; d. Paris, France, Aug. 31, 1997.

Diana, princess of Wales, enjoyed fame as a glamorous and often controversial personality whose every move was followed by the global media. Hours after her death following a car crash in Paris, it became obvious that her manifest empathy for the poor, the sick and dying, and the innocent victims of war had won much admiration. Prime Minister Tony Blair perhaps came closest to reflecting Great Britain's appreciation of Diana, and explaining the worldwide reaction to her untimely death, when he described her as "the people's princess." Her funeral in Westminster Abbey was watched by a worldwide audience estimated at more than 1 billion. Prior to the service, millions of flowers had been laid in tribute to Diana throughout London.

In life, the princess had an impact on the British monarchy and the reigning House of Windsor that only the passage of time may make it possible to measure. Before her marriage to Charles, prince of Wales, ended in divorce, she accused her husband of being unsuited to succeed to the throne and criticized other members of the royal family for their failure to groom her in her role as queen-in-waiting.

Background. Diana Frances Spencer was the third of four children of the 8th Earl Spencer and Frances Roche. She became Lady Diana Spencer on the death of her grandfather in 1975. Her childhood was disrupted by the separation of her parents when she was 6, and by their acrimonious divorce two years later. Educated at a girls' boarding school in Kent, Diana worked as a part-time kindergarten teacher.

Before her marriage on July 29, 1981, at the age of 20, to Charles, prince of Wales, she was little known to the British public. Her wedding in St. Paul's Cathedral attracted international attention. A son, Prince William, was born on June 21, 1982, and become the second in line to the throne, behind his father. A second son, Prince Henry (Harry), was born on Sept. 15, 1984.

With her invariably dazzling attire, Princess Diana became the personification of British fashion and began appearing on the covers of magazines in many countries. Her public profile was higher than that of Prince Charles, who sometimes found that his speeches went unreported while his wife's clothes attracted intense media attention. Within four or five years of their marriage,

Diana, Princess of Wales

© John Stillwell/Reuters/Archive Photos

strains between the royal couple were apparent. Increasingly, Charles and Diana began to make separate public appearances. In December 1992, Prime Minister John Major announced that the couple had separated. They were divorced on Aug. 28, 1996. As part of the divorce settlement, Diana was required to give up the title "Her Royal Highness," but was said by Buckingham Palace to remain a member of the royal family. The couple were given joint custody of their sons, and Diana continued to devote much time and energy to their upbringing. She tried hard to ensure that her sons were in contact with "ordinary life and ordinary people."

The princess' activities on behalf of more than 100 charities included work for the Red Cross and visits to leper hospitals in Africa, where she shook hands with patients. On a visit to New York City in 1989, she made headlines by embracing a person suffering from AIDS. In the final two years of her life, Diana took a lead in a world campaign to ban land mines and was photographed visiting areas where they had been laid. In October 1997 the Nobel Prize Committee announced that it was awarding the Nobel Peace Prize to the International Campaign to Ban Landmines and its coordinator, Jody Williams. The committee acknowledged Diana's commitment to the cause of banning such mines, but said it had no direct bearing on the award.

By the time of her death, she reportedly had formed a close attachment to Emad Mohamed (Dodi) al Fayed, heir to the owner of the London department store Harrods, who also died as a result of the Paris car crash. Freelance photographers reportedly were pursuing the car at the time of the high-speed crash, and several were detained in connection with the investigation into the accident.

ALEXANDER MACLEOD

MOTHER TERESA

Roman Catholic nun and Nobel Peace Prize winner: b. Skopje, now in Macedonia, Aug. 27, 1910; d. Calcutta, India, Sept. 5, 1997.

No other Roman Catholic woman of the 20th century achieved the level of veneration and respect gained by Mother Teresa of Calcutta. Although she was born in what now is Macedonia, most of her work was among the destitute dying of India, where she founded her religious congregation—the Missionaries of Charity. By the time of Mother Teresa's death, when most religious orders were suffering from dwindling membership, her order was a worldwide congregation of more than 5,000 women and men. A Nobel laureate, she had gained worldwide fame.

Background. Mother Teresa was born Agnes Gonxha Bojaxhiu on Aug. 27, 1910, to middle-class Albanian parents in Skopje. At age 18, she joined an Irish missionary congregation, the Sisters of Loreto. After studies in Dublin, Sister Teresa, as she now was known, was sent to India, where she began a seemingly routine career in the field of education. By 1946 she was principal of Loreto House, a convent school in Calcutta. Becoming increasingly uncomfortable with the contrast between the relative affluence of her school and the stark poverty surrounding her, Sister Teresa applied to the Vatican for permission to leave her congregation in order to work exclusively among the poor.

After two years her petition was granted and, with the blessing of the archbishop of Calcutta, she founded what would become the Missionaries of Charity. At first she and her followers worked at educating poor children, but the focus quickly changed to caring for the destitute sick, especially the dying, of all religious faiths. Members of her congregation took the vows of poverty, chastity, and obedience as well as a vow to serve the "poorest of the poor." In 1952, Mother Teresa opened Nirmal Hriday (Pure Heart) Home for Dying Destitutes. Many of her patients were picked up off the streets of Calcutta and brought to the home, where they at least could die with dignity. Five years later the sisters began caring for persons with leprosy.

It was a British journalist, Malcolm Muggeridge, who brought Mother Teresa to world attention. Muggeridge convinced her that a documentary on the work of her congregation would give publicity to the needs of the poor. The resulting documentary and 1971 book, *Something Beautiful for God*, made Mother Teresa of Calcutta an instant celebrity. Volun-

Mother Teresa

© Francis Apesteguy/Gamma-Liaison

teers flocked to her new congregation and funds poured in, enabling her to open homes and hospices—always in the poorest of districts—in 120 countries. In 1971 her order opened its first home in the United States—in New York City's Harlem.

Mother Teresa traveled the world, preaching a gospel of charity. In 1979 she was awarded the prestigious Nobel Peace Prize; in 1985 she received the U.S. Presidential Medal of Freedom, the nation's highest civilian award; and there were countless other honors. But amid the applause there were detractors as well. She cared for the poor but did not campaign for changes in social structures that may cause poverty, some said. Others attacked her uncompromising opposition to artificial birth control and abortion, which she regarded as "the greatest destroyer of peace today." Still others attacked her willingness to accept donations from persons of unsavory repute. But to the vast majority of the public she remained on a very high pedestal.

In spite of concern about Mother Teresa's health, her congregation reelected her superior in 1990. It was not until March 1997 that she relinquished the leadership of the Missionaries of Charity to an associate, Sister Nirmala Joshi. After Mother Teresa's death from cardiac arrest, India—her adopted country and a land where Christians are a small minority—accorded her the rare honor of a state funeral. Some of her admirers asked that the Roman Catholic Church declare her a saint immediately. In the end, Pope John Paul II said that the norms for canonization should be observed.

LOU BALDWIN

The following is a selected list of prominent persons who died during 1997. Articles on major figures appear in the preceding pages.

Agosti, Orlando (72), Argentine military commander; coleader of a coup against the democratically elected government of Isabel Perón in 1976. He and two others established a military regime (1976–85). When democracy was restored, he was sentenced to several years in prison: d. Buenos Aires, Argentina, Oct. 6.

Akii-Bua, John (47), Ugandan track star; set a new world record in the 400-m hurdles at the 1972 Munich Olympics. He is the only Ugandan ever to win an Olympic gold medal: d. Kampala, Uganda, June 20.

al-Fayed, Emad Mohammed (Dodi) (41), eldest son of the Saudi Arabian owner of Harrods department store in Britain and friend of Diana, princess of Wales. He was killed in the car crash that took Diana's life: d. Paris, France, Aug. 31.

Anderson, Eugenie M. (born Helen Eugenie Moore) (87), diplomat; the first woman named as a U.S. ambassador. A Democrat, she was appointed envoy to Denmark in 1949 by President Harry Truman. She later headed the U.S. delegation to the UN Trusteeship Council and represented the United States on the UN Committee for Decolonization: d. Red Wing, MN, March 31.

Arcaro, Eddie (born George Edward Arcaro) (81), jockey; during his 31-year career, won the Kentucky Derby five times and twice swept the Triple Crown events (1941 and 1948). He rode to victory at the Preakness and the Belmont Stakes six times each: d. Miami, FL, Nov. 14.

Arcos, Sebastián (65), Cuban dissident; fought against the totalitarian leadership of Fidel Castro and cofounded the Committee for Human Rights in Cuba (1981): d. Miami, FL, Dec. 22.

Ashburn, Richie (Don Richard) (70), professional-baseball player for the Philadelphia Phillies (1948–59), Chicago Cubs (1960–61), and New York Mets (1962–63); was inducted into baseball's Hall of Fame in 1995. He broadcast Phillies games from his retirement until the time of his death: d. New York City, Sept. 9.

Auerbach, Oscar (92), pathologist; was the first to document a physical link between smoking and lung cancer. His work was cited in the 1964 surgeon general's report that led to the requirement of a warning label on cigarette packages: d. Livingston, NJ, Jan. 15.

Awdry, Wilbert Vere (85), English author and minister; best known for the internationally popular "Thomas the Tank Engine" children's-book series, the basis for a PBS television series, *Shining Time Station*. He was honored with the Order of the British Empire in 1996: d. Stroud, Gloucestershire, England, March 21.

Baker, LaVern (born Delores Williams) (67), rhythm-and-blues singer; among her hits were "Tweedlee Dee" (1954), "Jim Dandy" (1957), and "I Cried a Tear" (1959). She was inducted into the Rock and Roll Hall of Fame in 1991: d. New York City, March 10.

Banda, Hastings Kamuzu (90s), Malawi political leader; led British Nyasaland to independence as Malawi in 1964, and declared himself president for life in 1971. He spurned movements toward black nationalism, appointed white foreigners to important posts, and maintained ties with South Africa during apartheid. He called elections under pressure in 1994 and was defeated. He was tried and acquitted for the 1983 murders of four government figures: d. Johannesburg, South Africa, Nov. 25.

Bao Dai (born Nguyen Vinh Thuy) (83), Vietnam's last emperor (1926–45); assumed control in 1932. He abdicated in 1945 following a communist revolution led by Ho Chi Minh, but returned in 1949 and regained power, with the help of the French government. He declared the country a colony of France, and served as head of state until being deposed by a 1955 referendum: d. Paris, France, July 31.

Barco Vargas, Virgilio (75), president of Colombia (1986–90); a U.S.-educated engineer, he came to power in a nation suffering from poverty and attacks by guerrilla groups demanding economic and political reform. His U.S.-backed effort to extradite drug traffickers led to a civil war: d. Bogotá, Colombia, May 20.

Bartels, John R. (99), U.S. district judge; the oldest sitting federal judge. He was appointed to the Eastern District of New York by President Dwight Eisenhower in 1959. He retired in 1973, but remained as a senior judge: d. Brooklyn, NY, Feb. 13.

Bauby, Jean-Dominique (44), French journalist and author; paralyzed by a stroke in 1995. Using blinking to communicate, he dictated a book about being paralyzed. *Le Scaphandre et Le Papillon* (The Diving Suit and the Butterfly) (1997) was praised by critics: d. Paris, France, March 9.

Berlin, Isaiah (88), Latvian-born English philosopher and writer; an advocate of pluralism, he was famed for his lectures and essays; all of his work evidenced his concern with liberty and with the right to dignity of human beings. Many of his writings treated 19th-century Russian thinkers. He was knighted in 1957 and named to Britain's Order of Merit in 1971: d. Oxford, England, Nov. 5.

Isaiah Berlin

© Gemma Levine/Camera Press/Globe Photos

Berry, Richard (61), songwriter; best known for the legendary pop hit "Louie Louie." The song caused a controversy after it was recorded in 1963 by the Kingsmen, when rumors circulated that the lyrics were obscene: d. Los Angeles, CA, Jan. 23.

Bertil Gustaf Oscar Carl Eugene (84), Swedish prince; son of King Gustaf VI of Sweden, he was presumptive heir to the throne from 1973–79: d. Sweden, Jan. 5.

Bibas, Frank P. (80), film producer and director; won an Oscar in 1961 for his direction of the documentary *Project Hope*: d. Fort Myers, FL, Oct. 16.

Bing, Sir Rudolf (95), general manager of the New York Metropolitan Opera (1950–72); with his hiring of ballerina Janet Collins and the debuts at the Met of Marian Anderson and Leontyne Price, he broke the Met's color barrier. He brought the world's best

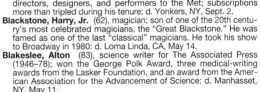

Sir Rudolf Bing

© Archive Photos

directors, designers, and performers to the Met; subscriptions more than tripled during his tenure: d. Yonkers, NY, Sept. 2.

Blackstone, Harry, Jr. (62), magician; son of one of the 20th century's most celebrated magicians, the "Great Blackstone." He was famed as one of the last "classical" magicians. He took his show to Broadway in 1980: d. Loma Linda, CA, May 14.

Blakeslee, Alton (83), science writer for The Associated Press (1946–78); won the George Polk Award, three medical-writing awards from the Lasker Foundation, and an award from the American Association for the Advancement of Science: d. Manhasset, NY, May 11.

Boban, Mate (57), Croatian nationalist; led the creation of an independent enclave in 1992 during the civil war in Bosnia and Herzegovina. He was suspected of participating in the killings of Muslim civilians and of ordering mass killings in Bosnia in 1993. A UN war-crimes tribunal was investigating, he was removed from power in 1994: d. Mostar, Bosnia and Herzegovina, July 7.

Bristol, Horace (88), photojournalist; one of *Life* magazine's first staff photographers, he was admired for his photos of Depression-era migrant workers. He came up with the idea for John Steinbeck's *Grapes of Wrath*, recruited Steinbeck to write the book, and accompanied him on his research trips: d. Ojai, CA, Aug. 4.

Brown, Roger (54), professional basketball player; after losing his college scholarship and being banned from NBA play in 1960 due to his associations with a convicted gambler, he became a star of the American Basketball Association's (ABA's) Indiana Pacers. He led the team to three championships (1970–73): d. Indianapolis, IN, March 4.

Brown, William Slater (100), writer; one of the last surviving members of the so-called "Lost Generation" of the post–World War I era. He authored ten books: d. Rockport, MA, June 22.

Buckley, Jeff (30), folk-rock singer; his first full-length album, *Grace* (1994), produced the minor hit "Last Goodbye." He was the son of the late folk musician Tim Buckley: d. Memphis, TN, May 29.

Burhoe, Ralph Wendell (85), educator and writer; highly regarded for his efforts to reconcile the tenets of religion and science. He was awarded the Templeton Prize for Progress in Religion in 1980: d. Chicago, IL, May 8.

Eddie Arcaro

© AP/Wide World Photos

Jeanne Calment

Burroughs, William S. (83), author; one of the 1950s' "Beat Generation" of writers, whose wild lifestyle was as famous as their books. His long struggle with drug addiction often was a theme in his works, the best known of which was the novel *Naked Lunch* (1959): d. Lawrence, KS, Aug. 2.

Caen, Herb (80), journalist; his column for the *San Francisco Chronicle* received a special Pulitzer Prize in 1996: d. San Francisco, CA, Feb. 1.

Calment, Jeanne Louise (122), French native recognized as the world's oldest person; gained celebrity in her last years, even releasing a CD and establishing a World Wide Web page: d. Arles, France, Aug. 4.

Calvin, Melvin (85), biochemist; won the Nobel Prize in chemistry in 1961 for his work on photosynthesis, and the National Medal of Science in 1989: d. Alta Bates, CA, Jan. 8.

Capps, Walter (63), member of the U.S. House of Representatives (D-CA, 1997); in only a few months in Congress, had become known as one of its most liberal members: d. Washington, DC, Oct. 28.

Carcani, Adil (75), premier of Albania (1982–91); the last of the nation's communist leaders, he was sentenced to five years in prison in 1994, which he served under house arrest: d. Tirane, Albania, Oct. 13.

Carpenter, Thelma (77), singer; first gained fame with the big bands of the 1940s. She appeared on Broadway in *Memphis Bound* (1944) and *Dolly!* (1968–69), among others; in the films *Hellzapoppin'* (1941), *The Wiz* (1978), and *The Cotton Club* (1984); and in the TV series *Barefoot in the Park* (1970): d. New York City, May 15.

Casali, Kim (55), New Zealand–born cartoonist; best known for her *Love Is...* cartoons, popular during the 1960s and 1970s: d. Surrey, England, June 15.

Chambers, George Michael (69), prime minister of Trinidad and Tobago (1981–86): d. Port-of-Spain, Trinidad, Nov. 4.

Chandler, Dorothy B. (96), philanthropist; helped finance and build the Music Center of Los Angeles County, whose auditorium is named for her. She was awarded the National Medal of Arts in 1985: d. Hollywood, CA, July 6.

Chaplin, Saul (85), musical composer, director, and producer; won Oscars for his work on *An American in Paris* (1951), *Seven Brides for Seven Brothers* (1954), and *West Side Story* (1961): d. Los Angeles, CA, Nov. 15.

Cheatham, Doc (born Adolphus Anthony Cheatham) (91), jazz trumpeter; played with Louis Armstrong and blues star Bessie Smith in the 1920s and with Cab Calloway's band in the 1930s. Early in 1997, *Doc Cheatham & Nicholas Payton*, a collaborative album, made the top-20 jazz-album charts: d. Washington, DC, June 2.

Christensen, L. Royal (82), microbiologist and epidemiologist; pioneered the use of streptokinase to treat heart attacks. He shared a 1949 Lasker Award: d. Madison, CT, March 22.

Clarke, Shirley (72), filmmaker; her 1962 documentary on Robert Frost, commissioned by President John F. Kennedy, won an Academy Award: d. Boston, MA, Sept. 23.

Claster, Nancy (82), teacher-host of television's *Romper Room* from shortly after its inception in 1953 until 1964; she also wrote much of the material: d. Baltimore, MD, April 25.

Coleman, Peter (77), governor of American Samoa (1978–85; 1989–93); the first popularly elected governor of the region. He had been appointed by the administration of U.S. President Dwight Eisenhower as governor of the unincorporated territory in 1956, serving until 1961: d. Honolulu, HI, April 28.

Cooke, Jack Kent (84), Canadian-born entrepreneur; worth approximately $825 million, he owned the Los Angeles Lakers basketball team and the Washington Redskins football team. Among his holdings was the Chrysler Building in New York City: d. Washington, DC, April 6.

Copeland, Johnny (60), blues musician; won a Grammy in 1986 for *Showdown*, with Albert Collins and Robert Cray: d. Teaneck, NJ, July 3.

Crocket, George William, Jr. (88), criminal-court judge and member of the U.S. House of Representatives (D-MI, 1981–91); notorious for his 1949 defense of 11 Communist Party members accused of conspiracy, in a case that landed him in prison for four months for contempt of court: d. Washington, DC, Sept. 7.

Danielian, Leon (75), ballet dancer; a star with the Ballet Russe de Monte Carlo during the 1940s and 1950s. He choreographed several ballets and served as director of the American Ballet Theatre School (1967–80): d. Canaan, CT, March 8.

Danilova, Alexandra (93), Russian-born ballerina; performed with the Ballets Russes and the Ballet Russe de Monte Carlo from the 1930s into the 1950s. She received the Capezio Award in 1958. She appeared in two Broadway productions and in the 1977 film *The Turning Point*: d. New York City, July 13.

Davis, Gail (born Betty Jeanne Grayson) (71), actress; starred in the TV series *Annie Oakley* (1955–58), the first Western series to star a woman: d. Burbank, CA, March 15.

Davis, Kingsley (88), sociologist and demographer; in the 1940s, advocated lower birthrates and a stable population and coined the term "zero population growth." However, toward the end of his career, he warned of dangers presented by the West's very low birthrate: d. Stanford, CA, Feb. 27.

Davis, Piper (born Lorenzo Davis) (79), player and manager in the Negro baseball leagues; helped develop several notable players, including Willie Mays. In 1950 he was the first black player to be signed by the major leagues' Boston Red Sox, but was released the same year. He also played basketball with the Harlem Globetrotters: d. Birmingham, AL, May 21.

Dederich, Charles E. (83), founder in 1958 of the drug-rehab program Synanon; in the mid-1980s, Synanon declared itself a religion, was condemned by the U.S. government, and was stripped of its tax-exempt status. Dederich was convicted in 1980 of conspiracy to commit murder: d. Visalia, CA, Feb. 28.

de Kooning, Willem (92), *see* SIDEBAR, page 119.

Denver, John (53), *see* SIDEBAR, page 374.

De Santis, Giuseppe (80), Italian film director; one of the fathers of Italy's post–World War II neorealist movement. Among his films were *Caccia Tragica* (Tragic Hunt) (1947), *Riso Amaro* (Bitter Rice) (1949), and *Non c'e pace fra gli ulivi* (Under the Olive Tree) (1950). He was presented with a life-time-achievement award at the 1995 Berlin Film Festival: d. Rome, Italy, May 17.

Dicke, Robert H. (80), physicist; an early proponent of the "Big Bang" theory. He was awarded the National Medal of Science in 1971: d. Princeton, NJ, March 4.

Dickerson, Nancy H. (70), television news reporter and producer; was the first woman correspondent for CBS. She was an original producer of CBS' *Face the Nation*. In 1960 she became a TV news correspondent and had her own radio show. During the 1970s and 1980s she worked as an independent producer; her 1982 documentary on President Richard Nixon won a Peabody Award: d. New York City, Oct. 18.

Nancy Dickerson

Dickey, James (73), poet and author; his poetry was noted for its use of plain, clear language. The collection *Buckdancer's Choice* received a 1966 National Book Award. He is best known for his first novel, *Deliverance* (1970), made into a 1972 film: d. Columbia, SC, Jan. 19.

James Dickey

Dixon, Jeane (79), astrologer; gained fame with her apparent prediction in 1956 of the death of President John F. Kennedy. She wrote several books and produced a syndicated astrology column, and regained the spotlight in the 1980s when it was revealed that she advised First Lady Nancy Reagan: d. Washington, DC, Jan. 25.

Dorris, Michael (52), author; won the National Book Award in 1989 for *The Broken Cord*, a nonfiction account of the life of his adopted Native American son, who suffered from fetal alcohol syndrome: d. Concord, NH, April 13.

Doyle, David (67), actor; best known for his role in the hit television series *Charlie's Angels* (1976–81). He also appeared on Broadway and in several films: d. Los Angeles, CA, Feb. 26.

Jeane Dixon

Duvalier, Simone (80s), Haitian political figure; the wife of Haitian dictator François (Papa Doc) Duvalier and mother of his successor, Jean-Claude (Baby Doc) Duvalier. She was regarded as the "power behind the throne": d. near Paris, France, Dec. 26.

Dwinell, Lane (90), governor of New Hampshire (1955–59); a Republican, he was known for his shrewd budgeting: d. Hanover, NH, March 27.

Eccles, Sir John Carew (94), Australian neurophysiologist; shared the 1963 Nobel Prize in physiology or medicine for his research on the stimulation of human nerve cells by electrical currents. He was knighted by Britain's Queen Elizabeth II in 1958: d. Contra, Switzerland, May 2.

Edel, (Joseph) Leon (89), author and critic; won a Pulitzer Prize and a National Book Award in 1963 for the third volume of his five-volume *The Henry James Biography*: d. Honolulu, HI, Sept. 5.

Esau, Katherine (99), Ukrainian-born botanist; laid the foundation for research into plant physiology and molecular biology. She was presented with the National Medal of Science in 1989: d. Santa Barbara, CA, June 4.

Farley, Chris (33), comedian and actor; during his five seasons on NBC's *Saturday Night Live*, he became known for his physical comedy and characterizations of overbearing, yet good-hearted characters. He appeared in several films, including *Black Sheep* (1996) and *Beverly Hills Ninja* (1997): d. Chicago, IL, Dec. 18.

Fassi, Carlo (67), Italian-born figure-skating coach; helped rebuild the U.S. figure-skating program after a 1961 tragedy in which 18 of the best U.S. skaters and several coaches, officials, and judges died in a plane crash en route to the world championships. Four of his skaters won Olympic gold medals: d. Lausanne, Switzerland, March 20.

Fela Anikulapo-Kuti (born Fela Ransome-Kuti) (58), Nigerian musician and political dissident; creator of Afro-beat music, a blend of jazz and traditional African rhythms: d. Lagos, Nigeria, Aug. 2.

Ferreri, Marco (68), Italian film director; his satiric films were noted for their shocking content. *The Wheelchair* (1960) and *La Grande Bouffe* (The Great Feast) (1973) each won the International Critics Prize at the Cannes Film Festival: d. Paris, France, May 9.

Figueroa Mateos, Gabriel (89), Mexican cinematographer; known for his dramatic landscape shots. He twice was honored (in 1946 and 1950) with a photography award at the Cannes Film Festival, and won Mexico's National Arts Prize in 1977; the American Society of Cinematographers gave him its lifetime-achievement award in 1995: d. Mexico City, Mexico, April 27.

Fisher, Clarkson S. (76), U.S. district judge; chief judge of the U.S. district courts in New Jersey (1979–87): d. Princeton, NJ, July 27.

Flood, Curt (59), former professional baseball player; an All-Star center fielder for the St. Louis Cardinals in the 1960s, he challenged the reserve system as a form of enslavement. When traded to Philadelphia in 1969, he refused to go and filed suit, triggering a dispute that led to the collapse of the reserve system and opened the era of free agency: d. Los Angeles, CA, Jan. 20.

Frankl, Viktor Emil (92), Austrian psychiatrist; founded "logotherapy," the study of how individuals find meaning within their life circumstances. His book *Man's Search for Meaning* (1946) sold more than 10 million copies worldwide: d. Vienna, Austria, Sept. 2.

Freedberg, Sydney J. (82), art historian; was awarded the National Medal of Arts in 1988—the only art historian to receive the honor. In addition, he received several British honors for his World War II espionage work: d. Washington, DC, May 6.

Frooks, Dorothy (99 or 103), attorney, political activist, and writer; became an unofficial military recruiter during World War I and received a gold medal from President Woodrow Wilson, who made her chief yeoman of the U.S. Navy; she thus became the highest-ranking woman in the U.S. military at the time: d. New York City, April 13.

Fuller, Samuel (85), film director, producer, screenwriter, and actor; known for low-budget urban dramas and gritty Westerns and war films, most notably 1980's *The Big Red One*. His antiracism film *White Dog* (1982) was deemed too controversial for release; it was given a limited run in 1991: d. Hollywood Hills, CA, Oct. 30.

Furgol, Ed (79), former professional golfer; named PGA golfer of the year in 1954, he won the U.S. Open in 1954 and five PGA Tour victories between 1944 and 1983: d. Miami, FL, March 7.

Gabor, Jolie (97), Hungarian-born businesswoman and socialite; best known for being the mother of actresses Eva, Zsa Zsa, and Magda Gabor: d. Rancho Mirage, CA, April 1.

Gabor, Magda (78), Hungarian-born actress; less famous than her sisters, Eva and Zsa Zsa, she was praised by critics for her role in the Gabors' Las Vegas stage act, *This Is Our Life* (1953): d. Rancho Mirage, CA, June 6.

Gairy, Sir Eric (75), prime minister of Grenada (1974–79); the nation's first premier after it gained independence from Great Britain. Amid charges of dictatorship and human-rights abuses, he was overthrown in a bloodless coup: d. Grand Anse, Grenada, Aug. 23.

Geneen, Harold (87), executive; as president and CEO of International Telephone & Telegraph (1959–77), helped build the company into a powerful international conglomerate: d. New York City, Nov. 21.

Gill, Brendan (83), author and architectural preservationist; known for his writings for *The New Yorker* magazine since 1936. He also authored 15 books, including a 1975 best-seller about *The New Yorker*. He was given the first Jacqueline Kennedy Onassis Award in 1994: d. New York City, Dec. 27.

Allen Ginsberg

Ginsberg, Allen (70), poet; a voice of the 1950s' "Beat Generation," and one of the most celebrated U.S. poets of his generation. He was prominent in the social upheaval and antiwar protests of the 1960s and 1970s. His long poem "Howl!" (1956) became a subject of free-speech and censorship arguments, with Ginsberg tried—and acquitted—on obscenity charges. He received the National Book Award (1974), the Robert Frost Medal (1986), and an American Book Award (1990): d. New York City, April 5.

Goizueta, Roberto C. (65), Cuban-born chairman and chief executive of the Coca-Cola Co.; during his tenure (1981–97), helped raise the company's stock value from $4.3 billion to $152 billion: d. Atlanta, GA, Oct. 18.

Goldsmith, Sir James M. (64), French-born British billionaire financier; a forceful opponent of European integration, he founded a political party in 1995 whose agenda was to force a referendum on Britain's role in the European Union. He maintained, from France, a European Parliament seat. He was knighted by Britain's Queen Elizabeth II in 1976 and made a knight of the French Legion of Honor in 1978: d. Torre de Tamores, Spain, July 18.

Green, Gilbert (born Gershon Greenberg) (90), U.S. Communist Party leader; head of the Young Communist League in the 1930s.

With 11 others, he was tried and convicted in 1949 of "conspiracy to teach and advocate" the violent overthrow of the U.S. government. He jumped bail but later surrendered and served six years in prison: d. Ann Arbor, MI, May 4.

Grivich, Hilary (19), gymnast; a member of the 1991 U.S. team, which she helped to a silver medal in the world championships. She later became a champion diver: d. Houston, TX, May 4.

Guetary, Georges (born Lambros Worlou) (82), French-born singer; appeared in several films, including a lead role in the Oscar-winning *An American in Paris* (1951). He won a Tony for *Arms and the Girl* (1950): d. Mougins, France, Sept. 13.

Hairston, Sam (77), professional baseball player; a Negro Leagues star in the 1940s, he became one of the two first black players for the Chicago White Sox: d. Birmingham, AL, Oct. 31.

Halpern, Seymour (83), member of the U.S. House of Representatives (R-NY, 1959–73); cosponsored or sponsored some 279 bills, including the 1964 Civil Rights Act and Medicare legislation of 1965: d. Southampton, NY, Jan. 10.

Hanff, Helene (80), writer; her collection of letters to a London bookstore was published in 1970 as *84, Charing Cross Road*. The book was adopted for the London stage and for Broadway, and was made into a 1987 film: d. New York City, April 9.

Hassan, Sir Joshua (81), Gibraltarian politician; the British colony's first elected mayor (1964–69), he later served as chief minister (1972–87). He had founded Gibraltar's leading political party, the leftist Association for the Advancement Civil Rights, in 1942. He was knighted in 1963: d. Gibraltar, July 1.

Hayes, Charles A. (79), member of the U.S. House of Representatives (D-IL, 1983–93); was defeated in the 1992 Democratic primary after it was revealed that he was among the congressmen who were overdrawn at the House bank: d. Chicago, IL, April 8.

Helmsley, Harry B. (87), real-estate executive and billionaire; built a real-estate empire in New York City, with his most famous purchase being the Empire State Building in 1961. In 1996 his fortune was estimated at $1.7 billion. He and his second wife, Leona, were charged with tax evasion in 1988; he was declared incompetent, but she was convicted: d. Scottsdale, AZ, Jan. 4.

Henry, Marguerite (95), children's author; best known for the classic *Misty of Chincoteague* (1947), for which she won the John Newbery Honor Award. She received the Newbery Medal for *King of the Wind* (1990): d. Rancho Santa Fe, CA, Nov. 26.

Henson, Maria Rosa (69), Philippine activist; helped draw attention to the fact that as many as 200,0000 Philippine women were forced during World War II to work in Japanese army brothels. Her announcement of her ordeal in 1992 encouraged other victims to step forward. She wrote an account of the situation, *Comfort Woman: Slave of Destiny* (1996): d. Manila, Philippines, in August.

Herman, Robert (82), physicist; in the 1940s, predicted the existence of an "echo" from the Big Bang. In the 1960s the echo was found to exist. He shared the Henry Draper Medal of the National Academy of Sciences in 1993: d. Austin, TX, Feb. 13.

Hershey, Alfred D. (88), scientific researcher who pioneered the field of molecular biology; in the 1940s, he and several colleagues began working with bacteriophages to find out how viruses replicate. In 1952 he and an assistant performed experiments proving that DNA carries genetic information. He shared the 1969 Nobel Prize in physiology or medicine: d. Syosset, NY, May 22.

Herzog, Chaim (78), president of Israel (1983–93); born in Ireland, he immigrated to Israel in 1935. He helped solve disagreements between the nation's two major political parties and spoke out for greater rights for the Arab and Druse people of Israel. He had served as Israel's first head of military intelligence and as a major general in the Israeli army: d. Tel Aviv, Israel, April 17.

Hines, John E. (86), Episcopal clergyman; the presiding bishop of the Episcopal Church from 1965 to 1974. He helped guide the church through the social upheavals of the 1960s and led major changes in structure and views. He worked against racism and urged the ordination of women and blacks, as well as their promotion in other church positions: d. Austin, TX, July 19.

Hogan, Ben (84), professional golfer; won nine major championships—six after a near-fatal car accident: d. Fort Worth, TX, July 25.

Roberto Goizueta

Hu, King (born Hu Jingquan) (65), Chinese film director; won fame for his martial-arts films. *A Touch of Zen* won the grand prize at the Cannes film festival in 1975: d. Taipei, Taiwan, Jan. 14.

Huggins, Charles (95), surgeon; won the 1966 Nobel Prize in medicine for research that led to the use of chemotherapy in cancer treatment: d. Chicago, IL, Jan. 12.

Hutchence, Michael (37), Australian rock musician; leader of the popular band INXS. The group had just completed its tenth album in 20 years. Among INXS' hits were "Need You Tonight," "Devil Inside," and "Suicide Blonde": d. Sydney, Australia, Nov. 22.

Hutson, Don (84), professional football player; one of the greatest wide receivers ever. He played for the Green Bay Packers (1935–45), helping the team to three championships—in 1936, 1939, and

Charles Kuralt

1944. He still holds five NFL records. He was a charter member of the College Football Hall of Fame (1951) and the Pro Football Hall of Fame (1963): d. Rancho Mirage, CA, June 26.

Huxley, Elspeth (89), English author; best known for *The Flame Trees of Thika* (1959). She was made a Commander of the British Empire in 1962: d. Gloucestershire, England, Jan. 10.

Ibuka, Masaru (89), Japanese industrialist and engineer; a cofounder of the Sony Corporation. Breaking the Japanese tradition of copying successful technology, Ibuka worked to develop completely new products—among them Sony's Trinitron color television, introduced in 1967: d. Tokyo, Japan, Dec. 19.

Ignatow, David (born David Ignatowsky) (83), poet; winner of the 1977 Bollingen Prize. He authored or edited 27 books. He also received an award from the National Institute of Arts and Letters and the Robert Frost Medal of the Poetry Society of America: d. East Hampton, NY, Nov. 17.

Irsay, Robert (73), owner, since 1972, of the National Football League (NFL) team the Indianapolis Colts; it was under his leadership that the team moved from Baltimore in 1984: d. Indianapolis, IN, Jan. 14.

Jacobs, Helen Hull (88), tennis champion; won nine Grand Slam championships, including four straight U.S. national singles titles (1932–35) and Wimbledon (1936). In 1934 she won the singles, doubles, and mixed doubles titles at the U.S. championship. She was elected to the International Tennis Hall of Fame in 1962: d. East Hampton, NY, June 2.

Jaeckel, Richard (70), actor; known for his tough-guy roles. Among his films were *The Dirty Dozen* (1967) and *Sometimes a Great Notion* (1972); he was nominated for an Oscar for the latter film. He appeared in the 1980s TV series *Spenser: For Hire* and the 1990s series *Baywatch*: d. Woodland Hills, CA, June 14.

Jaffe, Leo (88), film executive and philanthropist; as head of Columbia Pictures (1973–81), he helped build the studio into one of Hollywood's most successful. He received a special Oscar in 1978, and was honored by President Ronald Reagan for his work with the U.S. Information Agency: d. New York City, Aug. 20.

Jagan, Cheddi B. (78), president of Guyana (1992–97); cofounder of the first political party in British Guiana in 1950, he helped lead the nation to independence in 1966: d. Washington, DC, March 6.

al-Jamali, Mohammed (Mohd) Fadhil (94), Iraqi statesman; served as prime minister before the monarchy was overthrown in 1958. He was tried and sentenced to hang after the revolution, but Morocco interceded for him and he went into exile: d. Tunis, Tunisia, May 24.

James, Dennis (born Demie James Sposa) (79), television announcer and game-show host; served as host of more than ten game and variety shows. He also hosted many fund-raising programs, most notably the annual United Cerebral Palsy telethon, and was credited with helping raise more than $1 billion for charity: d. Palm Springs, CA, June 3.

Jewell, Stuart (84), photographer and cinematographer; noted for his time-lapse photography for the Disney nature film *The Living Desert* (1953), which won an Oscar for best documentary, and for Disney's *Secrets of Life* (1956): d. Costa Mesa, CA, July 13.

John, Otto (88), German official; was part of an unsuccessful plan to assassinate Adolf Hitler in 1944. He became head of West Germany's counterintelligence agency in 1950, but went to East Germany and denounced the West German government in 1954. He was sentenced in West Germany to four years in prison for treason. He was pardoned in 1958: d. Innsbruck, Austria, March 26.

Johnson, U(ral) Alexis (88), diplomat; during his more than 40 years in the foreign service, was ambassador to Czechoslovakia, Thailand, and Japan. An authority on arms control, he was the chief U.S. delegate to the negotiations with the USSR that led to the first strategic-arms-limitation treaty: d. Raleigh, NC, March 24.

Jones, Robert E., Jr. (84), member of the U.S. House of Representatives (D-AL, 1947–77): d. Florence, AL, June 4.

Kaplan, Edgar (72), champion bridge player; won 28 national titles. He wrote several influential bridge books and owned, published, and edited *Bridge World* magazine: d. New York City, Sept. 7.

Kaufman, Frank (81), U.S. district judge; appointed to the federal bench by President Lyndon B. Johnson in 1966. During his tenure, he presided over several major cases in the Baltimore area: d. Baltimore, MD, July 31.

Keith, Brian (75), film and television actor; best known for his role as the bachelor uncle in the television series *Family Affair* (1966–71). He also appeared in several movies—including *The Parent Trap* (1961) and *With Six You Get Eggroll* (1968)—and in the TV series *Hardcastle & McCormick* (1983–86): d. Malibu, CA, June 24.

Kelley, Clarence M. (85), head of the FBI (1973–78); taking over after his predecessor had admitted to helping cover up the Watergate burglary, he worked to eliminate corruption within the FBI. He was instrumental in the introduction of computers and modernized crime-fighting methods: d. Kansas City, MO, Aug. 5.

Kelly, Edna (91), member of the U.S. House of Representatives (D-NY, 1949–69); the first woman to represent Brooklyn in Congress: d. Alexandria, VA, Dec. 14.

Kempton, Murray (79), journalist and writer; wrote commentary in *The New York Post* and *Newsday* (Long Island, NY) for many years, and authored several books. He won two George Polk Memorial Awards (1967, 1988), a National Book Award (1974), and a Pulitzer Prize (1985): d. New York City, May 5.

Kendrew, Sir John Cowdery (80), British biochemist; shared the 1962 Nobel Prize in chemistry with Max Perutz for their research using X-ray crystallography to determine the molecular structure of hemoglobin and myoglobin: d. Cambridge, England, Aug. 23.

Khan, Nusrat Fateh Ali (48), Pakistani singer; considered the greatest "qawwali" singer of his generation. He was popular in the West, and had collaborated with several U.S. rock musicians: d. London, England, Aug. 16.

Koliqi, Cardinal Mikel (94), Albanian Roman Catholic cardinal; under the nation's repressive regime, he spent 38 years in jails and labor camps. He was elevated to the College of Cardinals in 1994—the first Albanian to be named a cardinal: d. Shkoder, Albania, Jan. 28.

Kuralt, Charles (62), television and radio journalist and author; for his popular "On the Road" reports for CBS, he traveled the country reporting on local news and highlighting the lives of small-town Americans. He anchored *Sunday Morning* from 1980 to 1994, when he retired. He returned early in 1997 to host "An American Moment" and the weekly series *I Remember*. He won three Peabody Awards and 12 Emmy Awards, and was awarded the George Polk Memorial Award for national television reporting in 1981; he was named Broadcaster of the Year in 1985 by the International Radio-Television Society: d. New York City, July 4.

Roy Lichtenstein

Lane, Arthur S. (86), U.S. district judge; appointed to the federal bench by President Dwight Eisenhower, he was the sole federal judge in the Trenton, NJ, district until he retired in 1967: d. Princeton, NJ, Oct. 23.

Lane, Burton (born Burton Levy) (84), musical composer; among his best-known works was the Broadway hit *Finian's Rainbow* (1947); he also cowrote Broadway's *On a Clear Day You Can See Forever* (1965) and wrote songs for several films: d. New York City, Jan. 5.

Lane, Ronnie (51), English rock musician; bass player and cofounder of the 1960s British band Small Faces, later known as The Faces: d. Trinidad, CO, June 4.

Larson, Nicolette (45), recording artist; her hits included "Lotta Love" and "Fool Me Again": d. Los Angeles, CA, Dec. 16.

Leighton, Robert B. (77), physicist; inventor of the "Leighton dish," which covers the gap between light and radio telescopes, enabling astronomers to see an unfamiliar portion of the electromagnetic spectrum. He also was in charge of the first successful Mars probe, in 1965: d. Pasadena, CA, March 9.

Lemare, Iris (94), English musical conductor; the first professional female conductor in that country, and the first woman to conduct the British Broadcasting Corporation's symphony orchestra (1936): d. London, England, April 23.

Leonard, Buck (born Walter Fenner Leonard) (90), baseball player in the Negro Leagues; the Leagues' greatest first baseman, he was inducted into the Baseball Hall of Fame in 1972, becoming the third Negro Leagues star to receive the honor: d. Rocky Mount, NC, Nov. 27.

Leonard, Sheldon (born Sheldon Leonard Bershad) (89), actor and television producer and director; produced *I Spy*, *The Dick Van Dyke Show*, *Gomer Pyle*, and *The Andy Griffith Show*. He earned two Emmys, in 1957 and 1961, for directing *The Danny Thomas Show*. In 1997 he was inducted into the Hall of Fame of the Academy of Television Arts and Sciences: d. Beverly Hills, CA, Jan. 10.

Levertov, Denise (74), English-born U.S. poet and political activist; a prominent member of the anti–Vietnam war and antinuclear movements. Among her awards were the $50,000 Lannan Prize: d. Seattle, WA, Dec. 19.

Leventritt, Peter A. (82), bridge champion; one of the greatest U.S. bridge players, he won 13 national titles: d. New York City, Dec. 6.

Lewis, Robert (88), acting teacher and director; cofounder in 1947 of the Actors Studio. He advocated the Stanislavsky system of acting, and disapproved of the "Method" technique. He directed several hit Broadway productions: d. New York City, Nov. 23.

Lichtenstein, Roy (73), artist; a leading figure of the pop-art movement of the 1960s. He was famed for his stylized, comic-strip-style paintings: d. New York City, Sept. 29.

Liman, Arthur L. (64), attorney; known for his roles in the investigation of the 1971 prison uprising at Attica and the 1980s Iran-contra scandal. He served as chief counsel to the Senate committee investigating the latter case: d. New York City, July 17.

Lindley, Audra (79), actress; known for her role in the 1970s television series *Three's Company* and its spin-off, *The Ropers*. She also appeared in several Broadway productions and films: d. Los Angeles, CA, Oct. 16.

Louis, Jean (born Jean Louis Berthault) (89), French-born fashion designer; designed fashions for hundreds of Hollywood stars of the 1940s, 1950s, and 1960s. He won a 1956 Academy Award for his costume designs for *The Solid Gold Cadillac*, and was nominated 13 more times: d. Palm Springs, CA, April 20.

Lukas, J. Anthony (64), journalist and author; his book *Common Ground: A Turbulent Decade in the Lives of Three American Families* (1986) won a Pulitzer Prize. As a reporter for *The New York Times*, he had won a Pulitzer in 1968. Among his other honors were the National Book Award in 1985 and the National Book Critics Circle Award in 1986: d. New York City, June 5.

Maar, Dora (born Henriette Theodora Markovic) (89), French-born artist's model and photographer; best known as the lover of Spanish artist Pablo Picasso. She was the subject for several of his paintings: d. Paris, France, July 16 (reported).

Macapagal, Diosdado (86), president of the Philippines (1961–65); liberalized import and foreign-exchange controls and tried to reform the country's system of landownership: d. Manila, Philippines, April 21.

Manley, Michael (72), prime minister of Jamaica (1972–80; 1989–92); worked to expand health care and education and reduce class divisions in Jamaican society: d. Kingston, Jamaica, March 6.

Marchais, Georges (77), French political figure; led the French Communist Party (1972–94). During his tenure the party's membership dwindled and it went from garnering 21.4% of the vote to only 9.2% in 1993. He was blamed for the marginalization of the party in French society: d. Paris, France, Nov. 16.

Martin, David T. (89), member of the U.S. House of Representatives (R-NE, 1963–75); advised George Bush's presidential campaign in 1988: d. Kearney, NE, May 15.

Mas Canosa, Jorge (58), Cuban-born leader of exiled Cubans; founded and chaired the Cuban-American National Foundation, one of Washington's most effective lobbying groups. His group urged against the easing of sanctions against Cuba and against the normalization of Cuban-U.S. relations. He advocated the creation of Radio Marti and TV Marti, as well as the passage of the controversial Helms-Burton Act: d. Miami, FL, Nov. 23.

© Walter Dhladhla/AP/Wide World Photos

Mobutu Sese Seko

Matthews, William (55), poet; won the National Book Critics Circle Award (1996), for *Time & Money: New Poems*, and the Modern Poetry Association's Ruth Lilly Award (1997): d. New York City, Nov. 12.

McNichols, Stephen L.R. (83), Democratic governor of Colorado (1957–63); worked to establish a state planning agency and modernize the state's government and tax structure, as well as to reform health care for the mentally ill: d. Denver, CO, Nov. 25.

McNichols, William Henry, Jr. (87), Democratic mayor of Denver, CO (1968–83); his actions to improve Denver's infrastructure and expand its cultural offerings helped spur the city's 1970s building boom and burgeoning popularity: d. Denver, CO, May 29.

Mehrtens, Warren (77), jockey; in 1946, became one of only ten jockeys ever to win racing's Triple Crown—the Kentucky Derby, Preakness Stakes, and Belmont Stakes: d. Sarasota, FL, Dec. 30.

Melvin, Harold (57), rhythm-and-blues musician; leader of the Blue Notes, whose 1950s hits included "My Hero," "Get Out," and "I Miss You." In the 1970s the group teamed up with Teddy Pendergrass and produced more hits: d. Philadelphia, PA, March 24.

Meredith, (Oliver) Burgess (89), actor; his films include *Of Mice and Men* (1939) and *Rocky* (1976). He won an Emmy in 1977 for his role in *Tail Gunner Joe*, and was famed for his role as the Penguin in the 1960s TV series *Batman*: d. Malibu, CA, Sept. 9.

Meyner, Helen (69), member of the U.S. House of Representatives (D-NJ, 1975–79); worked for women's rights and served on the Committee of International Relations: d. Fort Myers, FL, Nov. 2.

Michener, James A. (90), novelist; known for his best-selling historical novels following generations of characters. His first book, *Tales of the South Pacific* (1947), won a Pulitzer Prize and was made into a Broadway musical. Many of his more than 40 books were adapted into films and TV movies: d. Austin, TX, Oct. 16.

Mifune, Toshiro (77), Japanese actor; best known for his samurai roles. He starred in the Oscar-winning *Rashomon* (1950) and *The Seven Samurai* (1954). In the United States he gained fame for his role in the 1980 TV miniseries *Shogun*: d. Mitaka, Japan, Dec. 24.

Milburn, Rod (47), track-and-field star; won a gold medal in the 110–m hurdles at the 1972 Munich Olympics. He set or tied many world records: d. Port Hudson, LA, Nov. 11.

Mitchum, Robert (79), actor; appeared in more than 100 films. He won an Academy Award nomination for his first major role, in *The Story of G.I. Joe* (1945). Among his other films were *Out of the Past* (1947), *The Night of the Hunter* (1955), *Cape Fear* (1962), and *The Friends of Eddie Coyle* (1975). On television, he was best known for the 1983 miniseries *The Winds of War* and its 1988 sequel, *War and Remembrance*: d. Santa Barbara, CA, July 1.

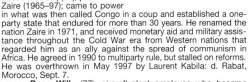

© Zigy Kaluzny/Gamma-Liaison

James Michener

Mobutu Sese Seko (born Joseph Désiré Mobutu) (66), president of Zaire (1965–97); came to power in what was then called Congo in a coup and established a one-party state that endured for more than 30 years. He renamed the nation Zaire in 1971, and received monetary aid and military assistance throughout the Cold War era from Western nations that regarded him as an ally against the spread of communism in Africa. He agreed in 1990 to multiparty rule, but stalled on reforms. He was overthrown in May 1997 by Laurent Kabila: d. Rabat, Morocco, Sept. 7.

Monroe, Rose Will (77), aircraft-plant employee who became famous during World War II as "Rosie the Riveter." She was featured in a widely distributed promotional film and in posters: d. Clarksville, IN, May 31.

Moore, Alvy (75), actor; best known for his role in the television series *Green Acres* (1965–71): d. Palm Desert, CA, May 4.

Moore, Audley L. (Queen Mother) (98), radical civil-rights activist and black-nationalist leader; a member of Marcus Garvey's Back to Africa movement. In 1996 she and 40 other African-American women were honored at the Corcoran Gallery of Art in Washington, DC: d. Brooklyn, NY, May 2.

Mosbacher, Emil (Bus), Jr. (75), diplomat, businessman, and yachtsman; twice led winning teams in the America's Cup race, in 1962 and 1968. He chaired the first Operation Sail in 1976 and helped organize two later events, in 1986 and 1992; these events brought a huge display of tall ships to New York Harbor to mark, respectively, the U.S. bicentennial, the centennial of the Statue of Liberty, and the 500th anniversary of Columbus' first voyage to the Americas: d. Greenwich, CT, Aug. 13.

Moss, John E. (84), member of the U.S. House of Representatives (D-CA, 1953–78); his fight against government secrecy led to the 1966 Freedom of Information Act: d. San Francisco, CA, Dec. 5.

Mullins, Rich (42), contemporary Christian musician; among his hits was "Our God Is an Awesome God": d. Lostant, IL, Sept. 19.

Najdorf, Miguel (born Moishe Najdorf) (87), Polish-born Argentinian chess grand master; won 52 international tournaments and took the Argentine national championship eight times: d. Málaga, Spain, July 4.

Notorious B.I.G. *See* Wallace, Christopher.

Nyro, Laura (born Laura Nigro) (49), singer and songwriter; wrote several ballads that became hits for the 1960s groups that recorded them. Among her songs were "Wedding Bell Blues," "Eli's Coming," and "And When I Die." She also made several albums of her own: d. Danbury, CT, April 8.

Okudzhava, Bulat S. (73), Russian poet and dissident during the communist era; his work helped establish the dissident literary community in the USSR in the 1950s. Although expelled from the Communist Party in 1972, he was never imprisoned. After the fall of the USSR, he continued to criticize Russia's policies. He won the Russian Booker Prize in 1994: d. Paris, France, June 12.

Parker, Tom (born Andreas Cornelius van Kuijk) (87), manager, known as "the Colonel," who "discovered" Elvis Presley and handled his career from 1955 until Presley's death in 1977: d. Las Vegas, NV, Jan. 21.

Parks, Lillian (100), writer of a best-selling book about life in the White House; *My Thirty Years Backstairs at the White House* (1961), written with Frances Spatz Leighton, was made into a miniseries in 1979: d. Washington, DC, Nov. 6.

Pastrana Borrero, Misael (73), president of Colombia (1970–74); the last president to be a member of the National Front coalition. Following his election, a guerrilla group was established that claimed the Front had stolen the election and that launched armed attacks on the government for the next 20 years: d. Bogotá, Colombia, Aug. 21.

Pastrano, Willie (62), boxing champion; held the light-heavyweight title (1963–65). He retired with a record of 63–13–8: d. New Orleans, LA, Dec. 6.

Paulsen, Pat (69), comedian and perennial U.S. presidential candidate; won an Emmy in 1968 for his appearances on *The Smothers Brothers Comedy Hour*. He appeared in several films: d. Tijuana, Mexico, April 25.

Payton, Lawrence (59), singer; a member of the Four Tops, a Motown vocal group that had many top-ten hits between 1964 and 1974. The group was inducted into the Rock and Roll Hall of Fame in 1990: d. Southfield, MI, June 20.

Peabody, Endicott (77), Democratic governor of Massachusetts (1963–65): d. Hollis, NH, Dec. 2.

Peng Zhen (95), Chinese hard-line political leader; one of the "eight immortals" of the Chinese Communist revolution. He served as Beijing's mayor (1951–66) and as chairman of the Congress (1981–88). A participant in the 1950s purges, he was brought down in 1966 by the Cultural Revolution. He was rehabilitated in 1978 and helped establish a new authoritarian legal framework. He strongly opposed Western influence and supported the imposition of martial law following the 1989 Tiananmen Square demonstrations: d. Beijing, China, April 26.

Picard, Henry (90), championship golfer; won 26 pro tournaments during the 1930s. He was a member of the Golf Hall of Fame: d. Charleston, SC, April 30.

Poletti, Cardinal Ugo (82), Italian Roman Catholic cardinal; as vicar general of Rome in the 1980s, he served as the pope's personal representative in that city: d. Rome, Italy, Feb. 24.

Porter, Keith R. (84), biologist; took the first pictures of tissue cells, using an electron microscope. He received the Horwitz Prize in 1970 and the National Medal of Science in 1977: d. Bryn Mawr, PA, May 2.

Pritchett, V(ictor) S(awdon) (96), English author; known for his masterful short stories about the daily lives of ordinary people. His literary criticisms and biographies also were admired. He was knighted in 1975: d. London, England, March 20.

Purcell, Edward M. (84), physicist; shared the 1952 Nobel Prize in physics for his discovery of a way to detect weak magnetism in the atomic nucleus. With an assistant, he succeeded in detecting radio emissions from hydrogen clouds in space. He was awarded the National Medal of Science in 1979: d. Cambridge, MA, March 7.

Rey, Luise King (83), big-band singer; part of a popular 1940s act known as the King Sisters. The group had a weekly TV program, *The King Family*, which ran in 1965 and was revived briefly in 1969: d. Sandy, UT, Aug. 4.

Reynolds, William (87), film editor; worked on some 70 films. He won two Academy Awards, for his work on *The Sound of Music* (1966) and *The Sting* (1973): d. South Pasadena, CA, July 16.

Richey, Charles R. (73), U.S. district judge; appointed to the federal bench by President Richard Nixon in 1971. He ruled on several Watergate-related cases, and not all of his decisions were favorable to the White House, although White House counsel John Dean testified before Congress that Richey had agreed secretly to help Nixon—a charge Richey strongly denied. In 1974 he blocked an effort by Nixon to claim ownership of audiotapes made in the White House while he was president: d. Chevy Chase, MD, March 19.

Robbins, Harold (81), best-selling author; among his best-known books were *The Carpetbaggers* (1961) and *The Betsy* (1971): d. Palm Springs, CA, Oct. 14.

Roberts, Louise (85), modern-dance producer; directed the Clark Center for the Performing Arts in New York City (1970–86). She won a Capezio Award in 1991: d. New York City, Jan. 17.

Rodríguez Pedotti, Carlos Andrés (72), Paraguayan political leader and military general; in 1989, led a military coup overthrowing dictator Gen. Alfredo Stroessner. He ruled democratically until 1993: d. New York City, April 21.

Rogers, Ralph Burton (87), founder of the Public Broadcasting Service (PBS) in 1972: d. Dallas, TX, Nov. 4.

Rosario, Edwin (34), boxing champion; held the World Boxing Council (WBC) lightweight title (1983–86) and the World Boxing Association (WBA) lightweight title (1986–90): d. Toa Baja, Puerto Rico, Dec. 1.

Rose, Margo (born Margaret Skewis) (94), puppeteer; with her husband, designed the "star" of the *Howdy Doody* children's television show (1947–60). The couple won a Peabody Award for their children's series *The Blue Ferry* (1957, 1958): d. New London, CT, Sept. 13.

Rossi, Aldo (66), Italian architect; his works were known for their monumental feel, yet also were noted for their simplicity. He received the 1990 Pritzker Prize: d. Milan, Italy, Sept. 4.

Royko, Mike (64), journalist; famed for his long-running column in Chicago newspapers. The widely syndicated column won a Pulitzer Prize in 1972. His prickly commentary was controversial and admired. He also wrote the best-seller *Boss: Richard J. Daley of Chicago* (1971): d. Chicago, IL, April 29.

Rudolph, Paul (78), architect; a modernist, he chaired Yale University's School of Architecture (1957–65) and in 1963 designed the university's controversial Art and Architecture building: d. New York City, Aug. 8.

Rugambwa, Laurean (85), Roman Catholic cardinal; in 1960, became the first African cardinal. Known for his work with the

Second Vatican Council and advocation of internationalism and ecumenism: d. Rome, Italy, Dec. 8.

Sager, Ruth (79), geneticist; discovered that genetic information is located throughout each cell rather than being enclosed in the nucleus. She received the Gilbert Morgan Smith Medal from the National Academy of Sciences: d. Brookline, MA, March 29.

Betty Shabazz

Sánchez Vilella, Roberto (84), governor of Puerto Rico (1964–68); campaigned for increased Puerto Rican autonomy and encouraged industrial development. In 1967 he ruined his career by announcing that he was divorcing his wife to marry his assistant: d. San Juan, Puerto Rico, March 25.

Sarnoff, Robert W. (78), television executive; while he was president of NBC (1956–65), the network aired the first televised presidential debate and hired the first black star of a prime-time series (Bill Cosby in *I Spy*): d. New York City, Feb. 22.

Saudek, Robert (85), television executive; created the "Omnibus" series of cultural programming (1952–61). He was the founding president of the Museum of Broadcasting in 1974. He won 11 Emmy Awards and seven Peabody Awards: d. Baltimore, MD, March 13.

Saw Maung (68), Myanmar military general; led the nation after heading a 1988 coup. During his tenure, the country at first moved toward democracy, but then the government forcibly rejected it. He resigned in 1992: d. Yangon (Rangoon), Myanmar, July 24.

Schaefer, George L. (76), television director and producer; received four Directors Guild Awards, as well as several Emmys. He earlier had several successful Broadway productions, most notably *The Teahouse of the August Moon* (1953), which won a Pulitzer Prize and a Tony Award: d. Los Angeles, CA, Sept. 10.

Scott, William L. (81), member of the U.S. House of Representatives (R-VA, 1967–73) and U.S. senator (1973–79); was the first Republican from Virginia to win a Senate seat since Reconstruction: d. Fairfax, VA, Feb. 14.

Sengstacke, John H. (84), publisher and civil-rights advocate; owned the *Chicago Daily Defender* as well as weekly papers in Detroit, Pittsburgh, and Memphis. He was influential behind the scenes in national and Chicago politics. He worked to found the Negro Newspaper Association, now known as the National Newspaper Publishers' Association: d. Chicago, IL, May 28.

Shabazz, Betty (61), civil-rights activist and widow of black activist Malcolm X; following her husband's assassination in 1965, she carried on his message, becoming important in her own right in the U.S. civil-rights movement: d. New York City, June 23.

Shanker, Albert (68), educator; leader since 1974 of the second-largest U.S. teachers' union, the American Federation of Teachers. He endorsed the concept of charter schools and stressed the need for high standards. He also served as vice-president of the AFL-CIO since 1973: d. New York City, Feb. 22.

Sheinwold, Alfred (85), English-born bridge expert; wrote 13 best-selling books on the subject. He was inducted into the Bridge Hall of Fame in 1996: d. Sherman Oaks, CA, March 8.

© Julia Jones/Sygma

© Bruce Hoertel/Gamma-Liaison

Albert Shanker

© AP/Wide World Photos

Red Skelton

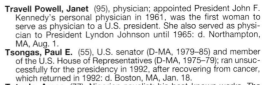

Shelton, Reid (72), actor and singer; created the role of Daddy Warbucks in the original Broadway production of *Annie* (1976).He appeared in other Broadway productions and on television, most notably in the HBO series *First and Ten*: d. Portland, OR, June 8.

Shoemaker, Eugene (69), planetary geologist who, with his wife, Carolyn, held the world record for discovering the largest number of comets—32. The two also discovered 1,125 asteroids. They discovered Comet Shoemaker-Levy, which in 1994 crashed spectacularly into Jupiter: d. Alice Springs, Australia, July 18.

Skelton, Red (Richard Bernard) (84), comedian and actor; noted for his routines incorporating slapstick and clowning, and for his comic personas. He hosted his own radio program in the 1940s and his own TV show, *The Red Skelton Show* (1950–70). He also appeared in more than 40 films. He was inducted into the Academy of Television Arts and Sciences' Hall of Fame in 1989: d. Rancho Mirage, CA, Sept. 17.

Smith, Frank E. (79), member of the U.S. House of Representatives (D-MS, 1951–63); voiced only muted opposition to civil-rights legislation but strongly supported the cotton industry. His staunch support of President John F. Kennedy finally led to his defeat: d. Jackson, MS, Aug. 2.

Smith, Mary L. (82), chairman of the Republican National Committee (1974–77); the first woman to serve in that post. She supported civil rights and abortion rights. Chosen by President Gerald Ford, she led the party after the damaging Watergate scandal. In 1981 she was named as vice-chair of the U.S. Civil Rights Commission by President Ronald Reagan: d. Des Moines, IA, Aug. 22.

Solti, Sir Georg (born Gyorgy Stern) (84), Hungarian-born musical conductor; served as conductor of the Chicago Symphony Orchestra (1969–91), music director of London's Royal Opera House (1961–71), chief conductor of the Orchèstre de Paris (1970–75), and principal conductor of the London Philharmonic (1979–83). He released some 250 albums and won more than 30 Grammy Awards, and was made a knight commander of the British Empire in 1972: d. Antibes, France, Sept. 5.

Spong, William B. (77), U.S. senator (D-VA, 1967–73): d. Portsmouth, VA, Oct. 8.

Stackpole, Peter (83), photographer; recorded the invasion of Saipan during World War II and the building of the Golden Gate Bridge and San Francisco–Oakland Bay Bridge. He won a George Polk Memorial Award in 1954: d. Novato, CA, May 11.

Starbuck, James (85), ballet dancer and choreographer; a principal dancer with the San Francisco Opera Ballet (1935–38) and the Ballet Russe de Monte Carlo (1938–44). He won several Emmy awards and choreographed the 1954 Broadway hit *Fanny*: d. Beverly Hills, CA, Aug. 13.

Steel, Dawn (51), film producer and executive; as president of production at Paramount in the early 1980s, she oversaw the development of hit films such as *Flashdance*, *Top Gun*, and *Fatal Attraction*. In 1987 she became the first woman to head a major Hollywood film studio, leading Columbia Studios until 1991: d. Los Angeles, CA, Dec. 20.

Stone, Jon (65), television writer, producer, and director; helped create the children's show *Sesame Street* in 1969. He served as director and executive producer for many years. He won 18 Emmy Awards, as well as an award from the Writer's Guild of America: d. New York City, March 30.

Tariki, Abdullah Ibn Hamoud al- (80), Saudi Arabian oil minister; the nation's first oil minister (1960–62), he was a founder of the Organization of Petroleum Exporting Countries (OPEC) in 1960: d. Cairo, Egypt, Sept. 7.

Tartikoff, Brandon (48), television-industry executive; as president of NBC's entertainment division (1980–91), he was the youngest person ever to head a TV network. He helped revive NBC's ratings and was instrumental in the development of some of the network's biggest hits. NBC topped the ratings for six consecutive seasons under his tenure: d. Los Angeles, CA, Aug. 27.

Tejeda, Frank (51), member of the U.S. House of Representatives (D-TX) since 1993; known for his defense of veterans and current armed-forces personnel and attempts to salvage his state's military installations: d. San Antonio, TX, Jan. 30.

Tikhonov, Nikolai A. (92), prime minister of the Soviet Union (1980–85); an apparent opponent of economic reform, he resigned shortly after Mikhail Gorbachev became the Communist Party's general secretary: d. Moscow, Russia, June 1.

Todd, Lord (born Alexander Robertus Todd) (89), Scottish biochemist; won the 1957 Nobel Prize in chemistry for his research on the makeup of genes. He focused on the elements that constitute DNA. He received a knighthood in 1954 and was made a life peer in 1962: d. Cambridge, England, Jan. 10.

Tombaugh, Clyde W. (90), astronomer; best known for discovering the planet Pluto in 1930: d. Las Cruces, NM, Jan. 17.

Tonypandy, Viscount (born Thomas George Thomas) (88), Welsh-born British government figure; served as speaker of the House of Commons (1976–83). He was named to the House of Lords—and thus given his title—in 1983: d. Cardiff, Wales, Sept. 22.

Tracy, Arthur (born Abba Tracovutsky) (98), Moldavian-born U.S. radio star of the 1930s and 1940s; known as the "Street Singer." A 1937 recording he made of "Pennies from Heaven" was used in the 1980s film of the same name, garnering him a new round of fame: d. New York City, Oct. 5.

Travell Powell, Janet (95), physician; appointed President John F. Kennedy's personal physician in 1961, was the first woman to serve as physician to a U.S. president. She also served as physician to President Lyndon Johnson until 1965: d. Northampton, MA, Aug. 1.

Tsongas, Paul E. (55), U.S. senator (D-MA, 1979–85) and member of the U.S. House of Representatives (D-MA, 1975–79); ran unsuccessfully for the presidency in 1992, after recovering from cancer, which returned in 1992: d. Boston, MA, Jan. 18.

Tutuola, Amos (77), Nigerian novelist; his best-known works, *The Palm-Wine Drinkard* (1952) and *My Life in the Bush of Ghosts* (1954), were adapted into plays: d. Ibadan, Nigeria, June 8.

Tyrwhitt, Brigadier Dame Mary Joan Caroline (93), founder of Britain's Women's Royal Army Corps (WRAC) in 1949. She was appointed an officer of the Order of the British Empire in 1946 and was made Dame Commander of the Order of the British Empire in 1949: d. England, Feb. 13.

Vander Meer, John S. (82), professional-baseball player (1937–43; 1946–51); was the only pitcher ever to throw consecutive no-hitters, in 1938 for the Cincinnati Reds: d. Tampa, FL, Oct. 6.

Van Zandt, Townes (52), country-music singer and songwriter; wrote "If I Needed You" and "Pancho and Lefty." The latter was made into a hit by Willie Nelson and Merle Haggard: d. Smyrna, TX, Jan. 1.

Vasarely, Victor (born Gyozo Vasarhelyi) (88), Hungarian-born artist; leader of the 1960s Op Art movement. He won a Guggenheim Prize in 1964: d. Paris, France, March 15.

Versace, Gianni (50), *see* SIDEBAR, page 241.

Wald, George (90), biologist; shared the 1967 Nobel Prize in Medicine or Physiology for his research on how the eye processes images: d. Cambridge, MA, April 12.

Wallace, Christopher (24), rap-music performer known as Biggie Smalls and Notorious B.I.G.; built his persona on his past as a drug dealer: d. Los Angeles, CA, March 9.

Wardenburg, Frederic A.C. 3d (92), executive and World War II hero; interrupted his career to work on a secret mission in Europe to discover how far along the Germans were in creating an atomic bomb. He was made an honorary member of the Order of the British Empire and was presented with the U.S. Medal of Freedom: d. Scottsdale, AZ, Aug. 10.

Wayne, Chuck (born Charles Jagelka) (74), jazz guitarist; helped pioneer the bebop style in the 1940s. He recorded with Dizzy Gillespie and Sarah Vaughan, and served as musical director for pop singer Tony Bennett (1954–57): d. Jackson, NJ, July 29.

Weaver, Robert (89), U.S. civil-rights activist; in 1966, was appointed as secretary of the newly formed Department of Housing and Urban Development—becoming the first African-American to serve as a cabinet member: d. New York City, July 17.

Werner, Charles (88), editorial cartoonist; was the youngest in his field ever to win a Pulitzer Prize. He won in 1938, when he was 29, for a cartoon inspired by the Munich Agreement between Britain and Germany: d. Indianapolis, IN, July 1.

Westwood, Jean (73), chairman of the Democratic Party (1972); the first woman to head a major U.S. political party. During her brief tenure, she suffered criticism for her role in the unsuccessful presidential campaign of George McGovern: d. American Fork, UT, Aug. 18.

Williams, Stanley (72), English-born teacher of male ballet dancers; taught at the Royal Danish ballet school and the School of American Ballet. He was knighted by Denmark in 1961 and won the Dance Magazine Award in 1981: d. New York City, Oct. 21.

Wohlstetter, Albert (83), adviser to U.S. presidents; advocated that there always should be alternatives to nuclear attack. He was awarded the Presidential Medal of Freedom in 1985: d. Los Angeles, CA, Jan. 9.

Wolfert, Ira (89), journalist and novelist; won a 1943 Pulitzer Prize for his articles about a sea battle near Guadalcanal in 1942: d. Margaretville, NY, Nov. 24.

Wu, Chien-Shiung (84), Chinese-born physicist; her groundbreaking experiment overthrew a fundamental law of physics known as the principle of conservation of parity. She won the 1957 Nobel Prize in physics, and was awarded the National Medal of Science and the Wolf Prize in physics: d. New York City, Feb. 16.

Wyeth, Henriette (89), artist; a daughter of the artist N.C. Wyeth and sister of painter Andrew Wyeth, she was a child prodigy especially noted for her portraits: d. Roswell, NM, April 3.

Yepes, Narciso (69), Spanish classical guitarist and musical composer; internationally praised for his interpretation and technique: d. Murcia, Spain, May 3.

Young, Coleman A. (79), Democratic mayor of Detroit (1974–93); the city's first African-American mayor, he worked to revitalize the city and to keep its financial problems from becoming insurmountable. He also was somewhat successful in decreasing tensions between black residents and police: d. Detroit, MI, Nov. 29.

Zale, Tony (born Anthony Florian Zaleski) (83), professional boxer; twice held the world middleweight championship (1940–47; 1948). He was elected to the Boxing Hall of Fame in 1958: d. Portage, IN, March 20.

Zinnemann, Fred (89), Austrian-born U.S. film director; won Academy Awards for direction for *From Here to Eternity* (1953) and *A Man for All Seasons* (1966), and was awarded France's Order of Arts and Letters in 1982: d. London, England, March 14.

© Gary Pyne/Gamma-Liaison

Paul Tsongas

OCEANOGRAPHY

The year 1997 was an important one for oceanography. Some new scientific hypotheses were proposed, an El Niño was developing, and two new research ships were added to the U.S. oceanographic fleet.

Research Results. In 1986 physicist Louis Frank suggested that so-called "small icy comets" were hitting the Earth and contributing an unanticipated supply of water to the atmosphere and ultimately to the ocean. He proposed that this process may have supplied several oceans' amount of water over geological time. At the time, Frank's hypothesis was challenged by many scientists and was unaccepted by most. Frank, however, developed imaging equipment that was used by the National Aeronautics and Space Administration (NASA) on its 1996 Polar satellite. The images obtained showed clear evidence of what may be icy comets—large snowballs may be a good analogy—reaching the Earth's atmosphere. It seemed that these "small comets" might be bringing water to Earth. In 1997, however, measurements of the ratio of isotopes in water molecules in the spectacular Hale-Bopp and several other comets showed a considerable difference when compared to those ratios in ocean water. Thus while the data was not yet supportive of Frank's original idea, his hypothesis was being considered again.

The small-scale turbulent mixing of deep ocean water always has been difficult to determine, but a series of measurements by scientists from the Woods Hole Oceanographic Institution has shown how such mixing is affected by bottom topography. For example, mixing over the smooth seafloor abyssal plains was found to be relatively slow compared to mixing over the rough and irregular topography of the Mid-Atlantic Ridge. This indicates that such mixing is influenced by the underlying bathymetry.

The interactions between the ocean and the atmosphere are beginning to be understood, but clearly the ocean has a considerable impact on the weather and climate of Earth. This is shown by the pattern of hurricanes. The initial hurricane forecasts for 1997 were for above-average activity. By late summer, however, the global weather picture seemed to be complicated by a series of satellite measurements showing that an El Niño condition was beginning. An El Niño—the expression is derived from the Spanish term for the Christ child—usually results when warm waters reach the west coast of South America around Christmastime. (The 1997 one was early.) An El Niño usually causes severe weather conditions, such as drought and heavy rains, in many areas of the world. Among the many effects of an El Niño can be a decline in hurricane activity along the southeastern coast of the United States; thus, forecasters downgraded their hurricane forecast for 1997. (*See also* METEOROLOGY.)

Research by scientists from Florida State University resulted in the discovery of a phenomenon called El Viejo—Spanish for "old man." An El Viejo is essentially the reverse of an El Niño phenomenon and occurs when colder than normal water is off western South America, rather than the warm water of an El Niño. The researchers noted that tornado activity can be several times higher in central parts of the United States following an El Viejo period.

New Oceanographic Ships. Two new vessels were added to the U.S. research fleet. Research Vessel (RV) *Atlantis* is based at the Woods Hole Oceanographic Institution in Woods Hole, MA. It is one of the most sophisticated research vessels afloat and will carry the submersible *Alvin* as well as the remotely controlled vehicles (ROVs) *JASON/Medea*—which was used in the exploration of the *Titanic*—and the new *Autonomous Benthic Explorer (ABE)*, an autonomous underwater vehicle (AUV). AUVs, usually less than 10 ft (3 m) long, can carry various acoustic, chemical, and physical sensors to make measurements in the deeper waters of the ocean. These vehicles have the capability to reach about 98% of the ocean's seafloor. They operate independently of the surface ship and can work in dangerous environments such as under the polar ice sheets or in marine caves. *Atlantis* is 274 ft (84 m) long and carries a complement of 23 officers and crew, 23 scientists, and 13 deep-submergence pilots and technicians.

The second new vessel, the RV *Ronald H. Brown*, belongs to the National Oceanic and Atmospheric Administration (NOAA) and was named after the late secretary of commerce. (NOAA is a division of the Department of Commerce.) The *Brown* is equipped to make sophisticated measurements both in the ocean and in the atmosphere, and it will be involved in various global-change research programs. *Atlantis* and the *Brown* are sister ships to the RV *Roger Revelle*, which was delivered to the Scripps Institution of Oceanography in 1996.

DAVID A. ROSS
Woods Hole Oceanographic Institution

PAKISTAN

Pakistan marked two milestones in 1997—the 50th anniversary of the country's creation and the fourth general elections in less than a decade. The new government faced major challenges.

Political Affairs. The February 3 national elections, occasioned by President Farooq Leghari's dismissal of former Prime Minister Benazir Bhutto three months earlier, returned to power Nawaz Sharif, who had served as prime minister from 1990 to 1993. His party, the Pakistan Muslim League, secured about two thirds of the 204 contested seats in the 217-seat National Assembly, while Bhutto's Pakistan People's Party was reduced to less than 10%. The fundamentalist Jamaati Islami boycotted the elections. Tehreeq-e-Insaaf, the fledgling party of former cricket star Imran Khan, failed to capture a seat. Although observers pronounced the elections free and fair, electoral turnout was only about 25%.

Nawaz Sharif's strong parliamentary majority enabled him to move quickly to strengthen the prime minister's position vis-à-vis the president and the military. By repealing the 8th Amendment to the Constitution, which had been imposed in 1985 by Gen. Zia ul-Haq, Sharif mitigated the power of the president to dismiss elected governments. He also acquired the power to appoint service chiefs. He eliminated the council of defense and national security, which President Leghari had created in January to give the military a direct advisory role in government.

Sharif had supported Chief Justice Sajjad Ali Shah in a 1996 confrontation with Bhutto over the right of the Supreme Court to appoint judges without political interference. However, he and Shah clashed in 1997 over several issues, including judicial appointments and a parliamentary attempt to reduce the size of the court. In early December a panel of ten judges removed the chief justice from office and named a successor. In turn, Leghari charged the prime minister with responsibility for the political crisis and resigned. At month's end, Mohammad Rafiq Tarar, a Sharif ally, was chosen president by the electoral college.

Earlier the prime minister instituted accountability procedures to highlight the misdeeds of his predecessor. Benazir Bhutto's husband, Asif Ali Zardari, was indicted in July, along with 18 associates, for conspiring in the 1996 murder of Mir Murtaza Bhutto, her brother and political rival. The Swiss government agreed to freeze $13.7 million in Bhutto-

© K. M. Choudary/AP/Wide World Photos

As Pakistan celebrated its 50th anniversary as a nation in August 1997, portraits of Mohammed Ali Jinnah—the nation's founder—and his sister, Fatima, were displayed throughout the country, above, and Britain's Queen Elizabeth II presented Prime Minister Nawaz Sharif with the Knight Grand Cross of St. Michael and St. George, below.

© B. K. Bangash/AP/Wide World Photos

family assets in Swiss banks, pending court findings over whether the wealth had resulted from corrupt practices. The anticorruption drive also empowered Sharif, with the approval of President Leghari and army chief Gen. Jehangir Karamat, to fire navy chief Admiral Mansur ul-Haq amid corruption charges. As the year ended, Zardari was taken

395

PAKISTAN • Information Highlights

Official Name: Islamic Republic of Pakistan.
Location: South Asia.
Area: 310,402 sq mi (803 940 km²).
Population (mid-1997 est.): 137,800,000.
Chief Cities (1981 census): Islamabad, the capital, 204,364; Karachi, 5,180,562.
Government: *Head of state,* Mohammad Rafiq Tarar, president (took office Jan. 1, 1998). *Head of government,* Nawaz Sharif, prime minister (took office February 1997). *Legislature*—Parliament: Senate and National Assembly.
Monetary Unit: Rupee (43.56 rupees equal U.S.$1, Dec. 31, 1997).
Gross Domestic Product (1995 est. U.S.$): $274,200,000,-000 (purchasing power parity).
Economic Index (1996, 1992 = 100): *Consumer Prices,* all items, 153.2; food, 157.8.
Foreign Trade (1996 U.S.$): *Imports,* $12,131,000,000; *exports,* $9,321,000,000.

from a Karachi jail and flown to Islamabad so that he could take the oath as a senator. He had been elected to the Senate in March.

Political violence increased not only in Karachi, where it had been endemic for several years, but also in Punjab, Pakistan's largest province. Most of the politically motivated murders in Karachi related to warfare between factions of the Muhajir Qaumi Movement (MQM). The death toll had passed 250 by midyear. The larger faction of the MQM changed its name in 1997 to Muttahida (United) Qaumi Movement to represent an intended broadening of its political base beyond the Muhajir (refugee) community.

In Punjab more than 150 people died during the first nine months of the year in sectarian conflict between militant Sunni and Shia groups. Mosques, buses, and public places were bombed; crowds at religious gatherings were sprayed with machine-gun fire; and prominent religious leaders were assassinated. Sharif countered this growing anarchy with the passage, in August, of an Anti-Terrorism Act that gave law-enforcement officials extraordinary authority. Curtailing the rights of the accused and giving police the right to shoot to kill on mere suspicion of violent crime raised protest from opposition parties and the press.

Economy. The new government inherited a sluggish economy, double-digit inflation, and a massive debt crisis. In February the country had only $770 million in foreign-exchange reserves—not even enough to pay three months of interest on the $30 billion in foreign debt. On March 28, Finance Minister Sartaj Aziz announced a package of economic reforms. Key features included cuts in personal-income taxes, import tariffs, and the general sales tax, and a promise to broaden the tax base. Only 800,000 Pakistanis pay income tax, out of a total population of approximately 135 million. The tax-cut package was received

positively by business and, significantly, by the International Monetary Fund, despite the possibility that lost revenues might result in even greater budget deficits than the more than 6% in the previous year. The IMF had pressured Pakistan to reduce deficits to 4%.

On June 13, Aziz announced the annual budget, which incorporated the reform package, combined with deep cuts in social spending. Overall spending was projected to increase by 10%, less than the current inflation rate of 13%. The budget projected 7% growth in industrial output, 5% in agriculture, 15% in exports, and 6% in gross domestic product (GDP). Achievement of these projections would be a real accomplishment, given the dismal performance of the previous year, when agricultural output grew by less than 1% and total manufacturing by less than 2%. By midyear, however, there were some positive signs: Exports and foreign-exchange holdings were up and bank borrowing was down. In July the IMF agreed to grant Pakistan a three-year Extended Structural Adjustment Facility (ESAF) loan of $1.6 billion.

Foreign Relations. As India and Pakistan jointly celebrated their half century of independence, the two nations appeared to be moving to improve relations. On March 29 talks between their foreign secretaries resumed after a hiatus of three years. Sharif and India's new Prime Minister I. K. Gujral met in the Maldives in May. Talks then continued in Islamabad at the foreign-secretary level in June. Eight separate commissions were established to deal with Kashmir and other issues. Both sides claimed tactical victories: Pakistan for getting India to agree to discuss an issue it previously had claimed to be an internal matter; India for Pakistan's willingness to discuss other issues at the same time. Confidence-building measures, including the release of about 400 people who had been detained in both countries for minor infractions, also were taken.

Relations with Afghanistan worsened in 1997. Pakistan had been a supporter of the Taliban militia, which spread its control over most of the country early in the year but then lost ground to an alliance of forces supported by Iran and Russia. Pakistan's attempts to encourage negotiations between Taliban and its opponents were unsuccessful. As Taliban became more distrustful of Pakistan's continued support, Pakistan became more aware of potential threats Taliban might present.

The United States welcomed and encouraged Sharif's economic reforms. Pakistan cooperated with U.S. agencies in capturing and returning to U.S. custody Mir Amal Kansi, accused of shooting two officials of the U.S. Central Intelligence Agency (CIA) in Virginia in 1993. These clandestine actions, without benefit of extradition proceedings, drew heavy criticism in Pakistan, especially in Quetta, where Kansi's family is prominent. Shortly after Kansi's conviction in November, four U.S. oil-firm employees and their Pakistani driver were gunned down in Karachi in apparent retaliation. Although U.S. residents in Pakistan were warned to take special precautions, U.S. Secretary of State Madeleine Albright visited Pakistan later in November.

WILLIAM L. RICHTER, *Kansas State University*

PARAGUAY • Information Highlights
Official Name: Republic of Paraguay.
Location: Central South America.
Area: 157,046 sq mi (406 750 km²).
Population (mid-1997 est.): 5,100,000.
Chief Cities (1992 census): Asunción, the capital, 502,426; Ciudad del Este, 133,896; San Lorenzo, 133,311.
Government: *Head of state and government,* Juan Carlos Wasmosy, president (sworn in Aug. 15, 1993). *Legislature*—Congress: Chamber of Senators and Chamber of Deputies.
Monetary Unit: Guaraní (2,190.0 guaraníes equal U.S.$1, market rate, July 1997).
Gross Domestic Product (1995 est. U.S.$): $17,000,000,-000 (purchasing power parity).
Economic Index (1995, 1992 = 100): *Consumer Prices,* all items, 164.2; food, 173.0.
Foreign Trade (1995 U.S.$): *Imports,* $3,144,000,000; *exports,* $919,000,000.

PARAGUAY

Paraguay prepared for 1998 presidential elections in 1997. Economic conditions improved but banking scandals proliferated.

Politics. By August the Authentic Radical Liberals had agreed with the National Encounter Party (PEN) on a ticket for the May 1998 elections. It would be headed by perennial presidential candidate Domingo Laíno, with Carlos Filizzola, a former mayor of Asunción, for the vice-presidency. In a September 7 party primary the Colorado Party chose retired Gen. Lino Oviedo and Raúl Alberto Cubas Grau as its 1998 standard-bearers, over factions headed by party stalwart Luis María Argaña and Carlos Facetti, the choice of President Juan Carlos Wasmosy.

After his primary victory, Oviedo traveled to Brazil and Argentina, where he accused Wasmosy of corruption and thievery, prompting the latter to order his arrest for being disrespectful of the president. A Paraguayan judge dismissed the case, ruling Oviedo no longer was subject to military regulations. Both Oviedo and Laíno were rejected in October as viable candidates by worker and peasant organizations.

Economy. An economic-growth rate of above 4% was forecast for Paraguay for 1997, with an inflation rate of 8.5%. In July the government approved the sale of its steel plant to a consortium of employees and suppliers for $35 million. Meanwhile an agreement on construction of a free zone and a $300 million cellulose plant on the Paraná River was signed in April. Its main foreign stockholders were from Canada, Austria, and the United States. The European Union announced a plan in February for studying the improvement of three Paraguayan ports on the Paraná-Paraguay Waterway. Paraguay arranged in April for the purchase of three European-type barges to transport liquefied petroleum gas on its rivers.

Union Bank—among the country's largest banks, with 1 million customers—was one of three banks that closed in June. It suddenly became insolvent, in spite of a $340 million bailout attempt by the government. Tito Scavone, its owner, was among six bankers arrested in July. Scavone told investigators that the bank's failure was caused by Public Works Minister Gustavo Pedrozo and a congressman from the ruling Colorados. Party factions demanded changes in the cabinet and also called for the resignation of President Wasmosy. The latter defended his economic team.

Ten banks and 25 currency-exchange houses were being investigated in March for their role in laundering about $900 million from the sale of fraudulent Brazilian bonds. Earlier a Paraguayan brokerage was taken over by the government for participating in the same bond scandal. Its exchange house at Ciudad del Este on the Brazilian border was used to launder $126 million from bond sales.

Foreign Relations. On June 19 in Asunción, President Wasmosy hosted the heads of state from Argentina, Brazil, and Uruguay—Paraguay's partners in Mercosur, a regional-integration pact. The presidents of Bolivia and Chile attended as observers. Widespread opposition to Brazil's financial restraints on trade with its partners dominated the event. Argentina's President Carlos Saúl Menem signed five bilateral agreements with Paraguay, embracing navigation on the Paraná and Paraguay rivers, a strengthened operation of the binational Yacyretá hydroelectric dam, and stricter border controls.

The South American Group of Río held a summit in Asunción on August 24 over rifts among its member states.

LARRY L. PIPPIN, *University of the Pacific*

People, Places, and Things

The following four pages recount the stories behind a selection of people, places, and things that may not have made the headlines in 1997 but that drew attention and created interest.

On May 2, 1997, the $48 million Franklin Delano Roosevelt Memorial, above, designed by Lawrence Halprin, was dedicated on the Mall in Washington, DC. In mid-January seven men who were denied Medals of Honor for World War II service because they were black were given the award. Joseph Vernon Black, below and inset, *the only one of the veterans still living, accepted his medal from President Bill Clinton. In June the president and First Lady Hillary Rodham Clinton watched proudly as their daughter, Chelsea, was graduated from Sidwell Friends School.*

© Sygma

After bailing out of a bullet-torn torpedo bomber over the Pacific Ocean during World War II, Lt. (j.g.) George Bush vowed that someday he would skydive for fun. Accordingly, in March the 72-year-old former president, *above*, jumped safely out of a plane 12,500 ft (3 810 m) above the Arizona desert. In May, Linda Finch, *right*, completed a 26,000-mi (41 843-km) round-the-world flight in a restored 1935 Lockheed two-engine plane. The Texas businesswoman was commemorating the 1937 flight of Amelia Earhart, who disappeared off Hawaii. In February, Frenchman Christophe Auguin, 38, broke the world record for nonstop solo circumnavigation of the world in a yacht. His time was 105 days, 20 hours, and 31 minutes.

© Sergey Shayevich/"Arizona Daily Star"/AP/Wide World Photos

© Bulcao-LeCorre/Gamma-Liaison

In March 1897, Pearl Bixby Wait, a carpenter who was looking to make a fortune in patent medicine, mixed fruit flavoring with gelatin. He then began selling the mixture, named "Jell-O" by his wife, door-to-door. Wait sold the Jell-O trademark for $450 in 1899. As Jell-O turned 100 in 1997, some 13 boxes of the product were sold every second in the United States. Germany's Felix Hoffmann, a Bayer chemist, synthesized a shelf-stable form of acetylsalicylic acid in 1897. The result, aspirin, was marketed in 1899 and became a best-seller. Despite the arrival of competing analgesic products in recent years, some 50 billion doses of aspirin were sold in its centennial year. In honor of its 200th birthday and after a $3^1/_2$-year restoration, the USS "Constitution"—one of the U.S. Navy's first warships, nicknamed Old Ironsides—sailed under its own power for the first time in 116 years.

© Mark Humphrey/AP/Wide World Photos

Twenty years after the death of Elvis Presley, the king of rock 'n' roll remained the subject of an extraordinary outpouring of devotion and interest. Thousands of persons flocked to Presley's Memphis, TN, home, Graceland, to visit his grave (above) and to purchase some of the Elvis-related items offered for sale. In June a replica of William Shakespeare's Globe Theater opened in London. The original Globe had been destroyed by fire in 1613. The late U.S. actor Sam Wanamaker, who moved to Britain after being blacklisted during the Joseph McCarthy era, was instrumental in the Globe's reconstruction. The new theater took four years to build and cost $13 million. It features a 20-sided polygon of green oak, plastered with ground limestone and goat's hair.

© Liz Gilbert/Sygma

© David Thomson/AP/Wide World Photos

PERU

A prolonged, high-stakes hostage crisis with a spectacular resolution made Peru the focus of worldwide attention throughout the first third of 1997. President Alberto Fujimori became increasingly intolerant of his critics, a stance that accelerated his rapid political decline later in the year.

Hostage Crisis. On Dec. 17, 1996, some 30 guerrillas from the Tupac Amaru Revolutionary Movement (MRTA), disguised as waiters, infiltrated a diplomatic reception at the residence of the Japanese ambassador in Lima. They blocked exits and brandished automatic weapons, taking hundreds of hostages, including the ambassadors of Brazil, Bolivia, Cuba, Uruguay, and Venezuela; Peruvian Foreign Minister Francisco Tudela; the chief of the Peruvian National Police; at least one Peruvian Supreme Court justice; and President Fujimori's mother, brother, and sister. MRTA leader Néstor Cerpa Cartolini—one of the captors—announced that the group would hold hostages until dozens of MRTA militants were released from prison. The guerrillas let most of the hostages go—including all the women and children—during the first week,

The popularity of Peru's President Alberto Fujimori, shown below participating in a tree-planting ceremony at the inauguration of a new school, fluctuated greatly during 1997.

© Ricardo Choy Kifox/AP/Wide World Photos

but held the 72 most influential captives for the duration. Fujimori, who owed much of his popular support to his success in combating terrorism, refused to consider releasing prisoners, despite guerrilla threats to execute hostages one by one.

MRTA was founded in 1984, as one of the most violent splinter groups of the rural communist revolutionary movements that date back to 1965. Never as large or active as the more notorious Shining Path, MRTA had concentrated on planting bombs in the metropolitan Lima-Callao region since the 1990s. Its founder, Víctor Polay, was arrested in 1992, and most other leaders and militants either surrendered or were captured the following year. Most observers considered the organization dead or dying before the embassy seizure, although the government continued to arrest its civilian supporters. One of those was Lori Helene Berenson, a U.S. citizen convicted in 1995 of raising funds for MRTA.

Archbishop Juan Luis Cipriani began to serve as a mediator in the crisis, and in January both sides agreed to recognize a commission to oversee talks. Negotiations began in February. In early March, Fujimori offered the rebels safe passage to Cuba if they would release the hostages, but MRTA rejected the plan, claiming that the government was digging a tunnel in preparation for an attack and could not be trusted. By late March it appeared that the two sides were close to agreement on a deal that would secure release of the hostages in exchange for asylum in Cuba, several million dollars in ransom, and a chance at early parole for MRTA prisoners. But in early April, Fujimori backed away from the deal, and on April 22, while the guerrillas were distracted by a soccer game, government soldiers stormed the residence from all directions, including the now-completed tunnel. Two soldiers and 14 guerrillas were killed, while all but one hostage—Supreme Court Justice Carlos Giusti Acuña, who died of a heart attack after being shot in the leg—were rescued.

Politics. The first reaction to the daring and spectacularly successful rescue was enthusiastic praise, both internationally and within Peru. The president's approval rating shot up to 67%, reversing a year and a half of slow decline. But some of the euphoria wore off quickly when it was revealed that soldiers taking part in the raid summarily had executed some of the guerrillas by shooting them in the back of the head. These executions came to be symbolic of the regime's brutal methods of dealing with its enemies. Within the next few months, Fujimori's increasingly authoritarian style of governing, coupled with unresolved economic problems, lost him his newfound popularity. Public-opinion polls showed that more and more Peruvians believed Fujimori was in league with the military and the universally hated de facto head of the National Intelligence Service, Vladimiro Montesinos. Montesinos—already a controversial figure because of alleged ties to drug traffickers—became the subject of renewed scandal in June when it was learned that he was drawing a government salary of $600,000 per year. Montesinos, referred to as "the Darth Vader of Peruvian politics" by writer and professor of Peruvian studies Carlos Iván Degregori, had claimed that he worked for a small token salary or even ad honorem. The intelligence service seemed even more sinister when former intelligence agent Leonor La Rosa Bustamante accused her employers of torturing her in retaliation for accusations of corruption and abuse. Her lawyer was suspended for "slandering" military tribunals trying her case. Another former agent, Mariella Barreto, was found dead and dismembered. Fujimori acknowledged these abuses in a press conference, but continued to back Montesinos, using the occasion to warn that "corrupt" journalists would be prosecuted by the state.

In May the pro-government majority in Congress dismissed three justices from the Constitutional Court—the same justices who, a few months earlier, had declared unconstitutional Congress' decision that Fujimori would be eligible for reelection in the year 2000. Opposition legislators later frustrated a government attempt to pack the court by increasing the number of justices from five to nine. Deputy Fernando Olivera Vega of the Independent Moralizing Front was suspended from Congress without pay for 90 days, allegedly for insulting the pro-government Congress president, Victor Joy Way.

The Fujimori administration was especially intolerant of opposition in the electronic media. One television reporter, César Hildebrandt—who attracted large audiences for his hard-hitting reports on corruption—consistently brought harassment down on any station that employed him. Hildebrandt had begun at the prominent Channel 4, but was marginalized by management in the early 1990s. When he moved to the smaller Channel 13, one of its affiliates was bombed promptly by two National Intelligence Service agents. By 1997 he was limited to the very small Channel 15. A more notorious case concerned Channel 2, "Frecuencia Latina," an influential

---

PERU • Information Highlights

Official Name: Republic of Peru.
Location: West coast of South America.
Area: 496,224 sq mi (1 285 220 km²).
Population (mid-1997 est.): 24,400,000.
Chief Cities (mid-1991 est.): Lima, the capital, 6,414,500 (metropolitan area); Arequipa, 624,500; Trujillo, 521,200.
Government: *Head of state,* Alberto Fujimori, president (took office July 28, 1990). *Head of government,* Alberto Pandolfi Arbulu, prime minister (sworn in April 3, 1996). *Legislature* (unicameral)—Congress.
Monetary Unit: New sol (2.697 new sols equal U.S.$1, official rate, Dec. 10, 1997).
Gross Domestic Product (1995 est. U.S.$): $87,000,000,-000 (purchasing power parity).
Economic Index (Lima, 1996; 1990 = 100): *Consumer Prices,* all items, 2,015.1; food, 1,663.8.
Foreign Trade (1996 U.S.$): *Imports,* $9,472,000,000; *exports,* $5,897,000,000.

---

broadcaster that always had been pro-Fujimori. In 1996, however, after the station switched to an opposition line, the government accused its largest shareholder, Baruch Ivcher, of selling arms to Ecuador, Peru's enemy in an unresolved border conflict. Ivcher was an Israeli-born, naturalized citizen of Peru, but the accusation of treason allowed the government to deprive him of Peruvian citizenship and bar him by law from being the majority owner of a television station. Control of Channel 2 passed to two minority shareholders who were supporters of Fujimori.

Fujimori tried to staunch his loss of support through a series of economic measures. In June he announced a $2.7 billion Focalized Strategy for the Struggle Against Poverty, to address criticism that unemployment was too high and wages too low. In August he decreed a 15% wage increase for public employees, free health insurance for public school students, and a low-income electricity subsidy. Economists estimated that the economy would grow 6% in 1997, with only 9% inflation.

The measures helped stop the loss of popular support for Fujimori. After his approval rating fell to 17% in late July, it rebounded to 33% in September. Among the elite, however, Fujimori grew increasingly isolated. U.S. Ambassador Dennis Jett called the dismissal of the justices "a step backward for democracy." The attempt against the Constitutional Court prompted both Foreign Minister Tudela and Constitutional Court President Ricardo Nugent to resign in protest. In July three deputies from the governing Change 90–New Majority Party alliance deserted to the opposition—an event without precedent in Fujimori's administration. An August poll asked influential Peruvians what was "the worst thing that could happen to Peru in the next three years." The majority answered, "the reelection of Fujimori." This opposition filtered down to the popular level somewhat; Fujimori consistently lost in early election polls. The front-runner was Alberto Andrade, Lima's opposition mayor, who revitalized the capital's downtown area. He branded the regime a "dictatorship."

Michael Coppedge, *University of Notre Dame*

PHILIPPINES

It was a politically and economically unsettling year for the Philippines in 1997, with the prospect of elections in May 1998 seeming to bring out the worst in national politics. President Fidel V. Ramos aggravated the process by being coy about whether or not he intended to try to stay in office beyond the single six-year term mandated by the constitution.

By attempting to amend the constitution, some Ramos supporters raised the specter of the long period of martial law and authoritarian rule under President Ferdinand Marcos (1972–86). A petition of 6 million signatures calling for a constitutional amendment to permit another term was rejected unanimously by the Supreme Court. A later move by the court to reconsider was defeated narrowly; some justices had changed their minds. There was also an attempt to turn the Congress itself into a constitutional assembly to revise the constitution. This, too, failed.

Supporters of Ramos continued to look for options, arguing that the incumbent president was indispensable to Philippine growth—an argument that had been more persuasive in 1996, when the economy was booming, the political process stable, and a peace accord with Muslim insurgents just had been signed. Those achievements, however, became tarnished in 1997, and opposition to constitutional revision soared. Ramos' predecessor, Corazon Aquino—who endorsed his 1992 candidacy—was active in the antirevision movement. Ramos—the first Protestant president—also was forced into another conflict with Cardinal Jaime Sin, the leader of the powerful Philippine Catholic Church. A political-risk report noting that political uncertainty was threatening future foreign investment made business leaders who supported Ramos more wary.

After a large antirevision rally in Manila, Ramos said he would not seek another term, but supported future efforts to amend the constitution. The issue abated somewhat, but took a toll on the president's popularity and that of his party, the Lakas-NUCD. The 69-year-old Ramos was reluctant to endorse anyone from his own party and had nothing good to say about other contenders.

Potential political alliances were tested in 1997, while parties continued to be nonideological. Foremost among Ramos' potential successors within his own party was Defense

In August 1997 thousands of Filipinos gathered in a Manila park to voice their opposition to a charter change that would have permitted President Fidel Ramos to seek reelection in 1998. Constitutionally, Filipino presidents can serve only one term.

© Romeo Ranoco/Reuters/Archive Photos

Secretary Renato de Villa, who shared the president's military background and pro-business stance. Another likely contender was Vice-President Joseph Estrada, a former actor with a populist following, but who was considered an intellectual lightweight in business and political circles. Miriam Defensor Santiago—leader of the People's Reform Party, who came in second in the 1992 election with little financing or grassroots organization—also was considered a major contender, drawing support from those disenchanted with traditional politics. Sen. Gloria Macapagal-Arroyo also had a popular following, but lacked a large party base. In June other opposition factions formed the Laban Ng Makabayang Masang Pilipino, as a united front against Ramos or his party successor. In December, Ramos surprised observers by endorsing House Speaker José de Venecia as his successor.

The forthcoming election encouraged more spending by Congress, as members jockeyed to reward constituents with tangible projects while placing on hold badly needed tax reform. Election issues were expected to include the stalled agrarian reform, the social-reform agenda languishing in Congress, and the perennial issues of crime and corruption.

A series of bombings and drive-by shootings in Manila shook confidence in the police. In an effort to appear tough on drug dealers, police cracked down on sellers; but some contended the safety of innocent bystanders was not guaranteed. A small girl was killed in the wake of one drug raid. Police collusion was blamed for the fact that kidnappings had become common; some people were kidnapped again and again. For years, wealthy Chinese were singled out for kidnapping and ransom, but in 1997 the practice spread. An average of one kidnapping a week—40 times the rate in Thailand, a nation of comparable size—led to the creation of vigilante groups.

An effort to democratize the universities, announced by the president in his state-of-the-nation address, was resisted bitterly by private-school administrators. The Magna Carta for Student Rights, which would have allowed for some student representation on school policy-making bodies, instead led to the closure of 2,000 private schools. The closures affected several million students.

Economy. The president's upbeat message of economic vigor in his July state-of-the-nation address highlighted a modest decline in unemployment—from 9.8% to 8.6%—during his administration, and significant drops in inflation, from 18.7% in 1991 to the current 4.6%. Ramos also cited a major increase in

per-capita income, from $840 to $1,250. Tourism grew more than 16% annually during the five years of Ramos' administration—the fastest percentage increase in Asia and the Pacific. The Philippines also exported 300 limousines to Japan, the result of a new joint venture with Japanese carmakers.

Other reports were less cheerful. The trade deficit was up more than 13%, and inflation was expected to increase. The results of agrarian reform, in the ninth year of its budgeted ten-year plan, had been dismal. On June 9, the anniversary of the Comprehensive Agrarian Reform Law (CARL), farmers and nongovernmental organizations (NGOs) staged an awards ceremony to mock CARL's failures.

In June the Philippines was to have "graduated" from International Monetary Fund (IMF) guidance, but a deteriorating economic situation postponed that milestone. The peso was devalued substantially, losing nearly 25% of its value against the dollar and other Western currencies. Newly Industrialized Country (NIC) status, which the president once had predicted would be achieved by the year 2000, now seemed like a mirage. Like other Southeast Asian countries, the Philippines suffered sharp drops in its stock market. Overcapacity, spiraling debt, and other regional problems seemed likely to continue.

Overseas workers' remittances had come to represent more than 5% of gross national product (GNP). But the number of these workers was declining, due to more opportunities at home and to the crackdown on illegal aliens in the region—especially in Malaysia, from which 150,000 undocumented Filipino workers may return.

A 1996 summit of NGOs and government agencies had focused on the president's social-reform agenda, including a wide range of issues from economic equity for women to

---

PHILIPPINES • Information Highlights

Official Name: Republic of the Philippines.
Location: Southeast Asia.
Area: 115,830 sq mi (300 000 km²).
Population (mid-1997 est.): 73,400,000.
Chief Cities (1995 census): Manila, the capital, 1,654,761; Quezon, 1,989,419; Caloocan, 1,023,159; Davao, 1,006,840.
Government: *Head of state and government,* Fidel V. Ramos, president (sworn in June 30, 1992). *Legislature*—Congress: Senate and House of Representatives.
Monetary Unit: Peso (35.07 pesos equal U.S. $1, floating rate, Dec. 10, 1997).
Gross Domestic Product (1995 est. U.S.$): $179,700,000,-000 (purchasing power parity).
Economic Indexes: *Consumer Prices* (1996, 1990 = 100): all items, 177.8; food, 170.4. *Industrial Production* (1995, 1990 = 100): 152.
Foreign Trade (1996 U.S.$): *Imports,* $34,122,000,000; *exports,* $20,417,000,000.

Low-lying areas in Manila and neighboring provinces of the Philippines were submerged in deep water as a result of torrential rains on the tail of a typhoon in August 1997. An earlier typhoon in May had taken the lives of 53 Filipinos.

antirape legislation to fisheries regulation. Little progress was made on the agenda in Congress in 1997, and only a few regulations were implemented by executive action.

Insurgencies. The most serious threat to political stability was renewed fighting between Muslim separatists and the military on the resource-rich island of Mindanao in the southern Philippines. In 1996 a peace accord was signed with the largest group, the Moro National Liberation Front (MNLF), but smaller, more radical groups did not sign. During 1997 the Muslim Islamic Liberation Front (MILF) and the smaller Abu Sayyaf rebels waged repeated attacks on government camps, inflicting and sustaining many casualties. The intense fighting sent thousands of refugees fleeing from central Mindanao. In February there were numerous attacks on Catholics, including the killing of Bishop Benjamin de Jesus of Jolo. Teachers were threatened, too. The instability froze efforts to develop investments in the region.

In 1997 the Philippines negotiated inconclusively with a former head of the communist New People's Army (NPA). José Sison—exiled in the Netherlands for years—was trying to arrange for amnesty in the Philippines, since the Dutch wanted him to leave. Another NPA leader joined the president's party.

Foreign Affairs. Ramos attempted to make a virtue of personal diplomacy after having been criticized bitterly for an unusual degree of globe-trotting. He insisted the visits to more than 17 countries in the first 11 months of 1997 reaped trade and investment dividends and protected overseas workers. The chief foreign-policy matter facing the Philippines was the ongoing dispute with China and several other nations over the Spratly Islands—presumed to have rich natural-gas resources.

In July the United States expressed disappointment about the decision made by the Philippines and other Association of Southeast Asian Nations (ASEAN) to admit Myanmar to ASEAN membership, given that country's poor human-rights record. The Philippines in turn was upset that the United States decided not to sign the anti-land-mine treaty of which the Philippines and nearly 100 other nations were signatories.

Disasters. From May 24–26, Typhoon Bining, the worst in a decade, struck the Philippines, leaving 53 dead and more than 77,000 homeless. Half of metropolitan Manila was flooded; the stock market and schools were closed. In August, Typhoon Ibiang intensified monsoons, bringing more floods to Manila. The Philippines also was affected by the smog and haze from burning Indonesian forests, although not as badly as were other countries in the region.

LINDA K. RICHTER, *Kansas State University*

PHOTOGRAPHY

The year 1997 marked a watershed for digital electronic photography—the year when it truly became "the next big thing." A developing consumer consciousness of digital imaging sparked an ongoing buying spree. From April 1996 to April 1997, 1 million digital cameras were sold worldwide—up from 400,000 in the same period one year earlier. Industry estimates projected yearly sales at 10 million units by the end of the 1990s, with annual volume near $4 billion. As a result, some photographic manufacturers have decided to concentrate almost entirely on digital-imaging equipment rather than conventional cameras.

The Computer Connection. Since the mid-1990s, more computers have been sold for use in the home than in business; most of these units, moreover, are sophisticated, memory-rich, Internet-ready machines. For a large and growing number of consumers, digital imaging thus has become as accessible as snapshot photography—given some type of capture device. The industry responded with a wide—and often confusing—array of digital cameras, with cutthroat competition driving prices down below $200 for bare-bones, low-resolution cameras. More-serious consumers, however, considered pixel count as well as price, as manufacturers finally made the $1,000 megapixel camera a reality. (A megapixel camera is capable of recording an image consisting of 1 million dots, which produces photographic quality in a 4-inch x 5-inch or 10-cm x 13-cm print.) A breakthrough camera appearing late in the year, the Olympus D-600L, could record images up to 1.4 million pixels and had a 3X zoom, through-lens viewing, and removable storage on cards of two to 16 megabytes, for a selling price of about $1,300.

Other factors encouraging digital snapshooting included a competitive market for home scanners, color inkjet printers, and image-manipulation software. The latter, exemplified by Adobe's PhotoDeluxe, typically sold for as little as $49 in 1997 and provided a level of sophistication nearly equal to that of programs costing many hundreds of dollars. Additionally, this type of software often provided automated functions such as elimination of "red-eye" in portraits taken by flash.

Professional applications of digital imaging continued to flourish. The Associated Press had reached a significant milestone in its photo coverage of the Democratic and Republican conventions and football's Super Bowl in 1996; these events were covered with-

Courtesy, Sony Corporation

In 1997, Sony introduced its Mavica, a digital camera that can transfer picture files on floppy discs from the camera to a computer. It also features a small preview and playback screen.

out the exposure of a single frame of conventional film. Finally, awareness of digital imaging got a boost with the transmission of images of the surface of Mars by the robot rover Sojourner. Millions of stargazers were able to view Martian landscapes on World Wide Web sites almost as soon as NASA scientists could. (*See also* SPACE EXPLORATION.)

Other Hardware and Software. Rumors of the death of silver-halide imaging, however, were exaggerated greatly; a stunning 21 billion conventional photographs were taken in the United States alone in 1996, with 35mm point-and-shoot cameras and single-use (disposable) cameras fueling the photo frenzy. It was a relatively quiet year for camera development, with most manufacturers content to tweak existing camera models with modest upgrades. One notable exception was the venerable house of Leica, whose surprise debut of the Leica R8 was its first ground-up design of a new SLR (single-lens reflex) since the Leicaflex SL2 of 1974. A thoroughly modern camera with multimode automation, the R8 also features an intriguing array of eight electronic contacts in the lensmount, leading to speculation about a future autofocus Leica SLR.

Canon, with its 300mm f/4 IS lens for the EOS line of autofocus cameras, made image stabilization a viable option for amateurs of moderate means. For under $1,500, photographers could obtain a telephoto lens that would allow them to hand-hold at two shutter speeds slower than they normally could, thanks to an internal optical stabilizer that counteracted blur due to camera shake. Nikon, meanwhile, brought out its 24–120mm f/3.5–5.6 zoom—the first "supernormal [all-purpose wide-to-telephoto zoom] lens" that starts at an extra-wide 24mm.

The Advanced Photo System (APS) continued modest—but not earth-shattering—sales. Tiny designer models like Canon's phenomenal ELPH continued their hold on the public imagination; a new pocketable Pentax APS model had quite similar specs and the rather derivative moniker "efina." Canon, meanwhile, introduced the ELPH Jr., a single-focal-length version believed to be the smallest reloadable camera in production, other than subminiature "spy" cameras.

The 35mm "posh point-and-shoot" segment of expensive, limited-production cameras saw the introduction of the Ricoh GR1, an industrial-looking, magnesium-alloy model whose 28mm f/2.8 lenses were individually factory adjusted for best resolution. One of the most influential point-and-shoot models of all time, the Olympus Infinity Stylus, was redesigned as the Stylus Epic with a faster f/2.8 lens, an even smaller "clamshell" body, and a metering system that could detect fluorescent light and compensate for it by adding fill flash.

The biggest news in film was Kodak's Gold Max, an 800-speed color-negative emulsion whose grain, sharpness, and color challenged 400-speed and even some 200-speed films. With a latitude for exposure error of two stops under- and five stops overexposure, Gold Max was positioned as the ideal film for both point-and-shoot as well as available-light photography. As expected, Fuji was set to introduce its own upgraded 800-speed color negative by the end of 1997. Both film giants now use 800-speed exclusively in their 35mm single-use cameras. Kodak, the only remaining maker of film for the ill-starred Disc camera, introduced in 1982, announced that production of Disc film would cease at the end of 1998.

Exhibitions and Publications. The celebrity presence continued in the world of photo collecting. André Kertèsz' "Mondrian's Pipe and Glasses, Paris" was auctioned at Christie's for $376,500 to a buyer reportedly representing singer-songwriter Elton John. And New York City's Museum of Modern Art's show of Cindy Sherman's "The Complete Untitled Film Stills" was underwritten by Madonna. Collectors and galleries stressed a new emphasis on works by Japanese photographers, World War II photographers of the

© Marc Riboud/Magnum Photos, Inc.

The historic photographs of Marc Riboud—which were taken in China over a 40-year period, including the 1965 one above—were exhibited in New York City and London as well as Beijing.

Axis countries, and those from the former Soviet Union and Eastern bloc. Of the latter, Yevgeny Khaldei, at age 80, received long-overdue recognition for his powerful, iconic images of World War II.

Also of historic note was the show "Marc Riboud in China: Forty Years of Photography," by the man who seemed, at times, to be the only Western eye behind the Bamboo Curtain. It was seen in Beijing, New York City, and London. Harry N. Abrams published the accompanying book. "Reunions: The Lost Children of Rwanda" showed that photographers have not deserted social concerns. Seamus Conlan and Tara Farrell's straightforward record portraits of children displaced by the ruinous civil war in Rwanda have helped reunite hundreds of children with their parents. The show was viewed in West Los Angeles and New York City. And Sebastião Salgado's dramatic book *Terra: Struggle of the Landless* (Phaidon Press/Chron-

·icle Books) was being used as a fund-raising tool to aid landless peasants in Brazil.

Other books that drew interest during 1997 included *LaChapelle Land* (Simon and Schuster), a collection of David LaChapelle's zany, sexy, and surreal takes on advertising and editorial photography, in an eye-popping style that has been dubbed "cybertrash." Nick Waplington's *The Wedding* (Aperture) continued the documentarian's unflinching but still affectionate record of a working-class English family. *Orbit: NASA Astronauts Photograph the Earth* (National Geographic) presents glorious color portraits of Mother Earth. And *The Killing Fields* (Twin Palms Publishers) is a selection of the portraits of doomed victims of Khmer Rouge mass murder in Cambodia.

The Paparazzi. The tragic death of Diana, princess of Wales, in Paris after a car crash that occurred while the car was being pursued by motorcycle-riding paparazzi cast a harsh light on tabloid photographers. Public outcry over intrusive or aggressive pursuit of celebrity photographs was vehement. Even newspapers that purchase celebrity-grab shots branded the practitioners "stalkerazzi." The incident was concurrent with a New York show, "Paparazzi," at the Roger Miller Gallery, which demonstrated that much of the "paparazzi aesthetic" has been assimilated into popular culture. *See also* PUBLISHING— *The Paparazzi.*

DAN RICHARDS, *"Popular Photography"*

PHYSICS

In 1997 new precision was achieved in atomic-parity-violation experiments; research with Bose-Einstein condensates came closer to achieving the development of an atom laser; and a new continuous-beam electron accelerator became fully operational.

Anapole Moment. Researchers at the Joint Institute for Laboratory Astrophysics (JILA) at the National Institute of Standards and Technology (NIST) and the University of Colorado—led by Carl Wieman—performed the most precise atomic-parity-violation experiment ever and confirmed the existence of the anapole moment—the internal electromagnetic moment in the nucleus that results due to the weak force.

In atomic transitions the electron interacts with the nucleus by exchanging a virtual photon. According to the Standard Model that unifies electromagnetic and weak interactions, a Z^0 (neutral intermediate vector boson) also will be exchanged. This exchange violates parity conservation (the process and its mirror image are different) and mixes S and P atomic states. In the experiment an electric field was applied—which also mixes S and P states— and induced a transition that conserved parity. The interference between the parity-violating term and the much larger parity-conserving term was measured and then repeated under mirror-image conditions to determine the difference between the transition rates. The results reduced the uncertainty in this difference by nearly an order of magnitude.

The anapole moment is not allowed by parity conservation. In 1980, Iosif Kriplovich and Victor Flambaum—then at the Budker Institute in Novosibirsk, Russia—predicted that the anapole moment would occur in parity-violating atomic transitions. Wick Haxton of the University of Washington at Seattle suggested that the anapole moment could be considered as an effective magnetic field created by the nucleus as a result of ordinary electromagnetic coupling plus the parity violation. The current causing the magnetic field is confined to a nuclear-sized donut shape, with the current spiraling due to the parity violation. The anapole moment depends on the hyperfine spin. The new experiments measured two different transition rates between two different spin states and confirmed the existence of the anapole moment.

Bose-Einstein Condensation. The state of matter called the Bose-Einstein (BE) condensate that was discovered in the mid-1990s remained a very active research area. Every particle has a wavelength associated with it, and as the temperature is lowered the wavelength increases. At very low temperatures, bosons (particles with integral spins) should act as one state, with the quantum effects extending over macroscopic distances. Such effects are observed in solids (superconductivity), liquids (superfluidity), and now in gases (BE condensation). This latter effect is interesting because for the condensation to occur in a gas the bosons must be so far apart that the other (chemical) interactions are not important, and thus pure quantum effects can be studied. These requirements make the formation of the BE condensate extremely difficult. The atoms must be cooled to 100 nanoKelvin, and then trapped.

Researchers at JILA and at the University of Colorado—led by Eric Cornell and Carl Wieman—succeeded in observing this new state of matter. The ultralow temperature was obtained through a combination of laser cooling (laser light slows down the atoms) and evaporative cooling (atoms are trapped in a shallow well by a combination of magnetic fields and faster-moving atoms are removed at the edge of the gas cloud). A cloud of rubidium-87 atoms was produced, with several thousand atoms in one quantum state. The signature of this new state was a sudden increase in the number of atoms with nearly zero velocity, which sat at the bottom of the trap. When the magnetic trap was turned off, the gas spread out slowly.

This new state of matter was observed at the Massachusetts Institute of Technology as well. A group led by Wolfgang Ketterle demonstrated that when two BE condensates were released from their traps and allowed to overlap, interference patterns resulted. This means that the BE condensates must be coherent, providing the key ingredient for an "atom laser" for fundamental research.

Neutrino Oscillations. Results of experiments at Los Alamos National Laboratory (LANL) in New Mexico suggested that neutrinos can change form. Detecting the neutral, nearly massless particles that interact very weakly with matter is very difficult. The solar-neutrino problem is the discrepancy between the number of neutrinos expected to be emitted by the Sun and the number actually measured. For more than a generation a series of experiments have confirmed the deficit. The latest and largest neutrino detector—the Super-Kamiokande detector—is located in a mine 186 mi (300 km) from Tokyo. This new system, in just a few months, "has more events than all previous solar-neutrino events have gotten in 30 years," according to John Bahcall of the Institute for Advanced Study in Princeton, NJ. Initial results confirmed the solar-neutrino deficit.

One proposed explanation was that neutrinos change in flight from one type of neutrino to another, according to a process called neutrino oscillation. In the new LANL experiment, proton beams from an 800-MeV accelerator struck a water target and generated many subatomic particles, including muon neutrinos. (Neutrinos come in three types, or flavors, and are labeled by the lepton with which they are associated.) The first key point was that only muon neutrinos were produced. Next there was a massive neutrino detector consisting of 50,000 gallons (189 270 l) of baby oil and liquid scintillator. The second key point was that this detector—the Liquid Scintillator Neutrino Detector (LSND)—was designed to detect only electron neutrinos. Therefore the observation of electron neutrinos would imply that the neutrinos changed in flight. New, more extensive data were consistent with the initial results: Electron neutrinos were observed. By fall 1997 there was no other conclusive experimental evidence to confirm neutrino oscillation.

Present and Future Accelerators. The Continuous Electron Beam Facility (CEBAF) at the newly named Thomas Jefferson National Accelerator Facility near Newport News, VA, was in operation in 1997. The 4-GeV electron accelerator provides a continuous beam of electrons, which will enable physicists to examine a much wider variety of reactions in more detail. That factor distinguishes the new facility from other electron accelerators— such as the Stanford Linear Accelerator Center (SLAC)—which provide short pulses of electrons.

The scientific motivation behind the new accelerator focuses on the quark-based description of nuclei. Quantum chromodynamics is thought to provide an exact theory of the strong (nuclear) interaction, but has been tested only at very high energies—corresponding to very short distances. At the energies available at the new laboratory, a variety of interesting phenomena occur. The goal is to use the well-understood electromagnetic interaction to study the so-called transition region between the "simple" high-energy world and the everyday world. An active user group with more than 1,000 members has been formed, and program-advisory committees have been meeting for a decade to plan how the facility can be used most efficiently.

Following the cancellation of the Superconducting Super Collider (SSC) project by the U.S. Congress in 1993, the only remaining prospective high-energy accelerator is the Large Hadron Collider (LHC) planned at CERN in Geneva, Switzerland. The United States agreed to contribute $500 million for its development. However, in 1997 the U.S. Congress questioned the details of the agreement, wishing assurance that U.S. physicists would have access to the facility and that the United States would play a role in technical and financial decisions regarding its development. The goals of the proposed accelerator, which would be the most powerful ever, are to search for the Higgs boson particle and for the twins of known particles that are predicted by the supersymmetry theory. These questions will not be answered quickly. Even with a fast-track production schedule, the LHC would not be fully operational until 2005, while a slower schedule would have the LHC reach full power in 2008.

GARY MITCHELL
North Carolina State University

POLAND

Natural disaster and political change did not deter significant advances in Poland's economic and international position during 1997.

Floods. An extraordinary amount of rain during June and July to western, southwestern, and parts of central Poland led to widespread flooding and massive destruction of houses, roads, and economic infrastructure. In one of Poland's worst disasters of the past century, at least 60 died, thousands lost their homes and possessions, and millions were affected—especially along the Oder (Odra) River and its tributaries. The Polish government, the World Bank, and the European Union (EU) provided assistance, but ineffective or delayed relief efforts had political repercussions. The leftist government of Prime Minister Wlodzimierz Cimoszewicz was the target of widespread public criticism, particularly for its failure to declare a prompt state of emergency.

Economy. In January the Polish statistical office reported that the 1996 inflation rate was 18.5%, a significant decrease from previous post-communist years. Increasing affluence was reflected in a 41% rise in automobile sales in Poland over 1995. The economic-growth rate remained around 6% throughout 1997, making Poland one of the most dynamic economies of Europe. Privatization and elimination of inefficient public enterprises continued.

The March 6 announcement that the Gdansk Shipyard—birthplace of Lech Walesa's Solidarity movement in 1980—would close prompted demonstrations in Gdansk and Warsaw over the consequent layoff of 3,800 workers. On March 20, Prime Minister Cimoszewicz announced a government bailout through the merger of the plant with other shipbuilding facilities; prospects remained dim, however. In May it was announced that one of the shipyard's empty production halls was to be rented to a nightclub to raise money.

Government and Politics. Deputy Premier and Finance Minister Grzegorz Kolodko resigned on February 4 and was replaced by a 45-year-old professor, Marek Belka. Tensions within the ruling leftist coalition increased. In an action spurred by the demands of protectionist small-farm operators, Roman Jagielinski—deputy prime minister and minister of agriculture—was forced out in late March. He was repudiated by the leadership of his own Peasant Party (PSL) and on April 25 was replaced by a PSL member more willing to bail out the farmers, Jaroslaw Kolinowski.

Marian Krzaklewski (below, front) led the Solidarity Electoral Action (AWS)—a conglomerate of 36 right and right-center political parties—to an impressive showing in September 1997 elections for the lower house of Poland's parliament (Sejm).

POLAND • Information Highlights

Official Name: Republic of Poland.
Location: Eastern Europe.
Area: 120,728 sq mi (312 683 km²).
Population (mid-1997 est.): 38,600,000.
Chief Cities (Dec. 31, 1995, est.): Warsaw, the capital, 1,635,112; Lodz, 823,215; Kraków, 744,987.
Government: *Head of state,* Aleksander Kwasniewski, president (took office December 1995). *Head of government,* Jerzy Buzek, prime minister (named Oct. 17, 1997). *Legislature*—National Assembly: Senat and Sejm.
Monetary Unit: Zloty (3.52 zlotys equal U.S.$1, Dec. 31, 1997).
Gross Domestic Product (1995 est. U.S.$): $226,700,000,000 (purchasing power parity).
Economic Indexes (1996, 1990 = 100): *Consumer Prices,* all items, 667.5; food, 550.2. *Industrial Production,* 134.
Foreign Trade (1996 U.S.$): *Imports,* $36,966,000,000; *exports,* $24,410,000,000.

On March 10, Gen. Tadeusz Wilecki was ousted as chief of Poland's general staff because of his unsympathetic view toward civilian control of the armed forces, a prerequisite of North Atlantic Treaty Organization (NATO) membership. He was succeeded by the deputy chief, Gen. Henryk Szumski.

On March 25, 42.9% of eligible Polish voters approved a new constitution by a margin of 52.7% to 45.9%. The new constitution replaced the 1952 communist-era one and continued the post-1989 parliamentary system, in which the prime minister heads a cabinet responsible to the popularly elected lower house (Sejm) and president. The president exercises general oversight and also acts as a ceremonial head of state. Most divisive issues relating to the passage of the new constitution centered on religious questions. The Catholic Church and its supporters wanted a total ban on abortion and a more influential position for Catholicism in Poland's public life—a view that coincided more closely with that of the right and center opposition than with the more secular leftist majority in parliament.

Ultimately, the constitution stopped short of outlawing abortion, while it did secure the autonomy of the church and provided for religious education in state-supported schools. It also outlawed homosexual marriages. The constitution affirmed a free-market economy in Poland but balanced it with guarantees of free education and health care as well as a state-enforced minimum wage.

On June 19 parliament enacted a "lustration" law, requiring public disclosure of past communist associations from all candidates for parliament and senior government posts. On July 3 it abolished the death penalty, effective Jan. 1, 1998. Parliamentary elections on September 21 shifted the balance of power away from the former communists' Alliance of the Democratic Left (SLD). Parties grouped around the former Solidarity movement, Solidarity Electoral Action (AWS), gained 33.9% of the vote; the SLD received 27.1%. The centrist Freedom Union won 13.4% and the old SLD ally, PSL, received 7.3%. The dominant personality in Polish parliamentary politics became Marian Krzaklewski, leader of the victorious AWS, a conglomerate of 36 right and right-center political parties, which gained 201 seats in the 460-seat lower house of parliament (Sejm). The SLD won 164 and the PSL took 27, while the Freedom Union won 60 seats. The remainder went to smaller parties. This was a marked difference from the 1993 elections, when the left-center coalition of the SLD and PSL garnered 303 seats, and jointly controlled 66% of the seats in the Sejm.

In mid-October, Jerzy Buzek, a 57-year-old professor and member of the Freedom Union, was named premier of a new center-right coalition government. Leszek Balcerowicz, an economic reformer during the early 1990s, returned as finance minister.

Pope John Paul II. Between May 31 and June 10, Pope John Paul II made his seventh visit since 1978 to his native Poland. Because of the 77-year-old pontiff's frail health, the visit was highly emotional for many, including the pope himself. Some feared it would be his last visit to his homeland. The pope made many public appearances and drew audiences estimated at several million. All political parties, including the former communists, led by President Aleksander Kwasniewski, attempted to identify themselves with the enormously popular pope.

The pontiff cautioned Polish Catholics about the spiritual dangers of a materialistic, Western-style, open society. He specifically condemned abortion. While generally supportive of post-communist democratization, he warned about the excessive mixing of politics with religion. During the pope's visit, a church-sponsored radio station, Radio Marya, became the subject of political controversy because of the apparent far-right, anti-Semitic content of some of its broadcasts.

In mid-October some 12,000 Polish pilgrims traveled to Rome to celebrate the 19th anniversary of John Paul II's papacy.

Foreign Affairs. In late April, Prime Minister Cimoszewicz visited the United States, promoting Poland's bid for entry into NATO. On June 12, U.S. President Bill Clinton announced support for the admission of Poland. The decision, supported by all 16 NATO member states, was seen as a recognition of Poland's relatively stable democratic government, free-market economy, and clear civilian control of the armed forces. Actual entry was slated for 1999. With estimated armed forces of 248,000 in 1996, Poland's military establishment would be the sixth largest in the NATO alliance, after the United States, Turkey, France, Germany, and Italy. (*See also* EUROPE—*NATO Expansion*.)

On July 16 the European Commission in Brussels announced on behalf of the European Union (EU) that five East European nations, including Poland, would be invited to apply for EU membership, with entry likely by the year 2002. Among the requirements set in the commission's report were the accelerated privatization of state enterprises, reduced inflation, modernization of financial markets, and the rooting out of political corruption.

President Kwasniewski met in Kiev with Ukrainian President Leonid Kuchma on May 21. They signed a reconciliation pact condemning the deportation of some 100,000 Ukrainians from South-Eastern Poland in 1947 and the killings of thousands of Poles by Ukrainian nationalists during World War II.

In mid-October an arms deal was announced between Poland and Israel, in which Israel would supply antitank missiles and upgrade the capabilities of Polish military helicopters. In December negotiations began with Russia on the possible production of Russian SU-39 attack aircraft in Poland.

ALEXANDER J. GROTH, *Professor Emeritus*
University of California, Davis

POLAR RESEARCH

The importance of the polar regions in understanding global problems was a dominant theme of much of the Arctic and Antarctic research in 1997. Great efforts continued to improve global climate models by incorporating the effects of sea ice, to establish more details of earlier environments from ice cores, to understand the effects of increasing ultraviolet radiation on ecosystems and people, and to establish baseline pollution levels against which worldwide change could be assessed.

Antarctic.   U.S. President Bill Clinton agreed with a high-level review of Antarctic research that found maintaining the present three year-round stations there served both national and international interests. He also accepted the recommendation that Amundsen-Scott Station at the South Pole be rebuilt to allow continued monitoring of greenhouse gases and to develop its contribution to astronomy. The very clean air, low temperature, and high altitude of the station make it better than anywhere else on Earth for astronomical research. Tourism continued to grow in the Antarctic, as did concern over its impact on the environment. A 13-year study by U.S. scientists comparing the breeding success of penguins in colonies visited once a year by scientists and those visited almost daily by tourists in managed groups showed that the tourist site was much more successful.

The springtime ozone hole continued to grow, with its effects felt well beyond the Antarctic. Research on the effects of increased ultraviolet radiation on both marine and terrestrial organisms showed that there can be serious damage to DNA unless protective pigments can be made. The breakup of another major ice shelf in the Antarctic Peninsula provided support for a pattern of significant regional warming. A major U.S. ice-drilling program successfully collected cores, which should determine if and when the West Antarctic ice sheet suddenly collapsed in the past. Such a collapse would have caused huge changes in world sea level.

Arctic. After six years of work, the international Arctic Monitoring and Assessment Program provided the first complete survey of pollution in the Arctic. It concluded that ozone depletion was increasing and that acidification and regional pollution were damaging many of the ecosystems seriously. There appeared to be no immediate threat from Russian reactors dumped in the Arctic Ocean, but there was great concern over the accumulation of mercury and persistent organic pollutants in the food chains, and a number of real threats to human health were found. PCB blood levels were two to four times higher than in more southerly populations, while DDT concentrations in mothers' milk exceeded levels believed to cause neurological disorders in infants.

There were also radiation increases that have led to genetic impacts in Russia. Volumes of long-classified Cold War data on the Arctic Ocean released jointly by the United States and Russia in January would allow accurate maps of the Arctic Basin sea to be made, greatly aiding in the modeling of water movements. The medical and family records of Iceland's small population also offered unrivaled opportunities for investigating the genetic causes of many common diseases. With the data, researchers in Reykjavík made great progress toward identifying genes linked to multiple sclerosis, inflammatory bowel disease, diabetes, and psoriasis.

DAVID W.H. WALTON, *British Antarctic Survey*

PORTUGAL

During 1997, Portugal's Prime Minister António Guterres, the pragmatic leader of the Socialist Party (PS), watched his popularity surge because of the nation's economic expansion—Europe's biggest after Finland—and decisive movement toward entry in the European economic and monetary union (EMU).

Political Affairs. Guterres' Socialist Party commanded 112 seats in the nation's 230-member legislature. Since their 1995 electoral triumph, the prime minister and his party had sought the support of the centrist Social Democratic Party (PSD) on controversial issues. In 1997 a growing economy helped smooth the tensions between these major parties, both of which endorsed Portugal's adopting the common European currency. Meanwhile, additional income enabled the Socialists to honor their campaign pledge to devote more resources to health and education. Portuguese President Jorge Sampãio saw eye to eye with fellow Socialist Guterres on most matters.

Following his loss to Sampãio, PSD candidate and former Prime Minister Aníbal Cavaco Silva had warned that PS control of the executive and legislative branches of government would give rise to a "dictatorship of the majority." This fear faded as the Socialists endeavored to find common political ground with the PSD and other opposition groups. In light of Portugal's robust economy and projections of even higher growth in 1998, the PS appeared in no hurry to call new parliamentary contests. Guterres believed that the continuing prosperity would enable the Socialists to increase their popularity further—with a payoff coming in additional legislative seats when voters next go to the polls.

Expansion of the gross domestic product (GDP) and the prospect of EMU affiliation eclipsed serious problems that continued to afflict the nation's public-health and social-security systems. Guterres and Sampãio, fearful that addressing these controversial issues in the near future would spark protests, planned to wait until after Portugal's inclusion in the EMU "launch group," planned for 1999.

In early June a judge sentenced 11 skinheads to 14- to 18-year prison terms for beating a young black man to death. The defendants numbered among 50 racial bigots who had rampaged through Lisbon's streets two years earlier, cursing and attacking blacks.

Economics. A bright economic picture augured well for Portugal's joining the EMU. Guterres trimmed government finances to bring the nation's fiscal deficit as a percentage

PORTUGAL • Information Highlights

Official Name: Portuguese Republic.
Location: Southwestern Europe.
Area: 35,552 sq mi (92 080 km²).
Population (mid-1997 est.): 9,900,000.
Chief Cities (1991 census): Lisbon, the capital, 681,063; Oporto, 309,485; Vila Nova de Gaia, 247,499.
Government: *Head of state,* Jorge Sampãio, president (took office March 1996). *Head of government,* António Guterres, prime minister (took office October 1995). *Legislature* (unicameral)—Assembly of the Republic.
Monetary Unit: Escudo (182.97 escudos equal U.S.$1, Dec. 31, 1997).
Gross Domestic Product (1995 est. U.S.$): $116,200,000,-000 (purchasing power parity).
Economic Indexes (1996): *Consumer Prices* (1991 = 100): all items, 131.1; food, 122.9. *Industrial Production* (1990 = 100): 101.
Foreign Trade (1996 U.S.$): *Imports,* $33,933,000,000; *exports,* $23,754,000,000.

of GDP to 3%—the target of the Maastricht Treaty. This success occurred amid a 3.5% rise in national income, while the inflation rate fell to 2.2%—down from 2.5% in 1996—and unemployment dipped below 7%. In mid-October, Finance Minister Antonio Sousa Franco unveiled a 1998 budget that contemplated an even lower fiscal deficit (2.5%) without raising taxes. Indeed, most economists predicted that faster growth, combined with a crackdown on tax evaders, would spur a 7.3% upswing in tax receipts. Although the PS was four seats short of a legislative majority, the budget was approved in November.

The major labor action of the year erupted in early June, when 50 trawlers and other vessels temporarily blockaded Lisbon's port. The move constituted a protest against the government's moratorium on Sunday fishing beyond the 12-mi (19-km) limit. Boat captains cried discrimination because the ban did not apply to the Spanish fleet, which fished the same waters. For their part, environmental authorities justified the initiative as a means of replenishing dwindling fish stocks.

While buffeted by international forces in October, shares on the Lisbon Stock Exchange shot up 65% during the first eight months of the year. At the same time, foreign investment expanded 5%—with technology, textiles, and footwear proving especially attractive targets of opportunity. Portugal's Telecom forged a strategic alliance with British Telecom and MCI to explore telecommunications opportunities in Brazil, which accounts for 40% of the mushrooming Latin American market. Lisbon-based Telecom already had a working relationship with its Brazilian counterpart, Telebras.

Foreign Relations. As Lisbon prepared to cede the island territory of Macao to China, Portuguese leaders carefully watched Great

Britain's handover of Hong Kong to Beijing. Meanwhile, Portugal began its two-year term on the United Nations Security Council on Jan. 1, 1997, after receiving votes from European allies and the Third World. The latter loomed important because Lisbon continued to maintain special economic and cultural ties with Brazil, Angola, Mozambique, and Guinea-Bissau. In April, President Sampãio and former President Mario Soares strengthened these bonds by attending the inauguration of the new president of Angola, a former Portuguese overseas dependency.

Soares also made headlines in April when he was named to head a commission investigating his country's gold dealings with Germany during World War II. Experts believed that, after Switzerland, Portugal was the second-largest buyer of gold from the Nazi regime.

GEORGE W. GRAYSON
College of William and Mary

PRISONS

Despite a downward trend in the rates of person-to-person violent and property crimes in the United States, the number of people in state and federal prisons continued to grow. As of Jan. 1, 1997, the number was 1,111,142. Three factors suggested that this number would continue to increase: The average minimum time to be served by new inmates continued to increase, up 3% in 1996; the release rates of prisoners eligible for parole had decreased, down 6% in 1996; and the percentage of newly admitted prison inmates who had served prior terms was increasing steadily (from 18% in 1980 to more than 35%). The disproportionate percentages of African-Americans and other minorities throughout the U.S. criminal-justice system continued to grow.

Prison Construction. The rise in the number of prison inmates has been accompanied

In January 1997 a U.S. magistrate in Montgomery, AL, ruled in a lawsuit that the Alabama prison system should not be allowed to chain prisoners to metal bars known as "hitching posts," left. State officials had maintained that the "restraining bars" were an appropriate form of discipline but were not punitive.

by a surge in prison construction. Between 1990 and 1995, 168 state and 45 federal prisons were built, bringing the number of these institutions to 1,500. Even with this construction, state prisons operated at an average 3% above capacity, and federal prisons were 24% above capacity. Staffing of prisons also increased between 1990 and 1995. The number of state and federal prison employees grew 31% to reach 337,320. At an overall cost of more than $30 billion per year, prisons continued to impose considerable financial burdens on state governments. To stabilize costs, most states contracted with outside agencies and businesses to provide essential services ranging from food and supplies to medical care.

Drug Offenses. Experts have disagreed about the reasons for the contrasting trends in rates of crime and imprisonment. Alfred Blumstein of Carnegie Mellon University has argued that the crimes that have led to the largest increase in incarceration—namely, narcotic-drug offenses—are not counted in the Federal Bureau of Investigation's (FBI's) indexes of violent and property crime. He has estimated that drug offenders have accounted for about half of the growth in the prison population. In this connection, it is noteworthy that the number of drug-abuse-violation arrests has risen about 60% since the mid-1980s, and now accounts for approximately 9% of all arrests.

Others have argued that the underlying rate of crime would have grown faster had so many people not been locked up. In one study, Steven Levitt of Harvard University found that states in which prisoner lawsuits were successful in reducing overcrowding—thereby causing release of felons—have rates of violent crime that exceed the national average by 10%.

African-Americans in Prison. A major area of concern is the disproportionate numbers in the prison population who are young (29 is the median age of admitted prisoners), male (94%), and black (46%). African-Americans make up 12% of the U.S. population. In most jurisdictions, however, black males make up a majority of those behind bars and on probation and parole. The percentage of prison admissions to state and federal prisons who are black grew from 39% in 1950 to 46% in 1992, the latest year for which such figures were available. While there are many reasons for this, one major factor is the racial disparity in drug-abuse-violation arrests. In 1992 the race-specific arrest rate for blacks under 18 was more than five times the rate for whites (483.9 per 100,000 versus 88.5); for blacks over 18 the rate also was more than five times as high (1,999.9 per 100,000 versus 381.3).

According to a report issued by the U.S. Justice Department's Bureau of Justice Statistics, almost 30% of black males can expect to serve a prison sentence in their lifetime. The rate for Hispanic men is 16%, and for white males, 4.4%. In January the Sentencing Project, a Washington-based organization monitoring incarceration trends, issued a report, *Intended and Unintended Consequences: State Racial Disparities in Imprisonment*, which addressed some side effects of the growing disparities in black-white incarceration rates and stated that the extremely high number of black males marked by the penal system should be examined. It indicated that contact, even a single arrest, with the criminal-justice system brings about a loss in income and a decrease in employment opportunities, affecting the individual, family, and community. For example, removing large numbers of males from neighborhoods to prisons severely reduces the wages available and undermines formal and informal organizations, from churches and block associations to family and neighborhood connections. This in turn further destabilizes the community and creates a cycle of despair.

Death Penalty. The number of executions in the United States reached a 40-year high in 1997, with 74 prisoners executed by mid-December. High-death-penalty states such as Texas, Virginia, Florida, Missouri, Louisiana, Georgia, Alabama, and Arkansas—which account for 80% of all executions in the United States—increased their use of capital punishment. And the states of Oregon and Kentucky conducted their first executions since 1962. By the end of 1998, Connecticut, New Jersey, Ohio, and Tennessee were expected to hold their first executions since the 1960s. Although the number of executions has remained small, judges have continued to employ the death sentence in homicide cases. The result has been an increase in the numbers of prisoners on death row. Between 1995 and 1997, these numbers had grown almost 10%—to reach a record 3,269 in August 1997. While racial disparity in executions long has been of concern to the courts, the demographics of the death-row population reflect those of the prison population: The largest percentage, 44%, are in the 30–39 age group; 99% are male; and 41% are black.

See also CRIME.

ROBERT L. BONN and DONALD GOODMAN
John Jay College of Criminal Justice

PRIZES AND AWARDS

© Jim Bourg/Gamma-Liaison

The six-year-old International Campaign to Ban Landmines and its coordinator, Jody Williams, above, of Putney, VT, were honored with the 1997 Nobel Peace Prize.

NOBEL PRIZES[1]

Chemistry (shared): Paul D. Boyer, University of California at Los Angeles, and John E. Walker, Medical Research Council Laboratory of Molecular Biology, Cambridge, England, for discovering the enzyme ATP synthase, which all living things use to produce the energy-storing molecule adenosine triphosphate, or ATP; Jens S. Skou, Aarhus University, Denmark, for discovering another enzyme involved in the chemistry of ATP, sodium-potassium stimulated adenosine triphosphatase

Economics (shared): Robert C. Merton, Harvard Business School; Myron S. Scholes, Stanford Business School; for developing "a pioneering formula for the valuation of stock options"

Literature: Dario Fo, Italy; for his "strength in the creation of texts that simultaneously amuse, engage, and provide perspectives....he opens our eyes to abuses and injustices in society"

Peace (shared): International Campaign to Ban Landmines; coordinator, Jody Williams, Putney, VT; for starting a "process which in the space of a few years changed a ban on anti-personnel mines from a vision to a feasible reality"

Physics (shared): Steven Chu, Stanford University; William D. Phillips, U.S. National Institute of Standards and Technology; Claude Cohen-Tannoudji, Collège de France and Ecole Normale Supérieure, France; for their "development of methods to cool and trap atoms with laser light." The new methods "have contributed greatly to increasing our knowledge of the interplay between radiation and matter"

Physiology or Medicine: Stanley B. Prusiner, University of California at San Francisco, for his discovery of prions, proteins that function as disease-causing agents; the finding provides insights into "understanding biological mechanisms underlying . . . dementia-related diseases . . . and establishes a foundation for drug development and new types of medical treatment strategies."

[1]approx. $1 million in each category

ART

American Academy and Institute of Arts and Letters Awards
Academy-Institute Awards: architecture—Daniel Libeskind; art—Enrique Chagoya, Tim Hawkinson, Bill Jensen, Harvey Quaytman, James Seawright; music—Curt Cacioppo, Brian Fennelly, Morris Rosenzweig, Marilyn Shrude
Award for Distinguished Service to the Arts: Kitty Carlisle Hart
Arnold W. Brunner Memorial Prize in Architecture: Henri Ciriani
Jimmy Ernst Award in Art: Anita Huffington
Gold Medal for Music: Gunther Schuller
Walter Hinrichsen Award in Music: Gustavo Leone
Charles Ives Fellowship in Music: Jennifer Higdon
Goddard Lieberson Fellowships in Music: Robert Maggio, Zhou Long
Wladimir and Rhoda Lakond Award in Music: David Lang
Louise Nevelson Award in Art: Michael Kareken
Richard and Hinda Rosenthal Foundation Award: Eve Aschheim
Canada Council Molson Prize for the Arts ($50,000): Mavis Gallant
Capezio Dance Award ($10,000): Mark Morris
U.S. Congressional Gold Medal: Frank Sinatra
Ditson Conductor's Award for the advance of American music ($1,000): David Zinman, musical director, Baltimore Symphony Orchestra
George and Ira Gershwin Award for lifetime musical achievement: Randy Newman
Dorothy and Lillian Gish Prize for outstanding contribution to the arts ($200,000): Bob Dylan
Grawemeyer Award for musical composition ($150,000): Simon Bainbridge, Great Britain
John F. Kennedy Center Honors for career achievement in the performing arts: Lauren Bacall, Bob Dylan, Charlton Heston, Jessye Norman, Edward Villella
National Academy of Recording Arts and Sciences Grammy Awards for excellence in phonograph records
Album of the year: Celine Dion, *Falling Into You*
Alternative performance: Beck, *Odelay*
Classical album: *Corigliano: Of Rage and Remembrance (Symphony No. 1, etc)*, Leonard Slatkin, conductor
Classical vocalist: Bryn Terfel, *Opera Arias (works of Mozart, Wagner, Borodin, etc.)*
Country album: Lyle Lovett, *The Road to Ensenada*
Country instrumental album: Chet Atkins, *Jam Man*
Country song (songwriter's award): Bill Mack, "Blue"
Country vocal collaboration: Vince Gill, featuring Alison Krauss and Union Station, "High Lonesome Sound"
Country vocalist: (female)—LeAnn Rimes, "Blue"; (male)—Vince Gill, "Worlds Apart"; (group or duo)—Brooks & Dunn, "My Maria"
Hard-rock album: Smashing Pumpkins, *Bullet With Butterfly Wings*
Jazz instrumental album: Michael Brecker, *Tales From the Hudson*
Jazz instrumental solo: Michael Brecker, "Cabin Fever"
Jazz vocalist: Cassandra Wilson, "New Moon Daughter"
Metal album: Rage Against the Machine, *Tire Me*
New artist: LeAnn Rimes
Pop album: Celine Dion, *Falling Into You*
Pop collaboration: Natalie Cole and Nat "King" Cole, "When I Fall in Love"
Pop instrumental album: Bela Fleck and the Flecktones, *The Sinister Minister*
Pop vocalist: (female)—Toni Braxton, "Un-Break My Heart"; (male)—Eric Clapton, "Change the World"; (group or duo)—Beatles, "Free as a Bird"
Rap album: Fugees, *The Score*
Rap duo or group: Bone Thugs-n-Harmony, "Tha Crossroads"
Rap solo performance: LL Cool J, "Hey Lover"
Record of the year: Eric Clapton, "Change the World"
Rhythm-and-blues album: Tony Rich Project, *Words*
Rhythm-and-blues song: Babyface, "Exhale (Shoop Shoop)"
Rhythm-and-blues vocalist: (female)—Toni Braxton, "You're Makin' Me High"; (male)—Luther Vandross, "Your Secret Love"; (group or duo)—Fugees, "Killing Me Softly With His Song"
Rock album: Sheryl Crow, *Sheryl Crow*
Rock instrumental album: Jimmie Vaughan, Eric Clapton, Bonnie Raitt, Robert Cray, B.B. King, Buddy Guy, Dr. John, and Art Neville, *SRV Shuffle*
Rock song (songwriters' award): Tracy Chapman, "Give Me One Reason"
Rock vocalist: (female)—Sheryl Crow, "If It Makes You Happy"; (male)—Beck, "Where It's At"; (group or duo)—Dave Matthews Band, "So Much to Say"
Song of the year (songwriter's award): Gordon Kennedy, Wayne Kirkpatrick, Tommy Sims, "Change the World"
National Humanities Medal (presented by President Bill Clinton on Sept. 29, 1997): Nina M. Archabal, David A. Berry, Richard J. Franke, William Friday, Don Henley, Maxine Hong Kingston, Luis Leal, Martin E. Marty, Paul Mellon, Studs Terkel
National Medal of Arts (presented by President Bill Clinton on Sept. 29, 1997): Louise Bourgeois; Betty Carter; Agnes Gund; Daniel Urban Kiley; Angela Lansbury; James Levine; The MacDowell Colony, Peterborough, NH; Tito Puente; Jason Robards; Edward Villella; Doc Watson
Praemium Imperiale for lifetime achievement in the arts ($150,000 ea.): Richard Meier, United States (architecture); Ravi Shankar, India (music); Gerhard Richter, Germany (painting); George Segal, United States (sculpture); Peter Brook, Great Britain (theater and film)
Pritzker Architecture Prize ($100,000): Sverre Fehn, Norway
Pulitzer Prize for Music: Wynton Marsalis, *Blood on the Fields*
Samuel H. Scripps/American Dance Festival Award ($25,000): Anna Halprin
TNN/Music City News Country Awards
Album: George Strait, *Blue Clear Sky*
Artist: (female)—Lorrie Morgan; (male)—Alan Jackson
Christian country artist: Ricky Van Shelton
Comedian: Jeff Foxworthy
Entertainer: Alan Jackson
Living legend: Charley Pride
Minnie Pearl Award for contributions to the country-music industry: George Lindsey
Single: Billy Ray Cyrus, "Trail of Tears"
Star of tomorrow: (female)—LeAnn Rimes; (male)—Wade Hayes
Video: Neal McCoy, "Then You Can Tell Me Goodbye"
Vocal band: Sawyer Brown
Vocal group: Statler Brothers
Vocal collaboration: Lorrie Morgan and Jon Randall, "By My Side"
Vocal duo: Brooks & Dunn

JOURNALISM

Maria Moors Cabot Prizes ($1,000 ea.): Gerardo Bedoya Borrero, editorial-page editor, *El País*, Cali, Colombia (posthumous); José de Cordoba, writer, *Wall Street Journal*; Jorge Fontevecchia, editor, *Noticias de la Semana*, Argentina; Julia Preston, Mexico correspondent, *The New York Times*; Hernando and Enrique Santos Castillo, editors, *El Tiempo*, Bogotá, Colombia
International Press Freedom Awards: Christine Anyanwu, editor in chief, *The Sunday Magazine*, Nigeria; Viktor Ivancic, editor in chief, *Feral Tribune*, Croatia; Yelena Masyuk, special correspondent, NTV (independent television station), Russia; Freedom Neruda,

© Charles Abel/"Springfield Union-News"/AP/Wide World Photos

"Blood on the Fields," a three-hour jazz oratorio about an African couple sold into slavery—composed by trumpeter Wynton Marsalis, 35—captured the Pulitzer Prize for music.

managing/senior editor, *La Voie*, Ivory Coast; Ying Chan and Shieh Chung-liang, *Yazhou Zhoukan* (*Asia Week*), Hong Kong; special award—Ted Koppel, *Nightline* (ABC)

National Magazine Awards
Design: *I.D.*
Essays and criticism: *The New Yorker*
Feature writing: *Sports Illustrated*
Fiction: *The New Yorker*
General excellence: *Vanity Fair, Outside, Wired, I.D.*
General excellence in new media: *Money*
Personal service: *Glamour*
Photography: *National Geographic*
Public interest: *Fortune*
Reporting: *Outside*
Single-topic issue: *Scientific American*
Special interest: *Smithsonian*

Overseas Press Club Awards
Business reporting from abroad (newspapers): *Chicago Tribune*
Hal Boyle Award: John-Thor Dahlburg, *The Los Angeles Times, Afghanistan: Legacy of Fear*
Robert Capa Gold Medal: Corrine Dufka, Reuters chief photographer—Africa, "Liberia: From a Dead Man's Wallet"
Madeline Dane Ross Award (for foreign reporting in any medium showing a concern for the human condition): *Chicago Tribune*
President's Award for lifetime achievement: Katharine Graham

George Polk Memorial Awards
Criticism: Blair Kamin, *Chicago Tribune*, for examinations of Chicago's architecture
Cultural reporting: Chuck Philips, *The Los Angeles Times*, for in-depth coverage of the inner workings of the music industry
Economics reporting: *The New York Times*, "Downsizing of America"
Foreign reporting: John F. Burns, *The New York Times*, for series on the takeover of Kabul, Afghanistan, by Taliban forces
Foreign television reporting: Christiane Amanpour and Anita Pratap, CNN, for a special on Afghanistan
Local reporting:Kevin Collison, *Buffalo* (NY) *News*
Magazine reporting: Anne-Marie Cusac, *The Progressive*, "Stunning Technology"
National reporting: Elizabeth Marchak, *Cleveland Plain Dealer*, for "The FAA and ValuJet Airlines"
National television reporting: *Inside Edition*, for "Door-to-Door Insurance" (syndicated)
Political reporting: *The Los Angeles Times*, "Money from Asia"
Transportation reporting: Byron Acohido, *Seattle Times*, "Safety at Issue: The 737"

Pulitzer Prizes
Beat reporting: Byron Acohido, *The Seattle Times*
Commentary: Eileen McNamara, *The Boston Globe*
Criticism: Tim Page, *The Washington Post*
Editorial cartooning: Walt Handelsman, *The Times-Picayune* (New Orleans, LA)
Editorial writing: Michael G. Gartner, *The Daily Tribune* (Ames, IA)
Explanatory journalism: Michael Vitez, April Saul, and Ron Cortes, *The Philadelphia Inquirer*
Feature photography: Alexander Zemlianichenko, The Associated Press
Feature writing: Lisa Pollak, *The Baltimore Sun*
International reporting: John F. Burns, *The New York Times*
Investigative reporting: Eric Nalder, Deborah Nelson, and Alex Tizon, *The Seattle Times*
National reporting: staff of *The Wall Street Journal*
Public service: *The Times-Picayune* (New Orleans, LA)
Spot news photography: Annie Wells, *The Press Democrat* (Santa Rosa, CA)
Spot news reporting: staff of *Newsday* (Long Island, NY)

LITERATURE
American Academy and Institute of Arts and Letters Awards
Academy-Institute Awards: Charles Baxter, Lane Dunlop, Allen Grossman, Maureen Howard, Jayne Anne Phillips, Luc Sante, Wallace Shawn, Jane Smiley
Award of Merit Medal for the Novel: Richard Ford
Michael Braude Award for Light Verse: Robert Conquest
Witter Bynner Prize for Poetry: Mark Doty
E.M. Forster Award in Literature: Glyn Maxwell
Gold Medal for Poetry: John Ashbery
Sue Kaufman Prize for First Fiction: Brad Watson, *Last Days of the Dog-Men*
Rome Fellowship in Literature: Fae Myenne Ng
Richard and Hinda Rosenthal Foundation Award: Mary Kay Zuravleff, *The Frequency of Souls*
Harold D. Vursell Memorial Award: Elizabeth McCracken, *The Giant's House*
Morton Dauwen Zabel Award: Wendy Lesser

Anisfield-Wolf Book Awards
Fiction: James McBride, *The Color of Water*
Lifetime achievement: Albert L. Murray
Nonfiction: Jamaica Kincaid, *The Autobiography of My Mother*

Bancroft Prizes in American history ($4,000 ea.)**:** David E. Kyvig, *Explicit and Authentic Acts: Amending the U.S. Constitution, 1776–1995*; James T. Patterson, *Grand Expectations: The United States, 1945–74*

Booker Prize (c. $32,000)**:** Arundhati Roy, *The God of Small Things*

Canada's Governor-General Literary Awards ($10,000 ea.)
English-language awards
Drama: Ian Ross, *fareWel*
Fiction: Jane Urquhart, *The Underpainter*
Nonfiction: Rachel Manley, *Drumblair: Memories of a Jamaican Childhood*
Poetry: Dionne Brand, *Land to Light On*
French-language awards
Drama: Yvan Bienvenue, *Dits et Inédits*
Fiction: Aude, *Cet imperceptible mouvement*
Nonfiction: Roland Viau, *Enfants du néant et mangeurs d'âmes—Guerre, culture et société en Iroquoisie ancienne*
Poetry: Pierre Nepveu, *Romans-fleuves*

Jerusalem Prize ($5,000): Jorge Semprun, Spain

Lannan Foundation prizes for distinctive literary merit
Fiction ($75,000 ea.): John Banville, Anne Michaels, Grace Paley
Lifetime achievement ($100,000): William Gass
Nonfiction ($75,000): David Quammen
Poetry ($75,000): Ken Smith

Mystery Writers of America/Edgar Allan Poe Awards
Critical or biographical work: Robert Polito, *Savage Art: A Biography of Jim Thompson*
Fact crime: Darcy O'Brien, *The Power to Hurt*
First novel: John Morgan Wilson, *Simple Justice*
Novel: Thomas A. Cook, *The Chatham School Affair*
Grandmaster award: Ruth Rendell
Motion-picture screenplay: Billy Bob Thornton, *Sling Blade*
Original paperback: Harlan Coben, *Fade Away*

National Book Awards ($10,000 ea.)
Medal for distinguished contribution to American letters: Studs Terkel
Fiction: Charles Frazier, *Cold Mountain*
Nonfiction: Joseph Ellis, *American Sphinx: The Character of Thomas Jefferson*
Poetry: William Meredith, *Effort at Speech: New and Selected Poems*
Young people's literature: Han Nolan, *Dancing on the Edge*

National Book Critics Circle Awards
Nona Balakian Citation for excellence in book reviewing: Dennis Drabelle
Biography/autobiography: Frank McCourt, *Angela's Ashes*
Criticism: William Gass, *Finding a Form*
Fiction: Gina Berriault, *Women in Their Beds*
Nonfiction: Jonathan Raban, *Bad Land: An American Romance*
Poetry: Robert Hass, *Sun Under Wood*
Ivan Sandrof Award for lifetime achievement: Albert Murray

PEN Literary Awards
Emerging writer prizes: Rita Williams-Garcia ($3,000); Judy Blunt ($4,000)
Essay ($5,000): Cynthia Ozick, *Fame and Folly*
First nonfiction: Mark Doty, *Heaven's Coast*
PEN/BOMC Translation Award: Arnold Pomeran, for translation of *The Letters of Vincent van Gogh*
PEN/Faulkner Award for fiction ($15,000): Gina Berriault, *Women in Their Beds*
PEN/Klein Book Editing Award: Kate Medina, Random House
PEN/Malamud Award for excellence in short fiction: Alice Munro, *Selected Stories*
PEN/Manheim Translation Medal: Robert Fagles, for lifetime achievement
Poetry in translation: Edward Snow for translation of Rilke's *Uncollected Poems*
Poggioli Emerging Translator Award: Ann McGarrell for translation of Vittoria Ronchey's *The Face of Isis*

Pulitzer Prizes
Biography: Frank McCourt, *Angela's Ashes*
Fiction: Steven Millhauser, *Martin Dressler: The Tale of an American Dreamer*
General nonfiction: Richard Kluger, *Ashes to Ashes: America's Hundred-Year Cigarette War, the Public Health, and the Unabashed Triumph of Philip Morris*

History: Jack N. Rakove, *Original Meanings: Politics and Ideas in the Making of the Constitution*
Poetry: Lisel Mueller, *Alive Together: New and Selected Poems*
Rea Award for the Short Story ($30,000): Gina Berriault
Tanning Prize for Poetry ($100,000): Anthony Hecht
Thurber Prize for American Humor ($5,000): Ian Frazier, *Coyote v. Acme*
Kingsley Tufts Poetry Award ($50,000): Campbell McGrath, *Spring Comes to Chicago*
U.S. Poet Laureate: Robert Pinsky
Whitbread Book of the Year Award ($34,000): Seamus Heaney, *The Spirit Level*

MOTION PICTURES

Academy of Motion Pictures Arts and Sciences ("Oscar") Awards
Actor—leading: Geoffrey Rush, *Shine*
Actor—supporting: Cuba Gooding, Jr., *Jerry Maguire*
Actress—leading: Frances McDormand, *Fargo*
Actress—supporting: Juliette Binoche, *The English Patient*
Art direction: *The English Patient*
Cinematography: *The English Patient*
Costume design: *The English Patient*
Director: Anthony Minghella, *The English Patient*
Documentary feature: *When We Were Kings*
Documentary short subject: *Breathing Lessons: The Life and Work of Mark O'Brien*
Film: *The English Patient*
Film editing: *The English Patient*
Foreign-language film: *Kolya* (Czech Republic)
Makeup: *The Nutty Professor*
Original dramatic score: Gabriel Yared, *The English Patient*
Original musical or comedy score: Rachel Portman, *Emma*
Original song: Andrew Lloyd Webber and Tim Rice, "You Must Love Me," (from *Evita*)
Screenplay—original: Joel and Ethan Coen, *Fargo*
Screenplay—adaptation: Billy Bob Thornton, *Sling Blade*
Short film (animated): *Quest*
Short film (live action): *Dear Diary*
Sound: *The English Patient*
Irving G. Thalberg Memorial Award: Saul Zaentz
Visual effects: *Independence Day*
American Film Institute's Life Achievement Award: Martin Scorsese
Cannes Film Festival Awards
Palme d'Or (best film) (shared): Shohei Imamura, *Unagi* (The Eel) (Japan); Abbas Kiarostami, *Taste of Cherry* (Iran)
Grand Prize: Atom Egoyan, *The Sweet Hereafter* (Canada)
Jury Prize: Manuel Poirier, *Western* (France)
Fiftieth-anniversary prize: Youssef Chahine, *Al Massir* (Destiny) (Egypt)
Best actor: Sean Penn, *She's So Lovely* (United States)
Best actress: Kathy Burke, *Nil by Mouth* (United States)
Best director: Wong Kar-Wai, *Happy Together* (Hong Kong)
Best screenplay: James Schamus, *The Ice Storm* (United States)
Directors Guild of America Awards
Documentary: Al Pacino, *Waiting for Richard*
Feature film: Anthony Minghella, *The English Patient*
D.W. Griffith Award: Stanley Kubrick
Golden Globe Awards
Actor—drama: Geoffrey Rush, *Shine*
Actress—drama: Brenda Blethyn, *Secrets & Lies*
Actor—musical or comedy: Tom Cruise, *Jerry Maguire*
Actress—musical or comedy: Madonna, *Evita*
Director: Milos Forman, *The People vs. Larry Flynt*
Drama: *The English Patient*
Musical or comedy: *Evita*
National Society of Film Critics Awards
Actor: Eddie Murphy, *The Nutty Professor*
Actress: Emily Watson, *Breaking the Waves*
Cinematography: Robby Muller, *Breaking the Waves*
Director: Lars von Trier, *Breaking the Waves*
Documentary: *When We Were Kings*
Film: *Breaking the Waves*
Foreign-language film: *La Cérémonie* (France)
Screenplay: Albert Brooks and Monica Johnson, *Mother*
Special award: James Katz and Robert Harris, restoration of *Vertigo*
Supporting actor: Martin Donovan, *The Portrait of a Lady*
Supporting actress: Barbara Hershey, *The Portrait of a Lady*

PUBLIC SERVICE

Africa Prize for Leadership for the sustainable end of hunger ($100,000 shared): Joaquim Chissano, president of Mozambique; Joyce Banda, founder, National Association of Business Women of Malawi
Charles A. Dana Foundation Awards for pioneering achievements in health and higher education ($50,000 ea.): health (shared)—Paul Greengard, professor and head, Laboratory of Molecular and Cellular Neuroscience, Rockefeller University, New York; Eric R. Kandel, University Professor, Columbia University, and senior investigator, Howard Hughes Medical Institute; education—Margot Stern Strom, executive director and president, Facing History and Ourselves National Foundation; distinguished achievement—U.S. Sen. Ted Stevens (R-AK)
Sidney Hillman Foundation Awards for pursuit of social justice and public policy for the common good:
General awards: William Julius Wilson, *When Work Disappears*; Rita Giordano and Alfred Lubrano, "Passyunk Homes: Welfare's Ground Zero," *The Philadelphia Inquirer*; Grace Kahng and Stone Phillips, "Toy Story," *Dateline* (NBC); Charles Bowden, "While You Were Sleeping," *Harper's Magazine*
Officers' Award for Public Service: Committee for a National Teach-In with Labor (Steve Fraser and Nelson Lichtenstein, co-conveners)
Officers' UNITE Award: Ed Krueger, Comité Fronteriza de Obreras
American Institute for Public Service Jefferson Awards
Benefiting the Disadvantaged: Oseola McCarty, benefactor, University of Southern Mississippi
Elected or Appointed Official: former U.S. Sen. Robert Dole (R-KS)
Private Citizen: Brian Lamb, C-SPA
Citizen 35 or Younger: Michael Danziger, founder, Steppingstone Foundation
John F. Kennedy Profile in Courage Award ($25,000): Charles Price, U.S. circuit-court judge, Alabama
Sara Lee Foundation Frontrunner Awards ($50,000 ea.):
Arts—Rita Dove, Commonwealth professor of English, University of Virginia
Business—Katharine Graham, chair, executive committee, The Washington Post Company
Government—Sandra Day O'Connor, associate justice, U.S. Supreme Court
Humanities—Sarah Brady, chair, Center to Prevent Handgun Violence
National Peace Foundation: Janet Reno, Desmond Tutu
Franklin D. Roosevelt Four Freedoms Awards: Katharine Graham, chair, executive committee, The Washington Post Company; former U.S. Sen. Mark Hatfield (R-OR); U.S. Sen. Daniel Inouye (D-HI); U.S. Rep. Sidney Yates (D-IL); Bill Gray, president, United Negro College Fund
Templeton Prize for Progress in Religion ($1,200,000): Pandurang Shastri Athavale, India
U.S. Congressional Medal of Honor (presented by President Bill Clinton on Jan. 13, 1997): Vernon Baker, Edward Carter, Jr. (posthumous), John Fox (posthumous), Willy James, Jr. (posthumous), Ruben Rivers (posthumous), Charles Thomas (posthumous), George Watson (posthumous)
U.S. Presidential Medal of Freedom (presented by President Bill Clinton on Jan. 14, 1997): William J. Perry; (presented by President Clinton on Jan. 17, 1997): Robert J. Dole

SCIENCE

Bristol-Myers Squibb Awards for distinguished achievement in medical research ($50,000 ea.): cancer: Stanley J. Korsmeyer, Howard Hughes Medical Institute, Washington University School of Medicine; cardiovascular: Oliver Smithies, University of North Carolina at Chapel Hill; infectious diseases: Stanley Falkow, Stanford University School of Medicine; neuroscience (shared): Eric Shooter, Stanford University School of Medicine; Hans Thoenen, Max-Planck Institute for Psychiatry, Martinsried, Germany; nutrition: Scott M. Grundy, University of Texas, Southwestern Medical Center at Dallas; orthopedic: Joseph A. Buckwalter, University of Iowa Hospitals and Clinics
John Bates Clark Medal (for the best U.S. economist under age 40): Kevin M. Murphy, University of Chicago
King Faisal International Prize for Medicine ($200,000): James Gusella, Cambridge, MA
Louisa Gross Horwitz Memorial Prize for research in biology or biochemistry ($22,000): Stanley B. Prusiner, University of California at San Francisco
General Motors Cancer Research Foundation Awards ($100,000 ea.)
Kettering Prize: Herman D. Suit, Massachusetts General Hospital and Harvard Medical School
Mott Prize: Judah Folkman, Harvard Medical School Children's Hospital
Sloan Prize: Paul Nurse, Imperial Cancer Research Fund, London, England
Albert Lasker Medical Research Awards:
Basic Research ($25,000): Mark S. Ptashne, Memorial Sloan-Kettering Cancer Center
Clinical Research ($10,000 ea.): Alfred Sommer, Johns Hopkins University
Special Achievement in Medical Science ($25,000): Victor A. McKusick, Johns Hopkins University
National Medal of Science (presented by President Bill Clinton on Dec. 16, 1997): William K. Estes, Darleane C. Hoffman, Harold S. Johnston, Marshall N. Rosenbluth, Martin Schwarzschild (posthumous), James D. Watson, Robert A. Weinberg, George W. Wetherill, Shing-Tung Yau
National Medal of Technology (presented by President Bill Clinton on Dec. 16, 1997): Norman R. Augustine, Ray M. Dolby, Robert S. Ledley, Vinton Gray Cerf and Robert E. Kahn (joint award)
Tyler Prize for Environmental Achievement ($150,000 shared): Biruté Galdikas, president, Orangutan Foundation International, and professor, Simon Fraser University, Vancouver, B.C., Canada; Jane Goodall, director, The Jane Goodall Institute for Wildlife Research, Education and Conservation; George B. Schaller, director for science, Wildlife Conservation Society
World Food Prize ($250,000 shared): Ray F. Smith and Perry L. Adkisson, for researching a new approach to agricultural pest control

TELEVISION AND RADIO

Academy of Television Arts and Sciences ("Emmy") Awards
Actor—comedy series: John Lithgow, *3rd Rock From the Sun* (NBC)

Actor—drama series: Dennis Franz, *NYPD Blue* (ABC)
Actor—miniseries or a special: Armand Assante, *Gotti* (HBO)
Actress—comedy series: Helen Hunt, *Mad About You* (NBC)
Actress—drama series: Gillian Anderson, *The X-Files* (Fox)
Actress—miniseries or a special: Alfre Woodard, *Miss Evers' Boys* (HBO)
Comedy series: *Frasier* (NBC)
Directing—comedy series: David Lee, "To Kill a Talking Bird," *Frasier* (NBC)
Directing—drama series: Mark Tinker, "Where's Swaldo?" *NYPD Blue* (ABC)
Directing—miniseries or a special: Andrei Konchalovsky, *The Odyssey: Parts I & II* (NBC)
Directing—variety or music program: Don Mischer, *Centennial Olympic Games: Opening Ceremonies* (NBC)
Drama series: *Law & Order* (NBC)
Individual performance—variety or music program: Bette Midler, *Bette Midler: Diva Las Vegas* (HBO)
Miniseries or a special: *Prime Suspect 5: Errors of Judgment* (PBS)
Movie made for television: *Miss Evers' Boys* (HBO)
President's Award: *Miss Evers' Boys* (HBO)
Supporting actor—comedy series: Michael Richards, *Seinfeld* (NBC)
Supporting actor—drama series: Hector Elizondo, *Chicago Hope* (CBS)
Supporting actor—miniseries or a special: Beau Bridges, *The Second Civil War* (HBO)
Supporting actress—comedy series: Kristen Johnston, *3rd Rock From the Sun* (NBC)
Supporting actress—drama series: Kim Delaney, *NYPD Blue* (ABC)
Supporting actress—miniseries or a special: Diana Rigg, *Rebecca* (PBS)
Variety, music, or comedy series: *Tracey Takes On...* (HBO)
Variety, music, or comedy special: *Chris Rock: Bring the Pain* (HBO)
Writing—comedy series: Ellen DeGeneres (story); Dava Savel, Tracy Newman, and Jonathan Stark (teleplay), "The Puppy Episode," *Ellen* (ABC)
Writing—drama series: David Milch, Stephen Gaghan, and Michael R. Perry, "Where's Swaldo?" *NYPD Blue* (ABC)
Writing—miniseries or a special: Horton Foote, *Hallmark Hall of Fame Presentation: William Faulkner's Old Man* (CBS)
Writing—variety or music program: Chris Rock, *Chris Rock: Bring the Pain* (HBO)

Golden Globe Awards
Drama series: *The X-Files* (Fox)
Musical or comedy series: *3rd Rock from the Sun* (NBC)
Humanitas Prizes (for film and TV scripts that enrich the lives of the viewing public)**:**
Feature film ($25,000): Mike Leigh, *Secrets & Lies*
Cable- or public-television production ($25,000): Walter Bernstein, *Miss Evers' Boys* (HBO)
Children's animated television production ($10,000): Alex Taub, *Life With Louie* (Fox)
Children's live-action television production ($10,000): Bruce Harmon, *Someone Had to Be Benny* (HBO)
Network television production (90-minute or longer) ($25,000): Horton Foote, *William Faulkner's "Old Man"* (CBS)
Network television production (60-minute) (15,000): David Mills, episode of *NYPD Blue* (ABC)
Network television production (30-minute) ($15,000): Bob Tischler, episode of *Something So Right* (NBC)
George Foster Peabody Awards
Radio: Radio Smithsonian, Washington, for Public Radio International, *Black Radio: Telling It Like It Was*; Sound Portrait Productions for National Public Radio, *Remorse: The 14 Stories of Eric Morse*; WBEZ-FM, Chicago, IL, *This American Life*
Television: WCVB, Boston, MA, *Who's Guarding the Guardians?*; BBC News, London, England, *Newsnight*, "Afghanistan"; WNBC, New York, *Passport to Kill*; Center for New American Media, Midnight Films and WETA, Washington, *Vote for Me: Politics in America*; Telling Pictures, HBO, Channel 4 in London, and ZDF-Arte (Germany/France), *The Celluloid Closet*; Long Bow Group Inc. and Independent Television Service for Frontline/WGBH, Boston, MA, *Frontline*, "The Gate of Heavenly Peace"; HBO, Creative Thinking International Ltd., *Paradise Lost: The Child Murders at Robin Hood Hills*; KOMO, Seattle, WA, for excellence in local programming; Frontline/WGBH, Boston, MA, and Helen Whitney Productions, *Frontline*, "The Choice '96"; Nova/WGBH, Boston, MA, Agaton Film and Television, Swedish Television, SVTI, ZDF-Arte (Germany/France), and Channel 4 in London, England, *Nova*, "Odyssey of Life"; BBC, London, England, and WGBH, Boston, MA, *People Century*; American Experience and Lennon Documentary Group/WGBH, Boston, MA, *The American Experience*, "The Battle Over Citizen Kane"; KCET, Los Angeles, CA, and BBC, London, England, *The Great War and the Shaping of the 20th Century*; Turner Entertainment Group, Atlanta, GA, and Steven Spielberg in association with Survivors of the Shoah Visual History Foundation, *Survivors of the Holocaust*; Fox, Ten Thirteen Productions in association with 20th Television, *The X-Files*; HBO Sports, *Journey of the African-American Athlete*; NBC, Wolf Films in association with Universal Television, *Law and Order*; A&E and BBC, London, England, *Pride and Prejudice*; Fox, Gracie Films, in association with 20th Television, *The Simpsons*; ABC, Steve Bochco Productions, *NYPD Blue*; BBC, London, England, and WGBH, Boston, MA, Mobil Masterpiece

© Joan Marcus

The highly praised 1997 staging of Henrik Ibsen's "A Doll's House" garnered four Tony awards, including one for best actress for Janet McTeer, above, of Great Britain.

Theatre, for *House of Cards*, *To Play the King*, and *The Final Cut*; HBO, *How Do You Spell God?*; Carlton Television for Channel 4 in London, England, *Wise Up!*; ABC, Tomlin & Wagner Theatricalz, Kurtz & Friends, *Edith Ann's Christmas*; WCCO, Minneapolis, MN, *One to One: Mentoring*; Bud Greenspan, for sports documentary filmmaking

THEATER
American Academy and Institute of Arts and Letters Awards
Marc Blitzstein Memorial Award for Musical Theater: Charles Kondek, *Librettist*
Richard Rodgers Awards for Musical Theater: production—Brian Crawley and Jeanine Tesori, *Violet*; staged readings—Mike Reid and Sarah Schlesinger, *The Ballad of Little Jo*; Fernando Rivas and Luis Santeiro, *Barrio Babies*
New York Drama Critics Circle Awards
Best foreign play: *Skylight*, by David Hare (England)
Best musical: *Violet*, music by Jeanine Tesori; book and lyrics by Brian Crawley
Best new play: *How I Learned to Drive*, by Paula Vogel
Special award: cast and creative team of *Chicago*
Outer Critics Circle Awards
Actor—play: Christopher Plummer, *Barrymore*
Actor—musical: Robert Cuccioli, *Jekyll & Hyde*
Actress—play: Janet McTeer, *A Doll's House*
Actress—musical: Bebe Neuwirth, *Chicago*
Choreography: Ann Reinking, *Chicago*
Director: Walter Bobbie, *Chicago*
Musical: Cy Coleman, *The Life*
Play: Alfred Uhry, *The Last Night of Ballyhoo*
Revival—musical: *Chicago*
Revival—play: *A Doll's House*
Antoinette Perry ("Tony") Awards
Actor—play: Christopher Plummer, *Barrymore*
Actor—musical: James Naughton, *Chicago*
Actress—play: Janet McTeer, *A Doll's House*
Actress—musical: Bebe Neuwirth, *Chicago*
Choreography: Ann Reinking, *Chicago*
Costume design: Judith Dolan, *Candide*
Director—play: Anthony Page, *A Doll's House*
Director—musical: Walter Bobbie, *Chicago*
Featured actor—play: Owen Teale, *A Doll's House*
Featured actor—musical: Chuck Cooper, *The Life*
Featured actress—play: Lynne Thigpen, *An American Daughter*
Featured actress—musical: Lillias White, *The Life*
Lifetime achievement: Bernard B. Jacobs
Lighting design: Ken Billington, *Chicago*
Musical: *Titanic*
Musical—book: Peter Stone, *Titanic*
Musical—score: Maury Yeston, *Titanic*
Orchestration: Jonathan Tunick, *Titanic*
Play: *The Last Night of Ballyhoo*
Regional theater award: Berkeley Repertory Theater, Berkeley, CA
Reproduction of a musical: *Chicago*
Reproduction of a play: *A Doll's House*
Scenic design: Stewart Laing, *Titanic*
Pulitzer Prize for Drama: no award

PUBLISHING

While book publishing in the United States continued to face difficult times in 1997, prosperity marked the nation's newspaper and magazine industries, as signs of healthy profits and surging advertising dollars continued. Books and magazines that focused on the tragic death of Great Britain's Princess Diana received a notable boost in second-half sales.

Books. Many U.S. book publishers bade a thankful farewell to 1996—a year of soaring returns of unsold copies, lackluster sales, and market uncertainty; but 1997 brought only slight improvement. Total 1996 book sales rose by about 4% to $20.75 billion, according to preliminary figures from the Association of American Publishers; however, these figures disguised recent declines in adult hardcover-book sales. The Book Industry Study Group (BISG) predicted total book sales would rise by approximately 5.3% during 1997—to about $21.32 billion—and that industry sales would increase by some 5% per year through 2000.

The memoirs of celebrities and other people attracted high levels of interest during 1997. The release of a new version of *Diana, Her True Story* following the death of the princess of Wales drew controversy—especially in the United Kingdom, where critics accused author Andrew Morton of profiteering. Morton revealed that Diana was the principal source for his 1992 book, which detailed her eating disorders, suicide attempts, and agony over the infidelity of her former husband, Prince Charles. Diana's death also helped push Kitty Kelley's *The Royals*—which featured gossip about Diana and others in the House of Windsor—to the top of best-seller lists. *Angela's Ashes*, the story of Frank McCourt's impoverished childhood in Ireland, remained a best-seller.

Television's Oprah Winfrey increased her considerable book-marketing influence. Jacquelyn Mitchard's *The Deep End of the Ocean*—the first selection of the talk-show host's monthly on-air reading club, which began in September 1996—became a Number 1 seller, as did subsequent selections.

In December 1996, Pearson PLC agreed to acquire the Putnam Berkley Group from Seagram Co. for $336 million, making Pearson the fourth-largest U.S. trade publisher. The merger helped to boost the value of major 1996 book-industry deals to $1.8 billion, a threefold increase from 1995. In February 1997 a federal judge approved the merger of the Thomson Corp. and West Publishing, two of the largest legal publishers. Textbook pub-

© New York Times Pictures

"The New York Times" underwent its biggest makeover since the 1970s. The introduction of full-color photographs, new and enlarged sections, and later deadlines were part of the change.

lisher Harcourt General paid $800 million for National Education Corp., majority owner of education-supplement supplier Steck-Vaughn Publishing.

HarperCollins' August decision to write off some $270 million in losses—about 35% of its value—reflected financial problems within the industry. It was quite possibly the largest such action in the history of English-language publishing. Earlier, the company had canceled more than 100 contracts with authors due to missed deadlines and anticipated weak sales.

During the fiscal year ending Jan. 31, 1997, the four major chains added 164 new superstores. Sales at these chains' superstores rose 36% during 1996, to $3.27 billion. Superstores held an estimated 30% of the retail book market, up from about 23% a year earlier. Bookstores remained the largest outlet for sales of adult books during 1996, but their share declined from 46% to 43% as food, drug, and discount stores showed big sales gains. Although apparently not yet profitable, Internet bookstores also experienced rapid growth. The largest, Amazon.com, reported almost $44 million in sales from its 2.5 million titles during the first half of 1997, compared with $3.1 million during the first six months of 1996. Barnes & Noble's new on-line store became Amazon's major competitor, but during the summer, Wal-Mart—which previously had sold only 350 on-line best-sellers—added 300,000 titles.

Many publishers cheered a June decision by the U.S. Supreme Court that struck down the Communications Decency Act. The ruling held that provisions of the Internet-related law banning "indecent" and "patently offensive" materials violated the 1st Amendment. In October the American Booksellers Association (ABA) won a $25 million settlement from Penguin Group USA over discounts Penguin offered to large retailers for speeding up payments. In 1995, as part of a settlement of an antitrust lawsuit filed by the ABA, Penguin had agreed not to favor large retailers with special discounts.

Magazines. During 1996 and early 1997, U.S. magazine revenues continued a seven-year climb. Advertising revenue of titles measured by the Publishers Information Bureau increased about 8.4% in 1996, while total magazine advertising pages declined slightly. Overall revenue for the first half of 1997 grew by 12.2%. As of late 1996, family/parenting, gardening, and personal-finance magazines saw especially strong circulations. In mid-1997 investment bankers Veronis, Suhler, & Associates predicted that ad spending on consumer magazines would grow by about 7.9% annually through 2001, but that circulation would remain flat.

By 1996 some 10,625 U.S. titles were being published. Two publications received by members of the American Association of Retired Persons (AARP)—*NRTA/AARP Bulletin* and *Modern Maturity*—remained circulation leaders, with more than 20 million each. *Reader's Digest*, *TV Guide*, and *National Geographic* followed.

Princess Diana's death caused September production upheavals as major weekly magazines scrambled to remake nearly completed editions in time for deadlines. The coverage may have boosted newsstand sales of such magazines as *Newsweek* and *Time* to the highest levels in history. Many titles published special editions, which sold briskly.

The magazine industry continued to move away from general-interest publications, with many new titles about special interests such as exotic pets or food. Acquisitions continued during 1997, with Rodale Press Inc. agreeing to purchase *New Woman* from K-III Communications Corp., and Reed Elsevier buying the Chilton Business Group from the Walt Disney Co. for $447 million. In a deal with Time, Inc., celebrity Martha Stewart gained control over the monthly *Martha Stewart Living*. In July,

Canberry Partners—which includes investment bank Wasserstein, Perella & Co.—purchased the company that publishes *The American Lawyer*. Observers described the growing tendency of investment banks to purchase publishing properties as a sign of prosperity.

In March the first issue of *Cosmopolitan* in 31 years that was not edited by Helen Gurley Brown appeared. The new editor in chief, Bonnie Fuller, doubled the number of pages devoted to beauty and fashion. After *Esquire* killed a short story about a gay man, allegedly due to possible advertising losses, the American Society of Magazine Editors expressed concerns that advance warning to advertisers about issue contents may encourage advertiser pressures.

Early in 1997, a judge upheld a challenge by *Penthouse* and other plaintiffs to a ban on sales of sexually explicit materials on U.S. military bases. The potential impact on tobacco ads of an agreement between cigarette companies and 40 states remained unclear. As part of the pact, which would shield tobacco companies from certain lawsuits, the industry agreed to restrict advertising. Some U.S. magazines benefited from a World Trade Organization (WTO) ruling that Canadian efforts to keep *Sports Illustrated* from printing a profitable Canadian edition violated international law. Canada had applied tariffs to split-run editions of U.S. titles to keep them from taking advertising away from native titles.

Newspapers. In many ways, good times continued for U.S. newspapers in 1997. Solid profits and growing advertising revenues overshadowed modest increases in the cost of newsprint. Advertising revenues rose 9.5% in the first half of 1997, according to the Newspaper Association of America (NAA). The growth, much stronger than was expected, was the largest since the late 1980s. Advertising spending rose 5.8% in 1996, with classified ads increasing 9.9%. In mid-1996, Veronis, Suhler, & Associates predicted 6.3% compound annual growth in daily-newspaper advertising and circulation spending through 2001. Weekly spending was expected to grow by 6.5%. The industry had grown at 4.5% annually since 1991.

The number of dailies fell slightly, to 1,520, during 1996 despite an increase in the number of morning papers. Circulation among daily newspapers fell, from about 58.2 million in 1995 to about 57 million, while circulation of morning papers continued to increase. Sunday circulation fell from about 61.5 million to about 60.8 million. *The Wall Street Journal* was still the daily circulation leader, with

The Paparazzi

The tragic death of Princess Diana following a car wreck in Paris, France, during the early hours of Aug. 31, 1997, turned the term "paparazzi" into a household word. Paparazzi refers to photographers who make a living by following famous people—in cars, boats, helicopters, and with long-range digital equipment—in the hopes of photographing them at an unguarded moment. Such pictures command huge sums of money from tabloid newspapers and magazines worldwide. The term was introduced following Federico Fellini's 1960 film *La Dolce Vita*. One of the film's characters was a photographer called *Paparazzo*—an Italian word meaning "buzzing insect."

The fact that Princess Diana died after fleeing from photographers in a chauffeur-driven automobile caused public outrage. Celebrities already had been objecting strongly to paparazzi methods. Diana's death also led to attempts to strengthen existing privacy laws. U.S. Rep. Sonny Bono (R-CA) introduced a bill in Congress that would make it a crime for photographers to "persistently physically follow" someone while taking commercial pictures. Existing U.S. civil privacy laws, however, already could make journalists who harass celebrities liable. In one famous case, Jacqueline Kennedy Onassis won an injunction against Ron Galella, a photographer who had hounded her persistently. Ironically, France has some of the most stringent privacy laws in Europe—which raised questions about the effectiveness of legal action in curbing the excesses of the paparazzi.

Observers continued to debate the ethics of the paparazzi. Some critics compared these journalists to parasites and argued that they were responsible in part for the princess' tragic death. Others, however, suggested that these photographers simply are giving the public what it wants. Celebrities often complain about media attention, they argued, yet encourage it by welcoming photographers when the publicity will be beneficial to them.

DAVID PERRY

---

about 1.78 million copies, followed by *USA Today*, *The New York Times*, and *The Los Angeles Times*. The NAA reported that some 7,915 weeklies, with total circulation of almost 81.6 million, were being published.

Faced with circulation declines, aging readership, and weakening ties between readers and newspapers, the industry experimented with innovations such as feature stories written by readers and front pages without full-length news stories. To encourage readership by the young —fewer than 50% of whom read newspapers daily—the NAA launched a national advertising campaign.

Mergers and acquisitions continued. In April, Knight-Ridder Inc. agreed to spend $1.65 billion to buy *The Kansas City Star*, the *Fort Worth Star-Telegram*, and two other dailies from the Walt Disney Co.; this was the largest all-newspaper purchase on record. In July the largest U.S. cable operator, Tele-Communications Inc., acquired the Kearns-Tribune Co., which owns *The Salt Lake Tribune*, Utah's biggest newspaper. During the summer, Knight-Ridder agreed to swap the Boulder, CO, *Daily Camera* to E.W. Scripps in exchange for two California dailies—*The Monterey County Herald* and the San Luis Obispo *Telegram-Tribune*—reflecting a trend among chains to concentrate their properties geographically. Similarly, Lee Enterprises augmented its northwestern holdings by acquiring Pacific Northwest Publishing Group from Disney for $185 million. The deal included two Oregon dailies—the *Albany Democrat-Herald* and the *Lebanon Express*—as well as 22 weekly and specialty publications.

Large newspaper chains tended to acquire smaller ones. In May, E.W. Scripps Co. agreed to spend up to $775 million for six dailies, including the *Corpus Christi Caller-Times* in Texas, and the broadcast operations of Hart-Hanks Communications Inc. In the wake of eased legal restrictions from the 1996 Telecommunications Reform Act, many chains sought television properties. For example, the biggest deal in the history of the Tribune Co.—its 1997 acquisition of Renaissance Communications Corp. for $1.13 billion—involved no newspapers. In June the Riverside, CA, *Press-Enterprise*, one of a dwindling number of family-owned newspapers, was sold to A.H. Belo Corp. In January the 116-year-old *Phoenix Gazette* published its last issue. The *Rochester* (NY) *Times-Union* disappeared in a July merger with its sister newspaper, the *Democrat and Chronicle*.

In February, after nearly two years, six striking unions offered to return to work at the *Detroit Free Press* and *The Detroit News*. Management agreed to take back as many strikers as possible, but only as jobs opened. The unions charged that they were locked out.

DAVID K. PERRY, *The University of Alabama*

REFUGEES AND IMMIGRATION

During 1997 the number of refugees worldwide declined, while the number of internally displaced people increased. Refugees are those persons who are displaced forcibly by persecution or war and who cross national borders to seek refuge, while the internally displaced are those persons who also are uprooted from their homes but who remain within their own countries, frequently without any assistance or protection.

The global total of refugees and asylum seekers, estimated at 14.5 million people in 1997, stood at its lowest level since 1988. While some of the decrease was due to improvement in the human-rights conditions that caused refugees to flee, the decline in refugee numbers also indicated that the availability of asylum was becoming more restricted, particularly as economic difficulties in regions with a tradition of long-term asylum were making local integration of refugees in host countries more difficult to achieve. It also is the case in the late 1990s that more refugees have little choice but to repatriate even if conditions back home are not really safe enough for them to do so.

In 1997 there were an estimated 30 million internally displaced people around the world. Sudan, Afghanistan, Angola, Sri Lanka, and Colombia, among other countries, had the greatest number. The number of internally displaced, and the ratio of internally displaced people to refugees, well may continue to increase as intrastate conflicts break out and environmental pressures intensify.

Continuing Crises in Africa. After the controversial return home in 1996 of more than 1 million Rwandan refugees from Zaire and Tanzania, the international community was faced in 1997 with a new repatriation crisis in the new Democratic Republic of the Congo (formerly Zaire). During the civil war that ousted Zairean President Mobutu Sese Seko, hundreds of thousands of Hutu refugees fled westward and dispersed into the forests. The UN High Commissioner for Refugees (UNHCR) and the International Committee of the Red Cross (ICRC) mounted rescue operations, and between May and September more than 65,000 refugees were airlifted back to Rwanda. Tens of thousands of others, however, died of hunger, exhaustion, disease, or fighting at the hands of military forces. Access to the remaining refugees still alive in the forests frequently was limited or denied.

There were repeated military attacks on refugee sites, and violence and mass killings of refugees were reported. UNHCR was confronted with the dilemma of repatriating Rwandans to some unsafe areas of western Rwanda or leaving them in the forests, where death was almost a certainty. In Rwanda itself, the earlier massive return of Hutu from Tanzania and the former Zaire contributed to tension and violence, particularly in the western region. Armed groups and political extremists operating from within western Rwanda added to the grave instability and insecurity there. Monitoring returnees in these areas was practically impossible, and several staff members of humanitarian agencies were killed while attempting to work in these areas.

New Problems and Positive Developments. There were at least two new refugee influxes during 1997. Following the breakup of Cambodia's coalition government of Hun Sen and Prince Norodom Ranariddh and renewed civil war in that nation, more than 40,000 Cambodians crossed the border into Thailand. Internal fighting in the Republic of Congo (Brazzaville) caused the flight of thousands of refugees, particularly to the neighboring Democratic Republic of the Congo.

Some older refugee problems also flared up again. In Afghanistan continued civil conflict and human-rights abuses, particularly against women, created new displacements and all but stopped the repatriation of Afghans from Iran and Pakistan. There were continuing threats to the security of Sudanese refugees in northern Uganda, and the anticipated resolution of Sierra Leone's refugee crisis was dashed when the elected government of that country was deposed in a military coup.

After seven years of continual conflict and refugee exodus, elections were held in Liberia in July, raising hopes that this would facilitate the repatriation of some 500,000 Liberian refugees, some of whom had returned home on their own. In addition, some 300,000 Togolese refugees, who had fled in 1993, were repatriated during 1997. In Central America there was progress on the repatriation of Guatemalan refugees from Mexico, and some 2,500 Guatemalan refugees were under consideration for naturalization in Mexico.

U.S. Immigration. In April, U.S. immigration legislation passed in 1996 became fully effective. In May 1997 the budget agreement reached between the Bill Clinton administration and the Republican congressional leadership revised the sections of the 1996 welfare law that barred certain basic benefits to legal aliens. However, immigrants who arrived after the passage of the welfare law remained ineligible for social benefits. Moreover, the prob-

© John Moore/AP/Wide World Photos

The United Nations and the Red Cross staged rescue operations after thousands of Rwandan Hutu refugees were stranded in deep forests in Zaire during that nation's civil war in the spring of 1997. Eventually some 65,000 refugees were airlifted back to Rwanda.

lem would grow since new immigrants would be barred from safety-net programs that protect other members of U.S. society.

Other stringent features of the 1996 immigration law—such as elimination of judicial review in many cases, restrictions on asylum, and retroactive application of the law— remained intact and were enforced by the Immigration and Naturalization Service (INS). These measures significantly inhibited the ability of individuals to seek asylum in the United States or to challenge decisions about their immigration status. For example, since the law took effect, INS officers had been permitted to decide, on the spot, whether a person arriving at a port of entry without proper documentation has a credible asylum claim. Even those able to apply for asylum had to convince an immigration officer of a "credible fear" of persecution within 48 hours or face immediate deportation. The new law was based on the presumption that those entering the United States without documentation, or with fraudulent papers, do not have legitimate asylum claims. In fact, individuals fleeing persecution often have no opportunity, or ability, to obtain proper documentation.

In one of the most far-reaching provisions of the new law, the important role of the federal courts in reviewing INS decisions was restricted severely. One section of the new law effectively bars class-action lawsuits against the INS, thus eliminating a crucial check on an agency with a reputation of being misman-

aged. Moreover, under the new law immigrants can be deported for misdemeanors committed years or decades earlier.

Debate over U.S. Citizenship. During the year a number of operational and managerial problems spurred congressional investigations into the activities of the INS. In addition, there was considerable pressure applied on the agency to undertake fundamental reforms. Congressional committees particularly criticized the INS' "Citizenship USA Program," under which hundreds of thousands of individuals had been naturalized since 1995. Operational problems caused the INS to confer citizenship on about 180,000 individuals without the proper background checks, resulting in the naturalization of about 16,000 persons who had at least one felony arrest. As a result, the INS announced in May that it would revoke the naturalization of about 5,000 individuals.

Expressing great dissatisfaction with the INS' failure to screen out criminals in the citizenship process, Congress refused to allocate the agency's request for $150 million in July to support its naturalization programs during the 1997–98 fiscal year. Consequently, INS had to slow the naturalization process for hundreds of thousands of new immigrants who wanted to become U.S. citizens. Demand for citizenship had increased dramatically—from fewer than 350,000 naturalization applications in 1992 to a projected 1.8 million in 1997.

Gil Loescher, *University of Notre Dame*

Religion

Overview

Religious groups faced persecution by several governments during 1997, while interfaith relations suffered some setbacks. The mass suicide by adherents of a fringe belief drew attention to anxieties over the approach of a new millennium.

Religious Persecution. A U.S. State Department report in July described persecution of Christians in 78 countries, including Burma, Iran, Russia, Saudi Arabia, and Sudan. The 83-page report drew particular attention to China's crackdown on unregistered organizations and places of worship. A Chinese foreign-ministry official responded by saying that the United States "lacks the necessary understanding about China's religious situation."

The report also cited a Russian bill to restrict non-Orthodox Christianity, including Roman Catholicism and evangelical Protestantism. In July, Russian President Boris Yeltsin vetoed the bill—the first time he publicly had rebuffed the Russian Orthodox Church on national policy. His veto, however, was criticized roundly in the Russian parliament, which then passed a similar bill in September. Yeltsin signed the new bill despite appeals from the U.S. government, the Vatican, and several organizations that monitor religious freedom.

German legal pressures on the Church of Scientology and nationwide government surveillance of the group also were criticized in the State Department report. Thirty-four prominent Americans in the entertainment industry drew comparisons to Nazi treatment of Jews in the 1930s.

Church-State. A 6–3 ruling in June by the U.S. Supreme Court struck down the four-year-old Religious Freedom Restoration Act, to the dismay of a broad coalition of religious and civil-liberties groups. The court said Congress had exceeded its authority by passing the law, which attempted to give additional protection to religious observances and was in response to a 1990 Supreme Court ruling that curtailed religious protections. Groups that had backed the law disagreed on whether to proceed with a constitutional amendment, a new federal law, or state statutes.

In another June case, the Supreme Court voted 5–4 to reverse a 12-year-old decision forbidding publicly financed teachers to tutor children in religious schools. Writing for the majority, Justice Sandra Day O'Connor said that "interaction between church and state is inevitable, and we have always tolerated some level of involvement between the two." The court said government programs do not impermissibly advance religion where they create no financial incentives to religious activity.

Ecumenical Relations. In June, Orthodox Ecumenical Patriarch Bartholomew I of Constantinople boycotted the Second European Ecumenical Assembly in Austria and canceled his church's participation in the Vatican celebration of the feast of Saints Peter and Paul. Russian Orthodox Patriarch Aleksy II also refused a meeting with Pope John Paul II. Difficulties over what the Orthodox interpreted as proselytizing led to the cancellations.

© Les Stone/Sygma

Mormons from around the world traveled by wagon train from the U.S. Midwest to Utah in 1997 to reenact the 1847 journey members of their faith took to escape persecution. With a worldwide membership of nearly 10 million, today's Mormon Church is one of the world's fastest-growing religions.

© Oleg Nikishin/AP/Wide World Photos

© Yuri Gripas/Reuters/Archive Photos

Russia's President Boris Yeltsin joined Orthodox Patriarch Aleksy II for ceremonies opening the square around the rebuilt Christ the Savior Cathedral, left, in Moscow. The 19th-century church had been destroyed by the Bolsheviks in the 1930s.

In May the Georgian Orthodox Church withdrew its membership from the World Council of Churches; it was the first such action since the 330-member organization was founded in 1948. The Georgian church said the council's policies failed to take Orthodox interests into account....On a more positive note, the Evangelical Lutheran Church in America approved a joint declaration with the Roman Catholic Church on the doctrine of justification at its August convention in Philadelphia.

Heaven's Gate. In March, 39 members of the Heaven's Gate group committed suicide in a San Diego suburban mansion. The group, assembled over 20 years by Marshall Applewhite, the son of a Presbyterian minister, blended elements of Christianity, Gnosticism, theosophy, and belief in extraterrestrial life. Scholars of millenarian beliefs considered the group an example of a preoccupation with apocalyptic prophecies. Members believed they were aliens planted on Earth by a UFO and that they would be transported after death to a spacecraft they thought was hiding behind Comet Hale-Bopp.

The Mormons. A group that had been considered a dangerous cult in the 19th century, the Church of Jesus Christ of Latter-day Saints, reenacted its 1,000-mi (1 610-km) migration to the West during 1997. About 300 people arrived at Big Mountain Pass, UT, in July, to retrace a pioneer trail traveled by some 70,000 Mormons between 1847 and 1869. Today, the church has a worldwide membership of 9.7 million, with more than half living outside the United States.

Publications and the Templeton Prize. *The Bible Code*, which made the best-seller lists in 1997, was the most prominent of several new books that deal with deciphering hidden messages in the text of the Hebrew Bible. Drawing on the work of Israeli mathematician Eliyahu Rips, author Michael Drosnin said the code contains references to the assassination of Israeli Prime Minister Yitzhak Rabin, the Oklahoma City bombing, the Holocaust, and Watergate. However, Rips repudiated Drosnin's use of his method and most of the book's conclusions....Evangelist Billy Graham, 79, published his long-awaited autobiography, *Just as I Am.*

Pandurang Shastri Athavale, 76, a Hindu who sparked a self-help movement among millions of poor villagers in India, won the $1.2 million Templeton Prize for Progress in Religion. The Swadhyaya, or "self-study," movement has no paid staff, budget, or headquarters but has helped to establish village farms and orchards and to provide boats to poor fishermen. "I have not advocated a new ideology or a new religion but merely tried and picked from human culture certain universally shared principles," Athavale said....A previous Templeton winner who was also a Nobel laureate, Mother Teresa of Calcutta, died in September at the age of 87. *See* OBITUARIES, page 386.

DARRELL TURNER, *Religion Writer "Journal Gazette," Fort Wayne, IN*

Far Eastern

The Dalai Lama was in the news more than usual in 1997.

The Dalai Lama. The Dalai Lama experienced a challenge to his leadership of Tibetan Buddhists from followers of Dorje Shugden, a 17th-century monk who was murdered in his palace. In 1996 the Dalai Lama had asked his followers to renounce Dorje Shugden, who has been considered a "protector deity" with the power to answer prayers. The Dalai Lama rejected belief in the monk as a deity and called him an evil spirit.

Police believed the controversy was the motive behind the slayings of three disciples of the Dalai Lama in February 1997 near the Tibetan leader's exile headquarters in Dharmsala, India. The Dorje Shugden Society in New Delhi denied involvement in the slayings and accused the Dalai Lama's administration of implicating the group in order to crush religious dissent. Cheme Tsering, a monk whom police named as a suspect in the slayings, said Dorje Shugden devotees may decide to seek citizenship in India. Such a move would represent a split in the ranks of Tibetan Buddhists, most of whom have preserved their refugee status as a symbol of hope of one day returning to Tibet, from which the Dalai Lama fled in 1959 with 120,000 followers. It was unclear how many Buddhists remained faithful to Dorje Shugden. Tsering claimed as many as 20,000, but the Dalai Lama's administration dismissed them as a fringe group.

In a March visit to Taiwan the Dalai Lama conferred with the nation's president, Lee Teng-hui. The Dalai Lama portrayed the visit as an attempt to promote "basic human values and religious harmony." Preaching from the pulpit of the Washington National Cathedral in April, the Dalai Lama declared that "all major religious traditions carry basically the same message—that is, love, compassion, and forgiveness." The service featured prayers by a Buddhist patriarch from Cambodia—the Venerable Samdech Preah Maha Ghosananda—and readings from Hindu, Jewish, and Christian scriptures.

Other Buddhism News. In another interfaith gesture, a Buddhist temple in Cambodia agreed to host the tomb of a Catholic bishop who died in a Khmer Rouge labor camp in 1977 and had been buried in a mass grave.

A U.S. immigration judge granted political asylum in the United States in June to a Thai Buddhist monk who said he feared persecution from the government of that country. The monk, Phra Winai La'Ongusuwan, had been charged with wearing a monk's robes despite being defrocked, offending the supreme Thai Buddhist patriarch. He also reportedly insulted governmental and religious officials by accusing the government of corruption, brutality, and complicity in drug trafficking and prostitution. The U.S. Immigration and Naturalization Service announced plans to appeal the granting of asylum to Winai, who had established a monastery in Lilac, CA, in 1995. It said the charges against him constituted "a grave criminal offense in Thailand."

Japan Court Ruling. Japan's Supreme Court ruled in April that a local government's use of tax money as offerings at a Shinto war shrine was unconstitutional. It ordered authorities in the Ehime prefecture to return 166,000 yen—about $1,360—to the public coffers for offerings made at Tokyo's Yasukuni Shrine between 1981 and 1986.

DARRELL J. TURNER

Islam

Army officers in both Turkey and Algeria took steps to rein in powerful Islamist movements in their countries during 1997. On several occasions, Muslim extremists attacked members of Egypt's Christian minority, while other advocates of an Islamic government initiated legal actions against public figures whose behavior they deemed un-Islamic. Conflict also erupted between the Turkic Muslim peoples of western China and the government, dominated by non-Muslim Chinese. In the midst of the annual pilgrimage to Mecca, a fire swept through a housing area, killing hundreds of worshippers. As Muslims in the United States continued to carve a niche for themselves in the country's religious mainstream, their organizations called attention to, and sought to end, practices that denigrated Islam.

Strife. Since assuming the prime ministership in Turkey's coalition government in 1996, Welfare Party leader Necmettin Erbakan had alarmed Turkish military officers by his willingness to inject Islam into the political process. In the spring the officers, who regard themselves as guardians of the secular republic created in the 1920s, pressured Erbakan to restrict the activity of Islamic organizations in the country and to close down Islamic schools. The generals' conclusion that these steps had failed to halt Turkey's drift toward Islamist rule led them to demand Erbakan's resignation. Although a new, and secular, prime minister was appointed without incident, the appropriate role of Islam in Turkish society remained a matter of debate.

Parliamentary elections in Algeria in June resulted in an overwhelming victory for supporters of the secular officers who seized power in 1992. Some Islamist parties were permitted to contest the elections, but the largest such organization, the Islamic Salvation Front (FIS), was not. Its leader, Abbasi Madani, was released from prison later in the summer, however. After the elections, members of the extremist Armed Islamic Group (GIA) stepped up an intense campaign to topple the government. Their brutal tactics, including massacres of civilians sympathetic to the government or to moderate Islamist groups, and the authorities' equally brutal responses resulted in thousands of deaths.

Armed assaults on Coptic Christians in southern Egypt resulted in more than 20 fatalities and belied government assertions that religious extremism had been brought fully under control. In Cairo, other Islamist leaders attempted to secure the removal of a Cairo University professor, claiming that his writing demeaned Islam. Changes in Egyptian law, following a similar incident in 1995, had made the successful prosecution of such cases more difficult, however.

Relations between Muslims and non-Muslims degenerated into violence in China's Xinjiang province, where Muslim Uygurs faced government opposition to their efforts to assert their Islamic identity. Widespread arrests early in the year precipitated riots in which several hundred Uygurs died. The Chinese authorities blamed Muslim activists for a subsequent series of explosions in the region's capital of Urümqi, as well as for a bomb that later destroyed a bus in Beijing.

Mecca Pilgrimage. More than 2 million Muslims gathered in Mecca, Saudi Arabia, in April to participate in the annual pilgrimage rituals. As had been its practice in recent years, Libya ignored an embargo on air travel to and from the country to ferry pilgrims to Mecca. Iraq, for the first time, also defied the ban on flights over its southern provinces by sending pilgrim flights to Saudi Arabia. Despite criticisms of these acts, the international community took no retaliatory measures out of respect for the important religious event. During the rituals, a fire erupted in an extensive tent encampment housing participants. At least 300 pilgrims, most of them from the Indian subcontinent, perished.

The United States. Muslim advocacy groups in the United States convinced the publishing firm of Simon & Schuster to withdraw copies of a children's biography of Muhammad that they considered demeaning and inaccurate. They also succeeded in persuading Nike to remove from the market athletic shoes with a design that seemed to replicate the Arabic word *Allah*. In March, U.S. Muslims petitioned the Supreme Court to remove an image of Muhammad from a marble frieze in its chambers. The Muslims noted that Islam rejects religious statuary and finds any such depiction of the prophet offensive. The court declined to meet the request, citing a statute forbidding any alteration in the appearance of the building.

KENNETH J. PERKINS
University of South Carolina

Judaism

The heading of the *New York* magazine cover story of July 14, 1997, said it all: "Declining Birth Rates. Rampant Intermarriage. The 'Seinfeld Effect.' Are American Jews Assimilating Themselves Out of Existence?" Concern about the potential erosion of Judaism characterized the year 1997, as did a sharpening battle between Orthodoxy and the non-Orthodox denominations.

Proposals for addressing the high rates of intermarriage and low fertility rates of Diaspora Jewish communities abounded. Two of the most widely discussed appeared in major new books. *The Vanishing American Jew: In Search of Jewish Identity for the Next Century*, by the noted Harvard law professor Alan M. Dershowitz, argues that Judaism needs to secularize itself to have any hope of maintaining its hold on coming generations. In striking contrast, former U.S. Assistant Secretary of State Elliott Abrams, in *Faith or Fear: How Jews Can Survive in a Christian America*, claims that the secularization of Jewish identity is exactly what has weakened the community, and that a return to traditional religion—even if that means cooperation with the Christian religious right—is the only hope for saving American Jewry.

Tensions in Israel. Interdenominational tensions centered on Israel, where the large number of non-Orthodox Jews tended to identify themselves as secular rather than as Reform or Conservative, and the tiny non-Orthodox movements had been struggling for some time against the official Jewish monopoly of the Orthodox chief rabbinate. A November 1995 court decision had opened the way for the recognition of non-Orthodox conversions to Judaism, and the Orthodox

The Museum of Jewish Heritage—A Living Memorial to the Holocaust, located at New York City's Battery Park, opened on Sept. 15, 1997. The museum seeks to tell the story of the culture of the Jewish people through 800 artifacts and more than 2,000 photographs.

parties in the Israeli governing coalition pushed legislation to override the ruling. Through 1997, Reform and Conservative groups in the United States complained bitterly over such a bill as a denial of basic human rights, even going so far as to threaten the withholding of donations to Israel. They successfully convinced the United Jewish Appeal, which raises and allocates money for Israel, to channel more funds to the non-Orthodox denominations there. Their anger increased when mixed groups of men and women, attempting to conduct non-Orthodox services near the Western Wall in Jerusalem, were mistreated by Orthodox onlookers and the police. At the end of the year, an interdenominational committee, set up by the Israeli government during the summer, was seeking a compromise solution.

Identity. Conflict between Orthodox and non-Orthodox accelerated even outside the Israeli context. Mounting self-confidence among the Orthodox in the United States, who were least affected by the negative demographic trends, was reflected in a public statement by the 600-member Union of Orthodox Rabbis of the United States and Canada that while non-Orthodox Jews are, as individuals, bona fide members of the faith, their forms of Judaism "are not Judaism at all." Other Orthodox organizations, appalled at the divisive implications of this sweeping declaration, were hard put to argue against its substance, since they, too, rejected a pluralistic approach to Judaism.

And at the opposite end of the American Jewish spectrum, a special committee set up by Reform Judaism endorsed rabbinical performance of gay marriages, and the president of the Reform rabbinic organization heaped public scorn on Orthodoxy, charging that it alienated more Jews than it attracted, and that the only contribution it made to Jewish life was its focus on Jewish study.

A similar cleavage erupted in Great Britain, where the Orthodox chief rabbi—the official representative of all of British Jewry—had declined to attend non-Orthodox funeral services for a Liberal (Reform) colleague in 1996 and wrote a letter, damning Reform, to an ultra-Orthodox rabbi; the letter was leaked. This embarrassment led to calls for dismantling the British chief rabbinate.

Women's Issues. A long-simmering fissure within U.S. Orthodoxy over the religious role of women broke into the open. Although no Orthodox rabbi would sanction the mingling of the sexes in prayer, a number of communities had "women's prayer groups" in which women, with no men present, would conduct the bulk of the services themselves. In 1997 the authorization by a rabbi in Queens, NY, of such a service—where a bat mitzvah girl would read from the Torah—sparked an uproar, as the Orthodox rabbinic council of the area voted overwhelmingly to disapprove the move on the ground that it deviated from tradition, even if there was no specific point of Jewish law that was violated. The bat mitzvah took place nonetheless.

Indeed, many women in the American Orthodox community appeared to be discovering feminism. More than 1,000 of them gathered in New York in February for a conference that led to the formation of an ongoing Jewish Orthodox Feminist Alliance in July.

LAWRENCE GROSSMAN
The American Jewish Committee

Orthodox Eastern

With the Greek Orthodox Archdiocese of America celebrating its 75th anniversary in 1997, Ecumenical Patriarch Bartholomew of Constantinople toured the United States. Meanwhile, rifts between various Orthodox churches widened.

U.S. Developments. Ecumenical Patriarch Bartholomew's monthlong tour of the United States, during which he conferred with President Bill Clinton and visited various dioceses, came amid widespread opposition to the policies and actions of the new primate of the Greek Orthodox Archdiocese in the United States, Archbishop Spyridon. Massive confusion and dissent arose as the new archbishop attempted major administrative and structural changes in the archdiocese. Foremost among such changes was the archbishop's dismissal of the president and three ranking professors at Hellenic College and Holy Cross Greek Orthodox School of Theology in Brookline, MA. Critics of the archbishop claimed that the dismissals violated school bylaws and were intended to cover up a sexual-harassment case. The archbishop denied such charges and said that the dismissals were intended to end "discord" at the school.

Archbishop Spyridon's refusal to accept his election as chairman of the Standing Conference of Orthodox Bishops in America (SCOBA) brought activities of the American bishops' conference to a standstill. Efforts by Metropolitan Theodosius of the Orthodox Church in America and Metropolitan Philip of the Antiochian Orthodox Christian Archdiocese of North America to reactivate the conference were unsuccessful. Archbishop Spyridon also took back leadership of International Orthodox Christian Charities (IOCC), an American philanthropic agency that Archbishop Iakovos had placed under SCOBA's governance.

The World Scene. Relations between Ecumenical Patriarch Bartholomew of Constantinople and Russian Orthodox Patriarch Aleksy II of Moscow improved in 1997. Meeting in Odessa during a symposium on the environment sponsored by Bartholomew, the two patriarchs agreed to support Metropolitan Vladimir of Kiev, a member of the Holy Synod of the Moscow Patriarchate, as sole legitimate leader of the divided Orthodox in Ukraine.

The Russian government passed a law giving full legal rights to religions historically present in Russia, primarily the Russian Orthodox Church, and gravely restricting rights and activities of religious groups having less than a 15-year history in the country. The law was criticized widely by defenders of religious freedom, with strong opposition coming from the United States and the Vatican. Defenders of the law claimed that it was necessary in order to limit unfair advantages of wealthy and powerful missionary and proselytizing movements coming from abroad.

Roman Catholic and Protestant missionary activities in former communist countries largely populated by Orthodox Christians have given rise to even stronger opposition to ecumenism than was present in the Orthodox Church. The Orthodox Church of Georgia officially withdrew from the World Council of Churches. Many other Orthodox Churches—including the Churches of Russia, Serbia, Greece, and Jerusalem—were considering the same course of action.

The Orthodox Church in Macedonia continued in schism from the Belgrade patriarchate. Disagreement persisted between the Russian Orthodox Church and the Romanian Orthodox Church over ecclesiastical authority in Moldavia. Tensions increased between the Romanian Orthodox Church and Vatican over the rights and activities of Greek Catholics in Romania. Schism again was dividing the Orthodox Church in Bulgaria, with the 90-year-old Pimen enjoying recognition from the country's new government and the not-much-younger incumbent Maxim being recognized by the Orthodox churches.

THOMAS HOPKO
St. Vladimir's Orthodox Theological Seminary

Protestantism

Protestant denominations had a mixed year on the ecumenical front in 1997. The year saw more turmoil among churches troubled by what stance to take toward practicing homosexuals. Donald P. Hodel and Randy Tate were chosen president and executive director, respectively, of the Christian Coalition (*see* SIDEBAR, page 433), and thousands of Promise Keepers assembled on the Mall in Washington, DC, in October (*see* SPECIAL REPORT, page 434).

Ecumenism. The 5.2-million-member Evangelical Lutheran Church in America (ELCA) voted at its assembly in Philadelphia in August 1997 to share full communion with three churches in the Reformed tradition—the 3.7-million-member Presbyterian Church (U.S.A.), the 300,000-member Reformed Church in America, and the 1.5-million-mem-

© Dan Loh/AP/Wide World Photos

In July 1997, Bishop Frank T. Griswold 3d, above, was elected presiding bishop of the Episcopal Church in the United States. Bishop Griswold, 59, was a member of the Chicago diocese.

ber United Church of Christ. A statement prepared by the heads of the four denominations said the agreement marked "a decisive milestone in our journey towards unity and signals the beginning of a new chapter in the history of these four churches of the 16th-century Reformation." Under the Formula of Agreement the churches retain their creeds and theological traditions but recognize one another's sacraments and support the exchange of clergy members.

Meanwhile, the ELCA assembly fell six votes short of approving a concordat with the 2.4-million-member Episcopal Church after several speakers expressed concern about the role of that church's "historic episcopate." While a resolution to reconsider the matter also failed, the Lutherans called for a revised proposal for full communion with the Episcopal Church to be brought to the ELCA's 1999 Churchwide Assembly.

Five churches in Wales announced plans to work toward appointing the world's first ecumenical bishop by Jan. 1, 2000. Representatives of the Church in Wales, the Presbyterian Church of Wales, the Methodist Church, the United Reformed, and the Covenanted Churches of the Baptist Union of Great Britain said the bishop could come from any one of them. But Gethin Abraham-Williams, general secretary of the Covenanted Churches in Wales, said it would not be a woman because of the "realities of the situation," as the Welsh Anglican denomination does not provide for women bishops.

Two denominations broke ties with the 285,000-member Christian Reformed Church (CRC) because of its 1995 decision to allow its 47 regional bodies the option of ordaining women ministers, elders, and evangelists. The 278,000-member Presbyterian Church in America voted in June in Colorado Springs to terminate immediately recognition of the CRC as a "church in ecclesiastical fellowship." A day earlier, the 22,000-member Orthodox Presbyterian Church had taken a similar action at its meeting in Beaver Falls, PA.

The World Alliance of Reformed Churches held its 23d General Council in Debrecen, Hungary, in August. It accepted three new member churches, bringing the total to 211 denominations in 104 countries.

Issues. As an amendment calling on officers of the Presbyterian Church (U.S.A.) to live "in fidelity within the covenant of marriage of a man and a woman or chastity in singleness" took effect, the denomination's General Assembly voted in Syracuse, NY, in June to approve a less restrictive measure. The new proposal, which would urge church officers to "demonstrate fidelity and integrity in marriage or singleness, and in all relationships of life," passed by a vote of 328 to 217. It then went to the presbyteries for approval as a replacement for the "fidelity and chastity" amendment.

The Episcopal Church rejected a proposal to create a blessing rite for gay and lesbian unions when the measure failed to receive majority votes from the church's lay and clergy delegations at its convention in Philadelphia in July. However, the convention issued a formal apology to homosexuals for what it called "years of rejection and maltreatment by the church." Bishop Frank T. Griswold 3d of Chicago was elected presiding bishop of the church. Calling himself an "orthodox theologian," he said both conservatives and liberals have "truth to tell."

The United Reformed Church in the United Kingdom agreed to accept practicing homosexuals as ministers if requested by local congregations. A measure implementing the policy was agreed to by a nearly two-to-one margin at the denomination's General Assembly in Portsmouth in July.

The 15.7-million-member Southern Baptist Convention approved a boycott of the Walt Disney Company and its affiliates at its convention in Dallas in June because of what it called the entertainment conglomerate's "gay-

The Christian Coalition

The Christian Coalition, an organization of religious conservatives formed by television evangelist Pat Robertson in 1989, changed leadership in 1997. Chairman Robertson named Randy Tate, a 31-year-old conservative Republican from the state of Washington who had served one term in the U.S. House of Representatives, as executive director, and Donald P. Hodel, a 62-year-old former U.S. secretary of the interior and secretary of energy, as president. They succeeded Ralph Reed, who earlier resigned as the coalition's executive director to become a campaign consultant. During his eight years at the helm, Reed had transformed the coalition from a loose array of evangelicals into a major force in Republican politics.

The new leadership took over as the Christian Coalition was facing federal investigation. The Federal Election Commission was examining whether the coalition had misused its tax-exempt status by supporting GOP candidates directly.

The Christian Coalition had 1.9 million members and more than 1,900 chapters in 1997. Its annual budget totaled $27 million. During the 1996 election campaign, the coalition distributed 45 million voter guides in 125,000 churches.

© Terry Ashe/Gamma-Liaison

Following the resignation of Ralph Reed (right) *as executive director of the Christian Coalition, Pat Robertson announced that Randy Tate* (second from right) *and Donald P. Hodel* (third from right) *would be the coalition's executive director and president, respectively.*

friendly" policies. A similar stance had been taken by other Protestant bodies, including the 1.3-million-member Assemblies of God and the 214,000-member National Association of Free Will Baptists. The Southern Baptists also implemented their most far-reaching reorganization since the denomination was founded in 1845, reducing the number of national agencies from 19 to 12.

The International Bible Society dropped plans to develop what it called a "gender-accurate" Bible translation in the United States in the wake of criticism from some fundamentalists and conservative evangelicals. The controversy was touched off by a March 29 report in *World* magazine, published in Asheville, NC, that plans for a "unisex" version of the New International Version were fueled by a feminist agenda. While the IBS said the report was inaccurate, the organization's president, Lars Dunberg, said that the board had concluded that to move ahead with the project "would cause division within the body of Christ."

The Promise Keepers

Hundreds of thousands of people filled the national Mall in Washington on Oct. 4, 1997. The predominantly male crowd sang, prayed, and prostrated themselves in what may have been the largest religious gathering in U.S. history. Confounding critics and journalists, the participants insisted they were not there to make demands on the government or to criticize feminists but acknowledge and repent of their sins.

The "Stand in the Gap" rally was put together by an organization that did not exist ten years earlier. Known as Promise Keepers, it was the fulfillment of a 1990 vision of Bill McCartney, then head football coach of the University of Colorado, and Dave Wardell, an official of the Fellowship of Christian Athletes. The two were preparing to travel from Boulder, CO, to Pueblo when McCartney was struck by a vision of stadiums filled with men who wanted to become committed Christians. In July 1991, 4,200 men gathered for the first Promise Keepers conference at the University of Colorado basketball arena. By the time of the 1997 rally, more than 2.6 million men had attended more than 60 stadium conferences.

The Movement's Mission. The movement's backbone consists of seven promises: (1) honoring Jesus Christ through prayer, worship, and obedience to God's Word in the power of the Holy Spirit; (2) pursuing vital relationships with a small group of men, understanding that a man needs brothers to help him keep his promises; (3) practicing spiritual, moral, ethical, and sexual purity; (4) building strong marriages and families through love, protection, and biblical values; (5) supporting the mission of one's church by honoring and praying for one's pastor and by actively giving one's time and resources; (6) reaching beyond any racial and denominational barriers to demonstrate the power of biblical unity; and (7) influencing one's world by obeying the Great Commandment (Mark 12:30–31) to love God completely and your neighbor as yourself and the Great Commission (Matthew 28:19–20) to "make disciples of all nations...."

McCartney announced in October that the movement was planning rallies on the steps of every state capitol on New Year's Day 2000. In the interim, the movement's stadium and arena

Hundreds of thousands of Promise Keepers, an all-male evangelical group, gathered on the Mall in Washington, DC, on Oct. 4, 1997, for a rally. The men were seeking forgiveness for failing to live up to their commitments to their families and communities.

© B. Kraft/Sygma

events would be free of charge, without the $60 admission charged in the past.

Praise and Criticism. The Promise Keepers movement has generated enthusiasm from wives of participants, who say their husbands have started assuming more family responsibilities after joining the movement.

Donna Minkowitz, a writer who attended a Promise Keepers rally undercover on assignment for *Ms.* magazine in 1995, wrote, "In some ways, I think they are changing men in a really good way that feminists would like." And Nation of Islam leader Louis Farrakhan said, "I have nothing but praise for the Promise Keepers."

However, the fairly new movement also has been the subject of considerable debate and criticism. The National Organization for Women passed a resolution in Memphis, TN, during July declaring Promise Keepers to be "the greatest danger to women's rights." And the General Association of Regular Baptist Churches, meeting in Grand Rapids, MI, during June, reflected the attitude of several fundamentalist Protestant groups in opposing "the·inclusive character of Promise Keepers, which minimizes doctrine and denomination distinctions in an attempt to achieve unity and fellowship."

DARRELL J. TURNER

Clergy. The Rev. Henry Lyons of St. Petersburg, FL, survived attempts to oust him from the presidency of the 8.5-million-member National Baptist Convention USA Inc., the largest black denomination in the United States. Lyons was the subject of state and federal investigations into his alleged misuse of church money that came to light after his wife, Deborah, was accused of setting fire to a $700,000 home owned by her husband and another woman. At the denomination's convention in September, members voted to allow Lyons to complete his term, which ends in 1999, after he appealed for forgiveness.

Bishop Christian Krause of Brunswick, Germany, was elected president of the Lutheran World Federation (LWF) at the organization's ninth assembly in Hong Kong in July. The federation, which celebrated its 50th anniversary in 1997, is made up of 122 Lutheran churches with more than 57 million members in 68 countries. The 2.6-million-member Lutheran Church–Missouri Synod, which is not a member of the LWF, celebrated its 150th anniversary with an extravaganza in St. Louis in August that drew 14,000 people.

DARRELL J. TURNER

Roman Catholicism

The activities of Pope John Paul II, the death of Mother Teresa, and a Synod of Bishops for the Americas were among 1997 highlights in Roman Catholicism.

The Papacy and World Developments. Pope John Paul II turned 77 in 1997—two years past the age when other Roman Catholic bishops are expected to submit their resignations. He kept a full schedule of meetings, audiences, and visits abroad. But it was a noticeably feebler pope who disembarked from the airplane for 1997 visits to Bosnia and Herzegovina, the Czech Republic, Lebanon, Poland, France, and Brazil.

If the pope was aging, so were the top administrators in the Curia, the Vatican's administrative arm. More than one third of the 40 cardinals and archbishops who headed Vatican departments had reached 75 by the end of 1997. The average age of the top administrators was 71. The net effect may be that, while Pope John Paul II's relatively long pontificate—19 years as of October 1997—has enabled him to put his personal stamp on the hierarchy, his team of administrators may not stay in place for long into the reign of the next pope.

Pope John Paul's April visit to Bosnia could have ended in disaster—23 mines and a radio-controlled detonator were found under a bridge near Sarajevo just hours before the arrival of the papal motorcade. Nevertheless, in an April 13 meeting with the Muslim community in Sarajevo, the pontiff said, "The time has come to overcome the hatred and vengeance which still hinders the reestablishment of genuine peace in Bosnia-Herzegovina." The first-ever papal trip to Fidel Castro's Cuba was scheduled for January 1998.

Mother Teresa of Calcutta died in India on September 5. The 87-year-old Nobel laureate and founder of the Missionaries of Charity was accorded the unusual honor of a state funeral by India (*see* OBITUARIES, page 386). In mid-March, Sister Nirmala, a 63-year-old former Hindu who had converted to Roman Catholicism, had been named to succeed Mother Teresa as head of the order of nuns.

On October 19, John Paul II proclaimed St. Thérèse of Lisieux (1873–97), who was a French cloistered nun, a "doctor of the church." Her new honor was unusual in several respects. She became the youngest of 33 such doctors, whose number include such learned teachers or mystics as Augustine, Thomas Aquinas, and Teresa of Avila. Thérèse joins the latter and Catherine of Siena as the only women to be named "doctors of the church." Her theological reputation rests upon a slender volume, her memoirs—*Story of a Soul*, which was published posthumously. The pope said, "Her spiritual journey was so mature and courageous, the intuitions about the faith were so vast and profound that she deserves to be placed among the great spiritual masters."

U.S. Developments. On November 16 the Synod for the Bishops of the Americas opened in Rome. Approximately 233 cardinals, bishops, and priests—representing the Catholic Church in North, South, and Central America and the Roman Curia—and about 70 other delegates met with Pope John Paul II for a monthlong series of meetings. This was to be the first of a series of regional synods called in preparation for the millennium. The synod concluded on December 12. In its final proposal the synod urged a renewed style of evangelization that promotes personal conversion and Gospel-based social action, including a preferential option for the poor. In Catholicism, synods, unlike councils, are consultative, rather than legislative. A worldwide synod was expected in 1999.

Bishop Charles J. Chaput, 52, a member of the Prairie Band Potawatomi tribe, became the first Native American to be named an archbishop. On February 18 he was appointed head of the archdiocese of Denver. Two months later, Archbishop Francis George, 60, was named archbishop of Chicago. The former archbishop of Portland, OR, succeeded Cardinal Joseph Bernardin, who died in November 1996.

The American bishops, through their Committee on Marriage and Family, reached out to homosexual Catholics in a statement made public in October. The statement asked parents of homosexuals to "accept and love your son or daughter." While the statement reaffirmed Catholic teaching that all persons are called to abstain from sexual activity outside of marriage, it said, "God does not love someone any less simply because he or she is homosexual."

On another issue, the American bishops pondered a turning back of the clock. During their November 10–12 meeting in Washington, the bishops approved a future study of ways to revive the penitential practices of fast-

© Bernard Bisson/Sygma

In March 1997, Sister Nirmala Joshi, who was born in 1934 in Bihar, India, was elected head of the Missionaries of Charity. She succeeded Mother Teresa, who died six months later.

ing from food and abstaining from meat on certain days of the year.

The Statistical Outlook. The Vatican's *1997 Statistical Yearbook of the Church* showed 989.4 million Catholics worldwide, but that figure did not include China and North Korea, where millions of Catholics are members of an underground church. The total, which represented year-end 1995, showed continued growth in the Second and Third worlds.

Brazil led with 134.8 million Catholics, followed by Mexico with 86.3 million. The Philippines moved up to third, with 58.7 million; the United States had 57 million; and Italy had 55.6 million. The position of the Catholic Church in China remained ambiguous. While the Chinese government only recognized the Patriotic Catholic Church, which had no visible ties with the Vatican, an underground Catholic Church loyal to the pope was estimated to number in the millions. Catholicism on Hong Kong, which has ties to Rome, appeared to be unaffected by the colony's reunification with China on July 1, 1997.

According to the yearbook, the number of priests worldwide stood at 404,750, up 289 from the previous year. But there was a wide disparity in numbers from country to country. Brazil had 8,708 Catholics for every priest, while Italy had 980 Catholics for every priest.

LOU BALDWIN
Reporter, "Catholic Standard and Times"

RETAILING

The Christmas-season *USA Today* headline "Shoppers hit malls, look for bargains" best may summarize retailing in 1997. The year was a mixed bag for the $1.8 trillion industry. Discount chains, upscale department stores, and specialty shops performed well, while the broad range of middle-line department stores had mediocre successes. Most analysts predicted that final retail-sales figures would show a moderate boost over 1996.

However, the 1997 Christmas season was a disappointing one for retailers. Since it was the third consecutive Christmas season of lackluster sales, analysts said that it now was up to the retailers to realize the diminishing role of Christmas in the retail picture. According to Bruce Van Kleeck, vice-president of the National Retail Federation, retail sales started off the Christmas season with a bang, "then had a lull," and, unfortunately, were not what was expected on the final weekend. According to Van Kleeck, "mainstream department stores were struggling. Discounters did reasonably well, as did luxury stores, but even the discounters said they saw weekend sales declining."

Consumer Confidence. When consumer-confidence levels are high, consumer spending—approximately two thirds of the U.S. economy—is usually brisk. Two significant measures of consumer confidence—the consumer-confidence index and the present-situation index—surged to record and near-record highs in 1997.

The consumer-confidence index—which is based on a comparison to the 1985 base of 100 by the Conference Board—soared to a 28-year high of 130.2 in September. After dipping to 123.4 in October, it rebounded in November to 128.3. These increases were noteworthy since, as recently as 1995, the index had dipped below 100.

The present-situation index, which measures consumers' current judgment of the economy, reached its highest level since 1969—158.9. Such optimism was generated by a robust economy, the lowest unemployment rate in 24 years, record stock-market levels, and predictions of exceptionally low inflation for 1998.

Potential Problems. Some analysts, however, approached 1998 with guarded optimism, stemming from uncertainty in the global market—most notably in Asia, where mid-1997 currency difficulties sent the U.S. stock market on a roller-coaster ride—and from the fact that consumer debt continued at astronomical levels. The debt load of U.S. consumers in 1997 was in excess of $1 trillion. Increasing numbers of consumers have become accustomed to high debt—behavior that can spell disaster for families with little savings. In fact, the United States had one of the lowest savings rates in the industrialized world.

Retail Sales. The discounters continued to exhibit strong growth figures, with retail giant Wal-Mart and upstart Dollar General Stores leading the way. Kmart and Dayton Hudson also had respectable gains. Conversely, major department stores like Sears, J.C. Penney, Federated, May, and Dillard's all posted more modest gains. Upscale department stores Neiman-Marcus and Saks were able to post slightly better performances. Many specialty stores had brisk business in 1997, with the Gap, Kohl's, and Ross Stores posting especially strong sales gains.

For the first time, a retailer—Wal-Mart—replaced General Motors (GM) as the largest corporate employer in the United States. Wal-Mart ranked fourth in total sales revenue behind GM, Ford, and Exxon. With plans to open 100 stores annually, it appeared that the retail giant could surpass GM in sales revenues in the foreseeable future. Montgomery Ward, the nation's oldest general-merchandise department store, filed for bankruptcy protection in July; in August, F.W. Woolworth, the nation's first discount variety store, founded in 1879, announced it was closing its 400 remaining U.S. stores. In December, Home Depot announced it was opening 61 new stores in California.

Cyberspace Shopping. Retailers spent an average of $8.7 million on technology in 1997—up 36% from 1996. High-tech improvements ranged from scanners to communications headsets to digital cameras for mall Santas. The marketing technology that appeared to have the most significant impact on the retail industry in 1997, however, was Internet shopping. Although 1997 Internet sales produced less than 1% of total retail revenues, most analysts predicted that cyberspace shopping would be the way many would shop in the near future. Some futurists predicted that shopping malls would become a thing of the past once Internet shopping became accepted widely. In fact, Americans were spending less time engaging in shopping as a form of recreation. Since 1982 the average shopping time decreased 25%, and the number of stores visited at malls decreased by 33%. Consumers apparently were looking for ways to cut shopping time further, and Internet buying may be the answer.

Internet sales for 1997 were estimated at a modest $1 billion–$2.5 billion. However, respected research companies like International Data Corporation predicted that sales would skyrocket to nearly $200 billion by the year 2000. Even the most conservative estimates predicted that sales figures would exceed $20 billion by the millennium.

The optimism for the future of Internet shopping was fueled further by the fact that major retailers were spending substantial amounts of resources for their Internet shopping sites. Retailers appeared to be endorsing this technological innovation because of the prospects of huge sales increases at comparatively lower costs per unit sold. Many larger retailers—including Wal-Mart, Sears, Spiegel, Barnes and Noble, J.C. Penney, and the Gap—have established Web sites.

Retailers believe that consumers will endorse Internet shopping because of its convenience, its virtually unlimited selection options, and its lower prices. There are no other sales "sites" that can offer the consumer the advantage of shopping 24 hours a day, seven days a week, from the comfort and safety of home. But by late 1997, Internet shopping had not yet received widespread acceptance from consumers. Consumers had credit-card-security concerns, were unwilling to shop for products that they could not hold physically, and were afraid of not getting the goods as promised. There also was the annoyance of returning merchandise, and price comparisons that were difficult or impossible to ascertain, since so many products were being offered by so many different retailers on the Internet.

To address consumer concerns, retailers and service companies were beginning to guarantee credit-card security, offer liberal return policies, and provide enhanced interactive Web sites so consumers better could visualize products. There also was a free service that allowed consumers to price-shop among many of the Internet retail offerings.

See also MARKETING TO KIDS, page 74.

MEL J. ZELENAK
University of Missouri-Columbia

ROMANIA

During 1997 the new Romanian government launched far-reaching domestic reforms, underscoring its commitment to capitalism. Substantial progress was made in foreign policy, and Romania narrowly missed inclusion in first-round North Atlantic Treaty Organization (NATO) enlargement into Eastern Europe.

Political Reform. The coalition government of Prime Minister Victor Ciorbea, which took office in late 1996, initiated various reforms aimed at economic restructuring and completion of the decommunization of Romanian society. In October a draft law was approved that permitted public access to the files of the communist-era secret police—the Securitate. Parliament restored the citizenship of former King Michael, who became an informal ambassador, petitioning for NATO membership.

Interethnic relations improved as the government included elected representatives of the largest Hungarian organization—the Democratic Union of Hungarians in Romania. In May, Parliament approved amendments to the education law eliminating provisions that discriminated against minorities. Negotiations began with Hungary to restore a Hungarian-language university in the Transylvanian city of Cluj. In recognition of Romania's progress, the Council of Europe's Parliamentary Assembly ended special monitoring of Bucharest's commitment to respect human rights.

Political opposition to the centrist government was in disarray throughout 1997. The Party for Social Democracy of Romania (PDSR), which controlled the previous government, split over growing dissatisfaction with the PDSR's leader, former President Ion Iliescu. The PDSR deputy chairman, former Foreign Minister Theodor Melescanu, established a new political party—Alianta Pentru Romania. Ultranationalist parties failed to gain significant public support. Despite austerity measures, President Emil Constantinescu remained highly popular.

As 1997 drew to a close, tensions between Romanians and ethnic Hungarians seeking

---

ROMANIA • Information Highlights

Official Name: Romania.

Location: Southeastern Europe.

Area: 91,699 sq mi (237 500 km²).

Population (mid-1997 est.): 22,500,000.

Chief Cities (July 1, 1994 est.): Bucharest, the capital, 2,080,363; Constanţa, 348,575; Iaşi, 339,989.

Government: *Head of state,* Emil Constantinescu, president (elected November 1996). *Head of government,* Victor Ciorbea, prime minister (named November 1996). *Legislature*—Parliament: Senate and House of Deputies.

Monetary Unit: Leu (7,354.0 lei equal U.S.$1, market rate, July 1997).

Gross Domestic Product (1995 est. U.S.$): $105,700,000,-000 (purchasing power parity).

Economic Index: *Consumer Prices* (1996, 1991 = 100): all items, 4,804.7; food, 4,987.3.

Foreign Trade (1996 U.S.$): *Imports,* $9,828,000,000; *exports,* $8,460,000,000.

© Alain Morvan/Gamma-Liaison

Romania's King Michael, who abdicated in 1947, visited his homeland for six days, Feb. 28–March 5, 1997. With his Romanian citizenship having been restored, the 75-year-old former monarch began lobbying for Romania's entry into NATO.

autonomy were increasing in Transylvania. The Hungarians claimed that Romanian politicians and news organizations were trying to assimilate the Hungarian minority by force. The Romanians in turn accused the Hungarians of having separatist ambitions. The Hungarian minority of 1.7 million people represents some 7% of the total population of Romania.

Economy. A "shock therapy" program of economic reform based on fiscal austerity, privatization, and openness to foreign investment was launched to implement marketization. The government cut subsidies for a range of goods and services, including fuel, public transportation, and telecommunications, and closed several unprofitable state enterprises—in particular, most mining operations. Strikes by miners protesting layoffs were defused when the government agreed to provide the workers with substantial compensation. Also approved were an ordinance for privatizing most state-owned companies and banks, as well as legislation to attract foreign investment. Foreigners also were permitted to buy real estate.

In recognition of Romania's bold reform program, the International Monetary Fund (IMF) approved a $400 million standby loan; the World Bank granted a $330 million assistance package; and the European Bank for Reconstruction and Development (EBRD) supplied $443 million. Although initial statistics showed high inflation, rising unemployment, and negative gross-domestic-product (GDP) growth, longer-term trends were positive. Economic growth was forecast to rebound in 1998—the result of privatization and foreign capital. The budget deficit was decreasing steadily.

International. In March, Bucharest signed a treaty of friendship and cooperation with Ukraine, renouncing all claims to Romanian territory incorporated into Soviet Ukraine after World War II. Romania became a member of the Central European Free Trade Agreement and strengthened its ties with the European Union (EU). Romania also became a serious contender for NATO membership, and Washington signaled that it was a front-runner for the second round of expansion after narrowly missing first-round incorporation. U.S. President Bill Clinton visited Bucharest in May and announced the creation of a "strategic partnership" between the two countries. In December, Romania proposed transporting 35 million tons of Azerbaijani oil to world markets through its territory.

JANUSZ BUGAJSKI
Center for Strategic and International Studies

Russia and the Commonwealth of Independent States

During much of 1997, Russian politics were in turmoil. The economy improved, but not as expected. Russia was unable to stem the eastward expansion of the North Atlantic Treaty Organization (NATO), a notable foreign-policy setback. By late fall, Russia found itself buffeted by the Asian financial crisis. And after recovering from illness, President Boris Yeltsin gave economic reformers in the government their head, only to witness one of his principal ministers awash in scandal. Still, despite appearances, it was a year in which Russia continued its gradual progress toward political and economic normalcy.

Political Developments. After recovering from heart bypass surgery in late 1996, President Yeltsin again fell ill in early January with double pneumonia. His new serious illness caused friend and foe alike to wonder about his ability to govern. With the reopening of parliament at midmonth, Yeltsin's Communist opposition in the State Duma, the lower house of parliament, launched an unusual campaign to impeach the president medically. This involved a rather novel reading of the constitution, but Yeltsin nevertheless took the challenge seriously and fought back through his press spokesman and legal and political advisers.

Complicating the situation, the president simultaneously was faced with the first organized effort to amend the 1993 constitution, which had conferred upon his office considerable powers. Unlike the Duma campaign, though, the drive for constitutional revision was led by respected, politically moderate politicians whom President Yeltsin normally counted on as his allies, namely Yegor Stroyev—speaker of the Federation Council, the upper house of the parliament—and President Mintimer Shaymiyev of the constituent Republic of Tatarstan. Thus, while the Communist challenge could be countered with bluntness and even counterthreat, the respectable constitutional movement to scale back presidential powers had to be dealt with tactfully and subtly.

By March, Yeltsin had regained his strength sufficiently to deliver the deferred State of the Nation speech, which was seen widely as a test of his political health. The speech was a success, showcasing the presi-

In Paris, France, on May 27, 1997, the leaders of the 16 NATO nations and Russia's President Boris Yeltsin (second from right) *signed the Founding Act on Mutual Relations, Cooperation, and Security. The agreement set up a permanent NATO-Russia council.*

dent once again as a take-charge leader. Subsequently, he was able to beat back the Communist attempt to impeach him medically, and to deflect until a later time the idea of amending the constitution.

To seal his effective return to full command, Yeltsin appointed two of the most able political managers in Russia as first deputy prime ministers and gave them a mandate to renew the momentum of economic reform. Yeltsin's stolid prime minister, Viktor Chernomyrdin, thus found himself flanked by the president's former chief of staff, Anatoly Chubais, and the former governor of the Nizhniy Novgorod region, Boris Nemtsov. Chubais had run Russia's successful privatization program from 1992 to 1996, while Nemtsov was considered one of the country's most successful reform-minded governors. To ensure the two younger men's domination of economic policy, the president also appointed Chubais the minister of finance, and additionally assigned Nemtsov the fuel and energy portfolio.

Although he again politically had survived illness as well as the opposition's attempt to oust him, Yeltsin's problems with the Duma had not lessened. The Communist Party and its parliamentary allies still controlled a working majority of deputies, making Russia's legislative-executive relationship a difficult one on certain issues. The first such contentious issue in the spring was the question of World War II "trophy" art, the art treasures of Germany and other countries occupied by the Nazi regime that had been captured by the Soviet army. These works long had been held by Soviet and now Russian museums. Yeltsin, who was planning a state visit to Germany, sought to return the art treasures to their rightful owners, but both houses of parliament strongly objected on the patriotic grounds that the "trophies" had been "purchased" with much Soviet blood. Parliament then passed a law barring the return of the artworks. The president vetoed the law but parliament overrode the veto, stymieing Yeltsin's restitution plan.

Another difficult issue was the bill on religious organizations in Russia, which parliament passed by a wide margin. Backed by the dominant Russian Orthodox Church, the bill restricted the activity of several minor religions in Russia, as well as various foreign evangelical groups. The religion bill was in conflict with the constitution, and the president predictably vetoed it. However, recognizing that his social ally, the Orthodox Church, strongly supported the measure,

---

RUSSIA • Information Highlights

Official Name: Russian Federation.
Location: Eastern Europe and northern Asia.
Area: 6,592,772 sq mi (17 075 200 km²).
Population (mid-1997 est.): 147,300,000.
Chief Cities (July 1, 1993, est.): Moscow, the capital, 8,526,750; St. Petersburg, 4,328,851; Nizhniy Novgorod (Gorky), 1,425,316; Novosibirsk, 1,423,860; Yekaterinburg (Sverdlovsk), 1,350,861.
Government: *Head of state*, Boris Yeltsin, president (took office June 1991). *Head of government*, Viktor Chernomyrdin, prime minister (took office December 1992). *Legislature*—Federal Assembly: Federation Council and State Duma.
Monetary Unit: Ruble (5,963.00 rubles equal U.S.$1, fixed rate, Dec. 31, 1997).
Gross Domestic Product (1995 est. U.S.$): $796,000,-000,000 (purchasing power parity).
Economic Index (1996, 1991 = 100): *Consumer Prices*, all items, 284,429.0; food, 287,151.0.
Foreign Trade (1996 U.S.$): *Imports*, $61,147,000,000; *exports*, $88,703,000,000.

Yeltsin chose his words in the veto message carefully. Later, with presidential blessing, a compromise version was agreed to, duly passed, and signed into law. In its final version, the law still contained aspects offensive to international human-rights standards.

Two other issues—the government's draft tax code and parliament's land-code bill—stirred conflict between the legislature and the executive. Russia had been badly in need of tax-law reform for several years. Its absence had discouraged foreign investment because of the uncertain financial climate associated with the nation's myriad taxes. The government's 1997 draft code promised to reduce the number of taxes to less than 30, but then got mired in parliamentary politics. By fall, approximately 4,500 amendments had been proposed, causing Yeltsin to order the draft recalled and reworked.

On the matter of a much-needed new land code, the battle lines had been drawn for the previous couple of years. The president favored legislating the constitutional right to buy and sell land as private property, while parliamentary majorities consistently opposed the free sale of land, especially agricultural land. Parliament staked out its position in a land-code bill that guaranteed the right to buy land, but placed an owner's right to sell his land under various restrictions. The bill passed by a comfortable margin and then was vetoed by the president as expected, but Yeltsin's veto was overridden by parliament. Normally, the president would be obliged to sign the returned bill into law, but Yeltsin refused on the grounds that improper legislative roll calls were used in overriding his veto. The deadlock on the land code continued.

At the subnational level of Russian politics, the executive branch continued to sign

For the separatist Russian republic of Chechnya, the year 1997 began with Aslan Maskhadov being elected president. Four months later, Russia and Chechnya signed a peace treaty.

bilateral power- and revenue-sharing treaties with constituent regions and republics, bringing the treaty total to 37 out of the 89 constituent governments. One republic, however, remained intransigent to any such agreement with Moscow. The Chechen Republic, which effectively won its internal war with Russia by virtue of the 1996 cease-fire, claimed full independence, which Russia in turn denied. Even after President Yeltsin and Chechen President Aslan Maskhadov signed a peace treaty in May 1997, each side held differing views about what the treaty meant: Russia maintained that Chechnya was part of Russia, and Chechnya maintained that it was fully independent. Nevertheless, President Yeltsin pledged that he never again would use force against Chechnya, and President Maskhadov vowed to crack down on hard-line Chechens. Negotiations between the sides continued.

Elsewhere in the Russian Federation, elections to 22 of the regional legislatures got under way in the latter half of 1997. November 7, the 80th anniversary of the Bolshevik Revolution, passed uneventfully, but by that point in time, Russia's post-Soviet government was in turmoil. Bitter that his bank and its partners lost out on a major privatization deal during the summer, Deputy National Security Adviser Boris Berezovsky blamed Chubais, who reacted by persuading the president to fire his critic. Not long after, a capital

newspaper allied with Berezovsky revealed that Chubais and three of his protégés in the privatization program had accepted $90,000 each to write chapters for a book on the history of privatization in Russia. The publisher involved was owned by a rival bank with much to gain by currying favor with the influential Chubais. President Yeltsin promptly fired Chubais' subordinates for their ethical lapses and put Chubais on warning by stripping him of his finance portfolio. By the end of the year, Russia's chief economic reformer's future remained clouded.

The Economy. In late 1996, both international financial institutions and internal Russian agencies cautiously had predicted that 1997 finally would be the turnaround year for the economy—a year of positive growth after contraction throughout the 1990s. By fall, it was apparent that the only thing that could be said with certainty about the Russian economy was that it at last had bottomed out, and that the year would turn out to be one of neither contraction nor growth.

There was some good news, however. A few Russian forecasters opined that there were indications of 0.2% gross-domestic-product (GDP) growth through the fall, but others suggested that the increase might be due to a change in the public-accounting system earlier in the year. Nonetheless, there was consensus that industrial output was up 1.5% after years of contraction; that inflation was down to 9.1% for the first three quarters, its lowest point since 1992; and that Russia continued to enjoy a foreign-trade surplus based heavily on exports of oil, armaments, and nuclear technology.

There was other good news as well—on privatization, unemployment, poverty, and the harvest. During the summer, the largest-yet privatization auction was held. Twenty-five percent of the shares in Svyazinvest, a state telecommunications giant, went on the block. The bidders were several conglomerates, led by Russia's most powerful banks. The auction generally was considered fair and free of undue insider influence, as had been experienced in the past, and the group with the highest bid won, paying the state the equivalent of $1.9 billion for the shares. Nonetheless, one of the losing groups, which involved the bank owned by Deputy National Security Adviser Berezovsky, took exception to the outcome, arguing that Chubais, as finance minister, had rigged the auction. The heretofore solid front among Russia's leading bankers quickly came apart as the losers unleashed their press and television subsidiaries to attack the winners, whose media in turn defended the outcome. By late fall, the dispute had escalated from a financial to a political donnybrook, costing Berezovsky and several privatization officials their government jobs.

In spite of the controversy, the disputed auction as well as other privatization auctions during the year resulted in a tenfold gain in revenue to the state for the sale of its property. Foreign direct investment also grew substantially, although it continued to be largely concentrated in just two regions of the country, Moscow and St. Petersburg. Other foreign investors remained cautious, preferring to wait until the new tax code was written, creating a more predictable and capital-friendly environment.

From January to June of 1997, unemployment fell slightly, to 9.1%, according to an estimate by the International Labor Organization (ILO) of Geneva, Switzerland. The number of people below the official poverty line also declined, from 22.6% to 20.9%, while at the other end of the spectrum the number of well-to-do people grew to 6 million by the criterion of earning the equivalent of $10,000 or more. By late November the grain harvest had come in at approximately 25% above the previous harvest, but well below the better years of the late Soviet period. Still, for the first time in decades, Russia managed to export grain.

As the year wound to an end, Russia's modest economic progress was threatened by the spreading Asian economic crisis. Speculators successfully attacked the Thai currency; this action soon had a domino effect on the economies of Hong Kong, Indonesia, South Korea, and other so-called "Asian tigers." What initially appeared to be a regional crisis soon sent all emerging countries, including Russia, into an abrupt downturn. The Russian stock market, which had ballooned nearly 300% since early 1996, deflated quickly as an estimated $4 billion was pulled out and sent out of the country.

Two other factors complicated Russia's incipient crisis. The first was Yeltsin's pending plan to revaluate and stabilize the ruble-dollar exchange rate within a defined trading range. The second was the government's chronic problem of not meeting International Monetary Fund (IMF) requirements for the periodic payments of its $10.2 billion multiyear loan. As the effects of the Asian crisis began to be felt in Russia, the ruble came under attack, causing the Central Bank to come to its defense by digging deeply into its foreign-currency reserves. In the same time frame, the

© Gleb Kosorukov/Gamma-Liaison

Open-air markets were part of the festivities as Muscovites celebrated the 850th anniversary of their city in 1997. Overall the Russian economy improved slightly during the year.

IMF suspended its third-quarter tranche of $700 million because of the government's failure to meet agreed-upon tax-revenue-collection benchmarks.

The shortfall of tax revenue at 52% of the projected goal further aggravated another chronic problem—the buildup of unpaid wages, salaries, and pensions. The arrearage problem no doubt contributed to the growing frequency of strikes observed in data from the first six months, when the number of strikes soared fivefold and the number of people involved tripled. By mid-December, First Deputy Prime Minister Chubais reportedly was negotiating separately with a consortium of Western commercial banks and the World Bank to obtain a short-term bridge loan to get the Russian economy through the end of the year. Late in the month, the IMF announced resumption of its loan, followed by large commitments from the World Bank—both of which helped ease Russia's immediate financial crisis.

Foreign Affairs. Aside from the unavoidable setback of having to countenance NATO expansion to its western border, Russian diplomacy was active, with varying degrees of success, in Asia, the Middle East, the Near

443

Abroad (a collective designation for neighboring former Soviet republics), and the United States. For several years, one of the main objectives of Russian foreign policy was to avoid the expansion of NATO into Eastern Europe. Every gambit was tried—including bluff, bluster, and even threats, such as Yeltsin's previous warning in Budapest of a "cold peace"—but all to no avail.

The Russians were up against three powerful counterforces. A number of Eastern European and Baltic states actively were lobbying for NATO admission in Washington, DC, at the organization's headquarters in Brussels, and in other European capitals. There was strong support for individual applicants in the various NATO capitals, including indications that Europe favored expansion as an alternative to early admission of Eastern European applicants into the European Union (EU). Finally, President Bill Clinton had been persuaded by foreign-policy advisers that NATO was key to securing the peace in postcommunist Eastern Europe, and hence the pressure for expansion from Washington was firm and steady.

Brushed aside in the West's rush to move its military frontier eastward was the fact that after the Russian military's defeat by the small, irregular Chechen forces, it was evident that Russia would not likely be a conventional military force to reckon with for some years to come. To soften the inevitable inclusion of Poland, the Czech Republic, and Hungary at the NATO summer meeting, the United States and NATO held several prior consultations with Russia during the spring of 1997. To signal NATO's nonthreatening intentions, Russia was persuaded to name a special representative to Brussels as its permanent liaison with the NATO staff. (*See also* EUROPE—*NATO Expansion*.)

Offsetting his policy toward the West, President Yeltsin turned eastward, taking steps to improve Russia's relations with Japan and China. In a meeting with the Japanese prime minister in the Russian Far East, Yeltsin and the prime minister agreed to move forward with negotiations on a peace treaty that finally would bring a formal end to World War II hostilities between their two countries by the year 2000. On a state visit to China, Russia's president and the Chinese leadership successfully resolved a 300-year-old border issue and agreed on other measures to improve relations. Russia's policy toward the Middle East during the year also probably was intended to counter Western moves in East Central Europe.

In search of needed export earnings, Russia agreed to sell Iran both nuclear and oil-drilling technology in spite of strong U.S. and Western objections. During the fall, as tensions with Iraq mounted over the United Nations (UN) weapons-inspection process and the United States threatened a punitive military response, Russia again broke ranks with the West. Foreign Minister Yevgeny Primakov, an old friend of Saddam Hussein, was dispatched to Baghdad to broker a compromise. On Primakov's return, the Moscow press crowed that Russia had prevented a second Gulf war.

Russian diplomacy in the Near Abroad was less successful. The Commonwealth of Independent States (CIS) was in disarray, with various member states reacting negatively to Russian initiatives for closer integration. Finally, Russia's relations with the United States were mixed. Presidents Clinton and Yeltsin met in Helsinki during the spring to deal with various issues. Among other things, it was an opportunity for President Yeltsin to demonstrate for both foreign and domestic consumption his newly regained health and fitness. Later in the fall, in spite of differences over Iran and Iraq, the United States became very concerned over the ripple effects of the Asian currency crisis on Russia's economic recovery and development, and brought its influence to bear on the international financial institutions to take prompt action in Asia, both to solve the problems there as well as to stem possible repercussions for Russia's still-fragile economy.

ROBERT SHARLET, *Union College*

Commonwealth of Independent States

The leaders of the nations of the Commonwealth of Independent States (CIS) met on March 28, 1997, in Moscow and again on October 9 in Kyrgyzstan's capital, Bishkek. A document on implementing a "Concept for the Integrated Economic Development of the CIS" was signed at the latter meeting by all those who attended except for Georgia, but little else was accomplished. Nor was much accomplished at the summit held in Chisinau, the capital of Moldova, on October 23. Indeed, the CIS and Russia were subjected to some serious criticism—the organization for its ineffectiveness, and Russia for its perceived desire to dominate the organization. Russian President Boris Yeltsin acknowledged that the CIS was ineffective and that Russia was partly to blame and promised that it would be reorganized.

In other areas of cooperation, the presidents of five Central Asian CIS countries—Kazakhstan, Kyrgyzstan, Tajikistan, Turkmenistan, and Uzbekistan—agreed to help the World Bank finance a fund to save the Aral Sea, which had shrunk to one quarter its former size because of irrigation projects; and Russia, Kazakhstan, Kyrgyzstan, and Tajikistan, along with China, signed an agreement to reduce military forces along their respective borders.

ARMENIA. In 1997, Armenia continued to deal with the conflict over Nagorno-Karabakh, the Armenian-controlled enclave within Azerbaijan, and with the political fallout from the controversial 1996 presidential election and the ensuing demonstrations. On March 20, President Levon Ter-Petrosyan named Robert Kocharyan as prime minister, replacing Armen Sarkissian, who had resigned for health reasons. Azerbaijan immediately condemned the appointment because Kocharyan had been president of Nagorno-Karabakh. In June five protesters who had been jailed for taking part in the disturbances that followed the 1996 election were released, but a member of the opposition Armenian Revolutionary Federation was found guilty of inciting the disturbances and given a two-year suspended sentence.

Azerbaijan Conflict. The conflict over Nagorno-Karabakh continued in 1997. In April, just two weeks after Armenians and Azerbaijanis met in Moscow for negotiations, fighting broke out in the enclave, as well as in Armenian-Azerbaijani border areas. Fighting erupted again in May. In March, Russian Defense Minister Igor Rodionov had confirmed that more than $1 billion worth of Russian arms had been shipped to Armenia over the past several years. The Armenian government denied that it had received these arms, and the Azerbaijani government condemned the shipments.

Despite the outbreaks of violence, President Ter-Petrosyan and Azerbaijan's President Geidar Aliyev agreed in October to continue to seek a peaceful solution to the conflict over Nagorno-Karabakh. They envisioned a solution that would leave the enclave part of Azerbaijan, but with autonomous status. However, the Armenian leaders of Nagorno-Karabakh called the plan unacceptable.

Economy. In February the Armenian National Assembly adopted a 1997 budget that included an estimated $277 million in revenues and $329 million in expenditures, leaving a deficit of $52 million. In August the World Bank approved $65 million worth of credits for Armenia, to be used to finance economic reform and the growth of the private sector. During that same month, President Ter-Petrosyan traveled to Moscow, where he signed an agreement to establish a joint Russian-Armenian natural-gas project. The project, once the construction of a network of new gas pipelines was completed, would provide Armenia with cheaper gas and allow gas to be exported by Russia to Turkey and other countries by way of Armenia.

AZERBAIJAN. During 1997, Azerbaijani and Armenian forces exchanged gunfire but the cease-fire generally held, and the two governments continued efforts to resolve the problem of Nagorno-Karabakh, the Armenian enclave within Azerbaijan. In the meantime, Azerbaijan moved steadily ahead in its effort to develop its Caspian Sea oil resources.

Economy. The Azerbaijani legislature in January approved 1997 expenditures of $753 million, with anticipated revenues of $591 million and a deficit of $162 million. Despite continuing budget deficits, Azerbaijanis could look forward to a much improved economy in the years ahead for one important reason—oil. In July, Azerbaijan signed contracts—worth $8 billion—with four U.S. oil companies to develop oil fields in the Azerbaijani sector of the Caspian Sea.

Politics. It was announced in January that a coup attempt in October 1996 had been foiled and that the leaders of the coup were former President Ayaz Mutalibov and former Prime Minister Surat Guseinov. Additional information released in February revealed that dozens of people had been arrested, and that the plotters had intended to assassinate President Geidar Aliyev and seize control of the country.

Armenia Conflict and Foreign Affairs. Fighting erupted in Nagorno-Karabakh and in Azerbaijani-Armenian border areas in April and again in May. Also in May, President Aliyev met with Turkish President Suleyman Demirel and signed a declaration of strategic partnership that included a condemnation of Armenian aggression in Nagorno-Karabakh. Nevertheless, Aliyev and President Ter-Petrosyan of Armenia announced in October that they would continue to seek a peaceful resolution of the long-standing conflict. The two presidents sought a solution that would keep Nagorno-Karabakh as part of Azerbaijan, but with a strong degree of autonomy. However,

At the Kremlin in Moscow on April 2, 1997, Russia's President Boris Yeltsin (right) and Belarus President Aleksandr Lukashenko initialed The Treaty on a Union, increasing "brotherhood, friendship, and cooperation" between the two nations.

the Armenians living in that enclave denounced such plans.

With Russia secretly arming Armenia, and a hostile Iran condemning Azerbaijan for unilaterally taking oil out of the Caspian Sea, Azerbaijan continued to use its huge reserves of oil as a political as well as an economic tool. By giving such foreign powers as the United States, Britain, and Russia a stake in the development of Azerbaijani oil, President Aliyev sought to bring a measure of stability to the region and to put pressure on the Armenians to settle the Nagorno-Karabakh dispute.

BELARUS. On April 2, President Aleksandr Lukashenko and Russian President Boris Yeltsin initialed The Treaty on a Union between Belarus and Russia, which pledged the two former Soviet republics to increase their "brotherhood, friendship, and cooperation." Under the terms of the treaty, neither country would relinquish any sovereignty, and it was not envisioned that a full merger would take place.

Belarus-Russia Pact. On May 23 the two presidents signed the "Charter of the Union," and on June 10 they signed the treaty into law after it was approved by both the Belarussian and Russian parliaments. The treaty gave Russians and Belarussians the right to unfettered travel between the two countries; the right to own property in either country; and the right to vote in local elections in either country.

Many Russians, including Foreign Minister Yevgeny Primakov, supported the reintegration of Russia and Belarus, considering it an appropriate response to the eastward expansion of the North Atlantic Treaty Organization (NATO). But other Russians, including liberal parliamentarians, opposed the treaty because of the rise of authoritarianism in Belarus and its perceived threat to Russian democracy. The most vociferous opponents, however, were Belarussians. On March 15 and again on April 2, thousands of protesters rallied in Minsk in opposition to the treaty.

Human Rights and Politics. The constitution of 1996, which gave President Lukashenko the power to rule by decree and also created new upper and lower houses of parliament that were stacked with Lukashenko supporters, was clear evidence that Soviet-style authoritarianism was on the increase in Belarus.

Lukashenko's authoritarianism brought condemnation from many Belarussians and others. On January 13 the parliamentary assembly of the Council of Europe suspended Belarus' guest status, stating that Belarus did not respect human rights. On March 21 the United States suspended $40 million in aid to Belarus because of its human-rights record. And in August, Human Rights Watch/Helsinki condemned Lukashenko's repression of opponents and the press. Despite the fact that Lukashenko restricted the rights of demonstrators on March 6,

10,000 government opponents rallied in Minsk on March 15 and again on March 23. Serge Alexandrov, first secretary at the U.S. embassy in Minsk, was expelled from Belarus for allegedly taking part in a rally against Lukashenko. In another confrontation, the U.S.-based Soros Foundation closed its doors in May after Peter Byrne, its Belarussian director, was accused of supporting the Belarussian political opposition and then was denied reentry into Belarus.

GEORGIA. It was reported in February 1997 that a conspiracy to assassinate Georgia's President Eduard Shevardnadze in October 1996 had been foiled and a number of arrests made. Meanwhile, Georgia continued to contend with the problems created by Abkhazia and South Ossetia, its two breakaway regions. Talks to resolve the problem with the Abkhazians were held in June and again in August. President Shevardnadze agreed to give Abkhazia substantial autonomy but stated that the region would have to remain an integral part of Georgia. This proposal was rejected by Abkhazian President Vladislav Ardzinba, who stated that Abkhazia was no longer part of Georgia. Despite the divergent points of view, both parties promised to continue talking in an effort to find a solution.

In the meantime, some 7,000 ethnic Georgians who had been forced to flee Abkhazia in 1993 held a rally in Tbilisi demanding that the CIS peacekeeping force in Abkhazia, as well as in South Ossetia, be removed. That force, made up primarily of Russian troops, was considered "an army of occupation" by the Georgians.

Economy. During 1997, Georgia continued to redirect its economy toward the West and away from Russia and the other CIS nations. By the start of the year, Turkey already had replaced Russia as Georgia's most important trading partner.

With help from the International Monetary Fund (IMF), Georgia was able to reduce inflation from 62% in 1994 to less than 2% in January 1997. Help also came from the International Finance Corporation (IFC), a member of the World Bank Group: In May the IFC announced that it would make its first investment in Georgia—$2.9 million to the Georgian Glass and Mineral Water Company (GGMW). GGMW produces Borjomi mineral water, which is famous and highly in demand throughout the CIS.

KAZAKHSTAN. On December 10, President Nursultan Nazarbayev officially declared the city of Akmola to be the nation's new capital. Located some 750 mi (1,200 km) north of Almaty, the former capital, Akmola is populated heavily by ethnic Russians. Some believed that the move reflected a desire on the part of the government to lure more ethnic Kazakhs to the area, while others believed that it was done to attract investment to the interior of

Nation	Population (in Millions)	Area (sq mi)	(km²)	Capital	Head of State and Government
Armenia	3.8	11,506	29 800	Yerevan	Levon Akopovich Ter-Petrosyan, president
Azerbaijan	7.6	33,436	86 600	Baku	Geidar A. Aliyev, president
Belarus	10.3	80,155	207 600	Minsk	Aleksandr Lukashenko, president
Georgia	5.4	26,911	69 700	Tbilisi	Eduard Shevardnadze, president
Kazakhstan	16.4	1,049,155	2 717 300	Almaty/Akmola	Nursultan A. Nazarbayev, president
Kyrgyzstan	4.6	76,641	198 500	Bishkek (Frunze)	Askar Akayev, president
Moldova	4.3	13,012	33 700	Chisinau (Kishinev)	Petru Lucinschi, president
Russia	147.3	6,592,772	17 075 200	Moscow	Boris Yeltsin, president
Tajikistan	6.0	55,251	143 100	Dushanbe	Emomili Rakhmonov, president
Turkmenistan	4.6	188,457	488 100	Ashkhabad	Saparmurad Niyazov, president
Ukraine	50.7	233,090	603 700	Kiev	Leonid Kuchma, president
Uzbekistan	23.7	172,742	447 400	Tashkent	Islam Karimov, president

COMMONWEALTH OF INDEPENDENT STATES • Information Highlights

During 1997, Akmola—a city of some 300,000 in north-central Kazakhstan—became the nation's new capital. Members of Kazakhstan's Republican Guard, left, participated in ceremonies transferring the symbols of state to the new government seat.

the country. Whatever the reason, few Kazakh government employees and even fewer members of the diplomatic community welcomed the move to the windswept city of Akmola.

Economy. The Akmola region also has a large ethnic German population, and in 1997 the German government continued to be Europe's major aid donor to Kazakhstan. One of the goals of German aid was to entice the Germans to stay in Kazakhstan and help in its economic development.

The most important economic news during the year was Kazakhstan's imminent emergence as an energy giant. In October it signed a $750 million contract with Turkey to develop oil in the northwestern part of the country. And in November it signed two multibillion-dollar agreements with nine foreign oil companies, including the U.S. firm of Texaco, to develop the offshore reserves in the Caspian Sea and onshore at the Karachaganak field. The reserves at Karachaganak are estimated at 2.4 billion barrels of crude oil and 16 trillion cubic feet of gas. Earlier in October an agreement was reached with China to build an 1,860-mi (3,000-km) oil pipeline to Xinjiang province. This would be in addition to pipelines already planned to run from Kazakhstan's Tengiz oil field on the Caspian Sea to a new Russian port on the Black Sea, and from Kazakhstan through Iran.

Government and Politics. Early in the year, in an effort to save money and reduce corruption, President Nazarbayev began cutting the number of government divisions and the number of government workers. By spring, 10,000 workers were dismissed and the number of government bodies was reduced from 47 to 24.

On October 10, President Nazarbayev dismissed Premier Azekhan Kazhegeldin, replacing him with Nurlan Balgimbayev, the former minister of oil and gas.

KYRGYZSTAN. During 1997 the Kyrgyzstan government continued to deal with the problems caused by the hundreds of thousands of refugees who had fled the fighting in neighboring Tajikistan. And it continued to consolidate its power by jailing journalists and other critics. But the government's main concern was the nation's economy. In July, President Askar Akayev traveled to Washington, DC, where he met with U.S. Vice-President Al Gore to discuss economic reforms, among other issues. And in the same month, the nation's new foreign minister, Muratbek Imanaliyev, made clear that Kyrgyzstan's foreign policy would be conducted so as to benefit its economy. Economic growth was Kyrgyzstan's major goal, and there were some good signs in this regard.

Economy. Kyrgyzstan's gross domestic product (GDP) for the first half of 1997 increased by 6.8% over the GDP for the first half of 1996. Industrial output alone rose more than 20% to about $538 million. However, exports of foodstuffs, textiles, and other products fell 12%, while imports fell by 31%. The increase in GDP and industrial output was attributed partially to the success of the Bishkek Free Economic Zone on the outskirts of the capital city. By late 1997 the zone, with 120 enterprises that enjoy preferential tax and other benefits, accounted for 5% of the GDP. Kyrgyzstan received credits totaling $13 million from the Islamic Bank of Development in Saudi Arabia and signed an agreement with the Export-Import Bank of the United States, which helps finance the purchase of U.S. goods.

MOLDOVA. On January 15, Petru Lucinschi, who had defeated Mircea Snegur in a runoff election in December 1996, was inaugurated as Moldova's new president. He immediately dealt with the ongoing problem of the secessionist Dnestr region along Moldova's border with Ukraine. The region is home primarily to ethnic Russians and Ukrainians. Igor Smirnov, who in January was inaugurated for a second term as president of the Dnestr region, held talks with Lucinschi in January and again in May in an effort to get negotiations back on track.

In May the two presidents signed a memorandum of understanding to continue negotiations within "the framework of a single state," but with the Dnestr region getting substantial autonomy. President Boris Yeltsin of Russia, who was present at the signing of the memorandum, said he would be willing to withdraw Russian peacekeeping troops from the Dnestr region "at any time." The troops first entered the region in 1992. Moldovan and Dnestr officials later agreed to establish groups and commissions to detail the special status of the region.

Politics and Economy. In February, just a month after Lucinschi's inauguration, his supporters established the

Movement for a Democratic and Prosperous Moldova, a centrist grouping whose aim was to promote Lucinschi's platform. A month later, Dumitru Motpan, leader of the Agrarian Democratic Party of Moldova (PDAM), succeeded Lucinschi as speaker of the Moldovan parliament, and in June he also was reelected leader of the PDAM. The parliament in March approved a $483 million budget.

TAJIKISTAN. The five-year-long civil war between the Russian-backed government of President Emomili Rakhmanov and the United Tajik Opposition (UTO), led by Said Abdullah Nuri, came to an end on June 27, when the two leaders signed a peace pact in Moscow. Incorporated in the treaty was the establishment of a National Reconciliation Committee, composed of 13 members from each side. In addition, the UTO was given 30% of the government posts and the right to bring a small armed force into the capital, Dushanbe, to protect UTO members of the National Reconciliation Committee. In September, Nuri ended his five-year exile in Iran and returned to Tajikistan to head the committee.

Continuing Violence. Despite the peace treaty, armed clashes, kidnappings, and other forms of violence were evidenced throughout the year. In February rebels under the command of Bakhran and Rizvon Sadirov seized a number of hostages—including Red Cross workers, UN military observers, Russian reporters, and even Tajik Interior Minister Saidamir Zukhurov, who had attempted to negotiate the hostages' release. The hostages were released later in the month, but the Tajik government and UTO forces cooperated to capture Bakhran Sadirov. In other violent incidents, President Rakhmanov was injured by a grenade in April; rival government factions fought in Dushanbe, the capital, during August; and masked gunmen killed 14 presidential guards in Dushanbe in October. But of greatest concern to the government was the initiation of a military campaign in August by Makhmud Khudoberdyev, a renegade Tajik army colonel who strongly opposed the June peace treaty. Government successes forced Khudoberdyev to flee to Uzbekistan.

TURKMENISTAN. During 1997, President Saparmurad Niyazov and other members of the government continued their efforts to halt the deterioration of the nation's economy, with particular attention being paid to the development of oil and natural-gas fields and the construction of pipelines.

Oil, Gas, and the Economy. During October and November, Turkmenistan made some important moves to ensure that it would receive its fair share of the oil and natural gas in the Caspian Sea. Turkmen Foreign Minister Boris Shikhmuradov and Iranian Foreign Minister Kamal Kharazi agreed to form a consortium to develop oil and gas fields in their respective areas of the Caspian Sea. Plans first formulated in 1996 to construct a $2 billion, 870-mi (1,400-km) natural-gas pipeline to Pakistan by way of war-torn Afghanistan got a boost when the Turkmen government substantially improved its relations with Taliban, the radical Islamic group that controlled most of Afghanistan. And Turkmenistan began exporting natural gas to Iran. It was expected that the volume of gas exported in 1998 would be 3 billion cubic meters, and that the figure would rise to 8 billion cubic meters over eight years.

Earlier in the year, the United States made clear that it would not stand in the way of the construction of a pipeline that would go from Turkmenistan to Turkey, despite the fact that it also would run through Iran.

In other economic news, the World Bank approved $64 million in loans to Turkmenistan for the improvement of urban transportation and water-supply and sanitation systems. About one third of the total was slated for the purchase of 130 buses and trolley buses. World Bank loans to Turkmenistan totaled $89.5 million.

UKRAINE. For the second year in a row, Ukraine's government underwent considerable change. During the last half of February, President Leonid Kuchma dismissed five ministers because of alleged governmental corruption. Then, on June 19, he dismissed Prime Minister Pavlo Lazarenko, in office just more than a year, for the same reason. President Kuchma nominated and the parliament approved Valeriy Pustovoytenko as prime minister. A former Communist Party official, he took office on July 17. Even before the ouster of Lazarenko, President Kuchma took a number of steps to reduce corruption, including the suspension of immunity for justices and parliamentarians suspected of corruption.

Economy. In July, after parliament approved a 1997 budget that included deficit spending of 5.7%, Ukraine was granted a $750 million standby loan by the International Monetary Fund (IMF). McDonald's opened two branches in Kiev, the capital.

Foreign Relations. On May 31, President Kuchma and Russian President Boris Yeltsin met in Kiev, where they signed a friendship treaty that included Russian acceptance of Ukrainian sovereignty over the Crimean peninsula. Three days earlier, Ukrainian Prime Minister Lazarenko and Russian Prime Minister Viktor Chernomyrdin had reached an agreement on the status of the Black Sea fleet and the port of Sevastopol. Under the terms of this pact, Russia will lease part of Sevastopol from Ukraine for $100 million annually for 20 years. In addition, Russia will credit Ukraine with an additional $526 million for the use of that part of the fleet that Ukraine had wanted. And a further credit of $200 million will be given to Ukraine for the 1992 transfer of its nuclear weapons to Russia. These payments and credits will go toward settling Ukraine's $3 billion debt to Russia.

Ukraine signed two other pacts during the year. One, signed in June with Romania, confirmed the existing boundary between the two nations. The second pact, signed in July with the North Atlantic Treaty Organization (NATO), was a mutual-cooperation agreement.

UZBEKISTAN. Uzbekistan President Islam Karimov signed agreements with Turkey and Russia. In November he traveled to Ankara, where he and Turkish President Suleyman Demirel signed agreements to cooperate in the fields of health, tourism, and science and technology. And Russian Prime Minister Viktor Chernomyrdin visited Karimov in December in Tashkent, where they signed agreements to encourage mutual investments and to cooperate in the areas of science and technology, the peaceful use of nuclear energy, and space exploration.

In October there were armed clashes on Uzbekistan's border with Tajikistan, probably initiated by Tajik rebels who had fled their homeland for the safety of Uzbekistan. But Uzbekistan's major problem was its economy.

Economy. By late 1997, South Korea's Daewoo Group had investments of more than $1.4 billion in Uzbekistan, and Japanese investments totaled an additional $1 billion. But because of corruption, nepotism, and currency controls, many other international investors were staying away, and there was little economic growth during 1997. The World Bank did approve a $75 million loan for a water-supply program and for improved sanitation, bringing its loan total to Uzbekistan to $327 million. But the International Monetary Fund suspended its $180 million loan program because of the government's propensity to print money instead of undertaking economic reforms.

See also BALTIC REPUBLICS.

WILLIAM E. SHAPIRO, *Freelance Writer*

SAUDI ARABIA

Saudi Arabia remained relatively tranquil in 1997 despite growing concern over its stability in light of terrorist attacks and declining oil prices.

International Relations. The United States and Saudi Arabia continued to try to determine the perpetrators of the June 25, 1996, Khobar bombing that killed 19 U.S. servicemen, even though friction between the two countries increased because of U.S. charges of insufficient Saudi cooperation. On Nov. 1, 1996, the Federal Bureau of Investigation (FBI) withdrew its team of investigators from Saudi Arabia, apparently frustrated by an inability to interview directly the 40 suspects detained in Saudi prisons. In December, Saudi Arabia again told the United States that Saudi Shiites trained in Lebanon and supported by Iran had been responsible. Iranian President Hashemi Rafsanjani denied that his country had been involved in the bombing.

In January 1997, FBI Director Louis Freeh and U.S. Attorney General Janet Reno criticized Saudi authorities for not allowing U.S. investigators to interrogate the bombing suspects directly. By June, Saudi Arabia provided the United States with videotapes and summaries of the interrogations.

On March 18, Canada arrested Hani Abdel Rahim al-Sayegh, a Saudi Shiite who had claimed political-refugee status since August 1996, on suspicion of involvement in the June 1996 bombing. After a Canadian report on March 27, 1997, said that al-Sayegh had links to Lebanon's Hezbollah Shiite organization and perhaps to Iran, he was deported to the United States on June 17. According to media reports, the United States agreed not to extradite al-Sayegh and to reduce charges against him in return for his providing full information, but on July 30, al-Sayegh pled not guilty to the lesser charges, which later were dismissed. In September, Saudi Arabia filed for his extradition as the United States continued to hold him amid uncertainty over his future.

The *Al-Hayat* newspaper published in London and owned by Saudi Prince Khalid bin Sultan, the leading Saudi military figure in the 1991 Persian Gulf war, became the target of anonymous attacks in 1997. In early January the newspaper's Riyadh headquarters discovered two letter bombs mailed from Egypt. In January, 13 letter bombs were addressed to the newspaper and found in its London, New York, and Washington, DC, offices. No group made any claims of responsibility for the bombs.

Saudi Arabia's tense international situation was shown in Iraq's abrupt decision on April 9 to fly 104 pilgrims to Mecca, thereby violating the United Nations (UN) air embargo. Saudi Interior Minister Prince Nayef said that even though Saudi Arabia disapproved of the flight, it decided for religious reasons to

Saudis enjoy a picnic at Al-Sooda Mountain—the nation's highest peak. For many Saudis, vacations in their homeland, instead of foreign travel, have become a trend.

allow the Iraqi pilgrims to land. They returned on April 22 to the Saudi-Iraqi border, where Iraqi helicopters—defying the UN-imposed southern no-fly zone ban—transported them home.

Saudi Arabia announced January 31 a possible acquisition of F-16 U.S. warplanes worth about $3 billion. On July 19 the Saudis fired the first locally made short-range surface-to-surface missiles, which could reach targets up to 37 mi (60 km) away.

Political Affairs. In an effort to allow some greater degree of participation in forming political decisions, King Fahd on July 7 changed the Majlis al-Shura, an appointed consultative council that advises him on policies. The all-male council was increased from 60 to 90 members. The king reappointed about one half of the original council members and added some 60 new members, most of whom were middle-aged, highly educated professionals and government employees. Fahd's choices represented a broad range of views, including both reformers and fundamentalists, as well as several Shiites.

In its January 1997 annual report on human rights, the U.S. State Department remained critical of Saudi Arabia's political and judicial systems, pointing out that there is no mechanism for citizens to change their government through elections and that the Saudi authorities commit and tolerate serious human-rights abuses.

The Saudis' management of the Muslim pilgrimage to Mecca came into question on April 15 when strong winds fanned a fire at Mina, causing a panic among some of the 2 million pilgrims assembled there. The fire caused more than 300 deaths.

A Saudi court considering the December 1996 murder of Yvonne Gilford, an Australian nurse working at the King Fahd Military Medical Center, convicted two British nurses of the crime. The family of the victim then was offered the standard Saudi option in such cases of deciding whether to insist on the application of strict punishments or to accept monetary compensation (which it did). Resident foreigners such as the nurses continued to play a large role in Saudi society in 1997, with more than 1 million Egyptians and millions of other foreign workers providing services and labor to the Saudi economy.

Economy. Higher oil prices provided an unexpected bonus for Saudi Arabia in 1996, but lower prices in 1997 cramped the Saudi economy and government. On Nov. 28, 1996, the Organization of the Petroleum Exporting Countries (OPEC), with the backing of Saudi Arabia, had renewed an agreement to keep oil-production quotas at 25 million barrels per day for the next six months. Higher-than-predicted oil revenues allowed Saudi Arabia's gross domestic product (GDP) to grow by 8.6% in 1996 as the government repaid $6 billion of internal debts. For the first time since 1982, the country had a current-account surplus. Nevertheless, the national budget announced on Dec. 31, 1996, cautiously predicted lower oil prices and a deficit of around $4.5 billion.

The 1996 production limits were renewed at the June 26, 1997, OPEC meeting in Vienna. Saudi Arabian Oil Minister Ali Naimi privately complained of overproduction by some countries, especially Venezuela, and threatened increased Saudi production so as to secure a greater market share and decrease the profits going to countries that had defied the OPEC quotas. Oil prices declined by one quarter between January and June, averaging about $19 per barrel by August. Saudi Arabia in 1997 pumped between 8.3 million and 8.5 million barrels per day, reflecting its 12% share of world production.

WILLIAM OCHSENWALD
Virginia Polytechnic Institute and State University

SINGAPORE

In 1997, Singaporeans went to the polls and gave a landslide victory to the ruling People's Action Party (PAP). Singapore's economy remained strong during the year, and the nation was not affected greatly by the financial crisis that hit other Southeast Asian nations.

Politics and Government. On January 2 the People's Action Party (PAP) captured 81 of 83 parliamentary seats with 67% of the vote, compared with 77 of 81 seats with 61% of the vote in 1991. Opposition seats went to the

Worker's Party and the Singapore People's Party. The government considers public order more important than individual liberties, and Prime Minister Goh Chok Tong noted that the voters had rejected Western-style liberal democracy and freedom. However, Singaporeans may have had other motives. The PAP had announced that a campaign to upgrade government flats in which much of the population lives might be withheld from constituencies that supported opposition candidates.

Defamation suits by the ruling party against opposition-party members continued. In May opposition politician Tang Liang Hong was ordered to pay $5.4 million plus costs to Prime Minister Goh and ten PAP leaders for calling them liars after they accused him of being an anti-Christian. And in September, J. B. Jeyaretnam, secretary-general of the opposition Worker's Party, was ordered to pay $13,150 to Prime Minister Goh because of alleged derogatory remarks he had made about Goh and other ruling-party members prior to the January election. Jeyaretnam had been given a parliamentary seat as a Non-Constituency MP (NCMP) under a provision allowing unsuccessful opposition-party members to serve in Parliament if there were fewer than three elected opposition members.

Society. The year produced new challenges as a result of Singapore's success. On August 24, Prime Minister Goh announced a worldwide talent search to attract the best and brightest to Singapore, "the new Global City." Many young Singaporeans have been choosing not to return after completing their studies abroad, and Singapore remains unable to fill some 7,000 high-paying positions each year. The country needs about 35,000 immigrants annually to keep pace. The government predicted a significant shortage even if Singaporeans came home in increasing numbers. However, an influx of immigrants could increase pressure on the government to establish a more democratic political system.

In early September, Singapore's air was polluted heavily by the haze emanating from uncontrolled fires on the Indonesian island of Sumatra and Kalimantan, the Indonesian half of Borneo. The government provided Jakarta with satellite photos indicating the location of the fires.

Economy. Singapore was not affected particularly by the financial crisis that hit Southeast Asia in 1997. The Singapore dollar depreciated little against the currencies of the global economic powers—Germany, Japan, and the United States. The government con-

© Renga/Reuters/Archive Photos

The year 1997 began on a positive note for Singapore's Prime Minister Goh Chok Tong, above. His People's Action Party scored a near sweep in general elections on January 2.

servatively predicted year-end growth in gross domestic product (GDP) at above 5%, which would put average adjusted income at almost $32,000 per year and give Singapore one of the highest standards of living in the world. The country continued to experience growth in foreign trade, no budget deficit, and a minimal shortfall in the current account. The government declared a onetime 10% income-tax rebate for 1997.

Foreign Relations. In March relations with Malaysia took a turn for the worse when disparaging remarks by former Prime Minister Lee Kuan Yew referring to Malaysia's Johor state as a place full of "muggings, carjackings, and shootings" were made public. Lee's apology did little to calm the waters, and the affair escalated. Unusually long delays developed on the Malaysian side of the border for Singa-

---

SINGAPORE • Information Highlights

Official Name: Republic of Singapore.
Location: Southeast Asia.
Area: 244 sq mi (632.6 km²).
Population (mid-1997 est.): 3,500,000.
Chief City: Singapore City, the capital.
Government: *Head of state,* Ong Teng Cheong, president (took office September 1993). *Head of government,* Goh Chok Tong, prime minister (took office November 1990). *Legislature* (unicameral)—Parliament.
Monetary Unit: Singapore dollar (1.6770 S. dollars equal U.S. $1, Dec. 31, 1997).
Gross Domestic Product (1995 est. U.S.$): $66,100,000,-000 (purchasing power parity).
Economic Index (1996, 1990 = 100): *Consumer Prices,* all items, 115.1; food, 112.2.
Foreign Trade (1996 U.S.$): *Imports,* $131,340,000,000; *exports,* $125,059,000,000.

poreans entering Johor, while Malaysian officials accused Singapore of telling its people not to visit their country. Substantive issues relating to Malaysia's plan to build a high-speed rail line into Singapore and the latter's need for assurance of a future water supply from across the causeway were affected. For the rail project to proceed, Singapore must agree to changes in the Points-of-Agreement, the framework for rail cooperation. Prime Minister Goh used this issue to bargain for reassurance on the water issue. Singapore continued to investigate the possibility of constructing a desalination plant as an alternate water source. Frayed relations or not, Singapore remained Malaysia's number-one foreign investor.

PATRICK M. MAYERCHAK
Virginia Military Institute

SLOVAKIA

In 1997, Slovakia's political life continued to be marked by conflict between Prime Minister Vladimir Mečiar and President Michal Kovač, and between the government and the opposition. Relations with Hungary remained troubled, and those with the Czech Republic worsened.

Domestic Affairs. Five opposition parties—the Democratic Union, Christian Democratic Party, Democratic Party, Social Democrat Party, and Green Party—formed a coalition in June 1997 and agreed to run candidates together in the 1998 elections. Opposition activists called for foreign monitors to ensure that these elections would be free and fair, but the prime minister refused these requests.

Talks between Prime Minister Mečiar and the opposition collapsed in July. The Constitutional Court ruled that month that the removal of František Gauliedér's parliamentary mandate when he left the prime minister's Movement for a Democratic Slovakia was unconstitutional. However, the parliament, which was dominated by deputies of the governing coalition, refused to reinstate Gauliedér in September. In October all of the opposition parties except the Party of the Democratic Left boycotted talks with the government.

Economy. Despite the political situation, Slovakia's economic recovery continued. Gross domestic product (GDP) increased by 5% in the first half of the year. Unemployment decreased to 12.5% by July and inflation increased somewhat—to 6.5% by midyear. However, government spending and foreign indebtedness increased significantly. Continued concern over the political situation resulted in low levels of foreign investment.

Foreign Affairs. Slovakia's relations with the Czech Republic worsened in 1997, when Slovak leaders criticized the Czech government's decision to give $580,000 to a Jewish foundation to settle a claim regarding the gold confiscated from Slovak Jews in World War II. Czech President Václav Havel's criticism of Prime Minister Mečiar's attitude toward expansion of the North Atlantic Treaty Organization (NATO) also increased tensions. Relations between Slovakia and Hungary continued to be troubled by the treatment of the Hungarian minority in Slovakia, especially when the leaders of the Slovak National Party, a member of the government coalition, continued to speak against that minority. The dispute over the controversial Gabčikovo dam project also continued. The International Court of Justice ruled that both Hungary and Slovakia had violated international law.

Both the prime minister and the president continued to affirm Slovakia's interest in joining the European Union (EU) and NATO. Slovakia, however, was not included in the group of former communist countries invited to join NATO at the Madrid NATO summit in July. U.S. officials linked Slovakia's failure to be included in the first wave of NATO expansion to continued problems with democracy. In May a referendum on joining NATO was declared invalid because it did not also include an approved question on direct presidential elections. The opposition boycotted the referendum, and only 10% of voters went to the polls.

EU officials reacted negatively to a number of developments in Slovakia, including the manipulation of the May referendum and the parliament's failure to reinstate Gauliedér. In July, EU officials criticized Slovakia's leaders

---

SLOVAKIA • Information Highlights

Official Name: Slovak Republic.
Location: East-central Europe.
Area: 18,859 sq mi (48 845 km²).
Population (mid-1997 est.): 5,400,000.
Chief Cities (Dec. 31, 1995 est.): Bratislava, the capital, 452,053; Kosice, 240,915.
Government: *Head of state,* Michal Kovač, president (took office February 1993). *Head of government,* Vladimir Mečiar, prime minister (took office December 1994). *Legislature* (unicameral)—National Parliament.
Monetary Unit: Koruna (34.78 koruny equal U.S.$1, Dec. 31, 1997).
Gross Domestic Product (1995 est. U.S.$): $39,000,000,-000 (purchasing power parity).
Economic Index: *Consumer Prices* (1996, 1991 = 100): all items, 178.6; food, 175.4.
Foreign Trade (1996 U.S.$): *Imports,* $10,911,000,000; *exports,* $8,841,000,000.

for failing to respect the constitution and for their treatment of the Hungarian minority. In September, however, Slovak leaders agreed to EU demands that they pass a minority-language law. The Organization for Security and Cooperation in Europe (OSCE) also called on Slovak leaders to adopt a law to protect the use of minority languages.

SHARON L. WOLCHIK
The George Washington University

SLOVENIA

In 1997, after the formation of a multiparty coalition government, Slovenia continued to exhibit political progress and stability. As a result, the country's international acceptance for future membership in both the North Atlantic Treaty Organization (NATO) and the European Union (EU) was enhanced.

Politics. In February, following two months of negotiations necessitated by the inconclusive results of the November 1996 parliamentary elections, Slovenia formed a new center-left government. Prime Minister Janez Drnovsek's Liberal Democratic Party entered into a coalition with the Slovene People's Party (SPP) and a number of smaller political groups. The SPP, led by Marjan Podobnik, had been one of the three major opposition groups belonging to the center-right Slovenian Spring coalition.

In November 1997 presidential elections, Milan Kucan won his second term in office after facing little credible opposition. A new Senate (upper house), representing the interests of specific occupational groups, also was installed.

The new parliament passed a number of important laws to bring the country into line with European standards. In July, for example, it amended the constitution to allow foreigners to own property in the country. Prime Minister Drnovsek and Archbishop Franc Rode also reached an agreement to return to the Roman Catholic Church property seized and nationalized by the Communists after World War II.

Economy. Slovenia has registered one of the healthiest economies and highest living standards in Eastern Europe. Nevertheless, in 1997 the government had to grapple with a number of negative trends, including a rising budget deficit fueled by a growth in state expenses and increasing unemployment among workers laid off from the unprofitable heavy-industry sector. The new state budget projected the annual inflation rate to remain

SLOVENIA • Information Highlights

Official Name: Republic of Slovenia.
Location: Southeastern Europe.
Area: 7,821 sq mi (20 256 km²).
Population (mid-1997 est.): 2,000,000.
Chief Cities (Dec. 31, 1994 est.): Ljubljana, the capital, 269,972; Maribor, 103,113.
Government: *Head of state,* Milan Kucan, president (took office April 22, 1990). *Head of government,* Janez Drnovsek, prime minister (took office May 14, 1992). *Legislature*—National Assembly and State Council.
Monetary Unit: Tolar (154.000 tolars equal U.S.$1, noncommercial rate, July 1997).
Gross Domestic Product (1995 est. U.S.$): $22,600,000,-000 (purchasing power parity).
Economic Indexes (1996): *Consumer Prices* (1991 = 100): all items, 616.1; food, 597.8. *Industrial Production* (1990 = 100): 81.
Foreign Trade (1996 U.S. $): *Imports,* $9,399,000,000; *exports,* $8,123,000,000.

in single digits and forecast a gross-domestic-product (GDP) growth of about 4%.

With the aim of substantially cutting government expenses, a major debate on the reform of the pension system was launched in parliament. In addition, the World Bank contributed $80 million for technical assistance and advice in restructuring Slovenia's bloated public sector.

Foreign Affairs. Slovenia was included with four other Central and East European countries for early negotiations for EU membership. Parliament ratified Slovenia's Association Agreement with the EU; it was the only former Yugoslav republic to have such an arrangement. The process of negotiation for EU entry was expected to begin early in 1998.

Ljubljana clearly was disappointed in July when the NATO summit in Madrid excluded Slovenia from the first wave of planned NATO enlargement into Central and Eastern Europe. Nevertheless, the country was singled out as a prime candidate for the second wave of NATO expansion early in the 21st century if it continued to pursue political and military reforms.

Slovenia largely settled its tense relations with both Italy and Croatia. Visa-free travel was arranged with Italy; Slovenia, Hungary, and Italy agreed to form a joint military brigade; and Italy strongly supported Slovenia's entry into NATO. Croatia and Slovenia finally agreed to seek international arbitration for their border dispute in the Gulf of Piran on the Adriatic Sea. The two countries also started a joint administration of the Krsko nuclear-power plant in Slovenia, ownership of which had been a subject of dispute between the two governments since they gained independence from Yugoslavia.

JANUSZ BUGAJSKI
Center for Strategic and International Studies

SOCIAL WELFARE

The U.S. economy remained on a healthy course in 1997 with low inflation and low unemployment. The robust economy, however, failed to improve the lives of tens of millions of Americans living in poverty. Internationally, social conditions remained dire in many parts of the developing world, where some 1.3 billion people lived on less than one U.S. dollar a day.

U.S. Developments

Income and Poverty. The annual U.S. Census Bureau survey of family income and poverty reported a rise in overall household income for a second consecutive year and a slight decrease in the number of Americans living below the poverty line. On the other hand, the report, released September 29, found that in 1996 the number of Americans considered "very poor"—those with incomes of less than half the poverty threshold—rose from 13.9 million in 1995 to 14.4 million in 1996. The poverty line was defined as a total income of $16,036 for a family of four. The survey found that some 36.5 million Americans—about 13.7% of the entire population—lived below the poverty line. That compared with 13.8% of the population living in poverty in 1995, 14.5% in 1994, and 15.1% in 1993.

Among ethnic groups, Hispanic Americans had the highest poverty rate: 29.4%—a slight decrease compared with 1995's all-time high of 30.3%, a figure that for the first time was higher than African-Americans' poverty rate. In 1996 some 28.4% of African-Americans lived below the poverty line. The poverty rate for whites was 11.2%. The survey found that 20.5% of all the nation's children and 32.6% of all single mothers were living in poverty. Median household income, which rose for all ethnic groups, increased 1.2% in 1996 to $35,492. The largest rise was among Hispanics: from $23,535 in 1995 to $24,906 in 1996.

According to a report issued in July by the National Council of La Raza, the nation's largest Hispanic-advocacy group, the size of the Hispanic middle class had increased 25% in the last ten years. The report also pointed out, however, that Hispanics remained the nation's poorest ethnic group, with a median family income amounting to only two thirds that of whites. "There is a significant portion of our community that is not benefiting from the nation's economic growth," said Sonia Perez, a La Raza researcher.

Welfare Reform. Aug. 22, 1997, marked the first anniversary of President Bill Clinton's signing of a far-reaching welfare-reform law that turned the national welfare program over to the states in the form of block grants, thereby ending the federal government's 60-year guarantee of assistance to needy families. The new law went into effect on Oct. 1, 1996. The states were given until July 1, 1997, to submit new welfare plans to the federal government.

Under the law, those plans had to follow new guidelines designed to cut welfare rolls

International agencies assisted North Korea as the nation of 24 million faced a severe food shortage. The Connecticut-based charity AmeriCares responded by sending some 30 tons of emergency aid, including infant formula, right.

and put welfare recipients in jobs. The guidelines required the states to reduce lifetime welfare assistance to five years; require the head of every family on welfare to work within two years or lose all benefits; deny welfare benefits and food stamps to most legal immigrants who were not American citizens; restrict childless adults aged 18 to 50 to three months of food stamps over three years; and establish a national child-support-payment system.

On August 11, Gov. Pete Wilson of California signed his state's welfare reform into law. The new California law, which contained the five-year lifetime limit, also restricted current California welfare recipients to 24 consecutive months of aid and new recipients to 18 consecutive months. In 1997 some 2.4 million Californians were on welfare, about 22% of the national total.

The federal government reported in August that some 10.7 million Americans were receiving welfare benefits—a decrease of some 1.45 million compared to a year earlier. The percentage of Americans on welfare stood at its lowest total since 1970. The situation was similar with food-stamp recipients. Throughout 1996 an average of more than 25 million Americans had received food stamps. That number dropped to 21.7 million by July 1997, according to the U.S. Department of Agriculture. "The debate is over," President Clinton said in August. "We now know that welfare reform works."

Other administration officials said the steep decline in welfare and food-stamp recipients was due only in part to the new welfare-reform laws. Health and Human Services Secretary Donna E. Shalala said that only about 31% of the decline in welfare recipients was linked to the welfare-reform measures. Other factors, including the robust economy, accounted for the balance, she said.

Many liberals, including those in Congress, and some religious groups who opposed the welfare-reform legislation said that some state laws were harming the nation's poor unfairly. Others said that most state laws did not contain harshly unfair provisions, and that the states, in general, did not cut back the amount of money spent on welfare significantly.

The Disabled. One controversial element of the 1996 welfare-reform law was a provision that ended Supplemental Security Income (SSI) payments to some 500,000 elderly and disabled legal immigrants. Those payments were restored in the balanced-budget bill President Clinton signed into law in July. Another controversial part of the 1996

welfare law—tightening eligibility requirements in order to reduce fraud and abuse in SSI payments to low-income children with disabilities—remained in effect in 1997. The law required the Social Security Administration to provide SSI children's disability payments only to those with children having "marked and severe functional limitations." In 1997 about 1 million children were receiving such payments, which averaged $426 a month. In August, Social Security Administration officials announced that after reviewing some 260,000 cases, benefits would be cut off for some 95,000 children. Most of those slated to lose disability benefits had what were termed "mental disorders."

There were various criticisms of the move by those who said that the Clinton administration used stricter standards than those required by the 1996 law. In Iowa, Kansas, Louisiana, Mississippi, Montana, and Texas more than 75% of the cases reviewed resulted in children losing their benefits. In the states of Hawaii, Michigan, Minnesota, and Nevada, less than 35% lost benefits. Commissioner of Social Security Kenneth Apfel announced that his agency would reexamine the cases of 60,000 of the 135,000 children whose benefits were denied since August 1996 because mistakes may have been made. He also said that other families would be given a chance to appeal his agency's decision to discontinue their children's disability payments.

The federal government in 1997 issued regulations called for by the seven-year-old Americans With Disabilities Act (ADA), which prohibited discrimination against the nation's physically and mentally disabled in the workplace and in public facilities. In April the Equal Employment Opportunity Commission (EEOC) issued a set of rules prohibiting employers from discriminating against qualified workers with mental illnesses. The new rules had two main provisions. First, prospective employers may not ask job applicants if they have a history of mental illness. Second, employers must take steps to accommodate employees with psychiatric or mental problems. Such accommodations could include "room dividers, partitions, or other soundproofing or visual barriers between work spaces" to help mentally ill employees who have difficulty concentrating. Advocates for the disabled praised the new rules, as did some business groups. Others had reservations about the guidelines. The new rules create "confusion for employers, especially small employers who don't have any special expertise," said Susan R. Meisinger of the Society for Human Resources Management, which represents personnel directors.

The EEOC reported in May that in 1996 nearly 18,000 disability complaints were filed with the agency. That compared with some 15,000 complaints filed in 1991, the first year after the ADA was passed, and a high of nearly 19,800 complaints filed in 1993.

International Conditions

Poverty. Hundreds of millions of people around the world faced severe poverty, malnutrition, and social dislocation in 1997. The annual report of the United Nations Development Program (UNDP), released in June, found that some 1.3 billion people—primarily in Brazil, Central America, China, Indochina, South Asia, and sub-Saharan Africa—lived on less than one U.S. dollar a day, and that living standards had declined in at least 30 countries since 1970. Two thirds of the people in developing countries lived on less than two dollars a day, according to UNDP statistics.

Regional Conflict. Civil and tribal wars and political upheaval remained a vexing social problem in many parts of Africa. In southwestern Sudan health officials reported a potentially catastrophic outbreak of sleeping sickness—a consequence of fighting between the nation's Arab Muslim government and the rebelling Sudan People's Liberation Army. International and local doctors fled when the civil conflict, which began its 15th year in 1997, entered the region in 1990. Health officials believed that thousands of people contracted the curable disease during that period. The fear was that many would die due to the ongoing fighting and the high cost of drugs.

In 1997 social dislocation was a growing and serious problem in Central Africa. Hundreds of thousands of men, women, and children throughout the region suffered dire problems due to a civil war between the Hutu and Tutsi tribal ethnic groups that began in Rwanda in 1994. Social conditions deteriorated following the overthrow in May of Zaire's President Mobuto Sese Seko by the forces of rebel leader Laurent Kabila. As many as 100,000 Rwandan Hutu refugees who had fled to Zaire in 1995 after Rwandan Tutsi won the civil war were hit by deadly disease and food shortages at the time of Mobuto's overthrow when they came under attack from Zairian rebels, a group dominated by ethnic Tutsi.

After Kabila seized power and renamed the nation the Democratic Republic of the Congo, ethnic violence continued throughout the region. Civilians often were the victims. The fighting was the worst in western Rwanda, where at least 4,000 people, mostly civilians, were killed between May and October. In the neighboring Republic of the Congo, a bloody four-month civil war ended in October with a victory by the rebellious forces under former President Denis Sassou-Nguesso. The fighting virtually destroyed Brazzaville, the nation's capital.

In Europe near-anarchic conditions reigned in Albania following the collapse in January of a pyramid investment scheme in which at least one fourth of the population had invested. A violent rebellion against the government ensued, primarily in the southern half of Europe's poorest nation, where most of the population earned between $40 and $60 per month.

The 24 million people of North Korea faced the world's worst social crisis. Severe food shortages had persisted in that nation since 1995. In 1997 a drought that caused the loss of 70% of the corn crop—combined with an isolated, repressive government—led to the possibility of famine. Relief officials said that widespread starvation would be avoided only by massive amounts of food aid from other nations.

Overall foreign aid to the world's poorest nations decreased by $3.8 billion in 1996, according to a report issued in October by the Organization for Economic Cooperation and Development (OECD). The $55.8 billion sent to developing nations in 1996 by the 21 member nations of that organization equaled one fourth of 1% of those countries' total gross domestic product. Private groups, on the other hand, increased foreign aid by $80 million in 1996, to a total of $234 billion. About 90% of the private investment went to China or to middle-income countries, according to data compiled by the UNDP. Less than 1% of the money given by private groups, UNDP said, went to the world's 50 poorest countries.

A report issued in October by a unit of the World Bank predicted that rising world grain prices could have disastrous consequences throughout South Asia and sub-Saharan Africa in the next 25 years. The International Food Policy Research Institute report said that the volume of imported food needed to make up for local production shortages and increasing food demand was growing. Most countries in sub-Saharan Africa and South Asia, the report said, "will require special assistance to avert widespread hunger."

See also VOLUNTEERISM, page 58.

MARC LEEPSON, *Freelance Writer*

SOUTH AFRICA

The South African political landscape began to change in significant ways during 1997, with high-profile resignations from all the major political parties: F.W. de Klerk, leader of the National Party (NP); Inkatha Freedom Party (IFP) National Chairman Frank Mdlalose and IFP Secretary-General Ziba Jiyane; and Gauteng province's Premier Tokyo Sexwale, of the African National Congress (ANC). Former Pan Africanist Congress (PAC) leader Clarence Makwetu was suspended from participating in PAC activities after he lost the presidency to former Methodist Church leader Bishop Stanley Mogoba. The most dramatic event occurred in July, when President Nelson Mandela announced, "The real ruler of South Africa, the de facto ruler, is [Deputy President] Thabo Mbeki. I am shifting everything to him, and he is doing remarkably well." This was a clear effort on Mandela's part to ease the country's concerns about his impending retirement in 1999.

A new party, the United Democratic Movement, was launched by former members of the NP and ANC in an attempt to appeal to a broader range of voters. There were exploratory talks among various political parties about other potential alliances to increase chances for success in the 1999 general election.

Resignations. At the end of August, de Klerk, 61, former president of South Africa, announced that as of September 9 he was resigning as leader of the NP—the country's major opposition party—and from politics. In 1990, de Klerk freed Mandela from prison, and subsequently shared the 1993 Nobel Peace Prize with Mandela for opening the way to major reforms leading to majority black rule and an end to apartheid. De Klerk said that he was resigning "...to open a door for the National Party to provide further proof of its dynamic break with the past," but was said to have been concerned about internal NP disputes over its future and about stinging criticism from within the party. He also had differences with the country's Truth and Reconciliation Commission (TRC), which questioned his role in the apartheid era.

De Klerk was succeeded by another NP member, political scientist Marthinus van Schalkwyk, 37, a surprise choice. As a law student at Rand Afrikaans University in the mid-1980s, van Schalkwyk had been involved in Jeugkrag (Youth Power)—a student organization later found to have been paid from covert funds from South African military intelligence to spy for the apartheid regime. Van Schalkwyk—who lacked de Klerk's stature and only

© Mohamed El-Dakhakhny/AP/Wide World Photos

Libya's Col. Muammar el-Qaddafi (right) welcomed President Nelson Mandela (left) to Tripoli on Oct. 22, 1997. Both Washington and London tried to dissuade the South African president from making the Libyan trip and a second one later in October.

had entered parliament in 1990—was selected after Hernus Kriel, premier of the Western Cape, decided not to run.

In June, Gauteng Premier Sexwale announced that he would end his term of office in January 1998 to work in the private sector. It was rumored that his real reason for resigning was because of a power struggle with Deputy President Mbeki. Mathole Motshekga succeeded Sexwale as premier. The transition was likely to be complicated, because such key members of the Gauteng cabinet as Jessie Duarte, Jabu Moleketi, and Amos Masondo had supported the Reverend Frank Chikane for the position.

United Democratic Movement. In September, Roelf Meyer and Bantu Holomisa launched a new political party, the United Democratic Movement, which they expected to take part in the 1999 election. Meyer—the former NP secretary-general, chief NP negotiator in the constitutional talks that led to the 1994 election, and potential heir to de Klerk—resigned in May from the NP because he felt that his efforts to widen the appeal of the party to attract black supporters had not been taken seriously. Holomisa, a former military leader of the Transkei homeland who won the most votes at the last ANC congress, was expelled from the ANC in 1996 after accusing several party leaders of corruption. The two said their new party would "seek to improve life for all South Africans through the pursuit of good governance and civil order." A number of liberal NP members defected to the new political party, confirming the widening split in the NP.

Truth and Reconciliation Commission. The TRC continued its hearings and provided a final opportunity in September for last-minute amnesty applications—8,000 of which already had been received by the earlier May dead-line. In its deliberations, the TRC heard from applicants representing all points in the political spectrum, including high-ranking ANC, NP, and IFP members. Several prominent leaders of the former NP government appeared before the commission—including former government ministers Piet Koornhof, Adriaan Vlok, and Pik Botha, as well as the former commander of the South African Defense Force, Gen. Constand Viljoen. Former President P.W. Botha refused to appear despite being subpoenaed to do so.

Former Foreign Minister Pik Botha testified that terms such as "elimination" should not be taken out of context and that cabinet members suspected that the police were engaged in such activities but never approved of them. "The question is whether we could have done more to ensure that it did not happen. I deeply regret this omission. God forgive me," said Botha. Former Minister of Law and Order Vlok told the TRC that words such as "eliminate" and "remove permanently from society" had been misinterpreted by his subordinates and that he had not been giving instructions to them to kill political opponents. While he acknowledged that counterrevolutionary tactics were employed, he insisted that the police implemented these in ways of which he was unaware.

As many as 25 ANC leaders sought amnesty for acts committed during the liberation struggle. They included Deputy President Mbeki, Defense Minister Joe Modise, Justice Minister Dullah Omar, Transport Minister Mac Maharaj, and Minister of Public Administration Zola Skweyiya.

In September, just before facing a special TRC inquiry, Winnie Madikizela-Mandela—former wife of President Mandela and an active candidate for the deputy presidency of the ANC—was linked to 18 incidents, eight of which were murders, including that of activist James (Stompie) Moeketsi Seipei, 14, in 1988. She also was connected to cases of abduction and assault. Although convicted in 1991 for assaulting and kidnapping Seipei, Madikizela-Mandela insisted that she was innocent and brought five witnesses whom she claimed would indicate that she had not committed murder or acts of violence. Other former supporters implicated her in the killings, however. Although the commission had no power to prosecute or to determine guilt, she subsequently requested a public hearing, ostensibly to clear her name, and, according to some, to revive her waning political career. During a weeklong hearing at the end of November, she was alleged to have slandered a Methodist

---

SOUTH AFRICA • Information Highlights

Official Name: Republic of South Africa.
Location: Southern tip of Africa.
Area: 471,008 sq mi (1 219 912 km²).
Population (mid-1997 est.): 42,500,000.
Chief Cities (1991 census, city proper): Pretoria, the administrative capital, 525,583; Cape Town, the legislative capital, 854,616; Durban, 715,669; Johannesburg, 712,507.
Government: *Head of state and government,* Nelson Mandela, president (took office May 10, 1994). *Legislature—* Parliament: National Assembly and National Council of Provinces.
Monetary Unit: Rand (4.8670 rands equal U.S.$1, Dec. 31, 1997).
Gross Domestic Product (1995 est. U.S.$): $215,000,000,-000 (purchasing power parity).
Economic Indexes (1996, 1990 = 100): *Consumer Prices,* all items, 183.2; food, 209.9. *Industrial Production,* 104.
Foreign Trade (1996 U.S.$): *Imports,* $29,105,000,000; *exports,* excluding exports of gold, $28,145,000,000.

minister she considered a political rival and to have been involved in numerous beatings and murders during the apartheid era. Although her political bid had the support of ANC women's organizations, she withdrew; KwaZulu-Natal leader Jacob Zuma became ANC deputy chairman.

In July, Peter and Linda Biehl—parents of Fulbright scholar Amy Biehl, who was killed in the township of Guguleto near Cape Town on Aug. 25, 1993—attended a TRC hearing at which her killers sought amnesty. The Biehls supported the amnesty. Amy, who was from California, had been killed by Mongezi Manqina, Ntobeko Peni, Easy Nofemela, and Vusumzi Ntamo after they had attended a meeting of the PAC's armed wing—the Azanian People's Liberation Army (APLA). At the meeting they had been urged to make South Africa ungovernable and to consider every white person as an enemy. One of the young men maintained that Amy—who was in the township during a period of considerable unrest—was killed because she was seen as a "white settler." The four men—who at their trial originally claimed to have no knowledge of the murder—received amnesty and were released from serving the remainder of their 18-year sentences.

In August, Janusz Walus and Clive Derby-Lewis—convicted of the April 10, 1993, killing of ANC and South African Communist Party leader Chris Hani—also petitioned for amnesty. Also in August the Dutch Reformed Church released an apology for its role in apartheid. Earlier in the year it decided against appearing before the TRC, preferring to have a member of its synod prepare a report.

Escalating Violence. In 1997 crime in South Africa was rampant, and the nation's largest city, Johannesburg, was reputed to have the highest murder and car-jacking rates in the world. Serious incidents of political violence also continued to plague the country. Aware that widespread lawlessness threatened foreign investment, tourism, and the transition to democracy, the government declared war on crime, committing $241 million to restructure the criminal-justice system over the next few years. Increased anticrime efforts in Gauteng province late in the year resulted in more than 43,000 arrests in a two-month period. Nonetheless, the South African Human Rights Commission expressed grave concern at the government's inability to control the spiral of criminal violence.

Budget. In March, Minister of Finance Trevor Manuel presented the 1997–98 budget to Parliament. He emphasized the need for economic growth, jobs, and the control of inflation. He also noted that in 1996 the South African economy had grown by 3.1% and inflation had declined to 7.4%, the lowest since 1972. He predicted that in 1997 the economy would grow by 2.5%. He also indicated that it was time for significant relaxation of exchange-control regulations. During the October Commonwealth meeting in Edinburgh, Scotland, Mandela emphasized that stable democracies could not be viable if there was rampant poverty. The statement was made in relation to an economic charter—Promoting Shared Prosperity, endorsed by the 54 Commonwealth nations at the conference—that advocated free-market principles and sought to promote trade and investment among member nations.

Foreign Relations. Warm diplomatic relations between South Africa and the United States were threatened by South Africa's continued contact with such states as Libya, Cuba, and Iran. An alleged arms deal with Syria—which the United States considered a supporter of international terrorism—to upgrade Syria's Russian-made T-72 battle tanks with a sophisticated new South African–developed firing-control system aroused particularly strong U.S. disapproval. South Africa delayed the sale under U.S. pressure. The decision whether or not to sell arms to Syria and some of its Arab neighbors was a difficult one because the multimillion-dollar sale would mean a significant boost to South Africa's foreign reserves and the creation of new jobs at a time when drastic cuts in the defense budget seriously threatened the future of the country's armaments industry.

In October, Mandela visited Libya on two occasions despite U.S. and British efforts to dissuade him. On both visits, he traveled by road to comply with a United Nations (UN) arms and air embargo imposed in 1992, when Libya refused to hand over two Libyans suspected of bombing a Pan Am jet over Lockerbie, Scotland, in 1988. On his official visit to Tripoli, Mandela called for sanctions to be lifted and for an international tribunal to investigate the bombing. On his second visit, on October 29, he conferred South Africa's highest award, the Order of Good Hope, on Col. Muammar el-Qaddafi because of his support during the struggle against apartheid. On his return to South Africa, Mandela was criticized severely by the Democratic Party and the NP for his recognition of Qaddafi.

PATRICK O'MEARA and N. BRIAN WINCHESTER
Indiana University

Sojourner, Mars Rover, and Pathfinder Spacecraft Designs and Images.

SPACE EXPLORATION

A close encounter by spacecraft with an asteroid and startling images of Jupiter's moon Europa and the surface of Mars high-lighted space exploration in 1997. The Cassini spacecraft was launched on a mission to Saturn. U.S.-Russian joint missions involved the docking of a shuttle with the beleaguered *Mir* space station (*see* SIDEBAR, page 462).

Shuttle Program. The National Aeronautics and Space Administration (NASA) launched eight shuttle missions, the most since 1992 (*see* page 461). The $3.1 billion 1997 shuttle budget—nearly a third less than in 1992—represented cost-cutting measures of United Space Alliance, the NASA-contracted commercial operator for the shuttle fleet. Three *Atlantis* flights to the Russian *Mir* space station provided a technical and cultural foundation for the construction of a 21st-century International Space Station (ISS). During the January *Atlantis* mission, astronaut John Blaha—who lived on *Mir* for 118 days—was replaced by Jerry Linenger. For four days, Russian and U.S. crews moved several tons of equipment, experiments, and drinking water—the largest such logistical transfer. *Atlantis* returned to Earth with the first plants to complete a life cycle in space.

Four planned extravehicular activities (EVAs) by astronauts during the February

After the U.S. Mars Pathfinder, an unmanned spacecraft, landed on Mars on July 4, 1997, the Sojourner—a roving robotic explorer, top—gathered data, including photos of the planet, above.

Discovery mission gave the Hubble Space Telescope (HST) state-of-the-art sensing abilities. The Goddard High Resolution Spectrograph and Faint Object Spectrograph were removed and replaced by a Space Telescope Imaging Spectrograph and a Near Infrared Camera and Multi-Object Spectrometer. Astronauts also installed a new digital tape recorder and a stabilization device. In an unscheduled fifth extravehicular activity (EVA), thermal-insulation blankets were placed on select spots. The HST was reboosted into a higher orbit.

The first flight of the Microgravity Science Laboratory-1 (MSL-1) in April aboard shuttle *Columbia* ran into trouble. Soon after the shuttle reached orbit, concern arose about one of three fuel cells, forcing mission controllers to curtail the flight. Despite the problem, work was performed using the German electromagnetic-levitation furnace facility, while other investigations focused on the roles that heat, pressure, and melting point play in creating new alloy combinations. Studies of fire in microgravity also were carried out. MSL-1 was reflown in July, completing various microgravity experiments.

During the August *Discovery* mission, the shuttle's robot arm was used to set the Cryogenic Infrared Spectrometers and Telescopes for the Atmosphere–Shuttle Pallet Satellite–2 (CRISTA-SPAS-2) adrift to survey the middle atmosphere with ultraviolet spectrometers. It was retrieved by the shuttle after nine days. During CRISTA-SPAS-2's flight, more than 60 U.S. and German minirockets and balloons were launched, to monitor the same regions of the atmosphere concurrently.

During November, *Columbia* astronauts deploying a Spartan solar observatory discovered that it had not received a crucial computer command. The problem was compounded when Spartan went into an uncontrollable spin during an attempted retrieval with the shuttle's robot arm. To recover the $10 million satellite, two astronauts caught the 3,000-lb (1 261-kg) Spartan with their gloved hands. The shuttle crew completed experiments constituting the fourth U.S. Microgravity Payload (USMP-4), including research into various industrial processes. They also tested a crane for use in building the ISS. A floating robotic camera—also for possible use on the space station—was released; it flew around *Columbia*, relaying imagery to the ground and crew.

Applications Satellites. On April 25 a U.S. GOES-10 geosynchronous meteorological satellite was launched by an Atlas-Centaur rocket from Cape Canaveral, to back up

---

1997 MANNED SPACEFLIGHTS

STS-81—U.S. Space Shuttle *Atlantis*. Jan. 12–22, 1997. **Crew:** Capt. Michael A. Baker (mission commander), Brent Jett, Marsha S. Ivins, Capt. Jerry L. Linenger, Dr. John M. Grunsfeld, Dr. Peter J.K. Wisoff. **Mission Highlights:** Linked with the Russian space station *Mir* and picked up John E. Blaha, who had been aboard *Mir* since September 1996. Linenger joined Russian astronauts Valery Korzun and Aleksandr Kaleri on *Mir*. The shuttle also delivered essential supplies and fresh water to the *Mir* crew.

Russia's Space Capsule *Soyuz TM-25*. Launched Feb. 10, 1997. **Crew:** Vasily Tsibliyev and Aleksandr Lazutkin of Russia and Dr. Reinhold Ewald of Germany. Tsibliyev and Lazutkin succeeded Valery Korzun and Aleksandr Kaleri aboard *Mir*. The latter two astronauts had been residents of *Mir* since August 1996, and had carried out more than 200 experiments in new scientific modules attached to *Mir*. They returned to Earth with Ewald aboard *Soyuz TM-24* on March 2.

STS-82—U.S. Space Shuttle *Discovery*. Feb. 11–21, 1997. **Crew:** Cmdr. Kenneth D. Bowersox (mission commander), Lt. Col. Scott J. Horowitz, Col. Mark C. Lee, Joseph R. Tanner, Gregory J. Harbaugh, Steven L. Smith, Steven A. Hawley. **Mission Highlights:** Repaired and serviced the Hubble Space Telescope. The crew raised Hubble's orbit by some 10 mi (16 km) and repaired tears in the telescope's insulation panels. New equipment to enhance the telescope's accuracy also was installed.

STS-83—U.S. Space Shuttle *Columbia*. April 4–8, 1997. **Crew:** Lt. Col. James D. Halsell, Jr. (mission commander), Lt. Cmdr. Susan L. Still, Dr. Janice Voss, Dr. Michael L. Gernhardt, Dr. Donald A. Thomas, Roger K. Crouch, Dr. Gregory T. Linteris. **Mission Highlights:** The first Microgravity Sciences Laboratory (MSL-1) mission conducted various experiments associated with the influence of gravity on daily life. Returned to Earth 12 days early due to a fuel-cell problem.

STS-84—U.S. Space Shuttle *Atlantis*. May 15–24, 1997. **Crew:** Charles J. Precourt (mission commander), Eileen M. Collins, Carlos I. Noriega, Edward T. Lu, Jean-François Clervoy of the European Space Agency, Russia's Elena V. Kondakova, and C. Michael Foale. **Mission Highlights:** Docked with Russia's *Mir* for five days. Jerry L. Linenger, who had been on *Mir* since mid-January, returned to Earth; Foale remained on board the space station.

STS-94—U.S. Space Shuttle *Columbia*. July 1–17, 1997. **Crew:** same as STS-83; mission was a reflight of STS-83, which had to be shortened. **Mission Highlights:** During a 6.2-million-mi (10-million-km) journey, laboratory research—including the growing of spinach, clover, and more than 700 protein crystals—was conducted. The mission carried out a host of materials-processing experiments using the Microgravity Sciences Laboratory (MSL-1).

Russia's Space Capsule *Soyuz TM-26*. Launched Aug. 5, 1997. **Crew:** Russia's Anatoly Solovyev and Pavel Vinogradov. They succeeded Vasily Tsibliyev and Aleksandr Lazutkin aboard *Mir*. The latter two astronauts had been residents of *Mir* since February and had faced a series of disasters, including a June crash of a supply ship into *Mir* that caused the space station to lose nearly half its power. They returned to Earth aboard *Soyuz TM-25* on August 14.

STS-85—U.S. Space Shuttle *Discovery*. Aug. 7–19, 1997. **Crew:** Comdr. Curtis L. Brown, Jr. (mission commander), Comdr. Kent V. Rominger, Lt. Cmdr. Robert L. Curbeam, Jr., N. Jan Davis, Stephen K. Robinson, and Bjarni V. Tryggvason of Canada. **Mission Highlights:** Released and retrieved the Cryogenic Infrared Spectrometers and Telescopes for the Atmosphere environmental satellite, which monitored gases in the Earth's ozone layer. Tested a robotic arm designed to perform precision tasks.

STS-86—U.S. Space Shuttle *Atlantis*. Sept. 25–Oct. 6, 1997. **Crew:** Cmdr. James D. Wetherbee (mission commander), Michael J. Bloomfield, Comdr. Wendy B. Lawrence, Scott E. Parazynski, Dr. David A. Wolf, Brig. Gen. Jean-Loup Chrétien of France, and Vladimir G. Titov of Russia. **Mission Highlights:** Linked with *Mir* and picked up C. Michael Foale, who had been aboard the space station since May. Wolf joined Russian astronauts Anatoly Solovyev and Pavel Vinogradov on *Mir*. The mission included a five-hour space walk by Parazynski and Titov—the first shuttle-based U.S.-Russian space walk. The shuttle also delivered supplies, including a new central computer, to *Mir*.

STS-87—U.S. Space Shuttle *Columbia*. Nov. 19–Dec. 5, 1997. **Crew:** Cmdr. Kevin R. Kregel (mission commander), Maj. Steven W. Lindsey, Capt. Winston E. Scott, Kalpana Chawla, Leonid K. Kadenyuk of the Ukraine, and Takao Doi of Japan. **Mission Highlights:** The Spartan science satellite accidentally was sent into a spin during its release, requiring a space-walk rescue. The AERcam/Sprint remote-control camera was tested for the first time, taking TV views of the shuttle from a distance of about 40 ft (12 m).

Difficult Times for *Mir*

For most of 1997, the orbiting Russian *Mir* space station became a test site for human survival skills. An onboard fire and decompression of a key station module, along with repeated computer breakdowns and loss of power, seemed to transform *Mir* into a space-age version of the *Titanic*.

Mir is Russia's seventh successful space station. Since 1986, when the first component of *Mir* was orbited, cosmonaut crews routinely have lived and worked there. Over a decade, five more station modules were added to the basic *Mir* core module. Starting in 1995, as a forerunner to building and operating the International Space Station (ISS), a shuttle-*Mir* program was established. This post–Cold War relationship between two former adversaries involved U.S. astronaut crews carrying out tours of several months' duration aboard *Mir*. Ultimately, this strengthening of cooperation was deemed by the National Aeronautics and Space Administration (NASA) as mandatory if the ISS is to be completed in the 21st century. Five NASA astronauts—Norman Thagard, Shannon Lucid, John Blaha, Jerry Linenger, and Michael Foale—accumulated 22 months of experience on *Mir*. In early October a sixth U.S. astronaut, David Wolf, moved from the docked shuttle *Atlantis* to begin his stint on the space station.

During 1997 both U.S. astronauts and Russian cosmonauts encountered a number of in-space glitches, several of them potentially life-threatening. On February 23 an oxygen-generation unit caught fire, filling the station with smoke and burning for nearly 14 minutes. Fire extinguishers proved ineffective against the blaze. The fire burned itself out, and none of the six men on board *Mir* was injured. Station personnel were advised to don goggles and masks for the day as protection against potentially damaging toxic chemicals. A few weeks later a set of oxygen generators failed, forcing the *Mir* crew to rely on the same type of oxygen-producing devices that had caught fire. In early April the *Mir* complex suffered cooling-system leaks and an air-purification-system failure.

Vasily Tsibliyev conducted a space walk, below, during his stressful six months on board "Mir" in 1997. The Russian cosmonaut later implied that the station's difficulties were caused by the Russian space agency's lack of resources.

© Johnson Space Center

The most serious incident for *Mir* and its joint U.S.-Russian crew was the June 25 crash of an out-of-control Progress supply vessel into the station. At the time, *Mir*'s cosmonaut commander, Vasily Tsibliyev, was controlling the Progress remotely in a practice rendezvous and docking. Smashing into a *Mir* solar panel, the errant vessel then struck the Spektr science module, breaching its exterior and causing precious air to rush out into space. In a race against time, crew members Foale and Aleksandr Lazutkin sealed off the Spektr module, a process that involved disconnecting power cables that fed electricity to the station from a set of solar panels. With *Mir*'s power level cut in half, a cascading set of problems then beset the crew, including the loss of proper orientation of the space station. Furthermore, the decompression of the Spektr module ruined a number of science experiments.

As crewmen worked to solve *Mir*'s problems over the next several months—both inside Spektr and outside the space station—a Soyuz return capsule stood ready to serve as a rescue craft. Slowly, *Mir* regained most of its lost power; a new computer and other hardware were sent to the station, further improving the prospects for regaining normal operations.

While Russian space officials continued to eye potential fixes, and teams of astronauts and cosmonauts worked to maintain *Mir*, members of the U.S. Congress began to question the safety of the Russian facility. Some key legislators called *Mir* a "bucket of bolts," labeling the series of mistakes, accidents, systems failures, and life-threatening incidents "Mir-haps." Critics argued that the safety of U.S. astronauts should not be placed in jeopardy on the Russian outpost. NASA's stay-the-course attitude prevailed, however, with the launch of U.S. astronaut David Wolf to *Mir* in September. The space agency pointed to valuable lessons learned in maintaining *Mir*. Shuttle-*Mir* flights, NASA argued, provided hands-on experience in an unforgiving environment—experience crucial to the construction and day-to-day operations of the planned ISS.

In addition, one of the most important commodities of spaceflight is the time astronauts

© NASA

C. Michael Foale exercised on a treadmill while on board "Mir" from May 16 to Sept. 28, 1997. The U.S. astronaut worked with his Russian counterparts to help repair the space station.

accumulate in orbit. The accumulated 22 months U.S. astronauts had gained by the end of Foale's stay aboard *Mir*, NASA argued, could not have been amassed any other way. By contrast, it took the U.S. space-shuttle fleet more than a dozen years and 60 flights to achieve an accumulated year in orbit. Through the cooperative venture, NASA pointed out, knowledge and experience were being gained that otherwise could not be achieved.

LEONARD DAVID

GOES-8 or GOES-9, should one become inoperational.

China placed the Fengyun 2 geosynchronous meteorological spacecraft into orbit June 10, on its Long March 3 rocket. India launched the IRS 1D on September 29 aboard the new Polar Satellite Launch Vehicle (PSLV-1C). On September 2 an Ariane 4 rocket launched from Kourou, French Guiana, placed Europe's METEOSAT 7 weather satellite into orbit. A U.S. ocean-monitoring spacecraft, OrbView 2, was launched August 1 by a Pegasus XL rocket. Its primary instrument—a color scanner called Sea-Viewing Wide Field-of-View Sensor (SeaWiFS)—was built to image phytoplankton growth and fish schools.

The U.S. Small Spacecraft Technology Initiative–Lewis (SSTI-Lewis) was launched on August 23 by the first successful boost of a Lockheed Martin Launch Vehicle. But shortly after reaching orbit, it spun out of control and was destroyed reentering Earth's atmosphere. Japan's Advanced Earth Observation Satellite (ADEOS), launched in August 1996, was crippled by a major power loss on June 30. The failure was a blow to scientists tracking the effects of El Niño. The maiden flight of Brazil's VLS-1 rocket—launched November 2 from the Alcantara launch center in northern Brazil—ended in failure.

Riding a Boeing Delta 2 rocket, the 28th and final satellite of the U.S. Air Force's NAVSTAR Global Positioning System (GPS), Bock IIA, was orbited November 5. GPS—a navigation satellite system—provides worldwide precision location guidance. A January 17 attempt to loft a GPS satellite on a Delta 2 from Cape Canaveral failed when the rocket exploded 13 seconds after liftoff, 1,477 ft (450 m) above its launchpad.

Communications Satellites. Arianespace— the private operator of the Ariane launcher— ordered an additional 20 Ariane 4 boosters; it will launch 42 satellites in the next few years, worth an estimated $3 billion. The company celebrated the 100th Ariane launch after an Intelsat 803 satellite reached orbit September 23. Among satellites lofted by Ariane in 1997 were Argentina's Nahuel 1A; a U.S. GE 2 and a Panamsat 6; Thailand's Thaicom 3; India's Insat 2D; Japan's JCSAT-5; and a European geosynchronous direct-TV spacecraft, Hot Bird 3. After its first successful flight on October 30, the Ariane 5 booster—which failed on its maiden 1996 flight—was transferred from the European Space Agency (ESA) to Arianespace. Dual operation of Ariane 4 and Ariane 5 rockets from the European Spaceport in Kourou was planned.

Worldwide competition was increasing among launch companies and satellite builders for a share of the $30 billion business—a figure expected to double by 2000.

Beginning in May, eight launches over eight months placed the majority of a planned 66-satellite Motorola Iridium global satellite system into orbit. The system will provide global, land-based wireless communications to subscribers, for handheld telephone and pager use. Some satellites had problems and might not be used in 1998, when the system was expected to be operational.

On February 17 a Japanese JCSAT-4 reached orbit aboard Lockheed Martin's commercial Atlas 2AS rocket from Cape Canaveral. An Atlas 2AS lofted the U.S. GE 3 into orbit on September 4, Japan's Superbird-C into geostationary orbit on July 28, and the U.S. Echostar 3 into space on October 5.

China's Long March 3B put Hong Kong's Apstar IIR into space on October 17. Russia's Proton booster was offered commercially through a joint venture between Lockheed Martin and Russia's Proton manufacturer, Khrunichev. Luxembourg's Astra-1G went into orbit aboard a commercial Proton on December 3.

Space Science. On July 4 the U.S. Mars Pathfinder bounced to a stop on the Martian surface, cushioned by air bags. Renamed the Sagan Memorial Station in honor of the late astronomer Carl Sagan, the lander deployed a "micro-rover" named Sojourner. From its locale in the Ares Vallis, the station operated nearly three times longer than its 30-day design lifetime, while Sojourner lasted 12 times its expected seven days. More than 16,000 lander and 500 rover images, as well as more than 15 chemical analyses of rocks and extensive wind and weather data, were relayed to Earth. Scientists concluded, based on the data, that Mars was much more Earth-like than first believed; it was likely to once have had flowing water; a thick, stable atmosphere; and much warmer temperatures, enhancing the prospects that the planet once may have had life. That life still might exist there remained a reasoned possibility; future robotic missions would address such speculation. Another Mars spacecraft—the Mars Global Surveyor (MGS)—swung into action September 11, circling the planet with a host of scientific instruments. But after 43 days, MGS encountered problems while employing aerobraking maneuvers. One of two solar panels never had deployed fully, and ground controllers saw indications that the array might threaten the spacecraft. Engineers hoped that by slowing the process of circularizing MGS' orbit—thus minimizing forces on the panel—a final mapping orbit could be achieved. Despite the snag, MGS began relaying images and data, and detected a weak magnetic field surrounding Mars.

Throughout 1997 the U.S. Galileo spacecraft relayed information and images about Jupiter and several of its moons. Striking pictures of Europa pointed to possible ice volcanoes and an ocean underneath the moon's icy surface. Heat necessary for volcanoes or geysers could mean that Europa's interior was suitable for life. Radio scientists analyzed Jupiter's atmosphere by measuring changes in Galileo's radio signal as it passed through the

The plutonium-powered Cassini orbiter and its attached Huygens probe were launched from Cape Canaveral on Oct. 15, 1997. The craft was headed for a seven-year journey to Saturn; the Huygens probe is to be dropped on Saturn's moon Titan.

Jovian atmosphere. Jupiter observations included those designed to study "brown barges," believed to contain a unique mixture of chemicals. Galileo's formal mission of orbiting Jupiter ended after two years, on December 7. A Galileo Europa Mission (GEM) began in December and was expected to continue through December 1999. In addition to eight Europa flybys, GEM involves flybys of Callisto and Io.

Japan lofted the HALCA radio-astronomy satellite on February 12 aboard Japan's M-5 rocket. Toting a 26-ft (8-m)-diameter wire-mesh dish, HALCA worked with ground-based radio telescopes to map deep-space objects.

In March, Pioneer 10—the first to encounter Jupiter, in 1973—left the known solar system; it was shut down March 31.

NASA suspended plans to carry out joint missions with Russia involving animals, after a monkey that flew on the Bion 11 mission died. On June 27 the U.S. Near Earth Asteroid Rendezvous (NEAR) spacecraft flew by asteroid Mathilde, returning hundreds of images that showed the asteroid to be heavily cratered. At least five craters larger than 12 mi (20 km) across were found on its 37-mi (60-km)-diameter surface, and scientists puzzled over how the asteroid stayed intact under such impacts. Launched in 1996, NEAR was en route to the asteroid Eros.

The U.S. Advanced Composition Explorer (ACE) reached orbit on August 25 on a Delta 2 rocket. ACE would monitor the Sun's magnetic field and solar wind. The U.S./ESA Solar and Heliospheric Observatory (SOHO) provided a wealth of information about the Sun, and spotted a comet moving toward the Sun that apparently was vaporized by the heat. SOHO also found a high-energy "magnetic carpet" of looping magnetic fields wrapping the Sun.

Amid protests, on October 15 a Titan 4B rocket launched the plutonium-powered Cassini from Cape Canaveral, on its seven-year journey to Saturn. The 13,889-lb (6 300-kg) Cassini's trajectory involves two flybys of Venus (April 21, 1998, and June 20, 1999), one of Earth (Aug. 16, 1999), and one of Jupiter (Dec. 30, 2000). After reaching its target, Cassini will conduct four years of intensive study and drop an ESA-built Huygens probe onto Saturn's moon Titan.

LEONARD DAVID
Space Data Resources & Information

Spaniards jammed the Basque town of Ermua for the funeral of Miguel Angel Blanco Garrido in July 1997. The 29-year-old Spanish council member who belonged to the ruling Popular Party had been murdered, allegedly by Basque militants.

SPAIN

Despite defections from the ruling coalition during 1997, Prime Minister José María Aznar's Popular Party (PP) enjoyed important regional-election victories in October, thanks to labor peace and improved economic conditions. Five days of torrential rains killed some 30 persons along the Spanish-Portuguese border in November.

Politics. Both the ruling PP and the opposition Spanish Socialist Workers' Party (PSOE) agreed that Spain should become one of the initial members of the European economic and monetary union (EMU). To avoid the uncertain effects of reforms on the economy, Prime Minister Aznar delayed revamping the troubled social-security and public-health systems until after the naming of a "launch group" for EMU affiliation.

Former Prime Minister Felipe González announced that he would not seek reelection after 13 years as secretary-general of the PSOE. González, who led the country from 1982 to 1996, lost to Aznar—in part because of his alleged implication in a "dirty war"

involving the deaths of 27 Basque separatists. González' replacement, Joaquín Almunia, pledged to follow a moderate-left course, seeking issue-by-issue alliances with responsible members of the United Left, the current communist party in Spain. Almunia wasted no time before attacking Aznar's inaction on employment, asylum rights, and other issues at the Amsterdam summit of the European Union (EU).

Aznar was unperturbed by such criticism. Although the PP, which held only 155 seats in the 350-member parliament (Cortés), saw its ruling margin decline to one seat with the defection of the Basque nationalists, it got a boost in the Galician regional elections held in mid-October—the first electoral test since its rise to power. The PP captured 41 of 75 seats in the local legislature; the Galician Nationalist Bloc finished second with 19 seats, followed by the Socialists—aligned with environmentalists and two leftist parties—with 15 seats. The show of strength was expected to ensure that the PP's partners—Catalán Nationalists and the Canary Island party—would remain in the precarious governing coalition.

During the 1996 political campaign, Aznar promised to end compulsory military service. Accordingly, he planned to phase out conscription by 2003, while redesigning the Spanish military into volunteer units. The armed forces announced it would sell $787 million worth of nonresidential property, operational headquarters, and other facilities to help raise funds for modernization.

Basque Terrorists.   Spain's campaign against Basque rebels gained momentum following the February assassination by Basque Homeland and Liberty (ETA) gunmen of a Supreme Court justice and the July kidnapping and slaying of PP councillor Miguel Angel Blanco Garrido. ETA terrorists demanded that Madrid move imprisoned members of their group closer to the Basque region. The Basque Nationalist Party, Basque Solidarity, and the United Left echoed these demands, which the PP and PSOE rejected.

Spain convinced the Dominican Republic to deport three Basque terrorists. The three men, including a former ETA second in command, had been serving as liaisons between the Spanish government and ETA leaders hiding in France. Pressure to repatriate the men mounted after the murder of Blanco.

In October the government charged 23 members of Herri Batasuna—a Basque minority party holding two Cortés seats—with cooperating with ETA. The party had used an ETA video in its advertisements during the 1996 election campaign.

Economy.   The economy grew by 3% in 1997, as Madrid neared the EMU launch-group requirements. Tourism boasted its best year ever; aided by the strong British sterling and U.S. dollar, Spain hosted an estimated 42 million visitors. The travel industry, which generates 10% of the country's economic activity, stood poised to set new records in 1997, buoyed in part by Spain's hosting the Ryder Cup golf classic.

Major economic indicators suggested that the economic upswing would continue through 1998—possibly by as much as 3.5%. The country's 1.4% rise in prices placed it below the EU average inflation rate of 1.6%. Surveys found corporate executives bullish, as a strong U.S. dollar strengthened the already dynamic rise of exports.

The country's public debt—while still a major problem—fell to 68% of gross domestic product (GDP), after exceeding 70% in 1996. Aznar remained confident that the debt level would continue to fall, facilitating Spain's compliance with most of the Maastricht Treaty requirements.

SPAIN • Information Highlights

Official Name: Kingdom of Spain.
Location: Iberian Peninsula in southwestern Europe.
Area: 194,884 sq mi (504 750 km²).
Population (mid-1997 est.): 39,300,000.
Chief Cities (Jan. 1, 1995 est., metropolitan areas): Madrid, the capital, 3,029,734; Barcelona, 1,614,571; Valencia, 763,299.
Government: *Head of state,* Juan Carlos I, king (took office Nov. 1975). *Head of government,* José María Aznar, prime minister (took office May 5, 1996). *Legislature*—Cortés Generales: Senate and Congress of Deputies.
Monetary Unit: Peseta (150.02 pesetas equal U.S.$1, Dec. 2, 1997).
Gross Domestic Product (1995 est. U.S.$): $565,000,-000,000 (purchasing power parity).
Economic Indexes (1996, 1990 = 100): *Consumer Prices,* all items, 133.2; food, 125.2. *Industrial Production,* 102.
Foreign Trade (1996 U.S.$): *Imports,* $121,793,000,000; *exports,* $102,000,000,000.

More disturbing, however, was the 20.9% jobless figure, Western Europe's highest. Prospects brightened when union and business leaders hammered out an agreement in late April. Management promised to hire more workers in return for labor's consent to four-year, renewable contracts. As a result, in mid-1997 job seekers found the shortest unemployment lines in 15 years. Unemployment fell 4% in the 12 months from July 1996 to July 1997. Only 2 million Spaniards were without work by the end of the year. Spain still boasted some of the most liberal unemployment benefits in the world.

Officials at Telefónica, the national telecommunications company, ended a conflict within the communications industry. Telefónica bought 25% of the large Antena 3TV cable network, and convinced the Central Hispano and Santander banks to increase their equity in the enterprise. The deal stabilized the media industry and ended a feud between Antena and fellow cable giant Prisa.

Foreign Relations.   Proposed changes in the NATO command structure would place a Spanish general in charge of the Southern Command, which embraces Gibraltar—Great Britain's last European colony. This reinforced Madrid's demand that Britain relinquish control of the strategic "rock." Madrid hosted the NATO expansion summit, at which U.S. President Bill Clinton praised Aznar's leadership.

Spain and France forged a pact on illegal immigration in the face of a large influx of undocumented North Africans. Spanish authorities arrested 2,000 illegals between Tarfa and Cádiz, and 4,000 more in Cádiz province, in the first seven months of 1997.

GEORGE W. GRAYSON
College of William and Mary

Sports

© Art Zeitz/Gamma-Liaison

Overview

Like any sports year, 1997 saw both the expected and the unexpected. In terms of the expected, the Chicago Bulls captured another National Basketball Association (NBA) crown; Tiger Woods won the Masters golf tournament; and football's Denver Broncos got off to another fine start as the fall season began. In terms of the unexpected, the five-year-old Florida Marlins won baseball's World Series; the Detroit Red Wings swept the Philadelphia Flyers in four games for their first Stanley Cup in 42 years; Pete Sampras lost at the U.S. Open after capturing the Australian Open and Wimbledon; a much-hyped race between Michael Johnson and Donovan Bailey proved to be a disappointment; and Tara Lipinski, only 14, dominated women's figure skating.

It was also a year of remembering. Major League Baseball dedicated its season to Jackie Robinson, who 50 years earlier had become the first black to play in the majors; and the status of women's athletics was analyzed—25 years after Washington enacted Title IX. Women's pro basketball was a hit as two new leagues made their debuts. Cynthia Cooper, *right*, led the Houston Comets to victory in the first WNBA title game. Meanwhile, tennis fans paused to recall the first African-American male to win the U.S. Open as the new

Arthur Ashe Stadium, *above*, was dedicated in Flushing Meadows–Corona Park, NY.

Jan Ullrich became the first German to win cycling's Tour de France....Martin Buser won the Iditarod Trail Sled Dog race for a third time....The sport of boxing came under renewed fire following an unsportsmanlike incident by Mike Tyson.

© Todd Warshaw/Allsport

Women in Sports

If the apparent explosion of public interest in women's sports in the United States had to be attributed to a single causative factor, it would be the passage of Title IX—a 1972 federal law that prohibits discrimination on the basis of gender in the provision of educational programs or activities by recipients of federal funds. In 1997 the nation was witnessing the result of 25 years of girls and women being given the opportunity to play sports.

Yesterday and Today. As the 20th century comes to an end, the United States is in the midst of a cultural change where the typical American female sees herself as strong, effective, competitive, and skilled rather than as a sex object or "twiggy." In 1970, only one in 27 high-school girls played varsity sports. That number today is one in three—one in two for boys. Today, more than 55 million women participate in sports and fitness activities regularly. Women represent more than 55% of all volleyball players, 43% of all runners, and 41% of all soccer players. Unlike American men, who traditionally have been forced into playing the major sports, women are not pressured to play a particular sport or perform at a certain level. Therefore, they try a wider variety of sports and are more eclectic than their male counterparts.

Women's sports now are entrenched deeply in core family values, with parents enthusiastically supporting the participation of their daughters as well as their sons in sports. Media support of sports for women has increased. Five new women's sports magazines came out between late 1995 and the summer of 1997. Most major women's magazines have a health/fitness editor on staff. Lifetime Television, a network dedicated to women's programming, began airing women's sports programs in prime time on Friday nights in 1997, and presented four one-hour specials on women's sports. ABC champions a similar "Passion to Play" series of women's sports specials. The number of women aged 18–34 who viewed the Olympic Games increased 40% from 1992 to 1996. The overall television-viewing audience for the 1996 Olympics was 65% female. The audience for women's sports programming is both male and female, and media exposure is driving public demand further.

Now, for the first time, there are large numbers of women competing in the Olympics and successful professional team-sports leagues. This increased level of female participation on the competitive level is a result of women receiving 15 to 20 years of coaching, access to weight rooms, college scholarships, and international competition. Four new women's professional leagues—the American Basketball League (ABL), the National Soccer Alliance (NSA), the Women's National Basketball Association (WNBA), and the Women's Professional Fastpitch (WPF) league in softball—have been announced in the United States since the end of 1994. The athletes on those teams will strengthen the grassroots base by serving as role models. Aspirational role models drive young girls' demands for sports opportunities.

A Spectator's Market and the Future. Men and women who have grown up appreciating female athletes now are supporting women's sports as a growing and lucrative spectator market. Men's professional sports have priced themselves out of many family markets and women's sports are stepping into that vacuum. Different people go to women's games than to men's sports events for the most part, so the two are not competing for the same audiences. The audience for women's sports appreciates the values women are bringing to sports—nonviolence, respect for and sincere admiration of their opponents, 100% effort, little or no arrogance, and a sincere appreciation for and sensitivity to their fan base of families and children.

However, realistically, there is still another 10 to 15 years of work to be done before the system embraces equal opportunity in sports for women. Male college athletes still receive $184 million more in athletic scholarships than do female athletes. Men's programs receive double the participation opportunities, double the sports operating budgets, and almost triple the recruiting budgets. Schools and colleges have reached only the halfway point in the march toward Title IX compliance. The bottom line is that while more needs to be done, women's sports have exploded upon the scene and are here to stay!

Donna A. Lopiano

Editor's Note. Dr. Donna A. Lopiano is executive director of the Women's Sports Foundation®. Based in East Meadow, NY, the organization is dedicated to promoting the lifelong participation of all girls and women in sports and fitness.

Auto Racing

Canada's Jacques Villeneuve won his first Formula One world driving championship in a close battle with Germany's Michael Schumacher. Villeneuve accumulated 81 points and Schumacher had 78 in the 17-race series that ended with a controversy at the European Grand Prix on Oct. 26, 1997, in Jerez, Spain, when Schumacher turned into Villeneuve's car on a curve and took his own Ferrari out of the race. Villeneuve, who then needed only a top-six finish to clinch the title, came in third as Finland's Mika Hakkinen won the race. Schumacher, needing to finish ahead of Villeneuve to win his third world title, placed 18th.

Jeff Gordon won ten Winston Cup stock-car races and his second points championship in three years. Gordon clinched the title with a 17th-place finish in the NAPA 500 on November 16. Gordon had 4,710 points to 4,696 for runner-up Dale Jarrett.

American open-wheel racing continued under two governing bodies, the Championship Auto Racing Teams (CART) and the two-year-old Indy Racing League (IRL). Italy's Alex Zanardi captured five races and four pole positions en route to the CART championship. His 195 points outdistanced Gil de Ferran of Brazil, who had 162.

Arie Luyendyk won the Indianapolis 500, held for the second time under the auspices of the IRL, beating Scott Goodyear by .57 of a second. Tony Stewart won the IRL points title by a 278–272 margin over Davey Hamilton.

STAN SUTTON, *"Louisville Courier-Journal"*

AUTO RACING

Major Race Winners, 1997
Indianapolis 500: Arie Luyendyk, United States
U.S. 500: Alex Zanardi, Italy
Daytona 500: Jeff Gordon, United States
Brickyard 400: Ricky Rudd, United States

1997 Champions
Formula One: Jacques Villeneuve, Canada
NASCAR: Jeff Gordon, United States
CART: Alex Zanardi, Italy
Indy Racing League: Tony Stewart, United States
IROC: Mark Martin, United States

Grand Prix for Formula One Cars, 1997
Australian: David Coulthard, Scotland
Brazilian: Jacques Villeneuve, Canada
Argentinian: Villeneuve
San Marino: Heinz-Harald Frentzen, Germany
Monaco: Michael Schumacher, Germany
Spanish: Villeneuve
Canadian: Schumacher
French: Schumacher
British: Villeneuve
German: Gerhard Berger, Austria
Hungarian: Villeneuve
Belgian: Schumacher
Italian: Coulthard
Austrian: Villeneuve
Luxembourg: Villeneuve
Japanese: Schumacher
European: Mika Hakkinen, Finland

Baseball

Baseball began the 1997 season by saluting Jackie Robinson. African-Americans had played professional baseball in the latter days of the 1800s, but it was Robinson who broke Major League Baseball's 20th-century color barrier (*see* SIDEBAR, page 473). Also in 1997 the game initiated its most radical and controversial innovation—interleague play (*see* SIDEBAR, page 471) and saw a wild-card team reach and win the World Series for the first time. In addition, the San Diego Padres, who took major-league baseball to Mexico in 1996, played the first games in Hawaii on April 19 and 20, when they hosted a three-game "Paradise Series" against the St. Louis Cardinals in Honolulu.

Play-offs and World Series. The Florida Marlins, fortified by an off-season spending spree approaching $100 million, advanced to the World Series in their fifth year after knocking off the heavily favored Atlanta Braves—a postseason participant for a record sixth consecutive time—in the Championship Series. The Braves had won 101 games, the most in the majors, and had the widest first-place margin—ending nine games ahead of

Florida's Livan Hernandez helped pitch the Marlins to a world title. The rookie was the most valuable player (MVP) of the National League Championship Series and the World Series.

© Gary Hershorn/Reuters/Archive Photo

the Marlins in the National League (NL) Eastern Division. Nevertheless, Florida reached the play-offs as the NL's wild-card winner. After Florida swept San Francisco, the NL Western Division winner, and Atlanta swept Houston, the NL Central champion, in the best-of-five Division Series, the Braves and Marlins met in the best-of-seven Championship Series.

Although Atlanta scored more runs and had a higher batting average and a better earned-run average (ERA) than the Marlins, Florida won Game 1, 5–3; Game 3, 5–2; Game 5, 2–1; and Game 6, 7–4. Atlanta won only Game 2, 7–1, and Game 4, 4–0. Florida rookie Livan Hernandez, who tied a Championship Series mark with 15 strikeouts in Game 5 after winning Game 3 in relief, was named most valuable player (MVP) of the series.

In the American League, the Baltimore Orioles won the most games and the AL Eastern Division crown, finishing two games ahead of the defending-world-champion New York Yankees. The Orioles advanced after winning three of four over the Seattle Mariners, champions of the AL West, in the Division Series, while the AL Central champion Cleveland Indians took the full five games to oust the wild-card Yankees in the preliminary round.

Although the Orioles were prohibitive favorites in the AL Championship Series (ALCS), Cleveland prevailed with a combination of timely hitting, strong defense, and surprising pitching. Baltimore sandwiched Game 1 (3–0) and Game 5 (4–2) victories around consecutive Cleveland victories—5–4, 2–1 in 12 innings, and 8–7. The Indians then won the decisive Game 6, 1–0, in 11 innings, when slap-hitting Tony Fernandez hit a rare home run. Marquis Grissom, acquired from Atlanta with David Justice in a profitable spring-training trade, was MVP of the ALCS.

The World Series, the first ever played in the Sunshine State, opened in Pro Player Park on October 18, with Florida—a wild-card winner—paired against Cleveland, a team with the worst regular-season record of any of the American League's four play-off qualifiers. In Game 1, with the rookie Hernandez on the mound, the Marlins won, 7–4. But Chad Ogea outpitched veteran Florida ace Kevin Brown to win Game 2, 6–1. With the Series moving to the cold temperatures of Jacobs Field, the Marlins won a wild 14–11 game marred by multiple miscues and walks. Florida broke a 7–7 tie with a seven-run ninth, then managed to hold on while Cleveland scored four in the home half.

© Jean-Marc Giboux/Gamma-Liaison

After leading the American League in home runs, RBIs, runs scored, total bases, extra base hits, and slugging, Seattle's Ken Griffey, Jr., was the unanimous choice as the league's MVP.

Cleveland evened the series again with a 10–3 win behind rookie Jaret Wright in Game 4, but the Marlins pulled out an 8–7 win in the pivotal Game 5, returning the fall classic to Florida's warmer temperatures. Ogea, a postseason standout after losing more than he won during the regular season, stunned Brown, 4–1, in Game 6. Ogea was also the hitting star, becoming the first pitcher since Detroit's Mickey Lolich in 1968 to get two hits and two RBIs in a World Series game. In Game 7—the first time a World Series had gone the limit since 1991—Florida spotted Cleveland's Wright an early 2–0 lead, then scored in the seventh, ninth, and 11th innings to win the game, 3–2, and the World Championship. Hernandez, who had defected from communist Cuba, was the only Marlin pitcher with two wins; he again received MVP honors.

Regular Season. The 1997 regular season featured some fine pitching performances. Kevin Brown of the Florida Marlins pitched the year's first no-hitter on June 10 in San Francisco, blanking the Giants, 9–0, and missing a perfect game when an eighth-inning 1–2

471

pitch grazed the leg of Marvin Benard. The year's only other no-hitter occurred on July 12, when Pittsburgh's Francisco Cordova and Ricardo Rincon combined for a 3–0, ten-inning gem against the Houston Astros at Three Rivers Stadium. It was the first combined, extra-inning no-hitter in history.

Randy Johnson, Seattle's flame-throwing southpaw, fanned 19 men in a game twice but surrendered the season's longest home run, a 538-ft (164-m) blast by Mark McGwire, in the first of those efforts, on June 24. Johnson won 20 games for the first time but finished second in the voting for the American League's Cy Young Award. Longtime Boston ace Roger Clemens, in his first year with the Toronto Blue Jays, led the league with 21 wins, a career-best 292 strikeouts, and a 2.05 ERA. In addition to winning his fourth strikeout title and fifth ERA crown, Clemens became the AL's first four-time Cy Young winner and the first American Leaguer to win the triple crown of pitching since Hall of Famer Hal Newhouser in 1945.

The National League's lone 20-game winner was Atlanta lefty Denny Neagle, but the Cy Young Award went to Montreal's Pedro Martinez, who led the NL with a 1.90 ERA and became the first ERA king since 1972 to also reach 300 strikeouts (305). Since Philadelphia's Curt Schilling fanned 319, tops in the majors, the National League had two 300-strikeout pitchers for the first time since Nolan Ryan and Steve Carlton did it in 1972.

Home-run hitter Mark McGwire got to face Cy Young contenders from both leagues. Oakland, uncertain of whether it would be able to re-sign McGwire, traded him to St. Louis on July 31. He finished the year with 58 home runs—three shy of the single-season record—and joined Babe Ruth as the only players to produce consecutive 50-homer campaigns.

Seattle's Ken Griffey, Jr., led the American League with a career-best 56 home runs and 147 runs batted in (RBIs), helping him win his first MVP award, while Colorado teammates Larry Walker and Andres Galarraga led the National League with 49 homers and 140 RBIs, respectively. Walker, the National League's MVP, had a .720 slugging percentage, joining Jeff Bagwell (.750 in 1994) as the only players to slug .700 since Stan Musial finished at .702 in 1948. Walker's 409 total bases were the most in the majors since Musial had 429 for the 1948 Cardinals.

Although the Rockies had a trio of teammates reach at least 40 homers for the second straight year and the third time in baseball history, the 1997 group produced a three-man record of 130—49 by Walker, 41 by Galarraga, and 40 by Vinny Castilla. Colorado also had four 30-homer teammates for the fourth straight year, joining the 1977 and 1997

BASEBALL

Professional—Major Leagues
Final Standings, 1997

AMERICAN LEAGUE Eastern Division				NATIONAL LEAGUE Eastern Division			
	W	L	Pct.		W	L	Pct.
Baltimore	98	64	.605	Atlanta	101	61	.623
New York	96	66	.593	Florida	92	70	.568
Detroit	79	83	.488	New York	88	74	.543
Boston	78	84	.481	Montreal	78	84	.481
Toronto	76	86	.469	Philadelphia	68	94	.420

Central Division				Central Division			
	W	L	Pct.		W	L	Pct.
Cleveland	86	75	.534	Houston	84	78	.519
Chicago	80	81	.497	Pittsburgh	79	83	.488
Milwaukee	78	83	.484	Cincinnati	76	86	.469
Minnesota	68	94	.420	St. Louis	73	89	.451
Kansas City	67	94	.416	Chicago	68	94	.420

Western Division				Western Division			
	W	L	Pct.		W	L	Pct.
Seattle	90	72	.556	San Francisco	90	72	.556
Anaheim	84	78	.519	Los Angeles	88	74	.543
Texas	77	85	.475	Colorado	83	79	.512
Oakland	65	97	.401	San Diego	76	86	.469

Play-offs—American League: Division Series—Baltimore defeated Seattle, 3 games to 1; Cleveland defeated New York, 3 games to 2. Championship Series—Cleveland defeated Baltimore, 4 games to 2. National League: Division Series—Atlanta defeated Houston, 3 games to 0; Florida defeated San Francisco, 3 games to 0. Championship Series—Florida defeated Atlanta, 4 games to 2.
World Series—Florida defeated Cleveland, 4 games to 3. First Game (Pro Player Stadium, Miami, Oct. 18, attendance 67,245): Florida 7, Cleveland 4; Second Game (Pro Player Stadium, Oct. 19, attendance 67,025): Cleveland 6, Florida 1; Third Game (Jacobs Field, Cleveland, Oct. 21, attendance 44,880): Florida 14, Cleveland 11; Fourth Game (Jacobs Field, Oct. 22, attendance 44,877): Cleveland 10, Florida 3; Fifth Game (Jacobs Field, Oct. 23, attendance 44,888): Florida 8, Cleveland 7; Sixth Game (Pro Player Stadium, Oct. 25, attendance 67,498): Cleveland 4, Florida 1; Seventh Game (Pro Player Stadium, Oct. 26, attendance 67,204): Florida 3, Cleveland 2.
All-Star Game (Jacobs Field, Cleveland, OH, July 8, attendance 44,916): American League 3, National League 1.
Most Valuable Players—American League: Ken Griffey, Jr., Seattle; National League: Larry Walker, Colorado.
Cy Young Memorial Awards (outstanding pitchers)—American League: Roger Clemens, Toronto; National League: Pedro Martinez, Montreal.
Managers of the Year—American League: Davey Johnson, Baltimore; National League: Dusty Baker, San Francisco.
Rookies of the Year—American League: Nomar Garciaparra, Boston; National League: Scott Rolen, Philadelphia.
Leading Hitters—(Percentage) American League: Frank Thomas, Chicago, .347; National League: Tony Gwynn, San Diego, .372. (Runs Batted In) American League: Ken Griffey, Jr., Seattle, 147; National League: Andres Galarraga, Colorado, 140. (Home Runs) American League: Griffey, 56; National League: Larry Walker, Colorado, 49. (Hits) American League: Nomar Garciaparra, Boston, 209; National League: Gwynn, 220. (Runs) American League: Griffey, 125; National League: Craig Biggio, Houston, 146. (Slugging Percentage) American League: Griffey, .646; National League: Walker, .720.
Leading Pitchers—(Earned Run Average) American League: Roger Clemens, Toronto, 2.05; National League: Pedro Martinez, Montreal, 1.90. (Victories) American League: Clemens, 21; National League: Denny Neagle, Atlanta, 20. (Strikeouts) American League: Clemens, 292; National League: Curt Schilling, Philadelphia, 319. (Shutouts) American League: Pat Hentgen, Toronto, 3 (tied); National League: Carlos Perez, Montreal, 5. (Saves) American League: Randy Myers, Baltimore, 45; National League: Jeff Shaw, Cincinnati, 42. (Innings) American League: Clemens, Hentgen, 264 (tied); National League: John Smoltz, 256.

Professional—Minor Leagues, Class AAA
American Association: Buffalo
International League: Rochester
Pacific Coast League: Edmonton

Amateur
NCAA: LSU
Little League World Series: Guadalupe, Mexico

Jackie Robinson and His Legacy

Major League Baseball dedicated its 1997 season to the late Jackie Robinson, the first African-American to play for a big-league team. On April 15, 1997—the 50th anniversary of Robinson's first game in the majors—President Bill Clinton made a mid-game presentation to Rachel Robinson, Jackie's widow, at New York's Shea Stadium. Acting Commissioner Allan H. (Bud) Selig announced that all teams would retire Robinson's Number 42 permanently. As part of the tribute, all players wore commemorative patches on their uniforms in 1997 and Major League Baseball contributed $1 million to the Jackie Robinson Foundation, which provides scholarships to minorities.

Robinson's Story. Jack Roosevelt Robinson was born in Cairo, GA, on Jan. 31, 1919. The grandson of a Georgia sharecropper, he earned letters in four sports at UCLA. He left UCLA without a degree, however, because of financial pressures. He played pro football for the Los Angeles Bulldogs before enlisting in the U.S. Army in 1942. In 1943, 2nd Lt. Robinson was court-martialed (and acquitted) for refusing to sit in the "colored" section of an army bus. After receiving an honorable discharge, he signed his first pro-baseball contract—with a Negro League team.

Although blacks were banned from the major leagues by an unwritten agreement among club owners, Branch Rickey, president of the Brooklyn Dodgers, was determined to break the color line; he selected Robinson for the job. Rickey warned Robinson he needed a ballplayer "with guts enough not to fight back" when taunted. Robinson accepted Rickey's challenge, reporting to the Montreal Royals, the Dodgers' top farm team, in 1946. On April 15, 1947, he played in his first game for Brooklyn. He collected his first major-league home run in his third contest, but nobody shook his hand when he returned to the dugout. In retrospect, Robinson played under more pressure than any other modern-day athlete. Despite a torrent of racial insults—including death threats—he kept his cool and his word to Rickey.

As a player, Robinson was an intimidator, capable of hitting for both average and power. He played with flair as he revived the art of base stealing. He won baseball's first rookie-of-the-year award in 1947 and most-valuable-player honors two years later. He finished his career with a ten-season batting average of .311, and was an all-star six times. As a fielder, Robinson was best known as the second-base half of a formidable double-play combination with Pee Wee Reese. It had been Reese, a Southerner, who diffused a potential anti-Robinson revolt among the Dodgers. In 1962, Robinson was elected to the Baseball Hall of Fame. He died on Oct. 24, 1972.

The Legacy. Some historians have hailed the end of the color line as the real beginning of major-league baseball. Numerous contributions by other African-Americans have had a lasting impact on the nation's pastime. Robinson's success was an inspiration to African-Americans not only in baseball but also in other sports.

DAN SCHLOSSBERG

Interleague Play

For years, baseball executives had debated the pros and cons of interleague play—teams from the American League playing against teams from the National League during the regular season. Traditionalists complained that the uniqueness of the World Series—previously a meeting of two teams that had not faced each other during the season—would be compromised. They also said that a hitter who excels against weak interleague pitching could wind up winning a batting title or home-run crown and that long-standing records could be unfairly toppled by interleague results. Skeptics concluded that there were few compelling reasons for interleague play aside from a handful of natural rivalries.

Despite such objections, club owners were so determined to create fan interest stilled by the player strike of 1994–95 and to increase revenue that interleague play was approved for 1997, with the consent of the Major League Baseball Players Association. Interleague games were played in mid-June and around the holiday weekends of Independence Day and Labor Day. The inter-league schedule consisted of 214 games over 18 days. The designated hitter was used only in games played in American League parks. The league of the home team provided the umpire crew. Teams in the four-team Western Divisions played 16 interleague games each, while all other teams played 15 games each.

National League teams won 117 of the interleague games, while American League teams took 97. Attendance averaged 33,407 fans—20.2% higher than for regular league games (27,800). The "subway series" in New York (the Mets against the Yankees) and the rivalry in Chicago (the Cubs facing the White Sox) set attendance records. Florida and Montreal finished with the best records, winning 12 times each for an .800 percentage; Anaheim had the most trouble, posting a 4–12 mark (.250).

Although interleague play would continue in 1998, its future beyond that would require the approval of the Major League Baseball Players Association.

DAN SCHLOSSBERG

Dodgers as the only teams ever to do that. Not surprisingly, the Rockies finished with 237 home runs, a National League record. In the American League, Griffey helped Seattle slug 264 homers—a major-league mark—one year after Baltimore broke the previous record with 257. In general, however, home-run hitting was not as prevalent in 1997 as it had been the year before. After hitting a record 4,962 homers in 1996 (2.19 per game), big-league hitters banged 4,640 in 1997 (2.05 per game)—a 6.5% decrease.

Frank Thomas, known as a home-run hitter, hit .347 to win the AL batting crown—the first by a member of the Chicago White Sox since Luke Appling in 1943. Nomar Garciaparra became the first freshman to lead the AL in hits since Kevin Seitzer in 1987. The Boston Red Sox shortstop was a unanimous choice as AL rookie of the year, while Philadelphia third baseman Scott Rolen won NL rookie honors. Garciaparra and Cleveland catcher Sandy Alomar, Jr., had the year's longest hitting streaks—30 games each. San Diego's Tony Gwynn (*see* BIOGRAPHY) led the major leagues in hits with 220, while winning his eighth batting title and fourth in a row.

Pittsburgh's Tony Womack led the NL with 60 stolen bases but Detroit's Brian Hunter, in his first American League season after a trade from Houston, led the majors with 74. It was the first time a Detroit player topped the AL since Cobb in 1917. In the All-Star Game July 8, Sandy Alomar, Jr., thrilled his hometown fans at Cleveland's Jacobs Field with a two-run, seventh-inning home run that snapped a 1–1 tie and gave the American League a 3–1 victory. By season's end, Baltimore third baseman Cal Ripken, Jr., had extended his record for consecutive games played to 2,478.

Fame and Expansion. On August 3 knuckleball pitcher Phil Niekro, second baseman Nellie Fox, longtime manager Tommy Lasorda, and Negro Leagues shortstop Willie Wells were inducted into the Baseball Hall of Fame.

On November 18 the existing teams participated in a player draft to stock two 1998 expansion entries, the Tampa Bay Devil Rays and Arizona Diamondbacks. Owners placed Tampa Bay in the AL East, pushing the Detroit Tigers to the AL Central and the Milwaukee Brewers to the National League Central—baseball's only six-team division. Every other division has five teams, except for the four-team AL West. Arizona was added to the NL West, giving the National League 16 teams and the American League 14.

DAN SCHLOSSBERG, *Baseball Writer*

Basketball

The Chicago Bulls won their second straight National Basketball Association (NBA) title and their fifth in seven years by downing the Utah Jazz in the final round of the league play-offs. The Bulls, behind the outstanding play of Michael Jordan, eliminated the Jazz in six games.

In college basketball, the University of Arizona, which did not even win its conference championship, rode a hot streak throughout the National Collegiate Athletic Association (NCAA) tournament and wound up winning the title by defeating defending champion Kentucky in the final game. The women's NCAA basketball championship went to defending champion Tennessee, which overran Old Dominion.

Two women's professional leagues—the American Basketball League (ABL), an independent group; and the Women's National Basketball Association (WNBA), which is sponsored by the NBA—completed their inaugural seasons.

The Professional Ranks

Headliners. The NBA season began with the Bulls a clear-cut choice to emerge once again as champions. The only question surrounding Chicago was that of the ongoing misadventures of unpredictable Dennis Rodman, whose contrary behavior threatened to disrupt team unity and consistency. But it seemed that as long as Jordan remained healthy, no other team was capable of beating out the Bulls for the title.

Rodman did his best to disrupt the team. He had four major incidents during the season. He was suspended by the Bulls for swearing during a live televised postgame interview. He was fined $25,000 and suspended for at least 11 games by the league for deliberately kicking a courtside photographer after failing to save a ball from going out of bounds. He was suspended for a game and fined $7,500 by the league for hitting Milwaukee's Joe Wolf. Then, during the final round of the play-offs against Utah, he made derogatory comments about the Mormon population in Utah and was fined $50,000, the largest such penalty in NBA history.

The schedule also was highlighted by a major free-agent move when center Shaquille O'Neal left Orlando and signed with the Los Angeles Lakers, immediately reducing the Magic to also-ran status. The Houston Rockets received a huge boost when perennial all-pro Charles Barkley was traded from Phoenix to join two other likely Hall of Famers, Clyde Drexler and Hakeem Olajuwon.

Regular Season. The Seattle SuperSonics were coming off a standout 1995–96 season and had high expectations for 1996–97. But although they wound up winning the Pacific Division of the Western Conference, they never played as consistently or as powerfully

The Chicago Bulls—with Steve Kerr (25), Michael Jordan, and Dennis Rodman (91)—defeated the Utah Jazz, led by Karl Malone (32), four games to two, for their fifth NBA championship in seven years. Jordan was the most valuable player (MVP) of the series; Malone had outpolled Jordan for season-MVP honors.

as they had hoped. They finished one game ahead of the Lakers, whose title hopes were diminished when O'Neal suffered a major knee injury midway through the season. He returned in time for the play-offs. Utah, behind longtime stars Karl Malone (*see also* BIOGRAPHY) and John Stockton, held off Houston in the Midwest Division. The Rockets were plagued throughout the season by injuries. The Jazz finished with the best record in the conference to secure home-court advantage during the play-offs' early rounds.

San Antonio's hopes ended when center David Robinson came down with a back injury that put him out for the season. The Minnesota Timberwolves, a former expansion club, enjoyed their finest season and made the play-offs, while Portland played well in the Pacific Division.

Chicago, which won a league-record 72 games in 1995–96, made a run at breaking that mark but fell short by winning only 69. The Bulls still were the dominant team in the eastern Conference and easily won home-court advantage and the Midwest Division title. Atlanta, boosted by the addition of free agent Dikembe Mutombo, bolted to second place in the division by winning 56 games. Detroit got off to a fast start behind Grant Hill before cooling off during the final two months. Miami, which had been one of the most active teams in the off-season, beat out New York in the Atlantic Division. The talents of Alonzo Mourning and Tim Hardaway led the Heat. The Knicks once again got stellar play from center Patrick Ewing and added Larry Johnson and Allan Houston to their roster. Orlando, without O'Neal, slumped to third place despite the good work of guard Penny Hardaway.

Jordan won his record ninth scoring crown, averaging 29.6 points. Rodman won his record sixth rebounding championship, averaging 16.1. But another perennial leader, Stockton, lost his assist title to Mark Jackson, who played for both Denver and Indiana during the season. Jackson averaged 11.4 assists to Stockton's 10.5. Stockton had won a record nine assist titles. Shawn Bradley of Dallas was the leading shot blocker (3.4), edging out three-time champion Mutombo. Mookie Blaylock of Atlanta averaged the most steals (2.72).

Malone, the major reason Utah had such a banner season, upset Jordan in the voting for most valuable player (MVP). It was the first time the Utah star had won the coveted award. Pat Riley of Miami was selected coach of the year, the third time he had been so hon-

PROFESSIONAL BASKETBALL

National Basketball Association
(Final Standings, 1996–97)

Eastern Conference

Atlantic Division	W	L	Pct.	Games Behind
*Miami	61	21	.744	—
*New York	57	25	.695	4
*Orlando	45	37	.549	16
*Washington	44	38	.537	17
New Jersey	26	56	.317	35
Philadelphia	22	60	.268	39
Boston	15	67	.183	46

Central Division				
*Chicago	69	13	.841	—
*Atlanta	56	26	.683	13
*Detroit	54	28	.659	15
*Charlotte	54	28	.659	15
Cleveland	42	40	.512	27
Indiana	39	43	.476	30
Milwaukee	33	49	.402	36
Toronto	30	52	.366	39

Western Conference

Midwest Division	W	L	Pct.	Games Behind
*Utah	64	18	.780	—
*Houston	57	25	.695	7
*Minnesota	40	42	.488	24
Dallas	24	58	.293	40
Denver	21	61	.256	43
San Antonio	20	62	.244	44
Vancouver	14	68	.171	50

Pacific Division				
*Seattle	57	25	.695	—
*Los Angeles Lakers	56	26	.683	1
*Portland	49	33	.598	8
*Phoenix	40	42	.488	17
*Los Angeles Clippers	36	46	.439	21
Sacramento	34	48	.415	23
Golden State	30	52	.366	27

*In play-offs

Play-offs

Eastern Conference

First Round	Atlanta	3 games	Detroit	2
	Chicago	3 games	Washington	0
	Miami	3 games	Orlando	2
	New York	3 games	Charlotte	0
Second Round	Chicago	4 games	Atlanta	1
	Miami	4 games	New York	3
Finals	Chicago	4 games	Miami	1

Western Conference

First Round	Houston	3 games	Minnesota	0
	L.A. Lakers	3 games	Portland	1
	Seattle	3 games	Phoenix	2
	Utah	3 games	L.A. Clippers	0
Second Round	Houston	4 games	Seattle	3
	Utah	4 games	LA. Lakers	1
Finals	Utah	4 games	Houston	2
Championship	Chicago	4 games	Utah	2
All-Star Game	East 132, West 120			

Individual Honors

Most Valuable Player: Karl Malone, Utah
Most Valuable Player (championship): Michael Jordan, Chicago
Most Valuable Player (All-Star Game): Glen Rice, Charlotte
Rookie of the Year: Allen Iverson, Philadelphia
Coach of the Year: Pat Riley, Miami
Defensive Player of the Year: Dikembe Mutombo, Atlanta
Sixth-Man Award: John Starks, New York
Most Improved Player: Isaac Austin, Miami
Leader in Scoring: Michael Jordan, 29.6 points per game
Leader in Assists: Mark Jackson, Indiana, 11.4 assists per game
Leader in Rebounds: Dennis Rodman, Chicago, 16.1 per game
Leader in Field-Goal Percentage: Gheorghe Muresan, Washington, .604
Leader in Three-Point-Shooting Percentage: Glen Rice, .470
Leader in Free-Throw Percentage: Mark Price, Golden State, .906
Leader in Steals: Mookie Blaylock, Atlanta, 2.72 per game
Leader in Blocked Shots: Shawn Bradley, Dallas, 3.4 per game

ored; Allen Iverson of the 76ers was named rookie of the year; Isaac Austin of Miami was picked as the most improved player; John Starks of New York was selected as the outstanding sixth man; and Bob Bass of Charlotte was chosen executive of the year. Malone, Jordan, Hill, Olajuwon, and Tim Hardaway were named to the NBA first team, while Scottie Pippen of Chicago, Glen Rice of Charlotte, Ewing of New York, Gary Payton of Seattle, and Mitch Richmond of Sacramento made second team.

There was an unprecedented postseason movement within the coaching ranks. The biggest hiring was made by the Celtics, who let M.L. Carr go and lured Rick Pitino from the University of Kentucky to take over their basketball operations. Former superstar Larry Bird took over in Indiana, where Larry Brown resigned. Brown later became the 76ers' coach. Chuck Daly, who guided the Pistons to two titles, became the Magic's head coach. The club had fired Brian Hill during the season and replaced him with Richie Adubato. Other coaches who were fired included Dick Motta of Denver, P.J. Carlisemo of Portland, Eddie Jordan of Sacramento, Rick Adelman of Golden State, and Johnny Davis of Philadelphia. Carlisemo wound up replacing Adelman; Mike Dunleavy succeeded Carlisemo at Portland; Brian Hill was named to replace Brian Winters at Vancouver; and Allen Bristow took over in Denver.

The Play-offs. Based on their regular season and the play of Michael Jordan, the Bulls were heavy favorites to repeat as champions, with the likelihood they would face Utah or Houston in the final round. The Bulls had very little trouble living up to these expectations. Chicago rolled over Washington in the first round of the Eastern Conference play-offs, then overcame some tough defense from Atlanta to coast by the Hawks before meeting Miami in the conference final. The Heat had survived by edging out New York after falling behind, 3–1, in their series. But key Knick players—including Starks, Ewing, and Johnson—were given suspensions for their involvement in a fight and the Heat took advantage of New York's manpower shortage. But the Heat were no match for Jordan and Pippen, and the Bulls eased into the championship round after winning the series, 4–1.

In the Western Conference, the most intense series was between Houston and Seattle. The clubs traded thrilling victories before the Rockets prevailed in seven games. They met Utah in the conference finals after the Jazz had breezed through its early rounds. In the final, the Rockets could not defend Malone and Stockton consistently and could not overcome the home-court advantage owned by Utah. The Jazz won in six games.

Utah then had the difficult task of trying to dethrone Chicago, which had won three straight titles before Jordan took two years off to pursue a baseball career. He led the Bulls to a fourth crown in 1995–96 and played better than ever in 1996–97. The Bulls opened the 1997 finals by pulling out the first game, 84–82, after the teams traded 23 lead changes. Pippen scored 27 points but the contest came down to the final seconds, when Malone missed two foul shots and Jordan hit a jumper at the buzzer for the win. Things were easier in Game 2 for Chicago, which led by 16 points at the half. Jordan finished with 38 in the 97–85 victory. Playing on its home court, Utah won Game 3, 104–93, behind standout play from its bench. The Jazz then evened the series at two apiece by scoring the game's last nine points to pull out a 78–73 triumph behind Malone's 23 points and Stockton's 17. The pivotal fifth game went to Chicago; it wound up being one of the most brilliant efforts of Jordan's incredible career. Sick with the flu, he could do little as Utah took a 16-point lead in the first half. But in the fourth period, he scored 15 points, including a three-pointer with the game tied at 85. He finished with 38 points, and the Bulls had a 90–88 win. They ended the series with Game 6, overcoming a ten-point deficit in the first half. Jordan fed Steve Kerr for the game-winner. Jordan was named series MVP for a record fifth time.

Women's Leagues. The increasing popularity of women's basketball was evidenced by the formation of rival professional leagues. The ABL made its debut during the fall of 1996 and played a longer schedule with higher-priced players than the WNBA, which had better television exposure and the backing of the NBA. The WNBA played throughout the summer in major markets, while the ABL decided to situate itself in smaller cities. The ABL averaged about 5,000 fans per game, meeting its first-year expectations. Its first championship was won by Columbus, behind the play of Nikki McCray, Katie Smith, and Tonya Edwards. Columbus downed Richmond in five games after winning the Eastern Conference title. Colorado had won the Western Conference's regular-season crown but lost in the play-offs.

Led by Cynthia Cooper—the WNBA's MVP and scoring leader—the Houston Comets defeated the New York Liberty, 65–51, to win the league's first title. Cooper had 25 points in the final. Houston and New York had beaten Charlotte and Phoenix, respectively, in the semifinals. The WNBA's regular-season attendance averaged 9,669 fans.

College Basketball

At the start of the 1996–97 college-basketball season, two teams—Cincinnati, featuring a tough, physical, veteran lineup; and Kansas, featuring the best starting five in the nation— stood out from the rest. They were considered odds-on favorites to win the national title. But Cincinnati never lived up to its expectations. The Bearcats stumbled early and often and fell out of the Number 1 ranking, giving way to Kansas. The Jayhawks, led by guard Jacque Vaughn and forward Raef LaFrentz, played extremely well throughout the season and seemed likely to emerge as winners of the NCAA tournament.

There also were other talented teams. North Carolina got off to a slow start, then returned to its place among the nation's elite. Wake Forest featured the country's best player, center Tim Duncan. Duke became yet another strong school out of the Atlantic Coast Conference. Utah dominated the mountain states behind the play of forward Keith Van Horn. UCLA's quickness enabled it to become a Pacific Ten power. South Carolina surprised by performing better than expected in the Southeastern Conference, which also produced strong Kentucky. Villanova was tough in the east, while Texas came on strong in the southwest.

Duncan was by far the best player. A strong scorer and rebounder, he was one of the few dominant players of 1996–97. Kansas' LaFrentz and Vaughn, Kentucky's Ron Mercer, Colorado's Chauncey Billups, Colgate's Adonal Foyle, Minnesota's Bobby Jackson, and Stanford's Brevin Knight also had exciting years. As usual, a large number of underclassmen chose to pass up their remaining eligibility and join the pro ranks. UCLA coach Jim Harrick was fired for rules violations. He later was hired as coach of Rhode Island. Meanwhile, North Carolina's Dean Smith became the "winningest" coach in NCAA history.

The NCAA Tournament. Along with Kansas and North Carolina, the top seeds in the tournament were Minnesota and defending champion Kentucky. The Jayhawks, who had been atop the polls most of the season, were heavy favorites to come away with the championship. But in the Southeast Regional, they ran into surprising Arizona, which barely had qualified for the tournament. The Wildcats won, 85–82, in a huge upset. Arizona then

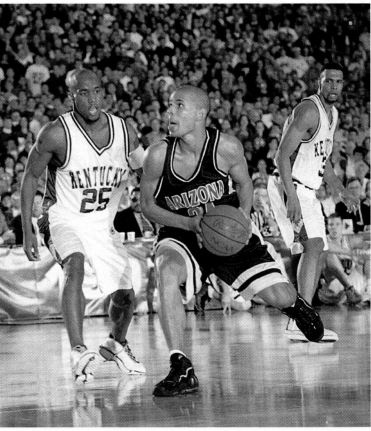

NCAA Photos

The University of Arizona thwarted Kentucky's hopes of capturing a second consecutive NCAA championship by defeating the Kentucky Wildcats, 84–79, in overtime in the tournament final. Arizona's Miles Simon (with ball) scored 30 points in the final and was named the tournament's outstanding player.

beat another upstart, Providence, in overtime to advance to the Final Four. North Carolina prevailed in the East Regional, while Minnesota emerged in the Midwest and Kentucky topped Utah in the West.

In the Final Four, Minnesota, which was a mostly veteran team, tried to run with Kentucky but could not keep pace and lost. In the other semifinal, North Carolina was favored to knock off Arizona, but the Tar Heels could not cope with the Wildcats' stars, Miles Simon and Mike Bibby, and fell.

In the championship game, Arizona needed overtime to register yet another upset, this time over Kentucky. Simon continued his outstanding performances, scoring 30 points as his quickness proved too much for Kentucky. Arizona appeared to have the game won in regulation, but Kentucky scored two three-point baskets in the final 63 seconds to force the extra period. Arizona got all ten of its points in overtime on free throws and wound

© Doug Pensinger/Allsport

DEAN SMITH

On March 15, 1997, University of North Carolina coach Dean Smith won the 877th game of his 36-year career, becoming the college-basketball coach with the most wins of all time. With a 73–56 victory over Colorado, Smith surpassed Adolph Rupp, who had won 876 games while at Kentucky for 41 years. The Tar Heels won two more NCAA tournament games. In October, Smith suddenly announced his retirement. His career mark as a coach was 879 victories and 254 losses. His teams appeared in 27 NCAA tournaments, reached the final four 11 times, and took two championships.

Born on Feb. 28, 1931, Dean Smith played several sports for the University of Kansas. After graduation, he served in the U.S. Air Force and later became an assistant coach to Frank McGuire at UNC. Smith took over as the college's head coach in 1961. His coaching innovations included the "four-corners offense" and the "run-and-jump defense." In addition, an unusually high percentage of Smith's players earned their degrees.

COLLEGE BASKETBALL

Conference Champions

American East: Boston University[r,t]
Atlantic Coast: Duke[r]; North Carolina[t]
Atlantic 10: St. Joseph's (Eastern Division)[r], Xavier, Ohio (Western Division)[r]; St. Joseph's[t]
Big East: Villanova and Boston College (tied, Big East 6)[r], Georgetown (Big East 7)[r]; Boston College[t]
Big Sky: North Arizona[r]; Montana[t]
Big South: North Carolina-Ashville[r]; Charleston Southern[t]
Big Ten: Minnesota
Big 12: Kansas (Northern Division)[r], Texas (Southern Division)[r]; Kansas[t]
Big West: Utah State, Nevada, New Mexico State (Eastern Division, tied)[r], Pacific (Western Division)[r]; Pacific[t]
Colonial: Old Dominion, N. C. Wilmington (tied)[r]; Old Dominion[t]
Conference USA: Tulane (Red Division)[r], Memphis, North Carolina, Charlotte (White Division, tied)[r], Cincinnati (Blue Division)[r]; Marquette[t]
Ivy League: Princeton
Metro Atlantic Athletic: Iona[r]; Fairfield[t]
Mid-American: Bowling Green, Miami, Ohio (tied)[r]; Miami, Ohio[t]
Mid-Continent: Valparaiso[r,t]
Mid-Eastern Athletic: Coppin State[r,t]
Midwestern: Butler[r,t]
Missouri Valley: Illinois State[r,t]
Northeast: Long Island University[r,t]
Ohio Valley: Austin Peay, Murray State (tied)[r]; Murray State[t]
Pacific Ten: UCLA
Patriot: Navy[r,t]
Southeastern: South Carolina (Eastern Division)[r], Mississippi (Western Division)[r]; Kentucky[t]
Southern: Davidson, Marshall (Northern Division, tied)[r], Tennessee Chattanooga (Southern Division)[r]; Tennessee Chattanooga[t]
Southland: Northeast Louisiana, McNeese State, Southwest Texas State (tied)[r]; Southwest Texas State[t]
Southwestern Athletic: Mississippi Valley State[r]; Jackson State[t]
Sun Belt: New Orleans, South Alabama (tied)[r]; South Alabama[t]
Trans America: College of Charleston (Eastern Division)[r], Samford (Western Division)[r]; College of Charleston[t]
West Coast: Santa Clara, St. Mary's (tied)[r]; St. Mary's[t]
Western Athletic: Utah (Mountain)[r], Hawaii, Fresno State (tied)[r]; Utah[t]

[r]regular-season winner
[t]conference-tournament winner

Tournaments

NCAA Division I: Arizona
NCAA Division II: Cal State Bakersfield
NCAA Division III: Illinois Wesleyan
NIT: Michigan
NAIA Division I (men): Life
NCAA Division I (women): Tennessee
NCAA Division II (women): North Dakota
NCAA Division III (women): New York University
NAIA Division I (women): Southern Nazarene

up making 34 of 41 foul shots for the game, compared with Kentucky's 9 of 17. Arizona had made two previous appearances in the championship game and lost in both. It was the school's first basketball title.

The Women. Defending champion Tennessee entered the NCAA tournament as an underdog to favored Connecticut, which entered the play-offs undefeated. But when they met in the Midwest Regionals, Tennessee pulled away to a 91–81 victory. Another upset was registered by Notre Dame, which advanced out of the East Regional despite not being a Number 1 seed. Old Dominion and Stanford also made it to the Final Four. In semifinal matchups, Old Dominion took a thriller against Stanford and All-American Kate Starbird, 83–82, while Tennessee handled Notre Dame, 80–66. Tennessee then rode the plays of sophomore Chamique Holdsclaw to a 68–59 triumph over Old Dominion for a second straight title. It was coach Pat Summitt's fifth national championship.

PAUL ATTNER, *"The Sporting News"*

Boxing

Boxing's heavyweight division, its reputation tainted for years, suffered further humiliation during 1997. The nadir was reached when challenger Mike Tyson bit a piece from the right ear of World Boxing Association (WBA) champion Evander Holyfield and then bit his left ear in their June 28 bout in Las Vegas, NV.

The other championship belts also were touched by controversy. Lennox Lewis retained his World Boxing Council (WBC) heavyweight crown when challenger Henry Akinwande was disqualified for excessive holding. Lewis had won the title earlier in the year from Oliver McCall after the bout was stopped in the fifth round because a distraught McCall refused to fight. McCall was not the only one who chose to quit fighting. Former world champion Riddick Bowe first announced his retirement in January, then decided to enlist in the U.S. Marines. After only nine days in boot camp at Parris Island, SC, however, Bowe decided again to throw in the towel and was discharged from the military upon his request.

Heavyweights. One of boxing's most awaited rematches became one of the sport's most embarrassing moments, especially when Tyson attempted to rationalize his uncivilized action by saying he had to defend himself from Holyfield's head butts. Holyfield had been leading on points when, with about 40 seconds left in the third round, Tyson bit off a chunk of the champion's right ear and spit it on the floor. Holyfield leaped in pain as his ear bled profusely. Dr. Flip Homansky examined the wound and referee Mills Lane, while announcing that two points were being subtracted from Tyson's score, allowed the fight to resume. Lane warned Tyson that another bite would cause disqualification, and when fighting resumed after a lengthy delay, Tyson again spit out his mouthpiece and bit the champion on the left ear. A melee ensued after referee Lane disqualified the former champion, who charged across the ring toward Holyfield's corner and hit a police officer before being pulled away. The missing part of the right ear was taken to Holyfield's dressing room after the fight and surgically reattached at a Las Vegas hospital.

Tyson had fought five outmatched opponents following his release in 1995 from an Indiana prison where he had served three years for rape. But Holyfield, an 8–1 underdog, had pummeled Tyson and scored an 11th-round technical knockout on Nov. 9, 1996.

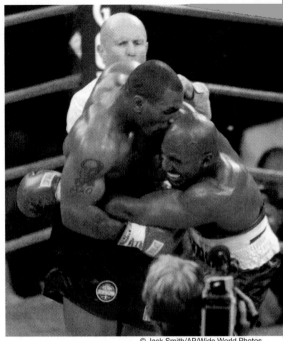

© Jack Smith/AP/Wide World Photos

The sport of boxing came under renewed attack after Mike Tyson (left) bit Evander Holyfield on both ears in a World Boxing Association (WBA) heavyweight title bout on June 28, 1997.

The Nevada State Athletic Commission, which sanctioned the June 28 bout in Las Vegas, investigated Tyson's action and subsequently fined him $3 million and banned him from boxing for at least one year, at which time the fighter would be able to apply for reinstatement.

Two weeks after the Holyfield-Tyson debacle, Akinwande and Lewis staged another ugly bout in Las Vegas that Lane also brought to an unique conclusion. Akinwande's constant holding caused his disqualification in the fifth round as a disgruntled crowd voiced its disapproval of the antics. The 6'7" (2-m) Akinwande was warned by Lane in the second round that he had to fight or the bout would be stopped. Nonetheless, he continued to wrap his long arms around the champion at every opportunity. The referee stopped the fight in the third, fourth, and fifth rounds to lecture Akinwande about not fighting. His trainer, Don Turner, also pleaded with the challenger to fight back. The Nevada commission reviewed the bout, decided disqualification was sufficient punishment, and awarded Akinwande his $1 million purse.

Lewis had won the title in Las Vegas on February 7, avenging a second-round knockout by McCall in England in 1994 that determined the championship claimed by Tyson before his imprisonment. The conclusion of the rematch may have been even more inconceivable than the Tyson or Akinwande bouts. Lane disqualified McCall 55 seconds into the fifth round after the WBC champion refused to throw punches in either the fourth or fifth rounds. Lane had visited McCall's corner after the fourth round and was told, "I want to fight. I need to fight." According to Lane, "It was almost like he wanted to be knocked out." The 237-lb (108-kg) McCall, who had spent the previous 18 months in and out of drug rehabilitation, broke down in tears at one point. Most of the last two rounds he walked in circles around the confused Lewis. McCall was credited with throwing only 75 punches, including two in the fourth round and a single jab in the fifth. After the jab, McCall turned his back and walked away and Lane stopped the fight. McCall's trainer, George Benton, said his boxer was acting like a "lunatic" and talking incoherently.

Andrew Golota, whose low blows twice cost him disqualifications to Bowe, did not last long enough with Lewis for another incident. Lewis knocked him out in the first round. At age 48, two-time world champion George Foreman lost a controversial decision to Shannon Briggs on November 22 and retired once again.

Holyfield added the International Boxing Federation (IBF) title to his collection on Nov. 9, 1997, with a convincing victory over Michael Moorer. Holyfield won the fight on an eighth-round technical knockout.

Lighter Divisions. In the lighter weights, two dominant fighters, Oscar De La Hoya and Roy Jones, Jr., kept their undefeated records unblemished. De La Hoya won the WBC welterweight title in April with a 12-round decision over Pernell Whitaker in Las Vegas. Two months later, De La Hoya defeated David Kamau in a second-round knockout in San Antonio on June 14, followed by an easy decision over Hector "Macho" Camacho in September. De La Hoya knocked Camacho down in the ninth round and staggered him several other times. Camacho, who had 69 professional bouts over 18 years, called De La Hoya the best he ever had fought. In his last bout of the year, De La Hoya stopped Wilfredo Rivera in a December 8 bout in Atlantic City, NJ, with a knockout in the eighth round. At year's end, De La Hoya's record stood at 27–0 with 22 knockouts.

Meanwhile, Jones knocked out Montel Griffin with a left hook in the first round to regain the WBC light-heavyweight championship on August 7. The crowd at Ledyard, CT, saw Griffin take a standing eight-count only 18 seconds into the contest. The fight ended at 2:31 of the round when a floored Griffin was unable to beat the count. With the win, Jones gained revenge for a March 21 fight in which he was disqualified for hitting Griffin twice while he was on one knee. Jones also improved his record to 35–1 with 25 knockouts.

In March, five-time champion Sugar Ray Leonard unwisely ended a six-year retirement to fight a bout against Camacho. Leonard was knocked out in the fifth round and announced his retirement again.

Legislation. Many provisions of the 1996 U.S. Professional Boxing Safety Act went into effect on July 1, 1997. The act set minimum safety standards for boxing and primarily was intended to protect boxers who travel across the United States and fight without medical supervision or in states without boxing commissions. The act requires that boxers pass a physical examination before fighting and carry health insurance. In addition, medical personnel must be present at all matches.

STAN SUTTON

WORLD BOXING CHAMPIONS *

Heavyweight: World Boxing Council (WBC)—Lennox Lewis, Great Britain, 1997; World Boxing Association (WBA)—Evander Holyfield, United States, 1996; International Boxing Federation (IBF)—Holyfield, 1997.

Cruiserweight: WBC—Marcelo Dominguez, Argentina, 1996; WBA—Fabrice Tiozzo, France, 1997; IBF—Imamu Mayfield, United States, 1997.

Light Heavyweight: WBC—Roy Jones, Jr., United States, 1997; WBA—Louis Del Valle, United States, 1997; IBF—William Guthrie, United States, 1997.

Super Middleweight: WBC—Thulane Malinga, South Africa, 1997; WBA—Frank Liles, United States, 1994; IBF—Charles Brewer, United States, 1997.

Middleweight: WBC—Keith Holmes, United States, 1996; WBA—Julio Cesar Green, Dominican Republic, 1997; IBF—Bernard Hopkins, United States, 1995.

Junior Middleweight: WBC—Keith Mullings, United States, 1997; WBA—Laurent Boudouani, France, 1996; IBF—Yori Boy Campas, Mexico, 1997.

Welterweight: WBC—Oscar De La Hoya, United States, 1997; WBA—Ike Quartey, Ghana, 1994; IBF—Felix Trinidad, Puerto Rico, 1993.

Junior Welterweight: WBC—vacant; WBA—Khalid Rahilou, France, 1997; IBF—Vincent Phillips, United States, 1997.

Lightweight: WBC—Steve Johnson, United States, 1997; WBA—Ulzubek Nazarov, Russia, 1993; IBF—Shane Mosley, United States, 1997.

Junior Lightweight: WBC—Genaro Hernandez, United States, 1997; WBA—Yongsoo Choi, South Korea, 1995; IBF—Arturo Gatti, United States, 1995.

Featherweight: WBC—Luisito Espinosa, Philippines, 1995; WBA—Wilfredo Vazquez, Puerto Rico, 1996; IBF—Hector Lizarraga, United States, 1997.

Junior Featherweight: WBC—Erik Morales, Mexico, 1997; WBA—vacant; IBF—Vuyani Bungu, South Africa, 1994.

Bantamweight: WBC—Sirimongkol Singmanassuk, Thailand, 1996; WBA—Nana Konadu, Ghana, 1997; IBF—Tim Austin, South Africa, 1997.

Junior Bantamweight: WBC—Gerry Peñalosa, Philippines, 1997; WBA—Satoshi Iida, Japan, 1997; IBF—Johnny Tapia, United States, 1997.

Flyweight: WBC—Chatchai Sasakul, Thailand, 1997; WBA—José Bonilla, Venezuela, 1997; IBF—Mark Johnson, United States, 1996.

Junior Flyweight: WBC—Saman Sorjaturong, Thailand, 1996; WBA—Pitchinoi Siriwat, Thailand, 1996; IBF—Mauricio Pastrana, Colombia, 1997.

Strawweight: WBC—Ricardo Lopez, Mexico, 1990; WBA—Rosendo Alvarez, Nicaragua, 1995; IBF—Rataanpol Vorapin, Thailand, 1993.

*As of Dec. 31, 1997. Date indicates year title was won.

© Mark J. Terrill/AP /Wide World Photos

Michigan cornerback Charles Woodson, winner of the 1997 Heisman Trophy, had a timely interception as the Wolverines defeated Washington State, 21–16, in the Rose Bowl. With the win, Michigan shared the national championship with Nebraska.

Football

The championship game of the 1997–98 National Football League (NFL) season matched the Green Bay Packers, the defending champs, against the Denver Broncos, who had not won a Super Bowl in four attempts. Both clubs won their conference championships on the road, with Green Bay beating San Francisco for the National Football Conference (NFC) crown, and Denver defeating Pittsburgh for the American Football Conference (AFC) title.

Before 68,912 fans at Qualcomm Stadium in San Diego on Jan. 25, 1998, the Broncos and their longtime star quarterback John Elway finally won a Super Bowl, defeating the Packers, 31–24. In a game that was really "super," Broncos running back Terrell Davis set a Super Bowl record by scoring three rushing touchdowns. He was named the game's most valuable player. With the win, Denver became only the second wild-card team to capture a Super Bowl. It also was the first AFC team since the Oakland Raiders in 1984 to take the big one.

In college football, the national championship was shared by the Michigan Wolverines and the Nebraska Cornhuskers—whose legendary coach, Tom Osborne, retired after his team beat Tennessee in the Orange Bowl. Michigan also finished undefeated after downing Washington State in the Rose Bowl.

The Toronto Argonauts once again won the Canadian Football League (CFL) title. They were led by quarterback Doug Flutie, who repeated as the CFL's regular-season and championship-game most valuable player. He later signed a contract with the Buffalo Bills of the NFL.

The Professional Season

NFL Developments. In a relatively calm off-season, the Seattle Seahawks were sold by Ken Behring to Paul Allen, owner of the Portland Trail Blazers and cofounder of Microsoft Corp. Owners in Denver, New England, and Minnesota still pushed for new stadiums. The Oilers made their debut in Tennessee, after moving from Houston following an unsuccessful attempt by owner Bud Adams to have taxpayers build a stadium. Tennessee voters agreed to construct a stadium in Nashville. Meanwhile, the Oilers played their 1997 games in Memphis, drawing poor support.

The most dynamic changes occurred in coaching. Bill Parcells left the New England

Patriots after losing Super Bowl XXXI and took over as coach and head of football operations for the New York Jets. George Seifert quit the San Francisco 49ers and was replaced by former University of California head coach Steve Mariucci—who never had been an NFL head coach. Two veteran coaches came out of retirement: Mike Ditka and Dick Vermeil signed on at New Orleans and St. Louis, respectively. Dan Reeves was released by the New York Giants and wound up in Atlanta. Joe Bugel became head coach at Oakland, while Jim Fassel took over the Giants, Bobby Ross the Detroit Lions, and Kevin Gilbride the Chargers. Just after the season began, Minnesota coach Dennis Green published a book in which he said he might try to become an owner of the team or sue the club.

Regular Season and Play-offs. The San Francisco 49ers in the NFC and the Kansas City Chiefs in the AFC finished the regular season with 13–3 records and secured home-field advantage for the play-offs. They both had to overcome major obstacles.

In their opening game, the 49ers lost star receiver Jerry Rice to a major knee injury. They still put together 11 straight victories behind a revitalized running game, a strong defense, and the standout play of veteran quarterback Steve Young. They easily won the NFC West Division title, after losing it in 1996 to the Carolina Panthers. The rest of the division was a disappointment. The Panthers were hurt by injuries and poor play from quarterback Kerry Collins, finishing with a 7–9 record. New Orleans was 6–10, and St. Louis was 5–11. Only the Falcons were a surprise, overcoming a poor start to put up a 7–9 mark.

The Chiefs were putting together a strong season when they lost quarterback Elvis Grbac to a broken collarbone. Grbac previously was Young's backup at San Francisco. Still, the Chiefs held off a challenge from Denver and took the NFC West title—thanks in part to Grbac's backup, Rich Gannon. The preseason-favorite Broncos lost three road games near the end of the schedule and managed a 12–4 record, despite the dynamic play of running back Terrell Davis.

The AFC East was the closest race. Parcells turned the Jets—the worst team in the league in 1996—into an immediate contender. They stayed in the play-off race until the final week, when they lost to the Detroit Lions, leaving first place to the New England Patriots and the Miami Dolphins. The Patriots won the season finale in Miami to grab the title with a 10–6 record—one game better than the Dolphins and Jets.

PROFESSIONAL FOOTBALL

National Football League
Final Standings, 1997

AMERICAN CONFERENCE

Eastern Division	W	L	T	Pct.	Points For	Against
New England	10	6	0	.625	369	289
Miami	9	7	0	.563	339	327
N.Y. Jets	9	7	0	.563	348	287
Buffalo	6	10	0	.375	255	367
Indianapolis	3	13	0	.188	313	401

Central Division	W	L	T	Pct.	Points For	Against
Pittsburgh	11	5	0	.688	372	307
Jacksonville	11	5	0	.688	394	318
Tennessee	8	8	0	.500	333	310
Cincinnati	7	9	0	.438	355	405
Baltimore	6	9	1	.406	326	345

Western Division	W	L	T	Pct.	Points For	Against
Kansas City	13	3	0	.813	375	232
Denver	12	4	0	.750	472	287
Seattle	8	8	0	.500	365	362
Oakland	4	12	0	.250	324	419
San Diego	4	12	0	.250	266	425

PLAY-OFFS
Denver 42, Jacksonville 17
New England 17, Miami 3
Denver 14, Kansas City 10
Pittsburgh 7, New England 6
Denver 24, Pittsburgh 21

NATIONAL CONFERENCE

Eastern Division	W	L	T	Pct.	Points For	Against
N.Y. Giants	10	5	1	.656	307	265
Washington	8	7	1	.531	327	289
Philadelphia	6	9	1	.406	317	372
Dallas	6	10	0	.375	304	314
Arizona	4	12	0	.250	283	379

Central Division	W	L	T	Pct.	Points For	Against
Green Bay	13	3	0	.813	422	282
Tampa Bay	10	6	0	.625	299	263
Detroit	9	7	0	.563	379	306
Minnesota	9	7	0	.563	354	359
Chicago	4	12	0	.250	263	421

Western Division	W	L	T	Pct.	Points For	Against
San Francisco	13	3	0	.813	375	265
Carolina	7	9	0	.438	265	314
Atlanta	7	9	0	.438	320	361
New Orleans	6	10	0	.375	237	327
St. Louis	5	11	0	.313	299	359

PLAY-OFFS
Tampa Bay 20, Detroit 10
Minnesota 23, New York 22
Green Bay 21, Tampa Bay 7
San Francisco 38, Minnesota 22
Green Bay 23, San Francisco 10

SUPER BOWL XXXII: Denver 31, Green Bay 24

Pittsburgh used first-year starter Kordell Stewart at quarterback, and he turned in a surprisingly good season to help the Steelers win the AFC Central. He was supported by big running back Jerome Bettis. The Jacksonville Jaguars opened the season without quarterback Mark Brunell, who injured his knee in the preseason. Brunell came back and the Jaguars—who lost the 1996 AFC play-off finals—ended with an 11–5 record.

In the NFC East, Fassel's tremendous first-year performance as the Giants' coach guided them to a 10–5–1 record—good enough to take first place over the preseason division favorite, the Washington Redskins. The Redskins ended out of the play-offs with an 8–7–1 record. The Dallas Cowboys—despite a veteran core of star players, including quarterback Troy Aikman and running back Emmitt Smith—were a big disappointment. They lost their last five games and had a 6–10 record. It was the first time in six years that they did not make the play-offs.

Defending NFL champion Green Bay had another successful season, overcoming an early challenge from the Tampa Bay Buccaneers to run away with the NFC Central title. The Bucs—in the play-offs for the first time in 15 years—were second, while the Lions also made the play-offs, thanks to the great effort of running back Barry Sanders.

In the play-offs, the Broncos played the Chiefs in Kansas City, where the Chiefs had not lost all season. But Davis scored two touchdowns, and the Broncos held off a last-minute Chiefs drive to come away with a 14–10 victory. That put Denver in the AFC championship game against Pittsburgh, which had beaten New England, 7–6, in the second round. The Broncos used a strong rushing game and timely defense to hold off the Steelers in Three Rivers Stadium, 24–21.

In the NFC the two favorites, the 49ers and the Packers, both made the conference championship. The Packers easily handled the Bucs in the semifinal round, while San Francisco romped over the Vikings. The Packers dominated what was supposed to be a highly competitive contest and cruised to a 23–10 win.

Individual Performances. For the third straight season, Packer quarterback Brett Favre was the NFL's most valuable player, sharing the honor with Barry Sanders. Favre threw for 35 touchdowns, the third straight season he recorded at least 30 scoring passes. Sanders was even more spectacular, rushing for 2,053 yards—the second-highest total in NFL history and only the third time anyone had passed the 2,000-yard mark. He beat out Terrell Davis for the rushing title. Davis also had a shot at the 2,000-yard mark, but a late-season injury left him short with 1,750 yards—best in the AFC. With Rice injured, the receiving title was shared by Detroit's Herman Moore and Tim Brown of Oakland, both with 104 receptions. Young was the top-rated passer (104.7). The top rookie was Tampa Bay running back Warrick Dunn. The best coaching jobs were turned in by Fassel, Reeves, Tampa Bay's Tony Dungy, Parcells, and the Chiefs' Marty Schottenheimer. Other standout players included 49er defensive tackle Dana Stubblefield, Buffalo defensive end Bruce Smith, Tennessee running back Eddie George, Pittsburgh running back Jerome Bet-tis, Minnesota defensive lineman John Randle, Arizona receiver Rob Moore, Green Bay runner Dorsey Levens, Jacksonville quarterback Brunell, Denver linebacker John Mobley, Giant linebacker Jessie Armstead, and Green Bay safety LeRoy Butler.

Off the Field. It was another painful year for NFL coaches. The Raiders' Bugel was fired soon after the season ended, then the Cowboys Barry Switzer—who had won a Super Bowl with Dallas—resigned. Coach Lindy Infante and general manager Bill Tobin were released in Indianapolis by team owner Jim Irsay, who replaced his father, Robert, who died during the season. Former Saints coach Jim Mora was hired by new general manager Bill Polian, formerly of Carolina, to replace Infante. Marv Levy, who had coached Buffalo to four Super Bowls, retired and was replaced by Wade Phillips.

The College Season

There were many preseason favorites for the collegiate championship, including Florida State, Colorado, Nebraska, and Florida. Other strong teams included North Carolina, Tennessee, Penn State, Michigan, Ohio State, UCLA, Texas, and Washington. Notre Dame started the season with a new coach, Bob Davie, who replaced the retired Lou Holtz.

Defensive back Charles Woodson of Michigan won the 1997 Heisman Trophy—the first-ever defensive player to win the award. He upset preseason favorite Peyton Manning of Tennessee, who finished second in the voting. Other standout players included Washington State quarterback Ryan Leaf, Texas running back Ricky Williams, Iowa return man Tim Dwight, Marshall receiver Randy Moss, Nebraska lineman Grant Wistrom, Kentucky quarterback Tim Couch, Louisiana Tech receiver Troy Edwards, and Nebraska running back Ahman Green.

Grambling coach Eddie Robinson retired as the "winningest" coach in college-football history; he had coached the team since 1941. He was replaced by former Grambling quarterback and NFL star Doug Williams. Nebraska coach Tom Osborne—one of the most successful coaches of all time—also retired.

The Bowl Games. In the third season under the so-called Bowl Alliance, the national title went to two teams. A showdown between Number 1–ranked Michigan and second-ranked Nebraska could not be arranged, since Michigan, the Big Ten champion, played in the Rose Bowl—not yet associated with the alliance.

Bill Kuharich (right), the general manager of the New Orleans Saints, honored Eddie Robinson (center) and his wife, Doris, prior to a Saints game at the Louisiana Superdome. Robinson had retired after 57 years as coach at Grambling University and as the "winningest" coach in NCAA history.

Michigan finished undefeated, holding off Washington State, 21–16, in the Rose Bowl. Quarterback Brian Griese—son of Pro Football Hall of Famer Bob Griese, the former Miami Dolphin—was the game's most valuable player. In the Orange Bowl, Nebraska gave Osborne a great send-off by routing Manning and third-ranked Tennessee, 42–17. In the final polls, The Associated Press (AP) rankings placed Michigan first, giving the Wolverines their first national crown since 1948. But in the coaches' poll, Nebraska replaced Michigan in first place. It was the Cornhuskers' second straight championship.

Florida State—which might have had the best talent of any team in the nation—won the Sugar Bowl to finish third. UCLA, which finished the year strongly, took the Cotton Bowl; and Florida, which had defeated Florida State in the regular season to cost the Seminoles the national title, captured the Citrus Bowl. North Carolina took the Gator Bowl title.

Michigan nosed out Ohio State for the Big Ten championship. Washington State and UCLA ruled over the Pacific Ten, while Tennessee won the Southeastern Conference championship. Nebraska won the Big Twelve championship, and Florida State beat out North Carolina for the Atlantic Coast title. Syracuse was the Big East's best team. Former powers Alabama and Texas had disappointing seasons. A late-season slump cost Penn State a run at the national title, while Notre Dame finished well under Davie.

PAUL ATTNER, *"The Sporting News"*

COLLEGE FOOTBALL

Conference Champions

Atlantic Coast—Florida State
Big Ten—Michigan
Big Twelve—Nebraska
Big West—(tie) Nevada, Utah State
Pacific Ten—Washington State
Southeastern—Tennessee
Western Athletic Conference—Colorado State

NCAA Champions

Division I-AA—Youngstown State (OH)
Division II—Northern Colorado
Division III—Mount Union (OH)

NAIA Champion: Findlay (OH)

Individual Honors

Heisman Trophy—Charles Woodson, Michigan
Lombardi Award—Grant Wistrom, Nebraska
Outland Trophy—Aaron Taylor, Nebraska

Major Bowl Games

Alamo Bowl (San Antonio, TX, Dec. 30)—Purdue 33, Oklahoma State 20
Aloha Bowl (Honolulu, HI, Dec. 25)—Washington 51, Michigan State 23
Blue-Gray Classic (Montgomery, AL, Dec. 25)—Gray 31, Blue 24
Carquest Bowl (Miami, FL, Dec. 29)—Georgia Tech 35, West Virginia 30
Citrus Bowl (Orlando, FL, Jan. 1)—Florida 21, Penn State 6
Cotton Bowl (Dallas, TX, Jan. 1)—UCLA 29, Texas A&M 23
Fiesta Bowl (Tempe, AZ, Dec. 31)—Kansas State 35, Syracuse 18
Gator Bowl (Jacksonville, FL, Jan. 1)—North Carolina 42, Virginia Tech 3
Heritage Bowl (Atlanta, GA, Dec. 27)—Southern University 34, South Carolina State 28
Holiday Bowl (San Diego, CA, Dec. 29)—Colorado State 35, Missouri 24
Humanitarian Bowl (Boise, ID, Dec. 29)—Cincinnati 35, Utah State 19
Independence Bowl (Shreveport, LA, Dec. 28)—LSU 27, Notre Dame 9
Insight.com Bowl (Tucson, AZ, Dec. 27)—Arizona 20, New Mexico 14
Las Vegas Bowl (Las Vegas, NV, Dec. 20)—Oregon 41, Air Force 13
Liberty Bowl (Memphis, TN, Dec. 31)—Southern Mississippi 41, Pittsburgh 7
Motor City Bowl (Pontiac, MI, Dec. 26)—Mississippi 34, Marshall 31
Orange Bowl (Miami, FL, Jan. 2)—Nebraska 42, Tennessee 17
Outback Bowl (Tampa, FL, Jan. 1)—Georgia 33, Wisconsin 6
Peach Bowl (Atlanta, GA, Jan. 2)—Auburn 21, Clemson 17
Rose Bowl (Pasadena, CA, Jan. 1)—Michigan 21, Washington State 16
Sugar Bowl (New Orleans, LA, Jan. 1)—Florida State 31, Ohio State 14
Sun Bowl (El Paso, TX, Dec. 31)—Arizona State 17, Iowa 7

Golf

The 1997 golf season began as the year of Eldrick ("Tiger") Woods, but other golfers, particularly Hale Irwin and Annika Sorenstam, took center stage as the season progressed into the summer and fall.

The year's big event was the 32d edition of the biennial Ryder Cup. In that competition, Europe held on to the cup with a $14\frac{1}{2}$–$13\frac{1}{2}$ victory over the United States at Valderrama in Sotogrande, Spain. Led by Bernhard Langer, Colin Montgomerie, and Constantino Rocca—each of whom won three matches—the European team dominated the second day of foursomes and four-balls and took a five-point lead into the final day. The United States rallied with seven wins in singles matches on Sunday, but it was too little, too late.

A New "Tiger" for the Game

Eldrick ("Tiger") Woods came on like a firestorm early in 1997, burning everything in his path. It was not a sudden explosion; the public had been hearing about Tiger since he won the first of three U.S. Golf Association Junior Championships in 1991 at the age of 15, and later after he won three consecutive U.S. Amateur Golf Championships. But nobody was quite prepared for his impact on the PGA Tour and on golf itself.

In the first seven months of 1997, Woods won four times, including a runaway victory at the Masters (*photo, right*), where he won by the largest margin in any major tournament. He struggled after that, failing to contend in any of the remaining three major championships and managing only two top-ten finishes in a limited schedule. He had a disappointing 1-3-1 record in the Ryder Cup. Although Woods wound up with a record money total and was named player of the year, his season ended on a down note. He blamed his performance on fatigue—he never had played that much golf in a single year—and pressure.

Since turning professional in late 1996, Woods had been showered with endorsement money—estimates ranged up to $100 million. That hauled him into the limelight in a hurry, and his early success intensified the attention. He was hounded by the media and the fans, young and old, of all races. Woods calls himself a "cablinasian" because of his multiracial ancestry—his mother is of Thai heritage, while his father is part black, part Native American, and part white. With such a diverse background, Woods quickly became a symbol for minorities, a beacon luring them toward the game. His galleries soon were filled with minorities, the very young, and others who never before would have considered setting foot on a golf course.

In total, Tiger's influence on the game and the public was enormous. Men and women who

© Steve Munday/Allsport

knew little about golf suddenly were glued to their televisions to watch the game's latest hero; children of all ages wanted to take up golf and emulate Tiger; and golf clubs and other merchandise associated with the sport enjoyed increased sales, including at Christmastime.

Whether Woods' impact would be sustained remained unclear. However, he was doing his part with the Tiger Woods Foundation, through which he conducted clinics for inner-city youngsters to help bring them into the game. Golf's major associations launched the First Tee program, which was designed to provide minorities more opportunities to learn and play golf. The success of these and other programs depended on the availability of money, teachers, clinics, and courses.

LARRY DENNIS

GOLF

Mercedes Championships: Tiger Woods (202)
Bob Hope Chrysler Classic: John Cook (327)
Phoenix Open: Steve Jones (258)
AT&T Pebble Beach National Pro-Am: Mark O'Meara (268)
Buick Invitational of California: Mark O'Meara (275)
United Airlines Hawaiian Open: Paul Stankowski (271)
Tucson Chrysler Classic: Jeff Sluman (275)
Nissan Open: Nick Faldo (272)
Doral-Ryder Open: Steve Elkington (275)
Honda Classic: Stuart Appleby (274)
Bay Hill Invitational: Phil Mickelson (272)
Players Championship: Steve Elkington (272)
Freeport-McDermott Classic: Brad Faxon (272)
Masters Tournament: Tiger Woods (270)
MCI Classic: Nick Price (269)
Andersen Consulting U.S. Championship: Davis Love III
Greater Greensboro Chrysler Classic: Frank Nobilo (274)
Shell Houston Open: Phil Blackmar (276)
BellSouth Classic: Scott McCarron (274)
GTE Byron Nelson Classic: Tiger Woods (263)
MasterCard Colonial: David Frost (265)
Memorial Tournament: Vijay Singh (202)
Kemper Open: Justin Leonard (274)
U.S. Open Championship: Ernie Els (276)
Buick Classic: Ernie Els (268)
FedEx St. Jude Classic: Greg Norman (268)
Motorola Western Open: Tiger Woods (275)
Quad City Classic: David Toms (265)
Deposit Guaranty Golf Classic: Billy Ray Brown (271)
Canon Greater Hartford Open: Stewart Cink (267)
Sprint International: Phil Mickelson (+48)
Buick Open: Vijay Singh (273)
PGA Championship: Davis Love III (269)
NEC World Series of Golf: Greg Norman (273)
Greater Vancouver Open: Mark Calcavecchia (265)
Greater Milwaukee Open: Scott Hoch (268)
Bell Canadian Open: Steve Jones (275)
CVS Charity Classic: Loren Roberts (266)
LaCantera Texas Open: Tim Herron (271)
B.C. Open: Gabriel Hjertstedt (275)
Buick Challenge: Davis Love III (267)
Michelob Championship at Kingsmill: David Duval (271)
Walt Disney World/Oldsmobile Classic: David Duval (270)
Las Vegas Invitational: Bill Glasson (340)
Tour Championship: David Duval (273)

Senior PGA Tour

MasterCard Championship: Hale Irwin (209)
Senior Skins Game: Raymond Floyd
Royal Caribbean Classic: Gibby Gilbert (202)
LG Championship: Hale Irwin (201)
GTE Classic: David Graham (204)
American Express Invitational: Bud Allin (205)
Senior Slam: Hale Irwin (131)
Toshiba Senior Classic: Bob Murphy (207)
Liberty Mutual Legends of Golf: John Bland/Graham Marsh (192)
Southwestern Bell Dominion: David Graham (206)
The Tradition: Gil Morgan (266)
PGA Seniors' Championship: Hale Irwin (274)
Las Vegas Senior Classic: Hale Irwin (207)
Bruno's Memorial Classic: Jay Sigel (205)
The Home Depot Invitational: Jim Dent (208)
Cadillac NFL Golf Classic: Bruce Crampton (210)
Bell Atlantic Classic: Bob Eastwood (135)
Ameritech Senior Open: Gil Morgan (210)
BellSouth Senior Classic at Opryland: Gil Morgan (202)
du Maurier Champions: Jack Kiefer (269)
Nationwide Championship: Graham Marsh (205)
U.S. Senior Open: Graham Marsh (280)
Kroger Senior Classic: Jay Sigel (195)
Ford Senior Players Championship: Larry Gilbert (274)
Burnet Senior Classic: Hale Irwin (199)
Franklin Quest Championship: Dave Stockton (201)
BankBoston Classic: Hale Irwin (203)
Northville Long Island Classic: Dana Quigley (204)
First of America Classic: Gil Morgan (207)
Saint Luke's Classic: Bruce Summerhays (199)
Pittsburgh Senior Classic: Hugh Baiocchi (206)
Bank One Classic: Vicente Fernandez (203)
Boone Valley Classic: Hale Irwin (200)
Comfort Classic: David Graham (200)
Emerald Coast Classic: Isao Aoki (196)
Vantage Championship: Hale Irwin (195)
The Transamerica: Dave Eichelberger (205)

Hyatt Regency Maui Kaanapali Classic: Hale Irwin (200)
Raley's Gold Rush Classic: Bob Eastwood (204)
Ralphs Senior Classic: Gil Morgan (198)
Energizer Senior Tour Championship: Gil Morgan (272)

LPGA Tour

Chrysler-Plymouth Tournament of Champions: Annika Sorenstam (272)
HealthSouth Inaugural: Michelle McGann (207)
Diet Dr. Pepper National Pro-Am: Kelly Robbins (271)
Los Angeles Women's Championship: Terry-Jo Myers (206)
Cup Noodles Hawaiian Ladies Open: Annika Sorenstam (206)
Alpine Australian Ladies Masters: Gail Graham (273)
Welch's/Circle K Championship: Donna Andrews (273)
Standard Register PING: Laura Davies (277)
Nabisco Dinah Shore: Betsy King (276)
Longs Drugs Challenge: Annika Sorenstam (285)
Susan G. Komen International: Karrie Webb (276)
Chick-fil-A Charity Championship: Nancy Lopez (137)
Sprint Titleholders Championship: Tammie Green (274)
Sara Lee Classic: Terry-Jo Myers (207)
McDonald's LPGA Championship: Chris Johnson (281)
LPGA Corning Classic: Rosie Jones (277)
JC Penney/LPGA Skins Game: Annika Sorenstam
Michelob Light Classic: Annika Sorenstam (277)
Oldsmobile Classic: Pat Hurst (279)
First Bank Presents Edina Realty LPGA Classic: Danielle Ammaccapane (208)
Rochester International: Penny Hammel (279)
ShopRite LPGA Classic: Michelle McGann (201)
Jamie Farr Kroger Classic: Kelly Robbins (265)
U.S. Women's Open: Alison Nicholas (274)
JAL Big Apple Classic: Michele Redman (272)
Giant Eagle LPGA Classic: Tammie Green (203)
du Maurier Classic: Colleen Walker (278)
Friendly's Classic: Deb Richard (277)
Weetabix Women's British Open: Karrie Webb (269)
Star Bank LPGA Classic: Colleen Walker (203)
State Farm Rail Classic: Cindy Figg-Currier (200)
The Safeway LPGA Golf Championship: Chris Johnson (206)
Safeco Classic: Karrie Webb (272)
Welch's Championship: Liselotte Neumann (276)
Fieldcrest Cannon Classic: Wendy Ward (265)
CoreStates Betsy King Classic: Annika Sorenstam (274)
Samsung World Championship of Women's Golf: Juli Inkster (280)
Nichirei International: United States (23 points)
Japan Queens Cup: Liselotte Neumann (205)
ITT LPGA Tour Championship: Annika Sorenstam (277)

Other Tournaments

British Open: Justin Leonard (272)
Ryder Cup: Europe 14½, United States 13½
Walker Cup: United States 18, Great Britain & Ireland 6
U.S. Women's Amateur Public Links: JoJo Robertson
U.S. Men's Amateur Public Links: Tim Clark
U.S. Junior Girls: Beth Bauer
U.S. Junior Boys: Jason Allred
U.S. Women's Amateur: Silvia Cavalleri
U.S. Men's Amateur: Matthew Kuchar
U.S. Women's Mid-Amateur: Carol Semple
U.S. Men's Mid-Amateur: Kenneth Bakst
U.S. Senior Women's Amateur: Nancy Fitzgerald
U.S. Senior Men's Amateur: Cliff Cunningham
World Cup of Golf: Ireland (Paul McGinley, Padraig Harrington) (545); Individual: Colin Montgomerie (266)
NCAA Men: Individual: Charles Warren, Clemson (279); Team: Pepperdine (1,148)
NCAA Women: Individual: Heather Bowie, University of Texas (285); Team: Arizona State (1,178)
British Amateur: Craig Watson
British Senior Amateur: Bud Bradley
British Senior Open: Gary Player (278)
Toyota World Match Play: Vijay Singh
Lincoln-Mercury Kapalua International: Davis Love III (268)
Grand Slam of Golf: Ernie Els (133)
Franklin Funds Shark Shootout: Bruce Lietzke/Scott McCarron (186)
JC Penney Classic: Amy Fruhwirth/Clarence Rose (264)
The Skins Game: Tom Lehman
Sun City Million Dollar Challenge: Nick Price (275)
Wendy's Three-Tour Challenge: PGA Tour (59 points)
Diner's Club Matches: PGA Tour—Steve Elkington/Jeff Maggert; Senior PGA Tour—Gil Morgan/Jay Sigel; LPGA—Dottie Pepper/Juli Inkster
Sarazen World Open Championship: Mark Calcavecchia (271)

PGA Tour. Woods, who came on the scene as the most highly touted new player since Jack Nicklaus, lived up to all expectations in the early going. He won the year's first tournament, the rain-shortened Mercedes Cham-pionships, in a one-hole play-off over Tom Lehman, then stunned the golf world with a record 12-stroke, 18-under-par victory in the Masters. The 21-year-old Woods added victo-ries at the GTE Byron Nelson Classic and the

Motorola Western Open, but he had only two top-ten finishes and no wins for the rest of the year. Still, his $2,066,833 in winnings was good for the PGA Tour money title and player-of-the-year honors.

His earnings mark barely surpassed that of the fast-closing David Duval, who won the first three titles of his three-year career in his last three events, including the rich season-ending Tour Championship. Duval finished second in the money race with $1,885,308. Davis Love III also had an outstanding year. Love, 33, won the PGA Championship at Winged Foot in Mamaroneck, NY, beating Justin Leonard with a dramatic final-round 66. Love led the Tour Championship in the final nine holes, but he faltered coming home and finished third. The winner's purse would have given him the money title over Woods.

Young players dominated the two remaining major championships. The 25-year-old Leonard fired a brilliant 65 on the last day to win the British Open at Royal Troon in Scotland. South Africa's Ernie Els, 27, won his second U.S. Open title in four years at the Congressional in Bethesda, MD.

Senior Tour. While Woods' earnings were a record for the PGA Tour, two players on the Senior PGA Tour surpassed him. Officially,

Irwin won a record-tying nine times and banked $2,343,364, the most money ever earned on any tour. That gave Irwin, whose victories included the PGA Seniors Championship, player-of-the-year honors. Close behind was Gil Morgan, who won six tournaments, starting with the Tradition, the first senior major. Morgan capped his year with a victory in the season-ending Energizer Senior Tour Championship, a triumph that boosted his year's earnings to $2,160,562.

In the other senior majors, Australian Graham Marsh survived a shoot-out with South African John Bland to win the U.S. Senior Open and Larry Gilbert won the Ford Senior Players Championship. Gilbert later was diagnosed with inoperable lung cancer, which he was battling at year's end. Other players on the tour also battled cancer during the year. Arnold Palmer and Jim Colbert both underwent successful surgery for prostate cancer, while Bruce Devlin was treated successfully for a cancerous kidney.

LPGA Tour. With a late-season play-off victory in the ITT LPGA Tour Championship, Sorenstam notched her sixth official win of 1997. Although she did not capture a major title, she earned the player-of-the-year award and won an LPGA record of $1,236,789.

Silver Charm (right) lost his bid to become the 12th Triple Crown champion as he was edged out at the wire by Touch Gold (center) at the 129th running of the Belmont Stakes on June 7, 1997. Free House (left) finished third.

HORSE RACING

Major U.S. Thoroughbred Races

Arkansas Derby: Crypto Star, $500,000
Arlington Million: Marlin, $1 million (total purse)
Belmont Stakes: Touch Gold, $721,000
Blue Grass Stakes: Pulpit, $700,000
Breeders' Cup Classic: Skip Away, $4 .4 million
Breeders' Cup Turf: Chief Bearhart, $1,832,000
Breeders' Cup Juvenile: Favorite Trick, $916,900
Breeders' Cup Juvenile Fillies: Countess Diana, $1, 030,000
Breeders' Cup Mile: Spinning World, $1,007,600
Breeders' Cup Distaff: Ajina, $916,000
Breeders' Cup Sprint: Elmhurst, $1,080,880
Champagne Stakes: Grand Slam, $400,000
Donn Handicap: Formal Gold, $300,000
Florida Derby: Captain Bodgit, $500,000
Haskell Invitational: Touch Gold, $1 million
Hollywood Gold Cup: Gentlemen, $1 million
Iselin Handicap: Formal Gold, $250,000
Jim Beam Stakes: Concerto, $600,000
Jockey Club Gold Cup: Skip Away, $1 million
Kentucky Derby: Silver Charm, $1 million
Kentucky Oaks: Blushing K.D., $584,700
Pacific Classic: Gentlemen, $1 million
Pegasus Handicap: Behrens, $1 million
Preakness Stakes: Silver Charm, $751,000
Santa Anita Derby: Free House, $750,000
Strub Stakes: Victory Speech, $500,000
Travers Stakes: Deputy Commander, $750,000

Woodbine Mile: Geri, $500,000
Wood Memorial: Captain Bodgit, $500,000
Woodward Stakes: Formal Gold, $500,000

Major North American Harness Races

Breeders Crown Open Pace: Extreme Velocity, $282,000
Breeders Crown Open Trot: Wesgate Crown, $540,000
Breeders Crown Mare Pace: Extreme Velocity, $282,500
Breeders Crown 2-year-old Filly Pace: Take Flight, $583,200
Breeders Crown 2-year-old Colt Pace: Artiscape, $665,145
Breeders Crown 2-year-old Filly Trot: My Dolly, $405,000
Breeders Crown 2-year-old Colt Trot: Catch as Catch Can, $405,000
Breeders Crown 3-year-old Filly Pace: Stienam's Place, $492,750
Breeders Crown 3-year-old Colt Pace: Village Jasper, $594,000
Breeders Crown 3-year-old Filly Trot: No Nonsense Woman, $438,750
Breeders Crown 3-year-old Colt Trot: Malabar Man, $594,000
Cane Pace: Western Dreamer, $540,000
Hambletonian: Malabar Man, $1 million
Hambletonian Oaks: Must Be Victory, $500,000
Little Brown Jug: Western Dreamer, $326,813
Meadowlands Pace: Dream Away, $1 million
Messenger Stakes: Western Dreamer, $331,300
Peter Haughton Memorial: Harry's Bar, $408,000
Sweetheart Pace: Clover Hanover, $604,800
Woodrow Wilson Pace: Real Artist, $765,750
World Trotting Derby: Lord Stormont, $565,000
Yonkers Trot: Lord Stormont, $291,948

Karrie Webb, a three-time winner, was second on the money list with $987,606. In the women's major championships, Betsy King won the Nabisco Dinah Shore, Chris Johnson won the McDonald's LPGA Championship, Alison Nicholas took the U.S. Women's Open in a down-to-the-wire fight with Nancy Lopez, and Colleen Walker captured the du Maurier Classic.

LARRY DENNIS
Founding Editor, "Senior Golfer" Magazine

Horse Racing

In the 1997 running of the $4.4 million Breeders' Cup Classic, Skip Away—which owners Sonny and Caroline Hine paid $480,000 to enter as a supplement—paid dividends by setting an event record with a time of 1:59 for 1.25 mi (2 km). The 4-year-old colt, ridden by jockey Mike Smith, beat a field of eight other horses by a Classic record of six lengths. The event was held at Hollywood Park in Inglewood, CA.

Favorite Trick made the $1 million Breeders' Cup Juvenile his eighth straight victory with a $5\frac{1}{2}$-length victory over the two longest shots in the field, Dawson's Legacy and Nationalore. Favorite Trick became the first 2-year-old champion to go unbeaten since Gilded Time won four races in 1992. The last time a 2-year-old won so many races was in 1952, when Native Dancer went nine for nine.

Smith also was aboard Ajina in her two-length victory over Sharp Cat in the $1 million Breeders' Cup Distaff. Ajina, owned by Allen and Madeline Paulson, failed to win in her

first four races of 1997, but trainer Bill Mott had the horse peaked for the $1\frac{1}{8}$-mile race. Chief Bearhart, 11th in the 1996 Breeders' Cup Turf, rebounded by winning the 1.5-mi (2.4-km) event by three quarters of a length over Borgia.

The Breeders' Cup Mile went to Spinning World, whose jockey, Cash Asmussen, ended a 20-race losing streak in Breeders' Cup events. Elmhurst, a 7-year-old gelding, came from last place under Corey Nakatani's whip to win the Breeders' Cup Sprint by a half length over Hesabull. Countess Diana won the Breeders' Cup Juvenile Fillies by $8\frac{1}{2}$ lengths over Career Collection.

Silver Charm beat Captain Bodgit by a head to win the 123d Kentucky Derby at Churchill Downs in Louisville, KY. He won over a field of 12 other three-year-olds in $2:02\frac{2}{5}$ for 1.25 miles (2 km). The win gave jockey Gary Stevens his third Derby victory. Free House was third. Silver Charm then edged Free House by a head to win the Preakness Stakes at Pimlico in Baltimore, MD, for owners Bob and Beverly Lewis. Silver Charm thus went to the Belmont Stakes in Elmont, NY, with a chance to become the 12th Triple Crown champion. But Touch Gold nipped Silver Charm at the wire to win the 1.5-mi (2.4-km) race in $2:28\frac{4}{5}$.

Harness Racing. Western Dreamer became the first pacer since 1983 to win harness racing's triple crown, taking top honors at the Little Brown Jug, Cane Pace, and Messenger Stakes. Malabar Man won the $1 million Hambletonian, the top event for trotters, and Dream Away took the Meadowlands Pace.

STAN SUTTON

Ice Hockey

The Detroit Red Wings ended a 42-year drought by taking the Stanley Cup championship in June 1997. They won the National Hockey League (NHL) crown with a smashing four-game sweep of the Philadelphia Flyers. It was the third consecutive season the finals were over in four games. In 1996, Colorado had blanked Florida, and the Wings had suffered the same fate as the Panthers in 1995, losing to New Jersey. In 1997, however, Detroit finished off a great run—losing only four play-off games in the four series it played. It was the seventh Stanley Cup for coach Scotty Bowman, with three different teams—Montreal, Pittsburgh, and Detroit. He was the first coach to accomplish that feat.

NHL Regular Season. Until the Wings' breakthrough, the big story of the season was Mario Lemieux, who, at the age of 31, announced his retirement after 12 seasons. Lemieux, who had been diagnosed with Hodgkins' disease in 1993 and missed the entire 1994–95 season, went on to win two of his six scoring championships after the illness (1996 and 1997). The Pittsburgh center finished his career with 1,494 points, sixth best in NHL history. He also was sixth in total goals, with 613 in only 745 games—the best ratio of goals to games of all time.

In a year when scoring was down significantly around the league, there was an all-time record set of 127 shutouts; the old record was 99. Lemieux won the scoring title with 122 points, the lowest total in 27 years. Hall of Fame defenseman Bobby Orr had 120 points in 1969–70. Only two players—Lemieux and Anaheim's Teemu Selanne (109)—had more than 100 points, the fewest number in 19 years. Phoenix captain Keith Tkachuk led the league with 52 goals. Only three others—Selanne (51), John LeClair of Philadelphia (50), and Lemieux (50)—reached that figure. The year before, eight players had done so. Three players—Pittsburgh's Joe Mullen, St. Louis' Brett Hull, and New Jersey's Dave Andreychuk—reached the magic 500-goal plateau. Mullen was the first U.S.-born player to obtain the milestone; in all, only 26 players have done so.

New Jersey's Martin Brodeur had ten shutouts and the lowest goal average (1.88) since Tony Esposito (1.77) in 1971–72. The reasons for lower scoring in the league ranged from better goaltending to more goals called back on a new wrinkle, video replay. If a player's skate was in the crease when the puck went into the net, it was disallowed. There also were few penalties called, lowering the number of power-play goals scored by the various teams.

Buffalo Sabres goalie Dominik Hasek scored a rare double in 1997—winning the Vezina Trophy as the NHL's best goalie as well as the Hart Trophy for most valuable player (MVP). His fellow players awarded him the Pearson Award for MVP as well.

Colorado won the Pacific Division with 107 points, the most of any team in the league and 22 points ahead of second-place Anaheim. Dallas took the Central Division with 104 points, while New Jersey edged Philadelphia by a point (104–103) to take the Atlantic. Buffalo was the surprise Northeast champ with 92 points. Boston missed the play-offs for the first time in 29 years.

Play-offs. The 1996 Stanley Cup–champion Colorado Avalanche went down to Detroit in the Western Conference final, continuing a trend. Only one team—Pittsburgh in 1992 and 1993—has repeated as champion since the Edmonton Oilers in 1987 and 1988. The team Colorado beat in the 1996 Stanley Cup finals, the Florida Panthers, was ousted in five games in the first round in the East by the New York Rangers.

There was one huge play-off upset when the Oilers, who had missed the play-offs in four consecutive years, knocked off the Dallas Stars in overtime in the seventh game of the first round in the West. The Oilers had finished with the seventh-best record of the regular season in the West, and the Stars, who had the second-best regular-season record in the division, had beaten them four straight times in league play. In other first-round Western matchups, the Avalanche got past Chicago in six games; Detroit beat St. Louis in six; and Anaheim, making its first-ever play-off appearance, squeaked past Phoenix in seven games. In the East, the Flyers bounced Lemieux's Penguins in five games; New Jersey took out Montreal in five; and Buffalo rallied to beat another first-time play-off team, Ottawa, in seven games.

In round two, Colorado ended the Oilers' play-off dream in five games; Avalanche winger Claude Lemieux's overtime goal in game four was the backbreaker against Edmonton. Detroit won three overtime games, including one that went to a third overtime before Slava Kozlov scored, and went on to oust Anaheim in four straight. In the East, the Flyers beat the Buffalo Sabres in five after Buffalo had to go without the league's most valuable player (MVP), Dominik Hasek, for three games when he was suspended for attacking a Buffalo columnist after a game. The New York Rangers shocked the New Jersey Devils in five, with Wayne Gretzky scoring a hat trick in one of the wins.

In the third round, the Avalanche were overwhelmed by the Wings. Colorado stole the first game on Patrick Roy's stellar goaltending and routed Detroit 6–0 in game five, but was no match for the determined Wings in

ICE HOCKEY

National Hockey League
(Final Standings, 1996–97)

Eastern Conference

Atlantic Division	W	L	T	Pts.	Goals For	Goals Against
*New Jersey	45	23	14	104	231	182
*Philadelphia	45	24	13	103	274	217
*Florida	35	28	19	89	221	201
*N.Y. Rangers	38	34	10	86	258	231
Washington	33	40	9	75	214	231
Tampa Bay	32	40	10	74	217	247
N.Y. Islanders	29	41	12	70	240	250

Northeast Division	W	L	T	Pts.	For	Against
*Buffalo	40	30	12	92	237	208
*Pittsburgh	38	36	8	84	285	280
*Ottawa	31	36	15	77	226	234
*Montreal	31	36	15	77	249	276
Hartford	32	39	11	75	226	256
Boston	26	47	9	61	234	300

Western Conference

Central Division	W	L	T	Pts.	Goals For	Goals Against
*Dallas	48	26	8	104	252	198
*Detroit	38	26	18	94	253	197
*Phoenix	38	37	7	83	240	243
*St. Louis	36	35	11	83	236	239
*Chicago	34	35	13	81	223	210
Toronto	30	44	8	68	230	273

Pacific Division	W	L	T	Pts.	For	Against
*Colorado	49	24	9	107	277	205
*Anaheim	36	33	13	85	245	233
*Edmonton	36	37	9	81	252	247
Vancouver	35	40	7	77	257	273
Calgary	32	41	9	73	214	239
Los Angeles	28	43	11	67	214	268
San Jose	27	47	8	62	211	278

*In play-offs

Stanley Cup Play-offs
Eastern Conference

Quarterfinals	Buffalo	4 games	Ottawa	3
	New Jersey	4 games	Montreal	1
	New York	4 games	Florida	1
	Philadelphia	4 games	Pittsburgh	1
Semifinals	New York	4 games	New Jersey	1
	Philadelphia	4 games	Buffalo	1
Finals	Philadelphia	4 games	New York	1

Western Conference

Quarterfinals	Anaheim	4 games	Phoenix	3
	Colorado	4 games	Chicago	2
	Detroit	4 games	St. Louis	2
	Edmonton	4 games	Dallas	3
Semifinals	Colorado	4 games	Edmonton	1
	Detroit	4 games	Anaheim	0
Finals	Detroit	4 games	Colorado	2

Stanley Cup Finals

Detroit   4 games   Philadelphia   0

Individual Honors

Hart Trophy (most valuable player): Dominik Hasek, Buffalo
Ross Trophy (leading scorer): Mario Lemieux, Pittsburgh
Vezina Trophy (top goaltender): Dominik Hasek
Norris Trophy (best defenseman): Brian Leetch, New York Rangers
Selke Trophy (best defensive forward): Mike Peca, Buffalo
Calder Trophy (rookie of the year): Bryan Berard, New York Islanders
Jennings Trophy (goals against average): Martin Brodeur and Mike Dunham, New Jersey
Lady Byng Trophy (most gentlemanly player): Paul Kariya, Anaheim
Conn Smythe Trophy (most valuable in play-offs): Mike Vernon, Detroit
Adams Award (coach of the year): Ted Nolan, Buffalo
King Clancy Trophy (humanitarian service): Trevor Linden, Vancouver
Bill Masterton Trophy (perseverance, sportsmanship, and dedication): Tony Granato, San Jose
Lester B. Pearson Award (outstanding player, voted by peers): Dominik Hasek

the other four games. Detroit avenged a six-game loss to Colorado in 1996, outshooting the Avalanche 42–16 in the final 3–1 win. In the East, Philadelphia's Eric Lindros had five goals in the final three games as the bigger

Flyers wore down the injury-riddled Rangers in five. Gretzky was New York's best player in the play-offs with 20 points—belying his age, 36. But Philadelphia won the last three games with Rod Brind'Amour helping Lindros with two goals in the final game.

Stanley Cup Finals. The Wings surprised the Flyers in Philadelphia in the first two games of the finals. Flyer goalie Ron Hextall, who had come under fire for poor play-off performances the previous few years, gave up a soft goal on a long slap shot by Wings captain Steve Yzerman in the first minute of the third period as Detroit held off a Flyer rally to win 4–2. In game two, it was the same story as Garth Snow, replacing Hextall, gave up a long shot to checker Kirk Maltby early in the second period to take the steam out of a Philadelphia comeback; Detroit won again, 4–2. In Detroit, the Wings defeated the Flyers 6–1 in the third game, with Sergei Fedorov scoring two goals and adding three assists. Detroit spotted the Flyers the first goal—by John LeClair—two minutes into the game, but roared back with six in a row. In the climax, Hextall gave up another weak goal, a long slap shot by Nicklas Lidstrom in the last minute of the first period, as the Wings went on to a 2–1 victory. So dominant was Detroit that the Flyers held the lead for a total of two of the 240 minutes played in the series.

Personnel Changes. Off the ice, it was a good winter and bad spring for coaches and general managers. Only two coaches, Pittsburgh's Eddie Johnston and St. Louis' Mike Keenan, were fired during the regular season. In the first six weeks after the season ended, however, Phoenix (Don Hay), Boston (Steve Kasper), San Jose (Al Sims), Washington (Jim Schoenfeld), Philadelphia (Terry Murray), and Anaheim (Ron Wilson) let their coaches go. In addition, Mario Tremblay (Montreal) and Pierre Page (Calgary) stepped down. In July, Lindy Ruff was named coach of the Buffalo Sabres. His predecessor, coach of the year Ted Nolan, had sought a long-term contract and rejected a one-year extension. The general managers—usually a very safe position in the NHL—saw their ranks thinned when David Poile (Washington), John Muckler (Buffalo), and Sam McMaster (Los Angeles) were terminated; Ron Caron (St. Louis) was reassigned after filling in when Keenan, who had the dual portfolio, was fired.

World Championships and NCAA. Canada captured its 21st World Ice Hockey Championship, with a 2–1 victory in a deciding third game against Sweden in May 1997. It was Canada's second championship in four years.

Earlier, Canada's women's team had defeated the United States in overtime to capture the World Women's Hockey Championship.

In the NCAA championship, the University of North Dakota won its first national crown in ten years—beating Boston University, 6–4. Boston had surprised the 1996 champion University of Michigan in the semifinals. Senior center Brendan Morrison of Michigan University won the Hobey Baker Award as the country's best college player.

JIM MATHESON, *"The Edmonton Journal"*

Ice Skating

In March 1997, Tara Lipinski, a 14-year-old from Houston, TX, became the youngest woman ever to win the World Figure Skating Championship. At the time of her triumph, Lipinski was one month younger than the legendary Sonja Henie of Norway had been when she won the first of her ten consecutive world titles in 1927. In capturing the world crown, Lipinski outskated runner-up Michelle Kwan of Torrance, CA, the 1996 world champion, and France's Vanessa Gusmeroli, who took the bronze. Earlier the 4'8" Lipinski had upset Kwan at the U.S. National Figure Skating Championships in Nashville, TN. Nicole Bobek, the 1995 U.S. champion, took the bronze.

In the men's competition, Todd Eldredge of Chatham, MA, won his fourth U.S. title but failed to repeat as the world champion. Canada's Elvis Stojko completed a superb, techni-

---

ICE SKATING

World Figure Skating Championships
Men: Elvis Stojko, Canada
Women: Tara Lipinski, United States
Pairs: Mandy Woetzel and Ingo Steuer, Germany
Dance: Oksana Gritschuk and Yevgeny Platov, Russia

U.S. National Figure Skating Championships
Men: Todd Eldredge
Women: Tara Lipinski
Pairs: Kyoko Ina and Jason Dungjen
Dance: Elizabeth Punsalan and Jerod Swallow

European Figure Skating Championships
Men: Alexei Urmanov, Russia
Women: Irina Slutskaya, Russia
Pairs: Marina Yeltsova and Andrei Bushkov, Russia
Dance: Oksana Gritschuk and Yevgeny Platov, Russia

Speed Skating World Cup—Final Points
Men's 500 meters: Hiroyasu Shimizu, Japan
Men's 1,000 meters: Manabu Horii, Japan
Men's 1,500 meters: Rintje Ritsma, Netherlands
Men's 5,000 meters/10,000 meters: Rintje Ritsma
Women's 500 meters: Ruihong Xue, China
Women's 1,000 meters: Franziska Schenk, Germany
Women's 1,500 meters: Gunda Niemann, Germany
Women's 3,000 meters/5,000 meters: Tonny de Jong, Netherlands

World Speed Skating Championships
Men's Overall: Ids Postma, Netherlands
Women's Overall: Gunda Niemann

---

victory in the slalom as well. The 26-year-old Swede, a former postal worker, was the only active skier to win races in all four Alpine World Cup disciplines.

Ending a successful 13-year skiing career, Hilary Lindh of Juneau, AK, captured the downhill and the super-giant slalom at the U.S. championships. Earlier the 27-year-old had won the downhill at the world championships. Tommy Moe, a fellow Alaskan, took the men's downhill and the super-giant slalom at the U.S. championships.

Italy's Deborah Campagnoni enjoyed a successful ski season, winning the World Cup giant slalom and the world championships' slalom and giant slalom. Utah repeated as the National Collegiate Athletic Association's ski champion.

Norway's Björn Dählie and Russia's Elena Välbe dominated 1997's Nordic competition.

© Jean-Loup Gautreau/Agence France Presse/Corbis-Bettmann

At 14, Tara Lipinski skated into the history books in 1997 by becoming the youngest woman to win the World Figure Skating (above) and the U.S. National Figure Skating championships.

cally demanding long program to edge Eldredge for the world crown. It was his third world title in four years. Aleksei Yagudin of Russia took the bronze medal at the world events; Michael Weiss of Washington, DC, and Dan Hollander of Royal Oak, MI, finished second and third, respectively, at the U.S. championships.

Speed Skating. Germany's veteran speed skater Gunda Niemann won an unprecedented sixth overall title at the World Speed Skating Championships in Japan. Ids Postma of the Netherlands clinched the men's overall title. Postma and Tonny de Jong, also of the Netherlands, took the men's and women's European all-around speed-skating championships, respectively, in January.

Skiing

In 1997, Luc Alphand, a 31-year-old father of two children who speaks five languages, became France's first skiing hero since Jean-Claude Killy. In 1968, Killy had won three Olympic gold medals and the overall World Cup title; 29 years later, Alphand took the World Cup downhill, super-giant slalom, and overall title. France's latest skiing hero announced in June, however, that he was retiring from competitive skiing.

Meanwhile, Pernilla Wiberg was the women's overall World Cup champion, with a

SKIING

Alpine World Cup

Men's Downhill: Luc Alphand, France
Men's Slalom: Thomas Sykora, Austria
Men's Giant Slalom: Michael Von Gruenigen, Switzerland
Men's Super-Giant Slalom: Luc Alphand
Men's Overall: Luc Alphand
Women's Downhill: Renate Goetschl, Austria
Women's Slalom:Pernilla Wiberg, Sweden
Women's Giant Slalom: Deborah Compagnoni, Italy
Women's Super-Giant Slalom: Hilde Gerg, Germany
Women's Overall: Pernilla Wiberg

Alpine U.S. Championships

Men's Combined: Chris Puckett, United States
Men's Downhill: Tommy Moe, United States
Men's Slalom: Martin Tichy, Czech Republic
Men's Giant Slalom: Sacha Gros, United States
Men's Super-Giant Slalom: Tommy Moe
Women's Combined: Carrie Sheinberg, United States
Women's Downhill: Hilary Lindh, United States
Women's Slalom: Kristina Koznick, United States
Women's Giant Slalom: Carrie Sheinberg
Women's Super-Giant Slalom: Hilary Lindh

Alpine World Championships

Men's Downhill: Bruno Kernen, Switzerland
Men's Slalom: Tom Stiansen, Norway
Men's Giant Slalom: Michael Von Gruenigen
Men's Super-Giant Slalom: Atle Skaardal, Norway
Men's Combined: Kjetil-Andre Aamodt, Norway
Women's Downhill: Hilary Lindh
Women's Slalom: Deborah Compagnoni
Women's Giant Slalom: Deborah Compagnoni
Women's Super-Giant Slalom: Isolde Kostner, Italy
Women's Combined: Renate Goetschl, Austria

NCAA Alpine Championships

Men's and Women's Team: University of Utah

Nordic World Championships

Men's 10 kilometers: Björn Dählie, Norway
Men's 15 kilometers: Björn Dählie
Men's 30 kilometers: Alexei Prokurorov, Russia
Men's 50 kilometers: Mika Myllylä, Finland
Men's Relay: Norway
Women's 5 kilometers: Elena Välbe, Russia
Women's 10 kilometers: Elena Välbe
Women's 15 kilometers: Elena Välbe
Women's 30 kilometers: Elena Välbe
Women's Relay: Russia
Jumping—90-m Hill: Janne Ahonen, Finland
Jumping—120-m Hill: Masahiko Harada, Japan
Jumping—Team: Finland
Combined Individual: Kenji Ogiwara, Japan
Combined Team: Norway

Nordic World Cup

Men's Overall: Björn Dählie
Women's Overall: Elena Välbe

Soccer

As 1997 drew to a close, the attention of soccer fans around the world was focused on the upcoming World Cup. In the United States, Major League Soccer (MLS) saw a successful close to its second season.

The 16th World Cup, the sport's quadrennial showpiece, was scheduled to take place in France for a month beginning in June 1998. The U.S. national team secured a bid to the 32-team tournament in November with a 3–0 defeat of Canada. The victory helped the U.S. squad clinch a second-place finish in regional competition behind Mexico.

International Play. In May new victors were crowned in each of the three most important European club competitions. Borussia Dortmund of Germany won the European Champions' Cup by upsetting defending champion Juventus of Turin, 3–1. In the Cup Winners Cup, Barcelona of Spain ended the reign of another defending champion, Paris–St. Germain, with a 1–0 victory. FC Schalke 04 of Germany defeated Italy's Inter Milan to win the Union of European Football Associations (UEFA) Cup. In South American club action, Cruzeiro of Brazil edged Peru's Sporting Cristal, 1–0, to win the Libertadores Cup.

In other international competition, Brazil won the Copa America in June with a 3–1 defeat over host Bolivia in the tournament finale. The win marked the fifth time that Brazil had captured the South American soccer championship. Earlier in the year, Mexico retained the U.S. Cup championship, an event in which the U.S. national team lost all three of its games and finished last.

Two biennial junior championships were held during 1997. In June, Argentina edged Uruguay, 2–1, to capture the under-20 world title, an event held in Kuala Lumpur, Malaysia. Three months later, Brazil defeated Ghana, 2–1, to take the under-17 world championship in Cairo, Egypt.

MLS. In the MLS championship game, which was played on October 27 before a sellout crowd of 57,431 at RFK Stadium in Washington, DC, the defending champions, D.C. United, defeated the upstart Colorado Rapids, 2–1. With one goal, United forward Jaime Moreno, the league's top goal-scorer in the regular season, was named the game's most valuable player (MVP). The game was viewed in more than 100 countries around the globe.

The league enjoyed a successful second season in 1997, despite a 16% drop in regular-season attendance from the previous year to an average of 14,616 fans per game. MLS officials announced the addition of two expansion teams, the Chicago Fire and the Miami Fusion, which would begin play in 1998. The league also inked a new six-year television contract guaranteeing the sport greater network exposure in years to come.

Women's Play. The U.S. squad swept Canada, Australia, and Italy in June to win the U.S. Cup championship. The dominating victory marked the third consecutive year that the U.S. women had won the tournament.

Collegiate Champions. In the National Collegiate Athletic Association (NCAA) men's-tournament final on December 14 in Richmond, VA, UCLA defeated Virginia, 2–0, for the title. One week earlier in Greensboro, NC, North Carolina had taken the women's crown by defeating Connecticut, 2–1.

GRAHAME L. JONES, *"Los Angeles Times"*

Swimming

Typically, post-Olympic years are slow in swimming, with established stars hanging up their suits and a new crop of youngsters struggling to rise to the top. But 1997 was anything but typical, with Olympians extending their careers and fireworks bursting both in and out of the pool.

Controversy raged anew around the drug issue when China's women reemerged to dominate the sport in October after two years in the doldrums. It flared again in December when three top Russian swimmers and a Brazilian tested positive for steroids. In Germany the trials of more than 100 former East German coaches, trainers, and physicians charged with administering steroids to their athletes grabbed headlines for months.

The Women. The dominant female swimmer was 1996 Olympic champion Claudia Poll of Costa Rica. At the Short Course (25-m pool) World Championships in Göteborg, Sweden, in April, Poll destroyed world records for the 200-m freestyle (1:54.17) and 400-m freestyle (4:00.03). The latter mark cut more than two seconds off the previous record. She remained unbeaten by repeating her triumphs at the year's most important long-course (50-m pool) meet, the Pan Pacific Championships, held in August in Japan.

Four other short-course world records were set by women in Göteborg. In the 100-m butterfly, Jenny Thompson of the United States raced to a time of 57.79, overtaking her teammate Misty Hyman in the final lap. Hyman earned some consolation by setting a world record for the 50-m butterfly (26.55) in the 100-m race. Chinese teams also set new marks in the 400-m freestyle relay (3:34.55) and 800-m freestyle relay (7:51.92). In November, Thompson erased Hyman's 50-m butterfly mark when she stroked 26.48 in a Toronto meet.

Two Chinese women—Chen Yan and Wu Yanyan—obliterated two long-course world records in October at the National Games in Shanghai; these achievements generated more accusations and suspicions than congratulations from other nations. Chen stroked the 400-m individual medley (IM) in 4:34.79, breaking the last mark set by an East German swimmer. Wu raced 2:09.72 in the last 200-m IM, carving almost two seconds off the old record. Neither woman had ranked in the top 50 in her event before the meet, and critics charged that they and other Chinese swimmers had been using performance-enhancing drugs. The Chinese athletes and their coaches denied the accusations.

The Men. Although the men's competition was fast and furious, only one world record was set during the year in long-course competition. In October, Australia's Michael Klim, 20, lowered the world mark for the 100-m butterfly to 52.15 seconds at the Australian swimming championships. Klim also ranked first globally in the 200-m freestyle.

Australia's Michael Klim celebrated after setting a world record of 52.15 seconds for the 100-m butterfly. The mark surpassed the one set by Russia's Denis Pankratov in 1996.

© Archives Photos

Lenny Krayzelburg of the United States, who emigrated from Ukraine and was naturalized as a U.S. citizen in 1995, twice broke the U.S. record in the 200-m backstroke during 1997. He set his second mark (1:57.87) while swimming to victory at Fukuoka. Also in August, Neil Walker cracked an 11-year-old U.S. record when he flew through the 100-m butterfly in 52.76. The old mark of 52.84 had been set by Pablo Morales in 1986.

At the European Championships in Seville, Spain, Russia's Alexander Popov demonstrated that he had recovered fully from a near-fatal stabbing in 1996, by winning his third straight European titles in both the 50-m and 100-m freestyle events.

Collegiate Championships. At the National Collegiate Athletic Association (NCAA) championship, the women's team from the University of Southern California (USC) edged Stanford for the team title. On the men's side, the team championship was captured by Auburn.

PHILLIP WHITTEN, *"Swimming World"*

Tennis

Martina Hingis and Pete Sampras looked down on their world from the heights with Number 1 rankings. A damaged knee limited the deposed top women's player, German Steffi Graf, to five tournaments. She won one title—upping her career total to 103—but suffered losses to Amanda Coetzer of South Africa in both majors she entered, the Australian and French.

In team competition, host Sweden humiliated a favored U.S. squad, 5–0, to take the Davis Cup for a sixth time. Sampras was forced to retire from the tournament due to a leg injury. On the women's side, Mary Pierce and Sandrine Testud powered France to its first Federation Cup title. France took the final with a 4–1 victory over the Netherlands, a team that dumped the reigning U.S. squad in the opening round.

The Women. Hingis, a Czechoslovak-born Swiss, became the youngest player to rise to a top ranking—achieving such eminence before her 17th birthday in September. She barely missed a Grand Slam, losing the French final—and a 41-match streak—in an upset by another teen, 19-year-old Iva Majoli of Croatia, 6–4, 6–2. But Hingis did collect 12 titles on a stunning 78–5 match record and captured the other three majors: the Australian over Pierce, 6–2, 6–2; Wimbledon over Czech Jana Novotna, 2–6, 6–3, 6–3; and the U.S. Open

© Gary M. Prior/Allsport

Martina Hingis, a 17-year-old Czechoslovak-born Swiss, dominated women's tennis in 1997, winning three major singles titles—the Australian Open, Wimbledon, and the U.S. Open.

over a startling Venus Williams, 6–0, 6–4. Williams, 17, became the all-time lowest ranked of U.S. Open finalists (Number 66).

TENNIS

Davis Cup: Sweden
Federation Cup: France

Major Tournaments
Australian Open—men's singles: Pete Sampras; men's doubles: Mark Woodforde (Australia) and Todd Woodbridge (Australia); women's singles: Martina Hingis (Switzerland); women's doubles: Martina Hingis (Switzerland) and Natasha Zvereva (Belarus); mixed doubles: Manon Bollegraf (Netherlands) and Rick Leach.
French Open—men's singles: Gustavo Kuerten (Brazil); men's doubles: Yevgeny Kafelnikov (Russia) and Daniel Vacek (Czech Republic); women's singles: Iva Majoli (Croatia); women's doubles: Gigi Fernandez and Natasha Zvereva (Belarus); mixed doubles: Rika Hiraki (Japan) and Mahesh Bhupathi (India).
Wimbledon—men's singles: Pete Sampras; men's doubles: Mark Woodforde (Australia) and Todd Woodbridge (Australia); women's singles: Martina Hingis (Switzerland); women's doubles: Gigi Fernandez and Natasha Zvereva (Belarus); mixed doubles: Cyril Suk (Czech Republic) and Helena Sukova (Czech Republic).
U.S. Open—men's singles: Patrick Rafter (Australia); men's doubles: Yevgeny Kafelnikov (Russia) and Daniel Vacek (Czech Republic); women's singles: Martina Hingis (Switzerland); women's doubles: Lindsay Davenport and Jana Novotna (Czech Republic); mixed doubles: Manon Bollegraf (Netherlands) and Rick Leach.

Important Tournaments
Lipton International Players Championships—men's singles: Thomas Muster (Austria); men's doubles: Mark Woodforde (Australia) and Todd Woodbridge (Australia); women's singles: Martina Hingis (Switzerland); women's doubles: Natasha Zvereva (Belarus) and Arantxa Sánchez Vicario (Spain).
Italian Open—men's singles: Alex Corretja (Spain); men's doubles: Mark Knowles (Bahamas) and Daniel Nestor (Canada); women's singles: Mary Pierce (France); women's doubles: Nicole Arendt and Manon Bollegraf (Netherlands).
ATP Finals—singles: Pete Sampras; doubles: Rick Leach and Jonathan Stark.
WTA Tour Championship—singles: Jana Novotna (Czech Republic); doubles: Lindsay Davenport and Jana Novotna (Czech Republic).
NCAA (Division I)—men's singles: Luke Smith (Australia), UNLV; men's doubles: Luke Smith (Australia) and Tim Blenkiron, UNLV; women's singles: Lilia Osterloh, Stanford; women's doubles: Dawn Buth and Stephanie Nickitas, Florida.

N.B. All players are from the United States unless otherwise noted.

The U.S. Open marked the opening of the new 22,547-seat Arthur Ashe Stadium, the centerpiece of a $300 million rejuvenation of Flushing Meadow, where record tennis crowds exceeding 500,000 congregated for the tournament. The Number 2 ranking went to Novotna, followed by Lindsay Davenport of the United States, who won six titles during the year.

The Men. Sampras, Number 1 since 1993, became the second man ever to earn five straight top rankings, tying fellow American Jimmy Connors. During 1997, Sampras racked up eight titles on a 55–12 record, among them two majors: a second Australian, over unseeded Carlos Moya, 6–2, 6–3, 6–3; and a fourth Wimbledon, over unseeded Frenchman Cedric Pioline. That lifted Sampras to ten majors, only two behind Australian legend Roy Emerson. Sampras, with 52 career titles, won the year-concluding ATP World Championship, beating Russian Yevgeny Kafelnikov, 6–3, 6–2, 6–2.

However, defender Sampras had been jolted earlier in the year in his quest for a fifth U.S. crown. He was upended in the fourth round by Czech lefty Petr Korda, 6–7 (4–7), 7–5, 7–6 (7–2), 3–6, 7–6 (7–3). That opened up the tournament for an unlikely but appealing attacking victor, 24-year-old Patrick Rafter, seeded 13th—the first Australian champ since John Newcombe won the tourney 24 years earlier. In a 6–3, 6–2, 4–6, 7–5 decision, Rafter—who finished the year at Number 2—overcame the huge serves of unseeded lefty Greg Rusedski, the first Briton in the final since 1936. Ranked Number 3 was Michael Chang of the United States, who finished the year with five tournament titles, a mark matched by Spaniard Felix Mantilla.

The year's most unlikely performance was the electrifying and nerveless play of Brazilian Gustavo Kuerten to win the French Open as an unseeded player. Ranked Number 66, Kuerten took the title in an unprecedented run through three champs: Thomas Muster (1995), defender Kafelnikov, and finally Sergi Bruguera (1993–94), 6–3, 6–4, 6–2.

See also BIOGRAPHY—*Sampras, Pete.*

BUD COLLINS, *"Boston Globe"/NBC*

Track and Field

Track fans were treated to another outstanding year in 1997.

Distance Records. The oldest record in track and field was eclipsed by Wilson Boit Kipketer of Denmark. The Kenyan-born Kipketer first tied Sebastian Coe's 16-year-old mark of 1:41.73 in July and then broke the record twice during August. For the latter mark, Kipketer ran 1:41.11 in Cologne, Germany, on August 24.

Haile Gebrselassie of Ethiopia captured a fleeting spot in the record books with impressive runs in two events. In the 10,000-m, he clocked 26:31.32 in July at the Bislett Games in Oslo, Norway, clipping nearly seven seconds off the year-old mark set by Salah Hissou of Morocco. The following month, Gebrselassie lowered his own 5,000-m record to 12:39.74 on August 22. That same day, his countryman Paul Tergat dropped the 10,000-m standard to 26:27.85.

The men's 3,000-m steeplechase record was broken twice during 1997. At Zurich, Kipketer ran the distance in 7:59.08, nipping the old mark set in 1995 by Moses Kiptanui of Kenya. The record took a larger hit in Cologne, where another Kenyan, Bernard Barmasai, lowered the standard to 7:55.72.

The Sprints. The year's most-publicized sprinting event was a 150-m duel between two Olympic champions—Michael Johnson of the United States and Donovan Bailey of Canada—for $1.5 million and bragging rights. In Atlanta, Bailey had set a world record of 9.84 for 100-m, while Johnson shattered the 200-m mark with a time of 19.32. Unfortunately, the June 1 race in Toronto, ON, settled little because Johnson slowed with a strained muscle as Bailey owned a slight lead, leaving the winner to claim his opponent had pulled up because he knew he would lose.

At the 1997 World Championships, held in Athens, Greece, two U.S. sprinters took the 100-m titles. Marion Jones took the women's race in 10.83, while Maurice Green beat all three medal winners from the 1996 Olympics with a time of 9.86. Both performances were the year's best in the event. In the 400-m dash, Michael Johnson ended a disappointing and injury-ridden year on an up note with a come-from-behind victory. Australia's Cathy Freeman captured the women's title in the event, becoming the first Aborigine to win a world championship.

In Berlin, Germany, U.S. sprinting legend Carl Lewis ran his last Grand Prix race. Lewis, winner of nine Olympic gold medals, anchored a 400-m relay team to victory, then proclaimed it a "fantastic farewell."

Field Record. The year's only field record was set in the women's hammer throw. In that event, Olga Kuzenkova of Russia upped the mark to 239′ 10″ (73.10 m) on June 22 in Munich, Germany. With a win in Athens,

Ukraine's legendary pole vaulter Sergei Bubka became the only person to win gold in each of the last six world championships.

Marathons. African marathon runners had a dominant year. In Boston, Lameck Aguta became the seventh consecutive Kenyan winner, with Fatuma Roba of Ethiopia winning the women's honors. In New York, Kenya's John Kagwe raced to victory, while Franziska Rochat-Moser of Switzerland took a controversial win. The year's best time was run by Khalid Khannouchi of Morocco, who raced the Chicago Marathon in 2:07:10, the fourth-fastest time in history for the distance.

STAN SUTTON

Yachting

A French team trimmed the round-the-world sailing record by more than three days in 1997. Sailing the 90-ft (27-m) trimaran *Sport-Elec*, a crew led by skipper Oliver de Kersauson circled the globe nonstop in 71 days, 14 hours, 22 minutes, and 8 seconds.

Other long-distance marks were set during the year. In the Transpac '97 competition—a 2,200-mi (3 500-km) race from Los Angeles to Honolulu, HI—new records were set in two classes. The French catamaran *Explorer* reached Hawaii in 5 days, 9 hours, slicing more than 30 hours off the two-year-old multihull mark. In the monohull division, the sloop *Pyewacket* finished the distance in 7 days, 15 hours, cutting about 15 hours off a record set a week earlier. A new standard also was set for the 153-mi (246-km) journey from Newport, RI, to New York City. A crew led by skipper Dawn Riley sailed the race in only 13 hours, 39 minutes, breaking the old mark by about seven hours.

In regatta competition, the 70-ft (21-m) sloop *Cynosure* raced to the fastest time in the Chicago-Mackinac Race, sailing the 333-mi (535-km) distance in 35 hours, 18 minutes. Due to handicap systems, however, two smaller craft won the event.

The celebrated Worrell 1000 race was revived in 1997 after an eight-year hiatus. The 1997 event, a 1,000-mi (1 600-km) journey from Florida to Virginia, was won by Randy Smyth and Jason Sneed on *Chick's Beach*.

Late in the year, attention in the sailing world was focused on the start of the quadrennial Whitbread Round the World Race. In September, ten boats began the grueling 36,365-mi (56 200-km) event, which was scheduled to end eight or nine months later.

PETER FLAX

SPORTS SUMMARIES[1]

ARCHERY—World Target Champions: men's Olympic bow: Kyung Ho Kim, South Korea; men's compound bow: Dee Wilde, Pocatello, ID; men's Olympic team: South Korea; women's Olympic bow: Du Ri Kim, South Korea; women's compound bow: Fabiola Palazzini, Italy; women's Olympic team: South Korea. **U.S. Intercollegiate Champions:** team: Texas A&M.

BADMINTON—U.S. Open: men's singles: Paul-Erik Hoyer-Larssen, Denmark; men's doubles: Dong Moon Kim and Tae Kwon Ho, South Korea; women's singles: Camilla Martin, Denmark; women's doubles: Young-Shu Tang and Yiyuan Qin, China; mixed doubles: D. Kim and Kyung Min Ra, South Korea. **World Champions:** men's singles: Peter Rasmussen, Denmark; men's doubles: Budiarto Sigit and Candra Wijawa, Indonesia; women's singles: Ye Zhaoying, China; women's doubles: Gu Jun and Gei Fi, China.

BEACH VOLLEYBALL—International Federation of Beach Volleyball (F.I.V.B.) World Champions: men's team: Para and Guilherme, Brazil; women's team: Sandra Pires and Jackie Silva, Brazil.

BIATHLON—World Champions: men's 10 k: Wilfried Pallhuber, Italy; men's 20 k: Ricco Gross, Germany; men's 12.5 k pursuit: Viktor Maigurov, Russia; men's 10 k team: Belarus; men's relay: Germany; women's 7.5 k: Olga Romasko, Russia; women's 15 k: Magdalena Forsberg, Sweden; women's 10 k pursuit: Magdalena Forsberg, Sweden; women's 7.5 k team: Norway; women's relay: Germany.

BILLIARDS—World Champions: men's 9-ball: Johnny Archer, Raleigh, NC; women's 9-ball: Allison Fisher, Charlotte, NC.

BOBSLEDDING—World Champions: 2-man: Reto Goetshi and Guido Acklin, Switzerland; 4-man: Germany (Wolfgang Hoppe).

BOWLING—Professional Bowlers Association Tour: Tournament of Champions: John Gant, Winston Salem, NC; PBA National Championship: Rick Steelsmith, Wichita, KS; PBA Senior Championship: Larry Laub, Tucson, AZ. **Ladies Professional Bowlers Tour:** Sam's Town Invitational: Kim Adler, Las Vegas, NV; International Bowling Congress Queens: Sandra Jo Odom, Coldwater, MI; Hammer Players Championship: Marianne Dirupo, Succasunna, NJ.

CANOEING—World Cup Slalom: men's canoe singles: Patrice Estanguet, France; men's canoe doubles: Frank Adisson and Wilfrid Forgues, France; men's kayak singles: Scott Shipley, United States; women's kayak singles: Irene Pavelkova, Czech Republic.

CASTING—World Champions: men's all-around: Steve Rajeff, Woodland, WA; women's all-around: Brenda Banks, St. Catharines, Ont. **U.S. Champions:** men's all-accuracy: Steve Rajeff; women's all-accuracy: Brenda Banks.

CAT SHOWS—The Cat Fanciers' Association, Inc.: Best cat: Grand Champion, National Winner Agonistes Commotion of Scrimshaw; Best kitten: Grand Champion, National Winner Becton's Queen-of-the-Desert.

CRICKET—The Ashes: Australia.

CROQUET—U.S. Croquet Association Champions: singles: Britt Ruby, Tyler, TX; doubles: John Osborn, Palm Beach, FL, and Mik Mehas, Palm Springs, CA.

CROSS-COUNTRY—World Champions: men: Paul Tergat, Kenya; women: Derartu Tulu, Ethiopia.

CURLING—World Champions: men: Peter Lindholm, Sweden; women: Sandra Schmirler, Canada.

CYCLING—Tour de France: Jan Ullrich, Germany; **World Cup:** overall: Michele Bartoli, Italy.

Ch. Parsifal Di Casa Netzer, a standard schnauzer who answers to the name "Pa," was judged best of show at the 1997 Westminster Kennel Club Dog Show in New York City. Rita Holloway and Gabrio Del Torre of Newark, DE, are the dog's owners.

© AP/Wide World Photos

DOG SHOWS—Westminster: best of show: Ch. Parsifal Di Casa Netzer, standard schnauzer, owned by Rita Holloway and Gabrio Del Torre, Newark, DE.

EQUESTRIAN—U.S. Champions: Grand Prix Dressage: Pikant, Shelly Francis, Woodstock, VT; Show Jumping: Imaginario, Beezie Patton, Cazenovia, NY; Three-day Event, Spring: Worth the Trust, Karen O'Connor, The Plains, VA; Three-day Event, Fall: Giltedge, David O'Connor, The Plains, VA.

FENCING—U.S. Champions: men's foil: Cliff Bayer, New York; men's saber: Terrence Lasker, Kansas City, MO; men's épée: John Normile, New York; women's foil: Iris Zimmerman, Rush, NY; women's épée: Jessica Burke, Pittsford, NY. **World Champions:** men's foil: Sergei Golubitsky, Ukraine; men's saber: Stanislaw Pozdniakov, Russia; men's épée: Eric Srecki, France; women's foil: Giovanna Trillini, Italy; women's épée: Miraide Garcia-Soto, Cuba; men's foil: Sergei Golubitsky, Ukraine; men's saber: Stanislaw Pozdniakov, Russia; men's épée: Eric Srecki, France; women's foil: Giovanna Trillini, Italy; women's épée: Miraide Garcia-Soto, Cuba. **NCAA:** team: Penn State.

FIELD HOCKEY—NCAA Division I: North Carolina. **World Champion:** men's champions trophy: Germany; women's champions trophy: Australia.

GYMNASTICS—World Champions: men's floor exercise: Aleksei Nemov, Russia; men's parallel bars: Zhang Jinjing, China; men's rings: Yuri Chechi, Italy; men's vault: Sergei Fedorchenko, Kazakhstan; men's pommel horse: Valeri Belenki, Germany; men's horizontal bar: Jani Tanskanen, Finland; men's all-around: Ivan Ivankov, Belarus; men's team: China; women's floor exercise: Gina Gogean, Romania; women's uneven bars: Svetlana Chorkina, Russia; women's balance beam: Gina Gogean; women's vault: Simona Amanar, Romania; women's all-around: Svetlana Chorkina; women's team: Romania. **NCAA:** men's all-around: Blaine Wilson, Ohio State; men's team: California; women's all-around: Kim Arnold, Georgia; women's team: UCLA.

HANDBALL—U.S. Handball Association: men's one-wall: Robert Sostre, New York; men's three-wall: Vincent Munoz, Commerce, CA; men's four-wall: Octavio Silveyra, Los Angeles; women's one-wall: Dori Ten, New York; women's three-wall: Allison Roberts, Chicago; women's four-wall: Lisa Fraser, Winnipeg.

HORSESHOE PITCHING—World Champions: men: Alan Francis, Defiance, OR; women: Beverly Nathe, St. Stephen, MN.

JAI ALAI—World Cup: Katxin and Barrondo, Spain.

JUDO—World Champions: men's 60 kg: Tadahiro Nomura, Japan; men's 65 kg: Kim Hyuk, South Korea; men's 71 kg: Kenzo Nakamura, Japan; men's 78 kg: In-chol Cho, South Korea; men's 86 kg: Ki-young Jeon, South Korea; men's 95 kg: Pavel Nastula, Poland; men's over 95 kg: David Douillet, France; men's open: Rafal Kubacki, Poland; women's 48 kg: Ryoko Tamura, Japan; women's 52 kg: Marie Claire Restoux, France; women's 56 kg: Isabel Fernandez, Spain; women's 61 kg: Severine Vandenhende, France; women's 66 kg: Kate Howey, Great Britain; women's 72 kg: Noriko Anno, Japan; women's over 72 kg: Christine Cicot, France; women's open: Dana Beltran, Cuba.

LACROSSE—NCAA Division I: men: Princeton; women: Maryland.

LUGE—World Champions: men: Georg Hackl, Germany; men's doubles: Tobias Schiegl and Markus Schiegl, Austria; team: Austria; women's singles: Susi Erdmann, Germany. **World Cup:** men's singles: Markus Prock, Austria; men's doubles: Chris Thorpe and Gordy Sheer, United States. **U.S. National Champions:** men's singles: Robert Pipkins, Bloomfield, NJ; women's singles: Maryann Baribault, La Canada, CA.

MODERN PENTATHLON—World Champions: men: Sebastien Deleigne, France; women: Yelizaveta Suvorova, Russia.

PADDLEBALL—U.S. Champions: men's open: Bob Groya, Bay City, MI; men's open doubles: Andy Mitchell and Andy Kasalo, Kalamazoo, MI; men's seniors: Gene McNabb, Ann Arbor, MI; women's open doubles: Sue Smith and Linda Brzezinski, Warsaw, WI.

PADDLE TENNIS—U.S. Champions: men's singles: Scott Freedman, Venice, CA; men's doubles: Sol Hauptman, Los Angeles, and Scott Freedman; mixed doubles: Scott Freedman and Ingrid Fields, Los Angeles.

POLO—U.S. Open: Isla Carroll, Atlanta.

RACQUETBALL—U.S. Champions: men: Dan Obremski, Pittsburgh; women: Michelle Gould, Boise, ID.

RODEO—Professional Rodeo Cowboys Association: world champion: Dan Mortensen, Manhattan, MT; steer wrestling: Brad Gleason, Ennis, MT; bull riding: Scott Mendes, Weatherford, TX; calf roping: Cody Ohl, Orchard, TX; saddle bronc riding: Dan Mortensen.

ROWING—World Champions: men's pair with coxswain: United States; men's double sculls: Germany; men's four: Great Britain; men's pair: France; men's single: United States; women's double sculls: Germany; women's four: Great Britain; women's pair: Canada; women's single: Belarus.

RUGBY—U.S. Champions: men's club: Gentlemen of Aspen, Aspen, CO; women's club: Berkeley Blues, Berkeley, CA.

SHOOTING—U.S. National Pistol Champions: men's air: Daryl Szarenski, Fort Benning, GA; men's rapid fire: Stan Hayes, Dallas; men's standard: Jerry Wilder, Lowell, IN; women's air: Elizabeth Callahan, Upper Marlboro, MD; women's sport: Elizabeth Callahan.

SLED DOG RACING: Iditarod: Martin Buser, Big Lake, AK; Yukon Quest: Rick Mackey, Nenana, AK.

SOFTBALL—U.S. Champions: men's major fast pitch: Green Bay All-Car; men's major slow pitch: Long Haul/TPS, Albertville, MN; women's major fast pitch: California Commotion, Woodland Hills, CA; women's major slow pitch: Taylor's, Glendale, MD.

TABLE TENNIS—World Champions: men's singles: Jan-Ove Waldner, Sweden; men's doubles: Kong Linghui and Liu Guoliang, China; men's team: China; women's singles: Deng Yaping, China; women's doubles: Deng Yaping and Yang Ying, China; women's team: China; mixed doubles: Liu Guoliang and Wu Na, China.

TEAM HANDBALL—World Champions: men: Russia; women: Denmark.

TRIATHLON—World Champions: men: Chris McCormack, Australia; men's ironman: Thomas Hellriegel, Germany; women: Emma Carney, Australia; women's ironman: Heather Fuhr, Canada.

VOLLEYBALL—International Champions: men's World League: Italy; women's Grand Prix: Russia. **NCAA Division I:** men: Stanford; women: Stanford.

WATER POLO—World Cup: men: United States; women: Netherlands.

WEIGHT LIFTING—U.S. Champions: men's 54 kg: Shelton Gilyard; men's 59 kg: Brian Okada; men's 64 kg: Bryan Jacob; men's 70 kg: Oscar Chaplin III; men's 76 kg: Tim McRae; men's 83 kg: Kevin Dittler; men's 91 kg: David Conragan; men's 99 kg: Tom Gough; men's 108 kg: Wes Barnett; men's 108 kg-plus: Shane Mamman; women's 46 kg: Andrea Lyons; women's 50 kg: Tara Nott; women's 54 kg: Melanie Pritchard; women's 59 kg: Christina Wilson; women's 64 kg: Lea Rentmeester; women's 70 kg: Cara Heads; women's 76 kg: Khadijah Hunter; women's 83 kg: Vikki Scaffe; women's 83 kg-plus: Decia Stenzel.

WRESTLING—World Champions: freestyle: men's 119 lbs: Wilfredo Garcia Quintana, Cuba; men's 127.75 lbs: Mohammad Talaee, Iran; men's 138.75 lbs: Abbas Haji Kenari, Iran; men's 152 lbs: Araik Gevorkian, Armenia; men's 167.5 lbs: Buvaisar Saitiev, Russia; men's 187.25 lbs: Les Gutches, Corvallis, OR; men's 213.75 lbs: Kuramagomed Kuramagomedov, Russia; men's 286 lbs: Zekeriya Guclu, Turkey; men's team: Russia; women's 101.25 lbs: Zhong Xiue, China; women's 112.25 lbs: Joanna Piasecka, Poland; women's 123.25 lbs: Anna Gomis, France; women's 136.5 lbs: Lisa Golliot, France; women's 149.75 lbs: Christine Nordhagen, Canada; women's 165.25 lbs: Kyoko Hamaguchi, Japan; men's team: Japan.

---

[1]Sports for which articles do not appear in pages 468–97.

SRI LANKA

The Sri Lankan economy improved in 1997, while constitutional reform stagnated and the 14-year-old ethnic conflict between the mainly Buddhist Sinhalese speakers and the mainly Hindu Tamil speakers wore on. The People's Alliance government under the leadership of President Chandrika Bandaranaike Kumaratunga continued to combine military action with promotion of its plan to devolve power to the regions. In October the Liberation Tigers of Tamil Eelam (LTTE) set off a truck bomb in Colombo, killing 18 and injuring 110—mostly foreigners. At the halfway point in its electoral term, the government sought ways of winning support from Tamil civilians.

The Civil War. After fierce fighting over military bases early in the year, the government launched a major offensive on May 13 in the Vanni region to control highway access to the Jaffna peninsula. During the next five months, some 1,500 to 2,500 were killed and 7,500 wounded on both sides. The Sri Lankan army's commander, Maj. Gen. Lionel Balagalle, appointed the year before, emphasized a policy of curbing human-rights abuses as part of a strategy to win back Tamil "hearts and minds," but in December the army suffered a major setback in heavy fighting. Although the LTTE appeared to have widespread support, it was not clear how much was from fear of retaliation. Some LTTE raids involved women and children as young as 10. The LTTE was accused of assassinating more than 20 political leaders, some from within its own ranks.

Politics. In January, Minister of Justice and Constitutional Affairs and Deputy Finance Minister Gamini Lakshman Peiris announced the government's intention to act on a devolution plan for a union of regions, which had been bottled up in committee since January 1996. In April the government—which had retained support in the local March elections—together with the United National Party (UNP) opposition, announced a bipartisan approach to resolving the ethnic conflict. In July the state of emergency imposed 15 months before was lifted in some areas, and in October, despite opposition from Buddhist clergy, Peiris announced that the government would push ahead with a realignment referendum in two eastern districts. The plan would join part of the districts to the Tamil-speaking north, while part would become a Muslim-majority region and the remainder would be merged with the Sinhalese-speaking Uva province in south-central Sri Lanka.

Economy. The economic situation—which was particularly bad in 1996—improved considerably in 1997, due to improved agricultural production, continued privatization, and large investments from international companies. The stock market—from its low in February at less than half the 1994 peak—was up sharply by May. By September, after privatizing 23 tea estates, Sri Lanka was poised to regain its position as the world's top tea exporter. Tonnage handled in Colombo's port was up; tourism was recovering; and the growth rate rose to about 6%. The top focus of foreign investment and earner of foreign exchange was the garment industry, which was accused of sweatshop practices involving women. Second in foreign exchange were the remittances from migrant workers overseas, including 700,000 in the Middle East, mainly women domestics. There also was an unpopular increase in the price of bread.

Foreign Affairs. The U.S. listing of LTTE as a terrorist organization in October—a designation for which Sri Lankans had lobbied for some time—was expected to restrict the LTTE's ability to raise support from Tamils living in the United States. In India, where the national government had outlawed the LTTE six years earlier, after the assassination of Prime Minister Rajiv Gandhi, accusations that the Tamil Nadu state government had been too supportive of the LTTE led to the fall of the national coalition government in late November. Sri Lanka continued to participate in meetings of the South Asian Association for Regional Cooperation (SAARC) and to deal with a variety of trade and immigration issues with India. In the United Nations (UN), Sri Lanka remained neutral on the issue of support for a permanent Indian seat on an expanded Security Council until the Non-Aligned Movement decides on an Asia nominee.

LELAH DUSHKIN, *Kansas State University*

SRI LANKA • Information Highlights

Official Name: Democratic Socialist Republic of Sri Lanka.
Location: South Asia.
Area: 25,332 sq mi (65 610 km²).
Population (mid-1997 est.): 18,700,000.
Chief Cities (mid-1990 est.): Colombo, the capital, 615,000; Dehiwala–Mount Lavinia, 196,000; Moratuwa, 170,000.
Government: *Head of state,* C.B. Kumaratunga, president (took office November 1994). *Head of government,* S. Bandaranaike, prime minister (appointed November 1994). *Legislature* (unicameral)—Parliament.
Monetary Unit: Rupee (59.422 rupees equal U.S.$1, market rate, July 1997).
Gross Domestic Product (1995 est. U.S.$): $65,600,000,-000 (purchasing power parity).
Economic Index (Colombo, 1996; 1990 = 100): *Consumer Prices,* all items, 189.0; food, 193.2.
Foreign Trade (1996 U.S.$): *Imports,* $5,412,000,000; *exports,* $4,095,000,000.

STAMPS AND STAMP COLLECTING

The first U.S. postage stamps, a 5-center featuring Benjamin Franklin and a 10-center depicting George Washington, were issued in 1847. To commemorate their 150th anniversary, the United States Postal Service (USPS) in 1997 produced two souvenir sheets containing reproductions of those stamps, but with new denominations: 50¢ and 60¢, respectively. The new stamps made their debut at Pacific '97, an international stamp exhibition held in San Francisco to mark the anniversary year, and were among 112 stamps and six postal cards issued by USPS in 1997.

It was a "monster" stamp year in 1997, both in the United States and abroad. USPS issued five Classic Movie Monsters stamps depicting actors in their best-known roles: Dracula, Frankenstein's monster, the Mummy, the Phantom of the Opera, and the Wolf Man. Dracula glowered out from stamps issued by Great Britain, Ireland, Romania, and Sierra Leone, as well. Hollywood also provided USPS with the subjects for a Bugs Bunny stamp—the first U.S. stamp to honor a cartoon character—and a stamp depicting actor Humphrey Bogart.

Several U.S. sets in addition to the Monsters featured multiple designs on a single sheet. These included 15 different dinosaur stamps that could be punched out of two miniature murals depicting prehistoric landscapes, 20 different classic American aircraft, and 15 classic American dolls.

Canada's 1997 stamp issues included blocks of four depicting saltwater fish and

Courtesy, U.S. Postal Service

scenic highways, and a picture of the new Confederation Bridge to Prince Edward Island. The United States and Sweden produced their first-ever triangular stamps. The U.S. triangles were a pair of commemoratives publicizing Pacific '97, while Sweden's were a set of six depicting elks. Hong Kong issued a set of "farewell" stamps June 30—the day before its transfer from British to Chinese control—that were valid for that day only. The death of Britain's Princess Diana in August brought a large number of memorial stamp issues from around the world.

As always, there were innovations in stamp technology. USPS issued two experimental self-adhesive coil stamps that had no backing paper and peeled off their rolls like tape. The Netherlands issued a set of "surprise" stamps with heart designs that the recipient could scratch off, revealing one of ten different messages. For the sender's benefit, each stamp's inscription was printed on a piece of detachable selvage.

GEORGE AMICK
Author, "Linn's U.S. Stamp Yearbook"

SELECTED U.S. STAMPS FOR 1997

Subject	Denomination	Date
Year of the Ox	32¢	Jan. 5
Benjamin O. Davis, Sr.	32¢	Jan. 28
Love Swans	32¢ & 55¢	Feb. 4
Helping Children Learn	32¢	Feb. 18
Merian Botanical Prints	32¢	March 3
Pacific '97 (triangles)	32¢	March 13
Thornton Wilder	32¢	April 17
Raoul Wallenberg	32¢	April 24
The World of Dinosaurs	32¢	May 1
Bugs Bunny	32¢	May 22
1847 Benjamin Franklin	50¢	May 29
1847 George Washington	60¢	May 30
Marshall Plan	32¢	June 4
Classic American Aircraft	32¢	July 19
Legendary Football Coaches	32¢	June 25
Classic American Dolls	32¢	July 28
Humphrey Bogart	32¢	July 31
The Stars and Stripes Forever	32¢	Aug. 21
Opera Singers	32¢	Sept 10
Classical Composers and Conductors	32¢	Sept. 12
Padre Felix Varela	32¢	Sept. 15
U.S. Air Force	23¢	Sept. 18
Classic Movie Monsters	32¢	Sept. 30
Supersonic Flight	32¢	Oct. 14
Kwanzaa	32¢	Oct. 22

States, U.S.

During 1997 the governorships of Arizona and Massachusetts changed hands due to resignations; Virginians chose a new chief executive; and New Jersey saw its incumbent governor barely reelected. Several big cities held mayoralty races, with many incumbents being returned. Educational funding, abortion, and gambling were major state issues, and capital punishment was implemented more widely. The economy generally was good. Record flooding caused heavy damage in various regions.

ALABAMA. The opening in 1997 of a new Mercedes-Benz AG sport-utility plant that would employ up to 1,500 people was viewed as an opportunity for economic renewal. Ancillary businesses resulted in 1,500 additional jobs. The plant also was expected to help improve the state's image. Former Gov. Guy Hunt was pardoned by the Alabama Board of Paroles and Pardons for his 1993 criminal conviction on charges of stealing $200,000 from a tax-free inaugural fund and using the money for personal items. Redding Pitt, the U.S. attorney in Montgomery, said he would ask a federal grand jury to look into Hunt's pardon application.

Health and Environmental Issues. President Bill Clinton officially apologized to family members of 399 black men from Tuskegee whose syphilis went untreated for decades as part of a federal study. The study was under-taken by the U.S. Public Health Service, which was observing the long-term effects of syphilis.

The Pittsburgh-based USX Corp. agreed to pay $2.75 million to clean up hazardous wastes it allegedly disposed of at its U.S. Steel plant near Birmingham.

Crime. Three men were executed in Alabama, bringing to 15 the number of people put to death there since the U.S. Supreme Court reinstated the death penalty in 1976. Walter Leroy Moody was sentenced to death for the 1989 mail-bomb killing of a federal judge, Robert S. Vance of the U.S. 11th Circuit Court of Appeals.

Other News. A U.S. District Court judge who was nominated to the U.S. Court of Appeals was found by the *Birmingham News* to have lied about his past. He had claimed he was the James Ware whose brother Virgil died in his arms after being shot by two teens in Birmingham in 1963. That James Ware, however, was actually a coal-company worker....A state judge garnered the backing of thousands on the Christian right as he fought for the right to display the Ten Commandments in his courtroom. Circuit Court Judge Roy Moore had been ordered to remove the plaque. Among his supporters was Republican Gov. Fob James, Jr.

KRISTI VAUGHAN

ALASKA. Laws dealing with abortion, child abuse, and teenage smoking were prominent issues in Alaska during 1997.

Legislation. In May, Gov. Tony Knowles vetoed two bills that would have restricted abortions, saying the bills were "clearly unconstitutional" and claiming they would "infringe on the choice and rights of Alaska women." The

As in any year, education issues were a major concern for the U.S. states in 1997. In August women enrolled at the Virginia Military Institute (VMI) for the first time. The U.S. Supreme Court had ordered VMI in 1996 to end its single-sex admissions policy.

© Andres R. Alonso

bills called for a ban on most late-term abortions and parental or judicial consent for minors seeking abortions.

Citing Alaska's "shameful distinction" of leading the nation in child abuse, Knowles, a Democrat, called for a $32 million-per-year program to promote the health and care of children. Included in the expenditures were $7 million to provide health insurance for children of low-income families who were not eligible for Medicaid. "This is not welfare," the governor said. "This is supporting working families."

The Alaska House of Representatives agreed to impose the nation's highest cigarette tax, at $1 per pack. Supporters said the tax—which boosted the cost of cigarettes to about $3—would help keep youngsters out of the tobacco market. Opponents preferred stricter enforcement of laws as a better way to reduce teenage smoking.

Other News. The U.S. Forest Service authorized extensive new logging in the Tongass National Forest, the nation's last expanse of old-growth temperate rain forest. The authorization—less than loggers wanted but more than environmental groups liked—called for cutting approximately 240 million board feet annually, enough to build 20,000 new homes.

In a move that seemed to pit the state against the federal government, Knowles said he planned to take the statehood-compact case to the U.S. Supreme Court. The suit, which seeks to allow Alaska to keep its 90% share of revenues from mineral leasing on federal lands, was rejected by the U.S. Court of Appeals in July. "The compact case seeks to uphold the very terms that were agreed to when Alaska joined the union," Knowles said. "A deal is a deal."

BRUCE JACOBY

ARIZONA. Secretary of State Jane Dee Hull, 62, succeeded to the governorship following the resignation of Gov. Fife Symington, 52. Hull, a Republican, as is Symington, was first in line of succession. On September 5, Symington was convicted of bank fraud for business dealings that occurred before he became governor in 1991. Hull, a former teacher who served as speaker of the House before her 1994 election as secretary of state, was expected to run for a full four-year term as governor in 1998.

Legislation. The regular session of the legislature, which adjourned in April, increased funding for education by $239 million for fiscal 1998, to a total level of $2.9 billion for kindergarten through university levels. A new program would reward all public-school teachers with quarterly bonuses based on the percentage of children who test well and on parental rankings of the schools. New crime laws treated violent juveniles as adults and required adult prisoners to complete their terms. The session passed a $110 million income-tax reduction, and the 1997 budget year ended with a surplus.

In other action, a state court in August rejected the school-finance plan passed in the April session. The legislature was required to come up with a constitutional school-aid plan by June 30, 1998, under a 1994 state Supreme Court ruling. In a November special session, the legislature agreed to have the state pick up more of the cost for long-term health care for the poor and disabled elderly. Counties had complained that they had to pay the entire $149 million required in order to receive $300 million in federal funds for the program. The state agreed to pay $5.7 million in the 1998 fiscal year and $103 million by fiscal 2006–07.

Arizona began implementing welfare reforms required by a 1996 federal law. State officials said that 4,176 of 5,500 Arizona mothers on welfare did not respond to letters warning them of a 25% cut in benefits unless they participated in job training or looked for work.

A federal judge in October struck down an Arizona law, passed in April, to ban partial-birth abortions. The court ruled the law violated a woman's right to abortion.

Other News. Rep. Jeff Groscost was elected the new speaker of the state House of Representatives by the Republican majority caucus on October 20. He replaced Don Aldridge, who resigned for health reasons....The University of Arizona basketball team beat the University of Kentucky to win the NCAA championship, 84–79 in overtime.

ELAINE STUART

ARKANSAS. The involvement of several Arkansas residents in the so-called "Whitewater affair" continued to dominate the news in 1997 as James B. McDougal, a former partner of President Bill Clinton in the Whitewater Development Corp., was sentenced to three years in federal prison for obtaining about $3 million in fraudulent loans in the mid-1980s. McDougal's former wife, Susan, and former Arkansas Gov. Jim Guy Tucker previously were sentenced for their roles. Clinton, meanwhile, chose the Little Rock campus of the University of Arkansas as the site of his presidential library.

Crime and Legal Issues. Arkansas officials carried out four executions, bringing to 15 the number of people executed in the state since the U.S. Supreme Court reinstated the death penalty in 1976. Three of those executions occurred on the same day, which state officials said was more efficient.

The U.S. Supreme Court heard arguments on whether public-television stations had the right to exclude lesser-known candidates for political debates on their stations.

Race Relations. President Clinton used a ceremony marking the 40th anniversary of the integration of public schools in Arkansas as the kickoff point for a renewed drive to improve U.S. race relations. The September 25 ceremony paid tribute to the nine black students who entered Little Rock's Central High School after the outlawing of racial segregation in U.S. public schools.

Disasters. Tornadoes killed at least 25 people in early March, while associated rains, floods, and tornadoes caused hundreds of millions of dollars in crop damage. Three firefighters were killed in a chemical explosion in West Helena as they were fighting a fire at the BPS plant.

KRISTI VAUGHAN

CALIFORNIA. In August 1997, California lawmakers approved legislation to implement the federal welfare law passed in 1996. That same month, after a seven-week impasse, Gov. Pete Wilson signed the state's $69.6 billion budget into law, while a ban on hiring and contracting preferences went into effect. A weeklong San Francisco transit strike in October was settled, giving workers a onetime lump sum of $3,000 and a 4% raise each year from 1998–2000.

Legislation. In August the state's ten-year-old law requiring teenage girls to get the approval of a parent or judge before having an abortion was overturned. California's legislative term-limit initiative, approved by 51% of the voters in 1990, was struck down on October 7 because voters had not been notified it would be a lifetime ban. In December the California Board of Education endorsed math standards for elementary- and high-school students that emphasized the importance of basic computational skills. A law banning cigarette smoking in bars, casinos, and nightclubs across the state went into effect Jan. 1, 1998; it was the toughest such law in the United States.

Other News. Dismissed state-highway employee Arturo Reyes Torres, 43, opened fire at his former workplace on December 18, killing four and injuring three before he was killed by police in a fierce gun battle. In September former high-school track coach Tony L. Ran-

In San Francisco, the American Conservatory Theater's production of "A Streetcar Named Desire" featured Marco Barricelli (left) as Stanley Kowalski and Sheila Kelley as Blanche DuBois. Fifty years earlier, the Tennessee Williams classic first opened on Broadway.

som, 37, was charged with the rape, robbery, and assault of four Oakland-area women.

Two veteran California Democratic representatives, Vic Fazio and Ronald V. Dellums, announced they would retire from the U.S. House of Representatives. In April, Los Angeles Mayor Richard Riordan was reelected overwhelmingly to a second term.

JOSEPH FERGUSON

COLORADO. From the 1996 JonBenet Ramsey murder—still unsolved—to the trial of Terry Nichols for his part in the Oklahoma City bombing, crime in Colorado made headlines during 1997.

Crime. Developments in the Ramsey case included a vow by the victim's father, John B. Ramsey, to intensify his family's independent investigation, even as Boulder District Attorney Alex Hunter said that Ramsey and his wife, Patricia, continued to be the focus of the official probe into the murder of the 6-year-old participant in children's beauty pageants. Meanwhile, Nichols was found guilty of conspiracy to commit terrorism, but was acquitted on the more serious charges of murder and the actual terrorist act.

Denver suffered a spate of hate killings; during one horrific week in November, attacks on civilians and police by skinheads left two people dead, one paralyzed, and parts of the city under siege. In a case featured in *Time* magazine, 19-year-old Nathan Thill shot and killed Mauritanian immigrant Oumar Dia, claiming after his arrest, "In a war, everyone wearing an enemy uniform is an enemy and should be taken out." Dia's "uniform" was apparently the color of his skin.

Gary Lee Davis, 53, became the first man executed in Colorado in 30 years. Davis and his wife, Rebecca, had been convicted of the 1986 murder of Virginia May, who

was abducted from her home in front of her two small children, raped, and shot 14 times. Rebecca Davis was sentenced to life in prison.

Summit of the Eight. The first Summit of the Eight met in Denver in June. Formerly known as the Group of Seven (G-7), this annual gathering of leaders from the world's major industrialized nations changed its name to accommodate the newest member, Russia. The other seven are the United States, England, Japan, France, Germany, Italy, and Canada.

BRUCE JACOBY

CONNECTICUT. Politics and the criminal courts vied for headlines in Connecticut during 1997.

Politics. Nine-term Democratic U.S. Congresswoman Barbara Kennelly announced her intention to leave Washington and run for governor in 1998; independent polls in June showed her in a dead heat with her presumed opponent, incumbent Republican John G. Rowland.

Rowland, meanwhile, claimed a huge political victory when he pushed through the Democratic House and Senate a two-year, $21 billion budget that included tax cuts and reductions in the state workforce. In April he suffered a public-relations setback, however, when he admitted to violating an ethics law by accepting tickets to six rock-music concerts; most of the tickets came from a lobbyist.

Kelly Trial. The story that captured front-page attention throughout the country was the retrial and conviction of Alex Kelly, a 30-year-old former high-school wrestling star. Accused in 1986 of raping a teenage girl, Kelly had fled the country on the eve of his trial. He lived abroad for eight years, traveling from one ski resort to another, apparently financed by his wealthy parents.

Kelly surrendered in Switzerland in 1995 as his passport was about to expire. Refusing a plea bargain that would have given him seven to eight years behind bars, Kelly was tried in 1996, but the trial ended in a hung jury. This time, though, a jury of three men and three women took only nine hours to reach a guilty verdict. Kelly was sentenced to 16 years and was denied bail while he awaited yet another trial, this time for a second rape allegedly committed only days after the first.

BRUCE JACOBY

DELAWARE. Delaware was cited for several environmental problems during 1997.

Environmental Issues. Scientists were trying to determine what was causing outbreaks of a microbe, *Pfiesteria piscicida*, that had killed thousands of fish in states from North Carolina to Delaware. Six states had joined together to share research on the toxic organism....Federal officials required a prominent development firm, Pettinaro Construction Co. of Newport, to restore 18 acres (7 ha) of wetlands it destroyed when building a 420-acre (170-ha) housing development. A $60,000 penalty was also levied....Delaware was one of 22 states told by the federal Environmental Protection Agency to reduce its nitrogen oxide emissions from coal-burning power plants.

Congressional Spending. Several U.S. congressional spending bills of 1997 were expected to help Delaware. These included an Amtrak reform bill that preserved the Wilmington station and the jobs of nearly 1,000 residents. Also benefiting Delaware were three military-construction projects, a beach-reconstruction project, a new Job Corps Center, $4 million to help study the causes of the *P. piscicida* outbreak, repayment for the new bridge over the Chesapeake & Delaware Canal, and $1.5 million toward a bus-maintenance facility.

Economy. A rejuvenated Delaware Park offered competition to the Pimlico racetrack in nearby Baltimore. Competition was especially strong because Delaware Park included slot machines and had earmarked a portion of the slot revenue toward racing purses.

Delaware's welfare reforms resulted in 20% fewer people on welfare. The 1995 reform law limited assistance to two years and did not offer an increase in benefits for children born after their parent had been in the program for ten months or more. It also required recipients to attend job-training and parenting classes.

KRISTI VAUGHAN

FLORIDA. Airline mishaps, political corruption, and the murder of a prominent fashion designer grabbed Florida's headlines in 1997.

Politics. Former Miami Mayor Xavier Suárez regained power in a runoff election against Mayor Joe Carollo, who claimed campaign fraud in collecting absentee ballots. Corruption and bribery charges were dropped against former Miami City Manager Cesar H. Odio after he pleaded guilty to one charge of obstruction of justice. City Commissioner Humberto Hernandez and 12 other people were charged in an alleged $8 million mortgage-fraud and money-laundering operation. The commissioner Hernandez had replaced, Miller Dawkins, was sentenced to 27 months in prison for soliciting $200,000 from a computer company in return for voting for a $20 million city contract. Hernandez was reelected city commissioner in November.

Miami voters rejected a move to merge with surrounding Dade county, a move proponents argued would help overcome poverty and mismanagement....John Ellis (Jeb) Bush, former President George Bush's son, announced that he would run again for governor in 1998.

Airline Crashes. The National Transportation Safety Board, in its final report on the 1996 crash of ValuJet Flight 592, said most of the blame could be attributed to the Federal Aviation Administration and ValuJet Airlines. Five people, including four crew members and one person on the ground, died when a DC-8 cargo plane belonging to Fine Air Services Inc. crashed in Miami moments after takeoff.

Economy. The economic forecast for Florida was bright, with population and income levels projected by NationsBank to increase at double-digit rates for the next decade....Florida's citrus farmers successfully battled a threat by Mediterranean fruit flies, only to face an outbreak of citric cancer. Critics charged that state and federal inspection programs were lax.

Crime. Harry Shapiro, a 31-year-old Orthodox Jew, was sentenced to ten years in prison for planting a pipe bomb at a Jacksonville synagogue before a February appearance by former Israeli Prime Minister Shimon Peres....Fashion designer Gianni Versace was shot and killed on July 15, allegedly by Andrew Philip Cunanan, a reputed homosexual gigolo wanted in connection with the spree killings of four other people. On July 27, Cunanan killed himself in a houseboat....Florida was cited as the biggest source of out-of-state guns seized in crimes, according to a U.S. congressional study, selling 1,234 of the 16,635 out-of-state guns used in crimes in 1996.

Other News. The Florida legislature approved nearly $3 billion in school construction and repair spending over the next five years in an effort to ease some of the nation's worst school overcrowding.

KRISTI VAUGHAN

GEORGIA. In 1997, Bill Campbell became the third consecutive African-American to be reelected to a second term as mayor of Atlanta, defeating City Council President Marvin S. Arrington. An African-American mayor, Chuck E. Burris, also was elected in Stone Mountain, a onetime gathering place of the Ku Klux Klan.

U.S. House Speaker Newt Gingrich (R-GA) was reprimanded and fined $300,000 for using tax-exempt donations for political purposes and submitting false information to the House Ethics Committee. Former Attorney General Michael J. Bowers, the leading candidate for governor in 1998, admitted that he had had an affair for more than a decade with a woman who once worked in his office. Bowers had stood up for upholding the state's laws on adultery, fornication, and sodomy.

Crime. A bomb exploded at a gay nightclub in February, injuring five people; it was the fourth such incident in seven months. Police were investigating the possibility that the bombings—including the 1996 bombing at Centennial Olympic Park and one at an abortion clinic in January 1996—were linked.

Twenty-six years after being blamed for her infant half brother's death, Tracy Rhame had her name cleared when her stepfather was convicted of the 1971 beating death of four-month-old Matthew Golder.

Other News. Richard A. Jewell, who had been the focus of an investigation into the Centennial Olympic Park bombing, was sworn in as one of five new members of the Luthersville Police Department. The U.S. Justice Department had cleared Jewell of any wrongdoing in 1996. Jewell, meanwhile, had reached several out-of-court settlements with news organizations that had reported on the bombing.

KRISTI VAUGHAN

HAWAII. In what some representatives hailed as the most successful session in many years, Hawaii's state government passed legislation in 1997 dealing with same-sex marriages, no-fault auto insurance, and the long-contested issue of legislative pensions. The success was attributed to the Senate's use of a collaborative leadership model, with bipartisan cochairs overseeing all committees.

The most controversial approved bill was one granting gay couples inheritance rights, the right to sue for wrongful death, and spousal benefits for insurance and state pensions. At the same time, a bill was passed calling for a 1998 ballot on a constitutional amendment to deny the legality of gay marriages—a move designed to reverse the 1993 State Supreme Court ruling allowing such unions. Gay-rights activists denounced both pieces of legislation; nonetheless, they were signed into law by Gov. Benjamin J. Cayetano.

Economy. The state legislature also had to turn toward dealing with economic problems. Hawaii was suffering its worst economic slump since becoming a state in 1959; the downturn was blamed in part on a sharp drop in tourism and a reduction in Japanese investments. Personal bankruptcies soared in 1997, property values dropped, and unemployment continued to grow. Remedies being considered included reducing the state income-tax rate and lowering corporate taxes.

Other News. A statewide teachers' strike in February was averted with only a half hour to spare, as the state's 11,700 teachers agreed to a new four-year contract. The contract called for a 17% pay increase and added seven days to the school calendar.

China's President Jiang Zemin began his trip to the United States with a stop in Hawaii, arriving October 26. He visited the USS *Arizona* memorial at Pearl Harbor, recalling his country's World War II alliance with the United States.

BRUCE JACOBY

IDAHO. Like many U.S. states, Idaho worked in 1997 to reduce its welfare rolls. Changes in the law resulted in a 70% decline in welfare applications by early December. The number of people seeking assistance at soup kitchens and shelters, however, was increasing.

Politics. Citing his age, Gov. Phil Batt, 70—who in 1994 became the state's first Republican governor in 24 years—announced that he would not seek reelection in 1998. A 1995 deal between Idaho and the federal government to remove radioactive waste from the Idaho National Energy and Environmental Labs moved closer to fruition with the preliminary approval by the U.S. Environmental Protection Agency of the opening of a plutonium waste site in New Mexico.

Ruby Ridge. Murder and assault charges were filed under Idaho law against Kevin L. Harris in connection with his involvement in the 1992 armed standoff at a white supremacist's Ruby Ridge cabin. Those charges were dismissed when a district judge ruled that Harris, who earlier had been acquitted of federal murder charges, could not be tried twice for the same crime. In other charges relating to the Ruby Ridge incident, Lon Horiuchi, a former Federal Bureau of Investigation (FBI) agent, was charged by the state of Idaho with involuntary manslaughter, and E. Michael Kahoe, a former senior FBI official, was sentenced to federal prison for covering up an incriminating report.

Court Cases. The U.S. Supreme Court ruled that the Coeur d'Alene tribe of American Indians could not sue the state of Idaho to claim ownership of a lakebed that was partially on the tribe's reservation. Meanwhile, the tribe was running a controversial Internet lottery game that it claimed was authorized under the Indian Gaming Regulatory Act of 1988. Opponents, however, said that act allows gaming only on Indian lands.

KRISTI VAUGHAN

ILLINOIS. Illinois Gov. Jim Edgar announced Aug. 20, 1997, that he planned to retire from public service at the end of his second term in January 1999. His announcement left open the seat for the 1998 November election. Edgar called a special legislative session for December, hoping to secure passage of school-funding reforms that had failed in the regular session. Edgar had proposed raising state income taxes and lowering property taxes to fund schools. The plan was aimed at correcting funding inequities, based on property wealth, among various school districts.

Legislation. In the regular legislative session, which adjourned May 31, the legislature let die bills to restrict health-maintenance organization (HMO) practices, reform campaign-finance laws, and deregulate electric utilities. New laws were passed to improve pension benefits for state employees, to reform welfare, to protect foster parents' privacy, to ban partial-birth abortions, and to guarantee a minimum hospital stay for mastectomy patients. In addition, a new law lowered the drunk-driving threshold from .10% to .08% blood-alcohol content. Effective in January 1998, convicted sex offenders could be committed for treatment indefinitely until they were considered no longer likely to commit a sex crime. A 1997 law forbid insurers and employers from discriminating on the basis of the results of genetic tests.

Economy and Other News. The state's cash balance stood at $806 million at the end of fiscal 1997—the highest surplus in Illinois history. The 1998 budget called for less than a 5% increase in state general-fund spending. Most of the increased funding was for education and human services, Medicaid, and public safety.

The owner of Arlington International Racecourse in Illinois announced he would close the track in suburban Chicago. He cited losses due to nearby casino gaming.

In other action, Governor Edgar on August 26 issued an executive order stiffening ethics rules for state workers. The reforms banned the giving of gifts valued at $50 or more to state employees, and required competitive bidding on state contracts valued at more than $25,000. The governor's action followed the conviction of one of his biggest campaign contributors for bribing state officials to secure a state contract. Earlier in the year, Edgar had been subpoenaed by the defense in the bribery case, but was not himself accused of any wrongdoing. He had become the first sitting Illinois governor in 75 years to testify in criminal proceedings.

James Heiple, 63, resigned in early May as chief justice of the state Supreme Court, although he retained his seat on the court. He was accused of using his position to try to escape speeding tickets; the state House of Representatives later voted not to impeach Heiple.

ELAINE STUART

INDIANA. The continuing strength of the state's economy was recognized in 1997 as Standard & Poor's upgraded the state's credit rating to AA+. The higher rating would enable the state to issue bonds at a lower rate.

Politics. U.S. Rep. Lee Hamilton, a Democrat who had represented Indiana's 9th District for 17 terms, announced that he would not seek reelection in 1998. Hamilton was known for his foreign-policy work, especially for leading congressional opposition in the 1980s to the funding of Nicaragua's anticommunist contra rebels.

Crime. The Indiana Court of Appeals barred the state's department of corrections from keeping a 16-year-old girl in an adult prison....Gary Burris, 40—the fifth person to be executed in Indiana since the death penalty was reinstated in 1976—was killed by lethal injection in November....A U.S. congressional study found that there was significant gun smuggling between Indiana and Illinois, as well as in other areas, and that many of the guns used in states with tough gun-control laws were acquired in states with less-restrictive laws.

THE U.S. STATES

	Population* (in millions)	Area (sq mi)	Area (km²)	Capital	Governor
Alabama	4.3	52,423	135 776	Montgomery	Fob James, Jr. (R)
Alaska	.6	656,424	1 700 130	Juneau	Tony Knowles (D)
Arizona	4.6	114,006	295 276	Phoenix	Jane Dee Hull (R)
Arkansas	2.5	53,182	137 741	Little Rock	Mike Huckabee (D)
California	32.3	163,707	424 001	Sacramento	Pete Wilson (R)
Colorado	3.9	104,100	269 619	Denver	Roy Romer (D)
Connecticut	3.3	5,544	14 359	Hartford	John Rowland (R)
Delaware	.7	2,489	6 447	Dover	Tom Carper (D)
Florida	14.7	65,758	170 313	Tallahassee	Lawton Chiles (D)
Georgia	7.5	59,441	153 952	Atlanta	Zell Miller (D)
Hawaii	1.2	10,932	28 314	Honolulu	Benjamin J. Cayetano (D)
Idaho	1.2	83,574	216 457	Boise	Philip Batt (R)
Illinois	11.9	57,918	150 008	Springfield	Jim Edgar (R)
Indiana	5.9	36,420	94 328	Indianapolis	Frank O'Bannon (D)
Iowa	2.9	56,276	145 755	Des Moines	Terry E. Branstad (R)
Kansas	2.6	82,282	213 110	Topeka	Bill Graves (R)
Kentucky	3.9	40,411	104 664	Frankfort	Paul Patton (D)
Louisiana	4.4	51,843	134 273	Baton Rouge	Mike Foster (D)
Maine	1.2	35,387	91 652	Augusta	Angus King, Jr. (I)
Maryland	5.1	12,407	32 134	Annapolis	Parris N. Glendening (D)
Massachusetts	6.1	10,555	27 337	Boston	Paul Cellucci (R)
Michigan	9.8	96,705	250 466	Lansing	John Engler (R)
Minnesota	4.7	86,943	225 182	St. Paul	Arne Carlson (R)
Mississippi	2.7	48,434	125 444	Jackson	Kirk Fordice (R)
Missouri	5.4	69,709	180 546	Jefferson City	Mel Carnahan (D)
Montana	.9	147,046	380 849	Helena	Marc Racicot (R)
Nebraska	1.7	77,358	200 357	Lincoln	E. Benjamin Nelson (D)
Nevada	1.7	110,567	286 369	Carson City	Bob Miller (D)
New Hampshire	1.2	9,351	24 219	Concord	Jeanne Shaheen (D)
New Jersey	8.1	8,722	22 590	Trenton	Christine Todd Whitman (R)
New Mexico	1.7	121,598	314 939	Santa Fe	Gary Johnson (R)
New York	18.1	54,556	141 300	Albany	George Pataki (R)
North Carolina	7.4	53,821	139 396	Raleigh	James B. Hunt, Jr. (D)
North Dakota	.6	70,704	183 123	Bismarck	Edward Schafer (R)
Ohio	11.2	44,828	116 105	Columbus	George V. Voinovich (R)
Oklahoma	3.3	69,903	181 049	Oklahoma City	Frank Keating (R)
Oregon	3.2	98,386	254 820	Salem	John Kitzhaber (D)
Pennsylvania	12.0	46,058	119 290	Harrisburg	Tom Ridge (R)
Rhode Island	1.0	1,545	4 002	Providence	Lincoln Almond (R)
South Carolina	3.8	32,008	82 901	Columbia	David Beasley (R)
South Dakota	.7	77,121	199 743	Pierre	William Janklow (R)
Tennessee	5.4	42,146	109 158	Nashville	Don Sundquist (R)
Texas	19.4	268,601	695 673	Austin	George W. Bush (R)
Utah	2.1	84,904	219 901	Salt Lake City	Michael O. Leavitt (R)
Vermont	.6	9,615	24,903	Montpelier	Howard Dean (D)
Virginia	6.7	42,777	110 792	Richmond	George F. Allen (R)
Washington	5.6	71,302	184 672	Olympia	Gary Locke (D)
West Virginia	1.8	24,231	62 758	Charleston	Cecil Underwood (R)
Wisconsin	5.2	65,499	169 642	Madison	Tommy G. Thompson (R)
Wyoming	.5	97,818	253 349	Cheyenne	Jim Geringer (R)

*July 1, 1997, estimate

Other News. The state department of agriculture took a new tack in its battle against the corn rootworm, a major insect pest of corn, when it sprayed a bait laced with a tiny dose of carbaryl insecticide on five test sites. The spraying was part of area-wide integrated pest management....The families of 27 victims of a 1994 Indiana air crash were awarded $10 million, to be paid by the air carrier and the plane's manufacturer....Navistar International Corp., a truck manufacturer, announced that it would close its Indianapolis casting factory in 1998, after the foundry's 650 workers refused to ratify a new labor contract.

KRISTI VAUGHAN

IOWA. During 1997, Iowa faced a shortage of teachers, and the 1998 gubernatorial race began to shape up. The state's economic picture was stable.

Business and Economics. In a nationwide comparison, Iowa had the second-lowest rate of growth in personal bankruptcy filings for 1997. During the year it also was announced that the state's welfare caseload had dropped to a 22-year low, with approximately 27,450 receiving aid.

To increase successful collection of unpaid court costs and fines, Iowa began seizing tax refunds of people who owe such fees. The program resulted in $62.3 million being collected.

Shaeffer Pen of Fort Madison announced that it had reached an agreement to sell to the Bic Corporation. Executives of Shaeffer were looking for financial backers to exercise their right of first refusal over the sale of the company.

In late summer the Iowa Racing and Gaming Commission held a hearing to determine whether it would revoke Prairie Meadows' gaming license due to its connection to the Polk county government. In a controversial vote, the board agreed not to revoke the license. Meanwhile, construction was scheduled to start on an $18 million expansion at the Meskwaki Bingo and Casino in Tama.

Education. A shortage of teachers forced the state to issue conditional licenses to approximately 1,600 new teachers. Meanwhile, West Des Moines schools were allowed to segregate classrooms by gender to test learning differences between boys and girls. It was ruled that this would not be deemed a violation of federal antidiscrimination laws.

In higher-education news, Grinnell College opened its $15 million Robert N. Noyce Science Center, and the University of Iowa opened a new medical facility to treat macular degeneration.

Other News. Republican Lt. Gov. Joy Corning and former U.S. Rep. Jim Lightfoot (R) announced their candidacies for the governor's office. Gov. Terry Branstad would not seek reelection in 1998....During the summer, Iowa began using a new correctional facility at Newton. County officials begin construction at midyear on the new 288-bed Pottawattamie County Jail north of Council Bluffs....In October, Federal Court Judge Harold Vietor rejected a free-speech claim brought by juice-bar owners who were challenging a new state law banning nude dancing at such establishments....Due to an increasing number of divorces, debate heightened over the issue of ending no-fault divorces, increasing fees to become married, and requiring couples to use mediation services before filing for divorce.

CRAIG BORLIN

KANSAS. Kansas gained a national park in June 1997 when the Tallgrass Prairie National Preserve in the Flint Hills was opened.

Crime. Female inmates were granted permission to join the state's only boot camp for criminal offenders. A total of 15 women were to be allowed at the Labette Correctional Conservation Camp....The U.S. Supreme Court upheld a Kansas law allowing the state to commit violent sex offenders to mental institutions even after the offenders had served prison terms....Michael Kolnhofer, a 79-year-old Kansas City man accused of being a Nazi death-camp guard, died ten weeks after being wounded in a police shoot-out. The incident had begun when reporters gathered at Kolnhofer's house to ask about U.S. Justice Department allegations that he was involved with the World War II German death camps. Kolnhofer had suffered brain damage during surgery for his wounds.

Business and Other News. A midwestern energy powerhouse was created when Western Resources Inc. and Kansas City Power and Light Co. agreed to merge. The new company serves more than 2 million customers. In other corporate news, the International Speedway Corporation reached an agreement with the Unified Government of Wyandotte County/Kansas City regarding a 1.5-mi (2.4-km) oval motor speedway in western Kansas City. The facility would seat 150,000 racing fans.

The Insurance Institute for Highway Safety reported that highway death rates had increased an average of 12% in Kansas and 11 other states that had raised their speed limits.

KRISTI VAUGHAN

KENTUCKY. In March 1997 five persons were killed in Falmouth, KY, when the Licking River flooded. A total of 16 were killed statewide in 1997's catastrophic spring floods.

Legislature and Government News. A special legislative session called by Kentucky Gov. Paul Patton ended Oct. 15, 1997, without any changes being made to 1994 health-insurance reforms. The governor had called the session because the 1994 law was under fire; critics claimed it made the state unattractive to out-of-state health insurers. As it stood, the legislation guaranteed all citizens access to health insurance.

Governor Patton was more successful in a special session that he called in May to make changes in the governance of the state's system of higher education. The legislature agreed with Patton's proposal to place the state's community colleges under a single governing board, removing control for community colleges from the state's major university—the University of Kentucky. Kentucky, which has biennial legislative sessions in even-numbered years, did not hold a regular legislative session in 1997.

In other government news, the director of the Legislative Ethics Commission, Earl Mackey, resigned in January, saying that 1996 changes to the ethics laws had gutted the commission's powers. Kent Downey, a legislative aide, was accused in a federal indictment of promoting illegal gaming and prostitution on private golf outings he ran that were attended by legislators. Downey pleaded not guilty September 25, after losing his state job.

Crime. The state was shocked when, on December 1, a teenager fired into a group of students attending a prayer service at Heath High School in West Paducah. Michael Carneal, 14, killed three students and wounded five others before giving himself up....Kentucky held its first execution in the last 35 years. Harold McQueen Jr., 44, died in the electric chair July 1. He received the death penalty for murdering a store clerk 17 years earlier....The state adopted an automatic telephone system to notify crime victims when their attackers are let out of jail. The system is designed to call registered victims for 24 hours or until the victim responds.

Sports News. The University of Kentucky (UK) basketball team lost its bid for a second consecutive National Collegiate Athletic Association (NCAA) championship to Arizona, 84–79 in overtime. After the season ended, the team lost its coach of eight years, Rick Pitino, who left to coach the National Basketball Association's (NBA's) Boston Celtics. Tubby Smith replaced Pitino, becoming the university's first African-American basketball coach.

Hal Mumme, in his first season as UK football coach, amassed a 5–6 record. In November, Ron Cooper accepted a $1 million buyout of his coaching contract for the University of Louisville football team after a 1–10 season.

ELAINE STUART

LOUISIANA. Education was a priority in Louisiana during 1997 as Gov. Mike Foster's education package was passed by the legislature.

Education. The state's legislature increased funding for Louisiana's schools, providing $66.5 million for pay raises for teachers and $22.5 million for raises for support staff. The budget for kindergarten through 12th grade was increased by 6%, to $2.1 billion, for fiscal 1998. In addition, the legislature approved $37 million for classroom technology and $30 million for improved instruction in reading and math. It also funded $1.3 million for charter schools, $11 million for classroom supplies, and $2.2 million to set higher education standards.

Despite the pay increase, Louisiana's average annual teacher salary of $29,500 continued to lag behind the southern-state average of $33,000 per year. Governor Foster in November said he would keep his 1995 campaign promise to give up his $95,000 annual salary until he succeeded in raising teacher pay to the regional average. The governor told union leaders his top priority for 1998 would be to get teachers a pay raise for a third consecutive year.

Budget and Other Legislation. The legislature let expire as scheduled in 1997 a 1% increase in the sales tax on certain foods and utilities and used $360 million in surplus funds to retire debt early. It also raised to the federal level the income threshold for filing state income-tax returns, thereby granting some relief to lower-income households.

Louisiana became the first state to establish voluntary covenant marriage, in which couples are required to undergo premarital counseling and face legal hurdles to divorce. The legislature also passed a reduction in auto-insurance premiums, as part of a law barring uninsured motorists from recovering the first $10,000 they suffer in bodily or property damage. Slot machines were approved for three racetracks, subject to the approval of local voters.

The American Civil Liberties Union in November said it planned to challenge a new Louisiana law mandating drug testing for elected officials, welfare recipients, state contractors and vendors, college students receiving state aid, and certain state employees. Drug testing was scheduled to begin in July 1998.

Other News. Governor Foster, elected as a gambling opponent, in November announced he would ask the state gaming-control board and the legislature to approve a deal to allow Harrah's to complete its bankrupt land-based casino in New Orleans. Harrah's agreed to provide the state with a $100 million annual tax guarantee.

The U.S. Supreme Court in October refused to review a Louisiana parental-consent law for abortion. Lower courts had found the 1995 law interfered with teens' rights, as it did not guarantee that judges could bypass the parental-permission requirement.

ELAINE STUART

MAINE. Once again in 1997, environmental issues were the big newsmakers in Maine.

Environment. In June the state imposed what federal officials claimed were the toughest regulations in the nation against toxic discharges of dioxins. The regulations, which sought to limit the amount of effluents from paper mills that entered the state's waterways, appeared to exceed new rules currently under consideration by the U.S. Environmental Protection Agency. However, environmental groups criticized the state legislature for not making the regulations tough enough.

In November voters rejected a compromise that would have limited the practice of clear-cutting in the state's 17-million-acre (6.9-million-ha) Maine Woods, the greatest swath of forest remaining in the Northeast. The compromise—which was agreed to by Gov. Angus King, major paper companies, and Maine's two largest environmental groups—failed to receive a majority for the second time in a statewide referendum. King bemoaned the defeat, having cited the bill as a national model for compromise between business executives and environmentalists.

Nuclear Plant. The controversial Maine Yankee nuclear-power plant was to be closed. It had been off-line since serious safety problems were identified in December 1996, and in 1997 it was determined that the cost of correcting the problems would be prohibitive. A spokesman for the Union of Concerned Scientists—the group that brought the problems to the public's attention—said, "The biggest question here is why the NRC [Nuclear Regulatory Commission] allowed Maine Yankee to operate for more than 17 years in violation of numerous safety regulations. How many other nuclear plants are putting the public in danger while the NRC looks the other way?"

BRUCE JACOBY

MARYLAND. The U.S. Army sex scandal, which centered on the Aberdeen Proving Ground, continued in 1997. Meanwhile, scientists were battling a toxic microbe that was killing thousands of fish in the state and surrounding area and was infecting people as well.

Environmental Issues. Scientists were trying to determine what was causing outbreaks of the microbe *Pfieste-*

ria piscicida, which had killed thousands of fish in Chesapeake Bay tributaries and had infected nearly 30 people. Much suspicion centered on the region's numerous poultry farms. Gov. Parris N. Glendening called for a summit of governors from surrounding states to discuss the problem and possible regional solutions. A U.S. congressional committee conducted a hearing in October on the status of research regarding *P. piscicida*.

Crime. Ruthann Aron, a 1994 Republican candidate for the Maryland Senate, was charged with conspiring to kill her husband and a Baltimore lawyer....Flint Gregory Hunt, convicted of killing a Baltimore police officer in 1985, became the second person in Maryland to be executed since the U.S. Supreme Court reinstated the death penalty in 1976....Staff Sgt. Delmar G. Simpson was sentenced by a military jury in May to 25 years in prison for raping six trainees under his charge at the Aberdeen Proving Ground in Maryland. The charges were part of a growing scandal regarding sexual misconduct in the armed forces....The state police in late November launched a new offensive against dangerous drivers. Their weapon was a Ford Bronco equipped with high-tech equipment allowing police to photograph and record incidences of dangerous driving and send written warnings to the drivers' homes. Initial efforts focused on the Capital Beltway.

KRISTI VAUGHAN

MASSACHUSETTS. Massachusetts was very much a player in national headlines in 1997.

Politics. In what many pundits viewed as politics at its ugliest, popular Gov. William F. Weld resigned in July to pursue his nomination as President Bill Clinton's ambassador to Mexico, only to see that nomination squashed by Sen. Jesse Helms (R-NC). Weld, a moderate Republican who won the state House with an astonishing 71% majority in 1994, was considered by Helms as being soft on drugs. With his power as chairman of the Senate Foreign Relations Committee, Helms refused to hold hearings on Weld's nomination, effectively blocking the appointment. On September 15, Weld withdrew his name from nomination, saying his case might jeopardize the Clinton administration's relations with representatives of Capitol Hill; this was an unusual statement, coming as it did from a Republican Party stalwart.

In a July 29 ceremony in Boston, Weld had turned over the governorship to Lt. Gov. Paul Cellucci, a Republican who had been elected in 1990 and 1994.

Meanwhile, U.S. Rep. Joseph P. Kennedy 2d (D), who was expected to run for the governorship in 1998, announced that he would not do so. Barraged with bad press following his former wife's allegations that he had bullied her into getting a Roman Catholic annulment of their marriage—and following even worse press when it was alleged that his brother Michael had had an affair with a teenage babysitter—Representative Kennedy concluded that the race "would focus not on issues but on personal and family pressures." However, he said that he would seek reelection to the House. The year ended on another tragic note for the Kennedy family as Michael Kennedy was killed in a skiing accident in Aspen, CO.

Other News. In the fall the trial of 19-year-old British au pair Louise Woodward drew much attention and debate about child care. After a jury in Middlesex county found Woodward guilty of second-degree murder in the death of Matthew Eappen, an eight-month-old baby for whom she had been caring, the judge in the case reduced the conviction to manslaughter (*see* FAMILY).

Boston Mayor Thomas Menino was reelected....The state House refused to reinstate the death penalty in Massachusetts....And the state's Supreme Judicial Court overturned a voter-approved law preventing candidates who had served eight years in the legislature or in constitutional office from having their names on election ballots.

BRUCE JACOBY

MICHIGAN. In an effort to reduce poverty in cities and rural areas, Michigan began testing "renaissance zones" in 11 areas across the state in 1997. In these zones, state property and income taxes were being eliminated for up to 15 years in the hope that businesses then would locate there, bringing jobs and prosperity. Detroit Mayor Dennis W. Archer easily won a second term. A federal judge struck down Michigan's ban on certain late-term abortions, saying that the statute was too vague and placed too much burden on women seeking abortions in the second trimester.

Economic Issues. General Motors Corp. said it would close its Buick City automobile factory in Flint in 1999, a move affecting 3,000 workers. Chrysler Corp. said it would spend $1.3 billion over five years to improve its Detroit auto plants and $750 million to increase production at the assembly plant that built the Jeep Grand Cherokee sport-utility vehicle.

A bitter 19-month-long strike against the *Detroit Free Press* and *Detroit News*—the longest newspaper strike in history—ended in February, when managers accepted unconditional return-to-work offers from six labor unions. Several months later the National Labor Relations Board ordered the papers to rehire workers.

Disasters and Necrology. An outbreak of hepatitis-A virus that affected an estimated 185 people in two Michigan counties was linked to tainted frozen strawberries served in school lunches. Sixteen people were killed and more than 100 people were injured during violent July thunderstorms in southern Michigan. A Michigan commuter plane crash killed 29 in January.

Coleman Young, the first black mayor of Detroit, died in November. He had served as mayor for 20 years, the longest term in the city's history. Although his tenure was marked by high levels of crime and unemployment, he was credited with revitalizing Detroit's waterfront and helping alleviate the city's financial troubles through pay cuts and income-tax increases.....George W. Crockett, Jr., a former five-term Democratic U.S. congressman, died in September. He was known for outspoken and controversial stands on civil-rights issues....A small-town bank president, Harold Englehardt, who died in April, left $12 million to make life better in Lowell, a town of about 4,000, 15 mi (24 km) east of Grand Rapids.

KRISTI VAUGHAN

MINNESOTA. Disaster struck parts of Minnesota and neighboring North Dakota in April when the Red River overflowed its banks. Described as a 500-year-flood, it forced the evacuation of at least 100,000 residents and caused billions of dollars in damage. Good news came in the form of $1.2 billion in federal disaster relief for North Dakota, South Dakota, and Minnesota and a $15 million gift by Joan Kroc—widow of McDonald's Corp. founder Ray Kroc—to help flood victims in East Grand Forks, MN, and Grand Forks, ND. (*See also* METEOROLOGY—*A Year of Unusual Floods.*)

Politics. Sharon Sayles Benton, a Democrat, won a second term as mayor of Minneapolis. She defeated Barbara Carlson, the former wife of Gov. Arne Carlson. Incumbent Norm Coleman won another term as mayor of St. Paul, defeating state Sen. Sandy Pappas. In 1996, Coleman had switched from the Democratic Party to the

Although snowfall was relatively light for much of the Northeast during the winter of 1996–97, 2 ft (.6 m) of snow fell on Boston in early April. It was a record for the month and the third-largest snowstorm ever to hit the Massachusetts capital.

© Bill Plowman/AP/Wide World Photos

The 50th Anniversary of the "Roswell Incident"

An estimated 40,000 visitors flocked to Roswell, NM, during the summer of 1997 to celebrate the 50th anniversary of UFO believers' Holy Grail: the "Roswell Incident," an alleged crash of an alien spacecraft followed by a 50-year government cover-up. No little green men showed up, but the faithful and irreverent alike attended lectures, bought souvenirs, and dressed in strange costumes for the swarm of media on hand to record the July 1–6 event. The visitors helped shine an international spotlight on the small plains town of 48,000 that, during quieter times, is better known for its cheese factory and a long-closed U.S. Air Force Base. For Roswell tourism, the affair was an unqualified success. But the event's visitors went away no closer to an answer to the questions surrounding the crash.

The Mystery and How It Grew. In July 1947, W.W. "Mac" Brazel, a local rancher, brought some debris to town that he had found on his ranch—metallic fabric and strange sticks. At this time the United States was in the midst of its first episode of flying-saucer mania; reports were coming in from all over the country, and no one was sure what the mysterious aerial objects might be. Officials at Roswell Army Air Field looked over Brazel's debris and issued a press release stating that it was the remains of a flying saucer—the first ever recovered. After sending the debris to an air base in Texas for further analysis, the military quickly retracted its claim, saying it was, after all, merely a crashed weather balloon.

The incident was forgotten for some 30 years, until Canadian-American UFO researcher Stanton Friedman began investigating. Friedman interviewed Jesse Marcel, the intelligence officer at the base in 1947 who had said the stuff found on Brazel's ranch was not of this world. A series of books by Friedman and others—as well as television programs like *Unsolved Mysteries*—moved the Roswell Incident to center stage of the UFO movement in the 1980s and 1990s. UFO researchers intriguingly claimed that top-secret government teams had recovered not only a spacecraft but also alien bodies, then had covered up the findings.

The Ongoing Debate. After nearly 20 years of investigation, UFO researchers still could not agree on many of the alleged incident's details, from the shape of the craft to the crash date; even the location of the crash site was in question. The lectures and debates at the 50th-anniversary observance failed to resolve the disputes. UFO researchers' accounts are based on the recollections of a handful of alleged eyewitnesses and a larger number of secondhand sources. The witnesses relate tales of visiting a crash site or of participating in military analysis of debris or alien corpses. Skeptics point to inconsistencies in witnesses' tales and to a more prosaic explanation for the debris—a top-secret military experiment called Project Mogul, in which radar reflectors were suspended from a string of weather balloons as part of a search for ways to listen for Soviet nuclear tests.

While believers reveled in the festivities at Roswell, their case took three big blows during the summer of 1997. The U.S. Air Force weighed in with a report, released ten days before the Roswell celebration, documenting balloon experiments conducted in the 1950s in which dummies were dropped from high altitude. The dummies, the service theorized, may have been mistaken by some witnesses for alien bodies. Believers mocked the report, noting that the dummy experiments occurred a decade after the 1947 incident. But skeptics said the events easily could have been confused in the haze of memory, given that the UFO researchers did not even begin interviewing Roswell witnesses until the 1970s and 1980s.

The second blow came from within the believers' ranks, when, in June 1997, airline pilot and UFO researcher Kent Jeffrey bailed out on the Roswell UFO theory. Jeffrey headed the International Roswell Initiative, a massive effort to pressure the U.S. government to release documents and information about the Roswell Incident and UFOs. After years of research, however, he went public with his conclusions that what crashed in Roswell was nothing more than a Mogul balloon.

The third blow came when Brandeis University anthropologists Benson Saler and Charles Ziegler, working with New Mexico scientist Charles Moore, who had been involved in Project Mogul, published a study analyzing the Roswell evidence from the perspective of cultural anthropology. Noting researchers' inability to converge toward a single, canonical version of the Roswell Incident, the authors concluded that the telling and retelling of the Roswell tale looked less like historical investigation than like an evolving modern myth.

JOHN FLECK

The area near Billings, MT, was hit with severe flooding and ice floes as 1997 began. Thousands of people had to leave their homes.

© Larry Mayer/Gamma-Liaison

GOP. In a ruling that could affect other states as well, the U.S. Supreme Court ruled that the state could bar individuals from running for political office as candidates from more than one party.

Legislation. In May, Governor Carlson signed the Omnibus Economic Development Bill, funding the budgets of many state agencies for the 1998–99 biennium. The law also sought to improve the business climate in the state. A law was passed requiring divorcing parents who argue over child custody or visitation issues to take a class on the effects of divorce on children.

Crime. A federal judge in Minneapolis dismissed charges against Qubilah Shabazz, the daughter of Malcolm X, the slain black nationalist leader. Shabazz had been accused of hiring a hit man to kill Nation of Islam leader Louis Farrakhan. The charges were dismissed as part of a probationary agreement that included having Shabazz' son, Malcolm, live with his grandmother, Betty Shabazz. The elder Shabazz died in June from burns suffered in a fire apparently set by the boy.

KRISTI VAUGHAN

MISSISSIPPI. Mississippi Attorney General Michael Moore claimed victory in 1997 when the state and four leading tobacco companies reached a settlement that called for the tobacco industry to pay Mississippi $3.4 billion over 25 years. Moore had been the first state attorney general to sue the tobacco industry.

Crime. In the city of Pearl in October, six teenagers were charged with murder conspiracy in connection with the stabbing death of the mother of one of the boys and the fatal shooting of two schoolmates. Although only one of the teens, a 16-year-old boy, allegedly stabbed his mother and went on the shooting rampage that killed two students and wounded seven, the other teens allegedly were involved in a plot to kill students at the local high school. According to an investigator at the sheriff's office in Rankin county, the boys were involved in a satanic cult.

Politics. In June, Harvey Johnson, a Democrat, became the first African-American to be elected mayor of Jackson, winning 70% of the vote. He defeated Charlotte Reeves.

The U.S. Supreme Court ruled in March that Mississippi must consult with the Justice Department to ensure the legality of its limited implementation of the 1993 "motor-voter" law. That law allows individuals who register to vote at state motor-vehicle departments and welfare offices to vote in federal elections. Other states also give such registrants the right to vote in local and state elections, but Mississippi limits it to federal elections. The Supreme Court wanted to ensure that Mississippi's implementation does not violate the Voting Rights Act of 1965.

Highway Deaths. The Insurance Institute for Highway Safety reported in October that Mississippi's highway death rate increased following an increase in the speed limit in 1996.

KRISTI VAUGHAN

MISSOURI. Tighter drunk-driving laws and debates over gambling occupied the news in Missouri in 1997; authorities also grappled with ways to curb the growth of methamphetamine manufacturers.

Gambling. The Eastern Shawnee tribe asked the federal Bureau of Indian Affairs to place land it owns in southwestern Missouri in trust. This would enable the tribe to build a casino there, something federal and state officials opposed, saying it violates a "riverboat gambling" law prohibiting landlocked casinos.

Crime. The legislature's new tighter drunk-driving laws made "vehicular manslaughter by an intoxicated person" a crime punishable by five to 15 years in prison, more than double the previous penalty....The Midwest fast was becoming a center for the illicit manufacturer of methamphetamine, which some call "the crack of the '90s." Missouri was a particularly hot area, with 333 labs raided in the first eight months of the year—nearly 50% more than in all of 1996.

A federal grand jury indicted five men on charges of conspiring and carrying out racial intimidation by placing a burning cross at the home of a Rushville family....Four persons were executed in Missouri in 1997, bringing to 28 the number executed in the state since the death penalty was reinstated in 1976.

Politics. Clarence Harmon, a former St. Louis police chief, became the second African-American mayor of St. Louis in April, defeating the city's first African-American mayor in a primary and two white challengers in the general election. A U.S. district judge ruled that blocking Planned Parenthood from receiving state family-planning funds violated a court injunction issued in 1996. Some legislators had sought restrictions in funding that effectively denied the organization money because it performed abortions.

Newspaper Purchase. Knight-Ridder Inc., the nation's second-largest newspaper company, announced plans to buy the *Kansas City Star* and three other newspapers from the Walt Disney Co.

KRISTI VAUGHAN

MONTANA. On Feb. 14, 1997, the Montana Senate rejected a plan to set a daytime speed limit on interstate highways. Montana remained the only state not to have such a limit. In October, however, the Insurance Institute for Highway Safety reported that in Montana and in 11 states that had raised their speed limits, the number of accidents between April and December 1996 had increased by some 500 over the corresponding period in 1995.

Montana became the second state in the nation—after California—to approve the use of "chemical castration" to reduce the sexual drive of sexual offenders who are about to be released from prison.

During 1997, Montana's welfare caseload dropped by about one third—one of the best records in the nation. Credit was given to a state plan that brought welfare recipients and businesses together in a unique way: The state offered businesses interest-free loans if they hired welfare recipients.

In March the U.S. Supreme Court reinstated a Montana law that was enacted in 1995, requiring teenage girls

to notify at least one parent or guardian before having an abortion.

The Bison Controversy. During the winter of 1996–97, in an effort to prevent bison from spreading brucellosis to cattle outside of Yellowstone National Park, federal and state officials shot or sent to slaughter nearly 1,000 of the animals. After a public outcry, the officials said they would end the slaughter and force the bison back into the park. But Gov. Marc Racicot (R), who called the situation a federal problem, condemned this plan, saying it would put Montana's cattle in danger of contracting the disease. A lawsuit to end the slaughter, filed by the Sierra Club and other conservationist groups, failed in a federal appeals court in March. In other conservation-related news, Governor Racicot declared April 25 as Arbor Day in Montana.

WILLIAM E. SHAPIRO

NEBRASKA. The state was surprised by a major snowstorm in October 1997 that caused heavy damage in some areas.

Politics. Democratic U.S. Sen. Bob Kerrey voiced concerns over an argument between federal judges and the U.S. attorney's office involving the limited available space in the new Hruska Federal Courthouse, and tried to mediate the use of the space. The building was being constructed on a smaller scale than originally planned, due to budget cuts. Nebraska's senators were divided over future military-base closings. Senator Kerrey voted to continue with the closings of bases no longer needed by the U.S. Department of Defense, while Republican Sen. Chuck Hagel voted against continued base closings. U.S. Rep. Jon Christensen (R) entered the 1998 gubernatorial race.

Weather and Other News. A major snowstorm hit Nebraska on October 26, causing widespread damage to trees and power lines. The storm was described by Omaha citizens as the worst in 20 years. An estimated 25% of the city's trees were lost and cleanup was expected to take several months. Gov. Ben Nelson declared 12 Nebraska counties to be disaster areas after the storm, and President Bill Clinton declared the state a federal disaster area, thus making it eligible for federal funds.

William Kleffman, a well-known Roman Catholic priest in Omaha, was found beaten to death inside the St. Agnes Church rectory in August. The suspected killer, Rogerio Gallegos, was released from custody by a judge during a preliminary hearing....The state board of education voted to close the Nebraska School for the Deaf, which was founded in 1869....Union Pacific Railroad found itself under investigation by federal officials during the year, due to the recent number of train crashes.

CRAIG BORLIN

NEVADA. In early January 1997, northern Nevada was hit by severe flooding, causing damage estimated at nearly $500 million. Gov. Bob Miller later authorized $1 million in emergency-relief funds for the victims.

Controversial Nuclear Storage. The U.S. Senate in April and the House of Representatives in October approved a bill to temporarily store some 40,000 tons of nuclear waste from 41 states in facilities near Yucca Mountain in the Nevada desert, about 100 mi (161 km) from Las Vegas. President Bill Clinton had vowed to veto such a bill, which Nevada's Democratic Senators Harry Reid and Richard Bryan also opposed. Congress adjourned without taking final action on the bill.

Politics. In June the legislature passed a bill to raise the salaries of the governor, lieutenant governor, secretary of state, and attorney general. Other bills passed during the 168-day legislative session included an education-reform bill requiring higher educational standards and allocating millions for teacher training and technology; a welfare-reform bill limiting benefits to two consecutive years with a five-year lifetime limit; and a measure allowing the establishment of charter schools that are free from a variety of state education regulations.

In August, Governor Miller, whose term in office would end in January 1999, endorsed Democratic Attorney General Frankie Sue Del Papa as his successor. Miller, who was mentioned as a possible future ambassador to Mexico, was given high marks by Nevada legislators for his ten-year tenure as governor. His accomplishments in 1997 included the reduction of class sizes to a student-teacher ratio of 19–1; a substantial increase in funds for mental health; and the establishment of a Family-to-Family program that will teach parents about parenting skills.

WILLIAM E. SHAPIRO

NEW HAMPSHIRE. In June 1997, New Hampshire Gov. Jeanne Shaheen signed into law a measure making the state the 11th in the nation to give lesbians and gay men protection against discrimination. "If we are to be true to our belief that all people are created equal, we must insure that all of our people enjoy the same basic rights under the law," the governor said. The law, which was to take effect on Jan. 1, 1998, provides protection in employment, housing, and public accommodation.

Crime and Law. The quiet northern town of Colebrook was the scene of bloodshed in August when Carl Drega, a 67-year-old militant antigovernment activist, opened fire on several town authorities. Apparently intent on settling a grudge stemming from a property-tax ruling, Drega killed a local newspaper editor, a lawyer, a state trooper, and a highway inspector; he wounded five others. The lawyer, Vickie Bunnel, was the associate judge who made the ruling against Drega several years earlier. According to friends, she lived in constant fear of Drega, even keeping a gun for protection. When she saw him, she screamed, "He's got a gun! Get out!" before being shot as she tried to flee. Drega himself was shot to death during the subsequent police chase.

Shirley Barron of Derry became one of the first people to test a new law allowing citizens to sue the Internal Revenue Service (IRS) for overly aggressive tactics. The so-called Traficant Amendment is designed to curb abuses by the IRS. Barron's husband, Bruce, committed suicide in August 1996 after a long history of what she claims was IRS harassment. His suicide note blamed his problems on the government agency.

BRUCE JACOBY

NEW JERSEY. Governor Christine Todd Whitman narrowly was elected to a second term in 1997, defeating Woodbridge Mayor and former state Sen. James E. McGreevy. Campaign issues were auto-insurance reform and property taxes. In other political news, Democratic Sen. Frank R. Lautenberg's campaign committee admitted that it improperly had accepted more than $20,000 from the Mercer County Democratic Committee during the 1994 reelection campaign.

Crime. Several New Jersey crimes gained national attention in 1997. In April two teens were charged with the thrill-seeking slaying of two pizza deliverymen. The teens, Jayson Vreeland, 17, and Thomas Koskovich, 18, allegedly ambushed the deliverymen and shot to them to death when they made their delivery to a deserted house. The death penalty was being sought against Koskovich but not against Vreeland, since the latter was a minor. Jesse Timmendequas was found guilty of raping and killing 7-year-old Megan Kanka and was sentenced to death in June. Kanka's death precipitated the passage of "Megan's laws" around the nation to protect children from sex offenders. In related news, a federal appeals court upheld the constitutionality of New Jersey's Megan's law, which allowed prosecutors to notify residents and community groups about sexual offenders in their neighborhoods.

In June a teenager was charged with murder after giving birth in a bathroom stall at her senior prom. Melissa Drexler allegedly choked the baby, put him in a plastic bag, threw the bag away, and returned to the dance floor. An 11-year-old boy was assaulted sexually and murdered in September while selling candy and wrapping paper for a school fund-raising drive.

Other Issues. The New Jersey Supreme Court ruled against Governor Whitman's plan to improve urban schools by emphasizing curriculum standards. In three decades no governor has come up with a plan to satisfy the courts. Whitman's subsequent state budget included an additional $246 million for public schools to help reduce the spending disparity among school districts. An overhaul of the state's welfare system, which would impose a five-year lifetime limit on cash benefits, was approved.

The city of Newark, meanwhile, hoped to reverse its poor reputation and dwindling economy with a 12-acre (5-ha), $180 million performing-arts complex, the New Jersey Performing Arts Center....Late in the year the legislature overrode Governor Whitman's veto of a measure banning late-term abortions.

KRISTI VAUGHAN

NEW MEXICO. New Mexico ended the 1997 fiscal year with a budget surplus of $77 million, up $22 million from the previous fiscal year. Among the concerns during 1997 was the state Supreme Court's overturning of New Mexico's welfare-to-work plan, on the grounds that it had been implemented illegally. As a result, it was announced on September 10 that cash payments to the state's nearly 59,000 welfare recipients might have to be cut.

Federal Appointments. U.S. Rep. Bill Richardson (D) was confirmed by the U.S. Senate on February 11 as ambassador to the United Nations. In a special election on May 13, minister and businessman Bill Redmond, a Republican, defeated Democrat Eric Serna to win the U.S. House seat vacated by Richardson. The Senate also approved the appointment of Gloria Tristani to the five-member Federal Communications Commission (FCC). She had been a member of New Mexico's state utility and insurance regulatory board.

The Roswell Incident's 50th Anniversary. On July 4, tens of thousands of visitors flocked to Roswell to celebrate the 50th anniversary of the alleged UFO sighting on July 4, 1947. Just ten days earlier, the U.S. Air Force had released a report saying that the sighting was a mirage and that the "space aliens" that people had reported seeing were in reality dummies used in an air-force test. (*See* SPECIAL REPORT, page 511.)

Other News. The state moved forward with plans in 1997 to regain control of its prisons, which had been under the control of the federal government since 1980....New Mexico became the 30th state to sue tobacco manufacturers....Traffic deaths not involving the use of alcohol climbed by one third during the first eight months of 1997. Most observers blamed the recent increase in the speed limit on interstate highways from 65 to 75....The Georgia O'Keeffe Museum opened in Santa Fe in July.

WILLIAM E. SHAPIRO

NEW YORK. Even for a state known for its contentious legislature, New York seemed to outdo itself in this regard in 1997.

Legislature. In one of the longest legislative sessions ever—210 days—Albany accomplished relatively little, other than making huge headlines. Among the more

Campaigning for reelection in mid-October, New Jersey Gov. Christine Todd Whitman addressed a Women for Whitman rally in East Brunswick. On election day the 51-year-old Republican won a second term in a close race with former state Sen. James E. McGreevey.

© Charles Rex Arbogast/AP/Wide World Photos

notable controversies were a measure to legalize gambling—which was defeated—and a battle over laws limiting rent increases, which was resolved in a last-minute compromise. The state budget was not passed until 126 days after the fiscal year began on April 1, eclipsing the 1996 tardiness record. The $68 billion budget included many spending cuts, but also an increase in school spending.

Politics. Lt. Gov. Betsy McCaughey Ross switched affiliations from the Republican to the Democratic Party. This followed a long history of public battles with her Republican boss, Gov. George Pataki, who earlier had announced his intention to drop Ross from his reelection ticket in 1998. In her statement, Ross claimed that experience with the Republicans convinced her that she no longer held the ideals of the party. "I decided it was better to change parties than to change my principles," she stated.

In New York City, Mayor Rudolph W. Giuliani won a second term.

Tobacco Settlement. New York was one of 22 states involved in a landmark settlement with a major tobacco company. Liggett Group, Inc.—the smallest of the five major U.S. tobacco companies—agreed in March to a plan that will cost them 25% of their pretax profits for the next 25 years; the money will go toward fighting smoking-related illnesses. In addition, Liggett conceded that cigarettes are addictive and cause cancer, a first for any tobacco manufacturer. Its brands—which include Chesterfield, L&M, Lark, and Eve—would carry a new warning: "Smoking Is Addictive."

BRUCE JACOBY

NORTH CAROLINA. Gov. Jim Hunt, serving his fourth term, signed bills into law for the first time in 1997, because North Carolina voters in November 1996 had approved giving the governor veto power. Under the constitutional amendment, if the governor does not sign or veto a bill within ten days of passage, it becomes law.

While Hunt did not veto any bill produced by the 1997 session, he did use his new authority to hold bill-signing ceremonies for major legislation.

Legislation. The governor hosted a media event June 24 to sign into law the Excellent Schools Act, which boosted teacher pay. The law laid out a plan for raising the pay of North Carolina's teachers to the national average, but required increased legislative appropriations each year to do so. The plan raised the minimum state salary, rewarded teachers with 25 years of experience, provided for increases in the third and fourth years of teaching, and offered incentives for teachers in schools that achieve certain standards.

Other new laws made it more difficult to get a drivers' license, raised standards for day care, required sex offenders to register, and limited the number of state patronage jobs. In response to environmental and health concerns, the state adopted a two-year moratorium on new hog farms. Large hog farms would be monitored more closely and would have to meet stricter sewage standards.

A welfare-reform law allowed a few counties to experiment with their own rules for welfare. The legislative fight over welfare held up passage of the budget for two months past its July 1 deadline. The state finally approved a $24 billion 1997–99 biennial budget.

The legislature also reduced the sales tax on food by 1% and agreed to spend an additional $23 million to expand Governor Hunt's Smart Start program statewide; the program provides early child-care and education programs.

ELAINE STUART

NORTH DAKOTA. In April 1997 melting snow from 13 winter storms contributed to the worst spring flooding in 500 years along the Red River from North Dakota to Canada. At Grand Forks the river rose more than 5 ft (1.5 m) above the 1979 record, with many locations about 2 ft (0.6 m) above previous records. Most levees failed, and thousands of residents were forced to evacuate their homes for weeks or months. Several blocks in Grand Forks' downtown burned on April 19–20 because the waters prevented effective fire fighting. Total damage in the vicinity of Grand Forks alone was put at between $1 billion and $2 billion, while 11 persons died. The U.S. government provided the region with $488 million in disaster relief, and President Bill Clinton directed the Federal Emergency Management Agency (FEMA) to reimburse 100% of the immediate cleanup effort, instead of the usual 75%. By December the relief price tag topped $950 million.

Other News. Several agricultural projects in North Dakota received federal funding, including $423,000 for environmentally compatible weed-control systems; $1.2 million for potato-disease and genetic research; $423,000 for rural-development and research-and-education programs; and $7.25 million for the Grand Forks Human Nutrition Center.

The American Medical Association's Education and Research Foundation provided more than $24,000 to the North Dakota School of Medicine to help it rebuild in the aftermath of the floods.

JOSEPH FERGUSON

OHIO. It was an active year in politics in Ohio in 1997. U.S. Sen. John Glenn, who first was elected to the Senate from Ohio in 1974, announced on February 20 that he would not seek reelection in 1998. In September the former astronaut, who made his first and only spaceflight in 1962, said that he would be interested in flying into space once again. "I'm ready to go today," he said. In January 1998 the National Aeronautics and Space Administration (NASA) granted Glenn his wish, scheduling him—at the age of 77—for an October 1998 flight aboard the space shuttle *Discovery.*

Another Ohioan, former Gov. Richard Celeste, was confirmed by the U.S. Senate on November 6 as U.S. ambassador to India. In a local election held November 4, Mayor Michael White (D) of Cleveland was reelected to a third term, handily defeating Councilwoman Helen Knipe Smith with 61% of the vote.

Flooding. Communities along the Ohio River suffered from heavy flooding during late February and early March. Gov. George Voinovich, who was heading a two-week trade mission to a number of Pacific Rim nations, rushed back to Ohio to direct disaster-relief efforts.

School Funding. In a 4–3 ruling in the spring, the Ohio Supreme Court declared the state's system of funding public schools unconstitutional. The court noted that property-rich school districts had substantially more to spend than did poor districts. Cleveland, for example, spent $6,500 yearly per student, while nearby Beachwood, a prosperous community, spent $12,000 per pupil.

During the year, Ohio continued to grapple with plans to pay for education and school-building construction. In July, Voinovich attended a meeting of the National Governors' Association in Las Vegas, NV, where gambling revenues provide funds for education. Voinovich, however, stated that, in 1996, the people of Ohio had turned down a plan to fund education with proceeds from riverboat gambling. One bright note was that the Ohio legislature came up with a plan to fund Central State University in Wilberforce, thus keeping it from closing its doors.

WILLIAM E. SHAPIRO

OKLAHOMA. The 1995 Oklahoma City bombing of the Alfred P. Murrah Federal Building continued to dominate the news in 1997.

Bombing Trials. The accused bombers, Timothy J. McVeigh and Terry L. Nichols, were tried separately in Denver, CO. McVeigh was found guilty of conspiracy and

murder on June 2 and later was sentenced to death. Nichols was found guilty on December 23 of conspiracy and involuntary manslaughter for his role in the bombing. Citing concerns that the convictions in the federal trials might be overturned, Oklahoma state officials said they planned to press state murder charges against McVeigh and Nichols.

Other News. On April 25 some 3,500 workers at a General Motors plant in Oklahoma City went on strike. The strike, which involved disputes over staffing and health and safety issues, lasted for seven weeks....Scott Dawn Carpenter, 22, was executed May 8 for the 1994 killing of a bait-shop owner near Eufaula Lake. Carpenter was the youngest person executed in the United States since the death penalty was reinstated by the U.S. Supreme Court in 1976....Leaders of the Cheyenne-Arapaho tribe invoked the 5th Amendment before a U.S. Senate panel on October 1 in refusing to answer questions about a $107,000 donation they had made to the Democratic Party in 1996. The committee was questioning the tribal officials to find out if the donation was made in exchange for a promise to return Native American land.

PATRICIA BEHAN

OREGON. A controversial decision was made by Oregon voters in 1997 when they refused to repeal an assisted-suicide law. The law first had been passed in 1997. Along with California and Washington, parts of Oregon had to cope with flooding as the year began.

The Death with Dignity Act. By an overwhelming margin, voters in the state reaffirmed the nation's first and only Death with Dignity Act, making assisted suicide by physicians protected under law. The action was met immediately with stern opposition from federal authorities. The U.S. Justice Department was reviewing the wording of the law, while the Drug Enforcement Agency (DEA) warned doctors in Oregon that they would face severe sanctions if they exercised their new privilege. Referring to this latter development, which was urged by two legislators—U.S. Sen. Orrin Hatch (R-UT) and U.S. Rep. Henry Hyde (R-IL)—a spokesman for Democratic Gov. John Kitzhaber (who is a doctor) said, "Our position is that the Feds are wrong. We think that what happened is that the DEA was pushed out on a limb by a couple of powerful conservatives." Indeed, the issue created a curious reversal of political posturing: Conservatives argued in favor of federal intervention, while liberals embraced states' rights. The referendum followed a U.S. Supreme Court ruling in June that stated there was no constitutional right to die, but that individual states were free to pursue "the earnest and profound debate about the morality, legality, and practicality" of the issue. (*See also* MEDICINE AND HEALTH—*Bioethics.*)

Cloning. Another news item that raised serious questions about medical ethics had to do with cloning. In March, Don Wolf, a scientist at the Oregon Regional Primate Research Center in Beaverton, announced that he and a team had created two monkey clones from embryo cells. The achievement marked the first time that close relatives of humans had been cloned; and—unlike the case with the cloned Scottish sheep, "Dolly"—the genetic material used came from an embryonic cell rather than from a more-developed adult cell.

Other News. Governor Kitzhaber signed into law a bill making approximately 20,000 workers eligible for state-subsidized health insurance. Under the plan, which Kitzhaber praised as a step toward universal health care, the state would pay up to 90% of premiums for low-income families. Funding for the program would come from higher cigarette taxes, which were approved by voters in November.

BRUCE JACOBY

PENNSYLVANIA. During 1997, Pennsylvania was host to two national events urging people to get involved in their communities.

Calls to Action. An estimated 300,000 to 500,000 people gathered in Philadelphia in October for the "Million Woman March," designed to encourage unity among women of African descent. It was viewed as a counterpart to 1995's "Million Man March." Philadelphia also was host in April to the Presidents' Summit for America's Future, during which President Bill Clinton asked Americans to get involved in public service.

Welfare Reform. A federal district judge ruled that states cannot pay new residents less than longtime residents in welfare benefits. The 1996 welfare law allowed states to calculate welfare benefits based on the rules of the state where new residents previously had lived. The court decision applied only to Pennsylvania but was expected to have wide-ranging effects.

Politics. Empire Sanitary Landfill pleaded guilty in October to illegally funneling $129,000 through straw donors to candidates in the 1996 federal elections, including to the presidential campaigns of both Clinton and former Sen. Robert Dole (R-KS). In a related matter, Pennsylvania state legislator Frank Serafini and others, including four Empire officials, faced charges of trying to hide illegal corporate contributions. Pennsylvania planned to computerize campaign-finance reports to provide greater public access. The information would be available through Pennsylvania's World Wide Web page.

On May 25, 1997, Strom Thurmond became the longest-serving senator in U.S. history—41 years and ten months. The South Carolina Republican celebrated his 95th birthday in December.

© Lou Krasky/AP/Wide World Photos

U.S. Rep. Thomas M. Foglietta (D) resigned to become U.S. ambassador to Italy.

Crime. John E. du Pont, heir to the chemical-company fortune, was sentenced to 13–30 years in prison for the slaying of Dave Shultz, an Olympic wrestler who lived on du Pont's estate. Some of the time was to be served in a mental hospital....More than 16 years after the mummified body of Holly Maddux was found in a trunk in her boyfriend Ira Einhorn's closet, Einhorn was captured by French police. He had been convicted in absentia of first-degree murder and faced life in prison.

KRISTI VAUGHAN

RHODE ISLAND. The Rhode Island legislature was very active in 1997.

Legislature. The legislature approved a $1.84 billion budget plan, which called for reducing the state income tax from 27.5% of federal liability to 25% over five years. In addition, cigarette taxes were raised by 10 cents a pack. In other legislative action, the state banned late-term abortions, adopted new formulas for distributing school aid, provided aid for legal immigrants scheduled to lose federal welfare benefits, and provided a $25 million increase for education.

The budget called for adoption of statewide academic performance standards and publication of yearly progress reports on student performance. The session passed legislation requiring more frequent property revaluations to improve property-tax rates.

After much debate, the legislature passed a bill to regulate hospitals seeking to convert from nonprofit to for-profit status. The action was taken in response to a proposal by a private firm to acquire a nonprofit medical center. Gov. Lincoln Almond vetoed the bill because it required for-profit hospitals to wait three years before acquiring additional nonprofit hospitals.

Politics. In January, Governor Almond, a Republican, appointed fellow Republican Bernard Jackvony to fill a vacancy in the office of lieutenant governor. Democrat Robert Weygand had left the post after he won election to the U.S. House of Representatives in November 1996. Following Jackvony's appointment, the Democratic legislature sought to appoint someone retroactively to the post, but the state Supreme Court in May ruled the retroactive provision was unconstitutional. Rhode Island thus had its first-ever appointed lieutenant governor.

Other News. Almond pulled Rhode Island out of negotiations to move the National Football League's (NFL's) New England Patriots from Foxborough, MA, to Rhode Island. The governor said the state could not offer more than $135 million to the team.

ELAINE STUART

SOUTH CAROLINA. The legislature of South Carolina extended its regular session in order to finish business.

Legislation. After the regular session ended June 5, the legislature assembled again and was successful in passing an auto-insurance plan, among other things. The new law eliminated fees paid by good drivers—recoupment fees—to subsidize auto-insurance rates for poor drivers. Another new law required drivers to wait until age 16 for a license, unless they pass a training course. Drivers under 17 would have to have an adult accompany them at night.

Gov. David Beasley failed in his attempt to get the legislature to agree to remove the Confederate battle flag from the statehouse dome and to relocate it elsewhere on the capitol grounds.

The state ended fiscal 1997 with a budget surplus of more than $297 million. The legislature passed a plan to establish a new infrastructure bank to pay for road projects, partially funded by new truck-license fees. Of the

© Steve Helber/AP/Wide World Photos

In Virginia on November 4, former state Attorney General James S. Gilmore 3d (R) easily defeated Lt. Gov. Donald S. Beyer, Jr., winning the right to succeed George F. Allen (R) as governor.

surplus, $65 million was directed to the new transportation-infrastructure bank, which would aid local governments in highway, bridge, and transit projects.

Other News. South Carolina in May became the first tobacco-growing state to join in suing tobacco companies. Attorney General Charles Condon said he wanted the state to share in any funds received as a result of multistate settlement talks.

On October 13 the state Supreme Court ruled that special-purpose governments could not levy taxes unless their members were chosen by voters. These districts provide sewer, water, and fire-protection services.

ELAINE STUART

SOUTH DAKOTA. Higher-education news was in the forefront in South Dakota in 1997. In October, Peggy Gordon Elliott was hired as the first woman president of South Dakota State University. She would replace Robert Wagner, who was retiring. Elliott had resigned as president of the University of Akron, OH, in the midst of a controversy involving an investigation by the Ohio attorney general's office.

It was announced in November that a $650,000 grant by the Kresge Foundation had been offered to the Oglala Lakota College, conditional on the college raising an additional $1.3 million within a little over a year. The money would be used to construct new buildings and furnish them with modern computer and communications equipment. In July, Arlynn Knudsen, the college's former vice-president, was sentenced for embezzling $2.6 million from the school.

Politics. During the second half of the year, U.S. Senators Tom Daschle (D) and Tim Johnson (D) tried to secure an additional $650,000 in federal funds for the Yankton Sioux tribe. Senator Johnson announced in September a federal grant of $3 million for housing renovation and water-well development at the Pine Ridge Indian Reservation.

Democratic state Sen. Bernie Hunhoff announced his candidacy for the 1998 gubernatorial race.

Economics. Net farm income in South Dakota totaled $1.33 billion in 1996, up dramatically from the 1995 level of $650 million. Other economic signs were positive, as well; as autumn approached, U.S. West hired an additional 200 workers at its new call center in Sioux Falls.

In the 1950s the U.S. Army built dams along the Missouri River that resulted in flooding in towns located on Indian reservations in the area. In 1997 the Crow Creek Sioux tribe received the first payment of a $27.5 million settlement from the federal government. This was in addition to the original settlement payments. Other tribes affected by the settlement negotiations included the Three Affiliated Tribes, Standing Rock, and the Lower Brule Sioux tribe.

Other News. In fall the South Dakota branch of the American Civil Liberties Union (ACLU) approved the state's decision to replace the State Penitentiary Law Library with an attorney who would help prison inmates file grievances....A $750,000 federal grant was given to the state health department, which planned to use the money to provide financial help for cancer screening to underinsured women....The state Supreme Court refused to hear the appeal of Robert Loftus, who was sentenced to eight life terms in 1995; he was believed to be serving the longest prison term ever imposed in South Dakota.

CRAIG BORLIN

TENNESSEE. On April 2, 1997, Tennessee became the last state to ratify the 15th Amendment to the U.S. Constitution, which guarantees U.S. citizens the right to vote regardless of "race, color, or previous condition of servitude." The amendment had been on the books for 127 years.

Crime and Legislation. David W. Lanier, 62, a Tennessee judge convicted in 1992 of federal civil-rights charges in connection with sexual assaults on women in his employ or who had cases before him, became a fugitive in August while free from prison pending an appeal. Lanier, who served two years and four months of a 25-year sentence, pleaded by mail to be spared what he called a virtual death sentence. Lanier—who was captured two months later in Mexico—pleaded guilty to running from the authorities on December 30 and could face an additional five years.

In February the state Senate approved, 27–1, a resolution urging homes, businesses, places of worship, and schools to post and observe the Ten Commandments, despite an opinion by State Attorney General Charles W. Burson that the resolution was unconstitutional. Burson later resigned to become Vice-President Al Gore's legal counsel.

Sports. The former Houston Oilers made their debut in Tennessee, where voters agreed to construct a stadium in Nashville. The Oilers—who played their 1997 games in Memphis—drew poor support and were criticized by Gov. Don Sundquist and Nashville Mayor Phil Bredesen for not changing their name. Oilers owner Bud Adams—who had said he would hold a contest to let fans pick a new name—said in November that any major change in identity or uniform would be timed to coincide with the 1999 opening of the new stadium.

JOSEPH FERGUSON

TEXAS. An armed standoff between state authorities and a separatist group that claimed Texas was still an independent nation topped the news in Texas in 1997. The Republic of Texas asserted that the state's annexation by the United States in 1845 was illegal. The group and its leader, Richard L. McLaren, also said that they represented the rightful government of Texas. The standoff began April 27 when the Republic of Texas took a married couple hostage in their home near the group's headquarters in the Davis Mountains of southwestern Texas. It ended May 3 with the group's surrender to police. Two Republic of Texas members fled. One later was killed in a shoot-out with police; the other escaped to an unknown location outside the United States.

Other News. U.S. Rep. Frank Tejeda (D) died January 30. His seat was filled in a runoff election on April 12, won by state Rep. Ciro Rodriguez (D).

On June 25 the U.S. Supreme Court struck down the 1993 Religious Freedom Restoration Act, which attempted to limit government interference in religious expression. In the 6–3 ruling, the court determined that Congress unlawfully had usurped powers from the judicial courts in passing the act. The case sprang from a zoning dispute between city planners and the Roman Catholic Church in Boerne.

President Bill Clinton blocked a Texas plan to have private companies administer the state's welfare, Medicaid, and food-stamp programs. The president's decision was seen widely as having been influenced by Texas labor unions, which strongly had opposed the plan. Gov. George W. Bush (R) declared that he would find a way to implement the plan without the federal government's support.

Tornadoes ripped through central Texas in May, killing 30 people. Hardest hit was Jarrell, a small town north of Austin. The twisters were the most destructive tornadoes to hit Texas in ten years.

Plans for the 1998 construction of the Sierra Blanca nuclear dump, 20 mi (32 km) from the Mexican border, drew protests from the Mexican government and from environmentalists, who said that the dump violated accords signed with Mexico and also that it would overlie a seismically active fault zone.

PATRICIA BEHAN

UTAH. The creation of the Grand Staircase–Escalante National Monument in Utah triggered some negative reactions during 1997.

National Monument. One year after President Bill Clinton and Secretary of the Interior Bruce Babbitt were hanged in effigy for announcing the creation of the Grand Staircase–Escalante National Monument, residents of Utah were beginning to accept it. The national-monument status of this Delaware-sized parcel of land in the southeastern part of the state cost the Democrats their sole seat in Congress in 1996; a preelection poll in 1997, however, showed that opposition stood at only 32%. Protesters had claimed that the national-monument status would curtail development severely, thereby hurting the state's economy.

In a related story, the Clinton administration announced in September that it had approved limited exploratory drilling for oil on a piece of that same land—a move that many viewed as running contrary to the purposes of the monument status. In Washington both the Fish and Wildlife Service and the Environmental Protection Agency (EPA) complained that the potential effects of the drilling were being ignored. Opponents now called for a more comprehensive study of the project. A decision on four more wells would wait until the results of the first test well were known.

Other News. Thomas K. Welch, the chief organizer of the 2002 Winter Olympic Games in Salt Lake City, resigned in July after being charged with domestic abuse. Welch's wife, Alma, the alleged victim of the assault, declined to press charges. The day after his resignation, the Salt Lake Olympic Organizing Committee recommended a $2 million compensation package for Welch, who had spent 12 years trying to bring the Games to the city.

BRUCE JACOBY

VERMONT. In 1997 federal legislation to insure children was introduced, modeled after a Vermont program. The state became part of a controversial radioactive-waste-disposal program in Texas.

Legislation. U.S. Sen. James M. Jeffords (R-VT) joined in introducing federal legislation that would expand access to health care for 5 million of the nation's uninsured children. Based on Vermont's "Dr. Dynasaur" program, the plan targeted families with a yearly income of less than $24,000 by encouraging states to expand Medicaid eligibility to families at 150% of the federal poverty level. The bill also would provide outreach funds to enlist the one third of all uninsured children who were eligible for but not currently enrolled in Medicaid.

Other News. Vermont would receive at least $360,000 in federal funds under a new program to help enforce its laws against underage drinking, according to U.S. Sen. Patrick Leahy (D-VT). The new program, which cleared Congress on November 13, offered grants that could be used for statewide law enforcement, including prosecutorial task forces, advertising, and "innovative efforts." Leahy said, "The highway deaths and all the other harm caused by underage drinking have made this program a very high priority in Vermont. These funds will help make sure we can treat it as a high priority."

In a unanimous vote, the U.S. House of Representatives Commerce Committee approved legislation to form the Maine-Texas-Vermont Compact, the nation's tenth low-level radioactive-waste-disposal compact. The dump, however, would be located close to the Mexican border and raised protests from the Mexican government and from environmentalists.

BRUCE JACOBY

VIRGINIA. Former State Attorney General James S. Gilmore 3d was elected governor in 1997, leading the first-ever GOP sweep of the state's three highest offices. He defeated Lt. Gov. Donald S. Beyer, Jr., winning on a promise to phase out the tax on automobiles.

Politics. Also elected in November were Lt. Gov. John Hager and State Attorney General Mark Earley. Paul Harris became the first black Republican elected to the Virginia General Assembly, winning the House of Delegates seat once held by Thomas Jefferson. The Virginia Senate voted to retire the state song, "Carry Me Back to Old Virginia," because of its racial references. The song was written by a black minstrel in 1875 but had not been played for more than two decades. Black-majority congressional-district lines were in flux, as the state's 3d District was struck down by a panel of three federal judges. Democratic Rep. Robert C. Scott had won in that district since 1992 and was the only black House member from Virginia since Reconstruction. State legislators were not expected to change district lines until 1998.

Crime. In northern Virginia authorities announced in July that the killings of three girls—the first in September 1996—appeared to be the work of the same individual or individuals....Several people were executed in Virginia, bringing to more than 44 the number of prisoners put to death there since the U.S. Supreme Court reinstated the death penalty in 1976....Sportscaster Marv Albert was placed on probation following his guilty plea to a misdemeanor assault. Charges had been brought by his former lover Vanessa Perhach that he had bitten her repeatedly and forced her to perform sex.

KRISTI VAUGHAN

WASHINGTON. Unemployment fell in Washington in 1997. Democrat Gary Locke was sworn in as the nation's first Chinese-American governor; he had been elected in November 1996.

Law and Politics. For the first time in 40 years, the state legislature adjourned on time in a budget-writing year, after enacting 456 new laws. Lawmakers doubled penalties for drug crimes near housing projects, required life sentences for child rape, and set tougher penalties for crimes with an element of terrorism. Big trucks no longer could use the left-hand lanes of some interstate highways, college tuition was hiked, and oil and gas exploration and production along the coast of the state were banned permanently.

In September the legislature held the shortest special session in state history, to restore the long-standing authority of law officers to run criminal background checks on motorists and pedestrians stopped for routine traffic violations.

In a special statewide election in June, 51% of the voters okayed a $425 million sports complex for the Seattle Seahawks football team. The team's owner and billionaire cofounder of Microsoft, Paul Allen, kicked in $100 million for the stadium and paid for the election.

Voters in the November election soundly defeated almost every statewide ballot proposal. They said no to trigger locks and safety licenses for handguns, to a ban on job discrimination against homosexuals, to marijuana for seriously ill patients, to required coverage of chiropractors and naturopaths by managed health-care plans, and to dental hygienists who wanted to practice without the supervision of a dentist. However, voters overwhelmingly endorsed a reduction in property taxes.

Economy. Washington's economy was hot in 1997, with statewide unemployment falling below national levels—although that prosperity bypassed many rural counties. The University of Washington reported that technology-based industries now accounted for one third of all jobs in the state, with aerospace jobs leading the pack, followed by computer software. Boeing profits took a short-term tumble when the company's ability to supply airplanes failed to keep up with growing orders.

Nature Takes a Toll. A late-December 1996 snowstorm, followed by heavy January rains, resulted in major mud slides in western Washington. A Bainbridge Island family of four died when their home tumbled into Puget Sound, and more than 130 landslides occurred in Seattle alone, causing millions of dollars in property damage.

MARY LOU COOPER

WEST VIRGINIA. Efforts were under way in 1997 to make this rural state more technologically competitive in the years to come.

Economic issues. Bell Atlantic announced plans to improve technological access through a new $20 million broadband telecommunications network. The improvement was expected to make the state more economically competitive and to improve communications access to schools, hospitals, and state agencies. Gov. Cecil Underwood and Samuel Tully, the state's chief technology officer, signed an agreement with Idaho Gov. Phil Batt, the Lockheed Martin Idaho Technologies Co., and PMG. Inc., to develop new technologies and spawn business.

Near the end of the year, U.S. Department of Energy figures showed that domestic coal production for the 25 coal-producing states was about 2.5% greater in 1997 than in 1996. West Virginia was among the highest-ranking producers.

Environmental News. The U.S. Environmental Protection Agency recognized Wheeling-Pittsburgh Steel Corporation for voluntarily reducing emissions of 11 chemicals. A proliferation of poultry farms in West Virginia was being blamed for reversing a comeback from decades of pollution in the Potomac River. American Rivers International placed the river on its "ten most endangered list," because of the tons of manure that run into the river.

Disaster Relief. The U.S. Department of Housing and Urban Development granted $3.45 million to communities that were affected by severe flooding along the Potomac and Shenandoah rivers caused by Hurricane Fran in September 1996, and by heavy spring rains and snowmelt from the Ohio and Monongahela river valleys in February and March 1997.

Other News. West Virginia's Division of Motor Vehicles began using a new photography system from Polaroid Corp. to reduce the number of fraudulent driver's licenses. The system uses digital photography and facial-recognition technology to match the features of an applicant who is renewing a license or seeking a duplicate with information stored in a central database.

KRISTI VAUGHAN

WISCONSIN. Gov. Tommy Thompson declared a state of emergency in Milwaukee, Waukesha, and Ozaukee counties after June 1997 floods caused some $43 million worth of damage. In August a building designed by the late architect Frank Lloyd Wright some 60 years earlier—the Monona Terrace Community and Convention Center—opened in Madison; construction of the $67 million building had been mired in controversy over its design and cost. Although the defending champion Green Bay Packers again made the Super Bowl in January 1998, they lost to the wild-card-entry Denver Broncos, 31–24. Two railroad tankers carrying petroleum gas derailed in Grand Chute, about 75 mi (121 km) northwest of Milwaukee on November 1, causing several thousand people to be evacuated from their homes.

Crime. In March military-surplus dealer Leo Anthony Piatz, 37, was convicted of masterminding the largest theft ever of defense equipment—$13 million worth—from a U.S. military base, including a tank and 17 armored personnel carriers. In June three accomplices also were convicted, while two were acquitted. Kevin Gillson, 18, of Port Washington, who had planned to marry his 15-year-old girlfriend, was convicted in April of sexual assault after the girl became pregnant during consensual sex. Gillson—who faced up to 40 years in prison and had to register as a sex offender—was sentenced to two years' probation and 100 hours of community service. On December 20 postal worker Anthony J. DeCulit, who had been disciplined earlier, fired a dozen shots in Milwaukee's main post office, killing one and injuring two others before killing himself.

JOSEPH FERGUSON

WYOMING. An October 1997 blizzard with 40-mph (64-km/hr) winds, accompanied by subzero wind-chill readings and drifts up to 7 ft (2 m) high, shut down 400 mi (644 km) of Interstate 80 from Rock Springs, WY, to Big Springs, NE.

Serial Killer. In November a judge rejected serial killer Keith Jesperson's attempt to block his extradition to Wyoming, where he could face execution if convicted of the January 1995 murder of Angela Subrize. Jesperson—known as the "Happy Face Killer" because of drawings on letters he sent to the media—had avoided the death penalty by pleading guilty to killing three women in Oregon and Washington; he was serving a life sentence in Oregon. In December, Jesperson—who had confessed to some 160 murders—recanted, and an early-1998 investigation by NBC's *Dateline* brought into question the validity of the confessions.

Other News. A federal judge in Wyoming ruled that a wolf-reintroduction program in the northern Rockies was illegal and ordered the removal of some 160 animals. Since these wolves were not protected from hunters, the plan would have allowed native wolves—which were protected—to be shot, according to the ruling.

President Bill Clinton appointed former Wyoming Secretary of State Kathy Karpan as director of Surface Mining Reclamation and Enforcement, in the U.S. Department of the Interior. Karpan, of Cheyenne, managed Karpan and White Law Offices and was president of Karpan and White Corporate Services.

JOSEPH FERGUSON

STOCKS AND BONDS

Wall Street's mighty bull market staged another full-speed-ahead gain in 1997, slowed only briefly by financial quakes in Asia and spells of volatility in U.S. stocks. U.S. stock indexes put together their first run of three consecutive double-digit-gain years since the mid-1960s as the Main Street economy continued to prosper and the boom in mutual funds showed no sign of fading.

Stocks. At the close of trading on December 31, the Dow Jones average of 30 industrial stocks stood at 7,908.25, up 1,459.98 points, or 22.64%, from the end of 1996. That showing came atop gains of 26.01% in 1996 and 33.45% in 1995. Among other prominent market gauges, Standard & Poor's 500-stock composite index chalked up a 1997 gain of 31.01%, and the Nasdaq composite index for the computer-screen-based trading realm previously known as the over-the-counter market climbed 21.64%. While all those indexes reached new highs, trading-volume records also were set in a year marked by the first billion-share day in New York Stock Exchange (NYSE) history, on October 28.

Along the way, the stock market weathered sharp setbacks in the early spring and again in the fall. The latter sell-off culminated in the biggest daily point loss ever for the Dow, 554.26 points on October 27, as fears mounted over the potential effects of financial troubles in Asia that had begun with Thailand a few months before and spread outward to several other nations in the Pacific Basin. However, the next day, October 28, the Dow rebounded 337.17 points on Big Board volume of almost 1.2 billion shares, far more than ever had been traded in a single session.

For as long as it lasted, the October 27 sell-off evoked some memories of the crash that occurred ten years earlier, when the Dow fell 508 points on Oct. 19, 1987. But on a percentage basis, there was no comparison between the two drops. "Blue Monday" in 1997 produced a decline of less than 8% in the Dow; by contrast, "Black Monday" in 1987, which started from a much lower level, drove the average down more than 22%.

Some of the shock-absorbing systems set up in the aftermath of the 1987 crash were subjected to a real-world test in the 1997 experience. On the afternoon of Blue Monday, so-called "circuit breakers" administered by the exchange prompted trading halts when the Dow's drop for the day reached 350 points, and again when it hit 550 points. In early December the NYSE proposed widening those limits and resetting them regularly, based on a percentage of the stock market's level. Opinions remained divided on Wall Street over whether the trading halts helped to restore calm.

George Stewart

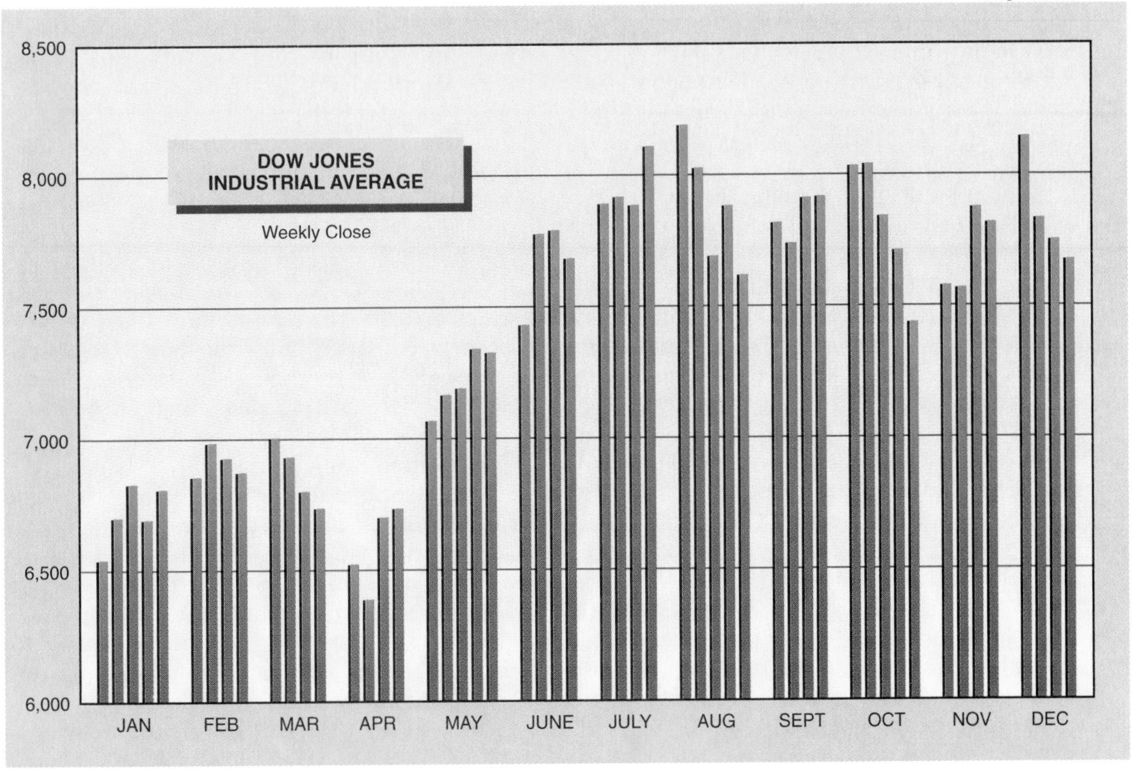

DOW JONES INDUSTRIAL AVERAGE

Weekly Close

As the year drew to a close, many questions still persisted about the possible effects of the "Asian flu" in currency and other financial markets, which was attributed mainly to overexuberant expansion in that fast-growing sector of the world economy. But most analysts voiced confidence that the damage inflicted on U.S. exports would not harm the U.S. economy severely, since it otherwise was in remarkably strong shape.

Both unemployment and inflation in the United States dropped to their lowest levels in a generation or more, even as measures of economic growth showed healthy gains in the range of 3.5% for the year and corporate profits kept rising. Over a stretch of more than 15 years dating back to the early 1980s, the U.S. economy had experienced just one recession, in 1990–91, and hopes remained high that no further business slumps loomed anywhere on the horizon.

Bonds. The U.S. bond market also enjoyed a good year, bolstered by evidence that inflation continued to subside even as business boomed. The yield on 30-year Treasury bonds, which began the year at about 6.6%, fell to about 6.0% as the year drew to a close. The Federal Reserve (the Fed) took one small step to tighten credit conditions early in the year, but held off on any further action through the second half despite repeated conjecture that it might apply the brakes. In the absence of any concerted push from the Fed, short-term interest rates fluctuated in a relatively narrow band all year, leaving yields on many short-term money-market investments in the 5% to 5.5% range. That proved good enough to spur steady growth in money-market mutual funds, whose aggregate assets surpassed $1 trillion for the first time.

Mutual Funds. The money funds' success was overshadowed in the fund industry by a continued boom in stock funds. As recently as the end of 1993, fund-industry assets were divided almost evenly among the three basic asset classes—stock funds, bond funds, and money funds. In 1997 stock funds' share of the industry had swelled to well over 50%. As of October 31, according to the Investment Company Institute, stock funds held $2.3 trillion of the industry total of $4,334,000,000,000 in assets. Money funds had $1,038,000,000,000, and bond funds totaled $996,200,000,000. Through the first ten months of 1997, stock funds had net inflows of $195,060,000,000 from investors—new share purchases minus the value of shares cashed in—slightly more than the net inflows of $192,690,000,000 in the comparable period of 1996.

The fund industry in late 1997 was more than four times as big as it had been just seven years before, in 1990, when total fund assets hit $1 trillion for the first time. As one fund firm, T. Rowe Price Associates Inc. of Baltimore, noted in a December meeting with the financial press, this onetime specialty business in a corner of the financial world now was accounting for 25% of U.S. household financial assets and generating more than $20 trillion a year in management fees.

More than one third of all the money entrusted to funds is invested through tax-favored retirement accounts, which are presumed to represent a strong stabilizing influence because they encourage regular investing for the long term. By all reports, the waves of volatility in the stock market in late October started no run-for-the-exits panic among fund investors. Indeed, some commentators suggested that the public, as represented by the actions of fund share owners, responded to the turmoil more calmly than did many professionals.

Foreign Markets. For all the commotion they touched off on Wall Street, the Asian financial troubles exerted an even more powerful pull on many overseas markets, in South America and Europe as well as in Asia itself. As the year neared a close, most European and South American markets still boasted healthy gains since 1997 began, but many Asian markets were left with severe net losses.

Among the best performers for the year, as reported by Birinyi Associates, were Mexico, which posted a 54.82% rise; Italy, up 58.9%; and Switzerland, up 58.83%—to rank considerably ahead of the U.S. market's 33.01% gain. Also in the plus column stood Germany, up 47.11%; Brazil, up 44.84%; the United Kingdom, up 24.69%; Canada, up 13.27%, and France, up 29.5%.

In Asia the gains and losses ranged from a gain of 18.08% in Taiwan to a whopping 55.18% loss in Thailand, where the trouble first surfaced. Japan, still struggling to pull out of a decade-long recession and trading at well below half its market index's high at the end of the 1980s, showed a loss for the year of 21.19%. Hong Kong, whose market began the year with impressive gains leading up to Britain's formal departure from its longtime colony, was down 20.29%. Other markets in the Pacific region showed the following results: Malaysia, down 51.98%; Indonesia, down 36.98%; the Philippines, down 41.04%; Singapore, down 30.99%; South Korea, down 42.39%; and Australia, up 7.91%.

CHET CURRIER, *The Associated Press*

SUDAN

Military conflict and negotiations to end the 14-year-old civil war dominated 1997 events in Sudan. Omar Hassan Ahmed al-Bashir and the National Islamic Front (NIF) led by Hassan al-Turabi remained in control of the government. Al-Turabi was speaker of the National Assembly. The process of defining the political system continued with the October appointment by presidential decree of a national committee for the permanent constitution.

Inflation and war costs continued to plague the economy; however, the development of petroleum resources moved forward with the creation of a consortium of Canadian, Malaysian, and Chinese companies. Sudan continued to rebuild relations with international financial institutions, and in October officials announced the resumption of technical and training aid from the World Bank and the International Monetary Fund (IMF).

Civil War. Opposition forces broadened the scope of their military activities. Early in January, armed forces of the National Democratic Alliance (NDA), a coalition of northern opposition parties, mounted the first major NDA military offensive against eastern Sudan from bases in Eritrea and Ethiopia. At the same time, the Sudan People's Liberation Army (SPLA), a southern Sudanese opposition group led by John Garang, captured frontier garrison towns in the north. Government control of road and rail routes between Khartoum and the Red Sea and of the Rossieres Dam—Khartoum's source of electricity—appeared threatened. By midyear, however, a military stalemate developed. In the south, SPLA forces won a series of victories. By September, SPLA leaders were talking about capturing Juba, the major government-controlled city in the region; but by late 1997, Juba remained under government control and the expanded opposition forces still were far from a military victory.

The government did negotiate a peace agreement with several opposition groups. In April 1997 six southern opposition groups signed a comprehensive peace agreement creating institutions of southern autonomy and prescribing procedures for a referendum for southern Sudanese self-determination after an interim of four years. The agreement allowed for the creation of a multiparty political system and of a South Sudan Defense Force, which would remain separate from the national army. In September, Lam Akol, leader of the Sudan People's Liberation Movement–

(SPLM-) United, accepted the agreement, leaving Garang's branch of the SPLM as the only southern group not accepting the accord.

Early in the year the government indicated willingness to talk with Garang. A scheduled meeting between Bashir and Garang in South Africa, to be hosted by South African President Nelson Mandela, did not take place. Instead, the government agreed to accept the 1994 Declaration of Principles (DOP)—an Inter-Governmental Authority on Drought and Development (IGADD) negotiation arrangement previously accepted only by opposition forces. IGADD is comprised of leaders of East African states actively working for a resolution to the Sudanese conflict. Bashir announced the Sudan government's acceptance of the DOP at a July summit of East African leaders. Despite partisan redefinition of terms on all sides, by the end of October delegations met in Nairobi to begin negotiations under the aegis of IGADD.

International Affairs. Sudan continued to be relatively isolated, but the civil-war negotiations helped build stronger relations with a number of African and Islamic states.

Strained relations with the United States continued. In early 1997 it was revealed that the Bill Clinton administration had granted Occidental Petroleum an exemption from the 1996 Anti-Terrorism Act—which bars U.S. companies from doing business with nations accused of supporting terrorism—to allow its participation in the petroleum consortium. But Sudan excluded Occidental when the United States announced that it was providing $20 million in military assistance to African countries supporting Sudanese opposition groups. In September the U.S. State Department announced that embassy staff would return to Khartoum, but retracted the statement following vigorous political opposition in Congress. The United States continued efforts to keep Sudan isolated diplomatically.

JOHN O. VOLL, *Georgetown University*

SUDAN • Information Highlights

Official Name: Republic of the Sudan.
Location: Northeast Africa.
Area: 967,494 sq mi (2 505 810 km²).
Population (mid-1997 est.): 27,900,000.
Chief Cities (1993 census—provisional): Khartoum, the capital, 924,505; Nyala, 1,267,077; Sharg en-Nil, 879,105.
Government: Head of state and government, Omar Hassan Ahmed al-Bashir, president (took power June 30, 1989). *Legislature* (unicameral)—National Assembly.
Monetary Unit: Pound (526.316 pounds equal U.S.$1, 1995).
Gross Domestic Product (1995 est. U.S.$): $25,000,000,-000 (purchasing power parity).
Foreign Trade (1995 U.S.$): *Imports,* $1,185,000,000; *exports,* $556,000,000.

SWEDEN

The Swedish government set full employment as its priority in anticipation of the mandatory 1998 general elections. Sweden planned to shut down nuclear-power plants in a change to renewable energy supplies. Economic growth improved.

European and Foreign Affairs. In June, Prime Minister Göran Persson said that Sweden would not join the European economic and monetary union (EMU) until after the next election, and only after membership was endorsed by another general election or by a referendum. The move was interpreted widely as barring membership until 2002, since elections only can be held every four years. Swedish polls held in August showed that 44% of the populace favored membership, while 30% was opposed.

Although Sweden does not participate in the Exchange Rate Mechanism—a prerequisite for membership in the EMU—five Swedish parties agreed to change the statutes of Sweden's central bank, the Riksbanken, giving it more independence and making price stability the overriding priority. The change would allow the Riksbanken to join the European Central Bank, which would be responsible for the new European Union (EU) common currency, the Euro.

A government-sponsored poll showed that more than 61% of Swedes wanted Sweden's future defense system integrated into a European structure; 33% rejected that idea—a complete reversal of attitudes five years earlier. Sweden still rejected North Atlantic Treaty Organization (NATO) membership in favor of expanding EU cooperation on security issues. But Carl Bildt, who served as the international community's representative in Bosnia, favored Sweden joining the new NATO. Swedish troops were serving under a U.S. NATO commander in Bosnia.

Politics. The ruling Social Democratic Party lost ground to opposition parties in 1997. Former Prime Minister Bildt returned from Bosnia to lead the conservative Moderates Party. Polls regularly reported that conservative support in the 1998 elections was widespread and that Bildt was twice as popular as Persson.

In February some 100 top business executives—including officials of telecommunications giant L.M. Ericsson, one of Sweden's most successful companies—declared they had lost confidence in the government and threatened to move their corporate headquarters out of Sweden. The executives protested the level of taxation, especially stock-market and wealth taxes. At 54% of gross domestic product (GDP), Sweden's tax rate is the highest in the world.

The business leaders also objected to Sweden's decision to decommission the nuclear-power industry, fearing dramatic increases in energy costs. The Conservative Party was campaigning on a tax-reduction platform and, in October, Finance Minister Erik Asbrink responded with plans to eliminate wealth taxes and cut low- and middle-income taxes. But Prime Minister Persson promised his party congress that he would abide by its decision to give full employment top priority, with more money for health, welfare, and schools.

The Swedish government announced in September that it would conduct a public inquiry into allegations that some 60,000 women with learning problems or non-Nordic ethnic backgrounds were sterilized forcibly from 1935 to 1976.

The Economy. The International Monetary Fund (IMF) August review of the Swedish economy noted that Sweden had been remarkably successful dealing with the deep economic recession of the early 1990s. The fiscal deficit was reduced from 12% to 2.5% of GDP from 1993 to 1996, and a small surplus was expected in 1998. The economic growth rate went from 1.1% in 1996 to 2.1% in 1997, with an estimated 3% in 1998. Unemployment remained at 8.4%, but the government was predicting a 4% rate by 2000.

Peter Wallenberg stepped down as chairman of Investor, the family investment vehicle, and was succeeded by Percy Barnevik of Asea, Brown, Boveri (ABB). Investor has controlling or major interests in Saab, Scania, and many other Swedish companies.

LEIF BECK FALLESEN, *Editor in Chief*
"Boersen," Copenhagen

SWEDEN • Information Highlights

Official Name: Kingdom of Sweden.
Location: Northern Europe.
Area: 173,732 sq mi (449 964 km²).
Population (mid-1997 est.): 8,900,000.
Chief Cities (Dec. 31, 1995 est.): Stockholm, the capital, 711,119; Göteborg, 449,189; Malmö, 245,699; Uppsala, 183,472.
Government: *Head of state,* Carl XVI Gustaf, king (acceded Sept. 1973). *Head of government,* Göran Persson, prime minister (took office March 1996). *Legislature* (unicameral)—Riksdag.
Monetary Unit: Krona (7.7773 kronor equal U.S.$1, Dec. 2, 1997).
Gross Domestic Product (1995 est. U.S.$): $177,300,000,-000 (purchasing power parity).
Economic Indexes (1996, 1990 = 100): *Consumer Prices,* all items, 123.3; food, 95.9. *Industrial Production,* 116.
Foreign Trade (1996 U.S.$): *Imports,* $66,619,000,000; *exports,* $84,517,000,000.

SWITZERLAND

In 1997, Switzerland was engulfed in a political, moral, and economic crisis over its relationship with Nazi Germany during World War II.

Nazi Relations. Several revelations were made in 1997 concerning the ongoing scandal of Switzerland's dealings with Nazi Germany, including details about the admitted sale of arms and manufactured goods, permission for unrestricted German use of Swiss rail lines, and the refusal to admit 30,000 of 50,000 Jewish World War II refugees. Swiss banks also allegedly bought and facilitated the international sale of Nazi gold bullion obtained from occupied countries and concentration-camp inmates.

On January 9 it was revealed that Christoph Meili, a bank guard at the Union Bank of Switzerland (UBS), had rescued documents slated for shredding that described bank dealings during World War II. The guard turned the documents over to a Jewish advocacy organization, which then turned them over to the police. Meili was fired for violating bank security and was threatened with criminal prosecution for stealing the documents. Critics charged that shredding the papers would have violated a new Swiss law prohibiting the destruction of documents related to Swiss dealings with Nazi Germany. On July 28 the government confirmed that the saved documents probably had bearing on the sale of Jewish property in Berlin during the war. Meili and his wife—harassed by threats of violence—fled to the United States, where they were granted permanent resident status. The Swiss government did not drop charges against Meili until October 2.

On January 30 a petition from more than 100 leading Swiss doctors, writers, lawyers, academics, and filmmakers accused the government of mishandling the crisis and damaging the nation's image. Signers asserted that Switzerland should own up to its past and recognize its moral obligation toward Holocaust victims. On February 5 some 5,000 people demonstrated in front of the Federal Government Building in Bern.

On February 23 three Swiss banks—Crédit Suisse, Swiss Bank Corporation, and UBS—announced that they would donate $70 million to establish a government-administered fund to support and compensate Holocaust victims. Businesses, organizations, and the government were encouraged to contribute; by the end of October the fund had grown to $190 million.

© Ruben Sprich/Reuters/Archive Photos

In March 1997, Switzerland's President Arnold Koller proposed establishing a foundation with Swiss gold reserves to aid people in need worldwide, including victims of Nazi genocide.

On March 5 the government, responding to demonstrators' demands, proposed establishing a Foundation for Solidarity. Foundation income would be used to aid victims of national disasters, poverty, and human-rights abuses throughout the world. Specifically included was aid to victims of the Nazi genocide. The government proposed that the foundation be funded by $5 billion from the sale of surplus gold bullion held by Swiss banks. This surplus would be created by changing the conservative official Swiss gold-bullion valuation of $3,170 per kg (2.2 lb) to one more in line with the $11,724-per-kg international market rate. On October 25 a government commission reported that such a revaluation would allow up to 1,400 tons of the 2,600 tons currently held to be sold without undermining the Swiss franc—although only the amount needed to generate the $5 billion endowment would be sold over a ten-year period. A constitutional amendment to change the value of gold was scheduled to go before the Swiss

Federal Assembly in 1998, with a national referendum likely in 1999.

Despite bankers' protestations of innocence, Swiss banks by January 1997 had located 775 pre-1945 dormant bank accounts registered to possible Holocaust victims and valued at $32 million. Further investigation was conducted under the direction of an international commission headed by former U.S. Federal Reserve Chairman Paul Volcker.

On May 8 a U.S. government report accused the Swiss of having followed a policy of "business as usual" during World War II. "Too often," the report said, "neutrality provided a pretext for avoiding moral considerations." The work of the Volcker commission and increasing pressure from foreign sources—particularly U.S. Senate Banking Committee Chairman Alfonse D'Amato (R-NY)—led the Swiss government to announce on June 25 that Swiss banks would waive normal account-secrecy regulations and would publish the names of domestic and foreign-held pre-1945 accounts that had seen no activity for at least ten years.

The new lists, published on July 23 and October 29, showed 5,443 such accounts, with an estimated value of $48 million. In addition, the existence of $8 million in more than 10,000 dormant pre-1945 accounts held by Swiss citizens (many thought to have acted as proxies for non-Swiss Jews) was revealed. These totals remained far below the $7 billion estimated by the World Jewish Congress—a figure Swiss bankers insisted had no basis in fact.

On October 15, California placed a ban on all state dealings with Swiss banks, while New York City Comptroller Alan Hevesi announced that he was dropping UBS from a banking group scheduled to back a city bond issue; he called for a December 8 general conference to discuss how U.S. public institutions should relate to Swiss banks. At the conference, U.S. Undersecretary of Commerce Stuart Eizenstat told state and local officials not to meddle in U.S. foreign policy and called for a 90-day moratorium on action against the Swiss.

A late-1997 report by an international historical commission on Swiss relations with Nazi Germany said that Swiss banks had received as much as $61.2 million in Nazi gold. In December representatives from some 40 nations gathered in London for a conference on wartime trade with Germany. A U.S. report delivered at the conference noted that, in addition to Switzerland, other countries that had been neutral during World War II continued to hold onto gold looted from Nazi Germany.

Economy. Nervousness over the long-term financial implications of the banking scandal was intensified by continued stagnation of the Swiss economy—which since 1990 had registered a cumulative –.5% in economic growth. Despite an August 28 UBS survey indicating that workers in Zurich and Geneva were the world's highest paid, unemployment—normally only 1%—reached 5.7% in February; 10% of the population was estimated to live below the poverty line.

Linked to these concerns was the resounding defeat in a June 8 national referendum of a Socialist Party proposal that would have banned the export of Swiss-manufactured arms or dual-use goods. Opponents cited the potential loss of some 120,000 jobs.

In one of the largest corporate deals ever, Swiss Bank Corporation and UBS merged into the world's second-largest bank in December. Some 6,000 Swiss jobs and another 6,000 from international operations were expected to be cut.

Other Events. A national referendum on September 28 to stop the distribution of heroin to addicts by state-run clinics was rejected by 71%. Critics called the policy a major step toward legalizing hard drugs; supporters cited studies showing a 90% reduction in crimes committed by those in the program, and significantly fewer AIDS and hepatitis cases.

Switzerland broke its tradition of neutrality on June 21 by becoming the 28th European nation to join the North Atlantic Treaty Organization (NATO) Partnership for Peace pact. The Swiss would not engage in armed NATO maneuvers, but agreed to participate in education, training, and rescue operations.

A September 1 post-office robbery in the city of Zurich netted the perpetrators an estimated $37 million—the biggest robbery in Swiss history.

A new airline, Swiss World Airways, planned to begin flights to New York and Miami in December.

PAUL C. HELMREICH, *Wheaton College (MA)*

SYRIA

Syria's internal politics and external stance changed little in 1997. President Hafiz al-Assad, in power since 1970, retained a firm grip on the country with an autocratic regime that made only a few gestures toward representative government. Assad did not budge from his long-held demand for the return of

© Mohsen Shandiz/Sygma

In August 1997, Syria's President Hafiz al-Assad (center) conferred with Iran's new president, Mohammed Khatami (right), as well as with the departing Iranian head of government, Hashemi Rafsanjani. Assad was the first world leader to met Iran's new president.

the Golan Heights before there could be peace with Israel. Technically, Syria has been in a state of war with Israel since 1967. Speculation about Assad's health and who might succeed him were rampant.

Domestic Affairs. In domestic affairs, there were signs that suggested change might be on the way—chief of which was the question of Assad's health. Like most autocratic regimes in the Middle East, Syria has no regular provision for selecting a successor to the president. The 66-year-old Assad physically had appeared to be in poor health for a number of years, and he was known to have had heart trouble in the early 1980s. On January 7 the Syrian news agency reported that Assad had undergone successful prostate surgery and would resume his duties "in a few days." In fact, he disappeared from public view for about a month. The London *Sunday Times* ran an article on February 9 that said Assad had been in a coma for two weeks in January, while Russian doctors strove to bring him back to consciousness. A Jordanian newspaper on February 14 described the state of his health as "grave." But at a news conference later in February, Assad appeared fit.

Succession had been a question since Assad's oldest son and heir apparent, Basil, died in a car accident in January 1994. Assad's second and only surviving son, Bashar—an ophthalmology student in Britain when Basil died—was brought home and sent to military school, ostensibly to groom him for the presidency. However, with no official confirmation of this view, speculation arose over other likely candidates, such as Vice-President Abdel-Halim Khaddam and armed forces Chief of Staff Hikmat Chehabi.

A series of Assad-family events heightened the mystery. In November 1996 officials closed an elegant Damascus restaurant owned by one of Assad's nephews, and in January 1997, Assad's brother Rifaat—nominally a vice-president—was brought back from a long exile in Paris but remained subject to strict surveillance. Another brother, Jemil, abruptly was sent off to Paris.

Foreign Affairs. Assad perceived the Israeli-Turkish agreement of February 1996, which provided for various forms of military

---

SYRIA • Information Highlights

Official Name: Syrian Arab Republic.
Location: Southwest Asia.
Area: 71,498 sq mi (185 180 km²).
Population (mid-1997 est.): 15,000,000.
Chief Cities (June 30, 1994 est.): Damascus, the capital, 1,444,138; Aleppo, 1,542,000; Homs, 558,000.
Government: *Head of state,* Gen. Hafiz al-Assad, president (took office officially March 1971). *Head of government,* Mahmoud Zubi, prime minister (took office November 1987). *Legislature* (unicameral)—People's Council.
Monetary Unit: Pound (11.225 pounds equal U.S.$1, principal rate, July 1997).
Gross Domestic Product (1995 est. U.S.$): $91,200,000,-000 (purchasing power parity).
Economic Index (Damascus, 1996; 1990 = 100): *Consumer Prices,* all items, 174.0; food, 160.0.
Foreign Trade (1996 U.S.$): *Imports,* $5,244,000,000; *exports,* $3,999,000,000.

and naval cooperation, as a threat to Syria—which lies between the two countries and had lost territory to both in the past. As a result, Syria pursued a much more active foreign policy, hoping to create a network of friendly cooperation with other Arab states to counterbalance the predominance of Israel and the United States in the Middle East. In order to maintain Syria's relationship with non-Arab Iran at the same time, the Syrian foreign minister was sent to mediate ongoing disputes between Iran and the Gulf states. At the end of July, Assad himself flew to Tehran to discuss reconciliation between Iran and the Arab states. He also met Ali Akbar Hashemi Rafsanjani, the outgoing Iranian president, and was the first national leader to meet his successor, Mohammed Khatami, after the Iranian election. This was Assad's second visit to Tehran; the first was in 1989.

A novel feature of Assad's foreign policy in 1997 was a cautious approach to reconciliation with Iraq. An Iraqi economic delegation was welcomed in Damascus in June, and further exchanges followed. Steps were taken toward free trade, although within United Nations (UN) guidelines.

During U.S. Secretary of State Madeleine Albright's first official trip to the Middle East in September, she spent three hours in Damascus conferring with Assad. Little came out of the meeting.

Despite Assad's cautious foreign policy, Syria began to devote considerably greater resources to its military in 1997, boosting military-budget expenditures from 25% to 37% of gross domestic product (GDP).

ARTHUR CAMPBELL TURNER
University of California, Riverside

TAIWAN

Three issues were at the forefront of political discourse in Taiwan's vibrant new democracy in 1997: reconstitution of the political system, the government's ability to deal with an increase in crime, and the future of Taiwan's economic and political relationship with mainland China. Taiwan's economy remained strong, with low unemployment, although figures fell slightly short of government projections.

Reconstitution. A 170-member National Development Conference held late in December 1996 recommended the reformation of Taiwan's political system through the strengthening of executive power at the expense of the legislature. Under the pro-posed system, the Legislative Yuan and the National Assembly would be combined into a new body of between 200 and 250 representatives. This new body no longer would have the power to appoint the prime minister, but could conduct a vote of no confidence in the prime minister or the president. The president, in turn, would have power to dissolve the legislature and call for new elections.

The conference also called for the elimination of the Chinese provincial government in Taiwan, triggering opposition from the New Party—a splinter of the Nationalist Party, which campaigns on a platform of reunification with the mainland; the Beijing authorities; and James Soong, the popular Nationalist Party governor of Taiwan. All argued that the elimination of the provincial government appeared to be a step in the direction of abandoning the idea that Taiwan is a province of China. New Party representatives walked out of the conference, while China issued a strong objection. The situation was complicated by the fact that the recommendations required approval by the National Assembly, effectively asking it to vote itself out of office. Despite the fact that the Assembly, in which the Nationalists were holding only a tenuous majority, held the reforms hostage while expressing disapproval of a range of other government initiatives, the reform package was adopted in July.

Social Disorder. Concern that crime was careening out of control and that the government had no plan to address the issue mounted in the late spring. In May the legislature—citing an 18% rise in the crime rate and three high-profile murder cases that remained unsolved—attempted a no-confidence vote in the legislature. Meanwhile, 50,000 people marched through the streets of Taipei to protest the government's apparent impotence in dealing with the crime surge.

TAIWAN • Information Highlights

Official Name: Taiwan.
Location: Island off the southeastern coast of mainland China.
Area: 13,892 sq mi (35 980 km²).
Population (mid-1997 est.): 21,500,000.
Chief Cities (Dec. 31, 1995 est.): Taipei, the capital, 2,632,863; Kaohsiung, 1,426,035; Taichung, 853,221; Tainan, 706,811; Panchiaio, 530,003.
Government: *Head of state,* Lee Teng-hui, president (took office January 1988). *Head of government,* Vincent Siew, prime minister (appointed August 1997). *Legislature* (unicameral)—Legislative Yuan; (unicameral)—National Assembly.
Monetary Unit: New Taiwan dollar (32.60 NT dollars equal U.S.$1, Dec. 31, 1997).
Gross Domestic Product (1995 est. U.S.$): $290,500,000,-000 (purchasing power parity).

Two weeks later, New Party delegates—demanding a public apology for the decline in public order—interrupted President Lee Teng-hui as he addressed the National Assembly. Ma Ying-jeou, the highly respected former justice minister, resigned from the cabinet, calling for Vice-President Lien Chan's resignation from his concurrent appointment as prime minister. Lien did resign in late August and was replaced by Vincent Siew, but few seemed satisfied. Popular dissatisfaction with the ruling party was manifested in the November local elections, in which the opposition Democratic Progressive Party (DPP) won 12 of the 23 contested municipalities; the Nationalists took eight. The Nationalists took their defeat very seriously; it was the first time that the opposition's overall popular vote (43%) exceeded theirs (42%).

Relations with the Mainland. Public opinion in 1997 gradually shifted away from advocating reunification toward favoring some form of independent existence for Taiwan, bringing into the mainstream what had been a radical view as recently as ten years earlier. The issue was given prominence with the transfer of sovereignty in Hong Kong in July; following the transfer, Chinese President Jiang Zemin stated that the first priority after Macau's "return to the motherland" in 1999 was reunification with Taiwan. Lee Teng-hui—who never formally had renounced the idea of reunification—insisted that substantial political changes must occur in China before closer political ties were possible. Lee increasingly became a voice of caution, arguing that direct communications links and excessive Taiwanese business investment on the mainland were a threat to the island's security.

In part, Lee's concern was triggered by Formosa Plastics, which ignored the opposition of Taiwan's government to its construction of a $3.2 billion coal-fired power plant in China's Fujian province. Formosa Plastics was one of more than 35,000 Taiwan firms that had invested some $16 billion in mainland enterprises, according to Beijing statistics. Total annual two-way trade between Taiwan and the mainland was approaching that same figure. In October, Lee's caution was attacked by Chang Jung-fa, chairman of the giant Evergreen transportation group. Chang was backed by a number of prominent Taiwan businessmen and members of Lee's administration who believed that restrictions on trade and investment were harmful to the development of the Taiwan economy.

Both Beijing and Taipei seemed ready by the end of 1997 to resume cross-strait talks,

© Dan Groshong/Sygma

The Dalai Lama was in Taiwan for the first time in March 1997. During his five-day visit, which angered mainland China, the Dalai Lama met with Taiwan's President Lee Teng-hui.

interrupted in 1995. The talks had been conducted by two nongovernmental organizations, the Strait Exchange Foundation (SEF) on the Taiwan side and the Association for Relations Across the Taiwan Strait (ARATS) on the Chinese side. SEF Deputy Secretary-General Lee Ching-ping visited the mainland in May and again in November; his ARATS counterpart, Liu Gangqi, visited Taiwan in July. It was speculated widely that talks would resume in the spring of 1998.

The Economy. Although the economy remained strong in 1997, growth fell short of the targeted rate. Whereas the government estimate for overall growth was 6.24%, the actual figure was projected to come in at 5.9%—the first time in many years it would fall below 6%. Foreign-trade growth also fell below government predictions. Although unemployment stood at a modest 3.2% at midyear, this figure was significantly higher than it had been in the recent past. Foreign-exchange reserves, which began the year at $100 billion, declined to $86.5 billion by the end of the third quarter. Despite these somewhat disappointing results, the Taiwan economy seemed better positioned than those of many of its Asian neighbors to survive the late-year economic upheaval.

JOHN BRYAN STARR, *Brown University*

TANZANIA

During 1997 both the ruling Chama Cha Mapinduzi (CCM) Party and the opposition faced major internal discord. These debates, however, did not detract from President Benjamin Mkapa's policy of economic reform, which once again attracted widespread international support.

Politics. Just prior to the 20th anniversary of the CCM, its former Secretary-General Horace Kolimba argued that, by giving up its socialist orientation, the ruling party had lost its direction. Party leaders denounced his criticism, although it did reflect the split between the older socialist members of the party, whose influence was declining, and its current leadership, which favors privatization, foreign investment, and smaller government. The CCM suffered another jolt when it lost a by-election to the National Convention for Construction and Reform (NCCR-Mageuzi). The United Democratic Party (UDP), led by John Cheyo, won a second by-election near Mwan-

za, which was thought to be a NCCR-Mageuzi stronghold. In May a rift between the national executive and the central committee led to a split in the NCCR-Mageuzi. The UDP experienced a split when Vice-Chairman Christopher Ngaiza resigned.

The Civic United Front (CUF) led the parliamentary opposition, although all of its members came from the islands of Pemba and Zanzibar, and few showed interest in mainland Tanzania's affairs. The CUF's relations with other opposition parties remained strained, and it refused to recognize the election of Salmin Amour as president of Zanzibar, boycotting the local parliament. Chadema—the final opposition party—also was plagued by infighting among its leadership and new members vying for influence.

Economy. Mkapa's commitment to economic liberalization and to the fight against corruption led to the signing of an agreement with the International Monetary Fund (IMF) and the World Bank. This agreement helped to restore international assistance and led to the writing off of $1 billion of Tanzania's $8 billion external debt. Debt service consumed 45% of recurrent expenditure; for every dollar spent on education, Tanzania spent $5 servicing debt. Tax collection virtually doubled, which enabled the minister of finance to propose no new domestic borrowing for the 1997 budget. Social services received 42% of the funds for development.

Tanzania's balance of payments remained strained, with commodity exports expected to be down by nearly 50% from 1996 because of inadequate rainfall. This resulted in a 41% increase in the trade deficit, although the export of cotton and nontraditional items, such as flowers, grew rapidly. Freight on the Tanzania-Zambia (TAZARA) railways, which once carried most of Zambia's external trade, fell by 40% due to competition from southern African routes and to the war in the Democratic Republic of the Congo. Fishing grew rapidly, as did mineral production, which was driven by Canadian and South African investors. Foreign investors also moved aggressively into the tobacco sector, although only R.J. Reynolds utilized Tanzanian tobacco in its production of cigarettes. A Kuwaiti and Danish consortium agreed to build an offshore duty-free area in Zanzibar.

Tanzania and Uganda agreed to merge their national airlines with Alliance Air, a regional consortium, which was profitable.

WILLIAM CYRUS REED
*The American University in Cairo
and Indiana University*

TANZANIA • Information Highlights

Official Name: United Republic of Tanzania.
Location: East coast of Africa.
Area: 364,900 sq mi (945 090 km²).
Population (mid-1997 est.): 29,500,000.
Chief Cities (1985 est.): Dar es Salaam, the capital, 1,096,000; Mwanza, 252,000; Tabora, 214,000.
Government: *Head of state,* Benjamin Mkapa, president (took office Nov. 23, 1995). *Head of government,* Frederick Sumaye, prime minister (appointed November 1995). *Legislature* (unicameral)—National Assembly.
Monetary Unit: Tanzanian shilling (624.810 shillings equal U.S.$1, official rate, July 1997).
Gross Domestic Product (1995 est. U.S.$): $23,100,000,000 (purchasing power parity).
Economic Index (Tanganyika, 1996; 1990 = 100): *Consumer Prices,* all items, 406.1; food, 417.5.
Foreign Trade (1996 U.S.$): *Imports,* $1,386,000,000; *exports,* $758,000,000.

TAXATION

The passage of the Tax Relief Act of 1997 (TRA-97) completed more than two and one-half years of acrimonious budget negotiations between the Republican-controlled Congress and President Bill Clinton. The ultimate purpose of these negotiations was to pass legislation that would balance the federal budget while providing tax relief. A primary feature of the TRA-97 is a net tax cut worth about $95 billion over five years. On a separate federal-tax issue, the Internal Revenue Service (IRS) came under increased scrutiny as the Senate held hearings into alleged abuses against taxpayers carried out by employees of the IRS. These hearings led several members of Congress to call for reform of the IRS. In response, President Clinton proposed and enacted reforms that were designed to increase IRS accountability.

Many states continued to enjoy the benefits of U.S. economic growth during fiscal year (FY) 1997 (Oct. 1, 1996–Sept. 30, 1997). For the third consecutive fiscal year, these gains were passed along through net state tax-revenue reductions. Legislatures in nearly half of the states passed modest individual- and business-tax cuts. Additional changes in state and local taxes resulted from ballot initiatives in several states that were designed to restrict the future growth of taxes or tax bases.

Federal. The individual-income, corporate, and social-insurance taxes and contributions for Social Security and Medicare dominated total U.S. federal receipts for FY 1997, making up more than 90% of federal-tax revenue. Of the estimated $1,505,400,000,000 in federal-tax collections, about 45% ($672 billion) came from individual income taxes, 36% ($536 billion) from social-insurance taxes and contributions for Social Security and Medicare, and 12% ($176 billion) from taxes on profits from corporations. Excise taxes, estate and gift taxes, customs duties, and miscellaneous receipts made up the remaining 7% of federal-tax collections.

Negotiations between Congress and the president over balancing the federal budget had begun in earnest after the Republicans gained control of both houses in 1994. Many of the successful Republican congressional candidates had campaigned with promises outlined in the Republican Party's Contract with America. Two of the promises were to balance the federal budget and to enact large federal-tax cuts. These twin goals of a balanced federal budget and significant tax reductions created substantial political tensions between the congressional Republicans and the Democratic president. Early on, these tensions led to two partial federal-government shutdowns during the latter part of 1995 and early 1996. During the next two years, Republican congressional leaders and the president continued to negotiate over the size of the tax cut and the timing of the balanced federal budget.

In the early months of 1997, three separate tax plans were offered by President Clinton, the House Republicans, and the Senate Republicans. Finally, in May, congressional

U.S. Sen. John Warner (R-VA) (right) listened attentively as Charles Rossotti (left) testified before the U.S. Senate Finance Committee. The U.S. Senate unanimously confirmed Rossotti, a 56-year-old computer-company executive, as commissioner of the Internal Revenue Service on Nov. 3, 1997.

leaders and the president agreed to the broad outlines of a budget package designed to achieve a balanced budget by the year 2002, including about $85 billion in tax cuts over the next five years and $250 billion over the next ten years. The largest tax breaks were to be concentrated in higher education, capital gains, and child tax credits. After the tax-writing committees in both houses drafted the specific tax bill and Congress passed it, the president signed the Tax Relief Act of 1997 (TRA-97) on August 5.

The main tax provisions of TRA-97 included more than $152 billion in tax cuts and about $56 billion in tax increases, for a net cut of about $95 billion over five years. The largest tax-cut provision is a $400-per-child tax credit, to start in 1998 and rise to $500 per child in 1999. This tax credit is aimed at lower-income taxpayers, as it is phased out for individuals with adjusted gross income of $75,000 and for couples at $110,000. Many low-income families who pay little or no federal income tax also qualify for the child tax credit. An additional tax cut came in the form of a credit against higher-education expenditures. Under TRA-97, families with children in college can qualify for up to a $1,500 tax credit for expenses in the first two years of college and $1,000 of expenses in the second two years. Education tax credits also are phased out for upper-income individuals and couples. Additional tax cuts came in the form of reductions in the capital-gains-tax rate. The maximum capital-gains-tax rate was reduced from 28% to 20% for individuals in the highest marginal income-tax bracket. The capital-gains-tax rate faced by individuals in the lower income-tax brackets was reduced from 15% to 10%.

Changes also were made to the tax provisions regarding the treatment of individual retirement accounts (IRAs). Old-style IRA accounts would remain, but income limits for tax-deductible contributions would be doubled over seven years. In addition, a new type of IRA was created in the TRA-97 that allows qualified individuals to pay taxes on contributions but not on accumulated principal or interest when funds are withdrawn for retirement or a first-time home purchase. In addition, IRAs were established for education expenses. Other phased-in tax cuts in the TRA-97 include an increase in the exemption for income subject to estate taxes, increased deductibility of health-insurance premiums for self-employed individuals to 100% by 2007, and an exemption from the corporate alternative minimum tax for small business. The TRA-97 also created or increased some

federal revenues. Federal taxes on cigarettes were to be increased by 10 cents per pack in 2000 and by an additional five cents per pack in 2002. The current 10% airline-ticket tax on domestic airline tickets would be cut to 9% in fiscal 1998, 8% in fiscal 1999, and 7.5% in fiscal 2000. A new per-passenger tax would be imposed on each segment of a domestic flight, beginning at $1 in fiscal 1998 and rising to $3 in fiscal 2002. The tax on international departures would rise from $6 to $12 and a new $12 tax would be imposed on international arrivals.

Although several members of Congress continued to call for a more radical overhaul of the federal-tax system toward one with more of a flat-rate structure, the current progressive rate structure of five marginal tax rates was maintained after the TRA-97. The 1998 tax schedules for couples filing joint returns would be: 15% for incomes not over $42,350; $6,352.50 plus 28% of the excess over $42,350 for incomes between $42,351 and $102,300; $23,138.50 plus 31% of the excess over $102,300 for incomes between $102,301 and $155,950; $39,770 plus 36% of the excess over $155,950 for incomes between $155,951 and $278,450; and $83,870 plus 39.6% of the excess over $278,450 for incomes above $278,450. The progressivity of the income tax is increased further with the federal Earned Income Tax Credit (EITC), which is a tax-credit subsidy to the earnings of low-income families. Since this credit is designed to help low-income working families, the EITC is phased out with higher family earnings. Provisions within the TRA-97 tightened eligibility for the EITC.

The fastest-growing portion of total federal revenue remained the social-insurance tax (payroll taxes). Given the projected growth in the social-insurance programs that this tax funds, this status would continue. The social-insurance tax is a flat statutory tax rate of 6.2% applied to all labor income. (E.g., interest and capital gains are not covered by this tax.) In 1997 no tax was paid on individual income beyond $65,400; in 1998 the limit would be $68,400. In addition to the employee's share, the employer also was responsible for 6.2% of the employee's labor income. An additional flat tax on the employer and employee of 1.45% on all labor income was designated for the medical-insurance program for the elderly (Medicare).

The IRS. The Internal Revenue Service (IRS) is the primary tax-collection agency of the federal government and, by most objective measures, it is effective in this role. In

1996 nearly $1.5 trillion was collected and more than 200 million tax returns were filed. With an operating cost of about $7.3 billion, collection efforts cost the IRS about 50 cents per $100 of revenue collected. Moreover, of the 102,000 employees hired by the IRS, there were 58 legal actions taken against employees and, of these, 32 were found guilty. However, even with these measures of effectiveness, the Senate Finance Committee held hearings during the summer over alleged IRS abuses of ordinary taxpayers.

The Senate Finance Committee heard testimony from four individuals who described extraordinary tactics taken by the IRS to collect back taxes and penalties. Employees of the IRS also testified to the illegal IRS practices of rewarding employee performance based on the level of tax collections and seizures and other forms of misconduct. This testimony of taxpayers and IRS employees was capped by the appearance before the committee of Michael Dolan, the acting IRS commissioner. During Dolan's testimony, he offered a formal public apology to the four taxpayers who had testified, as well as to all U.S. taxpayers, for this alleged misbehavior by IRS officials.

Prior to and immediately following these hearings, several reform proposals were considered by the House and Senate tax committees. These proposals ranged from abolishment of the IRS and replacement of the current income-tax structure with a national sales tax to more modest regulatory or oversight proposals. One proposal came directly from the recommendations from the National Commission on Restructuring the IRS. The bill would create a congressional oversight committee and establish an independent board of directors consisting of the Treasury secretary, an IRS union representative, and five private-sector professionals. It also would create employee-training programs and attempt to encourage electronic filing of tax returns. On October 10 the Clinton administration proposed a package of IRS reforms. Although smaller in scope than most of the congressional bills, the reforms had the advantage that many could be enacted immediately and did not require congressional approval. The administration's proposed reforms were designed to make the IRS more responsive to regular taxpayers and to make it more efficient. These proposals included opening the IRS telephone lines 24 hours a day, seven days a week, by 1999 and forcing the IRS to be more responsive through quicker refunds for wrongly assessed taxes and by expanding the use of a "taxpayer advocate" who would assist taxpayers and review complaints. Independent local citizens' panels would work with taxpayers to address their complaints and also would work with the taxpayer advocates to audit the performance of the regional IRS office. Meanwhile, Congress went forward with its own plans to overhaul the IRS, and on October 21 the Clinton administration said that it would support such legislation.

State and Local. State- and local-government tax revenues were projected to be about $1 trillion in FY 1997. The major sources of state-tax revenue are from taxes on individual income, sales, and corporate income. Many differences in tax structures and burdens exist from state to state. Seven states do not impose a personal-income tax, and, in the states that do, the numbers and levels of income-tax brackets vary widely, as do the levels of personal exemptions and deductions. In addition, a few states do not impose a general sales tax.

As a result of the continued strong U.S. economic growth, the states once again found themselves with a large budget surplus in FY 1997. Therefore, for the third consecutive year, nearly one half of the states were able to use their surpluses to reduce income taxes or to increase tax credits. Total state-tax cuts amounted to $1.4 billion, following reductions of $4 billion in FY 1996 and $3.3 billion in FY 1995. The largest of these tax cuts was the $931 million package passed in California. Minnesota also passed a large tax credit to rebate property taxes to home owners and renters.

Taxes remained important issues in the 1997 gubernatorial campaigns in New Jersey and Virginia. The victory of Republican candidate James S. Gilmore 3d in Virginia was based in large part on his proposal to phase out the state's personal-property tax, otherwise known as the "car tax." Because this is a large source of local revenue, the Virginia state legislature began considering alternative taxes to replace the car tax. Christine Todd Whitman, the incumbent governor in New Jersey, narrowly won reelection after she campaigned on her 30% income-tax cut during her first term in office. November ballot referenda in a few states also limited state and local taxation efforts. Colorado voters rejected proposed increases in the state's fuel taxes and registration fees, as well as a second proposal designed to increase sales taxes for mass transit. Voters in the state of Washington approved a ballot measure that reduces and limits property taxes.

THOMAS A. HUSTED, *American University*

TELEVISION AND RADIO

Television is often called the mirror—albeit perhaps a distorted one—of U.S. society, and that was never more true than in 1997. Trends in programming suggested a split national psyche. While the *Seinfeld* school of urban-singles sitcoms continued to treat sex more explicitly—and Ellen DeGeneres "outed" both her *Ellen* character and herself as being lesbian (*see* SIDEBAR, page 536)—a new genre of shows quietly moved in the opposite direction. These were shows with spiritual themes. Recognizing that "aging baby boomers are beginning to confront their own mortality... and seek the comfort of religion even on TV" (in the words of *Time* magazine), the TV industry shed its longtime caution about spirituality and embraced it with a lively (but perhaps financial) interest.

Touched by an Angel, a Columbia Broadcasting System (CBS) fantasy series with a career-resurrecting role for Della Reese as a down-to-earth angel, was among the Top 10 shows of 1996–97. It showcased such beloved guest stars as Carol Burnett and Bill Cosby (in an episode that aired, movingly, shortly after the murder of Cosby's son Ennis). *7th Heaven*, on the Warner Brothers (WB) network, was a melodrama about a minister's family, while *Promised Land* (CBS) was an *Angel* spin-off. *Soul Man*, on the American Broadcasting Companies (ABC), ironically cast Dan Aykroyd—a taboo-breaking writer-star of *Saturday Night Live* in the 1970s—as a priest.

Like any successful innovation, the spiritual shows spawned imitators. In the fall there was the irreverent *Teen Angel* (ABC) and the jokey *Good News* from United Paramount Network (UPN). The most serious—and most controversial—of the fall's new spiritual shows was *Nothing Sacred*, about Roman Catholic priests grappling with such issues as abortion, adultery, and their own weaknesses and doubts. The Catholic League, a conservative lay organization, condemned the low-rated show, while critics praised its courage and quality.

Sex, meanwhile, continued to "sell" far more than did spirituality across the spectrum of TV shows. A joint study by Children Now and the Kaiser Family Foundation found that three out of four shows during the "family hour" (between 8:00 P.M. and 9:00 P.M.) "contain sexually related talk or behavior"; this was a fourfold increase since 1976. Led by House Speaker Newt Gingrich, 100 members of Congress sent an open letter to the networks asking them to return to the family hour of wholesome programming.

Exploring the trend toward more adult-oriented shows, a *New York Times* article distinguished between shows that targeted adult audiences with a relatively sophisticated treatment of sex (NBC's *Frasier*, *Seinfeld*, and *Mad About You*, and Home Box Office's *The Larry Sanders Show*) and shows that reached younger and more impressionable audiences with smirky, titillating references (CBS' *The Nanny*; Fox's *Melrose Place*; NBC's *Friends*, *Third Rock from the Sun*, and *Men Behaving Badly*). Then, the *Times* observed, there were shows that occasionally could be just plain vulgar (as with Fox's *Martin*, which was canceled later in the year). In an in-between category, the *Times* also might have included *King of the Hill*, Fox's new animated hit series about a middlebrow suburban Texas family; the show was often crasser than *The Simpsons*

The success of CBS' "Touched by an Angel"—starring (l-r) Roma Downey, Della Reese, and John Dye as angels—touched off a trend toward religion-oriented shows on the other networks as well. "Angel" also engendered a 1997 spin-off, "Promised Land."

but shared the satirical edge of its Fox forebear.

Seinfeld's creator and star, Jerry Seinfeld, announced late in December that the show's current season—its ninth—was to be its last. Seinfeld reportedly had been offered up to $5 million an episode by NBC if he agreed to continue for another year. The comedy is considered to be one of the strongest ever on television, and was a sure source of revenue for the ratings-challenged NBC network.

The 1996–97 Broadcast Season. In May the A.C. Nielsen Company announced the results of its annual ratings race. NBC, powered by such hits as *Seinfeld* and *ER*, won for a second straight year with 10.5—its biggest margin of victory since 1986. (Each point represents 970,000 households.) CBS, led by *Angel*, struggled unsuccessfully to freshen its "old" audience demographics but held steady at 9.6. ABC, topped by *Home Improvement* and the slow-building *Drew Carey Show*, slipped from second to third, with 9.2. Fox was fourth but showed the strongest growth, partly due to enjoying both World Series and Super Bowl coverage and partly due to its youth-appeal Sunday lineup of *The Simpsons*, *King of the Hill*, and *The X-Files*.

Warner Brothers, with just three nights' programming, was a marginal ratings force but had a surprising mini-hit in *Buffy the Vampire Slayer*. Another popular show featuring an action-adventuress was the syndicated *Xena: Warrior Princess*.

As often happens, well-made dramas admired by critics—CBS' dark and gritty *EZ Street*, ABC's poignant *Relativity*—were canceled due to low ratings. However, a rare and encouraging combination of high quality and mass appeal was seen in *The Odyssey* (NBC), watched by 27 million viewers. The $32 million, four-hour adaptation of the classical Greek epic was minute-for-minute the most expensive TV program ever made.

And, as he has done since his 1990 landmark *The Civil War*, documentarian Ken Burns delivered rare high ratings to the Public Broadcasting Service (PBS) with burnished specials about Thomas Jefferson and—later, in the fall—the Lewis and Clark expedition.

Roseanne (ABC), closing out its nine-year run of feisty blue-collar attitude, was saluted by one critic for "playing a crucial role in defining social class in the 1990s and examining the flaws of family."

Cable. Perhaps the most striking proof of cable's coming of age was the performance of Home Box Office in the 1997 Emmy Awards; for the first time, HBO took more nominations (90) than any broadcast network. Nomi-

A PBS documentary on the Lewis and Clark expedition garnered high ratings in November 1997. The two-parter—written by Dayton Duncan (above, left), directed by Ken Burns (above, right), and with on-screen commentary by Duncan and historian Stephen Ambrose (above, center)—featured paintings of the era, such as the one at left by John Clymer.

"Ellen"

The saga of the ABC comedy *Ellen* had as many twists as a soap opera during its fourth season in 1996–97. For months it had been rumored that the show's lead character, played by comedian Ellen DeGeneres, would come out as a lesbian. Such a revelation—although it almost surely would boost ratings—could backfire among conservative viewers, since *Ellen* would become the first comedy series with a lesbian leading character.

Finally, the much-hyped "coming out" episode aired, on April 30, with guest stars including Laura Dern and Oprah Winfrey. The broadcast followed DeGeneres' announcement that she was gay in real life as well. The show drew 36 million viewers, almost triple *Ellen*'s average audience; it was the highest-rated ABC broadcast of the season other than the Academy Awards. The network increased the ratings bonanza by following the show with an airing of the newsmagazine *Prime Time Live*, featuring interviews with DeGeneres, her parents, and her brother.

The "coming out" episode drew prominent supporters (U.S. Vice-President Al Gore among them) as well as detractors; two Alabama stations, in fact, refused to air the episode, and various conservative groups spoke out against DeGeneres.

The controversy continued in the 1997–98 season, as the network kept a close watch on topics addressed on the show. A content rating of "TV-14" was added for the fall season. When ABC flashed a "parental discretion" advisory during an episode where DeGeneres' character gave another woman a comical kiss, the actress charged the network with "blatant discrimination" and threatened to walk off the show if ABC did not modify its position.

DAN HULBERT

© Everett Collection

nated HBO shows included *The Larry Sanders Show* (with 16, second only to NBC's *ER*, with 22), *Tracey* [Ullman] *Takes On...*; and the miniseries *Gotti* and *Miss Evers' Boys*.

Another HBO critics' darling was *Mr. Show*, an occasional sketch-comedy series hailed as "smart, savage, and often very goofy" by the World Wide Web magazine *Salon*. Showtime, meanwhile, enlisted heavyweight actors George C. Scott, Hume Cronyn, Jack Lemmon, and Edward James Olmos for a remake of the vintage 1950s courtroom drama *12 Angry Men*. And MTV introduced an experiment in video programming called *Amp*. The after-midnight combination of electronic "techno" music and eerie, computer-generated imagery commanded a substantial national audience of 400,000.

Other original cable shows launched in 1997 included *The Dish* (pop-culture news and gossip) on Lifetime; *The New Adventures of Robin Hood* (with a supernatural spin) on TNT; *La Femme Nikita* (espionage suspense) on USA; and *The Chris Rock Show* (outrageous comedy) on HBO.

Country Music Television (CMT) sparked audience involvement by asking viewers to vote by phone on their preference between

© Craig Blankenhorn/NBC/AP/Wide World Photos

Bryant Gumbel (center), who served for 15 years as host of NBC's "Today," received a standing ovation from his colleagues during a special two-hour tribute show on the occasion of his retirement from "Today" in January 1997.

two singers' new versions of the same song, played back-to-back for a week. Some 30,000 viewers—56% of the voters—preferred Trisha Yearwood's video of *How Do I Live* over LeAnn Rimes'.

Comedy Central grabbed some ink with *South Park*, an animated series about three third-grade boys that fell just short of MTV's *Beavis and Butt-head* on the crudeness scale, but featured a more bizarre imagination.

The Discovery Channel continued to build its reputation for multipart documentaries with *CIA: America's Secret Warriors*. Similarly admired was A&E's *Biography* series, which drew upon the resources of the CBS and ABC news departments. The series—treating subjects from Jesus Christ to Howard Stern—was so popular that it was scheduled to spin off into an all-*Biography* channel in 1998.

News and Personalities. The war between the network news departments and the corporate world they cover—which flared with the CBS–tobacco-industry skirmish of 1996—intensified in 1997. A federal jury ordered ABC to pay $5.5 million in damages to Food Lion for its 1992 *Prime Time Live* exposé on sanitary conditions in the supermarket chain. The jury found the network guilty of fraud for lying to get its undercover employees hired by Food Lion and for using secret cameras.

CBS' *60 Minutes* filmed, promoted—then decided not to air—an interview with Bill Cosby following the murder of his son and his revelation of an affair. Producer Don Hewitt explained, "I don't want to be part of America's soap opera." Critics were divided on whether the decision was a welcome reversal of the "tabloidization" of network news or a caving to pressure that some believed was exerted by Cosby.

Another clue that the tabloidization trend may have peaked was the trend of falling ratings for the sensationalistic syndicated shows *Inside Edition*, *Extra*, and *Hard Copy*.

The new MSNBC cable channel was dubbed the "cradle of the new punditry" by the *New York Times* Sunday magazine for its circle of diverse commentators (often under age 35), including neoconservative bombshell Laura Ingraham. And CBS became the last of the four broadcast networks to produce a cable channel: *Eye on People*, featuring follow-up and in-depth reports on news stories, with longer versions of interviews that had been edited for CBS news programs.

Bryant Gumbel—after an emotional send-off from his distinguished 15-year stint as anchor on NBC's *Today*—jumped to CBS to create *Public Eye*, TV's only newsmagazine with live segments. Cable News Network (CNN) also launched a newsmagazine, *Impact*, anchored by Bernard Shaw and Stephen Frazier; it was a joint operation with corporate cousin *Time* magazine. The show

TELEVISION • 1997

Some sample programs

About Us: The Dignity of Children—Special on children's thoughts and observations. Hosted by Oprah Winfrey. ABC, March 29.

The American Experience: Truman—Two-part documentary exploring the life of President Harry Truman. Narrated by Jason Robards. PBS, Oct. 5.

American Vision—Eight-part series on three centuries of America as seen through its art. PBS, May 28.

Any Mother's Son—Television movie based on the true story of the 1992 murder of a U.S. Navy sailor. With Bonnie Bedelia. Lifetime, Aug. 11.

Beyond Wall Street: The Art of Investing—Eight-part series on growing your money. PBS, Sept. 19.

Breaking the Code—Story of Alan Turing, a mathematical genius who designed the computer used to break the German Enigma code. PBS, Feb. 2.

Breaking the Surface: The Greg Louganis Story—About the Olympic diver. With Mario Lopez and Patrick David. USA, March 19.

Breast Men—Story of two fictional pioneers in breast-implant surgery. With David Schwimmer and Chris Cooper. HBO, Dec. 13.

Buffalo Soldiers—TV movie about the black cavalrymen who helped tame the West. With Danny Glover, Glynn Turman, and Carl Lumbly. TNT, Dec. 7.

Cadillac Desert—Four-part series on the struggle for water in the modern American West. PBS, July 6.

China: Born Under the Red Flag—Two-hour documentary on post-Mao China. PBS, July 9.

Color of Justice—Four black youths from the Bronx hijack a car driven by a white New Jersey woman. With F. Murray Abraham. Showtime, Sept. 7.

Daughters of the Troubles—Personal narratives by two working-class Belfast women. PBS, March 4.

David—Two-part biblical drama. With Nathaniel Parker, Jonathan Pryce, and Sheryl Lee. TNT, April 6.

A Day With...—Special on celebrities and their secrets. Lifetime, June 29.

Diana's Dresses—Stories behind the auctioned wardrobe of the late princess of Wales. PBS, Nov. 13.

Drop Dead Gorgeous—Story of stand-up comic Steve Moore, who refuses to let HIV get him down. HBO, June 16.

Ellis Island—Documentary on the human stories and the processing of 13 million immigrants. Narrated by Mandy Patinkin. History Channel, Jan. 19.

Emma—Television movie based on the Jane Austen novel. With Kate Beckinsale, Samantha Morton, and Olivia Williams. A&E, Feb. 16.

The Excellence Files—Tradition-breaking business practices. PBS, Sept. 2.

First-Time Felon—Drama about a Chicago gang member convicted of drug dealing. With Omar Epps and William Forsyth. HBO, Sept. 6.

Fonteyn and Nureyev: The Perfect Partnership—Story of a unique dance collaboration. PBS, Dec. 15.

Forbidden Territory: Stanley's Search for Livingstone—British journalist Henry Stanley travels to Africa to search for missionary David Livingstone. With Aidan Quinn, Nigel Hawthorne, and Fay Masterson. ABC, Dec. 7.

George Wallace—Two-part miniseries about the former Alabama governor. With Clarence Williams, Gary Sinise, and Mare Winningham. TNT, Aug. 24.

The GI Bill: The Law That Changed America—Dramatic story of the creation of a radical piece of legislation. PBS, Oct. 22.

Girls Like Us—Documentary about four working-class Philadelphia teenagers. PBS, July 22.

Great Books: Don Quixote and Great Expectations—Documentary series narrated by Donald Sutherland. The Learning Channel, June 28.

Great Performances: The Story of Gospel Music—Ninety-minute documentary with music by and stories about Mahalia Jackson, Sister Rosetta Tharpe, and Shirley Caesar and the Caravans. PBS, Feb. 5.

Great Ships: The Pirate Ships—Documentary on the exploration done by pirate ships. History Channel, Dec. 2.

Hitchhiking Vietnam: Letters from the Trail—Documentary about a 28-year-old woman's travels through Vietnam. PBS, Aug. 10.

Hostile Waters—Thriller about a collision between a U.S. submarine and a Soviet sub. With Martin Sheen, Rutger Hauer, and Max von Sydow. HBO, July 26.

In the Gloaming—A gay man returns home to die of AIDS. With David Strathairn, Glenn Close, Bridget Fonda, and Robert Sean Leonard. HBO, April 20.

Innovation—Three-part series on how biomedical technology is used to reengineer human beings. PBS, Dec. 16.

Judy Garland: Beyond the Rainbow—Biography of the singer and actress. A&E, March 23.

Knife to the Heart—Four-part series on transplant surgery. PBS, Jan. 27.

A Laugh, A Tear, A Mitzvah—What being Jewish means to U.S. Jews. PBS, March 10.

Lewis and Clark: The Journey of the Corps of Discovery—Two-part feature on the historical expedition and the friendship between the two explorers. PBS, Nov. 4.

Liberty! The American Revolution—Dramatic six-hour documentary on 26 years during the birth of the United States. PBS, Nov. 23.

The Living Edens: Namib, Africa's Burning Shore—Feature on this coastal desert. PBS, July 16.

Making Babies—Three-part documentary on reproduction and infertility. Discovery Channel, July 28.

Mandela and de Klerk—Television movie detailing the negotiations ending Nelson Mandela's 27-year imprisonment. With Sidney Poitier and Michael Caine. Showtime, Feb. 16.

Mario Puzo's "The Last Don"—Three-part miniseries based on Puzo's novel. With Kirstie Alley and Danny Aiello. CBS, May 11.

Midnight in Savannah—Documentary on a high-profile murder that shocked the Georgia city. A&E, Nov. 30.

Miss Evers' Boys—Story of a fictional nurse who tries to alleviate the suffering of men involved in a real-life study of syphilis and its treatments. HBO, Feb. 22.

Nature: Spirits of the Jaguar—Four-part series on the origins and natural and human history of Central America and the Caribbean. PBS, May 11.

Night Sins—Two-part series based on the novel by Tami Hoag. With Valerie Bertinelli and Harry Hamlin. CBS, Feb. 23.

Nova: Curse of T. Rex—The archaeological battles of one prospector in South Dakota. PBS, Feb. 25.

The Odyssey—Two-part miniseries based on Homer's epic. With Vanessa Williams and Armand Assante. NBC, May 18.

Old Man—The 1920s odyssey of a prison-farm inmate. With Arliss Howard and Jeanne Tripplehorn. CBS, Feb. 9.

Out in New York—Conversations and entertainment from authors, artists, historians, and others in New York City's gay and lesbian community. PBS, June 26.

Oz—Eight-episode police-drama series. With Ernie Hudson, Terry Kinney, and Eamonn Walker. HBO, July 12.

Path to Paradise—Docudrama about the 1993 bombing of the World Trade Center. With Art Malik, Ramzi Yousef, and Ned Eisenberg. HBO, June 14.

Philip Johnson: Diary of an Eccentric Architect—Documentary and tour of Johnson's "Glass House." PBS, Aug. 28.

Prime Suspect V: Errors of Judgement—Two-part Mobil Masterpiece Theatre story set in the gritty underworld of Manchester, England. With Helen Mirren. PBS, Feb 9.

Rebecca—Two-part Mobil Masterpiece Theatre story based on the Daphne du Maurier novel. With Diana Rigg, Charles Dance, and Emilia Fox. PBS, April 13.

Riot—Four stories on the 1992 Los Angeles riots. With Cicely Tyson, Mario Van Peebles, Melvin Van Peebles, Luke Perry, and Dante Basco. Showtime, April 27.

A Royal Scandal—An account of the disastrous 18th-century marriage of George, prince of Wales, and Princess Caroline of Brunswick. With Richard E. Grant and Susan Lynch. PBS, Jan. 12.

San Francisco Opera Gala Celebration—By repeating breakthrough performances, reunited performers celebrate days gone by. PBS, Dec. 10.

Simon Wiesenthal: Freedom Is Not a Gift from Heaven—The world's foremost Nazi hunter tells his life story. PBS, May 1.

The Snow Wolves—Yellowstone National Park attempts to reintroduce these endangered animals. PBS, Aug. 27.

Stephen Hawking's Universe—Six-part series that looks at the formation of the universe. PBS, Oct. 13.

Stomp Out Loud—Eight performers use trash-can lids, hammers, and basketballs in rooftops, alleys, and other New York City locations. HBO, Dec. 6.

Subway Stories—Ten tales from the underground. With Dennis Leary, Gregory Hines, Anne Heche, and Rosie Perez. HBO, Aug. 17.

Thomas Jefferson—Documentary on America's third president. PBS, Feb. 18.

Titanic: Anatomy of a Disaster—A look at the technical questions of why the "unsinkable" ship sank. Narrated by Martin Sheen. Discovery Channel, April 13.

12 Angry Men—Remake of Reginald Rose's 1954 drama. With Jack Lemmon, George C. Scott, Hume Cronyn, and Tony Danza. Showtime, Aug. 17.

20,000 Leagues Under the Sea—Two-part miniseries based on Jules Verne's book. With Michael Cain. ABC, May 11.

When Danger Follows You Home—Television movie about a social worker drawn to a troubled prison inmate. With Bill Switzer, JoBeth Williams, and Vanessa King. USA, Dec. 3.

was part of a CNN overhaul to bolster daily home viewership, which in midyear dipped to 284,000—the lowest in the channel's history and less than half the audience recorded during the O.J. Simpson trial coverage of 1995.

Murphy Brown again sparked debate about values. Once more the CBS comedy earned the displeasure of a high-level elected official—this time, Drug Enforcement Administrator Thomas Constantine—when the reporter played by Candice Bergen used marijuana to relieve nausea caused by chemotherapy for her breast cancer.

Among the beloved TV personalities who died in 1997 were oceanographer Jacques Cousteau, CBS newsman (with a touch of the poet) Charles Kuralt, and the great clown Red Skelton. (*See* OBITUARIES.)

New Fall Shows. In keeping with the trend of recent years, no new show immediately "broke out" with exceptional ratings from the ever-more-crowded field of new shows; there was an all-time high of 59 sitcoms, 18 of them new, on the broadcast networks.

However, *Veronica's Closet*, starring Kirstie Alley as a loose-tongued lingerie merchant, benefited from joining NBC's Thursday powerhouse lineup (between *Seinfeld* and *ER*) to score good ratings. There was also promising response to the young, dizzy, flawed, yet smart heroines of *Dharma & Greg* (ABC) and *Ally McBeal* (Fox). Modest critical praise came to *Fired Up* (NBC) and the police drama *Brooklyn South* (CBS). As the year drew to a close, new CBS vehicles for stars David Caruso (*Michael Hayes*), Gregory Hines (*The Gregory Hines Show*), and Danny Aiello (*Dellaventura*) were not performing consistently in the ratings.

In the late-night ratings race, *The Late Show with David Letterman* (CBS) not only slipped regularly behind its old runner-up, *The Tonight Show with Jay Leno* (NBC), but also occasionally lost to ABC's *Nightline*. *The Keenen Ivory Wayans Show*, starring the creator of the sketch-comedy show *In Living Color*, tried to resurrect the late-night talk-show format—targeted to young and racially mixed audiences—pioneered by Arsenio Hall in the early 1990s. Hall, meanwhile, resurfaced with a sitcom, *Arsenio*, on ABC.

Radio. Either because the radio "shock jocks" (Don Imus, Howard Stern) and provocative partisan commentators (Rush Limbaugh) toned down their rhetoric slightly or because audiences had become less easily shocked, there seemed to be fewer and milder controversies in the world of talk radio in 1997. Imus, in fact, was named by *Time* maga-

© Photofest

In NBC's new fall comedy "Veronica's Closet," Kirstie Alley (left) played the owner of a lingerie company, with Christopher McDonald (right) as her philandering husband.

zine as "one of America's most influential people," dismaying many readers.

One of the most talked-about episodes in radio instead involved "Dr. Laura" Schlessinger, the hugely popular Los Angeles–based on-air therapist. After being upbraided by a *Dallas Morning News* columnist for her allegedly arrogant behavior during a visit to address the Jewish Federation of Greater Dallas, Schlessinger—usually known for her stoic tone—broke down on the air, saying that the attack was causing her "a spiritual crisis."

A new radio niche was born when KGIL (1260 AM) in Hollywood created a 24-hour show-tunes format. With Florence Henderson (*The Brady Bunch*) and Gary Owens (*Laugh-In*) among the disk jockeys, the station played everything from classic musical scores to such collector's items as "Mack and Mabel" and "The Rothschilds."

DAN HULBERT
"The Atlanta Journal and Constitution"

TERRORISM

The United States experienced a diversity of terrorist-related events in 1997. These included several trials of domestic and foreign terrorists in the United States, the assassination of four American businessmen in Pakistan after a verdict was reached in one of these trials, and the resignation of the top general in the U.S. Air Force to protest the punishment of another air-force general for the 1996 bombing of a U.S. military housing complex in Dhahran, Saudi Arabia.

Terrorism Trials. The year 1997 would be remembered as one in which terrorists with a variety of political ideologies were brought to trial in the United States. The most dramatic and publicized trial was that of Timothy McVeigh, a right-wing extremist with ties to the militia movement who was arrested shortly after the April 19, 1995, bombing of the Alfred P. Murrah Federal Building in Oklahoma City, OK. The blast, which killed 168 people, was the worst act of terrorism ever on U.S. soil. It was charged that McVeigh committed the bombing in retaliation for the 1993 U.S. government raid on the Branch Davidian religious cult's compound in Waco, TX, that resulted in some 80 deaths. The bombing occurred on the second anniversary of that raid. Federal charges were brought against McVeigh for the murder of eight federal agents who were on duty when the 5,000-lb (2 268-kg) bomb exploded. The federal jury in Denver, CO, found McVeigh guilty of the eight murders and returned a death sentence in June. McVeigh also was found guilty by the same jury of conspiracy to use a weapon of mass destruction, using a weapon of mass destruction, and destruction of a federal building. McVeigh still could face state charges in Oklahoma.

McVeigh's alleged accomplice, Terry Nichols, faced similar charges in a separate federal trial. In December he was found guilty of conspiracy to use a weapon of mass destruction and involuntary manslaughter of the eight federal law-enforcement agents. However, he was found not guilty of the use of a weapon of mass destruction, not guilty of destruction by an explosive, and not guilty of first- or second-degree murder of the federal agents. Nichols had become friends with McVeigh while both were in the army in the late 1980s, and had allowed McVeigh to live for awhile on his farm in Decker, MI. Nichols and McVeigh reportedly attended militia meetings in Michigan and practiced setting off explosives on the farm. Prosecutors argued that Nichols helped build the bomb that exploded in front of the Oklahoma City federal building, including helping McVeigh pack barrels with fuel oil and ammonium nitrate and place them in the Ryder rental truck that was used in the bombing. In early 1998 the jury deadlocked on the death penalty for Nichols; the decision on Nichols' punishment was to be determined by the judge in the case.

Preparations for the trial of another suspected domestic terrorist, Theodore Kaczynski, began in 1997. Kaczynski was suspected of being the infamous Unabomber, a terrorist who committed 16 bombings over a 17-year period, beginning in 1978. Three people were killed and 23 were injured in the attacks, which originally began against university and airline targets, thereby leading the Federal Bureau of Investigation (FBI) to give the code name "Unabom" ("UN" for universities, "A" for airlines) to their investigation. The last bombing attributed to the Unabomber occurred in 1995, and Kaczynski was arrested in 1996 at a Montana cabin.

The trial in Sacramento would be for four separate bombs that Kaczynski allegedly sent from California or that exploded in California, killing two people and injuring four others. The motive for all the bombings was to protest technology and bring about a revolution against industrial society. Among the items found in Kaczynski's cabin were bomb components, a completed bomb, journal entries, and what authorities believe was the original draft of the Unabomber's manifesto, a 35,000-word antitechnology treatise that the Unabomber demanded be published in *The New York Times* and *The Washington Post* in return for a pledge to stop sending bombs. The manifesto was published and helped lead to Kaczynski's capture.

Mir Amal Kansi, a Pakistani, was convicted in November of ten charges in connection with the killing of two Central Intelligence Agency (CIA) employees and the wounding of three others in a shooting attack outside CIA headquarters in 1993. Kansi reportedly committed the killings to protest the U.S. bombing of Iraq during the Persian Gulf war. Following his conviction, four Americans working as auditors for U.S.-based Union Texas Petroleum were killed in Karachi, Pakistan, on November 12, along with their Pakistani driver, while they were on their way to work. It is believed that the assassinations may have been in retaliation for the Kansi verdict. Despite fears of additional attacks, the jury recommended a death sentence for Kansi a few days later.

In yet another significant terrorism trial, Ramzi Ahmed Yousef was found guilty in November of being the mastermind of the 1993 World Trade Center bombing in New York City that killed six persons and injured more than 1,000 others. The motive for the bombing was to protest U.S. policy in the Middle East. A U.S. secret-service agent testified that Yousef told him after his arrest in Pakistan in 1995 that he had hoped that the bomb would shear the support beams of the Trade Center, thereby toppling one of the towers and killing tens of thousands of people. Yousef also was convicted in 1996 of plotting to blow up several U.S. airliners in Asia. On Jan. 9, 1998, Yousef was sentenced to life plus 240 years in prison for both cases.

Eyad Ismoil also was found guilty for his part in the Trade Center bombing. Ismoil drove the van that carried the bomb into the underground garage of the Trade Center. Ismoil was to be sentenced in February 1998. He faced a possible life sentence. Four other defendants in the Trade Center bombing were convicted in 1994 and sentenced to prison terms of 240 years each.

TWA Flight 800 Investigation. The criminal investigation into the explosion of TWA Flight 800 officially ended on November 18, when the FBI announced that it had found no evidence that a criminal act downed the airliner in July 1996. All 230 people on board were killed when the plane exploded shortly after takeoff from Kennedy Airport in New York and crashed into the Atlantic Ocean. The FBI disputed speculation that a missile may have brought down the plane, stating that the streaks of light that many eyewitnesses saw the night of the crash actually were views of fuel burning after the center fuel tank exploded and the plane broke apart. The FBI also discounted the possibility that a bomb or some other act of sabotage downed the plane. The cause of the explosion remained unknown by the end of 1997.

The TWA crash had led to the formation of a White House Commission on Aviation Safety and Security that was chaired by Vice-President Al Gore. The commission issued its final report in February 1997 with more than 50 recommendations that focused on three general goals: reducing the rate of accidents by 80% within ten years; speeding up the timetable for implementing a modernized air-traffic-control system, known as the National Airspace System, from the year 2012 to 2005; and having the federal government treat aviation security as a national-security issue and provide substantial funding for capital improvements. Among the commission's antiterrorism recommendations were to have the FAA establish federally mandated standards for security enhancements, including standards for the use of Explosive Detection System machines, training programs for security personnel, use of automated luggage-match technology, development of manual and automated profiling programs, and deployment of explosive-detection canine teams.

Other Developments. Police raided a Brooklyn, NY, apartment on July 31 and arrested two Palestinian men, Ghazi Ibrahim Abu Maizar and Lafi Khalil, who they said planned to bomb a New York subway station and a commuter bus. Police found the makings of two pipe bombs in the apartment. Both men were shot and wounded during the police raid. Abu Maizar had been detained earlier in the year when he tried to sneak across the Canadian-U.S. border. He told U.S. immigration authorities at the time that Israel wrongly considered him a terrorist and asked for political asylum. He eventually dropped his request and was ordered to leave the United States by August 23.

Meanwhile, Gen. Ronald Fogleman, the air-force chief of staff, retired on September 1—a year before his four-year term was to expire—to protest the punishment of another air-force officer, Brig. Gen. Terryl Schwalier, for not providing adequate security at the Khobar Towers in Saudi Arabia. A truck bomb with the equivalent of 20,000 lbs (9 072 kg) of TNT exploded there in 1996, killing 19 U.S. airmen. Schwalier had been criticized in a Pentagon inquiry in 1996 but was cleared of any fault for the bombing in two separate air-force reports. But on July 31, Secretary of Defense William Cohen announced that he had recommended to President Bill Clinton that Schwalier's name be removed from the list of those to be appointed major general.

In October 1997 the U.S. State Department designated 30 foreign terrorist organizations as threats to the security of U.S. nationals or to the national security of the United States. This was in accordance with provisions of the Anti-Terrorism and Effective Death Penalty Act of 1996. Designating groups as such carries legal consequences for those who aid these organizations, for the organizations' funds, and for representatives and members who seek to enter the United States. Among the groups listed were the Abu Nidal Organization, Hamas, and Hezbollah.

JEFFREY D. SIMON
Author, "The Terrorist Trap"

THAILAND

The Thai economy collapsed in mid-1997, dampening enthusiasm over the adoption of a new democratic constitution.

Politics. Prime Minister Chavalit Yongchaiyudh's six-party coalition barely clung to power. Confidence plunged as doubts arose about the government's ability to stem economic disaster and civil unrest. A groundswell of support for the major reforms included in the proposed constitution, approved by the Constitution Drafting Assembly on August 15, contrasted with the government's "business-as-usual" image.

Despite concern that the government might reject or amend the new constitution—which for the first time in 65 years of constitutional monarchy involved public input—the parliament overwhelmingly approved it without change on September 17. The new constitution—signed by King Bhumibol Adulyadej and brought into force on October 11—was designed to reduce political corruption, promote fair elections, guarantee protection of civil rights, provide for greater accountability, and make local government more responsive.

As the economic crisis deepened, public protest and calls for broader government mounted. The threat of military intervention lurked in the background. In late October, Chavalit reshuffled his cabinet without changing the coalition's basic political configuration. To appease antigovernment clamor, he promised that after parliament passed new election laws, the government would be dissolved and new elections held as early as January 1998. But, unable to overcome the public mood, Chavalit stepped down on November 6. He was replaced by opposition leader and former Prime Minister Chuan Leekpai, who headed an eight-party coalition with a parliamentary majority of 13 seats. Chuan hinted at elections before the term of government ended in November 2000.

Economics. On July 2, 1997, the drain on its reserves forced Thailand to let its currency—the baht—float. In four months the baht lost nearly 60% of its value; the loss was followed by chaos in financial markets throughout Southeast Asia. The crisis grew out of a general loss of confidence in the health of the Thai economy, based largely on a 1996 current-account deficit that was 8% of the gross domestic product (GDP).

Thailand's external debt amounted to 50% of the GDP, of which 40% was short-term. The country's weak and poorly disciplined financial sector was caught in a liquidity crunch. As credit dried up and the real-estate market crashed, 58 of the country's 91 financial companies were suspended. Real economic growth in Thailand came to a halt, after slowing in 1996 to 6% from the 1991–95 rates of 8%–9.5%. For 1997 and 1998, growth estimates were less than 2%.

The Thai government turned to the International Monetary Fund (IMF) and World Bank. In August a rescue package valued at $17.2 billion was put together, with Japan's $4 billion the largest single component. The package came with stringent conditions—including a requirement that, in fiscal year 1998, Thailand run a budget surplus equal to 1% of GDP. This meant higher taxes and reduced government spending. Thailand also had to restructure its financial sector. When the restructuring program was presented in October, foreign investors and lenders were not impressed. Most analysts felt the plan did not go far enough, with the government responding more to domestic political pressure than to economic reality. A new tax on fuel oil was repealed only three days after it was announced, prompting the minister of finance to resign. As 1997 ended, the possibility of a debt moratorium was not ruled out.

Foreign Affairs. The most important foreign-policy issue in 1997 was the mobilization of international help for Thailand's economy. Although part of the Association of Southeast Asian Nations (ASEAN) mediation effort in Cambodia, Thailand kept a relatively low profile in that country, where it historically had vital interests. Border incidents continued to plague bilateral relations with Myanmar and Laos, despite protestations of regional cooperation.

DONALD E. WEATHERBEE
University of South Carolina

THAILAND • Information Highlights

Official Name: Kingdom of Thailand (conventional); Prathet Thai (Thai).
Location: Southeast Asia.
Area: 198,456 sq mi (514 000 km²).
Population (mid-1997 est.): 60,100,000.
Chief City (1990 census): Bangkok, the capital (metropolitan area), 5,876,000.
Government: *Head of state,* Bhumibol Adulyadej, king (acceded June 1946). *Head of government,* Chuan Leekpai, prime minister (took office November 1997). *Legislature*—National Assembly: Senate and House of Representatives.
Monetary Unit: Baht (46.95 baht equal U.S.$1, Dec. 31, 1997).
Gross Domestic Product (1995 est. U.S.$): $416,700,000,-000 (purchasing power parity).
Economic Index (Bangkok, 1996; 1990 = 100): *Consumer Prices,* all items, 134.0; food, 144.9.
Foreign Trade (1996 U.S.$): *Imports,* $71,843,000,000; *exports,* $55,526,000,000.

THEATER

During the 1996–97 season, attendance at Broadway shows reached its second-highest level in 20 years, while *Cats* (*see* SIDEBAR, page 546) became the longest-running show in Broadway history. Regional theaters, strapped by grant reductions and struggling to fill seats, became the focal point for racial issues, both on- and offstage.

Broadway. The Broadway season was full of twists and contradictions. Like the Japanese fable *Rashomon*, it supported radically different interpretations, depending on one's point of view.

One undeniable success was evidenced by the 10.6 million people who attended Broadway plays during the 1996–97 season. A 12% advance in attendance over 1995–96, it was the second-highest mark in the 20 years the figures had been tracked. Thirty-seven new shows opened, led by the entertaining *Chicago*. A robust figure by post-1980 standards, it still fell short of the lineups of earlier years, such as 1950. A relatively new, shifting roster of *New York Times* critics had not yet developed their predecessors' power to summarily "kill" a show, and so productions that they disliked (*Jekyll and Hyde*) or only mildly liked (*Titanic*, *The Life*) thrived on other warm notices and good word of mouth.

Unfortunately, the *Times* was right; these spring musicals were mediocre, and representative of the season. It was not the new crop of shows that made 1997 so commercially successful, but the year-by-year accumulation of long-runners, from 1988's *Phantom of the Opera* to 1996's *Bring in 'Da Noise, Bring in 'Da Funk* and *Rent*.

Titanic, an oddly becalmed musical considering its subject, with a pleasant but unremarkable score by Maury Yeston, did not even deliver a big visual payoff; its abstract sets hinted at the hugeness of the ocean liner without offering a genuine eyeful. Still, *Titanic* won five Tony Awards, including one for best musical, by default.

Also benefiting from thin competition was *The Last Night of Ballyhoo*, winner for best play. Alfred Uhry's second play since his Pulitzer Prize–winning first effort, *Driving Miss Daisy*, was a warm, well-made, romantic comedy set in 1939 Atlanta, loosely based on Uhry's own family history. It might have been too comfortably old-fashioned, if not for its sharp dramatic revelations of German-Jewish bigotry toward later-arriving Jews from Eastern Europe.

Another rare, outstanding new American play was Horton Foote's *The Young Man from Atlanta*, which cast Rip Torn and Shirley Knight as a 1950s Texas couple struggling to come to terms with the death—and an unspoken secret—of their son. Winner of the 1996 Pulitzer Prize, Foote's drama may have been too intimate and uncompromisingly melancholy for Broadway audiences; it closed after a brief run.

The 1997 Broadway musical "Titanic," based on the 1912 sinking of the "Titanic" cruise ship on its maiden voyage, captured five Tony Awards, including one for best musical. Maury Yeston, who wrote the score, also was honored with a Tony.

© Joan Marcus

"The Lion King," the adapted theatrical version of the Disney film, which reached Broadway in mid-November 1997, enjoyed record sales and was praised for its imaginative look. Elton John and Tim Rice wrote several new songs for the musical.

Wendy Wasserstein had a rare flop with *An American Daughter*, which attempted to show that a cynical Washington environment of media distortion and political subterfuge is especially toxic to women.

Actors from the British commonwealth dominated the Tonys even more than usual. Canada's Christopher Plummer (*see* BIOGRAPHY) won as best actor for his larger-than-life solo performance in *Barrymore*, beating out acclaimed rivals Antony Sher of South Africa as painter *Stanley* (Spencer) and Michael Gambon of Great Britain in David Hare's bracingly intelligent *Skylight*.

Janet McTeer of Great Britain won best actress for the London transfer of Ibsen's *A Doll's House*. By stressing Nora's sensuality—passionately expressed with Scotsman Owen Teale, who won for best supporting actor—McTeer made the heroine's pre-feminist transformation courageously wrenching and the abandonment of her seductive "doll's house" home, devastating.

Emblematic of the peculiar, mixed-success season was the fact that a 20-year-old work—John Kander and Fred Ebb's *Chicago*—was the hippest, most up-to-the-minute musical. Drolly evoking the trials of O.J. Simpson and the Menendez brothers with its rogues' gallery of celebrity criminals, lawyers, and reporters, *Chicago* was the most honored show at the Tonys, with six awards, including best revival, leading musical actor (James

Naughton), leading musical actress (Bebe Neuwirth), and choreography (Ann Reinking, adapting the slinky-smart original dances by Bob Fosse). Meanwhile, Kander and Ebb's newest show, *Steel Pier*, was a flop.

The stripped-down, film-noir look of *Chicago*, *Rent*, and *Funk*—together with the premature closing of Andrew Lloyd Webber's colossal *Sunset Boulevard*—suggested that the age of overproduced spectacles perhaps had run its course.

For Broadway's new fall season, *The Lion King* roared onto the stage, setting a new Broadway single-day record of $2.7 million in box-office sales. Elton John and Tim Rice expanded their award-winning movie score with several new songs. Critics marveled not just at the immediate mass appeal of an adapted Disney film (already proven by *Beauty and the Beast*) but at the daringly innovative approach of director/designer Julie Taymor. By costuming actors so that they looked like spectacular animal puppets—but without obscuring their natural faces—Taymor reimagined the fable with a rare combination of sophistication for adults and enchantment for children. *Lion*'s lustre was increased by the splendor of the New Amsterdam Theatre, the 1904 playhouse restored by Disney to its place as Broadway's grandest theater.

Triumph of Love, musicalized from a long-neglected, gender-disguised Marivaux comedy, received glowing notices (with the notable

BROADWAY OPENINGS • 1997

MUSICALS

Candide, adapted by Hugh Wheeler; music by Leonard Bernstein; lyrics by Richard Wilbur, Stephen Sondheim, and John Latouche; directed by Harold Prince; with Jim Dale, Andrea Martin, Jason Danieley, Harolyn Blackwell, Stacey Logan; April 29–July 26.

Jekyll and Hyde, book and lyrics by Leslie Bricusse; music by Frank Wildhorn; directed by Robin Phillips; based on the book by Robert Louis Stevenson; with Robert Cuccioli, Linda Eder, Christiane Noll; April 28– .

King David, book and lyrics by Tim Rice; music by Alan Menken; directed by Mike Ockrent; with Marcus Lovett, Alice Ripley, Stephen Bogardus, Peter Samuel, Martin Vidnovic; May 18–May 23.

The Life, book by David Newman, Cy Coleman, and Ira Gasman; lyrics by Gasman; music by Coleman; directed by Michael Blakemore; with Sam Harris, Pamela Isaacs, Kevin Ramsey, Katy Grenfell, Judine Richard, Mark Bove, Michael Gregory Gong, Rudy Roberson; April 26– .

The Lion King, book by Roger Allers and Irene Mecchi; lyrics by Tim Rice; music by Elton John. Additional songs by Hans Zimmer, Lebo M, Mark Mancina and Jay Rifkin; directed by Julie Taymor; with John Vickery, Samuel E. Wright, Geoff Hoyle, Tsidii Le Loka, Max Casella, Tom Alan Robbins, Jason Raize, Heather Headley, Stanley Wayne Mathis, Tracy Nicole Chapman, Kevin Cahoon, Scott Irby-Ranniar, Kajuana Shuford; Nov. 13– .

The Scarlet Pimpernel, book and lyrics by Nan Knighton; music by Frank Wildhorn; directed by Peter Hunt; based on novels by Baroness Orczy; with Douglas Sills, Christine Andreas, Terrence Mann; Nov. 9– .

1776, book by Peter Stone; music and lyrics by Sherman Edwards; directed by Scott Ellis; with Brent Spiner, Pat Hingle, Paul Michael Valley, Lauren Ward, Linda Emond; Aug. 14– .

Side Show, book and lyrics by Bill Russell; music by Henry Krieger; directed by Robert Longbottom; with Alice Ripley, Emily Skinner; Oct. 16– .

Steel Pier, book by David Thompson; music and lyrics by John Kander and Fred Ebb; directed by Scott Ellis; with Karen Ziemba, Ronn Carroll, Debra Monk, Gregory Harrison, Joel Blum, and Valerie Wright; April 24–June 28.

Titanic, book by Peter Stone; music and lyrics by Maury Yeston; directed by Richard Jones; with John Cunningham, Brian d'Arcy James, Allan Corduner, David Garrison, Michael Cerveris, Larry Keith, Alma Cuervo, Becky Ann Baker, Judith Blazer, Bill Buell, Victoria Clark, and Clarke Thorell; April 23– .

The Triumph of Love, book by James Magruder; music by Jeffrey Stock; lyrics by Susan Birkenhead; directed by Michael Mayer; based on the play by Marivaux; with Susan Egan, F. Murray Abraham, Betty Buckley; Oct. 23– .

PLAYS

An American Daughter, by Wendy Wasserstein; directed by Daniel Sullivan; with Kate Nelligan, Elizabeth Marvel, Lynne Thigpen, Peter Riegert, Bruce Norris, Cotter Smith, Hal Holbrook, Penny Fuller, and Andrew Dolan; April 13–June 29.

Barrymore, by William Luce; directed by Gene Saks; with Christopher Plummer; March 25–Nov. 2.

The Diary of Anne Frank, by Frances Goodrich and Albert Hackett, based on Anne Frank's diaries; directed by James Lapine; with Natalie Portman; Dec. 4– .

A Doll's House, by Henrik Ibsen; directed by Anthony Page; adapted by Frank McGuinness; with Janet McTeer, Owen Teale, Jan Maxwell, and Peter Gowen; April 2–Sept. 1.

The Gin Game, by D. L. Coburn; directed by Charles Nelson Reilly; with Julie Harris and Charles Durning; April 20–Aug. 31.

The Hairy Ape, by Eugene O'Neill; directed by Elizabeth LeCompte; with Willem Dafoe, Scott Renderer, Dave Shelley, and Kate Valk; April 3–May 25.

Jackie: An American Life, by Gip Hoppe; directed by Hoppe; with Margaret Colin; Nov. 10– .

The Last Night of Ballyhoo, by Alfred Uhry; directed by Ron Lagomarsino; with Jessica Hecht, Celia Weston, Dana Ivey, Terry Beaver, Paul Rudd, Arija Bareikis, and Stephen Largay; Feb. 27– .

London Assurance, by Dion L. Boucicault; directed by Joe Dowling; sets by Derek McLane; with John Horton, Robert Neill,

© T. Charles Erickson

Arija Bareikis and Paul Rudd were featured in "The Last Night of Ballyhoo," Alfred Uhry's comedy about intra-ethnic prejudice among Jewish families in Atlanta, GA, in 1939. The Broadway production was given the Tony Award for best play.

Brian Bedford, Helen Carey, Rainn Wilson, and David Schramm; April 30–June 29.

The Old Neighborhood, by David Mamet; directed by Scott Ziegler; with Peter Riegert, Patti LuPone; Nov. 19– .

One Flea Spare, by Naomi Wallace; directed by Ron Daniels; with Mischa Barton, Bill Camp, John De Vries, Dianne Wiest, and Paul Kandel; March 9–March 29.

Proposals, by Neil Simon; directed by Joe Mantello; with Dick Latessa, Kelly Bishop, Katie Finneran, L. Scott Caldwell; Nov. 6– .

Stanley, by Pam Gems; directed by John Caird; with Antony Sher, Deborah Findlay, Anna Chancellor, Ken Kliban, Barton Tinapp, Barbara Garrick, and Selina Cadell; Feb. 20–April 27.

Steward of Christendom, by Sebastian Barry; directed by Max Stafford-Clark; with Donal McCann, Ali White, Tina Kellegher, Aislin McGuckin, and Carl Brennan; Jan. 18–Feb. 23.

Stonewall Jackson's House, by Jonathan Reynolds; directed by Jamie Richards; with Lisa Louise Langford, R.E. Rodgers, Katherine Leask, Ron Faber, and Mimi Bensinger; Feb. 16–June 15.

Three Sisters, by Anton Chekhov; translated by Lanford Wilson; directed by Scott Elliott; with Billy Crudup, Calista Flockhart, Paul Giamatti, David Marshall Grant, Amy Irving, Jerry Stiller, Eric Stoltz, David Strathairn, Lili Taylor, and Jeanne Tripplehorn; Feb. 3–April 6.

The Sunshine Boys, by Neil Simon; directed by John Tillinger; with Jack Klugman, Tony Randall; Dec. 9– .

A View from the Bridge, by Arthur Miller; directed by Michael Mayer; with Anthony LaPaglia, Adam Trese, Allison Janey; Dec. 14– .

The Young Man from Atlanta, by Horton Foote; directed by Robert Falls; with Rip Torn, Shirley Knight, William Biff McGuire, and Marcus Giamatti; March 27–June 9.

OTHER ENTERTAINMENT

Forever Tango, created and directed by Luis Bravo; with Miriam Larici, Claudio Villagia; June 19– .

Street Corner Symphony, conceived, directed, and choreographed by Marion J. Caffey; with Carol Dennis, Victor Trent Cook, Eugene Fleming; Nov. 24– .

"Cats"—More Than Nine Lives

On June 19, 1997, when the curtain came down on the 6,138th performance of *Cats*, the widely popular musical based on poems by T.S. Eliot became the longest-running show in Broadway history.

Winner of seven Tony Awards in 1983, the production—directed by Trevor Nunn, with music by Andrew Lloyd Webber—had spent the previous 15 years at the Winter Garden Theater. One dancer, Marlene Danielle, had been with the show since opening night, racking up an impressive 5,481 performances.

The musical about life and salvation in a garbage dump from Eliot's *Old Possum's Book of Practical Cats* outlived such favorites as *A Chorus Line, Oh! Calcutta!,* and *Les Misérables,* and

was credited with introducing many children to the theater through its colorful and outrageous costumes. Large, spectacular, and replete with special effects, the show—which is devoid of "stars"—had been billed from the start as a special event.

On Broadway, *Cats* had grossed $329 million by the time it reached its milestone June performance, and had been seen by 8.25 million people. Worldwide, some 50 million people had spent $2.2 billion to see its various productions.

Cats, which opened Oct. 7, 1982, and was the first in a wave of megamusicals that reshaped Broadway, still was going strong by the close of 1997, with its claws firmly clutching the 1998 season.

exception of *The New York Times*), especially for actors Susan Egan, Betty Buckley, and F. Murray Abraham. It ran less than three months, however.

Even more unlikely and surprising was the respectful acclaim for *Side Show*, not only because it was based on the true story of vaudevillian female Siamese twins, but because the best-known member of the creative team, composer Henry Krieger, had not been heard from in theater circles since 1982's *Dreamgirls*. *Side Show*, too, closed early.

One of the few leading American playwrights to premiere a critically admired new work in 1997 was David Mamet. His *The Old Neighborhood*, starring Peter Riegert and Patti Lupone, was a spare, tingling, autobiographical drama of a middle-aged man's visit to reinvestigate scenes of his youth.

Off-Broadway. Good new American plays were rare off-Broadway, which meant an atypical "off" season for such companies as Manhattan Theatre Club, Playwrights Horizons, the New York Shakespeare Festival (NYSF), and Lincoln Center Theatre. There were off-Broadway critical hits by newcomers—Paula Vogel's *How I Learned to Drive*, a complex exploration of child molestation; Moises Kaufman's *Gross Indecency: The Three Trials of Oscar Wilde*; and a comeback play by Vietnam war chronicler David Rabe, *Question of Mercy*, about assisted suicide.

There also was renewed appreciation of Betty Comden and Adolph Green, creators of the book and lyrics of *On the Town*, with the 1940s sailors-on-leave musical enjoying a

moderately well-received NYSF revival in Central Park.

Some acclaimed performances of the off-Broadway season came from David Morse and Mary-Louise Parker (*How I Learned to Drive*), Michael Emerson (*Gross Indecency*), David Rasche (David Mamet's 1980 *Edmond*), and Fiona Shaw (the distinguished London thespian made her U.S. debut in a solo of T.S. Eliot's *The Waste Land*).

Commercial Tours. *Ragtime*, based on the 1975 E. L. Doctorow novel, was the newest musical epic from Toronto-based producer Garth Drabinsky and his Live Entertainment of Canada, known as Livent (*Kiss of the Spider Woman*). It had a good run in Los Angeles, and, at year's end, previewed in New York toward a projected opening in January 1998.

There were smash tours of *Beauty and the Beast*, a Hayley Mills *King and I*, and a Jasmine Guy/Charlotte D'Amboise *Chicago*. All three achieved box-office marks at Atlanta's Fox Theatre, topped only by *Phantom*.

Pace Theatrical Group, the dominant presenter of national tours, and Jujamcyn Theaters, a major Broadway landlord, merged, earning a front-page article in *The New York Times* because of the groups' complementary resources for developing and presenting productions for New York and "the road." The merger completed consolidation of commercial-theater power into five mega-companies—the others were the Shubert and Nederlander organizations, Livent, and Disney.

Regional Theater. Race was the galvanizing issue, on- and offstage, in the resident nonprofit theaters—commonly called regional theaters—across the United States. A public debate between two of the theater's most esteemed spokesmen—August Wilson, the two-time Pulitzer-winning, African-American playwright; and Robert Brustein, the white artistic director of American Repertory Theatre in Cambridge, MA, who, as theater critic for *The New Republic*, had disparaged Wilson's work—erupted over this touchy subject.

The debate grew out of a controversial address to a 1996 theater conference, in which Wilson accused philanthropists, corporate donors, and directors of major regional theaters of racist attitudes that left smaller black theaters underfunded. Wilson also angered many fellow blacks by criticizing the techniques of nontraditional casting, comparing blacks in white roles to the domestics or "house Negroes" of the slavery era. The debate raged in the pages of *American Theatre* and other periodicals, with Brustein offering evidence that funding in fact favored black institutions, and that Wilson's proposals to eliminate nontraditional casting and award grants by color instead of merit would constitute a "re-segregation" of American theater.

The two eloquent antagonists brought their debate to the stage of Manhattan's Town Hall, but observers felt that the January event was lukewarm and glossed over the chasm between two passionate schools of thought.

The Goodman Theatre of Chicago offered a sterling *Young Man from Atlanta* and coproduced its subsequent Broadway run; while in Cambridge, American Repertory Theatre's premiere of David Mamet's *The Old Neighborhood* was similarly acclaimed and was booked for New York.

Yale Repertory Theatre's lavishly praised mounting of *The Triumph of Love*, coproduced with Center Stage of Baltimore (which premiered it the previous year), launched the playfully musicalized 18th-century French comedy toward its Broadway run in the fall.

Barry Manilow tried his hand at musical theater at La Jolla (CA) Playhouse with *Harmony*, based on the story of a singing group of Jews and gentiles who ran afoul of Hitler. At Miami's Coconut Grove Playhouse, Jimmy Buffett also debuted as a legitimate composer with *Don't Stop the Carnival*, based on a Herman Wouk novel with a tropical setting.

Most regional theaters struggled to maintain audience levels. Nationwide attendance for 228 regional theaters was 17 million for 1996, down from 20 million in 1994. The figures suggested that audiences were spread more thinly among a greater number of smaller houses. In addition, regional theaters were strained by sharp reductions in National Endowment for the Arts grants (*see* UNITED STATES—*Funding the Arts*, page 565). Hartford Stage had the best-attended season in its 34-year history, playing to a 95% capacity audience of 120,400.

There was reshuffling of West Coast leaders. Artistic director Dan Sullivan, who had built the Seattle Repertory Theatre into one of America's most-admired resident playhouses, resigned to pursue an independent career. He was replaced by Sharon Ott, who had performed similar longtime service for Berkeley (CA) Repertory Theatre, leading it to the 1997 Special Tony Award for achievement by a regional theater. Ott's successor at the Rep was Tony Taccone, whose seven-year tenure at San Francisco's Eureka Theatre included the codirection of the world premiere of *Angels in America*.

In New Haven, CT, another of regional theater's father figures, Arvin Brown, retired after three decades as head of the Long Wharf Theatre. Douglas Hughes (*Question of Mercy*) succeeded him.

Racial issues came to a head again in the fall in two provocative Washington, DC, productions. At the Shakespeare Theatre, Patrick Stewart played the lead role in *Othello* amid a mostly black cast. He said the "photo-negative" approach was intended to make white audiences feel more keenly the isolation of the Moor. Although the production was well acted, the concept was flawed, since Shakespeare was not writing about some abstract "other" but a black man specifically, as seen through the prejudices of his time.

For *House Arrest: First Edition*, at Washington's Arena Stage, playwright Anna Deavere Smith interviewed 300 figures from politics and the media, including President Bill Clinton and *60 Minutes* anchor Ed Bradley. The sprawling subject of this three-hour documentary/fantasia—perhaps the most ambitious new work since Tony Kushner's *Angels in America*—was power, race, gender, and communication in the 1990s. Sometimes brilliant, but sometimes clumsy, *First Edition* was due for badly needed revisions as it proceeded in 1998 to its other, coproducing theaters: the Goodman of Chicago, the Mark Taper of Los Angeles, and the Intiman of Seattle.

DAN HULBERT
"The Atlanta Journal and Constitution"

TOBACCO. *See* BUSINESS AND CORPORATE AFFAIRS—*The Tobacco Industry*.

TRANSPORTATION

The majority of U.S. transportation companies thrived during 1997, with nearly all industries moving more goods and passengers. Most recorded increased profits as the U.S. economy remained strong, wages remained stable, and fuel costs declined. There was not the strong pressure to tighten aviation security and safety certification that there had been during 1996 in the wake of the Trans World Airlines (TWA) Flight 800 and ValuJet crashes. Mergers and alliances affected all corners of the industry.

Airlines. Propelled by a strong economy, U.S. airlines showed healthy increases in international and domestic traffic. Among major carriers, passenger-miles (one passenger transported one mile) were 4.7% higher for domestic travel and 5.1% higher for international travel through October than in the same period a year earlier. The number of passengers increased 2.9% on domestic routes and 4.1% internationally, indicating that travelers made longer trips on average. Air cargo ton-miles (one ton of freight or mail carried one mile) on scheduled airlines was 10% higher than in the previous year.

Strong volume growth and continued control of expenses boosted airline profits by some 50% over the $3.5 billion earned in 1996—a dramatic improvement from losses that had topped $13 billion between 1990 and 1994. Analysts predicted that growth in airline profits and traffic would moderate in 1998.

Meanwhile, smaller airlines such as Vanguard, Frontier, and Western Pacific struggled to reverse continued losses. Frontier and Western Pacific announced a merger, then called it off.

The year also saw increasing moves by regional carriers such as Comair and Atlantic Southeast Airlines to replace their turboprop aircraft with faster jets. Some analysts speculated that regional jets would revitalize service in smaller communities that had lost jet service in recent years.

While traffic and profits soared, the aviation industry enjoyed a safer year, with 613 U.S. fatalities reported by Oct. 31, 1997—more than a 50% reduction from 932 during the same period of 1996. After ten months, just one fatality was reported by major U.S. passenger airlines, compared with 342 in the same period of 1996. In December, however, another person was killed when United Flight 826 experienced severe turbulence and dropped 1,000 ft (305 m) over the Pacific, east of Tokyo. Fatalities among smaller airlines also declined for the first ten months of the year, from 84 in 1996 to 35 in 1997, although the number of accidents involving commercial

In the summer of 1997 the National Automated Highway System Consortium demonstrated the first automated highway system, in San Diego, CA. The high-tech plan for the future offers motorists a fast, safe alternative to highway gridlock.

airlines was higher (122 compared with 113 through ten months of 1996). The number of fatalities in noncommercial (general) aviation, however, rose from 506 to 539; meanwhile, general-aviation-accident totals—including personal, business, and instructional flights—dipped 4%, from 1,695 to 1,619, in the first ten months of 1997.

The most deadly accident occurred on August 5 in Guam, when a Korean Airlines 747 crashed, claiming more than 200 lives; 26 passengers survived. In December a ten-month-old Singapore Airline Boeing 737 with 104 on board, a Ukrainian aircraft carrying 70 passengers, and a Tajik plane with 86 aboard all crashed within the same week.

Final reports from the National Transportation Safety Board (NTSB) found that the May 1996 ValuJet Flight 592 accident was caused by improper handling of oxygen canisters, which ignited soon after the plane left Miami.

The most extensive air-crash investigation in U.S. history turned up no specific cause for the July 1996 TWA accident that killed 230 persons, but investigators ruled out sabotage or a missile as the reason for the crash of TWA Flight 800. They believed an electrical fault caused fuel and vapors in the center fuel tank to ignite. Federal officials and airplane manufacturers concentrated on steps to improve fuel-tank safety, including redesigning tanks, using different types of fuel in commercial aircraft, and developing new ways to prevent fuel-vapor flammability in airplane tanks.

Trucking. After two lean years, commercial motor carriers reported strong results, with profits of major companies 50% or more above 1996 figures. Total trucking tonnage reported by the American Trucking Associations by late 1997 was about 6% ahead of 1996. The gain was most prominent among less-than-truckload (LTL) carriers. Carriers whose workers were represented by the Teamsters Union generally suffered substantial losses in 1996, but in 1997 all four of the largest LTL companies were profitable—reporting 10% to 20% increases in tonnage and revenue.

Carriers handling full truckload shipments from a single customer posted smaller, but still healthy, increases. Loads were up 6% late in the year, with a 9% revenue increase.

Major union carriers began negotiations with the Teamsters Union on a new contract that would replace the four-year agreement that would expire in March 1998. A potential complication arose in November, when Team-

© Lennox McLendon/AP/Wide World Photos

Rodney E. Slater, above, former chairman of the Arkansas State Highway Commission and administrator of the Federal Highway Administration, became U.S. secretary of transportation in 1997.

sters President Ron Carey was disqualified from running for reelection in 1998 due to charges of improper fund-raising during his 1996 campaign. Carey appealed the decision in December.

The Teamsters reached a five-year agreement with the United Parcel Service (UPS) that ended a 16-day strike that had forced customers to find new ways to move more than 12 million parcels a day. Among those who took up the slack were the United States Postal Service, FedEx, air-cargo operators, motor carriers, and smaller package-delivery services. To better compete with UPS, FedEx agreed to acquire Caliber System and its ground-package-delivery subsidiary. Roadway Express teamed with Reimer Express Lines, a Canadian carrier, and Swift Transportation bought Direct Transit.

Strong market conditions prompted trucking companies to increase their purchases of freight-hauling tractors by more than 10%.

Government. Rodney Slater replaced Federico Peña as secretary of transportation in April, after Peña became secretary of energy. In June, President Bill Clinton announced the appointment of Jane Garvey as administrator of the Federal Aviation Administration (FAA); she was the first woman to hold the post.

Congress attempted to craft a new law to replace the Intermodal Surface Transportation Efficiency Act (ISTEA) of 1991—which determined federal transportation policy and spending levels—when it expired on Sept. 30, 1997. But replacing ISTEA proved difficult. Legislators debated issues such as devising a fair formula for allocating highway funds. Some states claimed the current formula was unfair because they paid more in federal gas taxes than they received in payments for highway improvements. Broad disagreement also existed over the proper level of federal spending for nonhighway uses such as bicycle trails. In November, Congress passed a stopgap measure to fund transportation projects through March 1998.

Bus. Greyhound passenger-miles traveled for the first three quarters of 1997 increased 12% over 1996. Revenue increased 10% during the same period, turning a 1996 operating loss of $7.7 million into a $3.8 million operating profit. The nationwide bus company agreed to acquire Carolina Trailways and Valley Transit and proposed pool service with Peter Pan Trailways and Colonial Trailways.

Amtrak and Greyhound continued to coordinate service with through ticketing and joint use of facilities on 30 routes. Greyhound and ValuJet created an intermodal alliance on some routes.

The charter and tour market—the fastest-growing segment of the bus industry—underwent consolidation after years as a "mom-and-pop" industry. Newcomer Coach USA used funds raised from stock sales and investment banks to purchase more than a dozen companies.

Water. Consolidation was also prominent in the ocean container industry. Two competing alliances composed of international shipping carriers based in Asia, Europe, and the United States were formed to minimize the effects of excess capacity. The alliances allowed companies to reduce total operating costs by transporting several companies' freight on one ship, while still preserving individual identities.

APL Limited, owner of the second-largest ocean carrier located in the United States, was acquired by Neptune Orient Lines, based in Singapore. CP Ships, a subsidiary of Canadian Pacific Limited, completed its purchase of Lykes Brothers Steamship Co. in a bankruptcy proceeding.

Another effort to partially deregulate the maritime industry failed in Congress, but the issue was expected to be taken up again by the House and Senate in 1998.

Rail. Consolidations—and their effects—continued to dominate events in the U.S. rail industry during 1997.

After an expensive and often bitter six-month takeover fight, CSX Corp. and Norfolk Southern (NS), Inc., agreed to divide up their Eastern rival, Conrail, Inc. The fight for control of Conrail began in October 1996, after Conrail announced plans to merge with CSX; within weeks, NS made a competing offer. In the end, NS acquired 58% of Conrail stock and CSX, the rest.

The two companies presented a joint application to the Surface Transportation Board for permission to take control of Conrail's assets and complete the acquisition, asserting that their breakup plan for Conrail could increase rail competition and improve service for customers on all three railroads. There was limited opposition to the Conrail purchase, although some critics predicted widespread job losses and higher prices.

A decision on the merger was expected in the summer of 1998. If the deal was approved, NS would own 21,000 mi (33 789 km) of railroad and CSX would control 22,500 mi (36 203 km), serving all major markets east of the Mississippi either directly or through connecting railroads. The battle for control forced both companies to raise offers, pushing Conrail stock from $71 a share before the 1996 agreement to $115 a share.

The total purchase price of $10.2 billion (all in cash) was the highest ever paid for a railroad, topping the $5.4 billion in cash, stock, and debt assumption that Union Pacific (UP) Corp. Railroad paid in 1996 for Southern Pacific Rail Corp. That combination formed the largest U.S. railway, with approximately 36,000 mi (57 924 km) of track.

The Union Pacific (UP)/Southern Pacific (SP) case approved by regulators in 1996 came back before the agency in the fall. A service crisis—the cause of which was in dispute—began in Texas on UP and spread to other parts of the company, affecting other carriers, which were asked to move delayed shipments. Trains and crews were unable to complete their trips on time and were late for their next assignments. Without enough extra people and equipment to take up the slack, parked trains often blocked other trains and problems snowballed. Customers claimed up to $1 billion in losses from plant shutdowns due to delayed delivery and the higher cost of alternative transportation.

Federal regulators issued a special service order that allowed the small Texas-Mexican Railway to operate over some Union Pacific

As the 1997 congressional session drew to a close, the U.S. Congress authorized funding for Amtrak—the national passenger railroad—through 2002. The $5.2 billion authorization provided for operating subsidies, capital improvements, and retirement funds.

© Bill Swersey/Gamma-Liaison

lines in Texas. Burlington Northern and Santa Fe Railway—itself created by a 1995 merger—was granted rights to UP tracks beyond those awarded in the 1995 Union Pacific merger. The crisis eased by the end of 1997, while customers and public agencies sought methods to assure that the western rail problems would not occur in the East if the Conrail breakup was approved.

Major railway traffic recorded modest gains. With the shipping year substantially completed, ton-miles were less than 1% ahead of 1996 levels. Rail-truck intermodal shipments were 7% higher. Profitability of major railroads lagged behind that of the airline and trucking industries. Net income of all railroads, excluding onetime charges, was barely 5% better than 1996 levels.

The Kansas City Southern Railway Co. added 402 mi (647 km) to its route system by receiving regulatory approval to purchase the Gateway Western Railway.

Privatization of rail lines in Mexico and other countries continued. A consortium of Mexican companies, joined by Union Pacific as minority owner, was awarded a 50-year concession to operate 4,000 mi (6 436 km) of rail lines. It was the second concession awarded in Mexico; the cost was $404 million, far below the $1.4 billion paid for the first portion of privately owned Mexican track.

During 1997, U.S. rail operators also made new purchases or increased their holdings in Great Britain, Australia, Guatemala, Chile, and Brazil. Overseas expansion opportunities for smaller U.S. rail companies overshadowed a generally weak market for domestic routes large carriers no longer wanted.

Conrail pulled back on plans to sell more than 1,800 mi (2 896 km) of track after the CSX-Norfolk Southern deal. Canadian Pacific Railway completed its spin-off of Midwest routes called the "corn lines" to a Montana-based company.

Rail safety remained a concern after summer collisions killed nearly a dozen persons. However, the number of accidents and injuries reported by carriers continued to decline. Rail-highway crossing accidents were down from 1996 by 9% during the first nine months. Federal Railroad Administration statistics showed virtually no change in injuries, but a 6% reduction in crossing-accident deaths.

Amtrak received a $2.3 billion infusion of federal funds to upgrade its fleet and infrastructure but remained under strong pressure to improve financial performance and service. Its efforts to wipe out enormous losses by carrying more cargo caused friction with freight railroads, which claimed Amtrak had an unfair advantage in attracting goods the freight companies normally carried.

A strike that would have shut down passenger rail service in the Northeast was averted by a last-minute agreement, but by year's end, Amtrak had just one signed labor contract and still was negotiating with 12 other unions. Amtrak President Thomas M. Downs resigned in December. George Warrington, who headed Amtrak's Northeast-corridor business unit, was made acting president during the search for a replacement.

See also AUTOMOBILES.

RIP WATSON
"The Journal of Commerce"

International tourism continued to increase in 1997. Preliminary figures showed a record $496 billion in tourist spending worldwide, making travel and tourism the world's largest industry, accounting for more than 10% of the gross domestic product (GDP). According to the U.S. Commerce Department, the United States ranked first in terms of spending by inbound travelers, with travel receipts projected to total $98 billion; it was second only to France in arrivals, with 48.9 million foreign visitors in 1997.

U.S. leisure travel also grew, with 1.2 billion person-trips of 100 mi (161 km) or more away from home. A record 42.9 million business travelers represented a 12% increase over the previous two years. The average business traveler took 5.3 trips of 3.3 days, with 3.8% booking tickets electronically. Corporate travel spending climbed 4.7%, with the largest increases in airline and hotel rates.

Growth in the rapidly expanding market niches of ecotourism (*see* SIDEBAR) and cultural tourism was attributed largely to growing interest in in-depth travel by affluent, well-traveled, and well-educated baby boomers. A Travel Industry Association survey showed that during 1997, 27% of the total U.S. adult population—53.6 million—took at least one cultural trip.

Domestic Travel. Despite higher personal earnings, more than 75% of pleasure travelers drove their cars on family vacations. They took shorter but more frequent trips, staying

Ecotourism

During the 1990s the world became a stage for one of the travel industry's most important trends—ecotourism, or, as it often is called, "green travel." This low-impact approach to exploring ecologically sensitive areas accounted for 25% to 30% of the travel market in 1997, and was predicted to influence mainstream travel significantly in the years ahead.

The Ecotourism Society defines the term as "responsible travel to natural areas that conserves the environment and sustains the well-being of local people." Ecotours encompass nature-based and "soft-adventure" travel, such as safaris, mountain-trekking, birding expeditions, and cruises to destinations like the Galápagos Islands, the African savanna, or the Amazon Basin.

Once offered only by conservation organizations and museums, ecotours now are provided by dozens of tour operators to travelers willing to take nothing but photographs and leave behind nothing but footprints. Even people who previously shunned group travel admit these well-researched excursions make sense. They tread lightly on the host country's culture and ecology, visit remote regions difficult to tour independently, are accompanied by knowledgeable local guides, and offer the companionship of people with similar goals.

Ecotourism works best in developing countries where the residents can see the results of preserving, rather than destroying, the environment. It can make a real contribution to the local economy by providing jobs and creating allied sources of revenue.

Although ecotourism is Africa's hottest growth business, much of the continent still is struggling to build it into a significant economic force. One private operator in the forefront of this type of tourism is Conservation Corporation of Africa (Conscorp), which operates 22 small, isolated, and expensive game lodges all over the continent for upscale clients who come to see African wildlife and culture. Forward-thinking Conscorp builds schools and clinics near its lodges for local people, tours locals through the lodge property, and trains and employs them in all aspects of the business—from being cooks and builders to guides and rangers. It buys seeds for farmers, teaches them to plant crops, and then buys the fruits and vegetables. It also buys materials for local artists and sells their work in curio shops. It hires people to clear trees, then buys the charcoal they produce from the wood.

Apparently this type of sustainable travel has translated into increased tourism. According to statistics from the World Tourism Organization (WTO), international arrivals to Africa rose by 7% in 1997, to 20.6 million, while tourism earnings increased by 15% to more than $8 billion. The continent's top visitor draw was South Africa (*photo, page 553*), followed by Zimbabwe, Kenya, Tanzania, and Zambia.

Today's responsible travelers are happy to endure some hardship and inconvenience to satisfy their curiosity about environmentally sensitive areas and cultures in all parts of the globe. They do not simply visit vanishing habitats—they care about helping to protect them. The Antarctica

© Bob Krist/The Stock Market

Project, an environmental group set up to monitor Antarctic tourism, maintains that most pollution problems stem from scientists stationed there, and not from the tourists, who are committed to protecting the land.

Central and South America are other favorite ecotour destinations. In fact, trips to the tropical forests, beaches, and national parks of Costa Rica are so popular that some people question whether the nation could be spoiled by its own success. But tourism, Costa Rica's main industry, has enabled the country to set aside 20% of its land as national parks. It also has helped schools to set up a corps of trained tourism workers.

Many islands in the Caribbean use tourism as a means of preserving their land and wildlife. The St. Croix Environmental Association (SEA) won the Caribbean Tourism Organization's Ecotourism Award for 1997, for setting aside 912 acres (369 ha) on the island's north shore as the Salt River Bay National Historical Park and Ecological Preserve, rather than having it developed as a hotel-condominium-marina project.

BARBARA J. BRAASCH

an average of seven nights on the road, down from 8.5 nights in 1996. The average cost per trip was $1,080—a slight increase over 1996. Favorite family destinations included beaches, lakes, large cities, and theme parks. Although many national parks doubled entry fees, the number of visitors was up nearly 5% over 1996. Florida, California, and Nevada remained the top vacation destinations for domestic and international travelers.

All types of transportation except Amtrak showed profits for the year, with airlines reaping more than $4 billion in net profits. Airline fares were 10% to 40% higher, and load factors climbed more than 70% during the summer months. Rates for the nation's 1.5 million rental cars were up 7%, with the highest rates in New York City; Washington, DC; New Haven, CT; and Baltimore. Rail travel sagged in 1997, with load factors of only 43.3% systemwide. The number of riders was up as much as 27% during the summer, but only Amtrak's Northeast Corridor route broke even for the fiscal year.

Hotel rates—averaging $106—were up in 1997, as were occupancy levels, which stood above 80%. San Francisco had the highest nationwide room rates, followed by Los Angeles, Boston, Orlando, and Denver.

International Travel. Bolstered by the U.S. dollar's continued strength, more than 54 million Americans vacationed outside the country in 1997. More than 13 million U.S. tourists traveled to Canada, while the European Travel Commission reported that 9 million U.S. travelers toured at least two countries. Great Britain was a hot spot, with U.S.-visitor counts up 18%. Package tours were down, because most travelers were repeat visitors who preferred to arrange their own itineraries. U.S. travel was up by as much as 20% to Greece, Turkey, Egypt, and Israel. Eastern Europe,

Southeast Asia, the South Pacific, and Asia also reported modest increases.

According to the U.S. International Trade Administration, Canadian and Mexican visitors represented 51% of total inbound travelers to the United States. Japan remained the overseas leader, with more than 5 million visitors, followed by Great Britain, Germany, France, Brazil, South Korea, and Italy.

Cruising. U.S. cruise sales were strong, with the industry recording 5 million passengers—up from 4.65 million in 1996—and its highest prices in three years. New ships, cruise-line consolidations, a strong economy, and consumer confidence spurred demand.

BARBARA J. BRAASCH, *Freelance Travel Writer*

TUNISIA

Tunisia's government released two Islamic dissidents from jail the day before 1997 began. Later in the year, however, it adopted a law that seemed to reaffirm the ban on Islamic fundamentalist groups.

Politics. On Dec. 31, 1996, Mohammad Moada, former secretary-general of the Movement of Social Democrats (MDS)—the main opposition group to the ruling Constitutional Democratic Party (RCD)—was released from jail on compassionate grounds. He had been sentenced to 11 years in prison in February 1996, after a court found him guilty of being a Libyan agent. The sentence had been condemned by Amnesty International, which said that clear evidence of his guilt had not been presented. Moada had been arrested after the MDS made public a letter he wrote to President Zine El Abidine Ben Ali, which criticized restrictions on political activity and the total control of the RCD. Moada's deputy, Khemais Chammari, who had been sentenced to five years in June 1996,

also was released. According to the World Organization Against Torture, Moada was subjected to various forms of harassment—including house arrest—since his release; on December 19 he was arrested without a warrant, then released and placed under house arrest. On December 20, the report said, he once again was arrested.

Another government opponent, Sheikh Mabrouk Zren—a member of the banned Renaissance Party and a founder of Tunisia's Islamic militant movement—died in prison on May 5, 1997. In August it was reported that yet another imprisoned government opponent, Ridha Khemeri, had died after a 40-day hunger strike.

In October the RCD-dominated Tunisian parliament adopted a law that gave the head of state the right to use referenda to amend the constitution and to obtain a mandate for important laws. The law also forbade the establishment of political parties based on religion, language, sex, or region. The latter aspect of the law was seen as a reaffirmation of the ban on Islamic fundamentalist parties.

The Economy. In October it was announced that a delegation of Tunisian businesspeople would visit Indonesia to find ways to revive trade between the two countries. In 1996 the two-way trade had dropped by 5.5%.

In December the Canadian-based Eurogas Corporation, an oil and gas company, announced that it would start drilling operations off the Tunisian coast in early 1998. One of its partners was a subsidiary of the U.S.-based Mobil Corporation.

WILLIAM E. SHAPIRO, *Freelance Writer*

TURKEY

The key events in Turkey during 1997 were the transition from an Islamist government to a broad, secularly based coalition cabinet; attempts to overcome high inflation and budget deficits; and continuing warfare against Kurdish insurgents.

Politics. A shaky governing coalition between Prime Minister Necmettin Erbakan's Islamist Welfare Party and former Prime Minister Tansu Ciller's True Path Party, formed in June 1996, was wracked by scandal in November 1996. Growing evidence of ties between organized-crime figures and police and pro-government parliamentarians caused Interior Minister Mehmet Agar to resign.

Even more troublesome to secular military and political leaders were Islamic fundamentalist measures in foreign policy and education

---

TUNISIA • Information Highlights

Official Name: Republic of Tunisia.
Location: North Africa.
Area: 63,170 sq mi (163 610 km²).
Population (mid-1997 est.): 9,300,000.
Chief Cities (1994 census): Tunis, the capital, 674,100; Sfax, 230,900.
Government: *Head of state,* Zine El Abidine Ben Ali, president (took office Nov. 7, 1987). *Head of government,* Hamed Karoui, prime minister (took office Sept. 27, 1989). *Legislature* (unicameral)—Chamber of Deputies.
Monetary Unit: Dinar (1.135 dinars equal U.S.$1, market rate, August 1997).
Gross Domestic Product (1994 est. U.S.$): $37,100,000,-000 (purchasing power parity).
Economic Indexes (1996, 1990 = 100): *Consumer Prices,* all items, 137.4; food, 137.0. *Industrial Production,* 105.
Foreign Trade (1996 U.S.$): *Imports,* $7,746,000,000; *exports,* $5,518,000,000.

undertaken by Erbakan's supporters. Conservative women in early 1997 now were free to wear Islamic attire in universities and government buildings, which resulted in a protest march by 8,000 women in Ankara on February 15, seeking the restoration of a ban on such clothing in public places.

The National Security Council issued an ultimatum to Erbakan on February 28, demanding adherence to the constitution's secular principles. The council wanted a prohibition against government hiring of Islamists, measures against Islamic mystic Sufis and the arming of private militias, and the closing of some Islamic schools. Although Erbakan accepted the demands in March, he tried to delay their being put into effect.

On May 11 a pro-Islamist rally in Istanbul drew 300,000 people. Secularists exerted great pressure to weaken the Welfare Party, even attempting to persuade the Constitutional Court to deny its right to exist. Defections from Ciller's True Path Party in May and June cost the coalition its parliamentary majority, leading to Erbakan's June 18 resignation.

Although Erbakan urged President Suleyman Demirel to give the task of forming a new cabinet to Ciller, Demirel asked former two-time Prime Minister Mesut Yilmaz, head of the Motherland Party, to form a coalition government. Yilmaz' broad-based cabinet received the official backing of the Democratic Left Party, the Democratic Turkey Party, and several smaller groups, as well as the unofficial support of the Republican Peoples Party. Yilmaz survived a July 12 confidence vote by 281–256.

On August 6, Yilmaz presented a plan designed to curb the influence of Islamic fundamentalists. His plan extended minimum public schooling from five to eight years, at an estimated cost of $4 billion; this cut the time Islamic schools could educate pupils from six to three years.

Economy. In December 1996 the Erbakan government introduced Turkey's first balanced budget—$45.9 billion. But 1997 revenue estimates were based on the unrealistic expectation of selling $8.5 billion in state assets to private industry. Hopes were high that, with rising employment and a 1996 growth of 8% in gross national product (GNP)—along with oil and natural-gas production, and commercial agreements with Iraq, Iran, Turkmenistan, Azerbaijan, and Russia—Turkey's economy was stabilizing.

Facing 80% inflation, however, the Yilmaz government introduced a new 1997 budget in July that abandoned the goal of balancing

---

TURKEY • Information Highlights

Official Name: Republic of Turkey.
Location: Southeastern Europe and southwestern Asia.
Area: 301,382 sq mi (780 580 km^2).
Population (mid-1997 est.): 63,700,000.
Chief Cities (mid-1994 est.): Ankara, the capital, 2,782,200; Istanbul, 7,615,500; Izmir, 1,985,300; Adana, 1,047,300.
Government: *Head of state,* Suleyman Demirel, president (took office May 16, 1993). *Head of government,* Mesut Yilmaz, prime minister (took office June 1997). *Legislature*— Grand National Assembly.
Monetary Unit: Lira (205,245.00 liras equal U.S. $1, Dec. 31, 1997).
Gross Domestic Product (1995 est. U.S.$): $345,700,000,-000 (purchasing power parity).
Economic Indexes (1996, 1990 = 100): *Consumer Prices,* all items, 3,359.1; food, 3,359.0. *Industrial Production* (1996, 1990 = 100): 123.
Foreign Trade (1996 U.S.$): *Imports,* $42,465,000,000; *exports,* $23,083,000,000.

---

expenditures and income, predicting a deficit of about $16 billion. Austerity measures announced in October called for higher taxes, reduced pensions, and privatization.

Military. Dealing with the Kurdish insurgency in the southeast was expensive for the Turkish government. About 200,000 troops faced 4,000–10,000 Kurdistan Workers Party (PKK) guerrillas, who operated from refuges outside of Turkey, particularly in northern Iraq. In late December 1996, and in May and September 1997, Turkish armed forces moved into Iraq to attack the PKK. In September extensive bombing accompanied the movement of 16,000 Turkish soldiers and 100 tanks into the mountainous region. The Turkish military claimed to have killed about 400 PKK partisans; some 26,000 have died on both sides since the Kurdish insurgency began in 1984. Despite continued fighting, the government ended martial law in three provinces on Oct. 2, 1997, keeping it in six others.

Turkey's links to the United States and Western Europe were strengthened further by a February 13 arrangement to buy new military helicopters.

Foreign Affairs. The center of Turkish foreign policy remained fixed on the international ramifications of the Kurdish guerrilla warfare and tense relations with Greece. At the same time, Turkey was drawing closer to Israel (*see* MIDDLE EAST).

On March 26, German Foreign Minister Klaus Kinkel said that Turkey would not be able to join the European Union (EU) "in the foreseeable future." Germany opposed Turkish entry because of alleged human-rights abuses, the continuing uncertainties of the Kurdish situation, and the strife with Greece—an EU member. Although Turkey was admitted to the European Customs Union in 1996, EU members favored the entry of other Eastern European countries first. EU leaders specifically excluded Turkey from EU membership in December.

U.S. Secretary of State Madeleine Albright helped bring about the signing of a Turkish-Greek nonaggression pact on July 8, whereby each country pledged to resolve problems peacefully, while recognizing their mutual interests in the Aegean Sea. U.S. mediation on Cyprus in August was inconclusive.

WILLIAM OCHSENWALD
Virginia Polytechnic Institute and State University

UGANDA

Rebel activities, which had continued to plague Uganda, were brought under control during 1997 with the help of alliances with factions in neighboring Sudan and the Democratic Republic of the Congo. Because of the victories, Uganda was able to devote money to expanding social services.

Security. The northern-based Christian fundamentalist Lord's Resistance Army (LRA), led by Joseph Kony, continued its ten-year war against the government. The LRA received extensive support from the Islamist government of Sudan. Cattle production—an economic mainstay of the north—all but collapsed, and security concerns led farmers to let bumper crops rot in the fields. Many international agencies predicted famine.

In the west the Allied Democratic Forces (ADF) were composed of remnants of the National Army for the Liberation of Uganda and members of the Islamic militant Tabliqs. In the central region many armed groups were said to exist, while in the far northwest the West Nile Bank Front (WNBF) was composed of loyalists to former dictator Idi Amin. Leaders of all the movements were said to be attempting to coordinate their operations.

The government of Uganda adopted a regional strategy to counter rebel activity. In the north, Gen. Salim Saleh, President Yoweri Museveni's brother, assumed direct control of operations along the border of Sudan and the former Zaire—now the Democratic Republic of the Congo—from which Ugandan troops could pursue rebels to their rear bases in neighboring countries. The operations helped ensure the success of Laurent Kabila's Alliance of Democratic Forces for the Liberation of Congo/Zaire (ADFL), which then drove the ADF into the Ruwenzori mountains. The Uganda-backed offensive by the Sudan People's Liberation Army (SPLA) into Sudan helped to cut supply lines for the LRA.

South Africa became Uganda's largest single military supplier and was granted greater access to Uganda's mineral wealth.

Gen. David Tinyefunza, one of Uganda's most popular officers, accused many senior colleagues of engaging in smuggling while rank-and-file members went without proper supplies. Soldiers remained poorly paid in spite of massive demobilizations and an increase in the defense budget. Despite a formal ban on soldiers engaging in private business, many did so openly. In December, Tinyefunza resigned.

In June remnants of the ADF, together with forces from the former government of Zaire and Rwanda's Interhamwe, invaded western Uganda and occupied Bundibugya.

Social Services. The various military victories and more effective military operations on the ground enabled the minister of finance to introduce a budget that shifted emphasis from security to social services. Universal primary education was introduced—and was expected to double enrollment—and programs were developed to help alleviate poverty. Salaries for civil servants and the budgets of most ministries were not increased. Revenues generated barely kept up with growth.

Uganda continued to service an external debt of $3.4 billion, most of which was inherited from previous dictatorships. Debt relief of $332 million under the Highly Indebted Poor Countries Initiative from the World Bank was criticized for how slowly it was being implemented. Uganda spent more on debt servicing than on primary health care or education.

Economic growth fell slightly from 8% in 1996, and inflation rose to 7.5%—largely because of a 30% increase in food costs.

WILLIAM CYRUS REED
The American University in Cairo
and Indiana University

UGANDA • Information Highlights

Official Name: Republic of Uganda.
Location: Interior of East Africa.
Area: 91,135 sq mi (236 040 km²).
Population (mid-1997 est.): 20,600,000.
Chief Cities (1991 census): Kampala, the capital, 773,463; Jinja, 60,979; Mbale, 53,634.
Government: *Head of state,* Yoweri Museveni, president (took office Jan. 29, 1986). *Head of government,* Kintu Musoke, prime minister (took office Nov. 18, 1994). *Legislature* (unicameral)—Constituent Assembly.
Monetary Unit: Uganda shilling (1,112.2 shillings equal U.S.$1, principal rate, August 1997).
Gross Domestic Product (1995 est. U.S.$): $16,800,000,-000 (purchasing power parity).
Economic Index (1996, 1990 = 100): *Consumer Prices,* all items, 260.5; food, 226.6.
Foreign Trade (1996 U.S.$): *Imports,* $1,189,000,000; *exports,* $588,000,000.

UNITED NATIONS

The United Nations (UN)—created in 1945 to prevent "the scourge of war" from being repeated—was in transition during 1997. With the end of the Cold War in the early 1990s, the UN's focus shifted from many small wars to subduing internal upheavals as nations adjusted to a different world order. While there were crises in 1997, there was nothing that threatened world peace. For the first time since the UN was created, it had the opportunity to look inward, while facing a problem that could mean its demise—a lack of finances.

The new UN secretary-general, Kofi Annan (*see* BIOGRAPHY), with decades of UN experience behind him, was inaugurated in January. On Staff Day, September 12, Annan told UN workers that reform was vital for the UN but that it should not obscure the broader picture—"our work for peace, development, and human rights."

The UN continued its work toward easing crises in the world, but decreased financing limited new UN peacekeeping operations. While there were many new conflicts throughout the world, in most cases the UN authorized regional groups to furnish peacekeepers.

Modernization. Reform was the UN's main occupation in 1997, and the 52d General Assembly became known as the "reform assembly." When newly elected assembly President Hennadiy Udovenko of Ukraine opened the three-month session on September 16, he said that there was no serious obstacle stopping the UN from becoming what it should be "in order to prevent it from becoming a historical monument in the midst of a changed and transformed world."

During the two weeks of the annual General Debate, which began September 23, representatives of 176 of the 185 UN members expressed their governments' views on the state of the world and the UN. All declared support and most were optimistic.

Annan divided the reform process into two tracks. The first included measures that he had authority to carry out, such as setting up for the first time a cabinet to advise him on policy issues; reducing budget and staff; and reducing documentation of UN meetings. The second track represented proposals that required General Assembly approval, such as creating a new deputy secretary-general position—which was approved by the General Assembly in December. The second track also included establishing a revolving fund from government contributions to help the UN through its financial crisis, and decentralizing the UN system by giving more authority to department heads.

General Assembly. Annan presented his reform package in July, and by late December—after intensive discussions—delegates passed two resolutions accepting in principle the listed reforms but putting off further decisions until after the first of the year.

Also on the 160-item General Assembly agenda in 1997 were disarmament and humanitarian issues, as well as political, economic, social, administrative, and budgetary questions. The assembly adopted 271 resolutions and a new scale of member dues, retaining the 25% ceiling for the top level, but lowering the floor to 0.001% to help poorer countries.

The General Assembly held its 19th Special Session from June 23–27, to review implementation of agreements reached during the 1992 UN Conference on Environment and Development in Rio. The 1997 summit revealed that world leaders lacked the political will to carry out earlier pledges.

The assembly moved closer to establishing a permanent International Criminal Court (ICC) to prosecute crimes against humanity, genocide, and serious war crimes. The UN earlier had set up temporary international tribunals in the former Yugoslavia and in Rwanda. The International Court of Justice in The Hague handles civilian disputes between states. The assembly also adopted an International Convention for the Suppression of Terrorist Bombing, which holds governments responsible for prosecuting or extraditing offenders. The former president of Ireland, Mary Robinson (*see* BIOGRAPHY), was named to the new position of High Commissioner for Human Rights and began by stating that she intended to be "a moral voice, independent and outspoken," and "to stand up to bullies."

While most members favored enlarging the Security Council—the UN's most powerful organ—there was little agreement on which countries would be added, whether they would be granted permanent seats, or if they would be given veto power. Discussions would continue in 1998.

The General Assembly held what had become an annual debate denouncing the U.S. embargo against Cuba. The 1997 vote was 143 in favor of repealing the embargo and three against (United States, Israel, and Uzbekistan), with 25 abstentions.

Finances. Despite praise and support from world leaders, the UN faced bankruptcy. By the end of 1997, there was $2.06 billion in

ORGANIZATION OF THE UNITED NATIONS

THE SECRETARIAT *Secretary-General:* Kofi Annan (until Dec. 31, 2001)
THE GENERAL ASSEMBLY (1997) *President:* Hennadiy Udovenko (Ukraine)

The 185 member nations were as follows:

Afghanistan	Central African	Germany	Lebanon	Nigeria	South Africa
Albania	Republic	Ghana	Lesotho	Norway	Spain
Algeria	Chad	Greece	Liberia	Oman	Sri Lanka
Andorra	Chile	Grenada	Libya	Pakistan	Sudan
Angola	China, People's	Guatemala	Liechtenstein	Palau	Suriname
Antigua and Barbuda	Republic of	Guinea	Lithuania	Panama	Swaziland
Argentina	Colombia	Guinea-Bissau	Luxembourg	Papua New Guinea	Sweden
Armenia	Comoros	Guyana	Macedonia, The For-	Paraguay	Syria
Australia	Congo	Haiti	mer Yugoslav	Peru	Tajikistan
Austria	Congo, Democratic	Honduras	Republic of	Philippines	Tanzania
Azerbaijan	Republic of the	Hungary	Madagascar	Poland	Thailand
Bahamas	Costa Rica	Iceland	Malawi	Portugal	Togo
Bahrain	Croatia	India	Malaysia	Qatar	Trinidad and Tobago
Bangladesh	Cuba	Indonesia	Maldives	Romania	Tunisia
Barbados	Cyprus	Iran	Mali	Russia	Turkey
Belarus	Czech Republic	Iraq	Malta	Rwanda	Turkmenistan
Belgium	Denmark	Ireland	Marshall Islands	Saint Kitts and Nevis	Uganda
Belize	Djibouti	Israel	Mauritania	Saint Lucia	Ukraine
Benin	Dominica	Italy	Mauritius	Saint Vincent and The	United Arab Emirates
Bhutan	Dominican Republic	Ivory Coast	Mexico	Grenadines	United Kingdom
Bolivia	Ecuador	Jamaica	Micronesia	Samoa	United States
Bosnia and Herzego-	Egypt	Japan	Moldova	San Marino	Uruguay
vina	El Salvador	Jordan	Monaco	São Tomé and	Uzbekistan
Botswana	Equatorial Guinea	Kazakhstan	Mongolia	Príncipe	Vanuatu
Brazil	Eritrea	Kenya	Morocco	Saudi Arabia	Venezuela
Brunei Darussalam	Estonia	Korea, Democratic	Mozambique	Senegal	Vietnam
Bulgaria	Ethiopia	People's Republic	Myanmar	Seychelles	Yemen
Burkina Faso	Fiji	of	Namibia	Sierra Leone	Yugoslavia
Burundi	Finland	Korea, Republic of	Nepal	Singapore	Zambia
Cambodia	France	Kuwait	Netherlands	Slovak Republic	Zimbabwe
Cameroon	Gabon	Kyrgyzstan	New Zealand	Slovenia	
Canada	Gambia	Laos	Nicaragua	Solomon Islands	
Cape Verde	Georgia	Latvia	Niger	Somalia	

COMMITTEES

General. Composed of 28 members as follows: The General Assembly president; the 21 General Assembly vice-presidents (heads of delegations or their deputies of China, Democratic Republic of the Congo, Egypt, Ethiopia, France, Greece, Guinea, Ireland, Jordan, Kyrgyzstan, Mexico, Mongolia, Panama, Qatar, Russian Federation, Saint Vincent and the Grenadines, South Africa, Togo, United Kingdom, United States, and Vietnam); and the chairmen of the main committees below, which are composed of all 185 member countries.

First (Disarmament and International Security): Mothusi D.C. Nkgowe (Botswana)

Second (Economic and Financial): Oscar de Rojas (Venezuela)

Third (Social, Humanitarian and Cultural): Alessandro Busacca (Italy)

Fourth (Special Political and Decolonization): Machivenyika Tobias Mapuranga (Zimbabwe)

Fifth (Administrative and Budgetary): Anwarul Karim Chowdhury (Bangladesh)

Sixth (Legal): Peter Tomka (Slovakia)

THE ECONOMIC AND SOCIAL COUNCIL

President: Karel Kovanda (Czech Republic)
Membership ends on December 31 of the year noted.

Algeria (2000)	France (1999)	Poland (2000)
Argentina (1998)	Gabon (1998)	Romania (1998)
Bangladesh (1998)	Gambia (1999)	Russia (1998)
Belarus (2000)	Germany (1999)	Saint Lucia (2000)
Belgium (2000)	Guyana (1998)	Sierra Leone (2000)
Brazil (2000)	Iceland (1999)	South Korea (1999)
Canada (1998)	India (2000)	Spain (1999)
Cape Verde (1999)	Italy (1999)	Sri Lanka (1999)
Central African	Japan (1999)	Sweden (1998)
Republic (1998)	Jordan (1998)	Togo (1998)
Chile (1999)	Latvia (1999)	Tunisia (1998)
China (1998)	Lebanon (1998)	Turkey (1999)
Colombia (2000)	Lesotho (2000)	United Kingdom
Comoros (2000)	Mauritius (2000)	(1998)
Cuba (1999)	Mexico (1999)	United States
Czech Republic	Mozambique (1999)	(2000)
(1998)	New Zealand (2000)	Vietnam (2000)
Djibouti (1999)	Nicaragua (1998)	Zambia (1999)
El Salvador (1999)	Oman (2000)	
Finland (1998)	Pakistan (2000)	

THE SECURITY COUNCIL

Membership ends on December 31 of the year noted; asterisks indicate permanent membership.

Bahrain (1999)	Gabon (1999)	Russia*
Brazil (1999)	Gambia (1999)	Slovenia (1999)
China*	Japan (1998)	Sweden (1998)
Costa Rica (1998)	Kenya (1998)	United Kingdom*
France*	Portugal (1998)	United States*

THE TRUSTEESHIP COUNCIL

Composed of the five permanent members of the Security Council: China, France, Russia, United Kingdom, United States. The Council amended its rules of procedure in 1994 to drop the obligation to meet annually and agreed to meet as occasion required.

THE INTERNATIONAL COURT OF JUSTICE

President: Stephen M. Schwebel (United States, 2006)
Vice-President: Christopher G. Weeramantry (Sri Lanka, 2000)
Membership ends on February 5 of the year noted.

Mohammed Bedjaoui (Algeria, 2006)
Carl-August Fleischhauer (Germany, 2003)
Gilbert Guillaume (France, 2000)
Géza Herczegh (Hungary, 2003)
Rosalyn Higgins (United Kingdom, 2000)
Pieter H. Kooijmans (Netherlands, 2006)
Abdul G. Koroma (Sierra Leone, 2003)

Shigeru Oda (Japan, 2003)
Gonzalo Parra-Aranguren (Venezuela, 2000)
Raymond Ranjeva (Madagascar, 2000)
José Francisco Rezek (Brazil, 2006)
Shi Jiuyong (China, 2003)
Vladen S. Vereshchetin (Russia, 2006)
Christopher G. Weeramantry (Sri Lanka, 2000)

INTERGOVERNMENTAL AGENCIES

Food and Agricultural Organization (FAO); International Atomic Energy Agency (IAEA); International Bank for Reconstruction and Development (World Bank); International Civil Aviation Organization (ICAO); International Fund for Agricultural Development (IFAD); International Labor Organization (ILO); International Maritime Organization (IMO); International Monetary Fund (IMF); International Telecommunication Union (ITU); United Nations Educational, Scientific and Cultural Organization (UNESCO); United Nations Industrial Development Organization (UNIDO); Universal Postal Union (UPU); World Health Organization (WHO); World Intellectual Property Organization (WIPO); World Meteorological Organization (WMO); World Trade Organization (WTO).

unpaid dues, with $1.3 billion owed by the United States. Out of desperation, the UN borrowed from its peacekeeping budget to continue functioning. But peacekeeping activities had been reduced, leaving less money to borrow. "We are perhaps facing the most serious cash crisis in our history," Annan said. In addition, the financial crisis prevented the UN from paying governments that contributed troops and equipment to peacekeeping operations. Should those governments suddenly demand payment—some $900 million—the UN would be bankrupt. The organization received a psychological lift on September 18 when Ted Turner, vice-chairman of Time-Warner, Inc., announced that he would donate $1 billion to UN humanitarian programs. The UN charter, however, permits only governments to pay the UN's budget.

UN-U.S. relations soured in 1997 over delinquent payments. Despite a promise to remit at least part of the debt if the UN put through reforms, Washington continued to hold back payment even after the UN implemented many changes long urged by the United States. Since dues are part of the treaty that governments sign when joining the organization, failure to pay is equivalent to breaking the treaty. Meanwhile, the United States insisted that its budgetary assessment be reduced from 25% to 22% by 1998; it also wanted its peacekeeping assessment reduced from 31% to 25%. European Union (EU) representative Jean-Louis Wolzfeld, ambassador of Luxembourg, rejected reducing the U.S. bill until Washington paid what it owed.

Peacekeeping. Although many intense wars were being waged, there was less interest among world powers in intervening. UN peacekeeping's major past contributor—the United States—rejected most new peacekeeping operations. Citing the 18 U.S. soldiers killed during the 1993 Somalia mission, it blamed the deaths on the UN. Annan rejected the charges, saying that "the operation that led to the deaths of the Americans was planned and ordered by U.S. forces acting independently of the UN."

At the end of 1997 the UN had 15 peacekeeping operations, with some 14,879 military and police personnel. In 1996 the UN oversaw 16 such operations and 24,919 personnel. With little money, the Security Council authorized regional organizations to send forces—such as the Italian-led European force in Albania and the Nigerian-led West African force in Sierra Leone.

Although the large UN peacekeeping operation in Cambodia from 1991 to 1993 ended fighting and organized democratic elections, a new civil war flared up there. While the UN attempted to negotiate a cease-fire among warring factions in Afghanistan, it conceded that as long as outside powers supported one side or the other, peace would be difficult to achieve. The picture was little better in Haiti, where the UN sent international police to train Haiti's police force. Haiti's difficult political scene continued to leave the country paralyzed, although the situation had improved since the Haitian people were freed from a military junta. Haiti now had a civilian president, René Préval, but had no luck in keeping a prime minister. Annan pointed out that the paralysis of governmental activity in Haiti blocked needed social and economic development. "Should this situation persist longer," he said, "the nascent democratic process itself could be brought into question and also could imperil the long-sustained international commitment to assist Haiti." Annan said that the police took the law into their own hands, and recommended continued UN assistance in training Haiti's police force.

After seven years of Security Council sanctions, Iraq grew defiant of the UN Special Commission (UNSCOM) set up to eliminate Iraqi weapons of mass destruction. When that was accomplished, the oil embargo could be lifted. Iraqi President Saddam Hussein said that U.S. UNSCOM inspectors personally were delaying the end of the sanctions through negative reports, and ousted all U.S. UNSCOM team members. The United States sent an armada to the area, threatening the use of force until Iraq retracted. That crisis barely had passed when Hussein barred UNSCOM from inspecting his many presidential palaces. The Security Council insisted that UNSCOM had the right to inspect any area it wished. The crisis continued into 1998. The new executive director of UNSCOM, Australian Ambassador Richard Butler, visited Baghdad in January 1998 in an effort to ease tensions.

The government of Angolan President José Eduardo dos Santos—faced with a 20-year-old civil war led by Jonas Savimbi and his National Union for the Total Independence of Angola (UNITA)—decided to end the fighting, after the governments of UNITA supporters Zaire (now the Democratic Republic of the Congo) and the Congo Republic were ousted with the help of Angola. Meanwhile, the UN tried to force Savimbi to live up to a 1994 peace agreement signed in Lusaka, Zambia.

RUTH PEARSON, *"Business Week"*

United States

"We have resolved for our time a great debate over the role of government," President Bill Clinton declared as he took the oath of office to start his second term in the White House on Jan. 20, 1997. "Today we can declare: Government is not the problem. And government is not the solution. We—the American people—we are the solution." With these words, the president sought to establish a tone of harmony and reconciliation in the nation—and in Washington particularly—appropriate to the results of the 1996 election. That balloting had left the Republicans in charge of Congress and, while giving Clinton a second term, had denied him the majority of the popular vote he sought.

In general, the year 1997 was a good one for the United States economically. Unemployment and inflation remained low. The stock market hit new heights but caused some anxious moments.

Relations with China, the enlargement of the North Atlantic Treaty Organization (NATO), an uncertain peace in Bosnia, and developments in the Middle East dominated the nation's diplomatic endeavors.

Domestic Affairs

The compromise and harmony of which President Clinton spoke in his second inaugural address was most evident during the summer, with the adoption of a fiscal plan that promised a balanced budget. However, as events in Washington demonstrated, sharp divisions—not only between Republicans and Democrats, but within each party—remained.

The Presidency. President Clinton sought to reinforce the moderate tone of his inaugural with his first substantive speech of the second term, the State of the Union address, which he delivered to a joint session of Congress on February 4. While he referred to his talk as "a call to action...to prepare America for the 21st century," he presented no sweeping new legislative initiatives. Instead the president focused on a package of relatively modest ideas, most of which he had broached during the 1996 presidential campaign. These included measures aimed at enlarging education opportunities, curbing crime, improving the environment, and expanding health-insurance coverage.

U.S. Sen. Frank Lautenberg (D-NJ) (left) and House Speaker Newt Gingrich joined President Bill Clinton and Vice-President Al Gore for an Aug. 5, 1997, ceremony on the White House lawn, marking the signing of a plan to balance the federal budget by 2002.

The president's hopes for compromise with the Republican opposition appeared to be borne out by his most significant achievement of the year—enactment of a five-year plan to balance the budget and cut taxes for families, students, investors, and the working poor. The agreement reached in July followed weeks of intense negotiations in which both parties dug in their heels until each realized it would be in their own interest to reach an accord.

In helping the Republicans take a giant step toward the balanced budget that had been a longtime GOP goal, Clinton gained some important objectives of his own. One was a multibillion-dollar plan to provide states with funds to finance health insurance for some of the 3.4 million children not covered currently by any health-care plan. A boost in the cigarette tax would finance the plan. Still another gain for Clinton was the Republican approval of his demand that welfare recipients required to work under the new welfare-reform law be paid minimum wage and also be covered by federal workplace laws.

Differences over the tax-cut package, a major bone of contention, were resolved by expanding the size of the cuts to $95 billion over the next five years—up from $85 billion in previous versions. The cuts included a tax credit for children under the age of 17, to reach $500 in 1999; expansion of the tax credit for the working poor; and reduction of the capital-gains tax. The plan also provided for two new individual retirement accounts, including one that would allow early withdrawals for first-time home buyers and another to help with education costs.

But the president's success on the budget in summer had to be balanced by the defeat he suffered in the fall when he was unable to get congressional approval for "fast-track" authority to negotiate trade agreements. Such authority, designed to expedite trade negotiations by limiting congressional power to amend trade pacts, had been granted to every chief executive since Gerald Ford. For Clinton, the rebuff was perhaps harder to take in that most of the opposition to the fast-track proposal was centered in his own party, particularly in the House of Representatives, where Democratic leader Richard Gephardt headed the opposition. The president and his allies contended that fast-track authority, by reaffirming the nation's free-trade stance, would stimulate commerce with other countries, thus creating more jobs and profits for U.S. workers and businesses. But critics of fast track, principally labor unions and environmental

UNITED STATES • Information Highlights

Official Name: United States of America.
Location: Central North America.
Area: 3,618,768 sq mi (9 372 610 km²).
Population (mid-1997 est.): 267,700,000.
Chief Cities (July 1, 1994 est.): Washington, DC, the capital, 567,094; New York, 7,333,253; Los Angeles, 3,448,613; Chicago, 2,731,743; Houston, 1,702,086; Philadelphia, 1,524,249; San Diego, 1,151,977.
Government: *Head of state and government,* Bill Clinton, president (took office Jan. 20, 1993). *Legislature*—Congress: Senate and House of Representatives.
Monetary Unit: Dollar.
Gross Domestic Product (1995): $7,247,700,000,000 (purchasing power parity).
Economic Indexes (1996, 1990 = 100): *Consumer Prices,* all items, 120.1; food, 116.4. *Industrial Production,* 116.
Foreign Trade (1996): *Imports,* $817,795,000,000; *exports,* $624,528,000,000.

groups, warned that the potential dangers from trade agreements with less developed countries outweighed the benefits.

Citing the impact of the North American Free Trade Agreement (NAFTA), approved in Clinton's first term, critics argued that such agreements required special safeguards to protect U.S. wage levels, workplace-safety standards, and environmental conditions from being undermined. In addition to these problems, analysts said Clinton hurt his own cause by claiming that he would win on the issue if the vote were held in secret, implying that opponents were inspired by fear of retaliation from special interests. He also said that a vote for the bill was "a no-brainer," suggesting that the opposition was totally without merit.

In addition, the dispute over trade suggested that, after more than four years of Clinton's leadership, the Democratic Party remained sharply divided between "New Democrats" like himself, who were more inclined to cater to business interests, and traditional Democrats such as Representative Gephardt, whose views were more weighted toward labor unions and consumers.

Along with problems with Democrats in Congress, the president had some trouble with Republicans, too, when it came to staffing his administration. An early wave of new appointments for his second term generally met with relatively easy approval. These included: former United Nations (UN) Ambassador Madeleine Albright as secretary of state; former U.S. Sen. William Cohen (R-ME) as secretary of defense; Chicago lawyer William Daley as commerce secretary; Andrew M. Cuomo as secretary of housing and urban development; Federico Peña, former transportation secretary, as secretary of energy; Rodney Slater, former federal highway administrator, as secretary of transportation; and Bill Richardson, former U.S. representative from New Mexico, to fill the UN post vacated by Albright. Alexis Herman was confirmed easily as secretary of labor after long hearings. However, the appointment of Anthony Lake as director of the Central Intelligence Agency (CIA) met with difficulty, and the former head of the National Security Council withdrew his nomination from consideration. The president then named George Tenet to the post.

Later in the year some of Clinton's nominees for posts outside the cabinet encountered difficulty. Republican William Weld, who gave up the governorship of Massachusetts after being picked by Clinton to be ambassador to Mexico, withdrew from consideration on September 15 after Senate Foreign Relations Committee Chairman Jesse Helms (R-NC) refused to hold a confirmation hearing. In Helms' view, Weld's stance on drug enforcement was too lax for the job. The nomination of Bill Lann Lee to head the civil-rights division of the Justice Department failed to win the approval of the Senate Judiciary Committee because of GOP opposition to Lee's support for affirmative action. In December, Clinton appointed Lee acting attorney general for civil rights and promised to resubmit the nomination when Congress returned in 1998. In another cabinet change, the president in July named Hershel W. Gober as secretary of veterans affairs after Jesse Brown resigned from the post. However, the nomination of Gober, who had been deputy secretary of veterans affairs, was withdrawn in view of a sexual-harassment complaint. Army Secretary Togo D. West, Jr., was to take over as acting secretary early in 1998, while his nomination went before Congress.

In a commencement address at the University of California at San Diego on June 14, Clinton launched a yearlong campaign of town-hall meetings, conferences, and reports to ease racial tensions. He called for reconciliation between the races, defended affirmative action, and pointed out that by the end of the next half century there no longer would be a majority race in America. His remarks drew criticism from both liberals and conservatives. On the left, the Rev. Jesse Jackson—who had sparred with Clinton over race-related issues for years—praised the president for setting "the right moral tone" in his speech. But he argued that Clinton's effort to encourage a "race discussion" could "divert attention away from our ability to, in fact, close the gap [between the whites and minorities] with real structure and investment." From the right, California Gov. Pete Wilson accused the president of undermining equality by backing affirmative-action programs, which Wilson argued resulted in reverse discrimination. And he assailed Clinton for ignoring evidence of the country's more open-minded attitude on racial matters.

Meanwhile a series of continuing scandals, including the Whitewater affair and the sexual-harassment case of Paula Jones, as well as a new inquiry into the campaign-financing practices of the president and Vice-President Al Gore in 1996, swirled around the executive branch. (*See* WHITE HOUSE SCANDAL—25 YEARS AFTER WATERGATE, page 36.)

Congress. The level of bipartisanship that reached a peak in the first session of the 105th Congress with the balanced-budget agreement later went careening downhill into an acrimonious collapse. The session's opening months were shaped by the widespread belief in both parties that voters in 1996 were demanding compromise and moderation when they ratified the division of power between a Democratic White House and Republican Congress. That conviction provided the impetus for the massive budget deal, but all the compromises required to seal that bargain produced a backlash among the ideological wings of the two parties—particularly conservative Republicans—who wanted to reemphasize the differences between the parties in the prelude to the 1998 election.

The result was a series of legislative standoffs from which both sides walked away almost empty-handed. On education, fierce resistance from House Republicans made Clinton delay his plan for voluntary national

On Jan. 7, 1997, Newt Gingrich narrowly was reelected speaker of the House. The Georgia Republican later was reprimanded and fined $300,000 for bringing discredit on the chamber.

© Brad Markel/Gamma-Liaison

In August 1997, President Clinton used the newly instituted line-item veto for the first time. He struck three special-interest provisions from the balanced-budget act.

Photos, © Ruth Fremson/AP/Wide World Photos

education tests. Likewise, Republican opposition to a Clinton proposal to use a new statistical method that would give more weight to minorities in the 2000 census forced postponement of a decision on design of the census until 1999. Similarly, campaign-finance reform died in the Senate amid dueling filibusters between Republicans resisting restrictions on "soft money"—i.e., donations intended for party-building activities and not individual candidates—and Democrats opposed to limits on political activity by unions.

President Clinton used the line-item veto for the first time to strike three special-interest provisions from the balanced-budget act. In June the U.S. Supreme Court had rejected a challenge brought by five members and one former member of Congress to the Line-Item Veto Act, which was enacted in 1996.

Like the White House, Congress, too, had to deal with ethical questions. A House Ethics subcommittee found in 1996 that House Speaker Newt Gingrich had violated House rules against using tax-exempt donations for political purposes. The subcommittee also held that Gingrich had given false information to the ethics probe. Gingrich admitted the charge but said his lapse had been unintentional. On Jan. 7, 1997, Gingrich won reelection to the speakership by the margin of 216 to 205, with nine Republicans voting against him. In accepting reelection, Gingrich offered an apology. "To whatever degree...that I brought controversy or inappropriate attention to the House, I apologize," he said.

As punishment the House voted to reprimand Gingrich formally and fine him $300,000. It was the first such sanction imposed on a speaker in the 208-year history of the House. But the matter did not end there. Gingrich initially announced that he would pay the fine off with money borrowed from 1996 Republican standard-bearer Robert Dole. But in the wake of public criticism that this arrangement amounted to a "sweetheart deal" between two veteran politicians, the committee imposed a more stringent arrangement on May 15. Under the new plan, which sliced the Dole loan in half, Gingrich had to pay $150,000 from personal funds—including $50,000 immediately. Following resolution of the Gingrich case, the House revised its ethics system to ban outsiders from bringing complaints against members. It was just such an outside complaint, brought by a former Democratic congressman, that had triggered the probe of Representative Gingrich.

In addition to the balanced-budget and tax-cut provisions, legislation enacted in 1997 included:

• *Adoption.* Congress approved legislation aimed at speeding adoptions for children in foster care and ensuring their health and safety during the process.

• *Amtrak.* Congress voted to overhaul operations of the passenger-rail system to allow for release of $2.3 billion in subsidies aimed at preventing Amtrak bankruptcy.

• *Chemical Weapons.* The Senate approved the Chemical Weapons Convention, negotiated by the Ronald Reagan and George Bush administrations to ban the development, production, sale, and use of chemical weapons.

© Carter Smith/Sygma

Presidents (r-l) Jimmy Carter, Gerald Ford, and Bill Clinton paid tribute to George Bush—the nation's 41st chief executive—as the George Bush Presidential Library and Museum was dedicated at Texas A&M University in College Station, TX, on Nov. 6, 1997.

• *Congressional Pay.* A 2.3% cost-of-living adjustment for members of Congress was approved.

• *Food and Drug Administration.* Congress agreed to modernize the Food and Drug Administration (FDA) and acted to reduce the amount of time required to approve prescription drugs and medical devices.

• *Immigration.* Congress approved legislation to restore some welfare benefits to illegal immigrants already in the country, to shield Central American refugees who fled their homes during civil wars from deportation, and to allow some illegal immigrants to remain in the United States while applying for permanent resident visas.

Politics. The off-year elections on November 4 brought mostly good news for Republicans. They won the four major prizes at stake—the governorships of New Jersey and Virginia, the mayoralty of New York City, and a special election for a seat in the House of Representatives from New York's Staten Island. But a close look at the returns offered little evidence that, from a national perspective, either Republicans or Democrats were poised to break the partisan deadlock and lay claim to a new electoral majority.

The most closely watched race of the day—the New Jersey gubernatorial contest—demonstrated a troublesome divisiveness in GOP ranks. Incumbent Gov. Christine Todd Whitman's gender and personality had stirred interest in her potential for national office, especially among those worried about the party's inability to attract more backing from women. But Whitman edged out her Democratic foe by only 1%. Her strong support of abortion rights aroused the wrath of staunch conservatives—many of whom deserted the Republican Party to vote for independent candidates opposed to abortion. The governor's abortion stance was given as a reason for the close vote.

Whitman's narrow margin of victory also demonstrated that tax cuts, such as the 30% income-tax reduction Whitman carried out early in her tenure, do not build lasting gratitude. Whitman failed to build on the initial accomplishment of the tax cut with other measures that affected the lives of the voters, analysts said. For example, she offered her own plan for cutting auto-insurance rates but failed to get it through the GOP-controlled legislature, creating an issue that the Democrats used against her in the campaign.

To be sure, the GOP proponents of tax-cutting took satisfaction from the results of Virginia's gubernatorial race, where former state Attorney General James Gilmore made his plan to phase out Virginia's annual tax on the value of personal vehicles the dominant issue of his campaign. Gilmore was to succeed Republican Gov. George F. Allen, who was barred by law from seeking reelection.

As Democrats were quick to point out, the Republican National Committee came to the aid of its candidates in Virginia, New Jersey, and Staten Island in a huge way, shelling out millions of dollars to pay for the type of "soft money" that was central to the controversy over fund-raising in the 1996 presidential campaign. The debt that the Democratic National Committee incurred dealing with legal inquiries into its 1996 fund-raising left it unable to respond to the GOP ad barrage in the fall of 1997.

Some Republicans saw hopes for a revival of their party in the nation's cities. The reelection of New York City's Republican Mayor Rudolph Giuliani came on top of the landslide reelection of Los Angeles' Republican Mayor Richard Riordan in April. But it was far from clear that Giuliani's success could be translated into a victory formula for Republicans in other urban areas. While Giuliani benefited from a dramatic reduction in crime during his first term, analysts pointed out that the crime rate has been declining in most of the nation's other cities, where Democrats generally are in control. In other big-city mayoral races, such Democratic mayors as Boston's Thomas Menino, Cleveland's Michael R. White, and Detroit's Dennis W. Archer won reelection.

In ballot-issue contests, Houston voters rejected a proposal to bar city agencies from using affirmative action in hiring and contracting; Oregon residents voted to keep the nation's only law allowing physician-assisted suicide; and Washington-state voters defeated a gun-control measure that would have required all handguns to be equipped with a trigger guard. Also defeated in Washington state were initiatives to bar discrimination against gays and to legalize the medicinal use of marijuana and other drugs. In December, Lee P. Brown became the first African-American to be elected mayor of Houston. In addition to the Republican victory in the special House election on November 4, the GOP was successful in one special election to fill a House vacancy and unsuccessful in another.

Trials. Two trials resulting from spectacular crimes captured national attention in 1997. On February 4 a Santa Monica, CA, civil jury found former football star O.J. Simpson liable for the 1994 stabbing deaths of his former

Funding the Arts

The federal government continued to provide funding for the arts in 1997 amid an ongoing debate over the role of government in artistic endeavors. After conservatives in the U.S. House of Representatives tried to eliminate all spending for the National Endowment for the Arts (NEA), the beleaguered agency received $98 million in operating funds for fiscal year 1998. The appropriation was part of a $13.8 billion Interior Department spending bill.

The controversy over federal support of the arts had been building since the late 1980s. Critics charged the NEA, which was created in 1965 to promote the arts, with subsidizing endeavors they said contained obscene or otherwise objectionable themes. The controversy escalated in 1990, and Congress passed a law requiring the NEA to consider "general standards of decency" when awarding cash grants to artists. Since 1990 conservative lawmakers also had tried repeatedly, and unsuccessfully, to garner enough votes to deny the NEA funding.

Conservative lawmakers tried again in 1997 to withhold funding from the NEA. They succeeded in the House of Representatives, but Senate supporters of the agency managed to win final approval of the $98 million appropriation. That amount was $38 million less than President Bill Clinton had requested and $72 million less than

the NEA had been allotted as recently as fiscal 1994.

The most outspoken champion of continued public funding of the arts was actress Jane Alexander. As head of the NEA from 1993 until her resignation in October 1997, Alexander fended off attacks against the agency while calling on the artistic community to reach out more aggressively to the public. She received various public-service awards for her efforts. In December it was announced that the president would nominate William Ivey, executive director of the Country Music Foundation, as Alexander's successor.

Shortly after the NEA received its reprieve for another year, the U.S. Supreme Court entered the fray over public funding of the arts by agreeing on November 26 to review a challenge to the federal decency standards. The case in question, *National Endowment for the Arts v. Finley*, stemmed from a suit against the NEA by actress Karen Finley and other artists who claimed the law violated their 1st Amendment rights to free speech. A federal appeals court in California had agreed with the plaintiffs' argument and struck down the law in 1996. Critics of the ruling countered that the decency standards imposed no limit on artists' constitutional freedoms, only on their access to public funds.

MARY H. COOPER

wife, Nicole Brown Simpson, and her friend Ronald Goldman. In October 1995, Simpson had been acquitted of murder in a criminal trial that millions of Americans followed on television and that sharply divided the country along racial lines. Announcement of the civil verdict competed for attention on television with President Clinton's State of the Union address given that night.

On June 2, Timothy J. McVeigh, a decorated veteran of the Persian Gulf war, was convicted by a federal-court jury of the April 19, 1995, bombing of the federal office building in Oklahoma City that killed 168 people. The jury sentenced McVeigh to death. In a separate trial later in the year, Terry Nichols, a friend of McVeigh, was found guilty of conspiracy to use a weapon of mass destruction and involuntary manslaughter of eight federal law-enforcement officers. He was found not guilty of several other charges. (*See also* TERRORISM.)

ROBERT SHOGAN
Washington Bureau, "The Los Angeles Times"

The Economy

The U.S. economy in 1997 confounded critics, surprised even those responsible for fiscal and monetary policy, and, in general, elated a public that had been warned not to expect too much.

The ambience was set early in the year when Congress was given a budget-deficit forecast far too pessimistic. The surprises continued as inflation remained much better contained than had been foreseen, and as some long-term interest rates—home mortgages included—fell. Corporate profits continued to rise and personal income edged higher throughout the year, while the jobless rate steadily declined. The stock market, which some seasoned analysts said was headed for another sharp decline, soared to one record high after another before justifying the doubts.

In general, performance overwhelmed doubts and uncertainties. The good news even included a tax cut that lowered the top capital-gains rate to 20% from 28% and allowed couples to exclude from taxes up to $500,000 in gains from the sale of a home. For such reasons, many people thought of 1997 as a magical year. As the year ended, however, latent concerns emerged more forcefully. They were intensified by the monetary collapse of East Asian nations, beginning in Thailand and spreading most seriously to Korea in November. Evidence of damage to U.S. exports began to show up as buying power shrank in affected nations, and fears grew that deflated Asian prices might hurt domestic producers. Spotty weaknesses appeared in U.S. corporate profits and, reflecting growing uncertainties, stock prices turned more volatile.

Typifying the earlier fears and eventual surprises, the Congressional Budget Office in January concluded that the U.S. budget deficit would rise to $124 billion for the year and to at least $158 billion in 2002. But when the fiscal year ended, the deficit had shrunk to below $25 billion, and President Bill Clinton confidently forecast a surplus in 2002. White House Budget Director Frank Raines called the 1997 deficit an "artificially low level."

Forecasts and Indicators. Early forecasts of price behavior were equally incorrect. Inflation remained in check in raw materials and at producer and consumer levels. For the first ten months of the year, the producer-price index fell at an annual rate of just below 1%, compared with a 2.8% rise during all of 1996, and consumer prices rose at a three-decade low of just 1.8%. Near the end of the year, the Commodity Research Bureau's price index of 13 raw industrial commodities was almost 10% lower than at its 1997 peak.

In view of rising output, employment, and worker earnings—up more than 4% in 12 months—as well as a jobless rate that fell in November to a 24-year low of just 4.6% of the civilian labor force, the price stability was hard to explain. Federal Reserve Chairman Alan Greenspan warned as the year was ending that "the economy has been on an unsustainable track." This, however, had become a familiar refrain, unsubstantiated by the monthly statistics. In spite of speculation that Greenspan would be forced to raise interest rates substantially, the federal funds rate remained at about 5.5%, the yield on the ten-year U.S. Treasury bond fell to a 19-month low of 5.95% in October, and the 30-year Treasury bond—the basis for calculating home-mortgage rates—dropped below 6%.

As the year ended, the national average for 30-year fixed-rate mortgages had fallen below 7.5%, and both refinancing and housing sales were strong. The strength in housing—existing home sales in October reached their highest level in at least 29 years, an annual rate of 4.4 million units, and new housing starts were at a rate of 1.49 million units during the third quarter—was helped by yearlong increases in personal income. Though it was the third straight year of higher incomes after a five-year hiatus, the household median income was just more than $36,000, and many households had yet to regain the relative buying power of the late 1980s. What some economists referred to as an unhealthy gap between rich and poor was becoming a growing political issue. Others were encouraged by what they said were real gains among the poor. Despite this, the savings rate remained near record lows—under 4%—throughout most the year, and credit-card-delinquency rates were near all-time highs.

Corporate profits remained strong and so did returns of stock-market investors. Earnings of the Standard & Poor's 500 stocks through the third quarter averaged about 9% higher than in 1996, and the S&P DRI division estimated post-tax cash flow of all corporations at an annual rate of more than $1 trillion. Companies handled their profits more conservatively than in the high-leverage days of the 1980s. They returned only slightly more than one third of profits as dividends, compared with one half of profits paid out as dividends in the preceding 20 years. Unlike in the 1980s, the corporate world planned to have funds in reserve for any downturn.

Productivity and Other Surprises. The explanation for the absence of inflation in spite of rising wages, low unemployment, continued strong profits, and high-capacity usage most often was attributed to rising productivity. Greenspan offered it as at least part of the explanation and suggested that methodology might be undercounting gains. And Michael Flament, economist at Wright Investors' Service, commented that while it might be hard to quantify, "the fact S&P Industrial earnings more than doubled over the last five years while sales increased just 20% makes productivity growth impossible to deny." Paine Webber, the securities firm, observed that U.S. patent applications in the latest two years averaged 70% over their annual pace in the 1980s, and that it could mean future gains in productivity along with low consumer-price inflation. The statistical evidence surfaced late in the year with the announcement that third-quarter nonfarm productivity gains rose to an annual rate of 4.1%, with manufacturing productivity soaring 9.1%—the highest since 1982. The Bureau of Labor Statistics reported in December that more than 200,000 manufacturing jobs had been added in little more than one year, with the greatest contributions coming in electronic components, industrial machinery, and aircraft parts.

There were other surprises. For the first time since March 1985, the price of gold fell below $300 an ounce in late November,

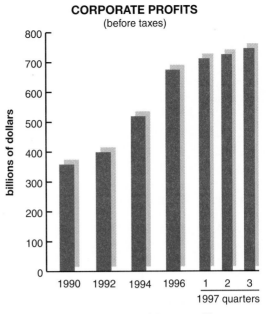

CORPORATE PROFITS
(before taxes)

billions of dollars

Source: Bureau of Economic Analysis, U.S. Department of Commerce

despite the monetary and economic turmoil in East Asia. It was a shocking turn of events for those who traditionally had sought security in gold during economic turmoil. The disenchantment was felt by both central banks and individual investors, who had seen the price rise to more than $800 an ounce during the 1980s. Meanwhile, silver futures rose in December to more than $5.40 an ounce on demand from filmmakers, and investors even viewed it as a temporary haven for funds. In contrast, nervous gold-mining companies in December bought options to sell at prices below $285 an ounce, and Newmont Mining's board cuts its dividend 75% to conserve cash.

To a large degree, the fate of gold resulted from diminishing inflation and growing faith in the strength of the U.S. economy and banking system. Reflecting this, the dollar rose near year's end to more than 130 Japanese yen, the first time it had reached that level since May 1992. Although it had weakened somewhat in August, and in spite of forecasts by traders of further weakening, the dollar was equal to 1.7964 German marks in December. A year before it had been at 1.55575 marks. The dollar's confidence was a direct consequence of the economy's surprising stability, a factor that also played a large role in the stock market's ascent.

Stocks and Asian Troubles. The Dow Jones industrial average, the most highly followed stock-market indicator, rose as high as 8,259.31 points, more than 24% above its 1996 high, but it was marked by increasing volatility. In spite of repeated warnings that the market was exceeding long-term valuation norms, investors continued to flood it with buy orders through 401(k) and corporate retirement plans, and individual retirement accounts (IRAs). Much of the money went into increasingly popular mutual funds, which numbered more than 6,000 and were valued at more than $4 trillion. Professional worries seemed justified when the worst October performance in ten years befell the market, underscored by a record one-day, 554-point sell-off in the Dow on October 27 that dropped it to a level of 7,161.15 points. It could have been worse, but New York Stock Exchange rules brought closing to an early halt. The decline then continued the next day, when more than 1.2 million shares changed hands on the Big Board. Thereafter, the market's volatility remained pronounced, though prices had regained most of the October loss by late November. (*See also* STOCKS AND BONDS.)

Weakness set in again before the end of the year as evidence built that the Asian monetary and economic collapses were having an impact on U.S. technological and agricultural exports, while simultaneously threatening to flood the country with low-priced imports. It brought renewed concern about the U.S. trade deficit, one of the major weaknesses and biggest disappointments of the economy. After only nine months, the deficit ran at an annual rate of $115.3 billion, even greater than the eight-year high of $111 billion in 1996. Fears grew that the Asian troubles were likely to exacerbate the situation, making Asian discounted goods more attractive to U.S. importers while leaving them less able to buy U.S. exports. The sharpest deficit rise was in trade with China, which vied with Japan as the nation with the greatest U.S. export-import imbalance.

While such concerns occupied the time and minds of economists and government officials, ordinary citizens were involved in more mundane pursuits. Help-wanted signs hung in the windows of fast-food and supermarket outlets, personal income had risen, confidence was high, and retailers enjoyed relatively strong holiday sales. And overall, the public had reason to be satisfied, having produced a total third-quarter domestic product of $7.2 trillion (in 1992 dollars)—3.8% higher than a year earlier. Still, an undercurrent of uncertainty ran closer and closer to the surface.

See also BUSINESS AND CORPORATE AFFAIRS; BIOGRAPHY—*Greenspan, Alan*; INTERNATIONAL TRADE AND FINANCE.

JOHN CUNNIFF, *The Associated Press*

Foreign Affairs

The Bill Clinton administration's main foreign-policy challenges in 1997 appeared to be in carrying through with the commitments and initiatives it had made during Clinton's first term and in the 1996 election. Whether in pushing the Oslo and Dayton peace processes in the Middle East and Bosnia, respectively; pursuing arms-control and trade-liberalization negotiations; implementing strategies for reduced hydrocarbon emissions; or dealing with China, the administration faced formidable dilemmas.

Foreign-policy issues remained highly politicized. Despite a U.S. trade deficit that reached more than $115 billion, Congress refused to pass "fast-track" trade authority, the ability to propose trade agreements and related legislation on an all-or-nothing basis (no amendments)—an authority granted to recent U.S. administrations. The president also had hoped to revive his first-term proposals for a Western Hemisphere free-trade pact. In May, Clinton dispatched a Commerce Department trade mission to South America and made his first trip to Central America to promote the idea, smoothing over border, immigration, and drug-enforcement conflicts in the process. In October he traveled widely in South America, encountering some resistance from the region's Mercosur trade group.

Delivering the Harvard commencement address in June, Secretary of State Madeleine Albright (*see* BIOGRAPHY) warned of isolationism and global indifference. She worked for bipartisan cooperation and ratification of the chemical-weapons treaty, seeking Russian cooperation and offering enough concessions to gain Senate confirmation—including a presidential promise to withdraw from the treaty if it threatened U.S. security and a promise of State Department reorganization. The Senate leadership nevertheless continued to delay ratification of other pending treaties, including the comprehensive nuclear-test ban. A raft of appointments for long-vacant diplomatic posts were approved in July, but Sen. Jesse Helms, chairman of the Foreign Relations Committee, refused hearings on the nomination of Gov. William Weld (R-MA) as ambassador to Mexico; the candidacy was withdrawn. Congress also pressed the administration to "get tough" on United Nations (UN) reform, on China's human-rights record, on Pentagon cooperation with the Chinese army, and on Chinese policies toward Tibet, Taiwan, and Hong Kong (which peacefully reverted to Chinese rule in July).

President Clinton was in San José, Costa Rica, in May 1997 for a summit of Central American leaders. The United States, Costa Rica, El Salvador, Guatemala, Honduras, Nicaragua, and Panama signed an "open-skies" agreement.

© Eugene Hoshiko/AP/Wide World Photos

Politics and Economics. Ironically, as many on Capitol Hill expressed concerns about threats to U.S. sovereignty from the UN and international agreements, French, Malaysian, and other national leaders openly blamed Washington for imposing its laws and brand of "ultra-capitalism" on the world in an effort to weaken competitors. Switzerland, for example, grudgingly complied with U.S. pressure to identify and repay Holocaust victims' funds that were deposited in Swiss banks by the Nazis during World War II.

Congressional and bureaucratic pressure, as well as international economic conflict, combined to create considerable tension between Washington and some of its closest allies. Canada was annoyed on a number of counts, ranging from a northwest-waters fishing dispute to tougher border-crossing requirements. Ottawa strongly criticized President Clinton's backing down from prior com-

mitments to a global treaty banning the use, development, and trade of antipersonnel land mines. Although Washington refused to sign the new pact, it still favored restrictions on land mines. The refusal was based on concerns over South Korea's defense.

A 1996 shipment of sophisticated computers for Russian nuclear labs also came under grand-jury investigation, which caused Russians to argue they had been deceived by supposed U.S. promises of such computers in return for signing the nuclear-test ban. The United States also opposed prospective Russian and South African arms sales to Syria, and Russian nuclear-reactor sales to India. France and Russia, as well as China, all felt heavy U.S. pressure against missile and technology trade with Iran, including threatened U.S. sanctions on companies involved.

Vice-President Al Gore visited Moscow for biennial talks in September, attempting to

smooth over issues related to plutonium production, nuclear proliferation, oil trade, and
religious freedom.This caused Euro-Ameri-
can friction and jarred Russia's shaky economy even as President Clinton had relatively
positive things to say about Iran's newly elected president and withdrew opposition to a
trans-Iranian gas pipeline. The mixed signals
represented internal administration debates
about how to treat the Iranian question and
enforce anti-Iran trade laws.

The final agreement for North Atlantic
Treaty Organization (NATO) "enlargement"
to allow for Hungarian, Czech, and Polish
membership also came in for economic and
inter-allied controversy. At the Madrid NATO
summit, Clinton held off European pressure
to admit other former East-bloc states while
fending off French demands to share in the
command of NATO forces in Europe. (*See*
Europe—*NATO Expansion.*)

Among the points raised at the June "Summit of Eight" (G-7 plus Russia) in Denver was
a trade-union petition to "humanize" globalization by emphasizing sustainable development and employment growth. The United
States strongly pushed its brand of economic
liberalization at the conference and suggested
free-trade and debt-relief measures to boost
African economies.

The tangle of economic and political issues
was epitomized by U.S.-China relations. At
their October summit, President Clinton,
faced with a substantial deficit in Chinese
trade, and President Jiang Zemin agreed to $3
billion of potential U.S. airliner sales and controversial moves to allow U.S. companies to
compete to sell nuclear reactors in China.
Progress on the human-rights question was
reported in February with a tentative deal for
China to sign two UN conventions and release
a group of dissidents; the best known of these,
Wei Jingsheng, reached Detroit and New
York in November. China was not happy
about the appointment of a special State
Department coordinator for Tibet nor about
the April U.S. visit of the Dalai Lama. Despite
proposing China for normal trade relations,
Clinton refused to take extraordinary measures to achieve that status or to help China
into the World Trade Organization. Nevertheless, China agreed to halt the sale of nuclear
technology to Iran and to return a powerful,
militarily useful U.S. supercomputer exported
illegally in 1996; the two sides also agreed to
establish a Beijing-Washington "hot line" for
crisis management, and President Clinton
accepted an invitation to visit China in late
1998. Attempts also were made to reassure

Beijing about enhanced U.S.-Japan security
arrangements.

Legislative agreements finally were
reached in November on a $12.8 billion for-
eign-operations bill; most of the amount was
for security and development assistance. Security assistance was approximately half the
total, and included foreign military financing
and economic support, aid to former Soviet
republics, and certain peacekeeping operations. Funding for a 60% payment on past UN
assessments (about $926 million) and for IMF
emergency aid to hard-hit East Asian
economies such as Thailand was deleted when
congressional efforts to deny global popula-
tion-planning assistance drew lively opposition from both the president and female legislators.

The failure to pay UN assessments and
efforts to downplay the organization, including the lukewarm reception given to a UN
human-rights monitor looking into the U.S.
use of the death penalty, were ironic given the
administration's strong condemnation of Saddam Hussein's autumn refusal to allow U.S.
arms inspectors to operate with their UN
counterparts in checking on Iraqi chemical
and biological weapons. Iraq tried to split the
UN Security Council coalition by playing on
Russian, French, and Chinese impatience with
the seven-year-old trade sanctions. However,
Washington was able to keep the coalition
together and extend travel restrictions on
Iraqi personnel, although threats to take military action against Baghdad were opposed by
the other UN powers and by moderate Arab
states. The crisis eased through the diplomacy
of UN Secretary-General Kofi Annan and
Russian Foreign Minister Yevgeny Primakov,
with inspectors returning to Baghdad and
indications of more oil trade.

The Wider Global Agenda. Despite the
image of lessened tensions in the post–Cold
War era, U.S. forces remained on active missions in more than 100 countries, ranging from
training in Haiti to peacekeeping in Bosnia,
from a heightened presence in the Persian
Gulf to Latin drug interdiction, from African
crisis rescue missions to monitoring the quiet
mountain passes of the Sinai peninsula.

Controversy about Israel's continued settlement-building and Jerusalem land developments led to renewed Palestinian protest,
Hamas violence, and Israeli border closures,
greatly complicating the task of moving to the
next steps of the peace process. Hoping to
bypass mutual distrust, and suspicious of
Prime Minister Benjamin Netanyahu's commitment to the process, the United States pro-

posed a quick move to the final stages of an agreement as well as a "time-out" in Israeli settlement-building. A number of moderate Arab states, including Egypt, boycotted a November economic meeting with Israel and Secretary Albright in Qatar out of their perception of a "double standard," whereby Iraq was condemned for violating UN Security Council resolutions while little was done about Israeli violations. As a signal of concern, President Clinton refused to see Netanyahu during his Washington stopover in November.

During the summer, the United States was able to press fairly successfully for local elections in Bosnia, in which refugees who could not yet safely move back to their hometowns nevertheless were allowed to vote there. However, Dayton Accords architect Richard Holbrooke was sent back to the region in August, as Washington signaled its displeasure at the pace of implementation by suspending contacts with Bosnia's ambassador. Concerned that no unified Bosnian government was emerging, the United States inserted itself forcefully into internal Serb politics, opposing the Bosnian Serb parliamentary group in Pale and favoring President Biljana Plavsic. In July, U.S. forces supported NATO's first attempt to arrest Serbian war criminals, resulting in one killing and one arrest. Meanwhile, after a threatened suspension of a $13 million loan to Croatia, Bosnian Croat leaders handed over some of their indicted officials for war crimes trials in The Hague. In December it was announced that President Clinton wanted the U.S. military stay in Bosnia to be extended past June 1998 in order to enforce the stalled peace accord. Some feared the potential for renewed fighting.

Secretary Albright also grew more serious about negotiating a settlement to the longstanding Cyprus conflict. Following quiet summer talks hosted in upstate New York, Holbrooke was assigned to convene major negotiations in Europe involving the Turkish and Greek Cypriot communities. Similarly, quiet U.S. diplomacy played into the attempts of Britain's new Labour government to reconvene Northern Irish peace talks.

Troubling African civil wars on the whole represented a setback for Clinton's policy of fostering democracy in developing countries. Zaire's decrepit Mobutu Sese Seko regime, long a U.S., French, and Belgian client, finally fell in the spring. It was uncertain what course the new Laurent Kabila government would follow in the renamed Democratic Republic of the Congo, as U.S. diplomats, unable to gain a free election, pressed for an accounting of war atrocities. This war also helped destabilize and devastate the neighboring Republic of the Congo; Bill Richardson, U.S. representative to the UN, toured the area in October, strongly pressing Angola and other neighbors to withdraw their troops. He also stopped in nearby Rwanda, which saw the return of thousands of Hutu refugees from Zaire. Rwanda was slow to try war criminals and to look into allegations of military atrocities against Hutu in Zaire, for fear of unleashing new bloodbaths.

Africa's troubling conflicts spread to Sierra Leone, where, among other places, U.S. military forces were employed for evacuation of civilians. U.S. officials continued to criticize human-rights violations in Nigeria despite that country's efforts to oust the rebels in Sierra Leone. South African President Nelson Mandela kept the impressive domestic "truth and reconciliation" process going and assisted in the Zaire transition, but strained U.S. relations by visiting Libyan leader Muammar el-Qaddafi in October.

Renewed U.S.-Japanese trade friction flared in September over the question of access to ports, and Washington moved to impose entry fines and close ports to Japanese cargo ships. The dispute eased through negotiations and with the greater concern about Asian economic stability, which was a primary topic at the late-November Asia-Pacific (APEC) summit in Vancouver.

Relations with East Asia also focused on key regional conflicts. Indonesia withdrew from U.S. military-assistance programs in June, protesting congressional human-rights criticism. In the spring, Washington suspended aid to Cambodia and dispatched envoy Stephen Solarz to seek free elections and military neutralization. En route to the July Association of Southeast Asian Nations (ASEAN) meetings in Malaysia, Secretary Albright pressed the organization to demand free Cambodian elections by May 1998; on human-rights grounds, she also objected to ASEAN's decision to admit Myanmar.

With reports of North Korean famine in June, Washington agreed to provide $27 million in food relief. The United States welcomed the August defection of North Korea's ambassador to Egypt. To protest the defection, North Korea withdrew from arms talks in New York, but the Clinton administration successfully pressed for North Korea's participation in subsequent peace talks with South Korea, China, and the United States.

FREDERIC S. PEARSON, *Wayne State University*

URUGUAY

A new constitution went into effect in Uruguay on Jan. 14, 1997. Signs of economic recovery were widespread, while diplomatic relations with Peru returned to normal.

Government and Politics. According to Uruguay's new constitution, each political party must choose only one presidential candidate in primary contests. When no candidate gains 50% of the popular vote in a general election, a runoff will follow. Legislators are chosen at the same time as the president, while municipal elections are held a year later. Executive power was increased, with the chief executive now empowered to remove public employees and Congress given less time to override a presidential veto. Public opinion was divided almost evenly on the new charter; of the nearly 2 million votes cast, 50.4% favored the changes.

Carlos Baraibar of the Broad Front was elected in February to preside over the lower house of Congress—the first leftist ever to have been chosen for that post. The Broad Front also controls the government of Montevideo, the capital city.

Economy. An economic turnaround was reflected in banking and tourism. Dollar deposits—83% of all funds deposited in the banking industry—amounted to $7.2 billion in August, of which about $460 million had been deposited since January. Tourist arrivals—70% from Argentina—were up by 17.5% over the previous season. Exports of beef, lamb, and wool were well above 1996 levels, with near-record car sales projected for the year. Monthly peso devaluations were lowered to 1% in August, and the inflation rate fell from 25% to 15%. A 5% growth rate for the year was forecast in July, and an improved credit rating facilitated a $300 million global bond issue in June. An outlay of $330 million was obtained from the Inter-American Development Bank to fund improvements in municipal governments, roads, and the social-security system.

Dissatisfaction with government privatizing and downsizing erupted into a general strike on January 13 that was supported heavily in Montevideo. Protests continued. One in Durazno, 100 mi (161 km) north of the capital, followed an attempt in June by President Julio Sanguinetti to blame the unrest on "old Communists" and opposition forces in the Broad Front coalition. Joining labor forces in Durazno were merchants and industrialists led by the conservative mayor. Unemployment hovered at 12%, and higher crime rates provoked an August expenditure of $1 million in crime-fighting equipment.

Foreign Relations. Ties with Peru were normalized in June, when the foreign ministry reassigned Uruguay's ambassador, Tabaré Bocalandro. Bocalandro had been taken hostage by the Tupac Amaru guerrillas and released on Dec. 24, 1996, after Uruguay freed two Tupac Amaru militants who had been detained since 1995. The swap of a hostage for prisoners angered Peruvian President Alberto Fujimori, and relations between the two countries had deteriorated.

In August a court acquitted Federico and Carlos Fassano of "insulting the honor" of Paraguayan president Juan Carlos Wasmosy. The Fassanos published articles in their Montevideo newspaper, *La República*, in April 1996, accusing businessman Wasmosy of engaging in corrupt practices before becoming president. The presiding judge ruled that Wasmosy was not in Uruguay when the accusations were published and that the offending articles did not pose a real threat to Uruguay's foreign relations.

LARRY L. PIPPIN, *University of the Pacific*

URUGUAY • Information Highlights

Official Name: Oriental Republic of Uruguay.
Location: Southeastern coast of South America.
Area: 68,039 sq mi (176 220 km²).
Population (mid-1997 est.): 3,200,000.
Chief City (1985 census): Montevideo, the capital, 1,251,647.
Government: *Head of state and government,* Julio Maria Sanguinetti, president (took office March 1995). *Legislature*—General Assembly: Chamber of Senators and Chamber of Representatives.
Monetary Unit: New peso (9.9600 new pesos equal U.S.$1, financial rate, Dec. 16, 1997).
Gross Domestic Product (1995 est. U.S.$): $24,400,-000,000 (purchasing power parity).
Economic Index (Montevideo, 1996; 1990 = 100): *Consumer Prices,* all items, 1,385.4; food, 1,104.9.
Foreign Trade (1996 U.S.$): *Imports,* $3,323,000,000; *exports,* $2,397,000,000.

VENEZUELA

In 1997 the Venezuelan economy began a modest recovery after the austere "Agenda Venezuela" economic program of 1996. In the political arena, strikes, intransigent partisan confrontation, violence, and border problems were growing concerns.

At least 81 persons were killed and some 500 were injured as the result of an earthquake in Sucre province in July.

Economy. The nation's economic performance improved in some respects since 1996, with economic growth at a modest rate of 4%, and inflation down from more than 100% to about 33%. President Rafael Caldera Rodríguez had hoped to bring inflation down to less than 25%, but succumbed to political pressure, postponing a gasoline price increase and granting a wage increase to public employees. These decisions followed two major strikes: one involving 22,000 doctors during 13 days in January; and the other involving a much larger number of teachers and professors in February and March. In June, Caldera signed a new Organic Labor Law that modified rules regarding dismissals, severance pay, social security, and the complex system of bonuses owed to Venezuelan workers. Some complained, however, that the new law was almost as confusing as the 1991 law it replaced. Despite the new law, wage increases, lower inflation, and the growing economy, a September poll reported that 74% disapproved of Caldera's performance. Majorities also disapproved of the performance of key government ministers.

Politics. The cooperation among major political parties, unions, and the private sector in the drafting and approval of the labor law did not extend to other issues. In March an odd legislative coalition called the Triple Alliance—composed of the center-right Social Christian Party (COPEI), the center-left Movement to Socialism (MAS), and the leftist La Causa R—managed to retain control of leadership positions in Congress after weeks of tense bargaining. This alliance first formed in early 1996 in order to reform the electoral law, but by late 1997 the law still had not been approved—in large part because of delaying tactics by the center-left Democratic Action Party (AD) in September and October.

The nation's political landscape grew more complex as new parties and candidates began to prepare for the December 1998 elections. The front-runner in the presidential race, according to early polls, was Irene Sáez, 35, the 1981 Miss Universe, who had earned a reputation for efficiency, honesty, and style as mayor of Chacao, a well-to-do district of Caracas. Sáez' popularity was so pervasive that leaders of several established parties hoped to recruit her as a presidential candidate. Another independent, former Gov. Henrique Salas Römer, had a sizable following based on a similar reputation.

Two new political movements formed as the result of party splits: Apertura ("Opening"), founded by Carlos Andrés Pérez (the nation's president, 1974–79 and 1989–93), who was forced to leave AD after his impeachment; and the leftist Fatherland For All

---

VENEZUELA • Information Highlights

Official Name: Republic of Venezuela.
Location: Northern coast of South America.
Area: 352,143 sq mi (912 050 km²).
Population (mid-1997 est.): 22,600,000.
Chief Cities (June 30, 1990 est.): Caracas, the capital (incl. suburbs), 3,435,795; Maracaibo, 1,400,643; Valencia, 1,274,354.
Government: Head of state and government, Rafael Caldera Rodríguez, president (inaugurated Feb. 2, 1994). Legislature—Congress of the Republic: Senate and Chamber of Deputies.
Monetary Unit: Bolívar (502.00 bolívares equal U.S.$1, official rate, Dec. 16, 1997).
Gross Domestic Product (1995 est. U.S.$): $195,500,-000,000 (purchasing power parity).
Economic Index (Caracas, 1996; 1990 = 100): Consumer Prices, all items, 1,233.7; food, 1,095.8.
Foreign Trade (1996 U.S.$): Imports, $9,788,000,000; exports, $20,725,000,000.

(Patria Para Todos—PPT), which broke away from La Causa R in July, during severe leadership disputes. The Bolivarian Revolutionary Movement (MBR-200) survived, but this vehicle of Hugo Chávez Frías—a leader of the February 1992 coup attempt—had lost much of its popular support.

Political violence returned to Venezuela in the second half of the year, when small pipe bombs were planted outside the headquarters of the Venezuelan Labor Confederation, the Supreme Electoral Council, the congressional office building, the Caracas Hilton, and two subway stations. The identity and motives of the bombers remained a mystery.

Along the border with Colombia, three bands of Colombian guerrillas launched raids into Venezuelan territory—seizing farms, attacking a paratrooper base, extorting funds, and kidnapping Venezuelans for ransom. In July one band, the Revolutionary Armed Forces of Colombia (FARC), requested peace talks, but the Venezuelan government instead mobilized 16,000 troops at the border in October. Drug traffickers also crossed the poorly monitored border with increasing frequency, bringing growing crime and corruption with them.

Clinton's Visit. During Bill Clinton's October visit to Venezuela, the U.S. president and President Caldera reaffirmed their determination to join forces against corruption and drug trafficking, as well as to promote trade and investment. Specifically, Venezuela and the United States signed an accord to share intelligence data on drug smuggling and to simplify the process of extraditing drug traffickers. President Clinton also addressed a crowd at Caracas' El Panetón Plaza, the site of the burial spot of Simón Bolívar.

MICHAEL COPPEDGE
University of Notre Dame

VIETNAM

New leaders chosen in 1997 by the Communist Party faced the task of strengthening Vietnam's economic reform and dealing with a weak banking system, corruption, and growing peasant unrest.

Politics. In June the Central Committee of the Communist Party chose First Deputy Prime Minister Phan Van Khai, 63, as the new prime minister. Khai was 11 years younger than his predecessor, Vo Van Kiet. Like Kiet, Khai was an active proponent of reform and favored less rigid party control over government decisions.

In September the Central Committee chose former engineer Tran Duc Luong, 60, to succeed the ailing 76-year-old Gen. Le Duc Anh as president. Tran Duc Luong was most likely a compromise choice, since senior defense and foreign-ministry officials had been vying for the job, which has overall responsibility for the armed forces.

General Secretary of the Communist Party Do Muoi, 80, was replaced in late December by Gen. Le Kha Phieu, 66, a hard-liner with no formal economic training, according to analysts. The choice was thought to reflect the leadership's concern over recent disturbances that have accompanied liberalization.

Economy. Despite an anticipated 1997 economic-growth rate of 8%—down from 9.3% in 1996—and 4% inflation, the new leaders faced a daunting array of economic problems. Major weakness in the banking system, widespread corruption, and growing unrest among peasant farmers who had not shared in the country's recent boom could drive off foreign investors and possibly undermine the stability of the regime.

The banking system was dominated by the four large state banks, which accounted for 80% of all loans. Most were to state enterprises, often based on politics. The banking system, which also included 52 small private banks, held $24 billion in bad loans, more than Vietnam's gross domestic product (GDP). Many of the $1.4 billion worth of letters of credit were unlikely to be paid on time. Since the state banks provided about half of Vietnam's revenue, officials resisted replacing them with a market-driven system. Although the system—in which poorly paid government officials control access to the economy— invites corruption, many officials blamed the private sector for the corruption.

Alarmed by the increase in social ills such as drug trafficking, Le Duc Anh warned of the "sin" of "individualism" that had been spawned by economic reform.

In June 1997, Madeleine Albright became the first U.S. secretary of state to visit Vietnam since the Vietnam war. She and Foreign Minister Nguyen Manh Cam (right) agreed to establish consulates in each other's countries and to a copyright pact.

© Richard Vogel/AP/Wide World Photos

VIETNAM • Information Highlights

Official Name: Socialist Republic of Vietnam.
Location: Southeast Asia.
Area: 127,243 sq mi (329 560 km²).
Population (mid-1997 est.): 75,100,000.
Chief Cities (April 1, 1989 census): Hanoi, the capital, 3,056,146; Ho Chi Minh City, 3,924,435; Haiphong, 1,447,523.
Government: *Head of state,* Tran Duc Luong, president (took office September 1997). *Head of government,* Phan Van Khai, prime minister (appointed June 1997). *Legislature*—National Assembly.
Monetary Unit: New dong (11,193 new dongs equal U.S.$1, 1995 average).
Gross Domestic Product (1995 est. U.S.$): $97,000,000,-000 (purchasing power parity).
Foreign Trade (1995 U.S.$): *Imports,* $7,500,000,000; *exports,* $5,200,000,000.

Vietnam was a growing market for heroin produced in the "golden triangle"—Laos, Thailand, and Myanmar—as well as a transit route for heroin exported to the West. A number of senior police officers were arrested in a crackdown that began in January, and at least two policemen were among those sentenced to death. A growing number of officials and businessmen also faced the firing squad for financial corruption.

Peasant farmers, who made up 75% of the population, became rebellious in some regions because of heavy taxes imposed by corrupt party officials. The farmers had annual incomes of $50 a year, while people living in the major cities made $1,000 a year. In February peasants clashed with police near Hanoi after officials pocketed money due to them from a Korean firm planning to build a golf course on the peasants' land. In May, 3,000 peasants staged a sit-in at the Communist Party office in Thai Binh province to protest corruption and increased taxes. The incident was largely peaceful, but reports indicated that farmers who later occupied the radio station in Thai Binh city were fired on by police. The protests reportedly were organized by war veterans, many of whom were unemployed after returning from Cambodia.

In the Mekong Delta, rice farmers—who paid middlemen exorbitant fees—faced crippling debt. In November the worst typhoon of the century struck Vietnam's southern coast, sinking hundreds of fishing boats and flattening thousands of homes.

Foreign Affairs. In March, Vietnam agreed to assume $140 million in debt owed to the United States by the former South Vietnamese government. U.S. Ambassador Douglas "Pete" Peterson—who had been a prisoner of war in Vietnam—arrived in Hanoi in May to prepare for Secretary of State Madeleine Albright's June visit. Albright laid the cornerstone of a new U.S. consulate in Ho Chi Minh City. In September the United States gave Vietnam a $400,000 grant to conduct a feasibility study for a direct-reduced iron plant—another step toward establishing full economic relations with Hanoi.

However, under U.S. law the United States cannot grant most-favored-nation trading status to Vietnam until the Vietnamese government demonstrates that it allows its people to leave Vietnam freely. In December, President Bill Clinton announced that he would seek a waiving of the restriction in 1998.

Vietnam's relations with China were relatively smooth in 1997, perhaps aided by the fact that Vietnam no longer was isolated politically and economically. Most issues concerning the land and sea border between the two countries were referred to a permanent panel of Vietnamese and Chinese diplomats. In November, Vietnam hosted a meeting of the heads of 49 French-speaking countries, known as *la Francophonie.*

PETER A. POOLE
Author, "Eight Presidents and Indochina"

WASHINGTON, DC

The District of Columbia, struggling for solvency in 1997, faced a takeover of most of its operations by an independent board formed to get the nation's capital on a sound financial footing.

Federal Intervention. The White House and Congress agreed on a plan in July to strip Mayor Marion Barry and other elected city officials of most of their power. Signed into law on Aug. 5, 1997, by President Bill Clinton, the legislation shifted control of Washington's major city agencies from the mayor and city council to the city's finance-control board. The plan put the Clinton-appointed control board in charge of much of the city government and called for the suspension of local-government power for at least four years to allow the board to restore the city to fiscal health.

Led by Andrew Brimmer, a former member of the Federal Reserve Board, the district board was to oversee functions such as public schools, police, fire, and emergency medical services. The mayor and city council retained control of such areas as recreation and tourism. The legislation—which included a federal promise to assume the city's liability for some $5 billion in pension payments—was a most serious blow to the home rule granted the district 25 years earlier by Congress. The district government had fought to keep control of the city as it struggled to climb out of fiscal chaos.

In Congress the legislation to provide federal money to help run the district ran into its own problems over providing school vouchers to poor children in the city, a step that would allow parents to choose what schools their children would attend. The provision called for providing up to $3,200 per child, based on greatest economic need. Critics said that was not enough money to send the students to most private schools in the area. The plan was pushed by conservatives such as House Majority Leader Dick Armey (R-TX). The conservatives, who support a nationwide voucher system, wanted to use the District of Columbia as an example of how such a system could work nationwide. Eventually, Congress approved legislation that did not include the controversial voucher plan.

Other Problems. District parents faced a three-week delay in the start of school—the third such delay in four years—because of a lawsuit charging that many schools were unsafe. A judge ordered the schools closed until all repairs were made, forcing parents to scramble to find baby-sitting and study sessions for their children.

An independent report by consultants Booz-Allen & Hamilton said that the city's police department was in disarray, plagued by mismanagement, wasteful spending, and lost evidence. The report found appalling conditions in the evidence warehouse.

Brimmer came under criticism, too, after he approved a $625,000 lease of a luxury suite requested by Barry for the district's Sports Commission at a new arena. Brimmer withdrew the approval after outraged congressional leaders threatened to block the deal.

JUDI HASSON
News Editor, "Congressional Quarterly"

WOMEN

Women made major domestic and international gains in 1997, with breakthroughs in medicine, politics, and the military.

Concerns over child care for working mothers intensified with the case of British au pair Louise Woodward, convicted of murdering eight-month-old Matthew Eappen, the boy she cared for in Newton, MA. After the verdict, the trial judge reduced the charge to manslaughter and jail time already served. The case highlighted the need for safe, available, and affordable child care for the growing number of working parents. President Bill Clinton promised that child care would be a priority in 1998, and members of Congress began working on a child-care bill that would help working families. (*See also* FAMILY.)

Military. Women made small gains in the military in 1997, although women in combat remained a divisive issue in the armed forces. The military continued to grapple with the issue of sexual harassment (*see also* THE NEW U.S. MILITARY—*Women in the Military*).

A private study by RAND's National Defense Research Institute found that the trickle of female troops into combat-related jobs had not hurt military readiness. But the report said that women continued to face a discriminatory "double standard" in the male-dominated force. The navy and air force had opened positions on many warships and combat aircraft to women, but the army and marine corps still excluded them from front-line fighting units.

The RAND study said a relatively small number of women had filled some of the tens of thousands of potential combat jobs opened to women in the previous five years. There were about 215,000 women in the military—14% of the total armed forces, according to the Pentagon.

After spending six years and millions of dollars fighting federal efforts to force it to accept women, Virginia Military Institute (VMI) took 30 women into its September 1997 freshman class. The school required all 1,200 cadets and 400 employees to complete a coed orientation and attend seminars on sexual harassment and fraternization.

The Women in Military Service for America Memorial was opened at Arlington Cemetery. One honoree was Frieda Hardin, 101, who joined the U.S. Navy in 1918.

Law and Medicine. Home Depot, the home-improvement discount chain, agreed to pay an $87.5 million settlement and reform its job procedures. A class-action lawsuit charged it had assigned women as clerks behind cash registers instead of putting them on the sales floor and promoting them. The company admitted no wrongdoing but agreed to reform promotion procedures at its 569 stores.

A new medical study found there was no increased risk of blood clots from the newest generation of oral contraceptives. The study, by McGill University in Canada, found no increased risk of heart attack among users of what is known as the third generation of birth-control pills. According to the report, "third-generation oral contraceptives are the first to be associated with no excess risk of [heart

Mary McAleese, a 46-year-old law professor and vice-chancellor at Queens University in Belfast, Northern Ireland, acknowledged her victory as the eighth president of the Irish Republic at Dublin Castle on Oct. 31, 1997.

© Sion Touhig/Sygma

attack]. A significantly lower risk is found when comparing use of third-generation oral contraceptives with use of second-generation oral contraceptives."

However, a study from the Emory University School of Medicine in Atlanta, GA, found that coronary heart disease was the leading cause of death among American women and could reach epidemic proportion as the study group ages.

The American Heart Association said women did not realize they were more likely to die from heart disease and stroke than from any other cause. A survey of women by the organization in 1997 found that 61% considered cancer to be their biggest threat; but in 1995, the association said, heart disease killed more than 500,000 U.S. women, outpacing cancer, diabetes, and accidents.

Politics. New Jersey Gov. Christine Todd Whitman narrowly won reelection after a bruising campaign defending her tax-cutting policies, while Jeanne Shaheen took office as governor of New Hampshire in 1997.

The National Women's Political Caucus said 81 women held statewide elected executive office posts in 1997—25% of the total. Forty-three states had women mayors of cities with populations of more than 30,000; California led the country with 54. In Congress there were a record nine women senators. Two states had two—California and Maine; in the latter state, Republican Susan Collins was elected in November 1996. In the House there were 50 women lawmakers—11.5% of the elected members.

As president, Clinton had named a record number of women to the executive branch.

Two women were appointed to his cabinet for his second term. In 1997, Madeleine Albright took office as secretary of state and Alexis Herman was the first African-American to become labor secretary (*see also* BIOGRAPHY). They joined two other women—Attorney General Janet Reno and Health and Human Services Secretary Donna Shalala—who remained in the cabinet.

International. Women continued to make political gains worldwide. Mary McAleese became the eighth president of Ireland, replacing Mary Robinson. Sweden and Norway were the only nations in which women held nearly as many ministerial posts as men.

The United Nations (UN) continued attempts to deal with the negative treatment of women and girls in Afghanistan, condemning restrictions that ban women from working or appearing in public unless accompanied by a male relative. The U.S.-based aid group CARE International suspended a feeding program for 10,000 widows in Kabul after religious police attacked five of its female employees and beat them with whips.

U.S. first lady Hillary Rodham Clinton, who turned 50 in October, renewed her campaign to help women around the world obtain more education and a better life. She traveled extensively to deliver her message of hope for women, urging leaders to toughen and enforce domestic-abuse laws. "Let us say as loudly and clearly as we possibly can, so that every abuser can hear us, we do not believe that violence against women is simply cultural. We believe it is simply criminal," she said.

JUDI HASSON
News Editor, "Congressional Quarterly"

YUGOSLAVIA, FEDERAL REPUBLIC OF

The Federal Republic of Yugoslavia—comprised of the republics of Serbia and Montenegro and the formerly autonomous regions of Kosovo and Vojvodina—faced political conflict, social unrest, and ethnic tension in 1997. An economic crisis reinforced calls for independence in Kosovo and Montenegro.

Serbia. In early 1997, Serb President Slobodan Milosevic was under enormous pressure from public protests and the Zajedno opposition coalition to introduce democratic reforms. Zajedno gained several local seats despite government obstruction; one of its leaders, Zoran Djindjic, head of the Serbian Democratic Party, became mayor of Belgrade. But by the end of the year, Milosevic managed to outflank the opposition—mainly by control of the mass media. Zajedno split over whether or not to boycott the elections, and Milosevic was able to oust Djindjic and other elected opposition leaders in October.

The ruling Socialists were unable to form a single-party government and entered into a coalition with the ultranationalist Radical Party. The federal assembly elected Milosevic as Yugoslav president after he was barred constitutionally from a third term in Serbia. No outright winner emerged in the September–October Serbian presidential elections, after Socialist candidate Zoran Lilic and Radical Party leader Vojislav Seselj both failed to gain more than 50% of the vote. In a December 21 runoff, Milan Milutinovic, the Yugoslav foreign minister and Milosevic protégé, was elected president. Again, no candidate had received the required percentage of the vote in the initial election on December 7.

The Serb and Yugoslav economy remained in dire straits, while the government failed to introduce essential structural reforms. Industrial production was about half the pre-breakup level. Economists predicted rampant 1998 inflation, caused by printing vast amounts of money to pay wages and pensions in the face of public unrest. Yugoslavia remained subject to U.S.-led sanctions that denied the country credits, investments, and access to international financial institutions.

Kosovo. Calls by the Albanian majority in Kosovo for independence from Serbia were not recognized by the international community, and the Albanians' mood seemed to be reaching a breaking point. The clandestine Kosovo Liberation Army staged several successful assassination attempts on Serb policemen and Albanian collaborators, while students in Pristina (the capital) and other towns staged protests against Belgrade's ban on Albanian schooling. The moderate Albanian leadership of President Ibrahim Rugova met with severe criticism from political opponents and young activists, frustrated by his insistence on passive resistance to Serbian rule.

Montenegro. The Montenegro government grew increasingly dissatisfied with Milosevic's policies and with Serbian rule. In October, Prime Minister Milo Djukanovic was elected president, defeating outgoing president and Milosevic loyalist Momir Bulatovic in a second-round ballot. Djukanovic favored broad autonomy for Montenegro and was frustrated by Belgrade's reluctance to conduct meaningful economic reforms. Earlier in the year, Montenegro launched an alternative economic program with sweeping privatization of state firms.

Montenegro promised to conduct a separate foreign policy if Serbia remained isolated in the international community—the first step toward a formal declaration of independence. The Montenegrin independence movement—associated with the major opposition parties—expanded its influence, enlisting support from Albanian and Muslim minorities.

JANUSZ BUGAJSKI
Center for Strategic and International Studies

YUGOSLAVIA • Information Highlights

Official Name: Federal Republic of Yugoslavia.
Location: Southeastern Europe.
Area: 39,518 sq mi (102 350 km²).
Population (mid-1997 est.): 10,600,000.
Chief Cities (1991 census): Belgrade, the capital, 1,168,454; Novi Sad, 179,626; Nis, 175,391.
Government: *Head of state,* Slobodan Milosevic, federal president (sworn in July 23, 1997). *Head of government,* Radoje Kontic, federal prime minister (took office Dec. 29, 1992). *Legislature*—Federal Assembly: Chamber of Republics and Chamber of Citizens.
Monetary Unit: New dinar (6.560 new dinars equal U.S.$1, July 1997).
Gross Domestic Product (1995 est. U.S.$): $20,600,000,-000.

ZAIRE. *See* CONGO, DEMOCRATIC REPUBLIC OF THE.

ZIMBABWE

In 1997 the government of Zimbabwe was the target of allegations of corruption and mismanagement. Widespread labor strikes in many industries were motivated by falling wages and a decline in real earnings.

On December 9 the country was crippled by a one-day general strike, the first nation-wide strike since independence in 1980. The strike, organized by the Zimbabwe Congress of Trade Unions, was called to protest higher taxes, which would have been used to finance compensation payments to war veterans.

Domestic Affairs. In June members of the ruling ZANU–Patriotic Front (PF) party refused to ratify a $110 million loan for the construction of a new airport in Harare. The bid had been awarded to Air Harbor Technologies of Cyprus, whose Zimbabwean representative was Leo Mugabe, President Robert Mugabe's nephew. A government board earlier had awarded the contract to a French company. Leo Mugabe also was involved in an earlier scandal in which a cellular-telephone franchise was awarded to Telecel, a foreign company in which the younger Mugabe owned interest. Parliament's refusal to ratify the airport loan was a surprise, since party members usually have been docile and supportive of the regime.

Mugabe was forced to end his speech abruptly at the August Heroes Day ceremony, honoring those who died during the liberation war, when hundreds of veterans disrupted the event. Protesters were seeking government compensation and action from an 11-member commission, appointed after July protests, to investigate the alleged misappropriation of money from the War Victims Compensation Fund. Cabinet ministers and Mugabe's brother-in-law were alleged to have received payments of nearly $65,000 each from the fund. A plan to compensate former combatants with money raised through higher taxation was withdrawn in the face of nationwide protests.

The supreme court of Zimbabwe ruled in February that the law giving the government wide powers to dismiss executives and take control of charitable and private organizations violated constitutional guarantees of freedom of association and expression. This effectively removed from the statute book the Private Voluntary Associations Act, which was alleged to have been used to silence organizations posing a threat to the ZANU-PF party.

A new report by Zimbabwe's Legal Resources Foundation and the Catholic Commission for Justice and Peace claimed that the army's Fifth Brigade massacred as many as 20,000 people in Southern Matabeleland in 1983 and 1984. The report said the killings had been intended to destroy support for the opposition Zimbabwe African People's Union (ZAPU) and recommended the creation of a fund to compensate victims and their families.

ZIMBABWE • Information Highlights

Official Name: Republic of Zimbabwe.
Location: Southern Africa.
Area: 150,803 sq mi (390 580 km²).
Population (mid-1997 est.): 11,400,000.
Chief Cities (1983 est.): Harare (formerly Salisbury), the capital, 681,000; Bulawayo, 429,000; Chitungwiza, 202,000.
Government: *Head of state and government,* Robert Mugabe, executive president (sworn in Dec. 31, 1987). *Legislature* (unicameral)—Parliament.
Monetary Unit: Zimbabwe dollar (13.0805 Z dollars equal U.S.$1, Nov. 17, 1997).
Gross Domestic Product (1995 est. U.S.$): $18,100,-000,000.
Economic Indexes: *Consumer Prices* (1996, 1990 = 100): all items, 406.9; food, 544.8. *Industrial Production* (1995, 1990 = 100): 89.
Foreign Trade (1995 U.S.$): *Imports,* $2,661,000,000; *exports,* $2,115,000,000.

The trial of Zimbabwe's former president, Canaan Banana, began in September in Harare. Banana was accused of numerous incidents of sexual abuse of security officers and students while he was in office. Perhaps more important than the trial itself was the accusation that high government officials were aware of the incidents but ignored complaints and engaged in a cover-up.

International Affairs. For the second consecutive year, the International Monetary Fund (IMF) continued to suspend balance-of-payment support to Zimbabwe because of the government's unwillingness to meet the bank's conditions—including bringing down inflation and lowering the budget deficit. Mugabe visited Paris and London in an effort to attract foreign investment, but investors remained wary of Zimbabwe's high inflation, declining currency, and widespread corruption, as well as of Mugabe's threats to white farmers and foreign-owned companies.

In 1997, Mugabe served as chairman of the Organization of African Unity (OAU), which held its 33d summit in Harare in May and June. From the OAU's 53 member states, 31 heads of state attended and pledged to promote democratization on the continent and to get tougher on human-rights violations.

The Convention on International Trade in Endangered Species (CITES), a regulatory body of the United Nations (UN), voted in June to allow Zimbabwe, Namibia, and Botswana to sell an annual ivory quota from excess elephant herds, subject to monitoring. Zimbabwe and others had argued for years that selectively rescinding the ban on the commercial ivory trade would allow countries to cull expanding elephant populations and use sales revenue to manage existing herds.

PATRICK O'MEARA and N. BRIAN WINCHESTER
Indiana University

ZOOS AND ZOOLOGY

Spring and summer 1997 were marked by a flurry of exhibit openings at U.S. zoos. Meanwhile, entomological researchers concluded that U.S. home owners who put up electric traps—commonly known as bug zappers—to rid their backyards of pesky mosquitoes might want to rethink their approach.

Exhibits. New wildlife displays in California and Florida both have an African safari as their theme. The Heart of Africa is a 30-acre (12-ha) forest and savanna complex at the San Diego (CA) Wild Animal Park. A dense tropical forest provides homes for okapis and duikers (small antelope). From the highlands, a stream flows to a large water hole, with island resting and nesting sites for flamingos and shoebill storks, as well as colobus and swamp monkeys. On the center island, visitors can stop at a research station and talk with scientists studying the birds and mammals. The open savannas are filled with rhino, wildebeests, cheetahs, crown cranes, and giraffes. Meanwhile, Busch Gardens in Tampa, FL, unveiled the Edge of Africa. This new 15-acre (6-ha) exhibit features a local fishing village and the riverine habitats of hippopotamuses and Nile crocodiles. Rock outcroppings and termite mounds provide sentry posts for vultures and meerkats.

The Tropical American Rain Forest opened in late June at Tulsa (OK) Zoo. The exhibit reflects the three zones of a tropical American rain forest: the flooded forest; the seasonal forest at altitudes below 3,000 ft (915 m); and the montane, or cloud forest, above 3,000 ft. Featured creatures include the jaguar, emerald tree boa, giant Amazon side-neck turtle, two-toed sloth, and scarlet ibis.

Several other notable exhibits debuted in 1997. The Minnesota Zoo brought the ocean to the Midwest with its new Discovery Bay: United Healthcare Marine Education Center. Visitors can see bottle-nosed dolphins, sharks, rays, and tropical fish from above and below water. And a mix of species inhabits the Regenstein Small Mammal/Reptile House at Chicago's Lincoln Park Zoo. Koalas, cottontop tamarins, and crocodiles share their habitats with other small mammals, birds, and reptiles from the same bioregions. Mountain and straw-colored fruit bats hang inside a huge baobab tree that measures 25 ft (7.6 m) in diameter. Oklahoma City (OK) Zoo shone its spotlight on felids in its new Cat Forest/Lion Overlook. In addition to lions, visitors can see nine other cat species.

Cleveland (OH) Metroparks Zoo focused on northern temperate wildlife in its new Wolf Wilderness: Wildlife of the Great Lakes exhibit. The Wolf Lodge shows visitors what a 19th-century trapper's home might have looked like. Visitors can use state-of-the-art computer technology to track the movements of radio-tagged wolves in the woods of Minnesota. The exhibit also is home to timber rattlesnakes, deer mice, bald eagles, and beavers.

Birds spread their wings over two new exhibits at the Bronx (NY) Zoo: BIG Birds highlights the world's ratites: ostriches, rheas, cassowaries, and emus. These biggest of birds are flightless but can move at high speed with their long legs. Visitors can try to outrun an

The new Edge of Africa exhibit at Busch Gardens in Tampa, FL, features many exotic animals—including the spotted hyena at right, who is visiting with former keeper Dr. Lawrence Frank of the University of California at Berkeley. Busch Gardens sponsors hyena research both at the university and in Kenya.

emu at the Emu Olympics and can look through a periscope to spot predators, much as an ostrich uses its long neck to see lions above the tall savanna grasses. Meanwhile, Magellanic penguins, Guanay cormorants, and Inca terns share a rugged Patagonian coastline habitat at the new Russell B. Aitken Seabird Colony, which replaces an 1899 aviary.

In September the completely revamped Central Park Children's Zoo in New York City was unveiled. The venerable 0.5-acre (0.2-ha) zoo—formally named the Tisch Children's Zoo—had undergone a $6 million redesign. The zoo's emphasis is on allowing children of prereading age to experience animals close up, and to learn about them through exploring mockups of their natural habitats. Children can crawl through hollow logs, climb on a "spiderweb," and leap onto giant lily pads.

Zoology. One particularly nasty component of pit-viper venom is an anticoagulant that prevents the victim's blood from clotting. Upon studying venoms from various pit-viper species, scientists at Merck Research Laboratories found a new family of proteins with anticoagulant properties; the researchers called these proteins disintegrins. To design a synthetic compound for use as an anticoagulant in humans, the scientists focused on the saw-scaled viper of Africa, which has a highly toxic venom. The result of their work is Aggrastat, which binds to receptor sites on blood cells, preventing them from linking together and forming clots. Aggrastat has been through clinical trials and soon may be approved for distribution.

Marine biologists reported that the northern elephant seal holds the titles for the longest and deepest dives of any pinniped. Alpha males travel about 12,000 mi (19 000 km) a year between rookeries on California's Channel Islands and feeding grounds in the eastern Aleutian Islands off Alaska. According to Brent S. Steward of the Hubbs–Sea World Research Institute in San Diego and Robert L. DeLong at the National Oceanic and Atmospheric Administration's (NOAA's) National Marine Mammal Laboratory in Seattle, WA, the seals make the trip twice a year, spending between 250 and 300 days a year at sea.

A Pacific green turtle dubbed "Wrong Way Corrigan" so far has made its incredible journey only once. The reptile turned up at the entrance to Prince William Sound, AK—thousands of miles from its normal range in the waters off South America. It is believed

© Lenny Ignelzi/AP/Wide World Photos

An African pelican investigates as workers complete the finishing touches at San Diego Wild Animal Park's Heart of Africa exhibit. The $7 million habitat opened in May 1997.

the turtle rode a thermal gyre of warm water to the north. Experts at Hubbs–Sea World Research Institute, where the turtle recuperated, released the animal into the ocean off San Diego in July, outfitting it with a satellite transmitter so its movements could be tracked.

According to University of Delaware entomologist Douglass Tallamy, bug zappers do indeed zap bugs; however, the glowing devices do not kill many mosquitoes. Tallamy and a student assistant installed six traps at homes in suburban Newark, DE, and returned periodically to collect and count the dead bugs. Their survey revealed that, of 13,789 insects killed, only 18 were female mosquitoes. (Female mosquitoes require a blood meal before they can lay eggs; male mosquitoes do not bite.) Another 13 were biting flies. Almost half the insects tallied were of the non-biting aquatic variety. Apparently the reason so few mosquitoes were zapped is that mosquitoes native to the United States are not attracted to the ultraviolet light that bug zappers use as bait.

DEBORAH A. BEHLER
"Wildlife Conservation" magazine

Statistical and Tabular Data

Nations of the World [1]
A Profile and Synopsis of Major 1997 Developments

Andorra, S.W. Europe

Population: 72,000   **Capital:** Andorra la Vella
Area: 174 sq mi (450 km²)
Government: Marc Forne Molne

In the February 16 general election, the ruling center-right Liberal Union (LU), led by Marc Forne Molne, president of the Executive Council (cabinet), won 18 seats in the 28-seat General Council of the Valleys, Andorra's legislature. This was the first time since 1993 that the LU won an outright majority, enabling it to govern without forming a coalition with smaller parties.

Angola, W. Africa

Population: 11,600,000 **Capital:** Luanda
Area: 481,354 sq mi (1 246 700 km²)
Government: José Eduardo dos Santos, president; Fernando José da Franca Dias van Dunem, prime minister

President José Eduardo dos Santos' ruling Popular Movement for the Liberation of Angola (MPLA) and Jonas Savimbi's rebel National Union for the Total Alliance of Angola (UNITA) inaugurated a government of national unity. (See also AFRICA.)

Antigua and Barbuda, Caribbean

Population: 100,000   **Capital:** St. John's
Area: 170 sq mi (440 km²)
Government: James B. Carlisle, governor-general; Lester Bird, prime minister

Bahamas, Caribbean

Population: 300,000   **Capital:** Nassau
Area: 5,382 sq mi (13 940 km²)
Government: Clifford Darling, governor-general; Hubert A. Ingraham, prime minister

In the March 14 elections, the ruling Free National Movement (FNM) won 34 seats in the 40-seat legislature, thus giving FNM leader Hubert Ingraham a second term as prime minister. The remaining six seats were won by the opposition Progressive Liberal Party (PLP).

Bahrain, W. Asia

Population: 600,000   **Capital:** Manama
Area: 239 sq mi (620 km²)
Government: Isa bin Salman Al Khalifa, emir; Khalifa bin Salman Al Khalifa, prime minister

Seventy Shiite Muslims, all members of the Iranian-backed Bahrain Party of God, were found guilty on March 26 of conspiring with a foreign nation to overthrow the Sunni-led government. In April the United States put its military forces in Bahrain on a high state of alert after intelligence information revealed that members of the Bahrain Party of God had made plans to attack U.S. military personnel.

Barbados, Caribbean

Population: 300,000   **Capital:** Bridgetown
Area: 166 sq mi (430 km²)
Government: Sir Clifford Husbands, governor-general; Owen Arthur, prime minister

Benin, W. Africa

Population: 5,900,000   **Capital:** Porto Novo
Area: 43,483 sq mi (112 620 km²)
Government: Mathieu Kérékou, president; Adrien Houngbedji, prime minister

Bhutan, S. Asia

Population: 800,000   **Capital:** Thimphu
Area: 18,147 sq mi (47 000 km²)
Government: Jigme Singye Wangchuck, king

Botswana, S. Africa

Population: 1,500,000   **Capital:** Gaborone
Area: 231,803 sq mi (600 370 km²)
Government: Ketumile Masire, president

In August the Botswana legislature passed a number of bills amending the constitution. The minimum voting age was reduced to 18 from 21; Botswanans living abroad were given the right to vote by absentee ballot; the total number of years a president could serve was limited to ten; and the vice-president was given automatic assumption of the presidency if the president resigned or died.

Brunei Darussalam, S.E. Asia

Population: 300,000   **Capital:** Bandar Seri Begawan
Area: 2,228 sq mi (5 770 km²)
Government: Hassanal Bolkiah, sultan and prime minister

Burkina Faso, W. Africa

Population: 10,900,000 **Capital:** Ouagadougou
Area: 105,869 sq mi (274 200 km²)
Government: Blaise Compaoré, president; Kadre Désiré Ouedraogo, prime minister

In January the legislature approved an increase of parliamentary seats from 107 to 111. In elections on May 11, President Blaise Compaoré's ruling Congress for Democracy and Progress (CDP) won 97 seats. It had held 88 seats in the previous parliament.

Burundi, E. Africa

Population: 6,100,000   **Capital:** Bujumbura
Area: 10,745 sq mi (27 830 km²)
Government: Pierre Buyoya, president; Pascal Firmin, prime minister

For Burundi, 1997 was a year of extreme turmoil and conflict. The Tutsi-dominated army, which seized power on July 25, 1996, was accused throughout 1997 of massacring thousands of Hutu. In March a plot to assassinate President Pierre Buyoya was uncovered, and Hutu rebels attacked villages in the nation's southern provinces. Fighting between rival Hutu groups erupted in August. And in October, Burundi's armed forces clashed with those of Tanzania after Tanzania expelled thousands of Burundian refugees. By year's end, there were an estimated 500,000 Burundian refugees. The Organization of African Unity (OAU) eased trade sanctions imposed on Burundi after the 1996 Tutsi coup.

Cameroon, Cen. Africa

Population: 13,900,000 **Capital:** Yaoundé
Area: 183,568 sq mi (475 440 km²)
Government: Paul Biya, president; Peter Mafany Musonge, prime minister

During 1997, Cameroonians went to the polls in May for legislative elections and in October for a presidential election. The results of both were condemned as fraudulent by parties in opposition to President Paul Biya's ruling Cameroon People's Democratic Movement (CPDM). The May 17 elections for the 180-seat legislature gave the CPDM 109 seats. And the October 12 presidential election returned Paul Biya to the presidency for a second seven-year term. The election was boycotted by the three main opposition parties. In December, Peter Mafany Musonge was appointed prime minister.

Cape Verde, W. Africa

Population: 400,000   **Capital:** Praia
Area: 1,556 sq mi (4 030 km²)
Government: Antonio Mascarenhas Monteiro, president; Carlos Wahnon Veiga, prime minister

Central African Republic, Cen. Africa

Population: 3,300,000   **Capital:** Bangui
Area: 240,533 sq mi (622 980 km²)
Government: Ange Patasse, president; Michel Gbezzera-Bria, prime minister

[1]Independent nations not covered in pages 94–581.

On January 25, President Ange Patasse and a group of some 200 soldiers who had mutinied in 1996 signed an agreement in Bangui, the capital, to end the conflict. The mutineers were given amnesty, and a government of national unity was created. Foreign Affairs Minister Michel Gbezzera-Bria was named prime minister. A 500-member African peacekeeping force, sent to the Central African Republic to monitor the agreement, clashed with the mutineers in March and again in June, but a cease-fire was signed in early July.

Chad, Cen. Africa

Population: 7,000,000   **Capital:** Ndjamena
Area: 495,753 sq mi (1 284 000 km²)
Government: Idriss Déby, president; Nassour Ouaidou Guelengdouksia, prime minister

In legislative elections held on January 5 and February 23, President Idriss Déby's ruling Patriotic Salvation Movement (MPS) won 55 seats in the 125-seat National Assembly. The main opposition party, the Union for Renewal and Democracy (URD), won 31 seats. President Déby substantially changed his cabinet on May 16; the many changes included the replacement of Prime Minister Djimasta Koibla with Nassour Ouaidou Guelengdouksia. In October the nation's three most important rebel groups met with government representatives in an effort to bring peace to the country.

Comoros, E. Africa

Population: 600,000   **Capital:** Moroni
Area: 838 sq mi (2 170 km²)
Government: Mohamed Taki Abdoulkarim, president; Tadjidine Ben Said Massoundi, prime minister

In early March a secessionist rebellion broke out on Anjouan, the largest of the Comoro Islands. Anjouan and the island of Mohéli declared their independence in July and announced their desire to be reunited with France. When troops loyal to the government attacked the Anjouan secessionists on September 3, they were beaten badly and forced to flee to Grand Comore, where the nation's capital, Moroni, is located. On October 25 the vast majority of the people of Anjouan voted to secede from Comoros. In Moroni crowds called for the resignation of President Mohamed Taki Abdoulkarim. Since gaining independence from France in 1975, Comorians had witnessed political unrest and economic decay.

Congo, Republic of, Cen. Africa

Population: 2,600,000   **Capital:** Brazzaville
Area: 132,046 sq mi (342 000 km²)
Government: Denis Sassou-Nguesso, president

See AFRICA.

Djibouti, E. Africa

Population: 600,000   **Capital:** Djibouti
Area: 8,494 sq mi (22 000 km²)
Government: Hassan Gouled Aptidon, president; Barkat Gourad Hamadou, prime minister

In March the Front for the Restoration of Unity and Democracy (FRUD), the former Afar rebel group, was recognized as a legal political party. In April, Eritrean troops entered Djibouti and clashed with Djiboutian troops.

Dominica, Caribbean

Population: 100,000   **Capital:** Roseau
Area: 290 sq mi (750 km²)
Government: Crispin Anselm Sorhaindo, president; Edison James, prime minister

Dominican Republic, Caribbean

Population: 8,200,000   **Capital:** Santo Domingo
Area: 18,815 sq mi (48 730 km²)
Government: Leonel Fernandez Reyna, president

In July about ten people in the northeastern part of the country were injured when security forces cracked down on strikers who were demanding improvements in the area's agricultural infrastructure and water and electricity supply. (See also CARIBBEAN.)

Equatorial Guinea, Cen. Africa

Population: 400,000   **Capital:** Malabo
Area: 10,830 sq mi (28 050 km²)
Government: Teodoro Obiang Nguema Mbasogo, president; Angel Serafin Seriche Dougan, prime minister

President Teodoro Obiang Nguema Mbasogo banned the Progress Party (PP), the main opposition party, after a ship carrying arms to Equatorial Guinea was intercepted by government forces. In July the PP dismissed its leader, Severo Moto, for attempting a coup.

Eritrea, E. Africa

Population: 3,600,000   **Capital:** Asmara
Area: 46,841 sq mi (121 320 km²)
Government: Issaias Afeworke, president

On May 23, Eritrea's Constitutional Assembly adopted the nation's first constitution. There was sporadic fighting during the year between the Eritrean army and pro-Sudanese forces along the borders of the two countries. The Texas-based Anadarko Petroleum Corp. announced that it had signed a production-sharing agreement with Eritrea in September. At midyear the government introduced a new currency, the nafka, to replace the Ethiopian birr.

Fiji, Oceania

Population: 800,000   **Capital:** Suva
Area: 7,054 sq mi (18 270 km²)
Government: Kamisese Mara, president; Sitiveni Rabuka, prime minister

In July, Fiji enacted the Constitution Amendment Bill to give the nation's large Indian population increased political power. The act increased Indian representation in the legislature and, for the first time, allowed a non-Melanesian Fijian to become prime minister.

Gabon, Cen. Africa

Population: 1,200,000   **Capital:** Libreville
Area: 103,348 sq mi (267 670 km²)
Government: El Hadj Omar Bongo, president; Paulin Obame, prime minister

In elections held in December 1996 and January 1997, the ruling Gabonese Democratic Party (PDG) won 82 of the 120 seats in the National Assembly.

Gambia, W. Africa

Population: 1,200,000   **Capital:** Banjul
Area: 4,363 sq mi (11 300 km²)
Government: Yahya Jammeh, head of state

In January 2 legislative elections, President Yahya Jammeh's ruling Patriotic Alliance for Reorientation and Construction (PARC) won 33 of the 45 seats in the nation's parliament. The election marked the return of civilian rule to Gambia.

Ghana, W. Africa

Population: 18,100,000 **Capital:** Accra
Area: 92,101 sq mi (238 540 km²)
Government: Jerry Rawlings, president

President Jerry Rawlings was sworn in for his second term on January 7. A value-added tax (VAT) was reintroduced in February.

Grenada, Caribbean

Population: 100,000   **Capital:** St. George's
Area: 131 sq mi (340 km²)
Government: Daniel Williams, governor-general; Keith Mitchell, prime minister

Daniel Williams took office as governor-general. (See also CARIBBEAN.)

Guinea, W. Africa

Population: 7,500,000   **Capital:** Conakry
Area: 94,927 sq mi (245 860 km²)
Government: Lansana Conté, president; Sidya Touré, prime minister

Three Belgians were arrested in April and accused of planning a coup against President Lansana Conté.

Guinea-Bissau, W. Africa

Population: 1,100,000   **Capital:** Bissau
Area: 13,946 sq mi (36 120 km²)
Government: João Bernardo Vieira, president; Carlos Correia, prime minister

President João Bernardo Vieira named Carlos Correia prime minister on June 5 following the dismissal of Manuel da Costa Saturnino.

583

Guyana, N.E. South America

Population: 800,000 **Capital:** Georgetown
Area: 83,000 sq mi (214 970 km²)
Government: Janet Jagan, president; Samuel Hinds, prime minister

Following the death of President Cheddi Jagan on March 6, Prime Minister Samuel Hinds was appointed interim president, and Janet Jagan, Cheddi Jagan's U.S.-born wife, was named the country's first woman prime minister. In presidential elections held on December 15, Mrs. Jagan defeated Desmond Hoyte. Hinds returned to the post of prime minister. Hoyte contested the election results, and hundreds of people protested in the streets of Georgetown.

Haiti, Caribbean

Population: 6,600,000 **Capital:** Port-au-Prince
Area: 10,714 sq mi (27 750 km²)
Government: René Préval, president

See CARIBBEAN.

Ivory Coast, W. Africa

Population: 15,000,000 **Capital:** Yamoussoukro
Area: 124,502 sq mi (322 460 km²)
Government: Henri Konan Bédié, president; Daniel Kablan Duncan, prime minister

Jamaica, Caribbean

Population: 2,600,000 **Capital:** Kingston
Area: 4,243 sq mi (10 990 km²)
Government: Howard Cooke, governor-general; P.J. Patterson, prime minister

In December 8 legislative elections, Prime Minister P.J. Patterson's ruling People's National Party won 49 seats in the 60-seat parliament. (See also CARIBBEAN.)

Kiribati, Oceania

Population: 81,000 **Capital:** Tarawa
Area: 277 sq mi (717 km²)
Government: Teburoro Tito, president

Kuwait, W. Asia

Population: 1,800,000 **Capital:** Kuwait
Area: 6,880 sq mi (17 820 km²)
Government: Jabir al-Ahmad al-Sabah, emir; Saad al-Abdallah al-Sabah, prime minister

A June 6 assassination attempt on liberal National Assembly member Abdullah al-Naybari was followed by the arrest of three Kuwaitis and two Iranians. They were charged with attempted murder.

Lesotho, S. Africa

Population: 2,000,000 **Capital:** Maseru
Area: 11,718 sq mi (30 350 km²)
Government: Letsie III, king; Ntsu Mokhehle, prime minister

Liberia, W. Africa

Population: 2,300,000 **Capital:** Monrovia
Area: 43,000 sq mi (111 370 km²)
Government: Charles Taylor, president

Following seven years of civil war, former warlord Charles Taylor was elected president of Liberia. (See also AFRICA.)

Liechtenstein, Cen. Europe

Population: 30,000 **Capital:** Vaduz
Area: 62 sq mi (160 km²)
Government: Hans Adam II, prince; Mario Frick, prime minister

In January 31 and February 2 elections, Prime Minister Mario Frick's Patriotic Union (VU) won 13 seats in the 25-seat legislature, and his coalition partner, the Progressive Citizens' Party (FPB), won ten seats. In March, however, the coalition government collapsed when the FPB pulled out. A new government, composed only of VU members, was formed on April 9.

Luxembourg, W. Europe

Population: 400,000 **Capital:** Luxembourg
Area: 998 sq mi (2 586 km²)
Government: Jean, grand duke; Jean-Claude Juncker, premier

On January 14, Cie. Luxembourgeoise de Télédiffusion and Bertelsmann AG of Germany merged their broadcasting operations. The new company, called CLT-UFA, became the world's third-largest media group, after Time Warner and the Walt Disney Company.

Madagascar, E. Africa

Population: 14,100,000 **Capital:** Antananarivo
Area: 226,656 sq mi (587 040 km²)
Government: Didier Ratsiraka, president; Pascal Rakotomavo, premier

On February 9, following his victory in the December 1996 election, former military dictator Didier Ratsiraka took office as president.

Malawi, E. Africa

Population: 9,600,000 **Capital:** Lilongwe
Area: 45,745 sq mi (118 480 km²)
Government: Bakili Muluzi, president

See AFRICA.

Maldives, S. Asia

Population: 300,000 **Capital:** Malé
Area: 116 sq mi (300 km²)
Government: Maumoon Abdul Gayoom, president

Mali, W. Africa

Population: 9,900,000 **Capital:** Bamako
Area: 478,764 sq mi (1 240 000 km²)
Government: Alpha Oumar Konare, president; Ibrahim Boubacar Keita, prime minister

In the May 11 presidential election, which was boycotted by almost all other candidates, President Alpha Oumar Konare was reelected. July 20 and August 3 legislative elections gave Konare's ruling Alliance for Democracy in Mali (ADEMA) 129 seats in the 147-seat National Assembly.

Malta, S. Europe

Population: 400,000 **Capital:** Valletta
Area: 124 sq mi (320 km²)
Government: Ugo Mifsud Bonnici, president; Alfred Sant, prime minister

On July 1 the government replaced the nation's value-added tax (VAT) with various customs and excise duties.

Marshall Islands, Pacific Ocean

Population: 100,000 **Capital:** Majuro
Area: 70 sq mi (181 km²)
Government: Imata Kabua, president

The legislature on January 14 elected Imata Kabua as president. He succeeded Amata Kabua, who had died in December 1996.

Mauritania, W. Africa

Population: 2,400,000 **Capital:** Nouakchott
Area: 397,954 sq mi (1 030 700 km²)
Government: Maaouya Ould Sid Ahmed Taya, president; Alavai Ould Mohamed Khouna, prime minister

Mauritius, E. Africa

Population: 1,100,000 **Capital:** Port Louis
Area: 718 sq mi (1 860 km²)
Government: Cassan Uteem, president; Navin Ramgoolam, prime minister

On June 21, Prime Minister Navin Ramgoolam dismissed Deputy Prime Minister Paul Raymond Berenger, a move that brought about the end of the coalition between the prime minister's Labour Party and the deputy prime minister's Mauritius Militant Movement. On July 2, Ramgoolam appointed a new cabinet, which consisted only of members of his Labour Party.

Micronesia, Federated States of, Pacific Ocean

Population: 100,000 **Capital:** Kolonia
Area: 271 sq mi (702 km²)
Government: Jacob Nena, president

President Bailey Olter resigned due to illness and was succeeded by Vice-President Jacob Nena.

Monaco, S. Europe

Population: 31,000 **Capital:** Monaco-Ville
Area: 0.7 sq mi (1.9 km²)
Government: Rainier III, prince; Michel Leveque, minister of state

Monaco marked the 700th anniversary of Grimaldi rule with celebrations that began in January and continued throughout the year.

Mongolia, N. Asia

Population: 2,400,000 **Capital:** Ulan Bator
Area: 604,247 sq mi (1 565 000 km²)
Government: Natsagiin Bagabandi, president; Mendsaikhan Enkhsaikhan, prime minister

Natsagiin Bagabandi, leader of the Mongolian People's Revolutionary Party (MPRP), won more than 60% of the vote to defeat incumbent Punsalmaagiyn Ochirbat in May 18 presidential elections. Formerly Mongolia's Communist Party, the MPRP had been ousted from power in 1996 by Ochirbat's Democratic Union Coalition.

Mozambique, E. Africa

Population: 18,400,000 **Capital:** Maputo
Area: 308,641 sq mi (799 380 km²)
Government: Joaquim Chissano, president; Pascoal Mocumbi, prime minister

In October, President Joaquim Chissano criticized the International Monetary Fund and the World Bank for delaying Mozambican debt relief until 1999.

Namibia, S.W. Africa

Population: 1,700,000 **Capital:** Windhoek
Area: 318,259 sq mi (824 290 km²)
Government: Sam Nujoma, president; Hage Geingob, prime minister

Nauru, Oceania

Population: 10,000 **Capital:** Nauru
Area: 8 sq mi (21 km²)
Government: Kinza Clodumar, president

After no-confidence votes toppled three presidents in three months, elections were held on February 8 for the 18-member parliament. The parliament in turn elected Kinza Clodumar as president.

Nepal, S. Asia

Population: 22,600,000 **Capital:** Katmandu
Area: 54,363 sq mi (140 800 km²)
Government: Birendra Bir Bikram Shah Deva, king; Surya Bahadur Thapa, prime minister

Prime Minister Sher Bahadur Deuba resigned on March 6 following a vote of no confidence in the legislature. Her successor, Lokendra Bahadur Chand, suffered a similar fate on October 4. On October 13, Surya Bahadur Thapa became prime minister.

Niger, W. Africa

Population: 9,800,000 **Capital:** Niamey
Area: 489,189 sq mi (1 267 000 km²)
Government: Ibrahim Maïnassara Baré, president; Ibrahim Assane Mayaki, prime minister

President Ibrahim Maïnassara Baré dissolved his government on April 1. A new government was formed on June 14, with Amadou Boubacar Cisse being reappointed prime minister. In turn, Ibrahim Assane Mayaki of the Niger Workers Union took over as prime minister in December after the latter government fell.

Oman, W. Asia

Population: 2,300,000 **Capital:** Muscat
Area: 82,031 sq mi (212 460 km²)
Government: Qaboos bin Said Al Said, sultan

On October 16, 164 candidates were elected as potential members of Oman's Consultative Council. In December, Sultan Qaboos bin Said Al Said chose 82 of the 164 to actually serve on the Consultative Council, which is strictly advisory and has no actual power.

Palau, N. Pacific Ocean

Population: 20,000 **Capital:** Koror
Area: 177 sq mi (458 km²)
Government: Kuniwo Nakamura, president

Papua New Guinea, Oceania

Population: 4,400,000 **Capital:** Port Moresby
Area: 178,259 sq mi (461 690 km²)
Government: Wiwa Korowi, governor-general; Bill Skate, prime minister

In an attempt to put down the nine-year-old separatist rebellion on the island of Bougainville, the government hired British and South African mercenaries early in the year. Street riots in Port Moresby and an army mutiny forced Prime Minister Julius Chan to suspend the government contract with the mercenaries and then to resign on March 26. A caretaker government was established. Chan resumed his position as prime minister at the beginning of June, but following the legislative elections later in the month, the new parliament elected Port Moresby Mayor Bill Skate as prime minister. Meanwhile, in New Zealand peace talks were carried on between the government and the Bougainville separatists.

Qatar, W. Asia

Population: 600,000 **Capital:** Doha
Area: 4,247 sq mi (11 000 km²)
Government: Hamad bin Khalifa Al Thani, emir; Abdallah bin Khalifa Al Thani, prime minister

In late 1996, Qatar made arrangements with its former ruler, Khalifa bin Hamad Al Thani, to get back billions of dollars that he had in European bank accounts. As as result, in January 1997, Hamad bin Khalifa Al Thani, the current emir and son of the former ruler, agreed to let his father return to the country.

Rwanda, E. Africa

Population: 7,700,000 **Capital:** Kigali
Area: 10,169 sq mi (26 337 km²)
Government: Pasteur Bizimungu, president; Pierre Celestin Rwigema, prime minister

In 1997, Rwanda continued to be the scene of bloodshed and bitter fighting between the ruling Tutsi and Hutu militants. It was estimated that, in January alone, more than 200 people were killed by Hutu militants and Tutsi reprisals. Many more lives were lost in December. A number of Hutu, convicted of genocide for their part in the slaughter of some 500,000 Tutsi and moderate Hutu in 1994, were sentenced to death. In July, Defense Minister Paul Kagame admitted that Rwanda had played a key role in the rebellion that in May overthrew dictator Mobutu Sese Seko in neighboring Zaire (Democratic Republic of the Congo). (See also AFRICA.)

Saint Kitts and Nevis, Caribbean

Population: 40,000 **Capital:** Basseterre
Area: 139 sq mi (360 km²)
Government: Clement Athelston Arrindell, governor-general; Denzil Douglas, prime minister

See CARIBBEAN.

Saint Lucia, Caribbean

Population: 100,000 **Capital:** Castries
Area: 239 sq mi (620 km²)
Government: Perlette Louisy, governor-general; Kenny Anthony, prime minister

In May 23 legislative elections, the center-left St. Lucia Labor Party (SLP) won 16 seats in the 17-seat parliament, defeating Prime Minister Vaughan Lewis and his ruling centrist United Workers' Party (UWP). SLP leader Kenny Anthony was sworn in as prime minister on May 26.

Saint Vincent and the Grenadines, Caribbean

Population: 100,000 **Capital:** Kingstown
Area: 131 sq mi (340 km²)
Government: David Jack, governor-general; James F. Mitchell, prime minister

After Jerome Joseph, a taxi driver, was found shot to death on the Grenadine island of Bequia in early October 1996, James and Penella Fletcher, two wealthy Americans, were charged with his murder. Prime Minister James Mitchell called the two "typically ugly Americans." U.S. President Bill Clinton called on Mitchell to ensure that the Fletchers were given a fair trial. At the trial, in Kingstown, judge Dunbar Cenac ruled that there was no evidence to support the murder charges, and they were acquitted on Aug. 8, 1997.

Samoa, Oceania

Population: 200,000 **Capital:** Apia
Area: 1,104 sq mi (2 860 km²)
Government: Tanumafili II Malietoa, head of state; Tofilau Eti Alesana, prime minister

On July 2, Western Samoa's legislature passed a constitutional amendment to change the country's name to Samoa.

San Marino, S. Europe

Population: 30,000 **Capital:** San Marino
Area: 23 sq mi (60 km²)
Government: Gabriele Gatti, head of state

São Tomé and Príncipe, W. Africa

Population: 100,000 **Capital:** São Tomé
Area: 371 sq mi (960 km²)
Government: Miguel Trovoada, president; Vaz d'Almeida, prime minister

Following the establishment of formal diplomatic ties between Taiwan and São Tomé and Príncipe in May, the government of the People's Republic of China suspended diplomatic relations with São Tomé and Príncipe on July 11.

Senegal, W. Africa

Population: 8,800,000 **Capital:** Dakar
Area: 75,749 sq mi (196 190 km²)
Government: Abdou Diouf, president; Habib Thiam, prime minister

Seychelles, E. Africa

Population: 100,000 **Capital:** Victoria
Area: 176 sq mi (455 km²)
Government: France Albert René, president

Sierra Leone, W. Africa

Population: 4,400,000 **Capital:** Freetown
Area: 27,699 sq mi (71 740 km²)
Government: Johnny Paul Kabbah, president

See AFRICA.

Solomon Islands, Oceania

Population: 400,000 **Capital:** Honiara
Area: 10,985 sq mi (28 450 km²)
Government: Sir Moses Pitakaka, governor-general; Bartholomew Ulufa'alu, prime minister

In August 6 elections for the 50-seat National Parliament, the ruling National Unity group won 21 seats, five short of a majority. The National Parliament elected Bartholomew Ulufa'alu, leader of the Liberal Party, prime minister on August 27.

Somalia, E. Africa

Population: 10,200,000 **Capital:** Mogadishu
Area: 246,202 sq mi (637 660 km²)
Government: No functioning government as of December 1997.

See AFRICA.

Suriname, S. America

Population: 400,000 **Capital:** Paramaribo
Area: 63,039 sq mi (163 270 km²)
Government: Jules Wijdenbosch, president

President Jules Wijdenbosch's ruling coalition government collapsed on August 26, when two parties—the Basis Party and the Renewed Progressive Party—defected because of a dispute over government spending. This left Wijdenbosch's National Democratic Party and its three other coalition allies with only 22 members in the 51-seat legislature. The crisis ended on September 5, when the Basis Party returned to the coalition, giving it a one-seat majority. On October 25, President Wijdenbosch announced that government security forces had thwarted a coup attempt.

Swaziland, S. Africa

Population: 1,000,000 **Capital:** Mbabane
Area: 6,703 sq mi (17 360 km²)
Government: Mswati III, king; Barnabas Sibusiso Dlamini, prime minister

The pro-democracy demonstrations and strikes that had erupted in 1996 were seen again in 1997. During a three-week strike that crippled the country's transportation system, police on February 12 forcibly broke up demonstrations and arrested union leaders. The Swaziland Federation of Trade Unions, which coordinated the strikes and protests, called for an end to King Mswati III's absolute rule.

Togo, W. Africa

Population: 4,700,000 **Capital:** Lomé
Area: 21,927 sq mi (56 790 km²)
Government: Gnassingbé Eyadéma, president; Klutse Kwassi, prime minister

Tonga, Oceania

Population: 106,000 **Capital:** Nuku'alofa
Area: 289 sq mi (748 km²)
Government: Taufa'ahau Tupou IV, king; Baron Vaea, prime minister

Trinidad and Tobago, Caribbean

Population: 1,300,000 **Capital:** Port-of-Spain
Area: 1,981 sq mi (5 130 km²)
Government: Arthur Robinson, president; Basdeo Panday, prime minister

Arthur Robinson, the minister for Tobago affairs and a former prime minister, was elected president on February 14.

Tuvalu, Oceania

Population: 10,000 **Capital:** Funafuti
Area: 10 sq mi (26 km²)
Government: Manuella Tulaga, governor-general; Bikenibeu Panieu, prime minister

Effective in February 1997, Tuvalu replaced its national flag with the one it had used from its independence in 1978 to September 1995.

United Arab Emirates, W. Asia

Population: 2,300,000 **Capital:** Abu Dhabi
Area: 32,278 sq mi (83 600 km²)
Government: Zayid bin Sultan Al Nuhayyan, president; Maktum bin Rashid Al Maktum, prime minister

After submitting the resignation of his government on March 16, Prime Minister Maktum bin Rashid Al Maktum formed a new cabinet.

Vanuatu, Oceania

Population: 200,000 **Capital:** Port-Vila
Area: 5,699 sq mi (14 760 km²)
Government: Jean-Marie Leye, president; Serge Vohor, prime minister

Serge Vohor, who had replaced Maxime Carlot Korman as prime minister in September 1996 and brought about a split in the ruling Union of Moderate Parties (UMP), reshuffled his cabinet on May 20. By bringing Korman supporters into the government, Vohor effectively ended the split in the party.

Vatican City, S. Europe

Population: 1,000 **Capital:** Vatican City
Area: 0.17 sq mi (0.438 km²)
Government: John Paul II, pope

Yemen, W. Asia

Population: 15,200,000 **Capital:** San'a
Area: 205,356 sq mi (531 870 km²)
Government: Ali Abdullah Saleh, president; Farag Said Ben Ghanim, prime minister

See MIDDLE EAST.

Zambia, E. Africa

Population: 9,400,000 **Capital:** Lusaka
Area: 290,583 sq mi (752 610 km²)
Government: Frederick Chiluba, president

In August former President Kenneth Kaunda was injured slightly when he was shot by a policeman at a political rally in Kabwe, a town north of Lusaka, the capital. An October 28 coup attempt against President Frederick Chiluba was put down by army troops. Kaunda ended the year under house arrest.

THE UNITED STATES GOVERNMENT

Executive Branch
(selected listing as of January 1998)

President: William J. (Bill) Clinton   **Vice-President:** Albert Gore, Jr.

Executive Office of the President
The White House

Chief of Staff to the President: Erskine Bowles

Senior Policy Adviser to the President: Rahm Emanuel

Assistant to the President and Deputy Chief of Staff: Sylvia Mathews

Assistant to the President and Deputy Chief of Staff: John Podesta

Assistant to the President and Director for Intergovernmental Affairs: Mickey Ibarra

Assistant to the President for Legislative Affairs: John Hilley

Assistant to the President for Communications: Ann Lewis

Assistant to the President and Deputy Counsel: Bruce R. Lindsey

Assistant to the President for Domestic Policy: Bruce Reed

Assistant to the President for Economic Policy: Gene Sperling

Assistant to the President for National Security Affairs: Samuel Berger

Assistant to the President for International Economic Affairs: Dan Tarullo

Counselor to the President: Douglas D. Sosnik

Deputy Assistant to the President and Press Secretary: Michael D. McCurry

Senior Adviser for Policy Development: Ira Magaziner

Office of Management and Budget, Director: Franklin D. Raines

Council of Economic Advisers, Chairman: Janet Yellen

Office of the United States Trade Representative, United States Trade Representative: Charlene Barshefsky

Office of Science and Technology Policy, Assistant to the President for Science and Technology and Director: John H. Gibbons

Office of National Drug Control Policy, Director: Barry R. McCaffrey

Office of Administration, Special Assistant to the President for Management and Director: Ada Posey

The Cabinet

Secretary of Agriculture: Dan Glickman

Secretary of Commerce: William M. Daley

Secretary of Defense: William S. Cohen
    Joint Chiefs of Staff, Chairman: Henry H. Shelton

Secretary of Education: Richard W. Riley

Secretary of Energy: Federico F. Peña

Secretary of Health and Human Services: Donna E. Shalala
    Surgeon General: David Satcher*
    Commissioner of Food and Drugs: Michael A. Friedman

Secretary of Housing and Urban Development: Andrew M. Cuomo

Secretary of Interior: Bruce Babbitt

Department of Justice, Attorney General: Janet Reno
    Federal Bureau of Investigation, Director: Louis Freeh

Secretary of Labor: Alexis M. Herman

Secretary of State: Madeleine K. Albright
    United Nations Representative: William Richardson

Secretary of Transportation: Rodney E. Slater

Secretary of the Treasury: Robert E. Rubin
    Internal Revenue Service, Commissioner: Charles O. Rossotti

Secretary of Veterans Affairs: Togo D. West, Jr.*

Independent Agencies (selected listing)

Central Intelligence Agency, Director: George J. Tenet

Consumer Product Safety Commission, Chairman: Ann Brown

Environmental Protection Agency, Administrator: Carol M. Browner

Equal Employment Opportunity Commission, Chairman: Paul M. Igasaki*

Export-Import Bank of the United States, President and Chairman: James A. Harmon

Farm Credit Administration, Chairman: Marsha Pyle Martin

Federal Communications Commission, Chairman: William E. Kennard

Federal Deposit Insurance Corporation, Chairman: Andrew C. Hove, Jr. (acting)

Federal Election Commission, Chairman: Joan D. Aikens

Federal Emergency Management Agency, Director: James Lee Witt

Federal Labor Relations Authority, Chairman: Phyllis N. Segal

Federal Maritime Commission, Chairman: Harold J. Creel, Jr.

Federal Mediation and Conciliation Service, Director: John Calhoun Wells

Federal Reserve System, Chairman: Alan Greenspan

Federal Trade Commission, Chairman: Robert Pitofsky

General Services Administrator: David J. Barram

National Aeronautics and Space Administration, Administrator: Daniel S. Goldin

National Foundation on the Arts and Humanities
    National Endowment for the Arts, Chairman: William Ivey*
    National Endowment for the Humanities, Chairman: William R. Ferris

National Labor Relations Board, Chairman: William B. Gould IV

National Science Foundation, Director: Neal F. Lane

National Transportation Safety Board, Chairman: James E. Hall

Nuclear Regulatory Commission, Chairman: Shirley A. Jackson

Office of Government Ethics, Director: Stephen D. Potts

Office of Personnel Management, Director: Janice R. Lachance

Peace Corps, Director: Mark Gearan

Postal Rate Commission, Chairman: Edward J. Gleiman

Securities and Exchange Commission, Chairman: Arthur Levitt

Selective Service System, Director: Gil Coronado

Small Business Administrator: Aida Alvarez

Social Security Administration, Commissioner: Kenneth S. Apfel

Tennessee Valley Authority, Chairman: Craven Crowell

U.S. Arms Control and Disarmament Agency, Director: John D. Holum

U.S. Commission on Civil Rights, Chairman: Mary Francis Berry

U.S. Information Agency, Director: Joseph D. Duffey

U.S. International Development Cooperation Agency, Director: J. Brian Atwood

U.S. International Trade Commission, Chairman: Marcia E. Miller

U.S. Postal Service, Postmaster General: Marvin Runyon

The Supreme Court

William H. Rehnquist, chief justice
John Paul Stevens
Sandra Day O'Connor

Antonin Scalia
Anthony M. Kennedy
David H. Souter

Clarence Thomas
Ruth Bader-Ginsburg
Stephen G. Breyer

*Nominated but not confirmed

The 105th CONGRESS
Second Session

SENATE MEMBERSHIP   *(As of January 1998: 55 Republicans, 45 Democrats.) Letters after names refer to party affiliation—D for Democrat, R for Republican, I for Independent. Single asterisk (*) denotes term expiring in January 1999; double asterisk (**), term expiring in January 2001; triple asterisk (***), term expiring in January 2003.*

Alabama
R. C. Shelby, R*
J.B. Sessions, III, R***

Alaska
T. Stevens, R***
F. H. Murkowski, R*

Arizona
J. McCain, R*
J. Kyl, R**

Arkansas
D. Bumpers, D*
T. Hutchinson, R***

California
D. Feinstein, D**
B. Boxer, D*

Colorado
B. N. Campbell, R*
W. Allard, R***

Connecticut
C. J. Dodd, D*
J. I. Lieberman, D**

Delaware
W. V. Roth, Jr., R**
J. R. Biden, Jr., D***

Florida
B. Graham, D*
C. Mack, R**

Georgia
P. D. Coverdell, R*
J. M. Cleland, D***

Hawaii
D. K. Inouye, D*
D. K. Akaka, D**

Idaho
L. E. Craig, R***
D. Kempthorne, R*

Illinois
C. Moseley-Braun, D*
R. J. Durbin, D***

Indiana
R. G. Lugar, R**
D. Coats, R*

Iowa
C. E. Grassley, R*
T. Harkin, D***

Kansas
S. Brownback, R*
P. Roberts, R***

Kentucky
W. H. Ford, D*
M. McConnell, R***

Louisiana
J. Breaux, D*
M. L. Landrieu, D***

Maine
O. J. Snowe, R**
S. Collins, R***

Maryland
P. S. Sarbanes, D**
B. A. Mikulski, D*

Massachusetts
E. M. Kennedy, D**
J. F. Kerry, D***

Michigan
C. M. Levin, D***
S. Abraham, R**

Minnesota
P. D. Wellstone, D***
R. Grams, R**

Mississippi
T. Cochran, R***
T. Lott, R**

Missouri
C. S. Bond, R*
J. D. Ashcroft, R**

Montana
M. Baucus, D***
C. Burns, R**

Nebraska
J. R. Kerrey, D**
C. Hagel, R***

Nevada
H. Reid, D*
R. H. Bryan, D**

New Hampshire
R. C. Smith, R***
J. Gregg, R*

New Jersey
F. R. Lautenberg, D**
R. G. Torricelli, D***

New Mexico
P. V. Domenici, R***
J. Bingaman, D**

New York
D. P. Moynihan, D**
A. M. D'Amato, R*

North Carolina
J. Helms, R***
L. Faircloth, R*

North Dakota
K. Conrad, D**
B. L. Dorgan, D*

Ohio
J. Glenn, D*
M. DeWine, R**

Oklahoma
D. Nickles, R*
J. M. Inhofe, R***

Oregon
R. Wyden, D*
G. H. Smith, R***

Pennsylvania
A. Specter, R*
R. J. Santorum, R**

Rhode Island
J. H. Chafee, R**
J. Reed, D***

South Carolina
S. Thurmond, R***
E. F. Hollings, D*

South Dakota
T. A. Daschle, D*
T. Johnson, D***

Tennessee
W. H. Frist, R**
F. Thompson, R***

Texas
P. Gramm, R***
K. B. Hutchison, R**

Utah
O. G. Hatch, R**
R. F. Bennett, R*

Vermont
P. J. Leahy, D*
J. M. Jeffords, R**

Virginia
J. W. Warner, R***
C. S. Robb, D**

Washington
S. Gorton, R**
P. Murray, D*

West Virginia
R. C. Byrd, D**
J. D. Rockefeller IV, D***

Wisconsin
H. Kohl, D**
R. Feingold, D*

Wyoming
C. Thomas, R**
M. B. Enzi, R***

HOUSE MEMBERSHIP   *(As of January 1998, 227 Republicans, 203 Democrats, 1 Independent, 4 vacancies.) "At-L." in place of congressional district number means "representative at large." *Indicates elected in special 1997 election. ** Pending resignation announced.*

Alabama
1. S. Callahan, R
2. T. Everett, R
3. R. Riley, R
4. R. Aderholt, R
5. B. Cramer, D
6. S. Bachus, R
7. E. F. Hilliard, D

Alaska
AT-L. D. E. Young, R

Arizona
1. M. Salmon, R
2. E. Pastor, D
3. B. Stump, R
4. J. B. Shadegg, R
5. J. Kolbe, R
6. J. D. Hayworth, Jr., R

Arkansas
1. M. Berry, D
2. V. Snyder, D
3. A. Hutchinson, R
4. J. Dickey, R

California
1. F. D. Riggs, R
2. W. Herger, R
3. V. Fazio, D
4. J. T. Doolittle, R
5. R. T. Matsui, D
6. L. Woolsey, D
7. G. Miller, D
8. N. Pelosi, D
9. R. V. Dellums, D**

10. E. Tauscher, D
11. R. W. Pombo, R
12. T. Lantos, D
13. F. P. Stark, D
14. A. G. Eshoo, D
15. T. Campbell, R
16. Z. Lofgren, D
17. S. Farr, D
18. G. A. Condit, D
19. G. Radanovich, R
20. C. M. Dooley, D
21. B. Thomas, R
22. Vacant
23. E. Gallegly, R
24. B. J. Sherman, D
25. H. P. McKeon, R
26. H. L. Berman, D
27. J. E. Rogan, R
28. D. Dreier, R
29. H. A. Waxman, D
30. X. Becerra, D
31. M. G. Martinez, Jr., D
32. J. C. Dixon, D
33. L. Roybal-Allard, D
34. E. E. Torres, D
35. M. Waters, D
36. J. Harman, D
37. J. Millender-McDonald, D
38. S. Horn, R
39. E. Royce, R
40. J. Lewis, R
41. J. Kim, R
42. G. E. Brown, Jr., D
43. K. Calvert, R
44. Vacant
45. D. Rohrabacher, R

46. L. Sanchez, D
47. C. Cox, R
48. R. Packard, R
49. B. Bilbray, R
50. B. Filner, D
51. R. Cunningham, R
52. D. Hunter, R

Colorado
1. D. L. DeGette, D
2. D. E. Skaggs, D
3. S. McInnis, R
4. B. Schaffer, R
5. J. Hefley, R
6. D. Schaefer, R

Connecticut
1. B. B. Kennelly, D
2. S. Gejdenson, D
3. R. L. DeLauro, D
4. C. Shays, R
5. J. H. Maloney, D
6. N. L. Johnson, R

Delaware
At-L. M. N. Castle, R

Florida
1. J. Scarborough, R
2. A. Boyd, Jr., D
3. C. Brown, D
4. T. Fowler, R
5. K. L. Thurman, D
6. C. B. Stearns, R
7. J. L. Mica, R
8. B. McCollum, R

9. M. Bilirakis, R
10. C. W. B. Young, R
11. J. Davis, D
12. C. T. Canady, R
13. D. Miller, R
14. P. J. Goss, R
15. D. Weldon, R
16. M. A. Foley, R
17. C. P. Meek, D
18. I. Ros-Lehtinen, R
19. R. Wexler, D
20. P. Deutsch, D
21. L. Diaz-Balart, R
22. E. C. Shaw, Jr., R
23. A. L. Hastings, D

Georgia
1. J. Kingston, R
2. S. Bishop, D
3. M. Collins, R
4. C. McKinney, D
5. J. Lewis, D
6. N. Gingrich, R
7. B. Barr, R
8. S. Chambliss, R
9. N. Deal, R
10. C. W. Norwood, Jr., R
11. J. Linder, R

Hawaii
1. N. Abercrombie, D
2. P. Mink, D

Idaho
1. H. P. Chenoweth, R
2. M. D. Crapo, R

Illinois
1. B. Rush, D
2. J. L. Jackson, Jr., D
3. W. O. Lipinski, D
4. L. V. Gutierrez, D
5. R. R. Blagojevich, D
6. H. J. Hyde, R
7. D. K. Davis, D
8. P. M. Crane, R
9. S. R. Yates, D
10. J. E. Porter, R
11. J. Weller, R
12. J. F. Costello, D
13. H. W. Fawell, R
14. J. D. Hastert, R
15. T.W. Ewing, R
16. D. Manzullo, R
17. L. Evans, D
18. R. LaHood, R
19. G. Poshard, D
20. J. M. Shimkus, R

Indiana
1. P. J. Visclosky, D
2. D. M. McIntosh, R
3. T. Roemer, D
4. M. E. Souder, R
5. S. Buyer, R
6. D. Burton, R
7. E. A. Pease, R
8. J. N. Hostettler, R
9. L. H. Hamilton, D
10. J. Carson, D

Iowa
1. J. A. Leach, R
2. J. Nussle, R
3. L. L. Boswell, D
4. G. Ganske, R
5. T. Latham, R

Kansas
1. J. Moran, R
2. J. Ryun, R
3. V. K. Snowbarger, R
4. T. Tiahrt, R

Kentucky
1. E. Whitfield, R
2. R. Lewis, R
3. A. M. Northup, R
4. J. Bunning, R
5. H. Rogers, R
6. S. Baesler, D

Louisiana
1. R. B. Livingston, R
2. W. J. Jefferson, D
3. W. J. Tauzin, R
4. J. McCrery, R
5. J. Cooksey, R
6. R. H. Baker, R
7. C. John, D

Maine
1. T. H. Allen, D
2. J. E. Baldacci, D

Maryland
1. W. T. Gilchrest, R
2. R. L. Ehrlich, Jr., R
3. B. L. Cardin, D
4. A. R. Wynn, D
5. S. H. Hoyer, D
6. R. G. Bartlett, R
7. E. E. Cummings, D
8. C. A. Morella, R

Massachusetts
1. J. W. Olver, D
2. R. E. Neal, D
3. J. McGovern, D
4. B. Frank, D
5. M. T. Meehan, D
6. J. F. Tierney, D
7. E. J. Markey, D
8. J. P. Kennedy II, D
9. J. J. Moakley, D
10. W. D. Delahunt, D

Michigan
1. B. T. Stupak, D
2. P. Hoekstra, R
3. V. J. Ehlers, R
4. D. Camp, R
5. J. A. Barcia, D
6. F. Upton, R
7. N. Smith, R
8. D. Stabenow, D
9. D. E. Kildee, D
10. D. E. Bonior, D
11. J. Knollenberg, R

12. S. M. Levin, D
13. L. N. Rivers, D
14. J. Conyers, Jr., D
15. C. C. Kilpatrick, D
16. J. D. Dingell, D

Minnesota
1. G. W. Gutknecht, R
2. D. Minge, D
3. J. Ramstad, R
4. B. F. Vento, D
5. M. O. Sabo, D
6. W. P. Luther, D
7. C. C. Peterson, D
8. J. L. Oberstar, D

Mississippi
1. R. F. Wicker, R
2. B. Thompson, D
3. C. W. Pickering, Jr., R
4. M. Parker, R
5. G. Taylor, D

Missouri
1. W. Clay, D
2. J. M. Talent, R
3. R. A. Gephardt, D
4. I. Skelton, D
5. K. McCarthy, D
6. P. Danner, D
7. R. D. Blunt, R
8. J. Emerson, R
9. K. Hulshof, R

Montana
At-L. R. Hill, R

Nebraska
1. D. Bereuter, R
2. J. Christensen, R
3. W. E. Barrett, R

Nevada
1. J. Ensign, R
2. J. A. Gibbons, R

New Hampshire
1. J. E. Sununu, R
2. C. F. Bass, R

New Jersey
1. R. E. Andrews, D
2. F. A. LoBiondo, R
3. J. Saxton, R
4. C. H. Smith, R
5. M. Roukema, R
6. F. Pallone, Jr., D
7. B. Franks, R
8. W. J. Pascrell, Jr., D
9. S. Rothman, D
10. D. M. Payne, D
11. R. P. Frelinghuysen, R
12. M. Pappas, R
13. R. Menendez, D

New Mexico
1. S. Schiff, R
2. J. R. Skeen, R
3. B. Redmond, R*

New York
1. M. P. Forbes, R
2. R. A. Lazio, R
3. P. T. King, R
4. C. McCarthy, D
5. G. L. Ackerman, D
6. Vacant
7. T. J. Manton, D
8. J. L. Nadler, D
9. C. E. Schumer, D
10. E. Towns, D
11. M. R. Owens, D
12. N. M. Velazquez, D
13. V. J. Fossella, Jr., R*
14. C. B. Maloney, D
15. C. B. Rangel, D
16. J. E. Serrano, D
17. E. L. Engel, D
18. N. M. Lowey, D
19. S. W. Kelly, R
20. B. A. Gilman, R
21. M. R. McNulty, D
22. G. B. H. Solomon, R
23. S. L. Boehlert, R
24. J. M. McHugh, R
25. J. T. Walsh, R
26. M. D. Hinchey, D
27. B. Paxon, R
28. L. M. Slaughter, D
29. J. J. LaFalce, D
30. J. Quinn, R
31. A. Houghton, R

North Carolina
1. E. Clayton, D
2. B. Etheridge, D
3. W. B. Jones, R
4. D. Price, D
5. R. Burr, R
6. H. Coble, R
7. M. McIntyre, D
8. W. G. Hefner, D
9. S. Myrick, R
10. C. Ballenger, R
11. C. H. Taylor, R
12. M. Watt, D

North Dakota
At-L. E. R. Pomeroy, D

Ohio
1. S. Chabot, R
2. R. Portman, R
3. T. P. Hall, D
4. M. G. Oxley, R
5. P. E. Gillmor, R
6. T. Strickland, D
7. D. L. Hobson, R
8. J. A. Boehner, R
9. M. Kaptur, D
10. D. Kucinich, D
11. L. Stokes, D
12. J. R. Kasich, R
13. S. Brown, D
14. T. C. Sawyer, D
15. D. Pryce, R
16. R. Regula, R
17. J. A. Traficant, Jr., D
18. R. W. Ney, R
19. S. C. LaTourette, R

Oklahoma
1. S. Largent, R
2. T. A. Coburn, R
3. W. Watkins, R
4. J. C. Watts, Jr., R
5. E. J. Istook, Jr., R
6. F. D. Lucas, R

Oregon
1. E. Furse, D
2. R. F. Smith, R
3. E. Blumenauer, D
4. P. A. DeFazio, D
5. D. Hooley, D

Pennsylvania
1. Vacant
2. C. Fattah, D
3. R. A. Borski, D
4. R. Klink, D
5. J. Peterson, R
6. T. Holden, D
7. C. Weldon, R
8. J. C. Greenwood, R
9. B. Shuster, R
10. J. M. McDade, R
11. P. E. Kanjorski, D
12. J. P. Murtha, D
13. J. D. Fox, R
14. W. J. Coyne, D
15. P. McHale, D
16. J. R. Pitts, R
17. G. Gekas, R
18. M. F. Doyle, D
19. W. F. Goodling, R
20. F. R. Mascara, D
21. P. S. English, R

Rhode Island
1. P. J. Kennedy, D
2. B. Weygand, D

South Carolina
1. M. C. Sanford, Jr., R
2. F. Spence, R
3. L. Graham, R
4. B. Inglis, R
5. J. M. Spratt, Jr., D
6. J. E. Clyburn, D

South Dakota
At-L. J. R. Thune, R

Tennessee
1. W. L. Jenkins, R
2. J. J. Duncan, Jr., R
3. Z. P. Wamp, R
4. V. Hilleary, R
5. B. Clement, D
6. B. Gordon, D
7. E. Bryant, R
8. J. S. Tanner, D
9. H. E. Ford, Jr., D

Texas
1. M. Sandlin, D
2. J. Turner, D
3. S. Johnson, R
4. R. M. Hall, D
5. P. Sessions, R
6. J. Barton, R
7. B. Archer, R
8. K. Brady, R
9. N. V. Lampson, D
10. L. Doggett, D
11. C. Edwards, D
12. K. Granger, R
13. W. M. Thornberry, R
14. R. E. Paul, R
15. R. Hinojosa, D
16. S. Reyes, D
17. C. W. Stenholm, D
18. S. J. Lee, D
19. L. Combest, R
20. H. B. Gonzalez, D
21. L. Smith, R
22. T. DeLay, R
23. H. Bonilla, R
24. M. Frost, D
25. K. F. Bentsen, Jr., D
26. D. Armey, R
27. S. P. Ortiz, D
28. C. Rodriguez, D*
29. G. Green, D
30. E. B. Johnson, D

Utah
1. J. V. Hansen, R
2. M. Cook, R
3. C. B. Cannon, R

Vermont
At-L. B. Sanders, I

Virginia
1. H. H. Bateman, R
2. O. B. Pickett, D
3. R. C. Scott, D
4. N. Sisisky, D
5. V. H. Goode, Jr., D
6. R. W. Goodlatte, R
7. T. J. Bliley, Jr., R
8. J. P. Moran, D
9. R. Boucher, D
10. F. R. Wolf, R
11. T. M. Davis, R

Washington
1. R. White, R
2. J. Metcalf, R
3. L. A. Smith, R
4. D. Hastings, R
5. G. R. Nethercutt, Jr., R
6. N. D. Dicks, D
7. J. McDermott, D
8. J. Dunn, R
9. A. Smith, D

West Virginia
1. A. B. Mollohan, D
2. R. E. Wise, Jr., D
3. N. Rahall II, D

Wisconsin
1. M. W. Neumann, R
2. S. Klug, R
3. R. Kind, D
4. G. D. Kleczka, D
5. T. M. Barrett, D
6. T. E. Petri, R
7. D. R. Obey, D
8. J. Johnson, D
9. F. J. Sensenbrenner, Jr., R

Wyoming
At-L. B. Cubin, R

AMERICAN SAMOA
Delegate, E. F. H. Faleomavaega, D

DISTRICT OF COLUMBIA
Delegate, Eleanor Holmes Norton, D

GUAM
Delegate, R. A. Underwood, D

PUERTO RICO
Resident Commissioner Carlos Romero-Barceló, New Progressive Party

VIRGIN ISLANDS
Delegate, Donna Christian-Green, D

589

MINING

Coal[a]
(thousand metric tons per month average)

	1995	1996
China	107,624	116,117
United States[r]	86,081[r]	88,574
India	22,131[r]	23,782[c]
South Africa	17,183[b]	16,923[b]
Australia	15,921[r]	16,558[b]
Russia	13,866	13,756[b]
Poland	11,347	11,796[b]
Kazakhstan	6,933	6,638[b]
Ukraine	6,717[r]	5,980[b]
Germany	4,905	4,428

Lignite[a]
(thousand metric tons per month average)

	1995	1996
Germany	16,058	14,921[e]
Russia	7,441[r]	7,520[b]
Poland	5,296	5,289[b]
Czech Rep.	4,829	5,039
Greece	4,539	5,024[b]
Australia	4,229[r]	4,183[b]
Turkey	4,402[r]	4,128[b]
Canada	3,028	3,181[b]
Romania	2,901	2,959[b]
Yugoslavia	3,328	2,949[b]

Natural Gas[a]
(terajoules per month average)

	1995	1996
Russia	1,936,092	1,567,221[b]
United States	1,683,692[r]	1,727,420
Canada	607,608	610,000[e]
United Kingdom	213,987	360,395
Indonesia	203,633[r]	291,490[b]
Netherlands	209,229	236,803
Mexico	143,224[b]	160,347[b]
Uzbekistan	141,891[r]	134,318[b]
Saudi Arabia	131,173	132,000[e]
Argentina	99,726[r]	116,620

Crude Oil[c]
(thousand barrels per day average)

	1995	1996[p]
Saudi Arabia	8,231	8,218
United States	6,560	6,471
Russia	5,995[r]	5,774
Iran	3,643	3,686
China	2,990[r]	3,131
Norway	2,768	3,104
Venezuela	2,750	3,053
Mexico	2,618	2,855
United Kingdom	2,489	2,568
United Arab Emirates	2,279[r]	2,278
World total	62,446[r]	63,999

Aluminum (primary smelter)[d]
(thousand metric tons)

	1995	1996
United States	3,375	3,577
Russia	2,722	2,800[e]
Canada	2,172	2,282
China[e]	1,870[r]	1,780
Australia	1,297	1,372
Brazil	1,188	1,190[e]
Norway	847	874
Venezuela	630	600[e]
Germany	575[r]	577[e]
India[f]	528[r]	518[e]
World total	19,900[r]	20,700

Bauxite[d,g]
(thousand metric tons)

	1995	1996
Australia	42,655	43,100
Guinea[e,h]	12,000[r]	14,000
Jamaica[h,i]	10,857	11,829
Brazil	9,700[r]	9,700
China[e]	5,000	6,200
Venezuela	5,184	5,600
India	5,163[r]	5,100[e]
Suriname	3,530	4,000[e]
Russia[e]	3,100	3,300
Kazakhstan	3,071[r]	3,140
World total[g]	107,000[r]	114,000

Cement[k] (thousand metric tons)

	1995	1996
China	475,910[r]	490,000
Japan	90,474	94,492
United States	78,320	80,000[e]
India[e]	70,000	75,000
Korea, South	55,130	57,334
Germany[e]	40,000	40,000
Thailand[e]	34,900[r]	35,000
Italy	33,715[r]	34,000[e]
Turkey	33,153	32,500[e]
Russia	36,500[r]	27,800
World total[l]	1,450,000[r]	1,480,000

Copper (mine)[m,n] (metric tons)

	1995	1996
Chile	2,488,600[r]	3,115,800
United States[o]	1,850,000	1,920,000
Canada	728,680	689,000
Peru	443,085[r]	572,402
Australia	419,900[r]	525,000[e]
Russia	525,000[e]	520,000[e]
Indonesia[o]	443,618	507,484
China	445,000[r,e]	439,100
Poland	383,600	422,000
Mexico	343,200[r]	340,710
World total	10,100,000[r]	11,000,000

Copper (refined primary and secondary)[m,n]
(metric tons)

	1995	1996
United States	2,280,000	2,340,000
Chile, primary	1,491,500[r]	1,748,200
Japan	1,187,959	1,251,373
China[e]	1,080,000[r]	1,120,000
Germany	616,300	671,000[e]
Russia	560,300	570,000[e]
Canada	572,600[r]	559,200
Poland	435,684	445,000[e]
Belgium[q]	376,000[r]	354,000
Peru	295,100	338,100
World total	11,900,000[r]	12,500,000

Iron Ore[m,s]
(thousand metric tons, metal content)

	1995	1996
Brazil	115,050[r]	117,000[e]
Australia	88,653	93,000
China[e]	75,000	75,000
India	42,700[r,e]	42,960
United States	39,600	39,200
Russia	41,700[r]	38,300[e]
Ukraine	27,700[r]	26,400[e]
Canada	23,416[r]	23,034
South Africa	19,806	19,115
Sweden	12,211[r]	12,975
World total	551,000[r]	549,000

Iron (crude steel)[m,t]
(thousand metric tons)

	1995	1996
China[e]	95,400[r]	100,000
Japan	101,640	98,801
United States	95,200	94,700
Russia[e]	51,300	49,200
Germany[e]	42,100	42,000
Korea, South	36,772	38,900[e]
Italy	27,766	28,000[e]
Brazil	25,076	25,700[e]
Ukraine	22,309	22,300[e]
India	20,291	20,000[e]
World total	754,000[r]	758,000

Lead (mine)[m,u] (metric tons)

	1995	1996
Australia	455,000	522,000
China[e]	520,000[r]	500,000
United States	394,000	436,000
Peru	237,597[r]	248,787
Canada	204,227[r]	240,835
Mexico	164,348	173,831
Sweden	100,070[r]	100,000[e]
South Africa	88,449[r]	88,613
Korea, North[e]	80,000	80,000
Morocco	67,706[r]	71,668
World total	2,780,000[r]	2,920,000

Lead (refined)[m,u] (metric tons)

	1995	1996
United States	1,390,000[r]	1,430,000
China[e]	608,000[r]	530,000
United Kingdom	320,704[r]	345,574
Germany[e]	335,000	340,000
Canada	281,391[r]	309,379
France	290,050[r]	295,000[e]
Japan	286,534	287,373
Australia	235,400	224,000[e]
Mexico[e]	170,000[r]	154,000
Italy	180,400[r]	143,000[e]
World total[g]	5,590,000[r]	5,480,000

Phosphate rock[m,v]
(thousand metric tons)

	1995	1996
United States	43,500	45,400[e]
China[e]	19,300[r]	21,000
Morocco	20,200	20,800[e]
Russia[e]	8,800	8,500
Tunisia	7,241	7,100[e]
Jordan	4,984	5,350[e]
Israel[w]	4,063	3,800[e]
Brazil	3,590[r]	3,600[e]
South Africa	2,790	2,700[e]
Togo[e]	2,560	2,600
World total	130,000[r]	133,000

Salt[m,n]
(thousand metric tons)

	1995	1996
United States	42,200[r]	42,300
China[e]	29,800[r]	28,900
Canada	10,957[r]	12,289
Germany[e]	10,800	10,800
India[e]	9,500	9,500
Mexico	7,670	8,508
Australia	8,148[r]	7,905
France	7,539[r]	7,660[e]
United Kingdom[e]	6,650[r]	6,700
Brazil	5,800[r]	5,900[e]
World total	192,000[r]	192,000

Sulfur (all forms)[m,x]
(thousand metric tons)

	1995	1996
United States[e]	11,800	12,000
Canada	9,010	9,014
China[e]	5,430[r]	5,470
Russia[e]	4,000	4,020
Mexico[e]	2,880	2,890
Japan[e]	2,810[r]	2,800
Saudi Arabia	2,200	2,000[e]
Poland	2,660[r,e]	1,769
France[e]	1,170[r]	1,200
Germany[e]	1,110[r]	1,110
World total	53,200[r]	52,400

Zinc (mine)[m,u] (metric tons)

	1995	1996
Canada	1,121,172[r]	1,235,274
Australia	937,000[r]	1,071,000
China[e]	1,010,000[r]	1,010,000
Peru	692,250[r]	760,563
United States	644,000	628,000
Mexico	363,658	377,599
Kazakhstan[e]	225,000[r]	225,000
Korea, North[e]	210,000	210,000
Spain	172,469[r]	170,000[e]
Ireland	184,118[r]	164,168
World total	7,240,000[r]	7,440,000

Zinc (smelter)[m,u] (metric tons)

	1995	1996
China[e]	1,080,000[r]	1,120,000
Canada	720,346[r]	715,553
Japan	716,900	642,200
United States	362,772	366,140
Spain	358,000[r]	350,000[e]
Australia[e]	325,000[r]	331,000
Germany	322,500[r]	327,000[e]
France[e]	290,000[r]	320,000
Belgium	301,100[r]	297,400
Korea, South	279,335	286,526
World total	7,550,000[r]	7,530,000

[a]Source: UN Dept. for Economic and Social Information and Policy Analysis. [b]Average of available monthly information. [c]Source: International Petroleum Statistics Report, U.S. Dept. of Energy, May 1997. [d]World totals and estimated data are rounded to three significant digits. [e]Estimated. [f]Primary ingot. [g]Table includes data available through June 25, 1997. [h]Dry bauxite equivalent of crude ore. [i]Bauxite processed for conversion to alumina in Jamaica plus kiln-dried ore prepared for export. [k]Table includes data available through Aug. 4, 1997. [l]World totals are rounded to three significant digits. [m]World totals, U.S. data, and estimated data are rounded to three significant digits. [n]Table includes data available through July 10, 1997. [o]Recoverable content. [p]Preliminary. [q]Includes leach cathode from former Zaire, which is processed. [r]Revised. [s]Table includes data available through July 16, 1997. [t]Table includes data available through June 10, 1997. [u]Table includes data available through July 1, 1997. [v]Table includes data available through May 8, 1997. [w]Beneficiated. [x]Table includes data available through August 1997.

Source: U.S. Geological Survey, U.S. Department of the Interior, unless otherwise indicated. **Note:** Numerals are annual production unless otherwise indicated.

Contributors

ADRIAN, CHARLES R., Professor Emeritus of Political Science, University of California, Riverside; Author, *A History of City Government: The Emergence of the Metropolis 1920–1945*; Coauthor, *State and Local Politics, A History of American City Government: The Formation of Traditions, 1775–1870, Governing Urban America*: ***Los Angeles***

AMICK, GEORGE, Author, *Linn's U.S. Stamp Yearbook*: ***Stamps and Stamp Collecting***

ARNOLD, ANTHONY, Author, *Afghanistan: The Soviet Invasion in Perspective, Afghanistan's Two-Party Communism: Parcham and Khalq, The Fateful Pebble: Afghanistan's Role in the Fall of the Soviet Empire*: ***Afghanistan***

ATTNER, PAUL, Senior Writer, *The Sporting News*: ***Biography***—*Karl Malone*; ***Sports***—*Basketball, Football*

BALDWIN, LOU, Staff Writer, *The Catholic Standard & Times*: ***Obituaries***—*Mother Teresa*; ***Religion***—*Roman Catholicism*

BATRA, PREM P., Professor of Biochemistry, Wright State University: ***Biochemistry***

BEHAN, PATRICIA A., Associate Editor, *The New Book of Knowledge Annual*: ***Canada***—*Northwest Territories; Yukon*; ***States, U.S.***—*(in part)*

BEHLER, DEBORAH A., Executive Editor, *Wildlife Conservation* magazine: ***Zoos and Zoology***

BEST, JOHN, Chief, *Canada World News*, Ottawa: ***Canada***—*New Brunswick, Prince Edward Island, Quebec*

BONN, ROBERT L., John Jay College of Criminal Justice, City University of New York: ***Prisons***

BORLIN, CRAIG H., Freelance Writer, Omaha, NE: ***States, U.S.***—*(in part)*

BOWER, BRUCE, Behavioral Sciences Editor, *Science News*: ***Anthropology; Archaeology; Medicine and Health***—*Mental Health*

BRAASCH, BARBARA, Freelance Travel Writer, Palo Alto, CA: ***Travel; Travel***—*Ecotourism*

BUGAJSKI, JANUSZ, Director of East European Studies, Center for Strategic and International Studies, Washington, DC; Author, *Ethnic Politics in Eastern Europe: A Guide to Nationality Policies, Organizations and Parties*: ***Albania; Bosnia and Herzegovina; Bulgaria; Croatia; Hungary; Macedonia; Romania; Slovenia; Yugoslavia (Serbia and Montenegro)***

BURK, DAN L., Professor, Seton Hall University, School of Law: ***Computers and Communications***—*The Internet*—*Legal Issues*

BURKS, ARDATH W., Professor Emeritus, Asian Studies, Rutgers University; Author, *Third Order of the Rising Sun*: ***Japan***

BUSH, GRAHAM W. A., Associate Professor of Political Studies, University of Auckland; Author, *Advance in Order: The Auckland City Council 1971–89*: ***New Zealand***

CHAMETZKY, PETER, Department of Art and Art History, Adelphi University: ***Art***

CHAYES, SARAH, Contributing Reporter, Paris, National Public Radio: ***Biography***—*Lionel Robert Jospin*; ***France; Morocco***

CHEMERINSKY, ERWIN, Professor, University of Southern California, Law Center: ***Law***—*Criminal v. Civil Law*

COLLINS, BUD, Sports Columnist, *The Boston Globe*; Author, *My Life With The Pros*: ***Sports***—*Tennis*

CONRADT, DAVID P., Professor of Political Science, East Carolina University; Author, *The German Polity, West European Politics*: ***Germany***

COOPER, ILENE, Children's Book Editor, *Booklist Magazine*: ***Literature***—*Children's*

COOPER, MARY H., Staff Writer, *CQ Researcher*; Author, *The Business of Drugs*: ***Abortion; Business***—*The Tobacco Industry*; ***Energy; United States***—*Funding the Arts*

COOPER, MARY LOU, Program and Public Relations Manager for Western Office, Council of State Governments: ***States, U.S.***—*(in part)*

COPPEDGE, MICHAEL, Helen Kellogg Institute for International Study, University of Notre Dame: ***Ecuador; Peru; Venezuela***

CUNNIFF, JOHN, Business News Analyst, The Associated Press; Author, *How to Stretch Your Dollar*: ***Business and Corporate Affairs; Industrial Production; United States***—*The Economy*

CURRIER, CHET, Financial Writer, The Associated Press; Author, *The Investor's Encyclopedia, The 15-Minute Investor*; Coauthor, *No-Cost/Low-Cost Investing*: ***Stocks and Bonds***

CURTIS, L. PERRY, Professor of History, Brown University: ***Ireland***

DAVID, LEONARD, Director, Space Data Resources and Information: ***Space Exploration; Space Exploration***—*Difficult Times for "Mir"*

DECKER, ANDREW, Contributing Editor, *ARTnews* magazine: ***Art***—*The Art Market*

DELZELL, CHARLES F., Professor of History Emeritus and Adjunct Professor, Vanderbilt University; Author, *Italy in the Twentieth Century, Mediterranean Fascism, Mussolini's Enemies*: ***Italy***

DENNIS, LARRY, Editor, *Senior Golfer* magazine: ***Sports***—*Golf; A New "Tiger" for the Game*

DUFF, ERNEST A., Professor of Politics, Randolph-Macon Woman's College; Author, *Agrarian Reform in Colombia, Violence and Repression in Latin America, Leader and Party in Latin America*: ***Colombia***

DUSHKIN, LELAH, Associate Professor of Sociology, Kansas State University: ***Sri Lanka***

DYER, RICHARD, Chief Classical Music Critic, *The Boston Globe*: ***Music***—*Classical*

EADINGTON, WILLIAM R., Director, Institute for the Study of Gambling and Commercial Gaming; Professor of Economics, University of Nevada, Reno; Author, *Gambling Behavior and Problem Gambling*: **Gambling; Gambling**—*Illegal Sports Betting*

EBERHART, GEORGE, *American Libraries* magazine, American Library Association: **Libraries**

ENSTAD, ROBERT, Writer, *Chicago Tribune*: **Chicago**

FALLESEN, LEIF BECK, Editor in Chief, *Boersen*, Copenhagen: **Denmark; Finland; Norway; Sweden**

FLAX, PETER A., Freelance Writer and Editor, Oakland, CA: **Biography**—*Pete Sampras, Andrew Weil*; **Sports**—*Yachting*

FLECK, JOHN, Reporter, *The Albuquerque Journal*: **States, U.S.**—*50th Anniversary of the "Roswell Incident"*

FRANCIS, DAVID R., Economy Page Editor, *The Christian Science Monitor*: **Biography**—*Alan Greenspan*; **International Trade and Finance**

FREEDMAN, ALLAN, Environmental Reporter, *Congressional Quarterly*: **Environment; Environment**—*Global Warming: A World Solution?*

GAILEY, HARRY A., Professor of History, San Jose State University; Author, *History of the Gambia, History of Africa, Road to Aba*: **Congo, Democratic Republic of the; Nigeria**

GOLDSTEIN, HARRY, Technical Insights: **Engineering, Civil**

GOODING, DUNHAM, President, American Alpine Institute: **Mount Everest**—*The Lure Continues*; **Mountain Climbing**—*The Sport Today*

GOODMAN, DONALD, Associate Professor of Sociology, John Jay College of Criminal Justice, City University of New York: **Prisons**

GORDON, MAYNARD M., Senior Editor, *Ward's Dealer Business* magazine; Author, *The Iacocca Management Technique*: **Automobiles; Automobiles**—*The Air Bag*

GRAYSON, GEORGE W., Class of 1938 Professor of Government, College of William and Mary; Author, *The Politics of Mexican Oil, The United States and Mexico: Patterns of Influence, Oil and Mexican Foreign Policy*: **Brazil; Mexico; Portugal; Spain**

GREGORY, BARBARA J., American Numismatic Association: **Coins and Coin Collecting**

GROSSMAN, LAWRENCE, Director of Publications, The American Jewish Committee: **Religion**—*Judaism*

GROTH, ALEXANDER J., Professor Emeritus of Political Science, University of California, Davis; Author, *People's Poland, Contemporary Politics: Europe, Comparative Resource Allocation, Public Policy Across Nations*: **Poland**

HARRIS, PHYLLIS LOUISE, Founder, Asian Culinary Arts Institutes Ltd.; Food Editor, *Asian Pages*: **America's Changing Taste Buds; Popular Dishes**

HASSON, JUDI, News Editor, *Congressional Quarterly*: **Biography**—*Fred Thompson*; **Washington, DC; Women**

HELMREICH, JONATHAN E., Professor of History, Allegheny College; Author, *Belgium and Europe: A Study in Small Power Diplomacy, Gathering Rare Ores: The Diplomacy of Uranium Acquisition, 1943–54*; Coauthor, *Rebirth: A History of Europe Since World War II*: **Belgium; Netherlands**

HELMREICH, PAUL C., Professor of History, Wheaton College; Author, *Wheaton College: The Seminary Years, 1834–1912, From Paris to Sèvres: The Partition of the Ottoman Empire at the Peace Conference of 1919–1920*; Coauthor, *Rebirth: A History of Europe Since World War II*: **Switzerland**

HOPKO, THE REV. THOMAS, Dean, St. Vladimir's Orthodox Theological Seminary, Crestwood, NY: **Religion**—*Orthodox Eastern*

HOYT, CHARLES K., Fellow, *American Institute of Architects*; Author, *More Places for People, Building for Commerce and Industry*: **Architecture**

HUFFMAN, GEORGE J., NASA/Science Systems and Applications: **Meteorology; Meteorology**—*A Year of Unusual Floods*

HULBERT, DAN, *Atlanta Journal & Constitution*: **Television and Radio; Television and Radio**—*"Ellen"*; **Theater**

HUSTED, THOMAS, Assistant Professor, Department of Economics, The American University: **Taxation**

JACKSON, PAUL CONRAD, Editor, *The Calgary Sun*; Author, *Battleground: The Social Assault on Grant Devine's Canadian Dream*: **Canada**—*Alberta*

JACOBY, BRUCE, Freelance Writer: **Biography**—*Garth Brooks, George Tenet*; **Food**—*The Bagel*; **States, U.S.**—*(in part)*

JENNERMANN, DONALD L., Director, University Honors Program, Indiana State University; Author, *Born of a Cretan Spring, Literature for Living*: **Literature**—*English*

JOHNSON, LONNIE, Author, *Central Europe: Enemies, Neighbors, Friends*: **Austria**

JONES, GRAHAME L., Soccer Columnist, *Los Angeles Times* and ESPN's *SportsZone*: **Sports**—*Soccer*

KARNES, THOMAS L., Professor of History Emeritus, Arizona State University; Author, *Latin American Policy of the United States, Failure of Union: Central America 1824–1960*: **Central America**

KESSLER, ANN, American Bankers Association: **Banking and Finance; Banking and Finance**—*Debit Cards*

KIM, HAN-KYO, University of Cincinnati; Author, *Korea and the Politics of Imperialism 1876–1910, Studies on Korea: A Scholar's Guide*: **Korea**

KING, PETER J., Professor of History, Carleton University, Ottawa; Author, *Utilitarian Jurisprudence in America*: **Canada**—*Ontario*

KINNEAR, MICHAEL, Professor of History, University of Manitoba; Author, *The Fall of Lloyd George, The British Voter*: **Canada**—*Manitoba*

KIRBY, DAVID, Professor of English, Florida State University: **Literature**—*American*

KISSELGOFF, ANNA, Chief Dance Critic, *The New York Times*: **Dance**

LAI, DAVID CHUENYAN, Professor of Geography, University of Victoria, British Columbia; Author, *The Forbidden City Within Victoria: Myth, Symbol and Streetscape of Canada's Earliest Chinatown*: **A Time of Change for Hong Kong**

LAWRENCE, ROBERT M., Professor of Political Science, Colorado State University; Author, *The Strategic Defense Initiative*: **The New U.S. Military; Women in the Military**—*An Update*; **Military Affairs**

LEEPSON, MARC, Freelance Writer: **Volunteerism**—*A Renewed Call to Serve; A Call to Give*; **Drugs and Alcohol; Social Welfare**

LEVINE, LOUIS, Professor, Department of Biology, City College of New York; Author, *Biology of the Gene, Biology for a Modern Society*: **Biotechnology; Biotechnology**—*Spotlight on Cloning*; **Genetics; Microbiology**

LEWIS, ANNE C., Education Policy Writer: **Education**

LOESCHER, GIL, Professor of International Relations, University of Notre Dame; Author, *Refugees and International Relations, The Global Refugee Crisis: A Reference Handbook, Beyond Charity: International Cooperation and the Global Refugee Crisis*: **Refugees and Immigration**

LOPIANO, DONNA, Executive Director, Women's Sports Foundation: **Sports**—*Women in Sports*

MacLEOD, ALEXANDER, British Isles Correspondent, *The Christian Science Monitor*, London: **Biography**—*Tony Blair*; **Great Britain; Great Britain**—*The Year of the "New" Labour*; **Obituaries**—*Princess Diana*

MAMMANA, DENNIS L., Reuben H. Fleet Space Center and Science Theater: *Astronomy; Astronomy—Comet Hale-Bopp*

MANDESE, JOE, Senior Vice-President, Editorial Director, *The Myers Reports*: *Advertising*

MARCOPOULOS, GEORGE J., Professor of History, Tufts University: *Cyprus; Greece*

MATHESON, JIM, Sportswriter, *Edmonton Journal*: *Sports—Ice Hockey*

MAYERCHAK, PATRICK M., Professor of Political Science, Virginia Military Institute; Author, *Scholar's Guide to Southeast Asia*; Coauthor, *Linkage or Bondage: US-ASEAN Economic Relations*: *Malaysia; Singapore*

McCORQUODALE, SUSAN, Professor of Political Science, Memorial University of Newfoundland: *Canada—Newfoundland*

McGEE, GLENN, Center for Bioethics, University of Pennsylvania School of Medicine; Author, *The Perfect Baby*: *Medicine and Health—Bioethics*

MICHIE, ARUNA NAYYAR, Department of Political Science, Kansas State University: *Bangladesh; India*

MILLER, RANDALL M., Department of History, St. Joseph's University; Author, *Shades of the Sunbelt: Essays on Ethnicity, Race and the Urban South*: *Ethnic Groups, U.S.*

MILWARD, JOHN, Freelance Writer and Critic: *Music—Popular and Jazz, John Denver*

MITCHELL, GARY, Professor of Physics, North Carolina State University: *Physics*

MORRIS, BERNADINE, Fashion Journalist; Author, *The Fashion Makers, American Fashion, Valentino, Scaasi*: *Fashion; Fashion—"Designermania," Gianni Versace*

MORTIMER, ROBERT A., Professor, Department of Political Science, Haverford College; Author, *The Third World Coalition in International Politics;* Coauthor, *Politics and Society in Contemporary Africa*: *Algeria*

MORTON, DESMOND, Director, McGill Institute for the Study of Canada; Author, *Working People: An Illustrated History of the Canadian Labour Movement, A Military History of Canada, Bloody Victory: Canadians and the D-Day Campaign, 1944*: *Canada*

OCHSENWALD, WILLIAM, Professor of History, Virginia Polytechnic Institute and State University; Author, *The Middle East: A History, The Hijaz Railroad, Religion, Society and the State in Arabia*: *Saudi Arabia; Turkey*

O'MEARA, PATRICK, Dean of International Programs, Indiana University; Coeditor, *Africa, International Politics in Southern Africa, Southern Africa, The Continuing Crisis*: *Africa; South Africa; Zimbabwe*

PAPER, HEATHER J., Freelance Interior Design Writer: *Interior Design*

PEARSON, FREDERIC S., Director, Center for Peace and Conflict Studies, Wayne State University, Detroit; Coauthor, *International Relations: The Global Condition, Fuel on the Fire? Effects of Armament During Warfare*: *United States—Foreign Affairs*

PEARSON, RUTH, United Nations Correspondent, *Business Week*: *Biography—Kofi Annan; United Nations*

PEIRIS, SARATH, Journalist, *Saskatoon Star-Phoenix*: *Canada—Saskatchewan*

PENDICK, DANIEL, Contributing Editor, *Earth Magazine*: *Geology*

PERETZ, DON, Professor Emeritus of Political Science, State University of New York at Binghamton; Author, *The West Bank—History, Politics, Society and Economy, Government and Politics of Israel, The Middle East Today*: *Egypt; Israel*

PERKINS, KENNETH J., Professor of History, University of South Carolina: *Libya; Religion—Islam*

PERRY, DAVID K., Associate Professor, Department of Journalism, The University of Alabama: *Publishing; Publishing—The Paparazzi*

PIPPIN, LARRY L., Professor of Political Science, University of the Pacific; Author, *The Remón Era*: *Argentina; Paraguay; Uruguay*

POOLE, PETER A., Author, *The Vietnamese in Thailand, Eight Presidents and Indochina*; Coauthor, *American Diplomacy*: *Vietnam*

REED, WILLIAM CYRUS, Director of African Studies, The American University in Cairo, Egypt; Department of African Studies, Indiana University: *Kenya; Tanzania; Uganda*

RICHARDS, DAN, Senior Editor, *Popular Photography*: *Photography*

RICHTER, LINDA K., Professor of Political Science, Kansas State University; Author, *Land Reform and Tourism Development, Policy-Making in the Philippines, The Politics of Tourism in Asia*: *Myanmar; Philippines*

RICHTER, WILLIAM L., Associate Provost for International Programs, Kansas State University: *Pakistan*

RIGGAN, WILLIAM, Associate Editor, *World Literature Today*, University of Oklahoma; Author, *Pícaros, Madmen, Naïfs, and Clowns, Comparative Literature and Literary Theory*: *Literature—World*

ROBERTS, SAM, *The New York Times*: *New York City*

ROSS, DAVID A., Senior Scientist, Woods Hole Oceanographic Institution; Author, *Introduction to Oceanography*: *Oceanography*

ROVNER, JULIE, Health-Policy Writer: *Medicine and Health—Health Care*

RUBIN, JIM, Washington Bureau, The Associated Press: *Crime; Crime—The FBI under Fire; Law*

RUFF, NORMAN J., Assistant Professor, Department of Political Science, University of Victoria, B.C.; Coauthor, *The Reins of Power: Governing British Columbia*: *Canada—British Columbia*

SCHLOSSBERG, DAN, Baseball Writer; Author, *The Baseball IQ Challenge, The Baseball Catalog, The Baseball Book of Why, Cooperstown: Baseball's Hall of Fame Players*: *Biography—Tony Gwynn; Sports—Baseball, Jackie Robinson and His Legacy*

SCHROEDER, RICHARD, Freelance Writer, Specialist on the Caribbean and Latin America: *Bolivia; Caribbean; Caribbean—Montserrat; Chile; Latin America*

SCHWAB, PETER, Professor of Political Science, Purchase College, State University of New York; Author, *Ethiopia: Politics, Economics, and Society, Human Rights: Cultural and Ideological Perspectives*: *Ethiopia*

SEIDERS, DAVID F., Chief Economist and Senior Staff Vice-President, National Association of Home Builders, Washington, DC: *Housing*

SENSER, ROBERT A., Freelance Writer: *Biography—Mary Robinson; Human Rights*

SERAFIN, BRUCE, Founding Editor, *Vancouver Review*: *Canada—The Arts; Literature—Canadian*

SETH, R. P., Professor Emeritus, Department of Economics, Mount Saint Vincent University, Halifax: *Canada—Nova Scotia*

SEYBOLD, PAUL G., Professor, Department of Chemistry, Wright State University: *Chemistry*

SHAPIRO, WILLIAM E., Freelance Writer and Editor, New York City: *Art—Willem de Kooning; Obituaries—William Brennan; Russia—The Commonwealth of Independent States; Tunisia; Nations of the World*

SHARLET, ROBERT, Chauncey Winters Professor of Political Science, Union College; Author, *Soviet Constitutional Crisis*: *Baltic Republics; Russia*

SHOGAN, ROBERT, National Political Correspondent, Washington Bureau, *The Los Angeles Times*; Author, *A Question of Judgment, Promises to Keep*: *White House Scandal—25 Years After Watergate; Independent Counsel; Biography—Madeleine Albright, Herman Cohen, Alexis Herman; United States—Domestic Affairs*

SIMON, JEFFREY D., Freelance Writer; Author, *The Terrorist Trap*: **Terrorism**

SIMON, SHELDON W., Professor of Political Science, Arizona State University–Tempe; Author, *The Future of Asian-Pacific Security Collaboration*: **Asia**

SNODSMITH, RALPH L., Ornamental Horticulturist; Author, *Ralph Snodsmith's Tips from the Garden Hotline*: **Gardening and Horticulture**

STARR, JOHN BRYAN, Managing Director, Annenberg Institute for School Reform, Brown University; Author, *Continuing the Revolution: The Political Thought of Mao*; Editor, *The Future of U.S.-China Relations*: **China: A New Era Begins; China; Obituaries**—Deng Xiaoping; **Taiwan**

STEIN, LANA, Associate Professor of Political Science, University of Missouri–St. Louis; Author, *Holding Bureaucrats Accountable: Politicians and Professionals in St. Louis*: **Cities and Urban Affairs**

STIEBER, JACK, Professor Emeritus, School of Labor and Industrial Relations, Michigan State University; Author, *U.S. Industrial Relations: The Next Twenty Years, Governing the UAW, Public Employee Unionism*: **Labor**

STUART, ELAINE, Managing Editor, *State Government News*: **States, U.S.**—(in part)

SUTTON, STAN, Sportswriter, *The Courier-Journal*, Louisville, KY: **Sports**—Auto Racing, Boxing, Horse Racing, Track and Field

TESAR, JENNY, Science and Medicine Writer; Author, *The New Webster's Computer Handbook, Introduction to Animals, Parents as Teachers*: **The Growing Popularity of Cosmetic Surgery; Popular Procedures; Chess; Computers and Communications; Medicine and Health**—Overview; **Obituaries**—Jacques-Yves Cousteau

TURNER, ARTHUR CAMPBELL, Professor Emeritus of Political Science, University of California, Riverside; Coauthor, *Ideology and Power in the Middle East*: **Biography**—Mohammed Khatami; **Iran; Iraq; Jordan; Lebanon; Middle East; Syria**

TURNER, DARRELL J., Religion Writer, *The Journal Gazette*, Fort Wayne, IN; Former Associate Editor, Religious News Service, New York, NY: **Religion**—Overview, Far Eastern, Protestantism, The Promise Keepers

VAN ZANDT, CHRISTINE, U.S. Government Analyst on East Asian Affairs, Washington, DC: **Cambodia; Laos**

VAUGHAN, KRISTI, Freelance Writer: **Biography**— Christopher Plummer, Jerry Seinfeld, Martha Stewart; **Family; Literature**—Overview; **States, U.S.**—(in part)

VOLL, JOHN O., Professor of History, University of New Hampshire; Author, *Islam: Continuity and Change in the Modern World*; Coauthor, *Sudan: Unity and Diversity in a Multicultural Society*; Editor, *Sudan: State and Society in Crisis*: **Sudan**

VOLSKY, GEORGE, Center for Advanced International Studies, University of Miami: **Cuba**

WALTON, DAVID, British Antarctic Survey; Author, *Antarctic Science*: **Polar Research**

WATSON, RIP, *The Journal of Commerce*: **Transportation**

WEATHERBEE, DONALD E., Department of Government, University of South Carolina: **Indonesia; Thailand**

WHITTEN, PHILLIP, Editor in Chief, *Swimming World*: **Sports**—Swimming

WILLIS, F. ROY, Professor of History, University of California, Davis; Author, *France, Germany and the New Europe, 1945–1968, Italy Chooses Europe, The French Paradox*: **Europe; Europe**—NATO Expansion, The Marshall Plan—50 Years Later

WINCHESTER, N. BRIAN, Center for the Study of Global Change and Former Director, African Studies Program, Indiana University: **Africa; South Africa; Zimbabwe**

WIPPMAN, DAVID, Associate Professor, Cornell Law School: **Law**—International

WISNER, ROBERT N., Professor, Iowa State University; Coeditor, *Marketing for Farmers*; Author, *World Food Trade and U.S. Agriculture*: **Agriculture; Food**

WOLCHIK, SHARON LEE, Director of the Russian and East European Studies Program and Professor of Political Science, George Washington University; Author, *The Social Legacy of Communism, Czechoslovakia in Transition: Politics, Economics and Society*: **Czech Republic; Slovakia**

WOLF, WILLIAM, New York University; Author, *The Marx Brothers, Landmark Films, The Cinema and Our Century*: **Motion Pictures; Motion Pictures**—Special Effects, Cannes Film Festival Turns 50; **Obituaries**— Jimmy Stewart

YATES, ANNA, Freelance Writer and Translator; Author, *Leifur Eiriksson and Vinland the Good*: **Iceland**

YOUNGER, R. M., Journalist and Author; Author, *Australia and the Australians, Australia! Australia! A Bicentennial Record*: **Australia**

ZELENAK, MEL J., Department of Family/Consumer Economics, University of Missouri-Columbia: **Marketing to Kids; Toy Fads; Consumer Affairs; Retailing**

Acknowledgments

We also wish to thank the following for their services: color separations and electronic file output, Gamma One, Inc.; text stock printed on Champion's 60# Courtland Matte; dust jacket and covers printed by Mid-City Lithographers; cover materials provided by Ecological Fibers, Inc.; and printing and binding by R.R. Donnelley & Sons, Co.

Index

Main article headings appear in this index as bold-faced capitals; subjects within articles appear as lower-case entries. Bold-faced page numbers indicate the location of the article about the subject. Both the general references and the subentries should be consulted for maximum usefulness of this index. Illustrations are indexed herein. Cross references are to the entries in this index.